Complete Guide to
CRUISING
& CRUISE SHIPS
2011

BY DOUGLAS WARD
President
The Maritime Evaluations Group

Editorial

Written by
Douglas Ward

Managing Editor
Brian Bell

Series Editor
Tony Halliday

Editorial address
Berlitz Publishing
PO Box 7910, London SE1 1WE
United Kingdom
berlitz@apaguide.co.uk

Distribution

North America
Langenscheidt Publishers, Inc.
36–36 33rd Street, 4th Floor
Long Island City, NY 11106
orders@langenscheidt.com

UK & Ireland
GeoCenter International Ltd
Meridian House, Churchill Way West
Basingstoke, Hants RG21 6YR
sales@geocenter.co.uk

Worldwide
Apa Publications GmbH & Co.
Verlag KG (Singapore branch)
7030 Ang Mo Kio Ave 5
08–65 Northstar @ AMK
Singapore 569880
apasin@signet.com.sg

©2010 Apa Publications GmbH & Co.
Verlag KG (Singapore branch)
All Rights Reserved

Printed by CTPS-China

*Berlitz Trademark Reg. U.S. Patent Office
and other countries. Marca Registrada.
Used under licence from the Berlitz
Investment Corporation*

First Edition 1985
Nineteenth Edition 2011

HOW TO FIND THE X-FACTOR

Douglas Ward introduces the "bible" of the cruising world

The cruise industry's marketing men are quick to advertise the fact that they have won this award or that award (Readers' Choice Poll is a favorite) from travel magazines, as the "Best Ship in the World," or "Best Cruise Line in the World," or "Best Large Cruise Ship" and so on.

In truth, these polls are only as good as the number of people who vote in them, the criteria established, its regulation and tabulation, and the number of ships included. For example, if a magazine in the United States initiates a readers' poll and no readers have cruised aboard a British or Japanese or German or Spanish-speaking cruise ship, that ship will get no votes. It stands to reason that the votes will go to the most traveled ships. The magazines never state the criteria for their decisions.

At Berlitz, we do. That's why *Berlitz Complete Guide to Cruising and Cruise Ships 2011* is the most authoritative guide you can buy. What's more, it is totally independent and in no way subsidized by advertising or sponsorship.

Value for money

The international cruise industry consists of around 75 ocean-going cruise ship operators carrying over 20 million passengers a year. It can provide safe and hassle-free vaca-

tions but offers an almost overwhelming choice. So how do you identify the "X-factor," that special quality that makes a ship stand out from the rest? What this book will do is help you choose the right ship, for the right reasons, and will leave you as well-informed as most specialists in the industry.

An uncertain economic outlook has led to much innovative marketing activity in the industry. Although standards suffered from cost-cutting as the major cruise lines tried to counter the industry's deep discounting (mostly in North America), the lines have since been adding new items to woo

Douglas Ward aboard *SeaDream I.*

WHAT THIS BOOK GIVES YOU

This book is divided into two main parts, followed by a short section of practical information and useful addresses. The first part helps you define what you are looking for in a cruise vacation and advises you on how to find it. It provides a wealth of information, including a look at life aboard ship and how to get the best from it. Specialist cruises are discussed, too, culminating with that ultimate travel experience: the around-the-world cruise.

The book's main section profiles 285 ocean-going cruise vessels. From large to small, from unabashed luxury and exclusivity to ships for the budget-minded, new and old, they are all here.

The ratings and evaluations are a painstaking documentation of the author's personal work. He travels constantly throughout the world, and is at sea for up to 200 days each year. All evaluations have been made objectively, without bias, partiality, or preju-

Evening entertainment in the lobby bar of *Carnival Dream*'s 11-deck-high atrium.

passengers. Examples include premium mattresses and bed linen, ship-wide wi-fi access, and larger spa and sports facilities. Whatever the compromises, it remains true that cruise companies can provide vacation experiences seldom matched in product delivery, cleanliness and friendliness by land-based resorts.

Some things once included in the basic fare now cost extra. The resulting "onboard revenue" helps to compensate the industry for the fact that basic prices are still extremely low, while the newest ships have far more novel features than even a few years ago, and many more dining choices. Discounted pricing has done one thing, however, and that is to open up cruising to a much wider range of

customers, including younger people and more families with children.

All the above changes have affected the ratings of some cruise ships and are reflected in this book.

My 5,600 days at sea

In welcoming new readers to this edition, I should mention my qualifications for assessing cruise ships on your behalf. I first fell in love with ships when, in 1965, I worked Cunard Line's 83,673-ton ocean liner *RMS Queen Elizabeth* – then the world's largest passenger ship. Over the next 17 years, I worked for eight companies, lastly as cruise director.

To date, I have completed over 5,600 days at sea, participating in more than 1,000 cruises, 155 trans-

atlantic crossings and countless Panama Canal transits, plus many shipyard visits, ship naming ceremonies and maiden voyages.

The first edition of this book, reviewing, testing and evaluating 120 ships, appeared in 1985, when cruising seemed to most people an expensive, rarefied experience. Today, the book is the most highly regarded source of comparative information not only for cruise purchasers, but also for cruise industry executives, crew members, and travel agents.

This book is a tribute to everyone who has made my seafaring experiences possible, and I thank the cruise lines for their assistance during the complex scheduling, sailing, inspection, evaluation and rating processes.

dice. In almost all instances, the ships have been visited recently by the author or one of his team in order to assess current status. Passenger comments are taken into account in the final evaluations *(see form on page 720)*.

Please note that, although price indicators are supplied for such things as alternative restaurants, spa treatments and other items, prices may have changed since this book went to press.

Most of the statistical informa-

tion contained in the ship profiles was supplied and checked by the cruise lines and ship owners. Any errors or updated information should be sent to the author at the address shown on the facing page.

Please note that the author's constant ship inspection schedule means he is infrequently on land, and is no longer able to answer letters. However, every comment received will be studied and will help maintain the authority of the next edition for the benefit of all.

CONTENTS

WHAT'S NEW FOR 2011

The trendsetting *Oasis of the Seas* and *Allure of the Seas* are redefining mass-market cruising – but watch out for the growing list of "cruise enhancements" that can cost the unwary a lot of money

Although the credit crunch affected everyone, more than 20 million people took a cruise in 2009. The cruise companies found the economic waters unpleasantly choppy, however. Some smaller ones had to be dismantled, absorbed into larger units, or were re-structured. Cost-cutting was the order of the day. Head offices reduced management and staff, squeezed suppliers and port costs, and tried to make their ships more efficient. The introduction of the hugely successful *Oasis of the Seas* was seen as an indication that things would improve, but 2010 remained a year of cautious growth. Some cruise lines moved ships away from low-profit regions such as Alaska and the Caribbean, and sent them to Europe and Southeast Asia, or Australia.

Heavily discounted pricing kept demand surprisingly buoyant during the worst of the credit crunch. But in spring 2010, some operators, led by Carnival Cruise Lines and Norwegian Cruise Line, raised their cruise prices by about 7%, partly because demand remained high, and partly because operating costs had risen and shareholders were demanding healthier dividends. The lines justified their higher fares by saying they were giving "added value" – in other words, putting back some of the items that had been taken away when the credit crunch began.

An additional pressure came from the cost of implementing the latest requirements of SOLAS (Safety of Life at Sea) in 2010. This meant that some ships had to be retired or sold for scrap. This was sad because some of the older ships (such as *Saga Rose*) had a lot of charm and character – something lacking in many of today's ships with their urban-decor interiors and squared-off, clinical exteriors.

After the credit crunch

One way of making fares seem more attractive was to charge less for the basics but then push hard to earn more onboard revenue from all the "extras" that many passengers don't want in the first place. Put another way, cruising aboard

the large resort ships is now like buying a new car, with so-called "cruise enhancements" being the equivalent of optional extras.

Cruise discounts such as "30%, 40%, 50% or more off brochure prices," or "two for one" prices are really marketing gimmicks used by people more used to selling used cars than vacations. It's better to concentrate on your vacation – where you want to go, what size of ship you want to sail aboard, and what kind of food and service are you willing to pay for – or accept.

The truth about low fares

Although bargains exist, read the small print. A highly discounted fare may apply only to certain dates and itin-eraries – for example, the eastern Caribbean instead of the more popular western Caribbean. They may be sub-ject to a booking deadline or, typically, are "cruise-only," which means you must arrange your own air transportation separately. This can prove expensive (to Alaska or Europe, for example). If air transportation *is* included, deviations may not be possible. Your cabin choice, grade and location may not be available. You could be limited to first seating at dinner (aboard a ship that operates two seatings), and some highly discounted

PRECEDING PAGES: a Lindblad expedition finds a false killer whale in Mexico's Sea of Cortez.
LEFT: *Oasis of the Seas*, the biggest cruise ship yet, salutes 20th-century transportation.
RIGHT: getting away from it all – the classic marketing promise of a cruise vacation.

Balconies offer an escape from the crowds on a large resort ship.

as the Irish airline Ryanair, which charges extra for making a reservation (handling charge), airport check-in, checked baggage, priority boarding, carry-on duty-free items, carrying sports equipment, and changing a flight. It has even proposed charging to use the toilet. There are so many *potential* extra charges, in fact, that it's probably cheaper to book a scheduled airline. Yet even several scheduled carriers are getting in on the act, charging economy passengers, for example, $7 for a pillow and blanket, $25 to check a first bag and $35 to check a second bag for flights within the US, Puerto Rico and the US Virgin Islands – though one bag can be checked free on international flights.

Once you strip all the "free" extras away and obtain the final per-person, per-day cost, you'll have a better idea of what's included, what's not, and how good the "price deal" really is.

Is cruising still good value?

It's never been better, thanks in part because the economic downturn forced cruise lines to offer more incentives – such as onboard credit, cabin upgrades, and other perks – in an effort to keep their companies afloat.

The price of your vacation is protected by advance pricing, so you know before you go that your major outgoings have already been set. A fuel surcharge is the only additional cost that may change at the last minute, although new laws in Australia and the European Union

fares may not apply to children. Port charges, handling fees, fuel surcharges or other taxes may cost extra.

As with low-cost airlines, it's add-ons such as government taxes and perhaps a non-refundable processing fee that take the glow off an apparent give-away price. The cruise lines have taken their cue from outfits such

---

BE PREPARED: SIX CRUISE LINE RIP-OFFS YOU SHOULD AVOID

❶ Currency conversion
Currency conversion is a game where cruise lines win from total control over your onboard account. Using a foreign credit card to pay this account means you could incur currency conversion charges, known in the trade as dynamic currency conversion (DCC). This is because cruise lines may have a "guaranteed exchange rate." When you to pay your bill, the price quoted is recalculated into a "guaranteed" price, which can be higher than the rate quoted by banks or other credit card companies. For example, if your onboard bill is in euros and you pay with a US dollar-based credit card, the cruise line will convert the amount at its convenience – not necessarily on the day of the transaction, but later in the month when conversion rates could change to your disadvantage. Many passengers are annoyed by this tactic, which they learn about only when they

Beware of double-tipping for spa treatments.

receive their credit card statements at home, weeks after their cruise.

❷ Extra gratuities
The major cruise lines typically imprint an *additional* gratuity line on signable receipts for such things as spa treatments or extra-cost coffees or other bar charges, *despite* a 15% gratuity having already been added to the actual cost of the item. Example: for an espresso coffee costing $1.50, a 15% gratuity of 23 cents is added, thus making the total cost $1.73. You are then asked to sign the receipt, but one line *above* the signature line says

"Additional Gratuity" – thus inviting you to pay a *double* gratuity. What a rip-off!

❸ Transfer buses
The cost of airport transfer buses in some ports, such as Athens, Barcelona, and Civitavecchia (the port for Rome).

❹ Mineral water
The cost of bottled mineral water for shore excursions. Example: Celebrity Cruises charges $4.50, but then adds another 15% gratuity "for your convenience."

❺ Navigation bridge tours
You'd like to see the view from the bridge? Princess Cruises charges $150 per person to be entered into a "raffle" to compete for just six available tickets to visit the ship's bridge. Still want to see it?

❻ Bingo cards
The cost of cards for a game of Bingo is rising dramatically. Example: NCL now charges $40 for a block of four cards.

require all add-on port charges, charged gratuities, taxes and fuel surcharges to be included in the advertised price ("single figure advertising").

How to get the best deal

● Find out what's available by reading newspaper advertising and checking the internet. Then identify a travel agency that *specializes* in cruises – they'll be bonded if they belong to the UK's Passenger Shipping Association. A good agent will get you the best price, as well as get you upgrades and other benefits you won't be able to get on your own.

● Big travel agency groups and consortiums often reserve large blocks of cabins, and smaller independent agencies can access extensive discounts not available on the internet. Because the cruise lines consider travel agents as their principal distribution system, they provide special discounts and value-added amenities that are not provided to internet sites.

● Cruise lines offer their best prices to those who book early. It's worth taking the bait to get the best choice of cabin and location, and the best chance of any upgrades, in case any are offered closer to your sailing date. Booking late may sometimes get you cheaper prices, too, perhaps due to cancellations, but you *won't* get a choice of cabins and locations, so you could end up with a tiny cupboard above the galley.

● If you're on a tight budget, book an interior (no view) cabin on one of the best ships, instead of an outside cabin on a less fancy ship. This buys you better food and entertainment for the same money.

● If you're on a tight budget, a number of ships feature drinks-inclusive pricing – this can save you a bundle in extra onboard costs and is particularly good for families with children.

● Savvy passengers join frequent passenger clubs to get maximum benefits. These offer additional perks (onboard credit, free wi-fi service, private cocktail parties), and further discounts for booking your next cruise while on board (at prices not available on the internet).

● Check to make sure that all port charges, government fees, and any fuel surcharges are included in an advertised price quote.

● If you find a highly dis-

Music and fun rule at the easyCruise end of the market.

Braving the weather on a *Queen Mary 2* voyage.

counted cruise rate on the internet, fine. But, if a cruise line suddenly offers special discounts for your sailing, or cabin upgrades, or things go wrong with your booking, your internet booking service may prove quite unfriendly (many are not licensed or bonded). Your specialist travel agent, however, can probably work magic in making those special discounts and upgrades work for you – and travel agents do not charge for their service.

● **...and a deal to avoid:** Don't fall for one of those automated telemarketing scams (mainly operated from the United States) which tell you "Congratulations! You've won a free two-night cruise" or, "If you just answer our 10-question survey we'll send you two boarding passes for a two-night Bahamas cruise". These are scams – nothing more – and are *not* connected to genuine cruise lines. Don't even *think* about giving your credit card details "for port taxes".

E-cruising arrives

The major cruise lines have decreed that we're now in the digital age – which means online check-in. This makes life difficult for anyone with arthritis or typing problems, or for households without a computer, and bad luck if there's a power outage, or if your router or computer gives up the ghost. There's a lot to be said for letting your travel agent do it all for you.

Inevitably, though, there will be a greater reliance on e-technology, and this means the reduction of the number of paper tickets. Only the really exclusive, upscale cruise lines, expedition companies and tall ship lines will provide boxes or wallets packed with documents, cruise tickets, leather (or faux-leather) luggage tags and colourful destination booklets – cruise lines operating large resorts ships have all but abandoned such niceties already. Aboard ship, e-technology will be increasingly prominent. Today, we are seeing the disappearance of printed news sheets and sports results, with news only available on in-cabin "interactive" television systems.

There's no escaping the internet and social networks.

Fewer new ships on the horizon

Following the economic meltdown of 2008–9, the cost of newbuilds – and the cost of borrowing money to finance them – went north. Several factors were to blame: the higher price of steel, the higher cost of labor; and the higher fees demanded by banks, private finance groups and others lending money for construction and shipbuilding guarantees. The good news for cruise lines is that, because there is space in shipyards for new orders, delivery times are more convenient since they don't like accepting ships in the middle of winter.

In 2011, some 42 ships measuring over 100,000 gross tonnage will be in service *(see page 157)*, but, as this book went to press, only 20 new ships were scheduled

for delivery between January 2011 and the end of 2014. Orders for new ships have slowed down because, while most cruise lines earn their money in US dollars, ships are built in Europe, where the relatively weak dollar buys fewer euros than it used to. However, the new ships will come complete with the latest fuel-efficient technology.

Some of the new large resort ships look rather top-heavy. This is because the space above the bridge is increasingly assigned to the "pay more, get more" passengers who want exclusivity – suites, larger cabins, "private" lounges, exclusive dining venues, and relaxation areas – within the body of a larger ship.

Unless cruise lines spend money on ship makeovers, the tonnage that was delivered in the past 10 years – 127 ships between January 2000 and the end of 2010 – can quickly become old and tired, particularly those ships used for short cruises, where more wear and tear is normal. Cruise lines will need to build new tonnage in order to stay ahead of the competition – or so the shipyards hope. Cruise lines with older ships will opt for refits or big refurbishment projects to keep them fresh in the face of competition from the latest generation of high-tech, high-efficiency ships.

Movies squeeze out music

Passengers have seen an increase in the number of ships with pay-extra in-cabin movies for their flat-screen TV sets, and the disappearance of separate music channels with their two or three piped-in channels (one rock/jazz, one contemporary, and, possibly, one classical channel).

Getting on the brandwagon

Ever image-conscious, cruise lines are jockeying to become the "greenest" brand. Size is a major factor and so each line touts the benefits of its particular size of ship. For that reason, choosing the right sized ship for your vacation is now more important than ever.

Rebranding sometimes involves a change

AT A GLANCE: THE LATEST TRENDS

How Disney Cruise Line announced it is getting into the Alaska market.

- More large resort ships, charging for "extras."
- More multi-generational cruising aboard the large resort ships.
- More single-parent cruising.
- More child-free ships, for those who have matured beyond noise and games.
- Small ship cruising, for those seeking to avoid large resort ships and crowds.

- More themed dining venues.
- More sophisticated spas and well-being treatment options.
- More "healthy eating" and "spa" menu choices.
- An increasing variety of active adventures ashore.
- Demand for smoking-free ships.
- More demand for longer cruises.
- More demand for short "getaway" cruises.

of name. Azamara Cruises, for example, has restyled itself more intimately as Azamara Club Cruises, while Seabourn Cruise Line sounds much more elegant as The Yachts of Seabourn.

The growth of shopping malls

Onboard "enhancement" items – such as luggage and tote bags, bed linen, personal amenities, wooden deck lounge (steamer) chairs, coffee tables and chairs, ship posters, cruise line memorabilia and collectibles, wine glasses, chocolate, flowers, and even mattresses – can now be purchased online from the major cruise lines (examples: www.carnivalcomfortbed .com; www.shop-hollandamerica.com). But such online shopping only works if you have a US address and credit card.

A floating playground

The world's "largest ever" cruise ships, Royal Caribbean International's *Oasis of the Seas* and *Allure of the Seas,* are redefining large resort ship cruising. With 16 passenger decks and a capacity of more than 6,000 passengers, they are innovative and exciting – which means they are not quiet and relaxing.

Being aboard such a floating playground can be like being in a large shopping mall, which does please some people. But waiting for an elevator can be frustrating. Disembarkation is a bit like getting out of a sports stadium at the end of a big game. After which, of course, you'll need to locate your luggage.

Mid-size ships benefit from the introduction of so many large resort ships because more and more experienced cruisegoers are downsizing to avoid the big ships' sanitized cruise experience and long lines.

Dining and service

"Alternative" restaurants are fashionable, particularly aboard the large resort ships, and are ideal for escaping from huge dining halls full of noise and singing, table-dancing waiters. These are typically à la carte restaurants where you must make a reservation, and pay to dine in small, intimate places with superior food cooked à la minute, good wines and service, and a less frenetic ambiance. But a couple each having two glasses of palatable wine could, with the cover charge, easily end up paying $100 for dinner.

Cruise lines stuck with traditional two-seating dining are looking for ways to be more flexible (without placing an extra burden on the staff). More ships offer flexible dining and 24-hour casual (get-your-own food) eateries, so you can eat or snack when you want. Although the concept is good, the delivery often is not; it is typically self-service eating, and not the dining and service experience most passengers envisage.

When big isn't better

Cruising's impact on local economies remains an unresolved issue. While cruise ships are good for island economies (in the Caribbean, for example), the large resort ships can double the population of small islands, swamping local resources and tour infrastructure. However quaint an island may sound in a brochure, it becomes markedly less so when thousands of passengers disembark. ❑

HOW CRUISE LINES CUT COSTS TO STAY AFLOAT

The trick is to save costs while still offering value for money. But of course there'll always be people who buy rock-bottom fares and then complain when they don't get lobster every night. Cruise lines have also trimmed costs by increasing efficiency – the latest ships have more efficient power-plants, for example – and some have reduced staff.

Food is a target for cost-cutting.

15 cost-cutting ploys:

- By reducing menu selections
- By reducing food portions in main dining venues
- By providing cheaper cuts of meat (pork instead of beef)
- By reducing the strength of "free" coffee
- By reducing the variety of green vegetables
- By removing trays from self-serve buffets (some lines) so you can't carry as much food
- By reducing service levels and giving minimal training
- By charging for ship postcards that used to be free
- By replacing live flowers with silk flowers
- By reducing in-cabin toiletries
- By cutting speed between ports
- By switching to lower-cost suppliers
- By removing free writing paper and postcards
- By taking advantage of bulk buying (across several brands)
- By "squeezing" port agents, berthing and handling charges

Adding "value"
Some major cruise lines are desperately trying to put back some of the things that the accountants did away with in the past few years and then boasting about "adding value."

DOES THE NEW QUEEN DESERVE ITS CROWN?

Queen Elizabeth 2 was a celebrity among ocean liners, commanding fierce loyalty from its passengers. How will the new *Queen Elizabeth* measure up?

The 1,728-passenger *QE2*, retired to Dubai in 2008 after almost 40 years as the world's fastest ocean liner, is a hard act to follow, and its legion of fans will look critically at the new 2,092-passenger *Queen Elizabeth*, which made its debut in October 2010.

The two ships have some things in common. One is the bright Cunard red and black funnel – a tradition since 1837 when the company was founded by Samuel Cunard in Halifax, Nova Scotia. Another is Cunard Line's esteemed brand name, traditionally associated with elegance and grandeur.

But there the comparisons end. To appreciate why, you have to understand why Cunard's parent, the Miami-based Carnival Corporation, sold *QE2*. The ship, built in 1969 to tackle both high-speed transatlantic crossings and occasional cruises, was becoming uneconomical as a cruise ship because of increasing competition from newer ships and because of rising fuel costs. In addition, it would have needed a lot of structural changes to comply with the latest SOLAS (Safety of Life at Sea) regulations and amendments that came into force on October 1, 2010.

Today, a very different Cunard ship, the *Queen Mary 2*, built in 2004, carries on the tradition of transatlantic crossings but, crucially, it is also designed to cater for leisurely cruising. For example, only 32 of *QE2*'s 950 cabins had private balconies, compared with 953 of *QM2*'s 1,310 cabins. So it is with the new *Queen Elizabeth*, a sister ship to *Queen Victoria*, which entered service in 2007 and whose 1,007 cabins include 718 with private balconies.

Although the new *QE* is not a classic ocean liner, it tries valiantly to evoke the image of one, and Cunard's brochures take care to refer to "voyages" rather than "cruises." Above all, that beautifully sculpted red and black funnel evokes the long-gone days when grandeur and elegance prevailed and a ship was a means of transportation rather than a resort at sea.

BELOW: the 92,000-ton *Queen Elizabeth*.

TOP: the Queens Room in the new ship has an art deco appeal.
ABOVE: *QE*'s 6,000-book library is run by two full-time librarians.

ABOVE: the 830-seat Royal Court Theatre is designed in the style of a classic opera house, with 20 private "royal boxes."

ABOVE: the *QE2* joined its namesake on a 1969 British postage stamp.

HOW THE TWO QUEENS DIFFER

QE2's interiors had public rooms that could be closed off by glass doors to create separate spaces, whereas the new *Queen Elizabeth* has "open architecture" that lets passengers float between one room and the next, encouraging them to feel they are not in a contained environment but are free to roam everywhere, as in a classless society. The only significant exception is a small lounge/club room restricted to occupants of the more exclusive Queens Grill accommodation.

Open architecture does have its drawbacks, especially when live music "bleeds" from one environment to the next. *QE* does, however, have some delightfully private spaces, such as a beautiful 6,000-book library (with spiral staircase), caringly stocked by the UK's Ocean Books, long familiar with the reading tastes of Cunard passengers.

QE2 had 10 interior stairways, each colored differently to help people identify exactly where they were, whereas *QE*'s three stairways have common-theme carpeting (which is easier to store and replace). Although SOLAS safety regulations don't encourage the use of real wood, both the old and new ships have ballroom-sized dance floors made of genuine wood, and there's still live music for proper dancing. The new ship has a three-deck high main entrance lobby/reception area, whereas *QE2*'s was a single deck in height.

QE2's cabins were certainly larger, and with higher ceilings, larger bathrooms and more drawer and storage space than those aboard the new ship, but then QE has a far larger proportion of cabins with private balconies than its predecessor. *QE2* had a baggage room to store luggage on long voyages, whereas *QE* expects you to bring less clothing since the emphasis is on slightly less formal attire. *QE2* had many single-occupancy cabins, but QE has none – a victim of corporate arithmetic that rates double-occupancy as more profitable.

QE2's service was legendary. The ship had – at least in the early days – real loose tea at teatime, and cloth napkins. And *QE*? It uses teabags and paper napkins.

ABOVE: *QE* being built in Italy at Fincantieri's Monfalcone yard.
BELOW: British-style bowls on *QE*'s games deck.

CRUISING'S UNSTOPPABLE GROWTH

When the first jet aircraft made many of the old
passengers liners redundant, some were scrapped
but others gave birth to the modern cruise industry

Twenty-six years ago, the first edition of this book listed 120 ships, about 30 of which are still operating in one form or another. Today, that number has grown to more than 280 (around 350 including the list of ships operating coastal cruises). Throughout the period, the cruise industry has maintained a global growth rate of over 7% each year. But many well-known cruise lines have also gone to the deep blue seabed in the past 25 years. Indeed, since 1990 more than 60 cruise lines have either merged, or been taken over, or simply gone out of business, including such well-liked companies as Royal Cruise Lines, Royal Viking Line, and Sun Line Cruises.

Some start-up lines, using older ships, and aimed at specific markets also came and went – operations like American Family Cruises, Fiesta Marina Cruises, Premier Cruise Lines and Regency Cruises. In came new shiny tonnage, complete with vanity logos and adornments painted on all-white

A classic Cunard Line poster.

WHO GOES CRUISING

The Maritime Evaluations Group has analyzed by nationality the breakdown of cruise line passengers:

United States	13,500,000
Europe (excluding UK)	2,900,000
UK	1,550,000
Asia (excluding Japan)	600,000
Canada	770,000
Australia/New Zealand	330,000
Scandinavia	200,000
Japan	180,000
Cyprus *	75,000
Freighter Passengers	3,000
Total	20,108,000

Local Cyprus market only.

Note: The above numbers include the approximately 1 million passengers who took a river/inland waterway cruise, but not the 300,000 passengers who took a coastal voyage aboard the Hurtigruten (Norwegian Coastal Voyages) ships. All figures are for 2009.

hulls – the attributes of the industry's emerging giants. Fresh thinking transformed the design of accommodation, the use of public spaces, and more food and entertainment venues.

Yield management, a term purloined from the airline industry, was introduced. These days company executives think of little else, because running a cruise company is all about economics.

Modern cruising is born

In the early 1960s, passenger-shipping directories listed over 100 passenger lines. Until the mid-1960s, it was cheaper to cross the Atlantic by ship than by plane, but the appearance of the jet aircraft changed that rapidly, particularly with the introduction of the Boeing 747 in the early 1970s. In 1962, more than 1 million people crossed the North Atlantic by ship; in 1970, that number was down to 250,000.

The success of the jumbo jets created a fleet of unprofitable and out-of-work passenger liners that appeared doomed for the scrap heap. Even the famous big "Queens," noted for their regular weekly transatlantic service, were at risk. Cunard White Star Line's *Queen Mary* (81,237 gross tonnage) was withdrawn in September 1967.

Cunard Line's sister ship *Queen Elizabeth*, at 83,673 gross tonnage the largest-ever passenger liner (until 1996), made its final crossing in November 1968.

Ships were sold for a fraction of their value. Many lines went out of business and ships were scrapped. Those that survived attempted to mix transatlantic crossings with voyages south to the sun. The Caribbean (including the Bahamas) became appealing, cruising became an alternative, and an entire new industry was born, with new lines being formed exclusively for cruising.

Then smaller, more specialized ships arrived, capable of getting into the tiny ports of developing Caribbean islands; there were no commercial airlines taking vacationers to the Caribbean then, and few hotels. Instead of cruising long distances south from more northerly ports such as New York, companies established their headquarters in Florida. This avoided the cold weather, choppy seas, and expense of the northern ports and saved fuel costs with shorter runs to the Caribbean.

Cruising was reborn. California became the base for cruises to the Mexican Riviera, and Vancouver on Canada's west coast was the focus for summer cruises to Alaska.

Flying passengers to embarkation ports was the next logical step, and soon a working relationship emerged between the cruise lines and the airlines. Air/sea and "sail and stay" packages thrived – joint cruise and hotel vacations with inclusive pricing. Some of the old liners came out of mothballs, purchased by emerging cruise lines and refurbished for warm-weather cruising operations, often with their interiors redesigned and refitted. During the late 1970s, the modern cruise industry grew at a rapid rate.

Detail from a classic Hamburg-Amerika Linie poster.

Cruising today

Today's cruise concept hasn't changed much from that of earlier days, although it has been improved, refined, expanded, and packaged for ease of consumption. No longer the domain of affluent, retired people, cruising today attracts passengers of *every* age and socio-economic background. It's no longer the shipping business, but the hospitality industry – although it has to be said that some cruise ship personnel appear to be in the hostility industry.

New ships are generally larger than their predeces-

BERLITZ RATES THE BEST AND WORST U.S. HOMELAND PORTS

Berlitz constantly receives complaints about the forceful tactics of baggage handlers (porters) at the Port of Miami, and Port Everglades (Fort Lauderdale). As passengers alight from buses from the airport (which often have a sign stating: "Tips Not Included"), the baggage handlers ask passengers to identify their baggage, which they then place into luggage cages. For this "service," passengers are asked to tip generously – for what is a simple "lift and move three feet" job.

So, do the math. If each baggage handler receives the requested $1–$2 per bag tip, and the ship carries 5,000 passengers, that's a lot of moolah. Be smart: *don't* let them bully you into thinking your luggage won't get to your ship in time for your cruise – a threat often used. They are responsible for making sure that all bags *do* go to the ship on time – yours included.

Coping with the giants

There's no reason why ports should be any more immune from terrorist attacks than air-

Queen Mary 2 sails from Brooklyn.

ports, but the need for sensible safety measures has been taken to extremes by overenthusiastic security personnel at some United States and Canadian ports. After many complaints, the Maritime Evaluations Group has built a picture of ports based on their user-friendliness and sense of hospitality. Maximum score is 100.

As a benchmark, the terminal facilities, luggage handling, user-friendliness and hospitality factor of personnel at the Port of Yokohama in Japan score an impressive 94 out of 100. The comparison with the typical experience in US homeland ports is telling.

What the berth marks mean

In allocating points, we took account of the following factors: terminals and appearance and cleanliness, security personnel, attitude, check-in, security control, luggage handling by porters (often seeking tips), ease of disembarkation, immigration and customs, security personnel, luggage storage and identification system, porters, and ease of access to transportation and car parks.

FACILITIES RATED OUT OF 100

Port	Total
Baltimore	63
Boston	60
Cape Liberty, Bayonne, New Jersey	57
Charleston	53
Fort Lauderdale (Port Everglades)	45
Galveston	45
Gulfport	44
Honolulu	54
Houston	52
Jacksonville	44
Los Angeles (Long Beach)	48
Los Angeles (San Pedro)	52
Miami	42
Montreal	53
New Orleans	50
New York (Brooklyn)	81
New York (Manhattan)	68
Norfolk	52
Philadelphia	49
Port Canaveral	54
St. Thomas	51
San Diego	55
San Francisco	49
San Juan	46
Seattle	59
Tampa	53
Vancouver	72

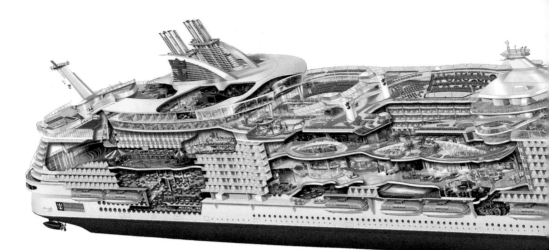

sors, yet cabin size is "standardized" to provide more space for entertainment and other public facilities. Today's ships boast air conditioning to keep out heat and humidity; stabilizers to keep the ship on an even keel; a high level of maintenance, safety, and hygiene; and more emphasis on health and fitness facilities.

Although ships have long been devoted to eating and relaxation in comfort, ships today offer more activities, and more learning and life-enriching experiences than before. For the same prices as a quarter of a century ago, you can cruise aboard the latest large resort ships that offer ice skating, rock climbing, golfing, roller blading, wave surfing, bowling, and so on while dining at fine restaurants that offer varied cuisines, being pampered in luxurious spas, and being entertained by high-quality production shows. And there are many more places you can visit on a cruise: from Antarctica to Acapulco, Bermuda to Bergen, Dakar to Dominica, Shanghai to St Thomas.

Cruising tomorrow

Current ship design follows two quite distinct paths: large resort ships or smaller niche-market ships.
● Large resort ships, where "economy of scale" helps the operator to keep the cost per passenger down. The first, *Carnival Destiny*, debuted in 1996, and today seven companies have ships measuring over 100,000 gross tonnage (see page 157). Some

---

WHAT'S NEW IN THE MODERN CRUISE INDUSTRY – BUT NOT ALWAYS AN IMPROVEMENT

- Cruise-only travel agents
- Pay-extra dining venues
- Vacuum (barking-dog) toilets
- "Art" auctions, jewelry shops
- Vibration-less "pod" propulsion systems
- On-line check in for some of the major cruise lines
- Balcony- and French-balcony, loft and lobby cabins
- Child-free ships
- Child-only playrooms and teen clubs
- More active and adventurous shore excursions
- Medivac helicopter lift for medical treatment
- Cashless cruising ("just sign here!")
- Electronic cabin key cards
- Pay-extra adult-only sanctuaries
- Pay-extra spa and wellness facilities
- Pay-extra tours to view the "Back of House"

Medivac rescues are a big plus.

- Personal safes
- Exclusive private accommodation areas (effectively gated communities)

- Multi-room suites for multi-generational families or friends
- Satellite-linked telephones in cabins
- Interactive touch- and flat screen cabin television sets
- Gratuities charged automatically to your onboard account or online pre-pay
- Much wider choice of dining venues, eateries, and food
- High-tech production shows, click-tracks
- Internet-connect centers, wi-fi, and e-mail facilities
- Large casinos, themed lounges and bars
- Huge self-serve stuff-your-face buffets (camping at sea)
- Better facilities for the frail and physically challenged
- "Private island" beach days
- Cruises for gays, singles, and themed groups
- More sports facilities (rock

- climbing walls, ice-skating rinks, golf simulators, bowling alleys, boxing rings, race car simulators, surf-riders)
- Deluge of sales flyers under cabin door
- Digital photographs and personal videos
- Lack of dress code
- Passengers with tattoos, and tracksuits
- A crew that can't speak your language
- Security personnel aboard ship who don't understand hospitality (but they're worse in the cruise terminals)
- Obnoxious port security staff for embarkation
- Sunbed hoggers
- Roll-over lifeboats
- Headline-making attacks of norovirus
- Overboards (whether for crime, accident, "assisted" suicide, or insurance money)

THE BIGGEST OF THE BIG

Oasis of the Seas and *Allure of the Seas* are floating cities, complete with parks and boulevards. Each ship can accommodate 6,296 passengers and 2,164 crew.

accommodate more than 5,000 passengers, with the "bigger is better" principle being pursued for all it's worth. Many are, however, too wide to transit the Panama Canal and so are designated non-Panamax.

● Small ships, where the "small is beautiful" concept has taken hold, particularly in the exclusive and luxury categories. Cruise lines offer high-quality ships of low capacity, which can provide a highly personalized range of quality services. This means better trained, more experienced staff (and more of them to serve fewer passengers), higher-quality food, and more meals cooked to order. Small ships can also visit the less overcrowded ports.

Other cruise lines have expanded by "stretching" their ships. This is accomplished literally by cutting a ship in half, and inserting a newly constructed midsection, thus instantly adding more accommodation and public rooms, while maintaining the same draft.

Ships that have been "stretched" (with year and length of "stretch") include: *Albatros* (1983, 27.7 meters), *Aquamarine* (1980, 26 meters), *Balmoral* (2007, 30 meters), *Black Watch* (1981, 27.7 meters), *Boudicca* (1982, 27.7 meters), *Braemar* (2008, 31.2 meters), *Enchantment of the Seas* (2005, 22.2 meters), *Louis Majesty* (1999, 30 meters), *Norwegian Dream* (1998, 40 meters), *Spirit of Adventure* (1986, 20 meters), *SuperStar Aquarius* (1998, 40 meters), and *Thomson Dream* (1990, 40 meters).

More exclusivity

Gated communities at sea are likely to proliferate. These areas are accessible only to those willing to pay extra to "live" in one of the larger suites, and gain access to "private" facilities, concierge lounges, and private sunbathing areas. Ships that have them: *MSC Fantasia, MSC Splendida, Norwegian Epic, Norwegian Gem, Norwegian Jade, Norwegian Pearl*. So two-class cruising (in some cases, three-class cruising) is back. ❑

HIGHLIGHTS OF THE PAST 25 YEARS

1985 The Chandris Group of Companies acquired Fantasy Cruises from GoGo Tours, renaming it Chandris Fantasy Cruises in the US and Chandris Cruises in the UK. *Achille Lauro* was hijacked in the Mediterranean by the Palestine Liberation Front.

1986 Direct-dial satellite calls were introduced. Cunard acquired Sea Goddess Cruises.

1987 *Queen Elizabeth 2* was converted from steam turbine to diesel-electric power.

1988 Royal Caribbean Cruise Line merged with Admiral Cruises to form Royal Admiral Cruises (later Royal Caribbean Cruises). Carnival Cruise Lines acquired Holland America Line. Seabourn Cruise Line's first ship, *Seabourn Pride*, entered service.

1989 The Chandris Group of Companies created Celebrity Cruises. The Panama Canal celebrated its 75th birthday.

1990 At the start of the Gulf War, the US government chartered *Cunard Princess* for six months as a rest and relaxation center for US service personnel in the Bahrain.

1991 Carnival Cruise Lines acquired a 25 percent stake in Seabourn Cruise Line.

1992 Chargeurs and Accor, the French property and leisure industries group, bought 23% of Costa Crociere, parent of Costa Cruises.

1993 Star Cruises was founded by Malaysia's Genting Group.

1994 Radisson Diamond Cruises and Seven Seas Cruise Line merged to become Radisson Seven Seas Cruises.

1995 British company Airtours purchased *Southward* from Norwegian Cruise Line and *Nordic Prince* from Royal Caribbean Cruises.

1996 Cunard (and parent company Trafalgar House) were bought by Kvaerner.

1997 Carnival Corporation, jointly with Airtours, purchased Costa Cruises. Royal Caribbean International bought Celebrity Cruises.

1998 Kvaerner sold Cunard to Carnival Corporation. Norwegian Cruise Line bought Orient Lines.

1999 Crown Cruise Line was reintroduced as an upscale part of Commodore Cruise Line.

2000 Star Cruises took full control of Norwegian Cruise Line (including Orient Lines) after buying the outstanding shares held by Carnival Corporation. P&O Group separated its cruising activities from the rest of the group. Costa Cruises became 100% owned by Carnival Corporation.

2001 Renaissance Cruises (10 ships) ceased operations after the September 11 terrorist attacks on the US – one of several casualties.

2002 SeaDream Yacht Club began with *SeaDream I* and *SeaDream II*.

2003 NCL America launched its US-flag operation.

2004 Carnival Corporation and P&O Princess plc merged to become the world's largest cruise company, with more than 60 ships and 13 brands.

2005 Orion Expedition Cruises launched with one ship, *Orion*.

2006 Radisson Seven Seas Cruises became Regent Seven Seas Cruises. Royal Caribbean International bought Pullmantur.

2007 Celebrity Cruises created a sub-brand, Azamara Cruises. *Queen Elizabeth 2* was sold for £50 million ($100 million) to a state investment company in Dubai, to be refitted and become a floating hotel and museum alongside the Palm Jumeirah.

2008 Fred Olsen Cruise Lines "stretched" its *Braemar* by 102ft (31.2 meters). Almost all cruise lines added or increased their fuel surcharges to future cruises in the face of rising oil prices. Most paddlewheel riverboats ceased operations in the USA.

2009 Island Cruises was acquired by TUI Travel's Thomson Cruises division. TUI Cruises started cruising with one ship. Imperial Majesty Cruise Line ceased operations, replaced by Celebration Cruise Line. Azamara Cruises was renamed Azamara Club Cruises. Seabourn Cruise Line changed its name to The Yachts of Seabourn.

2010 The Ocean Village brand disappears; its two ships join the P&O Cruises (Australia) fleet. Island Cruises becomes a sub-brand of Thomson Cruises. NCL America is merged into Norwegian Cruise Line (NCL).

WHAT THE BROCHURES DON'T ALWAYS TELL YOU

We answer frankly the questions about ocean cruising most frequently asked both by those new to this type of vacation and by experienced passengers

GENERAL DEFINITIONS

What exactly *is* a cruise?

A cruise is a vacation, an escape from the stress and strain of life ashore, a floating hotel where you have to unpack only once. It offers you a chance to relax and unwind in comfortable surroundings, with attentive service, good food, and a ship that changes the scenery for you. It can be a hassle-free, and, more importantly, a crime-free vacation. Everything's close to hand, and there are always polite people to help you. A cruise provides great value for money, variety (in ship size, destinations, facilities, cuisine, entertainment, activities and shore excursions), a chance to explore new places, meet new people, make friends, and, above all, provides the ingredients for a wonderful vacation.

More than 350 ocean-going cruise ships carrying

from 50 to more than 6,000 passengers visit almost 2,000 destinations throughout the world, and new ships are being constantly introduced. They range from under 200 ft (60 meters) to over 1,100 ft (330 meters) in length, and their shapes vary enormously. Facilities, food, and service vary from company to company, and according to the size of the ship.

Ambiance ranges from ultra-casual to very formal (starchy and reserved). Entertainment ranges from amateur dramatics to full-fledged high-tech production shows and circus-like theatrics, from the corner cabaret to a world-famous headliner.

How long does a cruise last?

The popular standard length is seven days, although cruises can vary from two-day party cruises to a slow exotic voyage around the world of up to 180 days. There are even passengers who stay aboard some ships all year round, and disembark only when the ship has to go into dry dock for refits. If you are new to cruising and want to "get your feet wet," try a short cruise first. Its length will depend on the time and money at your disposal and the degree of comfort you are seeking, but more leisurely cruises can last 14 days or more. To operate long, low-density voyages, cruise lines must charge high rates to cover the extensive preparations, high food and transportation costs, port operations, fuel, and so on.

Tall tale: *Carnival Pride* passes Maryland's *Pride of Baltimore II.*

WHO GOES CRUISING

Isn't cruising really meant for old people?

The average age of passengers gets younger each year, with the average age of first-timers now well under 40. But retirees find cruising a safe and comfortable way to travel and many have plenty of get-up-and-go.

On a typical cruise you're likely to meet singles, couples, families with

An active Quark Expeditions cruise to South Georgia.

children of all ages (including single parents and grand-parents), honeymooners (some second- or third-time around), groups of friends, and college buddies. You may even run across your next-door neighbors.

Won't I get bored?

Usually, it's the men who ask this question, but get them aboard and often there's not enough time in the day to try all the things they want to do – as long as you choose the right ship, for the right reasons.

There are more things to do aboard today's ships than there is on almost any Caribbean island. So, whether you want to lie back and be pampered, or be active non-stop, you can do it on a cruise, and you will have to pack and unpack only once.

Just being at sea provides an intoxicating sense of freedom that few places on dry land can offer. And, in case you think you may feel cut off without contact, almost all large resort ships (those carrying over 1,600 passengers) offer internet access, pay-per-view movies, digital music libraries, and ship-wide wi-fi access.

Isn't it all very regimented?

Some cruises simply aren't relaxing, despite cruise brochure claims that "you can do as much or as little as you want to." For example, the large resort ships carrying more than 1,600 passengers, and particularly those with 5,000-plus, cram lots of people into small cabins and provide nonstop activities that insult the intelligence and assault the wallet. The purpose of this book is to help you identify the cruise that's right for you.

Are there facilities for singles?

Yes. A cruise vacation is good for those traveling alone (over 25 percent of all passengers are solo travelers –

worldwide, that's over 4 million a year), because it is easy to meet other people in a non-competitive environment. Many ships have dedicated cabins for singles and special add-on rates for single occupancy of double cabins. Some cruise lines will even find a cabin mate for you to share with, if you so desire.

However, in cabins with three or four berths (two beds plus upper berths), personal privacy doesn't exist. Some companies sell two-bed cabins at a special single rate, forgetting that many people who cruise solo do so

I'M NEW TO THIS. WHERE DO I START?

First, think about where you want to go, how long a cruise you would like, and how much money you want to spend. How large a ship would you like to cruise aboard? Then, find a good travel agent who specialises in cruises and can match your needs, requirements, lifestyle, and personality. Ask the following questions:

❶ What size cruise ship would you recommend?
❷ What should I budget for the cruise?
❸ What is included in the cruise price?
❹ What extra costs can I expect to pay?
❺ Which destinations are included?
❻ What kind of accommodation would suit my tastes and budget?
❼ What is the ship's onboard ambience like?
❽ What facilities does the ship have?
❾ What kind of food and service does it provide?
❿ What kind of entertainment should I expect?

You can also research the internet, although you won't be able to ask those all-important questions.

because their partner has died, and the last thing they want is to be in a cabin with two beds.

Why is it so expensive for singles?

Because it's a couples world in most of the travel trade. Almost all cruise lines base their rates on double occupancy, as do hotels. Thus, when you travel alone, the cabin portion of your fare reflects an additional supplement. While almost all new ships are built with cabins for double occupancy, older ships have more single-occupancy cabins. Cruise line special offers are nearly always aimed at double-occupancy passengers.

Is there enough to keep kids busy?

A cruise provides families with more quality time than any other type of vacation, and family cruising is the industry's largest growth segment, with activities are tailored to various age groups. Responding to this trend, Disney Cruise Line is doubling, from two to four, its family-friendly fleet.

The Serenity adults-only retreat aboard *Carnival Dream*.

A cruise is also educational, allows children to interact in a crime-free environment, and takes them to destinations in comfortable, familiar surroundings. In fact, children have such a good time aboard ship and ashore, you may have difficulty getting them home after the cruise – as long as you have chosen the right ship.

If you cruise aboard one of the major cruise lines, you may find gratuities for your children automatically added to your onboard account – or you may be able to pre-pay on-line. NCL, for example, requests $6 per day from each child of 3–12 years, while those over 13 pay the adult rate of $10 per day.

● *See also Cruising for Families, pages 71–81.*

Are there child-free ships?

If you don't like crowds, noise, and long lines, try a small ship – a sail-cruise vessel or a river or barge cruise could also provide the right escape. Companies that operate child-free ships include P&O Cruises (*Adonia, Arcadia*) and Saga Cruises (*Spirit of Adventure, Saga Pearl II, Saga Ruby*).

DO CRUISES SUIT HONEYMOONERS?

Absolutely. A cruise is the ideal setting for romance, for shipboard weddings aboard ships with the right registry (they can also be arranged in some ports, depending on local regulations), receptions, and honeymoons. Most decisions are already made for you, so all you have to do is show up. Many ships have double, queen- or king-sized beds, too. And for those on a second honeymoon, many ships can perform a "renewal of vows" ceremony; some will make a charge for this service.

HEALTH ISSUES

Will I get seasick?

Today's ships have stabilizers – large underwater "fins" on each side of the hull – to counteract any rolling motion, and most cruises are in warm, calm waters. As a result, fewer than 3 percent of passengers become seasick. Yet it's possible to develop some symptoms – anything from slight nausea to vomiting.

Both old-time sailors and modern physicians have their own remedies, and you can take your choice or try them all (but not at the same time):

● When you notice the first movement of a ship, walk back and forth on the deck. You will find that your knees, which are our own form of stabilizer, will start getting their feel of balance and counteraction. This is known as "getting your sea legs."
● Get the sea breeze into your face (arguably the best antidote), and if nauseous, suck an orange or a lemon.
● Eat lightly. Do not make the mistake of thinking a heavy meal will keep your stomach anchored. It won't.
● When on deck, focus on a steady point, such as the horizon.

Drugs: Dramamine (dimenhydrinate, an anti-histamine and sedative introduced just after World War II) will be available aboard in tablet (chewable) form. A stronger version (Meclazine) is available on prescription (brand names: Antivert, Antrizine, Bonine, Meni-D). Ciba-Geigy's Scopoderm (or Transderm Scop), known as "The Patch," contains scopolamine and has proven effective. Possible side effects are dry mouth, blurred vision, drowsiness and problems with urinating.

If you are really distressed, the ship's doctor can give you, at extra cost, an injection to alleviate discomfort. It may make you drowsy, but the last thing on your mind will be staying awake during the movie.

A natural preventive is ginger in powder form. Mix half a teaspoon in a glass of warm water or milk, and drink it before sailing. This is said to settle any stomach for up to eight hours.

"Sea Bands" (or "Aquastraps") are a drug-free method of controlling motion sickness. These are slim bands (in varying colors) that are wrapped around the wrist, with a circular "button" that presses against the acupressure point Pericardium 6 (nei kuan) on the lower arm. Attach them a few minutes before you step aboard and wear on both wrists throughout the cruise.

Another drug-free remedy can be found in Relief-Band, a watch-like device worn on the wrist. First used for patients undergoing chemotherapy, it is said to "emit gentle electrical signals that interfere with nerves that cause nausea."

Can I go cruising if pregnant?

Yes, but most cruise lines will not allow a mother-to-be to cruise past her 28th week of pregnancy, and some set the limit at the 24th week. You may need to produce a doctor's certificate. Cruise lines simply aren't equipped to handle pre-term deliveries – the reason for the ruling. So, if you are in your third trimester, cancel your cruise and recover any money you've paid.

Is having hay fever a problem?

Actually, people who suffer from hay fever and pollen allergies benefit greatly from a cruise. Most sufferers I have talked to say that their problems simply disappear on a cruise – particularly when the ship is at sea.

Are hygiene standards high enough?

News reports often focus on hygiene and sanitation aboard cruise ships. In the 1980s, the North American

Exercise and fresh sea air promote good health.

cruise industry agreed with the Centers for Disease Control (CDC) that hygiene and sanitation inspections should be carried out once or twice yearly aboard all cruise ships carrying American passengers, and the Vessel Sanitation Program (VSP) was born. The original intention of the VSP was to achieve and maintain a level of sanitation that would lower the risk of gastro-intestinal disease outbreaks and assist the cruise industry to provide a healthy environment for passengers and crew.

It is a voluntary inspection, and cruise lines pay handsomely for each inspection. For a ship the size of *Queen Mary 2*, for example, the cost would be about $15,000; for a ship the size of *Azamara Journey*, it would be about $7,800). However, the 42 inspection points are accepted by the international cruise industry as a good system. Inspections cover two main areas:
● Water sanitation, including free chlorine residuals in the potable water system, swimming pool and hot tub filters.
● Food sanitation: food storage, preparation and serving areas, including bars and passenger service pantries.

The ships score extremely well – the ones that undergo inspections, that is. Some ships that don't call on US ports would possibly not pass the inspections every time. Older ships with outdated galley equipment and poor food storage facilities would have a harder time complying with the USPH inspection standards. Some other countries also have strict health inspection standards. However, if the same USPH inspection standards were applied to restaurants and hotels ashore, it is estimated that at least 90 percent or more would fail, consistently.

Anyone concerned about personal hygiene should note that some ships have fixed shower heads. A removable shower and hose are better for reaching those parts that fixed head showers can't. Check with your cruise provider *before* you book.

What about the Norovirus?

This temporary but highly contagious condition occurs worldwide. Humans are the only known hosts, and only the common cold is reported more frequently than viral gastroenteritis as a cause of illness in the USA. About 23 million Americans each year are diagnosed with the effects of the Norwalk-like virus (NLV gastroenteritis, sometimes known as winter vomiting virus or norovirus). It is more prevalent in adults and older children than in the very young.

Norovirus is part of the "calicivirus" family. The name derives from the chalice or calyx, meaning cuplike; this refers to the indentations of the surface of the virus. The condition itself is self-limiting, is mild, and is characterized by nausea, vomiting, diarrhoea, and abdominal pain. Although it can be transmitted by person-to-person contact, it is more likely to arrive via contaminated foods and water.

Shellfish (most notably clams and oysters), salad ingredients (particular salad dressings) and fruits are the foods most often implicated in Noroviral outbreaks.

Water can also be a common source of outbreaks – water aboard cruise ships stored in tanks, etc. A mild and brief illness typically occurs 24 to 48 hours after contaminated food or water has been consumed, and lasts for 24 to 72 hours. The virus can also be brought on board when passengers are ashore in foreign ports with poor hygiene standards. If you board a large resort ship after norovirus has struck, bread and bread rolls, butter, and salt and pepper shakers may not be placed on tables, but will be available on request during meals.

Note that only cruise ships are required to report every incidence of gastrointestinal illness. Nowhere else in the health system of the US are such viruses a reportable illness.

How can you avoid them? Don't drink from aircraft water dispensers on the way to join your cruise – they are seldom cleaned thoroughly. Always wash your hands after using the toilet.

Cuban cigars are banned in US ports.

Where is smoking allowed?

Some cruise lines allow smoking in cabins, while some permit it only in cabins with balconies. Almost all cruise lines prohibit smoking in restaurants and food service areas; almost no ships have smoking sections in dining rooms. If you are concerned, check with the cruise line or your travel agent before booking. Most ships now allow smoking only on the open decks. However, you could be sunbathing on an open deck and the person next to you can light up – not a healthy situation.

What about cigars?

Cigar smoking lounges are found aboard *Adventure of the Seas, Amadea, Asuka II, Bleu de France, Brilliance of the Seas, Crystal Serenity, Crystal Symphony, Europa, Explorer of the Seas, Freedom of the Seas, Grand Mistral, Independence of the Seas, Liberty of the Seas, Mariner of the Seas, MSC Armonia, MSC Fantasia, MSC Lirica, MSC Magnifica, MSC Musica, MSC Opera, MSC Orchestra, MSC Poesia, MSC Sinfonia, MSC Splendida, Navigator of the Seas, Norwegian Dawn, Norwegian Epic, Norwegian Gem, Norwegian Jewel, Norwegian Pearl, Norwegian Star, Norwegian Sun, Queen Elizabeth, Queen Mary 2, Queen Victoria, Radiance of the Seas, Seabourn Odyssey, Serenade of the Seas, Seven Seas Mariner, Seven Seas Voyager, Silver Shadow, Silver Spirit, Silver Whisper, SuperStar Virgo,* and *Voyager of the Seas.*

Note, however, that ships starting or ending their cruises in a United States port are not permitted to carry genuine Cuban cigars. Instead, most cigars will be made in the Dominican Republic.

Remember that, if you smoke a cigar in a ship's dedicated cigar lounge, the air purification system will often not be effective enough if someone comes in to smoke a cigarette, and you may suffer the consequences of inhaling second-hand cigarette smoke.

Compacting waste on board has given a significant boost to recycling.

Have there been murders during a cruise?

Violent crime is much less common on a cruise than during land-based vacations, but there have been a few suspicious deaths, and a number of passengers have gone missing, mainly in the Caribbean and on Mexican Riviera cruises. A small number have been thrown over a balcony by another passenger, typically after an alcohol-fueled argument.

Murder is hard to prove if no actual body is found (did he jump or was he pushed?). Another headache is that, if the alleged crime happens at sea, the jurisdiction responsible for investigating it will depend on the ship's registry, perhaps in Panama, Liberia or Malta.

CAN I BRING MY PETS?

Pets are not allowed aboard cruise ships, with one exception: the regular transatlantic crossings aboard Cunard Line's ocean liner *Queen Mary 2*, which has carried more than 500 pet animals since its debut in 2004. It provides air-conditioned kennels, plus a genuine British lamppost and New York fire hydrant for dogs' convenience, and cat containers.

WHAT CRUISING COSTS

Isn't cruising expensive?

Compare what it would cost on land to have all your meals and entertainment provided, as well as transportation, fitness and sports facilities, social activities, educational talks, parties, and other functions, and you can see the remarkable value of a cruise.

Cost provides a useful guideline to a ship's ambience, type of passengers, and degree of luxury, food, and service. What you pay determines the size, location, and style of accommodation. Be wary of huge discounts – it either means that the product was unrealistically priced or that quality will be reduced somewhere. Ships are as individual as fingerprints: each can change its "personality" from cruise to cruise, depending on the mix of passengers (and crew). The choice ranges from basic to luxury, so give yourself a budget, and ask your professional travel supplier how to make the best use of it.

Will a repositioning cruise be cheaper?

When ships move from one cruise region to another, it is termed repositioning. When ships move between the Caribbean and Europe, typically in April/May, or between Europe and the Caribbean (typically in October/November), for example, the cruise fares are usually discounted. The ships rarely sail full, and offer excellent value for money.

I've found a seven-day cruise advertised at a very cheap price. Is there a catch?

As a rule, yes. If the price is a fraction of what you might pay for a decent hotel room in London or New York without meals or entertainment, something is not quite as it seems. Before booking, read the fine print. Look at all the extra costs such as tips to cabin and dining room stewards, shore excursions, drinks, plus getting to and from the ship. The price per person advertised could well be for a four-berth cabin adjacent to the ship's laundry or above the disco, but in any event, not in a desirable location – just like a dirt-cheap hotel room in London or New York.

Is the brochure price firm?

No. A cruise's brochure price is set by the sales and marketing departments of cruise lines, rather like the "recommended retail price" of a new car is set by the manufacturer. It's the price they would like to achieve to cover themselves against currency fluctuations, international bonding schemes and the like. But, in the real world, discounts attract business, and so there is always some leeway. Also, travel agents receive a commission (typically 10–15%, plus special overrides for volume bookings). So, as a consumer, always ask for the "best price," watch for special offers in newspapers and magazines, and talk to your specialist travel agent.

European cruises cost more than in the Caribbean. Why?

There are several reasons. Almost all aspects of operations, including fuel costs, port charges, air transportation,

Key players: a music lesson aboard *Crystal Serenity*.

Cities like Copenhagen in Denmark can be costly.

supplying food to the ships, are higher. European-sourced food has more taste – eggs with real yellow yolks, and food free from chemical additives, coloring and flavoring – than is found in the processed foods that cruise lines often purchase from US-based suppliers.

Companies can make more money than in the cut-price Caribbean, where sun, sea, and sand are the main attractions, whereas sightseeing, architecture, culture, and other things are part of a more enriching cruise experience. The price of shore excursions in Europe is high. Admission prices to some historic sites and museums have risen recently.

How inclusive is "all-inclusive"?

That's like asking how much sand is on the beach. It usually means that transportation (often including flights), accommodation, food, and entertainment are wrapped up in one neat package. Today on land, however, "super clubs" offer everything "all-in" including drinks,

10 Smart Ways to Save Money

- Research online, but book through a real cruise-travel agency.
- Cut through the sales hype and get to the bottom line.
- Make sure that all taxes are included.
- Book early – the most desirable itineraries go soonest. If air travel is involved, remember that air fares tend to rise in peak seasons.
- Book early – the best cabins and locations go sooner rather than later.
- Book a cabin on a lower deck – the higher the deck, the more expensive will it be.
- An interior (no view) cabin is cheaper, if you can live without natural light.
- Be flexible with your dates – go off-season, when fares will be lower.
- Book an older (pre-1980) ship – the newest ships are more expensive.
- Do purchase travel cancelation insurance – your cruise is an investment, after all.

although mostly low-quality brands are provided, with a much smaller selection than aboard most cruise ships.

While that concept works better aboard small ships (those carrying fewer than 600 passengers), large cruise ships (those carrying more than 1,600 passengers) provide more facilities and more reasons for you to spend money on board. So "mostly inclusive" might be a better term to use, particularly as spa treatments and medical services are definitely *not* included.

Should I take a back-to-back cruise?

If you're considering two seven-day back-to-back cruises (for example: Eastern Caribbean/Western Caribbean), bear in mind that many aspects of the cruise – the seven-day menu cycle, one or more ports, all shows and cabaret entertainment, even the cruise director's jokes and spiel – may be duplicated.

Do cruise lines have their own credit cards?

Most don't. Among those that do: Carnival Cruise Lines, Celebrity Cruises, Disney Cruise Line, Holland America Line, Princess Cruises, Saga Cruises, The Yachts of Seabourn. You'll earn credits for any spending charged to the card. If you accrue enough points, you can exchange them for cruises, onboard credit, or discounted airfare.

Do ships have different classes?

Yes and no. Gone are the class distinctions and the pretensions of formality of the past. Differences are now found mainly in the type of accommodation chosen, in the price you pay for a larger cabin (or suite), the location of your cabin (or suite), and whether or not you have butler service.

Some cruise lines, including Holland America Line, MSC Cruises (*MSC Fantasia* and *MSC Splendida* only) and Royal Caribbean International (*Oasis-* and *Freedom-*class ships only), provide a "concierge lounge" which can be used only by occupants of accommodation designated as suites (thus re-creating a two-class system).

Private areas have been created by MSC Cruises (Yacht Club) and Norwegian Cruise Line (The Courtyard) for occupants of the top suites, in an effort to insulate them from the masses. The result is like a "ship within a ship."

Celebrity Cruises has, in essence, created three classes: 1) Suites; 2) Concierge Class (middle-level) mini-suites/cabins; 3) Standard (exterior view and interior – no view) cabins. Perhaps it's less complicated to think in general terms of "Balcony Class" and "Non-Balcony Class."

Cunard Line has always had several classes for transatlantic travel, but today's ships *(Queen Elizabeth, Queen Mary 2, Queen Victoria)* are classed according to the restaurant and accommodation grade chosen.

Cabins advertised in newspapers aren't always available. Why not?

Newspaper advertisements are written way ahead of publication. Meanwhile, some cabin price grades may have sold out. Often, the cheapest "lead-in" price is for a cabin that is small, or has obstructed views, or is in an "inconvenient" or "noisy" location.

What does a category guarantee mean?

It means you have purchased a specific grade of accommodation (just as in a hotel), although the actual cabin may not have been assigned to your booking yet. Your cabin may be assigned before you go, or when you arrive for embarkation.

What are port charges?

These are levied by ports visited, rather like city taxes imposed on hotel guests. They help pay for the infrastructure required to provide facilities including docks,

---

10 THINGS AN "ALL-INCLUSIVE" PRICE DOESN'T INCLUDE

- Dining in "alternative" restaurants
- Premium (vintage) wines
- Speciality ice creams and coffees
- Internet access (extra charge)
- Spa treatments
- Some fitness classes
- Laundry, pressing and dry cleaning
- Babysitting services
- Professional souvenir photographs
- Casino gaming

---

linesmen, security and operations personnel, and porters at embarkation and disembarkation ports.

FACILITIES ABOARD

Can I eat when I want to?

Yes, you can – well, almost. If you're hungry when you get aboard on the day of embarkation, you may want to head to the self-serve buffet – but, be warned that aboard the large resort ships, it'll probably be a bit of a free-for-all, with the frustrations of lining up for food, and then trying to find a place to sit and eat. And those buffets are only really good when they first open. It's more civilized aboard mid-sized and small ships.

Several major cruise lines offer "flexible dining" which allows you to choose (with some limitations) when you want to eat, and with whom you dine, during your cruise. Just like going out to restaurants ashore, reservations may be required, you may also have to wait in line at busy periods, and occupants of the most expensive suites get priority.

Aboard large resort ships (1,600-plus passengers) the big evening entertainment shows typically are staged twice each evening, so you end up with the equivalent of two-seating dining anyway.

What is "alternative" dining?

Mass-market dining isn't to everyone's taste, so some ships now have alternative dining spots other than the main restaurant. These à la carte restaurants usually cost extra – typically between $15 and $50 a person – but

---

A casual eatery on *Carnival Dream* offers a big choice.

the food quality, preparation and presentation are decidedly better, as is service and ambience. Most alternative dining spots are also more intimate, and much quieter than the main dining rooms. You may need to make a reservation. For more details, see pages 56–57.

What's the difference between an "outside" and an "interior" cabin?

An "outside" (or "exterior") cabin doesn't mean it's outside the ship; it simply means that it has a window (or porthole) with a view of the outside, or there is a private balcony for you to physically be – or look – outside. An "interior" (or "inside") cabin means that it does not have a view of the outside, but it will have artwork or curtains on one wall instead of a window or patio-like (balcony) door. Naturally, an outside cabin costs more than an interior cabin of the same size.

Should I tip for room service?

No. It's part of the normal onboard duties that the hotel staff are paid to carry out. For more on tipping other staff, see page 53.

Is it hard to find one's way around large resort ships?

Well, it can take at least a few hours in a ship such as *Oasis of the Seas*, which is more than one-fifth of a mile long, so wear good walking shoes. However, in general, remember that decks are horizontal, while stairs are vertical. The rest comes naturally, with practice. If you're arranging to meet one of the thousands of other passengers, you need to be very specific indeed about the rendezvous point.

Controlling the engines aboard *Oasis of the Seas*.

Tee time: a golf lesson aboard *Crystal Symphony*.

Isn't it very noisy aboard these giants?

It can be, because of the constant activities and music, and many announcements. Since some cruise lines and staff seem to think that high volume enhances ambience, anyone averse to loud noise should consider taking earplugs, just in case.

Do cruise ships vibrate?

Many ships built before 1990 suffer from vibration, usually at the stern. It is usually worse when the vessel is maneuvering at slow speed. So anyone occupying a cabin on the lowest decks at the stern is likely to be affected most. Vibration-free cruising is more possible aboard ships that have the latest "pod" propulsion system fitted (to check whether a particular ship has it, see the "Propulsion" entry in the ship's alphabetical listing in the ratings section of this book).

Can I visit the bridge?

Usually not, for insurance and security reasons. But NCL and Princess Cruises run extra-cost "Behind the Scenes" tours, and a background video on how the ship is run may be shown on your cabin TV system.

Are there any ships with walk-in pools (instead of steps)?

Not many, because of space considerations, although they can often be useful for older passengers. Some examples: *Aurora, Crystal Serenity, Crystal Symphony* and *Oriana*.

Can I bring golf clubs?

Yes, you can. However, although cruise lines do not charge for carrying them, some airlines do – worth checking if you have to fly to join your cruise because the "budget" airlines charge a fortune. Some ships cater for golfers with mini-golf courses on deck and electronically monitored practice areas.

Golf-themed cruises are popular, with "all-in" packages allowing participants to play on some of the world's most desirable courses. Hapag-Lloyd Cruises and Silversea Cruises, for example, operate a number of golf theme sailings each year, and if you take your own clubs, they will provide storage space and arrange everything.

What about my bicycle?

Most cruise lines will let you take your bike – preferably the folding variety because of lack of storage space. If you use a flight case, however, it may not be easy to find storage space for it.

Airlines will also charge you to transport your bike. Ask your travel provider to contact the cruise line for its rules.

Note that very few ships provide bicycles for free. Those that do include *Europa, Hanseatic* and *Hebridean Princess*.

Do cellular phones work on board?

Cruise passengers use cellular phones on open decks, in cabins, and, sadly, even in restaurants. Most cruise lines have contracts with land-based phone service companies – rates for usage vary, but you will typically pay international roaming rates. Mobile phone signals piggyback off systems that transmit internet data via satellite.

When your ship is in port, the ship's network may be switched off and you will pay the going local (country-specific) rate for mobile calls if you can access a local network.

Keeping in touch with children's whereabouts on a big resort ship can be expensive using mobile phones. It's permissible to use two-way radio transceivers (walkie-talkies) for this purpose; at sea they won't interfere with any public-service radio frequency.

Can I send and receive emails?

Aboard most ships, email facilities have now been added to some degree or other. Many ships have wi-fi, for a fee, allowing you to connect your own laptop. Several ships have an internet café, or internet-connect center, where you can log on for about 50¢ per minute. Note that connections and downloads are often very slow compared to land-based services (shipboard emails link through satellite systems, and are therefore more expensive than land-based connections). Attachments are not generally allowed. For many cruise companies, email has now become an important revenue generator.

Where can I watch movies?

Some – but not many – ships have a dedicated movie theater. The movies are provided by a licensed film dis-

Hanseatic is one of the few ships that provides free bicycles.

Big-screen entertainment aboard *Carnival Freedom*.

tribution/leasing service. Many newer ships have replaced or supplemented the movie theater with TV sets and DVD players in cabins, or with giant poolside screens for 24-hour viewing.

Do all cabins have flat-screen TV sets?

No. Many older cruise ships still have bulky CRT sets, but all the latest ships have flat-screen TVs. So, if you think you'll spend time in your cabin relaxing and watching movies, it's best to choose a ship that is less than five years old.

DESTINATIONS

Where can I go on a cruise?

As the saying goes: The world is your oyster! There are over 30,000 different cruises to choose from each year, and about 2,000 cruise destinations in the world. A cruise can also take you to places inaccessible by almost any other means, such as Antarctica, the North Cape, the South Sea islands, and so on. In fact, if you close your eyes and think of almost anywhere in the world where there's water, there's probably a cruise ship or river vessel to take you there. To get an idea of the choice available, see pages 31–43 and 91–8.

What is "homeland" cruising?

The term stems from cruise ships sailing out of an increased number of ports in the United States (more than 20 at last count, with over 4,000 cruises a year). While some, like Miami and Fort Lauderdale, have good facilities for checking in, many do not, and long lines are

the result, particularly when 50 motorcoaches arrive at virtually the same time *(see page 15 for rating of ports)*.

"Homeland" cruising has great appeal for people who can drive themselves to a local (regional) port of embarkation. The result, however, is that one ship sailing out of, say, Baltimore will attract many other people from the surrounding area, and that could mean you'll bump into any of your neighbors who've had the same idea as you. It also makes for particularly strong regional dialects aboard any given ship, and can even change the ways that cruise consumers act and dress.

What is expedition cruising?

Expedition cruises are operated by specialists such as Quark Expeditions *(see page 169)* using small ships that have ice-strengthened hulls or with specially constructed ice-breakers that enable them to reach areas totally inaccessible to "normal" cruise ships. The ships are typically converted to carry passengers in some degree of basic comfort, with comfortable accommodation and a relaxed, informal atmosphere, with expert lecturers and expedition leaders accompanying every cruise.

These cruises really are for small groups, and much care and attention is placed on minimizing the impact on the environment. More information: pages 91–4.

What is a Panamax ship?

This is one that conforms to the maximum dimensions possible for passage through the Panama Canal – useful particularly for around-the-world voyages. These dimensions are: 294 meters (964.56 ft) long, with a beam of 32.3 meters (105.97 ft); or below approximately 90,000 gross tonnage. Because of the locks, the 50-mile (80-km) journey takes from eight to nine hours. Most large resort cruise ships (examples: *Carnival*

Dream, Celebrity Solstice, MSC Fantasia, Queen Mary 2, Ruby Princess) are too big to go through the Panama Canal, and are thus classed as "post-Panamax" ships.

Is there a cruise that skips ports?

Yes, but it isn't really a cruise. It's a transatlantic crossing, from New York to Southampton, England (or vice versa), aboard *Queen Mary 2*. See page 99.

Can I shop in ports of call?

Yes, you can. Many passengers embrace retail therapy when visiting ports of call such as Dubai, Hong Kong, Singapore, St Maarten, and St Thomas, among many others. However, it's prudent to exercise self-control. Remember that you'll have to carry all those purchases home at the end of your cruise; duty-free liquor – a favorite, for example – is heavy.

Do I have to go ashore in each port?

Absolutely not. In fact, many passengers enjoy being aboard "their" ships when there are virtually no other passengers aboard. Also, if you have a spa treatment, it could be less expensive during this period than when the ship is at sea; some ships, such as *Queen Mary 2*, have price differentials for sea days and port days.

Zodiacs from *Hanseatic* on an expedition up the Amazon.

MAKING BOOKINGS

Can I fly in the day before or stay an extra day after the cruise?

Cruise lines often offer pre- and post-cruise stay packages at an additional cost. The advantage is that you don't have to do anything else. All will be taken care

Most people go ashore at ports of call, but they don't have to.

of, as they say. If you book a hotel on your own, however, you may have to pay an "air deviation" fee if you don't take the cruise line's air arrangements or you want to change them.

Can I pre-book seats on flights?

With packaged holidays such as cruises, it is normally not possible to reserve airline seats prior to check-in, and, although the cruise line will typically forward your requests for preferred seating, these may not be guaranteed. However, most airlines allow you to check-in online, access the seating plan and select a seat.

Should I book early?

The further ahead you book, the greater will be any discount applied by the cruise line. You'll also get the cabin you want, in the location you want, and you may even be upgraded. When you book late (close to the sailing date), you may get a low price, but you typically won't get the cabin or location you might like, or – worse still – in ships with two seatings for dinner, you won't be able to choose early or late seating.

What legal rights do I have?

Very few. After reading a cruise line's Passenger Ticket Contract, you'll see why. A 189-word sentence in one contract begins "The Carrier shall not be liable for…" and goes on to cover the legal waterfront (*see page 677*).

AND FINALLY…

What are cruising's downsides?

Much anticipated ports of call can be aborted or changed due to poor weather or other conditions. Some popular ports (particularly in the

Caribbean) can become extremely crowded – there can be up to 12 ships in St Thomas, or six in St Maarten at the same time, disgorging 20,000 people. Fellow passengers, and those lacking social manners can be irritating, notably in the dining room where you may have to share a table with strangers.

Many frequent irritations could be fixed if the cruise lines really tried. Entertainment, for instance, whether production shows or cabaret acts, is much the same aboard nearly every large resort ship and lack originality. Also, many aggressive, young, so-called "cruise directors" insist on interposing themselves into every part of your cruise, day and night, military-style through the public address system. Some of these cruise directors may make good cheerleaders, but seem unable to communicate with anyone over 25.

Where did all the money go?

Apart from the cruise fare itself, there could be other incidentals such as government taxes, port charges, air ticket tax, and fuel surcharges. On board, extra costs may include drinks, mini-bar items, cappuccino and espresso coffees, shore excursions (especially those involving flightseeing tours), internet access, sending or receiving email, beauty treatments, casino gaming, photographs, laundry and dry-cleaning, babysitting services, wine tasting, bottled water placed in your cabin, and medical services.

A cruise aboard a ship belonging to a major cruise line could be compared to buying a car, whereby motor manufacturers offer a basic model at a set price, and then tempt you with optional extras to inflate the price. Cruise lines say income generated on board helps to keep the basic cost of a cruise reasonable. In the end, it's up to your self-restraint to stop those little extras mounting up to a very large sum.

10 WAYS TO MANAGE ONBOARD SPENDING

- Plan spa treatments *(above)* for days when the ship is in port – when prices are usually lower.
- Buy a soda package only if you drink a lot of sodas, but buy individually if you have only one or two a day.
- Check and re-check anything you sign for on board.
- Say no to "souvenir" glasses that come with your cocktail.
- Say "no" to extra-cost name-brand ice creams at the pool.
- Don't use your cell phone (which can incur excessive roaming charges) except for emergencies.
- Forget the extra costs of internet and email access – you're on vacation.
- Don't use the ship's (extra charge) laundry services – wait until you get home.
- Be really selective about hiring watersports gear at "private island" beach calls.
- Use a debit card for payment of your onboard account (using a credit card could mean you pay more in interest if you don't pay off your card in full each month).

How are ships weighed?

They aren't. They are measured. Gross Tonnage is a measurement of the enclosed space within a ship's hull and superstructure (1 gross ton = 100 cubic feet).

How long do cruise ships last?

In general, a long time. For example, during the *QE2*'s almost 40-year service for Cunard Line, the ship sailed more than 5½ million nautical miles, carried 2½ million passengers, completed 25 full world cruises and crossed the Atlantic more than 800 times. But *QE2* was built with a very thick hull, whereas today's thin-hulled cruise ships probably won't last so long. Even so, the life expectancy is typically a healthy 30 years.

Where do old cruise ships go when they're scrapped?

They go to the beach. Actually, they are driven at speed onto a not very nice beach at Alang in India, or to Chittagong in Bangladesh, or to Pan Yo in China – the main shipbreaking places. Greenpeace has claimed that workers, including children, at some sites have to work under primitive conditions without adequate protective equipment. In 2009, a new IMO guideline – "International Convention for the Safe and Environmentally Sound Recycling of Ships" – was adopted. ❑

LEFT: Where does all the money go? Sometimes here.

WHERE TO?

Cruise lines currently visit around 2,000 destinations, from the Caribbean to Antarctica, from the Mediterranean to the Baltic, from Northern Europe to the South Pacific

Carnival guests visit Half Moon Cay in the Bahamas.

Because itineraries vary widely, it is wise to make as many comparisons as you can by reading the cruise brochures for descriptions of the ports of call. Several ships may offer the same or similar itineraries simply because these have been tried and tested. Narrow the choice further by noting the time spent at each port, and whether the ship actually docks in port or lies at anchor. Then, compare the size of each vessel and its facilities.

Caribbean cruises

There are over 7,000 islands in the Caribbean Sea, although many are small or uninhabited. Caribbean cruises are usually destination-intensive, cramming between four and eight ports into one week, depending on whether you sail from a Florida port or from a port already in the Caribbean, such as Barbados or San Juan. This means you could be visiting at least one port a day, with little time at sea for relaxation. This kind of island-hopping leaves little time to explore a destination (but you'd probably get bored after a few days on one island). Although you may see several places in a week, by the end of the cruise you may need another week to unwind.

Note that June 10 to November 30 is the official hurricane season in the Caribbean (including the Bahamas and Florida). Cruise ships can change course quickly to avoid weather problems, which can also mean a change of ports or itinerary. When that happens, cruise lines will generally not offer compensation, nor will travel insurance providers.
● **Eastern Caribbean** cruises include ports such as Antigua, Barbados, Dominica, Martinique, Puerto Rico, St Croix, St Kitts, St Maarten, St Lucia and St Thomas.
● **Western Caribbean** cruises typically include ports such as Calica, Cozumel, Grand Cayman, Grand Turk, Playa del Carmen, Ocho Rios, and Roatan Island.
● **Southern Caribbean** cruises include ports such as Antigua, Aruba, Barbados, La Guaira (Venezuela), Tortola, San Juan.

Private islands

Several cruise lines with Bahamas/Caribbean itineraries feature a "private island" (also called an "out-island"). NCL pioneered the trend when it bought a former military outpost in 1977, and it is currently spending $22 million to upgrade its facilities. These islands, most of which are leased from the owning governments, have all the ingredients to make an all-day beach party a "nice day out" – water sports, scuba, snorkeling, crystal-clear waters, warm sands, even a hammock or two, and, possibly, massage in a beach cabana. There are no reservations to make, no tickets to buy, no hassles with taxis. But you may be sharing your private island with more than 5,000 others from a single large resort ship anchored for a "beach barbecue."

One bonus is that a "private island" will not be

THE CRUISE LINES THAT OWN PRIVATE ISLANDS

Cruise Line	Name of Island	Location	First Used	Berlitz Rating (out of 10)
Celebrity Cruises	Catalina Island	Dominican Republic	1995	5.7
Costa Cruises	Serena Cay	Dominican Republic	1996	5.7
Disney Cruise Line	Castaway Cay	Bahamas	1998	8.6
Holland America Line	Half Moon Cay	Bahamas	1997	8.4
MSC Cruises	Cayo Levantado	Dominican Republic	2005	4.7
Norwegian Cruise Line	Great Stirrup Cay	Bahamas	1977	7.5
Princess Cruises	Princess Cays	Eleuthera, Bahamas	1992	7.8
Royal Caribbean Int.	Coco Cay	Bahamas	1990	6.4
Royal Caribbean Int.	Labadee	Haiti	1986	7.2

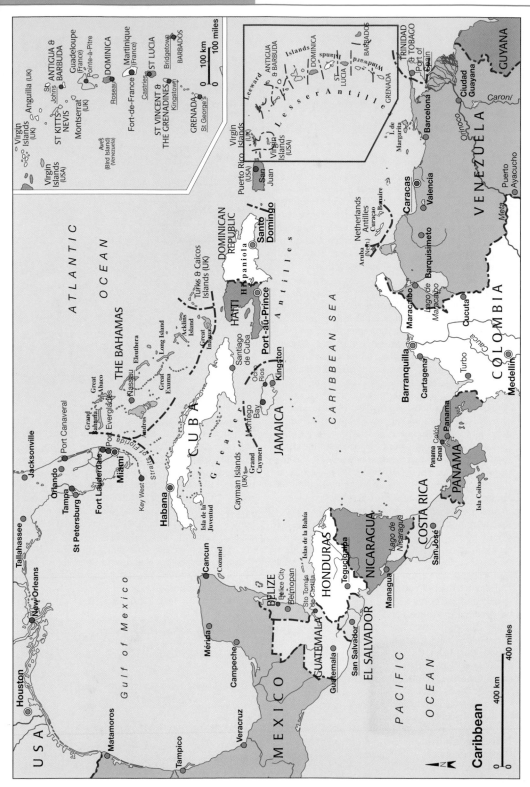

Caribbean

cluttered with hawkers and hustlers, as are so many Caribbean beaches. And, because they *are* private, there is security, and no fear of being mugged, as occurs in some islands. Reality can intrude, though, as it did in Royal Caribbean International's private resort of Labadee in Haiti which had a narrow escape during the devastating 2010 earthquake.

Private island beach days are not all-inclusive, however, and attract premium prices for snorkel gear (and mandatory swim vest), rental pleasure craft, and "banana" boat fun rides; it has become yet another way for cruise lines to increase revenue. But then it does cost a lot of money to develop a private island. Although private islands sound attractive, remember that many items cost extra and will be added to your onboard account. Examples: Sunfish sailboat rental, $40 per hour; snorkel gear rental, $10 per hour; floating foam mattress, $6; bottle of water, $2.50–$4; ice cream, $1.50–$3; water bicycle, $5–$10 per 15 minutes; use of hammock, $2.50–$5.

Alaska cruises

These are especially popular because:
● They offer the best way to see the state's magnificent shoreline and glaciers.
● Alaska is a vast, relatively unexplored region.
● There is a wide range of shore excursions, including many floatplane and helicopter tours, some going to glaciers and salmon fisheries.
● There are many excursions, including "dome car" rail journeys to Denali National Park to see North America's highest peak, Mt. McKinley.
● Pre- and post-cruise journeys to Banff and Jasper National Parks can be made from Vancouver.

There are two popular cruise routes:

Exploring Alaska on a Lindblad Expeditions cruise.

The Inside Passage Route, a 1,000-mile (1,600-km) stretch of protected waterways carved a million years ago by Ice Age glaciers. This usually includes visits to tidewater glaciers, such as those in Glacier Bay's Hubbard Glacier or Tracy Arm (just two of the 15 active glaciers along the 60-mile/100-km Glacier Bay coastline). Typical ports of call might include Juneau, Ketchikan, Skagway, and Haines.

The Glacier Route usually includes the Gulf of

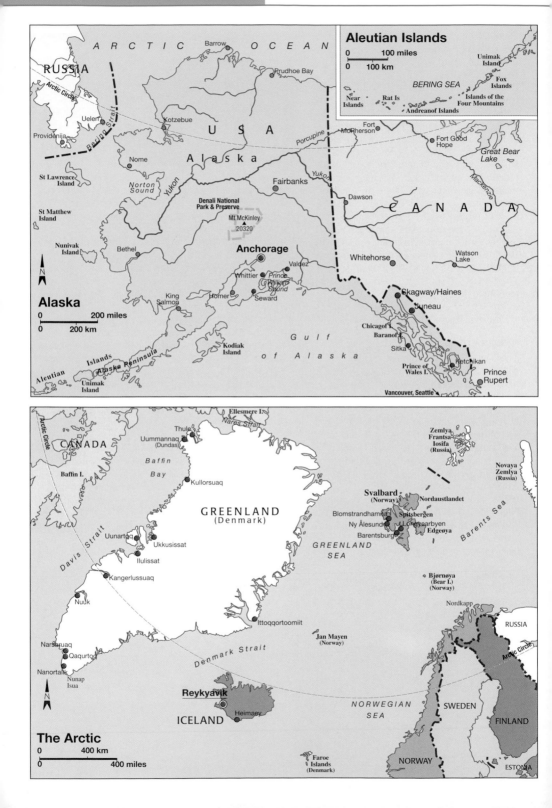

Aleutian Islands

0   100 miles
0   100 km

BERING SEA

Near Islands
Rat Is
Andreanof Islands
Islands of the Four Mountains
Fox Islands
Unimak Island

A R C T I C   O C E A N

RUSSIA
Arctic Circle
Uelen
Providenija

Barrow
Prudhoe Bay

Kotzebue
U S A
Alaska
Fort McPherson
Fort Good Hope
Great Bear Lake

Nome
Norton Sound
Fairbanks
Porcupine
Yukon
Dawson
C A N A D A
Mackenzie

St Lawrence Island
St Matthew Island

Nunivak Island
Bethel
Yukon
Denali National Park & Preserve
Mt McKinley 20320
Anchorage
Whitehorse
Watson Lake

N

Alaska

0   200 miles
0   200 km

King Salmon
Homer
Whittier
Valdez
Prince William Sound
Seward
Skagway/Haines
Juneau

Kodiak Island
G u l f
o f   A l a s k a
Chicagof I.
Baranof I.
Sitka
Prince of Wales I.
Ketchikan
Prince Rupert

Aleutian
Islands
Alaska Peninsula
Unimak Island
Vancouver, Seattle

Arctic Circle
CANADA
Ellesmere I.
Nares Strait
Thule
Uummannaq (Dundas)

Zemlya Frantsa Iosifa (Russia)
Novaya Zemlya (Russia)

Baffin I.
Baffin Bay
Kullorsuaq

Svalbard (Norway)
Nordaustlandet
Blomstrandhamna
Spitsbergen
Ny Ålesund
Longyearbyen
Barentsburg
Edgeøya
Barents Sea

GREENLAND (Denmark)

GREENLAND SEA

Davis Strait
Uunartoq
Ukkusissat
Ilulissat
Kangerlussuaq

Bjørnøya (Bear I.) (Norway)

Nuuk

Ittoqqortoormiit

Jan Mayen (Norway)

Nordkapp
RUSSIA
Arctic Circle

Narsaruaq
Qaqurtoq
Nanortalik
Nunap Isua

Denmark Strait

Reykjavik
Heimaey
ICELAND

NORWEGIAN SEA
SWEDEN
FINLAND

N

The Arctic

0   400 km
0   400 miles

Faroe Islands (Denmark)
NORWAY
ESTONIA

Alaska during a one-way cruise between Vancouver and Anchorage. Typical ports of call might include Seward, Sitka, and Valdez.

Holland America Line and Princess Cruises own many facilities in Alaska (hotels, tour buses, even trains), and between them have invested more than $300 million in the state. Indeed, Holland America Line-Westours is Alaska's largest private employer. Both companies take in excess of 250,000 passengers to Alaska each year. Other lines depend on what's left of the local transportation for their land tours.

In ports where docking space is limited, some ships anchor rather than dock. Many cruise brochures do not indicate which ports are known to be anchor (tender) ports.

With around 930,000 cruise passengers visiting Alaska in 2010 and several large resort ships likely to be in port on any given day, there's so much congestion in many of the small ports that avoiding crowded streets can be difficult. Even nature is retreating; with more people around, wildlife is harder to spot. And many of the same shops are now found in Alaska as well as in the Caribbean.

The more adventurous might consider one of the more unusual Alaska cruises to the far north, around the Pribilof Islands (superb for bird watching) and into the Bering Sea.

Finally, remember that Alaska isn't always good weather cruising – it can be very wet and windy and excursions may be canceled or changed. Even if it's sunny in port, remember that glaciers have their own weather systems and helicopter flightseeing excursions are vulnerable.

European & Mediterranean cruises

Traveling within Europe (including the Aegean, Baltic, Black Sea, Mediterranean, and Norwegian fjord areas) by cruise ship makes economic sense. Although no single cruise covers every port, cruise ships do offer a comfortable way of exploring a rich mix of destinations, cultures, history, architecture, lifestyles and cuisines – and without having to pack and unpack each day. For some, the appeal is to have a safe, virtually crime-free holiday.

These cruises have become increasingly popular because:
● So many of Europe's major cities – Amsterdam, Athens, Barcelona, Copenhagen, Genoa, Helsinki, Lisbon, London, Monte Carlo, Nice, Oslo, St. Petersburg, Stockholm, and Venice – are on the water. It is far less expensive to take a cruise than to fly and stay in decent hotels, paying extra for food and transport.
● You will not have to try to speak or understand different languages when you are aboard ship as you would ashore (if you choose the right ship).

● Aboard ship you use a single currency (typically US dollars, British pounds, or euros).
● A wide variety of shore excursions are offered.
● Lecture programs provide insights before you step ashore. Small ships are arguably better than large resort ships, as they can obtain berthing space (the large resort ships may have to anchor in more of the smaller ports, so it can take time to get to and from shore, and you'll probably have to wait for shore tender tickets). Many Greek islands are accessible only by shore tender. Some companies allow more time ashore than others, so compare itineraries in the brochures; it's probably best to choose a regional cruise line (such as Louis Cruises) for these destination-intensive cruises, for example.

Middle East cruises

Countries with cruise facilities and places of historic interest are: Bahrain, Egypt, Iran, Jordan, Oman, Yemen, and the seven sheikdoms of the United Arab Emirates (UAE). Note that different visas may be required for each of the emirates.

Dubai, which has the world's largest carbon footprint, is fast becoming a cruise base, although cruise terminal and handling facilities are still very limited. If you visit Dubai, though, note that displays of affection such as hand-holding or kissing are not permitted in public, and you can't drink alcohol in a public place. If you fly into Dubai and need to take

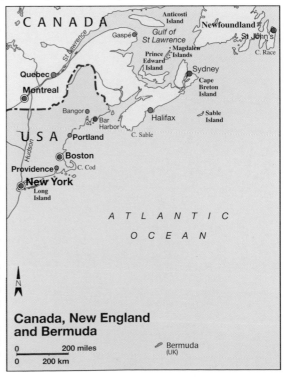

Canada, New England and Bermuda

0 ———— 200 miles

0 ———— 200 km

prescription medicines with you, make sure you have the appropriate, signed prescription. The authorities are extremely strict with drugs and medication.

South Africa and Indian Ocean cruises

The attractions here include cosmopolitan cities, wine tours, wildlife safaris, unspoiled landscapes, and uninhabited beaches. Itineraries (typically of 10–14 days) include sailings starting and finishing in Cape Town (in the same time zone as the UK), or from Cape Town to East African ports such as Port Elizabeth, Richards Bay, Durban, Zanzibar and Mombasa (Kenya). Longer itineraries, of 21 days or more, could include Madagascar, Mozambique and the Seychelles.

Mexican Riviera cruises

These typically sail from Los Angeles or San Diego, along Mexico's west coast, calling at ports such as Cabo San Lucas, Mazatlan, Puerto Vallarta, Manzanillo, Ixtapa/Zihuatanejo, and Acapulco. These cruises also typically include a call in the Baja Peninsula, Mexico's northernmost state.

Route Canal (Transcanal cruises)

These take you through the Panama Canal, constructed by the United States after the failure of a French effort which began in 1882 with a labor force of over 10,000 but was plagued by disease and financial problems (over 22,000 people died). The US took over the building effort in 1904 and the waterway opened on August 15, 1914, shaving over 7,900

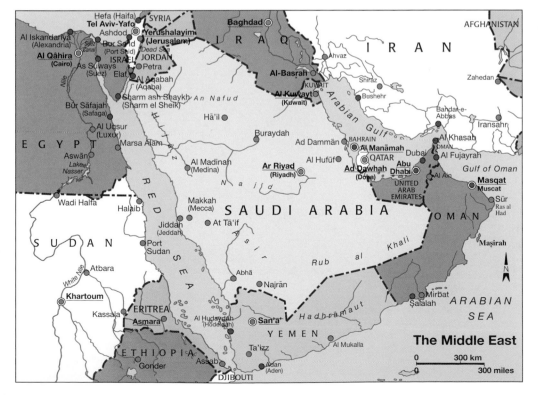

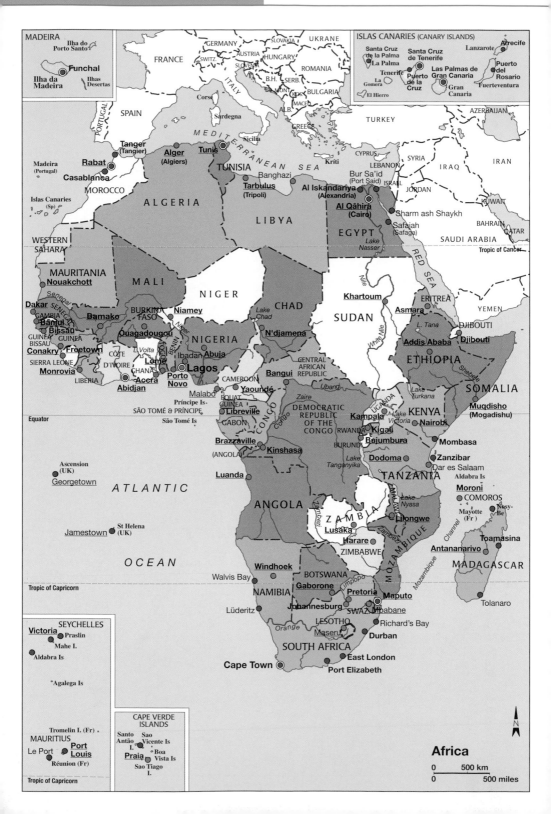

Africa

0   500 km

0   500 miles

nautical miles off the distance between New York and San Francisco. The Panama Canal runs from *northwest* to *southeast* (not west to east), covering 51 miles (82 km) of locks and gates and dams.

Control of the canal passed from the US to Panama in 2000. The $6 billion widening of the canal and new locks, to be built by 2014, will double its capacity, enabling the latest large resort ships to use it.

Between the Caribbean and the Pacific, a ship is lifted 85 ft (26 meters) in a continuous flight of three steps at Gatun Locks to Gatun Lake through which it travels to Gaillard Cut where the Canal slices through the Continental Divide. It is lowered at Pedro Miguel Locks 31 ft (9.4 meters) in one step to Miraflores Lake, then the remaining two steps to sea level at Miraflores Locks before passing into the Pacific.

Ships move through the locks under their own power, guided by towing locomotives. The 50-mile (80-km) trip takes 8–9 hours. What does it cost? Well, *Disney Magic* paid a record $331,200 for one transit of the canal in 2008.

Most Panama Canal cruises depart from Fort Lauderdale or San Juan, calling at islands such as Aruba or Curacao before entering the canal and ending in Acapulco, Los Angeles, or San Francisco. In 2008, the Inter-American Development Bank's (IDB) board of directors approved a $400 million loan to help finance the historic Panama Canal Expansion Program.

South America cruises

Cruises around Cape Horn between Santiago or Valpariso in Chile and Buenos Aires in Argentina are increasingly popular. The optimum season is November to March and most cruises last 14 days.

Sailing southbound, ports of call might include

Puerto Montt (Chile), the magnificent Chilean fjords, Punto Arenas (Chile), and Ushuaia (Argentina), the world's southernmost city (pop. 64,000) and the starting point for many cruises to the Antarctic Peninsula. Coming up the continent's west coast, ports of call might include Puerto Madryn (Argentina), and Montevideo (Uruguay). Slightly longer itineraries may include a call at Port Stanley in the Falkland Islands. Do watch for pickpockets in the major cities of South America.

A number of cruise lines also operate 7-day cruises from Rio de Janeiro, Brazil, mainly for Brazilians (who love to dance the night away and don't arise

Crystal Serenity squeezes through the Panama Canal.

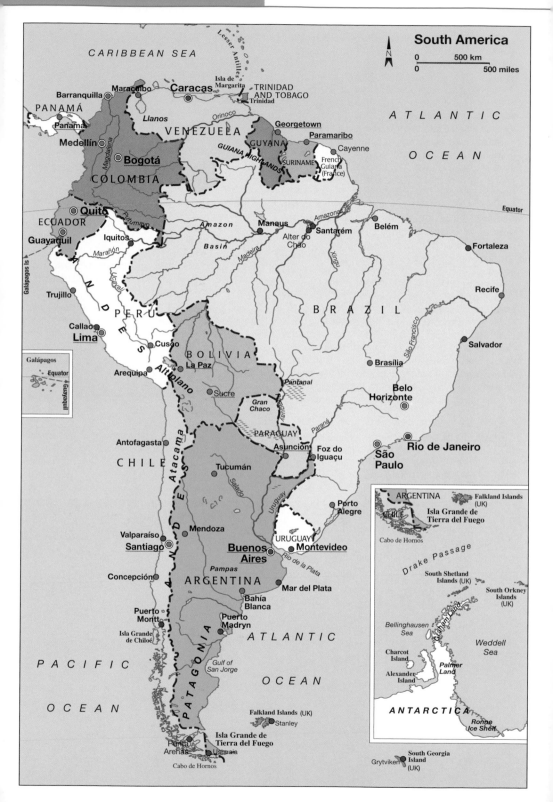

until nearly afternoon). Called "eat late, sleep late" cruises, these are typically aboard large resort ships chartered to local companies such as CVC.

The Great Lakes

Although an internal body of water bordering the United States and Canada, the Great Lakes – Ontario, Erie, Huron, Superior, and Michigan – are home to small ocean-going cruise ships such as *Clelia II* and *C. Columbus*, and so qualify for entry here. The lakes and all their connecting channels are part of the Great Lakes–St. Lawrence Seaway System (GLSLS), and the largest fresh water system in the world. An essential part of the North American transportation infrastructure, they hold more than one-fifth of the world's fresh water supply and are so large (more than 94,000 sq. miles) that they are visible from the moon.

There are about 30,000 islands within the Great Lakes system, the largest of which is Manitoulin Island, the largest island within any internal body of water and home to the world's largest lake within a lake, Lake Manitou. The Great Lakes ecosystem is rich in biodiversity, and has varied flora and fauna.

A cruise within the Great Lakes means a journey that requires crisscrossing from Canada to the US several times in a week-long journey, necessitating

An Aboriginal guide explains carvings on a tour of Australia.

multiple form-filling. In less bureaucratic times, Charles Dickens and Mark Twain crossed the lakes by steamer.

Australia, New Zealand and Orient cruises

If you live in Europe or North America, be aware that the flight to your port of embarkation will be long. It's advisable to arrive at least two days before the cruise, as time changes and jet lag can be severe. Economic constraints have depressed bookings in the past year, which is a shame because the region has so much to offer that it's worth taking a cruise of at least 14 days. Australia, New Zealand, the islands of the South Pacific, Hong Kong, China, Japan, Indonesia, Malaysia, Singapore, Thailand, and Vietnam are all fascinating. ❏

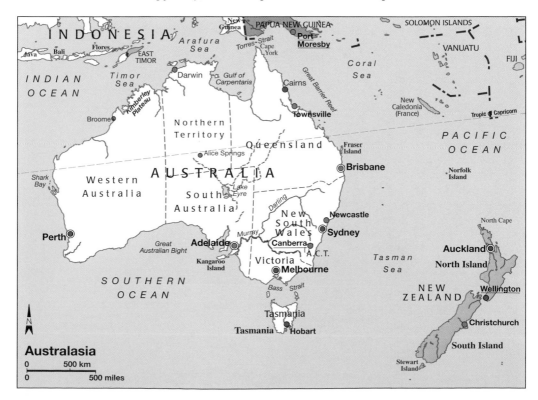

The Baltic and Northern Europe

Southeast Asia

HOW A NEW CRUISE SHIP IS PUT TOGETHER

Ships used to be constructed from the keel up. Today they are built in as many as 100 huge sections which are then joined together in a shipyard

It is the job of the shipyard, its marine architects, consultants, interior designers, and a mass of specialist suppliers to turn those dreams and concepts into a ship without unduly straining the laws of naval architecture, safety regulations, or budgets. Computers have simplified this complex process, although shipboard management and operations personnel often become frustrated with designers who are more idealistic than they are practical.

Today's ships begin life as huge sections – as many as 100 sections, each weighing up to 450 tons – for a resort ship such as *Carnival Freedom*. Most are extensively pre-outfitted and may not even be constructed in the shipyard – simply assembled there.

Formerly, passenger spaces were slotted in wherever there was space within a given hull. Today, computers provide targeted ship design, enabling a new ship to be built in two years instead of the four or five it used to take in the 1950s.

Maximum noise and vibration levels allowable in the accommodation spaces and recreation areas are stipulated in any owner's contract. Vibration tests, focusing on propellers and main engines, are carried out once a ship is built and launched.

Prefabricated cabin modules, including in situ bathrooms complete with toilets and plumbing, are used today. When the steel structure of the relevant deck is ready, with main lines and insulation installed, cabin modules are then affixed to the deck, and power lines and sanitary plumbing are swiftly connected. All waste and power connections, together with hot/cold water mixing valves, are arranged in the service area of the bathroom and can be reached from the passageway outside the cabin for maintenance.

TOP: Keel laying ceremony in Meyer Werft's German shipyard.
ABOVE: One of 55 ship blocks is moved into position.

Cloning a design

With the costs of developing new designs prohibitively expensive, some companies go into "clone" mode using the same basic platform, space and machinery configuration for the hull, but varying the upper structure and layout of public spaces. The best example of this is in the "Vista"-class ships, with the same basic platform shared by cruise lines belonging to the Carnival Corporation. Examples include *Carnival Legend, Carnival Miracle, Carnival Pride, Carnival Spirit* (Carnival Cruise Lines); *Costa Atlantica, Costa Luminoso, Costa Mediterranea* (Costa Cruises); *Eurodam, Nieuw Amsterdam, Oosterdam, Westerdam, Zuiderdam* (Holland America Line). More modified versions can be found in Cunard Line's *Queen Elizabeth* and *Queen Victoria*.

ABOVE: An engine unit is added. At this point the ship looks like a stack of containers bolted together – which is close to reality.

Who builds them

The major cruise ship builders are STX Europe (formerly Aker Yards) in Finland (Helsinki and Turku) and France (St Nazaire); Fincantieri in Italy (Ancona, Trieste and Venice); T. Mariotti in Genoa, Italy; Meyer Werft in Papenburg, Germany; and Mitsubishi in Kagoshima, Japan.

ABOVE: Today's ships are a compromise between a designer's ideal, maximizing use of interior space, and financial constraints.

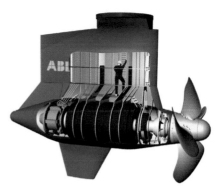

HOW THE LATEST CRUISE SHIPS ARE PROPELLED

The favored drivers are now eco-friendly diesel-electric or diesel-mechanical propulsion systems that propel ships at speeds of up to 28 knots (32mph). Only Cunard Line's *QM2*, with a top speed of more than 30 knots (34.8mph), is faster.

More than 70 cruise ships are now fitted with the "pod" propulsion system, first introduced to the industry in 1990. It resembles a huge outboard motor fitted below the waterline *(pictured above)*. It replaces the long-used conventional rudder, shaft and propeller mechanisms, saves valuable machinery space, and makes stern thrusters redundant.

The pods are compact, self-contained units powered by internal electric propulsion motors. They are turned by the hydraulic motors of the steering gear, and can turn through 360 degrees (azimuthing). This allows even the largest ships to maneuver into smaller spaces without help from tugs.

There are typically two "pods" for most ships, although some have three or even four units. Each pod typically weighs about 170 tons each. But the four pods attached to *Queen Mary 2* weigh 250 tons each – more than an empty Boeing 747 jumbo jet; two are fixed, two are of the azimuthing variety. Although they are at the stern, pod units pull, rather than push, a ship through the water, thanks to their forward facing propellers, and provide greater maneuvrability.

Ships with pod propulsion systems should have no noticeable vibration or engine noise at the stern, unlike ships with conventional propulsion systems. Competing manufacturers have different names for their pod systems – examples: Azipod, Dolphin, Mermaid. The design of the pods has been improved, resulting in slimmer, more efficient units, including safe access for maintenance.

ABOVE: The prefabricated bridge section is moved into position. Meyer Werft's massive cranes can carry 600 tons.

ABOVE: Gradually the 122,000-ton *Celebrity Solstice*, the biggest ship so far built in Germany, assumes its final shape.

ABOVE: The ship is towed away from the shipyard and towards its new marine life, initially cruising down the North Sea.

BELOW: The skies light up after a naming ceremony in Hamburg.

LIFE ABOARD

This A to Z survey covers the astonishing range of
facilities that modern cruise ships offer and
tells you how to make the most of them

Air-conditioning

Cabin temperature can be regulated by an individually
controlled thermostat, so you can adjust it to suit yourself. Public room temperatures are controlled automatically. Air temperatures are often kept cooler than you
may be used to. In some cases (e.g. "Vista"-class ships
*Arcadia, Carnival Legend, Carnival Miracle, Carnival
Pride, Carnival Spirit, Costa Atlantica, Costa Deliziosa,
Costa Luminosa, Costa Mediterranea, Eurodam, Nieuw
Amsterdam, Noordam, Oosterdam, Queen Elizabeth,
Queen Victoria, Westerdam, Zuiderdam*), the air-
conditioning can't be turned off.

Art auctions

Beware of these. Aboard most large resort ships, intrusive art auctions form part of the "entertainment"
program, with flyers, brochures, and forceful announcements that almost demand that you attend. They may be
fun participation events – though the "free champagne"
given to entice you is mostly sparkling wine and *not*
champagne – but don't expect to purchase an heirloom,
as most of the art pieces (lithographs and seriographs)
are rubbish. It's funny how so many identical pieces
can be found aboard so many ships.

Note that art "appraisal prices" are done in-house by
the art provider, a company that *pays* a cruise line to be
onboard. Watch out for the words: "retail replacement
value". Also, listen for phrases such as
"signed in the stone" – it means that the artists
did not sign the work – or "pochoire" (a sten-
cil print less valuable than an original etching
or lithograph). If the auctioneer tries to sell a
piece of art (particularly a "block" print or
wood cut/engraving) with an "authenticated
signature," don't buy it – when it's delivered
to your home and you have it appraised,
you'll probably find it's not genuine. Forged
signatures are not uncommon.

If you do buy something, do so because it
will look good on your wall, not as an investment. Read the fine print, and buy with caution. Remember that the cruise line takes
absolutely no responsibility for artwork that's
worthless – it acts only as the carrier, and the
art auction house is just a concession.

LEFT: atrium bar aboard *Carnival Conquest*.
RIGHT: an art auction aboard *Noordam*.

Baby-sitting

In some ships, stewards, stewardesses, and other staff
may be available as babysitters for an hourly fee.
Make arrangements at the reception desk. Aboard
some ships, evening baby-sitting services may not
start until late; check times and availability before you
book a cruise.

Beauty salon/Barber shop

Make appointments as soon after boarding as possible,
particularly on short cruises. Appointment times fill up
rapidly, especially before social events such as a captain's cocktail party. Charges are comparable to city
prices ashore. Typical services: haircut for men and
women, styling, permanent waving, coloring, manicure,
pedicure, leg waxing. *See Spas, pages 64–69.*

Cashless cruising

You simply settle your account with one payment (by
cash or credit card) before disembarking on the last day.
An imprint of your credit card is taken at embarkation or
when you register online, permitting you to sign for
everything. Before the end of the cruise, a detailed statement is delivered to your cabin.

Some cruise lines, irritatingly, discontinue their "cashless" system for the last day of the cruise. Some may add
a "currency conversion service charge" to your credit

The casino aboard Fred Olsen Cruise Lines' *Balmoral*.

card account if it is not in the currency of the cruise line.

Ships visiting a "private island" on a Bahamas or general Caribbean itinerary may ask you to pay cash for beverages, water sports and scuba diving gear, and other items that you purchase ashore.

Casino gaming

Many cruise ships have casinos, where the range of table games includes blackjack or 21, Caribbean stud poker, roulette, craps, and baccarat. Under-18s are not allowed in casinos, and photography is usually banned inside them. Customs regulations mean that casinos generally don't open when the ship is in port. Gaming casino operations aboard cruise ships are unregulated. However, some companies, such as Celebrity Cruises and Royal

Disembarking from large resort ships can be tedious.

Caribbean International, abide by Nevada Gaming Control Board regulations. Most table games have a $5 minimum and $200 maximum – but, for serious players, Carnival Cruise Lines' casinos have blackjack tables with a $25 minimum and $500 maximum.

Some cruise lines have "private gaming club" memberships, with regular newsletters, rebates and special offers (example: Star Cruises/Genting Hong Kong). Slot machines are also in evidence and make more than half a casino's profits.

Note that, for American citizens and resident aliens in the US, slot machine winnings may be subject to WG-2 tax withholding.

Comment cards

On the last day of the cruise you will be asked to fill out a company "comment card." Some lines offer "incentives" such as a bottle of champagne. Be truthful, as the form serves as a means of communication between you and the cruise line. Pressure from staff to write "excellent" for everything is rampant but, unless you highlight problems you have encountered, things are unlikely to improve.

Daily program

This contains a useful list of the day's activities, entertainment, and social events. It is normally delivered to your cabin the evening before the day that it covers.

Departure Tax

If you are disembarking in a foreign port and flying home, there could be a departure tax to pay, in local currency, at the airport.

Disembarkation

This can be the most trying part of any cruise. The cruise director will already have given an informal talk on customs, immigration, and disembarkation procedures. The night before the ship reaches its destination, you will be given a customs form. Include any duty-free items, whether purchased aboard or ashore. Save the receipts in case a customs officer asks for them.

The night before arrival, place your main baggage outside your cabin on retiring, or before 2am. It will be collected and off-loaded on arrival. Leave out fragile items and the clothes you intend to wear for disembarkation and onward travel – it is amazing just how many people pack absolutely everything. Anything left in your cabin will be considered hand luggage to be hand-carried off when you leave.

On disembarkation day, breakfast will probably be early. It might be better to miss breakfast and sleep later, providing announcements on the ship's public address system do not wake you (it may be possible to turn off such announcements). Even worse than early breakfast is the fact that aboard many ships you will be commanded – requested, if you are lucky – to leave your cabin early, only to wait in crowded public rooms, sometimes for hours. To add insult to injury, your cabin steward – after he has received his tip, of course – will knock on the door to take the sheets off the bed so the cabin can be made up for the incoming passengers. This will not happen aboard the smaller "upscale" ships.

Some companies, such as Princess Cruises, now offer a more relaxed system that allows you to stay in your cabin as long as you wish, or until your tag color is called, instead of waiting in public areas, where it's difficult to avoid the mass of wheeled luggage waiting to trip you up.

Before leaving the ship, remember to claim any items placed in your in-cabin safe. Passengers cannot go ashore until all baggage has been offloaded, and customs and/or immigration inspections or pre-inspections have been carried out. In most ports, this takes two to three hours after arrival. It is wise to leave at least three hours from the time of arrival to catch a connecting flight or other transportation. Once off the ship, you identify your baggage on the pier before going through customs inspection. Porters may be there to assist you.

Unseen by passengers: the engine room of *Oasis of the Seas*.

Duty-free liquor purchases

If you buy a box of "duty-free" liquor in the Caribbean, it will be taken from you at the gangway as you reboard and given back to you the day before you disembark. Also, if you fly home from a US airport after your cruise, you are not permitted to take any liquid items larger than 100ml in your hand luggage. Place liquor in your checked baggage, or it will be confiscated.

Engine room

For insurance and security reasons, visits to the engine room are seldom allowed. Some ships may have a tech-nical information leaflet. Aboard others, a Behind the Scenes video may be shown on the cabin TV system.

Gift shops

The gift shop/boutique/drugstore offers souvenirs, gifts, toiletries, logo and duty-free items, as well as a basic stock of essential items. Opening hours are posted at the store and in the Daily Program.

Internet access, email, and cell phones

The trend toward cell (mobile) phone use aboard ship is certainly growing, and most cruise ships built after 2000 are wired and ready for internet and cell phone use, albeit at a price. You can use your own device, but it must be set for roaming – and extra charges will apply. The calls are handled by a marine satellite provider, which will pass on the international roaming

Internet access typically costs 50–75 cents a minute.

Tenders transport passengers when a ship can't dock.

charges to your phone operator. Before you cruise, check with your phone operator for the international roaming rates applicable to your tariff.

As for internet use, most new ships have a room – often part of the library – with computers. The best wired ships also have strong signals to cabins and public areas, so you could use your own laptop in the privacy of your room or on deck (extra charges apply).

When a ship is close to antennae on land, or under the track of a passing telecommunications satellite, signals can be strong. But they can also fade in and out – typically just as you are finishing a long email. Waiting for web pages to appear on your computer screen can be frustrating.

The cost of internet time ranges from about 50 cents to 75 cents a minute. If you think you will use the internet a lot, perhaps for e-mails, it makes sense to buy a package of minutes. Typical charges are around $50 for 100 online minutes and $100 for 250 minutes.

Shipboard computers will ask you to establish a user name and password before you can access web sites or your email. Each ship-received email arrives separately (unlike on your home computer) and will take longer to load. This is because ships use different software to home-based systems, and you will be sharing the space with marine requirements.

The signal strength can vary substantially from hour to hour, minute to minute. The farther north you get, the closer the telecommunications satellite is to the horizon, so signals tend to fade in and out. Mountain ranges can get in the way, too. A few important tips:
● Remember to log off the computer when you are finished or your online charges will continue to accumulate.
● Peak demand for online time is on sea days, and just before and after the evening meal, slowing your connection. Avoid those times.
● Remember to take your user name and password for your favourite web sites.
● Some browsers have small print that says "click here

if you have a slow connection." Clicking on that may help speed the connection.
● If you can wait, an internet café ashore will be faster and cheaper.

Launch (shore tender) services

Enclosed or open motor launches ("tenders") are used when your cruise ship is unable to berth at a port or island. In such cases, a regular launch service is operated between ship and shore for the duration of the port call. Aboard the large resort ships, you'll need to obtain a tender ticket, usually given out in one of the lounges, unless you are on an organized excursion (these get priority). The procedure can take a long time.

When stepping on or off a tender, extend "forearm to forearm" to the person who is assisting you. Do not grip their hands because this has the unintentional effect of immobilizing the helper.

Laundry and dry cleaning

Most ships offer a full laundry and pressing service. Some ships may in addition offer dry cleaning facilities. A detailed list of services, and prices, can be

The library aboard *Celebrity Solstice*.

found in your cabin. Your steward will collect and deliver your clothes.

Some ships have self-service launderettes, well equipped with washers, dryers, and ironing facilities. There may be a charge for washing powder and for the use of the machines.

Library

Some cruise ships have a library offering a good selection of books, reference material, and periodicals. A small, refundable deposit may be required when you borrow a book. Aboard small luxury ships, the library is open 24 hours a day, and no deposit is required. Aboard the large resort ships, the library may be open only a couple of hours a day. *Aurora, Oriana, QM2, Queen Elizabeth* and *Queen Victoria* have full-time, qualified librarians provided by the dedicated specialist company Ocean Books, which also sells a superb range of specialist maritime books and memorabilia aboard the three Queens.

The reception desk is the information hub.

Sadly, libraries aboard some ships are like forgotten children, with books badly organized. Aboard most other ships a member of the cruise staff or entertainment staff – with little knowledge of books or authors – staffs the library. The library may also have board games such as Scrabble, backgammon and chess.

Lido

This is typically a deck devoted to swimming pools, hot tubs, showers, and general recreation, often with intrusive "background" music. Aboard most cruise ships, it has a self-serve buffet.

Lost property

Contact the reception desk immediately if you lose or find something aboard the ship.

Mail

You can buy stamps and mail letters aboard most ships, at the reception desk. Some ships use the postal privileges and stamps of their flag of registration, while others buy local stamps at ports of call. Mail is usually taken ashore by the ship's port agent just before the ship sails. You will receive a list of port agents and mailing addresses with your tickets and documents, so you can advise friends and family how they can send mail to you.

News/sports bulletins

Most ships have satellite TV for world news and sports coverage. Others print world news and sports results in the ship's newspaper or place details on a bulletin board near the reception desk or in the library. For sports results not listed, inquire at the reception desk.

Photographs

Professional photographers on board take digital pictures of passengers during embarkation and throughout the cruise. They cover all the main events and social functions, such as the captain's cocktail party. The pictures can be viewed without any obligation to buy, but the prices may surprise. The cost is likely to exceed $10 for a postcard-sized photograph, and a 10 x 8-inch embarkation photo aboard *Queen Mary 2* will set you back a whopping $27.50.

Postcards/stationery

These are typically available from the writing room, the library, or the reception desk. Some cruise lines now charge for them, although if you are in suite-grade accommodation, you may get stationery personalized with your name a suite number when you embark.

Pre-paid drinks

Most large resort ships offer drinks packages in an effort to "add value." However, although these booze-cruise packages mean you don't need to sign each time you order a drink, they really are a temptation to drink more. Some packages include wine, although the choice is the cruise lines' – not yours. If you travel on a low-budget ship that includes a drinks package, you could be in for a rowdy vacation.

Reception desk

This is also known as the Purser's Office, guest relations, or information desk. Centrally located, it is the nerve center of the ship for general passenger information and problems. Opening hours – in some ships, 24 hours a day – are posted outside the office and given in the Daily Program.

Religious services

Interdenominational services are conducted on board many ships, usually by the captain or staff captain. Costa Cruises' ships have a small private chapel.

Denominational services may be taken by clergy traveling as passengers.

Room service
Beverages and snacks are available at most times. Liquor is normally limited to the opening hours of the ship's bars. Some ships may charge for room service.

Sailing time
In each port of call, sailing and all-aboard times are posted at the gangway. The all-aboard time is usually half an hour before sailing (one hour in US ports). If you miss the ship, it's entirely your responsibility to get to the next port of call to re-join the vessel.

Shipboard etiquette
Here are a few points that are sometimes overlooked:
● In public rooms, smoking and nonsmoking sections are available. In the dining room, cigar and pipe smoking are banned.
● If you take a video camera with you, be aware that international copyright laws will prohibit you from recording any of the professional entertainment shows.
● It is all right to be casual but not to enter a ship's dining room in just a bathing suit, or with bare feet.
● If you are uncomfortable eating with the typical 10-piece dining room cutlery setting, some cruise lines have introduced etiquette classes to help you.

Shopping
A large resort ship with its captive audience afloat is something of a "padded sell" for retailers – hence the bargain basement stalls that spring up almost as soon as the ship sets sail. Even on formal nights, you'll see bazaar tables selling tee-shirts. It's all a bit tacky.

Many cruise lines operating in Alaska, the Bahamas, the Caribbean, and the Mexican Riviera engage an out-

Shopping in an Istanbul bazaar during a shore excursion.

side company that provides the services of a "shopping lecturer." This person promotes "selected" shops, goods, and services heavily, fully authorized by the cruise line (which receives a commission). This relieves the cruise director of responsibility, together with any questions concerning his involvement, credibility, and financial remuneration. Shopping maps, with "selected" stores highlighted, are placed in your cabin, and sometimes include a guarantee of satisfaction valid for 30 days.

During shore excursions, be wary of stores recommended by tour guides – they may be receiving commissions from the merchants. Shop around before you purchase. When buying local handicrafts, make sure they have indeed been made locally. Be wary of "bargain-priced" name brands, as they may be counterfeit. For watches, check the guarantee.

The ship's shops are also duty-free and, for the most part, competitive in price. They are closed while in port, however, due to international customs regulations. Worthwhile discounts are often offered on the last day of the cruise.

Some of the world's shopping havens put serious temptation in the way of cruise passengers. Top of the list are Hong Kong, Singapore and Dubai (especially in the new Mall of the Emirates – a shopping *resort* rather than a mall; and the Dubai Mall – with over 1,200 shops, including the only Bloomingdale's outside the USA).

Swimming pools
Most ships have outdoor or indoor swimming pools, or both. They may be closed in port owing to local health regulations or cleaning requirements. Diving is not allowed – pools are shallow.

Parents should note that most pools are unsu-

RCI organizes water sports off its resort of Labadee, Haiti.

pervised. Some ships use excessive chlorine or bleaching agent; these could cause bathing suit colors to run.

Telephone calls

Most ships have a direct-dial satellite link, so you can call from your cabin to anywhere in the world. All ships have an internationally recognized call sign, a combination of letters and digits (example: C6SE7). Satellite calls can also be made when the ship is in port. Satellite telephone calls cost between US$5 and $12 a minute, depending on the type of equipment the ship carries, and are charged to your onboard account.

To reach any ship dial the International Direct Dial (IDD) code for the country you are calling from, followed by the ship's telephone number.

Anyone without a direct-dial telephone should call the High Seas Operator (in the United States, dial 1-800-SEA-CALL). The operator will need the name of the ship, together with the ocean code (Atlantic East is 871; Pacific is 872; Indian Ocean is 873; Atlantic West/Caribbean/US is 874).

● *For cell phone usage, see Internet entry (page 49).*

Television

Programming is obtained from a mixture of satellite feeds and onboard videos. Some ships lock on to live international news programs such as CNN or BBC World, or to text only news services. Satellite TV reception can be poor because ships constantly move out of the narrow beam transmitted from the satellite.

Tipping

Aboard many ships, particularly the large resort ships, tipping appears to be mandatory rather than voluntary. Gratuities, typically at $10–$12 per person, per day, are added automatically to onboard accounts by almost all the major cruise lines, and may need to be converted to your local credit card currency at the prevailing rate, whether you have received extra service or not. However, many people, especially Europeans, don't like to be told when and how much to tip, and tipping is foreign to Asian cultures.

Gratuities are included in the cruise fare aboard a small number of ships, mainly those at the luxury end of the market, where no extra tipping is permitted – at least in theory. Even when cruise brochures state "tipping is not required," it will be expected by the staff. Aboard some ships, subtle suggestions are made regarding tips; in others, cruise directors get carried away and dictate rules.

Here are the accepted industry guidelines: dining room waiter, $3–$4 per person per day; busboy (assistant waiter), $1.50–$2 per day; cabin steward or stew-

ardess, $3–$3.50 per person per day; Butler: $5–$6 per person per day. Tips are normally given on the last evening of a cruise of up to 14 days' duration. For longer cruises, hand over half the tip halfway through and the rest on your last evening.

Aboard many ships, a gratuity of 10 or 15 percent is automatically added to your bar check, whether you get good service or not, and for spa treatments.

Valuables

Most ships have a small personal safe in each cabin, but items of special value should be kept in a safety deposit box in the purser's office. This is accessible during the cruise.

Water sports

Some small ships have a water sports platform that lowers from the ship's stern or side. These ships usually carry windsurfers, waterski boats, jet skis, water skis, and scuba and snorkel equipment, usually at no extra charge (except for scuba equipment).

Such facilities look good in brochures, but ships are often reluctant to use them. This is because many itineraries have too few useful anchor ports. Also, the sea must be in an almost flat calm condition – seldom the case. Insurance regulations can be restrictive too.

Wine and liquor

The cost of drinks on board is generally lower than on land, since ships have access to duty-free liquor. Drinks may be ordered in the dining room, at any of the ship's bars, or from room service. Dining rooms have extensive and reasonably priced wine lists.

Some ships sell duty-free wine and liquor to drink in your cabin. You can not normally bring these into the dining room or public rooms, nor any duty-free wine or liquor bought in port. These rules protect bar sales, a substantial source of onboard revenue. ❑

A wine appreciation session run by Regent Seven Seas Cruises.

CUISINE

Anyone determined to eat around the clock could do so aboard many ships, but the weight-conscious should exercise restraint, especially at self-service buffets

Conceited menus, rubberized duck, bitter gravy, rock-hard lobster, brittle pizza, elasticized croissants, grenade-quality fruit, coffee that tastes like army surplus paint… you can find all this and more in the cruise industry's global cafeteria. On the other hand, you can enjoy prime cuts of meat, really fresh fish and seafood, fine caviar, foie gras and vintage champagne – aboard the right ship.

The message to remember is this: generally speaking, as in most restaurants on land, you get what you pay for. High-quality food ingredients cost money, so it's pointless expecting low-cost cruises to offer anything other than low-cost food. It's not that the cruise lines don't try. They know that you will spend more time eating on board than doing anything else, so their intention is to cater as well as they can to your palate while keeping the cruise price competitive. They even boast about their food, but the reality is that meals aboard most ships are not gourmet affairs. How could they be when a kitchen has to turn out hundreds of meals at the same time? Most cruise-ship cuisine compares favorably with "banquet" food in a family restaurant – in other words, often tasteless and pedestrian. So what you can expect, therefore, is a good selection of palatable, pleasing, and complete meals served in comfortable surroundings. Maybe you will even dine by candlelight, which at least creates some atmosphere.

Menus are typically displayed outside the dining room each day so that you can preview each meal. Menus are delivered to suites.

Fresh versus frozen

Aboard low-priced cruises, you will typically be served portion-controlled frozen food that has been reheated. Fresh fish and the best cuts of meats cost the cruise lines more, and that cost is reflected in the cruise price. Aboard some ships, the "fresh" fish – often described as "Catch of the Day" (but *which* day?) – has clearly had no contact with the sea for quite some time.

Sushi bars are a recent fad but, in 90% of cases, fish used in sushi (with rice) is cooked, and raw (sashimi-style, without rice) fish is not available, as storage and preparation facilities are inadequate. The only ships with authentic sushi bars and authentic sushi/ sashimi are *Asuka II*, *Crystal Serenity*, *MSC Musica* and *MSC Poesia*.

Note also that many items of "fresh" fruit may have been treated with 1-MCP (methylcyclopropene) to make them last longer – apples, for example, may be up to a year old.

Bread and pastry

Most bread baked aboard cruise ships is unappealing because, with little time for fermentation of natural yeast, it is made instead with instant dough that contains dried yeast from packets. Many baked goods and pastry items will be made mostly from refined flours and sugars.

A typical day

From morning till night, food is offered to the point of overkill, even aboard the most modest cruise ship. Aboard the large resort ships, pizzas, hamburgers, hot dogs, ice-cream and frozen yoghurt are almost always available. If you're still hungry, there's 24-hour room service – which, aboard some large resort ships, may cost extra. Some ships also have extra-charge bistros, cafés and patisseries.

A Crystal Cruises head waiter prepares crêpes.

Carnival Dream's full-service Crimson Restaurant.

If you prefer to eat at set times rather than graze, these are the options:

● **6am:** hot coffee and tea on deck for early risers (or late-to-bed types).

● **Full breakfast:** typically with as many as 60 different items, in the main dining room. For a more casual meal, you can serve yourself buffet-style at an indoor/outdoor deck café, though the choice may be restricted.

● **Lunchtime:** with service in the dining room, buffet-style at a casual café, or at a separate grill for hot dogs and hamburgers, and a pizzeria, where you can watch the cooking.

● **4pm:** Afternoon tea, in the British tradition, complete with finger sandwiches and scones. This may be served in a main lounge to the accompaniment of live music (it may even be a "tea-dance") or recorded classical music.

● **Dinner:** the main event of the evening, and apart from the casualness of the first and last nights, it is generally formal in style.

● **Light Bites:** typically served in public rooms late at night. These have mostly replaced the traditional midnight buffet.

● **Gala Midnight Buffet:** It's almost extinct, but if there is one, it is usually held on the penultimate evening of a cruise when the chefs pull out all the stops. It features a grand, colorful spread, with much intricate decoration that can take up to 48 hours to prepare.

THE RISE OF CELEBRITY CHEFS

Several cruise lines have signed up well-known chefs to devise menus for their alternative dining venues. Celebrity Cruises, for example, worked with three-star Michelin chef Michel Roux from 1989 until 2007. The partnership worked because Roux insisted that the cruise line buy high-quality ingredients and make everything from scratch, avoiding pre-made sauces, soup mixes and the like.

P&O's Marco Pierre White.

The celebrity chef's ideal is to create food that can be mass produced, and not cooked à la minute, as on land. But because ingredients cannot be delivered daily, as on land, the choice of dishes can be a challenge. If he is fond of cooking over charcoal-flaming grills, he's out of luck. No open flames are allowed, though ships often use induction cooking instead to achieve a similar result.

Celebrated chefs have included Georges Blanc (Carnival Cruise Lines), Elizabeth Blau (Celebrity Cruises), Nobu Matsuhisa (Crystal Cruises), Todd English (Cunard Line), Mauro Uliassi (MSC Cruises), Gary Rhodes and Marco Pierre White (P&O Cruises), Charlie Palmer (Seabourn Cruise Line), Aldo Zilli (Thomson Cruises), and Joachim Splichal (Windstar Cruises).

Seating arrangements

● **Open Seating:** You can sit at any available table, with whomever you wish, at any time within dining room opening hours – just like going out to a restaurant ashore. You'll probably have a different waiter each time, because you'll be seated in different locations, so the attraction of your waiter learning your likes and dislikes is missing.

Unless you are with your own family or group of friends, you will be seated next to strangers. It is the responsibility of the restaurant manager – who is also known as the maître d'hôtel – to seat you with compatible fellow passengers. If a reservation has been arranged prior to boarding, you will find a table assignment/seating card in your cabin when you embark. If not, make your reservation with the restaurant manager or one of his assistants as soon as you embark.

Tables for two are a rarity; most tables seat

four, six, or eight. It is a good idea to ask in advance to be seated at a larger table, because if you are a couple seated at a table for four and you don't get along with your table partners, there is no one else to talk to. And remember, if the ship is full, it may be difficult to change tables once the cruise has started.

Depending on the size of the ship, it may have one, two or open seatings:

● **Single Seating** doesn't mean seating for single passengers. It means you can choose when you wish to eat (within dining room hours) but have the same table assigned for the cruise.

● **Two Seatings:** you are assigned (or choose) one of two seatings, early or late. Typical meal times for two-seating ships are: Breakfast: 6.30am–8.30am; Lunch: 12 noon–1.30pm; Dinner: 6.30pm–8.30pm.

Some ships operate two seatings for all meals and some just for dinner. Dinner hours may vary when the ship is in port to allow for the timing of shore excursions. Ships that operate in Europe and the Mediterranean or in South America may have later meal times to suit their clientele.

● Some ships operate a mix of open seating (dine when you want) or fixed dining times, for greater flexibility.

The captain's table

The captain usually occupies a large table in or near the center of the dining room on "formal" nights, although this tradition is disappearing as ships get bigger and more fun-oriented. The table seats eight or more people picked from the passenger or "commend" list by the hotel manager. If you are invited to the captain's table, it is gracious to accept, and you will have the chance to ask questions about shipboard life.

Multi-level dining aboard *Voyager of the Seas*.

Bolero's bar aboard RCI's *Oasis of the Seas*.

Alternative Dining

Extra-cost "alternative" restaurants were pioneered by RMS *Queen Mary* in 1936 and introduced in modern times by NCL in 1988 and Crystal Cruises in 1990. Now the large resort ships, never reluctant to embrace an additional source of revenue, have joined the trend, offering their customers an escape from the huge, noisy main dining rooms with their singing, table-dancing waiters who know little about food.

These specialist restaurants are typically smaller, à la carte venues where you must make a reservation, and pay an extra charge of between $6 and $30 a person. In return, you get better food, wines, service and ambi-

ence. The costs can soon add up, just as can happen when you dine out ashore.

As an example, take David's Supper Club aboard *Carnival Pride*. The food is good, and the ambiance is modestly refined. But a couple having two glasses of decent wine each can, with the cover charge, easily end up paying over $100 for dinner.

Molecular gastronomy

The term, invented in 1992 by the physicist Nicholas Kurti, signals food's collision with science to create molecularly synthesized food. The cuisine was first introduced to cruising by Italy's Emilio Bocchia in the extra-cost restaurants aboard some Costa Cruises ships.

To provide it, you'll need blast chillers, a Pacojet (a machine that can turn everyday ingredients into ice cream), liquid nitrogen, thickening gums (such as algin and xantham), malic acid, and flame retardants (such as gellan). You'll also need a serious qualification in molecular engineering.

The end result is rather like a plate of colorful toy portions of "foam food." It can look pretty, and is reassuringly expensive, but it still tastes like foam food. In the world of molecular gastronomy, bacon can be made to taste like melon. Britain's Heston Blumenthal became famous for his snail ice cream. This type of cooking is, in the most literal sense, a matter of taste.

Special needs

Cruise lines tend to cater to general tastes. If you are allergic to ingredients such as nuts or shellfish, let the cruise line know in writing well ahead of time and, once on board, check with the restaurant manager.

---

10 RECOMMENDED ALTERNATIVE DINING VENUES

Kaito *MSC Musica, MSC Poesia*
Le Champagne *Silver Spirit*
Le Cordon Bleu *Seven Seas Voyager*
Olympic Restaurant *Celebrity Millennium*
Palo's *Disney Dream, Disney Magic, Disney Wonder*
Prime 7 *Regent Seven Seas Cruises*
The Sushi Bar *Crystal Serenity*
Teppanyaki Grill *Norwegian Epic*
Two Stars *Europa*
Umihiko *Asuka II*

Vegetarians should make sure that soups are not made with a chicken stock, as I have in the past found many so-called "vegetarian" soups are aboard ships. I once came across a "vegetarian burger" with mozzarella cheese topping – but the cheese had been made with buffalo milk and animal rennet!

If you are vegetarian, vegan, macrobiotic, counting calories, want a salt-free, sugar-restricted, low-fat, low-cholesterol, or any other diet, advise your travel agent when you book, and get the cruise line to confirm that the ship can meet your needs. Cruise ship food tends to be liberally sprinkled with salt, and vegetables are often cooked with sauces containing dairy products, salt, and sugar.

Most cruise ships don't cope well with those on vegan or macrobiotic diets who regularly need fresh-squeezed juices; most large resort ships use commercial canned or bottled juices containing preservatives and can't provide really fresh juices in their bars.

A Silversea Cruises chef prepares a dainty dish.

MULTI-DECK DINING

Dining rooms with balcony levels include: *Amsterdam, Carnival Legend, Carnival Pride, Carnival Spirit, Celebrity Century, Celebrity Infinity, Celebrity Mercury, Celebrity Millennium, Celebrity Summit, Costa Atlantica, Costa Mediterranea, Dawn Princess, Empress, Eurodam, Legend of the Seas, Liberty of the Seas, Maasdam, Mein Schiff, Nieuw Amsterdam, Noordam, Oosterdam, Queen Elizabeth, Queen Victoria, Rotterdam, Ryndam, Sea Princess, Splendour of the Seas, Statendam, Sun Princess, Veendam, Volendam, Zaandam* and *Zuiderdam* have them.

Not to be outdone, *Adventurer of the Seas, Allure of the Seas, Explorer of the Seas, Freedom of the Seas, Independence of the Seas, Liberty of the Seas, Mariner of the Seas, Navigator of the Seas, Oasis of the Seas, Queen Mary 2* and *Voyager of the Seas* have dining halls that span three decks.

A selection of cheeses aboard *MSC Fantasia*.

at the same time and can eat together, rather than let their food become cold.

SILVER SERVICE: When the component parts are brought to the table separately, so that the diner, not the chef, can choose what goes on the plate and in what proportion. Silver service is best when there is plenty of time, and is rare aboard today's ships. What some cruise lines class as silver service is actually silver service of vegetables only, with the main item, whether it is fish, fowl, or meat, already on the plate.

Self-serve buffets

Most ships have self-serve buffets for breakfast and luncheon (some also for dinner), one of the effects of discounted fares and dumbing down – and fewer staff are needed. Strangely, passengers don't seem to mind lining up for self-service food (reminiscent of school lunches and army canteens) in scandalously overcrowded venues. But while buffets look fine when they are fresh, they don't after a few minutes of passengers helping themselves. And, one soon learns, otherwise sweet little old ladies can become ruthlessly competitive at opening time.

Passengers should not have to play guessing games when it comes to food, but many cruise lines forget to put proper labels on food items; this slows down any buffet line. Labels on salad dressings, sauces, cold cuts of meat and cheeses would be particularly useful.

What's not good is that if you ask anyone behind the self-serve buffet counters what kind of apples are in the fruit bowl they haven't a clue, "red" or "green" being the

Plate service versus silver service

PLATE SERVICE: When the food is presented as a complete dish, it is as the chef wants it to look. In most cruise ships, "plate service" is now the norm. It works well and means that most people seated at a table will be served

WHAT YOU'RE MOST LIKELY TO FIND ON A TRADITIONAL CRUISE SHIP MENU

APPETIZERS
Prawn Cocktail
Smoked Salmon or
    Graved Lax
Deep Fried Camembert
Cheese Croquets
Bacon-wrapped
    Asparagus Spears
Honeydew Melon with
    Proscuito (or Parma)
    Ham
Emmental Cheese Soufflé
Escargots Bougignone
Garlic-Sautéed Frog Legs
Forest Mushroom Terrine

SOUPS
French Onion Soup
Scotch Barley Broth
Cream of Spinach
Lobster Bisque
Fagioli Red Bean
Vegetable Minestrone
    Soup

Chicken Consommé
Louisiana Gumbo
Chilled Fruit Soup
Cock a Leekie Soup

MAIN COURSES
Prime Rib of Beef/Roast
    Sirloin of Beef
Roasted Pork Loin
Beef Wellington

Veal Cordon Bleu
Broiled Lobster Tail
Surf & Turf
Coq au Vin
Pan-Seared Darne of
    Salmon
Salmon Kulebiak
Duckling à L'Orange
Magret de Canard
Sautéed King Prawns

Herb-Crusted Rack
    of Lamb
London Mixed Grill
Osso Bucco
Beef (or Mushroom)
    Stroganoff
Fish, Chips and Mushy
    Peas
Roast Turkey with
    trimmings

Boneless Chicken Kiev
Grilled Sirloin Steak/
    Filet Mignon

SALADS
Caesar Salad
Cobb Salad
Tossed Spinach Salad
    with Bacon Bits
Tossed Garden Greens
Salad Niçoise

DESSERTS
Baked Alaska
Crème Brûlée
Apple Pie à la Mode
Black Forest Cake
Sticky Toffee
    Pudding
Amaretto Soufflé
Tiramisu
Pecan Pie
Lemon Cheesecake
Chocolate Chiffon Pie

usual answer (red apples, for example, could be Brae-burn, Calville, Egremont Russet, Gala, Pink Lady, Stark-ing Delicious, or Worcester Pearmain). Staff should know the most basic details about food on display.

Healthy eating

It's easy to gain weight when cruising – but not inevitable. In fact, taking a cruise could well be a reason to get serious about your well-being. Weight-conscious passengers should exercise self-restraint, particularly at self-service buffets. The same rule applies as on dry land: eat slowly and chew well.

Many ships' menus include "heart-healthy" or "lean and light" options, with calorie-filled sauces replaced by so-called "spa" cuisine. It may also be wise to choose grilled or poached fish (salmon, or sea bass, for exam-ple), rather than heavy meat dishes or chicken – which is typically loaded with hormones and antibiotics – or fried food items.

If you have a sensitive stomach, avoid the self-serve buffets. If you must use them (some cruise lines close their main dining rooms for lunch, leaving you with lit-tle choice), salads are a wise choice.

● **Fruit and vegetables:** Quality and variety are directly linked to the per-passenger budget set by each cruise line and are dictated by suppliers, regions and seasons. Companies operating large resort ships buy fruit at the lowest price, which can translate to unripe bananas, tasteless grapes, and hard-as-nails plums.

The smaller, more upscale ships usually carry bet-ter-quality ripe fruits as well as the more expensive varieties such as dragon fruit, carambola (star fruit), cherimoya, cactus pear, guava, kumquat, loquat, pas-

Emile's, *Carnival Liberty's* self-serve lido café.

---

sion fruit, persimmon, physalis (Cape gooseberry), rambutan, and sharon fruit.

Some cruise lines are also putting a greater emphasis on fresh vegetables, whole grains, and organic food. As well as being healthier, eating fruit regularly checks hunger pangs and so delays the need for heavier fare. If you take fruit from the buffet to your cabin, it would be wise to wash it because it may have been sprayed with pesticides and fungicides.

● **Exercise:** There are plenty of opportunities for exer-cise, either in the spa or gym, on the jogging track often found above the main swimming pool deck, or by sign-ing up for active shore excursions involving biking, hik-ing or river-rafting. Also, to encourage good digestion, forget about the elevator and take to the stairs – you'll skip those tedious lines for the elevator on large resort ships at peak times, and you'll feel fitter, too.

WHERE TO FIND REAL ALE

Most major cruise lines offer mainly canned lagers such as Becks, Budweiser, or Heineken. The best beer from the barrel and bottled beers are stocked by UK-based cruise lines such as Cunard Line, Fred Olsen Cruise Lines, P&O Cruises, Saga Cruises and Swan Hellenic Cruises – though the selection is generally unexciting. Of course, many real ales do not travel well.

A 33cl can of lager on a major cruise lines will cost you anything from $3.50 to $5 plus a 15% tip (a 17% tip on NCL).

Not for weight watchers: a spread aboard *Sapphire*.

National differences

Most cruise lines feature mainly American-style cuisine, or cuisine that is often described as international, while more European-style cuisine is typically provided aboard the ships of European cruise lines (examples: Cunard Line, Fred Olsen Cruise Lines, Hebridean Island Cruises, P&O Cruises, and TUI Cruises).

Note that beef, lamb and pork cuts are different on both sides of the Atlantic, so what you ordered may not be quite the cut, shape or size you thought it was going to be. For example, there are 15 British cuts of beef, 17 American cuts, and 24 French cuts. There are 6 American cuts of lamb, 8 British cuts, and 9 French cuts. There are 8 American cuts of pork, 10 British cuts, and 17 French cuts.

While American passengers typically like iced water, or a jug of iced tea at lunch, most European passengers don't like ice in their water, and few drink iced tea.

If you care about cutlery, note that only a few cruise

lines with large resort ships provide the correct, specially shaped fish knives, or the correct soup spoons (oval for thin bouillon-style soups and round for creamy soups).

Dining room and kitchen staff

Celebrity chefs *(see box on page 55)* make the headlines, but it's the executive chef who plans the menus, orders the food, organizes his staff, and arranges all the meals. Although he himself rarely cooks, he oversees everything about the galley operation. He makes sure that menus are not repeated, even on long cruises. On some cruises, he works with guest chefs from restaurants ashore to offer tastes of regional cuisine. He may also purchase fish, seafood, fruit, and various other local produce in "wayside" ports and incorporate them into the menu with a "special of the day" announcement.

The restaurant manager – also known as the maître d'hôtel and not to be confused with the ship's hotel manager – is an experienced host, with shrewd perceptions about compatibility. It is his responsibility to seat you with suitable fellow passengers. If a reservation has been arranged prior to boarding, you'll find a table assignment or seating card in your cabin when you embark. If not, make your reservation with the restaurant manager or an assistant as soon as you embark.

If you are unhappy with any aspect of the dining room operation, the sooner you tell someone the better. Don't wait until the cruise is over to send a scathing letter to the cruise line – it's too late then to do anything positive.

The best waiters are those trained in European hotels or catering schools. They provide fine service and quickly learn your likes and dislikes. They normally work aboard the best ships, where dignified professionalism is expected and living conditions are good.

Many lines contract the running and staffing of dining rooms to a specialist maritime catering organization.

DID YOU KNOW...

● that Holland America Line passengers consume around 1.3 million pounds (589,680 kg) of Alaska fish and seafood during the Alaska summer cruise season? These include wild salmon, halibut, crab, and scallops.
● that Cunard Line used to be the world's largest single buyer of Russian caviar – spending about $500,000 a year – after the Russian and Ukrainian governments? (Today the line buys American caviar from the lower-grade hackleback sturgeon.)
● that *Legend of the Seas* was christened in 1995 with the world's largest bottle of champagne? It had to be specially made, and was a "Sovereign-size" bottle (the equivalent of 34 bottles) of Moët & Chandon champagne.

Ships that cruise far from their home country find that professional caterers such as Hamburg-based Sea Chefs do a good job. However, ships that control their own catering staff and food often try very hard for good quality.

Hygiene standards

Galley equipment is in almost constant use, and regular inspections and maintenance help detect potential problems. There is continual cleaning of equipment, utensils, bulkheads, floors, and hands.

Cruise ships sailing from or visiting US ports are subject to in-port sanitation inspections. These are voluntary, not mandatory inspections, based on 42 inspection items, undertaken by the United States Public Health (USPH) Department of Health and Human Services, under the auspices of the Centers for Disease Control. The cruise line pays for each inspection. A similar process takes place in Britain under the Port Health Authority, which has even more stringent requirements.

A tour of the galley proves to be a highlight for some passengers, when a ship's insurance company permits. A video of Behind the Scenes, for use on in-cabin television, may be provided instead.

In accordance with international standards, all potable water brought on board, or produced by distillation aboard cruise ships, should contain a free chlorine or bromine residual equal to or greater than 0.2 ppm (parts

How to be aware of waiting times aboard *Oasis of the Seas*.

per million). This is why drinking water served in dining rooms often tastes of chlorine.

Smoking/nonsmoking areas

Most ships now have totally nonsmoking dining rooms, while some still provide smoking (cigarettes only, not cigars or pipes) and nonsmoking sections. Those wishing to sit in a no-smoking area should tell the restaurant manager when reserving a table.

At open seating breakfasts and luncheons in the dining room or at a casual self-serve buffet venue, smokers and nonsmokers may be seated close together. ❑

HOW THE MAJOR CRUISE LINES SCORE ON CUISINE AND SERVICE

Scores out of maximum 10. Note that these ratings do not reflect extra-cost "alternative" restaurants

Food	Carnival Cruise Lines	Celebrity Cruises	Costa Cruises	Cunard Line	Holland America Line	MSC Cruises	Norwegian Cruise Line	P&O Cruises	Princess Cruises	Royal Caribbean Int.	Star Cruises
Dining Room/Cuisine	5.7	7.3	5.9	7.7	7.1	7.0	6.0	6.5	7.4	4.8	6.0
Buffets/Informal Dining	5.8	7.0	5.6	7.1	6.3	6.4	6.2	6.0	6.8	6.1	5.9
Quality of Ingredients	6.0	7.1	6.0	7.5	6.7	7.5	6.1	6.6	6.8	5.8	6.4
Afternoon Tea/Snacks	4.0	6.6	4.6	7.4	5.6	6.6	4.5	6.5	6.3	4.0	5.2
Wine List	5.7	7.5	5.6	8.0	6.1	7.3	6.2	6.7	6.6	5.4	5.5
Overall Food Score	**5.44**	**7.10**	**5.54**	**7.54**	**6.36**	**6.96**	**5.80**	**6.46**	**6.78**	**5.22**	**5.80**
Service											
Dining Rooms	6.0	7.6	6.0	7.6	7.4	7.3	6.6	6.8	7.5	5.7	6.3
Bars	5.8	7.4	6.2	7.6	7.1	7.5	6.4	7.1	7.5	5.6	6.0
Cabins	6.0	7.6	6.8	7.7	7.5	7.5	6.2	7.6	7.3	6.2	6.1
Open Decks	5.5	7.2	5.6	7.4	6.6	7.2	6.0	6.2	6.8	5.6	6.0
Wines	5.0	7.5	5.2	8.0	6.1	7.4	6.0	6.0	6.2	5.2	5.2
Overall Service Score	**5.66**	**7.46**	**5.96**	**7.66**	**6.94**	**7.38**	**6.24**	**6.74**	**7.06**	**5.66**	**5.92**
Combined food/service	**5.55**	**7.28**	**5.75**	**7.60**	**6.65**	**7.17**	**6.02**	**6.60**	**6.85**	**5.44**	**5.86**

THAT'S ENTERTAINMENT?

After food, the most subjective part of any mainstream cruise is the entertainment, which tries to be diversified and innovative but never controversial

Many passengers, despite having paid so little for their cruise, expect to see top-notch entertainment, "headline" marquee-name cabaret artists, the world's most "popular" singers, and the most dazzling shows with slick special effects, just as one would find in the best venues in Las Vegas, London, or Paris. There are many reasons why it is not exactly so. International star acts invariably have an entourage that accompanies them to any venue: their personal manager, their musical director (often a pianist or conductor), a rhythm section (with bass player and drummer), even their hairdresser.

On land, one-night shows are possible, but with a ship, an artist cannot always disembark after just one night, especially when it involves moving equipment, costumes, and baggage. This makes the whole matter logistically and financially unattractive for all but the very largest ships on fixed itineraries, where a marquee-name act might be a marketing plus.

When you are at home you can bring the world's top talent into your home via television. Cruise ships are a different matter. Most entertainers don't like to be away from their "home base" for long periods, as they rely on telephone contact. They don't like the long contracts that most ships must offer in order to amortize the cost.

A certain sameness

So many acts working aboard cruise ships are interchangeable with so many other acts also working aboard cruise ships. Ever wonder why? Entertainers aboard ship must also *live* with their audiences for several days (sometimes weeks) – something unheard-of on land – as well as work on stages aboard older ships that weren't designed for live performances. However, there is no question that cruise ships are the new location for vaudeville acts, where a guaranteed audience is a bonus for many former club-date acts, as well as fresh acts trying to break in to the big time on land.

Entertainment in large resort ships is market-driven. In other words, it is directed toward that segment of the industry that marketing departments are specifically targeting. This is predominantly a family audience, so the fare must appeal to a broad age range. That partly accounts for the frequency of formulaic Cirque du Soleil-style acrobatic routines and rope climbing.

A cruise line with several ships will normally employ an entertainment director and several assistants, and most cruise lines use entertainment agencies that specialize in entertainment for cruise ships. Regular passengers will notice that they seem to see the same acts time after time on various ships.

Mistakes do happen. It is no use, for example, booking a juggler who needs a floor-to-ceiling height of 12 feet but finds that the ship has a show lounge with a height of just 7 feet (although I did overhear one cruise director ask if the act "couldn't juggle sideways"); or an acrobatic knife-throwing act (in a moving ship?); or a concert pianist when the ship only has an upright honky-tonk piano; or a singer who sings only in English when the passengers are German-speaking.

Trying to please everyone

The toughest audience is one of mixed nationalities (each of whom will expect entertainers to cater exclusively to their particular linguistic group). Given that cruise lines are now marketing to more international audiences in order to fill ever-larger ships, the problem of finding the right entertainment is far more acute.

The "luxury" cruise lines (typically those operating small ships) offer more classical music, even some light

---

There's a retro look to many cruise ship shows.

opera, more guest lecturers and top authors than the seven-day package cruises heading for the sun.

These performers and ship entertainers generally, need to enjoy socializing. Successful shipboard acts tend to be good mixers, are presentable when in public, do not do drugs or take excess alcohol, are not late for rehearsals, and must cooperate with the cruise director.

Part of the entertainment experience aboard large resort ships is the glamorous "production show," the kind of show you would expect to see in any good Las Vegas show palace – think flesh and feathers – with male and female lead singers and Madonna or Marilyn Monroe look-alike dancers, a production manager, lavish backdrops, extravagant sets, grand lighting, special effects, and stunning custom-designed costumes. Unfortunately, most cruise line executives, who know little or nothing about entertainment, still favor plumes and huge feather boas paraded by showgirls who *step*, but don't *dance*. Some cruise ships have coarse shows, and topless performances can be found aboard the ships of Star Cruises/Genting Hong Kong.

Book back-to-back seven-day cruises (on alternating eastern and western Caribbean itineraries, for example), and you will probably find the same two or three production shows and the same acts on the second week of your cruise. The way to avoid seeing everything twice is to pace yourself. Go to some shows during the first week and save the rest for the second week.

Sadly, entertainment has of late been a major target for some companies (particularly the smaller operators) who have targeted it as a major area

The Miss Teenage Hairspray show, *Oasis of the Seas*.

for cost-cutting. This translates to bringing on, for example, lower-cost singers (who often turn out to be vocally challenged) and bands that cannot read charts (musician-speak for musical arrangements).

Other entertainment

Most ships organize acts that, while not nationally known "names," can provide two or three different shows during a seven-day cruise. These will be singers, illusionists, puppeteers, reality TV show wannabees, hypnotists, and even circus acts, with wide age-range appeal.

Also, comedians who perform "clean" material can find employment year-round on the "cruise ship circuit." These popular comics enjoy good accommodation, are mini-stars while on board, and may go from ship to ship on a standard rotation every few days. There are raunchy, late-night "adults only" comedy acts in some of the ships with younger, "hip" audiences, but few have enough material for several shows. The larger a ship, the broader the entertainment program.

Playing the game

TV game shows could be the next audience participation event aboard the big resort ships with their large showlounges. These professionally produced game shows, licensed from TV companies, involve all passengers seated in the show lounge with interactive buttons wired into every seat. While they are expensive to mount, they provide something different from the expensive costumed production extravaganzas. ❏

THE COST OF STAGING A SHOW

In today's high-tech world, staging a lavish 50-minute production show can easily cost between $500,000 and $1 million, plus performers' pay, costume cleaning and repair, royalties, and so on. To justify that cost, shows must remain aboard for 18 to 24 months.

Some smaller operators see entertainment as an area for cost-cutting, so you could find yourself entertained by cheaper singers (who sound cheaper) and bands that can't read musical arrangements.

SPAS AND WELLNESS FACILITIES

The "feelgood factor" is alive and well aboard the latest cruise ships, which offer a growing array of beauty salons and body-pampering treatments – but the costs can quickly add up

As we constantly move in "fast-forward" mode we create stress, our energy becomes impaired. Muscles become taut and knotted. So, taking time out to pamper ourselves is a good way to combine "me" vacation time with moments of indulgence.

Land-based health spas have long provided a range of body treatments and services for those who wanted to hide away at a venue (health farm) in the countryside. With the increase in awareness of the body beautiful and the importance of well-being has come a whole new array of shipboard spas to rival those on land, particularly in the range of body-pampering treatments available. Today's cruise ships have elaborate spas where, for an extra fee, whole days of almost continuous treatments are on offer. Once the domain of adult women, spas now cater almost as equally to men.

A visit to the ship's spa will help you to relax and feel pampered. Many people not used to spas may find some of the terminology daunting: aromatherapy, hydrotherapy, ionithermie, rasul, thalassotherapy. Spa staff are used to first-time users, however, and will help you choose the massage or other treatment that best suits you and your needs. It's a good idea to visit the spa on embarkation day, when staff will be on hand to show you round, and answer your questions. Some cruise lines let you pre-book spa treatments online before your cruise. But take note of prices, which can soon add up.

Facilities

Large resort ships will have a large gymnasium with ocean views, saunas, steam rooms, rasul chamber, several body treatment rooms, thalassotherapy pool, relaxation area, changing/locker rooms, and a beauty salon. Some ships even have acupuncture treatment clinics, and some have a built-in juice bar.

Thermal suites

Thermal Suites (no, they're not specially insulated cabins) are private areas that provide a combination of various warm scented rain showers, saunas, steam rooms, thalassotherapy (saltwater) pools and relaxation zones offer the promise of ultimate relaxation. While most ships do not charge for use of the sauna or steam room, some make a per-day charge (examples: *MSC Musica* $30; *Norwegian Gem* $20; *Queen Mary 2*, $25). Note that some ships add a gratuity to a spa Day Pass, even though it is supposed to be included.

Spa suites

Some ships have "spa suites," which include spa access and even a treatment or two (whereas regular cabin occupants pay extra to use the sauna/steam room/relaxation rooms), and special spa amenities (examples: *Costa Concordia, Costa Luminosa, Costa Pacifica, Costa Serena, Europa*), and even a special spa-food-menu-only restaurant (examples: *Celebrity Eclipse, Celebrity Equinox, Celebrity Solstice, Costa Concordia, Costa Serena*).

Spa design

The latest sea-going spas have Asian-themed decor, with warm woods and gently flowing water to provide a soothing atmosphere, with therapy staff dressed in the appropriate attire. But interior designers often forget to include dimmers and mood lighting, particularly in reception areas, where lighting is often too bright.

Pampering treatments

Stress reducing and relaxation treatments are featured, combined with the use of seawater, which contains minerals, micronutrients, and vitamins. Massages might include Swedish remedial massage, shiatsu, and aromatherapy oils. You can even get a massage on your private balcony aboard some ships.

Too relaxed aboard *MSC Musica* to notice the view.

Keeping fit aboard an AIDA cruise.

Having body-pampering treatments aboard a cruise ship can be wonderful, as the ship can provide a serene environment in itself; so, when enhanced by something like a massage or facial, the benefits can be more therapeutic. Ship interior designers do, however, need to pay more attention to soundproofing so that facilities can be used at all hours (lighting dimmers are also essential – it's surprising how often this simple, but essential, item is overlooked). Examples of poor soundproofing include the treatment rooms aboard *Golden Princess, Grand Princess*, where they are located directly underneath a sports court. So, before you actually book your relaxing massage, find out if the treatment rooms are quiet enough.

Unfortunately, treatments are usually available only until about 8pm, whereas some passengers would welcome being able to have a massage late at night before retiring to bed (the problem is that most shipboard spas are run by concessions, with well-being treated as a daytime-only event). Also, be aware that the latest rip-off in the revenue game is to charge more for treatments on days at sea, and lower on port days. Check the daily program for "port day specials" and packages that make prices more palatable.

Some of the smaller, more upscale ships now offer "Spa Days" with a whole day of body-pampering treatments (often termed "wellness packages"). Expect to pay up to $500 a day in addition to the basic cruise cost.

Fitness centers

A typical large resort ship spa will include a gymnasium, probably with ocean-view win-

dows. Virtual-reality exercise machines are found in the techno-gyms aboard most large resort ships, with state-of-the-art muscle-pumping and body-strengthening equipment, universal stations, treadmills, bicycles, rowing machines, and free weights.

Most fitness centers are open only until early evening (one exception: NCL ships, whose gyms are open 24 hours a day). And if you've forgotten your workout clothes, you can probably purchase new items on board.

Typical exercise classes

These include aerobics (for beginners, intermediate, and advanced), high intensity/low impact aerobics, step aerobics, interval training, stretch and relax, super body sculpting, fab abdominals, sit and be fit, and walk-a-mile.

Group exercycling, kick-boxing, pilates and yoga classes, body composition analysis, and sessions with a personal trainer, will cost extra.

Massage

Having a massage aboard ship is a treat that more people are discovering. Today, many ships have suites and cabins with a "private" balcony, although you'll need a balcony with plenty of space in order to set up a proper portable massage table and allow the masseur/masseuse room to walk around it and work from all sides. It can be a real stress-busting experience, but if it's not right it can prove frustrating, and expensive.

Here are some of my favourite massages (always

10 EXCELLENT SHIPBOARD SPAS

AIDAbella/AIDAluna
Asuka II
Crystal Serenity
Europa
Mein Schiff
MSC Fantasia
Pacific Pearl
Queen Mary 2
Seabourn Odyssey
Silver Spirit

taken in the late afternoon or early evening, preferably just before sundown):

● Aboard *Celebrity Constellation, Celebrity Infinity, Celebrity Millennium, Celebrity Summit* (on the balcony of a Sky Suite).

● Aboard *Royal Clipper* (in a private massage hut on an outside deck).

● Aboard *SuperStar Virgo* (on the floor of a junior suite bedroom).

● Inside a beach cabana ashore on Castaway Cay or Half Moon Cay in the Bahamas, or as part of the beach, caviar and champagne experience of ships such as *SeaDream I* and *II* in the British Virgin Islands.

Make appointments for a massage as soon after embarkation as possible, so you can obtain the time and day of your choice. Large resort ships have more staff and offer more flexibility in appointment times, although cruises tend to be shorter than those aboard smaller, more upscale ships. The cost averages $2 a minute. In some ships, a massage service may be available in your cabin (or on your private balcony), if it is large enough to accommodate a portable massage table.

While it's easy to telephone and make an appointment for a massage or facial or two (some cruise lines let you do this online), do watch the cost. When you charge treatments to your onboard account, remember that gratuities are often added automatically (typically 10–15%). Elixirs of youth, lotions and potions, creams and scrubs – all are sold by therapists, typically at the end of your treatment, for you to use when you get home. But be warned, these are expensive items; beware of falling for subtle and flattering sales talk.

A whole range of treatments and styles has evolved

Best foot forward aboard *Costa Concordia*.

from the standard Swedish Remedial Massage. The most popular are:

Swedish Massage: There are two main effects of massage – a reflex effect and a mechanical effect. There are four basic movements in this general massage: effleurage (the stroking movements that benefit the circulation of lymphatic fluids and drainage), petrissage (the picking, kneading, rolling and wringing movements), friction (the application of circular pressure) and tapotement (percussive tapping, flicking and hacking movements that stimulate circulation).

Well-being Massage: This is really another term for general Swedish Massage but with more emphasis on effleurage movements, the use of complementary, warmed aromatic (aromatherapy) oils and four-hand massage (two therapists working rhythmically in unison).

Shiatsu Massage: This literally means "finger pressure" and in Japan for thousands of years has been applied to the pressure points of the body as a preventative measure. It typically promotes a peaceful awareness of both body and mind, and is administered in a calm, relaxed environment, without oil.

Hot Stones Massage: The therapist places 24 to 36 smooth basalt volcanic stones of varying sizes in a special oven. These are then applied to various key energy points of the body, using the stones to gently massage specific areas and muscles. The heated volcanic stones are then left in place while the therapist works on other parts of the body. The heat from the stones helps the body to achieve a sense of deep relaxation.

Ayurvedic Head Massage: Using a selection of warmed herbal oils, the therapist will apply

Hot stones massage helps produce a sense of deep relaxation.

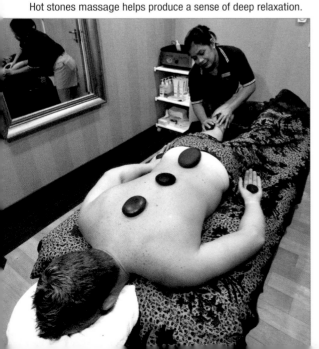

the oil to the scalp, neck and shoulders to stimulate circulation and nourish the hair (you'll need to wash your hair afterwards, as it will be extremely oily). Shirodhara is the form of Ayurvedic medicine that involves gently pouring warm oil (made from tulsi, or holy basil) over the forehead (including the "third eye"). Ayurveda is a compound word meaning life and knowledge. A shirodosha experience includes bathing and polishing the feet with Himalayan salts prior to an Ayurvedic head massage, followed by a full body massage using warm oils drizzled over the body.

Underwater Massage: You soak in a large tub of warm water, possibly with rose petals floating around you, while the therapist massages joints and muscles.

Sports Massage: Typically provided by a male therapist, sports massage is a deep-tissue massage designed to unlock the kinks and knots.

Lomi-Lomi Massage: This is a more rhythmic massage inspired by Hawaiian healing traditions that restore the free flow of "mana" or life force; it is typically given using warm aromatherapy oils, and may be a two-hand or four-hand massage.

Lymphatic Massage: This detox massage is designed to improve circulation by releasing body toxins and nodes that build up in key lymphatic points. It is usually recommended for those who have poor circulation.

Thai Massage: Uses pressure points and stretching techniques employed by the therapist, using both hands and feet, to stretch and relax muscles, improve circulation, and reduce stress. It is usually carried out on a mat or thin mattress which is laid out on the floor.

Chinese Tuina: This is a therapeutic massage based on a diagnostic evaluation, manipulation of the joints and muscle fibers, and identification and prevention of wrong body postures, habits and degenerative conditions.

Couples Massage: Sometimes known as a "duet massage," this is typically a 90-minute session for a couple that includes a hands-on lesson from a massage specialist on the art of massaging each other.

Ultimate Massage: Two therapists provide a synchronized full body massage, using Swedish massage movements to provide the ultimate in stress-busting relief. But it can be less than good if the two therapists are even slightly out of sync.

Recent variations of massage include a warm candle massage, and a bamboo tamping treatment. Aboard some ships (MSC Cruises, for example), combinations of Balinese massage and reflexology are popular.

THE 10 RULES OF SPA ETIQUETTE

❶ It is important to wear proper attire (including shoes) in the gym.

❷ Wipe the equipment off with a clean towel (or sanitized cloth) after you have used it.

❸ Limit your time on the equipment or in the hot tub to a maximum of 30 minutes when others are waiting.

❹ Most ships allow jogging on a designated deck or area at selected times which will be posted. Adhere to the times posted because cabins are usually located directly below the designated deck and you may disturb fellow passengers who are sleeping.

❺ If there's a mixed sauna, men should not shave in it – it's unclean, and uncool.

❻ Arrive at least 10 minutes before your appointment.

❼ Take a shower or wash off all suntan lotions or oils.

❽ It's better not to talk during a massage – simply close your eyes, relax and enjoy.

❾ Shipboard spas are no-smoking zones – so no quick drag in the sauna.

❿ You can cancel an appointment up to 24 hours before your treatment time without charge. If you cancel within the 24 hours before your appointment time, you will be charged for the treatment you booked.

OTHER TREATMENTS

While massage is the most popular shipboard spa treatment, some ships offer a whole range of body-pampering treatments, such as facials, manicures, pedicures, teeth whitening – even acupuncture. Most treatments are based on holistic Asian therapies. Some examples: Bali or Java, Indonesia (*ural* and *pijat* massage; mandi lulur, a scrub made from herbs, essential oils and rice to soften the skin; Balinese *boreh* (a warm herb, rice, spice, galangal water and oil body wrap for detoxification); China (*acupuncture*); Japan (shiatsu massage; enzyme baths made from warmed finely shaved cedar chips, rice bran and vegetable enzymes to improve the metabolic system); Malaysia (Malay massage, which focuses on the body's 600,666 nerves); Philippines (*Hilot* massage, using virgin coconut oil and banana leaves); Thailand (Thai massage, or *nuad boran*).

Typically, the spa will provide items such as towels, robes and slippers, but it's best to store valuables safely in your cabin prior to your appointment.

Don't worry about having to get naked; you'll typically change into a robe and slippers in the men's or women's changing rooms. You then go to the treatment room, and the therapist will leave while you disrobe and lie down, placing a towel over your body, ready for massage. Some spas offer disposable panties for body treatments such as a Body Salt Glow or Seaweed Wrap. They may be optional, or mandatory.

Acupuncture

This can be used to prevent and remedy many maladies. Moxibustion is the treatment which involves hair-thin needles and heat transfer based on a special plant, the Artemisa Capillaris, placed into one of the body's 1,100-plus acupuncture points.

Body scrub

The aim of this treatment is to cleanse and soften the skin, and to draw out impurities from within, using aromatic oils, creams, lotions, and perhaps sea salt, together with exfoliation (removal of dead skin cells) using skin brushing techniques.

Body wrap

Often called a body mask, this treatment typically includes the use of algae and seaweeds applied to the whole body. The body is then covered in aluminium foil and blankets. There are many variations on this theme, using mud from the Dead Sea or Mediterranean Sea, or sea salt and ginger, or cooling cucumber and aloe, or combinations of herbs and oils that leave you with a warm glow. The aim of this treatment is to detoxify, firm and tone the skin, and reduce cellulite.

Dry flotation

This hydrobath gives you the sensation of floating without getting wet; you lie on a plush warm blanket between your body and the water. A therapist then gently massages your head and neck.

Facials

Aromatherapy facial: This treatment typically uses aromatic oils such as lavender, sandalwood and geranium, plus a rejuvenating mask and accompanying creams and essences to "lift" the skin and facial muscles. **Rejuvenation facial:** Typically a classic French facial which utilizes the latest skin care products that may include essential plant and vitamin-rich oils. This facial aims to reduce lines and wrinkles.

Other popular treatments include eye lifting, volcanic mud mask, manicure with back and neck massage, and teeth whitening.

Rasul chamber

This is a steam chamber (also known as Hammam) that is typically fully tiled, with a domed roof and Moorish decor. When you enter, you paste yourself or your partner (it's a much better experience with a partner) with

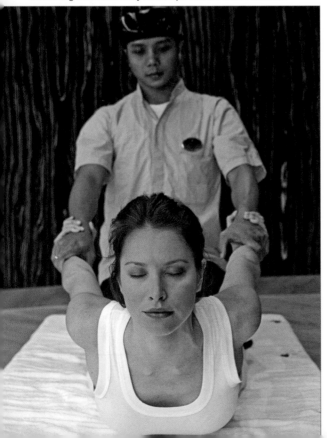
Stretching mind and body in the spa aboard *MSC Fantasia*.

Some RCI cruise ships have a full-size boxing ring.

three types of mud, and sit down while gentle steam surrounds you. The various types of mud become heated and then you're in a mud bath, after which you rub yourself (and each other) with large crystals of rock salt.

Reflexology

The body's energy meridians exist as reflex points on the soles of the feet. The therapist uses thumb pressure to stimulate these points to improve circulation and restore energy flow throughout the body.

Thalassotherapy

The use of seawater to promote well-being and healing dates back to ancient Greece. Today, shipboard spas have whole bath rituals involving water and flower petals, herbs or mineral salts.

Sample prices

Prices of body-pampering treatments have escalated recently, and are now equal to the prices you would find at land-based spas in the United States. You can expect to pay up to:

$200 for a 75-minute Hot Stones Massage
$125 for a 50 minute Well-Being Massage
$200 for a 75-minute Seaweed Wrap
$125 for a 50-minute Reflexology Session

Spa cuisine

Originally designed as low-fat, low-calorie (almost tasteless) meals for weight loss using grains, greens, and sprouts, spa cuisine now includes whole grains, seasonal fruits and vegetables, and lean proteins – ingredients low in saturated fats and cholesterol, low-fat dairy products, and reduced salt. They provide the basis for balanced nutrition and portion sizes while maintaining some flavor, texture and taste. Spa cuisine should be about using natural, not artificial, ingredients, flavor enhancers, coloring mediums, preservatives, or foods laden with sodium.

To eat healthier meals, choose steamed or grilled items rather than baked or fried items.

Sports facilities

Sports facilities might include basketball and paddle tennis (a sort of downsized tennis court), and electronic golf simulators. Some boutique/small "luxury" ships offer kayaking, water-skiing, jet skiing, and wake boarding for no extra charge. In reality, however, the watersports equipment is typically only used on one or two days (or part days) during a seven-day cruise. ❑

WHO RUNS THE SPAS

Aboard most ships, the spa and fitness areas are operated by a specialist concession, although each cruise line may have a separate name for the spa, such as AquaSpa (Celebrity Cruises), The Greenhouse Spa (Holland America Line), Lotus Spas (Princess Cruises), etc.

Aboard the large resort ships, spa staff tend to be young and enthusiastic "therapists" who will try hard to sell you own-brand beauty products, for a commission. Steiner Leisure is by far the largest concession, operating spas aboard more than 100 ships.

This company, founded in London in 1901 by Henry Steiner, began its ambitious growth in 1926 when Herman Steiner got involved in the family beauty salon on his father's death. He opened salons throughout England, became official cosmetician to Queen Elizabeth the Queen Mother, and won his first cruise ship contract in 1956.

The company closed its land-based salons in the 1990s as its cruise ship business burgeoned. It bought Elemis, a lifestyle range of plant-based beauty products, and acquired Mandara Spas, which it has developed in the US alongside its Elemis Spas. It runs 14 training schools. Steiner's corporate headquarters is now in the Bahamas.

Other shipboard concessions include Blue Ocean (MSC Cruises), Canyon Ranch At Sea (Cunard), Espace Elegance, Flair (Louis), Futuresse, and Harding Brothers (The Onboard Spa Company).

CRUISING FOR FAMILIES

Many cruise lines, recognizing the needs of
parents, have added a whole variety of
children's programs to their daily activities

More than 2 million children and teens a year take a cruise; Carnival Cruise Lines alone carries over 625,000. There are few better vacations for families than a ship cruise. Active parents can have the best of all worlds: family togetherness, social contact, and privacy. Cruise ships provide a virtually crime-free, encapsulated environment, and give young passengers a lot of freedom without parents having to be concerned about where their children are at all times. Because the days aboard are long, youngsters will be able to spend time with their parents or grandparents, as well as with their peers. They can also meet senior officers and learn about the navigation, radar, and communications equipment. They will be exposed to different environments, and experience many types of food. They will discover different cultures during shore excursions.

Although children may not like organized school-like clubs, they will probably make new friends quickly in the surroundings of a cruise ship. Whether you share a cabin with them or book an adjoining cabin, there will be plenty to keep them occupied.

Some cruise lines have token family programs, with limited activities and only a couple of general staff allocated to look after children, even though their brochures might claim otherwise. Other lines dedicate teams of counselors who run special programs off-limits to adults. They also provide practical facilities such as high chairs in the dining room, cots, and real playrooms.

Note that some ships provide children's programs and youth counselors only during the summer holidays, Christmas, New Year, and Easter. If you want to cruise at any other time, check whether the cruise line actually offers the right product for your needs.

Most of the cruise lines with large resort ships give out colored bracelets to children which must be worn at all times. These identify which muster station they belong to in the event of an emergency, as well as showing which children are enrolled in which activity programs.

Choosing a cabin

Families cruising together often find the hassle of shared cabins causes most distress. Teens need a place they can call their own, where they can put their stuff and retreat to when the world gets to be too much – in short, privacy. So, before booking, check the size of the cabin, and pace it out at home, remembering that the size quoted on ship deck plans *includes* the bathroom. If you are a large family, some ships (such as NCL's) have three-bedroom suites that can accommodate as many as 14.

Choose the largest cabin you can afford, because, if there's not enough storage space, expect to use your suitcase a lot for young children's dolls, games or toys, and for toddlers' diapers and baby food. If you have a large or extended family, cabins with interconnecting doors may be more practical.

If possible, opt for a cabin with a balcony. An interior (no view) cabin may be adequate for a short cruise, but could be claustrophobic on a 10-day Mediterranean vacation. To get access to fresh air without a balcony, you'd have to keep trudging up to the open deck, carrying the towels many large resort ships provide for use with deck chairs. If you have a baby, having a balcony gives you somewhere to escape to in the evening while keeping an eye on the sleeping infant.

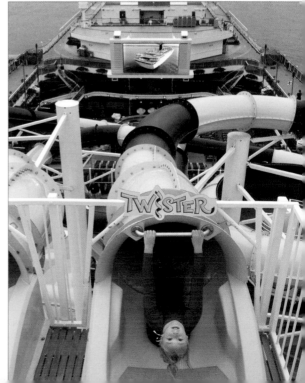

LEFT: P&O Cruises' *Arcadia* arrives in Venice.
RIGHT: Carnival caters well for children.

Some ships' play areas are generously stocked.

Many ships have family-friendly cabins with two lower beds, and one or two upper berths. But in some cabins, the two lower beds can't be pushed together to form a queen-sized bed for parents. This means mum and dad, and one or two children all have separate beds, – so families that cruise together can't always be sure they'll sleep together as they would wish.

If you have older children, consider two adjoining cabins. Larger cabins or suites have much more space, and may include sofa beds. Some ships, such as *Disney Dream, Disney Magic, Disney Wonder* and *Norwegian Epic,* have cabins with two bathrooms – good for families who want to get ready at the same time.

Caring for babies under three

Many new or recent parents understandably want to take their new babies with them when they cruise. Per-

THE GOOD PARENTING GUIDE

Parenting responsibilities don't end just because you're on vacation, and cruise lines will charge parents for any damage caused by their children and teens. Princess Cruises, for example, posts a short statement warning parents or guardians to supervise children and teens who are not taking part in the youth programs, to restrain children in public areas from running or engaging in loud or disruptive behavior, and to accompany children in elevators at all times. Here are a few rules worth laying down at the outset:

● Parents should establish a curfew, and stick to it.
● Children are not permitted to use the elevators unless accompanied by a parent or guardian.
● No shouting in passenger hallways.
● Tantrums should be confined to cabins, not restaurants or public areas.
● No urinating in the pool.
● No diaper changing on deck – many ships have diaper changing stations in both men's and women's toilets.

haps the most attractive thing is that you, as parent(s), need to pack and unpack the baby things only once, you'll get to see new destinations, and experience life on the ocean wave. You will, however, need to adjust your normal routines a little, given the way that ships operate at sea.

However, this can mean lots of baby strollers (baby buggies) cluttering up the open decks – and nowhere to store them. Some cruise lines prohibit babies under six months old from sailing (examples include: Carnival Cruise Lines, Royal Caribbean International). This is because of concerns over specialist medical attention for problems, and the fact that there have been many instances of "naughties" in paddling pools (even if toddlers are wearing swim diapers, or even if parents are with them), making them unusable for others.

Note that Disney Cruise Line is the only line that does allow toddlers in paddling pools – that's because of a special filtration system that is cleverly disguised in Mickey's face and ears painted into the bottom of the paddling pool aboard its ships.

It may be difficult to bathe small children in cabins with no bathtub but only a shower enclosure with a fixed-head shower. So check with your travel agent to make sure that your little one is not too little for the cruise line you choose.

It's important to check the ship's itinerary. Why? Because it's easier if a ship docks alongside in each port, rather than being at anchor, when shore tenders must be used (these may require you to go down a rigged ladder to a small boat waiting to take you ashore – not easy with an infant in tow).

Most cruise lines' children's programs start at age three, so if you have a toddler, you're generally on your own. And that can mean around-the-clock. But, some cruise lines do have nurseries, wading pools, babysitting services, and nappy-changing facilities. Children under three years old need to be potty trained to take part in group activities.

Some cruise ships will lend you key baby equipment,

such as bouncy seats, cribs, strollers, books and toys. Check with the cruise line or your travel agent *before* you book. Disposable nappies, wipes and sterilising fluid can be purchased aboard most child-friendly ships, but if you have very small children, you will be expected to bring your own supplies. Cots and bed guards are usually available on request (they can be pre-booked when you make your reservations).

If you do take baby (or babies) along, and you want some time to yourself, you'll need the services of a babysitter, so choose well. Some, but not all, ships have babysitting services; some have restricted hours (meaning you'll need to be back by midnight – or you'll change into a pumpkin); and some have only group babysitting and not in-cabin care.

From the viewpoint of a cruise line, babies do not bring much revenue (no alcohol, they don't play in the casino, or patronize the shop – except, perhaps, for diapers), and so many cruise lines would rather not bother with them. While some babies do travel well, others can also upset a lot of passengers who are older and don't want to be around them. Another reason that many cruise lines do not cater to passengers with babies is that the medical department simply isn't set up for paediatric services – nor is there a paediatrician on board, should a medical situation arise, because cruise ship doctors are generalists.

If you have a swim vest (the ones with "floaties" built into them are *not* life vests – they are made to help children learn to swim, not to actually keep their head above water, and are not recommended) for your toddler, it's a good idea to take it with you. That's because the life vest provided aboard a cruise ship is for emer-

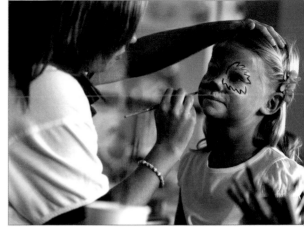

Trying on a new face aboard P&O Cruises' *Aurora*.

gency use only – you can't take it off the ship when you go to the beach, or on a boating excursion ashore.

Packing for infants

It's important to calculate how much ready-feed formula, baby food, diapers and wipes you'll need for the duration of the cruise. Most lines don't sell these products on board, and those that do sell diapers – such as Disney Cruise Line – charge exorbitant prices. If you normally give your baby ready-to-feed formula, consider using powder for the cruise, and buy bottled water from the ship's bar or in ports of call. Fruit is now available in unbreakable plastic containers. If you need to fly to join your cruise, decide whether to carry glass vegetable jars by hand, or risk possible breakage by bubble-wrapping and packing them.

In luggage for airline check-in, remember to pack items such as baby bottles and extra nipples, baby spoon and bib, swim diapers, medicines, pacifiers, insulated bag for keeping bottles cool, picture books and toys. And a thermometer might come in handy.

Berlitz Tip: Carnival Cruise Lines is one of the few operators to offer baby strollers for rent. If you take your own stroller, it's best to consider one with an integral umbrella – particularly useful for strong sunlight areas. These are collapsible and can be stored easily under the bed or in a corner.

The right food

Selected baby foods, along with cribs and high chairs, are stocked by ships catering to children, but ask your travel agent to check first and obtain confirmation in writing that they will be provided. Steamed or boiled vegetables such as steamed or boiled broccoli, carrots, cauliflower, pumpkin, and potatoes are

Children try their hand at baking cookies on a Crystal cruise.

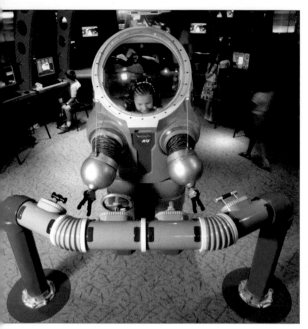

Disney Cruise Line's Oceaneer Lab keep kids busy.

usually available on request aboard, as are steamed chicken or fish, and white rice (brown rice can be more difficult to obtain unless requested in advance). Remember that children can eat later aboard ships – at the self-serve buffet – than they would at home.

If you need a special brand of baby food, or a high chair in the restaurant, let your travel agent know well in advance. Parents using organic baby foods, such as those obtained from health food stores, should be aware that cruise lines buy their supplies from major general food suppliers and not the smaller specialized food houses.

Children's entertainment

Most entertainment for children is designed to run simultaneously with adult programs; few ships have dedicated children's entertainers. For those cruising with very young children, baby-sitting services may be available. For example, *Queen Mary 2* has children's nurses and English nannies. *Aurora, Azura, Oceana, Oriana* and *Ventura* have a "night nursery" for two- to five-year-olds. Some ships have children's pools and play areas, as well as junior discos, video rooms, and teen "chill-out" centers off limits to parents.

AN ESSENTIAL CHECKLIST FOR PARENTS CRUISING WITH CHILDREN

The basics
● What are the age restrictions for the cruise line?
● Do your children's ages qualify them for a discount?
● Are discounts available for a third and/or fourth person in your cabin?
● Are the special activities and child care/teen centers open and available at the time you want to cruise?
● How big are the cabins?
● Will your children find the ports of call interesting? If not, is there enough to keep them happy aboard the ship?
● Is there a special place or playroom dedicated for children? For teens?

Accommodation
● Are cribs and/or day beds or cots available to put in the cabin?
● Are adjoining cabins available (for those with a large or extended family)?
● Do they have interconnecting doors? How large are the cabins?
● If there is no child's or infant's life vest in your cabin, see your steward right away and ask for one.
● Are bedrails (guardrails) available for the upper berths?

Computers for kids aboard an RCI ship.

Dining
● Does the menu offer the kind of food your children will eat? If not, are pizza and burgers and hot dogs available?
● Is a children's menu available for each meal?
● Is early seating available or does the ship feature "open" seating so that you can eat at a time close to when the children normally dine?
● Kids in the dining room can be even messier and more demanding than adults, so remember to tip accordingly.

Activities
● What activities are planned for children?
● Is there a children-only pool available on the ship?
● Will there be special movies or live entertainment that children will enjoy?
● Are any scheduled shore excursions geared toward children?
● Is a babysitting service available? If so, what are its hours and costs?
● Does the cruise lines provide after-midnight babysitting services?

Activity/Play Centers
● What are the requirements for placing a child in the center such as age, vaccinations, or toilet training?
● How are the children's areas supervised? Is the teen center supervised?
● What are the hours, costs, and restrictions on the centers?
● What security methods are used when a child is picked up from the center?
● What is the ratio of children to adult staff in the children's center?
● How are staff members trained for work in the children's center? Are they insured? Do they know how to perform CPR on children and infants?

The classic carousel aboard RCI's *Oasis of the Seas*.

In some ships, stewards, stewardesses, and other staff may be available as private babysitters for an hourly charge; otherwise, group babysitting may be offered. Make arrangements at the reception desk. Aboard some ships, evening baby-sitting services may not start until late – check details before booking.

Cruise lines serious about children typically divide them into distinct age groups: Toddlers (ages 2–4); Juniors (ages 5–7); Intermediate (ages 8–10); Tweens (ages 11–13); and Teens (ages 14–17). It often seems to be children under 12 who get the most from a cruise.

Activities for children

Although many ships have full programs for children during days at sea, these may be limited when the ship is in port. Ships expect you to take your children with you on organized excursions, which sometimes have lower prices for children. If the ship has a playroom, find out if it is open and supervised on all days of the cruise.

When going ashore, remember that if you want to take your children swimming or to the beach, it is wise to telephone ahead to a local hotel with a beach or pool. Many hotels will be happy to show off their property to you, hoping to gain your future business.

Some cruise ships in the Caribbean have the use of a "private" island for a day, including waterpark areas for children and adults. A lifeguard will be on duty, and there will be water sports and snorkeling equipment you can rent. But remember that the beaches on some "private" islands are fine for 200 passengers, but with 2,000 they quickly become crowded, forcing you to stand in line for beach barbecues and toilet facilities. Also, since operators take advantage of the captive market, rental of beach and watersports items can be very expensive.

Although the sun and warm sea might attract juniors to the Caribbean, many older children will find a Baltic, Black Sea, or Mediterranean cruise fascinating as they are exposed to different cultures.

Activities for pre-teens

Supervised group activities and activity/play centers mean that you won't have to be concerned, and will be able to go out and enjoy yourself, knowing that your children are in good hands. Some cruise lines issue beepers in case of problems. Activities would typically include scavenger hunts, make-up and cookery classes, and interactive computer programs.

Activities for teens

Many large resort ships have dedicated "no adults allowed" zones. Teen-only activities include deck parties, pool parties, games, karaoke, discos, dances, com-

---

SAFETY TIPS AT SEA

● In case children get lost or separated from their parents, most cruise lines provide them with colored wristbands, which must be worn at all times.

● Young children love to climb, so don't ever leave them on a balcony alone. On the open decks, ships have railings – these are either horizontal bars through which children cannot get their heads, or they are covered in glass/plexiglass under a thick wooden top rail.

● While children find their way around easily, walk with them between the playroom/activity and your cabin, so that all of you get to know the way.

● Discuss safety issues with them, and warn them not to walk into "Crew Only" areas at any time.

● Children's lifejackets are available aboard most cruise ships that carry children. However, check with your cabin steward as soon as you embark.

puter gaming consoles and talent shows. Some Royal Caribbean International ships provide musical instruments for jam sessions. Sports include rock-climbing and basketball. There's usually almost unlimited food, too, although some of it may not be very nutritious.

Cruising with teens provides a chance to meet other families who cruise with teens, and the other moms enjoy sharing thoughts and experiences while their teens and other kids are having fun together. But some ships simply are not big-kid friendly, so choose wisely. Teens also tend to eat a lot, so cruising aboard one of the large resort ships makes sense, and provides excellent value for money. Just think, your teenagers can eat themselves silly if they really want to.

Balancing adult needs with teenage desires can be challenging. Teens do really well for themselves on cruises. And, once they find others of a like age, you'll probably never see them again for the whole cruise. Teens can go almost anywhere aboard ship, and, although they can't play in the casino, or use reserved, "adult-only" sanctuary areas, and perhaps certain lounges. They will, however, probably end up spending most of their free time hanging out in "chill-out" rooms – just the job for truculent teens – maybe even practising their communication skills! It's best if you set limits and curfews *before* you leave home. Girls end up in gaggles, while boys end up in "cool" groups (or groups trying to *be* "cool.") And teens who go cruising almost always say how surprised they were at just how many other teens were also on board – and at just how fast a seven-day cruise goes by.

Getting meals right helps keep the kids contented.

Teens can get together in their own disco, games rooms, video arcades and activity clubs, and on deck for sports tournaments and basketball games, rock-climbing and roller-blading. With some cruise lines, the fun extends ashore, with beach barbecues and even some shore excursions aimed at younger passengers.

Note that if your teens are inclined to be messy at home, perhaps getting an adjoining cabin for them is a good idea – and will also give them a feeling of independence. Just be sure to set some limits to what they can and cannot do in their "home away from home."

A Major Teen Gripe: Understandably, teens often want to take a dip in the swimming pool late at night, but, aboard most large resort ships, this is simply not possible. Most pools are closed and netted over by 6pm. Why? Because it's the end of the crew working shift, and no one is assigned to take over in the evening. Keeping them open would mean paying for adequate supervision, or risking negligence claims. So pools get closed, and teens get frustrated. It's about time the cruise lines started catering to their customers – after all, today's teens could be tomorrow's suite occupants.

Disney goes cruising

In 1932, a Disney cartoon, *Steamboat Willy*, depicted Mickey Mouse at the wooden wheel of a ship. But it took another six decades until Disney decided to get into the family cruise market, creating Disney Cruise Line as an extension of its resort stay business, offering a "seamless vacation package."

In 1998, it introduced the first of two large resort ships to cater to families with children,

Carnival Cruise Lines provides hi-tech centers for teens.

for families with young children, one for families with more grown children and teens, and one for adults only. Each group has its own swimming pool and deck facilities. The cabin bathrooms are practical and have a separate toilet. Disney characters also appear at certain times, much to the delight of children, who can also book a breakfast with their favorite character – or be tucked up in bed by one. It's all a question of endless Disney magic. The ships also have three identically sized main restaurants (but with different Disney themes and decor), and passengers change restaurants daily, together with their waiters, keeping the same table number – ingenious, and very popular.

Facilities are highly organized for specific age groups, and each group gets its own daily program (Personal Navigator). Flounders Reef Nursery is for babies/kids aged three months to three years. Kids aged 3–8 get to play in the Oceaneer Club, a playroom themed on Captain Hook, with lots of crawling and climbing-centered activities. The Oceaneer Lab is an interactive center for 8–12-year-olds, where kids learn to about science, get to use microscopes, build things, act and direct their own TV commercials, and learn how animation works. Pre-teens and teens have their own chill-out spaces, and teen counselors. Each ship carries over 40 children's and youth counselors.

with cruises of 3, 4 and 7 days. *Disney Magic* and *Disney Wonder* carry 1,750 adults and 1,000 or more children, and the casino-free ships have ambitious entertainment programs, with everything centered around Disney and its superb stable of famous characters. Disney has its own art-deco passenger terminal and facilities at Port Canaveral, Florida, plus a fleet of motorcoaches.

Disney Cruise Line's success is due to the way in which the ships are designed to handle both children and adults well. Each ship has three distinct areas: one

Families preparing to sail on Disney Cruise Line with little ones (under three years of age) have access to an online service that allows you to order baby supplies in advance of their cruise and have them delivered to

THE SHIPS THAT CATER WELL FOR CHILDREN

These ships have been selected for the quality of their children's programs:
Aida Cruises: *AIDAaura, AIDAbella, AIDAblu, AIDA-cara, AIDAdiva, AIDAluna, AIDAsol, AIDAvita*
Carnival Cruise Lines: *Carnival Conquest, Carnival Destiny, Carnival Dream, Carnival Freedom, Carnival Glory, Carnival Legend, Carnival Liberty, Carnival Pride, Carnival Spirit, Carnival Splendor, Carnival Triumph, Carnival Valor, Carnival Victory, Carnival Ecstasy, Carnival Elation, Carnival Fantasy, Carnival Fascination, Carnival Imagination, Carnival Inspiration, Carnival Paradise, Carnival Sensation*
Celebrity Cruises: *Celebrity Constellation, Celebrity Eclipse, Celebrity Equinox, Celebrity Infinity, Celebrity Millennium, Celebrity Solstice, Celebrity Summit*

Some cruise lines are more child-friendly than others.

Costa Cruises: *Costa Atlantica, Costa Concordia, Costa Deliziosa, Costa Fortuna, Costa Luminosa, Costa Costa Magica, Costa Mediterranea, Costa Pacifica, Costa Serena*
Cunard Line: *Queen Elizabeth, Queen Mary 2, Queen Victoria*
MSC Cruises: *MSC Fantasia, MSC Magnifica, MSC Musica, MSC Opera, MSC Orchestra, MSC Poesia, MSC Splendida*
Disney Cruise Line: *Disney Dream,*

Disney Magic, Disney Wonder
Norwegian Cruise Line: *Norwegian Dawn, Norwegian Epic, Norwegian Gem, Norwegian Jade, Norwegian Jewel, Norwegian Pearl, Norwegian Spirit, Norwegian Star, Norwegian Sun*
P&O Cruises: *Aurora, Azura, Oceana, Oriana, Ventura*
Princess Cruises: *Crown Princess, Diamond Princess, Emerald Princess, Golden Princess, Grand Princess, Ruby Princess, Sapphire Princess, Star Princess*
Royal Caribbean International: *Adventure of the Seas, Allure of the Seas, Explorer of the Seas, Freedom of the Seas, Independence of the Seas, Liberty of the Seas, Mariner of the Seas, Navigator of the Seas, Oasis of the Seas, Voyager of the Seas*
Star Cruises: *SuperStar Virgo*
Thomson Cruises: *Thomson Celebration, Thomson Destiny, Thomson Dream, Thomson Spirit.*
TUI Cruises: *Mein Schiff*

Disney characters gather on the last night of a cruise.

their cabin. The service is exclusive to Disney Cruise Line passengers and is provided by Babies Travel Lite, an online retailer offering more than 1,000 brand-name baby products including diapers, baby food, infant formula and specialty travel items. On disneycruise.com, you can access a section of the Babies Travel Lite Web site where you can create orders for familiar brands in quantities customized to the length of your cruise.

One ship also sails in the Mediterranean in summer, from Barcelona, and in 2011 one ship will sail to Alaska during the summer. Disney has its own 1,000-acre private island experience on 3-, 4-, and 7-day Bahamas and Caribbean cruises. It's about 50 miles north of Nassau in the Bahamas, and called Castaway Cay – Disney's own private country, with its own ship docking pier. (Locals say it had a military landing strip that was once used by drug runners.) Beaches are divided into family-friendly and adults-only "quiet" sections.

Disney has two larger casino-free ships on order, for delivery in 2011 (*Disney Dream*) and 2012 (*Disney Fantasy*), each with the longest water slide at sea.

Single parents

Only a few cruise lines have introduced their versions of the "Single Parent Plan" (e.g. Disney Cruise Line, P&O Cruises). This offers an economical way for single parents to take their children on a cruise, with parent and child sharing a two-berth cabin, or parent and children sharing a three-berth cabin. Reduced rates may apply to children of single parents in the same cabin.

As a single parent, you should expect to pay about one-third the normal single-person rate for your children. However, as a single parent with just one child, you may have to pay for two adults (double occupancy), so it's important to check the pricing policy of each

ent, parent or guardian with a passport surname different to that of any child traveling with you. Without this form, which includes passport information of the child's legal parent, you will be denied boarding.

Family reunions

A cruise can provide the ideal place for a family get-together, with or without children. Let your travel agent make the arrangements and ask for a group discount if there are more than 15 of you.

Take care to choose a cruise line with a suitable ambience. Book 12 months in advance if possible so that you can arrange cabins close to each other. If the ship operates two dinner seatings, you may also wish to arrange for everyone to be at the same one.

With pricing that includes accommodations, meals, entertainment, use of most of the ship's recreational facilities, and travel from destination to destination, any cruise represents excellent value for money spent. Cruise lines also make special offers to groups. Depending on the company, these include reduced fares for groups as small as eight guests and free berths for one in every 10 to 15 paying passengers.

Family groups may have the option to ensure even greater value by purchasing everything in advance, from cruise fares to shore excursions, drinks packages, spa packages, and even pre-paid gratuities. Additional savings can be realized through reduced fares for third and fourth passengers in each stateroom and some cruise lines offer "kids sail free" programs.

cruise line you are interested in. It may also be better to take an adult friend and share the cost (in some cases, your child could travel free).

Confirming a guardian's identity

A Parent and Guardian Consent Form (PGCSA) will be needed at or before embarkation if you are a grandpar-

THE PROS AND CONS OF CRUISING WHEN PREGNANT

If your pregnancy is routine and healthy, there's no reason for you not to go on a cruise. Indeed, a cruise could be a great getaway before you deal with the things associated with an upcoming childbirth. However, if you are in your third trimester, you should cancel your cruise quickly, and recover any money you have already spent. Although some cruise lines may let you sail even in your 27th week of pregnancy, most will not allow you to do so if you have entered your 24th week of pregnancy.

Ask about any restrictions by your chosen cruise line. Do purchase travel insurance. Although most travel insurance won't cover cancellation penalties resulting from normal pregnancy, any claims arising from complications may be paid. And since you stand to lose much of your cruise fare for last-minute cancellations, insurance is a must – whether you paid for your cruise with money, or with award

Shore excursions in hot climates can be tiring.

points. Also, make sure that your medical insurance covers you in case of complications, either on board or in ports of call.

Berlitz's Pregnancy Tips:
● If you are heavily pregnant, standing in line at embarkation, with heavy carry-on bags could be stressful. Tell

a member of staff that you are heavily pregnant and ask for an expedited embarkation (but make sure all your documentation is correct before you do). Most cruise line personnel will whisk you through quickly so that you can get off your feet and rest.
● Don't be afraid to ask for extra pillows, in case your mattress is a bit worn or saggy – you'll need more support when pregnant. Your cabin steward will be happy to oblige.
● Shore excursions can be challenging for someone who is heavily pregnant – too much walking, not enough rest or comfort stops, etc.
● Don't even think of going scuba diving, parasailing, or water-skiing. Wine-tasting should be off-limits, too.
● Carry a re-usable water bottle when off the ship to keep your hydration levels high.
● Carry some healthy snack items when you are off the ship, either on your own or on a shore excursion.

Family reunions can provide opportunities for accommodation upgrades, private events and special shipboard credits and complimentary amenities ranging from free family photos to "Fountain Soda Cards" to special family meals, and some cruise lines offer personalized shore excursions and customized programs that fit the needs and requirements of a family reunion.

The diversity of itineraries and cruise experiences means there is a family-friendly cruise vacation for all interests and budgets. Some cruise lines offer vacations as short as a weekend, with an itinerary that meets your family reunion's needs. A professional travel agent – and this book – will guide you through the maze.

Birthday specials

If anyone in the group has a birthday or anniversary, tell your travel agent to arrange a special cake – most cruise lines don't charge extra for this. Private parties can also be arranged, at a price. Shore excursions, too, can be booked in advance for a group.

Finally, get everything confirmed in writing, particularly cabin assignments and locations.

Formal nights

Some ships have nights when "formal attire" is the required dress code. If you don't want your children to dress formally (some children really enjoy getting dressed up – it's a bit like going to a prom night), you can opt out of the festivities, and simply head for one of the casual dining options. Or, your kids may prefer to opt out and go to the children's clubs or teen rooms and hang out while *you* go to the captain's cocktail party.

Maybe your teenage dropouts don't want anything to do with formal dress. However, once they see many other teens dressed nicely, they may want to emulate them on their next cruise. Most like it – because, today, it's actually *different* – particularly when almost everyone has gone into "dress down" mode ashore. Again, that makes cruising different. But anyone with an image-conscious teenage daughter will anticipate that it will probably take them a *long* time to get ready.

Unfamiliar languages

If you book a cruise aboard one of the ships catering to more international passengers, such as Costa Cruises, MSC Cruises, or Star Cruises, your youngsters may find themselves surrounded by children who speak other languages. This could cause a degree of confusion, but in most cases it will prove to be an adventure in learning and communication. ❑

Holland America's Half Moon Cay in the Bahamas.

HOW GRANDPARENTS CAN BRIDGE THE GENERATION GAP

Many children love to go cruising with grandparents, perhaps because they anticipate fewer restrictions than they have at home. And busy parents like the idea, too, particularly if the grandparents make a contribution to the cost.

Having enrolled their grandchildren in age-related groups for daytime activities aboard ship, grandparents will be able to enjoy the adults-only facilities, such as the wellness and spa treatments. Not surprisingly, it's the large resort ships that provide the widest choice of facilities for both age groups. For those not averse to ubiquitous cartoon characters, Disney Cruise Line provides some facilities for adults and children in separate areas, but also allows them to mix in others.

Before you leave home

Grandparents should remember that their grandchildren will need their own passports. They should also bring along a letter signed by the parent authorizing any necessary medical attention. In some cases they may also need a notarized letter by a custodial parent granting permission for a child to travel with them.

Incipient architectural ambitions aboard *Enchantment of the Seas*.

Ground rules should be established with a child's parent(s) present to avoid potential problems. An important issue is whether a child will be allowed to roam the ship unsupervised, given that some cruise lines allow children as young as eight to sign themselves out of supervised programs. Walkie-talkies are a good solution to this issue. They work well aboard ships, and allow adults and children to stay in constant touch.

You should remember to pack a grandchild's favorite toys and any medications for your journey to the ship. If flying to an embarkation port, pack games, books, a bathing suit and a change of clothes for your grandchild in your carry-on, plus any important medication – just in case any checked-in luggage gets lost.

On embarkation day, it's wise to take essentials in a carry-on or tote bag, because your luggage may not be delivered to your cabin until several hours after you embark. This is especially so aboard the large resort ships.

On board

Most cruise lines offer scheduled activities from 9am to noon, 2–5pm and 7–10pm. This means you can drop your grandchild off after breakfast, relax by the pool, go to a lecture, or take part in other activities, and pick them up for lunch. After a couple of hours together, they can rejoin their friends while you enjoy an afternoon movie or siesta.

Dining: Flexibility is the key. Coaxing children out of a pool,

getting them dressed and ready to sit quietly through a four-course dinner every night can be tough. Work out a compromise by eating dinner together occasionally at the buffet. Most ships offer a tempting menu of children's favorites, and some ships have special mealtimes for children.

Children with special needs

If a grandchild has special needs, you'll need to advise the cruise line when you book. Children needing one-to-one care or assistance must be accompanied by a grandparent when in the children's play center.

Shore excursions

Consider your grandchild's interests before booking expensive shore excursions (example: flightseeing in Alaska). It's also best to avoid long bus rides, shopping trips and scenic tours, and better to choose excursions that feature water and/or animals. Examples include snorkeling, aquariums or nature walks. Remember to pack snacks. In some ports, it may be better to explore on your own. If your grandchildren are really young, full-day shore excursions are a bad idea.

Disembarkation

When it's time to go home, some grandparents like to minimize post-cruise blues for the children by adding on an extra couple of days' vacation ashore. If everybody genuinely enjoyed the cruise, that's a good time to get out the brochures and start planning next year's. ❑

CRUISING FOR SENIORS

People everywhere are living longer and healthier lives, and cruise lines are keen to cater for their needs

Although cruise lines have been striving, with some success, to embrace all age groups, the over-60s remain an important segment of the market. Group cruising for seniors, in fact, is growing in popularity and is a good way for like-minded people to vacation together. Nowhere is this more evident than in Japan's "Golden Week," a collection of four national holidays within seven days in late April/early May, when seniors clamor for available cabins.

One trend for seniors is towards longer cruises – even round-the-world cruises if they can afford them. Some opt for a child-free ship such as *Adonia* and *Arcadia* (both P&O Cruises); *Saga Pearl II*, *Saga Ruby* and *Spirit of Adventure* (all Saga Cruises).

There are bargains to be had, too. Organizations for seniors such as AARP in the United States and Saga in the UK often offer discount fares and upgrades.

Some seniors who may have had major surgery or have mobility problems cannot fly, or don't wish to.

They are aided by the trend toward "Homeland Cruising," which enables them to embark at and disembark from a nearby port in their home country. In the United States, the number of homeland ports increased dramatically following the terrorist attacks of September 2001. In the UK, some cruise ships sail from ports in both the north and south of the country. The same is true elsewhere, as language-specific cruise lines and ships proliferate.

But all is far from perfect. Some cruise lines have yet to recognize that, with seniors as with other groups, one size does *not* fit all. Only a few, for example, take the trouble to provide the kind of items that millions of seniors need, such as large-print editions of daily programs, menus, and other printed matter.

Special diets

While the wide range of cuisine aboard many ships is a big attraction, cruise lines understand that many

---

WHY SENIORS LIKE CRUISING – BUT CAN OFTEN FIND IT FRUSTRATING

THUMBS UP

● A cruise is an excellent choice for those who like to be independent while having the chance to meet other like-minded people.

● Cruising is stress-free and relaxing. You don't have to keep packing and unpacking as you do on a land-based tour.

● It's safe. You travel and dine in comfort and safety, while your floating hotel takes you to a choice of around 2,000 destinations all over the world.

● Lecturers and lessons in everything from golf to computing provide a chance to learn something new.

● There's plenty of entertainment – shows, cinema, casinos, games, dances.

● All main and self-serve buffet meals are included in the fare, and those on special diets can be easily accommodated.

● Senior singles, in particular, find it easy to meet others in a non-threatening environment. Some ships provide male dance hosts, screened and subject to a strict code of ethics, who can also act as escorts on shore excursions.

● Most ships have 24-hour room service and a 24-hour reception desk.

A senior moment aboard *Oasis of the Seas*.

● The disabled can find ships that cater for their needs.

● Ships carry a medical doctor and one or more trained nurses. In an emergency, treatment can be arranged.

THUMBS DOWN

● Online check-in procedures, and unreadable Passenger Ticket Conditions and Contracts that are provided only online.

● Credit-card sized electronic key cards to cabins that often don't make it clear which end to insert and penalize those passengers with poor eyesight.

● Booking events and meals via the in-cabin "interactive" television/keypad system; it is user-unfriendly for many seniors (all services should be readily accessible via telephone).

● Poor, difficult to read signage such as "You are here" deck plans unreadable from further away than an inch.

● Menus with small, hard-to-read typefaces and daily programs that require a magnifying glass.

● Buffets with plates only, requiring several visits, and cutlery too heavy to hold comfortably.

● Anything that requires a signature – for example: bar, shore excursions, spa bills with small print.

● Libraries that contain few books, if any, in large-print format – notably recent novels.

● The absence of a "concierge" for seniors.

● Public toilets not clearly marked.

● The lack of music-free lounges and bars for conversation and drinks.

Saga Cruises' expanded fleet caters for the over-50s.

passengers are on special diets. Lighter menu options *are* available aboard most ships, as well as vegetarian and vegan choices. Options include low sodium, low fat, low cholesterol, and sugar-free entrées, and desserts. A booking agent will ensure that special dietary needs are recorded.

Healthier eating

You don't have to put on weight during a cruise. Many health-conscious seniors prefer smaller portions of food with taste and nutritional value rather than the overflowing plates that emerge from the kitchens of large floating resorts. Heart-healthy diets are in demand, as are low-fat, low-carbohydrate, salt-free or low-salt foods and salad dressings. Denture wearers often request food that includes softer items.

Those seeking lighter fare should be aware that most cruise lines have an "always available" section of heart-healthy items that can be cooked plainly, such as grilled or steamed salmon, skinless chicken breast, lean sirloin steak, or baked potatoes.

Gentlemen hosts

Because more female than male seniors cruise, cruise lines have developed "gentlemen host" programs. Unescorted female seniors can select cruise lines that have such hosts to enhance their cruise experience. These are gentlemen, typically over 55 years of age, selected for their social skills and competence as dance partners, for dining table conversation, and for accompanying passengers on shore excursions.

Cruise lines with gentlemen host programs include: Celebrity Cruises, Crystal Cruises, Cunard Line, Holland America Line, P&O Cruises, Princess Cruises, Regent Seven Seas Cruises, Silversea Cruises, Swan Hellenic Cruises, The Yachts of Seabourn, and Voyages of Discovery Cruises.

Enrichment programs

Many seniors want to learn about the history and culture of a destination rather than be told which shops to visit ashore. Lecturers of academic quality can be found aboard some smaller ships such as *Aegean Odyssey* (Voyages to Antiquity), *Minerva* (Swan Hellenic Cruises), *Spirit of Adventure* and *Saga Ruby* (Saga Cruises). Some cruise lines also have special interest cruises and lecturers on topics such as archaeology, food and wine, ornithology, and military history.

Tips for seniors

● If you are traveling solo, it's important to check the price of any single supplements.
● If you take medication, make sure you have enough with you to cover all eventualities.
● Some ships are dressy, some are casual. Choose a ship according to your own lifestyle and tastes.
● If you have mobility difficulties, choose one of the newer ships that have public rooms with an "open-flow" style of interior design. Examples include *Arcadia, Balmoral, Nieuw Amsterdam, Oosterdam, Queen Elizabeth, Queen Mary 2, Queen Victoria, Westerdam, Zuiderdam*. Older ships such as *Marco Polo* often have "lips" or doors between public rooms.

Best facilities

Among the cruise lines that provide the facilities and onboard environment that seniors enjoy most are: American Cruise Lines, Azamara Club Cruises, Blount Small Ship Adventures, Classic International Cruises, Crystal Cruises, Delphin Cruises, Fred Olsen Cruise Lines, Hebridean Island Cruises, Holland America Line, Noble Caledonia, Oceania Cruises, P&O Cruises, Pearl Seas Cruises, Regent Seven Seas Cruises, Saga Cruises, Sea Cloud Cruises, The Yachts of Seabourn, Silversea Cruises, Swan Hellenic Cruises, Voyages of Discovery, and Voyages to Antiquity. ❑
● *For contact addresses, see page 719.*

CRUISING FOR ROMANTICS

No need to worry about getting to the church
on time – you can be married at sea, or
get engaged, or have a second honeymoon

Two famous TV shows, *The Love Boat* (US) and *Traumschiff* (Germany), boosted the concept of cruising as a romantic vacation, though the plots didn't always match reality. The real captain of one ship, when asked the difference between his job and that of the captain of *The Love Boat*, remarked: "On TV they can do a retake if things aren't right the first time around, whereas I have to get it right the first time."

Getting engaged aboard ship

Princess Cruises has a special "Engagement Under the Stars" package that allows you to propose to your loved one in a personal video that is then screened just before an evening movie at a large outdoor screen aboard some of the company's ship's. Current cost: $695.

Getting married at sea

Instead of the hassle of arranging flights, hotels, transportation and packages, you can let a specialist wedding planner do it all for you. As in all those old romantic

Getting hitched by the rockwall aboard *Freedom of the Seas*.

black-and-white movies, a ship's captain can indeed marry you when at sea if properly certified – unless the ship's country of registry prohibits or does not recognize such marriages. You first need to inquire in your country of domicile whether such a marriage is legal, and ascertain what paperwork and blood tests are required. The onus is on you to prove the validity of such a marriage. The captain could be held legally responsible if he married a couple not entitled to be wed.

It's relatively easy to get married aboard almost any cruise ship when it is alongside in port. Carnival Cruise Lines, Celebrity Cruises, Holland America Line, and Princess Cruises, among others, offer special wedding packages. These include the services of a minister to marry you, wedding cake, champagne, bridal bouquet and matching boutonnière for the bridal party, a band to perform at the ceremony, and an album of wedding photos. Note that US citizens and "green card" residents may need to pay sales tax on wedding packages.

Several cruise lines can arrange a marriage ceremony on a Caribbean beach. For example, Princess Cruises offers weddings on a beach in St. Thomas (prices range from $525 to $1,175 per package). Or how about a romantic wedding Disney-style on its private island, Castaway Cay?

Azamara Club Cruises, Celebrity Cruises and Princess Cruises offer weddings aboard many of their ship. The ceremonies can be performed by the captain, who is certified as a notary, when the ships' registry – Bermuda or Malta, for example – recognizes such unions.

Expect to pay about $2,500, plus about $500 for licensing fees. Harborside or shore-side packages vary according to the port. A wedding coordinator at the line handles all the details, enabling you to be married aboard ship and honeymoon aboard, too.

Even if you don't get married aboard ship, you could have your wedding reception aboard one. Contact the director of hotel services at the cruise line of your choice. The cruise line should go out of its way to help, especially if you follow the reception with a honeymoon cruise – and a cruise, of course, also makes a fine, no-worry honeymoon *(see facing page)*.

UK-based passengers should know that P&O Cruises hosts a series of cruises called the "Red-Letter Anniversary Collection" for those celebrating 10, 15, 20, 25, 30, 35, 40, 45, 50, 55, or

Two's company in an MSC Cruises spa.

60 years of marriage; the cruise comes with a complimentary gift, such as a brass carriage clock, leather photograph album, or free car parking at Southampton.

Getting married ashore

An alternative is to have a marriage ceremony in an exotic destination with your reception (and honeymoon) aboard ship afterwards. For example, you could get married on the beach in Barbados or Hawaii; on a glacier in Juneau, Alaska; in a villa in Rome or Venice; in an authentic Tahitian Village (Tahiti); or in Central Park, New York.

Renewal of vows

Many cruise lines now perform "renewal of vows" ceremonies. A cruise is a wonderful setting for reaffirming to one's partner the strength of commitment. A handful of ships have a small chapel where this ceremony can

PRACTICAL TIPS FOR HONEYMOONERS

Remember to take a copy of your marriage license or certificate, for immigration (or marriage) purposes, as your passports will not yet have been amended. Also, allow extra in your budget for things like drinks, shipboard gratuities, shore excursions, and spending money while ashore.

Since you will probably wish to share a large bed with your partner, check with your travel agent and cruise line to make sure the cabin you have booked has such a bed. Better still, book a suite if you can afford to. It's important to check and double-check to avoid disappointment.

If you plan to combine your honeymoon with getting married along the way – in Hawaii or Bermuda, for example – and need to take your wedding gown aboard, there is usually space to hang it in the dressing room next to the stage in the main showlounge, especially aboard the large resort ships.

take place; otherwise it can be anywhere aboard ship – a most romantic time is at sunrise or sunset on the open deck. The renewal of vows ceremony is conducted by the ship's captain, using a non-denominational text.

Although some companies, such as Carnival Cruise Lines, Celebrity Cruises, Holland America Line, P&O Cruises and Princess Cruises, have complete packages for purchase, which include music, champagne, hors d'oeuvres, certificate, corsages for the women, and so on, most other companies do not charge – yet.

Cruising for honeymooners

There are many advantages in honeymooning at sea: you pack and unpack only once; it is a hassle-free and safe environment; and you get special attention, if you want it. It is easy to budget in advance, as one price often includes airfare, cruise, food, entertainment, several destinations, shore excursions, and pre- and post-cruise hotel stays. Also, some cruise lines offer discounts if you book a future cruise to celebrate an anniversary.

Although no ship as yet provides bridal suites, many ships have suites with king- or queen-sized beds. Some also provide tables for two in the dining room should you wish to dine together without having to make friends with others. A variety of honeymoon packages is available; these might include champagne and caviar for breakfast, flowers in the suite or cabin, a complementary cake, and a private captain's cocktail party.

Some cruise ships feature Sunday departures, so couples can plan a Saturday wedding and reception before traveling to their ship. Pre- and post-cruise hotel accommodation can also be arranged.

Most large resort ships accommodate honeymoon couples well. However, couples averse to crwds crowds might try one of the smaller, yacht-like cruise vessels such as those of The Yachts of Seabourn, Regent Seven Seas Cruises, Silversea Cruises, or Windstar Cruises.

And for quiet moments? The deck to the forward part of a ship, near the bridge, is the most dimly lit part and the quietest – except perhaps for some wind noise. ❑

CRUISING FOR SOLO PASSENGERS

Cruise prices are geared towards couples. Yet more
than one in four cruise passengers travels alone
or as a single parent. How do they fare?

Many solo passengers are prejudiced against cruising because most lines charge them a single occupancy supplement. The reason is that the most precious commodity aboard any ship is space. Since a solo-occupancy cabin is often as large as a double and is just as expensive to build, cruise lines feel the premium price is justified, What's more, because solo-occupancy cabins are at a premium, they are unlikely to be discounted.

Single supplements

If you are not sharing a cabin, you'll be asked to pay either a flat rate or a single "supplement" if you occupy a double-occupancy cabin by yourself. Some lines charge a fixed amount – $250, for instance – as a supplement, no matter what the cabin category, ship, itinerary, or length of cruise. Such rates vary between lines, and sometimes between a line's ships. Because there are so few single-occupancy cabins, it's best to book as far ahead as you can.

Lines that charge low single supplements include Crystal Cruises, Peter Deilmann Ocean Cruises, and Voyages of Discovery. Only a few of the smaller cruise

lines, such as Saga Cruises and Voyages of Discovery, have no additional supplements for singles. A sneaky cruise line may try to charge you twice for port charges and government taxes (by including that non-existent second person in the cabin you occupy as a single), so check your cruise fare invoice carefully

Guaranteed singles rates

Some lines offer singles a set price for a double cabin but reserve the right to choose the cabin. So you could end up with a rotten cabin in a poor location or a wonderful stateroom that happened to be unallocated.

Guaranteed share programs

These allow you to pay what it would cost each half of a couple for a double-occupancy cabin, but the cruise line will find another passenger of the same sex (and preferences such as smoking or non-smoking) to share it with you. If the line does not find a cabin-mate, the single passenger may get the cabin to himself or herself at no extra charge. Some cruise lines do not advertise a guaranteed-share program in their brochures but will often try to accommodate such bookings at times when demand for space is comparatively light.

Solo dining

A common complaint concerns dining arrangements. Before you take your cruise, make sure that you request a table assignment based on your personal preferences; table sizes are typically for 2, 4, 6, or 8 people. Do you want to sit with other singles? Or do you like to sit with couples? Or perhaps with a mixture of both? Or with passengers who may not speak your language?

When you are on board, make sure that you are comfortable with the dining arrangements, particularly in ships with fixed table assignments, or ask the maître d' to move you to a different table. Aboard ships with open seating or with several different dining venues, you can choose which venue you want to eat in, and when; Norwegian Cruise Line (NCL) is an example of this arrangement, with its Freestyle Dining.

Cruising for single women

A cruise ship is at least as safe for single women as any major vacation destination, but of course that doesn't mean it is entirely hassle-free. It's easy to strike up conversations with other passengers,

Best foot forward at the disco, but the decibel level is high.

Awaiting a gentleman host aboard *Queen Mary 2*.

and cruising is not a "meat market" that keeps you under constant observation. The easiest way to meet other singles is to participate in scheduled activities. Single black women may find there is often a dearth of single black men for dancing or socializing with.

Beware of embarking on an easy affair with a ship's officer or crew member. They meet new people on every cruise and could transmit sexual diseases. Crews have been known to award an imaginary Golden Mattress award to whoever can bed the most passengers.

Gentlemen cruise hosts

The female-to-male passenger ratio is typically high, especially among older people, so some cruise lines provide male social hosts. They may host a table in the dining room, appear as dance partners at cocktail parties and dance classes, join bridge games, and accompany women on shore excursions.

These men, usually over 55 and retired, are outgoing, mingle easily, and are well groomed. First introduced aboard Cunard Line's *QE2* in the mid-1970s, gentlemen hosts are now employed by a number of cruise lines, including Crystal Cruises, Cunard Line, Holland America Line, Regent Seven Seas Cruises, and Silversea Cruises.

If you think you'd like such a job, do remember that you'll have to dance for several hours most nights, and be proficient in just about every kind of dance. ❑

THE BEST OPTIONS FOR GAYS AND LESBIANS

Several US companies specialize in ship charters or large group bookings for gay and lesbian passengers. These include the California-based Atlantis (tel: 310-859 8800; www.atlantis events.com), San Francisco's lesbian specialist Olivia (www.olivia.com) or New York's Pied Piper Travel (tel: 212-239 2412; http://home.att.net/~gaygroupcruises).

One drawback of gay charters is that they're as much as 20% more expensive than the equivalent general cruise. Another is that they have been greeted with hostility by church groups on some Caribbean islands such as Grand Cayman, Jamaica and Bermuda. One Atlantis cruise was even denied the right to dock. But their great advantage is that they provide an accepting environment and gay-geared entertainment, with some big-name comedians and singers.

Another idea is to join a gay affinity group on a regular cruise at normal prices; these groups may be offered amenities such as private dining

Rosie O'Donnell promotes a gay family cruise.

rooms and separate shore excursions.

Many gays, of course, have no wish to travel exclusively with other gays but may worry that, on a mainstream cruise, they might be seated for dinner with unsympathetic companions. They would prefer to sit where they want, when they want, and such open seating is offered by Norwegian Cruise Line

and Princess Cruises, and by upscale lines such as Crystal, Oceania, Regent, Silversea and Seabourn. Open seating is not offered by Carnival, Celebrity or Royal Caribbean International.

That doesn't mean that any of the major cruise companies are not gay-friendly – many hold regular "Friends of Dorothy" gatherings, sometimes scheduled and sometimes on request – though it would be prudent to realize that Disney Cruise Line, for example, will not really offer the ideal entertainment and ambience. Among the smaller companies, Windstar's sail-powered cruise yachts have a reputation for being gay-friendly.

Gay families are catered for by R Family Vacations (tel: 866-732 6822; www.rfamilyvacations.com), although it's not essential to bring children. Events may include seminars on adoption and discussion groups for teenagers in gay families. One of the company's founders was the former TV talk show host Rosie O'Donnell, herself a lesbian mother.

CRUISES TO SUIT SPECIAL NEEDS

Cruising for the physically challenged offers one of the
most hassle-free vacations possible. But it's important
to choose the right ship and to prepare in advance

Cruise ships have become much more accessible for people with most types of disabilities. Ships built in the past five to 10 years will have the most up-to-date suites/cabins and accessible shipboard facilities for those with special needs. Many new ships also have text telephones and listening device kits for the hearing-impaired (including show lounges aboard some ships). Special dietary needs can often be met, and many cabins have refrigerators – useful for those with diabetes who need to keep supplies of insulin cool.

Special cruises cater for dialysis patients (check out www.dialysisatsea.com; and www.dialysis-cruises.com) and for those who need oxygen regularly. Ask your cruise specialist if your chosen cruise line has a special needs brochure.

If you use a wheelchair, take it with you, as ships carry only a limited number for emergency hospital use only. An alternative is to rent an electric wheelchair, which can be delivered to the ship on your sailing date.

Arguably the weakest point of cruising for the mobility-limited is any shore tender operation. Ship tenders simply aren't designed properly for the wheelchair-bound. This is why it is important to make sure that the itinerary you have chosen will work for you if there are ports where the ship is at anchor and a tender operation takes place.

Six problems to consider

It is as well to begin with the disadvantages of a cruise for the physically challenged:

❶ Unless cabins and bathrooms are specifically designed, problem areas include the entrance, furniture configuration, closet hanging rails, beds, grab bars, height of toiletries cabinet, and wheel-in shower stall.

❷ Elevators: the width of the door is important; in older ships, controls often can't be reached from a wheelchair.

❸ Few ships have access-help lifts installed at swimming pools (exception: P&O Cruises) or angled steps with handrail, or thalassotherapy pools or shore tenders (exception: Holland America Line).

❹ It can be hard to access areas like self-serve buffets, and many large resort ships provide only oval plates (no trays) in their casual eateries. So you may need to ask for help. Also, because the plates are plastic, they're cold. Tip: Ask a supervisor to get you a "proper" china heated plate for hot food items.

❺ Some insurance companies may prohibit smaller ships from accepting passengers with severe disabilities.

❻ Only five cruise ships have direct access ramps to lifeboats: *Amadea, Asuka II, Crystal Serenity, Crystal Symphony* and *Europa*.

12 tips to avoid pitfalls

❶ Start by planning an itinerary and date, and find a travel agent who knows your needs. But follow up on all aspects of the booking yourself to avoid slip-ups; many cruise lines have a department or person to handle requests from disabled passengers.

❷ Choose a cruise line that lets you select a specific cabin, not just a price category. If the ship does not have any specially equipped cabins, book the best outside cabin in your price range, or choose another ship.

❸ Check whether your wheelchair will fit through your cabin's bathroom door, or into the shower area whether there is a "lip" at the door. Don't accept "I think so" as an answer. Get specific measurements.

❹ Choose a cabin close to an elevator. Not all elevators go to all decks, so check the deck

If you need a wheelchair, you should take one with you.

WHAT TO ASK BEFORE YOU BOOK

● Are any public rooms or public decks inaccessible to wheelchairs – for instance, it is sometimes difficult to obtain access to outdoor decks?
● Will you be guaranteed a good viewing place in the main showlounge from where you can see the shows if seated in a wheelchair?
● Will crew be on hand to help, or must the passengers rely on their own traveling companions?
● Will special transportation be provided to transfer you from airport to ship?
● If you need a collapsible wheelchair, can this be provided by the cruise line?
● Do passengers have to sign a medical release?
● Are the ship's tenders accessible to wheelchairs?
● How do you get from your cabin to lifeboats in an emergency if the elevators are out of action?
● Do passengers need a doctor's note to qualify for a cabin for the physically challenged?
● Does the cruise line's travel insurance (with a cancellation or trip interruption) cover you for any injuries while you are aboard ship?
● Most disabled cabins have twin beds or one queen-sized bed. Parents or grandparents with a disabled child should ask the cruise line whether a suitable portable bed can be moved in.

plan. Smaller and older vessels may not even have elevators, making access to even the dining room difficult. ❺ Avoid, at all costs, a cabin down a little alleyway shared by several other cabins, even if the price is attractive. It's hard to access a cabin in a wheelchair from such an alleyway.
❻ Cabins located amidships are less affected by vessel motion, so choose something in the middle of the ship if you are concerned about possible rough seas. The larger – and therefore more expensive – the cabin, the

more room you will have to maneuver in. And a tub provides more space than a shower.
❼ Hanging rails in the closets on most ships are positioned too high for someone in a wheelchair to reach – even the latest ships seem to repeat this basic error. Many cruise ships, however, have cabins specially fitted out to suit the mobility-limited. They are typically fitted with roll-in closets and have a pull-down facility to bring your clothes down to any height you want.
❽ Meals in some ships may be served in your cabin, on special request – an advantage should you wish to avoid dressing for every meal. But few ships have enough space in the cabin for dining tables. If you opt for a dining room with two fixed-time seatings for meals, choose the second – it's more leisurely. Alert the restaurant manager in advance that you would like a table that leaves plenty of room for your wheelchair.
❾ Hand-carry medical records. Once on board, tell the reception desk help may be needed in an emergency.
❿ Make sure that the contract specifically states that if, for any reason, the cabin is not available, that you will get a full refund and transportation back home as well as a refund on any hotel bills incurred.
⓫ Advise the cruise line of the need for proper transfer facilities such as buses or vans with wheelchair ramps or hydraulic lifts.
⓬ If you live near the port of embarkation, arrange to visit the ship to check its suitability (most cruise lines will be accommodating).

Coping with embarkation

The boarding process can pose problems. If you embark at ground level, the gangway may be level or inclined. It will depend on the embarkation deck of the ship and/or the tide in the port.
Alternatively, you may be required to embark from

WHY DOORS CAN PRESENT A PROBLEM FOR WHEELCHAIR USERS

The design of ships has traditionally worked against the mobility-limited. To keep water out or to prevent water escaping from a flooded area, raised edges ("lips") – unfriendly to wheelchairs – are often placed in doorways and across exit pathways. Also, cabin doorways, at a standard 24 inches (60cm) wide, are often not wide enough for wheelchairs – about 30 inches (76 cm) is needed.
Bathroom doors, whether they open outward or inward, similarly hinder maneuverability. An electrically operated sliding door would be better.
Bathrooms in many older ships are small and full of plumbing fixtures, often at odd angles, awkward when moving about in a wheelchair. Those aboard

The author tests accessibility around a ship.

new ships are more accessible, but the plumbing may be located beneath the complete prefabricated module, making the floor higher than that in the cabin, which means a ramp is needed.
Some cruise lines will, if given

advance notice, remove a bathroom door and hang a fabric curtain in its place. Many lines will provide ramps for the bathroom doorway if needed.
Access to outside decks is usually through doors that must be opened manually rather than via automatic electric-eye doors.
It's not cheap to provide facilities for wheelchair-bound passengers. Trained crew members are needed to assist them, which translates to two crew members per eight-hour shift. Thus, six crew members would be required according to the latest safety and evacuation regulations solely to provide the necessary support for one wheelchair-bound passenger – a big drain on the cruise ship's labor resources.

Elevators on newer ships have Braille text on buttons.

an upper level of a terminal, in which case the gangway could well be of the floating loading-bridge type, like those used at major airports. Some have flat floors; others may have raised lips at regular intervals. The lips can be awkward to negotiate in a wheelchair, especially if the gangway is made steeper by a rising tide.

Ship-to-shore launches

Cruise lines should – but don't always – provide an anchor emblem in brochures for those ports of call where a ship will be at anchor instead of alongside. If the ship is at anchor, the crew will lower you and your wheelchair into a waiting tender and then, after a short boat-ride, lift you out again onto a rigged gangway or integral platform. If the sea is calm, this maneuver proceeds uneventfully; if the sea is choppy, it could vary from exciting to somewhat harrowing.

This type of embarkation is rare except in a busy port with several ships sailing the same day. Holland America Line is one of the few companies to make shore tenders accessible to the disabled, with a special boarding ramp and scissor lift so that wheelchair passengers can see out of the shore tender's windows.

Help for the hearing impaired

Difficulties for such passengers include hearing announcements on the public address system; using the telephone; and poor acoustics in key areas such as boarding shore tenders.

Take a spare hearing aid battery. Some cruise lines have special "alert kits." These include "visual-tactile" devices for those unable to hear a knock on the door, a telephone ringing, or the sound of an alarm clock. Crystal Cruises' *Crystal Serenity* and *Crystal Symphony*, and Celebrity Cruises' *Celebrity Century* and *Celebrity Mercury* have movie theaters fitted with special headsets for those with hearing difficulties.

Finally, when going ashore, particularly on organized excursions, be aware that most destinations, particularly in Europe and Southeast Asia, are simply not equipped to handle people with hearing impairment.

Cruising blind

Any totally- or almost-blind persons must be accompanied by a fully able-bodied person, occupying the same cabin. A few lines will allow seeing-eye dogs. Taking an around-the-world cruise or long voyage aboard a cruise ship is one way for them to enjoy the sea, the aromas of the world, and to feel things that they are unable to at home.

Recent improvements

Many new ships now provide mobility-limited cabin bathrooms with collapsible shower stools mounted on shower walls, and bathroom toilets have collapsible arm guards and lower washbasin. Other cabin equipment may include a vibrating alarm clock, door beacon (light flashes when someone knock on the door), television with closed caption decoders, and a flashing light as fire alarm. Look out, too, for:

● Hearing-impaired kits on request.
● Dedicated wheelchair positions in the showlounge (including induction systems).
● Electrical hoist to access pool and hot tubs.
● All elevators and cabins have Braille text. The large resort ships *MSC Fantasia* and *MSC Splendida* even have Braille pads subtly hidden under each lower section of handrail in the main foyers – very user-friendly.   ❑

WHEELCHAIR ACCESSIBILITY
Each cruise ship reviewed in this book is rated in its data listing for wheelchair accessibility. The ratings are defined on page 191.

EXPEDITIONS AND NATURE CRUISES

Looking for adventure in remote places? Specialist
cruise companies provide it while taking care to
respect the environment and indigenous peoples

Passengers joining expeditions tend to be more
self-reliant and more interested in doing or learning than in being entertained. They become "participants" and take an active role in almost every aspect
of the voyage, which is destination-, exploration- and
nature-intensive.

Naturalists, historians, and lecturers (rather than
entertainers) are aboard each ship to provide background information and observations about wildlife.
Each participant receives a personal logbook, illustrated
and written by the wildlife artists and writers who
accompany each cruise – a fine souvenir.

You can walk on pack ice in the islands and land
masses in the Arctic Ocean and Arctic Circle, explore a
huge penguin rookery on an island in the Antarctic
Peninsula, the Falkland Islands or South Georgia, or
search for "lost" peoples in Melanesia. Or you can
cruise close to the source of the Amazon, gaze at species
of flora and fauna in the Galápagos Islands (Darwin's
laboratory), or watch a genuine dragon on the island of
Komodo – from a comfortable distance, of course.

Briefings and lectures bring cultural and intellectual
elements to expedition cruise vessels. There is no formal entertainment as such; participants enjoy this type
of cruise more for the camaraderie and learning experience, and being close to nature. The ships are designed
and equipped to sail in ice-laden waters, yet they

Kapitan Khlebnikov slices through the Antarctic ice.

have a shallow enough draft to glide over coral reefs.

Despite being rugged, expedition cruise vessels can
provide comfortable and even elegant surroundings for
up to 200 passengers, and offer good food and service.
Without traditional cruise ports at which to stop, a ship
must be self-sufficient, be capable of long-range cruising, and be totally environmentally friendly.

Wildlife migrations

Lars-Eric Lindblad pioneered expedition cruising in the
late 1960s. A Swedish American, he turned travel into
adventure by going to parts of the world tourists had
not visited. After chartering several vessels for voyages
to Antarctica, he organized the design and construction
of a small ship capable of going almost anywhere in
comfort and safety. In 1969, *Lindblad Explorer* was
launched; it soon earned an enviable reputation in
adventure travel. Others followed.

To put together cruise expeditions, companies turn to
knowledgeable sources and advisors. Scientific institutions are consulted; experienced world explorers and
naturalists provide up-to-date reports on wildlife sight-
ings, migrations, and other natural phenomena. Although
some days are scheduled for relaxation, participants are
kept physically and mentally active. Avoid such an
adventure cruise if you are not completely ambulatory.

Adventure cruise companies provide expedition
parkas and waterproof boots, but you will need to take
waterproof trousers for Antarctica and the Arctic.

A Zodiac from *Prince Albert II* explores the Antarctic.

Antarctica

While Arctic ice is only a few feet thick, the ice of Antarctica is thousands of feet thick. The continent was first sighted in 1820 by the American sealer Nathaniel Palmer, British naval officer Edward Bransfield, and Russian captain Fabian Bellingshausen.

For most, it is just a windswept frozen wasteland – it has been calculated that the ice mass contains almost 90 percent of the world's snow and ice, while its land mass is twice the size of Australia. For others, it represents the last pristine place on earth, empty of people, commerce, and pollution, yet offering awesome icescape scenery and a truly wonderful abundance of marine and bird life. There are no germs, and not a single tree.

As many as 36,000 people a year visit Antarctica, which has 24-hour sunshine during the austral summer but not a single permanent inhabitant. Its ice is as much as 2 miles (3km) thick, and its total land mass equals more than all the rivers and lakes on earth and exceeds that of China and India combined. Icebergs can easily be the size of Belgium. The region has a raw beauty.

It is, perhaps, the closest thing on earth to another planet, and it has an incredibly fragile ecosystem that needs international protection. It contains two-thirds of

THE LEADING EXPEDITION CRUISE VESSELS: HOW THEY RATE

Research Vessels/ True Expedition Vessels	Rating (Facilities max: 100)	Company/ Operator (1)	Built	Pass. Cabins	Max No. Passengers	Tonnage	Registry	Length (m)
50 Years of Victory (2)	90	Quark Expeditions	2007	66	128	23,439	Russia	159.00
Akademik Ioffe	48	Quark Expeditions	1988	55	110	6,460	Russia	117.10
Akademik Sergey Vavilov	50	Quark Expeditions	1988	40	110	6,231	Russia	117.80
Akademik Sholaskiy	44	Quark Expeditions	1982	22	44	2,140	Russia	71.56
Antarctic Dream	35	Antarctic Shipping	1959	39	78	2,180	Panama	83.00
Grigoriy Mikheev	46	Oceanwide Expeditions	1990	22	44	2,000	Russia	70.00
Kapitan Dranitsyn	50	Poseidon Arctic Voyages	1980	53	113	10,471	Russia	131.00
Kapitan Khlebnikov	51	Quark Expeditions	1981	54	112	12,288	Russia	132.49
Marina Svetaeva	45	Aurora Expeditions	1989	45	100	4,575	Russia	89.98
Polar Pioneer	47	Aurora Expeditions	1985	26	54	2,140	Russia	71.60
Professor Molchanov	44	Oceanwide Expeditions	1983	29	52	1,753	Russia	71.60
Professor Multanovskiy	44	Oceanwide Expeditions	1983	29	49	1,753	Russia	71.60
Ocean Nova	48	Quark Expeditions	1992	45	96	2,118	Greenland	73.00
Spirit of Enderby	44	Heritage Expeditions	1984	22	48	6,231	Russia	72.00
Other Expedition Cruise Ships								
Bremen	77	Hapag-Lloyd Cruises	1990	82	184	6,752	Bahamas	111.51
Clipper Adventurer	57	Quark Expeditions	1976	61	122	5,750	Bahamas	100.01
Expedition	55	G.A.P. Adventures	1972	58	120	6,336	Liberia	105.00
Hanseatic	84	Hapag-Lloyd Cruises	1993	92	194	8,378	Bahamas	122.80
Marco Polo	55	Cruise & Maritime Voyages	1965	425	915	22,080	Bahamas	176.28
Minerva	66	Swan Hellenic Cruises	1996	178	474	12,500	Bahamas	133.00
National Geographic Endeavour	51	Lindblad Expeditions	1966	62	110	3,132	Bahamas	89.20
National Geographic Explorer	45	Lindblad Expeditions	1982	81	148	6,200	Bahamas	
Orion	82	Orion Expedition Cruises	2003	53	139	4,050	Bahamas	102.70
Polar Star	56	Polar Star Expeditions	1969	45	105	4,998	Barbados	86.50
Plancius	41	Oceanwide Expeditions	1976	53	110	3,175	Holland	89.00
Quest	47	Noble Caledonia	1992	26	50	1,268	Bahamas	49.65
Ushuaia	40	Ushuaia Adventure Corp/ Antarpply Expeditions	1970	41	84	2,963	Argentina	84.73

NOTES: (1) = most expedition ships are sold by multiple expedition companies, or under full charter to one operator
(2) = nuclear-powered

A Quark Expeditions excursion focuses on a local.

all the fresh water on Earth (covered by ice, in September there are 8.5 million square miles of sea ice, but only 1.2 million in March).

Although visited by "soft" expedition cruise ships and even "normal"-sized cruise ships with ice-hardened hulls, the more remote "far side" – the Oates and Scott Coasts, McMurdo Sound, and the famous Ross Ice Shelf – can be visited only by genuine icebreakers such as the 114-passenger *Kapitan Khlebnikov*, the first vessel to circumnavigate Antarctica with passengers, as the katabatic winds can easily reach more than 100 mph (160 km/h).

Only 100 passengers per ship are allowed ashore at any given time, so if you sail aboard one of the larger ships that claim to include Antarctica on their itineraries, it will probably be to view it – but only from the ship. Indeed, cruise ships with more than 500 passengers will not be allowed to sail in Antarctic waters after August 2011, as the chances of rescue in the event of pack ice crushing a normal cruise ship hull are virtually nil. For real expedition cruising, choose a ship that includes a flotilla of Zodiac rubber inflatable landing craft, proper boot washing stations, and expedition equipment.

There are no docks in Antarctica, so venturing "ashore" is done by Zodiacs – an integral part of the experience. Avoid the large resort ships in this region – they don't carry Zodiacs, cannot dock anywhere, and you will almost certainly be disappointed.

Be aware that you can get stuck even aboard these specialized expedition ships, as did *Nordkapp*, which ran aground near Deception Island in 2007. In the same year, Canadian company GAP Expedi-

tions' *Explorer* hit an iceberg in Bransfield Strait off King George Island and sank; all 91 passengers, nine expedition staff and 54 crew members were rescued thanks to the coordination efforts of the British Coast Guard and the Hurtigruten cruise ship *Nordnorge*. In December 2008 the Antarpply Expeditions' Ushuaia was grounded; all 89 passengers were rescued by the

PROTECTING SENSITIVE ENVIRONMENTS

Polar bears are under threat.

In the future, only ships capable of meeting new "zero discharge" standards will be allowed to cross environmentally sensitive areas. Expedition cruise companies are concerned about the environment, and they spend much time and money in educating their crews and passengers about safe procedures.

They observe the "Antarctic Traveler's Code," based on 1978's Antarctic Conservation Act, designed to protect the region's ecosystem, flora, and fauna.

The Antarctic Treaty Meeting in Kyoto in 1994 made it unlawful, unless authorized by permit, to take native animals, birds, and certain native plants, introduce species, enter certain special pro-

tected areas (SPAs), or discharge or dispose of pollutants.

To "take" means to remove, harass, molest, harm, pursue, hunt, shoot, kill, trap, capture, restrain, or tag any native mammal or bird, or to attempt to do so. Violators face civil penalties, including a fine of up to $10,000 and one-year imprisonment for each violation. A copy of the Act can be found in the library of each adventure or expedition ship that visits the continent.

Ships carrying over 500 passengers are not allowed to land and are restricted to "scenic" cruising, so the likelihood of a single-hulled mega-ship zooming in on the penguins with 3,000-plus passengers is unlikely. Nor would it be possible to rescue so many passengers and crew in the event of an emergency. Also, the large resort ships burn heavy oil rather than the lighter oil used by the specialist expedition ships, which also have ice-strengthened hulls – so the danger of pollution arising from an "incident" is far greater.

Chilean navy vessel *Achiles*. In February 2009, Quark Expeditions' *Ocean Nova* was grounded. Tip: Passengers would be advised to wear an identification bracelet or belt at all times while on an Antarctic expedition cruise.

Wildlife you may see or come into contact with include orcas, dolphins, the six species of Antarctic seals, penguins, birds, and various species of lichen and flora, depending on the area visited.

Take plastic bags to cover your camera, so that condensation forms inside the bag and not on your camera when changing from the cold of the outside Antarctic air to the warmth of your expedition cruise vessel. Make sure you know how to operate your camera with gloves on – frostbite is a real danger.

The Arctic

Want some Northern Exposure? Try the Arctic. This is an ocean surrounded by continents, whereas Antarctica is an ice-covered continent surrounded by ocean. The Arctic Circle is located at 66 degrees, 33 minutes, and 3 seconds north, although this really designates where 24-hour days and nights begin.

The Arctic is best defined as that region north of which no trees grow, and where water is the primary feature of the landscape. It is technically a desert (receiving less than 10 inches of rainfall a year) but actually teems with wildlife, including polar bears, walruses, seals, and Arctic birds. It has short, cool summers; long, cold winters; and frequent high winds. Canada's Northwest Territories, which cover 1.3 million square miles, is part of the Arctic region, as are some of Russia's northernmost islands such as Franz Josef Land.

An iguana basks in the sun in the Galápagos Islands.

10 TOP EXPEDITIONS

Aleutian-Pribiloff Islands
Amazon (Manaus-Iquitos)
Antarctic Peninsula
Galapagos Islands
Islands of Micronesia
Northwest Passage
Northeast Passage
Papua New Guinea
Ross Ice Shelf in Antarctica
Solomon Islands

Passenger ships that have navigated the Northwest Passage linking the Atlantic and Pacific Oceans include *Lindblad Explorer* (1984), *World Discoverer* (1985), *Society Explorer* (1988), *Frontier Spirit* (1992), *Kapitan Khlebnikov* (1994, 1995, 1998, 2006, 2007, 2008), *Hanseatic* (1995, 1996, 1997, 1999, 2007) and *Bremen* (2009).

Greenland

The world's largest island, the inappropriately named Greenland, in the Arctic Circle, is 82 percent covered with ice – actually compressed snow – up to 11,000 feet thick (3,350 meters). Its rocks are among the world's oldest, and its ecosystem is one of the newest.

The glacier at Jacobshavn, also known as Ilulissat, is the world's fastest moving and creates a new iceberg every five minutes. Greenland, which was granted home rule by Denmark in 1978, makes its living from fishing. It is said to have more dogs than people – its population is 68,400 – and dogs are an important means of transport.

The Galápagos Islands

These islands, 600 miles (960km) off the coast of Ecuador in the Pacific Ocean, are a microcosm of our planet. More than 100 islands, plus mineral-rich and lava outcroppings make up the Galápagos, which are fed by the nutrient-rich Cromwell and Humboldt currents. The fertile waters can be cold, even on the equator.

The Ecuadorians jealously guard their islands and prohibit the movement of almost all non-Ecuadorian-registered cruise vessels within its boundaries. The best way to follow in the footsteps of Charles Darwin, who visited the islands in 1835 aboard the *Beagle*, is to fly to Quito and cruise aboard an Ecuadorian-registered vessel. Ecological fact: cruising leaves a smaller carbon footprint because it does not contribute to the building of hotels, restaurants, roads and cars.

The government of Ecuador set aside most of the islands as a wildlife sanctuary in 1934, while uninhabited areas were declared national parks in 1959. The national park includes approximately 97 per cent of the islands' landmass, together with 20,000 sq miles (50,000 sq km) of ocean. The Charles Darwin Research Station was established in 1964, and the government created the Galápagos Marine Resources Reserve in 1986.

The Galápagos National Park tax doubled to $200 per person in 2009. Smoking is prohibited on the islands, and no more than 50,000 visitors a year are admitted. Some cruise lines require vaccinations for cruises that include Ecuador, although the World Health Organization does not. ❑

COASTAL CRUISES

Being all at sea doesn't appeal? You can stay close
to dry land by journeying round the coasts of
Australia, Europe, and North and South America

AUSTRALIA

The marine wonderland of the Great Barrier Reef, a
World Heritage site off the northeast coast of Australia,
is the earth's largest living coral reef – it actually consists
of more than 2,800 individual coral reefs. It is visited by
around 70 local Australian boutique ship operators, who
mostly offer 1- to 4-night cruises to the reefs and Whit-
sunday Islands. The area is excellent for scuba diving
and snorkelers.

June through September is humpback whale-watching
season; the Reef shelters the young whales while the
adults nurture them in the shallow waters. Note that the
Australian government levies an environmental charge of
A$5 on everyone over four years of age visiting the Great
Barrier Reef and its environs.

NORWAY

There is year-round coastal cruising along the shores
of Norway to the Land of the Midnight Sun aboard the
ships of the Hurtigruten Group, formerly known as Norwegian Coastal Voyages. The fleet consists of small,
comfortable, working express coastal packet steamers
and contemporary cruise vessels that deliver mail, small
packaged goods, and foodstuffs, and take passengers, to
the communities spread on the shoreline.

Invariably dubbed "the world's most beautiful voy-

ABOVE: glass-bottomed boat on the Great Barrier Reef.

age." this is a 1,250-mile (2,000-km) journey from
Bergen in Norway to Kirkenes, close to the Russian border (half of which is north of the Arctic Circle) and takes
12 days. The service started in 1893, and the name Hurtigruten – meaning "fast route" – reflects the fact that
this coastal express was once the most reliable communication link between southern Norway and its remote
north. Today the company carries more than 300,000
passengers a year. It's a good way to meet Norwegians,
who treat the service like a bus.

You can join it at any of the 34 ports of call and stay
as long as you wish because the vessels, being working
ships, sail every day of the year. At the height of sum-

HURTIGRUTEN SHIPS			
Ship	Tonnage	Built	Berths
Finnmarken	15,000	2002	638
Fram	12,700	2007	328
Kong Harald	11,200	1993	490
Lofoten	2,621	1964	147
Midnatsol	16,053	2003	652
Nordkapp	11,386	1996	464
Nordlys	11,200	1994	482
Nordnorge	11,386	1997	455
Nordstjernen *	2,621	1956	114
Polar Star *	4,998	1969	100
Polarlys	12,000	1996	479
Richard With	11,205	1993	483
Trollfjord	15,000	2002	648
Vesteralen	6,261	1983	316

* for "soft" expedition voyages only

SMALL COASTAL CRUISE VESSELS (more than 10 cabins)

Ship	Cruise Line	Cabins	Region	Built
American Eagle	American Cruise Lines	27	USA Coastal Cruises	2000
American Glory	American Cruise Lines	27	USA Coastal Cruises	2002
American Spirit	American Cruise Lines	50	USA Coastal Cruises	2005
American Star	American Cruise Lines	52	USA Coastal Cruises	2007
Aranui 3	Campagnie Polynesienne de Transport Maritime	63	Tahiti/Marquesas	2003
Callisto	Travel Dynamics International	17	Greek Isles	1963
Celebrity Xpedition	Celebrity Cruises	47	Galápagos Islands	2001
CoCo Explorer	CoCo Explorer Cruises	56	Philippines	1967
Contessa	Majestic America Line	25	Alaska	1986
Coral Princess	Coral Princess Cruises	27	Australia (Great Barrier Reef)	1988
Corinthian	Ecoventura/Galápagos Network	45	Galápagos Islands	1967
Discovery	Panama Marine Adventures	12	Panama	2004
Disko II	Arctic Umiaq Line	26	Greenland	1992
Emeraude	Emeraude Classic Cruises	38	Halong Bay (Vietnam)	2003
Evolution	various	17	Galápagos Islands	2004
Galápagos Legend	GlobalQuest	57	Galápagos Islands	1963
Grande Caribe	Blount Small Ship Adventures	48	USA Coastal Cruises	1997
Grande Mariner	Blount Small Ship Adventures	50	USA Coastal Cruises	1999
Independence	American Cruise Lines	52	USA Coastal Cruises	2009
Isabela II	Metropolitan Touring	21	Galápagos Islands	1989
La Pinta	South American Experience	24	Galápagos Islands	2008
Lord of the Glens	Magna Carta Cruises	27	Scotland	1985
Lycianda	Blue Lagoon Cruises	21	Yasawa Islands (Fiji)	1984
Marco Polo	CroisiEurope	100	European Coast	2006
Mare Australis	Cruceros Australis	64	Chilean Fjords (Patagonia)	2002
Megastar Aries	Star Cruises	33	Southeast Asia	1992
Monet	Elegant Cruises & Tours	30	Croatian Coast	1970
Mystique Princess	Blue Lagoon Cruises	36	Yasawa Islands (Fiji)	1996
Nanuya Princess	Blue Lagoon Cruises	26	Yasawa Islands (Fiji)	1987
National Geographic Islander	Lindblad Expeditions/National Geographic	24	Galápagos Islands	1995
National Geographic Sea Bird	Lindblad Expeditions/National Geographic	35	Alaska, Baja	1981
National Geographic Sea Lion	Lindblad Expeditions/National Geographic	35	Alaska, Baja	1982
Oceanic Discoverer	Coral Princess Cruises	38	Australia (Great Barrier Reef)	2005
Pacific Aurora	British Columbia Discovery Voyages	34	British Columbia (Canada)	1962
Pacific Explorer	Cruise West	50	Central America	1970
Pearl Mist	Pearl Seas Cruises	108	USA Coastal Cruises	2010
Pegasus	various tour operators	23	Croatian Coast	1992
Reef Escape	Captain Cook Cruises	60	Australia	1987
Safari Explorer	American Safari Cruises	18	Alaska/Mexico Coast	1998
Safari Quest	American Safari Cruises	11	Alaska/Mexico Coast	1992
Santa Cruz	Metropolitan Touring	43	Galápagos Islands	1979
Sea Voyager	various tour operators	33	Central America	1982
Shearwater	various operators	40	Worldwide	1962
Skorpios III	GlobalQuest	50	Chilean Fjords	1988
Spirit of '98	Cruise West	48	Alaska	1984
Spirit of Alaska	Cruise West	39	Alaska	1980
Spirit of America	Cruise West	51	Alaska	1984
Spirit of Columbia	Cruise West	39	Alaska	1979
Spirit of Discovery	Cruise West	25	Alaska	1982
Spirit of Endeavor	Cruise West	51	Alaska	1983
Spirit of Oceanus	Cruise West	50	Alaska/South Pacific	1991
Spirit of Yorktown	Cruise West	69	Alaska	1988
Tu Moana	Bora Bora Cruises	20	Tahitian Islands	2003
True North	North Star Cruises	18	Australia (west coast)	2005
Via Australis	Cruceros Australis	64	Chilean Fjords (Patagonia)	2005

Gierangerfjord, one of Norway's stunning vistas.

mer, north of the Arctic Circle, there are 24 hours of daylight, and between November and February the northern lights create spectacular arcs across the sky. Some specialist voyages are aimed at birdwatchers and others include onboard concerts and lectures celebrating the work of Norwegian composer Edvard Grieg.

The ships can accommodate between 144 and 652 passengers. The newest ships have an elevator that can accommodate a wheelchair passenger, but otherwise, they are fairly plain and basic, practical vessels, with food that is more bistro than restaurant. Note that alcohol prices are extremely high, as they are throughout Norway, and that the currency is the Norwegian krone.

Archipelago hopping can be done along Sweden's eastern coast, too, by sailing in the daytime and staying overnight in one of the many small hotels. One vessel sails from Norrtalje, north of Stockholm, to Oskarshamn, near the Baltic island of Öland, right through the spectacular Swedish archipelago.

The Hurtigruten Group also operates utilitarian ships for expeditions to the Arctic, Antarctic, and Greenland.

SCOTLAND

The fishing town of Oban, two hours west of Glasgow by road, is the base for one of the world's finest cruise experiences. *Hebridean Princess* is a little gem, with Laura Ashley-style interiors – homely enough to have been chartered by Queen Elizabeth II for a family-only celebration of her 80th birthday in 2006. The food is excellent, and includes Scottish beef, local seafood and seasonal vegetables. There's fine personal service.

This ship, owned by Hebridean Island Cruises, carries up to 49 passengers around some of Scotland's most magnificent coastline and islands. If you cruise from Oban, you can be met at Glasgow airport or rail station and taken to the ship by motor coach. Take lots of warm clothing, however (layers are best), as the weather can be flexible and often unkind.

As an alternative, there's the 54-passenger *Lord of the Glens*, operated by Magna Carta Steamship Company, which cruises in style through Scotland's lakes and canals. Some 7- and 10-night high-season sailings are accompanied by historians and guest lecturers.

NORTH AMERICA

Coastal cruise ships flying the American flag offer a complete change of style from the large resort cruise ships. They are American-owned and American-crewed, and very informal. Being US-registered, they can start from and return to a US port without being required to call at a foreign port along the way – which a foreign-flagged cruise ship must do.

Accommodating up to 150 passengers, the ships are more like private family affairs, and are rarely out of sight of land. These cruises are low-key, low pace, and not for active, adventurous types. Their operators seek out lesser-known areas, offering in-depth visits to destinations inaccessible to larger ships, both along the eastern and western seaboards of the USA, including Alaska.

Most passengers are over 60, and many over 70. They may prefer not to fly, and wherever possible drive or take a train to join their ship. During the summer, you might see a couple of children on board, but in general small kids are not allowed. There are no facilities for them, and no staff to look after them.

Destinations: Eastern US and Canadian seaboard cruises include the St Lawrence River, Atlantic Coastal Waterways, New England (good for fall cruises), Cape Cod and the Islands (and Cape Cod Canal), the Great Lakes (and Welland Canal), the Colonial Deep South, and Florida waterways.

Western seaboard cruises cover Alaska, the Pacific Northwest, California Wine Country, and Baja California/Sea of Cortés. Cruises focus on historically-relevant destinations, nature and wildlife spotting, and coastal

Blount Small Ship Adventures' cruises feel like family outings.

American Safari Cruises finds bottlenose dolphins in Mexico's Sea of Cortés and whales in Alaska.

viewing. On some cruises, these boutique ships can dock adjacent to a town, allowing easy access on foot.

The ships: These "D-class" vessels are less than 2,500 gross tonnage, and are subject neither to bureaucratic regulations nor to union rules. They are restricted to cruising no more than 20 miles (32 km) offshore, at a comfortable 12 knots (13.8mph). Public room facilities are limited. Because the vessels are American-registered, there is no casino. They really are ultra-casual, no-frills ships with the most basic of facilities, no swimming pools, little artwork, and no glitz in interior decor. They usually have three or four decks and, except for the ships of American Cruise Lines, no elevator. Stairs can be steep and are not recommended for people with walking difficulties. Because of this, some ships have an electric chair-lift on indoor or outdoor stairways.

Cabins: Accommodation is in outside-view cabins, some of which open directly onto a walking deck – inconvenient when it rains. Each has a picture window and small bathroom. They are small and basic, with very limited closet space – perhaps just a curtain across a space with a hanging rod for clothes. Many do not have a TV set or telephone. There's no room service, and you may have to turn your own bed down. Cabins are closer to the engines and generators than aboard the large resort ships, so generator humming noises can be disturbing at night. The quietest cabins are at the ship's bows – although there could be noise if the ship is equipped with a bow thruster – and most cruising is done in the early morning so that passengers can sleep better at night.

Tall passengers should note that the overall length of beds rarely exceeds 6 ft (1.82 meters). While soap is provided, it's best to bring your own shampoo, conditioner, and other personal toiletries. The ships of Blount Small Ship Adventures do not have cabin keys.

Although some of the older ships are really basic, the latest ones, particularly those of American Cruise Lines, are very comfortable. Because they are not classified for open-water cruising, though, they don't have to conform to the same rigorous shipbuilding standards that larger ocean-going cruise ships do. You may find that hot and cold water lines run close to each other in your bathroom, thus delivering neither really hot nor really cold water. Sound insulation could be almost non-existent.

Activities: The principal evening event is dinner in the dining room, which accommodates all passengers at once. This can be a family-style affair, with passengers at long tables, and the food passed around.

The cuisine is decidedly American, with fresh local specialties. However, menus aboard the ships of Blount Small Ship Adventures and Cruise West are very limited, while those aboard the ships of American Cruise Lines offer slightly more variety, including seasonal items. You'll probably be asked in the morning to choose which of two main courses you would like for dinner.

Evening entertainment consists mainly of after-dinner conversation. Most vessels are in port during the time, so you can easily go ashore for the local nightlife, although most passengers simply go to bed early.

The cost: These cruises are expensive, with an average daily rate of $400–$800 a person. Suggested gratuities are high – typically about $125 per person, per 7-day cruise – but they are shared by all the personnel. ❑

COASTAL CRUISE LINES IN NORTH AMERICA

There are six cruise companies: American Cruise Lines, American Safari Cruises, Blount Small Ship Adventures, Cruise West, Lindblad Expeditions and Pearl Seas Cruises.

What differentiates them? American Cruise Lines, American Safari Cruises and Pearl Seas Cruises provide better food and service than the others. American Cruise Lines' ships have larger cabins, and more public rooms. Drinks are included aboard the ships of American Cruise Lines only. American Cruise Lines and Blount Small Ship Adventures operate on the USA's east coast; American Safari Cruises and Lindblad Expeditions operate on the USA's west coast and Alaska.

Pearl Seas Cruises, under the same ownership as American Cruise Lines, introduced its first new ship in 2010. Considerably larger than those of the other lines, it accommodates 210 passengers, has an all-American registry and crew, is certified for oceangoing voyages, has more lounges and facilities and much larger cabins, and aspires to the standards set by international boutique ships. Itineraries include cruises around Newfoundland, the Caribbean and Central America.

NORTH ATLANTIC CROSSINGS

You're facing the world's most unpredictable weather, but there's still something romantic about this classic ocean voyage

Crossing the 3,000 miles (4,800km) of the North Atlantic by passenger vessel can be considered an art. I have done it 155 times and always enjoy it immensely. I consider crossings as rests in musical parlance, for both are described as "passages." Indeed, musicians do often "hear" rests in between notes. So if ports of call are the musical notes of a voyage, then the rests are the days at sea – temporary interludes, when physical and mental indulgence become ends in themselves.

Experienced mariners say a ship behaves like a ship only when it is doing a crossing, for that's what a real ship is built for. Yet the days when ships were built specifically for crossings are almost gone. The only one offering a regularly scheduled transatlantic service is Cunard Line's *Queen Mary 2*, a 148,151-tonnage ship, built with a thick hull designed to survive the worst weather the North Atlantic has to offer. The world's most unpredictable weather, together with fog off the Grand Banks of Newfoundland, can confine the captain to torturous hours on the bridge, with little time for socializing.

When it is foggy, the crew of *Queen Mary 2* is often pestered by passengers wanting to know if the ship has yet approached latitude 41°46' north, longitude 50°14' west – where White Star Line's 43,326-ton *Titanic* struck an Arctic iceberg on that fateful April night in 1912.

A great tradition

There is something magical in "doing a crossing." It takes you back to the days when hordes of passengers turned up at the piers of the ports of New York, Southampton, Cherbourg, or Hamburg, accompanied by chauffeurs and steamer trunks, jewels and finery.

Even today, excitement and anticipation usually precede a crossing. First there is the hubbub and bustle of check-in, then the crossing of the threshold on the gangway before being welcomed into the calmness aboard, and finally escorted to one's accommodation.

Once the umbilical cord of the gangway is severed, bow and stern mooring lines are cast off, and with three long blasts on the ship's deep whistle, the *QM2* is pried gently from its berth. The ship sails silently down the waterway, away from the world, as serene as a Rolls-Royce. Passengers on deck often observe motorboats trying to keep up with the giant liner as it edges away from Brooklyn's excellent Red Hook Pier 12 terminal towards the Statue of Liberty, the restored Ellis Island, then under the Verrazano-Narrows Bridge, and out to the open sea. Coming westbound, arriving in New York by ship is one of the world's thrilling travel experiences.

The *QM2* has almost year-round scheduled crossings, whereas other cruise ships crossing the Atlantic are little more than repositioning cruises – a way of moving ships that cruise the Mediterranean in summer to the Caribbean in winter, and vice versa – they offer more chances to experience the romance and adventure of a crossing, usually in spring and fall. These satisfy those wanting uninterrupted days at sea and lots of leisure time.

Most cruise ships operating repositioning crossings cross the Atlantic using the "sunny southern route" – departing from southern ports such as Ft. Lauderdale, San Juan, or Barbados, and ending the journey in Lisbon, Genoa, or Copenhagen via the Azores or the Canary Islands off the coast of northern Africa. In this way, they avoid the more difficult weather often encountered in the North Atlantic. Such crossings take longer, however: between eight and 12 days. ❑

ABOVE: *Queen Mary 2* berthed in Liverpool, England.

SAILING SHIPS

Want to be free as the wind? Think about cruising under sail, with towering masts, the creak of taut ropes and gleaming white sails to power you along

There is simply nothing that beats the thrill of being aboard a multi-mast tall ship, sailing under thousands of square feet of canvas through waters that mariners have sailed for centuries. This is cruising in the traditional manner of seafaring, aboard authentic sailing ships, contemporary copies of clipper ships, or aboard high-tech cruise-sail ships. But it gives you a genuine sailing experience without sacrificing creature comforts

There are no rigid schedules, and life aboard equates to an unstructured lifestyle, apart from meal times. Weather conditions may often dictate whether a scheduled port visit will be made or not, but passengers sailing on these vessels are usually unconcerned. They would rather savor the thrill of being one with nature, albeit in a comfortable, civilized setting, and without having to do the work themselves. The more luxurious sailing ships are the closest most people will get to owning their own mega-yacht.

Sea Cloud appeals to those seeking a stately home with sails.

Real tall ships

While we have all been dreaming of adventure, a pocketful of designers and yachtsmen committed pen to paper, hand in pocket and rigging to mast, and came up with a potpourri of stunning vessels to delight the eye and refresh the spirit. Examples are *Royal Clipper, Sea Cloud, Sea Cloud II, Star Clipper*, and *Star Flyer*.

Of these, *Sea Cloud*, built in 1931 and restored in 1979, is the most romantic sailing ship afloat. It operates under charter for much of the year, and sails in both the Caribbean and the Mediterranean. A kind of stately home afloat, *Sea Cloud* remains one of the finest and most exhilarating travel experiences in the world.

The activities are few, so relaxation is the key, in a stylish but unpretentious setting. The food and service are good, as is the interaction between the 69 passengers and 60 crew, many of whom have worked aboard the ship for many years. One bonus is the fact that a doctor is available on board at no charge for emergencies or seasickness medication.

Although passengers may be able to participate occasionally in the furling and unfurling of the sails, they are not permitted to climb the rigging, as may be possible aboard some of the other, more modern tall ships.

Sea Cloud Cruises introduced a new, real tall ship in 2010, and Star Clippers is said to be thinking of building one.

Contemporary sail-cruise ships

To combine sailing with push-button automation, try *Club Med 2* (Club Mediterranée) or *Wind Surf* (Windstar Cruises) – with five tall aluminum masts, they are the world's largest sail-cruise ships – and *Wind Spirit* and *Wind Star* (Windstar Cruises), with four masts. Not a hand touches the sails; they are computer-controlled from the navigation bridge.

The traditional sense of sailing is almost absent in these oceangoing robots because the computer keeps the ship on an even keel. Also, some people find it hard to get used to the whine of the vessels' generators, which run the lighting and air-conditioning systems 24 hours a day.

From a yachtsman's viewpoint, the sail-to-power ratio is poor. That's why these cruise ships with sails have engine power to get them into and out of port. The *Sea Cloud* and *Star*

Clipper ships do it by sail alone, except when there is no wind, which doesn't happen all that often.

On some itineraries, when there is little wind, you could be motor-powered for most of the cruise, with only a few hours under sail. The three Windstar Cruises vessels and one Club Med ship are typically under sail for about 40 percent of the time.

The Windstar ships carry mainly North Americans and the Club Med vessel mainly French-speakers.

Another slightly smaller but chic vessel is *Le Ponant*. This three-mast ship caters to just 64 French-speaking passengers in elegant, yet casual, high-tech surroundings, advancing the technology of the original Windstar concept. The ship made news in 2008 when its crew was held to ransom by pirates off the Somali coast; no passengers were on board at the time.

When the engine cuts in

So, do you get to cruise under sail most of the time? Not really. Aboard the ships of Sea Cloud Cruises and Star Clippers, because they are real tall ships, you could be under sail for most of the night when the ships are under way, as long as there is wind, of course, and on the days or part days at sea.

The ship's small engine is used for maneuvering in and out of port. In the Caribbean, for example, the trade winds are good for most of the year, while in the Mediterranean and Southeast Asia the winds are not so potent. But the thrill for many passengers is getting involved and helping to furl and unfurl the sails, and being able to climb the rigging. Lying in the netting under the ship's bows is a memorable experience.

Aboard the ships of Windstar Cruises, however, the itineraries are so port-intensive that the computer-controlled sails are hardly ever used today – so the experience can be disappointing. ❑

In full sail: *Star Clipper* (left) and *Royal Clipper*.

HOW TO MEASURE WIND SPEEDS

Understanding wind patterns is important to sailing ships, but the numbering system for wind velocity can confuse. There are 12 velocities, known as "force" on the Beaufort scale, devised in 1805 by Sir Francis Beaufort *(left)*, an Irish-born hydrographer and officer in Britain's Royal Navy. It was adopted internationally in 1874 as the official means of recording wind velocity. They are as follows, with descriptions of the ocean surface:

Force 0 (0–1mph): Calm; glassy (like a mirror).
Force 1 (1–3mph): Light wind; rippled surface.
Force 2 (4–7mph): Light breeze; small wavelets.
Force 3 (8–12mph): Gentle breeze; large wavelets, scattered whitecaps.
Force 4 (13–18mph): Moderate breeze; small waves, frequent whitecaps.
Force 5 (19–24mph): Fresh breeze; moderate waves, numerous whitecaps.
Force 6 (25–31mph): Strong breeze; large waves, white foam crests.
Force 7 (32–38mph): Moderate gale; streaky white foam.
Force 8 (39–46mph): Fresh gale; moderate waves.
Force 9 (47–54mph): Strong gale; high waves.
Force 10 (55–63mph): Whole gale; very high waves, curling crests.
Force 11 (64–73mph): Violent storm; extremely high waves, froth and foam, poor visibility.
Force 12 (73+mph): Hurricane; huge waves, thundering white spray, visibility nil.

FREIGHTER TRAVEL

These slow voyages appeal to independent
types who don't require constant entertainment,
and the accommodation can be surprisingly comfortable

More than 3,000 passengers travel by freighter each year, and the number is growing as passengers become further disenchanted with the large resort ships that dominate the cruise industry. Traveling by freighter is also the ultimate way to travel for those seeking a totally unstructured voyage without entertainment or other diversions.

The experience has particular appeal for retirees, relocating executives, those with far-flung family connections, graduates returning home from an overseas college, or professors on sabbatical leave. Freighters travel the busiest trade routes, and you can even take one around around the world aboard the vessels of Bank Line; the round-trip takes about four months.

Cabins on most freighters are surprisingly comfortable.

About 300 cargo ships (freighters and container vessels) offer berths, with German operators accounting for more than half of them. True freighters –

the general breakbulk carrier ships and feeder container vessels – carry up to 12 passengers; the only exception is the Royal Mail Ship *RMS St. Helena*, which carries up to 128 passengers, animals such as goats and sheep, and goods from the UK to the island of Ascension, While *RMS St Helena* carries a doctor, freighters do not, and remember that they are working vessels, not cruise ships.

Freighter schedules change constantly, depending on the whim of the owner and the cargo to be carried, whereas container ships travel on regular schedules. For the sake of simplicity, they are all termed freighters. But freighters have changed dramatically as cost management and efficiency have become vital. Container ships are operated as passenger liners used to be: running line voyages on set schedules. You can also make a one-way voyage.

Most freighter companies don't allow children or pregnant women to travel, and won't accept accept anyone younger than five or older than 80. You'll need to be fully mobile – there are no elevators to connect the various decks. Because there are no medical facilities, anyone over 65 is usually required to produce a medical certificate of good health. Also, if your freighter visits a US port at any point, non-Americans will need a full US visa (freighters are not part of the visa-waiver program).

Freighter facilities

What do you get when you book a freighter voyage? You get a cabin with double or twin beds, a small writing table, and a private bathroom. You also get good company, cocktails with conversation, hearty food

(you'll eat in one seating with the ship's officers), an interesting voyage, a lot of water, and the allure of days at sea. What don't you get? Organized entertainment. You will certainly have time to relax and read books (some freighters have a small library), as well as observe the small crew as they help with loading, unloading, and constant upkeep, rust control and maintenance.

The accommodation will consist of a spacious, well-equipped outside-view cabin high above the water line, with a large window rather than a porthole, comfortable lounge/sitting area, and private facilities – far larger than most standard cruise ship cabins are.

How much does it cost?

On a per day basis, freighter travel costs between $125 and $200. Freighter cruise fares are mostly estimated, with final fares provided prior to sailing. If you book with a US specialist, and the freighter line is based in euros, there may be an additional cost depending on the rate of conversion when final payment is due.

A 28-day round-trip sailing aboard one of four CMA-CGM container vessels (Le Havre–Le Havre, France to Guadeloupe and Martinique), for example, costs just over $120 (£80) per person, per day in a twin-bedded cabin, and slightly more in a single-occupancy cabin, plus any expenses incurred in getting to/from the embarkation and disembarkation ports.

Remember that voyages last much longer – typically 30 days or more – so the cost can be considerable. Most are sold out more than a year ahead – two years for some routes – and the freighter fleet has been reduced as a result of the credit crunch, so plan wisely, and remember to purchase trip cancellation insurance.

What to bring

What to take with you? Casual clothing (check with the freighter line, as some require a jacket and tie for din-

ner), all medications, cosmetics, and toiletry items, hairdryer, multi-voltage converter plug, washing powder, and other sundry items such as soap, sun protection, insect repellent, and small flashlight. There may be a small "shop" on board (for the crew) carrying bare essentials like toothpaste.

Bring along your medical certificate, travel insurance details, money in cash, and some extra photos of yourself in case the ship makes unannounced port stops and visas are required. The only gratuities needed are for the waiter and cabin steward, which are generally set at about $1–$2 per day, per person.

New international security regulations mean that if you book a one-way voyage, you must have all onward travel documents with you. Check with embassies and consulates of the countries you will visit. Note that freighters visit cargo ports, so private transportation such as taxis will need to be arranged in advance.

Freighters sometimes have to cancel port calls for commercial reasons at short notice. Bear this in mind if you are attracted by a particular itinerary or port.❑

ABOVE: the *Hatsu Crystal* carries five passengers.
BELOW: *Aranui 3* plies between the islands of Polynesia.

RIVER CRUISING

More than 1 million people a year take a river or inland waterway cruise, making this one of the industry's fastest growing sectors

Whether you want to cruise down the Nile, along the mighty Amazon or the lesser Orinoco, the stately Volga or the magnificent Rhine or the "blue" Danube, along the mystical Ayeyarwady (formerly the Irrawaddy) or the "yellow" Yangtze – to say nothing of the Don and the Dnieper, the Elbe, or Australia's Murray – there are more than 1,000 river cruise vessels to choose from.

What sort of person enjoys cruising aboard these vessels? Well, anyone who survives well without formal dinners, bingo, casinos, discos, or lavish entertainment, and those who want a totally unstructured lifestyle.

The plus points

● You need pack and unpack only once.
● Rivercruise vessels to enable you to enjoy the ever-changing scenery (the "riverscape"), all at eye level.
● You'll wake up in a different place each day, often in the very heart of a city or town.
● You never have to take a tender ashore – you simply step off the vessel when it ties up.
● The atmosphere on board is friendly and informal, never stuffy or pretentious.

Cologne-based 1AVista Reisen permits dogs on certain cruises.

● Cruising along one of the world's rivers is a delightful way to unwind at a slow pace.
● The ride is typically silky smooth – there's no rolling like aboard many of the ocean-going cruise ships, so you won't suffer from seasickness.
● Good food and service are essential elements of a successful river cruise operation.
● All meals are provided, typically in a self-serve buffet arrangement for breakfast and lunch, with sit-down service for dinner. Additionally, basic table wines may also be included for lunch and dinner (included wines are typical of the German river cruise operators or cruise/tour packagers).
● Almost all cabins have outside views; there are virtually no interior (no view) cabins, as aboard most of the ocean-going cruise ships.
● A whole range of optional, extra-cost excursions is available, while some excursions may be included.
● You will typically sail by day, and dock at night (exceptions: Danube and Russian river cruises, where most vessels sail at night), so you can get a restful sleep without engine noise. However, bear in mind that, if your cabin is towards the aft, there may well be the soft humming of a generator, which supplies power for air-conditioning, heating, water supply, lighting and cooking.
● You can, if you wish, leave the vessel in the evening to go out to dinner, or to the cinema, theater or a concert (exceptions: Danube and Russian river cruises).
● Rivers provide a sense of continuity – difficult to achieve from a coach tour, where you may change lodgings each night, and encounter border crossings. Also, while on board, you deal in a single currency.
● The dress code is completely casual.
● There are no cars to drive, or park.
● There are no intrusive art auctions, bingo, wet T-shirt contests and the like.

The minus points

● The flow of water in almost all rivers cannot always be controlled, so there will be times when the water level is so low that even a specially constructed rivercruise vessel, with its shallow draft, cannot travel.
● If you are tall, note that the beds aboard most rivercruise vessels are less than 6 ft (1.8 meters) long.

Cochem, a town in the Mosel Valley on the Rhine.

● Don't wear white. Rivercruise vessels are long and low, which means that their funnels are also low. Soot, created by the emissions from diesel engines and generators, can be a problem, particularly at the stern of the vessel, and on the upper (open) deck.

● Aboard some of the vessels that have an aft, open but sheltered deck area, or an open upper deck – almost all rivercruise vessels have one – smokers may be seated next to you. Few vessels distinguish between smoking and non-smoking areas outdoors, though almost none allow smoking in the public rooms.

● Depending on the vessel, river, the operating company, and tour operators that send passengers to the vessels, there could be passengers of several nationalities. While this can make for interesting social interaction, communication could be a problem if you don't speak the same language.

European river cruising

Cruising down one of Europe's great waterways is a soothing experience – different from sailing on an open sea, where wave motion is a factor. These cruises provide a constant change of scenery, often passing through several countries, each with its own history and architecture, in a week-long journey.

River vessels are always close to land and provide a chance to visit cities and areas inaccessible to the large resort ships. A cruise along the Danube, for example, will take you through nine countries (Germany, Austria, Slovakia, Hungary, Croatia, Serbia, Romania, Bulgaria, Ukraine).

The Rhine–Main–Danube waterway, at 2,175 miles (3,500 km), is the longest waterway in Europe. It connects 14 countries, from Rotterdam on the North Sea to Sulina and Izmail on the Black Sea, and offers travelers varied and fascinating sights.

River vessels are long and low in the water, and their masts fold down in order to negotiate low bridges. Although small when compared to ocean-going cruise ships, they have a unique and friendly international atmosphere. The most modern are air-conditioned and offer the discreet luxury of a small floating hotel, with several public rooms including a dining room, observation lounge, bar, heated swimming "dip" pool (some even have a small heated indoor pool), sauna, solarium, whirlpool, gymnasium, massage, hairdresser, and shop kiosk.

Although the cabins may be small, with limited closet space (take casual clothing, as informality is the order of the day), they are functional. Almost all have an outside view (facing the river), with a private bath-

WHAT GENDER IS A RIVER?

Whether a river is known as a he or a she depends on its behaviour. Take the River Rhône, for example – almost always referred to in the masculine because the waters can be turbulent, bothersome and rough at times. The Saône, on the other hand, is a gentler kind of river – more beautiful, more tranquil – and is thus referred to as "she", as is the "beautiful" Blue Danube (although Napoleon described the Danube as the "king of the rivers of Europe"). The Rhine is male, always referred to as "Father Rhine". The Nile is also deemed a masculine river. The River Volga is always referred to as the "dear little mother" (even though it is the mightiest river in Europe).

Disembarking passengers are serenaded on the Volga river.

room, and will prove very comfortable for a one-week journey. Romantics may lament the fact that twin beds are the norm on the older vessels, but many cabins in the latest vessels have twin beds that can be converted to a queen-sized bed. They also have a personal safe, a mini-bar, flat-screen TV, and an alarm clock/radio.

River cruising in Europe has reached quite a sophisticated level, and you can be assured of good service and meals of a consistently good local standard. Dining is a pleasant although not a gourmet experience, although some companies (such as AMA Waterways and Avalon Waterways) are making strenuous efforts to provide fine cuisine. The best food is typically catered by Austrian, German or Swiss companies. While breakfast and lunch are generally a buffet affair, dinners feature a set menu consisting of three or four courses.

Typical fares for river cruises are from $800 to over $3,000 per person for a one-week cruise, including meals, cabin with private facilities, side trips, and airport/railway transfers. If you are already in Europe, many cruises can be purchased "cruise-only."

Theme cruises are gaining in popularity. For example, greenery lovers might enjoy the "Gardens of the Rhine," with visits to famous botanical gardens, arboretums and herbariums. There are cruises for classical and jazz music fans, gourmets (including a meal at a top restaurants in France, for example), and wine lovers. Christmas Markets cruises in Germany are popular.

Although just a few years ago rivercruise vessels were little more than floating buses, today they have become like sophisticated, floating boutique hotels. While most are of the single hull type (propulsion machinery, accommodation areas, and public rooms are all in one hull), new "twin-cruisers" have been introduced. These vessels have their power unit and navigation bridge located aft in a separate unit attached to the longer body that contains the accommodation areas and public rooms. Although this guarantees that every cabin will be ultra-quiet for sleeping, captains find that the vessels are not so easy to manoeuvre.

Tip: To ensure a degree of peace and quiet, it is best to go for a cabin on a deck that does not have a promenade deck walkway outside it. Normally, cabins on the lowest deck have a four-berth configuration. It does not matter which side of the vessel you are on, as you will see a riverbank and scenery on either side.

Russia's rivers

The "Waterways of the Tsars" are a well-developed network of rivers, lakes, and canals. Geographically, river routes for tourists are divided into three main areas: Central European Russia, Northwestern European Russia, and Asian Russia. There are more than 80 river cruise vessels carrying international tourists.

In the Central Basin, Moscow is the hub of river tourism, and the newly opened waterways between Moscow and St Petersburg allow a 7-day cruise link between the present and former capitals, including the transit of the Volga-Baltic Canal System and its many locks. The best-known Russian rivers are the Don, Moskva, Neva, and Volga, but the lesser known Belaya,

THE BEST TIME TO CRUISE IN EUROPE AND ON THE NILE

There are advantages and disadvantages to every season in Europe. Early spring and late summer will be less crowded and can have beautiful weather. In July and August the weather is often more reliable, though it can be too hot for some and there are more crowds.

It's possible to time a river cruise to coincide with, say, the Rhine in Flames festival in high summer, or the paprika harvest in Hungary, or the beautiful autumn colors along the Danube's Wachau Valley. Special winter cruises operate on the Rhine and Danube to take in the Christmas markets – if you're lucky you'll get crisp, cool weather and

snow on the ground, but rain and slush are just as likely.

Russia tends to be hot and humid in summer. Take insect repellent for travel in August and September, when midges can be a problem, and something warm to wear in the evening in spring and fall.

Nile cruises operate year-round, the peak months being January to March when it's cooler. August is really too hot for anybody except the most dedicated sun-worshipper. September is tolerable if you take things slowly, and there'll be hardly any crowds at the temples. Wearing shorts and a tank top might keep you cool, but they'll indicate a lack of respect if you wear them when visiting tombs and you may be hassled.

Dvina (and North Dvina) Irtysh, Kama, Ob (longest river in Siberia), Oka, Svir, Tura, and Vyatka connect Russia's vast system of rivers and lakes.

Many Russian vessels are chartered to foreign cruise wholesalers and tour packagers, and dedicated to a specific onboard language. The vessels do vary quite a lot in quality and facilities. Some are air-conditioned and most are clean. Cruises include the services of a cruise manager and lecturers. Recommended vessels: *Volga Dream, Viking Kirov* and *Viking Surkov.*

The Nile

The scenery has changed remarkably little in more than 2,000 years, and the best way to see it, of course, is from a river vessel. In all, there are over 7,000 departures every year aboard 300 or so Nile cruise vessels, which offer standards of comfort, food, and service that vary between very good and extremely poor. Most have a small, shallow "plunge" pool, lounge, piano bar, and disco.

A specialist lecturer in ancient Egyptian history accompanies almost all sailings, which cruise the 140 miles (220 km) between Aswân and Luxor in four or five days. Extended cruises, of seven or eight days, cover about 295 miles (475 km) and visit Dendera and Abydos. The longest cruises, of 10 to 12 days, cover 590 miles (950 km) and may include visits to Sohâg, El Amarna, Tuna El Gabal, and Ashmuneim, ending in Cairo.

Most Nile cruises include sightseeing excursions, accompanied by experienced guides who may reside on board, or who may meet the vessel at each call. Security in Egypt has been improved, but the terrorist threat remains, and it's wise to be vigilant. It's also prudent to subtract two stars from any rating provided in brochures or on cruise company and tour operator websites.

The best peak time to take a River Nile cruise is between December and February when the weather is hot but not quite so humid. However, if you go in March/

A Nile cruise vessel by the temple at Kom Ombo.

April or October/early November, you'll find that the major hotels are not so crowded and it will be easier to get around. However, the water level can be low between October and May to conserve water at the Aswan Dam, so getting through the locks at Esna can take a long time as rivercruise vessels compete with cargo vessels and feluccas to get through.

Gratuities are usually not included in the cruise fare, but any tips you give will be divided among all crew members. Some vessels accept credit cards for payment of your onboard account, but others accept only cash.

A few useful tips:

● When you visit the major historic sites and temples, note that there are few public toilet facilities. Toilet paper is not normally provided, so take tissues with you.

● Most Nile rivercruise vessels provide 220-volt outlets in cabins. If you have 110-volt appliances, take adapters (plugs have European-style two round pins).

● If you take a camera with you to any of the 62 tombs in the Valley of the Kings (only a few are open at any one time), you will need to buy a ticket for your camera, too. Museums and other major tourist sites also charge for the use of video and still cameras.

There are several operators, but do check on the facilities, meet-and-greet service, and the newness of the vessels before booking. The best time of the year to go is May–June, and late August–October (July and early August are extremely hot and humid). However, in the Yangtze Valley, temperatures between April and September can reach into 97°F (36°C), and summer rains can be torrential. Monsoons – seasonally changing winds – dominate the region's weather conditions.

River Murray, Australia

The fifth-largest river in the world, the Murray, was the lifeblood of the pioneers who lived on the driest continent on earth. Today, the river flows for more than 1,250 miles (2,760 km) across a third of Australia, its banks forming protected lagoons for an astonishing variety of bird and animal life. A paddlewheel boat such as *Murray Princess* even has six cabins for the physically disabled.

Barge cruising in Europe

Smaller and more intimate than river vessels and more accurately called boats, "cruise barges" ply the inland waterways and canals of Europe from spring to fall, when the weather is best. Barge cruises (usually lasting three to 13 days) offer a completely informal atmosphere, and a slow pace of life, for up to a dozen passengers. They chug along slowly in the daytime, and moor early each evening, giving you time to pay a visit to a local village and get a restful night's sleep.

Most cruise barges are comfortable and beautifully fitted out with rich wood paneling, full carpeting, custom-built furniture and tastefully chosen fabrics. Each has a dining room or lounge-bar. Captains take pride in their vessel, often displaying some rare memorabilia.

Locally grown fresh foods are usually purchased and prepared each day, allowing you to live well and feel like a houseguest. Dining ranges from home-style cook-

A Yangtse cruise boards on a typically misty morning.

China's rivers

More than 80 vessels offer cruises along the Yangtze, the world's third-longest river, particularly through the area known as the Three River Gorges, a 100-mile (160-km) stretch between Nanjin Pass in the east and White King City in the west.

The Yangtze stretches 3,900 miles (6,300 km) from Shanghai through the very heartland of China. The Three Gorges include the 47-mile-long (76-km) Xiling Gorge, the 25-mile-long (40-km) Wu Gorge, and the 28-mile-long (45-km) Qutang Gorge, known locally as "Wind Box Gorge." The Lesser Three Gorges (or Three Small Gorges) are also an impressive sight, often part of the main cruise but also reached by small vessels from Wushan. If possible, take a cabin with a balcony. It is worth the extra money, and the view is better.

Standards of hygiene are generally far lower than you may be used to at home. In China, rats and rivers often go together, and rat poison may well be found under your bed. Some vessels, such as those of Viking River Cruises, have Chinese- and western-style restaurants, a beauty salon, a small health club with sauna, and private mahjong and karaoke rooms. Fine Asian hospitality and service prevail, and cabins are kept supplied with fresh towels and hot tea.

Murray Princess paddles along Australia's Murray River.

Tranquillity on the Burgundy Canal in France.

ing to some outstanding nouvelle cuisine, with all the trimmings. Often, the barge's owner, or spouse, cooks.Most cruise barges can be chartered exclusively so you can just take your family and friends. The waterways of France especially offer beauty, tranquility, and a diversity of interests, and barge cruising is an excellent way of exploring an unfamiliar area. Most cruises include a visit to a famous vineyard and wine cellar, as well as side trips to places of historic, architectural, or scenic interest. Shopping opportunities are limited, evening entertainment is impromptu.

Barging on the canals often means going through a constant succession of locks. Nowhere is this more enjoyable and entertaining than in the Burgundy region of France where, between Dijon and Mâcon, for example, a barge can negotiate as many as 54 locks during a 6-day cruise. Interestingly, all lock-keepers in France are women.

Rates range from $600 to more than $3,000 per person for a 6-day cruise. I do not recommend taking children. Rates include a cabin with private facilities, all meals, good wine with lunch and dinner, all other beverages, use of bicycles, side trips, and airport or railway transfers.

Some operators provide a hotel the night before or after the cruise. Clothing is totally casual – but, at the beginning and end of the season, it's a good idea to take sweaters and rain gear.

United States

Although the former Delta Queen Steamboat Company no longer exists and the steamboats stopped operating in 2008, a small American company, American Cruise Lines, bought the *Columbia Queen, Empress of the North* and *Queen of the West* steamboats in 2009, and started operations in 2010 on the Columbia and Snake rivers in the Pacific Northwest. So, the (faux) steamboat era lives on – just not on the mighty Mississippi.   ❑

RIVER CRUISING: WHO TO CONTACT

This is a complicated sector, with product details changing frequently and river cruise operators chartering their vessels to many different tour operators. The websites below will help you find what's available in your preferred destination.

EUROPE	RUSSIA AND UKRAINE
A'Rosa Cruises	**Noble Caledonia**
www.arosa.de	www.noblecaledonia.com
AMA Waterways	**Uniworld**
www.amawaterways.com	www.uniworld.com
APT Waterways	**Viking River Cruises**
www.aptwaterways.com	www.vikingrivercruises.com
Avalon Waterways	
www.avalonwaterways.com	**CHINA (YANGTZE)**
CroisiEurope	
www.croisieurope.com	**Noble Caledonia**
Feenstra Rhine Line	www.noblecaledonia.com
www.feenstrarijnlijn.nl	**Uniworld**
Grand Circle Travel	www.uniworld.com
www.gct.com	**Victoria Cruises**
Leuftner Cruises	www.victoriacruises.com
www.leuftner-cruises.com	**Viking River Cruises**
Phoenix Reisen	www.vikingrivercruises.com
www.poenixreisen.com	
Scenic Tours	**EGYPT (THE NILE)**
www.scenictours.com	
Scylla Tours	**Hilton Hotels**
www.scylla-tours.com	www.hiltonhotels.com
Sea Cloud Cruises	**Movenpick**
www.seacloud.com	www.movenpick-nilecruises.com
Tauck Tours	**Nabila Tours**
www.tauck.com	www.nabila.com/en
Uniworld	**Noble Caledonia**
www.uniworld.com	www.noblecaledonia.com
Victoria Cruises	**Oberoi Hotels**
www.victoriacruises.com	www.oberoihotels.com/cruises.asp
Viking River Cruises	**Sonesta Hotels**
www.vikingrivercruises.com	www.sonesta.com/nilecruises

AROUND-THE-WORLD CRUISES

They sound like a great way to see the world without having to pack and unpack constantly. But choose carefully: some cruises spend very little time in ports

Since Cunard operated its first world cruise aboard the *Laconia* in 1922, this has become the ultimate classic voyage. It is defined as the complete circumnavigation of the earth in a continuous one-way voyage, typically including both the Panama and the Suez Canals. Ports of call are carefully planned for their interest and diversity, and the entire voyage can last six months or longer.

Galas, themed balls, special social events, top entertainers, and, typically, well-known lecturers are all part of the package. It's a great way of exchanging the northern winter for the southern sun in a grand voyage that is typically over 32,000 nautical miles long, following in the wake of Magellan, who made his round-the-world voyage in 1539.

Around-the-world cruises – they are considered voyages more than cruises – pursue the sun in a westbound direction. This gives an added bonus: that of gaining an hour each time a ship goes into the next time zone. Travel in an eastbound direction – between, for example, Europe and Australia – and you lose an hour each time.

A world cruise aboard a modern ship means experiencing stabilized, air-conditioned comfort in luxury cabins, combined with extraordinary sightseeing and excursions on shore and overland. Aboard some ships,

Ports of call: Lisbon, Portugal; Lima, Peru.

every passenger gets to dine with the captain at least once. Such a cruise is all about experiencing a special annual event – cruise lines typically operate only one world cruise a year – exchanging familiar environments with new ones, glamorous evening soirées, special social parties, black and white themed balls, and entertainment that ranges from intimate recitals to large-scale shows and headline cabaret specialty acts. It's also about socializing, meeting new friends – and perhaps old ones, if you have done it before. There are four aspects to a good world cruise: itinerary, price, ship, and the cruise line's experience.

Some of the most ambitious itineraries are those operated by the German cruise lines such as Delphin Seereisen, Hapag-Lloyd Cruises, Phoenix Reisen, and Transocean Tours. But check brochures and itineraries carefully because some ships spend surprisingly little time in port. On *Arcadia*'s 83-day grand voyage in 2011 (Southampton to Southampton), for example, only two port calls include an overnight stay.

World cruise segments

If you haven't the time or the funds for a full world cruise, it's possible to book a specific segment, flying to join the ship at one of its ports of call and disembarking at another port. If you want to experience everything an around-the-world cruise provides but don't have the three months needed, you should know that most lines offer the cruise in several "segments." This also allows you to "test" the ship and service levels before investing the time and money needed for a full circumnavigation. *Queen Mary 2*, for example, offers 21 segments on its 2011 around-the-world cruise, from 17 days to 96 days. The most popular length for a segment is around 30 days. "Segmenters," as they are often called, typically add on a stay pre- or post-cruise in a destination combining a cruise 'n' stay vacation.

In this way they can visit exotic destinations such as China, the South Pacific, the Indian Ocean, or South America while enjoying elegance, comfort, splendid food, and good company.

Bear in mind that you tend to get what you pay for.

PLANNING AND PREPARATION

For passengers, one of the most important decisions to make will be about what clothes to pack for different climates and conditions. What's really good is that once you have boarded the ship, you need unpack only once. Also, you can take as much luggage as you wish; if you need to fly to join the cruise, you can send your luggage on ahead with a courier service. Although all ships have laundries, some also have self-service launderettes (the place to go for all the inside gossip), so you can clean small items that you need to re-use quickly.

For an operator, planning a world cruise involves daunting organization. For example, more than 700,000 main meals will be prepared during a typical world cruise aboard *Queen Mary 2*. A ship of its size needs two major crew changes during a three-month-long voyage. Hundreds of professional entertainers, lecturers, bands, and musicians must be booked a year in advance.

Ships rated at four stars or more, for example, will probably include shuttle buses from your ship to town centers; ships rated three stars or less will not.

Ships that roam worldwide during the year offer the most experienced world cruises or segments. Most operate at about 75 percent capacity, providing much more space per person than they could normally expect.

Calculating the cost

Prices for a full world cruise vary depending on the cruise line, ship, and accommodation chosen. The following examples are taken from 2011 world cruise brochures (per person rates are quoted, based on double occupancy; single occupancy rates are typically available on request):

Ports: Sydney, Singapore, St Petersburg

- *Crystal Serenity* (108 days: $116,490–$572,510).
- *Pacific Princess* (107 days: from $21,495).
- *Queen Mary 2* (96 nights: £9,749–£112,499).
- *Saga Ruby* (110 nights: £21,449–£78,669).
- *Seabourn Odyssey* (108 days: $107,490–$509,490).

Naturally, substantial discounts (up to 50%) and special incentives are offered by many cruise lines, particularly if you book early (the earlier the better). In today's difficult economic times, it's the lowest grade cabins

that tend to sell out fastest. Some cruise lines quote only a "from" price as a lead-in rate, and provide the price for the large suites only on application.

Passengers who book a full world cruise will probably enjoy a pre-cruise 5-star hotel stay and extravagant dinner with the cruise line's top executives, onboard credit, plus other special events during the cruise (not available to "segmenters"). Note that some cruise lines reserve the right to add a surcharge if the NYNEX oil price exceeds $70 a barrel (read the fine print in the brochure). Also, the lowest prices may not include airfare, if any is required.

Some ships include alcoholic drinks and wine in their cruise fares (examples include *Seabourn Odyssey*, *Seven Seas Voyager*, *Silver Spirit*), but most do not. There will inevitably be the question of gratuities to staff (included for the 2011 world cruises aboard *Albatros*, *Amadea*, *Asuka II*, *Seabourn Odyssey*, *Seven Seas Voyager* and *Silver Spirit*). So you'll need to factor in about $10 per person, per day to your budget. On a 90-day world cruise, that's $1,800. If you are in one of the largest suites, it would be considerably more – allow about $3,000 per couple. ❑

AROUND THE WORLD CRUISES 2011

Ship	Company	Days	Date (Start)	From (Start)	Date (Finish)	To	Direction	No. of Ports
Albatros	Phoenix Reisen	140	Dec 12, 2010	Monte Carlo	May 1, 2011	Venice	Westbound	67
Albatros	Phoenix Reisen	119	Nov 11, 2011	Hamburg	Apr 15, 2012	Monte Carlo	Westbound	58
Amadea	Phoenix Reisen	137	Dec 22, 2010	Nice	May 5, 2011	Hamburg	Westbound	70
Amadea	Phoenix Reisen	139	Dec 18, 2011	Hamburg	May 5, 2012	Venice	Westbound	69
Amsterdam	Holland America Line	110	Jan 5, 2011	Fort Lauderdale	Apr 25, 2011	Funchal	Westbound	36
Asuka II	NYK Cruises	104	Apr 3, 2011	Yokohama	July 15, 2011	Kobe	Westbound	28
Balmoral	Fred Olsen Cruise Lines	107	Jan 5, 2011	Dover	Apr 21, 2011	Dover	Westbound	39
Columbus	Hapag-Lloyd Cruises	170	Jan 17, 2011	Buenos Aires	May 8, 2011	Venice	Westbound	78
Costa Deliziosa	Costa Cruises	100	Nov 1, 2010	Savona	Jan 1, 2012	Savona	Westbound	36
Crystal Serenity	Crystal Cruises	110	Jan 17, 2011	Los Angeles	May 8, 2011	London (Dover)	Westbound	42
Delphin Voyager	Delphin Cruises	128	Dec 9, 2010	Barcelona	Apr 4, 2011	Athens (Piraeus)	Westbound	75
Oriana	P&O Cruises	85	Sept 23, 2010	Southampton	Dec 17, 2010	Southampton	Westbound	30
Pacific Princess	Princess Cruises	107	Jan 19, 2011	Fort Lauderdale	May 6, 2011	Rome (Civitavecchia)	Westbound	42
Queen Mary 2	Cunard Line	103	Jan 13, 2011	New York	Apr 19, 2011	Southampton	Eastbound	29
Saga Ruby	Saga Cruises	110	Jan 5, 2011	Southampton	Apr 24, 2011	Southampton	Westbound	35
Seabourn Sojourn	The Yachts of Seabourn	111	Jan 5, 2011	Los Angeles	Apr 27, 2011	Southampton	Westbound	45
Seven Seas Voyager	Regent Seven Seas Cruises	145	Jan 13, 2011	San Francisco	June 7, 2011	Southampton	Westbound	61
Silver Spirit	Silversea Cruises	119	Jan 19, 2011	Los Angeles	May 19, 2011	Southampton	Westbound	60

OTHER LONG VOYAGES

Ship	Company	Days	Date (Start)	From (Start)	Date (Finish)	To	Direction	No. of Ports
Arcadia *	P&O Cruises	83	Jan 5, 2011	Southampton	Mar 29, 2011	Southampton	Westbound	26
Artemis **	P&O Cruises	99	Jan 4, 2011	Southampton	Apr 12, 2011	Southampton	Eastbound	37
Aurora ***	P&O Cruises	96	Jan 9, 2011	Southampton	Apr 14, 2011	Southampton	East/South	30
Queen Elizabeth *	Cunard Line	105	Jan 5, 2011	Southampton	Apr 19, 2011	Southampton	Westbound	35

* UK to Australia and back   ** Grand Asian Cruise   *** South America/Pacific Cruise

CHOOSING THE RIGHT SHIP

What's the difference between large and small ships? Are new ships better than older ones? Should you consider a maiden voyage? Is corporate cruising good value? Are theme cruises fun?

Which ship? There's something to suit virtually all tastes, so take into account your own personality and tastes. Ships are measured (not weighed) in gross tonnage (gt) and come in four principal size categories:

● **Large Resort Ships**: for over 1,600 passengers (typically measure 50,000–220,000 gross tonnage)
● **Mid-Size Ships**: for 600–1,600 passengers (typically measure 25,000–50,000 gross tonnage)
● **Small Ships**: for 200–600 passengers (typically measure 5,000–25,000 gross tonnage)
● **Boutique Ships**: for up to 200 passengers (typically measure 1,000–5,000 gross tonnage)

Whatever the physical dimensions, all cruise ships provide the same basic ingredients: accommodation, activities, entertainment, plenty of food, good service, and ports of call, although some do it much better than others (and charge more).

Space

For an idea of the amount of the space around you, check the Passenger Space Ratio given for each ship in the listings section (gross tonnage divided by number of passengers). A Passenger Space Ratio of **50 and above** is the ultimate; **30 to 50** is very spacious; **20 to 30** is reasonably spacious; **10 to 20** is high density; and **10 or below** is extremely cramped.

LARGE RESORT SHIPS (1,600–6,000+ passengers)

Choose a large resort ship if you enjoy being with lots of other people, in a bustling big-city environment, you enjoy being sociable, and like to experience plenty of entertainment and dining (no, make that eating) options. These ships balcony-rich provide a well packaged standard or premium cruise vacation, usually in a seven-day cruise. It is the interaction between passengers and crew that determines the quality of the onboard experience.

Large resort ships have extensive facilities and programs for families with children of all ages. But if you meet someone on the first day

and want to meet them again, make sure you appoint a very specific place and time, or you may not see them again (apart from the size of the ship, they may be at a different meal seating). These ships have a highly structured array of activities and passenger participation events each day, together with large entertainment venues, and the most lavish production shows at sea.

It is in the standard of service, entertainment, lecture programs, level of communication, and finesse in dining services that really can move these ships into high rating categories, but they must be exceptional to do so. Choose higher-priced suite accommodation and the service improves. In other words: pay more, get more.

Large resort ships are highly programmed. It is difficult, for example, to go swimming in the late evening, or after dinner (decks are cleaned and pools are often netted over by 6pm). Having champagne delivered to outdoor

LEFT: breakfast, *Seven Seas Voyager*.
RIGHT: the large resort ships stage the most lavish Vegas-style shows.

hot tubs late at night is virtually impossible. They have lost the flexibility for which cruise ships were once known, becoming victims of company "policy" legislation and insurance regulations. There can be a feeling of "conveyor-belt" cruising, with cultural offerings scarcely extending beyond rap, rock, alcohol and gambling.

LARGE RESORT SHIPS: Advantages

● Have the widest range of public rooms and facilities, often a walk-around promenade deck outdoors, and more space (but more passengers).
● Generally have more dining options.
● The newest ships have state-of-the-art electronic interactive entertainment facilities (good if you like computers and high-tech gadgetry).
● Generally sail well in open seas in bad weather.
● There are more facilities and activities for people of all ages, particularly for families with children.

LARGE RESORT SHIPS: Disadvantages

● Finding your way around the ship can be frustrating.
● Waiting in terminal holding areas between check-in and actual boarding.
● Lines to wait in: for embarkation, the information desk, elevators, informal buffet meals, fast food grills, shore tenders, shore excursions, security checkpoint (when returning to the ship), immigration, and disembarkation.
● They resemble floating hotels (but with constant announcements), and so many items cost extra. They are like retail parks surrounded by cabins.
● No matter how big your suite is, or how many public rooms the ship has, you can't help feeling like just one of the crowd, and the individual attention or recognition is

The sports deck on the new *Norwegian Epic*.

MSC Sinfonia, though large, still offers solitude.

missing. You also have to mingle with all the other (lesser paying) passengers in the public rooms.
● The itineraries may be limited by ship size, and there are typically too many tender ports wher you need to take a number, and sit in a lounge and wait, and wait.
● Signage is often confusing; there will be a lack of elevators at peak times.
● The larger the ship, the more impersonal the service (except for "butler" service in penthouse suites).
● You will probably have to use a sign-up sheet to use gym equipment such as treadmills or exercise bikes.
●There are too many announcements (they could be in several languages).
● Dining room staff is so trained to provide fast service, it is almost impossible to sit and dine in leisurely fashion.
● Food may well be bland (cooking for 5,000 is not quite the same as cooking for a dinner party of 8).
● Telephoning room service can be frustrating, particularly in ships with automatic telephone answering systems that state "your call will be answered by room service personnel in the order it was received."
● Room service breakfast is not generally available on the day of disembarkation.
● In early evening, the deck chairs are taken away, or strapped up so they can't be used.
● The in-cabin music aboard the latest ships is supplied through the television set, and it may be impossible to turn off the picture (so much for quiet, romantic late-night music, and darkened cabins).
● Some of the large resort ships have only two main passenger staircases. In an emergency, the evacua-

tion of more than 4,000 passengers could be difficult.

● Waiting for a tender to take you ashore in "anchor" ports can be frustrating.

● Immigration line-up in ports of call such as St Thomas.

MID-SIZE SHIPS (600–1,600 passengers)

These are well suited to the smaller ports of the Aegean and Mediterranean, and are more maneuverable than larger ships. Several operate around-the-world cruises and other long-distance itineraries to exotic destinations not really feasible aboard many of the ships in the small or large resort ship categories.

There is a big difference in the amount of space available. Accommodation varies from large "penthouse suites" complete with butler service to tiny interior (no-view) cabins. These ships will generally be more stable at sea than "small ships", due to their increased size and draft. They provide more facilities, more entertainment, and more dining options. There is some entertainment, and more structured activities than aboard small ships, but less than aboard the large resort ships.

MID-SIZE SHIPS: Advantages

● They are neither too large, nor too small; their size and facilities often strike a happy balance.

● It is easy to find one's way around.

● They generally sail well in areas of bad weather, being neither high-sided like the large resort ships, nor of too shallow draft like some of the small ships.

● Lines seldom form (except for ships approaching 1,600 passengers), but if they do, they are likely to be relatively short.

● They appear more like traditional ships than most of the larger vessels, which tend to be more "boxy" in shape and profile.

MID-SIZE SHIPS: Disadvantages

● They do not offer as wide a range of public rooms and facilities as do the large resort ships.

● Few have large show lounges for large-scale production shows; hence entertainment tends to be more of the cabaret variety.

BOUTIQUE SHIPS (50–200 passengers) and SMALL SHIPS (200–600 passengers)

Choose a boutique or small ship for an intimate cruise experience and a small number of passengers. Some of the most exclusive cruise ships in the world belong in this group (but so do most of the coastal vessels with basic, unpretentious amenities, sail-cruise ships, and the expedition-style cruise vessels that take passengers to see nature).

Select this size of ship if you do not need much entertainment, large resort ship facilities, gambling casinos, several restaurants, and if you don't like to wait in lines for anything. If you want to swim in the late evening, or have champagne in the hot tub at midnight, it is easier aboard boutique or small ships than aboard larger ships, where more rigid programs lead to inflexible, passenger-unfriendly thinking.

BOUTIQUE/SMALL SHIPS: Advantages

● More like small inns than mega-resorts.

● Easy to find your way around, and signage is usually clear and concise.

● At their best in warm weather areas.

● Capable of true culinary excellence, with fresh foods cooked individually to order.

● Most provide an "open seating" in the dining room;

Yoga class aboard the mid-size *Crystal Serenity*.

Boutique ships such as *Le Diamant* can get up close.

this means that you can sit with whomever you wish, whenever you wish, for all meals.

● Provide a totally unstructured lifestyle, offering a level of service not found aboard most of the larger ships, and no or almost no announcements.

● Provide an "open bridge" policy, allowing passengers to go to the navigational bridge when safe to do so.

● Some small ships have a hydraulic marina water sports platform located at the stern and carry equipment such as jet skis, windsurfers, a water ski powerboat, and scuba and snorkeling gear.

● Go to the more off-beat ports of call that larger ships can't get into.

● When the ship is at anchor, going ashore is easy and speedy, with a continuous tender service and no lines.

● Less crowded ports mean more exclusivity.

BOUTIQUE/SMALL SHIPS: Disadvantages

● Do not have the bulk, length, or beam to sail well in open seas in inclement weather conditions.

● Do not have the range of public rooms or open spaces that the large resort ships can provide. Options for entertainment, therefore, are limited.

What about age?

A ship built before 1990 is considered old. However, this really depends on the level of maintenance it has received, and whether it has operated on short or longer cruises (short cruises get more passenger throughput, and so more wear and tear). Yet many passengers like older ships, as they tend to have fewer synthetic materials in their interior decor. Although it is inevitable that some older tonnage cannot match the latest in high-tech, ships today are not constructed with the same loving care as in the past.

Most cruise advertising you'll see revolves around the newer, larger ships, but some older ships have much to offer if you don't want the latest trendy facilities and city high street feel. Indeed, some of the older, smaller ships have adequate facilities, tend to have more character, and provide a more relaxing vacation experience than the go-go-go contemporary ships, where you're just one of a crowd.

Newer ships (post-1990): Advantages

● Incorporate the latest in high-tech electronic equipment and in advanced ship design and construction.

● Meet the latest safety and operating standards.

● Typically have "pod" propulsion system, which replaces conventional propeller shafts, propellers and rudders, with the result that there is little or no vibration *(details: page 45)*.

● Have more interior public rooms, and maybe no exterior promenade deck.

● More standardized cabin layouts, fewer categories.

● Are more fuel-efficient.

● Have a shallower draft, which makes it easier for them to enter and leave ports.

● Have bow and stern thrusters, so they seldom require tug assistance in many ports, reducing operating costs.

● Have good plumbing and air-conditioning systems.

● Have the latest submersible lifeboats.

New ships: Disadvantages

● Do not "take the weather" as well as older ships (sailing across the North Atlantic in November on one of the new large resort ships can be unforgettable). Because of their shallow draft, these ships roll, even when there's the slightest puff of wind.

● Tend to have smaller standard cabins, which can mean narrow, short beds.

● Have decor made mostly from synthetic materials

(due to stringent regulations) and could cause problems for passengers sensitive to such materials.

● Have thin hulls and do not withstand the bangs and dents as well as older, more heavily plated vessels.

● Have toilets of the powerful vacuum suction "barking dog" type.

● Are powered mainly by diesel (or diesel-electric) engines, which can cause some vibration; although on the latest vessels, the engines are mounted on pliable, floating rubber cushions and are, therefore, virtually vibration-free.

● Have cabin windows that are completely sealed instead of portholes that can be opened.

Pre-1990 ships: Advantages

● Have strong, plated hulls that can withstand tremendously hard wear and tear; they "take the weather" well.

● Have large cabins with long, wide beds/berths, because passengers needed more space in the days when voyages were much longer.

● Have toilets that are of the "gentle flush" variety instead of today's "barking dog" vacuum toilets.

● Have interiors built from traditional materials such as wood and brass, with less use of synthetic fibers (less likely to affect anyone allergic to synthetics).

● Have deep drafts that help them to achieve a smooth ride in the open seas.

Pre-1990 ships: Disadvantages

● They are not so fuel-efficient and, therefore, are more expensive to operate than new ships.

● Need a larger crew, because of the more awkward, labor-intensive layouts of the ships.

● Have a deep draft (necessary for a smooth ride) but need tugs to negotiate ports and tight berths.

● Have a tough job complying with current international fire, safety, and environmental regulations.

● Are fitted with older-type open lifeboats.

The crew

You can estimate the standard of service by looking at the crew-to-passenger ratio (provided in the ship profiles in this book). The best service levels are aboard ships that have a ratio of one crew member to every two passengers, or higher. The best ships in the world, from the point of view of crew living and working conditions, also tend to be the most expensive ones (the adage "you get what you pay for" tends to be true).

Most ships now have multinational crews, with one or two exceptions. The crew mixture can resemble a miniature United Nations. However, if the crew is happy, the ship will be happy, too, and that will communicate itself to passengers.

RIGHT: most crews today are thoroughly multinational.

Corporate cruising

Corporate, incentive organizations and seagoing conferences provide a growing market for cruise companies. Ships of all sizes, types and styles can provide an exciting venue for between 50 and 3,000 participants. Corporate organizers like having such things as accommodation, food or entertainment for their delegates organized as one contract.

Cruise companies have specialized departments and personnel to deal with all the details. Corporate organizers don't even have to think about car rentals either. Many larger ships have almost identical cabin sizes and configurations, a bonus for incentive houses.

Once you have signed the contract and paid the deposit for a charter, no refund is possible (thus insurance is essential). Although you may need only 70% of the capacity of a ship for your purposes, you will have to pay for the whole ship if you want an *exclusive* charter.

If you want to charter a whole ship (popular among corporations and associations), where you have complete control over the utilization of public areas:

● Decide which part of the world you want to be in.

● Decide how long you want to cruise for.

● Estimate how many will be in your group.

● Make arrangements as early as possible (at least one year ahead, preferably more).

● Although you can contact cruise lines directly, I strongly recommend contacting www.seasite.com, which contains all cruise brands designed for event planners by the Miami-based ship charter specialists Landry & Kling.

Tennis lessons are available aboard some ships.

Maiden and inaugural voyages

It can be fun to take part in the maiden voyage of a new cruise ship, or in joining the inaugural voyage of a refurbished, reconstructed, or stretched vessel – if you have a degree of tolerance and don't mind some inconvenience, slow or nonexistent service in the dining room. Otherwise, wait until the ship has been in service for at least three months. Then again, if you book a cruise on the third or fourth voyage and the ship's introduction is delayed, you could find yourself on the maiden voyage.

One thing is certain: any maiden voyage is a collector's item, but Murphy's Law – "If anything can go wrong, it will" – can prevail. For example:

● Service aboard new or recently refurbished ships (or a new cruise line) is likely to be uncertain and could be a disaster. An existing cruise line may use experienced crew from its other vessels to help "bring out" a new ship, but they may be unfamiliar with the ship's layout and may have problems training other staff.

● Plumbing and electrical items tend to cause the most problems, particularly aboard reconstructed and refurbished vessels. Examples: toilets that don't flush or don't stop flushing; faucets incorrectly marked, where "hot" really means "cold"; and "automatic" telephones that refuse to function.

● The galley (kitchen) of a new ship if the right supplies don't turn up on time.

● Items such as menus, postcards, writing paper, or TV remote control units, door keys, towels, pillowcases, glassware, and even toilet paper may be lost in the bowels of the ship, or simply not ordered.

● In the entertainment department, items such as spare spotlight bulbs may not be in stock. Or what if the pianos arrive damaged, or "flip" charts for the lecturers didn't show up? Manuals for high-tech sound and lighting equipment may be in a foreign language.

Theme cruises

A wide variety of theme cruises is available, with a focus on many cultural, ecological, and educational subjects. Typical topics range from antiques to wine tasting, from archaeology to holistic health, from sports stars to music festivals, from gardening to square dancing. There are specially chartered voyages for nudists, as well as gay and lesbian cruises *(see page 87)*.

Signs you've chosen the wrong ship

● When, as you embark, a waiter hands you a drink in a tall plastic glass from a tray of drinks of identical color

Luggage handling separates the good ships from the bad.

Big-ship shows can be spectacular – but very loud.

and froth, then gives you a bill to sign without even saying "Welcome Aboard."

● When you wanted a quiet, restful cruise, but your travel agent booked you aboard a ship with 300 baseball fans and provided them all with signed baseball bats and boom boxes for their use on deck.

● When your "luxury" cabin has walls so thin you can hear your neighbors combing their hair.

● When the brochure's "full bathtub" turns out to be "a large washbasin" located at floor level.

● When you packed your tuxedo, but other passengers take "formal" attire to mean clean cut-off jeans and a less stained T-shirt.

● When the "medical facility" is located in the purser's office and consists of a box of adhesive bandages with instructions in a foreign language.

● When the gymnasium equipment is kept in the restaurant manager's office.

● When you have a cabin with an "obstructed view" (usually there is a lifeboat hanging outside it), and it is next to or below the disco. Or the laundry. Or the garbage disposal facility. Or the anchor.

● When "fresh selected greens" means a sprig of parsley on the entrée plate, at every lunch and dinner seating (boring even on a three-day cruise).

● When the cruise director tries to sell passengers a watch, or an artwork, over the public address system.

● When front-row seats at a rock concert would be quieter than a poolside deck chair at midday.

● When you hear the same rap tracks 10 times during the first morning.

● When you need shin pads to prevent injury caused by 600 children chasing through passageways.

● When the cruise brochure shows your cabin with flowers and champagne, but you get neither.

● When the bottled water on your dining room table incurs a bill as soon as you open the bottle.

● When the brochure says "Butler Service," but you

have to clean your own shoes, get your own ice, and still tip twice the amount you would for an "ordinary" cabin steward.

● When the Beer Drinking or Hog Calling Contest, Knobby Knees Contest, and Pajama Bingo are listed as "enrichment lectures."

● When the "fresh-squeezed orange juice" you just ordered means fresh-squeezed, but last week, on land, and poured into industrial-size containers, before transfer to your polystyrene or plastic cup on deck.

● When the brochure says tipping is not required, but your waiter and cabin steward insist otherwise.

● When the cruise director telephones you at 2.30am to let you know that the bingo jackpot is up to $1,000 and that an exciting art auction is about to start.

● When, on the final day, the words "early breakfast" means 5am, and "vacate your cabin by 7.30am" means you face the dismal prospect of spending three hours sitting in the show lounge waiting for disembarkation, with 500 available seats, your hand luggage, and up to 5,000 other passengers, probably playing bingo.

● When on deck, you notice a large hole in the bottom of one or more of the ship's lifeboats.

● When the cabin steward tries to sell you a cut-price time-share in his uncle's coal mine.

● When the proclaimed "five-course gourmet meal" is four courses of salty chicken soup and a potato.

● When the "Deck Buffet" means that there are no tables and chairs, only the deck, to eat off.

● When the brochure shows photos of smiling young couples, but you and your spouse/partner are the only passengers under 80.

● When the library is located in the engine room.

● When the captain tells you he is really a concert pianist and his professional diploma is really for the piano, not navigation. ❏

CHOOSING THE RIGHT CABIN

Does cabin size count? Are suites sweeter than cabins?
How desirable is a balcony? What about location?

Ideally, you should feel at home when at sea, so it is important to choose the right accommodation, even if most of your time in it is spent with your eyes shut. Accommodation sizes range from a whopping 4,390 sq.ft. (407 sq. meters) to a minuscule 60 sq.ft. (5.5 sq. meters). Like houses ashore, all cabins have good and bad points. Choose wisely, for if you find your cabin (incorrectly called a "stateroom" by some companies) is too small when you get to the ship, it may be impossible to change it or to upgrade, as the ship could be full. As for the best location, the upper decks are more expensive.

Cruise lines designate cabins only when deposits have been received (they may, however, guarantee the grade and rate requested). If this is not done, or if you find a disclaimer such as "All cabin assignments are confirmed upon embarkation of the vessel", get a guarantee in writing that your cabin will *not* be changed on embarkation.

There are three main types of accommodation, but many variations on each theme:
● **Suites**: (the largest living spaces, typically with a private balcony); and "junior" suites (with or without private balcony).

WHY PEOPLE LIKE BALCONIES

- You can get fresh air and listen to the waves.
- You get the maximum amount of natural light.
- You can have tea/coffee, or breakfast outside.
- See what the weather is like, to decide how to dress.
- You may see the stars (and shooting stars) at night.
- You can sunbathe in private – assuming the ship is in the right position and your balcony isn't overlooked.
- You can escape from the noise and hullabaloo of the major entertainment areas.

ABOVE: a balcony suite aboard *Black Watch*.

● **Outside-view cabins**: a large picture window or one or more portholes (with or without private balcony).
● **Interior (no-view) cabins**: so called because there is no window or porthole.

Are balconies worth it?

Romeo and Juliet thought so – and, once you've had one, you won't be able to do without one on your next cruise. A private balcony (or "veranda," or "terrace"), for which you pay a premium, is just that. It is a balcony (or mini-terrace) adjoining your cabin where you can sit, enjoy the view, dine, or even have a massage.

Some private balconies are not so private, however. Balconies not separated by full floor-to-ceiling partitions (examples: *Carnival Destiny, Carnival Triumph, Carnival Victory, Maasdam, Oriana, Queen Mary 2, Ryndam, Seven Seas Mariner, Seven Seas Voyager, Statendam,* and *Veendam*) don't quite cut it. You could get noise or smoke from your neighbor. Some ships have balconies with full floor-to-ceiling privacy partitions *and* an outside light (examples: *Celebrity Century, Celebrity Mercury*). Some partitions in *Celebrity Century,* and *Celebrity Mercury* are of the full type, while some are partial.

Note that many large resort ships have balconies too small to accommodate even two reclining chairs.

Some suites with forward-facing private balconies may not be so good, as the wind speed can make them all but unusable. And when the ship drops anchor in ports of call, the noise pollution can be deafening (examples, *Silver Cloud, Silver Wind*).

All private balconies (except French balconies – *see below*) have railings to lean on, but the balconies in some ships have solid steel plates between railing and deck, so you can't look out to sea when seated (examples: *Costa Classica*, *Costa Romantica*, *Dawn Princess*, *Oceana*, *Sea Princess*, and *Sun Princess*). Better are ships whose balconies have clear glass (examples: *Aurora*, *Brilliance of the Seas*, *Celebrity Century*, *Celebrity Mercury*, *Empress*, *Mein Schiff*, *Radiance of the Seas*, and *Serenade of the Seas*) or horizontal bars.

Balcony doors can be quite heavy and difficult to open. Many ships have doors that slide open (examples: *Celebrity Century, Crystal Serenity, Grand Princess, Norwegian Gem*); a few have doors that open inwards (examples: *Seabourn Legend, Seabourn Spirit, Silver Cloud, Silver Wind*); some have doors that open outwards (examples: *Eurodam, Legend of the Seas, Queen Victoria*).

A "French balcony" is one where the doors open to fresh air, but there's no balcony for you to step onto unless your feet are less than six inches long.

Upstairs and downstairs

With the introduction of *Oasis of the Seas* and sister ship *Allure of the Seas*, "loft" accommodation – living room downstairs and sleeping quarters upstairs – will become a "must have" among regulars. Although ships such as the retired *QE2, Sagafjord* and *Vistafjord* (now *Saga Ruby*) had such split suites, they never shouted the fact.

How much?

The cost of accommodation is directly related to the size of the cabin, its location, and the facilities and services.
● Each line implements its own system according to ship size, age, construction, and profit potential.
● Many cruise lines still do not give accurate cabin sizes in their brochures, but you will find the size range in the ship profiles in this book.
● It may be better to book a low-grade cabin on a good ship than a high-grade cabin on a poor ship.
● If you are in a party of three or more and do not mind sharing a cabin, you'll save a lot per person, so you may be able to afford a higher-grade cabin.

Cabin sizes

Cabins provide more or less the same facilities as hotel rooms, except space. Most owners favor large public rooms over cabins. In some smaller interior (no-view) and outside cabins, changing clothes is a challenge.

The latest ships have more standardized cabin sizes, because they are made in modular form (I consider 180 sq. ft/16.7sq. meters to be the *minimum* acceptable size for a "standard" cruise ship cabin today). They all have integrated bathrooms (mostly made from non-combustible phenolic-glass-reinforced plastics) fitted during the ships' construction. Ask your travel agent for the dimensions of the cabin you have selected.

Cabin location

● An "outside-view" cabin is recommended for first-time passengers: an "interior (no-view)" cabin has no portholes or windows, making it more difficult to orient you or to gauge the weather or time.
● Cabins in the center of a ship are more stable and tend to be noise and vibration-free. Ships powered by diesel engines (i.e. most modern vessels) create and transmit some vibration, especially at the stern.
● Take into account personal habits when choosing the cabin location. If you like to go to bed early, avoid a cabin close to the disco. If you have trouble walking, choose a cabin close to the elevator.
● Generally, the higher the deck, the higher the cabin price, and the better the service. This is an inheritance from transoceanic times, when upper-deck cabins and suites were sunnier and warmer.
● Cabins at the front of a ship are slightly crescent-shaped, given that the outer wall follows the curvature of the ship's hull. But they can be exposed to early-morning noises, such as the anchor being dropped at ports where the ship is too big to dock.
● Cabins with interconnecting doors are fine for families or close friends, but the dividing wall is usually so thin you can hear the conversation next door.
● Many brochures indicate cabins with "obstructed-views." Cabins on lower decks are closer to engine noise and heat, especially at the aft of the vessel and around the engine casing. In many older ships, elevators may not operate to the lowermost decks.

Facilities

Cabins provide some, or all, of the following:
● Private bathroom (generally small) with shower, washbasin, and toilet. Higher-grade cabins and suites may have full-size bathtubs. Some have a whirlpool bath and/or bidet, a hairdryer, and more space.
● Multi-channel radio, TV (regular satellite channels or closed circuit), and DVD player.
● Two beds or a lower and upper berth (possibly, another one or two upper berths) or a double-, queen- or king-size bed. In some ships, twin beds can be pushed together to form a double.
● Depending on cabin size, a chair, or chair and table, or

WHAT A BUTLER DOES

Butlers are really better trained waiters and personal assistants who can provide the connections to enable you to have a more enjoyable cruise. Simply tell the butler what you want, and he (or she) will arrange it. For example, if you want a full dinner served course by course from the dining room menu, the butler will serve it. Butlers can:
● Arrange a private cocktail party
● Book shore excursions
● Make dining venue reservations
● Make your shoes shine
● Provide afternoon tea
● Make your spa reservations
● Bring you menus for all dining venues

Typical Cabin Layouts

The following rates are typical of those you can expect to pay for ❶ a seven-day and ❷ a 10-day Caribbean cruise aboard a modern cruise ship. The rates are per person and include free roundtrip airfare or low-cost air add-ons from principal North American gateways

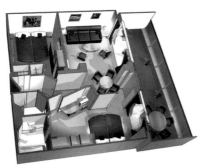

Luxury outside-view suite with private verandah, separate lounge area, vanity area, extra-large double or queen-sized bed, bathroom with tub, shower, and extensive closet and storage space.

❶ $1,750 ❷ $3,000

Large outside-view double with bed and convertible daytime sofabed, bathroom with shower, and good closet and drawer space. Typical size: 23 sq.meters/270 sq.ft.

❶ $1,000 ❷ $2,000

Junior suite with lounge, double or queen-size beds, bathroom with tub, shower, and ample closet and storage space. Typical size: 35 sq.meters/ 375 sq.ft.

❶ $1,500 ❷ $2,000

Luxury outside-view suite with private verandah, separate lounge, vanity area, king- or queen-sized bed, bathroom with full-sized tub and separate shower, and extensive walk-in closet and storage space (plus a guest bathroom). Typical size: 50 sq.meters/ 550 sq. ft.

❶ $2,000 ❷ $3,000

■ Note that in some ships, third- and fourth-person upper berths are available for families or friends wishing to share. The upper Pullman berths, not shown on these cabin layouts, are recessed into the wall or ceiling above the lower beds.

Interior no-view cabin with two lower beds convertible to queen-size bed (plus a possible upper third/fourth berth), bathroom with shower, and some closet space. Typical size: 15 sq.meters/160 sq.ft

❶ $600 ❷ $800

sofa and table, or even a separate lounge/ sitting area (higher accommodation grades).
● Phone, for inter-cabin or ship-to-shore calls.
● Refrigerator/wet bar (higher grades).
● Electrical outlets for personal appliances, usually 110 and/or 220 volts.
● Vanity/desk unit with chair or stool.
● Personal safe.
● Closet space, some drawer space, plus storage room under beds for suitcases.
● Bedside night stand/table unit.
● Towels, soap, shampoo, and conditioner. (Upscale ships provide a greater selection.)

Penthouse suite aboard the 2,852-passenger *Celebrity Solstice*.

Double beds are a comparative rarity except in the higher-priced suites. Aboard some ships you will find upper and lower berths. A "berth" is a nautical term for a bed held in a wooden or metal frame. A "Pullman berth" tucks away out of sight during the day, usually into the bulkhead or ceiling. You climb up a short ladder at night to get into an upper berth.

The suite life

Suites are the most luxurious and spacious of all shipboard accommodation, and typically come with butler service. A suite (which means a "suite of rooms") should measure a *minimum* 400 sq. ft. (37 sq. meters), and comprise a lounge or sitting room separated from a bedroom by a solid door (not just a curtain); a bedroom with a large bed; one or more bathrooms, and an abundance of closet, drawer, and other storage space.

The best suites have the most desirable position, and both privacy and good views should be standard.

Many cruise lines inaccurately describe some accommodation as suites, when they are nothing more than a large cabin with a curtain that divides sitting and sleeping areas.

Suites are best on long voyages with several days at sea. Be aware that, although the large resort ships may devote a whole deck or two to penthouses and suites, you will have to share the rest of the ship with those in lower-priced accommodation.

That means there is no preferential seating in the showroom, the dining rooms, or on sunbathing decks. You may, however, get separate check-in facilities and preferential treatment upon disembarkation, but your luggage will be lumped together with everyone else's. ❑

THE LARGEST SUITES AT SEA

Ship	Cruise Line	Total (sq. ft)	Total (sq. m)
Norwegian Dawn	Norwegian Cruise Line	4,390.0	407.8
Norwegian Gem	Norwegian Cruise Line	4,390.0	407.8
Norwegian Jade	Norwegian Cruise Line	4,390.0	407.8
Norwegian Jewel	Norwegian Cruise Line	4,390.0	407.8
Norwegian Pearl	Norwegian Cruise Line	4,390.0	407.8
Norwegian Star	Norwegian Cruise Line	4,390.0	407.8
Celebrity Constellation	Celebrity Cruises	2,530.0	235.0
Celebrity Infinity	Celebrity Cruises	2,530.0	235.0
Celebrity Millennium	Celebrity Cruises	2,530.0	235.0
Celebrity Summit	Celebrity Cruises	2,530.0	235.0
Queen Mary 2	Cunard Line	2,249.7	209.0
Freedom of the Seas	Royal Caribbean International	2,025.0	188.0
Independence of the Seas	Royal Caribbean International	2,025.0	188.0
Liberty of the Seas	Royal Caribbean International	2,025.0	188.0
Seven Seas Mariner	Regent Seven Seas Cruises	2,002.0	186.0
Silver Spirit	Silversea Cruises	1,614.0	150.0
Celebrity Century	Celebrity Cruises	1,514.5	140.7
Celebrity Mercury	Celebrity Cruises	1,514.5	140.7
Mein Schiff	TUI Cruises	1,514.5	140.7
Silver Shadow	Silversea Cruises	1,435.0	133.3
Silver Whisper	Silversea Cruises	1,435.0	133.3

NOTES: 1. Sizes shown include balconies. 2. Residents-only ships not included. 3. Most cruise lines measure the gross size, but in reality the net (interior) measurements will be slightly less.

Suites aboard *Silver Shadow*, (top), *Norwegian Dawn* (above), and *Freedom of the Seas* (below).

THE MAJOR CRUISE LINES

Is big necessarily better? We compare what the world's largest cruise companies, reviewed in alphabetical order, have to offer when it comes to facilities, cuisine, service and ambience

The mainstream cruise industry may appear diverse, but it is dominated by just a few conglomerates, principally Carnival Corporation and Royal Caribbean Cruises (see chart below). Dig deeper and you will find, for example, that two Carnival subsidiaries, Holland America Line and Princess Cruises, virtually control large resort ship cruising in Alaska, where they own hotels, lodges, tour companies and much land-based transportation (other operators have to buy their services). This came about in 2002–3 when Princess Cruises' parent company, P&O Group, sold its cruising division to the Carnival Corporation. It sounds monopolistic, although it is not really more so than some tour operators in Europe that own travel agency chains, hotels, an airline, and cruise ships.

Carnival Cruise Lines puts the emphasis on fun.

What makes them different

So how does one choose between the companies? The marketing tags they use in television advertising provide a clue: Carnival Cruise Lines (Ain't We Got Fun); Celebrity Cruises (Designed for You); Costa Cruises (Cruising Italian Style); Holland America Line (Signature of Excellence); Norwegian Cruise Line (Freestyle Cruising); P&O Cruises (Freedom); Princess Cruises (Escape Completely); and Royal Caribbean International (Way More than a Cruise). Cunard Line, MSC Cruises and Star Cruises do not advertise on television.

Ships belonging to the major cruise lines may look the same, but they differ not only in their layout, decor and passenger flow but also in such facilities as tea and coffee-making machines in passenger cabins (P&O Cruises provides them, as does RCI – but only aboard its UK-based ships). Even the size of towels varies widely – a trivial point for some, perhaps, though not for larger passengers. Some examples (in inches):

72" x 36"	P&O Cruises
70" x 36"	Cunard Line
60" x 38"	Holland America Line
56" x 36"	MSC Cruises
54" x 31"	Costa Cruises
54" x 28"	Celebrity Cruises, Royal Caribbean
54" x 27"	AIDA Cruises
50" x 28"	Carnival Cruise Lines
50" x 28"	Norwegian Cruise Line (NCL)
50" x 26"	Princess Cruises

Even aboard some ships of the same cruise line, there

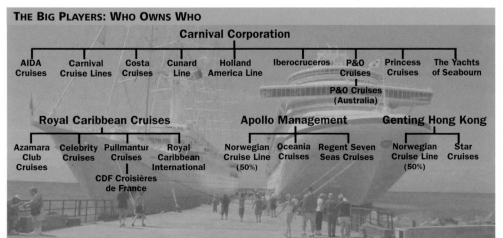

THE BIG PLAYERS: WHO OWNS WHO

Carnival Corporation

AIDA Cruises	Carnival Cruise Lines	Costa Cruises	Cunard Line	Holland America Line	Iberocruceros	P&O Cruises	Princess Cruises	The Yachts of Seabourn

P&O Cruises (Australia)

Royal Caribbean Cruises

Azamara Club Cruises	Celebrity Cruises	Pullmantur Cruises	Royal Caribbean International

CDF Croisières de France

Apollo Management

Norwegian Cruise Line (50%)	Oceania Cruises	Regent Seven Seas Cruises

Genting Hong Kong

Norwegian Cruise Line (50%)	Star Cruises

Cunard Line puts the emphasis on elegance.

counts, and "free" cruises (examples: Carnival Cruise Lines, Norwegian Cruise Line, Royal Caribbean International).

Standing in line for embarkation, disembarkation, shore tenders and for self-serve buffet meals is inevitable aboard all large resort ships. The ships do, however, differ in their characters, facilities, maintenance, space, crew-to-passenger ratio, food and service, crew training, and other aspects.

For example, you'll be escorted to your cabin aboard the ships of Cunard Line (suite-grade accommodation only), Holland America Line, MSC Cruises, and Star Cruises (VIP-club members only). Aboard other lines, staff at the entrance simply point you in the right direction – even if you have heavy carry-on luggage – and gangway staff may even try to give you a daily program, or spa details or other bumf.

There are other irritants common to most of the major cruise lines. Examples:
● Relaxation is not about music blaring over pool deck speakers 24 hours a day.
● Sterile passenger hallways.
● Bring back real cabin keys.
● Reception desk staff need to join the hospitality (not hostility) industry.
● There's a lack of port information for independent passengers who don't want to join organized excursions.
● Passengers are getting bigger, so the cruise lines should stop furnishing their ships with those stupid baby-sized tub chairs.
● The volume is too high at the poolside movies.

can be variations in towel sizes (example: RCI's *Oasis of the Seas* 54" x 27"; *Legend of the Seas* 45" x 27").

What they have in common

All offer one thing: a well-packaged cruise vacation (generally of seven days), typically with a mix of days at sea and days in port, plenty of food, reasonable service, large-scale production shows and trendy cabaret acts, plus large casinos, shopping malls, and extensive, busy spa and fitness facilities. Nine offer a variety of "drive to" embarkation ports within the US ("homeland cruising").

Their ships have a lot in common, too. All have art auctions (except MSC Cruises and Star Cruises), bingo, horse racing, shopping talks for ports of call (pushing "recommended" stores), programs for children and teens, wedding vows renewal programs, and wi-fi or internet connect centers (costing, typically, about 50 cents per minute). All except MSC Cruises still feature the "Peppermill Routine" (the waiter brings a huge peppermill to your table before you've even tasted the food), but only a few extra-charge dining venues offer tableside carving or flambée items.

Extra costs include port taxes, insurance, gratuities to staff, and use of the washer/dryers in self-serve launderettes. Some lines offer their own credit cards, with points useable for upgrades, dis-

---

MAJORS UNDER THE MICROSCOPE: WHO DOES WHAT BEST

● **Carnival Cruise Lines** is known for all-round fun, activities and casinos for the lively, no-sleep-needed youth market (although many passengers are over 45).
● **Celebrity Cruises** has the best food, the most elegant ships and spas, and its cruises are really underpriced.
● **Costa Cruises** has the edge on European style and lively ambiance, with multi-nationality passengers, but the swimming pools are full of noisy children in peak holiday periods.
● **Cunard Line** has one real ocean liner that provides a regularly scheduled transatlantic service, while its other ship is more about regular cruising. Both ships carry over some fine British traditions.
● **Holland America Line** has all the right touches for seniors and retirees: smiling service staff, lots of flowers, traditions of the past, good cooking demonstrations and alternative grill rooms.
● **MSC Cruises** tailors its onboard product to pan-European passengers of all ages, and displays fine Italian flair, with a high level of service and hospitality from a friendly, multilingual crew.
● **Norwegian Cruise Line** is good for a first cruise for families with children, with a great choice of eating places, good entertainment, and friendly service staff.
● **P&O Cruises** operates mainly ex-UK cruises for its predominantly UK-based passengers, with good facilities for families with children, as well as child-free ships, and a liking for Indian curries and cuisine.
● **Princess Cruises** has consistent product delivery, although the ships have decor that is rather bland, and passengers tend to be somewhat older.
● **Royal Caribbean International** is good for the Caribbean (naturally), for first-time cruisers and families, with a good variety of entertainment, and interesting programs designed for families with children.
● **Star Cruises**, with ships based in Southeast Asia, specializes in cruises for Asians, Australians, and British passengers, and offers a good choice of restaurants and ethnic cuisine.

CARNIVAL CRUISE LINES

Ships

Fantasy-class ships: *Carnival Ecstasy* (1991), *Carnival Elation* (1998), *Carnival Fantasy* (1990), *Carnival Fascination* (1994), *Carnival Imagination* (1995), *Carnival Inspiration* (1996), *Carnival Paradise* (1998), *Carnival Sensation* (1993)
Destiny-class ships: *Carnival Conquest* (2002), *Carnival Destiny* (1996), *Carnival Freedom* (2007), *Carnival Glory* (2003), *Carnival Liberty* (2005), *Carnival Splendor* (2008), *Carnival Triumph* (1999), *Carnival Valor* (2004), *Carnival Victory* (2000)
Dream-class ships: *Carnival Dream* (2009), *Carnival Magic* (2011)
Spirit-class ships: *Carnival Legend* (2002), *Carnival Miracle* (2004), *Carnival Pride* (2002), *Carnival Spirit* (2001)

About the company

Israel-born Ted Arison, whose ambition it was to be a concert pianist, founded Carnival Cruise Lines, now the world's largest and most successful single cruise line, in 1972 with one ship, *Mardi Gras* (formerly *Empress of Canada*). Carnival wanted to be different, youthful, and fun, and developed the "Fun Ship" concept. It worked, appealing to people of all ages and backgrounds.

The company's first new ship, *Tropicale*, debuted in 1982. In 1984 Carnival started advertising on television, introducing a wider public to the idea of cruising. It introduced the first cruise ship measuring over 100,000 gross tonnage, *Carnival Destiny* in 1996.

Today, the Carnival Corporation, parent company of

Two Carnival Cruise Line ships at Cozumel, Mexico.

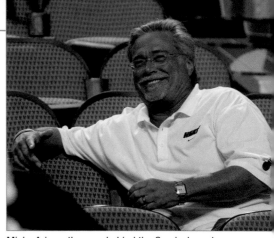

Micky Arison, the man behind the Carnival empire.

Carnival Cruise Lines, is run by Ted Arison's son, Micky Arison, who is chairman of the board – as well as owning the NBA's Miami Heat basketball team. More than 20 new ships have been introduced since the line was founded in 1972.

Self-dubbed the "fun ship" cruise line, the well organized company attracts passengers of all ages, although the majority are between 30 and 55. Carnival does not sell itself as a "luxury" or "premium" cruise line, which it certainly isn't. It consistently delivers exactly the well-packaged cruise vacation its brochures promise, for which there is a huge and growing first-time cruise market. Its smart ships have the latest high-tech entertainment facilities and features, and some include extra-cost alternative dining spots.

The line has upgraded some aspects of its operation and product. It needed to. The *Carnival Fantasy*-class ships are receiving an overdue multi-million dollar make-over, including an adults-only sunbathing area,

pool decks (a thatched roof over one of two hot tubs and the addition of palm trees and new mid-deck stairways), the creation of a new lobby bar, expanded children's and teens areas, more inter-connecting cabins, and balconies are being retro-fitted to 98 cabins; the *Fantasy*-class ship have few balcony cabins and no walk-around open promenade deck. Meanwhile, giant poolside movie screens have been fitted to most non-*Fantasy*-class ships.

In 2008 Carnival re-categorized cabin price grades based on the European model of charging more for those in prime position.

✪ **Frequent passengers' club:** Carnival Concierge Club.

So what's it really like?

It's an all-American experience: cruising for those with a low boredom threshold – exciting, noisy, challenging, but blood pressure-raising, organized fun, slickly packaged with about 60 itineraries.

Carnival's "fun" cruising is good for families with children and teens (anyone under 21 must be accompanied by a parent, relative or guardian) and youthful adults. Carnival ships are also good for whole-ship charters and incentive groups, for multi-generational passengers and for family reunions. Typically, about half of Carnival's passengers are taking their first cruise. About 30 percent are under the age of 35, 30 percent are over 55, the other 40 percent are between 35 and 55.

The dress code is ultra-casual – indeed, the waiters are better dressed than most passengers – particularly during youth-heavy holiday seasons and spring breaks, when clothes appear almost optional. Carnival is all about "happy" and "fun" – cruise directors actually tell passengers to "make some noise," so Camp Carnival is for adults as well as children. But it's a very impersonal cruise experience, overseen by young cruise directors who are fluent in "tongue-fu" and deliver the same jokes and banter on every trip. Solo cruisegoers can get lost in the crowds of doubles. It's all about towels shaped like animals, programmed participation activi-ties, yelling and screaming and having fun.

Perhaps the tone doesn't matter so much because this will be a first cruise for most passengers. Repeat cus-tomers, however, have a distinct sense of déjà vu, but carry a Gold Card for better recognition from hotel staff (Platinum for those who have cruised with Carnival more than 10 times).

The ships are clean and well maintained – if you don't peer too closely. Open deck space may look ade-quate when you board, but on days at sea you can expect your plastic deck chair, if you can find one that's free, to be kissing its neighbor – it's probably tied to it. There are no cushioned pads for the deck lounge chairs, which are hard to sit on, if you use just a towel, for any length of time.

You may well encounter lots of smokers, and masses

Carnival encourages its passengers to "make some noise."

of fellow passengers walking around in urban warfare clothing – passengers dress better on longer cruises such as Panama Canal sailings – clutching plastic sport drinks bottles at any time of the day or night. The decibel level is high: it is difficult to escape from noise and loud music, and "background" music is played even in cabin hall-ways and elevators 24 hours a day. Huge poolside movie screens are being fitted aboard Carnival's ships.

Expect to be subjected to a stream of flyers advertis-ing daily art auctions, "designer" watches, gold and sil-ver chains and other promotions, while "artworks" for auction are strewn throughout the ships. Also, expect intrusive announcements (particularly for activities that bring revenue), and waiters hustling you to have drinks.

Carnival Capers, the ship's daily program, is among the industry's poorest information sheets, in terms of lay-out and print quality, and most of it is devoted to per-suading you to spend money.

There are libraries but few books, and bookshelves are always locked by 6pm, because you are expected to be out in the (revenue-earning) public areas each evening. If you enjoy casino gaming at sea, you could join Carnival's Ocean Players Club, which brings ben-efits to frequent players, depending on your level of skill.

Between 2008 and 2010, a multimillion-dollar reno-vation added 98 small balconies to existing staterooms aboard the *Carnival Fantasy*-class ships. Also included: a new Circle "C" facility for 12- to 14-year-olds, a water park with water-spray area, and oversized umbrellas. An adults-only Serenity retreat was added to the aft area of Promenade Deck. The main pool now has more of a resort-style ambience.

● **Accommodation:** In 2008 Carnival reorganized some cabin categories, and, following the European way of

Sam's Piano Bar, a key venue aboard *Carnival Dream*.

doing things, cabins in the best locations now cost more. Note that balconies in many of the cabins with "private" balconies aren't so private – most can be overlooked from other cabins located on the deck above and from various public locations. You may have to carry a credit card to operate the personal safes – inconvenient. High-quality mattresses and bed linen, also available for sale, have been fitted to all beds.

● **Passenger niggles:** The most consistent complaints include the fact that most activities are geared around trying to sell you something. Free-to-enter onboard games have pint-sized "prizes," while the cost of playing bingo keeps rising. Many people object to the heavy sales pitches for products in spas. The intrusive photographers are almost impossible to escape. There's no listing of the free in-cabin TV movies – only those that are pay-per-view. The non-stop recorded poolside music is intrusive. Then there's disembarkation…

There is little finesse and not enough attention to individuals. Carnival operates from many "drive to" embarkation ports in the US, and promotes a "vacation guarantee program" that is almost useless (check the Carnival brochure for details).

Decor

The decor is very creative, although you probably wouldn't want to let the ships' interior designer loose in

Nightlife aboard *Carnival Freedom*.

your home. But there's no denying that Joe Farcus, the "neon-lithic" genius behind the decor, creates a dramatic impact, from the carpets to the ceiling, mixing more colors than a rainbow could aspire to. Strangely, the sensory overload works. It's pure magic, whimsical, and very entertaining.

So, if you love color, you'll be fine. If you prefer monochrome, take sunglasses. Excepted from the dazzle are the clinical public toilets, which could do with a little bit of cheering up – the designer clearly hasn't been in one lately.

Gratuities

These are added to your onboard account at $9.75 per person per day (the amount charged when this book went to press). You can have this amount adjusted if you visit the information desk. Additionally, 15% is added to your account for all bar, wine and spa charges (yes, even after high treatment prices). The onboard currency is the US dollar – and this applies even when a ship is operating in European waters.

Cuisine/Dining

All Carnival ships have one or two main dining rooms, and its "Your Choice Dining" program offers three dinner seating options, including "Your Time" open seating. Dining assignments are confirmed at time of booking. Menus are standardized across the fleet, and all the dining venues are non-smoking.

Don't even think about a quiet

table for two, or a candlelight dinner on deck – it's not Carnival's style – unless you pay extra at an "alternative" restaurant. Dining aboard a Carnival ship is all about table mates, social chat, lively meals, fast eating.

Tables are, however, nicely set with white tablecloths, plenty of silverware, and iced water/iced tea whenever you want it. Oh, and the tired old peppermill routine (where the waiter brings a huge peppermill to your table before you've even tasted the food) is all part of the show – delivered with friendly service that lacks polish but invites extra gratuities.

The main dining rooms marry food and show business. Waiters sing and dance, and there are constant waiter parades with flashing lights in an attempt to create some excitement.

Taste-filled food is not the company's strong point, but quantity, not quality, is – although consultant chef Georges Blanc has created daily "Georges Blanc Signature" menu items. The company has been striving to improve its cuisine and the menu choices often look good, but the actual food delivered is simply banquet-style catering, with its attendant standardization and production cooking.

While meats are of a decent quality, poultry, fish, seafood and desserts are disappointing. Sauces and gravies are used well as disguises, and there are few garnishes. The selection of fresh green vegetables, breads, rolls, cheese and ripe fruit is poor, and there is much use of canned fruit and jellied desserts, not to mention packets of jam, marmalade, butter, sugar – the same stuff you'd find in the average family eatery in the USA. It is virtually impossible to obtain anything remotely unusual or off-menu, and the "always available" items appear to have disappeared from the menus. Vegetarian and children's menus are available at all meals, but they wouldn't get a generous score for their nutritional content. Spa Carnival Fare has been introduced to provide healthy dining options.

The wine list is adequate, but there are no wine waiters or decent-sized wine glasses. Carnival also has a "wines by the glass" program, with good storage and presentation facilities that enable wines to be served properly in several locations and not just in the restaurants aboard each ship.

● **Alternative Dining Spots**

Carnival Conquest, Carnival Destiny, Carnival Dream, Carnival Freedom, Carnival Glory, Carnival Liberty, Carnival Miracle, Carnival Splendor, Carnival Triumph, Carnival Valor

These extra-cost restaurants feature fine table settings, china and silverware, and leather-bound menus. Menu favorites include prime American steaks such as filet mignon (9 ounces), porterhouse steak (24 ounces) and New York strip loin (be prepared for huge cuts of meat – shown to you at your table before you order), and broiled lobster tail, as well as stone crab claws from Joe's Stone Crabs of South Miami Beach.

Reservations are necessary, and a cover charge of $30 per person for service and gratuity is payable.

The food is good, and the ambience is reasonably quiet. But if you are a couple and you have just two glasses of wine each (Grgich Hills Chardonnay or Merlot, for example, at $12.50 a glass), and pay the cover charge, that's over $100 for dinner. Caviar (American) would cost around $30 for a 1-ounce serving.

Are alternative dining spots worth the extra money? Yes, I believe they are – the food's better, the service is slower, and it's less noisy.

● **Casual Eateries**

All ships also have large food court-style spaces for casual food, fast-food items, grilled meats, pizzas (each ship serves over 800 pizzas in a typical day), stir fry, deli and salad items. There are self-help beverage stands, coffee that looks like rusty water, and tea provided in paper cups with a teabag (tea dust, as far as I'm concerned), plastic or wooden stirrers (no teaspoons and no saucers), and packets of chemical "milk" or "creamer."

But some people are happy to have it that way, and it's actually better than what's offered aboard the ships of its competitor, Royal Caribbean International. Late-night "snacks" consist of greasy fast-food items instead of healthy alternatives such as light fruit bites, and are usually the same every night. Breakfast buffets are as repetitive as canned laughter on television.

● **The Coffee/Tea Factor**

Regular coffee is weak and poor, scoring 1 out of 10 (paper/foam cups in buffet areas). The espresso and cappuccino coffees score 2 out of 10 (served in paper or foam cups, in buffet areas).

Pizza is available 24 hours a day aboard Carnival's ships.

For Children:

Carnival is a fine family-friendly cruise line, carrying more than 575,000 children a year, and "Camp Carnival," the line's extensive child/youth program, is well organized and extensive. There are five age groups: Toddlers (ages 2–5); Juniors (6–8); Intermediate (9–11); Tweens (12–14, Circle C) and late Teens (15–17, with Club O2). Even the under-twos are now being catered to, with special programs aboard each ship. Meanwhile, Family Fun Nights are all about reconnecting parents to their children – something many can do only on vacation.

Soft-drinks packages can be bought for children (adults, too). Note that a babysitting service is not available after 10pm.

Best ships for children: *Carnival Conquest, Carnival Destiny, Carnival Dream, Carnival Freedom, Carnival Glory, Carnival Legend, Carnival Liberty, Carnival Miracle, Carnival Pride, Carnival Spirit, Carnival Splendor, Carnival Triumph, Carnival Valor,* and *Carnival Victory.*

Ships with fewer facilities: *Carnival Ecstasy, Carnival Elation, Carnival Fantasy, Carnival Fascination, Carnival Imagination, Carnival Inspiration, Carnival Paradise,* and *Carnival Sensation.*

Entertainment

The ships have big showlounges, all non-smoking, and large-scale flesh-and-feather production shows. On a

ABOVE: on *Carnival Elation*'s 660-ft jogging track.
BELOW: *Carnival Conquest*'s Monet Restaurant.

typical cruise, there will be one or two large-scale shows, with male and female lead singers and a clutch of dancers backed by a 10-piece live orchestra and supported by pre-recorded backing tracks.

These are loud, ritzy-glitzy, razzle-dazzle, Las Vegas-style revues with little or no story line or flow – lots of running around on stage and stepping in place, but little real dancing. The skimpy costumes are very colorful, as is the lighting, with extensive use of "color mover" lights. Stage "smoke" is much overused – to the irritation of anyone unfortunate enough to be seated in the front few rows.

Carnival often rotates entertainers aboard its ships, so that passengers see different acts each night, and specialty acts take center stage on nights when there is no production show. There's also live music in just about every bar and lounge – although there appears to be a trend to replace live music with more DJs – and there's also a strong trend toward smutty late-night adults-only comedy.

Cabaret acts include vocalists, magic acts, ventriloquists, and comedy jugglers. Each cruise has karaoke nights, a passenger talent show, and a discotheque with ear-splitting volumes and megaphones to enable you to converse with your partner.

Spa/Fitness Facilities

Spa/Fitness facilities are operated by Steiner Leisure, a specialist concession, whose young, revenue-conscious staff will try to sell you Steiner's own-brand beauty products. Some fitness classes are free; others, such as yoga and kick-boxing, cost extra (typically $10 per class), and you'll need to sign up to join.

Examples of treatments: Swedish Massage ($119 for 50 minutes); Aroma Stone Massage ($195 for 75 minutes); Couples Massage ($269 for 50 minutes); Facial ($119 for 50 minutes); Seaweed Body Wrap, with half-body massage ($195 for 90 minutes). It's prudent to book appointments early, and you can book more than 30 treatments online before your cruise.

The Spa Carnival layout spaces and facilities are identical to other ships in the same "class," as follows:

● *Carnival Legend, Carnival Miracle, Carnival Pride, Carnival Spirit*

SpaCarnival spans two decks, is located directly above the navigation bridge in the forward part of the ship and has 13,700 sq ft (1,272 sq meters) of space. Facilities on the lower level include a solarium, eight treatment rooms, lecture rooms, sauna and steam rooms for men and women, and a beauty parlor; the upper level consists of a large gymnasium with floor-to-ceiling windows on three sides, including forward-facing ocean views (with a large array of the latest in muscle-pumping electronic machines), and an aerobics room with instructor-led classes (the aerobics room and gymnasium together measure almost 6,000 sq ft/560 sq meters).

Carnival Elation's eye-catching atrium.

● *Carnival Conquest, Carnival Destiny, Carnival Freedom, Carnival Glory, Carnival Miracle, Carnival Splendor, Carnival Triumph, Carnival Valor*
SpaCarnival spans two decks (with a total area of 13,700 sq ft/1,272 sq meters), and is located directly above the navigation bridge in the forward part of the ship (accessible from the forward stairway). Facilities on the lower level include a solarium, eight treatment rooms, lecture rooms, sauna and steam rooms for men and women, and a beauty parlor; the upper level consists of a large gymnasium with floor-to-ceiling windows on three sides, including forward-facing ocean views. It has the latest in muscle-pumping electronic machines, and an aerobics room with instructor-led classes, some costing extra.

● *Carnival Dream, Carnival Magic*
The expansive 23,750-sq-ft (2,206 sq-meter) Serenity Spa, Carnival's largest and most elaborate health and wellness center, is positioned over three decks in the ship's front section. The uppermost deck is intended for indoor/outdoor private spa relaxation (at extra cost). A spiral staircase connects each deck, and the Steiner-operated spa offers a wide range of treatments.

● *Carnival Ecstasy, Carnival Elation, Carnival Fantasy, Carnival Fascination, Carnival Imagination, Carnival Inspiration, Carnival Paradise, Carnival Sensation*
SpaCarnival is located on Sports Deck, forward of the ship's mast, and accessed from the forward stairway. It consists of a gymnasium with ocean-view windows that look out over the ship's bow, and there's a good array of the latest in muscle-pumping electronic machines, an aerobics exercise room, men's and women's changing rooms (towels are provided), sauna and steam rooms, and beauty salon.

CELEBRITY CRUISES

Ships

Century-class ships: *Celebrity Century* (1995), *Celebrity Mercury* (1997)
Millennium-class ships: *Celebrity Constellation* (2002), *Celebrity Infinity* (2001), *Celebrity Millennium* (2000), *Celebrity Summit* (2001)
Solstice-class ships: *Celebrity Eclipse* (2010), *Celebrity Equinox* (2009), *Celebrity Silhouette* (2011), *Celebrity Solstice* (2008)
Other ships: *Celebrity Xpedition* (2001)

About the company

Celebrity Cruises was the brainchild of Harry H. Haralambopoulos and brothers John and Michael Chandris, the London-based Greek cargo ship owners and operators of the former Chandris Lines and Chandris Cruises. In 1989, as the cruise industry was gaining momentum, they determined to create a newer, better cruise line, with new ships, larger, more standard cabins, and focusing more on food and service in the European tradition.

In its formative years, Celebrity Cruises forged an alliance, since dissolved, with three-star Michelin chef Michel Roux. The company established an outstanding reputation for its cuisine, particularly in the main dining rooms, with a formal presentation and service.

Today it advertises itself as a "premium" line. There are aspects of the product that are no longer premium – for example, recorded "music" blaring over pool decks 24 hours a day is definitely not relaxing. But the term still sums up Celebrity reasonably well because the product delivery on board is superior to that of its parent company, Royal Caribbean International, which bought it in

1997 for $1.3 billion. The ships are recognizable, thanks to the "X" on the funnel denoting the third letter from the end of the Greek alphabet, the Greek "chi" or "C" in English, for Chandris, the founding family.

In 2007 Celebrity Cruises created a new company, **Azamara Cruises**, with mid-size ships, including *Azamara Journey* (2000) and *Azamara Quest* (2000). The idea is to focus on lesser-visited destinations, and offer better shore experiences. All hotel services and cruise operations are, however, operated by Celebrity Cruises. ✪ **Frequent passengers' club:** Captain's Club.

So what's it really like?

The ships are usually very clean and extremely well maintained. There are always lots of flowers and flower displays – some ships have flower shops, where you can buy fresh blooms for special occasions.

There is a lot of fine artwork aboard Celebrity's ships; it may not be to everybody's taste, but it is probably the most remarkable collection of contemporary art in the cruise industry. The company provides a lot of the niceties that other lines have long forgotten, although some are now playing "catch up": waiters who carry your trays when you obtain food from buffets or casual eateries; water spritzes on the pool deck. Sadly, stewards no longer escort you to your cabin on embarkation day. On days at sea in warm weather areas, if you are sunbathing on deck, someone will bring you a cold towel, and a sorbet, ice water or iced tea.

Regardless of the accommodation grade, Celebrity Cruises delivers a well-defined North American cruise experience at a modest price. Book a suite-category cabin for the extra benefits it brings – it's worth it. Strong points include the many European staff and the high level of service, fine spas with a good range of facilities and treatments, taste-filled food served in fine European dining tradition, a "zero announcement policy," cloth towels in public restrooms instead of the paper towels found aboard most major companies. Such touches differentiate Celebrity Cruises from its competitors.

Its ships have significantly more staff than other ships of comparable size and capacity, especially in the housekeeping and food and beverage departments. This helps create a superior product.

Celebrity's ships are best suited to well-educated, more sophisticated adult couples, families with older children and teenagers, and singles who like to mingle in a large ship setting with stylish surroundings, reasonably decent entertainment, and food and service that are extremely good, for a fare that's excellent value.

The waterfall pool aboard *Celebrity Millennium*.

Even so, such things as topless sunbathing spaces are now available aboard all ships (except *Azamara Journey, Azamara Quest, Celebrity Xpedition*). Meanwhile, what were formerly cigar smoking lounges have been turned into cozy jazz/piano lounges. Some cruises aboard some ships are child-free.

Sadly, background music is now played almost everywhere, and any lounge designated as "music-free" is typically full of activities and participation events, so it's hard to find a quiet corner to sit and read.

So, what's the difference between Celebrity Cruises and its parent, Royal Caribbean International? Here are a few examples relating to food items:

● **RCI** (*Brilliance of the Seas*)
Café: Seattle Coffee Company coffee in paper cups.
Dining Room Food: overcooked, poor quality (think leather briefcase) meat.
Dining Room: no tables for two.
In the Windjammer Café, waiters do not help passengers to tables with trays; plastic plates are used, cutlery is wrapped in paper napkins, melamine mugs for coffee/tea, tea selection disappointing, and poor-quality (Lipton) teas. Public restrooms have paper towels.

● Celebrity Cruises *(Celebrity Century)*:
Café el Bacio: Coffees/teas served in china cups and saucers, with doily and chocolate.
Dining Room Food: Good quality and presentation.
Dining Room: Tables for two are available.
Lido Cafe: Waiters line up to help passengers with trays to tables. Real china, white cloth napkins, polished cutlery, and a decent selection of teas are provided.
The public restrooms have cloth towels.

Decor

All ships: there are no glitzy atrium lobbies, rock-climbing walls, ice-skating rinks or other puffery – just good European style in the elegant interiors. The exception is in the casinos, which are simply coin boxes wrapped in garish, unfriendly lighting – like pachinko parlours.

Solstice-**class ships:** The layout is sensible, and the decor and colors are pleasing and elegant. There's also an abundance of designer chairs and sunloungers, including two-person clam-shell deck loungers.

Other ships: The decor is elegant – Greek, classical, minimalist, although some might find it a little antiseptic and cool in places.

Celebrity Cruises has some of the most eclectic sculptures and original artwork, from Picasso to Warhol, found at sea. The colors don't jar the senses, and cannot be said to be glitzy – except for the casinos, which are mostly vulgar.

The ships absorb people well, and the flow is, for the most part, good, except for entrances to showlounges and in photo galleries. Each public room subtly invites you to move on to the next.

Gratuities

US$11.95 per person per day is added to your onboard account. You can have this amount adjusted if you visit the guest relations desk before the end of

Celebrity Solstice sails year-round from Fort Lauderdale.

the cruise. Additionally, 15% is added for all bar and wine purchases – so, buy a bottle of mineral water at the bar and you'll be charged an extra 15% "for your convenience"; 10% for spa treatments (and receipts ask for an additional gratuity). The onboard currency is the US dollar.

For Children

Junior passengers are divided into Shipmates (3–6 years), Cadets (7–9), Ensigns (10–12), Teens (13–17).
● Best ships for children: *Celebrity Constellation, Celebrity Infinity, Celebrity Millennium, Celebrity Solstice, Celebrity Summit.* Almost as good: *Celebrity Century, Celebrity Mercury.*

Cuisine/Dining

The dining rooms aboard all ships are non-smoking areas. There are two seatings for dinner, and open seating for breakfast and lunch. Table settings are excellent, with fine quality linen, china and glassware. Tables for two are available – far more than by most other major lines. What sets Celebrity apart is the superior training

A Celebrity Cruises shore excursion on the Galápagos Islands.

Adventurous travelers return to *Celebrity Xpedition*.

and supervision of dining room waiters, and the service.

The food represents a range of culinary influences; it is based loosely on classic French cuisine, modified to appeal to North Americans and Europeans alike, and menus are standardized across the fleet and have been dumbed down since a new regime took over from Michel Roux – meatloaf, spaghetti, and striploin for dinner are pathetic for what is supposed to be a "premium" product. Items that can be made at home cannot be considered as acceptable. For better quality, Celebrity Cruises want you to pay extra to eat in the alternative venues. Sadly, the plot is being lost. Full service in-cabin dining is also available for all meals, including dinner.

The food is generally made from high-quality ingredients. Take croissants, for example. Those found aboard Celebrity ships are made fresh each morning, while

aboard most competitors' ships they are purchased ashore; there's a big difference in taste and consistency, depending on what kind of dough and butter are used.

Celebrity Cruises also has well-trained sommeliers and wine waiters who know their subject. *Celebrity Eclipse, Celebrity Equinox, Celebrity Silhouette* and *Celebrity Solstice* have a special wine room for tastings. *Celebrity Constellation, Celebrity Infinity, Celebrity Millennium* and *Celebrity Summit* have special wine rooms in their "alternative" restaurants that you can dine in, and fine wines that can cost thousands of dollars a bottle. But there are also wines that start at about $20.

● **Casual Eateries**

There are casual self-serve buffets aboard all Celebrity Cruises' ships. Except for *Celebrity Eclipse, Celebrity Equinox* and *Celebrity Solstice*, most are laid out in continuous straight lines, which can cause congestion when lines form at peak times. However, Celebrity is trying to be more creative with these buffets, and, like other cruise lines, has stations for pasta, faux sushi, salads, grilled and rotisserie items, and hot food items. A waiter will – or should – take your tray to a table. A bar trolley service for drinks and wines is provided at lunchtime, and wine waiters are always on hand to discuss and take wine orders for dinner. All the ships make great martinis.

● **The Coffee/Tea Factor**

Regular Coffee: Weak and poor. Score: 2 out of 10. Espresso/Cappuccino coffees: Score: 3 out of 10. If you order espresso/ cappuccino coffees in the dining room, there is a charge; they are treated like a bar item.

Café el Bacio: The cafés are in prominent locations, and provide an agreeable setting for those who like decent Italian coffees, pastries and cakes.

Entertainment

The company has little cohesive policy regarding big production shows, although *Celebrity Eclipse, Celebrity Equinox, Celebrity Silhouette* and *Celebrity Solstice* have better cirque-style acrobatic shows. Shows aboard some

ships are quite decent, with good costuming and lighting, but others look dated and lack story line, flow or connectivity. Each ship carries its own resident troupe of singers/dancers and audio-visual support staff. Bar service, available throughout shows, disrupts concentration. While some cabaret acts are good, they are the same ones seen aboard many ships. All showlounges are non-smoking.

Celebrity vessels have a variety of bands and small musical units, although there is very little music for social dancing, other than disco and pop music.

Then there are the summer camp-style audience participation events, games and talent shows that don't sit well with Celebrity's quality of food and service. There are also the inevitable country line dances and playschool routines.

On days at sea the program is crammed with things to do, though the emphasis is on revenue-enhancing activities such as art auctions, bingo, and horse racing.

Spa/Fitness Facilities

Celebrity Cruises, acknowledging the popularity of spas and fitness facilities, has been improving its offerings. Spa/fitness programs are staffed and operated by Steiner Leisure, a specialist concession, whose staff, who have sales targets as well as enthusiasm, will try to sell you Steiner's own-brand beauty products. Some fitness classes are free; others, such as yoga, and kickboxing, cost $10 per class. Being aboard will give you an opportunity to try some of the more exotic massages.

Massage (including exotic massages such as Aroma Stone massage, Chakra Balancing massage and other well-being massages), facials, pedicures, and beauty salon treatments cost extra. Examples: massage at $120 (50 minutes), facial at $120, seaweed wrap (75 minutes) $190 – to which you need to add a gratuity of 10 percent. Personal training sessions in the gymnasium cost $83 for one hour.

COSTA CRUISES

Ships

Atlantica-class ships: *Costa Atlantica* (2000), *Costa Deliziosa* (2010), *Costa Luminosa* (2009), *Costa Mediterranea* (2003)
Fortuna-class ships: *Costa Concordia* (2006), *Costa Fortuna* (2003), *Costa Magica* (2004), *Costa Pacifica* (2009), *Costa Serena* (2007)
Classica-class ships: *Costa Classica* (1992), *Costa Romantica* (1993)
Other ships: *Costa Allegra* (1992), *Costa Marina* (1990), *Costa Victoria* (1996)

About the company

Costa Cruises traces its history back to 1860 when Giacomo Costa started an olive oil business. The first

ship, in 1924, transported that oil. After he died in 1924, his sons, Federico, Eugenio and Enrico, inherited the business. In 1924 they bought *Ravenna*, a freighter to cut transport costs for their olive oil empire. In 1948 Costa's first passenger ship, the *Anna "C"*, carried passengers in style from Genoa to South America. In 1997, Costa Cruises was bought by the USA's Carnival Corporation and UK's Airtours plc. Three years later Carnival took full control.

Costa specializes in cruises for Europeans or passengers with European tastes, and particularly Italians, during the summer. Costa has initiated an aggressive newbuild policy in recent years, in order to modernize the company's aging fleet of different sized ships. The ships operate in three main markets: the Mediterranean, the Caribbean, and South America.

Most ships are well maintained, although there are inconsistencies throughout the fleet. The same is true of cleanliness – some ships are very clean, while others are a little dusty around the edges, as are its shore tenders. The ships have a laid-back European "feel" to their decor and manner of product delivery.

✪ **Frequent passengers' club:** Costa Club.

Setting the right tone at *Costa Classica*'s Grand Bar.

Costa ships incorporate eye-catching sculptures.

So what's it really like?

Costa is noted for its lively "Italian" ambience. There are few Italian crew members, however, although many officers are Italian. Nevertheless, Costa's lifestyle is perceived to be Italian – lively, very noisy, yet easygoing. The dress code is casual, even on formal nights.

Costa does a good job of providing first-time cruise passengers with a packaged holiday that is a mix of sophistication and basic fare, albeit accompanied by loud music. Most passengers are Italian, with a generous sprinkling of other Europeans. One night at the end of each cruise is reserved for a "Roman Bacchanal," when passengers dress up toga-style for dinner and beyond. This is a cruise line for those who like to party. If you want quiet, take earplugs – good ones.

On European and Mediterranean cruises, English will be the language least spoken, as most passengers will be Italian, Spanish, French and German. On Caribbean itineraries, a high percentage of passengers will speak Spanish, as the ships carry passengers from Latin American countries in addition to passengers from North America.

Expect to cruise with a lot of children of all ages if you book for peak holiday cruises – and remember that in Europe schoolchildren at certain times such as Easter have longer vacations. On some European itineraries, passengers embark and disembark in almost every port along the way, which makes for a disjointed cruise experience since there's almost no start or end to the cruise. There is almost no information for passengers who want to be independent in ports of call, and not take the ship's organized general excursions.

There is extensive smoking on board. No-smoking zones and signs are often ignored to the frustration of non-smoking passengers, and ashtrays are moved at whim; many of the officers and crew also smoke, even when moving through public rooms, so they don't bother to enforce the no-smoking zones.

The cabins tend to be on the mean side in size, but the decor is fresh and upbeat, and the bathrooms are very practical units. Some ships have cabin bathrooms with sliding doors – an excellent alternative to inward-openers that use up space.

Decor

Older Ships: *Costa Allegra, Costa Classica, Costa Marina, Costa Romantica, Costa Victoria* have a distinctively European feel. They are lively without being brash, or pastel-toned without being boring, depending on the ship you choose.

Newer, larger ships – *Costa Atlantica, Costa Concordia, Costa Deliziosa, Costa Fortuna, Costa Luminosa, Costa Magica, Costa Mediterranea, Costa Pacifica, Costa Serena* – have an "in-your-face" brashness similar to Carnival's ships, with grainy and unflattering digital artwork on walls and panels, and even inside elevators.

The "entertainment architecture," as designer Joe Farcus calls it, can't be ignored. There is an abundance of jazzy colors, fine or grotesque sculptures (depending on your taste) and huge murals that are both impressive and mind-numbing.

Gratuities

The onboard currency is the euro (Europe and Mediterranean cruises), or US dollar (Caribbean cruises). On the former, €32 per 7-day cruise per person is charged to your onboard account, plus 10% to all bar and wine orders. On Caribbean cruises, the figures are $53 per 7-day cruise per person and 15% for bar and wine orders. Many non-Italians would prefer to choose when to tip and how much. To have these amounts adjusted, you need to visit the information desk.

Cuisine/Dining

If you expect to be served by jovial Italian waiters, you'll be disappointed – although the restaurant managers might be Italian. All ships have two seatings for dinner; dining times on Europe/Mediterranean and South America cruises are usually later than those in the Caribbean because Europeans and Latin passengers eat much later than North Americans. Few tables for two are available, most being for four, six, or eight. All dining rooms are smoke-free – in theory.

The cuisine is best described as continental adequate, with many regional Italian dishes and much emphasis on pasta: 50 pasta dishes per cruise. Except for pasta dishes (made fresh on board) and cream sauces, presentation and food quality are not memorable, and are the subject of many negative comments from passengers. While the quality of meat is adequate, it is often disguised with gravies and rich sauces. Fish and seafood tend to lack taste, and are often overcooked. Green vegetables are hard to come by. Breads and bread rolls are usually good, but the desserts are of supermarket quality and lack taste.

There is a wine list but no wine waiters; table waiters are expected to serve both food and wine, which does not work well. Almost all wines are young – very young.

● **Alternative Dining**
If you opt for one of the "alternative" restaurants aboard the larger ships, note that a cover charge applies: €20 per person plus 10% service charge (Europe/Mediterranean cruises), or $20 per person plus 15% service charge (Caribbean cruises).

● **Casual Eateries**
All ships have self-serve lido buffets. In most, you have to move along with your tray, but the latest ships have more active stations and individual islands. The items available are quite basic. All ships except *Costa Europa* also have a pizzeria.

● **The Coffee/Tea Factor**
Regular Coffee: Decent and quite strong. Score: 5 out of 10.
Espresso/Cappuccino coffees (Lavazza) are among the best served by the major cruise lines: the main competition is from Celebrity Cruises' Café el Bacio; Star Cruises also serves Lavazza. All Costa ships have coffee machines in most lounges/bars. Score: 8 out of 10.

For children

Junior passengers are in four groups: Kids Club is for 3–6; Junior Club is for 7–12; Teen Club is for 13–17. The program varies by ship, itinerary and season. Group babysitting is available 6.30–11pm. During port days, babysitting is available generally 8.30am–12.30pm and 2.30–6.30pm.
● **Best ships for children:** *Costa Atlantica, Costa Concordia, Costa Fortuna, Costa Luminosa, Costa Magica, Costa Mediterranea, Costa Pacifica, Costa Serena.* But not: *Costa Allegra, Costa Classica, Costa Marina, Costa Romantica, Costa Victoria.*

Entertainment

Each ship carries its own resident troupe of singers/dancers and audio-visual support staff, but Costa Cruises is not known for the quality of its entertainment. What it does present tends to be of the "no finesse" variety, with revue-style shows that have little story line, poor choreography and execution, but plenty of fast-moving action – more stepping in place than dancing – and lots of volume. It's entertainment to pass the time rather than remember.

Cabaret acts (typically singers, magicians, comedy jugglers, ventriloquists, and so on) are entertaining but rather ho-hum. Most passenger participation activities include poolside games such as a "Belly Flop" competition, election of the "Ideal Couple," and other juvenile games – but some families love them. There are also dance classes, and the inevitable "Fine Art Auction."

Spa/Fitness Facilities

These vary according to ship and size. The newest and largest ships (*Costa Atlantica, Costa Concordia, Costa Fortuna, Costa Magica, Costa Mediterranea* and *Costa Serena*) have more space and better facilities, while the others (*Costa Allegra, Costa Marina*) have only basic facilities.

Spa/fitness facilities are staffed and operated by Steiner Leisure, a specialist concession, whose young staff will try to sell you Steiner's own-brand beauty products. Some fitness classes are free, while some, such as yoga, and kick-boxing, cost $10 per class.

However, being aboard will give you an opportunity to try some of the more exotic treatments, particularly some of the massages available. Massage (including exotic massages such as Aroma Stone mas-

Each Costa ship has a troupe of singers and dancers.

sage, Chakra Balancing massage and other well-being massages), facials, pedicures, and beauty salon treatments cost extra – massage, for example, costs about $2 per minute, plus gratuity.

Aboard *Costa Concordia* and *Costa Serena*, Samsara Spa accommodation grades benefit from Oriental-themed decor and Samsara bathroom amenities, and 12 Samsara Suites have direct access to the Samsara Spa facilities and special packages and concessions. To use the sauna/steam and relaxation areas aboard some of the ships, you'll need to buy a day pass, for €35 per person.

CUNARD LINE

Ships:
Queen Elizabeth (2010), *Queen Mary 2* (2004), *Queen Victoria* (2007).

About the company
Cunard Line was established in 1839, as the British and North American Steam Packet Company, to carry the Royal Mail and passengers from the Old World to the New. Its first ship, *Britannia*, sailed on its maiden voyage on American Independence Day in 1840. The author Charles Dickens crossed the Atlantic aboard the ship in 1842 together with 62 other passengers, 93 crew members, one cow, and, most important, Her Majesty's mails and despatches.

Cunard offers passengers a chance to brush up computer skills.

Since 1840, Cunard Line has always had ships built to sail across the North Atlantic. From 1850 until the arrival of *QE2* in 1969, all of the line's ships and those of White Star Line (with which Cunard merged in 1934) had several classes. Your luggage label, therefore, declared not only your name but also what you could afford. Today, there's no class distinction, other than by the grade of accommodation you choose. In other words, you get what you pay for, as on any cruise ship.

But one is still reminded of the company's illustrious history. For example, Cunard Line:
● was the first company to take passengers on regularly scheduled transatlantic crossings.
● introduced the first passenger ship to be lit by electricity (*Servia*, 1881).
● introduced the first steam turbine engines in an ocean liner (*Carmania*, 1905).
● introduced the first indoor swimming pool aboard a ship (*Aquitania*, 1914).
● pioneered an around-the-world cruise (*Laconia*, 1922).
● held the record for the largest passenger ship ever built (*Queen Elizabeth*, between 1940 and 1996).
● is presently the only company to sail regularly scheduled year-round transatlantic crossings (*Queen Mary 2*).
❍ **Frequent passengers' club:** Cunard World Club.

So what's it really like?
Sailing with Cunard Line is quite different to being aboard a standard cruise ship. The ships incorporate a lot of maritime history and the grand traditions of ocean liners – as opposed to the other ships, with their tendency to tacky high-street trappings.

Assuming your sea legs can cope with sometimes less than calm waters, a transatlantic crossing is supremely civilized, particularly if you can enjoy being cosseted in accommodation that allows you to dine in the "grill"-class restaurants with their fine cuisine and presentation. There's less pressure from staff to get you to purchase drinks than with other lines, and the itineraries are quite well spaced and not so hectic.

Cunard Line ships are best suited to a wide range of seasoned and well-traveled couples and single passengers who enjoy the cosmopolitan setting of an ocean liner, with their extensive array of facilities, public rooms, dining rooms, and lecture programs. Male social hosts – typically 10 on an around-the-world cruise – serve as dancing partners for women traveling alone.

Cunard Line is the only cruise line that allows you to take your dog or cat with you (*Queen Mary 2* transatlantic crossings only). Also, one of its most successful formulas is its adherence to formal dress codes – in contrast to the downward sartorial spiral of most cruise lines.

A starry night in *Queen Mary 2*'s planetarium.

Cuisine/Dining

Cunard Line provides good-quality ingredients (sourced in Europe and the USA). The cuisine is still of a mass market standard – you'll find butter in packets in some venues. However, at the self-serve buffets, salt and pepper are usually provided on each table. Espressos and cappuccinos are available in the dining rooms, and at extra cost in many bars. Cunard uses Colombian coffee (exception: *Queen Victoria*'s Café Carinthia, where Lavazzo is used for espressos/cappuccinos).

All ships have "grill rooms" as well as traditional large restaurants, and casual self-service dining venues. Grill rooms are more exclusive and some have à la carte menus, while the main restaurants have fixed menus. The grill rooms have seating dining at assigned tables, when you wish, while the main Britannia Restaurants in all ships have two seatings.

The cuisine includes many traditional British favorites, together with extensive French dishes as well as regional specialties from around the world, nicely presented on Wedgwood china.

For Children

Children's facilities are quite good, although not as extensive as aboard the former *Queen Elizabeth 2*. Youngsters are supervised by real English nannies.

Gratuities

The onboard currencies are the British pound and the US dollar, depending on the operating area. Gratuities are automatically charged to your onboard account – you will need to visit the information desk to change them. The amount is $13 per person per day (Grill Class accommodation, including children) or $11 per person per day (other accommodation). In addition, 15% is added to all bar and wine, and health spa/salon bills.

Entertainment

Production shows are colourful and visual, with pre-recorded backing tracks supplementing the showband. Other shows consist of cabaret acts – typically singers, magicians, mime artistes, comedy jugglers, and, occasionally, comedians – doing the cruise ship circuit. A number of bands and small musical units provide live music for dancing and listening.

Spa/Fitness Facilities

The spa/fitness centers are operated by Canyon Ranch (*QM2*) and Harding Brothers/Multitrax Maritime under the brand name The Onboard Spa Company (*Queen Elizabeth, Queen Victoria*), with prices that generally match those of land-based health resorts.

HOLLAND AMERICA LINE

Ships

Amsterdam (2000), *Eurodam* (2008), *Maasdam* (1993), *Nieuw Amsterdam* (2010), *Noordam* (2006), *Oosterdam* (2003), *Prinsendam* (1988), *Rotterdam* (1997), *Ryndam* (1994), *Statendam* (1993), *Veendam* (1996), *Volendam* (1999), *Westerdam* (2004), *Zaandam* (2000), *Zuiderdam* (2002).

About the company

Holland America Line was founded in 1873 as the Netherlands-America Steamship Company, shipping immigrants to the New World from Rotterdam. It moved its headquarters to New York in 1971. It bought into Alaskan hotels and transportation when it acquired Westours in 1983, and is one of the state's biggest employers. In 1989, it was acquired by Carnival Cruise Lines, but retained its Seattle-based headquarters.

HAL carries both traditional cruise passengers (senior citizens, alumni groups) and multi-generational families. It tries hard to keep its Dutch connections, with antique artefacts and traditional decor, as well as Indonesian stewards. It has a private island, Half Moon Cay, in the Bahamas.

✪ Frequent passengers' club: Mariner Society.

So what's it really like?

Fresh management with updated ideas, the line's "Signature of Excellence" program, the food variety and creativity have improved the HAL experience. The ships benefit from lots of fresh flowers, museum-quality art pieces, and more attention to detail than all the other major lines with the exception of Celebrity Cruises.

The brand encompasses basically two types of ship. Younger families with children and grandchildren are best suited to the newer, larger vessels such as *Eurodam, Nieuw Amsterdam, Noordam, Oosterdam, Westerdam,* and *Zuiderdam*, whereas those of senior years – HAL's traditional audience of repeat passengers from alumni groups – are best suited to ships that are smaller and less glitzy (*Amsterdam, Maasdam, Prinsendam, Rotterdam, Ryndam, Statendam, Veendam,* and *Zaandam*). All the ships are well maintained, and cleaning takes place constantly. All ships have teakwood outdoors promenade decks, whereas most rivals have artificial grass or some other form of indoor-outdoor carpeting. Explorations Cafés have been built into its ships as part of recent refurbishment programs.

Holland America Line has its own training school in Jakarta, Indonesia, and so is able to "pre-train" crew members who have never been to sea before. Many crew members have been promoted to supervisory positions due to a host of new ships introduced, but few of those promoted have the formal training, professional or management skills, or experience to do the job well. Internal promotion is fine, but decreased professionalism is not the price that passengers should pay. However, HAL's mainly Indonesian crew members are willing, polite, and smile a lot – particularly if extra tips are forthcoming – which is more than can be said for service staff on land today, particularly in western countries. That said, many struggle to communicate with passengers.

HAL is one of only three major cruise lines with cinemas built into all its ships. It also operates many theme-related cruises, and has an extensive "University at Sea" program of life-enrichment lecturers. The cinemas also have superb full demonstration kitchens built in for a "Culinary Arts" program that includes celebrity chefs, and interactive cooking demos.

HAL has established smoking and no-smoking areas throughout its ships, but there are many more smokers than you might expect, depending on ship and itinerary.

The ships are best suited to older couples and singles (and their grandchildren), who like to mingle in a large ship, in an unhurried setting with fine-quality surroundings, with plenty of eclectic antique artwork, decent – though not gourmet – food and service from a smiling Indonesian/Filipino crew who don't have the finesse many passengers expect from a "premium" product.

Decor

Aboard *Amsterdam, Maasdam, Nieuw Amsterdam, Prinsendam, Rotterdam, Ryndam, Statendam, Veendam, Volendam, Zaandam*, the decor is rather bland (restful), with eclectic artwork that is focused on Dutch artefacts, mainly from the 16th and 17th centuries.

As part of its "Signature of Excellence" program, which involves refreshing the ships, some vessels have received a new and trendy "Mix" lifestyle facility – an open area with three themed specialty bars: Champagne (serving champagne and sparkling wines from around the world), Martinis (in individual shakers), and Spirits & Ales (a sports bar with beer, baseball and basketball for the boys). Additionally, you can play checkers and chess, air hockey, and other sports games using Microsoft Surface touch-screen technology.

Aboard the newest ships (*Eurodam, Niuew Amsterdam, Oosterdam, Westerdam, Zuiderdam*) the decor is more lively – acceptable for families with children who like bright things such as large wall panels with digital "in-your-face" artwork that present an *Alice in Wonderland* look. You wouldn't go for it in your living room, but aboard these large resort ships it works. It is important, therefore, to choose the right ship for your personality type, and for the facilities that appeal.

Gratuities

$10 per person per day (the amount charged when this book went to press) is added to your onboard account. You can have this amount adjusted at the information desk to do so. Additionally, 15% is added to bar and wine accounts. The onboard currency is the US dollar.

An earlier era at sea: HAL ships display a wide range of artworks.

Master chef Rudi Sodamin, culinary consultant to HAL.

Cuisine/Dining

For dinner, Holland America Line features both open seating (on one level) or assigned tables (at fixed times, on the other level) in its dining rooms; it's called "As You Wish" dining. For breakfast and lunch in the main dining room, an open-seating policy applies. All dining venues are non-smoking.

Some tables for two are available, but most are for four, six, eight or 10. The larger tables are ideal for multi-generational families. Fine Rosenthal china and cutlery are used. Live music is provided for dinner. "Lighter option" meals are always available for the nutrition-conscious and the weight-conscious.

Holland America Line food was much upgraded when master chef Rudi Sodamin arrived in 2005 as a consultant; he introduced his "Wild About Salmon" and other creative ideas, and the "Culinary Arts Center" (with its own dedicated live interactive demonstration kitchen and guest chef program) has been a success story. In 2008 menus were revamped to include more regional cuisine and more local ingredients.

However, while the USDA beef is very good, poultry and most fish tend to be overcooked (except when the ships are in Alaska, where halibut and salmon are excellent). What are not "premium" are the packets of sugar, and packets (instead of glass jars) of supermarket-brand breakfast jams, marmalade and honey, sugar, and butter. Also, coffee and teas are poor-quality, except in the extra-charge Explorations Café. While packets may be suitable for a family diner, they do not belong aboard ships that claim "award-winning cuisine."

Dessert and pastry items are good, suited to American tastes, but canned fruit and jellied desserts are much in evidence. Most of the "international" cheeses are highly colored, processed cheese (cruises in Europe have better access to European cheeses).

HAL also offers complimentary ice cream during certain hours of the day, as well as hot hors d'oeuvres in all bars – something other major lines seem to have dropped, or charge extra for. Cabin service breakfasts are very basic, with only Continental breakfast available and few hot food items.

HAL can provide kosher meals. As the ships do not have kosher kitchens, these are prepared ashore, frozen, and brought to your table sealed in containers.

The wine list relies heavily on wines from California and Washington State, with few decent French or German wines, other than those found in a typical supermarket ashore. A Connoisseur List is available in the Pinnacle Grill.

● Alternative Dining

All HAL ships have "alternative dining" spots called "Pinnacle Grill" (or "Pinnacle Grill at the Odyssey Restaurant"), specializing in "Pacific Northwest Cuisine." Items include sesame-crusted halibut with ginger-miso; and an array of premium quality steaks, presented tableside prior to cooking. These are more intimate restaurants with tablecloths, linen napkins and decently sized wine glasses. The food is better than in the main dining rooms. There is a cover charge, and reservations

are required. Bulgari china, Frette linens, and Reidel glasses are part of this enhanced dining experience.

● **Casual Eateries**

All ships feature a Lido Deck self-serve buffet. Most are lines you move along with your tray, although the latest ships have more "active" stations (examples: omelets and pasta cooked to order) and individual islands. There are decent salad bars, dessert bars, regional specialties, and grilled fast-food items such as hamburgers, salmon burgers, hot dogs and French fries. These venues become overcrowded during breakfast and lunch.

● **The Coffee/Tea Factor**

Regular Coffee: Half decent, but weak (Score: 3 out of 10). Espresso/cappuccino coffees (Dutch) are adequate, served in proper china, but not quite up to the standard of Celebrity or Costa. Score: 6 out of 10.

For Children

Club HAL: Junior passengers are divided into three age-appropriate groups: 3–8, 9–12, and teens. Programming is based on the number of children booked on any given sailing, and children's counselors are provided accordingly. HAL's children's programs are not as extensive as those of Carnival Cruise Lines, for example, although they are improving with the latest ships.

● **Best ships for children:** *Eurodam, Nieuw Amsterdam,*

Perfecting a high-tech swing aboard *Prisendam.*

Noordam, Oosterdam, Westerdam, Zaandam, Zuiderdam, but not: *Amsterdam, Maasdam, Prinsendam, Rotterdam, Ryndam, Statendam, Veendam.*

Entertainment

Holland America Line is not known for lavish entertainment (the budgets aren't high enough). The production shows, while a good attempt, fall short on story line, choreography and performance, while colorful costuming and lighting hide the weak spots. Each ship carries its own resident troupe of singers and dancers and audiovisual support staff. HAL also offers a consistently good, tried and tested array of cabaret acts that constantly pop up on the cruise ship circuit. All showlounges are non-smoking venues.

A number of bands, a string ensemble and solo musicians present live music for dancing and listening in many of the lounges and bars. Each ship has a Crow's Nest Lounge (by day an observation lounge) for social dancing, and there is always serenading string music in the Explorer's Lounge and dining room.

Each cruise includes a Crew Show; these vary from poor to very entertaining, depending on your taste. Passengers always seem enthusiastic, because they like connecting staff that they know and have seen during their cruise.

Spa/Fitness Facilities

The Greenhouse Spa, beauty and fitness amenities named after the Texas-based facility, aboard all HAL ships are staffed and operated by Steiner Leisure, a specialist concession, whose young staff will try to sell you Steiner's own-brand Elemis beauty products. Some fitness classes are free; others, such as yoga, kickboxing or Pilates essentials, cost $11 per class (a special price is offered for unlimited classes).

Massages (including exotic massages such as Aroma Stone massage, Chakra Balancing massage and other well-being massages), facials, pedicures, and beauty treatments cost extra. Examples: well-being massage $109 for 50 minutes; hot stone therapy massage $175 for 75 minutes; reflexology $109 for 50 minutes; Japanese Silk Booster facial 129 for 75 minutes; personal fitness instruction $75 for 60 minutes (course of three for $191).

Holland America Line is not known for lavish shows.

MSC CRUISES

Ships

***Fantasia*-class ships:** *MSC Fantasia* (2008), *MSC Splendida* (2009)
***Lirica*-class ships:** *MSC Armonia* (2001), *MSC Lirica* (2003), *MSC Opera* (2004), *MSC Sinfonia* (2005)
***Musica*-class ships:** *MSC Magnifica* (2010), *MSC Musica* (2006), *MSC Orchestra* (2007), *MSC Poesia* (2008)
Other ships: *MSC Melody* (1982)

About the company

The HQ of the world's largest privately-owned cruise line is in Geneva, Switzerland, home of parent company Mediterranean Shipping Company, the world's second biggest container shipping company. Operations are based in Naples, Italy. It started in the passenger shipping business by acquiring the Italian company Star Lauro in 1995, together with two older ships, *Monterey* and *Rhapsody*. It expanded with the purchase of *Melody*, followed by almost new ships bought from the bankrupt Festival Cruises.

MSC Cruises has grown extremely fast, and has a number of large resort ships on order. It will have the world's youngest fleet by 2011. Also, it is owned by a shipping-based family, not a faceless corporation.

✪ **Frequent passengers' club:** MSC Club.

So what's it really like?

MSC Cruises' ships are really suited to adult couples and singles, and families with children. They are good for those who enjoy big city life, outdoor cafés, constant activity accompanied by plenty of live music, late nights, and food ranging from adequate to very good.

The company has evolved quickly as the "new kid on the block." Of all the major cruise lines, it's also the cleanest. It changes bed linen and towels the most; typically, bed linen is changed every second day, towels daily, and bathrobes in suites daily, unlike most other large cruise lines. MSC Cruises uses the most environmentally-friendly detergents and cleaning materials in its housekeeping department and laundries. It has drastically reduced the use of plastic items aboard its ships, and is aiming to eliminate them by the end of 2011.

The ships typically operate in five languages, with embarkation-day announcements in English, French, German, Italian, and Spanish. Thankfully, during the cruise, there are almost no announcements. Given this multilingual emphasis, production shows and other major entertainment displays are more visual than verbal. For the same reason, the ships do not generally carry lecturers. By culling news from 600 major newspapers around the world, in up to 36 languages, Newspapers Direct can supply you with a daily paper on board to your liking.

The roving band of photographers, taking your picture at every opportunity, can irritate, however. Particularly intrusive are the tacky photographs taken during dinner, when "pirates" and other costumed staff appear behind smartly dressed diners.

Cigar lovers will find a selection of Cuban (including Cohiba, Monte Cristo, Romeo e Juliet, Partagas), Dominican (Davidoff), and Italian (Toscana) smokes in the cigar lounges.

Decor

Except for the oldest ship, *MSC Melody*, the decor is decidedly European, with much understated elegance and really high-quality soft furnishings and other materials such as Italian marble. The latest ships are much brighter and more contemporary, albeit with restraint.

Gratuities

These are charged to your onboard cabin at €6 per person, per day. Note that 15% is added to all drinks and beverage orders; the price of drinks, however, is very reasonable. Onboard currency is the euro.

Cuisine/Dining

MSC Cruises provides better-quality ingredients, almost all sourced in Europe, than some other major cruise lines. The cuisine is still mainstream – you'll find butter in packets. However, at the self-serve buffets, salt and pepper are typically provided on each table, not in packets as on most cruise lines. Espresso and cappuccino

MSC Splendida's 4-D screenings add a new dimension.

MSC has introduced Italy's leisurely "slow food" concept to its fleet.

olds; Junior Club for 10–13s; Teenagers Club for those over 14 (a prepaid Teen Card is available). While the facilities and play areas are not as extensive as those aboard some other major lines, a "baby parking" service is useful when parents want to go ashore on excursions. MSC Cruises' mascot is Do-Re-Mi – the von Trapp family of *Sound of Music* fame would no doubt be delighted.

● **Best ships for children:** *MSC Fantasia, MSC Magnifica, MSC Musica, MSC Opera, MSC Orchestra, MSC Poesia, MSC Splendida*

Entertainment

Because of the multilingual passenger mix, production shows are colorful and visual, particularly aboard the newest ships. Other shows consist of unknown cabaret acts (typically singers, magicians, mime artistes, comedy jugglers, and others) doing the cruise ship circuit. The ship carries a number of bands and small musical units that provide live music for dancing or listening, but there is no show band, and production shows use pre-recorded backing tracks.

Spa/Fitness Facilities

The spas are operated as a concession by Blue Ocean – except *MSC Musica*, which is operated by Steiner Leisure. Treatments include acupuncture, massages, facials, and other beauty enhancement services.

(Segafredo brand Italian coffee) are available in the dining rooms, at extra cost, and in almost all bars – which also have coffees from Brasil, Costa Rica and Peru.

Aboard the newest ships, MSC Cruises has introduced the Italian "slow food" concept. Always available items include spaghetti, chicken breast, salmon fillet, and vegetables of the day. Refreshingly, the company spotlights regional Italian cuisine and wine, so daily dining room menus feature food from regions such as Calabria, Piedmont, Lazio, Puglia, and Sicily.

All pizza dough is made on board and risotto (featured daily) is a signature item for MSC Cruises and something the ships make really well. Spaghetti is always available, with a tomato sauce freshly made each day. Many varieties of Italian breads such as bruschetta, focaccia, and panettone, are provided.

● **Alternative dining:** The newest ships have an alternative specialty restaurant. Aboard *MSC Musica* and *MSC Poesia*, it is Kaito, an authentic Japanese restaurant and sushi bar with an extensive menu. Aboard *MSC Magnifica* and *MSC Orchestra* it is Shanghai, a Chinese restaurant with real wok cooking, dim sum, and other Chinese and Asian specialties. The quality is high, and it really is worth having at least one meal in these venues; the à la carte prices are quite reasonable.

● **Room service:** Continental breakfast is complimentary from 7.30 to 10am, while room service snacks can be bought at any other time. A basket of fruit is provided to all cabins at embarkation, and replenished daily for suite-grade accommodation.

For Children

Up to three children over two and under 12 can cruise free when sharing a cabin with two adults (they pay only port dues). Children are divided into three age groups, with facilities to match: Mini Club for 3–9-year-

NORWEGIAN CRUISE LINE

Ships

Norwegian Dawn (2002), *Norwegian Gem* (2007), *Norwegian Jade* (2006), *Norwegian Jewel* (2005), *Norwegian Pearl* (2006), *Norwegian Spirit* (1998), *Norwegian Star* (2002), *Norwegian Sun* (2001), *Pride of America* (2005) *Epic*-class: *Norwegian Epic* (2010),

About the company

Norwegian Cruise Line, the originator of contemporary cruising, was founded in 1966 by three Norwegian shipping companies as Klosters Sunward Ferries and was renamed Norwegian Caribbean Line in 1967. It was bought by Star Cruises in 2000, and has been replacing its older, smaller ships with brand new, larger vessels. NCL also operates one ship with mostly American crews and a base in Hawaii.

Freestyle Cruising is how NCL describes its operation – although it's hard to detect style in the onboard product. Its fleet is diverse, so the cruise experience can vary, although this makes for interesting character variation

The SpiegelTent aboard the new *Norwegian Epic*.

between the various ship categories. There is more standardization aboard the larger, newer ships. The senior officers are the only thing that's Norwegian.

Choose this line for a good all-round family cruise with a sporty, contemporary feel, interesting itineraries (many from "Homeland USA" ports) and lots of dining choices, particularly aboard the newest ships.

Most standard cabins are extremely small, though they have reasonably attractive decor and are functional. Closet and drawer space is limited aboard newer ships.
○ **Frequent passengers' club:** Latitudes.

So what's it really like?

If this is your first cruise, you should enjoy a good overall vacation in an lively, upbeat setting. The lifestyle is contemporary, fresh, creative and sporty, with a casualness typical of youthful city dwellers, and with its "eat when you want" philosophy, the shipboard ambiance is ultra-casual. The ambiance is best described as US-east coast "edgy." So is the dress code – indeed, the waiters are probably better dressed than many passengers. The staff is congenial, and you'll find a high percentage of females in cabin and restaurant service departments – more than most major cruise lines. However, revenue centers are everywhere, including "inch of gold," tee shirts, and sunscreen lotion, all sold at tables on the open decks adjacent to swimming pools.

All ships can provide an almost full-size newspaper from a wide

Scaling an NCL rock wall.

choice of US and European titles on the Multicast satellite delivery system (the cost: $3.95 per newspaper, per day). You can also request your favorite newspaper that's not in the list, although it may cost more.

NCL ships are best suited to first-time young and young-at-heart couples, single passengers, children and teenagers who want upbeat, color-rich surroundings, plenty of entertainment lounges and bars, and high-tech sophistication – all in one programmed but well packaged cruise vacation.

There's plenty of lively music, constant activity, entertainment, and food that's mainstream and acceptable but nothing more – unless you pay extra to eat in the "alternative" dining spots. All this is delivered by a smiling, very friendly service staff who lack polish but are willing. In the latest wheeze to extract revenue, NCL has started "Backstage Tours," costing $55 or $150 (depending on what's included).
● **NCL's Private Island (Great Stirrup Cay):** Only coffee and ice-water are free (there's no iced tea), and all other drinks are charged.

Decor

The newest ships have colorful, eye-catching designs on their hulls, differentiating them from the competition.

Gratuities

A fixed $12 per person per day service charge can be pre-paid, or it will be added to your onboard account. Children over 13 pay the full adult rate; those aged 3–12 pay $6 per day, and under-3s pay nothing. A 15% gratuity is added to bar and wine charges.

Some NCL ships have ten-pin bowling alleys.

Spa gratuities are a whopping 18%. Onboard currency: the US dollar.

Cuisine/Dining

NCL has recognized the increasing trend away from formal restaurants (purpose: dining) toward bistros (purpose: eating faster). For cruising, NCL has championed more choices in dining than any other cruise line, except parent company Star Cruises, which started "Freestyle Dining."

This allows you to try different types of cuisine, in different settings, when you want. In practice, however, it means that you have to make reservations, which can prove frustrating at times, and getting it just right takes a little planning and, often, waiting. Food in the main dining rooms is poor-to-average and marginally better in the extra-charge venues. (NCL is not known for good for good food – choose it because the itinerary appeals to you). Freestyle Dining works best aboard the ships that have been specially designed to accommodate it: *Norwegian Dawn, Norwegian Epic, Norwegian Gem, Norwegian Jade, Norwegian Jewel, Norwegian Pearl, Norwegian Spirit, Norwegian Star, Norwegian Sun,* and *Pride of America.*

On production show presentation nights, most people want to eat at the same time in order to see the shows, which causes massive prime-time congestion, slow service and utter frustration; pagers given out for anyone waiting for a table. The ships have plasma screens in various locations so you can make reservations when you want, and see at a glance the waiting times for a table; an updated version of its "Silverware" reservation program was introduced in 2009. The self-serve buffets are mostly chaotic, mob-scene affairs (and very repetitive) and should be avoided.

After-dinner espresso/cappuccino coffees are available in the dining rooms without extra charge – a nice feature. Once each cruise, there's a Chocoholics Buffet with paper plates and plastic cutlery.

The wine list is quite good, with many excellent wines in the $20–$30 range. But the wine is typically served by table waiters, whose knowledge of wines is poor.

Cabin service breakfasts are very basic, with only Continental breakfast available and no hot food items – for those, you'll need to go to a restaurant or self-serve buffet. The non-breakfast Room Service menu has only two hot items available throughout the day: Oriental soup and pizza – the rest is cold (salads and sandwiches).
● **The Coffee/Tea Factor:** Regular Coffee: Weak and poor. Score: 2 out of 10. Iced tea: pitiful.
Espresso/Cappuccino coffees: Score: 4 out of 10. Some bars have espresso/cappuccino machines, which are extra-charge items.

For Children

NCL's Junior Cruisers (Kids Crew) program divides children into three groups, according to age: Junior sailors (ages 2–5); First Mates and Navigators (6–12); Teens (13–17). Babysitting services are available (group only, not individual) at an extra change. Special packages are available for soft drinks.
● **Best ships for children:** *Norwegian Dawn, Norwegian Gem, Norwegian Jade, Norwegian Jewel, Norwegian Pearl, Norwegian Spirit, Norwegian Star, Norwegian Sun.*

Entertainment

NCL has good production shows that provide color and spectacle in a predictable – though now dated – format. Each ship has a resident troupe of singers/dancers. There are two or three production shows in a typical 7-day cruise.

They are all very colorful, high-energy, razzle-dazzle shows, with much use of laser and color-mover lights. They're not memorable but, it must be said, they're very entertaining. All showlounges are non-smoking.

Most activities and passenger participation events range from poor to extremely poor. Nintendo Wii interactive games are available on large screens.

Spa/Fitness Facilities

The spas are staffed and operated by the Hawaii-based Mandara Spa, owned by Steiner Leisure. Many of the staff are young, and will try to sell you Steiner's own-brand Elemis beauty products. Some fitness classes are free, while others, such as yoga and kick-boxing, cost $10 per class.

However, being aboard will give you an opportunity to try some of the more exotic treatments, particularly the various massages. Massage (including Aroma Stone massage, Chakra Balancing massage and other well-being massages), facials, pedicures, and beauty salon treatments cost extra, and an 18% gratuity is added. Examples: Lomi Lomi Massage ($99 for 50 minutes/$140 for 80 minutes); Mandara Four Hands Massage ($180 for 50 minutes; $280 for 80 minutes).

Aboard some ships, a "Thermal Suite" (sauna, steam room, aroma-showers and relaxation area) costs $20 per day, or $75 for a 7-day pass.

P&O CRUISES

Ships

Child-free ships: *Adonia* (2001), *Arcadia* (2005)
Family-friendly ships: *Aurora* (2000), *Azura* (2010), *Oceana* (2000); *Oriana* (1995), *Ventura* (2008)

About the company

Its full name is the Peninsular and Oriental Steam Navigation Company, though none of its ships is still operated by steam turbines. Based in Southampton, England, it was founded in 1837, just before Samuel Cunard established his company, and was awarded a UK government contract in 1840 to carry the mails from Gibraltar to Alexandria.

P&O Cruises acquired Princess Cruises in 1974, Swan Hellenic in 1982, and Sitmar Cruises in 1988. In 2000 it demerged from its parent to establish itself as P&O Princess plc. It was bought by Carnival Corporation in 2003.

So what's it really like?

P&O Cruises has always been a traditional British cruise company, never quite matching the quality aboard the Cunard Line ships, which have more international passengers. However, it has been reinventing itself, and the result is a contemporary onboard cruise product well aimed at the high-street traveler. It specializes in providing all the little things that British passengers have come to expect, including tea/coffee making sets in all cabins, and a choice of Indian-cuisine themed food.

Traditionally, P&O Cruises was known for British families who wanted to sail from a UK port – except for winter Caribbean cruises from Barbados. But now it's also known for having child-free ships, and so the two products differ widely in their communal spaces. It also makes an effort to provide theme cruises – antiques, art appreciation, classical music, comedy, cricket, gardening and horticulture, jazz, Scottish dance, etc. The ships typically carry ballroom dance instructors. Bed linen is not changed as often (twice a week) as on some lines, like MSC Cruises (every two days).

Decor

A mix of British "traditional" (think: comfy, dated armchairs, wood paneling, bistro-style food, non-glitzy). British artists are featured aboard all ships – *Ventura*, for example, displays works from more than 40 of them.

Gratuities

For gratuities, you should typically allow £3.50 ($5.20) per person, per day. Onboard currency: UK pound.

Cuisine/Dining

The cuisine is straightforward, no-nonsense British food, reasonably well presented well on nice Wedgwood china. But it tends to be rather bland and uninspiring. It is typical of mass banquet catering with standard fare comparable to that found in a family hotel in an English seaside town like Scarborough.

The ingredients of many meals are disguised by gravies and sauces, as in Indian curries – well liked, of course, by most British passengers. Bread, desserts and cakes are made well, and there is a wide variety. P&O Cruises always carries a decent selection of British, and some French, cheeses.

Most of the dining room staff are from India, and provide service with a warmth that many other nationals find hard to equal. Wine service is amateurish and the lack of knowledge is lamentable.

● **Alternative Dining**

Extra-cost restaurants with menus designed by some of Britain's well-known television celebrity chefs, such as Gary Rhodes and Marco Pierre-White, have been intro-

Noddy, familiar to English children, sails on P&O Cruises.

duced aboard the ships. They are a mix of trendy bistro-style venues, and restaurants with an Asia-Pacific theme.

● **Casual Eateries**

The self-serve buffets suffer from small, cramped facilities, and passengers complain of having to share them with the countless concession staff who take over tables and congregate in groups. In other words, the buffets are too small to accommodate the needs of most passengers today.

● **The Coffee/Tea Factor:** Regular Coffee: Weak, and poor. Score: 3 out of 10. 10. Good quality tea and coffee-making set-up is provided in all cabins. Self-serve beverage stations are provided at the buffets, but it's often difficult to find proper teaspoons – often only wooden stirrers are available. Espresso/cappuccino coffees in the extra-charge venues are slightly better, but not as good as aboard the ships of Costa Cruises or MSC Cruises, for example.

For Children

P&O Cruises really excels in looking after children. The ships – apart from the child-free ones, of course – have very good facilities and children's counselors, with lots of activities and participation events that make it a pleasure to take to take your kids with you.

Entertainment

P&O Cruises has always been known for its traditional, "end of pier" entertainment, with lots of pub-like sing-along sessions for the masses. These have been augmented with in-house production shows that provide lots of color, costume changes, and high-tech lighting. Each ship carries its own resident troupe of singers and dancers, called Headliners.

P&O Cruises does a good job in providing guest lecturers with varying themes, as well as occasional after-dinner speakers such as well-known television personalities and book authors.

Spa/Fitness Facilities

The spa/fitness facilities are operated by the UK concession Harding Brothers, which also provides a wide range of beauty products. Examples of prices: a full body massage is £60 for 50 minutes; an Indian head massage is £42 for 45 minutes; a holistic facial is £45 for 75 minutes. A manicure is £24 for 45 minutes, while a pedicure is £35 for 45 minutes.

PRINCESS CRUISES

Ships

Grand-class ships (over 100,000 gross tonnage): *Caribbean Princess* (2004), *Crown Princess* (2006), *Diamond Princess* (2004), *Emerald Princess* (2007), *Golden Princess* (2001), *Grand Princess* (1998), *Ruby Princess* (2008), *Sapphire Princess* (2005), *Star Princess* (2002)

Pacific-class ships: *Ocean Princess* (1999), *Pacific Princess* (1999)

Coral-class ships: *Coral Princess* (2002), *Island Princess* (2003)

Other ships: *Sea Princess* (1998), *Sun Princess* (1995)

About the company

Princess Cruises was founded by Stanley McDonald in 1965 with one ship, the former passenger ferry *Princess Patricia*, for cruises along the Mexican Rivera. In 1974, the company was bought by the UK's Peninsular and Oriental Steam Navigation Company (P&O), and in 1988 P&O/Princess Cruises merged with the Italian line Sitmar Cruises. In 2000, Carnival Corporation and Royal Caribbean Cruises fought a protracted battle to buy Princess Cruises. Carnival won.

Princess Cruises benefited hugely from its involvement in the American television series *The Love Boat*, and its brand became known as "The Love Boat Cruise Line." Today it provides comfortable mainstream cruising aboard a fleet of mainly large resort ships (plus two mid-sized ships), and covers the world. The ships have a higher-than-average Passenger Space Ratio than competitors Carnival or RCI, and the service is friendly without being showy. In 2010 the company converted to fully digital travel documents, so there are no more ticket document wallets and everything is online.

○ **Frequent passengers' club:** Captain's Circle.

So what's it really like?

Ships in both the mid-size and large resort categories are clean and always well maintained, and the open promenade decks of some ships have teak deck lounge chairs – others are plastic. Only

The atrium aboard P&O Cruises' *Oceana*.

Crown Princess heads for New York City.

Coral Princess and Island Princess have full walk-around open promenade decks; aboard all other Princess ships you cannot walk completely around the open promenade decks. The line also has a nice balance of officers, staff and crew members, and its British connections help it to achieve the feeling of calmness aboard its ships that some other lines lack.

Choose Princess Cruises if you enjoy being with families and fellow passengers of mid-50s and upwards, who want a well-organized cruise experience with unpretentious middle-of-the-road cuisine, a good range of entertainment, and an excellent shore excursion program – arguably the best run of any of the major cruise lines. There are proper cinemas aboard most ships as well as outdoor poolside mega-screens for showing "movies under the skies" in the evening.

Lines do form at peak times for elevators, the information office, and for open-seating breakfast and lunch in the main dining rooms. Lines for shore excursions and shore tenders are also a fact of life aboard large resort ships – although this doesn't apply to Ocean Princess or Pacific Princess.

All passengers receive turndown service and chocolates on pillows each night, as well as bathrobes (on request) and toiletry amenity kits – larger, naturally, for suite/mini-suite occupants – that typically include soap, shampoo, conditioner, and hand/body lotion. A hairdryer is provided in all cabins, sensibly located at a lounge area vanity desk unit.

If you want to keep up with the world, BBC World, CNN, CNBC, ESPN and TNT can be found on the in-cabin color TV system (when available).

Countless pieces of questionable "art" are encountered in almost every foyer and public room – an annoying reminder that cruising aboard large resort ships is like living in a bazaar of paintings surrounded by a ship.

The dress code is either formal – usually one formal night per 7-day cruise – or smart casual. The latter is interpreted by many as jeans or tracksuits and trainers.

The newest ships – Crown Princess, Emerald Princess, Ruby Princess – include an adults-only area called The Sanctuary, an extra-cost retreat at the top of the ship, forward of the mast. This provides a "private" place to relax and unwind and includes attendants to provide chilled face towels and deliver light bites. It has thick padded sunloungers both in the sun and in the shade, a swim-against-the-current pool, and there are also two outdoor cabanas for massages. I particularly recommend The Sanctuary in hot weather during Caribbean cruises. It's worth the extra $15 a head per half-day.

Princess's onboard product, especially the food and entertainment, is well established, and is totally geared to the North American market's west coast types. But British and other European nationalities should feel at home, as long as they realize that this is all about highly organized, packaged cruising, food and service, with an increasing emphasis on onboard revenue. So expect to be subjected to a stream of flyers advertising daily art auctions, "designer" watches, specialized classes (Princess Cruises' "ScholarShip@Sea" programs), and the like.

You'll also encounter many extra-charge items such as ice cream, non-standard coffees and pastry items taken in venues other than the restaurants, $4 per hour for group babysitting services. There's also a charge for using washers and dryers in self-service launderettes.

HOW TO GET HITCHED AT SEA

Princess Cruises has possibly the most extensive wedding program of any of the major lines, with its "Tie the Knot" wedding packages. The ship's captain can legally marry American couples at sea aboard its ships registered in Bermuda. This is by special dispensation, and should be verified when in the planning stage, and may vary according to where you reside.

The basic wedding at sea package costs $1,800, plus $450 for licensing fees, and includes a personal wedding coordinator. Live music, a candlelit celebration officiated by the captain, champagne, fresh floral arrangements, a bridal bouquet, boutinniere, a photographer and a wedding cake can all be

laid on, with the wedding to in an exclusive wedding chapel (or other location).

You'll also get keepsake champagne flutes, and keepsake wedding certificate. Tuxedo rental is available. Harborside or shore-side packages vary according to the port. For latest rates, see Princess Cruises' website or your travel agent.

Princess offers scuba diving classes on Caribbean cruises.

Princess Cruises' ships are best suited to couples, families with children and teenagers, and older singles who like to mingle in a large ship setting with sophisticated surroundings and lifestyle, reasonably good entertainment and fairly decent food and service, packaged affordably.

Sadly, the few staff members on duty at the gangway when you first arrive will merely point you in the direction of your deck, or to the ship's elevators instead of escorting you to your cabin – a practice now confined to MSC Cruises among the major lines. An "express check-in" option is available by completing certain documentation 40 days in advance of your cruise.

Decor

If Carnival's ships have the brightest decor imaginable, the decor aboard Princess Cruises' ships is almost the opposite – perhaps a little bland in places, with much use of neutral tones, calm colors and pastels. This really does suit the passengers who cruise with Princess.

Gratuities

Gratuities to staff are automatically added to your account, at $10.50 ($11 for suite occupants) per person, per day; gratuities for children are charged at the same rate. If you want to pay less, you'll need to go to the reception desk to have these charges adjusted (that could mean lining up with many other passengers wanting to do the same). Additionally, 15% is added to bar and wine bills. The onboard currency is the US dollar.

Cuisine/Dining

Although portions are generous, the food and its presentation are disappointing. Fish is often disguised by crumb or batter coating, the selection of fresh green vegetables is limited, and few garnishes are used. However, do remember that this is big-ship banquet catering, with all its attendant standardization and production cooking. Meats are of a decent quality, although often disguised by gravy-based sauces, and pasta dishes are accept-

able (though voluminous), and are typically served by section headwaiters who may also make "something special just for you" – in search of favorable comments and gratuities.

If you like desserts, order a sundae at dinner, as most other desserts are just so-so. Ice cream, when ordered in the dining room, is included, but costs extra elsewhere (Häagen Dazs can be found at poolside).

Specially designed dinnerware and good quality linens and silverware are used, such as Dudson of England dinnerware, Frette Egyptian cotton table linens, and silverware by Hepp of Germany. All dining rooms and eateries are smoke-free.

Themed dinners are a feature. On a 7-day cruise, a typical menu cycle will include a Sail-away Dinner, Captain's Welcome Dinner, Captain's Gala Dinner, and Landfall Dinner. An extra-cost "Chef's Table Dinner" is an indulgent, three-hour "foodertain-ment" event (at $75 per person, maximum 10 persons) in which the executive chef interacts with diners; appetizers and cocktails in the galley are followed by a multicourse tasting dinner with wines paired to the meal.

The wine list is reasonable, but not good, and there are no dedicated wine waiters.

Passengers in balcony-grade accommodation can enjoy a full-service "Balcony Dinner" for two at $50 per person extra, plus wine, and a truly indulgent Balcony Champagne Breakfast – superb value at $32 per couple.
● **Casual Eateries**: For casual eating, each ship has a Horizon Buffet (open almost round the clock), and, at night, provides an informal dinner setting with sit-down waiter service. A small, limited bistro menu is also available. The buffet displays are mostly repetitious, but far better than in past years. There is no finesse in presentation, however, as plastic plates are provided, instead of trays. The cabin service menu is quite limited, and the presentation of food items featured is poor.
● **The Coffee/Tea Factor:** Regular Coffee: Weak and poor. Score: 2 out of 10. Espresso/ Cappuccino coffees:

Princess Cruises has a wide range of supervised activities.

An art gallery on *Grand Princess* sells paintings.

Score: 3 out of 10. Except for beverage station at the serve-yourself buffets, coffees/teas in bars cost extra.

For Children

Children are divided into three age groups: Princess Pelicans (ages 2–5), Shockwaves (ages 8–12), and Off-Limits or Remix (13–17). The groups are split into age-related activities, and Princess Cruises has good children's counselors and supervised activities.
● **Best ships for children:** *Caribbean Princess, Coral Princess, Crown Princess, Dawn Princess, Diamond Princess, Emerald Princess, Golden Princess, Grand Princess, Island Princess, Ruby Princess, Sapphire Princess, Sea Princess, Star Princess, Sun Princess.* But not: *Ocean Princess, Pacific Princess*

Entertainment

Princess Cruises' production shows have always been aimed at its slightly older, more elegant passengers. The company prides itself on its glamorous all-American shows, and they should not disappoint. There are typically two or three shows during each 7-day cruise. Each ship has a resident troupe of singers and dancers.

Passenger participation events are put on by members of the cruise staff, who would be well advised to hang on to their day jobs. Most lounges and bars have live music. Musical units range from solo pianists to string quartets, from a cappella singers to bands that can provide music for ballroom dancing. Princess Cruises also provides a number of male hosts as dance partners for women traveling alone. Show lounges are non-smoking.

Spa/Fitness Facilities

All Lotus Spa/beauty treatments and fitness facilities are operated and staffed by the Steiner Leisure concession, whose offerings are similar to those already described for Celebrity Cruises and Costa Cruises. You can now make online reservations for spa treatments before your cruise. But be careful not to clash with shore excursions and other diversions. Days at sea are easiest to book online, and hardest to obtain on board.

ROYAL CARIBBEAN INTERNATIONAL

Ships
Oasis-class ships: *Oasis of the Seas* (2009), *Allure of the Seas* (2010)
Freedom-class ships: *Freedom of the Seas* (2006), *Independence of the Seas* (2008), *Liberty of the Seas* (2007)
Voyager-class ships: *Adventure of the Seas* (2001), *Explorer of the Seas* (2000), *Mariner of the Seas* (2004), *Navigator of the Seas* (2003), *Voyager of the Seas* (1999)
Radiance-class ships: *Brilliance of the Seas* (2002), *Jewel of the Seas* (2004), *Radiance of the Seas* (2001), *Serenade of the Seas* (2003)
Vision-class ships: *Enchantment of the Seas* (1997), *Grandeur of the Seas* (1996), *Legend of the Seas*(1995), *Rhapsody of the Seas* (1997), *Splendour of the Seas* (1996), *Vision of the Seas* (1998)
Sovereign-class ships: *Majesty of the Seas* (1992), *Monarch of the Seas* (1991)

About the company
Royal Caribbean Cruise Line (RCCL) was set up by three Norwegian shipping company dynasties in 1969: Arne Wilhelmsen, I.M. Skaugen, and Gotaas-Larsen (who was more of a sleeping partner). Its first ship, *Song of Norway*, debuted in 1970, followed by *Nordic Prince* and *Sun Viking*. Royal Caribbean was different to Carnival and NCL in that it launched its cruise operations with brand new ships, whereas the others had only older, pre-owned tonnage. In 1978 the cruise industry's first "chop-and-stretch" operation took place aboard *Song of Norway*, and 1988 saw the debut of the first really large cruise ship, *Sovereign of the Seas*.

In 1997 Royal Caribbean International bought Celebrity Cruises for $1.3 billion and in 2006 acquired Pullmantur Cruises for $889.9 million. In 2007 its Celebrity Cruises division created a new cruise line, Azamara Cruises, with two ships. In 2007 Royal Caribbean established CDF Croisières de France with one ship, diverted from the Pullmantur Cruises fleet.

At first the operation was excellent. But there are now shareholders to please, and the onboard product has

slipped to equal that of Carnival Cruise Lines (whose ships, in general, have larger standard cabins). RCI's ships are shapely, with well-rounded sterns, and interesting design profiles that make them instantly recognizable. Large, brightly lit casinos are provided, as are revenue-raising shopping galleries that passengers have to walk through to get almost anywhere else.
✪ **Frequent passengers club:** Crown and Anchor Society.

So what's it really like?

RCI provides a well-integrated, fine-tuned, and comfortable cruise experience, but there's nothing royal about it except the name. The product is consistent but homogenous. This is cruising for mainstream America. The ships are all quite pleasing, and some have really comfortable public rooms, lounges, bars, and innovative gimmicks such as ice-skating rinks.

The company competes directly with Carnival Cruise Lines, Norwegian Cruise Lines and Princess Cruises in terms of what's offered on board, as well as the hard sell for onboard revenue (the result of highly discounted pricing in the marketplace). But RCI ships have more glass area and connection with the outdoors and the sea than Carnival's ships, and are a better bet for families with children.

RCI's largest ships are termed *Oasis*-class (*Allure of the Seas, Oasis of the Seas*), *Freedom*-class (*Freedom of the Seas, Independence of the Seas, Liberty of the Seas*) and *Voyager*-class (*Adventure of the Seas, Explorer of the Seas, Mariner of the Seas, Navigator of the Seas, Voyager of the Seas*). They differ from other ships in the fleet – mainly in the internal layout – by having a large mall-like high street – the focal point for most passengers. Many public rooms, lounges and bars are located as adjuncts to the mall. It's rather like a mall with a ship built around it. Unfortunately, in placing so much emphasis on "active" outdoors areas, space has been taken away from the pool areas, leaving little room left just to sit and relax or sunbathe.

The next group of ships (*Brilliance of the Seas, Jewel of the Seas, Radiance of the Seas, Serenade of the Seas*) have lots of balcony cabins, and large expanses of glass. *Enchantment of the*

ABOVE: Caribbean musicians, *Rhapsody of the Seas*.
BELOW: *Oasis of the Seas* needs a horticulturalist.

Seas, Grandeur of the Seas, Legend of the Seas, Rhapsody of the Seas, Splendour of the Seas, and *Vision of the Seas* also have lots of glass in the public areas, but not so many balcony cabins. *Freedom of the Seas* pioneered a concierge lounge available only to suite occupants.

The oldest ships (*Majesty of the Seas, Monarch of the Seas*), innovative in the late 1980s, now look very dated. They have extremely small, barely adequate cabins, and tiny tub chairs in public rooms, for example, although the average passenger has become larger.

The onboard product is aimed at those with an active, lifestyle. All ships have a 30-ft (9-meter) high rock-climbing wall, with five separate climbing tracks. You'll need to plan what you want to take part in wisely as almost everything requires you to sign up in advance.

There are few quiet places to sit and read – almost everywhere has intrusive background music, played even in elevators and all passenger hallways. Bars also have very loud music. There are many, many intrusive announcements for activities that bring revenue, such as art auctions and bingo. Standing in line for embarkation, the reception desk, disembarkation, for port visits, shore tenders and for the self-serve buffet stations in the Windjammer Café is an inevitable aspect of cruising aboard large resort ships. It's often hard to escape the ship's photographers – they're everywhere. Take lots of extra pennies – you'll need them to pay for all the additional-cost items. Expect to be subjected to a stream of flyers advertising promotions, while "artworks" for auction are strewn throughout the ship, and frosted drinks in "souvenir" glasses are pushed to the hilt. There are no cushioned pads for the deck lounge chairs (they have plastic webbing and, even with a towel placed on them, soon become uncomfortable).

These niggles apart, RCI ships are liked by active, young-minded couples and singles of all ages, families with toddlers, children, and teenagers who enjoy mingling in a large ship setting with plenty of life, high-energy entertainment, and bright lighting everywhere. The food is more notable for quantity than quality – unless you pay extra for dining in an "alternative" restaurant (not all ships have them). Smoking is not allowed in cabins without a balcony.

Service personnel are friendly, but not many greet you when passing in the corridors, so the hospitality factor could be improved. The elevators talk to you, though "going up/going down" is informative but monotonous. However, the signage and illuminated picture displays of decks are good, particularly aboard the *Oasis*-class ships.

Occupants of the Presidential Family Suite, Royal Suite, Royal Family Suite, Owner's Suite and Grand Suite get a dedicated security line, where available. Royal and Presidential Family Suite occupants are welcomed by a senior officer and escorted aboard. Those in Grand Suites and higher categories get gold SeaPass

Loft accommodations on *Oasis of the Seas*.

cards for better staff recognition. On embarkation: free bottled water and a fruit plate, slippers, spa bathrobes, Vitality bathroom amenities, and Ghirardelli chocolates or petits fours at turndown. Free 24-hour room service, coffee and tea are available throughout the cruise, along with the option of ordering from the main dining room's full breakfast, lunch and dinner menus. There's also free garment pressing on formal evenings.

Other perks include a cocktail reception with the captain; reserved showlounge seating; and priority bookings for spa/salon appointments, tender tickets and excursions. On *Voyager*- and *Freedom*-class ships, suite guests get reserved seating poolside and at Studio B ice shows. During breakfast and lunch in the casual Windjammer buffet venue, there's reserved private seating in the adjacent specialty restaurants. Aboard *Radiance*-, *Voyager*- and *Freedom*-class ships, suite occupants receive a Concierge Club key. Junior Suite occupants get silver SeaPass cards for extra benefits.

Decor

Interior decor is bright and contemporary, but not as neon-intensive and glitzy as Carnival's ships. There is much Scandinavian design influence, with some eclectic sculpture and artwork. The "you are here" signage and deck plans are excellent. The furniture in public lounges tends to include small "tub" chairs that are often broken by large passengers.

Gratuities

Gratuities can be paid in cash or added to your onboard account daily at the suggested rate of $9 per person. Also, 15% is added to all bar, wine and spa charges. The onboard currency is the US dollar.

Cuisine/Dining

Most ships have large dining halls that are two or three decks high, giving a sense of space and grandeur. Few tables for two are available, most being for four, six, or

eight persons. All dining rooms and eateries are non-smoking. The efficient dining operation emphasizes highly programmed, extremely hurried service that many find insensitive. There are no fish knives.

"My Time Dining," rolled out fleetwide in 2009, means you can choose either a fixed dining time or any time you want to turn up. For this option, you'll need to prepay gratuities and enrol either on board or in advance through www.royalcaribbean.com or by asking your travel agent to arrange it via the reservations system.

The cuisine in the main dining rooms is typical of mass banquet catering, with mediocre standard fare. The food costs per passenger are below those for sister companies Azamara Club Cruises and Celebrity Cruises, so don't expect the same food quality. Dinner menus typically include a Welcome-Aboard Dinner, French Dinner, Italian Dinner, International Dinner, and Captain's Gala Dinner, and all offer plenty of choice. Menu descriptions sound tempting, but the food, although well enough prepared, is unmemorable. A decent selection of light meals is provided, and there is a vegetarian menu.

The quality of meat, particularly beef, is poor – unless you pay $14.95 extra for a "better" quality sirloin steak "cooked to order." Other meats are often disguised with gravies or heavy sauces. Most fish (except salmon) and seafood items tend to be overcooked and lack taste. Green vegetables are scarce – they're provided basically for decoration – but salad items are plentiful. Rice is often used

Brilliance of the Seas dwarfs Dubrovnik in Croatia.

as a source of carbohydrates, potatoes being more expensive. Breads and pastry items are generally good, although some items, such as croissants, may not be made on board. Dessert items are standardized and lack flavor, and the cheese selection and crackers are poor. The selection of breads, rolls, and fruit could be better. Caviar, once a standard menu item, is now lumpfish caviar – poor, incredibly salty and nothing to do with real caviar.

Although prices are moderate, the wine list is not extensive, and almost all wines are very young. Only small glasses are provided. The waiters are overly friendly for some tastes – particularly on the last night of the cruise, when tips are expected.

● **Alternative Dining Venues:** All *Freedom*, *Radiance* and *Voyager*-class ships have two additional dining venues: Chops Grille Steakhouse (for premium veal chops and steaks, cover charge $30 per person), and Portofino (for Italian-American cuisine; cover charge $25 per person). Both venues serve food of a much higher quality than that in the main dining room. Reservations are required in both venues. *Vision*-class ships have one extra-charge alternative dining venue, Portofino. Be prepared to eat Texas-sized portions, presented on large plates. Note that menus do not change throughout the cruise. *Oasis*-class ships have more extra-cost dining venues. The dress code is smart casual.

● **Casual Eateries:** All RCI ships have casual eateries called Windjammer Café or Windjammer Marketplace for fast-food items, salads, and other casual meals. Some are of the single-line type (move along with your tray), while the newer ships have individual islands for more variety and fewer lines. However, the actual quality of cooked food items is nutritionally poor, as are the rather tacky salad dressings.

Breakfast buffet items are virtually the same each day, monotonous and mostly below the standards of diner food. The same is true of lunchtime salad items. The beverage stations have only the most basic items. Hamburgers and hot dogs in self-

Taking a stroll along The Boardwalk, *Oasis of the Seas*.

serve buffet locations are generally left in steam tables. They are steamed rather than grilled, although you can ask for one to be grilled in front of you. Note that trays are not provided – only only oval plates – so if you are disabled or have mobility difficulties you may need to ask for help. Also, because the plates are plastic, it's impossible to get your food on a heated plate.

Almost all ships also have Johnny Rockets '50s-style diners ($3.95 extra charge, per person, whether you eat in or take out, and, while the food is included, shakes and drinks cost extra). These serve hamburgers, hot dogs, desserts and sodas, although the typical waiting time is about 30 minutes – pagers are provided, in case you want to wander off while waiting for a table.

Drinks packages are available in bars, in the form of cards or stickers so that you can pre-pay for a selection of soft drinks and alcoholic drinks. However, the rules for using the pre-paid packages are a bit cumbersome. There is a $3.95 charge for all cabin service deliveries between midnight and 5am.
● **The Coffee/Tea Factor:** Regular Coffee: Weak, poor quality. Score: 1 out of 10. Espresso/Cappuccino coffees (Seattle's Best brand): Score: 4 out of 10 – but it comes in paper cups.

For Children

Early 2009 saw the start of RCI's new youth programs, including My Family Time dining, and extra-cost packages such as a supervised "Lunch and Play" option. An in-cabin baby sitting service was introduced (at $10 per hour for two children or $15 for three).

Meanwhile, Adventure Ocean is RCI's "edutainment" area. Junior passengers are divided into four age-appropriate groups: Aquanaut Center (ages 3–5); Explorer Center (6–8); Voyager Center (9–12); and Optix Teen Center (13–17).

An unlimited soda and juice package for under-17s costs $4 a day. There are lots of activities, and a host of children's counselors.
● **Best ships for children:** *Adventure of the Seas, Allure of the Seas, Explorer of the Seas, Freedom of the Seas, Independence of the Seas, Liberty of the Seas, Mariner of the Seas, Navigator of the*

Seas, Oasis of the Seas, Voyager of the Seas. **Ships with fewer facilities:** *Brilliance of the Seas, Enchantment of the Seas, Grandeur of the Seas, Jewel of the Seas, Legend of the Seas, Radiance of the Seas, Rhapsody of the Seas, Serenade of the Seas, Splendour of the Seas, Vision of the Seas.* **Ships with poor facilities for children:** *Majesty of the Seas, Monarch of the Seas.*

Entertainment

The entertainment is upbeat, similar to what you would find in a resort hotel in Las Vegas. Production shows are colorful, fast-paced, high volume razzle-dazzle spectaculars, but with little or no storyline, poor linkage between themes and scenes, and basic choreography. The live band is augmented by prerecorded backing tracks to make it sound like a big, professional orchestra. Each ship has its resident troupe of singers and dancers.

Then there are silly audience participation (summer camp-style, but often funny) events and activities – something that RCI has always done well.

All showlounges are non-smoking venues.

Spa/Fitness Facilities

The Spa facilities in RCI ships are operated by the Steiner Leisure concession, whose offerings are similar to those already described for Celebrity Cruises and Costa Cruises. For the more sporting, all RCI ships have a rock-climbing wall, with several separate climb-

Size matters: *Freedom of the Seas* and a double-decker bus.

Soaking up the sun aboard *Superstar Libra*.

ing tracks. There is a 30-minute instruction period before anyone is allowed to climb, and this is done in pairs. It's free, and all safety gear is included, but you'll need to sign up. It's worth remembering that it's quieter on port days, but the hours of operation are limited – typically two hours each in the morning and afternoon. Playing a round of golf in the golf simulator costs $25 per hour (for up to four persons).

STAR CRUISES

Ships
MegaStar Aries (1991), *SuperStar Aquarius* (1993), *SuperStar Libra* (1988), *SuperStar Virgo* (1999)

About the company
Star Cruises, the world's third largest cruise operator, was set up in 1993 as a subsidiary of Genting Hong Kong, founded in 1965 in Malaysia as the Genting Group. The company operates ships dedicated to specific markets, and its brands include Star Cruises, Norwegian Cruise Line, and Cruise Ferries.

Star Cruises is one of only two cruise lines to have its own ship simulator (the other is MSC Cruises) – useful training tools when a captain these days may be in charge of a speeding vessel measuring more than 150,000 gross tonnage. It also owns the cruise terminal at its operations base in Port Klang, Malaysia, and the pier facility in Langkawi. Its marketing base is now in Hong Kong and the company is formally known as Star Cruises/Genting Hong Kong.

○ **Frequent passengers' club:** Star VIP Club.

So what's it really like?
Star Cruises' ships are best suited to adult couples and singles, and families with children. They are good particularly for Asians and Australians, and for those who enjoy big city life, gambling, and constant activity accompanied by plenty of music, late nights, and abundant food. Star Cruises was the originator of the "Freestyle Cruising" concept, which offered more flexibility and was later

adopted by NCL. A strictly casual dress code prevails aboard all the ships.

SuperStar Libra and *SuperStar Aquarius* are based in Hong Kong, mainly for the local gaming market, and specialize in short cruises. *SuperStar Virgo,* based in Hong Kong and Singapore, operates 2-, 3-, and 5-night cruises for the local market. Singapore-based *MegaStar Aries* and *MegaStar Taurus* are boutique ships available only for charter or private parties. All ships have gaming casinos, including members-only private gaming rooms for serious players – a major attraction for Asian passengers.

Decor
The ships have stunning Asian interior decor, with bright, fresh, happy, warm colors, and carpets with rich patterns. Many cabins have rich lacquered wood furniture and highly polished wood accents, with colorful soft furnishings as accompaniments. Some ships have original artwork costing millions.

Gratuities
Gratuities are included aboard all Star Cruises ships, and drink prices already include a service charge. Onboard currency: the Hong Kong dollar.

Cuisine/Dining
Star Cruises provides a wide variety of food to suit both Asian and Western tastes. However, the cuisine is still of a mainstream market standard – you'll find butter in packets. At self-serve buffets, salt and pepper are typically provided on each table, not in packets as aboard many other cruise lines. Espresso and cappuccino (Lavazza brand) Italian coffees are available fleet-wide, at extra cost. Service aboard the ships is usually by Asian staff, many from China and the Philippines.

Some ships have up to 10 restaurants and eateries; some are included in the fare, while others cost extra.
● **Room service:** Continental breakfast typically costs extra, and room service snacks are available at extra cost throughout the day. A basket of fruit is provided to all cabins at embarkation, and is replenished daily in suites.

For Children
Children are divided into three age groups, with facil-

Appealing to Asia: the Grand Piazza aboard *SuperStar Virgo*.

ities, activities and entertainment to match: for children from 6 to 9 years; for children 10–13; for teens 14–17. There's also a StarKids Club (for Singapore residents only), created for under-12s who sail aboard *SuperStar Virgo*. The facilities and play areas are extensive aboard *SuperStar Virgo*, and less so aboard the other ships.

Entertainment

The main production shows are colorful, visual shows, particularly aboard the largest ships. Brazilian dancers, Chinese acrobats, and many top Asian entertainers are featured. Small units provide live music for dancing or listening, but there is no real show band. Production shows are performed to pre-recorded backing tracks. Each ship has karaoke rooms for rent.

Spa/Fitness Facilities

The spas are an in-house operation, with Asian staff. Thai massage is the house specialty. Examples of prices: Thai Massage, S\$60 (60 minutes); Hot Stones Massage, S\$80 (75 minutes). A Singapore dollar is worth roughly 71 cents (US) or 47p (UK). ❑

THE BIGGEST OF THE BIG: CRUISE SHIPS OVER 100,000 GROSS TONNAGE

Ship Name	Cruise Line	Gross Tonnage	No. of Pass- engers	Passenger Space Ratio	Year Built
Allure of the Seas	Royal Caribbean Int.	225,282	5,400	41.2	2010
Oasis of the Seas	Royal Caribbean Int.	225,282	5,400	41.2	2009
Freedom of the Seas	Royal Caribbean Int.	154,407	3,634	42.0	2006
Independence of the Seas	Royal Caribbean Int.	154,407	3,634	42.0	2008
Liberty of the Seas	Royal Caribbean Int.	154,407	3,634	42.0	2007
Norwegian Epic	Norwegian Cruise Line	153,000	4,200	36.4	2010
Queen Mary 2	Cunard Line	148,528	2,620	56.6	2004
Explorer of the Seas	Royal Caribbean Int.	137,308	3,634	42.0	2000
Voyager of the Seas	Royal Caribbean Int.	137,280	3,634	42.0	1999
Adventure of the Seas	Royal Caribbean Int.	137,276	3,634	42.0	2001
Mariner of the Seas	Royal Caribbean Int.	137,276	3,634	42.0	2004
Navigator of the Seas	Royal Caribbean Int.	137,276	3,634	42.0	2003
MSC Fantasia	MSC Cruises	133,500	3,274	41.2	2008
MSC Splendida	MSC Cruises	133,500	3,274	41.2	2008
Carnival Dream	Carnival Cruise Lines	130,000	3,646	35.6	2009
Carnival Magic	Carnival Cruise Lines	130,000	3,646	35.6	2011
Disney Dream	Disney Cruise Lines	128,000	2,500	51.2	2011
Celebrity Eclipse	Celebrity Cruises	122,000	2,852	42.7	2010
Celebrity Equinox	Celebrity Cruises	122,000	2,852	42.7	2009
Celebrity Silhouette	Celebrity Cruises	122,000	2,852	42.7	2011
Celebrity Solstice	Celebrity Cruises	122,000	2,852	42.7	2008
Ventura	P&O Cruises	116,017	3,092	37.5	2008
Diamond Princess	Princess Cruises	115,875	2,674	43.3	2004
Sapphire Princess	Princess Cruises	115,875	2,674	43.3	2004
Azura	P&O Cruises	115,055	3,092	37.5	2010
Costa Favolosa	Costa Cruises	114,500	3,012	38.0	2011
Costa Serena	Costa Cruises	114,147	3,000	38.0	2007
Crown Princess	Princess Cruises	113,561	3,114	36.4	2006
Emerald Princess	Princess Cruises	113,561	3,114	36.4	2007
Ruby Princess	Princess Cruises	113,561	3,114	36.4	2008
Caribbean Princess	Princess Cruises	112,894	3,114	36.2	2004
Costa Concordia	Costa Cruises	112,000	3,000	37.3	2006
Carnival Conquest	Carnival Cruise Lines	110,239	2,974	37.0	2004
Carnival Splendor	Carnival Cruise Lines	110,239	2,974	37.0	2008
Carnival Freedom	Carnival Cruise Lines	110,239	2,974	37.0	2007
Carnival Glory	Carnival Cruise Lines	110,239	2,974	37.0	2003
Carnival Liberty	Carnival Cruise Lines	110,239	2,974	37.0	2005
Carnival Valor	Carnival Cruise Lines	110,239	2,974	37.0	2004
Star Princess	Princess Cruises	108,977	2,602	41.8	2002
Golden Princess	Princess Cruises	108,865	2,600	41.8	2001
Grand Princess	Princess Cruises	108,806	2,600	41.8	1998
Costa Fortuna	Costa Cruises	102,587	2,716	37.7	2003
Costa Magica	Costa Cruises	102,587	2,718	37.7	2004
Carnival Triumph	Carnival Cruise Lines	101,509	2,758	36.8	1999
Carnival Victory	Carnival Cruise Lines	101,509	2,758	36.8	2000
Carnival Destiny	Carnival Cruise Lines	101,353	2,642	38.3	1996

Oasis of the Seas

Queen Mary 2

MSC Fantasia

Ventura

Golden Princess

Costa Serena

THE BIG APPEAL OF SMALLER OPERATORS

While the major cruise lines dominate the mass market,
dozens of other companies cater for more specialist
tastes and can offer some exotic destinations

The international cruise industry is comprised of around 75 companies with ocean-going cruise ships providing vacations to more than 20 million passengers each year. Most major cruise lines are owned and operated by large corporations. Other operators are family-owned cruise lines. Still others are small, with just a couple of compact-sized ships. Some cruise companies don't own their own ships, but charter them from ship owning and ship management companies for year-round or seasonal operation – for example, specialized ships outfitted for Arctic and Antarctic expedition cruises only.

Some cruise lines are actually tour operators – vacation packagers, mostly in Europe, that put together airlines, hotels, car rentals, and cruises. Some own their own charter airlines. Tour operators have transferred some of their land-based tourists to the sea, aboard ships that move the destinations for them. These are the equivalent of the package vacation that first became popular in Europe in the 1970s – for example, Thomson Cruises.

These mini-profiles, in alphabetical order, include cruise lines with small- or mid-size ships and small fleets, those with a small number of large resort ships, those with tall ships (with either real working sail propulsion or computer-controlled assistance), those that specialize in hardy or "soft" expedition cruises, and those which cruise along coastal and inland waterways.

The major cruise companies are profiled on pages 124–57 and so are not included in this section.

Germany-oriented AIDA Cruises is yet another Carnival brand.

Abercrombie & Kent (A&K)

Geoffrey Kent started A&K as a safari company in 1962 – there was no Mr Abercrombie, it just sounded good – and then specialized in upscale train journeys around the globe for small groups. The company got started in the cruise business when it went into a marketing agreement with the long-defunct Society Expeditions in 1990.

Two years later it bought the little expedition ship *Society Explorer* (formerly *Lindblad Explorer*) when Society Expeditions ceased operations. The ship, renamed *National Geographic Explorer*, now belongs to Lindblad Expeditions. Today, A&K specializes in escorted educational and nature cruises, and charters various ships, such as those of Swan Hellenic Cruises, for its cruise programs, taking passengers to the more remote destinations such as the Antarctic, in relative comfort. The company is also involved in river cruises and hotel barges, for which it acts as sales agents. Gratuities are not included in the cruise fare.

AIDA Cruises

The former East German shipping company Deutsche Seereederei (DSR) and its marketing arm Seetours (Deutsche Seetouristik) were assigned the traditional cruise ship *Arkona* as part of the east-west integration in 1985, which included a contractual agreement with the Treuhandanstalt to build a new ship. It did this in 1996 with the newly built *Aida*, designed to appeal to young, active German-speaking families. The concept was to create a seagoing version of the popular Robinson Clubs – a sort of German Club Med concept. When *Aida* first debuted, there were almost no passengers and the company struggled.

In 1998 the company was sold to Norwegian Cruise Line, which sold it back to its original Rostock-based owners. P&O acquired it in 1999 and it is now a very successful multi-ship brand belonging to the Carnival Corporation. It is well-known in German-speaking countries for its *über*-casual cruising, with two main self-serve buffet restaurants instead of the traditional sit-down-and-be-served method of cruising – the tablecloth-less method of eating, a bit like camping at sea – with little contact with the small staff numbers.

The entertainment is extremely good, however, and is provided in conjunction with the Schmidt Theatre in Hamburg. Gratuities are not included in the cruise fare.

American Safari Cruises reaches deep into Alaska.

American Cruise Lines

ACL was originally formed in 1974, at the beginning of American coastal passenger shipping, but it went bankrupt in 1989, the ships were sold off, and the company lay dormant. The original owner, Charles Robertson, a renowned yachtsman who used to race 12-meter America's Cup yachts, resurrected it in 2000, and built its own ships in its own wholly owned small shipyard in Salisbury, Maryland, on the Chesapeake Bay.

ACL's ships *(American Glory, American Spirit, American Star, Independence)* ply the inter-coastal waterways and rivers of the USA's east coast (between Maine and Florida), and provide an up-close, intimate experience for passengers who don't need luxury or much pampering, but do like American history and culture. The "D-class" vessels are less than 2,500 gross tonnage, and are subject neither to bureaucratic regulations nor to union rules. The company also formed Pearl Seas Cruises, whose single ship was built in Canada. In 2010, the company also started operating *Queen of the West*, a 120-passenger paddlewheel (replica steamboat) on rivers in the USA's Pacific Northwest. Gratuities are not included in the company's cruise fares.

American Safari Cruises

This micro-cruise line, founded in 2001, was purchased in 2008 by InnerSea Discoveries, owned by the former chief executive officer of American Safari Cruises, Dan Blanchard. ASC has a fleet of very small vessels for 6–36 passengers for expensive up-close-and-personal cruises in Alaska and the Pacific Northwest. While the vessels are decent, the onboard facilities are few and the one-seat dining experience is very casual, with little choice. The advantage of these intimate vessels is that they really can take you up close to fascinating parts of Alaska that the large resort ships can't reach. Gratuities are not included in the cruise fare.

Aurora Expeditions

This Australian company was founded in 1993 by Australian Mount Everest veteran and geologist Greg Mortimer and adventure travel specialist Margaret Werner. The company, which specializes in small-group expeditions, uses the chartered expedition ship *Polar Pioneer* for its Antarctic expedition cruise programs. Other destinations include Papua New Guinea, Australia's Kimberley region, and the Russian Far East, for which the ship is the chartered Russian expedition vessel *Marina Svaetana*. Gratuities are not included in the fare.

Azamara Club Cruises

This company, formerly Azamara Cruises, is an offshoot of Celebrity Cruises, and was created in 2007. It consists of two 700-passenger ships, taking people to smaller ports that some of the large resort ships cannot get into. The company specializes in providing high-quality dining. Its ships are in direct competition with those of Oceania Cruises – except that Oceania does not charge extra to dine in its speciality restaurants.

The onboard experience is similar to that aboard the

American Cruise Lines' *Queen of the West* paddlewheel.

Azamara Journey berths near London's Tower Bridge.

ships of parent company Celebrity Cruises (including tacky art auctions), but modified to suit those who want a more personal cruise experience aboard smaller ships. Its strengths are the food and European-style service, and each ship has two extra-charge restaurants in addition to the main dining venues. Gratuities to dining and housekeeping staff, wine with lunch and dinner, coffee and tea 24 hours a day, and shuttle buses in ports of call, where needed, are all included in the fare.

Blount Small Ship Adventures

Founded in 1966 by the late Luther H. Blount, an engineer and inventor of the American Steam Trawler, who built his cruise vessels in his own shipyard in Warren, Rhode Island, the company started as as a family-run venture. Today, as the oldest US-flag cruise line still operating, it is run by his daughter, Nancy Blount.

Cruises are operated like private family outings, using two unpretentious ships that were specially constructed to operate in close-in coastal areas and inland waterways of the eastern US seaboard, with forays to the Bahamas and Caribbean during the winter.

The onboard experience is strictly no-frills cruising in very, very basic, down-to-earth surroundings that have a 1950s feel. Its early-to-bed passengers – average age 72 years – are typical of those who don't like glitz or trendy, and don't need much other than basic American food. Bring your own if you want a drink – the line supplies only tonic and soft drinks – so forget wine with dinner unless you supply your own bottle. Gratuities are not included in the cruise fare.

CDF Croisières de France

Founded and wholly owned by Royal Caribbean Cruise Line (RCCL), CDF Croisières de France was created in 2007, with headquarters in Paris. The brand is now under the overall control of Pullmantur Cruises, also owned by RCCL. The company devotes all its resources to cruising for French-speaking passengers, with one ship, *Bleu de France* (the former *Europa*). The empha-

sis is on fine French cuisine and all-inclusive pricing. Gratuities are included in the cruise fare.

Celebration Cruise Line

This company, a one-ship operation, is owned by Celebration Cruise Holdings, which also owned the now defuct Imperial Majesty Cruise Line, whose reputation suffered from high-pressure telemarketing campaigns. Its *Bahamas Celebration* operates two-night cruises from the Port of Palm Beach to the Bahamas. Despite the company's claims to "international gourmet dining," the ship provides a highly programmed but absolutely basic party getaway cruise with very standard food, and with much pressure for onboard revenue from its dining, casino and shore excursion operations.

Classic International Cruises

This small, family-owned company is based in Lisbon, Portugal. It buys or charters older (pre-owned) deep-draft ships that have "traditional" decor and lovingly refurbishes them. George Potamianos, an engineer who loves restoring ships' engine rooms, and his two sons run the company, which either operates the ships itself, or charters them to low-cost cruise/tour operators. Nau-

Chile-based Cruceros Australis runs expedition cruises.

tical officers and most service staff are Portuguese, known for their warm-hearted service. The ships may be old, but they are "traditional" ships that are well maintained, and provide the kind of seagoing experiences not found aboard the large resort ships of the world. Gratuities are not included in the cruise fare.

Club Med Cruises

Club Med became renowned for providing hassle-free vacations for the whole family. The first Club Med village was started in 1950 on the island of Mallorca, but the concept became so popular that it grew to more than 100 vacation villages throughout the world.

Club Med Cruises, an offshoot of the French all-inclusive vacation clubs, it introduced its first ocean-going cruise vessel in 1990, the computer-controlled sail-cruise ship *Club Med II* (extensively refurbished in 2008). Aboard the all-inclusive ship, it's the Gentils Ordinaires, who serve as both super-cruise staff and "rah-rah" cheerleaders for the mainly French-speaking passengers. *Club Med II* has a sister ship, Windstar Cruises' *Wind Surf*, which also provides a relaxed onboard experience. Gratuities are included in the cruise fare.

Cruceros Australis

Cruceros Australis, based in Santiago, Chile, operates cruise ships on soft expedition cruises to the Chilean fjords, Patagonia and Tierra del Fuego – some of the world's most fascinating but hostile environments. Catering increasingly to an international clientele, with Spanish as the official onboard language, cruising with this company is all about Chile and its truly dramatic coastline. Don't expect high standards aboard its two ships, but service is very friendly and its organization and operations are extremely good. The onboard languages are English and Spanish. The company introduced a brand new ship in 2010, the 210-passenger *Stella Australis*, and now operates a three-ship fleet. The other two ships are *Mare Australis* and *Via*

Kayaking in Mexico with Cruise West.

Australis (see the Coastal Cruises chart on page 96). Its cruises are "all-inclusive" with an open bar for all beverages, including wine, and gratuities included.

Cruise and Maritime Voyages

This UK-based company, which has existed for many years as a sales and marketing organization representing several small cruise lines, now charters two older ships owned by other companies. The company, whose owners originally worked for the now-defunct CTC Cruises, specializes in child-free (16 and over) cruises from UK ports, and provides traditional cruise features such as mid-morning bouillon, and captain's welcome and farewell dinners. The onboard product is at the lower end of the market, particularly where food is concerned. *Marco Polo* and *Ocean Countess* are the featured ships for ex-UK cruises. Gratuities are not included in the cruise fare.

Cruise West

Former bush pilot Chuck West founded Cruise West in 1954. He chartered two small ships, *Glacier Queen* and *Yukon Star*, for Alaska cruises. The cruises were marketed by Alaska Cruise Line, with offices in Seattle, Washington. Their hulls – they were converted ex-Canadian Navy corvettes – were painted black, and the superstructure blue and gold.

In 1971, he sold Westours to Holland America Line. In 1973, he set up Alaska Sightseeing, dedicated to small ship travel; this became Cruise West in 1983. Since then the company has expanded its operations to include Mexico, Costa Rica, and America's east coast from Florida to Maine.

The young, mostly college-age service staff are willing, but lack finesse and knowledge about the food served. Because, under US maritime procedures, its ships measure under 100 gross tonnage, the company is allowed to enter Alaska's Glacier Bay without having to bargain for the limited number of entry permits granted each year. Passengers participate rather than just cruise. Gratuities are not included in the cruise fare.

Crystal Cruises

Crystal Cruises was founded in 1988 by Nippon Yusen Kaisha (NYK), the world's largest freighter and transportation logistics company with more than 700 ships. The American-managed company is based in Century City, Los Angeles. *Crystal Harmony*, the company's first ship, was built in Japan, and debuted in New York in May 1990 to great acclaim. Meanwhile, Crystal Cruises introduced two new ships, *Crystal Symphony* in 1995, and *Crystal Serenity* in 2000, one built in Finland, the other in France.

In 2006 *Crystal Harmony* was transferred to parent company NYK as *Asuka II* for its Asuka Cruise division, for Japanese speakers. Crystal Cruises continues to provide excellent food and service aboard its two spacious ships (*Crystal Serenity* and *Crystal Symphony*), including a Nobu sushi/sashimi bar aboard *Crystal Serenity*.

The ships operate worldwide itineraries with flair. Both ships are superbly maintained, and passengers who seek fine food in a sophisticated setting should be delighted with their choice of ship and company. Open-

No mice in sight: *Disney Wonder*'s art nouveau atrium.

seating dining is being introduced in January 2011 for the first time, or passengers can opt for a choice of fixed-time dining. Gratuities are not included in the cruise fare.

Delphin Cruises

Founded by Heinz Herbert Hey, and based in Offenbach, Germany, this small cruise line specializes in providing superb itineraries for its German-speaking passengers. The company owns one ship, *Delphin*, and operates another ship, *Delphin Voyager*, under a long-term charter agreement. Passengers like the friendly staff and service, as well as the destination-rich itineraries, coupled with the fact that most cruises are of 14 days or longer. Some of the company's cruises are jointly marketed by Dephin Cruises and Hamburg-based Hansa Cruises. Gratuities are not included in the cruise fare.

Disney Cruise Line

In 1932, a Disney cartoon, Steamboat Willy, depicted Mickey Mouse at the wheel of a ship, but it took 60 years until Disney decided to get into the cruise business, as an extension of its resort stay business, offering a "seamless vacation package."

It was Lawrence (Larry) P. Murphy, executive vice-president of the Walt Disney Company, who was the guiding light in the early 1990s behind the expansion of the company into the cruise business. Previously, the company had flirted with cruising by participating in a licensing agreement with a Florida-based cruise line, the now-defunct Premier Cruise Lines, with three vintage ships based in Port Canaveral. Murphy and other Disney executives explored the possibility of creating their

Crystal Serenity's sushi stars Nobu Matsuhisa and Chef Tamba.

own ships when the licensing agreement ran out. They concluded that pairing with an established cruise line wouldn't work because of Disney's policy of generous spending on the guest experience.

The solution: create a new cruise line, wholly owned and controlled by Disney and to be known as Disney Cruise Line. The company committed an astonishing $1 billion to the project.

Its two large resort ships, *Disney Magic* (1998) and *Disney Wonder* (1999), the first cruise ships since the 1950s to be built with two funnels, cater to loyal Disney followers, and everything aboard the ships is Disney – every song, every piece of artwork, every movie and production show, and Mickey's ears adorn the ships' funnels. But there's no casino (hooray!), and no library (boo!). However, its "rotation dining" concept proved to be completely Disneylogical; you move, together with your waiter, to each of three identically-sized restaurant – each with different decor – in turn.

Disney is all about families with children, and the ships cater to both. You can buy a package combining a short stay at a Disney resort and a cruise. Disney has its own cruise terminal at Port Canaveral, Florida, its design bein g a close copy of the Ocean Terminal in Southampton, UK, used by yesteryear's ocean liners. Two new, larger ships, *Disney Dream* and *Disney Fantasy*, will join the fleet in 2011 and 2012. Gratuities are not included in the cruise fare.

easyCruise.com

Sir Stelios Haji-Iouannou, founder of many "easy" businesses including the successful airline easyJet, started easyCruise.com as an antidote to regular cruise lines. The company was acquired in summer 2009 by Hellenic Seaways, and its single ship, *easyCruise Life,* operates in the Greek Islands. It provides no-frills cruises, with a minimum stay of two nights.

The secondhand former Russian ship was refitted to easyCruise.com's minimalist design, although the original concept has been somewhat modified recently, and *easyCruise Life* now operates more in a traditional cruise manner. But, with almost no carpeting and minimal soft furnishings, it's all noise and no poise – more of a waterborne bus service, really, although it's useful for getting around bits of Greece from Piraeus. Gratuities are not included in the cruise fare.

Fred Olsen Cruise Line

This is a Norwegian family-owned and family-run company which was founded in Hvitstein, a town on Oslofjord, Norway, in 1848. Today, a fifth-generation Olsen, Fred Jr., runs the company from its headquarters in Suffolk, England. The group also has interests in the hotels, aviation, shipbuilding, ferries, and offshore industries. The company specializes in cruises for adults who are usually retired and of senior years – typically over 65. Aboard the ships, interior design reflects traditional design features, and dressing for dinner is expected on four nights during a two-week cruise. Many theme cruises, such as gardening and horticulture, and Scottish country dancing, hosted by recognised television celebrities, are regular features. The company welcomes solo passengers as well as couples.

The first ship dedicated exclusively to cruising debuted in 1987, and now ships cruise year-round out of the UK ports of Dover, Southampton, Liverpool, Newcastle, Greenock, Leith, Belfast and Dublin (ideal for anyone based in the UK to join one of the ships without having to fly), with some ships operating out of Caribbean ports during the winter. Coffee and tea-making facilities – much appreciated, particularly by its older passengers – are provided in each cabin. Smoking is allowed only on the open decks, and nowhere inside the ships. Gratuities are not included in the cruise fare.

Fred Olsen Cruise Line's *Boudicca* in Valletta, Malta.

Galápagos Cruises

Metropolitan Touring, Ecuador's foremost tour and travel company, is based in Quito, Ecuador, and sells its cruises through general sales agents such as the USA's Dallas-based Adventure Associates. Its boutique ships, the well-run *Isabella* and *Santa Cruz*, visit the Galápagos Islands, with all-Ecuadorean crew and food. Go because of the nature-filled destination, not for the ships, which are old and have few facilities. Gratuities are not included in the cruise fare.

Hansa Cruises

Founded in the late 1990s, Hansa Cruises (Hansa Kreutzfahrten) is based in Bremen, Germany. It typically charters low-budget cruise ships for cruises for a cost-conscious German-speaking clientele, and also markets cruises aboard the nicely-presented ships of Delphin Seereisen (Delphin Cruises). The ships have basic but comfortable facilities, with adequate and reasonable food. The onboard service, though friendly, is limited by the low fares, but the cruises do provide good value for money, particularly for German-speaking passengers who would simply not want to cruise aboard larger ships. Gratuities are not included in the cruise fare.

Hapag-Lloyd Cruises

Germany's two most famous ocean liner companies, the Bremen-based Norddeutscher Lloyd and the Hamburg-based Hamburg America Line, merged in 1970 to become Hapag-Lloyd. Today, Hapag-Lloyd operates four ships for three quite different market segments. Two small ships are in the specialized expedition cruise market (*Bremen* and *Hanseatic*); one is in the mid-priced market (*C. Columbus*), and one ship (*Europa*) is in the luxury market. All feature destination-intensive cruises aimed at the German-speaking market, with occasional

Hapag-Lloyd's *Bremen* explores the Antarctic.

cruises for the English-speaking market. Hapag Lloyd Cruises is a member of IAATO (Association of Antarctica Tour Operators), an association committed to the highest standards of responsible tourism to Antarctica. Gratuities are not included in the cruise fare.

Happy Cruises

Formerly known as Quail Cruises, this is part of Spain's Quail Travel Group. The company, a well-known tour operator, started its cruise division in 2008 by chartering one of the original Love Boats (Pacific). After several changes of ships, Happy Cruises now has one ship, *Ocean Pearl* (originally *Song of Norway*) under charter. It offers "all-inclusive" pricing and is marketed to families with children, with cruises from Barcelona and Valencia, Spain. Gratuities are included in the cruise fare.

Hebridean Island Cruises

Hebridean Island Cruises (formerly Hebridean International Cruises) was set up in 1989 under the Thatcher government's British Enterprise Scheme. Its headquarters is in Skipton, Yorkshire. The company operates one all-inclusive boutique ship, *Hebridean Princess*, which conveys the atmosphere of English country-house life – think Laura Ashley fabrics and soft furnishings – and specializes in cruises for mature adults. Gratuities and all port taxes are included, as are most excursions. The ship runs cruises around the Scottish islands, with an occasional sailing to English ports, the Channel Islands and Norway. Each cabin has coffee and tea-making facilities. Gratuities are not included in the cruise fare.

Hurtigruten

The company is an amalgamation of two shipping companies (OVDS and TVDS) and provides year-round service along the Norwegian coast, calling at 33 ports in 11 days. Hurtigruten, formerly known as the Norwegian Coastal Voyage, has also recently developed expedition-

Hebridean Princess cruises around Scotland's islands.

style cruises, albeit aboard ships that have been converted for the purpose, rather than aboard ships specifically built for expedition cruises. So, as long as you think utilitarian and modest decor, you'll get the idea of life aboard one of the Hurtigruten ships, which are practical rather than beautiful. Crown Princess Mette-Marit of Norway was the godmother of the company's newest ship, the *Fram*, a 318-berth expedition vessel built for cruising in Greenland. Even aboard the newest ships, the food and service are fairly basic – there's a lack of green vegetables – but the ships provide a great way to see many, many ports along the coast of Norway in a comfortable manner.

Iberocruceros

Founded originally as one of the Iberojet (tour-operator) companies, 75% of the venture company is owned by the Carnival Corporation, and 25% by the Orizonia Corporation. The company's ships operate well organized, all-inclusive cruises for the Spanish-speaking market, in direct competition to Pullmantur Cruises. The onboard product has developed well in the past couple of years, and now provides a well-established style of cruise and service for the family cruise segment of Spain's growing cruise market, with four ships: *Grand Celebration, Grand Holiday, Grand Mistral* and *Grand Voyager*. Gratuities are included in the cruise fare.

Island Cruises

Island Cruises was founded as a joint venture between Royal Caribbean Cruises and the British low-cost tour operator First Choice Holidays. Its first ship started operations in 2002. However, in 2007, First Choice merged with Germany's largest travel company TUI, to become TUI Travel. Its two-ship fleet was reduced to one ship (*Island Escape*) in 2009, and the company is now oper-

ated as a sub-brand of Thomson Cruises. It provides its mainly British passengers with an active cruise experience in ultra-casual, lager-lout-style surroundings. Its self-serve, self-carry buffet meals from an always-busy, congested café are the mainstay of the "culinary" offerings, although slightly better food can be had in a smaller extra-cost dining venue. Gratuities are not included in the cruise fare.

Kristina Cruises

This Finnish Partanan family-owned company was founded in 1985 as Rannikkolinjat to operate short cruises on Lake Saimaa. In 1987 the company purchased its first ship and started to open Baltic and Russian-owned ports on the Gulf of Finland to international cruise passengers. Today, Kristina Cruises owns and operates one vintage-style ship (*Kristina Brahe*), and one modern cruise vessel (*Kristina Katarina*), principally on cruises in the Baltic and Mediterranean, and continues to preserve nautical traditions on board. Gratuities are not included in the cruise fare.

Lindblad Expeditions

Lars-Eric Lindblad started the whole concept of expedition cruising with a single ship, *Lindblad Explorer*, in 1969, taking adventurous travellers to remote regions of the world. Today, his son, Sven-Olof Lindblad, runs the company, but with an array of small ships. It's all about wilderness, wildlife, off-the-beaten-path adventures, and learning. Zodiac inflatable craft are used to ferry participants ashore in remote areas such as the Arctic and Antarctic sub-continents.

The ships carry excellent lecturers, who are more academic than entertaining. In partnership with the National Geographic Society, the company operates the wholly owned *National Geographic Endeavour, National Geographic Explorer, National Geographic Islander* and

National Geographic Polaris, together with other small ships for coastal or soft expedition-style cruising. Gratuities are not included in the cruise fare.

Louis Cruises

In the 1930s and '40s, Louis Loizou became the undisputed father of tourism in Cyprus. His venture into sea tourism started with the charter of ships transferring immigrants from Cyprus to other continents. His son, Costakis Loizou, who took over the running of the company after his death in 1971, started organizing short cruises from Cyprus and in 1986 Louis Cruises was officially founded with the acquisition of the company's first fully owned ship, *Princesa Marissa*.

Today, Louis Group owns 20 four- and five-star hotels in the Greek islands and Cyprus. Louis Cruises has a 12-ship fleet, comprising small- to medium-sized vessels – ideal for small island-hopping itineraries – and operates principally from Greece and ports in the Mediterranean and Indian Ocean. Louis Cruises charters two of its ships to TUI Travels' UK-based Thomson Cruises and has, over the years, chartered some of its ships to many well known UK and European tour operators.

Gratuities are not included in the cruise fare.

Mano Cruise

The company, founded by Moshe Mano, caters mainly to Israeli and Russian passengers and the onboard product is tailored to their requirements. The company has small and mid-size ships and specializes in Mediterranean cruises. While most of passengers are Israeli, the ships also carry an increasing number of Russian tourists. The onboard ambience is quite sound, but basic. Gratuities are not included in the cruise fare.

Mediterranean Classic Cruises

The company, formerly Monarch Classic Cruises and Majestic International Cruises, was formed in 2006 by Andreas Potamianos and the Kollakis Group; it is a Greek-owned company, based in Piraeus. It charters its mid-size ships (*Ocean Countess* and *Ocean Majesty*) car-

Lindblad Expeditions finds a brown bear in Alaska.

rying up to 800 passengers, with service by a mainly Greek crew, to various European tour operators. Gratuities are not included in the cruise fare.

Mitsui OSK Passenger Line

Osaka Shosen Kaisha was founded in 1884 in Osaka, Japan. In 1964 it merged with Mitsui Steamship, to become Mitsui OSK. It is now one of the oldest and largest shipping companies in the world.

It entered cruise shipping in 1989 with *Fuji Maru*, the first cruise ship in the Japanese-speaking domestic market. The company specialized in incentive, meetings and groups at sea rather than cruising for individuals. But the company (now known as MOPAS) steadily changed to more cruises for individuals. The company operates two ships, *Fuji Maru* and *Nippon Maru* (extensively refurbished in 2010), both based in Japan for Japanese-speaking passengers, with *Fuju Maru* dedicated exclusively to the corporate and charter market.

Gratuities are included in the cruise fare.

Noble Caledonia

Based in London, Noble Caledonia owns two boutique-sized sister ships, *Corinthian II* and *Island Sky*, but sells cruises aboard a wide range of small and specialist expedition cruise companies as well as river cruises. It targets British passengers of mature years, and operates cruises with cultural interest themes (not recommended for children). The company has an excellent reputation for providing well organized cruises and tours, accompanied by good lecturers. Gratuities are not included in the cruise fare.

NYK Line

Nippon Yusen Kaisha (NYK Line) is the largest shipping company in the world, and owns the well-known US-based upscale

Colorful cocktails aboard Louis Cruises' *Cristal*.

brand, Crystal Cruises. It created its own NYK Cruise division – today branded as Asuka Cruise – in 1989 with one Mitsubishi-built ship, *Asuka*, for Japanese-speaking passengers. In 2006, the company sold the original *Asuka* to Germany's Phoenix Reisen, and the former *Crystal Harmony* was transferred from Crystal Cruises to become *Asuka II*. The ship, known for its excellent Japanese and western food, operates an annual around-the-world cruise, plus a wide array of both short and long cruises in the Asia-Pacific region. Coffee/tea-making facilities are provided in each cabin. Gratuities are included in the cruise fare.

Oceania Cruises

The company's ships provide faux English charm in a country-club atmosphere ideal for middle-aged and older couples seeking relaxation. Cruises are usually 10–14 days. Its trademarks are fine dining, comfortable accommodations and warm, attentive service.

In 2006, Oceania Cruises was bought by Apollo Management, a private equity company that owns Regent Seven Seas Cruises, and 50% of NCL. The brand was placed under the umbrella of Apollo's cruise brand, Prestige Cruise Holdings. With *Insignia, Nautica* and *Regatta* now operating, and two new, much larger and faster ships on order (the first, the 1,200-passenger *Marina* was delivered in 2010, while the second, *Riviera*, follows in 2011), the company is set to grow.

With multiple-choice dining at no extra cost (the line is good for foodies), the present 700-passenger ships suit people who prefer mid-sized ships to the large resort vessels. Gratuities are not included in the cruise fare.

Orion Expedition Cruises

This Australia-based expedition cruise company was created in 2004 by Sarina Bratton, specifically for soft expedition-style cruises to Antarctica, Australia's Kimberley region, and Papua New Guinea and its islands. The ship,

Orion, built in Germany, is a little gem, with hand-crafted cabinetry in every cabin, together with marble bathrooms and a health spa and gymnasium. Shore excursions range from camel safaris to snorkeling over pristine coral formations. In 2008, the company was sold to the US-based KSL Capital Partners. It will acquire a second ship, the 100-passenger *Clelia II* (chartered from Travel Dynamics International), scheduled to begin cruises in Southeast Asia in June 2011. Gratuities are not included in the cruise fare.

P&O Cruises (Australia)

This Australian division of P&O Cruises was founded in 1932. Today it provides fun in the sand and sun cruises for the beer and bikini brigade and their families, although the line is growing up to become more of a mainstream operator. With a maturing market, the company has larger, more contemporary hand-me-down ships from Carnival Corporation companies (mainly from the P&O Cruises stable), and continues to thrive, specializing in cruises in the Pacific and to New Zealand, with "Your Choice" dining. Coffee/tea-making facilities are provided in each cabin, and passengers will be pleased to learn that, in October 2010, the company scrapped automatic tipping on all ships.

Page & Moy Cruises

This travel company, based in Leicester in the UK, does not own any ships, but traditionally charters small ships for its many loyal passengers who want to travel widely aboard a ship with intimate dimensions. The company has long been booking and providing cruises and tour packages for low-budget passengers of mature years. Today it acts as a booking agency for cruises on many different lines and also sells river cruises. Gratuities are not included in the cruise fare.

Paul Gauguin Cruises

Created by Boston based tour operator Grand Circle Travel, Paul Gauguin Cruises took over the marketing and operation of *Paul Gauguin* in 2009 from Regent

Orion has a rendezvous with a seaplane in Australia.

Le Ponant is a sleek sail-cruise ship with three masts.

Seven Seas Cruises, who had operated the ship since its inception. Also in 2009, the ship was purchased by the Tahiti-based investor Richard Bailey, and his company Pacific Beachcomber, which owns Polynesian resort hotels (including four InterContinental Hotels). Gratuities are not included in the cruise fare.

Pearl Seas Cruises

Connecticut-based Pearl Seas Cruises, a sister company to American Cruise Lines, was founded to build and operate a ship for the upscale coastal cruising sector, but also usable in international waters. Being 2010 SOLAS-compliant (Safety of Life at Sea), it carries more passengers and is more luxurious than the ACL ships. Pearl Seas Cruises' first ship, the much-delayed *Pearl Mist*, made its debut in 2010 . The order for a second ship, originally to be built at the same Canadian shipyard, was canceled. The onboard service is provided by an international crew, unlike ACL's all-American crew. Gratuities are not included in the cruise fare.

Phoenix Reisen

Based in Bonn, Germany, the company for many years operated low-budget, tour-operator-style destination-intensive cruises for German speakers. It now has a loyal, more upscale audience and more contemporary ships, with better food and service (aboard *Amadea*). The company is praised for its extremely good itineraries, particularly on its world cruises, and is excellent value for money. In 2011 Phoenix will acquire another ship, *Artania* (formerly *Artemis* for P&O Cruises, but originally called *Royal Princess*). Gratuities are included in the cruise fare.

Plantours & Partner

This company, based in Bremen, Germany, provides low-budget cruises aboard its single small, chartered cruise ship, *Vistamar*, for German speakers. The Spanish-built ship suffers from poor build quality. The onboard food and service are well-meaning, but of only the most basic standard. The company also sells cruises on the rivers of Europe and Russia. Gratuities are not included in the cruise fare.

Plein Cap Cruises

The company (Plein Cap Croisières in French) was created in 1985 as part of the French TVL Voyages group, founded in 1981. It specializes in cruises and land vacations with a cultural bias toward French-speaking participants. Its cruise division chartered *Adriana* for many years, but in 2010 instead chartered a small ship, *Vistamar*. The company also sells river cruises.

Ponant Cruises

The company was founded in 1988 by Videau and Jean Emmanuel Sauve. It started life as La Compagnie des Iles du Ponant, is a subsidiary of CMA CGM (Compagnie Maritime Atlantique/Compagnie Générale Transatlantique, both of which started life in 1855, but which merged in 1977 to become the world's third largest container shipping company. The cruise company, whose head office is in Marseille, France, was created in 1988, and operates three boutique-sized ships – *Le Diamant, Le Levant*, and *Le Ponant* – for the French-speaking market. In 2004, the company acquired the Paris-based tour operator, Tapis Rouge International, which specializes in upscale travel. Two new ships – *Le Boreal*, introduced in 2010, and *L'Austral*, set to debut in 2011 – provide more space and more options for their passengers. Gratuities are not included in the cruise fare.

Pullmantur Cruises

The company was set up as part of Pullmantur, the Spain-based holiday tour operator founded in 1971. Its cruising division was established in 2000 when it bought *Oceanic* from the long-defunct Florida-based operator Premier Cruise Lines. In 2006, Pullmantur Cruises was purchased by Royal Caribbean Cruises. The company, mainly serving the Spanish-speaking market, operates

Quark Expeditions breaks the ice in Spitsbergen, Norway.

all-inclusive cruises for families with children to the Caribbean, Europe and, during the South American summer, serves the Brazilian market. While most passengers are Spanish, the company now also markets heavily to US and other cruisegoers. Gratuities are included in the cruise fare.

Quark Expeditions

The company was founded in 1991 by Lars Wikander, and silent-partner Christer Salen (formerly of Salen-Lindblad Cruises). It is based in Darien, Connecticut, and specializes in providing up-close-and-personal expedition cruises to some of the world's most remote regions and inaccessible areas.

In its formative years, Quark Expeditions chartered Russian ice-breakers to take adventurous, hardy outdoor types to the Polar regions, and has years of experience in taking participants to Antarctica. Quark Expeditions has always been committed to minimizing the environmental impact of operating in ecologically sensitive areas.

In 2007, it was sold to the UK's First Choice Holidays (founded in 1973), merged with Peregrine Shipping, and then in 2007 was bought, along with First Choice, by the large German travel company TUI.

Cruising with Quark Expeditions is all about being close to nature, wilderness, wildlife, off-the-beaten-path adventures, and learning. The company, an associate member of IAATO (Association of Antarctica Tour Operators), an association committed to the highest standards of responsible tourism to Antarctica, Quark Expeditions still specializes in chartering nuclear- and diesel-powered Russian icebreakers, the most powerful in the world, to provide participants with a truly memorable expedition experience. This is adventure cruising for toughies. Gratuities are not included in the cruise fare.

Regent Seven Seas Cruises

The company has a complicated history. It was born out of Seven Seas Cruises, which was originally based in San Francisco to market the cruise ship *Song of Flower* (belonging to "K"-Line, a cargo operator based in New Jersey) as well as expedition cruises aboard the chartered *Hanseatic* (then belonging to Hanseatic Tours). The lyre, logo of that ship, became RSSC's logo.

For many years, the company was part of the Carlson group, and operated as Radisson Seven Seas Cruises. Carlson Hospitality Worldwide ventured into cruising via its Radisson Hotels International division – hence, Radisson Diamond Cruises (when Radisson Diamond joined in 1992). In 1994 Radisson Diamond Cruises and Seven Seas Cruise Line merged to become Radisson Seven Seas Cruises, and in 2007 it became Regent Seven Seas Cruises.

It strives to pay close attention to detail and provide high-quality service aboard its small fleet of three small- and mid-sized cruise ships (*Seven Seas Mariner, Seven Seas Navigator,* and *Seven Seas Voyager*) operating world-wide itineraries.

In 2007 the company was bought by US-based investment group Apollo Management, and, together with Oceania Cruises, was placed under the umbrella of its Prestige Cruise Holdings. The company spent $40 million to refurbish its three ships in 2009–10.

It provides drinks-inclusive cruising, which means that drinks *and* gratuities are included in the fare. Passengers have to pay extra only for laundry services,

Regent Seven Seas Cruises employs a team of guest lecturers.

beauty services, casino and other personal expenditure. Shore excursions, however, are not included.

Saga Cruises

Saga, based in Folkestone, England, was created by Sydney de Haan as a company offering financial services and holidays to the over-60s (reduced to the over-50s in 1995 as the company's success grew). Its popular travel flourished because it was good at providing extra personal attention and competent staff. Instead of sending passengers to ships operated by other companies, it decided to purchase its own ships and market its own product under the Saga Holidays brand.

Saga Shipping (Saga Cruises), the cruising division of Saga Holidays, was set up in 1997 when it purchased *Saga Rose* (ex-*Sagafjord*), followed not long after by *Saga Ruby* (ex-*Vistafjord*) and, in 2010, *Saga Pearl II* (formerly *Astoria*).

Another brand, Spirit of Adventure, was added in 2006, the year that parent company Saga and Britain's Automobile Association merged. The cruise company is run mainly by former Cunard executives, with strong British seamanship and training, and its fleet manages to retain the feel of traditional, elegant, child-free cruising aboard *Saga Pearl II* and *Saga Ruby*. Saga Cruises offers single-seating dining, friendly, attentive service from a mainly Filipino hotel service crew, and its ships have many single-occupancy cabins. It takes care of all the many little details other lines have long forgotten.

Coffee and tea-making facilities are provided in each cabin. All gratuities are included in the cruise fare.

Sea Cloud Cruises

The company was founded in 1979 by a consortium of shipowners and investors known as the Hansa Treuhand (active in commercial vessel management, engineering, and construction), and has its headquarters in Hamburg, Germany. It owns and operates two tall ships (sailing vessels), the legendary *Sea Cloud* and *Sea Cloud II*, and two European rivercruise boats, *River Cloud I* and *River Cloud II*. Its latest tall ship, *Sea Cloud Hussar*, debuted in 2010.

The company has many corporate clients who charter the two tall ships, while a number of upscale cruise and travel companies sell cruises to individuals. The onboard style and product delivery is quite upscale, with elegant retro decor and fine food and service. Gratuities are not included in the cruise fare.

SeaDream Yacht Cruises

Larry Pimentel and his business partner Atle Brynestad jointly created the cruise line (Brynestad formerly founded Seabourn Cruise Line), purchasing the former Sea Goddess Cruises' ships and introducing them in 2002 to an audience anxious for exclusivity, personal pampering, and cuisine that is prepared à la minute.

The two ships, *SeaDream I* and *SeaDream II*, have been refreshed several times, and are often chartered by

TOP: the majestic *Royal Clipper* has 42 sails.
ABOVE: getting ready for lunch on *Silver Wind*.

companies or private individuals who appreciate the refined, elegant, but casual atmosphere on board. The 100-passenger ships operate year-round in the Caribbean and Mediterranean, and provide all-inclusive beverages and open-seating dining at all times, and a high degree of personalized service, all in a cozy, club-like atmosphere, with great attention to detail and personal idiosyncrasies. Atle Brynestad is now the company's chairman and sole owner. Gratuities are included in the cruise fare.

Silversea Cruises has generated a tremendous amount of loyalty from its frequent passengers, who view the ships as their own. All four Silversea ships feature teak verandas, and all-inclusive beverages. Open-seating dining prevails at all times, and the company is known for its partnership with the hospitality organization, Relais et Châteaux. A new, larger, 540-passenger all-suite luxury ship, *Silver Spirit*, debuted at the end of 2009.

Gratuities are included in the cruise fare.

Star Clippers

Swedish-born yachtsman Mikhail Krafft founded Star Clippers in 1991 with *Star Flyer* and then *Star Clipper*, both true tall ships. The company went on to build the largest tall ship presently sailing, the five-mast *Royal Clipper*. It is now building an even bigger tall ship. Good food and friendly service in a casual, laid-back setting, under the romance of sail (when there is enough wind), is what Star Clippers are all about – but the food variety and quality is extremely good.

The tall ships sail in the Caribbean, Mediterranean and Southeast Asia. Gratuities are not included in the cruise fare.

Swan Hellenic Cruises

Founded in 1954 By R.K. Swan, the company chartered small cruise ships for years. The company was purchased by P&O Cruises in 1982, and then it changed hands when Carnival Corporation merged with P&O in April 2004. In 2007, the Carnival Corporation disbanded Swan Hellenic, and its single ship (*Minerva II*) was transferred to the Princess Cruises fleet to become *Royal Princess* (now P&O Cruises' *Adonia*). Some months later, a semi-retired Lord Sterling purchased the brand from the Carnival Corporation and joined partners with the UK's Voyages of Discovery to be operated as a separate brand. So, the "swanners," as its intellectual passengers are called, now have their very own ship (*Minerva*).

The company's strengths are its program of highly academic lecturers and speakers, in a small ship setting that is unpretentious but comfortable, and includes gratuities, drinks (on Antarctic voyages), tailor-made shore excursions, and entrance fees to museums and places of interest. The company operates special-interest themes such as archaeology, history, nature and wildlife. Coffee and tea-making facilities are provided in each cabin. Gratuities are included in the cruise fare.

The Yachts of Seabourn

Originally founded in 1986 as Signet Cruise Line, the company, then owned by Norwegian industrialist Atle Brynestad, had to change its name in 1988 as a result of a lawsuit brought by a Texas ferry company that had already registered the name Signet Cruise Lines (no ships were ever built for cruising, however). Indeed, the company's first brochure was released under the Signet Cruise Lines name.

Silversea Cruises

Silversea Cruises is a mostly privately owned cruise line. It was founded in 1992 by the Lefebvre D'Ovidio family from Rome (previously co-owners of Sitmar Cruises: 90% partners being the Lefebvre D'Ovidio; 10% by V-Ships), and is based in Monaco.

Antonio Lefebvre D'Ovidio was a maritime lawyer and professor of maritime law before acquiring and operating cargo ships and ferries in the Adriatic. He took the family into partnership with Boris Vlasov's Vlasov Group (V-Ships) to co-own Sitmar Cruises until that company merged with Princess Cruises in 1988.

An unconventional shore excursion by The Yachts of Seabourn.

ring instead to leave ship operations, management and catering to specialist maritime companies. The company operates cruises for the whole family aboard its small fleet of ships. It also operates sub-brand Island Cruises, with just one ship for the ultra-casual market. The onboard currency is the British pound, and basic gratuities are included in the cruise price. The company owns its own airline, Thomsonfly (part of the TUI Travel group).

Transocean Cruises

Founded in 1954, Transocean Cruises (formerly Transocean Tours) has headquarters in Bremen, Germany. The company specializes in providing low-cost but high-value cruises aboard a ship under long-term charter (*Astor*), with traditional decor and excellent itineraries. Gratuities and port charges are included. In 2008, *Marco Polo*, a ship known for operating destination-intensive "soft-expedition" style cruises, was introduced. The company also sells river cruises, operated by chartered vessels under the banner of Transocean River Cruises. Gratuities are included in the cruise fare.

Travel Dynamics International

Founded by brothers George and Vasos Papagapitos, the company specializes in providing small and boutique cruise ships to culturally minded passengers. Long a provider of vacations and cruises to university alumni, cultural associations, and museum groups, the company seeks out unusual itineraries and destinations according to a group's interest or travel theme. The company is also known for its US Great Lakes cruises, and cruises to remote regions, as well as for its academically-trained lecturers. Gratuities are not included in the cruise fare.

In 1998, a consortium, which included the Carnival Corporation and Norwegian investors, bought Seabourn Cruise Line and merged its operations into Cunard Line, which was acquired from Kvaerner. The fleet then included its three present ships plus *Seabourn Goddess I* and *Seabourn Goddess II* (bought by SeaDream Yacht Cruises in 2002 and named *SeaDream I* and *SeaDream II*) and *Seabourn Sun* (which became Holland America Line's *Prinsendam*). The Carnival Corporation acquired 100% of Seabourn Cruise Line in 1999.

The company aims its product at affluent, sophisticated, well travelled North Americans, with small ships providing a high level of European-style service, open-seating dining, all-inclusive drinks, great attention to detail and personal pampering. Three new, larger ships join the company between 2009 and 2011. All three have an aft watersports platform, as well as more dining and spa options, more space, and more passengers. Seabourn Cruise Line was rebranded as The Yachts of Seabourn in 2009–10. Gratuities are included in the cruise fare.

Thomson Cruises

Thomson Cruises' first foray into cruising was in 1973 when it chartered two ships, *Calypso* and *Ithaca* (Ulysses Line). It was not a success, and the company withdrew from cruising two years later. Ulysses Line became known as Useless Line.

The company started again in 2002 after seeing rival tour operator Airtours operate ships successfully. Unlike Airtours' Sun Cruises, which no longer exists, Thomson Cruises charters its ships instead of owning them outright, prefer-

From sails to oars: *Wind Spirit* appeals to watersports devotees.

Zegrahm Expeditions organizes trips to Antarctica.

TUI Cruises

The German-owned TUI Group has several divisions, but started its own cruise line in 2009 with *Mein Schiff*, a large resort ship (ex *Celebrity Galaxy*) which underwent a massive reconstruction program. Targeted to families with children, the onboard product (particularly the food and service) is markedly superior to that of competitor AIDA Cruises. All cabins, for example, have their own espresso machine, and there is a wide choice of dining venues and food styles, with an emphasis on healthy eating. Much emphasis has also been placed on the wellness facilities. Gratuities are included in the cruise fare.

Venus Cruise

Founded in 1988, the company's headquarters are in Osaka, Japan. Venus Cruise was first known as Japan Cruise Line, which is owned by four ferry companies: Shin Nipponkai Ferry, Kyowa Shoji, Hankyu Ferry, and Kanko Kisen. As Japan Cruise Line, the company at first operated company and incentive charter cruises before branching out into cruises for individuals. The company, catering exclusively to Japanese speakers, has one ship, *Pacific Venus*, which operating an annual around-the-world cruise as well as shorter Asia-Pacific cruises. Gratuities are included in the cruise fare.

Voyages of Discovery

UK-based Roger Allard and Dudley Smith jointly founded the company to offer low-cost cruises aboard comfortable, roomy mid-sized ships, to UK-based passengers, but with good food and service. The company's *Discovery* is one of the former "Love Boats" of US television fame. The company went public in 2006 and, with the help of Lord Sterling of Plaistow, purchased Swan Hellenic Cruises. It now operates both brands from its headquarters in the south of England.

Windstar Cruises

Founded by New York-based Karl Andren in 1984 as Windstar Sail Cruises, the company built high-class sail-cruise ships with computer-controlled sails, outfitting them in a contemporary decor designed by Marc Held. The first ship, *Wind Star*, debuted in 1986 to much acclaim, and was followed by *Wind Spirit* (1988) and *Wind Surf* (1990).

Windstar Cruises was sold to Holland America Line in 1988. The company, with headquarters in Seattle, USA, was sold again in 2007 to the Ambassadors Cruise Group, wholly owned by Ambassadors International.

The onboard style is casual and unregimented, but smart, with service by Indonesian and Filipino crew. The ships carry watersports equipment, accessed from a retractable stern platform. Itineraries include off-the-beaten track ports not frequented by large resort ships. The onboard product is decidedly American casual, with unfussy bistro-style cuisine, and service that lacks finesse and the small details that could make it much better. Gratuities are not included in the cruise fare.

Zegrahm Expeditions

This small expeditions cruise company, which takes inquisitive travelers to remote or unusual destinations, including the Arctic and Antarctica, was founded in 1990 and bought in 2009 by TUI Travel. Although it doesn't own any ships, it charters high-quality specialized vessels. It also sells cruises operated by other expedition companies and operates safaris and small-group adventure vacations. Two- or three-week expedition cruises are headed by experienced leaders and expert naturalists. Gratuities are not included in the cruise fare. ❏

LIVING IN LUXURY

Of the 75-plus cruise lines operating internationally,
only a handful provide the kind of stylish ships
aboard which the word "no" is virtually unheard

L uxury cruises versus premium and standard (large resort ship) cruises are like the difference between a Bentley and a Hyundai. "Luxury cruising" should be a flawless combination of ship, facilities, food and service. Unfortunately, the word has been degraded by marketing people – you can even buy a "luxury" burger today – but the panel on the facing page tells you what the term ought to mean in a cruise ship.

Little and large

Size is important. Boutique and small ships can get into ports that larger ships can't. They can also get closer to the center of large cities. For example, in St. Petersburg, Russia large and mid-sized ships (such as those of Crystal Cruises and Regent Seven Seas Cruises) dock about one hour from the city center, while boutique ships such as those of Hapag-Lloyd Cruises, Silversea Cruises or The Yachts of Seabourn can dock right next to the Hermitage Museum in the heart of the city.

One area where "luxury" ships differ least from large resort ships is in shore excursions, particularly in the Caribbean and Alaska, where almost all cruise operators are obliged to use the same specialist tour operators ashore – simply because "luxury" is virtually unknown in these regions and local tour operators consider all cruise passengers to be the same. For example, when I checked a fleet of minivan vehicles in the Caribbean island of Grenada, several vehicles had wheel nuts missing; and when I checked two 45-passenger tour buses in Philadelphia, neither had a first aid kit on board. I have a whole bagful of similar examples.

SeaDream's yachts provide a setting for personal indulgence.

THE CRÈME DE LA CRÈME

These 18 ships (listed alphabetically, by company) belong to six cruise lines, and are the "cream" of the cruise industry in terms of style, finesse, staff training, cuisine, service, hospitality and finesse. Their individual facilities are fully reviewed in the ratings section of this book, and the Berlitz ratings awarded for accommodation, food, service, entertainment and so on indicate their particular strengths.

● CRYSTAL CRUISES
  Crystal Serenity, Crystal Symphony
● HAPAG-LLOYD CRUISES
  Europa
● REGENT SEVEN SEAS CRUISES
  Seven Seas Mariner, Seven Seas Navigator, Seven Seas Voyager
● SEADREAM YACHT CRUISES
  SeaDream I, SeaDream II
● SILVERSEA CRUISES
  Silver Cloud, Silver Shadow, Silver Spirit, Silver Whisper, Silver Wind
● THE YACHTS OF SEABOURN
  Seabourn Legend, Seabourn Odyssey, Seabourn Pride, Seabourn Sojourn, Seabourn Spirit

Large resort ships (those carrying more than 1,600 passengers) simply cannot provide the kind of personal service and attention to detail that the boutique/small ships can. Although you can book one of the largest suites afloat aboard a large ship, once you leave your "private living space" you'll have to mix with all other passengers, particularly if you want to go to a show, disembark at ports of call (think of the long lines at the gangway security checkpoint), or go on organized shore excursions. That's when you appreciate the fact that smaller may suit you better.

These are ships suited to those not seeking the active, family- and entertainment-driven cruise experiences that large ships resort offer. The ships, companies, and comparisons in this section provide ships, facilities and service levels hard to find elsewhere. While most of them boast about being the best, or boast the awards they receive annually from various magazines (whose respondents are almost never global in scope), not all provide the same degree of luxury, and there *are* differences in the cruise product delivered.

So, what are the differences?

Once you know the main differences, you'll be better equipped to choose the right cruise line and ship to provide the level of onboard food and service you are looking for. While most of the differences are immediately visible when you sail aboard (and compare) them all, some of the variations in style and service are more subtle. One thing is certain: the word "no" will be virtually unheard.

Some have more crew per passenger. Some have more expensive European crew than others. Some have better food and service. Some have entertainment, some don't. Some have more public space per passenger. It's important to weigh up the differences, so that you choose the right ship for the right reasons.

For example, the following facilities and services are found aboard the ships of Hapag-Lloyd Cruises, Sea-Dream Yacht Cruises and The Yachts of Seabourn, but not aboard the ships of Crystal Cruises, Regent Seven Seas Cruises, or Silversea Cruises.

● Anticipation is more widely practiced aboard the smaller ships, where staff training is better in terms of passenger recognition (remembering your name).
● Waiters escort female guests (waitresses escort male guests) to the dining table and to the dining room exit after meals.
● Relaxed embarkation/disembarkation at your leisure.
● Cabin stewardesses leave hand-written notes.
● There are no announcements, and no mindless background music in public rooms, accommodation hallways or elevators.
● The chef invites passengers to accompany him on visits to local food markets.

More space, better service

All 18 ships have an excellent amount of open deck and lounging space, and a high Passenger Space Ratio (almost all are above 40) when compared to large resort ships (which are typically under 35), the two Sea-Dreams being the exception.

Caribbean idyll: *Crystal Symphony* in St Thomas.

Almost all have a better Crew to Passenger Ratio than the large resort ships. In warm weather areas, the ships of SeaDream Yacht Cruises and The Yachts of Seabourn (all have fold-down platforms at the stern of each ship) provide jet skis, kayaks, snorkeling gear, windsurfers and the like at no extra cost, typically for one day each cruise (the others do not).

Hapag-Lloyd's *Europa* also has a fleet of Zodiac rigid inflatable craft for in-depth exploration and shore adventures, plus an ice-hardened hull and a crew who understand the culture of the passengers. And mattresses that are 7 ft (2.1 meters) long.

Dining

Fine dining is the highlight of ships in this category, and is more of an entertainment feature than the entertainment itself – if there is any. Good company and conversation are crucial. You can expect to find plenty of tables for two, a calm refined dining atmosphere, open or one seating dining, by candlelight (when permitted), high-quality china and silverware, large wine glasses, fresh flowers, a connoisseur wine list, and sommeliers who can discuss fine wines.

It's really about non-repetitive, highly creative menus, high-quality ingredients, moderate portions and attractive presentation, with fresh local fish and other items provided (when available) and cooked à la minute (not in batches), and meat of the highest grade. Caviar, foie gras, black/white truffles and other exotic foods, and fresh green vegetables (instead of frozen or canned vegetables) are provided. Caviar aboard *Europa* is from French farmed sturgeon, and is excellent, while caviar aboard most other ships in this category is from the American farmed hackleback variety of sturgeon (not as good). There should also be a choice of sea salt from different regions of the world; and olive oil from countries such as Greece, Italy, and Spain, for example.

Almost all the ships provide cloches for extra "wow" effect in the dining room service of main courses. Additionally, passengers are often invited to

The Yachts of Seabourn provide personal pampering.

visit local markets with the chef aboard the ships of Hapag-Lloyd Cruises, SeaDream Yacht Cruises, and The Yachts of Seabourn.

Some luxury ships provide even more special touches. *Europa,* for example, makes its own breakfast preserves. Strangely, Regent Seven Seas Cruises does not have fish knives – needed if you like to debone the Dover Sole yourself. *Europa* uses only loose tea (over 30 types) – all the others use teabags.

Typically, lunch and dinner menus are provided in your suite/cabin in advance, and special orders (ordering off menu) are often possible. Room service menus are extensive, and meals can be served, course by

HOW THE LUXURY SHIPS COMPARE

Ship	Company	Tonnage	Size	Pod Propulsion	Passenger space ratio
Crystal Serenity	Crystal Cruises	68,870	Mid-Size	Yes	62.6
Crystal Symphony	Crystal Cruises	51,044	Mid-Size	No	53.1
Europa	Hapag-Lloyd Cruises	28,437	Small	Yes	69.6
Seabourn Legend *	The Yachts of Seabourn	9.961	Boutique	No	46.9
Seabourn Odyssey	The Yachts of Seabourn	32,009	Small	No	71.1
Seabourn Pride *	The Yachts of Seabourn	9,975	Boutique	No	46.9
Seabourn Sojourn	The Yachts of Seabourn	32,000	Small	No	71.1
Seabourn Spirit *	The Yachts of Seabourn	9,975	Boutique	No	46.9
SeaDream I	SeaDream Yacht Cruises	4,253	Boutique	No	39.4
SeaDream II	SeaDream Yacht Cruises	4,253	Boutique	No	39.4
Seven Seas Mariner	Regent Seven Seas Cruises	48,015	Mid-Size	Yes	67.8
Seven Seas Navigator	Regent Seven Seas Cruises	28,550	Mid-Size	No	58.2
Seven Seas Voyager	Regent Seven Seas Cruises	41,827	Mid-Size	Yes	59.0
Silver Cloud	Silversea Cruises	16,927	Small	No	57.1
Silver Shadow	Silversea Cruises	28,258	Small	No	72.8
Silver Spirit	Silversea Cruises	36,009	Small	No	66.6
Silver Whisper	Silversea Cruises	28,258	Small	No	72.8
Silver Wind	Silversea Cruises	16,927	Small	No	57.1

* These ships also have a number of "French" balcony cabins with floor-to-ceiling doors that open for fresh air (the actual "balcony" is only about 12 inches/30 cm deep)

all alcoholic beverages. Crystal Cruises includes soft drinks. Regent, SeaDream, Seabourn and Silversea include all drinks (but only standard brands). Hapag-Lloyd Cruises does not include alcoholic drinks, because its passengers know and want their favorite brands, many of which are well above the level of standard brands carried by those cruise lines that do include alcoholic beverages, which are normally tailored to suit North American tastes.

Other differences

Aboard the ships of Regent Seven Seas Cruises and The Yachts of Seabourn, white plastic deck lounge chairs are provided. Aboard the ships of SeaDream Yacht Cruises they are made of teak (or other hardwood), and aboard Hapag-Lloyd Cruises' *Europa* they are made of aluminum and wood, and aboard the ships of Silversea Cruises they are made of aluminum.

Crystal Serenity, Crystal Symphony, Seven Seas Mariner, Seven Seas Navigator, and *Seven Seas Voyager* are mid-size ships (600–1,600 passengers) that include entertainment with production shows and cabaret acts. To a lesser extent, so do the Seabourn ships and Hapag-Lloyd's *Europa,* but the other ships do not have entertainment as such, but instead rely on their intimacy and friendliness, and promote after-dinner conversation or, aboard the ships of Silversea Cruises, individual specialist cabaret acts.

Regrettably, *Crystal Serenity* and *Crystal Symphony* hold art auctions, which seriously detract from the otherwise fine facilities, food and service, although they do have good-quality bistros (which none of the other ships do). ❑

course, in your suite/cabin, either on the balcony or inside on special portable tables (some ships do this better than others). It is also possible to have a special dinner set up on deck (wonderful in the right location), with all the finery and individual service you would expect of private dining.

Drinks: included or not?

Regent Seven Seas Cruises, SeaDream Yacht Cruises, The Yachts of Seabourn, and Silversea Cruises provide wine with dinner (Seabourn and Silversea also include wine with lunch), although the wines are typically young, and not from first-class houses. However, real premium brands and classic vintage wines cost extra.

Crystal Cruises and Hapag-Lloyd Cruises charge for

Crew to passenger ratio	Cabins (double)	Cabins w/balcony	Largest Suite (sq. m)	Smallest Cabin (sq. m)	Tips incl.	Water Sports Toys	Hand-held showers	Toiletries
1.7	550	466	125.0	21.0	No	No	Yes	Aveda
1.7	480	276	91.2	18.7	No	No	Yes	Aveda
1.5	204	168	85.0	33.0	Yes	No	Yes	Own brand
1.3	106	6	53.5	25.7	Yes	Yes	Yes	Therapies (Molton Brown)
1.3	225	199	133.6	27.5	Yes	Yes	Yes	Therapies (Molton Brown)
1.3	106	6	53.4	25.7	Yes	Yes	Yes	Therapies (Molton Brown)
1.3	225	199	133.6	27.5	Yes	Yes	Yes	Therapies (Molton Brown)
1.3	106	6	53.4	25.7	Yes	Yes	Yes	Therapies (Molton Brown)
1.2	54	0	45.5	18.1	Yes	Yes	Yes	Bulgari
1.2	54	0	45.5	18.1	Yes	Yes	Yes	Bulgari
1.6	354	354	142.0	28.0	Yes	No	Yes	Canyon Ranch
1.5	245	196	109.0	28.0	Yes	No	Yes	Canyon Ranch
1.6	354	354	130.0	33.0	Yes	No	Yes	Canyon Ranch
1.4	148	110	122.0	22.2	Yes	No	No	Bulgari
1.3	194	157	133.3	26.6	Yes	No	No	Bulgari
1.4	270	258	150.0	29.0	Yes	No	No	Bulgari
1.3	194	157	133.3	26.6	Yes	No	No	Bulgari
1.4	148	110	122.0	22.2	Yes	No	No	Bulgari

NOTE: Only *Europa* gives the true net (interior) measurement.
All the others provide gross measurements for their suites

THE BEST SHORE EXCURSIONS

Escorted tours in ports of call cost extra, but they are often
the best way to get a nutshell view of a destination and
make the most efficient use of your limited time ashore

Shore excursions used to be limited to city tours and venues that offered folkloric dances by local troupes. Today's excursions are almost limitless, and are very active, encompassing crocodile hunting in the Amazon, kayaking in Alaska, elephant riding in Thailand, or flying over Moscow in a MiG jet (fare $28,000). It's easily possible to spend far more on shore excursions on than on buying the cruise.

Most excursions are escorted by ship's staff, who will usually carry first-aid kits. If you explore independently and need medical help, you could risk missing the ship when it sails. Unless the destination is a familiar one, first-time cruisegoers are probably safer booking excursions organized by the ship and vetted by the cruise line. Also, if you have a problem during a tour, the cruise line should be able to sort it out on the spot.

If you do go it alone, always take the ship's port agent and telephone numbers with you, in case of emergencies (they are normally printed in the Daily Program). Allow plenty of time to get back to your ship before sailing time – the ship won't wait. Make sure your travel insurance covers you fully.

Note that if you book tours on your own, and it's a tender port where the ship has to remain at anchor offshore, you will need to wait until the ship's organized tours have been offloaded – which can take two or more hours aboard some of the large resort ships.

A TICKET TO RIDE

Many companies with large resort ships typically charge extra for shuttle buses to take you from the port or other docking area to a local city or town center. The port with the highest charge is Venice, Italy, where the transport is by motorboat, between the cruise terminals and St. Mark's Square.

How tiring are excursions?

Most tours will involve some degree of walking, and some require extensive walking. Most cruise lines grade their excursions with visual symbols to indicate the degree of fitness required.

Are there private excursions?

Yes, aboard some of the more upscale ships such as those of Hebridean Island Cruises, Hapag-Lloyd Cruises, Regent Seven Seas Cruises, SeaDream Yacht Cruises, The Yachts of Seabourn and Silversea Cruises, you can have shore excursions tailored to your specific needs. But even large resort ship lines like Norwegian Cruise Line (NCL) can book something special under its Freestyle Private Touring program.

What if my first choice is sold out?

Some excursions do sell out, owing to limited space or transport, but there can be last-minute cancellations. Check with the shore excursion manager on board.

What should I take with me?

Only what's necessary; leave any valuables aboard ship, together with any money and credit cards you do not plan to use. Groups of people are often targets for pickpockets in popular sightseeing destinations. Also, beware of excursion guides who give you a colored disk to wear for "identification" – they may be marking you as a "rich" tourist for local shopkeepers. It's always prudent to wear comfortable rubber-soled shoes, particularly in older ports when there may be cobblestones or other uneven surfaces.

How can I make a booking?

Aboard some ships, where shore excursions can be booked before the sailing date via the internet, they can sell out fast. So book early. Payment aboard ship is normally made via a ship's central billing system.

If you need to cancel a shore excursion, you

Venice, though crowded, is a perennially popular port of call.

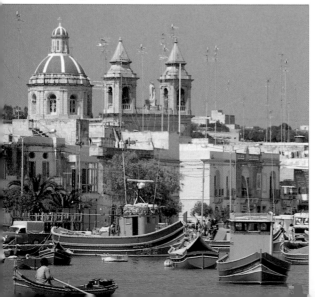

A street market in Ho Chi Minh City, Vietnam.

usually need to do so at least 24 hours before its advertised departure time. Otherwise, refunds are at the discretion of the cruise line, and refunds of pre-paid tickets booked over the internet can take a long time to make and incur currency losses. In many cases, you will be able to sell your ticket to another passenger. Tickets do not normally have names or cabin numbers on them, except those that involve flights or overland arrangements. Check with the shore excursion manager to make sure it's okay to resell.

How can I know which are good?

If it's your first cruise, try to attend the shore excursion briefing. Read the excursion literature and circle tours that appeal to you. Then go to the shore excursion office and ask any other questions you may have before you book.

A few helpful tips:

● Shore excursions are put together for general interest. If you want to see something that is not described in the excursion literature, do not take it. Go on your own or with friends.

● Brochure descriptions of shore excursions, often written by personnel who haven't visited the ports of call, can be imprecise. All cruise lines should adopt the following definitions in their descriptive literature and for their lectures and presentations: The term "visit" should mean actually entering the place or building concerned. The term "see" should mean viewing from the outside – as from a bus, for example.

● City excursions are basically superficial. To get to know a city intimately, go alone or with a small group. Go by taxi or bus, or explore on foot.

● If you do not want to miss the major sightseeing attractions in each port, organized shore excursions provide a good solution. They also allow you to meet fellow passengers with similar interests.

● In the Caribbean, many sightseeing tours cover the same ground, regardless of the cruise line you sail with. Choose one and then do something different in the next port. The same is true of the history and archaeology excursions in the Greek Islands, where the same ancient gods will put in frequent appearances.

What if I lose my ticket?

Report lost or misplaced tickets to the shore excursion manager. Aboard most ships, excursion tickets, once sold, become the sole responsibility of the buyer, and the cruise line is not generally able to issue replacements. ❑

GOING ASHORE INDEPENDENTLY – AND SAFELY

If you hire a taxi for sightseeing, negotiate the price in advance, and don't pay until you get back to the ship or to your destination. If you are with friends, hiring a taxi for a full- or half-day sightseeing trip can often work out far cheaper than renting a car – and it's probably safer. Try to find a driver who speaks your language.

Exploring independently is ideal in the major cruise ports of Alaska, the Bahamas, Bermuda, the Caribbean, the Mexican Riviera, the Canary Islands, the Mediterranean, Aegean ports, and the South Pacific's islands. If you don't speak the local language, carry some identification (but not your passport, unless required), the name of your ship and the area in which it is docked. If the ship is anchored and you take a launch tender ashore, observe landmarks near the landing place, and write down the location. This will help if you get lost and need to take a taxi back to the launch.

Some small ships provide an identification tag or boarding pass at the reception desk or gangway, to be handed in each time you return to the ship. Remember that ships have schedules – and sometimes tides – to meet, and they won't wait for you if you return late. If you are in a launch port in a tropical area and the weather changes for the worse, the ship's captain could well make a decision to depart early to avoid being hemmed in by an approaching storm; it has happened, especially in the Caribbean. If it does, locate the ship's agent in the port – he's likely to be carrying a walkie-talkie – who will try to get you back.

Planning on going to a quiet, secluded beach to swim? First check with the cruise director or shore excursion manager, as certain beaches may be considered off-limits because of a dangerous undertow, drug pushers, or persistent hawkers. And don't even think of going diving alone – even if you know the area well.

100 POPULAR SHORE EXCURSIONS AROUND THE WORLD

THE CARIBBEAN

Antigua
❶ Tour to Shirley Heights and Nelson's Dockyard
Aruba, Netherlands Antilles
❷ Full-day Jeep eco-adventure trip
Barbados
Party cruise aboard the *Jolly Roger* pirate boat
Grand Cayman
❸ Go snorkeling with the sting rays at Sting Ray City
Grenada
❹ Eco-hiking tour to the Seven Sisters waterfall
Hamilton, Bermuda
❺ Guided Walking Tour of the former capital, St George's
Jamaica
❻ Excursion to Dunn's River Falls and Prospect Plantation (Ocho Rios)
❼ Horseback riding on the beach (Montego Bay, Ocho Rios)
❽ Zip-line forest canopy tour
Nassau, Bahamas
❾ Go swimming with the dolphins
San Juan, Puerto Rico
❿ El Yunque Rain Forest Tour & Hike
St Lucia
⓫ Jungle Eco-Tour by Jeep
St Maarten, Netherlands Antilles
⓬ Join the America's Cup Regatta Adventure tour and compete in an actual yacht race
St Thomas, US Virgin Islands
⓭ The Coral World Underwater Aquarium and Island Drive Tour
⓮ "Screemin' Eagle" Jet Boat thrill ride
Tortola, British Virgin Islands
⓯ Hiking tour to the peak of Sage Mountain (National Park)
Virgin Gorda, British Virgin Islands
⓰ Trip to "The Baths," exotic pools and grottos formed by giant boulders

MEXICO / CENTRAL AMERICA

Acapulco, Mexico
⓱ Excursion to see the rock divers
⓲ Tour to the Silver City of Taxco
Belize, Central America
⓳ Horseback riding and more in the jungles of Belize
Cabo San Lucas, Mexico
⓴ Personal dolphin encounter (for children) at the Cabo Dolphin Center

Ziplining in Belize during a Norwegian Cruise Line shore excursion.

Cozumel, Mexico
㉑ Tour to 12th-century Mayan ruins of Tulum and Xel-Ha national park

EUROPE AND THE BALTIC

Amsterdam, Holland
㉒ Go to the Anne Frank Museum
Athens (Piraeus, the port for Athens), Greece
㉓ Tour to the Acroplis and museums of ancient Athens
Barcelona, Spain
㉔ City tour to see Gaudi's architecture, the Sagrada Familia cathedral, and the Ramblas
Casablanca, Morocco
㉕ Casablanca, including the Hassan II Grand Mosque, and Rabat
Catania/Messina, Sicily
㉖ Visit to Mt. Etna and Taormina
㉗ Sicilian Cooking Class tour
Copenhagen, Denmark
㉘ Guided walking tour of the famed Tivoli Gardens
Dublin, Ireland
㉙ Visit the original Guinness brewery
Dubrovnik, Croatia
㉚ Walking tour of the old walled city
Edinburgh, Scotland
㉛ Visit Edinburgh Castle and the city
㉜ The Whisky Distillery Tour
Flam/Gudvangen
㉝ Take the mountain railway excursion from Flam to Gudvangen
Helsinki, Finland
㉞ Art, city highlights and Sibelius concert tour

Istanbul, Turkey
㉟ Tour to Topkapi Palace and the Grand Bazaar
Kusadasi
㊱ Tour to historic Ephesus, and the house of the Virgin Mary
La Coruna, Spain
㊲ Tour to Santiago de Compostela, home to the mystery of St James
Lisbon, Portugal
㊳ Tour to the Alfama (old) quarter of Lisbon and the Maritime Museum
Livorno, Italy
㊴ Full-day tour to Florence and the Leaning Tower of Pisa
London, England
㊵ River cruise along the historic River Thames for a different view of London
㊶ London by Night, including a West End musical or play
Madeira, Portugal
㊷ The toboggan ride excursion
Monte Carlo, Monaco
㊸ Tour to the Royal Palace and Grand Casino (jacket and tie required)
Naples, Italy
㊹ Tour to the Isle of Capri by boat to visit the famous Blue Grotto caves
Nice, France
㊺ Tour to the medieval hilltop village of Eze and the Corniche
Palma de Mallorca
㊻ Tour to former Carthusian monastery of Valldemosa (Frederick Chopin and George Sand lived here in 1838)
Rhodes, Greece
㊼ Follow in the footsteps of St Paul

Rome (Civitavecchia, the port for Rome), Italy
㊽ Guided "Roman Holiday" walking tour, including the Colosseum
㊾ Visit the Vatican's Sistine Chapel
Santorini, Greece
㊿ Donkey ride tour up the hillside
Sorrento, Italy
51 Visit to the ruins of Pompeii, the Amalfi Coast and Sorrento
St Petersburg, Russia
52 Guided walking tour through the Hermitage Museum
53 Excursion to St Catherine's Summer Palace
54 Night tour to a ballet or classical music concert at the Mariinsky Theater
Stockholm, Sweden
55 Tour to the Nobel Prize Museum
56 Tour to the Viking Museum and the warship *Wasa*
Venice, Italy
57 Romantic gondola ride excursion
58 Guided walking tour to the Guggenheim Museum
Warnemunde, Germany
59 Excursion to Berlin and the Brandenburg Gate

Reykyavik, Iceland
60 Tour to the warm geothermal waters of the Blue Lagoon

Aqaba, Jordan
61 Tour to the "Rose Red City" of Petra
Dubai, United Arab Emirates
62 4 x 4 Dune Drive Safari Tour
Male, Seychelles
63 Flightseeing of the atolls and inlets
Mumbai, India
64 Mumbai City Sights
65 Buddhist Trail tour to Kanheri Caves
Alexandria or Port Said, Egypt
66 Tour to the amazing temple of Karnak in Luxor
Sharm el Sheik, Egypt
67 Go diving and snorkeling
Tripoli, Libya
68 Tour to historic Leptis Magna and Tripoli's Medina

Hilo, Hawaii
69 Kilauea Volcano tour in Volcanoes National Park

Juneau, Alaska
70 Flightseeing trip to Mendenhall Glacier, and Alaska salmon bake
Ketchikan, Alaska
71 Misty Fjords flightseeing trip
Key West, Florida
72 The Conch Train Tour in Ernest Hemingway's favorite city
Los Angeles, California
73 Tour past the Hollywood homes of top movie stars
New York City
74 Take a Circle Line boat cruise around Manhattan
Skagway, Alaska
75 The historic White Pass & Yukon Route Railway train tour
Sitka, Alaska
76 Sea Otter and Wildlife Quest

Auckland, New Zealand
77 Tour to one of West Auckland's wineries and micro-breweries
Hamilton Island, Australia
78 Cruise/tour to Great Barrier Reef
Melbourne, Australia
79 Guided walking and tram tour, including the Gold Treasury
80 Shark diving in the aquarium tour on the banks of the Yarra River

Floatplane rides are popular in Alaska.

Sydney, Australia
81 Full-day catamaran tour taking in the Blue Mountains and Featherdale Wildlife Park

Bali, Indonesia
82 Balinese music and dance show
Bangkok (Laem Chabang, the port for Bangkok), Thailand
83 Tour to the Royal Palace and the sacred halls of Wat Phra Kaew
Ha Long Bay, Vietnam
84 Junk tour through the misty waters and limestone monuments
Ho Chi Minh City, Vietnam
85 Tour to the (Vietnam) War Museum
Hong Kong, China
86 The Harbour Bay cruise tour
Kuala Lumpur, Malaysia
87 Visit the Petronas Twin Tower building and night market
Osaka, Japan
88 Tour to Kyoto, Japan's former capital, and the monuments of the ancient city, now a Unesco World Heritage site
Singapore
89 The Night Safari Tour
Yokohama, Japan
90 Tour to the famous Ginza shopping area in Tokyo
91 Kabuki Theater Performance tour

Rio de Janeiro, Brazil
92 Tour to Sugar Loaf Mountain
93 Corcovado Tour & Christ the Redeemer Monument
94 **Buenos Aires, Argentina**
Steak and Tango night tour
Ushuaia, Argentina
95 Ride world's southernmost train
Puerto Madryn, Chile
96 The Penguin Safari tour (encounter 250,000 penguins, and the landscape of Patagonia)

Cape Town, South Africa
97 Cape Town/Table Top Mountain
98 Vintage car tour to Mount Nelson Hotel for afternoon tea
Mombasa, Kenya
99 Tour to Tsavo National Park (Kenya's oldest game preserve)
Walvis Bay, Namibia
100 Moon landscape and Welwitschia Plains Tour

THIS YEAR'S STAR PERFORMERS

Having reviewed 285 cruise ships, Berlitz names
the top-rating ships for 2011 and explains
why they scored as highly as they did

THE WORLD'S HIGHEST RATED CRUISE SHIP

Despite constant cruise company claims that theirs has been named the "Best Cruise Line" or "Best Cruise Ship," *there really is no such thing* – only what's right for you. Most ship owners want to be a "luxury" cruise operator, and most passengers want to sail aboard one of the top-rated "luxury" ships. But few operators can really deliver a ship, product, and crew worthy of five Berlitz stars. For this 2011 edition, only one ship has achieved the score required for it to be awarded membership in this most exclusive club.

Europa   (Hapag Lloyd Cruises)   1,853 points   ★★★★★+

Why? Because there is outstanding cuisine and attentive, friendly, very attentive, yet unobtrusive personal service from a staff dedicated to working aboard the world's finest cruise ship. But it's not just the ship itself and its facilities and appointments that contribute to the ship's high rating – it's also in the extensive array of details and personal attention from a fine, dedicated crew. It all adds up to the very best cruise ship and cruise experience available today – unless you own a private motor yacht. Also, thanks to the pod propulsion system, there is absolutely no vibration anywhere.

Naturally, *Europa* is not a cheap ship, but one of the reasons for its continuing success is that the food is creatively produced using high-quality ingredients. The ship also delivers excellent itineraries, taking passengers to many ports of call off the beaten track and inaccessible to larger cruise ships. Although *Europa* is now 11 years old, it looks almost new, thanks to the dedication of its crew and owners.

THE TOP 10 LARGE RESORT SHIPS		
(more than 1,600 passengers)		
Queen Mary 2 (Grill Class)	1,702	★★★★★
Queen Victoria (Grill Class)	1,671	★★★★★
Celebrity Eclipse	1,612	★★★★★
Celebrity Equinox	1,611	★★★★★
Celebrity Solstice	1,611	★★★★★
MSC Fantasia (Yacht Club)	1,570	★★★★★
MSC Splendida (Yacht Club)	1,570	★★★★★
Celebrity Constellation	1,568	★★★★★
Celebrity Millennium	1,568	★★★★★
Celebrity Summit	1,568	★★★★★

THE TOP 10 MID-SIZE SHIPS		
(600–1,600 passengers)		
Crystal Serenity	1,702	★★★★★
Crystal Symphony	1,701	★★★★★
Asuka II	1,685	★★★★★
Seven Seas Voyager	1,654	★★★★★
Seven Seas Mariner	1,651	★★★★★
Prinsendam	1,642	★★★★★
Amadea	1,600	★★★★★
Nautica	1,575	★★★★★
Insignia	1,574	★★★★★
Regatta	1,572	★★★★★

ABOVE: *Queen Victoria*'s captain.
LEFT: *Europa* has a driving range and a golf simulator room.

THE TOP 10 SMALL SHIPS		
(200–600 passengers)		
Europa	1,853	★★★★★+
Seabourn Odyssey	1,787	★★★★★
Seabourn Sojourn	1,787	★★★★★
Seabourn Legend	1,774	★★★★★
Silver Spirit	1,772	★★★★★
Seabourn Spirit	1,770	★★★★★
Seabourn Pride	1,769	★★★★★
Silver Whisper	1,753	★★★★★
Silver Shadow	1,750	★★★★★
Silver Wind	1,669	★★★★★
Silver Cloud	1,664	★★★★★

THE TOP 10 BOUTIQUE SHIPS		
(50–200 passengers)		
SeaDream II	1,788	★★★★★
SeaDream I	1,786	★★★★★
Hanseatic	1,746	★★★★★
Sea Cloud	1,704	★★★★★
Sea Cloud II	1,702	★★★★★
Prince Albert II	1,684	★★★★★
Hebridean Princess	1,680	★★★★★
Orion	1,612	★★★★★
Corinthian II	1,546	★★★★
Island Sky	1,540	★★★★

HOW WE EVALUATE THE SHIPS

Their facilities count, of course, but just as important are the standards of food, service, staff and hospitality

I have been evaluating and rating cruise ships and the onboard product professionally since 1980. In addition, I receive regular reports from my team of five trained assessors. The ratings are conducted with *total objectivity*, from a set of predetermined criteria and a modus operandi designed to work *globally*, not just regionally, across the entire spectrum of ocean-going cruise ships today, in all segments of the marketplace.

There really is no "best cruise line in the world" or "best cruise ship" – only the ship and cruise that is right for you. After all, it's the overall enjoyment of a cruise as a vacation that's really important. Therefore, different criteria are applied to ships of different sizes, styles, and market segments throughout the world (people of different nationalities seek different things in their vacation).

The evaluation and rating of cruise ships is about as contrary to football as you can get. In football, the goalposts are always in the same place. But with cruise ships, they keep changing as the industry evolves and matures. Ship owners, cruise operators, wholesalers and tour packagers keep redefining their product, pricing, and marketing strategies in order to fill ships and make a profit.

This section includes 285 oceangoing cruise ships in service (or due to enter service) and chosen by the author for inclusion when this book was completed. Almost all except the newest ships have been carefully evaluated, taking into account around 400 separate items based on personal cruises, visits and revisits to ships, as well as observations and comments from my team. These are channeled into 20 major areas, each with a possible 100 points. The maximum possible score for any ship is therefore 2,000 points.

For the sake of clarity and user-friendliness, scores are further channeled into five main sections (Ship, Accommodation, Food, Service, and Cruise Operation).

Cruise lines, ship owners, and operators should note that the ratings may be adjusted annually as a result of increased competition, the introduction of newer ships with better facilities, and other market- or passenger-driven factors.

The ratings more reflect the *standards* of the cruise product delivered to passengers (the software: dining experience, and the service and hospitality aspects of the cruise), and less the physical plant (the hardware). Thus, although a ship may be the latest, most stunning vessel in the world in terms of design and decor, if the food, service, staff, and hospitality are not so good, the scores and ratings will reflect these aspects more clearly.

The stars beside the name of the ship at the top of each page relate directly to the Overall Rating. The highest number of stars awarded is **five stars** (★★★★★), and the lowest is one star. This system is universally recognized throughout the hospitality industry. A plus (+) indicates that a ship deserves just that little bit more than the number of stars attained. However, I must emphasize that it is the number of points achieved rather than the number of stars attained that perhaps is more meaningful to anyone comparing ships.

The star system

★★★★★+	1,851–2,000 points
★★★★★	1,701–1850 points
★★★★+	1,551–1,700 points
★★★★	1,401–1,550 points
★★★+	1,251–1,400 points
★★★	1,101–1,250 points
★★+	951–1,100 points
★★	801–950 points
★+	650–800 points
★	501–650 points

What the ratings mean

1,851–2,000 points   ★★★★★ +
You can expect an outstanding top-class cruise experience – it doesn't get any better than this. It should be truly memorable, and with the highest attention to detail, finesse, and personal service (how important you are made to feel is critical). The decor

The award-winning *Europa* in Hamburg, Germany.

The Cellarmasters Bar aboard *Celebrity Solstice*.

must be elegant and tasteful, measured by restraint and not flashiness, with fresh flowers and other decorative touches in abundance, and the layout of the public rooms might well follow *feng shui* principles.

Any ship with this rating must be just about unsurpassable in the cruise industry, and it has to be very, very special, with service and hospitality levels to match. There must be the very highest quality surroundings, comfort and service levels, the finest and freshest quality foods, including all breads and rolls baked on board. Highly creative menus, regional cuisine, and dining alternatives should provide maximum choice and variety, and special orders will be part of the dining ritual.

Dining room meals (particularly dinners) are expected to be grand, memorable affairs, correctly served on the finest china, with a choice of wines of suitable character and vintage available, and served in the correct-sized sommelier glasses of the highest quality (Reidel or Schott).

The service staff will take pleasure in providing you with the ultimate personal, yet unobtrusive, attention with the utmost of finesse, and the word "no" should not be in their vocabulary. This really is the very best of the best in terms of refined, unstructured living at sea, but it is seriously expensive.

1,701–1,850 points ★★★★★
You can expect a truly excellent and memorable cruise experience, with the finesse and attention to detail commensurate with the amount of money paid. The service and hospitality levels will be extremely high from all levels of officers and staff, with strong emphasis on fine hospitality training (all service personnel members *must* make you feel important).

The food will be commensurate with the high level expected from what is virtually the best possible, while the service should be very attentive yet unobtrusive. The cuisine should be memorable, with ample taste. Special orders should never be a problem, with a creative cuisine of a very high standard. There must be a varied selection of wines, which should be served in glasses of the correct size (not simply a standard size glass for white and one for red wines).

Entertainment is expected to be of prime quality and variety. Again, the word "no" should not be in the vocabulary of any member of staff aboard a ship with this rating. A cruise aboard a ship with this high rating may well cause damage to your bank statement, particularly if you choose the most spacious grades of accommodation. Few things will cost extra once you are on board, and brochures should be more "truthful" than those for ships with a lower rating.

1,551–1,700 points ★★★★ +
You should expect to have a high-quality cruise experience that will be quite memorable, and just a little short of being excellent in all aspects. Perhaps the personal service and attention to detail could be slightly better, but, nonetheless, this should prove to be a fine all-round cruise experience, in a setting that is extremely clean and comfortable, with few lines anywhere, a caring attitude from service personnel, and a good standard of entertainment that appeals to a mainstream market.

The cuisine and service will be well rounded, with mostly fresh ingredients and varied menus that should appeal to almost anyone, served on high quality china.

All in all, this should prove to be an extremely well rounded cruise experience, probably in a ship that is new or almost new. There will probably be less "extra cost" items than ships with a slightly lower rating, but you get what you pay for these days.

1,401–1,550 points ★★★★

You should expect to have a very good quality all-round cruise experience, most probably aboard a modern, highly comfortable ship that will provide a good range of facilities and services. The food and service will be quite decent overall, although decidedly not as "gourmet" and fanciful as the brochures with the always-smiling faces might have you believe.

The service on board will be well organized, although it may be a little robotic and impersonal at times, and only as good as the cruise line's training program allows. You may notice a lot of things cost extra once you are on board, although the typically vague brochure tells you that the things are "available" or are an "option." However, you should have a good time, and your bank account will be only moderately damaged.

1,251–1,400 points ★★★ +

You should expect to have a decent quality cruise experience, from a ship where the service levels should be good, but perhaps without the finesse that could be expected from a more upscale environment. The crew aboard any ship achieving this score should reflect a positive attitude with regard to hospitality, and a willingness to accommodate your needs, up to a point. Staff training will probably be in need of more attention to detail and flexibility.

Food and service levels in the dining room(s) should be reasonably good, although special or unusual orders might prove more difficult. There will probably be a number of extra-cost items you thought were included in the price of your cruise – although the brochure typically is vague and tells you that the things are "available" or are an "option."

1,101–1,250 points ★★★

You can expect a reasonably decent, middle-of-the-

Having a decently sized balcony enhances the cruise.

road cruise experience, with a moderate amount of space and quality in furnishings, fixtures, and fittings. The cabins are likely to be a little on the small side (dimensionally challenged). The food and service levels will be quite acceptable, although not at all memorable, and somewhat inflexible with regard to special orders, as almost everything is standardized.

Crew attitude could certainly be improved, the level of hospitality and cleanliness will be moderate but little more, and the entertainment provided will probably be weak. A good option, however, for those looking for the reasonable comforts of home without pretentious attitudes, and little damage to their bank statement.

951–1,100 points ★★ +

You should expect to have a cruise experience that will be average in terms of accommodation (typically with cabins that are dimensionally challenged), quality of the ship's facilities, food, wine list, service, and hospitality levels, in surroundings that are unpretentious. In particular, the food and its service will probably be disappointing.

There will be little flexibility in the levels of service, hospitality, staff training and supevision, which will be no better than poor. Thus, the overall experience will be commensurate with the small amount of money you paid for the cruise.

801–950 points ★★

You should expect to have a cruise experience of modest quality aboard a ship that is probably in need of more attention to maintenance and service levels, not to mention hospitality. The food may be quite tasteless and homogenized, and of low quality, and service will leave much to be desired in terms of attitude, which will tend to be mediocre at best. Staff training is likely to be minimal, and turnover may be high. The "end-of-pier" entertainment could well leave you wanting to read a good book.

651–800 points ★ +

You can expect to have only the most basic cruise experience, with little or no attention to detail, from a poorly trained staff that is probably paid low wages and to whom you are just another body. The ship will, in many cases, probably be in need of much maintenance and upgrading, and will probably have few facilities.

Cleanliness and hygiene may well be questionable, and there will be absolutely no finesse in personal service levels, with poor attitude from the crew, and dismal entertainment as significant factors in the low score and rating. On the other hand, the price of a cruise is probably alluringly low.

501–650 points ★

You can expect to have a cruise experience that is the absolute bottom of the barrel, with almost nothing in

RCI's Flowrider is a neat feature aboard some ships.

terms of hospitality or finesse. You can forget about attention to detail – there won't be any. This will be the kind of experience that would equal a stay in the most basic motel, with few facilities, a poorly trained, uncaring staff, and a ship that is in need of better maintenance and upgrading.

The low cost of a cruise aboard any cruise ship with this rating should provide a strong clue to the complete absence of any quality. This will be particularly evident in the areas of food, service, and entertainment. In other words, this could well be a totally forgettable cruise experience.

Distribution of points

These are the percentage of the total points available which are allocated to each of the main areas evaluated:

- **The Ship**   25%
- **Accommodation**   10%
- **Cuisine**   20%
- **Service**   20%
- **Entertainment**   5%
- **The Cruise Experience**   20%

These last two categories may be combined for boutique ships, tall ships, and expedition ships.

The Ship

Hardware/Maintenance/Safety

This score reflects the general profile and condition of the ship (hardware), its age and maintenance, hull condition, exterior paint, decking and caulking, swimming pool and surrounds, deck furniture, shore tenders, lifeboats, life rafts, and other safety items. It also reflects interior cleanliness (public restrooms, elevators, floor coverings, wall coverings, stairways, passageways, and doorways), food preparation areas, refrigerators, garbage handling, compacting, and incineration, and waste disposal facilities.

Outdoor Facilities/Space

This score reflects the overall space per passenger on open decks, crowding, swimming pools/ whirlpools and their surrounds, lido deck areas, number and type of deck lounge chairs (with or without cushioned pads) and other deck furniture, outdoor sports facilities, shower enclosures and changing facilities, towels, and quiet areas (those without music).

Interior Facilities/Space/Flow

This score reflects the use of common interior public spaces, including enclosed promenades; passenger flow and points of congestion; ceiling height; lobby areas, stairways, and all passenger hallways; elevators; public restrooms and facilities; signage, lighting, air-conditioning and ventilation; and degree of comfort and density.

Decor/Furnishings/Artwork

This score reflects the overall interior decor and color scheme; hard and soft furnishings, wood (real, imitation, or veneer) paneling, carpeting (tuft density, color, and practicality), fit and finish (seams and edging), chairs (comfort, height, and support), ceilings and decor treatments, reflective surfaces, artwork (paintings, sculptures, and atrium centerpieces), and lighting.

Spa/Fitness Facilities

This score reflects any health spa, wellness center, and fitness facilities; location, accessibility and noise levels; lighting and flooring materials; fitness and muscle-training machines and other equipment; fitness programs; sports and games facilities; indoor swimming pools; whirlpools; grand baths; aqua-spa pools; saunas and steam rooms; rasul, the various types of massage, and other treatment rooms; changing facilities; jogging and walking tracks; and promenades.

Accommodation

Cabins: Suites and Deluxe Grades

This score reflects the design and layout of all grades of suites and deluxe grade cabins, private balconies (whether full floor-to-ceiling partition or part partitions,

Cabin aboard *Carnival Freedom*, which scores ★★★+.

balcony lighting, balcony furniture). Also beds/berths, furniture (its placement and practicality), cabinetry, and other fittings; closets and other hanging space, drawer space, and bedside tables; vanity unit, bathroom facilities, washbasin, cabinets, and toiletries storage; lighting, air-conditioning, and ventilation; audiovisual facilities; quality and degree of luxury; artwork; bulkhead insulation, noise, and vibration levels. Suites should not be so designated unless the sleeping room is completely separate from the living area.

Some large resort ships now have whole decks devoted to superior grade accommodation, with a significant difference between this accommodation and that of "standard" cabins.

Also the soft furnishings and details such as the information manual (list of services); paper and postcards (including personalized stationery); telephone directory; laundry lists; tea- and coffeemaking equipment; flowers (if any); fruit (if any); bathroom personal amenities kits, bathrobes, slippers, and the size, thickness, quality, and material content of towels.

Cabins: Standard Sizes

This score reflects the design and layout (whether outside or inside), beds/berths, furniture (its placement and practicality), and other fittings. Also taken into account: closets and other hanging space, drawer space, bedside tables, and vanity unit; bathroom facilities, washbasin, cabinets, and toiletries storage; lighting, air-conditioning and ventilation; audiovisual facilities; quality and degree of fittings and furnishings; artwork; bulkhead insulation, noise, and vibration levels.

In addition, we have taken into account the usefulness of the information manual (directory of services); paper and postcards (including stationery); telephone directory; laundry lists; tea- and coffee-

making equipment; flowers (if any); fruit (if any); and bathroom amenities kits, bathrobes, slippers, and the size, thickness, quality, and material content of towels.

Cuisine

Food is one of the main features of most vacations. Cruise lines put maximum emphasis on promising passengers how good their food will be, often to the point of being unable to deliver what is promised. Generally, the standard of food is good. The rule of thumb is: if you were to eat out in a good restaurant, what would you expect? Does the ship meet your expectations? Would you come back again for the food?

There are perhaps as many different tastes as there are passengers. The "standard" market cruise lines cater to a wide range of tastes, while the more exclusive

Douglas Ward checks the quality of spa towels.

cruise lines can offer better quality food, cooked individually to your taste. As in any good restaurant, you get what you pay for.

Dining Room/Cuisine

This score reflects the physical structure of dining rooms; window treatments; seating (alcoves and individual chairs, with or without armrests); lighting and ambience; table set-ups; the quality and condition of linen, china, and cutlery; and table centerpieces (flowers). It also reflects menus, food quality, presentation, food combinations, culinary creativity, variety, design concepts, appeal, taste, texture, palatability, freshness, color, balance, garnishes, and decorations; appetizers, soups, pastas, flambeaus, tableside cooking; fresh fruit and cakes; the wine list (and connoisseur wine list), price range, and wine service. Alternative dining venues are also checked for menu variety, food and service quality, decor, seating and noise levels.

The Yachts of Seabourn offer tempting hors d'oeuvres.

Informal Dining/Buffets

This score reflects the hardware (including the provision of hot and cold display units, sneeze guards, "active" stations, tongs, ice containers and ladles, and serving utensils); buffet displays (which have become quite disappointing and institutionalized); presentation; trays and set-ups; correct food temperatures; food labeling; breakfast, luncheon, deck buffets, midnight buffets, and late-night snacks; decorative elements such as ice carvings; and staff attitude, service, and communication skills.

Quality of Ingredients

This score reflects the overall quality of ingredients used, including consistency and portion size; grades of meat, fish, and fowl; and the price paid by the cruise line for its food product per passenger per day. It is the quality of ingredients that most dictates the eventual presentation and quality of the finished product as well as its taste. Also included is the quality of tea and coffee (better quality ships are expected to provide more palatable tea and coffee).

Tea/Coffee/Bar Snacks

This score reflects the quality and variety of teas and coffees available (including afternoon teas/coffees and their presentation); whether mugs or cups and saucers are presented or available; whether milk is served in the correct open containers or in sealed packets; whether self-service or graciously served. The quality of such items as cakes, scones, and pastries, as well as bar/lounge snacks, hot and cold canapés, and hors d'oeuvres also forms part of this section.

Service

Dining Room

This score reflects the professionalism of the restaurant staff: the maître d'hotel, dining room managers, head section waiters, waiters and assistant waiters (busboys), and sommeliers and wine waiters. It includes place settings and correct service (serving, taking from the correct side), communication skills, attitude, flair, dress sense (uniform), and finesse. Waiters should note whether passengers are right- or left-handed and, aboard ships with assigned table places, make sure that the cutlery and glasses are placed on the side of preference. Cutlery and wine glasses are also included.

Bars

This score reflects the lighting and ambience; overall service in bars and lounges; seating, noise levels; communication skills (between bartenders and bar staff and passengers); staff attitude, personality, flair and finesse; correct use of glasses (and correct size of glasses); billing and attitude when presenting the bill (aboard those ships where a charge is made).

Cabins

This score reflects the cleaning and housekeeping staff, butlers (for penthouse and suite passengers), cabin stewards/stewardesses and their supervisory staff, attention to detail and cleanliness, in-cabin food service, linen and bathrobe changes, and language and communication skills.

Open Decks

This score reflects steward/stewardess service for beverages and food items around the open decks; service for placement and replacement of towels on deck lounge chairs, self-help towels, emptying of used towel bins; and general tidiness of all associated deck equipment.

Entertainment

Aboard specialist ships, such as those offering expedition cruises, or tall ships, where entertainment is not a feature, it is the lecture program that forms this portion of the evaluations.

The score reflects the overall entertainment program and content as designed and targeted to specific passenger demographics. The entertainment has to appeal to passengers of many ages and types. Included is the physical plant (stage/bandstand) of the main showlounge; technical support, lighting, follow spotlight operation and set/ backdrop design; sound and light systems (including laser shows); recorded click-tracks and all special effects; variety and quality of large-scale production shows (including story, plot, content, cohesion, creativeness of costumes, relevancy, quality, choreography, and vocal content); cabaret; variety shows; game shows, singers; visual acts; bands and solo musicians.

Carnival Dream's 18-hole miniature golf course.

The cruise experience

Activities Program

This score reflects the daytime activities and events. It includes the cruise director and staff (their visibility, availability, ability, and professionalism), sports and watersports programs, participation games, special interest programs, port and shopping lecturers, and mind-enrichment lecturers. This score also reflects the extent and quality of any water sports equipment car-

ried), instruction programs, overall staff supervision, the marina or side-retractable water sports platforms, and any enclosed swimming area.

Movies/Television Programming

This score reflects movies screened in onboard theaters, picture and sound quality; videos provided on the in-cabin system; other programming, including a ship's own TV station programming; content; and entertainment value. Cabin TV audio channels are included.

WHAT THE DESCRIPTIONS MEAN

Ship Size
- ● Large Resort Ship (1,600–6,000+ passengers)
- ● Mid-Size Ship (600–1,600 passengers)
- ● Small Ship (200–600 passengers)
- ● Boutique Ship (50–200 passengers)

Lifestyle

Designated as Standard, Premium, or Luxury, according to a general classification into which segment of the market the ship falls. This should help you choose the right size ship and cruise experience to fit your lifestyle.
- ● **Standard**: the least expensive, offering the basic amenities, food and service.
- ● **Premium**: more expensive than Standard, have generally better food, service, facilities, amenities, more attention to detail, and differentiation of suites (with butler service) and standard accommodation.
- ● **Luxury**: more expensive than Premium or Standard, and provide more personal comfort, space, open or one-seating dining, much better food (no processed items, more menu creativity, and everything made fresh), and highly trained staff.

The Oatmeal Factor: Luxury by Degree

The Oatmeal Factor shows how various cruise ships will provide a passenger with a basic item such as a bowl of oatmeal. The difference can be found in its presentation. There are ships that provide one of four levels of oatmeal presentation, as follows.

Standard: Hot oatmeal (supermarket brand oats) mixed with water, with little or no chance of obtaining tahini to add taste to the oatmeal. You get it from a soup tureen at the buffet, and put it into a plastic or inexpensive china bowl yourself (or it may be served in

the dining room by a waiter/waitress); it is eaten with plastic or basic canteen cutlery. It's basic, basic, basic.
Premium: Hot oatmeal, water, salt and little olive oil; served in a higher quality bowl, by a waiter or waitress, with hotel-quality (or better) cutlery. It's possible that the ship will have tahini, to add taste and creaminess. It's also possible that the waiter/waitress will ask if you'd like hot or cold milk with your oatmeal. There may even be a doily between the oatmeal bowl and base plate.
Luxury: Hot oatmeal (medium or large flakes), water, salt, tahini, a little (extra virgin) olive oil and nutmeg, with a dash of blended Scotch (whisky); served in a high quality brand name bowl (Versace), with base plate and doily, and Hepp- or Robbe & Berking-quality silverware. Naturally, the waiter/waitress will ask if you'd like hot or cold milk with your oatmeal.
Incomparable: Hot Scottish (large flakes, hand ground) oatmeal, water, sea salt, tahini, and nutmeg (grated at the table), high-quality cold-pressed olive oil and a layer of rare single malt Scotch; served in small production hand-made china, with base plate and doily, and sterling silver cutlery. The waiter/waitress will ask if you'd like hot or cold milk (or anything else) with your oatmeal.

Naturally, there are variations and some crossover depending on the ship, supplies available, staff training, etc. The setting and presentation play a large part. Noise level, decor, chairs, table height, table settings, and overall comfort are all part of the evaluation process.

Cruise Line

The cruise line and the operator may be different if the company that owns the vessel does not routinely market and operate it. Tour operators often charter ships for their exclusive use (e.g. Thomson Cruises).

Notes on the rating results

Cruise ship evaluations and ratings have become much more complex. Although a ship may be the newest, with all the latest high-tech facilities possible, it is the onboard food and service that often disappoints, as well as standing in lines and signing up for activities.

Cruise companies say that food quality is a trade-off against lower prices. However, this implies a downward spiral that affects food quality as well as service, quality of personnel, crew training, safety, and maintenance.

Cruise companies hope that passengers won't notice cuts in food quality and employing cheaper crew members. However, in the final analysis, it is the little things that add to points lost on the great scorecard.

The ratings are intended to help the cruise companies evaluate their product, listen to their income-generating passengers, and revive some of the items and the finesse that have disappeared from the cruise experience over the past two decades, while adjusting fares to better reflect the long-term growth of this good value-for-money vacation. ❑

Hospitality Standard

This score reflects the level of hospitality of the crew; the professionalism of senior officers, middle management, supervisors, cruise staff, and general crew; social contact, appearance, and dress codes or uniforms; motivation; communication skills (most important); the general atmosphere and ambience and the attention to detail.

Overall Product Delivery

This score reflects the quality of the overall cruise as a vacation – what the brochure states and promises (real or implied), and the onboard hospitality and services.

First Entered Service

Where two dates are given, the first is the ship's maiden passenger voyage when it was new, and the second is the date it began service for the current operator.

Propulsion

The type of propulsion is given (i.e. gas turbine, diesel, diesel-electric, or steam turbine), together with the output (at 100 percent), expressed as MW (megawatts) or kW (kilowatts) generated.

Propellers

Number of propellers or fixed or azimuthing pods (see page 45 for a description of how pods work).

Passenger Capacity

This is based on:
● Two lower beds/berths per cabin, plus all cabins for single occupancy.
● All available beds/berths filled (Note: This figure may not always be accurate, as cruise lines often make changes by adding or taking away third/fourth berths according to demand).

Passenger Space Ratio (Gross Tonnage Per Passenger)

Achieved by dividing the gross tonnage by the number of passengers.

Crew to Passenger Ratio

Achieved by dividing the number of passengers by the number of crew (lower beds/all possible beds and berths filled).

Cabin Size Range

From the smallest cabin to the largest suite (including "private" balconies/verandahs), these are provided in square feet and square meters, rounded up to the nearest number.

Wheelchair-accessible Cabins and Ratings

Cabins designed to accommodate passengers with limited mobility.
There are four wheelchair accessibility ratings:
Best: the ship is recommended as being most suitable for wheelchair passengers.
Good: reasonably accessible.
Fair: moderately accessible.
None: the ship is not suitable.

Dedicated Cinema/seats

A "yes" means that there is a separate cinema dedicatedly solely to showing large-screen movies throughout the day and during the evening. This is distinct from a show lounge that may be used to screen movies during the day (afternoon) and live shows in the evening, or poolside screens. The number of seats is provided where known.

A Note About Prices

Some price examples are given throughout the ship reviews (for massage, the cover price for "alternative" restaurants, for internet access, or gratuities added to your onboard account, for example), but please note that these are provided only as a guideline, and may have changed since this book was completed. Always check with the cruise line, onboard concession or your travel provider for the latest prices.

KEEPING TRACK OF THE SEA CHANGES

A number of well-known ships have been withdrawn
from service in the past year. In many cases it's because
they didn't comply with tough new safety regulations

You have fond memories of a cruise a few years ago and you are about to book a cabin aboard the same ship for your next vacation. Then you suddenly find that, although the name is the same, the ship is entirely different. Alternatively, you might find yourself aboard a ship, supposedly for the first time – but then it begins to look strangely familiar and you find you have sailed aboard this ship before when it had a different name, and probably a different owner.

Welcome to the volatile world of cruising. To help regular readers keep ahead of the game, I provide updates by email *(see page 720)* and encourage them to invest in a new edition of the book each year.

A year of change

The year 2011 will be regarded as a milestone in the modern cruise industry. One reason is that new regulations, brought in under SOLAS 2010 (Safety of Life at Sea), allow the use of only a tiny percentage of real wood in new cruise ship interiors. The adoption of these rules by all 136 countries of the United Nations means that ships that no longer comply must be withdrawn from service and retired. Alternatively, they will be sold to become floating hotels, or training centers. Some ships will also be retired by their owners simply because, in today's tough economic climate, they are too costly to operate or too expensive to restructure.

Withdrawals started in late 2008 with the retirement of such illustrious ships as *Queen Elizabeth 2 (QE2)*. This was followed by the withdrawal from the international market of *Black Prince, Blue Monarch, Ivory, Kristina*

Regina, New Flamenco, Ocean Majesty, Oceanic, Princesa Marissa, Regal Empress and *Saga Rose*.

Some ships, however, will have been withdrawn or retired simply because they have been sold to other owners, or will begin a new life under a new name or brand. Examples include: *Celebrity Galaxy*, now *Mein Schiff* for TUI Cruises; *MSC Rhapsody*, now *Golden Iris* for Mano Cruise; *The Iris*, now *Kristina Katarina*, and *World Discoverer*, now *Prince Albert II* for Silversea Expedition Cruises. Meanwhile, Fred Olsen Cruise Line's *Black Prince* was sold in May 2009 to a Venezuelan buyer for service in domestic waters only.

Still others will simply change names as they are acquired by tour operators for language-specific markets – a burgeoning sector of the cruise market – or for new entrants into the international cruise marketplace. It's the constantly changing world of cruising.

Facts you can believe in

Discrepancies regarding ships often exist on websites. Cruise lines often round-up technical details (length, beam, tonnage, for example) for marketing and brochure purposes. We attempt (where possible) to source the correct technical specifications. Another example is in brochure or online deck plans, where some cruise lines have fewer cabins than are stated in this book. This is because some cruise lines may or may not deduct some cabins for entertainers from passenger deck plans. We at Berlitz aim to be as accurate as possible, but, occasionally, there will be variances.

Of course, some ship details may have changed since this book was completed. When these are significant, I will try to include the latest details in my quarterly emailed Cruiseletter *(see page 720)*.

What's in a name?

Sometimes cruise lines like to rebrand themselves in the hope that a change of name will bring their operations back into focus and attract media attention. Some recent examples: Azamara Cruises is now rebranded as Azamara Club Cruises; Seabourn Cruise Line is now The Yachts of Seabourn; Transocean Tours has become Transocean Cruises; and Quail Cruises has anticipated its passengers' level of satisfaction by renaming itself Happy Cruises. ❑

The new *Queen Elizabeth* takes shape at Italy's Monfalcone shipyard.

Adonia
NOT YET RATED

Size:	Mid-Size Ship	Passenger Decks:	9	Cabins (with private balcony):	258
Tonnage:	30,277	Total Crew:	300	Cabins (wheelchair accessible):	4
Lifestyle:	Standard	Passengers		Wheelchair accessibility	Good
Cruise Line:	P & O Cruises	(lower beds/all berths):	710/838	Cabin Current:	110 and 220 volts
Former Names:	*Royal Princess,*	Passenger Space Ratio		Elevators:	4
	Minerva II, R8	(lower beds/all berths):	42.6/36.1	Casino (gaming tables):	Yes
Builder: .Chantiers de l'Atlantique (France)		Crew/Passenger Ratio		Slot Machines:	Yes
Original Cost:	$150 million	(lower beds/all berths):	1.8/2.2	Swimming Pools (outdoors):	1
Entered Service:	Feb 2001/May 2011	Cabins (total):	355	Swimming Pools (indoors):	0
Registry:	Bermuda	Size Range (sq ft/m):	145.3–968.7/	Whirlpools:	2 (+ 1 thalassaotherapy)
Length (ft/m):	592.0/180.45		13.5–90.0	Self-Service Launderette:	Yes
Beam (ft/m):	83.5/25.46	Cabins (outside view):	332	Dedicated Cinema/Seats:	No
Draft (ft/m):	19.5/6.0	Cabins (interior/no view):	23	Library:	Yes
Propulsion/Propellers: diesel (18,600 kW)/2		Cabins (for one person):	0		

OVERALL SCORE: NYR OUT OF A POSSIBLE 2,000 POINTS

OVERVIEW. *Adonia*, formerly *Royal Princess* and *Minerva II* and originally Renaissance Cruises' simply named *R8*, was the last in a series of eight almost identical ships built for the defunct Renaissance Cruises. The ship's square funnel has P & O's trademark buff colored funnel to balance the ship's all-white hull, white superstructure, and high sides. An outside lido deck has a swimming pool and good sunbathing space; one of the aft decks has a thalasso-therapy pool.

Although there is no walk-around promenade deck outdoors, there is a small jogging track above the perimeter of the swimming pool, and you can also stroll on open decks on the port and starboard sides. There are no wooden decks outdoors; they are instead covered by Bolidt, a sand-colored rubberized material. The stairways, although carpeted, sound tinny.

The interior decor, designed by a Scotsman, John McNeece, is quite elegant, a throwback to the dark woods-style of ship decor of the ocean liners of the 1920s and '30s. It includes detailed ceiling cornices, both real and faux wrought-iron staircase railings, wood and leather paneled walls, trompe l'oeil ceilings, rich carpeting in hallways with an Oriental rug-look center section, and many other interesting and expensive-looking decorative touches. The overall feel is of an informal old-world country club – warm, comfortable, cosseting, and homely.

The ship's public rooms are basically spread over three decks. The reception hall (lobby) has a staircase with intricate, real wrought-iron railings, but these are cleverly painted on plasti-glass panels on the stairways on other decks – a copy of the staircase aboard SS *Titanic*.

BERLITZ'S RATINGS		
	Possible	Achieved
Ship	500	NYR
Accommodation	200	NYR
Food	400	NYR
Service	400	NYR
Entertainment	100	NYR
Cruise	400	NYR

A Crow's Nest Lounge is located high atop the ship, with great views from its floor-to-ceiling windows. The room has a long bar which faces forward – the barmen actually have the best view – and very comfortable seating. There is a small central bandstand and wooden dance floor forward of the bar, while the aft section on the port side has six internet-connect computer terminals, although there's little privacy.

In 2007, a casino was re-instated during the conversion from *Minerva II* to *Royal Princess*, but P&O Cruises has thoughtfully changed this into the gentleman's club-like Anderson's Lounge, a P&O Cruises favorite – like those aboard *Aurora* and *Oriana*. Anderson's is a delightful wood-paneled lounge with a fireplace, and a long bar.

Other public rooms: The Cabaret Lounge is used principally for evening theatrical shows and musical performances. There are several bars – including one in each of the restaurant entrances. The Library is a beautiful, grand, restful room – perhaps the nicest public room – designed in the Regency style. It has a fireplace, a high, indented, trompe l'oeil ceiling, and a collection of about 4,000 books, plus some very comfortable wingback chairs with footstools, and sofas you can fall asleep on.

P&O Cruises provides good cruise and tour programs, geared specifically to British passengers, and expert lecturers will be part of each cruise. You should experience a fine, hassle-free cruise vacation aboard this child-free ship. There may not be marble bathroom fittings, or other expensive niceties, but the value for money is good. The onboard currency is the British pound. The price of drinks is quite reasonable.

Note that the score and rating for the ship are expected to be similar to that for *Pacific Princess*, a close sister. A score will be applied in the next edition of this book.

ACCOMMODATION. There are six basic cabin size categories, but 20 different price categories (14 for double occupancy and 6 for single occupancy). The price you pay will depend on the grade, size, location and deck. The cabin size categories include: Owner's Suites (6), Master Suites (4), Deluxe with balcony, Superior Plus with balcony, Superior with balcony, and Standard Outside View/Standard Interior (no view) cabins. Some cabins have interconnecting doors – good for families with children – while 18 cabins on Deck 6 have lifeboat-obstructed views. All suites and cabins have tea and coffee making facilities.

There are two interior accommodation passageways.
Standard Outside-View and Interior (no view) Cabins: All the standard interior (no view) and outside-view cabins – the lowest four grades – are compact units, and tight for two persons, particularly for cruises longer than five days. They have twin beds or queen-sized bed, with good under-bed storage areas, personal safe, vanity desk with large mirror, good closet and drawer space in rich, dark woods, and waffle-pattern bathrobe. TV sets carry a major news channel, where obtainable, plus sport and several movie channels.
Cabins with Private Balcony: Cabins with private balconies – about 66 percent of all cabins – have partial, and not full, balcony partitions, sliding glass doors, and, due to good design and layout, only 14 cabins on Deck 6 have lifeboat-obstructed views. The bathrooms, which have tiled floors and plain walls, are compact, standard units, and include a shower stall with a removable hand-held shower unit, wall-mounted hairdryer, 100% cotton towels, toiletries storage shelves, and retractable clothesline. Toiletries include soap, shampoo, body lotion, and shower cap.
Owner's Suites/Master Suites: The six Owner's Suites and four Master Suites provide the most spacious accommodation – in my view, well worth the extra cost. These are fine, large living spaces located in the forward-most and aft-most sections of the accommodation decks. Particularly nice are those that overlook the stern, on Deck 6, 7 and 8. They have more extensive private balconies that really are private and cannot be overlooked by anyone on the decks above. There is an entrance foyer, living room, bedroom (the bed faces the sea, which can be seen through the floor-to-ceiling windows and sliding glass door), CD player with selection of audio discs, bathroom with Jacuzzi bathtub, and a small guest bathroom.

CUISINE. There are three proper restaurants to choose from, plus a casual self-serve buffet-style venue:

The Club Restaurant, the most formal, has 338 seats, a raised central section, and is located in the aft section of the ship. It has large ocean-view windows on three sides, several prime tables overlooking the stern, and a small bandstand for occasional live music. The menu changes daily for lunch and dinner. However, the noise level in this main dining room can be high, due to its single-deck-height ceiling, and noisy waiter stations. Immediately in front of the restaurant entrance is the Club Bar – a cosy, open lounge and bar, with an attractive fireplace.

Sterling Steakhouse, with ocean-view windows along two sides, serves steak and seafood dishes. There is a $20 cover charge, and reservations are needed.

A reservations-only Italian trattoria-style venue features Italian cuisine and has a cover charge.

While all restaurants have open-seating dining, reservations are necessary in the Italian Trattoria and Sterling Steakhouse, both of which are of the same size, are L-shaped and have ocean-view windows along two sides and at the stern; tables are mostly for four or six.

The Panorama Buffet has both indoor and outdoor seating, and is the ship's casual dining spot, in a self-serve buffet style. It is open for breakfast, lunch and casual dinners – the dinner menu is the same as that in the formal Dining Room. Additionally, there is a Poolside Grill for casual fast food items.

ENTERTAINMENT. The Cabaret Lounge, forward on Deck 5, is the venue for all main entertainment events, and occasional some social functions. The entertainment consists mainly of small production shows – with the accompaniment of pre-recorded tracks – and cabaret shows.

A Crow's Nest Lounge, which sits atop the ship at the front, has good forward views; it includes a dance floor and live music.

SPA/FITNESS. The Oasis Spa has a gymnasium with some muscle-toning equipment, a thalassotherapy pool, steam rooms for men and women (there are no saunas), several treatment rooms, and a beauty salon. A spa concession provides beauty and wellness treatments, as well as exercise classes – some of which may cost extra. Out on deck, there is a small swimming pool, two hot tubs, a jogging track, a golf practice net and shuffleboard courts.

● **For more extensive general information on what the P & O Cruises experience is like, see pages 147–8.**

Adventure of the Seas
★★★★

Size: . . . . .Large Resort Ship	Passenger Decks: 14	Cabins (with private balcony): 765
Tonnage: 137,276	Total Crew: 1,185	Cabins (wheelchair accessible): 26
Lifestyle: . . . . .Standard	Passengers	Wheelchair accessibility . . . . .Best
Cruise Line: Royal Caribbean International	(lower beds/all berths): 3,114/3,838	Cabin Current: . . . . .110 volts
Former Names: . . . . .none	Passenger Space Ratio	Elevators: . . . . .14 (6 glass-enclosed)
Builder: . . .Kvaerner Masa-Yards (Finland)	(lower beds/all berths): 44.0/35.7	Casino (gaming tables): . . . . .Yes
Original Cost: . . . .$500 million	Crew/Passenger Ratio	Slot Machines: . . . . .Yes
Entered Service: . . . . .Nov 2001	(lower beds/all berths): 2.6/3.2	Swimming Pools (outdoors): 3
Registry: . . . . .The Bahamas	Cabins (total): 1,557	Swimming Pools (indoors): 0
Length (ft/m): 1,020.6/311.1	Size Range (sq ft/m): 151.0–1,358.0/	Whirlpools: 6
Beam (ft/m): 155.5/47.4	14.0–126.1	Self-Service Launderette: . . . . .No
Draft (ft/m): 28.8/8.8	Cabins (outside view): 939	Dedicated Cinema/Seats: . . . . .No
Propulsion/Propellers: . . . . .diesel-electric	Cabins (interior/no view): 618	Library: . . . . .Yes
(75,600kW)/3 pods	Cabins (for one person): 0	

OVERALL SCORE: 1,454 OUT OF A POSSIBLE 2,000 POINTS

OVERVIEW. *Adventure of the Seas* is a large, floating, family-friendly leisure resort (sister to *Explorer of the Seas*, *Mariner of the Seas*, *Navigator of the Seas,* and *Voyager of the Seas*). The propulsion is derived from three pod units – two azimuthing, and one fixed at the centerline – powered by electric motors instead of conventional rudders and propellers *(see page 45 for details)*.

With large proportions, the ship provides an abundance of facilities and options, rather like a small town, yet it manages to have a healthy passenger space ratio (the amount of space per passenger). It is too large to go through the Panama Canal, thus limiting its itineraries almost exclusively to the Caribbean, where only a few islands can accept it, or for use as a floating island resort. Spend the first few hours exploring all the many facilities and public spaces aboard this vessel and it will be time well spent.

Although *Adventure of the Seas* is a large ship, the cabin hallways are warm and attractive, with artwork cabinets and wavy lines to lead you along and break up the monotony. In fact, there are plenty of colorful, even whimsical, decorative touches to avoid what could be a very clinical environment.

Embarkation and disembarkation typically take place through two access points, designed to minimize the inevitable lines – that's over 1,500 people for each access point. Once inside the ship, you'll need good walking shoes – it really is quite a long way from one end to the other.

A four-decks-high Royal Promenade is the main interior focal point; it's a good place to hang out, to meet someone, or to arrange to meet someone. The length of two football fields (American football, that is), it has two internal lobbies rising through 11 decks. Cafés, shops, and entertainment

BERLITZ'S RATINGS

	Possible	Achieved
Ship	500	419
Accommodation	200	149
Food	400	222
Service	400	281
Entertainment	100	82
Cruise	400	301

locations front this winding street and interior "with-view" cabins look into it from above. It is an imaginative piece of design work, and those who like shopping malls enjoy it immensely.

The long super-atrium houses a "traditional" pub. There is also a Champagne Bar, a Sidewalk Café (for continental breakfast, all-day pizzas, speciality coffees, and desserts), Sprinkles (for round-the-clock ice cream and yoghurt), and a sports bar. There are also several shops – jewelry shop, gift shop, liquor shop, perfume shop, and a logo souvenir shop. Comedy art has its place here, too, for example in the *trompe l'oeil* painter climbing up the walls.

The Guest Reception and Shore Excursion counters are located at the aft end of the promenade, as is an ATM machine. Things to watch for: look up to see the large moving, asteroid-like sculpture (constantly growing and contracting). At times, street entertainers appear, and parades are staged, while at other (carefully orchestrated) times it's difficult to walk through the area as it is filled to the brim with tacky shopping items – like a cheap bazaar.

Arched across the promenade is a captain's balcony, and in the center of the promenade a stairway connects you to the deck below, where you'll find the Schooner Bar (a piano lounge that is a feature of all RCI ships) and the flashy Casino Royale. Gaming includes blackjack, Caribbean stud poker, roulette, and craps, as well as 300 slot machines.

Aft of the casino is the Aquarium Bar, while close by are some neat displays of oceanographic interest. Royal Caribbean International has teamed up with the University of Miami's Rosenstiel School of Marine and Atmospheric Science to study the ocean and the atmosphere. A small onboard laboratory is part of the project.

There's a regulation-size ice-skating rink (Studio B), with real ice, with "bleacher" seating for up to 900, and the latest in broadcast facilities. Superb Ice Follies shows are presented here. A stunning two-deck library is open 24 hours a day, and $12 million was spent on permanent artwork. Drinking places include a neat Aquarium Bar, with with 50 tons of glass and water in four large aquariums.

Other drinking places include the small and intimate Champagne Bar, Crown & Anchor Pub, and Connoisseur Club – for cigars and cognacs. Lovers of jazz might appreciate Blue Moon, an intimate room for cool music atop the ship in the Viking Crown Lounge. Golfers might enjoy the 19th Hole – a golf bar, as they play the Adventure Links.

There is a TV studio with high-tech broadcast facilities, located adjacent to rooms that can be used for trade show exhibit space, with a conference center seating 400 and a multi-media screening room that seats 60. High atop the ship, you can tie the knot in a wedding chapel in the sky, the Skylight Chapel; located on the upper level of the Viking Crown Lounge, it has wheelchair access via an electric stairlift. Outdoors, the pool and open deck areas provide a resort-like environment. If possible, visit the Helicopter deck at the front of the ship for great starry-sky views at night.

Families with children are also well catered for, as facilities for children and teenagers are quite extensive. "Aquanauts" is for 3–5 year olds; "Explorers" is for 6–8 year olds; "Voyagers" is for 9–12 year olds. Optix is a dedicated area for teenagers, including a daytime club (with several computers), soda bar, and dance floor. "Challenger's Arcade" features an array of the latest video games. Paint and Clay is an arts and crafts center for younger children. Adjacent is Adventure Beach, an area for all the family; it includes swimming pools, a water slide and game areas outdoors.

Passenger niggles include having to negotiate the "sale" bazaar tables along the Royal Promenade; the lunchtime chaos in the Windjammer Café on embarkation day (before you have access to your cabin); and the problem of getting a table in the extra-cost dining venues.

ACCOMMODATION. There is an extensive range of 22 cabin categories in four major groupings: Premium ocean-view suites and cabins, Promenade-view (interior-view) cabins, Ocean-view cabins, and Interior (no view) cabins. Many cabins are of a similar size – good for incentives groups and other large groups, and 300 have interconnecting doors – useful for families. For a more detailed explanation, see entry for *Voyager of the Seas* on page 682.

CUISINE. The main dining room (total capacity 1,919) is massive, and is set on three levels, each named after a composer (Mozart, Strauss, Vivaldi). A dramatic staircase connects all three levels, and huge, fat support pillars obstruct the sight lines. All three levels have exactly the same menus.

Two small private wings serve private groups: La Cetra and La Notte, each seating 58 persons. All dining venues are non-smoking. Choose one of two seatings, or "My Time Dining" (eat when you want during dining room hours) when you book. Tables are for four, six, eight, 10 or 12.

The place settings, china and cutlery are of good quality. **Alternative Dining Options:** These are for casual and informal meals, and include:

● *Café Promenade:* for continental breakfast, all-day pizzas, pastries, desserts and specialty coffees (sadly provided in paper cups).

● *Windjammer Café:* for casual buffet-style breakfast, lunch and light dinner (except the last night of the cruise).

● *Island Grill:* (this is actually a section inside the Windjammer Cafe), for casual dinner (no reservations necessary) featuring a grill and open kitchen.

● *Portofino:* this is the ship's "upscale" (non-smoking) Euro-Italian restaurant, open for dinner only. Reservations are required, and there is a $20 per person cover charge. The food and its presentation are better than in the main dining room, although the venue is too small for all passengers to try even once during a cruise. Choices include: antipasti, soup, salad, pasta, main dish, dessert, cheese and coffee.

● *Johnny Rockets*, a retro 1950s all-day, all-night diner-style eatery that features hamburgers, malt shakes (at extra cost), and jukebox hits, with both indoor and outdoor seating (all indoor tables feature a mini-jukebox; dimes are provided for you to make your selection of vintage records), and all-singing, all-dancing waitresses that'll knock your socks off, if you can stand the high volume.

● *Sprinkles:* for round-the-clock ice cream and yoghurt.

ENTERTAINMENT. The 1,350-seat Lyric Showlounge is a stunning room located at the forward end of the ship. It spans the height of five decks, with only a few slim pillars and almost no disruption of sight lines from almost any seat in the house. There's also an array of up-and-coming cabaret acts and late-night adults-only comedy.

Entertainment is always upbeat. There is even background music in all corridors and elevators, and constant music outdoors on the pool deck. If you want a quiet relaxing holiday, this is not the right ship for you.

SPA/FITNESS. The ShipShape health spa is reasonably large, and measures 15,000 sq. ft (1,400 sq. meters). It includes an aerobics room, fitness center (with the usual stairmasters, treadmills, stationary bikes, weight machines and free weights), treatment rooms, men's and women's sauna/ steam rooms, while another 10,000 sq. ft (930 sq. meters) is devoted to a Solarium (with magrodome sliding glass-domed roof) for relaxation after you've exercised.

There's a 32.8-ft (10-meter) rock-climbing wall at the aft end of the funnel, with five climbing tracks. You'll get a great "buzz" being 200 ft (60 meters) above the ocean while the ship is moving. Other sports facilities include a roller-blading track, a dive-and-snorkel shop, a full-size basketball court and 9-hole, par 26 golf course. A dive-and-snorkel shop provides equipment for rental, and diving classes.

● **For more extensive general information about a Royal Caribbean cruise experience, see pages 151–6, and for more detailed information about the *Voyager*-class ships, see *Voyager of the Seas* (page 682).**

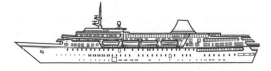

Aegean Odyssey
NOT YET RATED

Size: ....Small Ship	Propulsion/Propellers: ....diesel	Cabins (for one person):.......................18
Tonnage: 11,563	(10,296kW)/2	Cabins (with private balcony):..............42
Lifestyle:....................................Standard	Passenger Decks: 8	Cabins (wheelchair accessible): 2
Cruise Line:............Voyages to Antiquity	Total Crew: 200	Wheelchair accessibility: ....Fair
Golden Star Cruises	Passengers	Cabin Current: ....220 volts
Former Names:...........*Aegean I, Aegean*	(lower beds/all berths):..............378/388	Elevators: 2
Dolphin, Dolphin, Alkyon, Narcis	Passenger Space Ratio	Casino (gaming tables): ....Yes
Builder:......Santierul N. Galatz (Romania)	(lower beds/all berths):............30.5/ 29.8	Slot Machines:...................................Yes
Original Cost: ....n/a	Crew/Passenger Ratio	Swimming Pools (outdoors): 1
Entered Service:.............1974/May 2010	(lower beds/all berths):.................1.8/1.9	Swimming Pools (indoors): 0
Registry:....................................Greece	Cabins (total):.....................................198	Whirlpools: 0
Length (ft/m):.......................460.9/140.5	Size Range (sq ft/m): 130.0–550.0/	Self-Service Launderette:...................No
Beam (ft/m):............................67.2/20.5	12.0–51.0	Dedicated Cinema/Seats: ....No
Draft (ft/m): 20.3/6.2	Cabins (outside view):.......................153	Library: ....Yes
	Cabins (interior/no view):.....................45	

BERLITZ'S OVERALL SCORE: NYR OUT OF A POSSIBLE 2,000 POINTS

OVERVIEW. This small ship's profile is quite smart, with a nicely-shaped funnel that balances the rather angular stern – the result of a $26 million "chop and stretch" operation some years ago. The present operator, Voyages to Antiquity, purchased the ship in December 2007 then set about a painstaking, extensive refit and refurbishment program that ended up more like a complete rebuild, because the ship looks so much nicer than it ever did before.

BERLITZ'S RATINGS		
	Possible	Achieved
Ship	500	NYR
Accommodation	200	NYR
Food	400	NYR
Service	400	NYR
Entertainment	100	NYR
Cruise	400	NYR

Originally built to carry ammunition, the ship's hull is really strong. The passenger capacity has been significantly reduced – from 650 to 378, with a subsequent increase in the passenger space ratio – in what can only be described a skilful, well thought-out conversion, refit and refurbishment. As a result, the open deck space, all of it covered in teak, is extremely good, and measures 37,674 sq. ft (3,500 sq. meters) – a lot for a small ship. The vessel has been opened up a lot, almost creating a ship of light compared to what it used to be.

Inside, the Promenade Deck houses most of the public rooms. There is a forward observation lounge, with many windows providing plenty of natural light. The Rendez-Vous Square – actually a large lounge with a large dance floor – is quite stunning, with its classy black and red decor.

Some materials in public rooms are held together by the "patch and fix" method, but the subtle, pleasing, homely color combinations – most with earth tones – help to create a spacious, light, and open feel.

The company focuses on the cultural aspects of its cruises, which are typically of 14 days' duration. Indeed, the whole credo is based on history, ancient civilizations and

learning, so it's more like cruising for academics. Outstanding lecturers are an intrinsic part of all Voyages to Antiquity cruises, and a good-sized library is an important part of the facilities. Itineraries include several port overnights. Note that cellphone use inside the ship is, wisely, not permitted.

The onboard currency is the euro, although you can pay final bill in either US$ or UK£. Gratuities to dining and cabin staff are included in the fare, and so are most shore excursions, together with selected wines with dinner (or beer/soft drinks); otherwise, 12½% is added to bar accounts.

SUITABLE FOR: *Aegean Odyssey* is best suited couples and single travelers who want a learning and life enrichment cruise experience in a smart, yet somewhat traditional classic ship environment.

ACCOMMODATION. There are 14 cabin price grades, half of which are designated as Concierge Class, and some 42 cabins have a private balcony. The accommodation numbering system is nautically incorrect, however, with even numbered cabins on the starboard side instead of on the port, or left, side of the ship. Most cabins, however, do have an outside view, with similar sizes and configuration. All have a small refrigerator. They are reasonably spacious, considering the size of the ship, and pleasantly decorated, although closet, drawer and luggage storage space for two is limited in the lower grade cabins, particularly for longer cruises. Most of the bathrooms are partly tiled, and come with a decent amount of storage space for toiletries.

Single travellers have a choice of 18 single-occupancy cabins, most of which are quite spacious.

There are two owner's suites, located forward on Sun Deck. These are rather nice and have forward ocean views over the ship's bow, and include a narrow balcony on either port or starboard side. They have a separate bedroom, a walk-in closet, and a bathroom with a tub-shower combination.

CUISINE. The Marco Polo Restaurant, the ship's main dining room, is located on the lowest passenger deck. It has restful colors, and seating is mostly at large tables – there are no tables for two – in an open-seating arrangement that allows you to dine when you want and with whom you want. The amount of space around each table is good. Portholes on both sides, rather than windows, are set high up, and allow some natural light during the day. A smaller, more intimate alternative dining venue is found in the Yacht Club, for which there is no extra charge.

The cuisine is a mixture of Continental and Greek, but the selection of breads, cheeses and fruits is limited. Meats, fish and poultry items are not of high quality. For casual meals, self-serve breakfast and lunch buffets are available at the Terrace Café, aft on Promenade Deck, with indoor-outdoor seating that includes a Tapas Bar each evening ("Tapas on the Terrace").

ENTERTAINMENT. The Ambassador Lounge is a single-level showlounge, with a bar at one end, and seating that is mainly in tub-style chairs. The sightlines to the "stage" from many seats are obstructed, however, because of several support pillars. While the occasional cabaret act is presented for entertainment, this room serves as a lecture room for the specialist speakers carried as part of the in-depth enrichment cruises.

SPA/FITNESS. The wellness facilities have been reconstructed and provide a very attractive area, and include a separate sauna and changing area for males and females, plus a fitness area with aft-facing views. A separate Beauty Salon is located on a lower deck.

WHO'S WHO IN SHIPBOARD ENTERTAINMENT

Although production companies differ in their approach, the following gives some idea of the various people involved behind the scenes.

Executive Producer
Transfers the show's concept from design to reality. First, the brief from the cruise line's director of entertainment might be for a new production show (the average being two major shows per seven-day cruise). After deciding on an initial concept, they then call in the choreographer, vocal coach, and musical arranger.

Choreographer
Responsible for auditioning the dancers and for creating, selecting, and teaching the routines.

Musical Director
Coordinates all musical scores and arrangements; trains the singers in voice and microphone tech-niques, projection, accenting, phrasing, mem-ory, and general presentation; and oversees session singers and musicians for the recording sessions.

Musical Arranger
After the music has been selected, the musical arrangements must be made. Just one song can cost more than $2,000 for a single arrangement for a 12-piece orchestra.

Costume Designer
Provides creative original designs for a minimum of seven costume changes in one show lasting 45 minutes. The costumes must also be practical, as they will be used repeatedly.

Costume Maker
Buys all materials, and must be able to produce all required costumes in time for a show.

Graphic Designer
Provides all the set designs, whether they are physical one- two- or three-dimensional sets for the stage, or photographic images created on slide film, video, laser disk, or other electronic media.

Lighting Designer
Creates lighting patterns and effects for a production show. Sequences and action on stage must be carefully lit to the best advantage. The completed lighting plot is computerized.

Bands/Musicians
Before the big production shows and artists can be booked, bands and musicians must be hired, often for long contracts. Naturally, live musicians are favored for a ship's show band, as they are ex–cellent music readers (necessary for all visiting cabaret artists and for big production shows). Big bands are often placed in some of the larger ships for special sailings, or for world cruises, on which ballroom dancing plays a large part. Most musicians work to contracts of about six months.

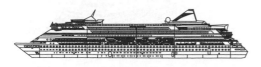

AIDAaura
★★★ +

Size:	Mid-size Ship
Tonnage:	42,289
Lifestyle:	Standard
Cruise Line:	AIDA Cruises
Former Names:	none
Builder:	Aker MTW (Germany)
Original Cost:	$350 million
Entered Service:	April 2003
Registry:	Italy
Length (ft/m):	665.5/202.8
Beam (ft/m):	92.2/28.1
Draft (ft/m):	20.3/6.2
Propulsion/Propellers:	diesel-electric (27,150kW)/2
Passenger Decks:	10
Total Crew:	389
Passengers (lower beds/all berths):	1,266/1,582
Passenger Space Ratio (lower beds/all berths):	33.4/26.7
Crew/Passenger Ratio (lower beds/all berths):	3.0/3.7
Cabins (total):	633
Size Range (sq ft/m):	145.3–344.4/13.5–32.0
Cabins (outside view):	422
Cabins (interior/no view):	211
Cabins (for one person):	0
Cabins (with private balcony):	60
Cabins (wheelchair accessible):	4
Wheelchair accessibility	Good
Cabin Current:	220 volts
Elevators:	6
Casino (gaming tables):	No
Slot Machines:	No
Swimming Pools (outdoors):	2
Swimming Pools (indoors):	0
Whirlpools:	5
Self-Service Launderette:	Yes
Dedicated Cinema/Seats:	No
Library:	Yes

OVERALL SCORE: 1,380

BERLITZ'S RATINGS

	Possible	Achieved
Ship	500	368
Accommodation	200	131
Food	400	259
Service	400	269
Entertainment	100	72
Cruise	400	281

Because the facilities and cruise experience offered aboard the AIDA Cruises fleet are reasonably similar, we have combined our assessment for all eight ships.

OVERVIEW.

The ships of AIDA Cruises have smart, contemporary profiles that are quite well proportioned, and each has a swept-back funnel and wedge-shaped stern. The bows display the red lips, as well as the blue eyes, of *Aïda* (from Verdi's opera, written to commemorate the opening of the Suez Canal in 1871). AIDA Cruises is part of Costa Cruises, which is itself part of the giant Carnival Corporation.

The AIDA-class ships (known as AIDA Clubships) all evolved from the first, and smallest ship, *AIDA* (over 10 years old and now named *AIDAcara*), in which the central idea was to get passengers into the public areas to participate in activities together, as in the Robinson Club concept on land. This led to "open plan" interiors and the feeling that the ship is one large space, but cleverly split into intimate rooms, although, in reality, rooms "flow" into each other at each fire zone section (a length of 157ft/48 meters).

One thing that is really noticeable aboard these ships is the fact that most of the chairs, counter stools and bar seats are really quite small, designed for thin young passengers, typically under the age of 40. There is constant high street music everywhere, so these ships are not for those wanting a "quiet escape" vacation, even though volume levels are well controlled.

AIDA Cruises has really grown up over the past few years, and no longer focuses on summer-camp style participation events. The ships have become more sophisticated, entertaining venues, and the old animateurs – somewhat like the *gentils ordinaires* of Club Med, but better – have grown up and morphed into what is now known as Club Teams. They, along with other staff, also interact with passengers throughout the ship.

About 20 nationalities are represented among the crew, who are upbeat and cheerful. Staff hospitality training is now at a high level in all departments, and AIDA Cruises has its own training schools in several countries, plus a recognized training academy in Rostock.

The company's brochure accurately describes the casual, active urban lifestyle. Sport biking is part of its youthful image, with three different levels of cycling to suit differing fitness levels. AIDA Cruises has also successfully embraced golfing, with special golf-theme packages, cruises, and golfing excursions ashore in many ports of call.

The open deck space is very tight, but sunbathing space includes some rather pleasant, reasonably quiet space above the navigation bridge. Dip pools and hot tubs, plus seating areas, are provided in a cascading, tiered setting atop the ship on the pool deck, providing a decent amount of sunbathing space. It's all designed to be in a "beach-like" environment, with splash and play areas.

There are three pricing levels – Aida Premium, Aida Vario, and Just Aida – depending on what you want to be included in your cruise vacation, plus differences in price according to the accommodation size and grade you choose, and the itinerary. Choose the basic, price-driven Just Aida package and the cruise line chooses the ship, itinerary and accommodation for you – sort of a pot luck cruise, based on or close to the dates you choose.

The dress code is simple: casual (no ties) at all times – there are no formal nights on board. All port taxes and gratuities are included in all packages,

AIDAbella
★★★★

Size:	.Large Resort Ship
Tonnage:	.69,200
Lifestyle:	.Standard
Cruise Line:	.AIDA Cruises
Former Names:	.none
Builder:	.Meyer Werft (Germany)
Original Cost:	.$390 million
Entered Service:	.Apr 2008
Registry:	.Italy
Length (ft/m):	.826.7/252.0
Beam (ft/m):	.105.6/32.2
Draft (ft/m):	.24.6/7.5
Propulsion/Propellers:	.diesel-electric (36,000 kW)/2
Passenger Decks:	.13
Total Crew:	.646
Passengers	
(lower beds/all berths):	.2,050/2,500
Passenger Space Ratio	
(lower beds/all berths):	.33.7/27.6
Crew/Passenger Ratio	
(lower beds/all berths):	.3.1/3.8
Cabins (total):	.1,025
Size Range (sq ft/m):	.145.3–473.2/ 13.5–44
Cabins (outside view):	.666
Cabins (interior/no view):	.359
Cabins (for one person):	.0
Cabins (with private balcony):	.480
Cabins (wheelchair accessible):	.11
Wheelchair accessibility	.Good
Cabin Voltage:	.110 volts
Lifts:	.10
Casino (gaming tables):	.Yes
Slot Machines:	.No
Swimming Pools (outdoors):	.3
Swimming Pools (indoors):	.0
Whirlpools:	.0
Self-Service Launderette:	.Yes
Dedicated Cinema/Seats:	.No
Library:	.Yes

OVERALL SCORE: 1,485

BERLITZ'S RATINGS

	Possible	Achieved
Ship	500	406
Accommodation	200	144
Food	400	280
Service	400	284
Entertainment	100	73
Cruise	400	298

/continued from previous page

and, with very attractive rates, a cruise provides much better value than almost any land-based vacation. The euro is the onboard currency.

These really are family-friendly ships. Children are split into four age groups: Seepferdchen (4–6 years), Delfin (7–9), Orcas (10–12), and Teens (14–17). Each has its own play area. There is a diverse selection of children's and youth programs in a holiday camp atmosphere, and special Club Team members dedicated to making at all happen. Supervised by a chef, children can make their own menus for the week, and visit the galley to make cookies and other items – a novel idea more ships could adopt.

A growing fleet of ships means that AIDA Cruises can offer a wide choice of itineraries that include the Middle East and Asia. There are differences between the various ships, due to their size and configuration, but all share the same basic concept, with self-service eateries being the mainstay. The oldest (*AIDAcara*) was the first ship, and the company has developed subsequent ships after observing the popularity of certain areas and the flow of passengers through the public rooms, and the needs of those new to cruising.

Overall, this really is cruising for high street and urban dwellers, and for those that don't mind busy places and lines. An AIDA cruise isn't cheap, but you do get a lot of high-tech entertainment, and there's always plenty of food. Some frustration occurs when shore excursions are sold out, when lines form after shore excursion buses return to the ship and you are required to go through the slow security check – and at peak times in the self-serve restaurants, and for shore tenders.

● *AIDAcara*. The original ship, from whence the concept developed. The open deck space is tight and there's not enough restaurant seating capacity at peak times, making a cruise aboard this ship a comfortable, but slightly cramped, experience.

● *AIDAaura, AIDAvita*. These ships' layout is much the same as for *AIDAcara*, but in a slightly rearranged manner that provides more space and seating in the Markt Restaurant, and adds more seating to the balcony level of Das Theater (the showlounge).

● *AIDAbella, AIDAblu, AIDAdiva, AIDAluna, AIDAsol*. Each has a small casino with blackjack, roulette and poker gaming tables and slot machines. There are many more balcony cabins, a separate aft sports deck , a "no music" observation lounge, and an art gallery. The embarkation entryway is really innovative, and has a bar, lookout balcony, and is cheerfully painted to look like a street scene in a city such as Copenhagen (*AIDAbella*). It is totally different to the utilitarian gangway entry areas found aboard regular cruise ships – it's a very welcoming environment and helps to calm tempers after waiting in a line to go through the security process for embarkation or in ports of call. *AIDAsol* is a sister to *AIDAblu* and close sister to *AIDAbella*, *AIDAluna* (but in a slightly modified form). *AIDAblu* and *AIDAsol* both have a microbrewery.

SUITABLE FOR:
The ships of AIDA Cruises are for youthful German-speaking couples, singles, and particularly families seeking good value for money in a fun, upbeat party-like environment, with excellent entertainment.

AIDAblu (2010)
AIDAsol (2011)

NOT YET RATED
These two new ships are sister ships of *AIDAbella* (see above) and have virtually the same specifications and facilites.

AIDAcara
★★★ +

THE SHIPS.

In all the ships, several decks of public rooms and facilities are positioned above the accommodation decks. Public rooms that have become common aboard all the ships are: Aida Bar, the main social gathering place, whose principal feature is a star-shaped bar (whose combined length per ship makes them the longest at sea).

The ships have good sport and wellness facilities. Each has a bike excursion counter, dive or golf excursion counter, golf simulator (not *AIDAbella, AIDAblu, AIDAluna, AIDAsol*), shore excursion counter, library, seminar rooms, duty-free shop, Nordic Walking machines, several bars and lounges, and eateries.

ACCOMMODATION.

There are eight or nine grades, from deluxe suites to interior (no view) cabins, depending on the ship, which keeps your cabin choice simple. Accommodation ranges in size, as follows:

AIDAaura (145.3–344.4 sq.ft/13.5–32 sq. meters)
AIDAbella (145.3–473.6/13.5–44 sq. meters)
AIDAblu (145.3–473.6/13.5–44 sq. meters)
AIDAcara (145.3–376.7/13.5–35 sq. meters)
AIDAdiva (145.3–473.6/13.5–44 sq. meters)
AIDAluna (145.3–473.6/13.5–44 sq. meters)
AIDAsol (145.3–473.6/13.5–44 sq. meters)
AIDAvita (145.3–344.4 sq.ft/13.5–32 sq. meters)

Contrary to maritime traditions (even-numbered cabins on the port side, odd-numbered cabins on the starboard side), cabin numbers progress numerically (example: 8201–8276 on the port side; 8101–8176 on the starboard side).

All suites and cabins have two beds (convertible to queen-sized bed). Some cabins also have two extra beds/berths for children, and some cabins have interconnecting doors (useful for families).

The decor in all accommodation grades is bright, youthful, rather minimalist, and slightly whimsical. All are accented with multi-patterned fabrics, wood-trimmed cabinetry (with nicely rounded edges) and rattan or wood-look furniture. Beds have duvets and a colorful fabric canopy that goes from the headboard to the ceiling. The windows have full pull-down blackout blinds (useful in destinations with long daylight hours). Some cabins in the ship's center (*AIDAaura, AIDAcara, AIDAvita*) may have views obstructed by lifeboats.

The bathrooms are compact, practical units; they have a shower enclosure, small washbasin, and small toilet. As in the most basic hotels and motels, only a wall-mounted body wash/shampoo dispenser is provided, so take your own conditioner, hand lotion, and other personal toiletries if you use them.

Thick 100% cotton bathrobes are provided for all grades of accommodation (*AIDAbella, AIDAblu, AIDAdiva, AIDAluna, AIDAsol*) and for suite-grade accommodation only (*AIDAaura, AIDAcara, AIDAvita*, although non-suite grade passengers can obtain one from the spa). Two towels are provided – a face towel and a "bath" towel, in two different colors. The "bath" towels are not very large, at 54 by 27 inches – compared to 72 by 36 inches aboard the P&O Cruises' *Ventura*, for example. Although the bathrooms do not have a hairdryer, one is located in the vanity unit in the cabin. Note that night-time turn-down service is *not* provided, and there is no cabin service after 3pm.

Cabins with balconies have a sliding door that is easy to open and does not impinge on balcony space; a small drinks table and two small, light chairs

Size:	Mid-size Ship
Tonnage:	38,557
Lifestyle:	Standard
Cruise Line:	AIDA Cruises
Former Names:	*Aida, Das Clubschiff*
Builder:	Kvaerner Masa-Yards (Finland)
Original Cost:	DM300 million
Entered Service:	June 1996
Registry:	Italy
Length (ft/m):	634.1/193.3
Beam (ft/m):	90.5/27.6
Draft (ft/m):	19.6/6.0
Propulsion/Propellers:	diesel(21,720kw)/2
Passenger Decks:	9
Total Crew:	370
Passengers	
(lower beds/all berths):	1,180/1,339
Passenger Space Ratio	
(lower beds/all berths):	32.6/27.5
Crew/Passenger Ratio	
(lower beds/all berths):	3.1/3.7
Cabins (total):	590
Size Range (sq ft/m):	145.3–376.7/ 13.5–35.0
Cabins (outside view):	390
Cabins (interior/no view):	200
Cabins (for one person):	0
Cabins (with private balcony):	48
Cabins (wheelchair accessible):	6
Wheelchair accessibility	Good
Cabin Current:	110 and 220 volts
Elevators:	5
Casino (gaming tables):	No
Slot Machines:	No
Swimming Pools (outdoors):	1
Swimming Pools (indoors):	0
Whirlpools:	2
Self-Service Launderette:	Yes
Dedicated Cinema/Seats:	No
Library:	Yes

OVERALL SCORE: 1,367

BERLITZ'S RATINGS

	Possible	Achieved
Ship	500	355
Accommodation	200	131
Food	400	259
Service	400	269
Entertainment	100	72
Cruise	400	281

AIDAdiva
★★★★

Size:	.Large Resort Ship
Tonnage:	.69,200
Lifestyle:	.Standard
Cruise Line:	.AIDA Cruises
Former Names:	.none
Builder:	.Meyer Werft (Germany)
Original Cost:	.$390 million
Entered Service:	.Apr 2007
Registry:	.Italy
Length (ft/m):	.826.7/252.0
Beam (ft/m):	.105.6/32.2
Draft (ft/m):	.24.6/7.5
Propulsion/Propellers:	.diesel-electric (36,000 kW)/2
Passenger Decks:	.13
Total Crew:	.646
Passengers (lower beds/all berths):	.2,050/2,500
Passenger Space Ratio (lower beds/all berths):	.33.7/27.6
Crew/Passenger Ratio (lower beds/all berths):	.3.1/3.8
Cabins (total):	.1,025
Size Range (sq ft/m):	.145.3–473.2/ 13.5–44
Cabins (outside view):	.666
Cabins (interior/no view):	.359
Cabins (for one person):	.0
Cabins (with private balcony):	.480
Cabins (wheelchair accessible):	.11
Wheelchair accessibility	.Good
Cabin Voltage:	.110 volts
Lifts:	.10
Casino (gaming tables):	.Yes
Slot Machines:	.No
Swimming Pools (outdoors):	.3
Swimming Pools (indoors):	.0
Whirlpools:	.0
Self-Service Launderette:	.Yes
Dedicated Cinema/Seats:	.No
Library:	.Yes

OVERALL SCORE: 1,484

BERLITZ'S RATINGS

	Possible	Achieved
Ship	500	405
Accommodation	200	144
Food	400	280
Service	400	284
Entertainment	100	73
Cruise	400	298

/continued from previous page

are provided. Note that balconies on the lowest deck can be overlooked by anyone occupying a balcony on the decks above. Balcony cabins aboard AIDAbella, AIDAdiva, AIDAluna) have a hammock as standard, although it only accommodates just one (thin) person. Some cabins (forward on Deck 5 – Nos 5103, 5104, 5105, 5106, 5203, 5204, 5206) aboard these ships have cabins with an outside view (well, outside light), but they are totally obstructed by steel bulkheads that form the front section of the ship.

Naturally, suite-grade accommodation offers more space, including more drawer and storage space, better quality furniture and furnishings, a larger lounge area and a slightly larger bathroom with a tub – and, of course, a larger balcony (those at the front and stern of the ship have the best).

CUISINE.
Principal restaurants:
Aboard AIDAaura, AIDAcara and AIDAvita two standard (included) eateries are the self-serve Markt and Karibik restaurants, plus Rossini – a decent enough à la carte (extra charge) tablecloth dining spot that serves high-quality meals cooked à la minute, and has friendly waiter service.

Aboard the larger AIDAbella, AIDAblu, AIDAdiva, AIDAluna and AIDAsol there are three self-serve eateries: Markt (Market), Bella Vista, and Weite Welt (Wide World) restaurants plus a Buffalo Steakhouse (for excellent steaks), Rossini, a Sushi Bar, and a Pizzeria. The restaurants are open at set times only (there are no 24 hours a day outlets, because there is no demand), although in the evening, the Pizzeria is typically open until midnight.

Beverage stations are open only during restaurant opening hours, unless you go to the extra-cost coffee bar. Aboard AIDAbella, AIDAdiva and AIDAluna there are also some vending machines for out-of-hours snacks.

The meal concept is simple: main meals are taken when you want them in one of the large self-serve buffet-style restaurants, with open seating at tables (of four, six or eight) where cutlery is provided hanging in a rack (but there are no soup spoons, only dessert spoons). Beer is available at the push of a button or a pull of the tap, and table wine – of the sort that would make a good drain cleaner – is usually provided in carafes on each table for lunch and dinner. It's very casual and easy-going mass catering, so think food court eating – it certainly can't be called dining, and is more like camping at sea.

The standard of food at the self-serve buffet islands ranges from adequate to quite good, with creative displays and presentation, and table-clearing service that is sometimes efficient, mostly not.

The many food islands and active stations cut down on the waiting time for food. There is always a big selection of breads, cheeses, cold cuts, fruits and make-your-own teas – with a choice of more than 30 types of loose-leaf regular and herbal teas – and coffee. A range of food, comprising more than 1,200 items, is offered. The fish section of AIDAbella, AIDAdiva, AIDAluna has its own fish smoking unit (which resembles a wine cabinet).

In addition, one à la carte option is available in all the ship: the "Rossini Restaurant", with waiter and sommelier service.

You can sit where you want, when you want, and with whom you want, so eating is a socially interactive occasion (in fact it's hard to be a couple and

AIDAluna
★★★★

Size:	Large Resort Ship
Tonnage:	69,200
Lifestyle:	Standard
Cruise Line:	AIDA Cruises
Former Names:	none
Builder:	Meyer Werft (Germany)
Original Cost:	$390 million
Entered Service:	Apr 2009
Registry:	Italy
Length (ft/m):	826.7/252.0
Beam (ft/m):	105.6/32.2
Draft (ft/m):	24.6/7.5
Propulsion/Propellers:	diesel-electric (36,000 kW)/2
Passenger Decks:	13
Total Crew:	646
Passengers (lower beds/all berths):	2,050/2,500
Passenger Space Ratio (lower beds/all berths):	33.7/27.6
Crew/Passenger Ratio (lower beds/all berths):	3.1/3.8
Cabins (total):	1,025
Size Range (sq ft/m):	145.3 –473.2/ 13.5–44
Cabins (outside view):	666
Cabins (interior/no view):	359
Cabins (for one person):	0
Cabins (with private balcony):	480
Cabins (wheelchair accessible):	11
Wheelchair accessibility	Good
Cabin Voltage:	110 volts
Lifts:	10
Casino (gaming tables):	Yes
Slot Machines:	No
Swimming Pools (outdoors):	3
Swimming Pools (indoors):	0
Whirlpools:	0
Self-Service Launderette:	Yes
Dedicated Cinema/Seats:	No
Library:	Yes

have a table for only two). However, at peak times, the venues may remind you of roadside cafés (albeit elegant ones), with all their attendant noise. Because of the large buffet rooms and self-serve dining concept, the crew to passenger ratio looks poor; but this is because there are no waiters as such (except in the à la carte venues), only staff for clearing tables.

Alternative (Extra Cost) Dining:

The **Rossini Restaurant** (à la carte), with mostly high-back seats, has an intimate atmosphere. It is open for dinner only, and has a set five- or six-course menu (plus daily specials). There is no cover charge, but an extra charge applies to everything on the à la carte menu (such as caviar, chateaubriand, rib-eye steak), and for wines. Reservations are needed. Tablecloths are provided, the food is very good, and service is sound.

Buffalo Steakhouse (*AIDAbella, AIDAblu, AIDAdiva, AIDAluna, AIDAsol*) has an open "display" kitchen, and features various steak cuts and sizes (Delmonico, New York Strip Loin, Porterhouse and Filet, plus bison steaks), and roast lamb rack. There is also a daily special – a prix-fix meal (example: a 180 kg filet steak, house salad, and dessert). It's just like going out to eat in a decent restaurant ashore – but there are no tablecloths. Wine is extra.

Sushi Bar (*AIDAbella, AIDAblu, AIDAdiva, AIDAluna, AIDAsol*). The 12-seater sushi counter is for Japanese-style sushi and sashimi dishes. While the counter provides stool seating, two low-slung tables with well-type seating are difficult to sit at and get up from (notice to females: avoid wearing a short skirt). The sushi is "commercial" and uninspiring, but typical of what you'd expect in a sushi bar not run by Japanese sushi masters. While the presentation is appetizing, the actual fare is mediocre and light on taste – and you can be subjected to intense noise level from the adjacent "open-plan" showlounge.

Vinotheque. The wine bar, located in front of the Weide Welt (Wide World) Restaurant, has a surprisingly good list of premium wines, and Davidoff cigars (although you can't smoke them at the bar – or anywhere inside the ship).

Pizzeria provides ever popular – and overcooked – pizzas

ENTERTAINMENT.

The Theater, the main venue for all shows and most cabaret, is two decks high aboard *AIDAaura, AIDAcara, AIDAvita*. It has a raised stage, and amphitheater-style bench seating on all levels. The benches have back rests, and are quite comfortable, and sight lines are good from most seats, with the exception of port and starboard balcony sections, where sight lines are interrupted by thick safety railings.

Aboard *AIDAbella, AIDAblu, AIDAdiva, AIDAluna* and *AIDAsol,* the Theater (called a Theatrium) is in the center of the ship, is open to the main foyer and other public areas, on three levels (Decks 9, 10, 11), and topped by a glass dome. It has amphitheater-style seating on three decks (the bench seating on the two upper levels has back supports, but not on the lower level), plus standing tables, although sight lines to the raised thrust stage area are less than good from many seats.

Also, the layout means that people constantly walk through the area, distracting you from what's on the stage. For the performers, it's a bit like being

OVERALL SCORE: 1,485

BERLITZ'S RATINGS

	Possible	Achieved
Ship	500	406
Accommodation	200	144
Food	400	280
Service	400	284
Entertainment	100	73
Cruise	400	298

AIDAvita
★★★ +

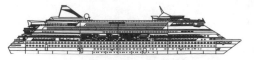

Size:	Mid-size Ship
Tonnage:	42,289
Lifestyle:	Standard
Cruise Line:	AIDA Cruises
Former Names:	none
Builder:	Aker MTW (Germany)
Original Cost:	$350 million
Entered Service:	Apr 2002
Registry:	Italy
Length (ft/m):	666.5/202.85
Beam (ft/m):	92.2/28.1
Draft (ft/m):	20.7/6.3
Propulsion/Propellers:	diesel-electric/2
Passenger Decks:	10
Total Crew:	389
Passengers	
(lower beds/all berths):	1,266/1,582
Passenger Space Ratio	
(lower beds/all berths):	33.4/26.7
Crew/Passenger Ratio	
(lower beds/all berths):	3.0/3.7
Cabins (total):	633
Size Range (sq ft/m):	145.3–344.4/
	13.5–32.0
Cabins (outside view):	422
Cabins (interior/no view):	211
Cabins (for one person):	0
Cabins (with private balcony):	60
Cabins (wheelchair accessible):	4
Wheelchair accessibility	Good
Cabin Current:	220 volts
Elevators:	6
Casino (gaming tables):	No
Slot Machines:	No
Swimming Pools (outdoors):	2
Swimming Pools (indoors):	0
Whirlpools:	5
Self-Service Launderette:	Yes
Dedicated Cinema/Seats:	No
Library:	Yes

OVERALL SCORE: 1,381

BERLITZ'S RATINGS

	Possible	Achieved
Ship	500	368
Accommodation	200	131
Food	400	259
Service	400	269
Entertainment	100	72
Cruise	400	282

/continued from previous page

in a TV studio, and trying to perform in front of the cameras, but with the audience in a different location. It doesn't really work well (passengers can watch the rehearsals), but, hey, this is really all about an active/interactive lifestyle, and it's a fresh way of presenting professional entertainment.

The shows are produced by AIDA Cruises' in-house department in a joint venture with SeeLive (Hamburg's Schmidt's Tivoli Theater), and typically consist of 12 performers. All vocals in the shows are performed live, to pre-recorded backing tracks that provide a mix of recorded live music and synthesized sound. The shows are trendy, upbeat, fun, and very entertaining. The whole entertainment experience is lively and fun – in fact, it's a little like going to the circus.

In addition, there is a live band in the Aida Bar, the only room with a large dance floor (except for the disco).

SPA/FITNESS.
The Wellness spas, fitness and sports programming are among the most extensive in the cruise industry. Several types of massage and body pampering treatments are offered. Examples of prices: Swedish Massage, €69 for 50 minutes; Shiatsu Massage, €79 for 50 minutes; Hot Stone Massage, €119 for 90 minutes.

"Sport Bikes" (mountain bikes with tough front and rear suspension units) are provided for conducted biking excursions in each port of call, a concession run by of Austrian downhill champion skier Erwin Resch. You can book biking, diving, and golfing excursions.

● *AIDAaura, AIDAcara, AIDAvita:*
The Body and Soul Spa, is located forward on Deck 11. It measures 11,840 sq. ft (1,100 sq. meters), and contains two saunas (one dry, one wet, both with seats for more than 20 persons, and glass walls that look onto the deck), massage and other treatment rooms, and a large lounging area. There are also showers, and two whole "ice walls" to use when you come out of the saunas (simply lean into the ice wall for maximum effect). Forward and outside the wellness center, is an FKK (FreiKoerperKultur) nude sunbathing deck, on two levels. A beauty and hair salon is located just behind the balcony level of the showlounge (*AIDAcara*).

● *AIDAbella, AIDAblu, AIDAdiva, AIDAluna, AIDAsol:*
The Body and Soul wellness/oasis area is located on two decks (connected by a stairway), and encompasses some 2,300 sq. meters (24,757 sq. ft). There is also an open air wellness deck for (FKK) relaxation/nude sunbathing in an area atop the ship forward of the ship's mast. In keeping with the times, all the trendy treatments are featured in an appealing contemporary setting. Each ship has a different design decor theme (*AIDAbella* is Africa, *AIDAdiva* is the Tropics, while *AIDAluna* is India).

There are saunas and steam rooms, and 14 rooms for massage and other treatments (most named after places associated with the design theme), neat showers, funky changing rooms and a tropical garden with real (waxed) palm trees and relaxation loungers. Sporting types can play golf in the electronic simulator, or billiards, or volleyball, or squash, or go jogging.

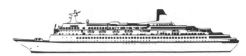

Albatros
★★★

Size	Mid-Size Ship	Propulsion/Propellers:diesel (13,400 kW)/2		Cabins (for one person):	.0
Tonnage:	.28,078	Passenger Decks:	.8	Cabins (with private balcony):	.9
Lifestyle:	Standard	Total Crew:	.340	Cabins (wheelchair accessible):	.0
Cruise Line:	Phoenix Reisen	Passengers		Wheelchair accessibility	Fair
Former Names:	Crown,	(lower beds/all berths):	.884/1,100	Cabin Current:	110 and 220 volts
	Norwegian Star I,	Passenger Space Ratio		Elevators:	.5
	Royal Odyssey, Royal Viking Sea	(lower beds/all berths):	.31.7/25.5	Casino (gaming tables):	Yes
Builder:	Wartsila (Finland)	Crew/Passenger Ratio		Slot Machines:	Yes
Original Cost:	$22.5 million	(lower beds/all berths):	.2.6/3.2	Swimming Pools (outdoors):	.1
Entered Service:	Nov 1973/Apr 2004	Cabins (total):	.442	Swimming Pools (indoors):	.0
Registry:	The Bahamas	Size Range (sq ft/m):	.123.7– 679.2/	Whirlpools:	.3
Length (ft/m):	.674.2/205.50		11.8–63.1	Self-Service Launderette:	No
Beam (ft/m):	.82.0/25.00	Cabins (outside view):	.380	Dedicated Cinema/Seats:	Yes/156
Draft (ft/m):	.23.9/7.30	Cabins (interior/no view):	.57	Library:	Yes

OVERALL SCORE: 1,194 OUT OF A POSSIBLE 2,000 POINTS

OVERVIEW. *Albatros* was built for long-distance cruising for the long-defunct Royal Viking Line and is now under long-term charter to Germany's Phoenix Reisen. It was refurbished in 2004 prior to replacing Phoenix Reisen's much loved but outdated *Albatros*. There is plenty of open deck and sunbathing space, although the popular aft swimming pool can become crowded.

The ship has a wide array of public rooms, including many lounges and bars, most of which are quite elegant and have high, indented ceilings. The Observation Lounge is a particularly pleasant place. Wide stairways and foyers give a sense of space, even when the ship is full.

Phoenix Reisen offers extensive destination-intensive itineraries. Friendly staff help with shore excursions and onboard activities. There is a very informal atmosphere aboard, and a relaxed, casual dress code.

Albatros performs well in most sea conditions, and the onboard product is very good value for money. Where passengers are required to fly to join their cruises, the airline most used by Phoenix Reisen is LTU. The onboard currency is the euro. A 7% gratuity is added to bar accounts.

SUITABLE FOR: *Albatros* is best suited to older German-speaking adults and families who seek a low-budget value-for-money vacation in fairly contemporary surroundings rather than in a brand new cruise ship.

ACCOMMODATION. There are more than 20 price grades, from expansive suites with private balcony to standard outside-view cabins and small interior (no view) cabins. A Captain's Suite is located at the front, directly under the navigation

BERLITZ'S RATINGS

	Possible	Achieved
Ship	500	310
Accommodation	200	128
Food	400	208
Service	400	237
Entertainment	100	60
Cruise	400	251

bridge, with fine forward-facing views. Nine other Penthouse Suites include a private balcony (with separate bedroom and living area). Most other cabins have an outside view and are quite well appointed, and there is a good amount of storage space; however, some bathrooms in the lower categories have awkward access. All cabins have a TV, bathrobe, and personal safe. Suites and "comfort cabins" also have a minibar.

Occupants of eight (mostly suite) accommodation grades receive Phoenix VIP service.

CUISINE. Two dining rooms (Mowe and Pelikan) have high ceilings, and are quite spacious. Dining is in one seating, at assigned tables for two, four, six or eight. Breakfast and luncheon can be taken in the dining room or outdoors in a self-service buffet by the swimming pool. Mid-morning bouillon is a Phoenix seagoing tradition, as is a Captain's Dinner (formal night), and Buffet Magnifique.

The service, by mainly Filipino waiters, is friendly and attentive, although there is little finesse. Table wines are included for lunch and dinner, although the quality is not good. Slightly better quality wines can be purchased.

The food itself is best described as "down home" simple. Casual eateries include a pizzeria at the (aft) pool bar.

ENTERTAINMENT. The large Pacific Lounge seats about 500, but thick pillars obstruct some sightlines. The entertainment consists of small-scale production shows presented by a small team of resident singers/dancers, and cabaret acts.

SPA/FITNESS. There's a gymnasium and sauna, two steam rooms, body treatment rooms, and a beauty salon.

Alexander von Humboldt
NOT YET RATED

Size:...................................Small Ship	Passenger Decks:.................................7	Cabins (wheelchair accessible):............0
Tonnage:.......................................15,343	Total Crew:...240	Wheelchair accessibility ....None
Lifestyle:.......................................Standard	Passengers	Cabin Voltage:..............................110 volts
Cruise Line:......................Phoenix Reisen	(lower beds/all berths):...............508/560	Lifts:...4
Former Names: ....*Jules Verne, Walrus,*	Passenger Space Ratio	Casino (gaming tables):......................Yes
Crown Monarch	(lower beds/all berths):............30.2/27.3	Slot Machines:....................................Yes
Builder:..............Union de Levante (Spain)	Crew/Passenger Ratio	Swimming Pools (outdoors):.................1
Original Cost:............................$95 million	(lower beds/all berths):.................2.3/2.6	Swimming Pools (indoors):.................0
Entered Service:.......Dec 1990/May 2010	Cabins (total):.....................................254	Whirlpools:..2
Registry:.............................The Bahamas	Size Range (sq ft/m):139.9–398.2/13.0–37	Self-Service Launderette:....................No
Length (ft/m):......................494.4/150.72	Cabins (outside view):........................225	Dedicated Cinema/Seats: ....No
Beam (ft/m):...........................67.6/20.62	Cabins (interior/no view):....................30	Library: ....Yes
Draft:.......................................18.7/5.7	Cabins (for one person):........................0	
Propulsion/Propellers: ....diesel	Cabins (with private balcony):.............10	

BERLITZ'S OVERALL SCORE: NYR (OUT OF A POSSIBLE 2,000 POINTS)

OVERVIEW. *Alexander von Humboldt*, formerly owned by the now-defunct Dutch company Club Cruise but purchased at auction by the UK's All Leisure company in 2009, serves the UK and German-speaking markets. Named after a German explorer and naturalist, it is under charter to Phoenix Reisen from May to October each year. Its profile is decent and balanced, though angular, and it has a squat, swept-back funnel. The "swimming pool" is really a dip pool, but it is flanked by two hot tubs, although there is little open deck space. There's more sunbathing space on the deck above. The Passenger Space Ratio is reasonable for the ship's size, and it carries several zodiac inflatable craft for shore landings and explorations.

Most public rooms are located on one deck. The focal point of the social life is the elegant Harry's Bar – a high-ceilinged lifestyle lounge/bar, off to one side of which is the Jules Verne library/card playing area, but the library is poor.

In typical Phoenix style, it's an almost all-inclusive product and excellent value-for-money. There should be enough space per passenger, because Phoenix keeps the capacity to 470. Most of the hotel service crew is Filipino. The onboard currency is the euro, and all gratuities are included. Those who want a little extra can buy silver and gold packages.

SUITABLE FOR: The ship is best suited to adult German-speaking couples and singles seeking soft-adventure and enrichment-style cruising in a small ship environment.

ACCOMMODATION. There are 18 cabin price grades – a lot for this small ship. Aft of the bridge are 10 fairly spacious suites, each with a private balcony. The sleeping area, which includes a small sofa and drinks table, and ample drawer space, can be

BERLITZ'S RATINGS

	Possible	Achieved
Ship	500	NYR
Accommodation	200	NYR
Food	400	NYR
Service	400	NYR
Entertainment	n/a	NYR
Cruise	500	NYR

curtained off from the lounge area, which includes a mini-fridge. There are two balcony doors (one each from the bedroom and the lounge). The small bathrooms have a Jacuzzi tub/shower combination.

The standard cabins have all the basics, including twin beds that convert to a double, a small vanity desk and small chair, and flat-screen TV set. Bathrooms have a shower enclosure, toilet, and washbasin. There is not much drawer space, and the soundproofing between cabins could be better. Many cabins close to the engine casing are noisy. Cabins on the lowest decks have portholes, while those on upper decks have windows.

CUISINE. The 280-seat Fier Jahreszeiten (Four Seasons Restaurant) is quite attractive, with a slightly raised center section. Seating is at tables for two, four, six, or eight. It's an open, one-seating arrangement. Table wines are included for lunch and dinner. Alternatively, casual, serve-yourself buffet-style meals (including dinner) can be taken in the Veranda indoor-outdoor eatery, although in the indoor section, windows have views obstructed by lifeboats. In warm weather, the seating at tables outdoors is very popular.

ENTERTAINMENT. The Music Lounge seats around 300 in banquette-style seating, and has decent sightlines to the wooden dance floor/stage, except for seats that are located behind the substantial support columns. A discotheque/late night spot is located adjacent to the fitness centre.

SPA/FITNESS. A wellness center is located aft of the discotheque on the uppermost deck overlooking the stern, while a beauty salon is located several decks below, as is a small unisex sauna and relaxation area.

Allure of the Seas
NOT YET RATED

Size:............................Large Resort Ship	Passenger Decks: 16	Cabins (with private balcony):.........1,956
Tonnage: 225,282	Total Crew: 2,164	Cabins (wheelchair accessible): 46
Lifestyle: ....Standard	Passengers	Wheelchair accessibility ....Good
Cruise Line:.Royal Caribbean International	(lower beds/all berths):........5,408 /6,360	Cabin Current: ....110 volts
Former Names: ....none	Passenger Space Ratio	Elevators: 24
Builder:.....................Aker Yards (Finland)	(lower beds/all berths):............41.6 /35.4	Casino (gaming tables):......................Yes
Original Cost:.........................$1. 5 billion	Crew/Passenger Ratio	Slot Machines:...................................Yes
Entered Service: ....Dec 2010	(lower beds/all berths):................2.4/2.9	Swimming Pools (outdoors): 6
Registry:...........................The Bahamas	Cabins (total):...................................2,704	Swimming Pools (indoors): 0
Length (ft/m):......................1181.1/360.0	Size Range (sq ft/m): 150.6–1,517.7/	Whirlpools:.......................................10
Beam (ft/m):.........................216.5 /66.0	14.0–141.0	Self-Service Launderette:...................No
Draft (ft/m): 30.0/9.15	Cabins (outside view):....................2,210	Dedicated Cinema/Seats: ....No
Propulsion/Propellers:.......diesel-electric	Cabins (interior/no view):...................496	Library: ....Yes
(97.2 MW)/3 pods	Cabins (for one person):........................0	

BERLITZ'S OVERALL SCORE: NYR (OUT OF A POSSIBLE 2,000 POINTS)

OVERVIEW. The world's largest cruise ship yet – a designation shared with sister ship *Oasis of the Seas* – is built as a "Moveable Resort Vacation" for families with children.

Because it is a close sister ship to *Oasis of the Seas*, the same general comments apply. However, some of the public room names are different, and even some of the onboard features are slightly different, or set in a slightly different location. *Allure of the Seas* is equipped with a 3-D movie screen (to be fitted into *Oasis* in January 2011). A few changes have been applied to The Boardwalk, as follows: Rita's Cantina replaces what is the Seafood Shack aboard *Oasis*; this serves casual Mexican fare, and there is a cover charge of around $5 per person. Where the Donut Hut is on the Boardwalk of *Oasis*, here aboard *Allure* it's the Boardwalk Dog House

BERLITZ'S RATINGS

	Possible	Achieved
Ship	500	NYR
Accommodation	200	NYR
Food	400	NYR
Service	400	NYR
Entertainment	100	NYR
Cruise	400	NYR

and serves hot dogs, wieners, bratwurst and sausages – a sort of pork haven. Meanwhile, the Donut Shop is positioned adjacent to the Ice Cream Shoppe.

DreamWorks Animation Studios will be introduced first aboard *Allure of the Seas*. It will provide interactive shows featuring popular animation characters such as Shrek, King Fu Panda, Madagascar, and How To Train Your Dragon. Also new aboard *Allure* is the provision of an iPod dock in all cabins.

The score for this ship is expected to be similar to the 1,524 achieved by *Oasis of the Seas*, which is reviewed on pages 510–3.

● **For more extensive general information on what an RCI cruise is like, see pages 151–6.**

Amadea
★★★★ +

Size:	Mid-Size Ship	Passenger Decks:	8	Cabins (with private balcony):	108

Size: ....Mid-Size Ship
Tonnage: 28,856
Lifestyle: ....Standard
Cruise Line: ....Phoenix Reisen
Former Names: ....*Asuka*
Builder: ..Mitsubishi Heavy Industries (Japan)
Original Cost: ....$150 million
Entered Service: ......Dec 1991/Mar 2006
Registry: ....The Bahamas
Length (ft/m): 632.5/192.81
Beam (ft/m): 81.0/24.70
Draft (ft/m): 21.6/6.6
Propulsion/Propellers: ....diesel
(17,300kW)/2

Passenger Decks: 8
Total Crew: 292
Passengers
(lower beds/all berths): 606/624
Passenger Space Ratio
(lower beds/all berths): 48.0/46.6
Crew/Passenger Ratio
(lower beds/all berths): 2.3/2.3
Cabins (total): 303
Size Range (sq ft/m): 182.9–649.0/
17.0–60.3
Cabins (outside view): 300
Cabins (interior/no view): 3
Cabins (for one person): 0

Cabins (with private balcony): 108
Cabins (wheelchair accessible): 2
Wheelchair accessibility ....Fair
Cabin Current: ....110 volts
Elevators: 5
Casino (gaming tables): ....No
Slot Machines: ....No
Swimming Pools (outdoors): 1
Swimming Pools (indoors): 0
Whirlpools: 3
Self-Service Launderette: ....Yes
Dedicated Cinema/Seats: Yes/97
Library: ....Yes

BERLITZ'S OVERALL SCORE: 1,600 OUT OF A POSSIBLE 2,000 POINTS

OVERVIEW. When introduced in 1991 as *Asuka*, it was the first all-new large ship specially designed for the domestic market, and the largest cruise ship built in Japan for the local market. The ship was sold to Phoenix Reisen in 2005 and started cruising for German-speaking passengers in March 2006.

The ship, which is a more upscale vessel compared to the other ships in the Phoenix Reisen fleet, has pleasing exterior styling and a contemporary profile, with a large, rounded, but squat funnel. There is a generous amount of open deck and sunbathing space, plus a wide walk-around teakwood promenade deck outdoors, good for strolling.

The "cake-layer" stacking of the public rooms hampers passenger flow and makes it somewhat disjointed, although passengers will like the separation of public rooms from the accommodation areas. There are many intimate public rooms, plenty of space and lots of light. So, because the ship absorbs people well, so there is never a feeling of crowding.

The interior decor is understated but elegant, with pleasing color combinations, quality fabrics and fine soft furnishings. There's some fascinating Japanese artwork, including Noriko Tamura's "Song of the Seasons," a four-deck-high mural on the wall of the main foyer staircase.

Harry's Bar is a bar and lounge decorated in the style of a contemporary gentleman's club with wood paneled walls, burgundy leather chairs, and a bar. This popular drinking spot has a light, airy feel.

As for the dress code, there is a mix of formal and informal nights, while during the day the dress code is very casual. In case you want to do your own laundry, there is a

BERLITZ'S RATINGS		
	Possible	Achieved
Ship	500	398
Accommodation	200	160
Food	400	336
Service	400	327
Entertainment	100	77
Cruise	400	302

self-service launderette, which has eight washing machines (useful for long voyages). The ship provides an extremely comfortable and serene environment in which to cruise.

The onboard currency is the euro, and all gratuities are included.

SUITABLE FOR: *Amadea* is best suited to German-speaking couples, single travelers and families with children, who enjoy cruising in very comfortable surroundings aboard a contemporary ship.

ACCOMMODATION. There are several price categories, although in reality there are just five types of suites and cabins. Three decks (8, 9 and 10) have suites and cabins with a private balcony (note that the floor is laid with green simulated turf, and there is no outside light).

No matter what grade you choose, all suites and cabins have ocean views, although some are slightly obstructed by the ship's gangway, when it is in the raised (stowed) position.

In all grades, cherry wood cabinetry, which is in beautiful condition, has nicely rounded edges. Cabin soundproofing is excellent, and there is a good amount of closet and drawer space (including lockable drawers), refrigerator, and personal safe.

All grades have bathrooms with full, deep bathtubs (while the suite bathrooms are of generous proportions, the "standard" bathrooms are practical but small), and all have a tiled floor and bath/shower area.

Two suites provide the largest accommodation (one is decorated in blue, the other in salmon); these are larger versions of the "A" grade cabins. Each has a separate bedroom, with walk-in closet that includes a luggage deck, and twin beds that convert to a queen-sized bed), sofa, two chairs and coffee table, large vanity desk, plenty of drawer space, and large color TV set. The marble-clad bathroom is large and has a whirlpool bathtub set alongside large ocean-view windows overlooking the private balcony, and twin washbasins set in a marble surround; a living room, and separate guest bathroom. The private balcony is quite large and has a tall tropical plant set in a glass display enclosure.

The top grade cabins are excellent living spaces, and have twice the size and space of the standard cabins. They are very nicely decorated and outfitted, and have twin beds (convertible to a queen-sized bed), sofa, two chairs and coffee table, large vanity desk, plenty of drawer space, and large color television. However, when in its twin bed configuration, the room's *feng shui* is poor, as one of the beds is facing a large mirror at the writing/vanity desk – a negative for some people.

Many cabins have a private balcony (with full floor-to-ceiling partition and a green synthetic turf floor (but no outside light) with floor-to-ceiling sliding door (the door handles are awkward).

There's also an illuminated walk-in closet (with long hanging rail and plenty of drawer space). The bathrooms are partly tiled and of generous proportions, and include a glass-fronted (plastic) toiletries cabinet, and two washbasins set in a thick marble surround.

CUISINE. There are two principal restaurants (Four Seasons and Amadea); both are non-smoking and both operate an open-seating basis for all meals. The Four Seasons Restaurant has two sections; there are ocean-view windows along one side of the aft section, and along two sides of the forward section. The Amadea Restaurant is located on a higher deck, with ocean view windows on two sides. The cuisine – and therefore the menu choice – is the same in both venues. For casual breakfasts and lunches, an informal self-serve Lido Café is provided, with plenty of outdoor seating adjacent to a small pool and hot tub.

With this ship, Phoenix Reisen has taken its cuisine and service to a much higher level in relation to that served aboard the company's other ships, by spending more money per passenger per day (this is also reflected in the cruise fare).

ENTERTAINMENT. The Atlantic Lounge is the venue for most entertainment events, including shows, social functions, and lectures. The room spans two decks, with seating on both main and balcony levels, and an extra-large wooden dance floor is provided for social dancing.

SPA/FITNESS. There is a spacious wellness center. It has large ocean-view windows, two baths, one hot tub, a sauna, steam room with wood floor; there are several shower enclosures, plus a changing area with vanity counter. Two massage rooms, however, are in a different location, although they are on the same deck.

LATITUDE AND LONGITUDE

Latitude signifies the distance north or south of the equator, while **longitude** signifies distance east or west of the 0 degree at Greenwich Observatory in London ("where time begins"). Both are recorded in degrees, minutes, and seconds. At the equator, one minute of longitude is equal to one nautical mile, but as the meridians converge after leaving the equator and meeting at the poles, the size of a degree becomes smaller. It was in 1714 that an Act of Parliament established a Board of Commissioners for the Discovery of Longitude at Sea. A prize of £20,000, then a huge sum, was set. The English clockmaker John Harrison (1693–1776) won it for his highly accurate chronometer. Indeed, none other than Captain Cook used a Harrison-designed chronometer on one of his voyages to the Pacific in 1775.

American Eagle
★★

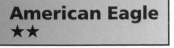

Size: . . . . .Boutique Ship	Total Crew: 22
Tonnage: .1,287	Passengers
Lifestyle: . . . . .Standard	(lower beds/all berths): 49/49
Cruise Line: . . . . . .American Cruise Lines	Passenger Space Ratio
Former Names: . . . . .none	(lower beds/all berths): 26.2/26.2
Builder: . .Chesapeake Shipbuilding (USA)	Crew/Passenger Ratio
Original Cost: . . . . .n/a	(lower beds/all berths): 2.2/2.2
Entered Service: . . . . .Apr 2000	Cabins (total): 27
Registry: . . . . .USA	Size Range (sq ft/m): 176.0–382.0/
Length (ft/m): 174.0/53.00	16.3–35.4
Beam (ft/m): 40.5/12.30	Cabins (outside view): 27
Draft (ft/m): 6.5/1.98	Cabins (interior/no view): 0
Propulsion/Propellers: diesel/2	Cabins (for one person): 5
Passenger Decks: 4	Cabins (with private balcony): 6

Cabins (wheelchair accessible): 2
Wheelchair accessibility . . . . .None
Cabin Current: . . . . .110 volts
Elevators: 1
Casino (gaming tables): . . . . .No
Slot Machines: . . . . .No
Swimming Pools (outdoors): 0
Swimming Pools (indoors): 0
Whirlpools: 0
Self-Service Launderette: . . . . .No
Dedicated Cinema/Seats: . . . . .No
Library: . . . . .No

OVERALL SCORE: 830 OUT OF A POSSIBLE 2,000 POINTS

OVERVIEW. American Cruise Lines is the resurrection of a company with the same name that existed between 1974 and 1989. It now features intra-coastal waterway cruising, as well as sailings in New England and the Hudson River Valley. *American Eagle* was built specifically for coastal cruising and cannot venture far into open seas away from the coastline (a sister vessel is planned, with more balcony cabins). The ship's uppermost deck is open (good for scenery observation), and there are tables and chairs, a few sunloungers, and a small putting green.

There are just two public lounges. The larger – the observation lounge – is located forward, with windows on three sides (an open bar is set up each afternoon). This is the main meeting place for passengers. A second, smaller lounge is sandwiched between cabins on the same deck.

The whole point of a cruise aboard this ship is to get close to the inland areas, cities and town of America's intra-coastal waterways and coastline. There's no waiting in line – you can board whenever you want. The ship docks in the center, or within walking distance of most towns on the itineraries. The dress code is "no ties casual".

It really is *extremely* expensive for what you get, compared even to ships of a similar size and purpose (although this is a new ship and the cabins are of a larger size and are slightly better equipped). There is an elevator, but it doesn't go to the uppermost deck (Sun Deck). The limited choice of food is very disappointing.

SUITABLE FOR: *American Eagle* is best suited to couples and single travelers sharing a cabin who are of mature years and want to cruise in an all-American environment aboard

BERLITZ'S RATINGS

	Possible	Achieved
Ship	500	249
Accommodation	200	110
Food	400	199
Service	400	170
Entertainment	n/a	n/a
Cruise	500	102

a small ship where the itineraries and destinations are more important than food, service or entertainment.

ACCOMMODATION. There are cabins for couples and singles, six suites, and two wheelchair-accessible cabins. All cabins have twin beds, color TV, a small desk with chair, and clothes hanging space. The six suites also have a VCR and compact disc (audio) player. All cabins have a private bathroom with separate shower enclosure, washbasin and toilet (none of the cabins has a bathtub), as well as windows that open.

CUISINE. The dining salon has large, panoramic picture windows on three of its sides. It has open seating (no assigned tables). There are no tables for two, and the chairs do not have armrests. The cuisine is very much American fare – good and wholesome, featuring regional cuisines, and presented and served in a basic, unfussy manner. Note that there is little choice of entrées, appetizers, or soups, although it has been improved in the past year. There is no wine list, although basic white and red low-quality American table wines are included in the cruise fare. On the last morning of each cruise, only continental breakfast is available.

ENTERTAINMENT. There is no formal entertainment, although dinner and after-dinner conversation with fellow passengers in the ship's lounge/bar really becomes the entertainment each evening.

SPA/FITNESS. There are no health spa facilities. Also, there are no medical facilities (but then the vessel is always close to land).

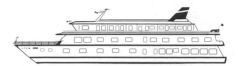

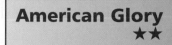

American Glory
★★

Size: . . . . .Boutique Ship	Total Crew: 22	Cabins (wheelchair accessible): 3
Tonnage: 1,287	Passengers	Wheelchair accessibility . . . . .None
Lifestyle: . . . . .Standard	(lower beds/all berths): 49/49	Cabin Current: . . . . .110 volts
Cruise Line: . . . . . .American Cruise Lines	Passenger Space Ratio	Elevators: 1
Former Names: . . . . .none	(lower beds/all berths): 26.2/26.2	Casino (gaming tables): . . . . .No
Builder: . .Chesapeake Shipbuilding (USA)	Crew/Passenger Ratio	Slot Machines: .No
Original Cost: .n/a	(lower beds/all berths): 2.2/2.2	Swimming Pools (outdoors): 0
Entered Service: . . . . .July 2002	Cabins (total): .27	Swimming Pools (indoors): 0
Registry: . . . . .USA	Size Range (sq ft/m): 176.0–382.0/	Whirlpools: 0
Length (ft/m): 174.0/53.00	16.3–35.4	Self-Service Launderette: . . . . .No
Beam (ft/m): 40.5/12.30	Cabins (outside view): 27	Dedicated Cinema/Seats: . . . . .No
Draft (ft/m): 6.5/1.98	Cabins (interior/no view): 0	Library: . . . . .No
Propulsion/Propellers: diesel/2	Cabins (for one person): 5	
Passenger Decks: 4	Cabins (with private balcony): 14	

OVERALL SCORE: 835 OUT OF A POSSIBLE 2,000 POINTS

OVERVIEW. American Cruise Lines is the resurrection of a company with the same name that existed between 1974 and 1989. It now features intra-coastal waterway cruising, as well as sailings in New England and the Hudson River Valley. *American Glory* was built specifically for coastal cruising and cannot venture far from the coastline. The ship's uppermost deck is open (good for views), and there are tables and chairs, a few sunloungers, and a small putting green.

There are two public lounges. The main one – the observation lounge – is located forward, with windows on three sides (an open bar is set up each afternoon). A second, smaller lounge is sandwiched between cabins on the same deck.

The point is to get close to the inland areas, cities and town of America's intra-coastal waterways and coastline. There's no waiting in line – you can board whenever you want. The ship docks in the center, or within walking distance of most towns on the itineraries. The dress code is "no ties casual". The score is marginally better than for sister ship *American Eagle* due to some improvements in construction and the addition of more balcony cabins.

It really is *extremely* expensive for what you get, compared even to ships of a similar size and purpose (although this is a new ship and the cabins are of a better size and are slightly better equipped). There is an elevator, which goes to all decks.

SUITABLE FOR: *American Glory* is best suited to couples and single travelers sharing a cabin who are of mature years and want to cruise in an all-American environment aboard a small ship where the itineraries and destinations are more important than food, service or entertainment.

BERLITZ'S RATINGS

	Possible	Achieved
Ship	500	267
Accommodation	200	110
Food	400	196
Service	400	170
Entertainment	n/a	n/a
Cruise	500	102

ACCOMMODATION. There are cabins for couples and singles, seven suites, and five wheelchair-accessible cabins. All cabins have twin beds (which can be converted to a king-size bed), color TV, a small desk with chair, and clothes hanging space. The seven most expensive cabins also have a VCR and compact disc (audio) player. All cabins have a private bathroom with separate shower enclosure, washbasin and toilet (none of the cabins has a bathtub), as well as windows that open. Accommodation designated as suites also have a private balcony; although this is narrow, it does have two chairs and a small drinks table.

CUISINE. The dining salon, located in the latter third of the vessel, has large, panoramic picture windows on three of its sides. There's open seating (no assigned tables). There are no tables for two, and the chairs do not have armrests The food is very much American fare – good and wholesome, featuring regional cuisines.

There is little choice of entrées, appetizers, or soups, although it has been improved in the past year. There is no wine list, although basic white and red low-quality American table wines are included. On the last morning of each cruise, only continental breakfast is available.

ENTERTAINMENT. There is no formal entertainment, although dinner and after-dinner conversation with fellow passengers in the ship's lounge/bar really becomes the entertainment each evening. Otherwise, take a good book.

SPA/FITNESS. There are no health spa facilities, and no medical facilities (the ship is almost always close to land).

American Spirit
★★

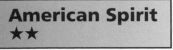

Size: . . . . .Boutique Ship	Total Crew: 27	Cabins (wheelchair accessible): 1
Tonnage: 99	Passengers	Wheelchair accessibility . . . . .None
Lifestyle: . . . . .Standard	(lower beds/all berths): 92/92	Cabin Current: . . . . .110 volts
Cruise Line: . . . . . .American Cruise Lines	Passenger Space Ratio	Elevators: 1
Former Names: . . . . .none	(lower beds/all berths): 1.0/1.0	Casino (gaming tables): . . . . .No
Builder: . .Chesapeake Shipbuilding (USA)	Crew/Passenger Ratio	Slot Machines: . . . . .No
Original Cost: . . . . .n/a	(lower beds/all berths): 3.4/3.4	Swimming Pools (outdoors): 0
Entered Service: . . . . .June 2005	Cabins (total): 51	Swimming Pools (indoors): 0
Registry: . . . . .USA	Size Range (sq ft/m): 204.0-240.0/	Whirlpools: 0
Length (ft/m): 220.0/67.0	18.9-22.2	Self-Service Launderette: . . . . .No
Beam (ft/m): 46.0/14.0	Cabins (outside view): 51	Dedicated Cinema/Seats: . . . . .No
Draft (ft/m): 8.2/2.5	Cabins (interior/no view): 0	Library: . . . . .Yes
Propulsion/Propellers: diesel/2	Cabins (for one person): 5	
Passenger Decks: 4	Cabins (with private balcony): 23	

BERLITZ'S OVERALL SCORE: 922 OUT OF A POSSIBLE 2,000 POINTS

OVERVIEW. *American Spirit* is the third vessel in the growing fleet of American Cruise Lines (which builds the vessels in its shipyard in Chesapeake, Maryland). It is the resurrection of a company with the same name that existed between 1974 and 1989. The company features intracoastal waterway cruising, as well as sailings in New England and the Hudson River Valley. *American Spirit* is built specifically for coastal cruising and cannot venture far from the coastline. Its uppermost deck is open (good for views) behind the forward windbreaker, and the expansive open deck sports many sunloungers, and a small putting green.

Inside, the public rooms include an observation lounge, with views forward and on starboard side (complimentary cocktails and hors d'oeuvres are offered before dinner); a library/lounge; a small midships lounge; and an elevator that goes to all decks.

Cruises are typically of seven days' duration. There's no waiting in line – you can board whenever you want. The ship docks in the center, or within walking distance of most towns on the itineraries. The dress code is "no ties casual". It really is extremely expensive for what you get (although this is a new ship and the cabins are of a better size and are slightly better equipped than those of smaller half-sisters *American Eagle* and *American Glory*). A sister ship, *American Star*, is entered service in June 2007.

SUITABLE FOR: *American Spirit* is best suited to couples and single travelers sharing a cabin who are of mature years and want to cruise in an all-American environment aboard a small ship where the itineraries and destinations are more important than food, service or entertainment.

BERLITZ'S RATINGS

	Possible	Achieved
Ship	500	287
Accommodation	200	125
Food	400	210
Service	400	175
Entertainment	n/a	n/a
Cruise	500	125

ACCOMMODATION. There are five cabin price grades (four are doubles, one is for singles). All cabins have twin beds (convertible to a king-size bed), a small desk with chair, color TV, and clothes hanging space. The seven most expensive cabins also have a DVD and CD player. All cabins have a private (modular) bathroom with separate shower enclosure, washbasin and toilet (none has a tub), plus windows that open, and satellite-feed TV sets. Accommodation designated as suites also have a private balcony; although this is narrow, it has two chairs and a small drinks table. Some 23 cabins have a French balcony (you can open the door for fresh air, but it's too narrow to place chairs on).

CUISINE. The dining salon, in the latter third of the vessel, has large, panoramic picture windows on three of its sides. There's open seating (no assigned tables) and all passengers dine at a single seating, at large tables, allowing you to get to know your fellow passengers. The food is very much American fare – good and wholesome, with regional cuisines. There is a limited choice of entrées, appetizers, and soups. There is no wine list, although basic white and red low-quality US table wines are included. On the last morning of each cruise, only continental breakfast is available.

ENTERTAINMENT. There is no formal entertainment, although dinner and after-dinner conversation with fellow passengers in the ship's lounge/bar really becomes the entertainment each evening. Otherwise, take a good book.

SPA/FITNESS. There is a small fitness room with a few bicycles and other exercise machines.

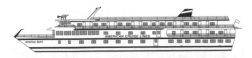

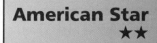

American Star
★★

Size: . . . . .Boutique Ship	Total Crew: 27	Cabins (wheelchair accessible): 1
Tonnage: 99	Passengers	Wheelchair accessibility . . . . .None
Lifestyle: . . . . .Standard	(lower beds/all berths): 94/100	Cabin Current: . . . . .110 volts
Cruise Line: . . . . . .American Cruise Lines	Passenger Space Ratio	Elevators: 1
Former Names: . . . . .none	(lower beds/all berths): 1.0/0.9	Casino (gaming tables): . . . . .No
Builder: . .Chesapeake Shipbuilding (USA)	Crew/Passenger Ratio	Slot Machines: .No
Original Cost: .n/a	(lower beds/all berths): 3.4/3.4	Swimming Pools (outdoors): 0
Entered Service: . . . . .June 2007	Cabins (total): .52	Swimming Pools (indoors): 0
Registry: . . . . .USA	Size Range (sq ft/m): 204.0-240.0/	Whirlpools: 0
Length (ft/m): 220.0/67.0	18.9-22.2	Self-Service Launderette: . . . . .No
Beam (ft/m): 46.0/14.0	Cabins (outside view): 51	Dedicated Cinema/Seats: . . . . .No
Draft (ft/m): 8.2/2.5	Cabins (interior/no view): 0	Library: . . . . .Yes
Propulsion/Propellers: diesel/2	Cabins (for one person): 5	
Passenger Decks: 4	Cabins (with private balcony): 23	

BERLITZ'S OVERALL SCORE: 925 OUT OF A POSSIBLE 2,000 POINTS

OVERVIEW. *American Star* is the fourth vessel in the growing fleet of American Cruise Lines (which builds the ships in its own shipyard in Chesapeake, Maryland), and the company's best vessel by far. The company features intra-coastal waterway cruising, as well as sailings in New England and the Hudson River Valley. *American Star* is built specifically for coastal and inland cruising to destinations unreachable by large cruise ships, in a relaxed, unregimented environment. The uppermost deck is open (good for views) behind a forward windbreaker; many sunloungers are provided, as is a small golf putting green.

The public rooms include an observation lounge, with views forward and to port and starboard side (complimentary cocktails and hors d'oeuvres are offered before dinner); a library/lounge; a small midships lounge, and an elevator that goes to all decks (including the outdoor sun deck).

Cruises are typically of 7–14 days' duration. The ship docks in the center, or within walking distance of most towns and ports. The dress code is "no ties casual." It is extremely expensive for what you get – although this is a new ship and the cabins are larger and slightly better equipped than those of smaller half-sisters *American Eagle* and *American Glory*. There are no additional costs, except for gratuities and port charges, because it's all included (quite different to big-ship cruising).

SUITABLE FOR: Couples and single travelers of mature years sharing a cabin and wishing to cruise in an all-American environment aboard a small ship where the destinations are more important than food, service or entertainment.

BERLITZ'S RATINGS

	Possible	Achieved
Ship	500	287
Accommodation	200	125
Food	400	210
Service	400	178
Entertainment	n/a	n/a
Cruise	500	125

ACCOMMODATION. There are five cabin price grades (four are doubles, one is for singles). All cabins have twin beds (convertible to a king-size bed), a small desk with chair, flat-screen TV set, DVD player and internet access, and clothes hanging space. All cabins have internet access, a private (modular) bathroom with separate shower enclosure, washbasin and toilet (no cabin has a bathtub), windows that open, and satellite-feed television sets. Accommodation incorrectly designated as suites (23) also have a private balcony; although narrow, it does have two chairs and a small drinks table.

CUISINE. The dining salon, in the latter third of the vessel, has large, panoramic picture windows on three of its sides. All passengers dine at a single (open) seating – there are no assigned tables – at large tables, so you can get to know your fellow passengers. The cuisine is American: simple, honest food featuring regional specialties. The choice of entrées, appetizers, and soups is limited, however. There is no wine list, although basic white and red American table wines are included. On the last morning of each cruise, only continental breakfast is available.

ENTERTAINMENT. There is no formal entertainment, although dinner and after-dinner conversation with fellow passengers in the ship's lounge/bar really becomes the entertainment each evening. Otherwise, take a good book.

SPA/FITNESS. There is a tiny fitness room with a few bicycles and other exercise machines.

Amsterdam
★★★★

Size: . . . . .Mid-size Ship	Passenger Decks: 12	Cabins (with private balcony): 172
Tonnage: .61,000	Total Crew: 600	Cabins (wheelchair accessible): 20
Lifestyle: . . . . .Premium	Passengers	Wheelchair accessibility . . . . .Good
Cruise Line: . . . . . . .Holland America Line	(lower beds/all berths): 1,380/1,653	Cabin Current: . . . . .110 and 220 volts
Former Names: . . . . .none	Passenger Space Ratio	Elevators: 12
Builder: . . . . .Fincantieri (Italy)	(lower beds/all berths): 44.2/36.9	Casino (gaming tables): . . . . .Yes
Original Cost: . . . .$400 million	Crew/Passenger	Slot Machines: . . . . .Yes
Entered Service: . . . . .Oct 2000	Ratio (lower beds/all berths): 2.3/2.7	Swimming Pools (outdoors): 1
Registry: . . . . .The Netherlands	Cabins (total): 690	Swimming Pools (indoors): 1
Length (ft/m): 780.8/238.00	Size Range (sq ft/m): 184.0–1,124.8/	(magrodome cover)
Beam (ft/m): 105.8/32.25	17.1–104.5	Whirlpools: 2
Draft (ft/m): 25.5/7.80	Cabins (outside view): 557	Self-Service Launderette: . . . . .Yes
Propulsion/Propellers: . . . . .diesel-electric	Cabins (interior/no view): 133	Dedicated Cinema/Seats: Yes/235
(37,500 kW)/2 x 15.5 MW azimuthing pods	Cabins (for one person): 0	Library: . . . . .Yes

OVERALL SCORE: 1,537 OUT OF A POSSIBLE 2,000 POINTS

OVERVIEW. *Amsterdam*, a close sister ship to *Rotterdam*, has a nicely raked bow, as well as the familiar interior flow and design style. It was the first ship in the Holland America Line fleet to feature an azimuthing pod propulsion system *(see page 45 for details)*. The pods are powered by a diesel-electric system.

The decor retains much of the traditional ocean liner detailing so loved by frequent Holland America Line passengers, with some use of medium and dark wood panelling. However, some color combinations – particularly for the chairs and soft furnishings – are rather wacky. Much of the artwork reflects Holland America Line's glorious past, as well as items depicting the city of Amsterdam's history.

The interior focal point is a three-deck high atrium, in an oval, instead of circular, shape. A whimsical "Astrolobe" is the featured centerpiece in this atrium. Also clustered in the atrium lobby are the reception desk, shore excursion desk, photo shop and photo gallery.

The ship has three principal passenger stairways – so much better than two from the viewpoint of safety, flow and accessibility. There is a magrodome-covered pool on the Lido Deck between the mast and the twin funnels, watched over by a sculpture of a brown bear catching salmon.

There are children's and teens' play areas (token gestures by a company that traditionally does not cater well to children). Popcorn is available at the Wajang Theater for moviegoers, while adjacent is the popular Java Cafe. The casino, in the middle of a major passenger flow on one of the entertainment decks, has blackjack, roulette, poker and dice tables alongside the requisite rows of slot machines.

BERLITZ'S RATINGS

	Possible	Achieved
Ship	500	430
Accommodation	200	165
Food	400	281
Service	400	273
Entertainment	100	78
Cruise	400	310

Amsterdam is an extremely comfortable ship, with some fine, elegant and luxurious decorative features. However, these are marred by the poor quality of food and service and the lack of understanding of what it takes to make a "luxury" cruise experience, despite what is touted in the company's brochures.

Holland America Line also provides cappuccino and espresso coffees and free ice cream during certain hours of the day aboard its ships, as well as hot hors d'oeuvres in all bars – something other major lines seem to have dropped, or charge extra for.

The onboard currency is the US dollar. Perhaps the ship's best asset is its friendly and personable Filipino and Indonesian crew, although communication can prove frustrating at times.

With one whole deck of suites (and a dedicated, private concierge lounge, with preferential passenger treatment), the company has in effect created a two-class ship. The charge to use the washing machines and dryers in the self-service launderette is petty and irritating, particularly for the occupants of high-priced cabins.

Communication (in English) with many of the staff, particularly in the dining room and informal buffet areas, can prove frustrating. The room service menu is limited, and room service is very basic.

ACCOMMODATION. This is spread over five decks (some cabins have full or partially obstructed views), and is in 16 grades: 11 with outside views, and 5 interior grades (no view). There are four penthouse suites, and 50 suites (14 more than aboard sister ship *Rotterdam*). No cabin is more than 130 feet (40 meters) from a stairway, which makes it very easy to find your way from your cabin to the public rooms. Although 81% of cabins have outside views, only 25% of those have balconies.

All of the "standard" interior and outside-view cabins are tastefully furnished, and have twin beds that convert to a queen-sized bed (but the space is a little tight for walking between beds and the vanity unit). There is a decent amount of closet and drawer space, although this will prove tight for longer voyages. The fully tiled bathrooms are disappointingly small (particularly on long cruises), the shower tubs are very small, and the storage for one's personal toiletries is quite basic. There is little detailing to distinguish the bathrooms from those aboard the *Statendam*-class ships. All cabin televisions carry CNN and TNT, as well as movies, and ship information and shopping channels.

There are 50 Verandah Suites and four Penthouse Suites on Navigation Deck. The suites all share a private Concierge Lounge with a concierge to handle such things as special dining arrangements, shore excursions and special requests, although strangely there are no butlers for these suites, as aboard ships with similar facilities. The lounge, with its wood detailing and private library is accessible only by private key-card.

Four Penthouse Suites are extremely civilized. Each has a separate steward's entrance, as well as a separate bedroom with king-sized bed, vanity desk, large walk-in closet with excellent drawer and hanging space, living room, dining room (seating up to eight), wet bar, and pantry. The bathroom is large, and has a big oval Jacuzzi bathtub, separate shower enclosure, two washbasins, separate toilet and bidet. There is also a guest bathroom with toilet and washbasin. There is a good-sized private balcony. Suite occupants get personal stationary, complimentary laundry and ironing, cocktail-hour hors d'oeuvres and other goodies, as well as priority embarkation and disembarkation.

CUISINE. The La Fontaine Dining Room seats 747, spans two decks, and has a huge stained-glass ceiling measuring almost 1,500 sq. ft (140 sq. meters), with a floral motif and fibre-optic lighting. There are tables for two, four, six or eight (there are few tables for two). Both open seating and fixed (assigned tables and times) seating are available, while breakfast and lunch are open-seating (you'll be seated by restaurant staff when you enter). Rosenthal china and fine cutlery are provided. The dining room is a non-smoking venue.

Alternative (Reservations Required) Dining Spot
The 88-seat Pinnacle Grill is available to all passengers on a reservation-only basis (priority reservations are given to those in suite grades). There is an extra charge for dining here ($10 for lunch, $20 for dinner), but there's better food and presentation than in the main dining room (it's open for lunch and dinner). The whimsically surreal artwork fea-

tures scenic landscapes. The cuisine is California-Italian in style, with small portions and few vegetables. The wine list is good (and wines are served in the correct stemware).

Another alternative, the Lido Buffet Restaurant, is open for casual dinners on all except the last night of each cruise, in an open-seating arrangement. Tables are set with crisp linens, flatware and standard stemware. A set menu is featured, and this includes a choice of four entrées.

For casual breakfasts and lunches, the Lido Buffet Restaurant provides old-style, stand-in-line serve-yourself canteen food – adequate for anyone used to TV dinner food, but most definitely not as lavish as the brochures claim. Although the salad items appear adequate when displayed, they are too cold and quite devoid of taste. The constant supply of iceberg lettuce doesn't seem to go away (but there is little choice of other, more suitable, lettuces and greens).

ENTERTAINMENT. The 577-seat Queen's Lounge is the venue for all production shows, strong cabaret, and other entertainment. It is two decks high (with main and balcony level seating). The stage has hydraulic lifts and three video screens, and closed-loop system for the hearing-impaired.

While Holland America Line is not known for its fine entertainment (the budgets aren't high enough), what the line does offer is a consistently good, tried and tested array of cabaret acts. The production shows, while a good attempt, fall short on storyline, choreography and performance, with colorful costuming and lighting hiding the weak spots.

A number of bands, a string ensemble and solo musicians present live music for dancing and listening in many of the lounges and bars. There's dancing in the Crows Nest (atop the navigation bridge), and serenading string music in the Explorer's Lounge, among other venues.

SPA/FITNESS. The Ocean Spa is located one deck above the navigation bridge at the very forward part of the ship. It includes a gymnasium (with all the latest muscle-pumping exercise machines, including an abundance of treadmills) with forward views over the ship's bows, an aerobics exercise area, large beauty salon with ocean-view windows to the port side, several treatment rooms, and men's and women's saunas, steam rooms and changing areas.

The spa is operated by Steiner, a specialist concession, whose young staff will try to sell you Steiner's own-brand Elemis beauty products. Some fitness classes are free, while some, such as yoga, and kick-boxing, cost $10 per class. Massage facials, pedicures, and beauty salon treatments cost extra (massage, for example, costs about $2 per minute, plus gratuity).

For the sports-minded, two paddle-tennis courts are located at the aft of the Sports Deck.

● **For more extensive general information about a Holland America Line cruise, see pages 139–42.**

Aquamarine
★★ +

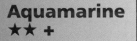

Size: . . . . Mid-Sized Ship	Passenger Decks: 7	Cabins (with private balcony): 0
Tonnage:. 23,149	Total Crew: 432	Cabins (wheelchair accessible): 0
Lifestyle: . . . . Standard	Passengers	Wheelchair accessibility . . . . .None
Cruise Line: . . . . Louis Cruises	(lower beds/all berths): 1,050/1,158	Cabin Current: . . . . 110/220 volts
Former Names: . . . . *Arielle, Aquamarine,*	Passenger Space Ratio	Elevators: 4
Carousel, Nordic Prince	(lower beds/all berths): 22.0/19.9	Casino (gaming tables): . . . . Yes
Builder: . . . . Wartsila (Finland)	Crew/Passenger Ratio	Slot Machines: . . . . Yes
Original Cost: . . . . $13.5 million	(lower beds/all berths): 2.4/2.6	Swimming Pools (outdoors): 1
Entered Service: . . . July 1971/May 2008	Cabins (total): 525	Swimming Pools (indoors): 0
Registry: . . . . Cyprus	Size Range (sq ft/m): 119.4–482.2/	Whirlpools: 0
Length (ft/m): 637.4/194.3	11.1–44.8	Self-Service Launderette: . . . . No
Beam (ft/m): 78.8/24.03	Cabins (outside view): 339	Dedicated Cinema/Seats: . . . . No
Draft (ft/m): 21.9/6.70	Cabins (interior/no view): 186	Library: . . . . Yes
Propulsion/Propellers: diesel 3,400kW/2	Cabins (for one person): 0	

BERLITZ'S OVERALL SCORE: 1,090 OUT OF A POSSIBLE 2,000 POINTS

OVERVIEW. *Aquamarine*, originally built for Royal Caribbean International, underwent a "shop and stretch" operation as *Nordic Prince* in 1980 that added a mid-section, including more public rooms and cabins. It began its present life with Louis Cruises in 2005, and now operates cruises from Greece.

There is a polished walk-around promenade deck outdoors (slippery when wet) and nicely varnished wooden railings. The main open deck space for sunbathing is limited and noisy when the ship is full, although there are quieter spots forward and aft. The interior layout and passenger flow is sound, with rather tired 1970s decor, including some wood paneling and bright metal accenting. But note that the accommodation deck hallways are extremely narrow and poorly lit. The major public rooms – showlounge, restaurant, buffet restaurant, card room/library and small casino – are conveniently located on one deck – the horizontal flow making it easy to find your way around.

The onboard currency is the euro, and gratuities to staff are not included in the fare. There are many children aboard during peak holiday periods, and under-17s cruise free (when in the same cabin as two adults), although children's facilities are extremely limited.

Aquamarine is all about no-frills destination-intensive cruising, with the ship essentially a floating hotel. However, the food is rather good, as is the food service.

SUITABLE FOR: *Aquamarine* is best suited to younger couples, singles, and young families who are used to package holidays and tight budgets. Good for a first cruise, in reasonably comfortable, but almost basic surroundings, with a fair array of facilities plus low cost food and entertainment.

BERLITZ'S RATINGS

	Possible	Achieved
Ship	500	258
Accommodation	200	104
Food	400	221
Service	400	241
Entertainment	100	54
Cruise	400	212

ACCOMMODATION. Most cabins are extremely small, and soundproofing between them is poor, but do remember that this ship is almost 40 years old. The cabins also have little closet and storage space, although all have a small TV (larger in accommodation designated as suites), radio, personal safe, hairdryer, and telephone. Many cabins have pull-down upper berths (good, but tight, for families). The bathrooms are small. Only the two top grades have bathrooms with a tub; all other cabins have showers.

There are two L-shaped suites, both located on Promenade Deck; these consist of a lounge/living area, separate bedroom and bathroom, but there is no private balcony.

CUISINE. The 610-seat Aquamarine Restaurant, which operates in two seatings, is quite large, with tables for four, six or eight. The food is basic, no-frills cuisine, but there's plenty of it. There is an adequate, but limited, wine list. Well-presented casual meals can be taken in the self-serve Bistro buffet, located aft. Alternatively, fast food and grilled items are served at a poolside Taverna.

ENTERTAINMENT. The Aquamarine Lounge has a "thrust" stage and hardwood dance floor, but some seats have obtructed sight lines. The single-level room best suits cabaret acts. Shows are typically revue or variety style, with an energetic troupe of young singers and dancers who may double as cruise staff. There are also professional cabaret acts.

SPA/FITNESS. There is a beauty salon, fitness room, and sauna (all in different locations). Treatment prices are quite moderate.

Arcadia
★★★★

Size: . . . . .Large Resort Ship	(34,000 kW)/ 2 azimuthing pods	Cabins (for one person): 0
Tonnage: .82,972	Passenger Decks: 10	Cabins (with private balcony): 677
Lifestyle: . . . . .Standard	Total Crew: 886	Cabins (wheelchair accessible): 30
Cruise Line: . . . . .P&O Cruises	Passengers	Wheelchair accessibility . . . . .Good
Former Names: . . . . .none	(lower beds/all berths): 2,064/2,628	Cabin Current: . . . . 110/220 volts
Builder: . . . . .Fincantieri (Italy)	Passenger Space Ratio	Elevators: 14
Original Cost: . . . .$400 million	(lower beds/all berths): 41.5/32.4	Casino (gaming tables): . . . . .Yes
Entered Service: . . . . .April 2005	Crew/Passenger Ratio	Slot Machines: . . . . .Yes
Registry: . . . . .Bermuda	(lower beds/all berths): 2.3/2.9	Swimming Pools (outdoors): 2
Length (ft/m): 936.0/285.3	Cabins (total): 1,032	Swimming Pools (indoors): 0
Beam (ft/m): 105.0/32.0	Size Range (sq ft/m): . .170–516.6/15.7–48	Whirlpools: 5
Draft (ft/m): 25.5/7.8	Cabins (outside view): 690	Self-Service Launderette: . . . . .Yes
Propulsion/Propellers: . . . . .diesel-electric	Cabins (interior/no view): 342	Dedicated Cinema/Seats: . . . . .Yes

OVERALL SCORE: 1,490 OUT OF A POSSIBLE 2,000 POINTS

OVERVIEW. P&O's *Arcadia* was intended to be Cunard Line's *Queen Victoria* for the British cruise market, but was transferred to the P&O Cruises brand (both are owned by the Carnival Corporation). *Arcadia* can also transit the Panama Canal.

Outdoors facilities include a walk-around promenade deck (covered in the ship's forward section), with plenty of sunloungers (and cushioned pads). A large Lido Deck pool has a moveable glass domed cover – useful in poor weather. Panoramic exterior glass-wall elevators grace the central foyer to port and starboard and travel between all 10 passenger decks. Pod propulsion is provided *(see page 45)*.

The layout provides a horizontal flow, with most public rooms, shops, bars and lounges set open-plan style on two principal decks, so finding your way around is relatively easy. However, the layout of upper public room decks is not so good. The interior decor is geared towards those with youthful, contemporary – even trendy British – tastes, and can best be described as "traditionally modern." It is, however, restrained and welcoming (if a bit bland), and has many warm, earthy pastel colors, assisted by 3,000 works of art (some outstanding) by contemporary British artists, at a cost of $4 million. Although *Arcadia* is one of the Carnival Corporation's Vista-class ships, the decor is perhaps the most refined of them all, and both passenger flow and signage are generally good.

Facilities include a forward-facing Crow's Nest observation lounge high atop the ship (in a contemporary setting); a florist; a gift shop arcade; and a Monte Carlo casino, a library (with leather armchairs and a Waterstone's section for paperback sales), a 30-seat boutique screening room which replaced the cyberstudy in a 2008 refit, and The Retreat (a

BERLITZ'S RATINGS

	Possible	Achieved
Ship	500	420
Accommodation	200	150
Food	400	258
Service	400	292
Entertainment	100	81
Cruise	400	289

good place to meet and chill out). The 14 bars include the Spinnaker Bar (good for ship buffs, with its fine display of ship models), a "traditional" English pub (The Rising Sun, with Boddington's draught beer), plus a bar overlooking a very modest three decks-high atrium lobby. The lobby (there isn't one, really) is small and disappointing, particularly when compared to *Oceana*.

Arcadia, strictly a child-free ship (no under-18s allowed), blends traditional British cruising with contemporary facilities for adults, although it really is a completely different type of ship to the more traditional *Aurora, Oceana* or *Oriana*. The ship is registered in Bermuda, so UK and US passport holders can be legally married by the ship's captain (check with P&O Cruises for the latest requirements). You can also renew your vows in a special ceremony (£250 per couple).

The New Horizons lecture program provides an array of lectures on a range of subjects (introductory sessions at no charge; more in-depth subject matter study in smaller groups, at an additional cost, typically £5 or £10 per class).

Arcadia is the latest generation of trendy, contemporary cruise ships, based year-round in Southampton, England (so there's no flying involved for UK passengers). The onboard currency is the UK pound. However, many extra onboard revenue centers have now appeared aboard P&O Cruises' ships, including *Arcadia* – such as paying for lectures and thalassotherapy pool use. Also, smoking is permitted only on cabin balconies and in designated spots on the open decks – the interior space is a non-smoking environment.

Some niggles: there is no room for card games such as bridge; the ship's dance floor space is pitiful; and the embarkation system keeps people waiting in a lounge after lines at the check-in desks and security until boarding card letters are called. The small public toilets lack touches like flowers and hand towels; poolside gala reception lacks atmosphere (and "nibbles"); pre-dinner announcements are robotic, too; and there are no towels at poolside (you must take them from your cabin). The often noisy air conditioning cannot be turned off in cabins or bathrooms.

SUITABLE FOR: *Arcadia* is best suited to couples and singles seeking to cruise in a large, modern, child-free ship, with entertainment geared for British tastes, with an informal setting and plenty of public rooms to play in.

ACCOMMODATION. There are 26 price grades of accommodation (in seven types of suites/cabins); the choice includes 23 suites, 24 mini-suites, and 685 outside view cabins with a private balcony. While there are plenty of price grades, there are really only five types of accommodation: suites, mini-suites, cabins with private balcony, and twin-bedded cabins with or without a window. All cabin doors and elevators have numbers in Braille.

There are 67 suites and mini-suites. All accommodation has duvets as standard (blankets and pillows if you prefer), flat-screen TV sets, tea/coffee making sets (with Tetley teabags and long-life milk) , small refrigerator, vanity/writing desk, personal safe, hairdryer; bathrooms have half-sized tubs/shower/washbasin and toilet. High quality personal toiletries are by Temple Spa, with larger bottles and more selection choice provided for suite occupants.

Also standard are stylish bed runners, Slumberland 8-inch sprung mattresses, 10.5 tog duvets (blankets and pillows if you prefer), Egyptian cotton towels and robes, improved tea/coffee making facilities with speciality teas (long-life is provided) and a Nick Munro-designed bespoke tray, as well as in-cabin toning and fitness facilities for passengers who would prefer to exercise in private.

In twin-bedded cabin grades (approximately 170 sq.ft.), when the beds are pushed together, there's little room to maneuver, but they are otherwise quite practical units.

Accommodation designated as suites (approximately 516 sq.ft. including balcony) and mini-suites (approximately 384 sq.ft. including balcony) benefit from more space (some are really just the size of two cabins), king-sized bed, trouser press, ironing board and iron, three-seat sofa (suites) or two-seat sofa (mini-suites), wall clock, binoculars. The bathrooms are larger, and include an aqua-jet bathtub, two washbasins, toilet, and separate shower enclosure (suites only), and a boxed set of Molton Brown personal toiletry items. So-called "butler" service is provided, but, unlike most lines with these kinds of grades, bottled water costs extra, as do soft drinks.

Passenger niggles include the space-hogging coffee/tea-making set on the small vanity desk in standard cabin grades, although the set is comprehensive. Other gripes (standard cabins) include: closets with hanging space too narrow for the width of a man's jacket; little drawer space; poor-quality plastic hangars and the hanging system, and no hooks for belts.

Room service breakfast choice is limited, but is available between 7am and 11am.

CUISINE. The Meridian Restaurant, located aft, is two decks high (the two decks are connected by a spiral staircase); it has 11 superb glass/fibre optic ceiling chandeliers (created by Neil Wilkin), and a podium with grand piano graces the upper level. There are two seatings in both restaurants, and tables are for two, four, six, or eight.

Alternative (extra charge) restaurants. Arcadian Rhodes (£15 per person), and the Orchid Restaurant (£10 per person) provide smaller, more intimate dining settings as an escape from the main dining rooms. Arcadian Rhodes was Gary Rhodes's first seagoing restaurant; he created the menu and the chefs/cooks were trained in his London restaurant. The decor is rather uninspiring, however, and banquette seating doesn't suit fine dining. The Orchid Restaurant (on Deck 11) has fine panoramic views, and is an alternative, eatery with Asian-fusion (heavy on the spices) cuisine, and its own bar for pre-meal drinks. Reservations are required in both venues.

For casual meals and snacks, there's a self-serve 24-hour food-court-style eatery (Belvedere), a section of which becomes another dining venue at night, serving Indian cuisine. There's also an open deck Neptune Grill (for burgers and other fast food items), and Caffe Vivo (for coffees and pastries, at extra cost).

ENTERTAINMENT. The Palladium show lounge is an entertainment palace with three seating tiers and the latest in high-tech staging, lighting, and sound systems. Seating is in both banquette-style and individual tub chairs, and the sightlines to the stage are generally good. There are several major production shows –some with a Cirque du Soleil feel to them – complete with major bungee-diving acrobatics and fine adagio dancers. In addition, the ship has an array of cabaret acts. Classical concerts are scheduled for many cruises (typically in the Crows Nest).

Ballroom dance aficionados should note that there are few wooden dance floors aboard this ship (P&O Cruises typically carries professional dance hosts and teachers).

SPA/FITNESS. The Ocean Spa includes a gymnasium with great forward ocean views, 10 body-pampering treatment rooms, a thermal suite that incorporates a hydrotherapy pool, sauna and steam room (£10 for two hours, in five timed sessions per day), and two very small multi-gender saunas at no charge, but in a location that discourages their use (the thermal suite is better), well away from the changing rooms. Additionally, The Retreat is a cool space for relation, and for calming classes like tai chi, and yoga (£5 per class). The spa is operated by the UK-based Harding Brothers. Sports facilities include a sports court for racquet or football games, a golf driving range, and the traditional shuffleboard and ring toss.

● **For more extensive general information about a P&O cruise, see pages 147–8.**

Arion
★★

Size: ....Small Ship	Passenger Decks: 5	Cabins (wheelchair accessible): 0
Tonnage: 5,885	Total Crew: 120	Wheelchair accessibility ....None
Lifestyle: ....Standard	Passengers	Cabin Current: ....220 volts
Cruise Line: .Classic International Cruises	(lower beds/all berths): 334/340	Elevators: 1
Former Names: ....*Astra I, Istra*	Passenger Space Ratio	Casino (gaming tables): ....Yes
Builder: .....Brodgradiliste (Yugoslavia)	(lower beds/all berths): 17.6/17.3	Slot Machines: ....Yes
Original Cost: ....n/a	Crew/Passenger Ratio	Swimming Pools (outdoors): 1
Entered Service: 1965/1999	(lower beds/all berths): 2.7/2.8	Swimming Pools (indoors): 0
Registry: ....Madeira	Cabins (total): 169	Whirlpools: 0
Length (ft/m): 387.1/118.0	Size Range (sq ft/m): 80.7–161.4/7.5–15.0	Self-Service Launderette: ....No
Beam (ft/m): 54.1/16.5	Cabins (outside view): 142	Dedicated Cinema/Seats: ....No
Draft (ft/m): 18.3/5.6	Cabins (interior/no view): 27	Library: ....Yes
Propulsion/Propellers: ....diesel	Cabins (for one person): 4	
(11,030kW)/2	Cabins (with private balcony): 0	

OVERALL SCORE: 902 OUT OF A POSSIBLE 2,000 POINTS

OVERVIEW. *Arion* is a charming little ship, originally built for weekly service between Venice and Egypt. It underwent a $15 million reconstruction by Classic International Cruises (even the navigation bridge was relocated forward) after the company bought the ship at auction in Haifa in 1999, and emerged in its present form in May 2000.

The ship is operated under charter to various tour operators, and thus attracts an international mix of passengers who like smaller ships with some character.

The ship features interesting itineraries, at low prices. It is particularly suited to the "nooks and crannies" style of cruising along the Dalmatian coast. The dress code is extremely casual, there is a relaxed ambiance, and the service staff are warm and friendly.

This is a small, but charming, lovingly reconstructed ship, but there are few public rooms and facilities, and little open deck space – although sunloungers do have cushioned pads. The interior passageways are narrow, the public rooms are always busy and it is difficult to avoid smokers. The ship is not suitable for disabled passengers.

SUITABLE FOR: *Arion* is best suited to adult couples, typically over 50, looking for a basic cruise holiday, in a traditional ship. This could be good for your first cruise experience, in a setting that provides basic comforts, and at a price that provides fair value for money.

ACCOMMODATION. There are 12 cabin price grades, though this may depend on tour operators that charter the vessel. Except for the top two grades, the cabins are modest in size and features, and one would not want to spend much time

BERLITZ'S RATINGS

	Possible	Achieved
Ship	500	186
Accommodation	200	90
Food	400	182
Service	400	225
Entertainment	100	40
Cruise	400	179

in them. Cabins 1–8, which have windows, have lifeboat-obstructed views. Cabins on the higher decks have windows, while others have portholes.

Each cabin has a small TV set, personal safe, and hairdryer. There is little closet and storage space (so take the minimal amount of clothing), although each cabin does have a set of bedside drawers. Some cabins have a twin bed arrangement (side by side), while others are "L"-shaped (only 13 cabins have a double bed). Some cabins have a third, or third and fourth berth. The bathrooms are tiny and basic, yet adequate.

CUISINE. The 352-seat restaurant is warm and cosy; there are ocean-view windows on two sides, and standard place settings. There are tables (quite close together) for four, six or eight. The chairs do not have armrests. All passengers dine together in one seating.

The menus are limited, although there is a good choice of breads and bread rolls. Dinner menus typically consist of one or two appetizers, two soups, and three entrées. The wine list is quite basic, and the wine glasses are small. The all-Portuguese waiters are friendly and attentive. Casual breakfasts and luncheons can be taken in the Lido Lounge, just forward of the swimming pool and the open deck aft.

ENTERTAINMENT. There is little entertainment, and what is provided is of the cabaret variety. There is a band for dancing and a pianist in the piano bar, located just aft of the main lounge, and Lido Bar.

SPA/FITNESS. None, although there is a small beauty salon. The small swimming pool is really only a "dip" pool.

Artemis
★★★ +

Size: . . . . .Mid-Size Ship	Total Crew: .520	Cabins (wheelchair accessible): 4
Tonnage: .44,348	Passengers	Wheelchair accessibility . . . . .Good
Lifestyle: . . . . .Standard	(lower beds/all berths): 1,200/1,260	Cabin Current: . . . . .110 & 220 volts
Cruise Line: . . . . .P&O Cruises	Passenger Space Ratio	Elevators: 6
Former Names: . . . . .Royal Princess	(lower beds/all berths): 36.9/35.1	Casino (gaming tables): . . . . .Yes
Builder: . . . . .Wartsila (Finland)	Crew/Passenger Ratio	Slot Machines: . . . . .Yes
Original Cost: . . . .$165 million	(lower beds/all berths): 2.3/2.4	Swimming Pools (outdoors): 2
Entered Service: . . . . Nov 1984/Jun 2005	Cabins (total): .600	(+2 splash pools)
Registry: . . . . .Bermuda	Size Range (sq ft/m): 186.0–1,126.0/	Swimming Pools (indoors): 0
Length (ft/m): 754.5/230.0	17.2–104.5	Whirlpools: 2
Beam (ft/m): 95.8/29.2	Cabins (outside view): 600	Fitness Center: . . . . .Yes
Draft (ft/m): 25.5/7.8	Cabins (interior/no view): 0	Self-Service Launderette: . . . . .Yes
Propulsion/Propellers: diesel (29,160kW)/2	Cabins (for one person): 0	Dedicated Cinema/Seats: Yes/150
Passenger Decks: 9	Cabins (with private balcony): 152	Library: . . . . .Yes

BERLITZ'S OVERALL SCORE: 1,385 OUT OF A POSSIBLE 2,000 POINTS

OVERVIEW. *Artemis* (formerly Princess Cruises' *Royal Princess*) is named after the Greek goddess Artemis and was dedicated in November 1984 by Diana, Princess of Wales. In April 2011 the ship will be transferred to Phoenix Reisen to become *Artania* for the German-speaking market, as a running mate to *Amadea*, and a restaurant will be added in order to accommodate all passengers in a single seating. P&O Cruises will replace *Artemis* with *Adonia* in May 2011.

The ship – the smallest and oldest in the P&O Cruises fleet – has reasonably contemporary outer styling that is almost handsome, and is currently committed to the British child-free cruise market. In May 2005, *Artemis* underwent a name change and a £10.5 million transformation from its former self as *Royal Princess*. In the refit, the Monte Carlo casino was made smaller in order to accommodate a new internet center; a Future Cruise Sales office and Portunus Club room replaced what was formerly a business center. The outdoor deck and sunbathing space is moderate, and there is a traditional wrap-around teak deck.

The well-designed, though slightly unconventional, interior layout features passenger cabins located above the public room decks. The interior decor is not the least bit garish, but rather reflects the feeling of space, openness and light; the passenger flow is good. For fans of P&O Cruises' "smaller" ships, *Artemis* has replaced the much loved *Victoria*, and, if you've cruised aboard *Aurora* and/or *Oriana*, you'll probably really like *Artemis*, which combines the traditions of cruising with the bonus of a child-free environment. There are several large, nicely appointed public rooms, spacious passageways and imposing staircases. Overall, however, the ship is well worn, and looks tired in several places.

BERLITZ'S RATINGS

	Possible	Achieved
Ship	500	346
Accommodation	200	141
Food	400	256
Service	400	279
Entertainment	100	72
Cruise	400	291

A Horizon Lounge, set around the funnel base, has fine views and a peaceful environment during the day, while at night it transforms into a disco for the late-night set. When this ship debuted, it was state-of-the-art, but now lags behind the latest ships in several ways, and looks tired. One nice feature is the dedicated movie theater (few new ships have them). *Artemis* will provide you with a decent cruise experience in reasonably spacious, almost elegant surroundings, at a decent price.

Many of the cruises are themed, and carry out the theme in the form of the company's New Horizons program (introductory classes are free of charge, but more in-depth classes are at extra cost, typically £5 or £10).

Smoking is permitted only on cabin balconies and in designated spots on the open decks – the interior space is a non-smoking environment.

The ship is registered in Bermuda, so UK and USA passport holders can be legally married by the ship's captain (do check with P&O Cruises for the latest requirements and details). You can also renew your vows in a special ceremony costing £250 per couple.

SUITABLE FOR: *Artemis* is best suited to couples and singles seeking to cruise in a modern *child-free* ship, with entertainment geared specifically for British tastes in a large ship, with an informal setting and plenty of public rooms to play in.

ACCOMMODATION. The all-outside view cabins (152 with private balcony) represent just four accommodation types (including suites), although there are 25 price categories.

All cabins (most have twin beds) are comfortable and well appointed, although they are a trifle bland. Note that many cabins have mirrors placed opposite beds (which will not please *feng shui* practitioners).

All cabins have a combination bathtub and shower, three-sided mirrors, color TV set, and British three-pin sockets. Also standard are stylish bed runners, Slumberland 8-inch sprung mattresses, 10.5 tog duvets (blankets and pillows if you prefer), Egyptian cotton towels and robes, improved tea/coffee making facilities with speciality teas (long-life is provided) and a Nick Munro-designed bespoke tray, as well as in-cabin toning and fitness facilities for passengers who would prefer to exercise in private. High quality personal toiletries are by Temple Spa, an upgrade from what was previously provided aboard the ships of P&O Cruises (with larger bottles and more selection choice provided for suite occupants).

Molton Brown personal toiletries are provided (suite occupants get more), as are bathrobes and chocolates on your pillow each night. Prompt, attentive room service is available 24 hours a day.

Some cabins on both Baja Deck and "C" Deck have full or partial lifeboat and safety equipment-obstructed views. Some cabins have extra berths fitted. Note that the in-cabin service menu is really quite basic.

The *Canberra* and *Oriana* suites are the largest, and they are quite attractive, although not that large by today's standards (the balcony is also small). All suite occupants get butler service, an expanded range of personal toiletries, complimentary mineral water, a larger breakfast menu, and the possibility of ordering anything from the full restaurant menu for lunch and dinner.

CUISINE. The elegant Coral Dining Room is set low down, and is conveniently adjacent to the lobby. There are two seatings for dinner, at tables for two, four, six or eight. The well-orchestrated service, by staff from India and Goa, is friendly. The Conservatory is an indoor-outdoor Lido Deck self-serve eatery for casual meals and snacks, and is open 24 hours a day; at night one section becomes The Grill at The Conservatory.

ENTERTAINMENT. The International Lounge is the venue for shows, drama presentations, main cabaret acts, and some social functions. It is an amphitheater-shaped room with good sightlines from the majority of seats, although it is only one deck high – more for cabaret acts than large-scale production shows. P&O Cruises always provides plenty of live music for the various bars and lounges, and volume is normally kept to an acceptable level.

SPA/FITNESS. The Oasis Spa is located on one of the uppermost decks, clustered around the base of the funnel housing. It contains a gymnasium with some decent muscle-toning equipment and large picture windows that overlook one of the swimming pools, saunas and changing rooms for men and women, and beauty salon (on a different deck), as well as a display of exercise clothing for sale.

The spa is operated by Harding Brothers, a UK-based concession that provides the staff and a wide range of beauty and wellness treatments. Examples of treatments include: Body Toning (detox for the body); Seaweed Wrap; Collagen Velvet Facial Mask; and a range of aromatherapy treatments.

Examples of prices: a full body massage is £60 (50 minutes); an Indian head massage is £42 (45 minutes); a holistic facial is £45 (75 minutes). A manicure is £24 (45 minutes), while a pedicure is £35 (45 minutes).

Note that if you want to book spa treatments (massage, facial, hairdressing), it is wise to do so as soon after you embark as possible, as time slots do fill up quickly aboard large ships such as this – particularly on the shorter cruises.

● **For more extensive general information about a P&O cruise experience, see pages 147–8.**

WIND SPEEDS

A navigational announcement to passengers is normally made once or twice a day, giving the ship's position, temperature, and weather information.

Various winds affect the world's weather patterns. Such well-known winds as the Bora, Mistral, Northwind, and Sirocco, among others, play an important part in the makeup of weather at and above sea level. Wind velocity is measured on the Beaufort scale, a method that was devised in 1805 by Commodore Francis Beaufort, later Admiral and Knight Commander of the Bath, for measuring the force of wind at sea. Originally, it measured the effect of the wind on a fully rigged man-of-war (which was usually laden with cannon and heavy ammunition). It became the official way of recording wind velocity in 1874, when the International Meteorological Committee adopted it.

Astor
★★★ +

Size:	Mid-Size Ship	Passenger Decks:	7	Cabins (wheelchair accessible):	0
Tonnage:	20,606	Total Crew:	300	Wheelchair accessibility	Fair
Lifestyle:	Standard	Passengers		Cabin Current:	220 volts
Cruise Line:	Transocean Cruises	(lower beds/all berths):	590/650	Elevators:	3
Former Names:	Fedor Dostoyevskiy,	Passenger Space Ratio		Casino (gaming tables):	Yes
	Astor (II)	(lower beds/all berths):	34.9/31.7	Slot Machines:	Yes
Builder:	Howaldtswerke Deutsche	Crew/Passenger Ratio		Swimming Pools (outdoors):	1
	Werft (Germany)	(lower beds/all berths):	1.9/2.1	Swimming Pools (indoors):	1
Original Cost:	$65 million	Cabins (total):	295	Whirlpools:	0
Entered Service:	Feb 1987/Apr 1997	Size Range (sq ft/m):	140.0–280.0/	Self-Service Launderette:	No
Registry:	The Bahamas		13.0–26.0		(ironing room)
Length (ft/m):	579.0/176.50	Cabins (outside view):	199	Dedicated Cinema/Seats:	No
Beam (ft/m):	74.1/22.61	Cabins (interior/no view):	96	Library:	Yes
Draft (ft/m):	20.0/6.10	Cabins (for one person):	0		
Propulsion/Propellers: diesel (15,400kW)/2		Cabins (with private balcony):	0		

OVERALL SCORE: 1,370 OUT OF A POSSIBLE 2,000 POINTS

OVERVIEW. *Astor* was the original name for this ship, the larger of two ships bearing this same name in the 1980s (the other being the former Transocean Cruises ship *Astoria*), originally built for the now-defunct Astor Cruises. Its previous owners, the also defunct Aqua-Marin Cruises, brought back the ship's name to *Astor* from its previous name *Fedor Dostoyevskiy*.

This is an attractive modern ship with a raked bow, a large square funnel and a nicely balanced almost contemporary profile. The ship is slightly larger than the first *Astor* (presently renamed *Astoria*), and has been well maintained and refurbished throughout the years. Introduced by Transocean Tours (as it then was called) in 1997, this ship was placed under a long-term charter agreement until 2011, when the ship will be almost 30 years old, from its present owners, Premicon.

Astor and its (slightly smaller) sister ship *Astoria* now operate in tandem as one product – two ships of a similar size and with very similar facilities (even built in the same shipyard, with the same bathroom fittings and washbasins), the same conservative decor and ambiance.

This ship represents a good mix of traditional and modern styling, with restful decor that does not jar the senses in any way (though some say it's a little too dark). Built to a high standard in Germany, fine teakwood decking and polished wood railings are seen outside almost everywhere.

There is an excellent amount of open deck and sunbathing space, as well as cushioned pads for the sun-loungers. There is a basketball court for active passengers, as well as a large deck chess game on an aft deck, and the usual shuffleboard courts.

BERLITZ'S RATINGS		
	Possible	Achieved
Ship	500	354
Accommodation	200	139
Food	400	257
Service	400	286
Entertainment	100	62
Cruise	400	272

The interior fittings are of extremely fine quality. There is a supremely comfortable and varied array of public rooms and conference facilities, most of which have high ceilings. Apart from a show lounge, public rooms include a Captain's Club lounge, a library and card room, and two large boutiques. The wood-paneled Hanse Bar (with good German lager on draft) is a fine retreat, and extremely popular as a late-night drinking club.

Transocean Cruises has interesting and well-designed destination-intensive worldwide itineraries, and cruises are provided at a very attractive price. The mainly European hotel staff are friendly without being obtrusive.

This ship, which caters exclusively to German-speaking passengers, provides a certain degree of style, comfort and elegance, and a fine leisurely cruise experience in a relaxed, spacious setting that is less formal than a ship such as *Europa*. There is no crowding anywhere and no annoying background music in hallways or elevators.

The ship represents a good choice for those people who are looking for a well-packaged cruise in traditional ship surroundings. Transocean Cruises staff can be found aboard every cruise, some of which are designated as special-theme cruises. As aboard all German-speaking ships, Fruhschoppen (free beer, sausages and carved meats) is one event not to be missed.

The currency aboard *Astor* is the euro. Port taxes, insurance and gratuities to staff are all included in the cruise fare. The drinks prices are inexpensive, particularly when compared to land-based prices.

A service provided by ABX Logistics will collect your

luggage from your house, and transport it to the ship for you; when you return, the service will collect it from the ship and bring it to your house – all for a nominal fee (this service is only available to/from certain ports).

SUITABLE FOR: *Astor* is best suited to German-speaking couples, and single travelers of mature years who seek a good value for money holiday in a traditional cruise ship setting, with appealing itineraries and destinations, good food and friendly service.

ACCOMMODATION. The accommodation, spanning 18 price categories, is spread over three decks, and comprises 32 suites and 263 outside-view and interior (no view) cabins. No matter what grade of accommodation is chosen, rosewood cabinetry and plain beige walls is the norm – a restful environment. All suites and cabins with outside-view windows have blackout blinds (good for cruises to the land of the midnight sun).

Suites: The suites (279.8 sq.ft/26 sq. meters) are tastefully decorated in pastel colors, and have rosewood cabinetry and accents. Each has a separate bedroom (with brass clock), lounge/living room (another brass clock), with mini-bar/refrigerator and personal safe (in a user-unfriendly position, almost at floor level). The bathroom is small but has a decent-sized cabinet for personal toiletry items, as well as a sit-in bathtub/shower combination, toilet, and a white enamel washbasin. A wide array of bathroom amenities is provided, including built-in hairdryer, soap, shampoo, shower cap, comb, sewing kit, shoe polish, shoehorn, clothes lint collector, nail file, matches, and a basket of fruit, replenished daily.

Outside-view and Interior (No View) Cabins: These cabins (139.9 sq. ft/13 sq. meters) are well appointed and tastefully decorated in fresh pastel colors, and have dark wood accents and cabinetry, making them very restful. There is plenty of closet and drawer space, as well as some underbed storage space for luggage. The bathrooms are very practical, and each has a decent sized cabinet for personal toiletry items, as well as all the necessary fittings, including a white enamel washbasin.

Outside-view Family (4-Berth) Cabins: These large cabins (258.3 sq.ft/24 sq. meters) have two lower beds, one upper berth and one sofa bed – good for families with children. The tiled bathroom has a shower enclosure, white enamel washbasin and toilet.

No matter what grade of accommodation you choose, all passengers get European duvets, 100% cotton towels, 100% cotton bathrobe, soap, shampoo, shower cap, sewing kit and a basket of fruit. The cabin service menu is very limited and could be better, although German-speaking passengers in general seldom use room service for food items. There is an extra charge for sandwiches, and little else is available. However, there is plenty of food elsewhere around the ship. Note that there is an extra charge for freshly-squeezed orange juice, as aboard all ships in the German-speaking market. The bathroom towels are too small.

CUISINE. The no-smoking Waldorf Dining Room is reasonably elegant, well laid-out, and operates two seatings. It also has one small wing (good for private parties or groups of up to 30). The service throughout is friendly and unpretentious, and the food quality and presentation has received some attention from the food caterer, although remember that you get what you pay for, and food is not a particularly high priority for Transocean Cruises. The menus are reasonably attractive, and both quality and presentation are acceptable standard fare, but nothing special – there's certainly no "wow" factor. In addition to the regular entrées (typically three entrées for dinner), there may also be a pasta dish, and a vegetarian specialty dish. The wine list contains a decent selection of wines from many regions, and all at inexpensive to moderate price levels, but wine glasses are small.

A small alternative dining venue featuring Italian cuisine is a reservations-only, extra-cost dining spot for those wanting something a little more special and as an alternative to the main dining room. Larger wine glasses are provided.

Casual breakfast and lunch buffets (both in the restaurant and another lounge) are reasonably well presented, and constantly refreshed, although they tend to be somewhat repetitive; the choice of foods is limited and there is room for improvement. In typical German style, a Fruhschoppen with the appropriate music, Bavarian sausages and complimentary beer is presented on the open lido deck once each cruise.

ENTERTAINMENT. The Showlounge is a single-level room (14 pillars unfortunately obstruct the sightlines) better suited to cabaret and mini-concerts than large-scale staged production shows. The stage itself is also the dance floor, (it cannot be raised for shows). The entertainment possibilities, therefore, are limited, with singers, magicians, and other visual acts providing the bulk of the shows.

SPA/FITNESS. The Wellness Oasis is located on the lowest passenger deck, and contains a sauna (there is no steam room), solarium, indoor swimming pool, beauty salon, treatment rooms and changing areas. Massage, facials, manicures and pedicures are some of the services offered. A separate fitness center, equipped with techno-machinery and exer-cycles, is located on an upper deck (Bridge Deck), complete with ocean views.

Asuka II
★★★★ +

Size: . . . . .Mid-Size Ship
Tonnage: 50,142
Lifestyle: . . . . .Luxury/Premium
Cruise Line: . . . . .Asuka Cruises
Former Names: . . . .*Crystal Harmony*
Builder:Mitsubishi Heavy Industries, Japan
Original Cost: . . . .$240 million
Entered Service: . . . July1990/May 2006
Registry: .Japan
Length (ft/m): 790.5/240.96
Beam (ft/m): 97.1/29.60
Draft (ft/m): 24.6/7.50
Propulsion/Propellers: . . . .diesel-electric
(32,800kW)/2

Passenger Decks: 8
Total Crew: .470
Passengers
(lower beds/all berths): 800/1,010
Passenger Space Ratio
(lower beds/all berths): 52.0/45.2
Crew/Passenger Ratio
(lower beds/all berths): 1.7/1.8
Cabins (total): 462
Size Range (sq ft/m): 198.1–949.4/
18.4–88.2
Cabins (outside view): 462
Cabins (interior/no view): 0
Cabins (for one person): 0

Cabins (with private balcony): 260
Cabins (wheelchair accessible): 4
Wheelchair accessibility . . . . .Best
Cabin Current: . . . . . . .115 and 220 volts
Elevators: 8
Casino (gaming tables): . . . . .Yes
Slot Machines: . . . . .Yes
Swimming Pools (outdoors): 1
Swimming Pools (indoors): 0
Whirlpools: 1
Self-Service Launderette: . . . . .Yes
Dedicated Cinema/Seats: Yes/263
Library: . . . . .Yes

BERLITZ'S OVERALL SCORE: 1,685 OUT OF A POSSIBLE 2,000 POINTS

OVERVIEW. *Asuka II,* formerly *Crystal Harmony,* is a handsome, well-balanced contemporary ship with raked clipper bow,sleek lines, and NYK's double red band on the funnel. There is almost no sense of crowding anywhere aboard this ship, a good example of form follows function (comfort by design). There is a wrap-around teakwood deck for walking, and an abundance of open deck and sunbathing space. Although now 20 years old, *Asuka II* underwent a four-month long drydocking and refit in 2005–06, and further refurbishment in 2009.

Inside, the layout is completely different to the previous *Asuka* in that there is a horizontal flow through the public rooms, with a design that combines some large ship facilities with the intimacy of rooms found aboard many smaller ships. There is a wide assortment of public entertainment lounges and small intimate rooms, and passenger flow is excellent. Fine-quality fabrics and soft furnishings, china, flatware and silver are used throughout.

Outstanding are the Vista (observation) Lounge and the tranquil, elegant Palm Court, one of the nicest rooms afloat, while adjacent are a computer (internet) room and a Washitsu (Japanese 12-tatami mat room). Other public rooms and facilities include the Mariner's Club Lounge (piano bar/lounge), Cigar Bar, Bistro Café, Casino Corner, Mahjong Room with eight tables, Compass Room (meeting and activities room), a book/video library, and Stars karaoke bar. The theater is a dedicated room with high-definition video projection. There is a self-service launderette on each deck – practical for long voyages.

It is the attention to detail that makes a cruise aboard this ship so pleasant, such as almost no announcements, and lit-

BERLITZ'S RATINGS		
	Possible	Achieved
Ship	500	427
Accommodation	200	160
Food	400	341
Service	400	337
Entertainment	100	83
Cruise	400	337

tle background music. The company pays attention to its repeat passengers, particularly those in Deck 10 accommodation. Although longer than the previous *Asuka,* the horizontal (rather than vertical) passenger flow (public rooms laid out horizontally) is better for NYK's typical passenger age range.

Asuka II is a hotel afloat and provides abundant choices and flexibility. It has just about everything for the discerning traveler prepared to pay for high style, space, and the comfort and the facilities of a mid-size vessel capable of long voyages. This is cruising in a well-tuned, well-run service-oriented ship, approximately the equivalent of Tokyo's Imperial Hotel. Unfortunately, dining is in two seatings, which makes it highly structured in terms of timing – although this works well in the Japanese market. The onboard currency is the Japanese Yen, and all gratuities are included.

Your evenings will be necessarily time-structured due to the fact that there are two seatings for dinner (unless you eat in the alternative dining spot), and two shows (the showlounge cannot seat all passengers at once). This detracts from the otherwise fine setting of the ship and the professionalism of its staff.

SUITABLE FOR: *Asuka II* is best suited to Japanese-speaking travellers, typically over 60, seeking a sophisticated ship with fine-quality fittings and furnishings, a wide range of public rooms and facilities, and excellent food and service from a well trained staff that enjoys providing hospitality.

ACCOMMODATION. There are five categories of suites and cabins (including four Royal Suites with private balcony;

26 Asuka Suites with balcony; 32 Suites with balcony; 202 Cabins with balcony; 172 Cabins without balcony. Regardless of the category, duvets and down pillows are provided, as are lots of other niceties. All cabins have a color TV set, DVD player, mini-refrigerator, personal safe, small couch and coffee table, excellent soundproofing, a refrigerator and mini-bar, full tea-making set, satellite-linked telephone, hairdryer, and slippers. A full range of personal toiletries (including Shiseido shampoo, hair rinse, shower cap, soap, toothbrush/toothpaste, cotton pads, razor set, hairbrush, and more) is provided, and plenty of cotton towels.

Deck 10 Penthouses: Four Royal Suites (whose entrance doorway has a door phone and camera) measure 949.4 sq. ft (88.2 sq. meters) and have a large private balcony and lounge with elegant walnut furniture, new soft furnishings, and audio-visual entertainment center (Bose audio system, Blu-Ray player); separate master bedroom with twin beds (flat-screen TV) , large walk-in closets, and excellent ocean-view Japanese-style bathrooms (with German quality fittings that include a large overhead shower) that come with jet bathtub, two washbasins, and plenty of storage space for personal toiletry items (a range of L'Occitane toiletries is provided). These fine, private, pampered living spaces at sea were totally refurbished in 2010, and come with perks such as priority service, free laundry service, a wide variety of alcoholic beverages and other goodies – in fact, almost anything you require.

Other Deck 10 Suites. All the other suites on this deck are worth the asking price, have plenty of space (all have a private balcony, with outside light), including a separate lounge with large couch, coffee table and chairs, large TV set, and a separate sleeping area that can be curtained off (thick drapes mean you can sleep totally in the dark). The bathrooms are quite large, and extremely well appointed. All deck 10 suites/cabins are attended by social officers, and complimentary in-room dining service is offered.

Deck 9/8/7/5 Cabins: Many of the cabins have a private balcony (in fact, 50 percent of all cabins have private balconies, with outside lights), and are extremely comfortable, although a little tight for space. They are very compact units, with one-way traffic past the bed, but there is a reasonable amount of drawer and storage space (the drawers are small, however) although the closet hanging space (as well as storage space for shoes) is extremely limited for long voyages. Some cabins have lifeboat-obstructed views, so it's best to check the deck plan carefully.

The bathrooms (except for those in Deck 10 accommodation), although well appointed, are of the "you first, me next" variety (and size), but they do come with generously sized personal toiletries and amenities, and all bathrooms are fitted with electric "washlet" high-cleanse toilets.

CUISINE. There are several choices. The non-smoking Four Seasons Dining Room is quite elegant, with plenty of space around each table, well-placed waiter service stations and a number of tables for two, as well as tables for four, six or eight. It can be noisy, particularly in the raised, center section, making it hard to carry on a conversation.

Dinner in the main dining room is in two seatings, with no set table assignments. Afternoon tea (and coffee) can be taken in the Vista Lounge – a restful venue.

Alternative (extra charge) Dining: *Umihiko* is a reservations required Japanese specialty restaurant, complete with a totally authentic sushi bar and live fish tanks (for absolutely fresh sashimi). It specializes in sushi and authentic sashimi dishes, and provides a refined, intimate dining experience with fine ocean views.

Prego, which has 40 seats with fine ocean views to starboard and aft, is for occupants of the Royal Suites and Asuka Suites. The menu is the same as the main dining room, but with more intensive waiter service.

For casual meals, beverages and ice cream, the Lido Café, which was completely reconstructed in the refit, has an extensive self-serve buffet area; it is located high up in the ship, and with ocean views from large picture windows. For casual meals, there is also a Lido Garden Grill, a large area with wooden tables and chairs, and bar.

Additionally, The Bistro, located on the upper level of the two-deck-high lobby, is a casual spot for coffees and pastries, served in the style and atmosphere of a European street café.

ENTERTAINMENT. The Grand Hall is the ship's showlounge; it is a large room on one level (with a tiered floor). The sightlines are good from most seats, although there are a few pillars that obstruct the view from some seats. Both banquette and individual seating is provided.

In addition, there are often good-caliber cabaret acts that change constantly. The bands and musical units are also, for the most part, of a high standard, and there is plenty of music for social dancing.

SPA/FITNESS. The Grand Spa includes a large Grand Bath/ cleansing center (one for men, one for women), with integral sauna and steam room. Other facilities include the first Shiseido Salon and Spa at sea, with five treatment rooms (longevity, water, wind, prosperity, harmony) including one for couples; other facilities include a separate sauna, steam rooms, changing rooms for men and women, a beauty salon, and a relaxation area. Another part of the spa houses the gymnasium, with ocean-view windows on one side.

Shiseido operates the spa and the staff offers a wide range of body pampering treatments using the brand products of Qi Estherapy, Carita and Decleor. Sample prices: Qi Energy Full Body Massage: 120 minutes, ¥21,000 (about $182); Qi Tenderness Body Massage: 90 minutes, ¥21,000 (about $182); Decleor Aromatic Body Massage: 120 minutes, ¥24,150 (about $210); Carita Body Treatment: 90 minutes, ¥29,400 (about $255); Carita Facial: 70 minutes, ¥14,700 (about $127). The spa also offers a kimono dressing service, which costs ¥12,600 (about $110).

There is an excellent amount of open deck space (including a swimming pool that is one of the longest aboard any cruise ship), and sports facilities that include a full-size paddle tennis court, putting green, and golf driving range.

Athena
★★ +

Size: ....Small Ship	Propulsion/Propellers: diesel (14,500kW)/2	Cabins (with private balcony): 8
Tonnage: 16,144	Passenger Decks: 7	Cabins (wheelchair accessible): 0
Lifestyle: ....Standard	Total Crew: 280	Wheelchair accessibility ....None
Cruise Line: ....Phoenix Reisen	Passengers	Cabin Current: ....220 volts
Former Names: ...*Vision Athena, Athena,*	(lower beds/all berths): 556/640	Elevators: 2
Caribe, Valtur Prima, Italia Prima, Italia I,	Passenger Space Ratio	Casino (gaming tables): ....Yes
Positano, Surriento, Fridtjof Nansen,	(lower beds/all berths): 29.0/25.2	Slot Machines: ....Yes
Volker, Volkerfreundschaft, Stockholm	Crew/Passenger Ratio	Swimming Pools (outdoors): 1
Builder: ....Varco Chiapella (Italy)	(lower beds/all berths): 1.7/2.0	Swimming Pools (indoors): 0
Original Cost: $150 million (reconstruction)	Cabins (total): 277	Whirlpools: 1
Entered Service: ....Feb 1948/May 2008	Size Range (sq ft/m): 129.2–376.7/	Self-Service Launderette: ....No
Registry: ....Madeira	12.0–35.0	Dedicated Cinema/Seats: ....No
Length (ft/m): 525.2/160.10	Cabins (outside view): 230	Library: ....Yes
Beam (ft/m): 68.8/21.04	Cabins (interior/no view): 47	
Draft (ft/m): 24.9/7.6	Cabins (for one person): 2	

BERLITZ'S OVERALL SCORE: 1,092 OUT OF A POSSIBLE 2,000 POINTS

OVERVIEW. *Vision Athena* has had many incarnations, names and operators, and was a transatlantic "liner" before being converted into a cruise ship in 1994. It has a large "sponson" stern apron, added to aid stability. Classic International Cruises' owner, George Potamianos, has an engineering background and loves older ships. The ship is often chartered to various tour operators when not operating under the CIC brand.

The sturdily built ship, a lovingly maintained classic, holds a special charm for those not seeking the newest large resort ships. Outdoors facilities include a walk-around teakwood promenade deck and many real wooden sunloungers are provided (although open deck sunbathing space is extremely limited). The cheerful, bright colors make the interiors feel quite contemporary.

There is a good selection of public rooms, including a 400-seat auditorium for meetings, and some smart boutiques, and most public rooms are conveniently located on one deck. However, *Athena* is a high-density ship, leaving little space to move around in, and its fixed gangway may be steep, depending on the port and tidal conditions. The small swimming pool is really just a "dip" or "plunge" pool. Book "Diplomat Suite" service and get VIP priority service and other niceties (welcome bottle of cava, flowers, bathrobe, chocolates, and room service). The currency aboard is the euro. Gratuities are not included.

SUITABLE FOR: *Athena* is best for adults and families with children, who seek an inexpensive first cruise in traditional non-glitzy surroundings with limited facilities, food and simple entertainment.

BERLITZ'S RATINGS		
	Possible	Achieved
Ship	500	258
Accommodation	200	121
Food	400	208
Service	400	238
Entertainment	100	50
Cruise	400	217

ACCOMMODATION. There are 12 cabin price grades. All cabins have a mini-bar, TV set, and safe. Bathrooms have a combination tub/shower, as well as a good amount of indented space for toiletries. Eight suites each have a small private balcony. Each has a separate lounge/living area, with table and chairs; the bedroom's twin beds convert to a queen-sized bed. The bathrooms in the suites and junior suites have whirlpool bathtubs with showers, toilet, washbasin and bidet.

Some cabins (on Promenade Deck) have lifeboat-obstructed views, and some on Mediterranean Deck may pick up noise from the public rooms on the deck above. The accommodation passageways are very narrow.

CUISINE. The 520-seat Grand Restaurant Olissipo is quite attractive, and has tables for two, four, six and eight, and 520 seats. There are normally two seatings for dinner. Continental cuisine is featured, with some regional specialties. The food quality is in line with the low cruise cost. One port-side section of the restaurant has been enclosed to create a separate environment for VIP/Diplomat Suite passengers, in a more exclusive setting. There is also a self-serve buffet for breakfast and lunch in the Lotus Buffet Restaurant, although the selection is really basic.

ENTERTAINMENT. Many sightlines in the Main Lounge, which presents basic shows and cabaret acts, are obstructed, and there's a large bar in the aft of the room.

SPA/FITNESS. There's a workout room, sauna, steam room, body therapy rooms, and beauty salon.

Aurora
★★★★

Size:	Large Resort Ship	Total Crew:	816	Cabins (wheelchair accessible):	22

Size: . . . . .Large Resort Ship
Tonnage: .76,152
Lifestyle: . . . . .Standard
Cruise Line: . . . . .P&O Cruises
Former Names: . . . . .none
Builder: . . . . .Meyer Werft (Germany)
Original Cost: . . . .$375 million
Entered Service: . . . . .May 2000
Registry: . . . . .Great Britain
Length (ft/m): 885.8/270.0
Beam (ft/m): 105.6/32.2
Draft (ft/m): 25.9/7.9
Propulsion/Propellers: . . . . .diesel-electric
(40,000kW)/2
Passenger Decks: 10

Total Crew: .816
Passengers
(lower beds/all berths): 1,868/1,975
Passenger Space Ratio
(lower beds/all berths): 40.7/38.5
Crew/Passenger Ratio
(lower beds/all berths): 2.2/2.4
Cabins (total): 934
Size Range (sq ft/m): 150.6–953.0/
14.0–88.5
Cabins (outside view): 655
Cabins (interior/no view): 279
Cabins (for one person): 0
Cabins (with private balcony): 406

Cabins (wheelchair accessible): 22
(8 with private balcony)
Wheelchair accessibility . . . . .Good
Cabin Current: . . . . . . .110 and 220 volts
Elevators: 10
Casino (gaming tables): . . . . .Yes
Slot Machines: . . . . .Yes
Swimming Pools (outdoors): 3
(1 with magrodome)
Swimming Pools (indoors): 0
Whirlpools: 5
Self-Service Launderette: . . . . .Yes
Dedicated Cinema/Seats: Yes/200
Library: . . . . .Yes

OVERALL SCORE: 1,503 OUT OF A POSSIBLE 2,000 POINTS

OVERVIEW. *Aurora* is named after the goddess of the dawn in Greek, Melanesian and Slavonic mythologies. Or perhaps the carnation Dianthus Aurora. Or it could be the famous Northern and Southern Lights, aurora borealis and aurora australis. At any rate, it was built specifically for Britain's growing traditional cruise market.

As ships evolve, slight differences in layout occur, as is the case with *Aurora* compared to earlier close sister *Oriana*. One big difference can be found in the addition of a large, magrodome-covered indoor/outdoor swimming pool (good in all weathers). The stern superstructure is nicely rounded and has several tiers that overlook the aft decks, pool and children's outdoor facilities. There is a good amount of open deck and sunbathing space, an important plus for the outdoors-loving mainly British passengers. There is an extra-wide wrap-around promenade deck outdoors, with plenty of white plastic sunloungers (cushioned pads are available).

The ship's interiors are gentle, welcoming and restrained, with warm colors and combinations that don't clash. The public rooms and areas have been designed in such a way that each room is individual, and yet there appears to be an open, yet cohesive flow throughout all of the public areas – something difficult to achieve when a number of designers are involved. There is good horizontal passenger flow, and wide passageways help to avoid congestion. Very noticeable are the fine, detailed ceiling treatments.

As it is a ship for all types of people, specific areas have been designed to attract different age groups and lifestyles. The focal point is a four-decks-high atrium lobby and a dramatic, calming, 35-ft (10.6-meter) high, Lalique-style

BERLITZ'S RATINGS

	Possible	Achieved
Ship	500	406
Accommodation	200	160
Food	400	256
Service	400	307
Entertainment	100	76
Cruise	400	298

sculpture (it's actually made of fiberglass) of two mythical figures behind a veil of water. At the top of the atrium is the ship's library.

The carpeting throughout is excellent, much custom designed and made of long-lasting 100% wool. Original artworks by British artists include several tapestries and sculptures. For a weird experience, try standing on the midships staircase and look at the oil on canvas paintings by Nicholas Hely Hutchinson – they are curved – this has a dramatic effect on one's ability not to be seasick while cruising through the Bay of Biscay.

Other features include a virtual reality games room, 12 lounges/bars (among the nicest are Anderson's – similar to Anderson's aboard *Oriana*, with a fireplace and mahogany paneling, and the Crow's Nest – complete with a lovely one-sided model of one of P&O's former liners: *Strathnaver* of 1931, scrapped in Hong Kong in 1962. There is also a cinema that doubles as a concert and lecture hall.

There are special facilities and rooms for children and teens. Toybox is the playroom for 2–5 year olds, Jumpin' Jack's for 6–9 year olds, Quarterdeck for 10–13 year olds, and Decibels for 14–17 year olds. and a whole deck outdoors to play on (swimming pools and whirlpools included just for the youngsters). Children and teens have "Club Aurora" programs with their own rooms and their own outdoor pool. Children can be entertained until 10pm, which gives parents time to have dinner and go dancing. All cabins also have a baby-listening device. A night nursery for small children (ages 2–5) is available (6pm–midnight, no charge; from midnight to 2am there is a charge), as well as slumber parties for 6–9 year olds, In addition, 16 passenger cabins have interconnecting doors – good for families with children (or maid). Note that at peak holiday times (summer, Christmas, Easter) there could be 400 or more children on board. However, the ship absorbs them well, and the children's programming helps keep them occupied.

The library has several writing desks, large leather audio listening chairs, a good range of hardbacks (and a librarian), and skillfully crafted inlaid wood tables. On the second day of almost any cruise, however, it will have been almost stripped of books by word-hungry passengers. The library also sells some nautical books. An internet-connect center is located on the port side, aft of the popular Crow's Nest observation lounge (but sending emails can be expensive).

In this ship, P&O Cruises has improved on the facilities of older sister ship *Oriana*, with larger cabins and suites and with more dining options and choice of public areas. *Aurora* provides a decent, standardized cruise experience – good value for money – for its mainly British passengers (of all dialects) and may be ideal for those who don't want to fly to join a cruise, as the ship sails from Southampton. Each year, the *Aurora* undertakes an around-the-world cruise; this is excellent value for money.

However, in the quest for more onboard revenue (and shareholder value), even birthday cakes now cost extra, as do espressos and cappuccinos (fake ones, made from instant coffee, are available in the dining rooms). Also at extra cost are ice creams, and bottled water (this can add up to a considerable amount on an around-the-world cruise). The onboard currency is the British pound. For gratuities, you should allow £3.50 ($5.25) per person, per day.

A British brass band send-off accompanies all sailings. Other touches include church bells that sound throughout the ship for the interdenominational Sunday church service. A coach service for passengers embarking or disembarking in Southampton covers much of the UK. Car parking is available (one rate for undercover parking, one rate for an open compound).

The ship's layout is a little disjointed in certain places, and there are several dead-ends and some poor signage. The reception desk's opening hours (7am–8pm) are too short. Shuttle buses, once provided in the various ports, are no longer free when provided (except on the around-the-world cruise). Standing in line for embarkation, disembarkation, shore tenders, and for self-serve buffet meals is inevitable. "Cashless Cruising" doesn't include tips (for an around-the-world cruise, this means carrying more than $750 in cash).

Passenger niggles include noisy air-conditioning in cabins, and the proliferation of extra-charge activities.

SUITABLE FOR: *Aurora* is best for adults of all ages (although most cruises attract the over-50s), and families with children of all ages who want a cruise that starts and ends in the UK, aboard a large ship with all the facilities of a small resort, with food and service that are very acceptable, though not as good as aboard some other cruise ships.

ACCOMMODATION. There are five main grades of cabins, in 26 price categories (location and size govern price).

Included are 2 two-level penthouses, 10 suites with balconies, 18 mini-suites with balconies, 368 cabins with balconies, 225 standard outside-view cabins, 16 interconnecting family cabins, and 279 interior (no view) cabins.

All grades, from the largest to the smallest, provide the following common features: polished cherry wood laminate cabinetry, full-length mirror, personal safe, refrigerator, television, individually controlled air conditioning; twin beds that convert to a queen-size double bed, sofa and coffee table. Also standard are stylish bed runners, Slumberland 8-inch sprung mattresses, 10.5 tog duvets (blankets and pillows if you prefer), Egyptian cotton towels and robes, improved tea/coffee making facilities with speciality teas (long-life is provided) and a Nick Munro-designed bespoke tray, as well as in-cabin toning and fitness facilities for passengers who prefer to exercise in private.

There are four whole decks of cabins with private balconies (about 40% of all cabins), and these feature easy-to-open sliding glass floor-to-ceiling doors; the partitions are of the almost full floor-to-ceiling type – so they really are quite private – and cannot be overlooked from above.

Cabin insulation could better (the magnetic catches in drawers and on the closet doors are noisy). Also, the TV sets provide only monaural sound. Although most doorways are 26 inches (66 cm) wide, the measurement of actual access is 2 inches (5 cm) less because of the doorframe; however, some doorways are only 21.5 inches (55 cm) wide.

A range of Molton Brown products is provided in penthouse suites, suites or mini-suites. For all other cabins, only soap is provided, plus a "sport wash" combination soap and shampoo in a dispenser in the shower (so take your favorite shampoo and conditioner), and a small pouch of assorted personal-care items. All grades get 100% cotton bathrobes, and 100% cotton towels. Except for the suites, no cabins have illuminated closets, and cabin ceilings are very plain.

Penthouse Suites: The largest cabins consist of two penthouse suites (named Library Suite and Piano Suite), each 953 sq. ft (88.5 sq. meters). They have forward-facing views, being located directly underneath the navigation bridge (the blinds must be drawn at night so as not to affect navigation). Each is spread over two decks in height, and connected by a beautiful wood curved staircase. One suite has a baby grand piano (which can be played manually or electronically), while the other has a private library. The living area is on the lower deck (Deck 10), and incorporates a dining suite (a first in a P&O ship) and a small private balcony. In the bedroom, upstairs, there is a walk-in closet, while the bathroom is decked out in porcelain and polished granite, with twin basins, bathtub and separate shower enclosure. There is also a small private balcony.

Suites: The suites (there are 10 of them) measure about 445 sq. ft (41.3 sq. meters). They have a separate bedroom with two lower beds that convert to a queen-sized bed. There is a walk-in dressing area and closet, with plenty of drawer space, a trouser press and ironing board. The lounge has a sofa, armchairs, dining table and chairs, writing desk, television, radio and stereo system. The marble-clad bathroom has a whirlpool bath, shower and toilet. The private balcony has space for two sunloungers, plus two chairs and two tables. Butler service is provided.

Mini-Suites: These measure 325 sq. ft (30.1 sq. meters), and have a separate bedroom area with two lower beds that convert to a queen-sized bed. There's one double and two single closets, a good amount of drawer space, binoculars, a trouser press and ironing board. Each private balcony has a blue plastic deck covering, one deck lounge chair, one chair and table, and exterior light.

Standard Outside-view/Interior (No View) Cabins: Any cabin designated as a double with private balcony measure about 175 sq. ft (16.2 sq. meters). They have two lower beds that convert to a queen-sized bed. The sitting area has a sofa and table. There's also a vanity table/writing desk, and a private balcony with blue plastic deck covering, two chairs (with only a small recline) and a small table. Note that a 110-volt (American) socket is located underneath the vanity desk drawer – in a difficult to access position.

Outside-view or Interior (with no view) Cabins have two lower beds that convert to a queen-sized bed, closet (but few drawers), and are 150 sq. ft (14 sq. meters). The bathroom has a mini-bath/shower and toilet, or shower and toilet.

All bathrooms in all grades (except those designated as suites) are compact, modular units, and have mirror-fronted cabinets, although the lighting is quite soft, and, in cabins with bathtubs, the retractable clothesline is located too high for most people to reach. High-quality personal toiletries are by Temple Spa.

There are 22 wheelchair-accessible cabins, well outfitted for the physically challenged passenger and almost all within easy access to lifts. However, one cabin (D165 on Deck 8) is located between forward and mid-ships stairways, and it is difficult to access the public rooms on Deck 8 without first going to the deck below, due to several steps and tight corners. All other wheelchair-accessible cabins are well positioned, and eight have a private balcony.

CUISINE. The two main dining rooms (each seats about 525) have tables for 2, 4, 6, 8 and 10, in two seatings. The mid-ships Medina has a vaguely Moorish theme, while Alexandria, with windows on three sides, has Egyptian decor. Both have more tables for two than in the equivalent restaurants aboard close sister ship *Oriana*. The china is Wedgwood, the silverware is by Elkington, the food by P&O.

The typical menu cycle is 14 days; anyone on a long voyage may find it quite repetitive. The cuisine is very British – a little adventurous at times, but always with plenty of curry dishes and other standard British items.

You should not expect exquisite dining, though – this is British hotel catering that doesn't pretend to offer foie gras and other gourmet foods. But what it does present is attractive and tasty, with some excellent gravies and sauces to accompany all dining room meals. In keeping with the Britishness of P&O Cruises, the desserts and cakes are good. The service is provided by a team of friendly stewards from India, with which P&O has had a long relationship.

There are several other dining options. You can, for example, also have dinner in the 24-hour, 120-seat French bistro-style restaurant, Cafe Bordeaux, for which there is a cover charge (for dinner only), with menus designed by Marco Pierre-White, the TV chef who starred in *Hell's Kitchen*. Breakfasts and lunches are also served here, as are several coffees: espresso, cappuccino, latte, ristretto, as well as flavored coffees. So, if you want a croque-monsieur (a toasted ham and Gruyère cheese sandwich) at 5am, you can have it. For £9.50 you can try the "Tasting Menu" – a selection of small cosmopolitan dishes, with three different menus per cruise.

Casual, self-serve breakfasts and lunches can be taken from the buffet in a colorful eatery named "The Orangery", which has fine ocean views. Other casual dining spots include the Sidewalk Cafe (for fast food items poolside), champagne bar and, in a first for a P&O cruise ship, Raffles coffee and chocolate bar (but without the ceiling fans). All dining rooms are non-smoking.

ENTERTAINMENT. There is a wide variety of mainly British entertainment, from production shows to top British "name" and lesser name cabaret artists. The Headliners Theater Company is a group of resident actors, singers and dancers. They provide theater-style presentations such as mini versions of well-known musicals, "book" shows, revues, and drama presentations. There is also a program of theme cruises – antiques, art appreciation, classical music, comedy, cricket, gardening, jazz, Scottish dance, etc.

Ballroom dance fans will make use of the four good-sized wooden dance floors. The ship always carries a professional dance couple as hosts and teachers, and plenty of dancing time is included in the programming.

SPA/FITNESS. The Oasis Spa is midships on Lido Deck – almost at the top of the ship, just forward of the Crystal swimming pool. It is moderately large, and facilities include a gymnasium with the latest high-tech muscle-pumping and body toning equipment. There is also a sauna and steam room (both unisex, so you'll need a bathing suit). There's a beauty salon, a spiral staircase, and a relaxation area overlooking the forward Riviera swimming pool.

The spa is operated by Harding Brothers, a UK concession that provides the staff and a wide range of beauty and wellness treatments. Examples of treatments include: Body Toning (detox for the body); Seaweed Wrap; Collagen Velvet Facial Mask, and a range of aromatherapy treatments. Book spa treatments as soon after you embark as possible, as time slots fill up quickly aboard large ships such as this. Examples of prices: a full body massage is £60 for 50 minutes; an Indian head massage is £42 for 45 minutes; a holistic facial is £45 for 75 minutes. A manicure is £24 for 45 minutes, while a pedicure is £35 for 45 minutes.

A sports court incorporates a golf practice cage and a golf simulator, for which there is an extra charge.

● **For more extensive general information about a P&O cruise experience, see pages 147–8.**

Azamara Journey
★★★★

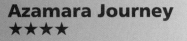

Size: ....Mid-Size Ship	Total Crew: 390	Cabins (wheelchair accessible): 6
Tonnage: 30,277	Passengers	Wheelchair accessibility ....Fair
Lifestyle: ....Premium	(lower beds/all berths): 676/866	Cabin Current: ....110 and 220 volts
Cruise Line: ......Azamara Club Cruises	Passenger Space Ratio	Elevators: 4
Former Names: .Blue Star, Blue Dream, R6	(lower beds/all berths): 42.7/34.9	Casino (gaming tables): ....Yes
Builder: .Chantiers de l'Atlantique (France)	Crew/Passenger Ratio	Slot Machines: ....Yes
Original Cost: ....$150 million	(lower beds/all berths): 1.8/2.2	Swimming Pools (outdoors): 1
Entered Service: ....Feb 2000/May 2007	Cabins (total): 338	Swimming Pools (indoors): 0
Registry: ....Malta	Size Range (sq ft/m): 151.0–818.0/	Whirlpools: 2 (+ 1 thalassotherapy hot tub)
Length (ft/m): 593.7/181.0	14.0–76.0	Self-Service Launderette: ....Yes
Beam (ft/m): 95.1/29.0	Cabins (outside view): 312	Dedicated Cinema/Seats: ....No
Draft (ft/m): 19.85/6.0	Cabins (interior/no view): 26	Library: ....Yes
Propulsion/Propellers: diesel 18,600kW)/2	Cabins (for one person): 0	
Passenger Decks: 9	Cabins (with private balcony): 249	

BERLITZ'S OVERALL SCORE: 1,465 OUT OF A POSSIBLE 2,000 POINTS

OVERVIEW. The all-white *Azamara Journey,* virtually identical to *Azamara Quest* in features and fittings, is a contemporary ship, whose exterior design balances the ship's high sides by combining a deep blue hull with the white superstructure and large, square blue funnel. A lido deck has a tiny – and I mean tiny – swimming pool, and good sunbathing space. There is no outdoor walk-around promenade deck, although a short jogging track encircles the pool deck (but one deck above it). The uppermost outdoors deck includes a golf driving net and shuffleboard court. There are no wooden decks outdoors; instead, they are covered by a sand-colored rubberized material.

The interior decor is in good taste, and is a throwback to ship decor of the ocean liners of the 1920s and '30s. The overall feel is of a members-only country club.

The public rooms are spread over three decks. The reception hall (lobby) has a staircase with intricate wrought-iron railings. A large observation lounge (The Looking Glass) is high atop the ship. This has a long bar with forward views (for the barmen, that is, as passengers sitting at the bar face aft). There's a bar in each of the restaurant entrances, as well as a Martini Bar. There's also a Michael's Club – a jazz/piano lounge, and, of course, a Luxe Casino, and a shop (Boutique C). Internet connectivity is provided at Online@Celebrity. Unfortunately, tacky art auctions spoil the experience.

The Library is a beautiful, grand, restful room (perhaps the nicest public room), and is designed in the Regency style. It has a fireplace, a high, indented, *trompe l'oeil* ceiling, and a good selection of books, comfortable wingback chairs with footstools, and sofas you could sleep on. Smoking is permitted only on cabin balconies and in designated spots on the open decks – the interior space is non-smoking.

The onboard currency is the US dollar. Gratuities to housekeeping and dining staff are included in the fare. Shuttle buses are provided free when needed in ports of call.

SUITABLE FOR: Mature couples seeking to get away from the crowds aboard a contemporary ship with a wide range of bars and lounges, in the setting of a mid-size ship, at a slightly lower cost than the luxury lines but with many of the same features.

ACCOMMODATION. There are eight cabin price grades; three suite-grades and five other grades. All have so-called butler service (merely better dressed cabin stewards). All of the standard interior (no view) and outside-view cabins (the lowest four grades) are extremely compact units – Azamara calls them staterooms (a real misnomer), but they are simply cabins – and rather tight for two persons, particularly during cruises longer than seven days. The bathrooms are postage-stamp-sized and you'll be fighting with the shower curtain, as well as storage space for toiletries. The standard cabins cannot, in any sense, be considered luxury, and even premium is stretching it a bit. But all suites/cabins receive "butler" service.

For the extra cost, it's wise to choose a suite or cabin with a balcony. Some cabins have interconnecting doors (good for families with children) while 18 cabins on Deck 6 have lifeboat-obstructed views. No matter what grade of accommodation you choose, all have TV sets that carry European news, sports channel (where obtainable), and several movie channels.

BERLITZ'S RATINGS

	Possible	Achieved
Ship	500	417
Accommodation	200	157
Food	400	256
Service	400	283
Entertainment	100	72
Cruise	400	280

Standard Interior (No View)/ Standard Outside-view Cabins: These have twin beds (convertible to a queen-size bed), with good under-bed storage areas, safe, vanity desk with large mirror, good closet and drawer space.

Ocean-view Cabins: Features: two lower beds convertible to queen size (some have an extra sofa bed); flat-screen TV; refrigerator with mini-bar; thermostat-controlled air conditioning; direct-dial telephone and voicemail; desk; in-room safe; hand-held hairdryer. Approximate size: 161 sq.ft.

Some cabins have a panorama window with an obstructed view. Those on the lowest deck have just a porthole.

Deluxe Ocean-view Cabins with Balcony: Features two lower beds convertible to queen size; floor-to-ceiling sliding glass doors; sitting area with sofa bed; private veranda; flat-screen television; refrigerator with mini-bar; thermostat-controlled air conditioning; direct-dial telephone and voicemail; desk; in-room safe; hand-held hairdryer. Approximate size: 215 sq.ft.; balcony 38 sq.ft.

Sunset Verandah Cabins: Features two lower beds convertible to queen size; floor-to-ceiling sliding glass doors; sitting area with sofa bed; private veranda; flat-screen television; refrigerator with mini-bar; thermostat-controlled air conditioning; direct-dial telephone and voicemail; desk; in-room safe; hand-held hairdryer. Approximate size: 215 sq.ft.; balcony 154 sq.ft.

Sky Suites: Superior Exterior View Cabins with Balcony: The cabins with private balconies, have partial balcony partitions, and sliding glass doors. The bathrooms, with tiled floors and plain walls, are compact units, and include either a tub/shower or a shower stall with a strong, removable hand-held shower unit, hairdryer, 100 percent cotton towels, toiletries storage shelves and retractable clothesline. Approximate size: 323 sq.ft.; balcony 57 sq.ft.

Royal Suites (Decks 6, 7): In reality these are large cabins, as the sleeping and lounge areas are not divided. The bathrooms have a good-sized tub and ample space for toiletries. The living area has a refrigerated mini-bar, lounge area with breakfast table, and a balcony with two plastic chairs and a table. Approximate size: 538 sq.ft.; balcony 173 sq.ft.

Penthouse De-Luxe Suite with Balcony: These provide the most spacious accommodation, and are fine, large living spaces located in the forward-most and aft-most sections of the accommodation decks (particularly nice are those that overlook the stern, on Deck 6, Deck 7 and Deck 8). An entrance foyer leads to a living room, bedroom (the bed faces the sea, which can be seen through the floor-to-ceiling windows and sliding glass door), CD player (with selection of audio discs), bathroom with Jacuzzi bathtub, and a small guest bathroom. They have more extensive private balconies that really are private. Approximate size: 603 sq.ft.; balcony 215 sq.ft.

Suite occupants get priority boarding, tender service, alternative dining venue reservations, and light bites at 4pm, in-suite spa treatments, in-suite portrait sitting, free espressos/cappuccinos, bottled water, and silk-wrapped hangers. All suites/cabins located at the stern can suffer from vibration and noise, particularly when the ship is proceeding at or close to full speed, or maneuvering in port.

CUISINE. Discoveries, the ship's main dining room, has around 340 seats, a raised central section (conversation at these tables may be difficult, due to its low ceiling height), and open-seating dining. There are large ocean-view windows on three sides, several prime tables overlooking the stern, and a small bandstand for live dinner music. Some tables for two are so close to adjacent tables for four that privacy is non-existent. The menu changes daily for lunch and dinner, and wine is included. Adjacent to the restaurant is a cosy Martini Bar, with a cozy fireplace.

Alternative Dining Spots (make reservations early):

● The *Restaurant* (service charge $5) is at the aft of the ship on the port side of Deck 10; it has 96 seats, windows along two sides, and serves Mediterranean cuisine. A $50 per person Tasting Menu includes wine.

● *Prime C* (service charge $5), at the aft of the ship on the starboard side of Deck 10, has grill food items such as steaks and seafood. It has 98 seats, windows along two sides and a set menu. Reservations are required.

● The *Windows Café* has indoor seating for just over 150 (not really enough when cruising in cold areas or in the winter months), and 186 seats outdoors. Many tables do, however, have ocean views. It is open for breakfast, lunch and casual dinners, and incorporates a small Sushi Café.

All dining venues have open-seating dining, although reservations are needed in the Aqualina Restaurant and Prime C, where there are mostly tables for four or six (there are few tables for two). Suite-grade occupants get two nights free, while other accommodation categories get one night free in one of the two alternative venues. All cappuccino and espresso coffees cost extra, even in the restaurants.

A Cova Café serves fine Italian coffees, as well as teas and pastries. And a Wine Bar with an extensive cellar has wine-and-food pairings, wine tasting sessions, and wines by the glass or bottle. Additionally, a Poolside Grill provides fast-food items. Some items are grilled to order. A self-serve soft ice cream machine is located adjacent to a beverage station. Coffee and tea are free 24 hours a day

ENTERTAINMENT. Celebrity Cabaret, located forward, is the venue for all main entertainment events. In the evenings, the entertainment consists of a mix of classical concerts, revues, as well as comedy and drama. The entertainment has a cultural tone to it. Additionally, local entertainers are brought on board in various destinations.

SPA/FITNESS. The AquaSpa has a gymnasium with some high-tech muscle toning equipment, an extra-cost thalassotherapy pool (outside, forward on deck), and several treatment rooms. Outside on deck, there is a small swimming pool, two hot tubs, and a jogging track (one deck above the pool). The spa is staffed and operated by Steiner Leisure, a specialist concession. An "Acupuncture at Sea" clinic provides treatments that are operated independently of the spa (but also as a concession). Spa treatments are possible in your suite, too. Outside on the Lido Deck, there is a small swimming pool, two hot tubs, and a jogging track (one deck above the pool).

Azamara Quest
★★★★

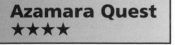

Size: . . . . .Mid-Size Ship	Passenger Decks: 9	Cabins (with private balcony): 232
Tonnage: 30,277	Total Crew: 306	Cabins (wheelchair accessible): 4
Lifestyle: . . . . .Premium	Passengers	Wheelchair accessibility . . . . .Fair
Cruise Line: . . . . . . .Azamara Club Cruises	(lower beds/all berths): 716/777	Cabin Current: . . . . .110 and 220 volts
Former Names: . . . . . .*Blue Moon, Delphin*	Passenger Space Ratio	Elevators: 4
Renaissance, R7	(lower beds/all berths): 42.2/38.9	Casino (gaming tables): . . . . .No
Builder: .Chantiers de l'Atlantique (France)	Crew/Passenger Ratio	Slot Machines: .No
Original Cost: . . . .$150 million	(lower beds/all berths): 2.3/2.5	Swimming Pools (outdoors): 1
Entered Service: . . . . .Oct 2000/Oct 2007	Cabins (total): .358	Swimming Pools (indoors): 0
Registry: . . . . .Malta	Size Range (sq ft/m): 156.0–484.3/	Whirlpools: 2 (+ 1 thalassotherapy hot tub)
Length (ft/m): 591.8/180.4	14.5–45.0	Self-Service Launderette: . . . . .Yes
Beam (ft/m): 83.3/25.4	Cabins (outside view): 332	Dedicated Cinema/Seats: . . . . .No
Draft (ft/m): 19.0/5.8	Cabins (interior/no view): 26	Library: . . . . .Yes
Propulsion/Propellers: diesel 18,600kW)/2	Cabins (for one person): 0	

BERLITZ'S OVERALL SCORE: 1,466 OUT OF A POSSIBLE 2,000 POINTS

OVERVIEW. *Azamara Quest* was originally *R7*, one of a series of eight almost identical ships in the now defunct Renaissance Cruises fleet (when it was in operation, between 1998 and 2001, it was the cruise industry's only totally no-smoking cruise line). It was purchased by Pullmantur in 2006, but transferred in 2007 to Celebrity Cruises' new mid-sized ship brand, Azamara Cruises (renamed Azamara Club Cruises in 2009). Before entering service, the ship underwent an almost $20 million make-over. The ship has a sister in *Azamura Journey* (ex-*R6*).

An outdoors lido deck has a swimming pool, and good sunbathing space, while one of the aft decks has a thalassaotherapy pool. The exterior decks are covered with a rubber and sand-like surface (teak, although very expensive, would be much better, and more in keeping with the decor of the ship). The uppermost outdoors deck includes a golf driving net and shuffleboard court.

The interior decor is quite elegant, in the style of the ocean liner decor of the 1920s and '30s. This includes

BERLITZ'S RATINGS

	Possible	Achieved
Ship	500	418
Accommodation	200	157
Food	400	256
Service	400	283
Entertainment	100	72
Cruise	400	280

detailed ceiling cornices, both real and faux wrought-iron staircase railings, leather paneled walls, *trompe l'oeil* ceilings, rich carpeting in hallways with an Oriental rug-look center section, and other interesting (and expensive-looking, but faux) decorative touches.

The overall ambiance is that of an old-world country club. The staircase in the main, two-deck-high foyer will remind you of something similar in a blockbuster hit about a certain iconic ship in which movie stars Kate Winslet and Leonardo di Caprio made their melodramatic voyage.

Passengers should be pleased with the ship's tasteful, traditional-style interiors, and with the variety of public rooms, basically spread over three decks.

For other comments regarding this ship, see the preceding entry for *Azamara Journey*. Some public rooms have different names to those of *Azamara Journey* (Breeze instead of Windows Café, for example, which changes, for some unknown reason, to Breeza in the evening). Note the 18% gratuity on drinks.

Azura
★★★★

Size: . . . . .Large Resort Ship	Passenger Decks: 14	Cabins (with private balcony): 910
Tonnage: .115,055	Total Crew: 1,239	Cabins (wheelchair accessible): 25
Lifestyle: . . . . .Standard	Passengers	Wheelchair accessibility . . . . .Good
Cruise Line: . . . . .P&O Cruises	(lower beds/all berths): 3,096/3,574	Cabin Voltage: . . . . .220/110 volts
Former Names: . . . . .none	Passenger Space Ratio	Elevators: 12
Builder: . . . . .Fincantieri (Italy)	(lower beds/all berths): 37.2/32.1	Casino (gaming tables): . . . . .Yes
Original Cost: . . . .€535 million	Crew/Passenger Ratio	Slot Machines: . . . . .Yes
Entered Service: . . . . .Apr 2010	(lower beds/all berths): 2.4/2.8	Swimming Pools (outdoors): 3
Registry: . . . . .Bermuda	Cabins (total): 1,557	Swimming Pools (indoors): 0
Length (ft/m): 951.4/290.0	Size Range (sq ft/m): 134.5–534.0/	Whirlpools: 6
Beam (ft/m): 118.1/36.0	12.5–49.6	Self-Service Launderette: . . . . .Yes
Draft (ft/m): 27.8/8.5	Cabins (outside view): 1,117	Dedicated Cinema/Seats: . . . . .No
Propulsion/Propellers: . . . . .diesel-electric	Cabins (interior/no view): 440	Library: . . . . .Yes
(42,000kW)/2	Cabins (for one person): 18	

BERLITZ'S OVERALL SCORE: 1,512 OUT OF A POSSIBLE 2,000 POINTS

OVERVIEW. *Azura* and sister ship *Ventura*, which debuted in 2008, are the largest cruise ships yet built specifically for British passengers and are P&O's version of Princess Cruises' Grand-class ships. With its flat stern, *Azura* looks a bit like a giant hatchback, but its side profile is softer and more balanced. Promenade walking decks are to port and starboard sides, underneath the lifeboats. You can't walk completely around, however; it's narrow in some places, and you'll need to negotiate past a number of deck lounge chairs.

There are three main pools: two on the pool deck, one at the stern. If your cabin is towards the front of the ship, it's a long walk to get to the pool at the stern. Considering the number of passengers carried, there's not a lot of outdoor deck space – unless you pay extra to go into a covered, child-free zone called The Retreat, with its faux-grass floor, private cabanas and personal waiter service. What's new is a huge open-air movie screen, the aptly-named SeaScreen, forward of the funnel by the Aqua Pool.

Inside, the three-deck atrium, with integral dance floor, is the focal point. It's a bit like a town center at sea. Four large, three-decks-high black granite archways, specially sourced from India, provide "gateways" to the center. It's certainly the place to see and be seen – as are the "alternative" dining venues – and a good location to arrange to meet friends. Also in the atrium are a smallish open-plan library that isn't at all intimate or good for reading in, particularly when noisy events are happening in the atrium; the library includes several computer workstations for internet access; and Java coffee corner for coffees, teas, cakes, pastries and snacks.

Other rooms, bars and lounges include the casino, The Exchange, an urban "warehouse" bar; the Blue Bar, the

BERLITZ'S RATINGS

	Possible	Achieved
Ship	500	426
Accommodation	200	166
Food	400	250
Service	400	287
Entertainment	100	77
Cruise	400	306

ship's social hub; a "traditional" British pub, The Marquis; and the Planet Bar, set high in the ship, featuring a video wall. There are 7,000 pieces of art on board, sourced from 55 British artists; naturally, there's an art gallery so you can also buy so-called "artwork."

Azura is child-friendly. There are clubs for the under-2s up to 17 years, plus a rock 'n' roll school. Children between 2 and 4 will find Noddy, the popular Enid Blyton character, on board. Youngsters can also enjoy a dedicated Wii room; Scalextric at sea with Grand Prix-style track; 3D cinema; and interactive classes. Family shore programs include aqua and "theme parks." There's a useful Night Nursery for under-5s.

Active types can participate in circus-like activities, including juggling, acro-balancing, tight-wire walking, stilt walking, and clowning. The area has bungee trampolines and a flying trapeze – high up on Sky Deck. If you tire of acrobatics, there are plenty of lounges to escape to.

Azura is P&O Cruises' most advanced cruise ship to date, and has a good passenger space ratio. The onboard currency is the British pound. Gratuities are recommended at £3.75 per person, per day. Smoking is permitted only on cabin balconies and in designated spots on the open decks.

Niggles include the low passenger space ratio, and the charge for shuttle buses in many ports. The upper-deck public room layout means you can't go from one end of the ship to the other without first going down, along and up. Those with mobility problems will need to plan their journey and use the most appropriate of three elevator banks.

SUITABLE FOR: *Azura* is best suited to families with children and adult couples who want to spend time together, and are seeking a big-ship environment with comfortable, unstuffy surroundings, lots of options, and a British flavor.

ACCOMMODATION. There are 27 price grades, according to size and location, but really just five types of accommodation: suite with balcony; family suite with balcony; outside-view twin/queen with balcony; outside-view twin/queen; interior no-view cabin. Although there are more balconies than aboard *Ventura*, more than a third of all cabins are of the interior no-view variety. Some have extra third/fourth berths that fold down from the ceiling.

Most welcome are 18 single-occupancy cabins, a first for P&O Cruises. They are located in a small section on the port side, adjacent to the casino. Also new are spa cabins, with added amenities and direct access to the ship's spa, and two large suites for extended families or groups of friends.

While the suites are reasonably spacious, they really are small when compared to those aboard some other cruise lines, such as Celebrity Cruises or Norwegian Cruise Line, whose top suites are four or five times the size. Most cabins are intelligently laid out, and manage to provide a feeling of space – well, sort of.

Standard in all cabins: bed runners, 10.5 tog duvets, Slumberland 8-inch sprung mattresses, Egyptian cotton towels and robes, and tea/coffee making facilities (plastic and basic). But getting fresh milk requires ingenuity – try the self-serve buffet. There are UK three-pin sockets plus US-style 110-volt sockets for electrical devices.

Open closets (no doors – a money saver), provide easy access, but many passengers dislike the "no trust" attached hangars. Balcony cabins have wooden railings atop glass dividers, green plastic floors, a couple of small chairs and drinks table, and an outside light. Most cabin bathrooms are small, beige modular units lacking in personality, with a shower enclosure that would prove challenging for anyone who wears clothes of size "X" or larger. The shower head is fixed – there is no hand-held shower hose unless you occupy suite-grade accommodation.

Wheelchair-accessible cabins, which have a large, user-friendly shower enclosure, are mostly located in the front section of the ship, but one of the main restaurants is aft. So be prepared for lots of wheeling time, and waiting time at the elevators. Wheelchair users should note that breakfast in the three main restaurants typically ends at 9.30am on sea days and 9am on port days. To take breakfast in the self-serve casual eatery, they will need to wheel across the decks containing the forward and midship pools and lots of deck chairs – not easy. Alternatively, they can order room service breakfast – typically cold items only.

There is no room service breakfast on disembarkation day, when the company want you out of your cabin by 8am.

CUISINE. P&O's marketing blurb claims that there are 10 restaurants. There aren't. There are five genuine restaurants (Peninsular, Oriental, Meridian, Sindhu, and Seventeen), the rest are eateries or fast food joints. The three main dining rooms, Peninsular, Oriental and Meridian, all have the same menus. Peninsular and Oriental offer fixed seating dining,

with assigned tables (typical seating times: 6:30pm or 8:30pm). In the Amber restaurant, you can dine when you want, with whomever you want, between 6pm and 10pm – P&O calls it "Freedom Dining," although at peak times, there can be a bit of a wait. Once or twice per cruise, additional special dinners will be served in the main dining rooms, one of which is a Chaîne des Rôtisseurs culinary dining event. **Alternative dining venues:** Sindhu is a dedicated Indian (reservation-only) extra-charge, à la carte restaurant. This is a first aboard a P&O Cruises ship and is a natural, given the UK passenger profile for this company and its links with India. It is overseen by Michelin-star chef Atul Kochhar, whose specialty is British and Indian fusion cuisine. The food is cooked to order, unlike in the main dining rooms. The design of the venue is poor, however, with some cold stone flooring. Table seating includes several alcove-style areas that make it impossible for waiters to serve food correctly without reaching across others at the same table. When I was aboard, it was difficult to read the menu outside the venue because colored inks are used, but can't be read in the bright lights of the passageway.

For the Glass House, TV wine expert Olly Smith has helped create a "Select Dining" restaurant and wine bar venue. The venue offers seafood and grilled items, paired with wines chosen by Smith. You can, of course, simply have just a glass of wine, without food.

Seventeen is a reservations-only, extra charge, à la carte fine dining restaurant in a quiet, refined setting.

Venezia is the ship's large, casual, self-serve buffet eatery/food court, open almost around the clock, with indoor-outdoor seating for thousands – well, hundreds – but the table tops are very high for most people. On the same deck, adjacent to the forward pool, are a poolside grill and pizzeria. Verona is a family-friendly self-service eatery.

In addition, 24-hour room service is available in cabins.

ENTERTAINMENT. The 800-seat Playhouse Theatre, which spans two decks and is located at the front of the ship, is an excellent venue for shows and, with two large video screens on either side of the stage; the sightlines are very good from all seats. Malabar is the ship's multicultural night venue, with its decor based on the hotels on Marine Drive, Mumbai. Cabaret, live bands and dancing are featured here. Meanwhile, the Planet Bar, a nightclub and entertainment venue, is an activities room by day and a club by night.

SPA/FITNESS. The Oasis Spa – located forward, almost atop the ship – has a gymnasium, aerobics room, beauty salon, separate male and female sauna and steam rooms (no charge), and 11 treatment rooms. An internal stairway connects to the deck below, which contains an extra-charge Thermal Suite (£15 per person, per day, or a composite price per cruise). Harding Brothers provide the spa staff and services. Treatments include special packages for couples, and the SilverSpa Generation.

● **For more extensive general information about a P&O cruise experience, see pages 147–8.**

Bahamas Celebration
★★ +

Size: ....Mid-Size Ship	Passenger Decks: 7	Cabins (wheelchair accessible): 0
Tonnage: 35,855	Total Crew: 360	Wheelchair accessibility ....None
Lifestyle: ....Standard	Passengers	Cabin Current: ....220 volts
Cruise Line: ....Celebration Cruise Line	(lower beds/all berths):......... 1,030/1875	Elevators: 4
Former Names:..........*Princesse Ragnhild*	Passenger Space Ratio	Casino (gaming tables):......................Yes
Builder: ....HDW (Germany)	(lower beds/all berths):............ 34.8/19.1	Slot Machines:....................................Yes
Original Cost: ....n/a	Crew/Passenger Ratio	Swimming Pools (outdoors): 1
Entered Service: 1981/Mar 2009	(lower beds/all berths):................ 4.1/5.2	(+1 child pool)
Registry:....................................Bahamas	Cabins (total):....................................515	Swimming Pools (indoors): 0
Length (ft/m):......................673.2/202.25	Size Range (sq ft/m): ....n/a	Whirlpools: 2
Beam (ft/m):.............................87.4/26.6	Cabins (outside view):.......................331	Self-Service Launderette: ....No
Draft (ft/m):................................20.0/6.1	Cabins (interior/no view):...................184	Dedicated Cinema/Seats: ....No
Propulsion/Propellers: .... diesel/	Cabins (for one person):.........................0	Library: ....No
(36,356kW/2	Cabins (with private balcony):............... 0	

OVERALL SCORE: 1,035 OUT OF A POSSIBLE 2,000 POINTS

OVERVIEW. This ship, now with a bright blue hull and sponson ducktail stern, was originally constructed as a ferry and operated in Scandinavia by Jahre Line until 1990, and then Color Line until 2008 (some Color Line signage can still be found). In 1992, it was extensively reconstructed and lengthened by the addition of a 35.25-meter section. Celebration Cruise Line – which isn't really a cruise "line" but a one-ship company – is owned by Celebration Cruise Holdings, once the parent company of Imperial Majesty Cruise Line. The ship underwent a further extensive refit and refurbishment before starting its new life as a short-cruise ship, based in the Port of Palm Beach, Florida.

Bahamas Celebration retains its bow and stern loading doors, and has an extremely unsightly exterior ducktail (sponson) skirt – the aft part is large enough to hold a small party on. Because it was built as a ferry, it has a rather boxy, slab-sided look, and the open deck space is *extremely* limited, with plastic chairs everywhere. Consequently, the Passenger Ratio is a very poor 23.6 (and that's with two per cabin), while crew to passenger ratio is the worst in the cruise industry, at 4.1.

The pool deck, with port and starboard hot tubs and twin Tiki bars, is pleasant, but there is simply not enough outdoor seating for the aft-positioned self-serve buffet. However, it's good to find shuffleboard courts on deck.

Inside, a glass-walled atrium spans six decks. Public rooms include a rather large casino, cutely named Wynmore, with a double-height ceiling, but most other public rooms have low ceilings. A small library and card room exist, but there's almost no time to use them on such short cruises. Note that many of the chairs in the lounges/bars

BERLITZ'S RATINGS

	Possible	Achieved
Ship	500	276
Accommodation	200	111
Food	400	185
Service	400	207
Entertainment	100	54
Cruise	400	202

are of the small, Scandinavian tub chair type – too cramped for many people today and with little back support. There are many support pillars in odd locations throughout the public rooms in this ship, a throwback to its construction as a ferry.

One neat feature is a cut-away model of the ship, adjacent to elevators on the main deck (Deck 4). Overall, the interiors have the same kind of Scandinavian feel as the Royal Caribbean Cruise Line ships from the early 1970s. You can even see the transport decks of the original design in the model, so you can compare the old with the new. Indeed, throughout the ship, there is evidence of its original life, with signs to the trailer deck, Color Line emblems and other items remaining as a tribute to the ship's days as *Princess Ragnhild*.

Perhaps the most popular room is the warm, inviting Pub 437, with its rather comfortable leather chairs and Victorian English decor and feel.

As for cruising with kids, the ship has reasonably decent facilities for its size. It features Island Club Coconuts, a club for ages 4–10, while Club Wave is for 11–14 year olds. A number of counselors keep the children busy, and a waterpark-style aft deck outside features a 180-ft waterslide in an area called "Kids of the Caribbean."

This ship operates cheap and cheerful two- and three-night get-away "party" cruises from the Port of Palm Beach that masquerade as real cruises. Fellow passengers will typically walk around with a bottle of drink in their hands. Overall, it's an easy way to take a trip for a couple of days.

ACCOMMODATION. There are nine cabin price grades, the price depending on location and size. When the ship was built as a cold-water Baltic ferry, it contained tiny cabins built for truckers doing an overnight sailing. These still exist, and are called Oceanview Couch cabins. Upper berths have a posted weight limit of 200lbs. Note that all cabins have European-style round-pin electrical sockets, so you may need a convertor plug for anything electrical such as phone chargers, adaptors, etc.

Most cabins are small, with plain, minimalist decor that is practical. There's room under beds to store luggage, however. Note that bedside reading lights in most cabins are poor. The bathrooms are of the extremely compact "you first, me next" variety, with a shower, washbasin and toilet.

Six "suites" face forward and have views over the bow (there's no balcony), while four others face aft. These have more space – although there's no separation of sleeping and lounge areas, so they are not real suites – larger bathrooms (with tiny bath), and more storage space.

CUISINE. There are several dining venue. The Crystal Dining Room is the ship's main dining room, with reserved tables; the restaurant entrance has beautifully polished parquet wood flooring. It's a nice room, although the chairs have "sit-up-and-beg" backs without armrests. Wine is served by the waiters. The cuisine is strictly American.

For better cuisine and slightly better service, The Cove, located between the Crystal Dining Room and the Wynmore Casino, is an intimate, extra-charge, reservations-only venue open for dinner only, with a $25 per person cover charge. Make your reservations as soon as possible – there are so few tables.

Rio's is a self-serve all-you-can-east Brazilian-style buffet venue, open for breakfast, lunch and dinner, and serves meat carved by Brazilian staff as they move from table to table. Other items are taken from a self-serve buffet display.

The Trattoria Di Gerry is a casual Italian-style eatery, with plain, uninspiring, bland decor, with wooden, school classroom-style chairs do not have armrests. However, it is lively, extremely popular, and is included in the basic cruise fare, although some items cost extra.

ENTERTAINMENT. The "View" is the ship's 630-seat showlounge/nightclub and disco. Entertainment is of the ear-splitting, in-your-face variety.

SPA/FITNESS. The Fountain of Youth "spa" – it's not much of a spa – includes a "Mussel Beach" fitness room with muscle-pumping equipment.

WHERE NAUTICAL EXPRESSIONS COME FROM

If you've ever wondered where some terms or phrases came from, you have only to look to the sea, ships, and seamen.

Above board

This term for honesty originated in the days when pirates would hide most of their crews below decks, to trick an unsuspecting victim. A ship that sh6wed its crew openly on the deck, aboveboard, was obviously an honest merchantman.

All Above Board

"All above board referred to the fact that boards or planking which made up the decks are in plain view;

hence, anything that was stored above board was in plain view of everyone. T6day we tend to use "going overboard" in the sense of going to far in our reaction or in some venture. "All above board" has come to be synonymous with honest dealings.

All hands on deck

Everyone should gather together to their positions and prepare for action. It is used nowadays to mean "to gather together for some task or other."

As the crow flies

British coastal vessels customarily

carried a cage of crows. These birds hate wide expanses of water and head, "as straight as the crow flies," to the nearest land when released at sea. This was useful to vessels lost in foggy coastal weather before the days of radar. The lookout perch on sailing vessels became known as the crow's nest.

Bale out

The term is typically used in the sense of getting out of some situation - particularly a financial one. However, the verb to bale out, means to remove water, and comes from the old name 'boyle' for a bucket.

Balmoral
★★★ +

Size: ....Mid-Size Ship	Passenger Decks: 10	Cabins (for one person): 91
Tonnage: 43,537	Total Crew: 471	Cabins (with private balcony): 121
Lifestyle: ....Standard	Passengers	Cabins (wheelchair accessible): 9
Cruise Line: .....Fred Olsen Cruise Lines	(lower beds/all berths): 1,340/1,930	Wheelchair accessibility ....Good
Former Names: ......Norwegian Crown,	+ 350 (after stretch)	Cabin Current: ....110/220 AC
Crown Odyssey	Passenger Space Ratio	Elevators: 4
Builder: ....Meyer Werft (Germany)	(lower beds/all berths):........31.1/31.1	Casino (gaming tables): ....Yes
Original Cost: ....$178 million	Crew/Passenger Ratio	Slot Machines: ....Yes
Entered Service: .....Jun 1988/Jan 2008	(lower beds/all berths): 3.03/3.03	Swimming Pools (outdoors): 2
Registry: ....The Bahamas	Cabins (total): 744	Swimming Pools (indoors): 0
Length (ft/m): 715.2/218.18	Size Range (sq ft/m): 153.9–613.5/	Whirlpools: 4
Beam (ft/m): 92.5/28.2	14.3–57.0	Self-Service Launderette: ....Yes
Draft (ft/m): 23.8/7.26	Cabins (outside view): 562	Dedicated Cinema/Seats: ....No
Propulsion/Propellers: diesel (21,330kW)/2	Cabins (interior/no view): 182	Library: ....Yes

BERLITZ'S OVERALL SCORE: 1,398 OUT OF A POSSIBLE 2,000 POINTS

OVERVIEW. *Balmoral,* formerly *Norwegian Crown,* is a well-designed and built ship, originally constructed for the long defunct Royal Cruise Line. Norwegian Cruise Line then operated the ship for many years, before it was transferred to Orient Lines in 2000, and then back to Norwegian Cruise Line in September 2003.

Fred Olsen Cruise Lines bought the ship in 2007 and, after a major refurbishment, including a "chop and stretch" operation involving the addition of a 99-ft (30.2-meter) mid-section, it entered service in January 2008. Although the company's logo includes the Norwegian flag, the ship is registered in the Bahamas.

The all-white ship has a relatively handsome, nicely balanced exterior profile, and one of its plus features is its full, walk-around teak promenade deck outdoors, although it becomes a little narrow in the forward section of the vessel. There are many nicely polished wood railings on balconies and open decks of the ship, and there is a jogging track on the uppermost deck outdoors. Atop the ship is the Observatory Lounge, with fine ocean views, central dance floor, and bar. Out on deck, there is a heated saltwater pool, but little shade (no glass dome for inclement weather).

The main public room spaces are on Lounge Deck. At the front of the ship is the Neptune Lounge, the main showlounge, with an integral bar at the back of the room; the raised stage and wood dance floor are surrounded by amphitheatre-style seating in banquettes with small drinks tables. Aft of the showlounge are the shops – a curved staircase connects this deck with the reception lobby on the deck below.

Next is the Braemar Lounge, alongside a lifestyle area

BERLITZ'S RATINGS

	Possible	Achieved
Ship	500	387
Accommodation	200	150
Food	400	258
Service	400	265
Entertainment	100	65
Cruise	400	273

that includes an internet center with good separation for privacy; there's also a library, and separate card room. Aft of the Braemar Lounge is the Morning Light Pub (named after the very first Fred Olsen ship, *Morning Light*). This venue is more like a lounge than a real pub, although it does have draught beers. Aft is the Palms Café, the ship's casual self-service buffet-style café.

The high lobby has a large gold sculpture in the shape of a globe of the world by the famous sculpture artist Arnaldo Pomodoro (called Microcosm, Macrocosm); it used to revolve.

Balmoral offers a wide range of itineraries, which keeps people coming back to this very comfortable ship; passengers also receive a log of each cruise to take home. Niggles include poor reception desk staff, the inflexible bed layout in some cabins, and the fact that the decor in some of the older cabins looks dated

The onboard currency is the British pound, and port taxes are included for UK passengers. Gratuities of £4 ($6) per passenger, per day, are suggested. The drinks prices are very reasonable, but laundry/dry-cleaning prices are quite high.

A piece of trivia for ship buffs: a bar at the back of the showlounge was originally named Theo's bar after one of the former Royal Cruise Line's most popular bartenders.

SUITABLE FOR: *Balmoral* is best suited to British couples and single travelers wanting destination-intensive cruising in a ship that has European quality, style, and character, a sense of space, comfortable surroundings, decent facilities, realistic pricing and good value for money, with British food and entertainment. A friendly and accommodating, mostly Filipino crew should help to make a cruise aboard the ship a pleasant, no-hassle experience.

ACCOMMODATION. There are 21 price categories; typically the higher the deck, the more expensive will be your accommodation. Most cabins are of the same size and layout, have blond wood cabinetry and accents, an abundance of mirrors, and closet and drawer space, and are very well equipped. All accommodation grades have a color television, a hairdryer, music console (plus a button that can be used to turn announcements on or off), personal safe, and private bathroom with shower (many upper-grade cabins have a good-sized bathtub).

All towels are 100% cotton, although they could be larger; soap, shampoo, conditioner, body lotion, shower cap and sewing kit are the amenities provided. Duvets (single) are standard, blankets and bed linen is available on request, as are double-bed size duvets. On-demand movies are £2.95 from the in-cabin Infotainment System.

The cabin soundproofing is generally good. Some cabins have interconnecting doors, so that they can make a two-room suite – good for families with children.

The largest accommodations are the suites on Highland Deck 10. They are quite spacious units, and provide a sleeping area and separate living room, including some nicely finished wood cabinetry and a large amount of closet and drawer space, together with a large, white marble-clad bathroom with a full-sized tub and integral shower. There is a large private balcony, although some balconies can be overlooked from the deck above.

There are nine wheelchair-accessible cabins; these provide plenty of space to maneuver, and all include a bathroom with roll-in shower. But wheelchair accessibility in some ports on the many itineraries operated by this ship – particularly in Europe – may prove quite frustrating and wheelchair-accessible transportation may be limited.

Cabins in the new mid-section have attractive, contemporary decor that is light and airy. Some of those on the upper decks (Deck 8, 9) have bathrooms with a vertical window with a direct view from the large shower enclosure through the sleeping space to the outside, and thus provide an enhanced feeling of spaciousness. Bathrooms have shower enclosures rather than tub/shower combinations (some have two washbasins), and enough storage space for personal toiletries.

CUISINE. The Ballindalloch Restaurant, in the aft third section of the ship, is the main dining room. It has ocean-view windows on port and starboard sides, and operates two seatings. It has comfortable seating at tables for two, four, six or eight. However, the waiter stations are exposed and can be extremely noisy; indeed, the noise level in this main restaurant is high, and trying to hold a conversation can be frustrating.

Two more intimate dining spots: Avon Restaurant and Spey Restaurant, both named after rivers, are located aft on Highland Deck 10 – the deck that contains the higher-priced suites. The floor-to-ceiling windows provide lots of light. The decor is contemporary and minimalist, and the noise level is low, which makes for comfortable conversation. However, these venues also operate two seatings.

The 70-seat Palms Café is an alternative, more intimate venue for informal self-serve meals.

All venues have open seating for breakfast and lunch.

ENTERTAINMENT. The Neptune Lounge is the venue for all entertainment shows, cabaret acts, lectures, and some social functions. It is a single level room with tiered seating levels. Sightlines are generally good, but could be better.

Revue-style production shows are staged by a resident troupe of singers and dancers, and there are cabaret acts. The quality of the shows, however, is average. Cabaret acts – typically singers, magicians, ventriloquists, comedy jugglers, and comedians – perform individually or as part of the revues.

SPA/FITNESS. There is a reasonably decent – but not large enough – indoor wellness center, which includes a fitness room with ocean views, plenty of muscle-pumping equipment, and several beauty treatment rooms. The wellness facilities and treatment staff are provided by The Onboard Spa Company.

Size: . . . . .Mid-Size Ship	Passenger Decks: 8	Cabins (with private balcony): 43
Tonnage: 28,613	Total Crew: .350	Cabins (wheelchair accessible): 4
Lifestyle: . . . . .Standard	Passengers	Wheelchair accessibility . . . . .Fair
Cruise Line: . . . . .Fred Olsen Cruise Lines	(lower beds/all berths): 804/868	Cabin Current: . . . . . . .110 and 220 volts
Former Names: . . . . .Star Odyssey,	Passenger Space Ratio	Elevators: 4
Westward, Royal Viking Star	(lower beds/all berths): 35.5/32.9	Casino (gaming tables): . . . . .Yes
Builder: . . . . .Wartsila (Finland)	Crew/Passenger Ratio	Slot Machines: . . . . .Yes
Original Cost: . . . .$22.5 million	(lower beds/all berths): 2.2/2.4	Swimming Pools (outdoors): 2
Entered Service: . . . June 1972/Nov 1996	Cabins (total): 421	Swimming Pools (indoors): 0
Registry: . . . . .The Bahamas	Size Range (sq ft/m): 135.6–819.1/	Whirlpools: 3
Length (ft/m): 674.1/205.47	12.6–76.1	Self-Service Launderette: . . . . .Yes
Beam (ft/m): 82.6/25.20	Cabins (outside view): 383	Dedicated Cinema/Seats: Yes/156
Draft (ft/m): 24.7/7.55	Cabins (interior/no view): 48	Library: . . . . .Yes
Propulsion/Propellers: diesel (13,400kW)/2	Cabins (for one person): 38	

OVERALL SCORE: 1,339 OUT OF A POSSIBLE 2,000 POINTS

OVERVIEW. The ship's name is taken from the famous Scottish Black Watch regiment, although the ship itself is all-white. There is a good amount of open deck and sunbathing space, and a decent health-fitness area high atop the ship, as well as a wide wrap-around teakwood promenade deck with wind-breaker on the aft part of the deck.

The interior decor is quiet and rest-ful, with wide stairways and foyers, soft lighting and no glitz anywhere, though many passengers find the artwork a little drab – it is, in reality, rather more Scandinavian eclectic than anything. In general, good materials, fabrics (including the use of the Black Watch tartan) and soft furnishings give a pleasant ambiance and comfortable feeling to the public rooms. Most of these are quite spacious, with high, indented ceil-ings, and most (including the main dining room) are located on one deck in a user-friendly horizontal layout.

An observation lounge (The Observatory) high atop the ship, displays nautical memorabilia and has commanding views. Draft beers are available, as in all bars. The whole ship indoors is a smoke-free zone.

There is a good cinema (few ships today have a dedi-cated cinema) with a steeply tiered floor, and a pleasant library with an adjacent room containing two computer terminals for internet access.

A popular meeting place is the Braemar Room, a large lounge close to the restaurant; it has a self-help beverage corner for coffees and teas (open 24 hours a day, although it does become overly busy during afternoon tea time), comfortable chairs, and large ocean-view windows along one side. The Library and Card Room is a very pleasant facility. A self-serve launderette (useful on the longer

BERLITZ'S RATINGS

	Possible	Achieved
Ship	500	346
Accommodation	200	141
Food	400	248
Service	400	273
Entertainment	100	63
Cruise	400	268

cruises) has four washing machines, five dryers, and a couple of irons in a large user-friendly room.

Black Watch is a comfortable (not luxurious) ship, with a moderate stan-dard of food and service from a friendly, mostly Filipino staff that provides decent, though not faultless, service. There is ample space per passenger, even when the ship is full. Cruises are well organized, with interesting itiner-aries, and free shuttle buses in many ports of call. The onboard currency is the British pound, and port taxes are included for UK passengers.

The National Express bus operator works in conjunc-tion with Fred Olsen Cruise Lines to provide a dedicated Cruiselink service via London's Victoria Coach Station to the UK departure ports of Dover or Southampton.

Although it is being well maintained, do remember that this ship will soon be 40 years old, which means that little problems such as gurgling plumbing, creaking joints, and other idiosyncrasies can occur, and air conditioning is not be all that it should be in some cabins. The company sug-gests gratuities of £4 per passenger per day, which, to some, seems a lot. Only a few suites have private balconies.

Passenger niggles include: noticeable cutbacks in food variety and quality; an increase in the use of paper nap-kins, packets of butter, margarine and preserves; the lack of choice of sugar; very poor coffee; long lines at the cramped buffet; poor wine service (not enough wine waiters); and too few staff for the increased passenger numbers follow-ing the addition of more cabins.

SUITABLE FOR: *Black Watch* is best suited to the older UK traveler who enjoys seeking out the world's duty-free shops and wants a British cruise environment, in comfortable surroundings, and relatively formal attire.

ACCOMMODATION. There are 18 price categories of cabins (plus one for the owner's suite, whose price is not listed in the brochure). These include four grades of cabin, spread around most of the decks, for those traveling solo. The wide range of cabins provides something for everyone, from spacious suites with separate bedrooms, to small (interior – no view) cabins. While most cabins are for two persons, some can accommodate a third, fourth, or even a fifth person.

In all grades, duvets are provided, and the decently sized bathroom towels are 100% cotton. A hairdryer and a package of Gilchrist & Soames personal toiletries is supplied to all passengers. Occupants of suite grades also get a cotton bathrobe and cold canapés each evening (as well as priority seating in the dining rooms).

The room service menu is quite limited and could be improved. The suites and cabins on Decks 7, 8, and 9 are quiet units. A number of cabins in the aft section of Decks 3, 4 and 5 can prove to be uncomfortable, with noise from throbbing engines and generator units a major distraction, particularly in the cabins adjacent to the engine casing.

Outside-view/Interior (No View) Cabins: Spread across Decks 3, 4, 5, 7 and 8, all cabins are quite well equipped, and there is plenty of good (illuminated) closet, drawer and storage space. Some cabin bathrooms have awkward access, and insulation between some of the lower grade cabins could be better. The bathrooms are of a decent size. Some cabins have a small bathtub, although many have only a shower enclosure.

Deluxe/Bridge/Junior Suites: These suites, on Decks 7 and 8, have a large sleeping area and lounge area with ocean-view picture windows and refrigerator, plenty of hooks for hanging bathrobes, outerwear and luggage; and a bathroom with bathtub and shower (cabin 8019 is the exception, with a shower instead of a bathtub).

Marquee Suites: These suites have a large sleeping area and lounge area with bigger ocean-view picture windows and a refrigerator, more hooks for hanging bathrobes, outerwear and luggage; and a bathroom with tub and shower.

Premier Suites: Each of these nine suites is named after a place: Amalfi (9006), Lindos (9002), Nice (9004), each measuring 547.7 sq. ft/50.8 sq. meters; Seville (9001), Singapore (9003), Carmel (9005), Bergen (9007), Waterford (9009), each measuring 341.7 sq ft/31.7 sq. meters; and Windsor (9008), measuring 574.8 sq. ft/53.4 sq. meters. They have a separate bedroom with ample closet and other storage space, a lounge with large windows (with large television and VCR, refrigerator and mini-bar), and bathroom with full-size bathtub and shower, and separate toilet.

Owner's Suite: This measures 819.1 sq. ft/76.1 sq. meters, including a large balcony. It consists of a foyer leading into a lounge, with sofa, table and chairs, audio center (TV set, DVD player), refrigerator and mini-bar. A separate bedroom has a double bed, and ample closet and drawer space. A second bedroom has two bunk beds – good for families with children. The bathroom is large and has a full-size tub, sep-

arate shower enclosure, toilet, and two washbasins. The balcony has space enough for a table and six chairs, plus a couple of sunloungers. It is located just aft of the navigation bridge on the starboard side of the ship.

CUISINE. The Glentanar Dining Room has a high ceiling, a white sail-like focal point at its center, and ample space at each table. The chairs have armrests, and are quite comfortable. The Orchid Room is a smaller offshoot of the dining room, which can be reserved for a more intimate, quieter dining experience. While breakfast is typically in an open seating arrangement, there are two seatings for lunch and dinner. Passengers help themselves from two cold food display counters during breakfast and lunch.

The Garden Cafe is a small, more casual dining spot with a light, breezy decor reminiscent of a garden conservatory. It sometimes has themed dinners, such as French, Indian, or Thai. There is a self-help salad bar and hot food display. The room is also the place for late-night snacks.

Fred Olsen Cruise Lines has above-average cuisine that is attractively presented, with a good range of fish, seafood, meat and chicken dishes, and has a good selection of cheeses as well as vegetarian options. The food is generally of good quality, with a decent selection of main course items to suit most British tastes. Breakfast buffets tend to be quite repetitious, although they appear to satisfy most.

There is a reasonably decent range of wines, at moderate prices, but few of the wine stewards have much knowledge of wines. Communication with the Filipino waiters can sometimes be a little frustrating.

Coffee and tea are always available in the Braemar Room, adjacent to, and aft of, the Glentanar Restaurant.

ENTERTAINMENT. The Neptune Lounge, the ship's showlounge, seats about 400, although some sightlines are obstructed by pillars. The entertainment mainly consists of small-scale production shows presented by a small team of resident singers/dancers, and cabaret acts. Standards are quite poor, and the cast self-congratulatory. There are also cabaret acts. To be fair, passengers who cruise aboard this ship are not really looking for first-rate entertainment, but rather something to fill the time after dinner, which is the main event for most.

There is plenty of live music for dancing and listening in several lounges, and there are good British sing-alongs.

SPA/FITNESS. The spa/fitness facilities are located at the top and front of the ship (inaccessible for wheelchair users). There is a combined gymnasium/aerobics room, while a door provides access to steam rooms, saunas, and changing rooms. Sample treatment prices: Elemis Aromapure facial: £29; Well-being massage (50 minutes): £35; Personal Training Session (60 minutes): £20. Sports facilities include a large paddle tennis court, golf practice nets, shuffleboard, and ring toss. Steiner's staff will try to sell their own-brand Elemis beauty products. Some fitness classes are free, while some, such as yoga and kick-boxing, cost extra. It's prudent to make appointments as early as possible.

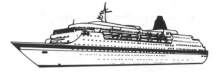

Bleu de France
★★★ +

Size: . . . . .Mid-Size Ship	Passenger Decks: 10	Cabins (with private balcony): 6
Tonnage: .37,301	Total Crew: 406	Cabins (wheelchair accessible): 2
Lifestyle: . . . . .Standard	Passengers	Wheelchair accessibility . . . . .Good
Cruise Line: . . .CDF Croisières de France	(lower beds/all berths): 752/1,158	Cabin Current: . . . . . . .110 and 220 volts
Former Names: Holiday Dream, SuperStar	Passenger Space Ratio	Elevators: 4
Aries, SuperStar Europe, Europa	(lower beds/all berths): 49.6/32.2	Casino (gaming tables): . . . . .Yes
Builder: . . . . . . .Bremer Vulkan (Germany)	Crew/Passenger Ratio	Slot Machines: . . . . .Yes
Original Cost: . . . .$120 million	(lower beds/all berths): 1.8/2.8	Swimming Pools (outdoors): 2
Entered Service: . . . . Jan 1982/Nov 2009	Cabins (total): 374	(1 magrodome)
Registry: . . . . .The Bahamas	Size Range (sq ft/m): 161.4–678.1/	Swimming Pools (indoors): 1 (fresh water)
Length (ft/m): 654.9/199.63	15.0–63.0	Whirlpools: 3
Beam (ft/m): 93.8/28.60	Cabins (outside view): 309	Self-Service Launderette: . . . . .Yes
Draft (ft/m): 27.6/8.42	Cabins (interior/no view): 65	Dedicated Cinema/Seats: . . . . .No
Propulsion/Propellers: diesel(21,270 kW)/2	Cabins (for one person): 0	Library: . . . . .Yes

BERLITZ'S OVERALL SCORE: 1,396 OUT OF A POSSIBLE 2,000 POINTS

OVERVIEW. The ship's name, *Bleu de France*, sounds more like a cheese than a ship. Originally sailing as the former *Europa* (No. 5) for Hapag-Lloyd Cruises, it was for many years the flagship of the German cruise industry. Star Cruises, having bought it in April 1998, leased it back to Hapag-Lloyd until 1999, when the new, current *Europa* debuted; it went into drydock for a $15 million refit and renovation prior to service for Star Cruises in 2002 for cruises to Thailand and China.

In 2004 it was sold to Spain-based tour operator Pullmantur Cruises, who kept it for four years, and then to CDF Croisières de France (a sub-brand of Pullmantur Cruises, which in turn is owned by Royal Caribbean Cruises). After a €30 million refit/transformation program that included facelifts to public rooms, and dining facilities were adapted to the growing French-speaking market, it made its latest debut in 2008, with the hospitality and the range and variety of food tailored to its new clientele.

The ship has a deep blue hull and white upper structure, and a sponson stern – a kind of "skirt" added in order to comply with stability regulations. But it still maintains its moderately handsome, balanced profile. There is a good amount of outdoor deck and sunbathing space, including a solarium on what was previously a nude bathing deck (perhaps it still is), and the ship has both outdoor and outdoor/indoor pools; the latter, which includes a Lido Deck bar, can be covered by a glass dome. While there is no walk-around outdoors promenade deck, there are half-length teak port and starboard promenades.

Bleu de France has a wide range of good-sized public rooms. Facilities include a casino, library/internet center,

BERLITZ'S RATINGS

	Possible	Achieved
Ship	500	382
Accommodation	200	143
Food	400	256
Service	400	284
Entertainment	100	64
Cruise	400	267

karaoke room, and children's play room. Restful colors were applied to many public rooms and cabins, and subtle, hidden lighting was used throughout, particularly on the wide, spacious stairways. The public rooms are located aft in a "cake-layer" stacking, with accommodation located forward, thus separating noisy areas from quieter ones.

The interior decor has splashes of bright colors, motifs, and helpful signage. The ship, which has an all drinks-inclusive policy, provides an informal, relaxed, yet quite elegant setting, with a casual dress code. You will typically find a lot of smokers aboard. *Bleu de France* operates with all-inclusive pricing, and drinks and table wines are included in all venues). Children are split into different age groups.

The onboard currency is the euro.

SUITABLE FOR: This ship is geared to French-speaking couples, singles, and families with children of all ages who want a first cruise experience in a traditional – but not new – ship, with plenty of public rooms and a lively atmosphere, food that is quantity rather than quality, at low cost.

ACCOMMODATION. There is a wide range of suites and cabins, in 15 price grades. All of the original cabins are quite spacious, and all have illuminated closets, dark wood cabinetry with rounded edges, full-length mirrors, color TV/DVD player, mini-bar/refrigerator, personal safe, hairdryer, and good cabin insulation. Most cabins can accommodate one or two additional persons, which mean the ship's original spacious feel has been greatly eroded in order to cater more to families with children. The port and starboard passenger hallways have different colors, and so do the fore and aft foyers, making it easy for first-time passengers to find their way around.

Most bathrooms have deep tubs (cabins without bathtub have a large shower enclosure), a three-head shower unit, two deep washbasins (not all cabins), large toiletries cabinet and handsome personal toiletries.

The largest living spaces are suites that were added during the 1999 refit. However, because of their location – they were created from former bridge officers' cabins – they have lifeboat-obstructed views. Six other suites had private balconies added; all provide generous living spaces. There is a separate bedroom with either queen-sized or twin beds, illuminated closets, and vanity desk. The lounge includes a wet bar with refrigerator and glass cabinets and large audio-visual center complete with large-screen TV set and DVD player. The marble-clad bathroom has a large shower enclosure, with retractable clothesline.

CUISINE. Le Flamboyant, the main restaurant, is large, with ocean-view windows on two sides, and a good amount of space around each table. There are two seatings for meals; dinner is at 7:15pm and 9:30pm. There is also a large, extremely varied self-serve cold table for all meals, with colorful displays of a wide variety of foods. All meals are included in the price, as is table wine (white, red or rosé).

For casual meals, self-serve breakfasts, luncheons and supper buffets are provided at Le Panorama self-serve buffet, located aft, with excellent ocean views.

Additionally, there is the Olive Bistro for light Mediterranean fare, located at the glass dome-covered center pool (open 11am–10pm), as well as Millesime (for cigars and quality spirits), and the Le Café Crème Bar.

ENTERTAINMENT. The main lounge (Le Grand Salon) is the venue for major events. The sightlines in the show lounge are quite poor from many seats – the room was originally built more for use as a single-level concert salon than a room for shows – although the setting is elegant.

The shows consist of a troupe of showgirl dancers, together with a host of cabaret acts, including singers, magicians, and comedians, among others, and are very much geared to the family audience that this ship carries. There is also plenty of live music for listening or dancing to in various bars and lounges, and there is the inevitable discotheque. A delightful observation lounge, Acajou, also hosts music and special acts.

SPA/FITNESS. The 800-sq. meter (8,611 sq. ft) Aqua-Marine Spa is really an extremely good indoor wellness center, and is located together with an indoor swimming pool that is larger than most outdoor pools you find nowadays aboard new, much bigger ships.

Adjacent facilities include three saunas (Finnish, hammam, herbal), fitness/exercise centre, hydrotherapy bath, 12 treatment rooms, and beauty salon. A solarium is located outdoors atop the ship.

WHERE NAUTICAL EXPRESSIONS COME FROM

If you've ever wondered where some terms or phrases came from, you have only to look to the sea, ships, and seamen.

Bamboozle

Today, when you intentionally deceive someone, usually as a joke, you are said to have bamboozled them. The word also was used in the days of sail, but then it meant to deceive a passing vessel as to your ship's origin or nationality by flying an ensign other than your own – a common practice by pirates. From the 17th century, it described the Spanish custom of hoisting false flags to deceive (bamboozle) enemies.

Batten down the hatches

The real hatches are the things that cover the hatchways: gratings and close-hatches. A great deal of water can come aboard either from the sea of the sky or both, so they used to cover those hatches with tarpaulins. The crew typically took battens – stout laths of wood that fit against the coaming (the raised rim of the hatchway) – and pinned the tarpaulin down to cleats on the deck, drum tight.

Barge in

The word barge has two nautical meanings. First as a term applied to a flag officer's boat or highly decorated vessel used for ceremonial occasions. The second usage refers to the more common, flat-bottomed work boat which is hard to maneuver and difficult to control. Hence the term "barge in."

Bigwigs

The senior officers in the English Navy, who once wore huge wigs, were referred to a "bigwigs."

Bitter End

If a sailor were to lay out all of the anchor warp (chain or rope) until he reached the bitter end, then he would have no more to give out. The bitter end also refers to the end of the "starter" (a short rope knotted at on end) used for punishment. Today we talk of having reached the "bitter end" when we mean that we can go no further in a task. The landlubber's phrase "stick it to the bitter end" and "faithful to the bitter end" are derivations of the nautical term and refer to anyone who insists in adhering to a course of action without regard to consequences.

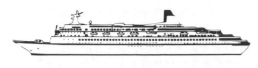

Boudicca
★★★ +

Size: ....Mid-Size Ship	Draft (ft/m): 24.7/7.55	Cabins (for one person): 35
Tonnage: 28,388	Propulsion/Propellers: diesel 13,400kW/2 (CP)	Cabins (with private balcony): 59
Lifestyle: ....Standard	Passenger Decks: 8	Cabins (wheelchair accessible): 4
Cruise Line: ....Fred Olsen Cruise Lines	Total Crew: 320	Wheelchair accessibility ....Fair
Former Names: ......Grand Latino, SuperStar	Passengers	Cabin Current: ....110 and 220 volts
Capricorn, Hyundai Keumgang, SuperStar	(lower beds/all berths): 839/900	Elevators: 5
Capricorn, Golden Princess, Sunward,	Passenger Space Ratio	Casino (gaming tables): ....Yes
Birka Queen, Sunward, Royal Viking Sky	(lower beds/all berths): 33.8/31.5	Slot Machines: ....Yes
Builder: ....Wartsila (Finland)	Crew/Passenger Ratio	Swimming Pools (outdoors): 2
Original Cost: ....$22.5 million	(lower beds/all berths): 2.3/2.5	Swimming Pools (indoors): 0
Entered Service: ....June 1973/Feb 2006	Cabins (total): 437	Whirlpools: 2
Registry: ....The Bahamas	Size Range (sq ft/m): ..135.6–579.1/12.6–53.8	Self-Service Launderette: ....Yes
Length (ft/m): 674.1/205.47	Cabins (outside view): 363	Dedicated Cinema/Seats: ....No
Beam (ft/m): 82.6/25.20	Cabins (interior/no view): 39	Library: ....Yes

BERLITZ'S OVERALL SCORE: 1,357 OUT OF A POSSIBLE 2,000 POINTS

OVERVIEW. Acquired by Fred Olsen Cruise Lines in 2005, this well-proportioned ship, originally built for long-distance cruising for the now-defunct Royal Viking Line (it was built for one of the three original shipping partners who formed the line – Bergenske Dampskibsselskab), has a sharply raked bow and a sleek appearance. The ship was "stretched" in 1982 with the addition of a 27.7-meter (91-ft) mid section.

The outer styling is quite handsome for an early 1970s-built vessel. The single funnel bears the company's starfish logo, and balances the profile of this attractive (now contemporary-classic) ship. The name *Boudicca* (pronounced Boodicker) comes from the Queen of the Iceni tribe that occupied England's East Anglia; she led a dramatic revolt against the Romans in AD61, and her body is supposedly buried under Platform 10 of London's King's Cross Station.

The ship has a good amount of open deck and sunbathing space; in fact, there is plenty of space everywhere and little sense of crowding because the ship absorbs passengers well. There are port and starboard walking teak promenade decks outdoors, although they no longer wrap around the front of the ship. Before the ship began cruising as *Boudicca*, it was given an extensive refit, which included creating a number of cabins for solo travelers, and re-engining.

The interior decor is restful, with a mix of English and Norwegian styles (particularly the artwork) with wide stairways and foyers, good passenger flow, soft lighting and no glitz anywhere. In general, good materials, fabrics and soft furnishings add to a pleasant ambience and comfortable feeling experienced throughout the public rooms, most of which are quite spacious and have high, indented ceilings.

BERLITZ'S RATINGS		
	Possible	Achieved
Ship	500	342
Accommodation	200	154
Food	400	258
Service	400	274
Entertainment	100	65
Cruise	400	264

There are lots of (small) public rooms, bars and lounges to play in, unlike the newer (larger) ships built today, including a delightful observation lounge, a small casino, card room, large library, and the Secret Garden Lounge (with its integral café.

Boudicca is an extremely comfortable ship in which to cruise, with a moderate standard of food and service from a friendly, mostly Filipino staff, featuring extremely good value for money cruises in a relaxed environment that provides passengers with many of the comforts of home.

For the ship's mainly British passengers, the National Express bus operator works in conjunction with Fred Olsen Cruise Lines to provide a dedicated Cruiselink service via London's Victoria Coach Station to the UK departure ports of Dover or Southampton.

Although the ship has benefited from an extensive refit and refurbishment, do remember that it is more than 30 years old, which means that little problems such as gurgling plumbing, creaking joints, and other idiosyncrasies can occur, and air conditioning may not be all that it should be. The onboard currency is the British pound and port taxes are included for UK passengers. Gratuities of £4 ($6) per passenger, per day, are suggested.

Passenger niggles include: noticeable cutbacks in food variety and quality, an increase in the use of paper napkins, packets of butter, margarine and preserves, the lack of choice of sugar, very poor coffee, long lines at the cramped buffet, and poor wine service (not enough wine waiters). Other gripes: Not enough staff for the increased passenger numbers after more cabin additions, and declining service standards.

SUITABLE FOR: *Boudicca* is best suited to British couples and single travelers looking for a ship with some sense of space, comfortable surroundings, decent facilities, realistic pricing and good value for money, with British food and entertainment. Good for passengers without tattoos.

ACCOMMODATION. There is something for every taste and wallet, from spacious family suites to small interior (no view) cabins. While most cabins are for two persons, some can accommodate a third, fourth, or even a fifth person. There are 20 price categories of cabins (plus one for the owner's suite, whose price is not listed in the brochure), including four grades of cabin for those traveling solo (these are spread across most of the cabin decks, and not just the lower decks, as is the case with some cruise lines), and three of these have a private balcony. While most cabins have bathtubs, some lower grades have only a shower enclosure.

Some of the quietest cabins are those located just under the navigation bridge, on Lido Deck, as well as those suites and cabins on Bridge Deck. In the refit, a vacuum toilet system was fitted.

In all grades, duvets are provided, the bathroom towels are 100% cotton and are quite large, and a hairdryer is provided. A package of Gilchrist & Soames personal toiletry items (bath gel, shampoo/conditioner, sewing kit, shower cap) is supplied to all passengers. Occupants of suite grades also get a cotton bathrobe and cold canapés each evening, as well as priority seating in the dining rooms.

The room service menu is quite limited and could be improved, although there is an abundance of food available at most times of the day. All cabins have had a facelift. Only a few suites have private balconies.

Outside-view/Inside (No View) Cabins: These are quite well equipped, and there is plenty of good (illuminated) closet, drawer and storage space, but insulation between some of the lower grade cabins could be better. While most cabin bathrooms are of a decent size, some have awkward access. Some have a small tub, although many have only a shower enclosure.

Deluxe/Bridge/Junior Suites: These suites, on Decks 7 and 8, have a large sleeping area and lounge area with ocean-view picture windows and refrigerator, plenty of hooks for hanging bathrobes, outerwear and luggage; and a bathroom with bathtub and shower.

Marquee Suites: These suites have a large sleeping area and lounge area with bigger ocean view picture windows and a refrigerator, more hooks for hanging bathrobes, outerwear and luggage; and a bathroom with tub and shower.

Premier Suites: Anyone wanting the most space should consider one of these suites (each is named after a place). These have a separate bedroom with ample closet and other storage space, a lounge with large windows (with large tele-vision/video player, refrigerator/mini-bar), and bathroom with full-size bathtub and shower, and a separate toilet.

CUISINE. The main dining room is divided into three venues: Heligan, Tintagel, and Four Seasons; each has a high ceiling, and ample space at each table. Although the decor is bland, the chairs, which have armrests, are comfortable. Window-side tables for two are the most sought after, naturally.

While breakfast is typically in an open seating arrangement, there are two seatings for lunch and dinner. Cold food display counters are provided for passengers to help themselves to breakfast and lunch items.

Fred Olsen Cruise Lines has above-average cuisine that is attractively presented and includes a good range of fish, seafood, meat and chicken dishes, as well as vegetarian options, and a wide selection of cheeses, to suit most British tastes. You'll also find a number of popular British pub standards such as bangers and mash, toad in the hole, and spotted dick. Breakfast buffets tend to be quite repetitious, although they appear to satisfy most passengers. There is a reasonably decent range of wines, at moderate prices.

Coffee and tea are available in the Secret Garden Café (part of the Secret Garden Lounge), just aft of the main dining venues – but, sadly, not around-the-clock.

Casual self-serve deck buffets are provided outdoors at the Poolside Café, while fast food items can be obtained from the Marquee Bar (also outdoors).

ENTERTAINMENT. The Neptune Lounge is the venue for shows, cabaret acts, and lectures. It is a large room that seats about 400, although some pillars obstruct sight lines from some seats. The entertainment consists of small-scale production shows presented by a small team of resident singers/dancers, and cabaret acts (these typically rotate around many cruise ships of the same standard).

There is plenty of live music for social dancing (many of the musicians are Filipino) and listening in several lounges, and good British sing-alongs are a feature on each cruise.

SPA/FITNESS. A decent amount of (window-less) space is given to providing health and fitness facilities (on Atlantic Deck). However, they are split in three separate areas (on Atlantic Deck). Forward are the sauna/steam rooms; the center section contains a gymnasium/aerobics room, changing rooms; while the aft section houses a beauty salon.

Some fitness classes are free, while some, such as yoga and kick-boxing, cost extra.

It's best to make appointments as early as possible as treatment time slots go quickly. Sports facilities include a large paddle tennis court, golf practice nets, shuffleboard, and ring toss.

Braemar
★★★ +

Size: .Mid-Size Ship	Propulsion/Propellers: diesel (13,200kW)/2	Cabins (for one person): 38
Tonnage: 24,344	Passenger Decks: 7	Cabins (with private balcony): 70
Lifestyle: . . . . .Standard	Total Crew: 371	Cabins (wheelchair accessible): 4
Cruise Line: . . . . .Fred Olsen Cruise Lines	Passengers	Wheelchair accessibility . . . . .Fair
Former Names: . . . .*Crown Dynasty*,	(lower beds/all berths): 930/930	Cabin Current: . . . . .110 and 220 volts
Norwegian Dynasty, Crown Majesty,	Passenger Space Ratio	Elevators: 5
Cunard Dynasty, Crown Dynasty	(lower beds/all berths): 25.9/25.9	Casino (gaming tables): . . . . .Yes
Builder: . .Union Navale de Levante (Spain)	Crew/Passenger Ratio	Slot Machines: . . . . .Yes
Original Cost: . . . .$100 million	(lower beds/all berths): 2.3/2.3	Swimming Pools (outdoors): 2
Entered Service: . . . .July 1993/Aug 2001	Cabins (total): .484	Swimming Pools (indoors): 0
Registry: . . . . .The Bahamas	Size Range (sq ft/m): 139.9–349.8/	Whirlpools: 2
Length (ft/m): 639.7/195.01	13.0–32.5	Self-Service Launderette: . . . . .Yes
Beam (ft/m): 73.8/22.50	Cabins (outside view): 373	Dedicated Cinema/Seats: . . . . .No
Draft (ft/m): 17.7/5.40	Cabins (interior/no view): 110	Library: . . . . .Yes

OVERALL SCORE: 1,315 OUT OF A POSSIBLE 2,000 POINTS

OVERVIEW. This ship was purchased by Fred Olsen Cruise Lines in spring 2001 and renamed *Braemar*. Following an extensive refurbishment, it started operating cruises targeted mostly at British and Scandinavian passengers.

A handsome-looking mid-sized ship for casual cruising, it has attractive exterior styling, and a lot of glass space. It's a refreshing change for those who don't want to cruise aboard larger, warehouse-size ships. But the ship does roll somewhat, probably due to its shallow draft design, meant for warm weather cruise areas.

There is a good amount of open deck and sunbathing space for its size, and this includes two outdoors bars – one aft and one midships adjacent to the two swimming pools and paddling pool – that have Boddington's and Stella Artois beers on draught. Four open decks, located aft of the funnel, provide good, quiet places to sit and read.

The teak promenade deck is a complete walk-around deck, wrapping around Lounge Deck. Passengers can also go right to the ship's bow – good for photographs. Faux teak floor covering is used on the pool deck, where two pools are located ; it looks tacky, but works well in the heat of the Caribbean, where the ship was meant to spend much of its time.

Inside, there is a pleasant five-deck-high, glass-walled atrium on the starboard side. Off-center stairways add a sense of spaciousness to a clever interior design that surrounds passengers with light. The interior decor in public spaces is warm and inviting, with contemporary, but not brash, art-deco color combinations. The artwork is quite colorful and pleasant, in the Nordic manner.

The Morning Light Club is an open-plan lounge, with its

BERLITZ'S RATINGS

	Possible	Achieved
Ship	500	356
Accommodation	200	133
Food	400	235
Service	400	254
Entertainment	100	62
Cruise	400	275

own bar, split by a walkway that leads to the showlounge (forward), the library/card room/internet center and the boutique (midships). Despite being open, it has cozy seating areas and is very comfortable, with a tartan carpet. A model of the first Fred Olsen ship named *Braemar* (4,775 gross tonnage) is displayed in the center of the room, as is a large carved wood plaque bearing the name Braemar Castle in Scotland.

The mostly Filipino staff is friendly and attentive, and the hospitality factor is good. This is noticeable in the restaurant and other food service areas. The company has come a long way from its humble beginnings, and now offers extremely good value for money cruises in a relaxed, welcoming environment that provides passengers with many of the comforts of home. The dress code is casual. The onboard currency is the British pound.

In 2008, a 102.3-ft (31.2-meter) mid-section extension was added, providing additional cabins and balcony "suites" and a capacity increase. Facilities added or changed include a second swimming pool and more sunbathing space, an observatory lounge, a new restaurant and a pub-style bar. All indoor areas are now no-smoking.

There can be a bit of a wait for shore tenders, and for the few elevators aboard this ship. British passengers should note that no suites or cabins have bathtubs.

Passenger gripes include: lines at the cramped self-service buffet; poor wine service (not enough wine waiters); an increase in the use of paper napkins, packets of butter, margarine and preserves; the lack of choice of sugar; and weak coffee. There is now a self-service launderette (£2 for wash and dry) – and the company usually charges for shuttle buses in some ports of call.

SUITABLE FOR: *Braemar* is geared specifically toward the middle-aged and older British passenger who wants to cruise in a casual, unstuffy environment, and who appears to enjoy seeking out the world's duty-free shops, in a ship with British food and entertainment.

ACCOMMODATION. There are 16 cabin price categories, and, the higher the deck, the higher the price. All grades have a small television and hairdryer (some are awkward to retract from their wall-mount holders), plus European-style duvets. The large bathroom towels are 100% cotton (bathrobes are available upon request in suite-grade cabins). Gilchrist & Soames toiletry items are provided. There is no separate audio system in the cabin, but music can be obtained from one of the TV channels, although you'll have to leave the picture on (suites, however, do have a CD music system).

Standard (Outside-view)/Inside (No View) Cabin Grades: The standard outside-view and interior (no view) cabins, almost all of which are the same size, are really quite small, although they are nicely furnished. Most have broad picture windows (some deluxe cabins on Deck 6 and Deck 7 have lifeboat-obstructed views). They are practical and comfortable, with blond wood-trimmed accents and multi-colored soft furnishings, but there is very little drawer space, and the closet (hanging) space is extremely limited (the ship was purpose-built originally for 7-day cruises). So, as there is little room for luggage, take only the clothing that you think necessary. Each of the outside-view cabins on Deck 4 has a large picture window, while those on the lower Decks 2 and 3 have a porthole. They are quite well equipped, with a small vanity desk unit, a minimal amount of drawer space, curtained windows, and personal safe (hard to reach).

Each cabin has a private bathroom (of the "me first, you next" variety) with a tiled floor, small shower enclosure, toiletries cupboard, washbasin, and low-height toilet (of the barking dog vacuum variety), and some under-basin storage space, and an electrical socket for shavers.

When the ship was bought by Fred Olsen Cruise Lines a number of cabins were changed from double-occupancy units to cabins for the single traveler.

Some cabins do unfortunately suffer from inadequate soundproofing; passengers in cabins on Deck 4 in particular are disturbed by anyone running or jogging on the promenade deck above. Note that cabins on the lowest deck (Deck 2) in the center of the ship are subject to some noise from the adjacent engine room.

Suites: On Deck 7, suites have city names such as Rio de Janeiro and Toronto. While they are not large, the suites do feature a sleeping area that can be curtained off from the living area. All of the suites are decorated in individual styles befitting their name, and each has its own small CD player/music system.

CUISINE. The Thistle Restaurant is a pleasing and attractive venue, with large ocean-view windows on three sides and a focal point of a large oil painting on a wall behind the buffet food display counter. However, space is tight, and tables are extremely close together, making proper service difficult. There are tables for two, four, six or eight; the Porsgrund china has the familiar Venus pattern. The ambiance, however, is warm, and service is friendly and attentive.

There are two seatings for dinner, and an open seating for breakfast and lunch. The menu is varied. Salad items are quite poor and very basic, with little variety, although there is a decent choice of dessert items. For breakfast and lunch the dual food counters are functional, but at peak times these create much congestion (the layout is not ideal). The Grampian Restaurant is an additional dining venue, located aft at the top of the ship, with some fine aft views.

Casual breakfasts and luncheons can also be taken in the self-service buffet located in the Palms Cafe, although these tend to be repetitive and poorly supervised (dishes not replaced or refreshed properly), with indoor and outdoor seating. Although it is the casual dining spot, tablecloths are provided. The indoor flooring is wood, which makes it rather a noisy room, and some tables adjacent to the galley entrance are to be avoided at all costs.

Out on the pool deck, there is a barbecue grill for casual eating – welcome when the ship is in warm weather areas.

ENTERTAINMENT. The Neptune Showlounge sits longitudinally along one side of the ship, with amphitheater-style seating in several tiers, but its layout is less than ideal for either shows or cocktail parties. There is often congestion between first- and second-seating passengers at the entrance.

Unfortunately, 15 pillars obstruct sightlines to the stage, and the banquet and individual tub chair seating arrangement is actually quite poor.

The entertainment mainly consists of small-scale production shows and mini-musicals presented by a small troupe of resident singers/dancers, and cabaret acts. They are rather amateurish, but enjoyable. Apart from the production shows, there are the typical cabaret acts which are found on the cruise ship circuit.

SPA/FITNESS. The health spa facilities are limited. It includes a combined gymnasium/aerobics room, and a separate room for women and men, with sauna, steam room and small changing area. Spa Rituals treatments are provided by Steiner. Some fitness classes are free; others, such as yoga and kick-boxing, cost extra.

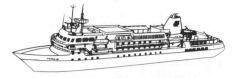

Bremen
★★★★

Size: ....Boutique Ship	Total Crew: 94	Cabins (wheelchair accessible): 2
Tonnage: 6,752	Passengers	Wheelchair accessibility ....None
Lifestyle: ....Premium	(lower beds/all berths): 164/184	Cabin Current: ....110 and 220 volts
Cruise Line:Hapag-Lloyd Expedition Cruises	Passenger Space Ratio	Elevators: 2
Former Names: ....*Frontier Spirit*	(lower beds/all berths): 41.1/36.6	Casino (gaming tables): ....No
Builder: Mitsubishi Heavy Industries (Japan)	Crew/Passenger Ratio	Slot Machines: ....No
Original Cost: ....$42 million	(lower beds/all berths): 1.7/1.9	Swimming Pools (outdoors): 1
Entered Service: .....Nov 1990/Nov 1993	Cabins (total): 82	Swimming Pools (indoors): 0
Registry: ....The Bahamas	Size Range (sq ft/m): 174.3–322.9/	Whirlpools: 0
Length (ft/m): 365.8/111.51	16.2–30.0	Self-Service Launderette: ....No
Beam (ft/m): 55.7/17.00	Cabins (outside view): 82	Lecture/Film Room: ......Yes (seats 164)
Draft (ft/m): 15.7/4.80	Cabins (interior/no view): 0	Library: ....Yes (open 24 hours)
Propulsion/Propellers: .diesel (4,855kW)/2	Cabins (for one person): 0	Zodiacs: 12
Passenger Decks: 6	Cabins (with private balcony): 18	Helicopter Pad: ....Yes

OVERALL SCORE: 1,461 OUT OF A POSSIBLE 2,000 POINTS

OVERVIEW. This purpose-built all-white expedition cruise vessel (formerly *Frontier Spirit*, for the now defunct US-based Frontier Cruises) has a handsome, wide, though squat, contemporary profile and decent equipment. Its wide beam provides decent stability and the vessel's long cruising range and ice-hardened hull provides the ship with access to remote destinations. The ship carries the highest ice classification for passenger vessels. In 1993 Hapag-Lloyd spent $2 million to reconfigure the restaurant and make other changes to the ship.

Zero-discharge of waste matter is fiercely practiced; this means that absolutely nothing is discharged into the ocean that does not meet with the international conventions on ocean pollution (MARPOL). Equipment for in-depth marine and shore excursions is provided, including a boot-washing station with three water hoses and boot cleaning brushes.

An "invitation to the bridge" policy applies. There is almost a walk-around deck (you must go up and down steps at the front of the deck to complete the "walk"). A large open deck aft of the mast provides a good viewing platform (also useful for sunbathing on warm-weather cruises).

The ship has a good number of public rooms for its size, including a forward-facing observation lounge/lecture room, and a main lounge (the Club) with a high ceiling, bandstand, dance floor and large bar, and an adjacent library with 12 bookcases (most books are in German).

Bremen has superb, well-planned destination-intensive itineraries, with good documentation, port information, and maps. It provides a good degree of comfort (although it is not as luxurious as the slightly larger sister ship *Hanseatic*). There is a reception desk (open 24 hours a

BERLITZ'S RATINGS

	Possible	Achieved
Ship	500	349
Accommodation	200	150
Food	400	298
Service	400	311
Entertainment	n/a	n/a
Cruise	500	353

day), a fine array of expert lecturers, and a friendly crew. The ship has two microscopes, and a plankton-collection net for in-depth studies.

Bremen is a practical expedition cruise vessel, nicely refurbished in 2009 when flat-screen TV sets were placed in all cabins, and the number of internet-connect computers was increased to four. Arguably, it is a better expedition vessel than *Hanseatic*, and, although not as luxurious in its interiors and appointments, the ship has a very loyal following. Its cruises will provide you with a fine learning and expedition experience, particularly its Antarctic cruises. All shore landings and tours are included, as is seasickness medication.

The onboard ambiance is completely casual, comfortable, unstuffy (no tux needed), friendly, and very accommodating. Passengers also appreciate the fact that there is no television on expedition cruises – although there are videos daily – and no music in hallways or on open decks.

Arctic/Antarctic Cruises: Red parkas (waterproof outdoor jackets) are supplied, as are waterproof rubber (Wellington) boots. You should, however, take some waterproof trousers and several pairs of thick socks, plus "thermal" underwear. Each of the fleet of 12 Zodiacs (rubber-inflatable landing craft) is named after a place or region: Amazon, Antarctic, Asmat, Bora Bora, Cape Horn, Deception, Jan Mayen, Luzon, Pitcairn, San Blas, Spitzbergen, and Ushuaia. On Arctic and Antarctic cruises, it is particularly pleasing to go to the bridge wings late at night to stargaze under pollution-free skies – the watch officers will be pleased to explain the night skies.

Special sailings may be under the auspices of various tour operators, although the ship is operated by Hapag-Lloyd

Expedition Cruises. Thus, your fellow passengers (I prefer to refer to them as expedition voyage participants) may well be from many different countries. Insurance, port taxes and all staff gratuities are typically included in the cruise fare, and an expedition cruise logbook is provided at the end of each expedition cruise for all participants – a reminder of what's been seen and done during the course of the adventure. The onboard currency is the euro.

The ship does not have a "bulbous bow" and so is liable to pitching in some sea conditions; it does, however, have stabilizers. The swimming pool is small, as is the open deck space around it, although there are both shaded and open areas. In-cabin announcements cannot be turned off (on cruises in the Arctic and Antarctic regions, announcements are often made at or before 7am on days when shore landings are permitted). Sadly, the ship was not built with good cabin soundproofing. Bathrooms are subject to gurgling plumbing noises between the washbasin and shower enclosure as a result of their design and construction.

SUITABLE FOR: *Bremen* is best suited to travelers (rather than cruise passengers) who would not dream of cruising aboard large, glitzy cruise ships. This is for anyone who enjoys nature and the natural world, and traveling off the beaten path to sample what the world has to offer in the more remote and unspoiled (a relative term) regions of the world, in moderate comfort, yet venturing on the wild side of cruising. It is for those who do not need entertainment, bingo, horse racing, art auctions, or parlour games.

ACCOMMODATION. There are just four different configurations. All cabins have an outside view (the cabins on the lowest deck have portholes; all others have good-sized picture windows). All cabins are well equipped for the size of the vessel. Each has wood accenting, a color TV (small) for videos, telephone, refrigerator (soft drinks are provided free and replenished daily), vanity desk with 110v American-style and 220v European-style electrical sockets, sitting area with small drinks table, and W-LAN access.

Cabins have either twin beds (convertible to a queen-sized bed, but with individual European cotton duvets) or double bed, according to location, bedside reading lights and alarm clock. There is also a small indented area for outerwear and rubber boots, while a small drawer above the refrigerator unit provides warmth when needed for such things as wet socks and gloves.

Each cabin has a private bathroom (of the "me first, you next" variety) with a tiled floor, shower enclosure with curtain, toiletries cupboard, washbasin (located quite low) and low-height toilet (vacuum type, with delay), a decent amount of under-basin storage space, and an electrical socket for shavers. Large towels and 100% cotton bathrobes are provided, as is a range of personal toiletries (shampoo, body lotion, shower gel, soap, and shower cap).

Each cabin has a moderate amount of illuminated closet space (large enough for two weeks for two persons, but tight for longer cruises), although the drawer space is limited – suitcases can be stored under the beds. Some Sun Deck and Bridge Deck cabins also have a small balcony (the first expedition cruise vessel to have them) with blue plastic (easily cleanable) decking and wooden handrail, but no exterior light. The balconies have two teak chairs and a small drinks table, but are small and narrow, with partial partitions and doors that open outwards onto the balcony, taking up space.

Two Sun Deck suites have a separate lounge area with sofa and coffee table, bedroom (with large wall clock), large walk-in closet, and bathroom with a bathtub and two washbasins.

CUISINE. The dining room has open seating when operating for mixed German and international passenger cruises, and open seating for breakfast and lunch, with one seating for dinner (assigned seats) when operated only as German-speaking cruises. It is fairly attractive, with pleasing decor and pastel colors; it also has big picture windows and 12 pillars placed in inconvenient positions – the result of old shipbuilding techniques.

The food, made with high-quality ingredients, is extremely good. Although the portions are small, the presentation is appealing to the eye – and you can always ask for more. There is an excellent choice of freshly made breads and pastries, and a good selection of cheeses and fruits.

Dinner typically includes a choice of two appetizers, two soups, an entremets (in-between course), two entrées (main courses) and two or three desserts, plus a cheese board (note that Europeans typically have cheese before dessert). There is always a vegetarian specialty, as well as a healthy (light) eating option. The service is also good, with smartly dressed bi-lingual (German- and English-speaking) waiters and waitresses.

As an alternative to the dining room, breakfast and luncheon buffets are available in "The Club", or outside on the Lido Deck (weather permitting), where "The Starboard Bar/Grill" provides items of grilled food.

ENTERTAINMENT. Although there is a small main lounge, this is used as a gathering place after meals and before expedition landings ashore. There is no formal entertainment as such, lectures being the principal feature of any expedition cruise aboard this ship (unless under charter), as are after-dinner recaps of the day. Occasionally, the crew may put on a little amateur dramatics event, or a seaman's choir. And at the end of each expedition cruise, the ship's chart is auctioned off one evening to the highest bidder, and profits are sent to a charity organization.

SPA/FITNESS. There is a small fitness room, a large sauna, and beauty salon (with integral massage table). Out on the open deck is a small swimming pool, which is heated when the ship sailing in cold weather regions such as the Arctic or Antarctica.

Brilliance of the Seas
★★★★

Size: . . . . .Large Resort Ship	Passenger Decks: 12	Cabins (with private balcony): 577
Tonnage: .90,090	Total Crew: 869	Cabins (wheelchair accessible): 24
Lifestyle: . . . . .Standard	Passengers	Wheelchair accessibility . . . . .Good
Cruise Line: Royal Caribbean International	(lower beds/all berths): 2,112/2,500	Cabin Current: . . . . .110/220 volts
Former Names: . . . . .none	Passenger Space Ratio	Elevators: 9
Builder: . . . . .Meyer Werft (Germany)	(lower beds/all berths): 42.6/36.0	Casino (gaming tables): . . . . .Yes
Original Cost: . . . .$350 million	Crew/Passenger Ratio	Slot Machines: . . . . .Yes
Entered Service: . . . . .July 2002	(lower beds/all berths): 2.5/2.8	Swimming Pools (outdoors): 2
Registry: . . . . .The Bahamas	Cabins (total): 1,056	Swimming Pools (indoors): 0
Length (ft/m): 961.9/293.2	Size Range (sq ft/m): 165.8–1,216.3/	Whirlpools: 3
Beam (ft/m): 105.6/32.2	15.4–113.0	Self-Service Launderette: . . . . .No
Draft (ft/m): 27.8/8.5	Cabins (outside view): 818	Dedicated Cinema/Seats: Yes/40
Propulsion/Propellers: . . . . . .Gas turbine/	Cabins (interior/no view): 238	Library: . . . . .Yes
2 pods (19.5 MW each)	Cabins (for one person): 0	

OVERALL SCORE: 1,446 OUT OF A POSSIBLE 2,000 POINTS

OVERVIEW. This is a streamlined contemporary ship, built in 66 blocks, and has a two-deck-high wrap-around structure in the forward section of the funnel. Along the ship's port side, a central glass wall protrudes, giving great views (cabins with balconies occupy the space directly opposite on the starboard side). The gently rounded stern has nicely tiered decks, which gives the ship an extremely well-balanced look. As is common aboard all Royal Caribbean International vessels, the navigation bridge is of the fully enclosed type (good for cold-weather areas). One of two swimming pools can be covered by a large glass dome (called a magrodome) for use as an indoor/outdoor pool.

The interior decor is contemporary, yet elegant and cheerful, designed for active, young and trendy types. The artwork is abundant and truly eclectic. A nine-deck high atrium lobby has glass-walled lifts (on the port side) that travel through 12 decks, face the sea and provide a link with nature and the ocean. The Centrum (as the atrium is called) has several public rooms connected to it: the guest relations (the erstwhile purser's office) and shore excursions desks, a Lobby Bar, Champagne Bar, the Library, Royal Caribbean Online, the Concierge Club, and a Crown & Anchor Lounge. A great view can be had of the atrium by looking down through the flat glass dome high above it.

There's also a Champagne Bar, and a large Schooner Bar that houses maritime art in an integral art gallery, not to mention the Casino Royale. There's also a small, deeply tiered, dedicated movie screening room (with space for two wheelchairs), as well as a 194-seat conference center, a business center, and several conference rooms.

A Viking Crown Lounge is set around the ship's funnel.

BERLITZ'S RATINGS

	Possible	Achieved
Ship	500	415
Accommodation	200	154
Food	400	238
Service	400	262
Entertainment	100	78
Cruise	400	299

This functions as an observation lounge during the daytime; in the evening, the space hosts Starquest, a futuristic, high-energy dance club, and Hollywood Odyssey, a more intimate and relaxed entertainment venue for softer mood music and "black-box" theater.

Youth facilities include Adventure Ocean, an "edutainment" area with four separate age-appropriate sections for junior passengers: Aquanaut Center (for ages 3–5); Explorer Center (6–8); Voyager Center (9–12); and the Optix Teen Center (13–17). Adventure Beach includes a splash pool with waterslide; Surfside has computer lab stations with entertaining software; and Ocean Arcade is a video games hangout.

This ship was constructed for longer itineraries, with more space and comfortable public areas, larger cabins and more dining options – for the young, active, and trendy set. A computer business center has 12 PCs with high-speed internet access for sending and receiving emails. The onboard currency is the US dollar, and gratuities are automatically charged to your onboard account.

ACCOMMODATION. A wide range of suites and standard outside-view and interior (no view) cabins comes in 10 categories and 19 price groups.

Apart from the six largest suites (called owner's suites), which have king-sized beds, almost all other cabins have twin beds that convert to a queen-sized bed (all sheets are 100% Egyptian cotton, although the blankets are of nylon). All cabins have rich (faux) wood cabinetry, including a vanity desk (with hairdryer), faux wood drawers that close silently (hooray), television, personal safe, and three-sided mirrors. Some cabins have ceiling recessed, pull-down berths for third and fourth persons, although closet and drawer space would be extremely tight for four persons (even if two are children), and some have interconnecting doors. Audio channels are available through the TV set, so if you want to go to sleep with soft music playing you'll need to put a towel over the television screen.

Most bathrooms have tiled accenting and a terrazzo-style tiled floor, and a half-moon shower enclosure (it is rather small, however), 100% Egyptian cotton towels, a small cabinet for personal toiletries and a small shelf. There is little space to stow personal toiletries for two (or more).

The largest cabins consist of a family suite with two bedrooms. One bedroom has twin beds (convertible to queen-sized bed), while a second has two lower beds and two upper Pullman berths, a combination that can sleep up to eight persons (good for large families).

Occupants of cabins designated as suites also get the use of a private Concierge Lounge (where priority dining room reservations, shore excursion bookings and beauty salon/ spa appointments can be made).

Many of the "private" balcony cabins are not very private, as they can be overlooked from the port and starboard wings of the Solarium, and from other locations.

CUISINE. Minstrel, the main dining room, spans two decks (the upper deck level has floor-to-ceiling windows, while the lower deck level has windows). It seats 1,104, and has Middle Ages music as its themed decor. There are tables for two, four, six, eight or 10 in two seatings for dinner. Two small private dining rooms (Zephyr, with 94 seats and Lute, with 30 seats) are located off the main dining room. Smoking is banned in all dining venues.

Choose one of two seatings, or "My Time Dining" (eat when you want during dining room hours) when you book. Minstrel is closed for lunch on most days, which leaves passengers scrambling for food and seating in the Windjammer Café – an awful prospect after passengers return from morning excursions.

The cuisine in the main dining room is typical of mass banquet catering that offers standard fare comparable to that found in American family-style restaurants ashore – mostly disappointing and without much taste. However, a decent selection of light meals is provided, and a vegetarian menu is available. Caviar, once a standard menu item, incurs a hefty extra charge. Special orders, tableside carving and flambéed items are not offered.

Menus typically include a "Welcome Aboard" Dinner, French Dinner, Italian Dinner, International Dinner, Captain's Gala Dinner.

There are two alternative dining spots: "Portofino", with 112 seats, has Italian-American cuisine (choices include antipasti, soup, salad, pasta, main dish, dessert, cheese and coffee); and "Chops Grille Steakhouse", with 95 seats and an open (show) kitchen, has premium veal chops and steaks (New York Striploin Steak, Filet Mignon, Prime Rib of Beef). Both these spots have food that is of a much higher quality than in the main dining room. There is an additional charge of $20 per person for Portofino, and $25 for Chops Grille, including gratuities. Both venues, which are typically open between 6pm and 11pm, require reservations.

Be prepared to eat a lot of food (perhaps this justifies the cover charge), as these are Texas-sized portions presented on large plates. Menus don't change throughout the cruise. The dress code is smart casual.

Also, casual meals can be taken (for breakfast, lunch and dinner) in the self-serve, buffet-style Windjammer Cafe, which can be accessed directly from the pool deck. It has a peculiar layout, and has several islands – so you may have to hunt for the items you like. It is impossible to get a hot plate for hot food because the plates are plastic, so things go cold quickly. The selection of cold cuts of meat is poor, cheeses have absolutely no taste, and salad items almost always look unappetizing.

Additionally, the Seaview Café is open for lunch and dinner. Choose from the self-serve buffet, or from the menu for fast-food seafood items, hamburgers and hot dogs. The decor, naturally, is marine- and ocean-related.

ENTERTAINMENT. The Pacifica Theatre, the main show-lounge, is three decks high, has 874 seats, including 24 stations for wheelchairs, and good sightlines from most seats.

SPA/FITNESS. The ShipShape Spa's health, fitness and spa facilities have themed decor, and include a 10,176 sq.-ft (945 sq.-meter) solarium with whirlpool and counter current swimming under a retractable magrodome roof, a gymnasium (with 44 cardiovascular machines), 50-person aerobics room, sauna and steam rooms, and therapy treatment rooms. All are located on two of the uppermost decks of the ship, forward of the mast.

Examples of treatment prices include Swedish Massage ($99 for 50 mins); Aroma Stone Massage ($159 for 75 mins); Lime and Ginger Salt Glow with half body massage ($127 for 50 mins); Aromapure Facial $99 for 50 mins); Cellulite Reduction Program ($132 for 50 mins).

For the more sporting, youthful passengers, there is activity galore – including a rock-climbing wall that's 30-ft (9 meters) high, with five separate climbing tracks. It is located outdoors at the aft end of the funnel. Other sports facilities include a golf course, jogging track, basketball court, 9-hole miniature golf course with novel decorative ornaments, and an indoor/outdoor country club with golf simulator. There is also an exterior jogging track.

● **For more extensive general information about a Royal Caribbean cruise experience, see pages 151–6.**

C. Columbus
★★★ +

Size: ....Small Ship	Passenger Decks: 6	Cabins (with private balcony): 2
Tonnage: 14,903	Total Crew: 170	Cabins (wheelchair accessible): 2
Lifestyle: ....Standard	Passengers	Wheelchair accessibility ....Fair
Cruise Line: ....Hapag-Lloyd Cruises	(lower beds/all berths): 408/421	Cabin Current: ....220 volts
Former Names: ....none	Passenger Space Ratio	Elevators: 2
Builder: ....MTW Schiffswerft (Germany)	(lower beds/all berths): 36.5/35.3	Casino (gaming tables): ....No
Original Cost: ....$69 million	Crew/Passenger Ratio	Slot Machines: ....No
Entered Service: ....July 1997	(lower beds/all berths): 2.4/2.4	Swimming Pools (outdoors): 1
Registry: ....The Bahamas	Cabins (total): 205	Swimming Pools (indoors): 0
Length (ft/m): 472.8/144.13	Size Range (sq ft/m): 139.9–339.0/	Whirlpools: 0
Beam (ft/m): 70.5/21.50	13.0–31.5	Self-Service Launderette: ....No
Draft (ft/m): 16.8/5.15	Cabins (outside view): 158	Dedicated Cinema/Seats: ....No
Propulsion/Propellers: ....diesel	Cabins (interior/no view): 47	Library: ....Yes
(10,560kW)/2	Cabins (for one person): 2	

BERLITZ'S OVERALL SCORE: 1,398 OUT OF A POSSIBLE 2,000 POINTS

OVERVIEW. *C. Columbus* has a smart contemporary profile, with a single, large funnel painted in Hapag-Lloyd's orange/blue colors. The Hamburg-based Hapag-Lloyd Cruises has chartered the ship from the German company Conti Reederei, the owner.

The ship also has an ice-hardened hull, which is useful for cold-weather cruise areas. In addition, the bridge "wings" can be folded inwards (as can the overhang lights) flush with the ship's side so that the vessel can enter the locks in the US/Canada Great Lakes region, including the St. Lawrence Seaway and Welland Canal, for which the ship was specifically built. There's a choice of well-planned itineraries and destination-intensive cruises.

The ship has a good passenger space ratio. Each deck has a distinctly different color scheme and carpeting, making it easy to find one's way around. There is a reasonable range of public rooms to choose from, most of which are located in a "cake-layer" vertical stacking aft of the accommodation. Although the ceilings in the public rooms are plain and unimaginative (except for the Palm Garden), the decor is really bright and upbeat, and very different to all other ships in the Hapag-Lloyd fleet. The most popular room is arguably the delightful multi-function Palm Garden, which is also the ship's forward-facing observation lounge. There are four internet-connect computers.

The fit and finish of the ship's interiors can best be described as a little utilitarian – the mottled gray walls are somewhat cold, but a contrast to the splashes of color found in carpeting and other decorative touches. The artwork chosen is, for the most part, minimal and uncoordinated, yet it all works together to provide cheerful surroundings. Ship buffs

BERLITZ'S RATINGS

	Possible	Achieved
Ship	500	342
Accommodation	200	145
Food	400	283
Service	400	297
Entertainment	100	61
Cruise	400	270

will be pleased to find some superb original photographs from the Hapag-Lloyd archives adorning the stairways.

You should know that the level of "luxury" is below that of Hapag-Lloyd's *Europa* and *Hanseatic*, and the experience aboard this very informal ship is different (so, of course, is the cruise price). However, the food is extremely good, and the service and housekeeping staff are well trained, so the overall onboard experience is excellent value for money, and better than you might expect. Indeed, the ship really delivers a four-star experience based on a three-and-a-half star price. The onboard currency is the euro. Gratuities are extra and are recommended at €5–€6 per person per day.

First-time cruise passengers in particular will find this a fresh, comfortable, casual and unpretentious ship for a cruise vacation. You don't need to buy a new wardrobe, and you can leave your tuxedo at home; for this ship you need only informal and casual clothes.

While it's a comfortable, trendy ship, note that the swimming pool is small (it's more like a "dip" pool), as is the open deck space, and there is no walk-around promenade deck outdoors. One of the main reasons to cruise aboard this ship is the excellent dining experience in a relaxed, one-seating environment. The ship also carries 12 bicycles for passenger use, free of charge.

SUITABLE FOR: *C. Columbus* is best suited to youthful-minded German-speaking couples and single travelers who are seeking good value for money on a first cruise, aboard a ship with contemporary, comfortable (but not pretentious or luxurious) surroundings, and good itineraries, at a very modest price.

ACCOMMODATION. The standard cabins are really small, and many are interior (no view) cabins. All but 10 cabins have lower berths, but the 16 price grades established really are a lot for this size of ship. Except for two forward-facing suites, there are no balcony cabins, and no room service (except for accommodation designated as suites). There are also two single-occupancy cabins.

The cabin decor is bright and upbeat, and a good amount of closet and shelf space is provided. The bathrooms are fully tiled and have large shower stalls (none have tubs). All cabins have a mini-bar/refrigerator (all items cost extra, as in hotels ashore), flat-screen TV, personal safe, and hairdryer. Bathrobes can be requested, at a small surcharge.

There are eight suites (each is at least double the size of a standard cabin), and each has a curtained partition between its lounge and sleeping areas, with a wall unit that houses a television that can be turned 360 degrees for viewing from either the lounge or bedroom.

Two suites at the bow each have a narrow private veranda (with two teak lounge chairs and coffee table), bedroom (with large wall clock) and lounge area separated by a curtain, two TV sets, and an excellent amount of closet, drawer and shelf space. The cabinetry, with its walnut-finish and bird's-eye pattern, makes these suites feel warm and luxurious.

All the suites have a small room service menu. The bathrooms have a large shower (it is big enough for two), hairdryer, and under-sink storage space.

CUISINE. There is one large main dining room, located at the stern, with large ocean-view windows on three sides, and all passengers can be seated in a single seating, at assigned tables. There are just two tables for two, but other tables can accommodate up to 16 – good for family reunions. The cuisine, which is presented in an unstuffy way, is extremely good, though the menu choice is small (there are typically two or three entrée options for dinner). There is an excellent selection of fresh-baked breads and rolls every day, and a good selection of cold cuts and cheeses daily. Creatively themed dinners, as well as an extensive array of late-night snacks, make dining a delight, and well beyond most passengers' expectations.

Breakfast and lunch can be taken in the bright, but casual, setting of the Palm Garden, which is also the ship's very comfortable observation lounge. Light dinners also can be taken in the Palm Garden, where a small dance floor adds another dimension.

ENTERTAINMENT. The Columbus Lounge is a single level, H-shaped room that is quite large, with banquette and individual seating in tub chairs, and a bar is situated on the port side in the aft corner of the room. Because the apron stage is in the center of the room, the sightlines from many seats are not that good. Entertainment consists mainly of cabaret acts typical of the cruise ship circuit. Plenty of live music, for dancing, is also provided.

SPA/FITNESS. A fitness room is located forward on the uppermost deck of the ship. A sauna is located on the lowest passenger deck, next to the beauty salon, and massage/facial treatments are available.

WHERE NAUTICAL EXPRESSIONS CAME FROM

Brass monkeys

Ever wondered where the expression "Cold enough to freeze the balls off a brass monkey" came from? Well, maritime history tells us that in the days when war ships and most freighters carried cannons (and round cannon balls) made of iron. In order to keep a supply of supply of cannon balls near each cannon, a method of keeping them from rolling around had to be found.

The best storage device consisted of a square-based pyramid. One cannon ball rested on top of four others, which rested on top of nine other, which rested on a base of sixteen. Thus, a supply of 30 cannon

balls could be stacked in a small area. There was, however, a small problem – how to prevent the bottom layer from rolling out from under the others on a moving ship. The solution was a metal plate called a "monkey." It had 16 round indentations – one for each of the 16 "base layer" of cannon balls.

If the "monkey" were made of iron, the cannon balls placed on it would rust to it; the solution was to make the "monkey" out of brass. However, brass contracts more than iron when it is chilled. Unfortunately, when the temperature dipped too far, the brass indentations would shrink so much that the iron cannon balls would come adrift from the "monkey." It was, thus,

a case of being "cold enough to freeze the balls off a brass monkey."

He let the cat out of the bag

On board a square-rigger 150 years ago, this would have sent shudders through one's spine – for it meant that a sailor had committed an offense serious enough to have the "cat o' nine tails" extracted from its bag.

The "cat" was a whip made of nine lengths of cord, each being about 18 inches (45 cm) long with three knots at the end, all fixed to a rope handle. It could seriously injure, or even kill, the victim. It was finally outlawed by the US Congress in 1850, and then by Britain's Royal Navy in 1879.

Caribbean Princess
★★★★

Size:	Large Resort Ship	Passenger Decks:	15	Cabins (with private balcony):	.881
Tonnage:	112,894	Total Crew:	1,163	Cabins (wheelchair accessible):	.25
Lifestyle:	Standard	Passengers		Wheelchair accessibility	Good
Cruise Line:	Princess Cruises	(lower beds/all berths):	3,114/3,622	Cabin Voltage:	110 volts
Former Names:	None	Passenger Space Ratio		Elevators:	.14
Builder:	Fincantieri (Italy)	(lower beds/all berths):	36.2/31.1	Casino (gaming tables):	Yes
Original Cost:	$500 million	Crew/Passenger Ratio		Slot Machines:	Yes
Entered Service:	Apr 2004	(lower beds/all berths):	2.6/3.1	Swimming Pools (outdoors):	.4
Registry:	Bermuda	Cabins (total):	1,557	Swimming Pools (indoors):	.0
Length (ft/m):	951.4/290.0	Size Range (sq ft/m):	163-1,279/	Whirlpools:	.9
Beam (ft/m):	118.1/36.0		15.1-118.8	Self-Service Launderette:	Yes
Draft (ft/m):	28.3/8.6	Cabins (outside view):	1,105	Dedicated Cinema/Seats:	No
Propulsion/Propellers:	diesel-electric	Cabins (interior/no view):	.452	Library:	Yes
	(42,000kW)/2	Cabins (for one person):	.0		

OVERALL SCORE: 1,539 OUT OF A POSSIBLE 2,000 POINTS

OVERVIEW. Designed to be a (somewhat smaller) competitor to Royal Caribbean International's *Voyager*-class ships (but with a similar passenger carry), *Caribbean Princess* has the same profile as half-sisters *Golden Princess, Grand Princess,* and *Star Princess.* This ship accommodates many more passengers than half-sisters due to an additional deck (Riviera Deck) full of cabins, and the fact that two of the ship's 17 upper decks are made of aluminum; although lighter than steel, it does tend to "harden" over time.

Although the ship accommodates over 500 more passengers, the outdoor deck space remains the same, as do the number of elevators – so waiting time increases during peak usage. The Passenger Space Ratio is also reduced considerably compared to that of its half-sisters.

There is a good sheltered faux-teak promenade deck – it's actually painted steel – which almost wraps around the ship (three times round equals one mile). The outdoor pools have various beach-like surroundings, and "Movies Under the Skies" and major sporting events are shown on a 300-sq-ft (28-sq-meter) movie screen located at the pool in front of the large funnel structure in what, aboard *Golden, Grand* and *Star Princess* would be The Conservatory. Movies afloat in the open are a big hit with passengers (they remind many of drive-in movies, which have mostly disappeared from land-based venues).

Unlike the outside decks, there is plenty of space inside (but there are also plenty of passengers), and a wide array of public rooms to choose from, with many "intimate" (a relative word) spaces and places to play. The passenger flow is well thought-out, and there is little congestion, except the wait for elevators at peak times.

BERLITZ'S RATINGS

	Possible	Achieved
Ship	500	431
Accommodation	200	165
Food	400	254
Service	400	293
Entertainment	100	82
Cruise	400	314

High atop the stern of the ship is a ship-wide glass-walled disco pod. It looks like an aerodynamic "spoiler" and is positioned high above the water, with spectacular views from the extreme port and starboard side windows (it would make a great penthouse).

The interior decor is attractive, with lots of earth tones (well suited to both American and European tastes). In fact, this is a culmination of the best of all that Princess Cruises has to offer from its many years of operating what is now a well-tuned, good-quality product.

An extensive collection of artworks has been chosen, and this complements the interior design and colors well. If you see something you like, you will probably be able to purchase it on board – it's almost all for sale.

Caribbean Princess also includes a Wedding Chapel, and a live web-cam can relay ceremonies via the internet. The captain can legally marry American couples, thanks to the ship's Bermuda registry and a special dispensation (which should be verified when in the planning stage, according to where you reside). But to get married and take your close family members and entourage with you on your honeymoon is going to cost a lot. The "Hearts & Minds" chapel is also useful for "renewal of vows" ceremonies.

For children, there is a large playroom, teen room, and a host of specially trained counselors. Children have their own pools, hot tubs, and open deck area at the stern of the ship, thankfully away from adult areas. There are good netted-in areas; one section has a dip pool, while another has a mini-basketball court.

Gamblers should enjoy what is presently one of the largest casinos at sea (Grand Casino), with more than 260 slot machines, and blackjack, craps and roulette tables, plus newer games such as Let It Ride Bonus, Spanish 21 and Caribbean Draw Progressive. But the highlight could well be the specially linked slot machines that provide a combined payout.

Other features include a small library and internet-connect room. Ship lovers should enjoy the wood-paneled Wheelhouse Bar, finely decorated with memorabilia and ship models tracing part of parent company P&O's history (this ship highlights the 1950-built cargo ship *Ganges*). Churchill's cigar/sports bar has several television screens. A high-tech hospital is provided, with SeaMed tele-medicine link-ups to specialists at the Cedars-Sinai Medical Center in Los Angeles, who are available for emergency help.

The ship is a stunning, grand resort playground in which to roam when you are not ashore. Princess Cruises delivers a consistently fine, well-packaged vacation product, always with a good degree of style, at an attractive, highly competitive price. Whether this really can be considered a relaxing holiday is a moot point, but with so many choices and "small" rooms to enjoy, the ship has been extremely well designed, and the odds are that you'll have an enjoyable cruise vacation.

If you are not used to large ships, it will take you some time to find your way around this one, despite the company's claim that it offers passengers a "small ship feel, big ship choice."

ACCOMMODATION. There are six principal types of cabins and configurations: (a) grand suite, (b) suite, (c) mini-suite, (d) outside-view double cabins with balcony, (e) outside-view double cabins, and (f) interior (no view) double cabins. These come in 35 different brochure price categories. The choice is quite bewildering for both travel agents and passengers; pricing will depend on two things, size and location. By comparison, the largest suite is slightly smaller, and the smallest interior (no-view) cabin is slightly larger than the equivalent suite/cabins aboard *Golden, Grand* and *Star Princess.*

Cabin bath towels are small, and drawer space is very limited. There are no butlers – even for the top-grade suites, which are not really large in comparison to similar suites aboard some other ships. Cabin attendants have too many cabins to look after (typically 20), which does not translate to fine personal service.

(a) The largest, most lavish suite is the Grand Suite (A750, located at the ship's stern). It has a large bedroom with queen-sized bed, huge walk-in (illuminated) closets, two bathrooms, a lounge (with fireplace and sofa bed) with wet bar and refrigerator, and a large private balcony on the port side (with hot tub that can be accessed from both balcony and bedroom).

(b/c) Suites (with a semi-private balcony) have a separate living room (with sofa bed) and bedroom (with a television in each). The bathroom is quite large and has both a tub and shower stall. The mini-suites also have a private balcony, and a separate living and sleeping area (with a television in each). The differences between the suites and mini-suites

are basically in the size and appointments, the suite being more of a square shape while mini-suites are more rectangular, and have few drawers. Both suites and mini-suites have plush bathrobes, and fully tiled bathrooms with ample open shelf storage space. Suite and mini-suite passengers receive greater attention, including priority embarkation and dis-embarkation privileges. What is not good is that the most expensive accommodation has only semi-private balconies that can be seen from above and so there is little privacy (Suites C401, 402, 404, 406, 408, 410, 412, 401, 405, 411, 415 and 417 on Riviera Deck 14). Also, the suites D105 and D106 (Dolphin Deck 9), which are extremely large, have balconies that are overlooked from above.

(d/e/f). Both interior (no view) and outside-view (the outsides come either with or without private balcony) cabins are of a functional, practical, design, although almost no drawers are provided. They are quite attractive, with warm, pleasing decor and fine soft furnishing fabrics; 80 percent of the outside-view cabins have a private balcony. Interior (no view) cabins measure 163 sq. ft (15.1 sq. meters).

The 28 wheelchair-accessible cabins measure 250–385 sq. ft (23.2–35.7 sq. meters); surprisingly, there is no mirror for dressing, and no full-length hanging space for long dresses (yes, some passengers in wheelchairs do also use mirrors and full-length clothing). Additionally, two family suites consist of two suites with an interconnecting door, plus a large balcony. These can sleep up to 10 (if at least four are children) or up to eight people (if all are adults).

All cabins receive turndown service and chocolates on pillows each night, bathrobes (on request) and toiletry amenity kits (larger, naturally, for suite/mini-suite occupants) that typically include soap, shampoo, conditioner, and hand/body lotion. A hairdryer is provided in all cabins, sensibly located at the vanity desk unit in the living area. All bathrooms have tiled floors, and there is a decent amount of open shelf storage space for personal toiletries, although the plain beige decor is very basic and unappealing.

Most outside-view cabins on Emerald Deck have views obstructed by the lifeboats. There are no cabins for singles. Your name is placed outside your suite or cabin in a documents holder – making it simple for delivery service personnel but also diminishing privacy. There is 24-hour room service – but some items on the room service menu are not available during early morning hours.

Some cabins can accommodate a third and fourth person in upper berths. However, in such cabins, the lower beds cannot then be pushed together to make queen-sized bed.

Almost all balcony suites and cabins can be overlooked both from the navigation bridge wing, as well as from the port and starboard sections of the ship's discotheque – high above the ship at the stern. Cabins with balconies on Dolphin, Caribe and Baja decks can be overlooked by passengers on balconies on the deck above. They are, therefore, not private.

Also, passengers occupying some the most expensive suites with balconies at the stern of the vessel may experience some vibration during certain ship maneuvers.

CUISINE. As befits the size of the ship, there are a variety of dining options. There are three main dining rooms, plus Sterling Steakhouse, and Sabatini's Trattoria.

The three principal dining rooms for formal dining are Coral, Island, and Palm. The Palm Dining Room has traditional two seating dining, while "anytime dining" (you choose when and with whom you want to eat) is featured in Coral and Island. All are no-smoking and split into multi-tier sections in a non-symmetrical design that breaks what are quite large spaces into smaller sections for better ambiance. Each dining room has its own galley. While four elevators go to Fiesta Deck, where the Coral and Island restaurants are located, only two go to Plaza Deck 5, where the Palm Restaurant is located (this can cause waiting problems at peak times, particularly for anyone in a wheelchair).

Specially designed dinnerware (by Dudson of England), high-quality linens and silverware, Frette Egyptian cotton table linens, and silverware by Hepp of Germany are used in the main dining rooms. Note that 15% is added to all beverage bills, including wines.

Alternative (Extra Charge) Dining Options: There are three: Sabatini's, Tequila's, and Sterling Steakhouse. All are open for lunch and dinner on days at sea. Sabatini's is an Italian eatery, with colorful tiled Mediterranean-style decor; it is named after Trattoria Sabatini, the 200-year old institution in Florence (where there is no cover charge). It has Italian-style pizzas and pastas, with a variety of sauces, as well as Italian-style entrées including tiger prawns and lobster tail – all provided with flair and entertainment from by the staff of waiters (by reservation only, with a cover charge of $20 per person, for lunch or dinner).

Sterling Steakhouse is located just aft of the upper level of the Princess Theater, adjacent to the Internet Café and shops, in a somewhat open area, to tempt you as you pass by, with people walking through as you eat – not a particularly comfortable arrangement. The cover charge is $20.

The cuisine in the alternative dining spots is decidedly better than in the three main dining rooms, with better quality ingredients and more attention to presentation and taste.

Casual eateries include a poolside hamburger grill and pizza bar (no additional charge), while extra charges do apply if you order items to eat at the coffee bar/ patisserie, or the caviar/champagne bar. Other casual meals can be taken in the Horizon Court, which is open 24 hours a day. It has large ocean-view on port and starboard sides and direct access to the two principal swimming pools and lido deck. There is no real finesse in presentation, however, as plastic plates are provided.

Ultimate Balcony Dinner/Breakfast: For something different, you could try a private dinner on your balcony, an all-inclusive evening featuring cocktails, fresh flowers, champagne and a deluxe four-course meal including Caribbean lobster tail – all served by a member of the dining staff; of course, it costs extra: $50 per person (or $25 per person for the Ultimate Balcony Breakfast).

ENTERTAINMENT. The Princess Theater (showlounge) is the main entertainment venue; it spans two decks and has comfortable seating on both main and balcony levels. It has $3 million worth of sound and light equipment, plus a 9-piece orchestra, and a scenery loading bay that connects directly from stage to a hull door for direct transfer to the dockside.

The ship carries its own resident troupe of 19 singers and dancers, plus audio-visual support staff.

Club Fusion is a second entertainment lounge (located aft). It features cabaret acts (magicians, comedy jugglers, ventriloquists and others) at night, and lectures, bingo and horse racing during the day. Explorers, a third entertainment lounge, can also host cabaret acts and dance bands. A variety of other lounges and bars have live music, and Princess Cruises employs a number of male dance hosts as partners for women traveling alone.

SPA/FITNESS/RECREATION. The Lotus Spa is located forward on Sun Deck – one of the uppermost decks. Separate facilities for men and women include a sauna, steam room, and changing rooms; common facilities include a relaxation/waiting zone, body-pampering treatment rooms, and a gymnasium with packed with the latest high-tech muscle-pumping, cardio-vascular equipment, and great ocean views. Some fitness classes are free, while some cost extra.

● **For more extensive general information on what a Princess Cruises cruise is like, see pages 148–51.**

Carnival Conquest
★★★ +

Size:	.Large Resort Ship	Total Crew:	1,160	Wheelchair accessibility .... .Good
Tonnage:	110,239	Passengers		Cabin Current: .... .110 volts
Lifestyle:	.Standard	(lower beds/all berths):	2,974/3,700	Elevators: .... .14
Cruise Line:	.Carnival Cruise Lines	Passenger Space Ratio		Casino (gaming tables): .... .Yes
Former Names:	.none	(lower beds/all berths):	37.0/29.7	Slot Machines: .... .Yes
Builder:	.Fincantieri (Italy)	Crew/Passenger Ratio		Swimming Pools (outdoors): 2
Original Cost:	.$500 million	(lower beds/all berths):	2.5/3.1	(+1 with magrodome)
Entered Service:	.Dec 2002	Cabins (total):	1,487	Swimming Pools (indoors): 0
Registry:	.Panama	Size Range (sq ft/m):	179.7–482.2/	Whirlpools: 7
Length (ft/m):	.951.4/290.0		16.7–44.8	Fitness Center: .... .Yes
Beam (ft/m):	.116.4/35.5	Cabins (outside view):	.917	Sauna/Steam Room: .... .Yes/Yes
Draft (ft/m):	.27.0/8.2	Cabins (interior/no view):	.570	Massage: .... .Yes
Propulsion/Propellers:	.diesel-electric	Cabins (for one person):	0	Self-Service Launderette: .... .Yes
	(63,400kW)/2	Cabins (with private balcony):	.574	Dedicated Cinema/Seats: .... .No
Passenger Decks:	.13	Cabins (wheelchair accessible):	.25	Library: .... .Yes

OVERALL SCORE: 1,385 OUT OF A POSSIBLE 2,000 POINTS

OVERVIEW. *Carnival Conquest* is the 19th new-build for this very successful cruise line. It has the same well-balanced profile as its sisters: *Carnival Destiny, Carnival Freedom, Carnival Glory, Carnival Liberty, Carnival Triumph* and *Carnival Victory*. The ship, whose bows are extremely short, has the distinctive, large, swept-back wing-tipped funnel that is the trademark of Carnival Cruise Lines, in the company colors of red, white and blue. However, due to its size, the ship is unable to transit the Panama Canal, and is thus dedicated to itineraries in the Caribbean.

This is quite a stunning ship, built to impress at every turn. Amidships on the open deck is a long water slide (200 ft/60 meters in length), as well as tiered sunbathing decks positioned between two swimming pools, several hot tubs and a giant poolside (Seaside Theater) movie screen. The layout of the ship is quite logical, so finding your way around is not difficult. The decor is all about the world's great Impressionist painters, such as Degas, Monet and Van Gogh. You'll also find large Murano glass flowers on antiqued brass stems in several public areas. It is very imaginative, and a fantasy land for the senses – though it isn't as glitzy as the *Fantasy*-class ships.

As for public areas, there are three decks full of lounges, 10 bars and lots of rooms to play in. There are two atriums: the largest, the Atelier Atrium (in the forward third of the ship) goes through nine decks, while the aft atrium goes through three decks. The ship has a doublewide indoor promenade, nine-deck-high, and a glass-domed rotunda atrium lobby.

For those who like to gamble, the Tahiti casino is cer-

BERLITZ'S RATINGS		
	Possible	Achieved
Ship	500	412
Accommodation	200	157
Food	400	218
Service	400	259
Entertainment	100	82
Cruise	400	257

tainly large and action-packed; there are also more than 320 slot machines. There are several other nightspots for just about every musical taste (except for opera, ballet and classical music lovers).

Children are provided with good facilities, including a two-level Children's Club (with an outdoor pool), and are well cared for with "Camp Carnival", the line's extensive children's program.

It is difficult to escape from noise and loud music (it's even played in cabin hallways and lifts), not to mention smokers, and masses of people walking around in unsuitable clothing, clutching plastic sport drinks bottles, at any time of the day or night. You have to carry a credit card to operate the personal safes, which is inconvenient.

The many pillars in the dining room make it difficult for proper food service by the waiters. The public toilets are spartan and could do with some cheering up.

ACCOMMODATION. There are 21 cabin price categories, in seven different grades: suites with private balcony; deluxe outside-view cabin with private balcony; outside-view cabin with private balcony; outside-view cabin with window; cabin with a porthole instead of a window; interior (no-view) cabin; interior (no-view cabin) with upper and lower berths. The price you pay will depend on the grade, location and size you choose.

There are five decks of cabins with private balcony – over 150 more than *Carnival Destiny, Carnival Triumph* or *Carnival Victory*, for example. Many of the private balconies are not so private, and can be overlooked from various public locations.

There are even "fitness" cabins aboard this ship – in a block of 18 cabins located directly around and behind the SpaCarnival; so, fitness devotees can get out of bed and go straight to the treadmill without having to go through any of the public rooms first.

The standard cabins are of good size and are equipped with all the basics, although the furniture is rather angular, with no rounded edges. Three decks of cabins (eight on each deck, each with private balcony) overlook the stern. Most cabins with twin beds can be converted to a queen-size bed format. A gift basket is provided in all grades of cabins; it includes aloe soap, shampoo, conditioner, deodorant, breath mints, candy, and pain relief tablets (all in sample sizes).

Note: If you book one of the suites (Category 11 or 12 in the Carnival Cruise Lines brochure) you automatically qualify for "Skipper's Club" priority check-in at any US homeland port – useful for getting ahead of the crowd.

CUISINE. There are two principal dining rooms: the Renoir Restaurant, with 744 seats, and the larger Monet Restaurant, with 1,044 seats. Both are two decks high, and both have a balcony level for diners (the balcony level in the Monet Restaurant is larger). Two additional wings in the Renoir Restaurant, named Cassat and Pissaro, provide room to accommodate large groups in a private dining arrangement. There's a choice of either fixed time dining (6pm or 8:15pm), or flexible dining (any time between 5:45pm and 9:30pm). Although the menu choice looks good, the cuisine delivered is typically adequate, but quite unmemorable.

The Cezanne Restaurant is the ship's casual self-serve international food court-style lido deck eatery, which has a capacity of over 1,200. Its decor reflects the style of a 19th-century French cafe. It has two main serving lines; it is adjacent to the aft pool and can be covered by a magrodome glass cover in inclement weather. Included in this eating mall are Paul's Deli, PC's Wok (Chinese cuisine, with wok preparation), a 24-hour pizzeria, and a patisserie (there's an extra charge for yummy pastries, however), as well as a grill for fast foods such as hamburgers and hot dogs. Each night, the Cezanne Restaurant is turned into the "Seaview Bistro", and provides a casual (dress down) alternative to eating in the main dining rooms, serving pasta, steaks, salads and desserts (typically between 6pm and 9pm). And, if you are still hungry, there's always a midnight buffet around the corner.

Alternative (Reservations-Only, Extra Cost) Dining: The Point is the name of the reservations-only, extra cost, alternative dining spot. The decor includes wall murals in the style of Seurat's famous Le Cirque (The Circus). Fine table settings, china and silverware are featured, as well as leather-bound menus.

ENTERTAINMENT. The Toulouse-Lautrec Showlounge is a multi-deck showroom seating 1,400, and serves as the main entertainment venue. It has a revolving stage, hydraulic orchestra pit, superb sound, and seating on three levels (the upper levels being tiered through two decks). There is a proscenium over the stage that acts as a scenery loft.

SPA/FITNESS. SpaCarnival is a large health, fitness and spa complex that spans two decks (the walls display hand-painted reproductions of the artist's poster work). It is located directly above the navigation bridge in the forward part of the ship (and is accessed from the forward stairway).

Facilities on the lower level include a solarium, eight treatment rooms, lecture rooms, sauna and steam rooms for men and women, and a beauty parlor. The upper level consists of a large gymnasium with floor-to-ceiling windows on three sides, including forward-facing ocean views, and an aerobics room with instructor-led classes (some at extra cost).

● **For more extensive general information on what a Carnival cruise is like, see pages 126–31.**

Carnival Destiny
★★★ +

Size: . . . . .Large Resort Ship	Passenger Decks: 12	Cabins (with private balcony): 418
Tonnage: .101,353	Total Crew: .1,000	Cabins (wheelchair accessible): 25
Lifestyle: . . . . .Standard	Passengers	Wheelchair accessibility . . . . .Good
Cruise Line: . . . . . . .Carnival Cruise Lines	(lower beds/all berths): 2,642/3,400	Cabin Current: . . . . .110 volts
Former Names: . . . . .none	Passenger Space Ratio	Elevators: 14
Builder: . . . . .Fincantieri (Italy)	(lower beds/all berths): 38.3/29.8	Casino (gaming tables): . . . . .Yes
Original Cost: . . . .$400 million	Crew/Passenger Ratio	Slot Machines: . . . . .Yes
Entered Service: . . . . .Nov 1996	(lower beds/all berths): 2.6/3.4	Swimming Pools (outdoors): 2
Registry: . . . . .The Bahamas	Cabins (total): 1,321	(+1 with magrodome)
Length (ft/m): 892.3/272.0	Size Range (sq ft/m): 179.7–482.2/	Swimming Pools (indoors): 0
Beam (ft/m): 116.0/35.3	16.7–44.8	Whirlpools: 7
Draft (ft/m): 27.0/8.2	Cabins (outside view): 806	Self-Service Launderette: . . . . .Yes
Propulsion/Propellers: . . . . .diesel-electric	Cabins (interior/no view): 515	Dedicated Cinema/Seats: . . . . .No
(63,400kW)/2	Cabins (for one person): 0	Library: . . . . .Yes

OVERALL SCORE: 1,361 OUT OF A POSSIBLE 2,000 POINTS

OVERVIEW. *Carnival Destiny* is the 11th new ship for this very successful cruise line. However, because of its size, the ship is unable to transit the Panama Canal, and is thus dedicated to itineraries in the Caribbean. The ship, whose bows are extremely short, has the distinctive, large, swept-back wing-tipped funnel that is the trademark of Carnival Cruise Lines, in the company colors of red, white and blue.

This is quite a stunning ship, built to impress at every turn, with the most balanced profile of all the ships in the Carnival fleet. Amidships on the open deck is a very long water slide (200 ft/60 meters in length), as well as tiered sunbathing decks positioned between two swimming pools, several hot tubs, and a giant poolside movie screen.

Inside, Joe Farcus, the designer who creates all the interiors for the ships of Carnival Cruise Lines, has done a fine job. The decor is a fantasyland for the senses (though nowhere near as glitzy as the *Fantasy*-class ships). The layout is logical, so finding your way around is easy. As for public areas, there are three decks full of lounges, 10 bars and lots of rooms to play in. The ship has a double-wide indoor promenade, nine decks high, and a glass-domed rotunda atrium lobby. For those who like to gamble, the Millionaire's Club Casino is certainly large and action-packed; there are also more than 320 slot machines.

An additional feature that this ship has which the *Fantasy*-class ships do not have is the Flagship Bar, located in the Rotunda (atrium), which faces forward to glass-walled lifts. Another feature is the All Star Bar – a sports bar with tables that include sporting memorabilia.

Youngsters are provided with good facilities, including

BERLITZ'S RATINGS

	Possible	Achieved
Ship	500	399
Accommodation	200	157
Food	400	218
Service	400	253
Entertainment	100	81
Cruise	400	253

their own two-level Children's Club (including an outdoor pool), and are well cared for with "Camp Carnival", the line's extensive children's program.

From the viewpoint of safety, passengers can embark directly into the lifeboats from their secured position without having to wait for them to be lowered, thus saving time in the event of a real emergency.

The terraced pool deck is cluttered, and there are no cushioned pads for the deck chairs. Getting away from people and noise is difficult. The Photo Gallery, adjacent to the atrium/purser's office, becomes extremely congested when photos are on display.

There is no escape from repetitious announcements (for activities that bring revenue, such as art auctions, bingo, and horse racing) that intrude constantly into your cruise. There is also much hustling for drinks, although accomplished with a knowing smile.

ACCOMMODATION. There are 19 price grades. The price you pay depends on grade, size and location. Over half of all cabins have an ocean-view, and at 225 sq. ft./21 sq. meters they are the largest in the standard market. The cabins are spread over four decks and have private balconies (with glass rather than steel balustrades, for better, unobstructed ocean views), extending over the ship's side. The balconies have bright fluorescent lighting.

The standard cabins are of good size and come equipped with all the basics, although the furniture is rather angular, with no rounded edges. Three decks of cabins (eight on each deck, each with private balcony) overlook the stern. With three days at sea on each of two alternating itineraries, vibration is kept to a minimum.

There are eight penthouse suites, and each has a large private balcony. Although they are quite lavish in their appointments, at only 483 sq. ft (44.8 sq. meters), they are really quite modest when compared to the best suites even in many smaller ships. There are also 40 other suites, each of which has a decent sized bathroom, and a good amount of lounge space, although they are nothing special.

In those cabins with balconies (more cabins have balconies aboard this ship than those that do not), the partition between each balcony is open at top and bottom, so you can hear noise from neighbors (or smell their cigarettes). It is disappointing to see three categories of cabins (both outside and interior) with upper and lower bunk beds (lower beds are far more preferable, but this is how the ship accommodates an extra 600 people over and above the lower bed capacity).

The cabins have soft color schemes and soft furnishings in more attractive fabrics than some other ships in the fleet. Interactive "Fun Vision" technology lets you choose movies on demand (for a fee). The bathrooms, which have good-sized showers, have good storage space in the toiletries cabinet. A gift basket is provided in all grades; it includes aloe soap, shampoo, conditioner, deodorant, breath mints, candy, and pain relief tablets (albeit all in sample sizes).

If you book one of the suites (Category 11 or 12 in the Carnival Cruise Lines brochure) you automatically qualify for "Skipper's Club" priority check-in at any US homeland port – useful for getting ahead of the crowd.

CUISINE. The ship has two dining rooms: the Galaxy, forward, with windows on two sides, has 706 seats; and the Universe, aft, with windows on three sides, has 1,090 seats). Both are non-smoking. Each spans two decks (a first for any Carnival ship), and incorporate a dozen pyramid-shaped domes and chandeliers, and a soft, mellow peachy color scheme.

The Universe dining room has a two-deck-high wall of glass overlooking the stern. There are tables for four, six and eight (and even a few tables for two that the line tries to keep for honeymooners). There's a choice of either fixed time dining (6pm or 8:15pm), or flexible dining (any time between 5:45 and 9:30pm). Although the menu choices look good, the actual cuisine delivered is adequate, but quite unmemorable.

Casual eaters will find a serve-yourself Lido Buffet – open for breakfast and lunch, while for dinner this turns into the Seaview Bistro for use as an alternative eatery – for those that do not want to dress to go to the formal dining rooms (between 6pm and 9pm). These include specialty stations where you can order omelets, eggs, fajitas, Chicken Caesar salad, pasta and stir-fry items. If you are still hungry, there's always a midnight buffet around the corner.

The dining room entrances have comfortable drinking areas for pre-dinner cocktails. There are also many options for casual dining, particularly during the daytime. The Sun and Sea Restaurant is two decks high; it is the ship's informal international food court-style eatery, which is adjacent to the aft pool and can be covered by a magrodome glass cover in inclement weather. Included in this eating mall are a Trattoria (for Italian cuisine, with made-to-order pasta dishes), Happy Valley (Chinese cuisine, with wok preparation), a 24-hour pizzeria, and a patisserie (extra charge for pastries), as well as a grill (for fast foods such as hamburgers and hot dogs).

At night, the area becomes the "Seaview Bistro" (it typically operates 6pm–9pm), providing a casual (dress down) alternative to eating in the main dining rooms. It serves pasta, steaks, salads and desserts. The good thing is that, if you really want to eat 24 hours a day, you can do it aboard this ship, which has something for (almost) everyone.

ENTERTAINMENT. The three-level (non-smoking) Palladium showlounge, the setting for all production shows and large-scale cabaret acts, is quite stunning, and has a revolving stage, hydraulic orchestra pit, superb sound, and seating on three levels (the upper levels being tiered through two decks). There is a proscenium over the stage that acts as a scenery loft.

SPA/FITNESS. SpaCarnival spans two decks (with a total area of 13,700 sq. ft/1,272 sq. meters), and is located directly above the navigation bridge in the forward part of the ship (it is accessed from the forward stairway). Facilities on the lower level include a solarium, eight treatment rooms, lecture rooms, sauna and steam rooms for men and women, and a beauty parlor; the upper level consists of a large gymnasium with floor-to-ceiling windows on three sides, including forward-facing ocean views, and an aerobics room with instructor-led classes (some at extra cost).

● **For more extensive general information on what a Carnival cruise is like, see pages 126–31.**

Carnival Dream
★★★ +

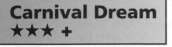

Size: . . . . .Large Resort Ship	Passenger Decks: 13	Cabins (with private balcony): 887
Tonnage: 128,251	Total Crew: 1,367	Cabins (wheelchair accessible): 35
Lifestyle: . . . . .Standard	Passengers	Wheelchair accessibility . . . . .Good
Cruise Line: . . . . . . .Carnival Cruise Lines	(lower beds/all berths): 3,646/4,631	Cabin Voltage: . . . . .110 volts
Former Names: . . . . .none	Passenger Space Ratio	Elevators: 14
Builder: . . . . .Fincantieri (Italy)	(lower beds/all berths): 35.1/27.6	Casino (gaming tables): . . . . .Yes
Original Cost: . . . .$740 million	Crew/Passenger Ratio	Slot Machines: . . . . .Yes
Entered Service: . . . . .Sept 2009	(lower beds/all berths): 2.6/3.3	Swimming Pools (outdoors): 2
Registry: . . . . .Panama	Cabins (total): 1,823	Swimming Pools (indoors): 0
Length (ft/m): 1,004.0/306.0	Size Range (sq ft/m): 185.0–430.5/	Whirlpools: 7
Beam (ft/m): 158.0/48.0	17.1–40.0	Self-Service Launderette: . . . . .Yes
Draft (ft/m): 26.2/8.0	Cabins (outside view): 1,145	Dedicated Cinema/Seats: . . . . .No
Propulsion/Propellers:	Cabins (interior/no view): 678	Library: . . . . .Yes
Diesel-electric (75.6 mW)/2	Cabins (for one person): 0	

BERLITZ'S OVERALL SCORE: 1,395 OUT OF A POSSIBLE 2,000 POINTS

OVERVIEW. This is the largest "fun ship" yet for this expansive cruise line, and will be followed in 2011 by a sister, *Carnival Magic*. Although its bows are short, the ship's profile is actually nicely balanced, with a rakish front and more rounded stern than previous Carnival ships. The propulsion system consists of the conventional twin rudder, with twin (six-blade) propellers.

There are numerous pools and open-deck nooks and crannies. One thing that stands out, however, is the ship's really big, and long Twister Water Slide – part of The Waterworks on pool deck. There's also a Serenity adults-only, extra charge retreat, and numerous other features. However, the general open deck space is really not enough for the number of passengers carried, so your sunbed loungers will be packed in tightly.

Carnival Dream is the first (and only) Carnival ship to have a full walk-around open promenade deck, which is lined with deck chairs (which are sometimes challenging to walk round). Four scenic hot tubs are cantilevered over the ship's side. Along the outdoor promenade, four "scenic whirlpools" are cantilevered over the sea, and provide fine sea views. Higher up, Lido Deck 10 offers the best open-deck area of any Carnival ship with a tropical, resort-style main pool complete with a giant Seaside Theatre LED screen for outdoor movies. *Carnival Dream* is the first Carnival ship to have a laser light show outdoors – which the AIDA Cruises' ships have featured since 1996.

The interior decor is bright, but well executed. Most public rooms, lounges and bars are on Dream Street or Upper Dream Street. The stunning Dream Lobby is the connection point for ship functions and people and is the main lobby. Take the glass-walled elevators for a neat view

BERLITZ'S RATINGS

	Possible	Achieved
Ship	500	415
Accommodation	200	157
Food	400	218
Service	400	260
Entertainment	100	82
Cruise	400	263

– but you may need sunglasses. It's good to note that there are three main elevator towers: forward, midships, and aft. This is in contrast to larger ships such as *Oasis of the Seas*, which, although it carries many more passengers, has only two main elevator banks. Well done, Carnival, good for safety.

The Ocean Plaza, a new feature for Carnival, is designed to be a comfortable place by day and a trendy entertainment venue by night. The indoor/outdoor café and live music venue has a bandstand where a variety of musical genres are showcased, and a large circular dance floor, and around 190 seats. An adjacent bar also offers espresso and cappuccino coffees, gelato ice creams, and pastries.

A wide variety of lounges, bars and nightspots, including a dance club with a twist, offering indoor/outdoor access, are accessible via an 11-deck-high atrium whose ground level has a neatly cantilevered bandstand atop a massive dance floor. The Page Turner (great name) is the ship's library, while Jackpot is – you guessed it – the colourful, large, lively and noisy casino. Other rooms include The Song (Jazz Bar), and Ocean Plaza, a sort of quiet area during the day, but lively at night with live entertainment. There are 36 internet-connect computer terminals refreshingly scattered throughout the ship, although most have no privacy. There's also a 232-capacity conference room, The Chambers.

Naturally, to get to the showlounge, you need to walk through the shops and casino. This is a ship that encourages you to spend money on all the extras you'll need.

Although passenger flow is generally sound, the ship's layout is rather disjointed. There is much congestion just prior to the second seating, on both Upper and Lower Dream Streets, both of which are located on the starboard side. Further congestion appears around the photo gallery, which surrounds the atrium lobby. Passenger niggles center around barely warm food in the two main dining rooms, poorly trained and rude staff, lines forming, particularly for self-serve food items, and congestion in the public areas just before second-seating dinner.

The ship's homeport is Port Canaveral, and the ship operates year-round Caribbean cruises. The onboard currency is the US dollar, and gratuities are automatically charged to your onboard account.

CHILDREN: There are plenty of facilities for the families with children, purpose-built for the line's three age-related children's programs: "Camp Carnival" for kids aged 2–11, "Circle C" for 12- to 14-year-olds, and "Club O2" for teens ages 15 to 17, together with a full schedule of morning-to-night activities catering to each age group. About 5,000 sq.ft. of space has been devoted to junior cruisers. Also, Carnival WaterWorks, an expansive aqua park offering exhilarating water slides and various water spray apparatus, should be a hit with active children.

ACCOMMODATION. There are 19 cabin price categories, but just 6 cabin types, to choose from. The price will depend on the accommodation grade you choose, and its location. But whether you go for high end or low end, all accommodation includes the Carnival Comfort Bed with plush mattresses, good-quality duvets and linens and pillows. However, the straight accommodation deck hallways create rather a cell block look – and they are bright, very bright – even at night. There are also lot of interior (no view) cabins. But the cabins to go for are those at the stern of the ship, with great rearward ocean views on Decks 6, 7, 8 and 9.

"Deluxe" ocean-view cabins, with two bathrooms, provide comfort and convenience for families. In addition to twin beds that convert to a king, decent closet space and elegant decor, the two-bathroom configuration includes one full bathroom and a second bathroom containing a small tub with shower and sink.

Some cabins can accommodate five persons – a rarity in new ships but useful for families. There is a wide selection of balcony cabins and suites, including "Cove Balcony" cabins that are the closest to the waterline.

Additionally, adjacent to the Serenity Spa are 65 "Cloud 9" spa cabins, designated as no-smoking. They provide a number of "exclusive" amenities and privileges. Twenty of these are positioned directly aft of the lower level of the spa, with direct access to it. Some cabins located directly over loud late-night venues (such as Encore), with poor soundproofing, have resulted in many restless nights. Also, cabins on Deck 12 are subject to lots of noise from kids having fun on the deck above – so afternoon naps are out.

CUISINE. There are two main restaurants: the 1,180-seat Crimson (mid-ships) and the smaller 828-seat Scarlet (aft). Each has two levels: main and balcony (stairways connect both levels), with the galley set on the lower level. Forward of The Crimson are two small restaurant annexes, which

can be reserved by small groups as a private dining room.

The Gathering is the ship's self-serve buffet facility, with indoor/outdoor seating areas on the lower (main) level, and indoor-only seating on the upper level. A number of designated areas serve different types of ethnic cuisine, including a Mongolian Wok and Pasta Bar on the upper level, open 6pm–9pm for tablecloth-free, candle-less (bare table top) buffet dinners. The layout invites congestion around the beverage stands. Go off-peak and it's much better.

Alternative (Reservations-Only, Extra-Cost) Dining:
The Chef's Art Supper Club (and bar) seats 139, has great views to port and starboard from its aft location high up on Spa Deck 12, and an à la carte menu. It features fine table settings, china and silverware, as well as leather-bound menus. The featured specialties are steaks and seafood items. It's worth paying the cover charge to get a taste of what Carnival can really deliver in terms of food that is of better quality than that served in the main dining rooms. It's also the place to go for celebrating something special, or just to get away from the noise of the large dining rooms.

Wasabi is the ship's tribute-to-sushi venue; note the large fish behind the sushi bar.

ENTERTAINMENT. The 1,964-seat Encore Showlounge spans three decks at the front of the ship, with seating set in a horseshoe shape around a large proscenium arched stage; the sightlines are generally good, except from some of the seats at the back of the lowest level. Large-scale production shows, with lots of feathers and skimpy costumes, are staged, together with snappy cabaret acts, all with a live showband as accompaniment.

The 425-seat Burgundy Lounge, at the aft end of the ship (opposite to the showlounge, at the front), has a stage, dance floor, large bar, and is a comedy venue, including late-night in-your-face, raunchy "adult comedy."

Caliente is the ship's hot club; it provides Latin music for vibrant dancing and hot-foot style and is very loud.

SPA/FITNESS. The expansive 23,750-sq-ft (2,206 sq-meter) Cloud 9 Spa is Carnival's largest and most elaborate health and wellness center to date. It is positioned over three decks in the front section of the ship. The uppermost deck includes indoor/outdoor private spa relaxation areas (at extra cost). A spiral staircase connects the two decks, and the Steiner-operated spa offers a wide range of treatments.

There are 10 treatment rooms, including a VIP room, a large massage room for couples, and a Rasul mud treatment room, plus two dry flotation rooms. A "Thermal Suite" (extra charge) comes with the typical sensory-enhanced soothing heated chambers: Laconium, Tepidarium, Aroma and Oriental steam baths.

There are two steam rooms, one each for men and women, and a small unisex sauna with a floor-to-ceiling window on its starboard side. *Carnival Dream* is the first "Fun Ship" to include a two-level miniature golf course.

● **For more extensive general information on what a Carnival cruise is like, see pages 126–31.**

Carnival Ecstasy
Carnival Elation
Carnival Fantasy
Carnival Fascination
★★★

Size: . . . . .Large Resort Ships	Propulsion/Propellers: . . . . .diesel-electric	Cabins (interior/no view): 408
Tonnage: .70,367	(42,240kW)/2 *(Ecstasy, Fantasy,*	Cabins (for one person): 0
Lifestyle: . . . . .Standard	*Fascination),* diesel-electric 42,842 kW)/	Cabins (with private balcony): 52 *(Ecstasy),*
Cruise Line: . . . . . . .Carnival Cruise Lines	2 azimuthing pods (14 MW each) *(Elation)*	152 *(Elation, Fantasy),* 250 *(Fascination)*
Former Names: . . . .*Ecstasy, Elation,*	Passenger Decks: 10	Cabins (wheelchair accessible): 22
Fantasy, Fascination	Total Crew: 920	Wheelchair accessibility . . . . .Fair
Builder: . . .Kvaerner Masa-Yards (Finland)	Passengers	Cabin Current: . . . . .110 volts
Original Cost: . . . .$225 million	(lower beds/all berths): 2,056/2,634	Elevators: 14
Entered Service: . . . .June 1991 *(Ecstasy),*	Passenger Space Ratio	Casino (gaming tables): . . . . .Yes
Mar 1998 *(Elation),* Mar 1990 *(Fantasy),*	(lower beds/all berths): 34.4/26.7	Slot Machines: . . . . .Yes
July 1994 *(Fascination)*	Crew/Passenger Ratio	Swimming Pools (outdoors): 3
Registry: . . . . . .Panama *(Ecstasy, Elation,*	(lower beds/all berths): 2.2/2.8	Swimming Pools (indoors): 0
Fantasy), The Bahamas *(Fascination)*	Cabins (total): . . . . .1,026 or 1,028	Whirlpools: 6
Length (ft/m): 855.8/263.6	Size Range (sq ft/m): 173.2–409.7/	Self-Service Launderette: . . . . .Yes
Beam (ft/m): 103.0/31.4	16.0–38.0	Dedicated Cinema/Seats: . . . . .No
Draft (ft/m): 25.9/7.9	Cabins (outside view): . . . . . . .618 or 620	Library: . . . . .Yes

BERLITZ'S OVERALL SCORE: 1,247 OUT OF A POSSIBLE 2,000 POINTS

OVERVIEW. Externally angular and not at all handsome, these ships belong to Carnival Cruise Lines' *Fantasy*-class series of almost identical, very successful ships, along with *Carnival Imagination, Carnival Inspiration, Carnival Paradise* and *Carnival Sensation.* They are aimed at the mainstream first-time cruise market, and most operate cruises shorter than a week. There are fewer of the much sought-after balcony cabins than in the company's newer ships.

BERLITZ'S RATINGS		
	Possible	Achieved
Ship	500	318
Accommodation	200	138
Food	400	213
Service	400	262
Entertainment	100	73
Cruise	400	243

The ships, whose bows are extremely short, have the distinctive, large, swept-back wing-tipped funnel that is the trademark of Carnival Cruise Lines, in the company colors of red, white and blue. They have reasonable open deck areas, which quickly become inadequate when the ships are full and everyone wants to be out on deck. The aft decks tend to be less noisy, whereas all the activities are focused around the main swimming pool and hot tubs (one with a thatched shade). There's also a topless sunbathing area for those who prefer European-style sunning. There is no walk-around open promenade deck, although there is a short jogging track. The lifeboats (six of which double as twin screw shore tenders) are positioned high atop the ships.

The interior spaces are well utilized. The general passenger flow is good, and the interior design – the work of Miami-based creative genius Joe Farcus – is clever, functional, and extremely colourful. He calls it "entertainment architecture," and considers every part of a ship as a piece

of a giant jigsaw puzzle. Each of the ships has an interior design theme. For example, *Carnival Fantasy*'s is mythical muses, and composers and their compositions. The interior focal (and gathering) point is an "open" atrium lobby, whose balconied shape recalls some of the world's great opera houses; it spans six decks, and is topped by a large glass dome.

The lowest level is where you'll find the Purser's Desk and Shore Excursion Desk. The original neon lighting in the lobby has gone, replaced by softer, more elegant design elements; the sculpture has also gone, replaced by a lobby bar (and live music); it's the most central place to meet.

There are public entertainment lounges, bars and clubs galore, with something for everyone (except quiet space). The public rooms, connected by a double-width indoor boulevard combine a colorful mix of classic and contemporary design elements that beg your indulgence. Most public rooms and attractions lead off from this boulevard – a sort of shipboard "Main Street" which runs between the showlounge (forward) and lounge/nightclub (aft). A large casino has almost non-stop action. Conversely, there is also a fine looking library and reading room, but few books.

Kids will, I am sure, enjoy "Children's World", a 2,500 sq. ft (230 sq. meter) play-area with games and fun stuff for youngsters of all ages, including Apple computers loaded with educational software, and an arts and crafts area with spin and sand art machines. A group babysitting service is available ($6 per hour for the first child; $4 per hour for each additional child of the same immediate family).

While the cuisine is just so-so, the real fun begins at sundown when Carnival really excels in sound, lights, razzle-dazzle shows and late-night high volume sounds. From venues such as Electricity Disco to Cleopatra's Bar, these ships' interior decor will entertain you. However, the ships are not for those who seeking a quiet, relaxing cruise experience. There are simply too many annoying announcements, and the never-ending hustling to get you to buy drinks and many other things. Shore excursions can be booked via the in-cabin "Fun Vision" television system, but obtaining advice and suggestions isn't easy. In fact, getting anyone to answer your questions can be frustrating.

Onboard enhancements for all eight of the "Carnival Fantasy"-class ships in their 2007–9 refurbishments included: an expansive children's water park; updated design style and features for pool areas, and the creation of the Serenity adults-only deck area; a nine-hole miniature golf course on Sun Deck as well as a new Café (a patisserie serving specialty coffees and sweets, located along the Promenade Deck); a teen club (for the line's popular "Club O2" teen program), plus a new 1,600-sq-ft (149-sq-meter) Children's World play area, located on Verandah Deck, to enhance the Camp Carnival children's program.

Other additions included an art gallery, a photo gallery, an Atrium Bar, a New York-style deli in the Lido restaurant, a better internet café, and a 1,200-sq-ft (111-sq-meter) conference room. Suites/cabins include flat screen TVs, new decor and remodeled bathrooms; 98 cabins received a small balcony. Spa Carnival got new private treatment rooms, and updated exercise equipment.

ACCOMMODATION. There are 13 grades of accommodation. The price you pay will depend on grade, size and location. The standard outside-view and interior (no view) cabins have decor that is rather plain and unmemorable. They are marginally comfortable, yet spacious enough and practical (most are of the same size and appointments), with good storage space and practical, well-designed no-nonsense bathrooms. However, if you have a queen-bed configuration instead of the standard twin-bed layout, note that one person has to clamber over the bed – an ungainly exercise for those of a heavier build.

Anyone booking one of the outside suites will find more space, whirlpool bathtubs, and some fascinating, rather eclectic decor and furniture. These are mildly attractive, but nothing special, and they are much smaller than those aboard the ships of a similar size of several competing companies. A gift basket is provided in all grades of accommodation; it includes aloe soap, shampoo, conditioner, deodorant, breath mints, candy, and pain relief tablets (all in sample sizes).

If you book accommodation in a suite (Category 11 or 12 in the Carnival Cruise Lines brochure), you automatically qualify for "Skipper's Club" priority check-in at any US homeland port – useful for getting ahead of the crowd.

Room service items are available 24 hours a day, although in standard cabins, only cold food is available, while those in suite-grade accommodation get a greater range of items (both hot and cold) to choose from.

CUISINE. The two large main dining rooms, located mid-ships and aft and both non-smoking, are called Wind Star and Wind Song in *Carnival Ecstasy*, Imagination and Inspiration in *Carnival Elation*, Celebration and Jubilee in *Carnival Fantasy*, and Sensation and Imagination in *Carnival Fascination*. All have ocean-view windows, and are noisy, but the decor is attractive, although extremely bright. There's a choice of either fixed-time dining (6pm or 8:15pm), or flexible dining (any time between 5:45 and 9:30pm).

The food is adequate. While the menu items sound good, their presentation is simple, and few garnishes are used. Many meat and fowl dishes are disguised with gravies and sauces. The selection of fresh green vegetables, breads, rolls, cheeses and fruits is limited, and there is much use of canned fruit and jellied desserts. There's a decent wine list, but no wine waiters. The waiters sing and dance, and there are constant waiter parades.

At night, the "Seaview Bistro", as the Windows on the Sea lido self-serve buffet restaurant is known in the evenings, provides a casual (dress down) alternative to eating in the main dining rooms, serving pasta, steaks, salads and desserts – it typically operates only between 6pm and 9pm. Although the food selection is very limited, it does make a change from the large, crowded main dining rooms.

A patisserie offers specialty coffees and sweets (extra charge), and a so-called sushi bar on Promenade Deck is open prior to dinner; if you know anything about sushi, don't expect authenticity.

Carnival Fantasy-class ships do not have "alternative" (extra-charge) dining spots.

ENTERTAINMENT. A main showlounge is the principal venue for large-scale production shows and major cabaret acts – although 20 pillars obstruct some views. In a typical 3- or 4-day cruise, there will be one or two, large-scale, trend-setting production shows, with a cast of two lead singers and a clutch of dancers, backed by a 10-piece live orchestra.

SPA/FITNESS. A large, glass-wrapped health, fitness and spa complex is located on the uppermost interior deck, forward of the ship's mast; it is typically open from 6am to 8pm daily. It consists of a gymnasium with oceanview windows that look out over the bow and the latest in muscle-pumping electronic machines, an aerobics exercise room, men's and women's changing rooms, sauna and steam rooms, and beauty salon. A common complaint is that there aren't enough staff to keep the area clean and tidy, and used towels are often strewn around the changing rooms.

Sporting types can play basketball or volleyball, or ping-pong. There is also a "banked" jogging track outdoors on the deck above the spa.

● **For more extensive general information on what a Carnival cruise is like, see pages 126–31.**

Carnival Freedom
★★★ +

Size:	Large Resort Ship	Passenger Decks:	13	Cabins (with private balcony):	574
Tonnage:	110,239	Total Crew:	1,150	Cabins (wheelchair accessible):	25
Lifestyle:	Standard	Passengers		Wheelchair accessibility	Good
Cruise Line:	Carnival Cruise Lines	(lower beds/all berths):	2,974/3,700	Cabin Current:	110 volts
Former Names:	none	Passenger Space Ratio		Elevators:	14
Builder:	Fincantieri (Italy)	(lower beds/all berths):	37.0/29.7	Casino (gaming tables):	Yes
Original Cost:	$500 million	Crew/Passenger Ratio		Slot Machines:	Yes
Entered Service:	Feb 2007	(lower beds/all berths):	2.5/3.1	Swimming Pools (outdoors):	2
Registry:	Panama	Cabins (total):	1,487	(+1 with magrodome)	
Length (ft/m):	951.4/290.0	Size Range (sq ft/m):	179.7–484.2/	Swimming Pools (indoors):	0
Beam (ft/m):	105.6/32.2		16.7–44.8	Whirlpools:	7
Draft (ft/m):	27.2/8.3	Cabins (outside view):	917	Self-Service Launderette:	Yes
Propulsion/Propellers:	diesel-electric	Cabins (interior/no view):	570	Dedicated Cinema/Seats:	No
	(63,400kW)/2	Cabins (for one person):	0	Library:	Yes

OVERALL SCORE: 1,390 OUT OF A POSSIBLE 2,000 POINTS

OVERVIEW. *Carnival Freedom* is the 24th new ship ordered by this incredibly successful cruise line that bases its success on the "Fun Ship" concept. It shares the same generally balanced profile as sisters *Carnival Conquest, Carnival Destiny, Carnival Glory, Carnival Liberty, Carnival Triumph, Carnival Valor*, and *Carnival Victory*. Being a non-Panamax ship, it is unable to transit the Panama Canal, due to its size. Immediately recognizable is the ship's swept-back, red, white and blue wingtip funnel – the trademark of all Carnival's ships.

The ship's interior decor is a kaleidoscopic blend of colors that stimulate and excite the senses, and is dedicated to time, and the decades. The deck and public room layout is logical, and finding your way around is quite easy. Most of the public rooms are located on one deck off a main interior boulevard, above a deck which contains the two main dining rooms. The public rooms include a large casino (gaming includes blackjack, craps, roulette, three-card poker, Caribbean Stud poker, Face Up, Let it Ride, Bonus, and Wheel of Madness, and more than 300 slot machines).

If you like movies on big screens in the open air (remember drive-in movie theaters?), Carnival's Seaside Theatre for movies on deck should do it for you (seating is in tiered rows and the movie screen faces forward). The ship has bow-to-stern wi-fi internet access, including all passenger cabins.

Youngsters are provided with their own Camp Carnival children's club (with its own small outdoor pool), and are well cared for with the line's extensive children's program. Camp Carnival is located on Sun Deck, out of the way of older passengers.

Minor niggles include the fact that many pillars obstruct

BERLITZ'S RATINGS		
	Possible	Achieved
Ship	500	414
Accommodation	200	157
Food	400	218
Service	400	260
Entertainment	100	82
Cruise	400	259

passenger flow, particularly in the dining room, where they make it difficult for the waiters to serve food properly.

ACCOMMODATION. There are 20 cabin price categories, in 7 different suite/cabin types, sizes and grades. These include suites with private balcony; deluxe outside-view cabins with private balcony; outside-view cabins with private balcony; outside-view cabins with window; cabins with a porthole instead of a window; interior (no-view) cabins; and interior (no-view cabins) with upper and lower berths.

There are five decks of cabins with private balconies. Standard cabins are of good size and come equipped with all the basics, although the furniture is rather square and angular, with no rounded edges. Three decks of cabins (eight on each deck, each with private balcony) overlook the stern. Most cabins with twin beds can be converted to a queen-size bed format.

Book one of the suites (Category 11 or 12 in the Carnival Cruise Lines brochure) and you'll get "Skipper's Club" priority check-in at any US homeland port – useful for getting ahead of the crowd.

There are even "spa" cabins aboard this ship – a grouping of 18 cabins that are located directly around and behind SpaCarnival; so fitness devotees can get out of bed and go straight to the treadmill without having to go through any of the public rooms first.

A gift basket of personal toiletries is provided in all grades of cabins; it includes aloe soap, shampoo, conditioner, deodorant, breath mints, candy, and pain relief tablets (all in sample sizes – and most in paper packets that are difficult, sometimes frustrating, to open).

CUISINE. There are two principal dining rooms (Chic 744, located midships; and Posh, aft, seating 1,122). Both are two decks high and have a balcony level (the balcony level in Posh is larger than the one in Chic). There's a choice of either fixed time dining (6pm or 8:15pm), or flexible dining (any time between 5:45pm and 9:30pm).

There are few table for two, but my favourites are the two tables for two right at the very back of the restaurant, with ocean views astern.

Alternative (Reservations-Only, Extra Cost) Dining: There is one reservations-only, extra-cost dining spot, the Sun King Supper Club. It features fine table settings, china and silverware, as well as leather-bound menus. The featured specialties are steaks and seafood items. It's worth paying the cover charge to get a taste of what Carnival can really deliver in terms of food that is of better quality than that served in the main dining rooms.

Casual Eateries: The Freedom Restaurant is a casual self-serve international food court-style lido deck eatery. It has two main serving lines. Included in this eating mall are a deli, an Asian eatery (with wok preparation), a 24-hour pizzeria, and a grill for fast foods such as hamburgers and hot dogs. Each night, the Freedom Restaurant morphs into the "Seaview Bistro," and provides a casual (dress down) alternative to eating in the main dining rooms, serving pasta, steaks, salads and desserts (typically between 6pm and 9pm).

Other "nooks and crannies" (extra cost) food and drink-related places include the Nouveau Wine Bar, the Viennese Café, and the cute little Meiji Sushi Bar. All are located on Promenade Deck.

ENTERTAINMENT. The Victoriana Theater (named after England's Queen Victoria) is the ship's multi-deck showroom. This large showlounge seats up to 1,400, and serves as the principal entertainment venue for the ship's colourful large-scale entertainment, including Las-Vegas-style production shows and major cabaret acts. It has a revolving stage, hydraulic orchestra pit, superb sound, and seating on three levels (the upper levels being tiered through two decks). A proscenium over the stage acts as a scenery loft.

The decor is medieval (drinks tables are made to look like shields, for example; and towers with stained-glass windows, shields, and coats of armor flank the stage).

An alternative entertainment venue is the aft lounge, which seats 425 and typically features live music and late-night cabaret acts including smutty adult comedy.

Body-throbbing loud music sensations can be found in the ship's discotheque; it includes a video wall with live projections from the dance floor. Meanwhile piano bar lovers should enjoy the 100-seat Lindy Hop piano bar.

SPA/FITNESS. SpaCarnival spans two decks (with a total area of approximately 13,300 sq. ft/1,235 sq. meters), and is located directly above the navigation bridge in the forward part of the ship (it is accessed from the forward stairway. Facilities on the lower level include a solarium, eight treatment rooms, lecture rooms, sauna and steam rooms for men and women, and a beauty parlor; the upper level consists of a large gymnasium with floor-to-ceiling windows on three sides, including forward-facing ocean views, and an aerobics room with instructor-led classes (some at extra cost) for which you'll need to sign up.

● **For more extensive general information on what a Carnival cruise is like, see pages 126–31.**

Carnival Glory
★★★ +

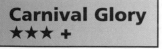

Size: . . . . .Large Resort Ship	Passenger Decks: 13	Cabins (with private balcony): 590
Tonnage: 110,239	Total Crew: .1,160	Cabins (wheelchair accessible): 25
Lifestyle: . . . . .Standard	Passengers	Wheelchair accessibility . . . . .Good
Cruise Line: . . . . . . .Carnival Cruise Lines	(lower beds/all berths): 2,974/3,700	Cabin Current: . . . . .110 volts
Former Names: . . . . .none	Passenger Space Ratio	Elevators: 14
Builder: . . . . .Fincantieri (Italy)	(lower beds/all berths): 37.0/29.7	Casino (gaming tables): . . . . .Yes
Original Cost: . . . .$500 million	Crew/Passenger Ratio	Slot Machines: . . . . .Yes
Entered Service: . . . . .July 2003	(lower beds/all berths): 2.5/3.1	Swimming Pools (outdoors): 2
Registry: . . . . .Panama	Cabins (total): 1,487	(+1 with magrodome)
Length (ft/m): 951.4/290.0	Size Range (sq ft/m): 179.7–482.2/	Swimming Pools (indoors): 0
Beam (ft/m): 116.4/35.5	16.7–44.8	Whirlpools: 7
Draft (ft/m): 27.0/8.2	Cabins (outside view): 917	Self-Service Launderette: . . . . .Yes
Propulsion/Propellers: . . . . .diesel-electric	Cabins (interior/no view): 570	Dedicated Cinema/Seats: . . . . .No
(63,400kW)/2	Cabins (for one person): 0	Library: . . . . .Yes

OVERALL SCORE: 1,380 OUT OF A POSSIBLE 2,000 POINTS

OVERVIEW. *Carnival Glory* is the 20th new ship for this very successful cruise line. It is, together with sister ship *Carnival Conquest*, the largest ship in the Carnival Cruise Lines fleet, and has the same generally well-balanced profile profile as its sisters: *Carnival Destiny Carnival Freedom, Carnival Glory, Carnival Liberty, Carnival Triumph* and *Carnival Victory*.

The ship is too big to transit the Panama Canal. With extremely short bows, it has the distinctive, large, swept-back wing-tipped funnel that is the trademark of Carnival Cruise Lines, in the company colors of red, white and blue. Outdoors on the pool deck is a giant poolside (Seaside Theater) movie screen.

The ship's interior decor is truly a fantasyland of colors (the central design theme), and every hue of the rainbow (and a few more) is represented in the public rooms and hallways throughout this ship. Also, the layout is logical, so finding your way around is easy. Most public rooms are located off the Kaleidoscope Boulevard, or main interior promenade (great for strolling and people-watching).

As for public areas, there are three decks full of lounges, 10 bars and lots of rooms to play in. There are two atriums: the largest, called The Colors Lobby, in the forward third of the ship (check out the interpretative paintings of US flags at the Color Bar) goes through nine decks – the colors on the towering atrium wall really are kaleidoscopic – while the aft atrium goes through three decks.

There are nightspots for just about every musical taste (except for opera, ballet and classical music lovers), and for those who like to gamble, the Camel Club Casino, with its Egyptian motif, is certainly large and action-packed; there are also more than 320 slot machines.

BERLITZ'S RATINGS		
	Possible	Achieved
Ship	500	408
Accommodation	200	157
Food	400	218
Service	400	259
Entertainment	100	82
Cruise	400	256

Youngsters are provided with good facilities, including their own two-level Children's Club (including an outdoor pool), and are well cared for with "Camp Carnival", the line's extensive children's program. Teens have a "Circle C" club of their own. Note that soft-drinks packages can be purchased for children (and adults).

Many pillars obstruct passengers flow. Those in the dining room, for example, make it difficult for the waiters to serve food properly. The public toilets are spartan and could do with some cheering up.

ACCOMMODATION. There are 20 cabin price categories, in 7 different grades: suites with private balcony; deluxe outside-view cabins with private balcony; outside-view cabins with private balcony; outside-view cabins with window; cabins with a porthole instead of a window; interior (no-view) cabins; and interior (no-view cabins) with upper and lower berths. There are five decks of cabins with private balcony – like sister ship *Carnival Conquest*. The price will depend on the grade, location and size you choose.

The standard cabins are of good size and come equipped with all the basics, although the furniture is rather square and angular, with no rounded edges. Three decks of cabins (eight on each deck, each with private balcony) overlook the stern. Most cabins with twin beds can be converted to a queen-size bed format. If you book one of the suites (Category 11 or 12 in the Carnival Cruise Lines brochure) you qualify for "Skipper's Club" priority check-in at any US homeland port – useful for getting ahead of the crowd.

There are even "fitness" cabins – in a block of 18 cabins located directly around and behind the SpaCarnival; so, fitness devotees can get out of bed and go straight to the tread-mill without having to go through any of the public rooms.

A gift basket is provided in all grades of cabins; it includes aloe soap, shampoo, conditioner, deodorant, breath mints, candy, and pain relief tablets (albeit all in sample sizes).

CUISINE. There are two principal dining rooms (Golden and Platinum). Both are two decks high, and both have a balcony level for diners (the balcony level in the aft dining room is larger than the other). The decor is interesting and includes wall coverings featuring a pattern of Japanese bonsai trees. Two additional wings provide room to accommodate large groups in a private dining arrangement.

There's a choice of either fixed time dining (6pm or 8:15pm), or flexible dining (any time between 5:45pm and 9:30pm). Although the menu choice looks good, the cuisine delivered is typically adequate, and quite unmemorable.

There is also a casual self-serve international food court-style lido deck eatery, the two-level Red Sail Restaurant. It has two main serving lines; it is adjacent to the aft pool and can be covered by a magrodome glass cover in inclement weather. Included in this eating mall are Paul's Deli, Mongolian Wok (pseudo-Chinese cuisine, with wok preparation), a 24-hour pizzeria, and a patisserie (there's an extra charge for yummy pastries, however), as well as a grill for fast foods such as hamburgers and hot dogs. Each night, the Cézanne Restaurant is turned into the "Seaview Bistro," and provides a casual (dress down) alternative to eating in the main dining rooms, serving pasta, steaks, salads and desserts (typically between 6pm and 9pm).
Alternative (Reservations-Only, Extra Cost) Dining: There is one reservations-only, extra cost, alternative dining spot, the Emerald Room. Fine table settings, china and silver-ware are featured, as well as leather-bound menus, cobalt-blue walls and lighting fixtures resembling giant emeralds.

ENTERTAINMENT. The Amber Palace Showlounge (named after Russia's great Amber Room, a gift by Frederick the Great in 1715) is a multi-deck showroom seating up to 1,400, and serves as the principal entertainment venue for large-scale entertainment, including Las-Vegas-style pro-duction shows and major cabaret acts. It has a revolving stage, hydraulic orchestra pit, superb sound, and seating on three levels (the upper levels being tiered through two decks). There is a proscenium over the stage that acts as a scenery loft.

For those who enjoy the body-throbbing sensations of loud music, the White Heat Dance Club is the ship's dis-cotheque, with its "Liberace-like" tall candelabra, and a video wall with projections live from the dance floor. Jazz lovers should enjoy the Bar Blue, while those whoe enjoy the sounds of the piano can do so in the Cinn-A-Bar, with its curved aluminum walls.

SPA/FITNESS. SpaCarnival spans two decks (with a total area of approximately 13,300 sq. ft/1,235 sq. meters), and is located directly above the navigation bridge in the forward part of the ship (it is accessed from the for-ward stairway). The area's decor is Polynesian in style, a theme that incorporates lush foliage, teak flooring, and a waterfall.

Facilities on the lower level include a solarium, eight treatment rooms, lecture rooms, sauna and steam rooms for men and women, and a beauty parlor; the upper level consists of a large gymnasium with floor-to-ceiling win-dows on three sides, including forward-facing ocean views, and an aerobics room with instructor-led classes (some at extra cost).

● **For more extensive general information on what a Carnival cruise is like, see pages 126–31.**

PLIMSOLL MARK

The safety of ships at sea and all those aboard owes much to the 19th-century social reformer Samuel Plimsoll, a member of the British Parliament concerned about the frequent loss of ships due to overloading. In those days, some shipowners would load their vessels down to the gunwales to squeeze every ounce of revenue out of them. They gambled on good weather, good fortune, and good seamanship to bring them safely into port. Consequently, many ships went to the bottom of the sea – the result of their buoyancy being seriously impaired by overloading.

Plimsoll helped to enact legis-lation that came to be known as the Merchant Shipping Act of 1875. This required shipowners to mark their vessels with a circular disc 12 inches (30 cm) long bisected by a line 18 inches (46 cm) long, as a measure of their maximum draft; that is, the depth to which a ship's hull could be safely immersed at sea.

The Merchant Shipping Act of 1890 went even further, and required the Plimsoll mark (or line) to be positioned on the sides of vessels in accordance with tables drawn up by competent authorities.

The Plimsoll mark is now found on the ships of every nation. The Plimsoll mark indicates three different depths: the depth to which a vessel can be loaded in fresh water, which is less buoyant than salt water; the depth in summer, when seas are generally calmer; and the depth in winter, when seas are much rougher.

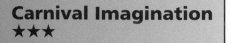

Carnival Imagination
★★★

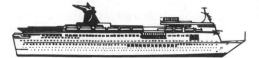

Size: . . . . .Large Resort Ship	Passenger Decks: 10	Cabins (wheelchair accessible): 22
Tonnage: 70,367	Total Crew: 920	Wheelchair accessibility . . . . .Fair
Lifestyle: . . . . .Standard	Passengers	Cabin Current: . . . . .110 volts
Cruise Line: . . . . . . .Carnival Cruise Lines	(lower beds/all berths): 2,056/2,634	Elevators: 14
Former Names: . . . . .Imagination	Passenger Space Ratio	Casino (gaming tables): . . . . .Yes
Builder: . . .Kvaerner Masa-Yards (Finland)	(lower beds/all berths): 34.4/26.7	Slot Machines: . . . . .Yes
Original Cost: . . . .$330 million	Crew/Passenger Ratio	Swimming Pools (outdoors): 3
Entered Service: . . . . .July 1995	(lower beds/all berths): 2.2/2.8	Swimming Pools (indoors): 0
Registry: . . . . .The Bahamas	Cabins (total): 1,028	Whirlpools: 6
Length (ft/m): 855.0/260.6	Size Range (sq ft/m): .173.2–409.7/16–38	Self-Service Launderette: . . . . .Yes
Beam (ft/m): 103.0/31.4	Cabins (outside view): 620	Dedicated Cinema/Seats: . . . . .No
Draft (ft/m): 25.9/7.9	Cabins (interior/no view): 408	Library: . . . . .Yes
Propulsion/Propellers: . . . . .diesel-electric	Cabins (for one person): 0	
(42,240 kW)/2	Cabins (with private balcony): 152	

OVERALL SCORE: 1,226 OUT OF A POSSIBLE 2,000 POINTS

OVERVIEW. *Carnival Imagination* has an angular appearance typical of today's space-creative designs. This is the fifth in a series of eight identically sized *Fantasy*-class Carnival ships. Almost vibration-free service is provided by the diesel electric propulsion system.

BERLITZ'S RATINGS

	Possible	Achieved
Ship	500	297
Accommodation	200	138
Food	400	213
Service	400	262
Entertainment	100	73
Cruise	400	243

The ship has expansive open deck areas (sadly, there is no walk-around open promenade deck), but they are inadequate when it is full and everyone wants to be out on deck. The aft decks tend to be less noisy, whereas all the activities focus on the main swimming pool and hot tubs (one with a thatched roof for shade). There is a "banked" jogging track outdoors on the deck above a large, glass-enclosed health spa.

The general passenger flow is good, and the interior design is clever, functional, and extremely colorful. The theme of the interior decor is musical muses and classical mythology. There is also a $1 million art collection. There are public entertainment lounges, bars and clubs galore, with something for everyone – except quiet space.

The public rooms, connected by a wide indoor boulevard, are a colorful mix of classic and contemporary design elements. There is a dramatic six-deck-high atrium, topped by a large glass dome. The large casino has almost non-stop action; an ATM machine is located outside it.

The Victorian-style library is a curious room, with intentionally mismatched furnishings (it reminds one of *Alice in Wonderland*), fine oriental rugs, and even a few books.

ACCOMMODATION. There are 13 price grades, linked to grade, size and location. See *Carnival Fantasy* for details.

CUISINE. There are two large, colorful, noisy dining rooms

(Pride, located midships, and Spirit, located aft, with the galley between the two). Both are non-smoking. Shorts are permitted in the dining room for one dinner each cruise. There's a choice of either fixed time dining (6pm or 8:15pm), or flexible dining (any time between 5:45pm and 9:30pm).

The Lido Cafe self-serve buffets are very basic, as is the selection of breads, rolls, fruit and cheeses. At night, the "Seaview Bistro", as the Lido Cafe becomes known, provides a casual (dress down) alternative to eating in the main dining rooms, serving pasta, steaks, salads and desserts (usually 6–9pm).

There's also a Pizzeria, open round the clock and typically serving over 500 pizzas every single day.

ENTERTAINMENT. The Dynasty Showlounge is the principal venue for large-scale production shows and major cabaret acts, but 20 pillars obstruct the views from several seats.

SPA/FITNESS. The Nautica Spa is a large glass-wrapped health, fitness and spa complex consisting of a gymnasium with oceanview windows, an aerobics exercise room, men's and women's changing rooms, sauna and steam rooms, and beauty salon.

A common complaint from passengers is that there are not enough staff to keep the area clean and tidy, and used towels are often strewn around the changing rooms, particularly on the men's side.

● **For more extensive information on what a Carnival cruise is like, see pages 126–31, and for more information on the Fantasy-class ships, see *Carnival Fantasy*.**

Carnival Inspiration
★★★

Size:	.Large Resort Ship	Passenger Decks:	.10
Tonnage:	.70,367	Total Crew:	.920
Lifestyle:	.Standard	Passengers	
Cruise Line:	.Carnival Cruise Lines	(lower beds/all berths):	.2,056/2,634
Former Names:	.Inspiration	Passenger Space Ratio	
Builder:	.Kvaerner Masa-Yards (Finland)	(lower beds/all berths):	.34.4/26.7
Original Cost:	.$270 million	Crew/Passenger Ratio	
Entered Service:	.Apr 1996	(lower beds/all berths):	.2.2/2.8
Registry:	.The Bahamas	Cabins (total):	.1,028
Length (ft/m):	.855.0/260.6	Size Range (sq ft/m):	.173.2–409.7/16–38
Beam (ft/m):	.103.0/31.4	Cabins (outside view):	.620
Draft (ft/m):	.25.9/7.9	Cabins (interior/no view):	.408
Propulsion/Propellers:	.diesel-electric	Cabins (for one person):	.0
	(42,240 kW)/2	Cabins (with private balcony):	.152

Cabins (wheelchair accessible):	.22
Wheelchair accessibility	.Fair
Cabin Current:	.110 volts
Elevators:	.14
Casino (gaming tables):	.Yes
Slot Machines:	.Yes
Swimming Pools (outdoors):	.3
Swimming Pools (indoors):	.0
Whirlpools:	.6
Self-Service Launderette:	.Yes
Dedicated Cinema/Seats:	.No
Library:	.Yes

OVERALL SCORE: 1,223 OUT OF A POSSIBLE 2,000 POINTS

OVERVIEW. The ship has expansive open deck areas (sadly, there is no walk-around open promenade deck), but they quickly become inadequate when it is full and everyone wants to be out on deck (the aft decks are less noisy, because all the activities are focused on the main swimming pool and hot tubs). Almost vibration-free service is provided by the diesel electric propulsion system.

The general passenger flow is good, and the interior design is clever, functional, and extremely colorful. There is lots of neon lighting, and the color combinations are quite vivid. The decor itself is themed after the arts (in an art nouveau style) and literature. There is also a $1 million art collection. Particularly interesting is an avant-garde rendition of the famed *Mona Lisa*, in Pablo's Lounge. There are public entertainment lounges, bars and clubs galore. Most lead off from a wide indoor boulevard.

As in its sister ships, there is a six-deck-high atrium, topped by a large glass dome. The atrium has scrolled shapes resembling the necks and heads of violins, and a marble staircase. The Shakespeare Library is a fine, stately room (25 of his quotations adorn the oak veneer), but there are few books. Another dazzling room is the Rock and Roll Discotheque, with its guitar-shaped dance floor and video dance club and dozens of video monitors.

ACCOMMODATION. There are 13 grades. The price you pay will depend on the grade, size and location you choose. For a detailed explanation, see the entry for *Carnival Fantasy*.

CUISINE. There are two large, rather noisy – or perhaps one should say "lively" – dining rooms (Mardi Gras, located

BERLITZ'S RATINGS

	Possible	Achieved
Ship	500	295
Accommodation	200	138
Food	400	213
Service	400	262
Entertainment	100	73
Cruise	400	242

midships, and Carnival, located aft, with the galley between them), both of which are non-smoking. The service is attentive, but far too fast and assertive, and lacks any kind of finesse. There's a choice of either fixed time dining (6pm or 8:15pm), or flexible dining (any time between 5:45 and 9:30pm).

Carnival meals stress quantity, not quality, although the company constantly works hard to improve the cuisine. However, food and its taste are still not the company's strongest points (you get what you pay for, remember).

Casual meals can be taken at informal food outlets such as the Brasserie Bar and Grill, which also includes an always-open Pizzeria (it serves over 500 every single day). At night, the "Seaview Bistro," as the Lido Café becomes known, provides a casual (dress down) alternative to eating in the main dining rooms, serving pasta, steaks, salads and desserts (it typically is in operation from 6pm to 9pm).

ENTERTAINMENT. The Paris Showlounge is the principal venue for large-scale production shows and major cabaret acts, although 20 pillars obstruct views from some seats.

SPA/FITNESS. The Nautica Spa is a large glass-enclosed complex consisting of a gymnasium with a large array of the latest in muscle-pumping electronic machines, an aerobics exercise room, men's and women's changing rooms, sauna and steam rooms, and beauty salon.

● For more extensive information on what a Carnival cruise is like, see pages 126–31, and for more information on the Fantasy-class ships, see *Carnival Fantasy*.

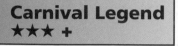

Carnival Legend
★★★ +

Size: . . . . .Large Resort Ship	Passenger Decks: 12	Wheelchair accessibility . . . . .Good
Tonnage: .85,920	Total Crew: 1,030	Cabin Current: . . . . .110 volts
Lifestyle: . . . . .Standard	Passengers	Elevators: 15
Cruise Line: . . . . . . .Carnival Cruise Lines	(lower beds/all berths): 2,124/2,680	Casino (gaming tables): . . . . .Yes
Former Names: . . . . .none	Passenger Space Ratio	Slot Machines: . . . . .Yes
Builder: . . . . .Kvaerner Masa-Yards	(lower beds/all berths): 40.4/32.0	Swimming Pools (outdoors): . . . . .2+1
Original Cost: . . . .$375 million	Crew/Passenger Ratio	children's pool
Entered Service: . . . . .Aug 2002	(lower beds/all berths): 2.2/2.6	Swimming Pools (indoors): 1
Registry: . . . . .Panama	Cabins (total): 1,062	(indoor/outdoor)
Length (ft/m): 959.6/292.5	Size Range (sq ft/m): .185–490/17.1–45.5	Whirlpools: 5
Beam (ft/m): 105.6/32.2	Cabins (outside view): 849	Self-Service Launderette: . . . . .Yes
Draft (ft/m): 25.5/7.8	Cabins (interior/no view): 213	Dedicated Cinema/Seats: . . . . .No
Propulsion/Propellers: . . . . .diesel-electric	Cabins (for one person): 0	Library: . . . . .Yes
(62,370 kW)/2 azimuthing pods	Cabins (with private balcony): 750	
(17.6 MW each)	Cabins (wheelchair accessible): 16	

OVERALL SCORE: 1,388 OUT OF A POSSIBLE 2,000 POINTS

OVERVIEW. *Carnival Legend* (sister ship to *Carnival Miracle, Carnival Pride* and *Carnival Spirit*) is the 18th new ship for this very successful cruise line. Its launch made headlines in 2002 when actress Dame Judi Dench, the celebrity chosen to break the traditional bottle of champagne on its hull, had difficulty doing so; a final hefty heave smashed the bottle, drenching Dame Judi with champagne. The ship, whose bows are extremely short, has the distinctive, large, swept-back wing-tipped funnel that is the Carnival's trademark, in the company colors of red, white and blue.

This ship is longer than the company's larger quintet (*Carnival Conquest, Carnival Destiny, Carnival Glory, Carnival Triumph,* and *Carnival Victory*). The colourful atrium lobby, spanning eight decks, has a wall decoration best seen from any of the multiple viewing balconies on any deck above the main lobby floor level. Take a drink from the lobby bar and look upwards – the surroundings are stunning, with a mural of the Colossus of Rhodes the focal point.

The interior decor is dedicated to the world's great legends, from wonders of the ancient world and heroes of antiquity to 20th-century jazz masters and great athletes – an eclectic mix that somehow works well. There are two entertainment/public room decks, the upper with an exterior promenade deck – something new for this fun cruise line.

Without doubt, the most dramatic room aboard this ship is the Follies Showlounge. Spanning three decks in the forward section of the ship, it recalls the movie palaces of the 1920s. Spiral stairways at the back of the lounge connect all three levels. Stage shows are best seen from the upper three levels, from where the sight lines are reasonably good.

BERLITZ'S RATINGS

	Possible	Achieved
Ship	500	401
Accommodation	200	148
Food	400	229
Service	400	252
Entertainment	100	81
Cruise	400	277

Directly underneath is the Firebird Lounge, which has a bar in its starboard aft section.

A small wedding chapel is forward of the uppermost level of the two main entertainment decks, adjacent to the library and internet center. Other facilities include a winding shopping street with several boutique stores, photo gallery, video games room, an observation balcony in the center of the vessel (at the top of the multi-deck atrium), and the large Club Merlin Casino, with its castle-like atmosphere (damsels, knights and wizards are painted on the walls).

In the medical department, Tele-Radiology is installed. This system enables shipboard physicians to digitally transmit X-rays and other patient information to shore-side facilities – useful for peace of mind for passengers and crew.

The information desk in the lobby is quite small, and can become congested. It is hard to escape from noise and loud music (it's even played in cabin hallways and lifts), not to mention smokers, and masses of people walking around in unsuitable clothing, clutching plastic sport drinks bottles, at any time of the day or night. Many private balconies are not so private, and can be overlooked from public locations.

Many pillars obstruct passenger flow (those in the dining room, for example, make it difficult for proper food service by the waiters). Books and computers are cohabitants in the ship's library/internet center, but anyone wanting a book has to lean over others who may be using a computer – an awkward arrangement.

ACCOMMODATION. There are 20 cabin categories, priced by grade, location and size. The range of cabins includes suites (with private balcony), outside-view cabins with private balcony, 68 ocean view cabins with French doors (pseudo balconies that have doors which open, but no balcony to step out onto), and a healthy proportion of standard outside-view to interior (no view) cabins.

All cabins have spy-hole doors, and have twin beds that can be converted into a queen-sized bed, individually controlled air-conditioning, television, and telephone. A number of cabins on the lowest deck have views that are obstructed by lifeboats. Some cabins can accommodate a third and fourth person, but have little closet space, and there's only one personal safe. There is no separate radio in each cabin – instead, audio channels are provided on the in-cabin TV system, but you can't turn the picture off. Nor can you turn off the air conditioning in cabins or bathrooms.

A gift basket of (sample sized) personal amenities is provided in all grades.

If you book one of the suites (Category 11 or 12 in the Carnival Cruise Lines brochure), you automatically qualify for "Skipper's Club" priority check-in at any US homeland port – useful for getting ahead of the crowd.

Among the most desirable suites and cabins are those on five of the aft-facing decks; these have private balconies overlooking the stern and ship's wash. You might think that these units would suffer from vibration, but they don't – a bonus provided by the pod propulsion system *(see page 45)*.

For the ultimate in extra space, it would be worth your while trying one of the large deluxe balcony suites on Deck 6, with its own private teakwood balcony. These tend to be quiet suites, with a large lounge and sleeping areas, a good-sized bathroom with twin washbasins, toilet and bidet, and whirlpool bathtub. They have twin beds that convert to a queen-sized bed, three (illuminated) closets, and a huge amount of drawer space. The balcony has an outside light, and a wide teakwood deck with smoked glass and wood railing (you could easily seat 10 people here).

Even the largest suites, however, are quite small compared with suites aboard other ships of a similar size – for example, Celebrity Cruises' *Constellation, Infinity, Millennium*, and *Summit*, where penthouse suites measure up to 2,530 sq. ft (235 sq. meters). Carnival Cruise Lines has fallen behind in the move to larger living spaces, and, with this ship, lost an opportunity to provide more space. But Carnival's philosophy has always been to get its passengers out into public areas to socialize and spend money.

CUISINE. This ship has a single, large, two-decks-high, 1,300-seat main dining room, Truffles Restaurant, with seating on both upper and main levels. Its huge ceiling has large murals of a china pattern made famous by Royal Copenhagen, and wall-mounted glass display cases contain fine china. The galley is located underneath the restaurant, with waiter access by escalators. There are tables for two, four, six or eight, and small rooms on both upper and lower levels can be closed off for groups of up to 60. finesse. There's a choice of either fixed time dining (6pm or 8:15pm), or flexible dining (between 5:45pm and 9:30pm)

For casual eaters, while there is no lido cafe, the Unicorn Cafe is an extensive eatery that forms the aft third of Deck 9 (part of it also wraps around the upper section of the huge atrium). Murals of unicorns are everywhere. The cafe includes a central area with small buffet counters (deli sandwich corner, Asian corner, rotisserie, and International counter); there are salad counters, a dessert counter, and a 24-hour Pizzeria counter, all of which form a large eatery with both indoor and outdoor seating. Movement around the buffet area is slow, and you have to stand in line for everything. Each night, the Unicorn Cafe becomes Seaview Bistro, for casual, serve-yourself dinners (typically open 6pm–9.30pm).

Alternative (Reservations-Only, Extra Cost) Dining: The Golden Fleece Supper Club is a more upscale dining spot atop the ship, with just 156 seats and a show kitchen. It is located on two of the uppermost decks of the ship, above the Unicorn, in the lower, forward section of the funnel housing, with great views over the multi-deck atrium. The decor is set around the Greek legend of Jason and the Argonauts. The bar is the setting for a large sculpture of the Golden Fleece. Fine table settings, china and silverware are featured, as well as leather-bound menus.

ENTERTAINMENT. The Follies Showlounge is the ship's principal venue for large-scale production shows and cabaret shows. Stage shows are best seen from the upper three levels. Directly underneath the showlounge is the Firebird Lounge, which has a bar in its starboard aft section.

Almost every lounge/bar, including Billie's Bar (a piano lounge), and Satchmo's Club (a nightclub with bar and dance floor) has live music in the evening. Finally, for the very lively, there's the disco; and there's always karaoke as well as a Passenger Talent Show during each cruise.

SPA/FITNESS. SpaCarnival spans two decks, is located directly above the navigation bridge in the forward part of the ship and has 13,700 sq. ft (1,272 sq. meters) of space. Facilities on the lower level include a solarium, eight treatment rooms, lecture rooms, sauna and steam rooms for men and women, and a beauty parlor; the upper level consists of a large gymnasium with floor-to-ceiling windows on three sides, including forward-facing ocean views, and an aerobics room with instructor-led classes.

There are two centrally located swimming pools outdoors, and one can be used in inclement weather due to its retractable glass dome. There are two whirlpool tubs, adjacent to the swimming pools. A winding water slide that spans two decks in height is located at an aft, upper deck. Another smaller pool is available for children. An outdoor jogging track is located around the ship's mast and the forward third of the ship; it doesn't go around the whole ship, but it's long enough for some serious walking.

● **For more extensive general information on what a Carnival cruise is like, see pages 126–31.**

Carnival Liberty
★★★ +

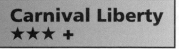

Size:	Large Resort Ship	Passenger Decks:	13
Tonnage:	110,239	Total Crew:	1,160
Lifestyle:	Standard	Passengers	
Cruise Line:	Carnival Cruise Lines	(lower beds/all berths):	2,974/3,700
Former Names:	none	Passenger Space Ratio	
Builder:	Fincantieri (Italy)	(lower beds/all berths):	37.0/29.7
Original Cost:	$500 million	Crew/Passenger Ratio	
Entered Service:	July 2005	(lower beds/all berths):	2.5/3.1
Registry:	Panama	Cabins (total):	1,487
Length (ft/m):	951.4/290.0	Size Range (sq ft/m):	179.7–482.2/
Beam (ft/m):	116.4/35.5		16.7–44.8
Draft (ft/m):	27.0/8.2	Cabins (outside view):	917
Propulsion/Propellers:	diesel-electric	Cabins (interior/no view):	570
	(63,400kW)/2	Cabins (for one person):	0

Cabins (with private balcony):	574
Cabins (wheelchair accessible):	25
Wheelchair accessibility	Good
Cabin Current:	110 volts
Elevators:	14
Casino (gaming tables):	Yes
Slot Machines:	Yes
Swimming Pools (outdoors):	2
	(+1 with magrodome)
Swimming Pools (indoors):	0
Whirlpools:	7
Self-Service Launderette:	Yes
Dedicated Cinema/Seats:	No
Library:	Yes

OVERALL SCORE: 1,383 OUT OF A POSSIBLE 2,000 POINTS

OVERVIEW. *Carnival Liberty* is the 23rd new ship for this incredibly successful cruise line. It shares the same generally well-balanced profile as sisters *Carnival Conquest, Carnival Destiny, Carnival Freedom, Carnival Glory, Carnival Triumph, Carnival Valor* and *Carnival Victory*. The ship is unable to transit the Panama Canal, due to its size, so it's called a non-Panamax ship. With extremely short bows, it has the distinctive, large, swept-back wing-tipped funnel that is the trademark of Carnival Cruise Lines, in the company colors of red, white and blue. A giant Seaside Theater LED movie screen adorns the open pool deck.

The ship's decor, in the public rooms, hallways and atrium, features a design theme that salutes the master trades, like ironwork, masonry, pottery and painting. The layout is logical, so finding your way around is easy. Most public rooms are located off one main boulevard (an interior promenade that is great for strolling and people watching – particularly from the Jardin Café or Promenade Bar). Other hangouts and drinking places include The Stage (live music/karaoke lounge), the Flower Bar (main lobby), Gloves Bar (sports Bar), Paparazzi (wine bar), and The Cabinet.

As for public areas, there are three decks full of lounges, 10 bars and lots of rooms to play in. There are two atriums: the largest, in the forward third of the ship goes through nine decks (the Grand Villa Garden Atrium combines all four of the design themes), while a small aft atrium spans three decks.

There are nightspots for just about every musical taste (except for opera, ballet and classical music lovers), and for those who like to gamble, the Czar's Palace Casino, with its Russian motifs and theme, is certainly large and

BERLITZ'S RATINGS

	Possible	Achieved
Ship	500	411
Accommodation	200	157
Food	400	218
Service	400	257
Entertainment	100	82
Cruise	400	258

action-packed; there are more than 320 slot machines.

Youngsters are provided with good facilities, including their own two-level Children's Club (including an outdoor pool), and are well cared for with "Camp Carnival", the line's extensive children's program. Soft-drinks packages can be purchased for children (and adults).

Many pillars obstruct passenger flow, and those in the two main restaurants constrain the waiters. The public toilets are spartan and could do with some cheering up.

ACCOMMODATION. There are 20 cabin price categories, in 7 different grades: suites with private balcony; deluxe outside-view cabins with private balcony; outside-view cabins with private balcony; outside-view cabins with window; cabins with a porthole instead of a window; interior (no-view) cabins; and interior (no-view cabins) with upper and lower berths. There are five decks of cabins with private balconies. The price depends on the grade, location and size you choose.

The standard cabins are of good size and come equipped with all the basics, although the furniture is rather square and angular, with no rounded edges. Three decks of cabins (eight on each deck, each with private balcony) overlook the stern. Most cabins with twin beds can be converted to a queen-size bed format.

Book one of the suites (Category 11 or 12 in the Carnival Cruise Lines brochure) and you qualify for "Skipper's Club" priority check-in at any US homeland port – useful for getting ahead of the crowd.

There are even "fitness" cabins aboard this ship – in a block of 18 cabins located directly around and behind

SpaCarnival; so, fitness devotees can get out of bed and go straight to the treadmill without having to go through any of the public rooms first.

A gift basket is provided in all grades; it includes aloe soap, shampoo, conditioner, deodorant, breath mints, candy, and pain relief tablets (albeit all in sample sizes).

CUISINE. There are two principal dining rooms (Golden Olympian Restaurant, forward, seating 744: and Silver Olympian Restaurant, aft, seating 1,122). Both are two decks high, and both include a balcony level for diners (the balcony level in the aft dining room is larger than the other). Two additional wings (the Persian Room and Satin Room) have room to accommodate large groups in a private dining arrangement. arrangement. There's a choice of either fixed time dining (6pm or 8:15pm), or flexible dining (any time between 5:45pm and 9:30pm). Although the menu choice looks good, the actual cuisine delivered is typically adequate, and quite unmemorable.

There is also a casual self-serve international food court-style lido deck eatery, the two-level Emile's. It has two main serving lines; it is adjacent to the aft pool and can be covered by a magrodome glass cover in inclement weather. Included in this eating mall are a deli, Chinese cuisine eatery, with wok preparation, a 24-hour pizzeria, and a patisserie (there's an extra charge for yummy pastries, however), as well as a grill for fast foods such as hamburgers and hot dogs. Each night, Emilie's morphs into the "Seaview Bistro", and provides a casual (dress down) alternative to eating in the main dining rooms, serving pasta, steaks, salads and desserts (typically 6pm–9pm).

Alternative (Reservations-Only, Extra Cost) Dining: There is one reservations-only, extra cost, alternative dining spot, Harry's. Fine table settings, china and silverware are featured, as well as leather-bound menus, cobalt-blue walls and lighting fixtures resembling giant emeralds.

ENTERTAINMENT. The Venetian Palace Showlounge is a multi-deck showroom seating up to 1,400, and serves as the principal entertainment venue for large-scale entertainment, including Las-Vegas-style production shows and major cabaret acts. It has a revolving stage, hydraulic orchestra pit, superb sound, and seating on three levels (the upper levels being tiered through two decks). There is a proscenium over the stage that acts as a scenery loft.

The Victoria Lounge, located aft, seats 425 and typically features live music and late-night cabaret acts, including adult comedy.

Body-throbbing loud music sensations can be found in the Tattooed Lady Dance Club is the ship's discotheque; it includes a video wall with projections live from the dance floor. Piano bar lovers should enjoy the 100-seat Piano Man piano bar.

SPA/FITNESS. SpaCarnival spans two decks (with a total area of approximately 13,300 sq. ft/1,235 sq. meters), and is located directly above the navigation bridge in the forward part of the ship (it is accessed from the forward stairway). The decor is Polynesian in style, a theme that incorporates lush foliage, teak flooring, and a waterfall.

Facilities on the lower level include a solarium, eight treatment rooms, lecture rooms, sauna and steam rooms for men and women, and a beauty parlor; the upper level consists of a large gymnasium with floor-to-ceiling windows on three sides, including forward-facing ocean views, and an aerobics room with instructor-led classes (some cost extra). It is always a good idea to book sessions as far in advance as possible.

● **For more extensive general information on what a Carnival cruise is like, see pages 126–31.**

Carnival Magic
NOT YET RATED

Size: ....Large Resort Ship	Passenger Decks: 13	Cabins (with private balcony):...........887
Tonnage: 128,251	Total Crew: 1,367	Cabins (wheelchair accessible): 35
Lifestyle:......................................Standard	Passengers	Wheelchair accessibility ....Good
Cruise Line: ....Carnival Cruise Lines	(lower beds/all berths):........3,646/4,631	Cabin Current: ....110 volts
Former Names: ....none	Passenger Space Ratio	Elevators: 14
Builder:.........................Fincantieri (Italy)	(lower beds/all berths):............35.1/27.6	Casino (gaming tables):......................Yes
Original Cost:.......................$740 million	Crew/Passenger Ratio	Slot Machines:...................................Yes
Entered Service:.......................Jun 2011	(lower beds/all berths):................2.6/3.3	Swimming Pools (outdoors):.................2
Registry:.....................................Panama	Cabins (total):.................................1,823	Swimming Pools (indoors): 0
Length (ft/m):....................1,004.0/306.0	Size Range (sq ft/m): 185.0–430.5/	Whirlpools: 7
Beam (ft/m):............................158.0/48.0	17.1–40.0	Self-Service Launderette:..................Yes
Draft (ft/m):............................26.2/8.0	Cabins (outside view):....................1,145	Dedicated Cinema/Seats: ....No
Propulsion/Propellers: ......Diesel-electric	Cabins (interior/no view):..................678	Library: ....Yes
(75.6 MW)/2	Cabins (for one person):........................0	

OVERALL SCORE: NYR OUT OF A POSSIBLE 2,000 POINTS

OVERVIEW. *Carnival Magic* is a sister ship to *Carnival Dream,* introduced in 2010, and both are 13% larger than their close sister *Carnival Splendour.* Although the ship's bows are short, the ship's profile is actually nicely balanced, with a rakish front and more rounded stern than previous Carnival ships. The propulsion system consists of the conventional twin rudder, with twin (six-blade) propellers. However, the ship is based on the original design for *Carnival Destiny,* the first cruise ship to top 100,000 tons in measurement, and includes some of the design flaws of the *Destiny*-class, with a passenger capacity that has been increased by just over 1,000. Strangely, the cabin numbering system – even numbers, starboard side; odd numbers, port side – goes against the maritime tradition that places even-numbered cabins on the port, or left, side; and odd-numbered cabins on the starboard, or right, side.

There are numerous pools and open deck nooks and crannies – but one less pool than the original *Carnival Destiny.* One thing that stands out, however, is the long Twister Water Slide, part of The Waterworks on pool deck. There's also an adults-only, extra-charge retreat called Serenity, and numerous other features. However, the general open deck space is really not enough for the number of passengers, so sunbed loungers are tightly packed together with no room for drinks tables.

The ship has a full walk-around open promenade deck, which is lined with deck chairs. Four scenic hot tubs are cantilevered over the ship's side. Along the outdoor promenade, four "scenic whirlpools" are cantilevered over the sea, and provide fine sea views. Higher up, Lido Deck 10 offers a very good open-deck area, with a tropical,

BERLITZ'S RATINGS		
	Possible	Achieved
Ship	500	NYR
Accommodation	200	NYR
Food	400	NYR
Service	400	NYR
Entertainment	100	NYR
Cruise	400	NYR

resort-style main pool and giant Seaside Theatre LED screen for outdoor movies. *Carnival Magic* is the second Carnival ship to stage a laser light show outdoors – which the AIDA Cruises' ships have had since 1996.

The interior decor is vivid. The stunning main lobby is the connection point for ship functions and people. Take the glass-walled elevators for a neat view, though you may need sunglasses. It's good to see there are three main elevator towers: forward, midships, and aft, unlike larger ships such as *Oasis of the Seas,* which, although it carries many more passengers, has only two main elevator towers. So, well done Carnival, better for safety.

The Ocean Plaza, a new feature for Carnival, is designed to be a comfortable place by day and a trendy entertainment venue by night. The indoor/outdoor café and live music venue has a bandstand where a variety of musical genres will be showcased, and a large circular dance floor, and around 190 seats. A floor-to-ceiling curved glass wall separates the room, dividing indoor and outdoor seating areas. An adjacent bar also offers espresso and cappuccino coffees, gelato ice creams, and pastries.

A wide variety of lounges, bars and nightspots, including a dance club with a twist, offering indoor/outdoor access, are accessible via an 11-deck-high atrium whose ground level has a neatly cantilevered bandstand atop a massive dance floor. The Page Turner (great name) is the ship's library, while Jackpot is – you guessed it – the colourful, large, lively and noisy casino. Other rooms include The Song (Jazz Bar); Ocean Plaza (a sort of quiet area during the day, but lively at night with live entertainment); internet-connect computer terminals are refreshingly scattered throughout the ship – although most have no privacy. There's also a 232-capacity conference room called The Chambers.

There is much congestion just prior to the second seating, on both Upper- and Lower Dream Streets, both of which are located on the starboard side. Further congestion appears around the photo gallery, which surrounds the atrium lobby. All in all, this is a ship designed to encourage you to spend money on all the extras you'll need – especially if have children with you.

The onboard currency is the US dollar, and gratuities are automatically charged to your onboard account.

CHILDREN: There are plenty of facilities, purpose-built for the line's three age-related children's programs: "Camp Carnival" for ages 2–11, "Circle C" for 12- to 14-year-olds, and "Club O2" for teens 15–17, together with a full schedule of morning-to-night activities catering to each age group. About 5,000 sq.ft. of space has been devoted to junior cruisers. Also, Carnival WaterWorks, an expansive aqua park offering exhilarating water slides and various water spray apparatus, should be a hit with active kids.

ACCOMMODATION. There are 19 cabin price categories, but just six cabin types, to choose from. But, whether you go for high end or low end, all accommodation includes the Carnival Comfort Bed with plush mattresses, good-quality duvets and linens and pillows. However, the straight accommodation deck hallways create rather a cell block look – and they are bright, very bright, even at night. There are also lot of interior (no view) cabins. But the cabins to go for are those at the stern of the ship, with great rearward ocean views on Decks 6, 7, 8 and 9.

"Deluxe" ocean-view cabins, with two bathrooms, provide comfort and convenience for families. In addition to twin beds that convert to a king, decent closet space and elegant decor, the two-bathroom configuration includes one full bathroom and a second bathroom containing a small tub with shower and sink. Some cabins can accommodate five persons, useful for families. There is a wide selection of balcony cabins and suites, including "Cove Balcony" cabins that are the closest to the waterline.

Additionally, adjacent to the Cloud 9 Spa, are 65 "Cloud 9" spa cabins, designated as no-smoking. They provide a number of "exclusive" amenities and privileges. You should be aware that some cabins are located directly over loud late-night venues, with poor soundproofing. Also, cabins on Deck 12 are subject to lots of noise from kids having fun on the deck above – so afternoon naps are out.

CUISINE. There are two main restaurants: a 1,180-seat midships dining room, and a smaller 828-seat aft dining room. Each has two levels: main and balcony, with the galley set on the lower level. Two small restaurant annexes can be reserved by small groups as a private dining room.

The Lido Restaurant, the ship's poorly-lit self-serve lido buffet facility, has indoor/outdoor seating areas on the lower (main) level, and indoor-only seating on the upper level. A number of designated areas serve different types of ethnic cuisine, including a Mongolian Wok and Pasta Bar on the upper level, which is open between 6pm and 9pm for tablecloth-free buffet dinners.

The layout invites congestion around the beverage stands. Go off-peak and it's much better.

Alternative (Reservations-Only, Extra-Cost) Dining: The extra-charge Supper Club (and bar) seats 139, has great views to port and starboard from its aft location high up on Spa Deck 12, and an à la carte menu. It has fine table settings, china and silverware, as well as leather-bound menus. The featured specialties are steaks and seafood items. It's worth paying the cover charge to get a taste of what Carnival can really deliver in terms of food that is of better quality than that served in the main dining rooms. It's also the place to go for celebrating something special, or just to get away from the noise of the large dining rooms.

There's also a sushi venue; note the large fish behind the sushi bar.

ENTERTAINMENT. The 1,964-seat showlounge spans three decks at the front of the ship, with seating set in a horseshoe shape around a large proscenium arched stage; the sightlines are generally good, except from some of the seats at the back of the lowest level. Large-scale production shows, with lots of feathers and skimpy costumes are staged, together with snappy cabaret acts, all with a live showband as accompaniment.

The 425-seat Burgundy Lounge, at the aft end of the ship – opposite to the showlounge, at the front – has a stage, dance floor, large bar, and is a comedy venue, including late-night raunchy "adult comedy." Caliente is the ship's hot club; it provides Latin music for vibrant dancing and hot-foot style, but at ear-splitting volume.

SPA/FITNESS. The expansive 23,750-sq-ft (2,206 sq-meter) Cloud 9 Spa is a large and elaborate health and wellness center; it is positioned over three decks in the front section of the ship and well appointed. The uppermost deck includes indoor/outdoor private spa relaxation areas, at extra cost. A spiral staircase connects the two decks, and the Steiner-operated spa offers a wide range of treatments.

There are 10 treatment rooms, including a VIP room, a large massage room for couples, and a Rasul mud treatment room, plus two dry flotation rooms. A "Thermal Suite" (extra charge) comes with the typical sensory-enhanced soothing heated chambers: Laconium, Tepidarium, Aroma and Oriental steam baths.

There are two steam rooms, one each for men and women, and a small unisex sauna with a floor-to-ceiling window on its starboard side. As for sports facilities, *Carnival Magic* is the second "Fun Ship" to include a two-level miniature golf course.

● **For more extensive general information on what a Carnival cruise is like, see pages 126–31.**

Carnival Miracle
★★★ +

Size:	Large Resort Ship	Passenger Decks:	13	Cabins (wheelchair accessible):	16
Tonnage:	85,920	Total Crew:	961	Wheelchair accessibility	Good
Lifestyle:	Standard	Passengers		Cabin Current:	110 volts
Cruise Line:	Carnival Cruise Lines	(lower beds/all berths):	2,124/2,680	Elevators:	15
Former Names:	none	Passenger Space Ratio		Casino (gaming tables):	Yes
Builder:	Kvaerner Masa-Yards	(lower beds/all berths):	40.4/32.0	Slot Machines:	Yes
Original Cost:	$375 million	Crew/Passenger Ratio		Swimming Pools (outdoors):	2+1
Entered Service:	April 2004	(lower beds/all berths):	2.2/2.7		children's pool
Registry:	Panama	Cabins (total):	1,062	Swimming Pools (indoors):	1
Length (ft/m):	959.6/292.5	Size Range (sq ft/m):	185.0–490.0/		(indoor/outdoor)
Beam (ft/m):	105.6/32.2		17.1–45.5	Whirlpools:	5
Draft (ft/m):	25.5/7.8	Cabins (outside view):	849	Self-Service Launderette:	Yes
Propulsion/Propellers:	diesel-electric	Cabins (interior/no view):	213	Dedicated Cinema/Seats:	No
	(62,370 kW)/2 azimuthing pods	Cabins (for one person):	0	Library:	Yes)
	(17.6 MW each)	Cabins (with private balcony):	750		

OVERALL SCORE: 1,387 OUT OF A POSSIBLE 2,000 POINTS

OVERVIEW. *Carnival Miracle* (sister to *Carnival Legend, Carnival Pride* and *Carnival Spirit*) is the 21st new ship for this very successful cruise line. Built from more than 100 blocks (each weighing up to 450 tons), the ship, whose bows are extremely short, has the distinctive, large, swept-back wing-tipped funnel that is the trademark of Carnival Cruise Lines, in the company colors of red, white and blue. The ship is longer than the company's larger quintet (*Carnival Conquest, Carnival Destiny, Carnival Glory, Carnival Triumph,* and *Carnival Victory*).

BERLITZ'S RATINGS		
	Possible	Achieved
Ship	500	401
Accommodation	200	148
Food	400	229
Service	400	251
Entertainment	100	81
Cruise	400	277

The interior decor is very artistic (and overwhelmingly colorful – there are no restful colors), with "fictional icons" as the design theme, with such luminaries as the Phantom of the Opera, Sherlock Holmes, Philip Marlowe, and Captain Ahab among the many art images (bronze statues of Orpheis, Sirenes, and Ulysses adorn the swimming pools).

The dramatic atrium lobby space spans eight decks and presents a stunning wall decoration best seen from any of the multiple viewing balconies on each deck above the main lobby floor level. Take a drink from the lobby bar and look upwards – the surroundings are simply stunning, with a mural of the Colossus of Rhodes, one of the seven wonders of the world. The interior decor is dedicated to the world's great legends, from wonders of the ancient world and heroes of antiquity to 20th-century jazz masters and great athletes – an eclectic mix of "entertainment architecture" that somehow works well.

There are two whole entertainment/public room decks, the upper of which also has an exterior promenade deck – something new for this fun cruise line. A small wedding chapel is forward of the uppermost level of the two main entertainment decks, adjacent to the library and internet center. Other facilities include a winding shopping street with several boutique stores (including those selling the usual Carnival logo items), photo gallery, video games room, an observation balcony in the center of the vessel (at the top of the multi-deck atrium), and a large Club Merlin Casino, with its castle-like atmosphere (damsels, knights and wizards are painted on the walls).

In the medical department, Tele-Radiology is installed. This system enables shipboard physicians to digitally transmit X-rays and other patient information to shore-side facilities – useful for peace of mind for passengers and crew.

The information desk in the lobby is really quite small, and can become quite congested. It is difficult to escape from noise and loud music (it's even played in cabin hallways and lifts), not to mention smokers, and masses of people walking around in unsuitable clothing, clutching plastic sport drinks bottles, at any time of the day or night. Many of the private balconies aren't so private, and can be overlooked from public locations. A stream of flyers advertises daily art auctions and other promotions, while "artworks" for auction are strewn throughout the ship.

Many pillars obstruct passengers flow. Those in the dining room, for example, make it hard for proper food service by the waiters. Books and computers are cohabitants in the ship's library/internet center, but anyone wanting a book has to lean over others who may be using a computer – a very awkward arrangement. Public toilets are spartan and could do with cheering up.

ACCOMMODATION. There are 20 cabin categories, priced according to grade, location and size. The range of cabins includes suites (with private balcony), outside-view cabins with private balcony, 68 ocean view cabins with French doors (pseudo balconies that have doors which open, but no balcony to step out onto), and a healthy proportion of standard outside-view to interior (no view) cabins. All cabins have original motifs of nature, plant life and lake views.

All cabins have spy-hole doors, and twin beds that can be converted into a queen-sized bed, individually controlled air-conditioning, TV, and telephone. Some cabins on the lowest deck have views obstructed by lifeboats. Some cabins that can accommodate a third and fourth person have very little closet space, and there's only one personal safe. There is no separate radio in each cabin – instead, audio channels are provided on the in-cabin television system (however, you can't turn the picture off). A gift basket of (sample sized) personal amenities is provided in all grades.

If you book one of the suites (Category 11 or 12 in the Carnival Cruise Lines brochure), you automatically qualify for "Skipper's Club" priority check-in at any US homeland port – useful for getting ahead of the crowd.

Among the most desirable suites and cabins are those on five of the aft-facing decks; these have private balconies overlooking the stern and ship's wash. You might think that these units would suffer from vibration, but they don't – a bonus provided by the pod propulsion system *(see page 45).*

For the ultimate in extra space, it would be worth your while trying one of the large deluxe balcony suites on Deck 6, with its own private teakwood balcony. These tend to be quiet suites, with a large lounge and sleeping areas, a good-sized bathroom with twin (his 'n' hers) washbasins, toilet and bidet, and whirlpool bathtub. These suites have twin beds that convert to a queen-sized bed, three (illuminated) closets, and a huge amount of drawer space. The balcony has an outside light, and a wide teakwood deck with smoked glass and wood railing (you could easily seat 10 people with comfort and still have space left over).

Even the largest suites are quite small, however, compared with suites aboard other ships of a similar size – for example, Celebrity Cruises' *Constellation, Infinity, Millennium,* and *Summit,* where penthouse suites measure up to 2,530 sq. ft (235 sq. meters). Carnival Cruise Lines has fallen behind in the move to larger living spaces, and, with this ship, lost an opportunity to provide more space for those seeking it.

CUISINE. This ship has a single, large, two-decks-high, 1,300-seat main dining room called the Bacchus Restaurant, with seating on both upper and main levels. Its huge ceiling has large murals of a china pattern made famous by Royal Copenhagen, and wall-mounted glass display cases feature fine china. There are tables for two, four, six or eight, and small rooms on both upper and lower levels can be closed off for groups of up to 60. There's a choice of either fixed time dining (6pm or 8:15pm), or flexible dining (any time between 5:45pm and 9:30pm), while breakfast is in an open-seating arrangement.

For casual eaters, while there is no lido cafe, Horatio's Cafe is an extensive eatery that forms the aft third of Deck 9 (part of it also wraps around the upper section of the huge atrium). Murals of unicorns are everywhere. The cafe includes a central area with small buffet counters (deli sandwich corner, Asian corner, rotisserie, and International counter); there are salad counters, a dessert counter, and a 24-hour Pizzeria counter, all of which form a large eatery with both indoor and outdoor seating. Movement around the buffet area is slow, and you have to stand in line for everything. At night, the cafe becomes Seaview Bistro, for casual, serve-yourself dinners (typically open 6pm–9.30pm). **Alternative (Reservations-Only, Extra Cost) Dining:** Nick and Nora's Supper Club is a more upscale dining spot, with just 156 seats and a show kitchen. It is located on two of the uppermost decks of the ship, above the Unicorn Grille, in the lower, forward section of the funnel housing, with great views over the multi-deck atrium. The decor is set around the Greek legend of Jason and the Argonauts. Fine table settings, china and silverware are featured, as well as leather-bound menus.

ENTERTAINMENT. The Mad Hatter's Ball Showlounge is the ship's principal venue for large-scale production shows and other evening cabaret shows. Stage shows are best seen from the upper three levels, from where the sight lines are reasonable. Directly underneath the showlounge is the Phantom Lounge, which has a bar in its starboard aft section. Stage smoke appears to be in constant use during the production shows, and volumes are of the ear-splitting type.

SPA/FITNESS. SpaCarnival spans two decks, is located directly above the navigation bridge in the forward part of the ship, and has 13,700 sq. ft (1,272 sq. meters) of space. Facilities on the lower level include a solarium, eight treatment rooms, lecture rooms, sauna and steam rooms for men and women, and a beauty parlor; the upper level consists of a large gymnasium with floor-to-ceiling windows on three sides, including forward-facing ocean views, and an aerobics room with instructor-led classes.

There are two centrally located swimming pools outdoors, and one of the pools can be used in inclement weather due to its retractable glass dome. There are two whirlpool tubs, located adjacent to the swimming pools. A winding water slide that spans two decks in height is located at an aft, upper deck. Another smaller pool is available for children. There is an additional whirlpool tub outdoors.

A jogging track is located around the mast and the forward third of the ship. Although it doesn't go around the whole ship, it's long enough for some serious walking.

● **For more extensive general information on what a Carnival cruise is like, see pages 126–31.**

Carnival Paradise
★★★

Size:	Large Resort Ship	Passenger Decks:	10
Tonnage:	70,367	Total Crew:	920
Lifestyle:	Standard	Passengers	
Cruise Line:	Carnival Cruise Lines	(lower beds/all berths):	2,052/2,594
Former Names:	Paradise	Passenger Space Ratio	
Builder:	Kvaerner Masa-Yards (Finland)	(lower beds/all berths):	34.2/26.7
Original Cost:	$300 million	Crew/Passenger Ratio	
Entered Service:	Nov 1998	(lower beds/all berths):	2.2/2.8
Registry:	Panama	Cabins (total):	1,026
Length (ft/m):	855.0/260.6	Size Range (sq ft/m):	173.2–409.7/16–38
Beam (ft/m):	103.3/31.5	Cabins (outside view):	618
Draft (ft/m):	25.9/7.9	Cabins (interior/no view):	408
Propulsion/Propellers:	diesel-electric	Cabins (for one person):	0
	(42,842 kW)/2 azimuthing pods	Cabins (with private balcony):	152

Cabins (wheelchair accessible):	22
Wheelchair accessibility	Fair
Cabin Current:	110 volts
Elevators:	14
Casino (gaming tables):	Yes
Slot Machines:	Yes
Swimming Pools (outdoors):	3
Swimming Pools (indoors):	0
Whirlpools:	6
Self-Service Launderette:	Yes
Dedicated Cinema/Seats:	No
Library:	Yes

OVERALL SCORE: 1,222 OUT OF A POSSIBLE 2,000 POINTS

OVERVIEW. *Carnival Paradise* is the eighth (and final) in a series of eight ships of the same series of eight *Carnival Fantasy*-class ships, with the same internal configuration and layout. It is good for first-time passengers and those seeking party-style cruising. The ship has a forthright, angular appearance typical of today's space-creative designs. It is one of only two of the *Carnival Fantasy*-class ships – the other is *Carnival Elation* – to have been provided with a "pod" propulsion system *(technical details: page 45)*.

The ship has expansive open deck areas (there is no walk-around open promenade deck), but they quickly become inadequate when it is full and everyone wants to be out on deck. The aft decks tend to be less noisy, whereas all the activities are focused around the main swimming pool and hot tubs.

The interior decor includes splashy, showy, public rooms and interior colors – pure Las Vegas, ideal for some tastes. Public entertainment lounges, bars and clubs galore offer something for everyone, including a large children's playroom. Some busy colors and design themes abound in the handsome public rooms. Much of the eclectic art collection is bright and eye-catching. The Blue Riband library: nice room, few books, but there are models of ocean liners.

Good hangout place: the atrium lobby bar, with live music. Facilities include a shop stuffed with low-quality merchandise; a large casino with gaming tables for blackjack, craps, roulette, Caribbean stud poker, plus slot machines.

ACCOMMODATION. There are 13 grades, priced according to grade, size and location. See *Carnival Fantasy* for a more detailed description.

BERLITZ'S RATINGS

	Possible	Achieved
Ship	500	296
Accommodation	200	138
Food	400	213
Service	400	260
Entertainment	100	73
Cruise	400	242

CUISINE/DINING. There are two dining rooms (Destiny, aft; and Elation, midships), both non-smoking. They have splashy decor, and are large, crowded and very noisy. While menu descriptions sound inviting, the food may prove disappointing. You get what you pay for, and this company pays very little for food. There's a choice of either fixed time dining (6pm or 8:15pm), or flexible dining (between 5:45pm and 9:30pm).

For casual meals, there's the Lido Cafe, which, aboard this ship, has some improvements and additions worthy of note, such as: an orange juice machine, where you put in oranges and out comes fresh juice (better than the concentrate stuff supplied in the dining room). The Pizzeria is open 24 hours a day. There's also a small sushi bar. At night, the "Seaview Bistro", as the Lido Cafe becomes known, provides a casual (dress down) venue.

ENTERTAINMENT. The Normandie Showlounge seats 1,010, and is the principal venue for large-scale production shows and cabaret acts (20 pillars obstruct some sightlines).

SPA/FITNESS. SpaCarnival is a large health, fitness and spa complex on the uppermost interior deck, forward of the ship's mast. It consists of a gymnasium with ocean-view windows that look out over the ship's bow (it has the latest in muscle-pumping electronic machines), an aerobics exercise room, men's and women's changing rooms, sauna and steam rooms, and beauty salon.

● **For more extensive information on what a Carnival cruise is like, see pages 126–31, and for more information on the Fantasy-class ships, see *Carnival Fantasy*.**

Carnival Pride
★★★ +

Size: . . . . .Large Resort Ship	Passenger Decks: 12	Cabins (wheelchair accessible): 16
Tonnage: 85,920	Total Crew: 1,029	Wheelchair accessibility . . . . .Good
Lifestyle: . . . . .Standard	Passengers	Cabin Current: . . . . .110 volts
Cruise Line: . . . . . . .Carnival Cruise Lines	(lower beds/all berths): 2,124/2,680	Elevators: 15
Former Names: . . . . .none	Passenger Space Ratio	Casino (gaming tables): . . . . .Yes
Builder: . . . . .Kvaerner Masa-Yards	(lower beds/all berths): 40.4/32.0	Slot Machines: . . . . .Yes
Original Cost: . . . .$375 million	Crew/Passenger Ratio	Swimming Pools (outdoors): . . . . .2+1
Entered Service: . . . . .Jan 2002	(lower beds/all berths): 2.2/2.6	children's pool
Registry: .Panama	Cabins (total): 1,062	Swimming Pools (indoors): 1
Length (ft/m): 959.6/292.5	Size Range (sq ft/m): 185.0–490.0/	(indoor/outdoor)
Beam (ft/m): 105.6/32.2	17.1–45.5	Whirlpools: 5
Draft (ft/m): 25.5/7.8	Cabins (outside view): 849	Self-Service Launderette: . . . . .Yes
Propulsion/Propellers: . . . . .diesel-electric	Cabins (interior/no view): 213	Dedicated Cinema/Seats: . . . . .No
(62,370 kW)/2 azimuthing pods	Cabins (for one person): 0	Library: . . . . .Yes
(17.6 MW each)	Cabins (with private balcony): 750	

OVERALL SCORE: 1,386 OUT OF A POSSIBLE 2,000 POINTS

OVERVIEW. *Carnival Pride* (sister to *Carnival Legend, Carnival Miracle* and *Carnival Spirit,* all of which can transit the Panama Canal) is the 17th new ship for this very successful cruise line. The ship, whose bows are extremely short, has the distinctive, large, swept-back wing-tipped funnel that is the trademark of Carnival Cruise Lines, in the company colors of red, white and blue. The ship is longer than the company's larger quintet (*Carnival Conquest, Carnival Destiny, Carnival Glory, Carnival Triumph,* and *Carnival Victory,* all of which measure over 100,000 tons).

The lobby is immense, spanning eight decks, and the decor includes lots of larger than life women's breasts, bums, and nude men – all reproductions from the Renaissance period. The atrium lobby has a stunning 37-ft high (11-meter) reproduction of Raphael's Nymph Galatea that is best seen from any of the multiple viewing balconies on each deck above the main lobby floor level. There's no question about it – the surroundings are quite stunning.

The decor is extremely artistic (eclectic, in fact), with art being the theme throughout the ship – even elevator doors and interiors display reproductions (blown-up, over-grainy photographic copies) of some of the great Renaissance masters such as Gauguin, Matisse and Vignali.

There are two whole entertainment/public room decks, the upper of which also has an exterior promenade deck – something new for this cruise line. Although it doesn't go around the whole ship, it's long enough to do some serious walking on. There is also a jogging track outdoors, located around the ship's mast and the forward third of the ship.

A small wedding chapel is forward of the uppermost level

BERLITZ'S RATINGS

	Possible	Achieved
Ship	500	401
Accommodation	200	148
Food	400	229
Service	400	251
Entertainment	100	81
Cruise	400	276

of the two main entertainment decks, adjacent to the library and internet center. Other facilities include a winding shopping street with boutique sections for brands such as Fendi, Fossil, Tommy Hilfiger, plus Carnival logo items. There's a photo gallery, video games room, an observation balcony in the center of the vessel (at the top of the multi-deck atrium), and a large casino, with gaming tables, slot machines, bar and entertainment.

The information desk in the lobby is quite small, and can become congested. You need a credit card to operate the personal safe, an inconvenience. You'll endure a stream of flyers advertising daily promotions, while "artworks" for auction are strewn throughout the ship. Many pillars obstruct passenger flow. Those in the dining room, for example, make it difficult for proper food service by the waiters.

Books and computers are cohabitants in the library/internet center, but to get a book you have to lean over those using a computer – an awkward arrangement. Public toilets are spartan and could do with some cheering up.

ACCOMMODATION. There are 20 cabin price categories, in 6 different grades, with the price depending on grade, location and size. The range of cabins includes suites (with private balcony), outside-view cabins with private balcony (many are not really private, and can be overlooked from above), 68 ocean view cabins with French doors (pseudo-balconies that have doors which open, but no balcony to step out onto – although you do get fresh air), and a healthy proportion of standard outside-view to interior (no view) cabins. While the smallest cabin measures a very decent 185 sq. ft (17.1 sq.

meters), the largest suite measures only 490 sq. ft (45.5 sq. meters) – small when compared with many other ships of a similar size, although still a healthy chunk of living space.

While the bathrooms are quite compact, they do include a shower enclosure, several shelves, a shaving mirror, and 100% cotton towels. A gift basket of (sample sized) personal amenities is provided in all grades; it includes aloe soap, shampoo and conditioner sachets, deodorant, breath mints, candy, and pain relief tablets.

All cabins have spy-hole doors, and have twin beds that can be converted into a queen-sized bed, individually controlled air-conditioning, TV, telephone, hairdryer (in the vanity desk), and neat, yellow glass bedside lights that might remind you of Tin Man in *The Wizard of Oz*. Some cabins on the lowest cabin deck (Main Deck) have views obstructed by lifeboats. Some cabins that can accommodate a third and fourth person have very little closet space, and there's only one personal safe. There is no separate radio in each cabin – instead, audio channels are provided on the in-cabin television system – but you can't turn the picture off. Nor can you turn off the air conditioning in cabins or bathrooms.

Among the most desirable suites and cabins are those on five of the aft-facing decks; these have private balconies with views over the stern and ship's wash. You might think that these units would suffer from vibration, but they don't, thanks to the two-pod propulsion system *(see page 45)*.

For the ultimate in extra space, try one of the large deluxe balcony suites on Deck 6 with large private teak deck balcony. These tend to be quiet suites, with a large lounge and sleeping areas, large bathroom with twin (his 'n' hers) washbasins, toilet and bidet, and whirlpool bathtub. These suites have twin beds that convert to a queen-sized bed, three (illuminated) closets, and a huge amount of drawer space.

The balcony has an outside light, and wide teak deck with smoked glass and wood railing (you could seat 10 people with comfort and still have space left over).

To keep things in perspective, note that even the largest suites are small compared with suites aboard other ships of a similar size – for example, Celebrity Cruises' *Constellation, Infinity, Millennium,* and *Summit,* where penthouse suites measure up to 2,530 sq. ft (235 sq. meters). Carnival Cruise Lines has fallen behind in the move to larger living spaces. However, Carnival's philosophy has always been to get its passengers out into public areas to socialize, and spend money (this is, after all, a holiday).

If you book one of the suites (Category 11 or 12 in the Carnival Cruise Lines brochure) you automatically qualify for "Skipper's Club" priority check-in at any US homeland port – useful for getting ahead of the crowd.

CUISINE. This ship has a single, large, two-decks-high, 1,300-seat main dining room called the Normandie Restaurant, with seating on both upper and main levels. The decor is designed to give the impression that you are dining in the grand style of the famous French liner *Normandie,* although ship buffs would probably be critical of the results. The galley is located underneath the restaurant, with waiter access by escalators. There are tables are for two, four, six or eight, and small rooms on both upper and lower levels can be closed off for groups of up to 60. food. There's a choice of either fixed time dining (6pm or 8:15pm), or flexible dining (any time between 5:45pm and 9:30pm), while breakfast is in an open seating arrangement.

For casual meals, there is the extensive Mermaid's Grille is the equivalent of a lido cafe – which is an eatery that forms the aft third of Deck 9 (part of it also wraps around the upper section of the huge atrium). It includes a central area with small buffet counters (deli sandwich corner, Asian corner, rotisserie, and International counter) in an eclectic mix; there are salad counters, a dessert counter, and a 24-hour Pizzeria counter, all of which form a large eatery with both indoor and outdoor seating. There is plenty of variety, although it's uninspiring. Movement around the buffet area is very slow. Each night, Mermaid's Grille changes its name to Seaview Bistro, for casual, serve-yourself dinners in a dress-down setting (typically open 6pm–9.30pm).

Alternative (Reservations-Only, Extra Cost) Dining: David's Supper Club is a more upscale dining spot located on two of the uppermost decks, under a huge glass dome, with seating for approximately 150. It has a show kitchen where chefs can be seen preparing their masterpieces. It is directly above Mermaid's Grille (the self-serve buffet area), in the lower, forward section of the funnel housing, with superb views over the multi-deck atrium, as well as to the sea. The decor includes a 12-ft (3.7-meter) replica of Michaelangelo's *David.* Fine table settings, china and silverware are featured, as are well as leather-bound menus.

ENTERTAINMENT. The 1,170-seat Taj Mahal Showlounge (the venue for large-scale production shows and major cabaret acts) is a dramatic room that spans three decks in the forward section. Spiral stairways at the back of the lounge connect all three levels. Stage shows are best seen from the upper three levels. Directly underneath the showlounge is Butterflies, a large lounge with its own bar.

SPA/FITNESS. SpaCarnival is quite large, spans two decks, is located directly above the navigation bridge in the forward part of the ship and has 13,700 sq. ft (1,272 sq. meters) of space. Facilities on the lower level include a solarium, eight treatment rooms, lecture rooms, sauna and steam rooms for men and women, and a beauty parlor; the upper level consists of a large gymnasium with floor-to-ceiling windows on three sides, including forward-facing ocean views, and an aerobics room with instructor-led classes.

One of the two centrally located outdoor swimming pools can be used in inclement weather due to its retractable glass dome. There are two whirlpool tubs, located adjacent to the swimming pools. A winding water slide that spans two decks in height is located at an aft, upper deck. Another smaller pool is available for children. There is also an additional whirlpool tub outdoors.

● **For more extensive general information on what a Carnival cruise is like, see pages 126–31.**

Carnival Sensation
★★★

Size:	Large Resort Ship	Passenger Decks:	10	Cabins (with private balcony):	152
Tonnage:	70,367	Total Crew:	920	Cabins (wheelchair accessible):	20
Lifestyle:	Standard	Passengers		Wheelchair accessibility	Fair
Cruise Line:	Carnival Cruise Lines	(lower beds/all berths):	2,040/2,594	Cabin Current:	110 volts
Former Names:	Sensation	Passenger Space Ratio		Elevators:	14
Builder:	Kvaerner Masa-Yards (Finland)	(lower beds/all berths):	34.4/26.7	Casino (gaming tables):	Yes
Original Cost:	$300 million	Crew/Passenger Ratio		Slot Machines:	Yes
Entered Service:	Nov 1993	(lower beds/all berths):	2.2/2.8	Swimming Pools (outdoors):	3
Registry:	The Bahamas	Cabins (total):	1,020	Swimming Pools (indoors):	0
Length (ft/m):	855.0/260.6	Size Range (sq ft/m):	173.2–409.7/	Whirlpools:	6
Beam (ft/m):	104.0/31.4		16.0–38.0	Self-Service Launderette:	Yes
Draft (ft/m):	25.9/7.9	Cabins (outside view):	618	Dedicated Cinema/Seats:	No
Propulsion/Propellers:	diesel-electric	Cabins (interior/no view):	402	Library:	Yes
	(42,240kW)/2	Cabins (for one person):	0		

OVERALL SCORE: 1,244 OUT OF A POSSIBLE 2,000 POINTS

OVERVIEW. *Carnival Sensation*, whose bows are extremely short, has a distinctive, large, swept-back wing-tipped funnel, the trademark of Carnival Cruise Lines. The ship, which is almost vibration-free, has expansive open deck areas (sadly, there is no walk-around open promenade deck), but they quickly become inadequate when it is full and everyone wants to be out on deck.

After a six-month charter to the US government as emergency housing in the wake of Hurricane Katrina, the ship was extensively refurbished in 2007, which provided a facelift for the ship's tired interiors. A new nine-hole miniature golf course was added, as was a 1,600-sq-ft (148-sq-meter) Children's World play area; a 'Circle C' tweens area (for 12-14 year-olds); a new "art" gallery, photo gallery, and a 1,200-sq-ft (111-sq-meter) conference room. Additionally, all cabins were completely refurbished and given flat-screen TVs (the bathrooms were also updated). A new New York-style deli counter and a patisserie were added to the Lido Café, and the internet café was redesigned.

Inside, the general passenger flow is good, and the interior design is clever, functional, and extremely colorful. A dramatic six-deck-high atrium, with cool marble and hot neon, is topped by a large colored glass dome.

The library is a lovely room, but there are few books. The Michelangelo Lounge is a creative thinker's delight, while Fingers Lounge is sheer sensory stimulation. The casino has plenty of gaming tables and slot machines.

ACCOMMODATION. There are 13 price grades. See *Carnival Fantasy* for more detailed information. In 2009, another 98 balconies were added to cabins in mid- and aft sections

BERLITZ'S RATINGS	Possible	Achieved
Ship	500	317
Accommodation	200	138
Food	400	213
Service	400	261
Entertainment	100	73
Cruise	400	242

of the ship; some suite balconies were also enlarged.

CUISINE. There are two huge, noisy dining rooms (Ecstasy and Fantasy, both no-smoking) with the usual efficient, assertive service. There's a choice of either fixed time dining (6pm or 8:15pm), or flexible dining (any time between 5:45pm and 9:30pm).

The Lido Cafe self-serve buffets are very basic, as is the selection of breads, rolls, fruit and cheeses. At night, the "Seaview Bistro", as the Lido Cafe becomes known, provides a casual (dress down) alternative to the main dining rooms, serving pasta, steaks, salads and desserts (typically between 6pm and 9pm). The Pizzeria is open 24 hours a day.

ENTERTAINMENT. The Fantasia Showlounge is the main venue for large-scale production shows and cabaret acts, although 20 pillars obstruct the views from several seats.

SPA/FITNESS. The Nautica Spa is a large health, fitness and spa complex that is located on the uppermost interior deck, forward of the ship's mast, and accessed from the forward stairway. It consists of a gymnasium with oceanview windows that look out over the ship's bow, an aerobics exercise room, men's and women's changing rooms, sauna and steam rooms, and beauty salon.

There is a "banked" jogging track outdoors on the deck above the spa.

● For more extensive information on what a Carnival cruise is like, see pages 126–31, and for more information on the Fantasy-class ships, see *Carnival Fantasy*.

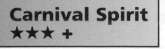

Carnival Spirit
★★★ +

Size:	.Large Resort Ship	Passenger Decks:	.12	Cabins (wheelchair accessible):	.16
Tonnage:	.85,920	Total Crew:	.930	Wheelchair accessibility	.Good
Lifestyle:	.Standard	Passengers		Cabin Current:	.110 volts
Cruise Line:	.Carnival Cruise Lines	(lower beds/all berths):	.2,124/2,680	Elevators:	.15
Former Names:	.none	Passenger Space Ratio		Casino (gaming tables):	.Yes
Builder:	.Kvaerner Masa-Yards	(lower beds/all berths):	.40.4/32.0	Slot Machines:	.Yes
Original Cost:	.$375 million	Crew/Passenger Ratio		Swimming Pools (outdoors):	.2+1
Entered Service:	.Apr 2001	(lower beds/all berths):	.2.2/2.6		children's pool
Registry:	.Panama	Cabins (total):	.1,062	Swimming Pools (indoors):	.1
Length (ft/m):	.959.6/292.5	Size Range (sq ft/m):	.185.0–490.0/		(indoor/outdoor)
Beam (ft/m):	.105.6/32.2		17.1–45.5	Whirlpools:	.5
Draft (ft/m):	.25.5/7.8	Cabins (outside view):	.849	Self-Service Launderette:	.Yes
Propulsion/Propellers:	.diesel-electric	Cabins (interior/no view):	.213	Dedicated Cinema/Seats:	.No
(62,370 kW)/2 azimuthing pods		Cabins (for one person):	.0	Library:	.Yes
(17.6 MW each)		Cabins (with private balcony):	.750		

OVERALL SCORE: 1,390 OUT OF A POSSIBLE 2,000 POINTS

OVERVIEW. *Carnival Spirit* was the 16th new ship for this very successful cruise line. It has Carnival's trademark large wing-tipped funnel in the Miami-based company's red, white and blue colors. The design makes the ship look much sleeker than any other in the Carnival Cruise Lines fleet (except for its sister ships), a process of continuing ship design and evolvement.

Sister ships in the same class and internal layout and design are *Carnival Legend, Carnival Miracle* and *Carnival Pride*, and all can transit the Panama Canal.

There are two centrally located swimming pools outdoors, and one can be used in inclement weather due to its retractable glass-dome cover. Two whirlpool tubs, adjacent to the swimming pools, are abridged by a bar. Another smaller pool is available for children; it incorporates a winding water slide that spans two decks in height. There is also a whirlpool tub outdoors.

The interior design theme is a tribute to the world's great architecture, from art nouveau to postmodern. The immense lobby space spans eight decks. The atrium lobby, with its two grand stairways, presents a stunning wall decoration best seen from any of the multiple viewing balconies on each deck above the main lobby floor level.

There are two entertainment/public room decks, the upper of which also has an exterior promenade deck – something new for this fun cruise line. Although it doesn't extend around the whole ship, it's long enough for some serious walking. There is also a jogging track outdoors, around the ship's mast and the forward third of the ship.

A winding shopping street contains several boutique

BERLITZ'S RATINGS

	Possible	Achieved
Ship	500	402
Accommodation	200	148
Food	400	229
Service	400	252
Entertainment	100	81
Cruise	400	278

stores selling the usual Carnival logo items. A small wedding chapel is located forward of the uppermost level of the two main entertainment decks, adjacent to the combined library and internet center. Other facilities include a photo gallery, video games room, an observation balcony in the center of the vessel, and a piano lounge/bar. The casino is large (one has to walk through it to get from the restaurant to the showlounge on one of the entertainments decks), and it has all the gaming paraphernalia and array of slot machines you can imagine.

There is a "tele-radiology" system that enables shipboard physicians to digitally transmit X-rays and other patient information to shore-side facilities – useful for peace of mind for passengers and crew.

The information desk in the lobby is quite small, and can become quite congested. It is difficult to escape from smokers, noise and loud music – it's even played in cabin hallways and elevators. Many private balconies are not so private, being overlooked from various public locations. You'll need to carry a credit card to operate the personal safe in your suite or cabin – an inconvenience. You'll endure a stream of flyers advertising various products.

Books and computers are cohabitants in the ship's library/internet center, but anyone wanting a book has to lean over others who may be using a computer – a very awkward arrangement. Public toilets are dull and spartan.

ACCOMMODATION. There are 20 cabin categories, priced according to grade, location and size. The range of cabins includes suites (with private balcony), outside-view cabins with private balcony, 68 ocean view cabins with French doors (pseudo balconies that have doors which open, but no balcony to step out onto), and a healthy proportion of standard outside-view to interior (no view) cabins. While the smallest cabin measures a very decent 185 sq. ft (17.1 sq. meters), the largest suite measures only 490 sq. ft (45.5 sq. meters) – small compared with many similar ships.

The bathrooms are quite compact, but include a circular shower enclosure, several shelves, a shaving mirror, and 100% cotton towels. A gift basket of (sample sized) personal amenities is provided in all grades; it includes aloe soap, shampoo, conditioner, deodorant, breath mints, candy, and pain relief tablets.

Regardless of the grade of cabin chosen, all cabins have spy-hole doors, and have twin beds that can be converted into a queen-sized bed, individually controlled air-conditioning, television, and telephone. A number of cabins on the lowest cabin deck have views obstructed by lifeboats. Some cabins that can accommodate a third and fourth person have very little closet space, and there's only one personal safe. There is no separate radio in each cabin – instead, audio channels are provided on the in-cabin television system – but you can't turn off the picture. Nor can you turn off the air conditioning in cabins or bathrooms.

If you book one of the suites (Category 11 or 12 in the Carnival Cruise Lines brochure), you automatically qualify for "Skipper's Club" priority check-in at any US homeland port – useful for getting ahead of the crowd.

Among the most desirable suites and cabins are those on five of the aft-facing decks; these have private balconies overlooking the stern and ship's wash. You might think that these units would suffer from vibration, but they don't – a bonus provided by the pod propulsion system *(see page 45)*.

For the ultimate in extra space, try one of the large deluxe balcony suites on Deck 6 with large private teak balcony. These tend to be quiet, with a large lounge and sleeping areas, a large bathroom with twin (his 'n' hers) washbasins, toilet and bidet, and whirlpool bathtub. These suites have twin beds that convert to a queen-sized bed, three (illuminated) closets, and a huge amount of drawer space. The balcony has an outside light, and a wide teak deck with smoked glass and wood railing (you could seat 10 people with comfort and still have space left over).

To keep things in perspective, note that even the largest suites are small compared with suites aboard other ships of a similar size – for example, Celebrity Cruises' *Constellation, Infinity, Millennium,* and *Summit,* where penthouse suites measure up to 2,530 sq. ft (235 sq. meters). Carnival Cruise Lines has fallen behind in the move to larger living spaces, and, with this ship, lost an opportunity to provide more space for those seeking it.

CUISINE. This ship has a single, large, two-decks-high, 1,300-seat main dining room called the Empire Restaurant, with seating on both upper and main levels. The decor is heavily "Napoleonic" (early 19th-century French) style. The galley is located underneath the restaurant, with waiter access by escalators. There are tables for two, four, six or eight, and small rooms on both upper and lower levels can be closed off for groups of up to 60. There's a choice of either fixed time dining (6pm or 8:15pm), or flexible dining (any time between 5:45pm and 9:30pm), while breakfast is in an open seating arrangement.

For casual eaters, while there is no lido cafe, there is the extensive La Playa Grille, which forms the aft third of Deck 9 (part of it also wraps around the upper section of the huge atrium). It includes a central area with small buffet counters (deli sandwich corner, Asian corner, rotisserie, and International counter); there are salad counters, a dessert counter, and a 24-hour Pizzeria counter, all forming a large eatery with both indoor and outdoor seating. Movement around the buffet area is very slow, with frequent lines. Each night, La Playa Grille becomes Seaview Bistro, for casual, serve-yourself dinners (typically open 6pm–9.30pm).

There is an outdoor self-serve buffet (adjacent to the fantail pool), which serves fast-food items such as hamburgers and hot dogs, chicken and fries, as well as two smaller buffets adjacent to the midships pool area. If you want to eat 24 hours a day, you can do it aboard this ship, which has something for (almost) everyone.

Alternative (Reservations-Only, Extra Cost) Dining: The Nouveau Supper Club is a more upscale dining spot located on two of the uppermost decks of the ship under a huge glass dome, with seating for approximately 150. It has a open-view kitchen where chefs can be seen preparing their masterpieces. It is located directly above La Playa Grille Mermaid's Grille, in the lower, forward section of the funnel housing, with some superb views over the multi-deck atrium, as well as to the sea. Fine table settings, china and silverware are used, as well as leather-bound menus. The decor has a floral pattern and there is a stained-glass balcony on the upper level. There is also a stage and dance floor.

ENTERTAINMENT. The 1,170-seat Pharaoh's Palace Show-lounge is a dramatic room which spans three decks in the forward section of the ship. Spiral stairways at the back of the lounge connect all levels. Stage shows are best seen from the upper three levels, from where the sight lines are reasonably good. Directly underneath the showlounge is the Versailles Lounge (in the highy decorative manner of 18th-century France), a large lounge with its own bar.

SPA/FITNESS. A large Nautica health spa, spanning two decks, is located directly above the navigation bridge in the forward part of the ship and has 13,700 sq. ft (1,272 sq. meters) of space. Facilities on the lower level include a solarium, eight treatment rooms, lecture rooms, sauna and steam rooms for men and women, and a beauty parlor; the upper level consists of a large gymnasium with floor-to-ceiling windows on three sides, including forward-facing ocean views, and an aerobics room with instructor-led classes (some at extra cost).

● **For more extensive general information on what a Carnival cruise is like, see pages 126–31.**

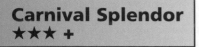

Carnival Splendor
★★★ +

Size: . . . . .Large Resort Ship	Passenger Decks: 13	Cabins (with private balcony): 574
Tonnage: .110,239	Total Crew: 1,150	Cabins (wheelchair accessible): 25
Lifestyle: . . . . .Standard	Passengers	Wheelchair accessibility . . . . .Good
Cruise Line: . . . . . . .Carnival Cruise Lines	(lower beds/all berths): 2,974/3,700	Cabin Current: . . . . .110 volts
Former Names: . . . . .none	Passenger Space Ratio	Elevators: 18
Builder: . . . . .Fincantieri (Italy)	(lower beds/all berths): 37.0/29.7	Casino (gaming tables): . . . . .Yes
Original Cost: . . . .$500 million	Crew/Passenger Ratio	Slot Machines: . . . . .Yes
Entered Service: . . . . .July 2008	(lower beds/all berths): 2.5/3.1	Swimming Pools (outdoors): 3
Registry: . . . . .Panama	Cabins (total): 1,487	(+1 with magrodome)
Length (ft/m): 951.4/290.0	Size Range (sq ft/m): 179.7–484.2/	Swimming Pools (indoors): 0
Beam (ft/m): 105.6/32.2	16.7–44.8	Whirlpools: 7
Draft (ft/m): 27.2/8.3	Cabins (outside view): 917	Self-Service Launderette: . . . . .Yes
Propulsion/Propellers: . . . . .diesel-electric	Cabins (interior/no view): 570	Dedicated Cinema/Seats: . . . . .No
(63,400kW)/2	Cabins (for one person): 0	Library: . . . . .Yes

BERLITZ'S OVERALL SCORE: 1,393 OUT OF A POSSIBLE 2,000 POINTS

OVERVIEW. *Carnival Splendor* was the 25th new ship ordered by this "Fun Ship" cruise line. It shares the same generally balanced profile as sisters *Carnival Conquest, Carnival Destiny, Carnival Freedom, Carnival Glory, Carnival Liberty, Carnival Triumph, Carnival Valor,* and *Carnival Victory.* It is unable to transit the Panama Canal, due to its size. Immediately recognizable is the ship's swept-back, red, white and blue wingtip funnel – the trademark of all Carnival's ships.

The ship's interior decor contains a vivid palette of colors that stimulate and excite the senses. The deck and public room layout is logical, and finding your way around is relatively easy. Most of the public rooms are located on one deck off a main interior boulevard, above a deck which contains the two main dining rooms. The public rooms include the large Royal Flush Casino (gaming includes blackjack, craps, roulette, three-card poker, Caribbean Stud poker, Face Up, Let it Ride, Bonus, and Wheel of Madness, and more than 300 slot machines).

If you like movies on big screens in the open air (remember drive-in movie theaters?), Carnival's Seaside Theater for movies on deck should do it for you (seating is in tiered rows and the movie screen faces forward). The ship has bow-to-stern wi-fi internet access (including all passenger cabins).

Youngsters are provided with their own Camp Carnival children's club (with its own small outdoor pool), and are well cared for with the line's extensive children's program. Camp Carnival is located on Sun Deck (out of the way of older passengers).

Minor niggles include the fact that many pillars obstruct passenger flow, particularly in the dining room, where they

BERLITZ'S RATINGS		
	Possible	Achieved
Ship	500	414
Accommodation	200	157
Food	400	218
Service	400	260
Entertainment	100	82
Cruise	400	262

make it difficult for the waiters to serve food properly.

ACCOMMODATION. There are 20 cabin price categories, in 7 different suite/cabin types, sizes and grades. These include suites with private balcony; deluxe outside-view cabins with private balcony; outside-view cabins with private balcony; outside-view cabins with window; cabins with a porthole instead of a window; interior (no-view) cabins; and interior (no-view cabins) with upper and lower berths. There are five decks of cabins with private balconies.

The standard cabins are of good size and come equipped with all the basics, although the furniture is rather square and angular, with no rounded edges. Three decks of cabins (eight on each deck, each with private balcony) overlook the stern. Most cabins with twin beds can be converted to a queen-size bed format. Book one of the suites (Category 11 or 12 in the Carnival Cruise Lines brochure) and you'll get "Skipper's Club" priority check-in at any US homeland port – useful for getting ahead of the crowd.

There are even "spa" cabins aboard this ship – a grouping of 18 cabins that are located directly around and behind SpaCarnival; so fitness devotees can get out of bed and go straight to the treadmill without having to go through any of the public rooms first.

A gift basket of personal toiletry items is provided in all grades of cabins; it includes aloe soap, shampoo, conditioner, deodorant, breath mints, candy, and pain relief tablets (all in sample sizes – and most in paper packets that are difficult, sometimes frustrating, to open).

CUISINE. There are two principal dining rooms (Black Pearl, seating 744, located midships; and Gold Pearl, located aft, seating 1,122). Both are two decks high and have a balcony level (the balcony level in Gold Pearl is larger than the one in Black Pearl). There's a choice of either fixed time dining (6pm or 8:15pm), or flexible dining (any time between 5:45pm and 9:30pm).

There are few tables for two, but my favourites are the two tables for two right at the very back of the Gold Pearl restaurant, with ocean views astern.

Alternative (Reservations-Only, Extra Cost) Dining: There is one reservations-only, extra-cost dining spot, the Pinnacle. It has fine table settings, china and silverware, as well as leather-bound menus. The featured specialties are USDA dry-aged prime steaks and seafood items. It's worth paying the cover charge to get a taste of what Carnival can really deliver in terms of food that is of better quality than that served in the main dining rooms.

Casual Eateries: The Lido Restaurant is a casual self-serve international food court-style eatery. It has two main serving lines and several stand-alone sections. Included in this eating mall are a New York-style deli, a 24-hour pizzeria, and a grill for fast foods such as hamburgers and hot dogs; one section has a Tandoori oven for Indian-themes items. Each night, the venue morphs into the "Seaview Bistro," and provides a casual (dress down) alternative to eating in the main dining rooms, serving pasta, steaks, salads and desserts (typically between 6pm and 9pm). An upstairs Rotisserie offers chicken.

ENTERTAINMENT. The large, multi-deck Spectacular Showlounge seats up to 1,400, and serves as the principal entertainment venue for the ship's colourful large-scale entertainment including Las-Vegas-style production shows and major cabaret acts. It has a revolving stage, hydraulic orchestra pit, superb sound, and seating on three levels (the upper levels being tiered through two decks).

An alternative entertainment venue is the El Morocco, a 425-seat lounge located aft; this typically features live music and late-night cabaret acts including smutty adult comedy. Adjacent is the Grand Piano Lounge/Bar.

SPA/FITNESS. The Cloud 9 Spa spans two decks (with a total area of approximately 40,000 sq. ft/3,715 sq. meters including the 16 spa suites – or 13,000 sq.ft./1,235 sq. m excluding the spa suites), and is located directly above the navigation bridge in the forward part of the ship (it is accessed from the forward stairway.

Facilities on the lower level include a gymnasium, solarium, a thermal suite (a number of saunas and steam rooms – some infused with herbal aromas), thalassotherapy pool (check out the huge Chinese dogs), and a beauty salon; the upper level houses 17 treatment rooms including two VIP suites (one for couples, one specially configured for wheelchair access), rasul (Mediterranean mud treatment – best for couples) chamber, floatation therapy room, several treatment rooms and outdoor relaxation areas (on both port and starboard sides) with integrated massage cabana.

This is Carnival's most extensive spa, and using it will cost you lots of pennies if you have several treatments – or even if you simply want to use the thermal suite – there's a charge for everything.

● **For more extensive general information on what a Carnival cruise is like, see pages 126–31.**

DID YOU KNOW...

● that Fred Olsen Cruise Lines' entire fleet is comprised of ships that have been "stretched"? It's only the second line that can claim so; the first was Royal Viking Line, with all three of its ships having been stretched (Fred Olsen Cruise Lines operate two of the former Royal Viking Line ships, and the third is operated by Phoenix Reisen).

● that shore power has been available in Juneau since 2001 and in Seattle since 2005?

● that the first cruise ship to have an outdoor laser light show was the original *AIDA* (since renamed *AIDAcara*, which debuted in 1996?

● that tickets for production shows were first issued by Celebrity Cruises in the early 1990s? They were given out by the waiters in the dining rooms aboard *Century, Galaxy* and *Mercury*.

● that the first passenger ship to have a children's carousel was the *Ile de France*?

● that Cunard introduced the first gymnasium and health center aboard a ship (*Franconia,* 1911)?

● that Cunard Line's *Aquitania* of 1913 was the first ship to have an indoor swimming pool?

● that Nowegian America Line's *Sagafjord* was the first ship to have a central plug-in vacuum system?

● that Karin Stahre Janson was the first female cruise ship captain? Born in Sweden, she took command of RCI's *Monarch of the Seas* in 2007 at the age of 38.

● that when sailing from England to the Caribbean in "the old days" a rule of thumb was to sail south until the butter melts, then proceed west?

● that the word "buccaneer" comes from the French word *boucanier,* which means: "to cure meat on a bucan (barbeque)?" Since pirates often used this method of cooking, they became known as buccaneers. The word buccaneer, strictly speaking, was used to denote pirates in the Caribbean.

● that in 1992 Carnival Cruise Lines used its original ship *Mardi Gras* as an accommodation ship? It was for senior executives and staff who were made homeless when Hurricane Andrew hit Miami in August that year.

Carnival Triumph
Carnival Valor
Carnival Victory
★★★ +

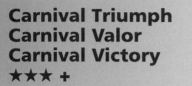

Size: . . . . .Large Resort Ships	Draft (ft/m): 27.0/8.2	Cabins (interior/no view): 526
Tonnage: . . . . .101,509 *(Triumph, Victory)*	Propulsion/Propellers: . . . . .diesel-electric	Cabins (for one person): 0
110,239 *(Valor)*	(34,000 kW)/2 azimuthing pods	Cabins (with private balcony): 508
Lifestyle: . . . . .Standard	(17.6 MW each)	Cabins (wheelchair accessible): 25
Cruise Line: . . . . . . .Carnival Cruise Lines	Passenger Decks: 13	Wheelchair accessibility . . . . .Good
Former Names: . . . . .none	Total Crew: .1,100	Cabin Current: . . . . .110 volts
Builder: . . . . .Fincantieri (Italy)	Passengers	Elevators: 14
Original Cost: . . . .$420 *(Triumph)*,	(lower beds/all berths): 2,758/3,473	Casino (gaming tables): . . . . .Yes
$500 million *(Valor)*, $410 million *(Victory)*	Passenger Space Ratio	Slot Machines: . . . . .Yes
Entered Service: . . . . .Oct 1999 *(Triumph)*,	(lower beds/all berths): 36.8/29.2	Swimming Pools (outdoors): 2
Dec 2004 *(Valor)*, Aug 2000 *(Victory)*	Crew/Passenger Ratio	(+1 with magrodome)
Registry: . . . . . . .The Bahamas *(Triumph)*,	(lower beds/all berths): 2.3/3.0	Swimming Pools (indoors): 0
Panama *(Valor, Victory)*	Cabins (total): 1,379	Whirlpools: 7
Length (ft/m): . . . . .893.0/272.2 *(Triumph,*	Size Range (sq ft/m): 179.7–482.2/	Self-Service Launderette: . . . . .Yes
Victory), 951.4/290.0 *(Valor)*	16.7–44.8	Dedicated Cinema/Seats: . . . . .No
Beam (ft/m): 116.0/35.3	Cabins (outside view): 853	Library: . . . . .Yes

OVERALL SCORES: 1,379 (TRIUMPH), 1,380 (VALOR), 1,369 (VICTORY)

OVERVIEW. These three ships belong to Carnival Cruise Lines' *Destiny* class, along with *Carnival Conquest, Carnival Destiny, Carnival Freedom, Carnival Glory* and *Carnival Liberty*. They are quite stunning, built to impress at every turn, and, with extremely short bows, have the most balanced profile of all the ships in the Carnival fleet. However, they are too big transit the Panama Canal.

BERLITZ'S RATINGS

	Possible	Triumph	Valor	Victory
Ship	500	409	410	407
Accommodation	200	157	157	157
Food	400	218	218	218
Service	400	259	260	249
Entertainment	100	82	82	81
Cruise	400	255	253	257

There are three decks full of lounges, 10 bars and lots of rooms to play in. Like their smaller (though still large) predecessors, these ships have a doublewide indoor promenade, nine decks high, with statues of Neptune at both ends, and a glass-domed rotunda atrium lobby. Amidships on the open deck is the longest water slide at sea – 200 ft /60 meters in length, it travels from just aft of the ship's mast – as well as tiered sunbathing decks positioned between two small swimming pools and several hot tubs.

The decor is quite tasteful, nowhere near as glitzy as the *Fantasy*-class ships, and public rooms are given a visual theme. On *Carnival Triumph* this is great cities such as Rome and Paris, on *Carnival Valor* it's famous names such as Josephine Baker and Charles Lindbergh, and on *Carnival Victory* it's oceans of the world, with seahorses, corals and shells prominent throughout the design. The layout is logical, so finding your way around is fairly simple.

Children have good facilities, including their own two-level Children's Club, including an outdoor pool, and are well cared for with "Camp Carnival," the cruise line's extensive children's program.

The terraced pool deck is really cluttered, and there are no cushioned pads for the deck chairs. Although the outdoor deck space has been improved, there is still much crowding when the ship is full and at sea. Getting away from people and noise is extremely difficult. The photo gallery becomes extremely congested when photographs are on display.

An extra feature the *Fantasy*-class ships do not have is a square-shaped bar, located in the atrium, which faces forward to the glass-walled lifts and sits under the 10-deck-high dome. A sports bar has tables featuring sports memorabilia.

From a safety viewpoint, passengers can embark directly into the lifeboats from their secured position without hav-

HOW THE SHIPS DIFFER

Carnival Valor differs from *Carnival Triumph* and *Carnival Victory* in a few ways not covered in the initial data (above). Its propulsion is diesel-electric (63,400kW/2). It carries up to 3,700 passengers (2,974 in lower beds) to give a crew/passenger ratio for lower beds/all berths of 2.5/3.1. It has 917 cabins with an outside view, and 574 cabins with a private balcony.

ing to wait for them to be lowered, thus saving time in the event of a real emergency. Well done.

ACCOMMODATION. There are 20 price categories, depending on grade, location and size. Over half of all cabins are outside, and at 225 sq. ft./21 sq. meters they are among the largest in the standard market. They are spread over four decks and have private balconies (with glass rather than steel balustrades, for unobstructed ocean views) extending from the ship's side. The balconies have bright fluorescent lighting. The standard cabins are of good size and have all the basics, although the furniture is angular, with no rounded edges. Three decks of cabins – eight on each deck, each with private balcony – overlook the stern.

There are eight penthouse suites, each with a large private balcony. Although they are quite lavish in their appointments, at only 483 sq. ft (44.8 sq. meters), they are really quite small when compared to the best suites even in many smaller ships. There are also 40 other suites, each of which has a decently sized bathroom, and a good amount of lounge space, although they are nothing special.

In cabins with balconies, the partition between each balcony is open at top and bottom, so you may well hear noise from neighbors or smell their cigarettes. It is disappointing to see three categories of cabins (both outside and interior) with upper and lower bunk beds – lower beds are far more preferable, but this is how the ships absorb hundreds of extra passengers over and above the lower bed capacity.

The cabins have soft color schemes and more soft furnishings in more attractive fabrics than other ships in the fleet. Interactive "Fun Vision" technology lets you choose movies on demand, for a fee. The bathrooms, which have good-sized showers, have good storage space in the toiletries cabinet. A gift basket is provided in all grades; it includes aloe soap, shampoo, conditioner, deodorant, breath mints, candy, and pain relief tablets – albeit all in sample sizes.

If you book one of the suites (Category 11 or 12 in the Carnival Cruise Lines brochure), you automatically qualify for "Skipper's Club" priority check-in at any US homeland port – useful for getting ahead of the crowd.

CUISINE. The ships have two main dining rooms, both non-smoking: one forward, with windows on two sides and 706 seats, and the other aft, with windows on three sides and 1,090 seats). Each dining room spans two decks, and incorporate a dozen domes and chandeliers. The aft dining room has a two-deck-high wall of glass overlooking the stern. There are tables for four, six and eight, and even a few tables for two that the line tries to keep for honeymooners.

There's a choice of either fixed-time dining (6pm or 8:15pm), or flexible dining (any time between 5:45pm and 9:30pm). This gives you very little time to "dine" – although it should give you some idea of what to expect from your dining experience. Although the menu choice looks good, the actual cuisine delivered is adequate, but quite unmemorable.

The dining room entrances have comfortable drinking areas for pre-dinner cocktails. There are also many options for casual dining, particularly during the day.

An informal international self-serve buffet-style eatery, has seating on two levels. Included in this eatery are a New York-style deli (open 11am–1pm), a Chinese restaurant, with wok preparation, and a 24-hour pizzeria which typically serves an average of more than 800 pizzas every day.

At night, one restaurant is turned into the "Seaview Bistro" and provides a casual (dress down) alternative to eating in the main dining rooms, serving pasta, steaks, salads and desserts. There is also a barbecue for fast grilled foods such as chicken, hamburgers and hot dogs, and a salad bar. In addition, there is a self-serve ice cream and frozen yogurt station, at no extra charge. If you want to eat 24 hours a day, you can do it aboard these ships, which have something for (almost) everyone.

Alternative (Reservations-Only, Extra Cost) Dining: There is one reservations-only, extra-cost dining spot, Scarlett's, aboard *Carnival Valor*. It has fine table settings, china and silverware, as well as leather-bound menus, and a design theme set around Scarlett O'Hara, the heroine of Margaret Mitchell's classic novel *Gone With the Wind*.

ENTERTAINMENT. The three-level showlounges are stunning, with a revolving stage, hydraulic orchestra pit, superb sound, and seating on three levels, the upper levels being tiered through two decks. There is a proscenium over the stage that acts as a scenery loft.

SPA/FITNESS. SpaCarnival spans two decks (with a total area of 13,700 sq. ft/1,272 sq. meters), and is located directly above the navigation bridge in the forward part of the ship; it is accessed from the forward stairway. Facilities on the lower level include a solarium, eight treatment rooms, lecture rooms, sauna and steam rooms for men and women, and a beauty parlor; the upper level consists of a large gymnasium with floor-to-ceiling windows on three sides, including forward-facing ocean views, and an aerobics room with instructor-led classes, some at extra cost.

● **For more extensive general information on what a Carnival cruise is like, see pages 126–31.**

Celebrity Century
★★★★

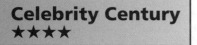
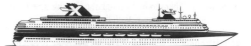

Size: . . . . .Large Resort Ship	Passenger Decks: 10	Cabins (with private balcony): 386
Tonnage: .71,545	Total Crew: .858	Cabins (wheelchair accessible): 8
Lifestyle: . . . . .Premium	Passengers	Wheelchair accessibility . . . . .Good
Cruise Line: . . . . .Celebrity Cruises	(lower beds/all berths): 1,750/2,150	Cabin Current: . . . . .110 and 220 volts
Former Names: . . . . .Century	Passenger Space Ratio	Elevators: 9
Builder: . . . . .Meyer Werft (Germany)	(lower beds/all berths): 40.8/33.2	Casino (gaming tables): . . . . .Yes
Original Cost: . . . .$320 million	Crew/Passenger Ratio	Slot Machines: . . . . .Yes
Entered Service: . . . . .Dec 1995	(lower beds/all berths): 2.0/2.5	Swimming Pools (outdoors): 2
Registry: . . . . .Malta	Cabins (total): 907	Swimming Pools (indoors): . . .1 hydropool
Length (ft/m): 807.1/246.0	Size Range (sq ft/m): 168.9–1,514.5/	Whirlpools: 4
Beam (ft/m): 105.6/32.2	15.7–140.7	Self-Service Launderette: . . . . .No
Draft (ft/m): 24.6/7.5	Cabins (outside view): 590	Dedicated Cinema/Seats: Yes/190
Propulsion/Propellers: . . . . .diesel	Cabins (interior/no view): 317	Library: . . . . .Yes
(29,250kW)/2	Cabins (for one person): 0	

OVERALL SCORE: 1,545 OUT OF A POSSIBLE 2,000 POINTS

OVERVIEW. This ship's exterior profile is quite well balanced despite its squared-off stern, and carries the distinctive Celebrity Cruises' "X" funnel ("X" being the Greek letter "C" – for Chandris, the former owning company, before Royal Caribbean purchased it). With a high passenger space ratio for such a large ship, there is no real sense of crowding, passenger flow is very good, and the high crew/passenger ratio provides a sound basis for good passenger service.

There is a good amount of open deck space, a three-quarter, two-level teak wood promenade deck, and a wrap-around jogging track atop the ship. The interior decor is elegant and understated, and the ship absorbs passengers really well. A small, dedicated cinema doubles as a conference and meeting center with the latest audio-visual technology. The atrium is calm and refreshing, not glitzy.

The former cigar club (Michael's Club) has been converted into a piano lounge; this triangular-shaped room, a favorite watering hole, has large comfortable chairs and the feel of a real gentlemen's club. Those who like gambling will find a large casino tightly packed with slot machines and gaming tables.

Children and teens are well catered for, too. X-Treme, within the Kid's Fun Factory area, is a new hangout for teens. Children's counselors are aboard for every cruise.

Outstanding are the 500 pieces of art that adorn the ship – a $3.8 million art collection that includes many Warhol favorites and fascinating contemporary sculptures (look for the colored violins on Deck Seven). The "Century Collection" includes a comprehensive survey of the most important artists and the major developments in art since the 1960s, and embraces Abstract Expressionism, Pop, Conceptualism,

BERLITZ'S RATINGS

	Possible	Achieved
Ship	500	411
Accommodation	200	175
Food	400	290
Service	400	298
Entertainment	100	72
Cruise	400	299

Minimalism and Neo-Expressionism.

Overall, this is a fine vessel for a big-ship cruise vacation, but instances of wear and tear and sloppy maintenance show in some areas, although general cleanliness is excellent. Gratifyingly, there are few annoying announcements. Gratuities are charged to your onboard account daily, and a 15% gratuity is added to all bar and wine accounts. The onboard currency is the US dollar.

Embarkation and disembarkation remain weak links in the Celebrity Cruises operation, and the cruise staff is unpolished and has little finesse. Standing in line for embarkation, disembarkation, shore tenders and for self-serve buffet meals is an inevitable aspect of cruising aboard all large ships. The interactive TV system is frustrating to use, and the larger suites have three remotes for TV/audio equipment (one would be better).

In 2006, *Celebrity Century* underwent a $55 million make-over that added 314 balconies, 14 new "Sky Suites" and 10 other cabins. The self-serve buffet area was expanded; an "Acupuncture at Sea" facility has been added, as has Murano – a specialty extra-charge restaurant, more shop space, an art gallery for art auctions, more internet-connect computers plus ship-wide wi-fi, and a neat ice-walled bar that is part of the Martini Bar. In short, the refit makes the ship more like the larger Millennium-class ships.

ACCOMMODATION. There are 12 different grades. The price depends on the grade, size and location. The wide variety of cabin types includes 18 family cabins, each with two lower beds, two foldaway beds and one upper berth. However, in the 2006 refit, new minimalist washbasins were installed in cabin bathrooms; however, they are not user-friendly as water splashes everywhere.

All cabins have wood cabinetry and accenting, personal safe, mini-bar/refrigerator (there is a charge if you use anything, of course), and interactive flat-screen TVs and entertainment systems (you can shop, book shore excursions or play casino games interactively in English, German, French, Italian or Spanish). Bathrooms have hairdryers, 100% cotton towels and large shower enclosures. However, the standard 24-hour cabin menu is disappointing, and very limited. There are no cabins for single occupancy.

The cabins are nicely equipped and decorated, with warm wood-finish furniture, and none of the boxy feel of cabins in many ships, due to the angled placement of vanity and audio-video consoles. In addition, all suites on Deck 10 (and the Sky Deck suites on Deck 12) have butler service and in-cabin dining facilities. Suites that have private balconies also have floor-to-ceiling windows and sliding doors to balconies (a few have outward opening doors).

For the largest living space aboard, choose one of two beautifully decorated Presidential Suites, each 1,173 sq. ft (109 sq. meters). These are located amidships in the most desirable position (each can be combined with the adjacent mini-suite via an inter-connecting door, to provide a living space of 1,515 sq. ft (140.7 sq. meters). Each suite has a marble-floored foyer, a living room with mahogany wood floor and hand-woven rug. Other features include a separate dining area with six-seat dining table; butler's pantry with wet bar; a wine bar with private label stock, refrigerator and microwave. A large private balcony has a dining table for two, chaise lounge chairs with cushioned pads, hot tub and dimmer-controlled lighting; master bedroom with king-sized bed, dressed with fine fabrics and draperies, and walk-in closet with abundant storage space. The all-marble bathroom has a jet-spray shower and whirlpool bath.

All cabins designated as suites have European duvets instead of sheets/blankets, fresh flowers, VCR, and butler service. Electrically operated blinds and other goodies are also standard in some suites.

CUISINE. A grand staircase connects the upper and lower levels of the splendid two-level, no-smoking Grand Dining Room. Huge windows overlook the stern. Each of the two levels has a separate finishing galley. There are two seatings for dinner (open seating for breakfast and lunch), at tables for two, four, six, eight or 10. The design of the two galleys is good, so food that should be hot does arrive hot at the table. The heavy dining room chairs should, but do not, have armrests.

All meals, including full dinners, can be served, course-by-course, in all suites and cabins, no matter what grade you choose. For those who can't live without them, freshly baked pizzas (boxed) can be delivered, in an insulated pouch, to your cabin.

Celebrity Cruises has an enviable reputation for fine dining aboard its ships. All meals are made from scratch, with nothing pre-cooked or pre-packaged ashore. However, the food served as room-service items is decidedly below the standard of food featured in the dining room.

There is also a large indoor/outdoor Lido Café (called "Islands") with four separate self-service buffet lines (included is a 76-seat sushi café), as well as two-grill serving stations located adjacent to the swimming pools outdoors.
Alternative Dining. Murano, a new reservations-only specialty restaurant off the main lobby, is a fine dining experience that takes about three hours, in a small, intimate setting – ideal for celebrating a birthday or anniversary, with refined service and specializing in à la minute tableside cooking and flambé items. The wine list is extensive.
Cova Café di Milano. This is a signature item aboard all the ships of Celebrity Cruises, and a seagoing version of the original Café di Milano opened in 1817 next to La Scala Opera House in Milan. The café is placed in a prominent position, on the second level of the atrium lobby, and a display case shows off the extensive range of Cova coffee, chocolates and alcoholic digestives. It is a fine meeting place for those who appreciate fine Italian coffees, pastries and superb cakes in an elegant, refined setting.

ENTERTAINMENT. The Celebrity Theater is a two-level, 1,000-seat showlounge/theater with side balconies. It has a large stage, a split orchestra pit (hydraulic), and the latest in high-tech lighting and sound equipment. Unfortunately, the production shows are not nearly as lavish. In fact, compared to some of the other major cruise lines, the shows are a letdown, and not in keeping with the elegant nature of the interior decor. Bar service, supplied continuously during shows, can prove irritating.

While there are some good cabaret acts, they are the same ones seen aboard many ships of the major cruise lines. In other words, it is disappointing to note that there is absolutely nothing to distinguish Celebrity Cruises in the entertainment department. The ship does have a number of bands, although there is very little music for social dancing, other than disco and pop music.

SPA/FITNESS. The AquaSpa has 9,040 sq. ft (840 sq. meters) of space dedicated to well-being and body treatments, all set in a calming environment. It includes a large fitness/exercise area, complete with all the latest high-tech muscle machines, thalassotherapy pool, and 10 treatment rooms. The spa has some of the more unusual wellness treatments, including an Acupuncture at Sea clinic, and a Rasul – a mud and gentle steam bathing room.

The spa is operated by Steiner, a specialist concession. Some fitness classes are free, while some, such as yoga and kick-boxing, cost $10 per class. Massage (including Aroma Stone massage, Chakra Balancing massage and other well-being massages), facials, manicures, pedicures, and beauty salon treatments cost extra. Examples of treatment costs: Hot Stone Massage, $175 for 75 minutes; facial, $130 for 50 minutes; plus a 10% gratuity.

● **For more extensive general information on what a Celebrity cruise is like, see pages 131–5.**

Celebrity Constellation
★★★★ +

Size:	Large Resort Ship	Passenger Decks:	11	Cabins (wheelchair accessible):	26
Tonnage:	90,228	Total Crew:	999		(17 with private balcony)
Lifestyle:	Premium	Passengers		Wheelchair accessibility	Best
Cruise Line:	Celebrity Cruises	(lower beds/all berths):	1,950/2,450	Cabin Current:	110 and 220 volts
Former Names:	Constellation	Passenger Space Ratio		Elevators:	10
Builder:	Chantiers de l'Atlantique	(lower beds/all berths):	46.2/36.8	Casino (gaming tables):	Yes
	(France)	Crew/Passenger Ratio		Slot Machines:	Yes
Original Cost:	$350 million	(lower beds/all berths):	1.9/2.4	Swimming Pools (outdoors):	2
Entered Service:	May 2002	Cabins (total):	975	Swimming Pools (indoors):	1
Registry:	Malta	Size Range (sq ft/m):	165.1–2,530.0/		(with magrodome)
Length (ft/m):	964.5/294.0		15.34–235.0	Whirlpools:	4
Beam (ft/m):	105.6/32.2	Cabins (outside view):	780	Self-Service Launderette:	No
Draft (ft/m):	26.2/8.0	Cabins (interior/no view):	195	Dedicated Cinema/Seats:	Yes/368
Propulsion/Propellers:	gas turbine/2	Cabins (for one person):	0	Library:	Yes
	azimuthing pods (39,000kW)	Cabins (with private balcony):	590		

BERLITZ'S OVERALL SCORE: 1,568 OUT OF A POSSIBLE 2,000 POINTS

OVERVIEW. *Celebrity Constellation* is a sister ship to *Celebrity Infinity, Celebrity Millennium*, and *Celebrity Summit* (the *Celebrity Millennium*-class ships). Jon Bannenberg, the famous mega-yacht designer, dreamed up the exterior featuring a royal blue and white hull, and racy lines in red, blue and gold – although it has turned out to look quite ungainly. This is the fourth Celebrity Cruises ship to be fitted with the "pod" propulsion system (*see page 45*) coupled with a quiet, smokeless, energy-efficient gas turbine powerplant (two GE gas turbines provide engine power while a single GE steam turbine drives the electricity generators).

BERLITZ'S RATINGS		
	Possible	Achieved
Ship	500	427
Accommodation	200	178
Food	400	291
Service	400	298
Entertainment	100	74
Cruise	400	300

On one side of Sky Deck, there is a huge bronze sculpture of a gorilla holding a fish under its arm; created by Angus Fairhurst, it is titled "A couple of differences between thinking and feeling."

One delightful feature is a large conservatory located in a glasshouse and spreading across a whole foyer. It includes a botanical environment with flowers, plants, tress, minigardens and fountains, all designed by the award-winning floral designer Emilio Robba of Paris. It is directly in front of the main funnel and a section of it has glass walls overlooking the ship's side.

Inside, the ship has a similar standard of decor and materials, and public rooms that have made the existing ships in the fleet so user-friendly. The atrium, with separately enclosed room for shore excursions, is three decks high and houses the reception desk, tour operator's desk, and bank. Four dramatic glass-walled elevators travel through the ship's exterior (port) side, connecting the atrium with another seven decks, thus traveling through 10 passenger decks, including the tender stations – a nice ride.

Facilities include a combination Cinema/Conference Center, an expansive shopping arcade with 14,447 sq. ft (1,300 sq. meters) of retail store space (with trendy brand name labels such as Fendi, Fossil, Hugo Boss, and Versace), a lavish four-decks-high showlounge with the latest in staging and lighting equipment, a two-level library (one level for English-language books; a second for books in other languages and reference material), card room, music listening room, and an observation lounge/ discotheque with outstanding views.

Michael's Club (originally a cigar smoker's haven), is now a piano lounge/ bar. An internet cafe has almost 20 computers with custom-made wood-surround flat-screen monitors and internet access.

The artwork throughout the ship (particularly the sculptures) is eclectic, provocative, thoughtful, and intelligent, and at almost every turn another piece appears to break the monotony associated with large spaces.

Gaming sports include the ship's overly large Fortunes Casino, with blackjack, roulette, and slot machines, and lots of bright lights and action. Families with children will appreciate the Fun Factory (for children) and The Tower (for teenagers). Children's counselors and youth activities staff provide a wide range of supervized activities.

After the downturn in business following 2001's terrorist attacks on the US, new management was brought in to restore Celebrity Cruises to the premium product envisioned when the company first started. Improvements introduced in 2003 have restored the art of hospitality and provide a taste of luxury for all. For example, on days at sea (in warm weather areas) if you are sunbathing on deck, someone will bring you a cold towel, and a sorbet, ice water and iced tea. Little touches like this differentiate Celebrity Cruises from other major cruise lines.

A cruise aboard a large ship such as this provides a wide range of choices and possibilities. If you travel in one of the suites, the benefits include the highest level of personal service, while cruising in non-suite accommodation is almost like in any large ship. One thing really is certain: cruising in a hassle-free environment such as this is hard to beat no matter how much or how little you pay. The onboard currency is the US dollar. A 15% gratuity is added to all bar and wine accounts.

Note that there is, sadly, no wrap-around wooden promenade deck outdoors. Standing in line for embarkation, disembarkation, shore tenders and for self-serve buffet meals is an inevitable aspect of cruising aboard all large ships (however, more flexible embarkation hours do help to spread the flow), but the worst time is when large numbers of passengers return from shore excursions and have to wait to go through a security check; the result being long lines outside the ship. The ship's two seating dining and two shows detract from an otherwise excellent product, and this ship (together with sister ships *Celebrity Infinity, Celebrity Millennium* and *Celebrity Summit*) can be said to provide the very best of the ships in the Premium segment of the marketplace, providing a taste of luxury for those who book in the largest suites.

ACCOMMODATION. There are 20 different grades from which to choose, depending on your preference for the grade, size and location of your living space. Almost half of the ship's cabins feature a "private" balcony; approximately 80 percent are outside-view suites and cabins, and 20 percent are interior (no view) cabins. The cabins are extremely comfortable throughout this ship, regardless of which cabin grade you choose. Suites, naturally, have more space, butler service (whether you want it or not), more and better amenities and more personal service than if you choose any of the standard cabin grades. There are several categories of suites, but those at the stern of the ship are in a prime location and have huge balconies that are really private and not overlooked from above.

Regardless of the grade you choose, all suites and cabins have wood cabinetry and accenting, interactive television and entertainment systems (you can go shopping, book shore excursions, play casino games interactively, and even watch soft porn movies). The bathrooms have hairdryers and 100% cotton towels.

Penthouse Suites: Two Penthouse Suites (on Penthouse Deck) are the largest cabins aboard this ship. Each occupies one half of the beam (width) of the ship, overlooking the ship's stern. Each measures a huge 2,530 sq. ft (235 sq. meters), consisting of 1,431.6 sq. ft (133 sq. meters) of living space, plus a huge wrap-around terrace measuring 1,098 sq. ft (102 sq. meters) with 180-degree views. This terrace includes a wet bar, hot tub and whirlpool tub – but much of

it can be overlooked by passengers on other decks above. Features include a marble foyer, a separate living room (complete with ebony baby grand piano – bring your own pianist if you don't play yourself – and a formal dining room. The master bedroom has a large walk-in closet, personal exercise equipment, dressing room with vanity desk, exercise equipment, marble-clad master bathroom with twin washbasins, deep whirlpool bathtub, separate shower, toilet and bidet areas, flat-screen televisions (one in the bedroom and one in the lounge), and electronically controlled drapes. Butler service is standard, and a butler's pantry, with separate entry door, has a full-size refrigerator, temperature-controlled wine cabinet, microwave oven and good-sized food preparation and storage areas. For even more space, an interconnecting door can be opened into the adjacent suite (ideal for multi-generation families).

Royal Suites: Eight Royal Suites, each measuring 733 sq ft (68 sq. meters), are located towards the aft of the ship (four each on the port and starboard sides). Each has a separate living room with dining and lounge areas (with refrigerator, mini-bar and Bang & Olufson CD sound system), and a separate bedroom. There are two entertainment centers with DVD players, and two flat-screen televisions (one in the living area, one in the bedroom), and a large walk-in closet with vanity desk. The marble-clad bathroom has a whirlpool bathtub with integral shower, and there is also a separate shower enclosure, two washbasins and toilet. The teakwood decked balcony is extensive (large enough for on-deck massage) and also has a whirlpool hot tub.

Celebrity Suites: Eight Celebrity Suites, each 467 sq. ft (44 sq. meters), have floor-to-ceiling windows, a separate living room with dining and lounge areas, two entertainment centers with flat-screen televisions (one in the living room, one in the bedroom), and a walk-in closet with vanity desk. The marble-clad bathroom has a whirlpool bathtub with integral shower (a window with movable blind lets you look out of the bathroom through the lounge to the large ocean-view windows). Interconnecting doors allow two suites to be used as a family unit; as there is no balcony, these suites are ideal for families with small children. These suites overhang the starboard side of the ship (they are located opposite a group of glass-walled lifts), and provide stunning ocean views from the glass-walled sitting/dining area, which extends out from the ship's side. A personal computer with wood-surround screen allows direct internet connectivity. Butler service is standard.

Sky Suites: There are 30 Sky Suites, each 308 sq. ft (28.6 sq. meters), including the private balcony (note that some balconies may be larger than others, depending on the location). Although these are designated as suites, they are really just larger cabins that feature a marble-clad bathroom with bathtub/shower combination. The suites also have a VCR player in addition to a TV set, and have a larger lounge area (than standard cabins) and sleeping area. Butler service is standard.

Butler Service: Butler service in all cabins designated as suites includes full breakfast, in-suite lunch and dinner service (as required), afternoon tea service, evening hors d'oeuvres, complimentary espresso and cappuccino, daily news delivery, shoeshine service, and other personal touches.

Suite occupants in Penthouse, Royal, Celebrity and Sky suites also get welcome champagne; a full personal computer in each suite, including a printer and internet access (on request in the Sky Suites); choice of films from a video library; personalized stationery; tote bag; priority dining room seating preferences; private portrait sitting, bathrobe; and in-suite massage service.

Standard Outside-View/Interior (No View) Cabins: All other outside-view and interior (no view) cabins have a lounge area with sofa or convertible sofa bed, sleeping area with twin beds that can convert to a double bed, a good amount of closet and drawer space, personal safe, mini-bar/refrigerator (extra cost), interactive television, and private bathroom. The cabins are nicely decorated with warm wood-finish furniture, and there is none of the boxy feel of cabins in so many ships, due to the angled placement of vanity and audio-video consoles. Even the smallest cabin has a good-sized bathroom and shower enclosure.

Wheelchair-Accessible Suites/Cabins: Wheelchair accessibility is provided in six Sky Suites, three premium outside-view, eight deluxe ocean-view, four standard ocean-view and five interior (no view) cabins measuring 347–362 sq. ft (32.2–33.6 sq. meters). They are located in the most practical parts of the ship and close to lifts for good accessibility – all have doorways and bathroom doorways, and showers are wheelchair-accessible. Some cabins have extra berths for third or third and fourth occupants. Note, however, that there is only one safe for personal belongings, which must be shared.

CUISINE. The 1,198-seat San Marco Restaurant is the ship's formal dining room. It is two decks high, has a grand staircase connecting the two levels (on the upper level of which is a musicians' gallery), and a huge glass wall overlooking the sea at the stern of the ship (electrically operated blinds provide several different backdrops). There are two seatings for dinner (with open seating for breakfast and lunch), at tables for two, four, six, eight or 10. The dining room, like all large dining halls, can be extremely noisy.

The menu variety is good, the food is tasty, and it is very attractively presented and served in a well orchestrated operation that displays fine European traditions and training. Full service in-cabin dining is also available for all meals (including dinner).

For casual eating, the Seaside Cafe & Grill is a self-serve buffet area, with six principal serving lines, and around 750 seats; there is also a grill and pizza bar. Each

evening, casual alternative dining takes place here (reservations are needed, although there's no additional charge), with tablecloths on tables and a modicum of service.

Alternative (Reservations-Only, Extra Cost) Dining: Ocean Liners Restaurant is the ship's alternative dining salon; it is adjacent to the main lobby. The decor includes some lacquered paneling from the famed 1920s French ocean liner *Ile de France*. Fine tableside preparation is the feature of this alternative dining room, whose classic French cuisine and service is very good. This is haute cuisine at the height of professionalism, for this is, indeed, a room for a full savoring, and not merely for dinner, featuring the French culinary arts of découpage and flambé. However, with just 115 seats, not all passengers are able to experience it even once during a one-week cruise (reservations are necessary, and a cover charge of $30 per person applies). There's a dine-in wine cellar (with more than 200 labels from around the world).

Café al Bacio and Gelateria: Located on the third level of the atrium lobby and formerly called Cova Café, is the place to see and be seen, for coffees (espresso, cappuccino, latte), pastries, cakes, and gelato, in a trendy setting.

ENTERTAINMENT. The 900-seat Celebrity Theatre is the three-deck-high venue for the ship's production shows and major cabaret acts. It is located in the forward part of the ship, with seating on the main level and two balcony levels. The large stage is equipped with a full fly loft behind its traditional proscenium.

SPA/FITNESS. Wellness facilities include a large AquaSpa measuring 24,219 sq. ft (2,250 sq. meters). It has a large thalassotherapy pool under a huge solarium dome, complete with health bar for light breakfast and lunch items and fresh squeezed fruit and vegetable juices.

There are 16 treatment rooms, plus eight treatment rooms with showers and one treatment room specifically designed for wheelchair passengers, an aerobics room, gymnasium with over 40 exercise machines, large male and female saunas (with a large ocean-view porthole window), a unisex thermal suite for $20 a day (containing several steam and shower mist rooms with different fragrances such as chamomile, eucalyptus and mint, and a glacial ice fountain), and beauty salon.

Sports facilities include a full-size basketball court, compact football, paddle tennis and volleyball, golf simulator, shuffleboard (on two different decks) and a jogging track.

● **For more extensive general information on what a Celebrity cruise is like, see pages 131–5.**

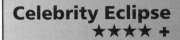

Celebrity Eclipse
★★★★ +

Size: . . . . .Large Resort Ship	Passenger Decks: 14	Cabins (with private balcony): 1,216
Tonnage: 122,000	Total Crew: 1,253	Cabins (wheelchair accessible): 30
Lifestyle: . . . . .Premium	Passengers	Wheelchair accessibility . . . . .Best
Cruise Line: . . . . .Celebrity Cruises	(lower beds/all berths): 2,852/3,145	Cabin Voltage: . . . . .110/220 volts
Former Names: . . . . .none	Passenger Space Ratio	Lifts: 12
Builder: . . . . .Meyer Werft (Germany)	(lower beds/all berths): 42.7/38.7	Casino (gaming tables): . . . . .Yes
Original Cost: . . . .$641 million	Crew/Passenger Ratio	Slot Machines: . . . . .Yes
Entered Service: . . . . Jun 2010	(lower beds/all berths): 2.2/2.5	Swimming Pools (outdoors): 2
Registry: .Malta	Cabins (total): 1,426	Swimming Pools (indoors): 1
Length (ft/m): 1,033.4/315.0	Size Range (sq ft/m): 182.9–668.4/	Whirlpools: 6
Beam (ft/m): 120.7/36.8	17.0–155.0	Self-Service Launderette: . . . . .No
Draft (ft/m): 27.2/8.3	Cabins (outside view): 1,286	Dedicated Cinema/Seats: . . . . .No
Propulsion/Propellers: . . . . .diesel	Cabins (interior/no view): 140	Library: . . . . .Yes
(67.2 MW)/2 pods	Cabins (for one person): 0	

OVERALL SCORE: 1,612 OUT OF A POSSIBLE 2,000 POINTS

OVERVIEW. Since it was founded in 1989, Celebrity Cruises has favored celestial names for its ships. *Celebrity Eclipse* is a sister ship to *Celebrity Equinox* (2009), *Celebrity Silhouette* (2011) and *Celebrity Solstice* (2008). For detailed information about its facilities, see the entries for those ships on pages 294, 304 and 305. At a cost of around $641 million when ordered, it's not as expensive as that other ship named *Eclipse*, Roman Abramovich's yacht, which cost an estimated $1 billion – for a much smaller ship.

The distinctive "X" (third letter of the Greek alphabet) is displayed on both sides of the ship, as well as on the forward funnel (one of two slim funnels), as part of a design that highlights the cruise line's origins as a Greek family-owned company.

Celebrity Eclipse has a steeply sloping stern – which includes a mega-yacht-style ducktail platform above the propulsion pods, is attractive, and nicely balances the ship's contemporary profile, with its two slim funnels, set one

BERLITZ'S RATINGS		
	Possible	Achieved
Ship	500	433
Accommodation	200	178
Food	400	303
Service	400	309
Entertainment	100	78
Cruise	400	311

behind the other. The ship's name is installed directly under the navigation bridge and not forward on the bows (for space reasons), and the bows were rounded to accommodate a helicopter landing pad.

One thing that's cool is an Apple "iLounge" equipped with 26 Apple Mac-Book Pro work stations. You can also buy Apple products.

CUISINE. Although this ship has almost the same dining venues as sister ships *Celebrity Equinox* and *Celebrity Solstice*, one venue is different. Called Qsine, it tries hard to present traditional and contemporary unordinary food from around the world, in a trendy setting. Note the waiters' jackets with their square buttons. The cover charge is $30 per person, reservations are required, and it's open for dinner only.

● **For more extensive general information on what a Celebrity cruise is like, see pages 131–5.**

Celebrity Equinox
★★★★ +

Size: . . . . Large Resort Ship	Passenger Decks: 14	Cabins (with private balcony): 1,216
Tonnage: 122,000	Total Crew: 1,253	Cabins (wheelchair accessible): 30
Lifestyle: . . . . .Premium	Passengers	Wheelchair accessibility . . . . .Best
Cruise Line: . . . . .Celebrity Cruises	(lower beds/all berths): 2,852/3,145	Cabin Voltage: . . . . .110/220 volts
Former Names: . . . . .none	Passenger Space Ratio	Lifts: 12
Builder: . . . . .Meyer Werft (Germany)	(lower beds/all berths): 42.7/38.7	Casino (gaming tables): . . . . .Yes
Original Cost: . . . .$641 million	Crew/Passenger Ratio	Slot Machines: . . . . .Yes
Entered Service: . . . . Aug 2009	(lower beds/all berths): 2.2/2.5	Swimming Pools (outdoors): 2
Registry: . . . . .Malta	Cabins (total): 1,426	Swimming Pools (indoors): 1
Length (ft/m): 1,033.4/315.0	Size Range (sq ft/m): . . . .182.9 –1,668.4/	Whirlpools: 6
Beam (ft/m): 120.7/36.8	17.0–155.0	Self-Service Launderette: . . . . .No
Draft (ft/m): 27.2/8.3	Cabins (outside view): 1,286	Dedicated Cinema/Seats: . . . . .No
Propulsion/Propellers: . . . . .diesel	Cabins (interior/no view): 140	Library: . . . . .Yes
(67.2 MW)/2 pods	Cabins (for one person): 0	

BERLITZ'S OVERALL SCORE: 1,611 OUT OF A POSSIBLE 2,000 POINTS

OVERVIEW. This is a sister ship to *Celebrity Eclipse, Celebrity Silhouette,* and *Celebrity Solstice.* The steeply sloping stern, which includes a mega-yacht-style ducktail platform above the propulsion pods, is very attractive, and nicely balances the ship's contemporary profile. The bows have been rounded to accommodate a helicopter platform.

Two rather slim funnels, set one behind the other distinguish the new ship from previous (single-funnel) Celebrity ships. Between the two funnels is a grass outdoor area, the Lawn Club. This is the real stuff – not green Astroturf – so let's hope it likes the salty air. The Lawn Club is open to all, so you can go putting, play croquet or bocce ball (like bowling or French boules), have a picnic on the grass, or perhaps sleep on it.

There are several pool and water-play areas on Resort Deck: one in a solarium (with glass roof), a sports pool, a family pool, and a wet zone. However, the deck space around the two pools is not large enough for the number of passengers carried.

Inside, the decor is elegant, yet contemporary. Michael's Club is an intimate, quiet lounge with classic English leather chairs, a dramatic black glass chandelier, a grand fireplace and some contemporary artwork. Rich furnishings help create a warm atmosphere, amidst a backdrop of piano and jazz music, as well as single malt scotch and cognacs for tastings.

Other attractions include a wine bar with a sommelier, a pre-dinner cocktail lounge that reflects the jazz music of the 1930s and '40s; a bar with the look of an ocean-going yacht; Quasar, a bar with designs from the 1960s and '70s and large screens that create a nightly light show synchro-

BERLITZ'S RATINGS		
	Possible	Achieved
Ship	500	433
Accommodation	200	178
Food	400	302
Service	400	310
Entertainment	100	78
Cruise	400	310

nized to music; and an observation lounge with a dance floor.

Celebrity's signature Martini Bar, which has a frosted bar – and more than 100 varieties of vodka as well as martinis – has a small alcove called Crush with an ice-filled table where you can participate in caviar and vodka tasting, or host a private party. This is a trendy, extremely noisy bar, which also makes the whole area congested.

Fortunes Casino (non-smoking) has 16 gaming tables and 200 slot machines. The ship also has a delightful two-deck library, but books on the upper shelves – it is 12 shelves high – are impossible to reach. An innovative Hot Glass Show, created in collaboration with Corning Museum of Glass, includes demonstrations and a narrated performance of glass-blowing, housed in an outdoor studio on the open deck as part of the Lawn Club. Three resident glass-blowing artists host workshops – but after you've seen it once, it's enough.

Passenger niggles include lack of usable drawer space in cabins; inadequate children's facilities and staff during the school holiday periods; utter congestion caused by a bottleneck when you exit the showlounge; and noise in all areas of the lobby when the martini bar is busy.

Also, don't bother looking for a deck chair after 8am – they'll be gone.

Good points include elevators call buttons located in a floor-stand "pod" so that, when the elevator arrives, a glass panel above it turns from blue to pink. Also, the ship has a good collection of designer chairs and sunloungers in various locations.

The onboard currency is the US dollar, and gratuities are automatically charged to your onboard account.

ACCOMMODATION. About 90% of the accommodation is in outside-view cabins. Of these, 85% have a balcony; indeed, this ship has more balcony cabins than any other cruise ship to date and, due to its slender width, there are very few interior (no-view) cabins. There are four suite-grade categories: Royal Suite, Celebrity Suite, Sky Suite, and Penthouse Suite. If you can afford it, book a suite-category cabin for the extra benefits it brings.

All grades of accommodation include: twin beds convertible to a queen-sized bed, sitting area, vanity desk with hairdryer, but there's very little drawer space. Also standard in all cabins: 32-inch flat-screen TVs (larger screens in suites), wireless internet access (for a fee), premium bedding. However, although the closets have good hanging space, there is no shelving on which to place folded items, and drawers in the vanity desk can't accommodate such items. The bathroom has a shower enclosure, toilet, and tiny washbasin but no soap dish. Accommodation designated as suites have more space, larger balconies with good-quality sunloungers, and more personal amenities.

Like other cruise lines, Celebrity has added "Spa-Class" accommodation. Some 130 AquaSpa-class cabins share the relaxation room of the AquaSpa itself, incorporate select spa elements into the cabins, and allow for specialized access to the AquaSpa's Thermal Relaxation Room and a Persian Garden (with aromatherapy/steam rooms) on the same deck. Features include: a choice of four pillows (conformance, body, goose, Isotonic); express luggage delivery; shoeshine; Frette bathrobes; dining and seating preferences in other alternative dining venues; and early embarkation and disembarkation. Bathrooms include a tub plus a separate shower enclosure. Occupants also get assigned seating at the exclusive 130-seat Restaurant Blu.

Other accommodation grades are named Veranda-class; Sunset-Veranda-class; Concierge-class; Family oceanview with veranda; Deluxe Oceanview with veranda; Standard Oceanview; and Standard Interior (no view) cabins.

Cabins 1551–1597 on the port side, and 1556–1602 on the starboard side on Penthouse Deck (Deck 11) suffer from "aircraft carrier" syndrome because they are directly under the huge overhanging Resort Deck. they have little exposure to sun or light, so private balcony sunbathing is out of the question. Many thick supporting struts ruin the view from these cabins, which are otherwise pleasantly fitted out.

CUISINE. Silhouette, the ship's balconied main dining room (included in the cruise price), has ocean views on the port and starboard sides. The design is stunning and contemporary. At the forward end, a two-deck-high wine tower provides a stunning focal point. As for the food, it is a bit of a let-down – the decreased quality is all too obvious to repeat Celebrity passengers. Shame!

The following four dining venues are all located one deck above the main restaurant and galley (on Deck 5), and occupy the aft section of the ship:

● Murano is an extra-cost, reservations-required venue ($30 for dinner) offering high-quality traditional dining with a French flair and exquisite table settings, including large Reidel wine glasses. Food and service are very good.

● Blu is a 130-seat specialty restaurant designated just for the occupants of AquaClass cabins. The room has pleasing (but rather cold) blue decor.

● The Tuscan Grille, an extra-cost venue ($30 for dinner), serves Kobe beef and premium quality steaks, and features beautifully curved archways – it's like walking into a high-tech winery. Great views from huge aft-view windows.

● Silk Harvest is a Southeast Asian extra-cost dining venue ($20 for dinner) serving pan-Asian fusion cuisine that is unmemorable. The venue has wood-topped tables.

For snacks and less ambitious meals, the options are:

● Bistro on Five (Deck 5, that is) is for coffee, cakes, crêpes, pastries, and more. It gets busy at times and the serving counter is small, so it's a congested area.

● Café al Bacio & Gelateria is a coffeehouse serving Lavazza Italian coffee. It is on one side of the main lobby, but it's small and lines quickly form at peak times. The seating is mostly in large, very comfortable armchairs.

● Oceanview Café and Grill is the expansive, tray-less, casual self-serve buffet venue. There are a number of food "islands" rather than those awful straight buffet counters, but the signage is reasonably good. However, it's impossible to get a warm plate for so-called hot food items, and condiments are hard to find.

● The AquaSpa Café is for light, healthier options (solarium fare), but the selections are bland and boring.

● The Mast Bar Grill and Bar is an outside venue that offers fast-food items.

ENTERTAINMENT. The 1,115-seat Equinox Theater, the ship's principal showlounge, has a main level and two balconied sections positioned amphitheatre-style around a stage with music lofts set on either side. Three circus-themed production shows highlight in-your-face, formulaic acrobatics.

Colorful theme nights are held in the Sky Observation Lounge, whose daytime bland and minimalist decor comes alive at night thanks to mood lighting effects. The 200-seat Celebrity Central hosts stand-up comedy, cooking demonstrations, enrichment lectures and feature films.

An Entertainment Court showcases street performers, psychics and caricaturists, and is in the center of the ship, linked to the adjacent Quasar nightclub, with its decor harking back to the 1960s and '70s. The Ensemble Lounge is a big-band era cocktail lounge with live jazz-styled music, set adjacent to the specialty restaurant, Murano.

SPA/FITNESS. The large AquaSpa is operated by concessionaire Steiner Leisure. The fitness center includes kinesis (pulleys against gravity) workout equipment, plus the familiar favorite muscle-pumping cardio-vascular machinery. There's also a relaxation area, AquaSpa station, and acupuncture center. Massages include fashionable things such as a Herbal Poultice massage and a Bamboo Massage using bamboo shoots and essential oils.

● **For more extensive general information on what a Celebrity cruise is like, see pages 131–5.**

Celebrity Infinity
★★★★ +

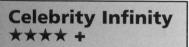

Size: . . . . .Large Resort Ship	Passenger Decks: 11	Cabins (wheelchair accessible): 26
Tonnage: 90,228	Total Crew: 999	(17 with private balcony)
Lifestyle: . . . . .Premium	Passengers	Wheelchair accessibility . . . . .Best
Cruise Line: . . . . .Celebrity Cruises	(lower beds/all berths): 1,950/2,450	Cabin Current: . . . . . . .110 and 220 volts
Former Names: . . . .*Infinity*	Passenger Space Ratio	Elevators: 10
Builder: . . . . . . .Chantiers de l'Atlantique	(lower beds/all berths): 46.2/36.8	Casino (gaming tables): . . . . .Yes
(France)	Crew/Passenger Ratio	Slot Machines: . . . . .Yes
Original Cost: . . . .$350 million	(lower beds/all berths): 1.9/2.4	Swimming Pools (outdoors): 2
Entered Service: . . . . .Mar 2001	Cabins (total): 975	Swimming Pools (indoors): 1
Registry: . . . . .Malta	Size Range (sq ft/m): 165.1–2,530.0/	(with magrodome)
Length (ft/m): 964.5/294.0	15.34–235.0	Whirlpools: 4
Beam (ft/m): 105.6/32.2	Cabins (outside view): 780	Self-Service Launderette: . . . . .No
Draft (ft/m): 26.2/8.0	Cabins (interior/no view): 195	Dedicated Cinema/Seats: Yes/368
Propulsion/Propellers: . . . . .gas turbine/2	Cabins (for one person): 0	Library: . . . . .Yes
azimuthing pods (39,000 kW)	Cabins (with private balcony): 590	

OVERALL SCORE: 1,566 OUT OF A POSSIBLE 2,000 POINTS

OVERVIEW. *Celebrity Infinity* is a sister ship to *Celebrity Constellation, Celebrity Millennium* and *Celebrity Summit.* Jon Bannenberg, famous for his mega-yacht designs, designed the exterior that features a royal blue and white hull, and racy lines in red, blue and gold. This is the second Celebrity Cruises ship to be fitted with a "pod" propulsion system *(see page 45)* coupled with a quiet, smokeless, energy-efficient gas turbine powerplant – two GE gas turbines pro-

(see page 45)

BERLITZ'S RATINGS		
	Possible	Achieved
Ship	500	425
Accommodation	200	178
Food	400	291
Service	400	298
Entertainment	100	74
Cruise	400	300

vide engine power while a single GE steam turbine drives the electricity generators.

One neat feature is a conservatory with seating, set in a botanical environment of flowers, plants, trees, mini-gardens and fountains, designed by the award-winning floral designer Emilio Robba of Paris. It is located directly in front of the main funnel. It has fresh flowers for any occasion, and a selection of Emilio Robba glass and flower creations, as well as pot pourri and other flora and fauna items.

Inside, the ship features the same high-class decor and materials, and public rooms that have made the existing ships in the fleet so popular and user-friendly. The atrium (with separately enclosed room for shore excursions) is three decks high and houses the reception desk, tour operator's desk, and bank. Four dramatic glass-walled elevators travel through the ship's exterior (port) side, connecting the atrium with another seven decks, thus traveling through 10 passenger decks, including the tender stations – a nice ride.

Facilities include a combination Cinema and Conference Center, an expansive shopping arcade with a 14,447 sq.-ft (1,300 sq.-meter) retail store space (including H. Stern, Donna Karan, Fossil), a four-decks-high showlounge , a two-

level library (one level for English-language books; a second level for other languages); card room; compact disc listening room; art auction center (with seating that look rather more like a small chapel); Cosmos, a combination observation lounge/discotheque; an Internet Center with 18 computer stations. Michael's Club, originally a cigar smoker's haven, has now become a piano lounge/bar.

Gaming sports include the ship's overly large Fortunes Casino, with blackjack, roulette, and slot machines, and lots of bright lights and action. Families with children will like the Fun Factory (for young children) and The Tower (for teenagers). Children's counselors and youth activities staff provide a wide range of supervised activities.

Hospitality prevails. For example, on days at sea in warm weather areas, if you are sunbathing on deck, someone will bring you a cold towel, and a sorbet, ice water and iced tea. Little touches like this differentiate Celebrity Cruises from other major cruise lines.

A cruise aboard a large ship such as this provides a wide range of choices and possibilities. If you travel in one of the suites, the benefits provide you with the highest level of personal service, while cruising in non-suite accommodation is almost like in any large ship – you'll be one of a number, with little access to the niceties and benefits of "upper class" cruising. It all depends how much you are willing to pay. The onboard currency is the US dollar. A 15% gratuity is added to bar and wine accounts. The ship's two-seating dining and two shows sadly detract from an otherwise excellent product.

There is, sadly, no walk-around wooden promenade deck

outdoors. There are cushioned pads for poolside sun-loungers only, but not for chairs on other outside decks. Trying to reach Cabin Service or the Guest Relations Desk to answer the phone (to order breakfast, for example, if you don't want to do so via the interactive television) is a matter of luck, timing and patience.

ACCOMMODATION. There are 20 different price grades. Almost half of the ship's accommodation features a "private" balcony; approximately 80% are outside-view suites and cabins, and 20 percent are interior (no view) cabins. The accommodation is extremely comfortable throughout this ship. Suites, naturally, have more space, butler service (whether you want it or not), more and better amenities and more personal service than any of the standard cabin grades. There are several categories of suites, but those at the stern of the ship are in a prime location and have huge balconies that are very private and not overlooked from above.

All suites and cabins have wood cabinetry and accenting, interactive television and entertainment systems (you can go shopping, book shore excursions, play casino games, interactively, and even watch soft porn movies). Bathrooms have hairdryers, and 100% cotton towels.

Penthouse Suites: Two Penthouse Suites (on Penthouse Deck) are the largest accommodation aboard. Each occupies one half of the beam (width) of the ship, overlooking the ship's stern. Each measures a huge 2,530 sq. ft (235 sq. meters): 1,431.6 sq. ft (133 sq. meters) of living space, plus a huge wrap-around balcony measuring 1,098 sq. ft (102 sq, meters) with 180° views, which occupies one half of the beam (width) of the ship, overlooking the stern (it includes a wet bar, hot tub and whirlpool tub); however, much of this terrace can be overlooked from other decks above.

Features include a marble foyer, a separate living room (complete with ebony baby grand piano – bring your own pianist if you don't play yourself) and a formal dining room. The master bedroom has a large walk-in closet; personal exercise equipment; dressing room with vanity desk; exercise equipment; marble-clad master bathroom with twin washbasins; deep whirlpool bathtub; separate shower; toilet and bidet areas; flat-screen televisions (one in the bedroom and one in the lounge); and electronically controlled drapes. Butler service is standard, and a butler's pantry, with separate entry door, features a full-size refrigerator, temperature-controlled wine cabinet, microwave oven and good-sized food preparation and storage areas. For even more space, an interconnecting door can be opened into the adjacent suite.

Royal Suites: Eight Royal Suites, each measuring 733 sq. ft (68 sq. meters), are located towards the aft of the ship (four each on the port and starboard sides). Each features a separate living room with dining and lounge areas (with refrigerator, mini-bar and a Bang & Olufsen CD sound system), and a separate bedroom. There are two entertainment centers with DVD players, and two flat-screen televisions (one in the living area, one in the bedroom), and a large walk-in closet with vanity desk. The marble-clad bathroom has a whirlpool bathtub with integral shower, and there is also a separate shower enclosure, two washbasins and toilet. The

teakwood decked balcony is extensive (large enough for on-deck massage) and also features a whirlpool hot tub.

Celebrity Suites: Eight Celebrity Suites, each measuring 467 sq. ft (44 sq. meters), have floor-to-ceiling windows, a separate living room with dining and lounge areas, two entertainment centers with flat-screen televisions (one in the living room, one in the bedroom), and a walk-in closet with vanity desk. The marble-clad bathroom has a whirlpool bathtub with integral shower (a window with movable shade lets you look out of the bathroom through the lounge to the large ocean-view windows).

Interconnecting doors allow two suites to be used as a family unit (as there is no balcony, these suites are ideal for families with small children). These suites overhang the starboard side of the ship (they are located opposite a group of glass-walled elevators), and provide stunning ocean views from the glass-walled sitting/dining area, which extends out from the ship's side. A personal computer with wood-surround screen allows direct internet connectivity. Butler service is standard.

Sky Suites: There are 30 Sky Suites, each measuring 308 sq. ft (28.6 sq. meters), including the private balcony (some balconies may be larger than others, depending on the location). Although these are designated as suites, they are really just larger cabins that feature a marble-clad bathroom with bathtub/shower combination. The suites also have a VCR player in addition to a television, and have a larger lounge area and sleeping area than standard cabins. Butler service is standard.

Butler Service: Butler service (in all accommodation designated as suites) includes full breakfast, in-suite lunch and dinner service (as required), afternoon tea service, evening hors d'oeuvres, complimentary espresso and cappuccino, daily news delivery, and shoeshine service.

Suite occupants in Penthouse, Royal, Celebrity and Sky suites also get welcome champagne; a full personal computer in each suite, including a printer and internet access (on request in the Sky Suites); choice of films from a video library; personalized stationery; tote bag; priority dining room seating preferences; private portrait sitting; bathrobe; and in-suite massage service.

Concierge Class: In 2003, Celebrity Cruises added a third service "class" to some of the accommodation grades aboard this ship. Positioned between the top grade suite grades and standard cabin grades, Concierge Class adds value to these "middle-class" cabins.

Enhanced facilities include priority embarkation, disembarkation, tender tickets, alternative dining and spa reservations. Here's what you get in the Concierge Class cabins that others don't (except for the suites): European duvet; double bed overlay (no more falling "between the cracks" for couples); choice of four pillows (goose down pillow, isotonic pillow, body pillow, conformance pillow); eight-vial flower vase on vanity desk; throw pillows on sofa; fruit basket; binoculars; golf umbrella; leather telephone notepad; larger beach towels; hand-held hairdryer. The balcony gets better furniture. In the bathrooms: plusher Frette bathrobes; larger towels in sea green and pink (alternating days); flower in silver vase. It all adds up to excellent value for money.

Standard Outside-View/Interior (No View) Cabins: All other outside-view and interior (no view) cabins feature a lounge area with sofa or convertible sofa bed, sleeping area with twin beds that can convert to a double bed, a good amount of closet and drawer space, personal safe, mini-bar/refrigerator (extra cost), interactive television, and private bathroom. The cabins are nicely decorated with warm wood-finish furniture, and there is none of the boxy feel of cabins in so many ships, due to the angled placement of vanity and audio-video consoles. Even the smallest cabin has a good-sized bathroom and shower enclosure.

Wheelchair-Accessible Accommodation: Wheelchair-accessible accommodation is available in six Sky Suites, three premium outside-view, eight deluxe ocean-view, four standard ocean-view and five interior (no view) cabins measure 347 sq. ft to 362 sq. ft (32.2–33.6 sq. meters) and are located in the most practical parts of the ship and close to elevators for good accessibility (all doorways and bathroom doorways and showers are wheelchair-accessible). Some cabins have extra berths for third or third and fourth occupants (note, however, that there is only one safe for personal belongings, which must be shared).

CUISINE. The Thellis Restaurant is the ship's 1,170-seat formal dining room. It is two decks high, has a grand staircase connecting the two levels, a huge glass wall overlooking the sea at the stern of the ship (electrically operated shades provide several different backdrops), and a musician's gallery on the upper level (typically for a string quartet/quintet). There are two seatings for dinner (open seating for breakfast and lunch), at tables for two, four, six, eight or 10. The dining room is a totally no-smoking area, and, you should note, that, like all large dining halls, it can prove to be extremely noisy. The menu variety is good, the food has taste, and it is very attractively presented and served in a well orchestrated operation that displays fine European traditions and training. Full service in-cabin dining is also available for all meals, including dinner.

Besides this principal restaurant, there are several other dining options, particularly for those seeking more casual dining, or for an extra-special (extra cost) meal in a more intimate (and quiet) setting.

For casual eating, the Las Olas Café and Grill is a self-serve buffet area, with six principal serving lines, and seating for 754; there is also a grill and pizza bar. For champagne and caviar lovers, not to mention martinis, Carlisle's is the place to see and be seen.

Alternative (Reservations-Only, Extra Cost) Dining Option: The United States Restaurant, the ship's alternative dining salon, is adjacent to the main lobby. Actual glass panelling from the former United States Lines liner *United States* is featured (in 1952, the *United States* made the fastest transatlantic crossing by a passenger ship, and took the famed "Blue Riband" from the Cunard's *Queen Mary*). The United States Restaurant is not nearly as luxurious as the alternative dining salons aboard sister ships *Celebrity Constellation*, *Celebrity Millennium* or *Celebrity Summit*.

A team of 10 chefs prepares the cuisine exclusively for this restaurant. Fine tableside preparation is the attraction of this alternative dining room, whose classic French cuisine (but including some menu items from the *United States*) and service are very good. This is haute cuisine at the height of professionalism, for this is, indeed, a room for a full degustation, and not merely a dinner. However, with just 134 seats, not all passengers will be able to experience it even once during a one-week cruise (reservations are necessary, and a cover charge of $30 per person applies). A dine-in wine cellar is also a feature, as is a demonstration galley.

Café al Bacio and Gelateria: Located on the third level of the atrium lobby and formerly called Cova Café, is the place to see and be seen, for coffees (espresso, cappuccino, latte), pastries, cakes, and gelato, in a trendy setting.

ENTERTAINMENT. The 900-seat Celebrity Theater is the three-deck-high venue for production shows and major cabaret acts. It is located in the forward part of the ship, with seating on main, and two balcony levels. The large stage has a full fly loft behind its traditional proscenium.

SPA/FITNESS. There is a large AquaSpa measuring 24,219 sq. ft (2,250 sq. meters). It features a large thalassotherapy pool under a huge solarium dome, complete with health bar for light breakfast and lunch items and fresh squeezed fruit and vegetable juices.

Spa facilities include 16 treatment rooms, plus eight treatment rooms with showers and one treatment room specifically designed for wheelchair passengers, aerobics room, gymnasium with over 40 exercise machines, large men's and women's saunas (with large ocean-view porthole window), a unisex thermal suite for $20 a day (containing several steam and shower mist rooms with different fragrances such as chamomile, eucalyptus and mint, and a glacial ice fountain), and beauty salon.

The spa is operated by Steiner, a specialist concession. Sports facilities include a full-size basketball court, compact football, paddle tennis and volleyball, golf simulator, shuffleboard (on two different decks) and a jogging track.

● **For more extensive general information on what a Celebrity cruise is like, see pages 131–5.**

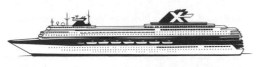

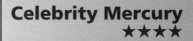

Celebrity Mercury
★★★★

Size: . . . . .Large Resort Ship	Passenger Decks: 10	Cabins (with private balcony): 220
Tonnage: 77,713	Total Crew: 909	Cabins (wheelchair accessible): 8
Lifestyle: . . . . .Premium	Passengers	Wheelchair accessibility . . . . .Good
Cruise Line: . . . . .Celebrity Cruises	(lower beds/all berths): 1,870/2,681	Cabin Current: . . . . .110 and 220 volts
Former Names: . . . .*Mercury*	Passenger Space Ratio	Elevators: 10
Builder: . . . . .Meyer Werft (Germany)	(lower beds/all berths): 41.5/28.9	Casino (gaming tables): . . . . .Yes
Original Cost: . . . .$320 million	Crew/Passenger Ratio	Slot Machines: . . . . .Yes
Entered Service: . . . . .Nov 1997	(lower beds/all berths): 2.0/2.9	Swimming Pools (outdoors): 2
Registry: . . . . .Malta	Cabins (total): 935	Swimming Pools (indoors): 1
Length (ft/m): 865.8/263.90	Size Range (sq ft/m): 171.0–1,219.0/	indoor/outdoor (magrodome)
Beam (ft/m): 105.6/32.20	15.8–113.2	Whirlpools: 4
Draft (ft/m): 25.2/7.70	Cabins (outside view): 639	Self-Service Launderette: . . . . .No
Propulsion/Propellers: . . . . .diesel	Cabins (interior/no view): 296	Dedicated Cinema/Seats: Yes/183
(31,500 kW)/2	Cabins (for one person): 0	Library: . . . . .Yes

OVERALL SCORE: 1,518 OUT OF A POSSIBLE 2,000 POINTS

OVERVIEW. *Celebrity Mercury,* which will be become *Mein Schiff II* when it is transferred to TUI Cruises in March 2011, is a good ship, inside and outside. The profile is quite well balanced despite its squared-off stern. It has the distinctive Celebrity Cruises' "X" funnel ("X" being the Greek letter "C" which stands for Chandris, the former owning company, before Royal Caribbean bought it). With a high passenger space ratio for such a large ship, there is no real sense of crowding, and the passenger flow is good, but *Celebrity Mercury* is now looking tired in places.

Facilities include a three-deck-high main foyer with marble floored lobby and waterfall; more than 190,000 sq. ft (18,000 sq. mcters) of open deck space (poolside lounge chairs have cushioned pads, those on other decks do not); a magrodome-covered indoor-outdoor pool; AquaSpa thalassotherapy pool with several "active" water jet stations, and assorted treatment rooms including a "rasul" mud treatment room.

Other facilities include "Michael's Club", a cigar/cognac room on Promenade Deck that overlooks the atrium, a small but luxurious cinema, a large casino (this is extremely glitzy, with confusing and congested layout). The children's facilities are good. As well as the "Fun Factory," there's an outdoor play area and a paddling pool.

The interior decor is elegant and understated. It includes plenty of wood (or wood-look) paneling and accenting throughout, and many refinements have been made during the three-ship "Century Series" that Celebrity Cruises has introduced in the past few years.

The ship also houses a $3.5 million living art collection with true, museum-quality pieces. The health and fit-

BERLITZ'S RATINGS

	Possible	Achieved
Ship	500	406
Accommodation	200	162
Food	400	278
Service	400	306
Entertainment	100	71
Cruise	400	295

ness facilities are among the nicest aboard any ship, and have been well thought-out and designed for quiet, efficient operation, with everything in just the right place.

This ship will provide you with a well-packaged cruise vacation in elegant surroundings. It is efficiently run. There are more crew members per passenger than would be found aboard other ships of the same size in the premium category, and hence service in general is very good indeed. Note that a 15% gratuity is added to all bar and wine accounts.

After Celebrity Cruises was bought by Royal Caribbean International, the standard of product delivery aboard all the ships in the Celebrity Cruises fleet went down as cuts were made by the new owner, and this reflected in the ship's revised score. The onboard currency is the US dollar.

Trying to reach Cabin Service or the Guest Relations Desk to answer the phone (to order breakfast, for example, if you don't want to do so via the interactive television) is a matter of luck, timing and patience – a sad reminder of the automated age, and lack of personal contact. The library is disappointingly small, and poorly located away from the main flow of passengers. There is a charge for using the Aquaspa/sauna/steam room complex. The room-service menu is poor, and food items are below the standards of food featured in the dining room. Standing in line for embarkation, disembarkation, shore tenders and for self-serve buffet meals is an inevitable aspect of cruising aboard all large ships.

While under the direction of its former owner, John Chandris, Celebrity Cruises managed to create a superb quality cruise holiday product virtually unbeatable at the prices charged in the Alaska and Caribbean markets, representing outstanding value for money. However, given the subtle changes that have occurred since Celebrity Cruises was integrated into the Royal Caribbean Cruises family in 1997, it has become evident that some slippage of product delivery standards and staff have occurred and the ship looks a bit tired in places.

SUITABLE FOR: *Mercury* is best suited to well-traveled couples and singles of 40 and above (not particularly recommended for children and teenagers) seeking a large ship with a sophisticated environment, good itineraries, fine food and good European-style service from a well-trained crew that cares and delivers an onboard product that is well above average.

ACCOMMODATION. There are 13 different grades. The price you pay will depend on the grade, size and location. The accommodation is extremely comfortable, regardless of which cabin grade you choose. Naturally, if you select a suite, you will find more space, butler service (whether you want it or not), more and better amenities and more personal service than if you choose any of the standard cabin grades.

Occupants of all accommodation designated as suites get gold cards (and priority service throughout the ship, free cappuccino/espresso coffees when served by a butler, welcome champagne, flowers, and video recorder. All occupants of standard (interior no view and outside-view) cabins have white cards. Suites that have private balconies also have floor-to-ceiling windows and sliding doors to balconies (a few suites have outward opening doors).

Two Presidential Suites are located amidships. These provide spectacular living spaces, perhaps even better than those in *Celebrity Century* and *Celebrity Galaxy*, depending on your personal taste. There is a separate bedroom (with high-tech Sony multimedia entertainment center), large lounge (complete with dining table), huge walk-in closet with mountains of drawers, and king-sized marble-tiled bathroom with every appointment necessary.

There is in-suite dining for the two Presidential and 12 Century Suites, as well as for the 24 Sky Suites (1202, 1203, 1236 and 1237 have enormous fully private balconies, while the others are only semi-private). All suites feature full butler service, personalized stationery, and business cards. If you choose one of the forward-most Sky Deck suites, however, be warned that you may well be subject to constant music and noise from the pool deck (one deck below) between 8am and 6pm (not good if you want to relax). The closet and drawer space provided in these suites is superb. In the bathrooms of the Sky Suites, the shaving mirror is positioned too high, and in the bedroom, the TV set cannot be viewed from the bed. Push-button bell and privacy curtains should be provided, but are not. In-suite massage is available (this really is pleasant when provided on the balcony of the Sky Suites).

The standard (interior and outside) cabins are quite spacious and nicely decorated with cheerful fabrics, and marble-topped vanity unit. The bathrooms are generous with space, tiled from floor to ceiling, and the power showers are extremely practical units.

All cabins have interactive TV for booking shore excursions, ordering cabin service items and purchasing goods from the ship's boutiques, so you don't have to leave your quarters, especially if you dislike the ports of call. The system works in English, French, German, Italian and Spanish. There are five channels of music – all available from the TV set (therefore you cannot have music without having a picture). All cabins are also equipped with a "baby monitoring telephone system" which allows you to telephone your cabin whilst you are elsewhere, and have a two-way intercom to "listen in". Automatic "wake-up" calls can also be dialed in. All accommodation designated as suites has duvets on the beds instead of sheets and blankets.

CUISINE. The two-level formal Manhattan Restaurant, located at the ship's stern, is quite grand and elegant (each level has its own full galley); a grand staircase connects the two levels. Large picture windows provide sea views on three sides; at night, large shades (with scenes of Manhattan, the name of the dining room) roll down electronically to cover the stern-facing windows. There are two seatings for dinner (open seating for breakfast and lunch), at tables for two, four, six, eight or 10, and the dining room is a totally no-smoking area.

Fine cuisine made Celebrity Cruises the shining star of the contemporary cruise industry. The menus are creative and the food is very attractively presented. There is also an excellent wine list, and real wine waiters (unlike so many other large cruise companies), although prices are high – particularly for good champagne – and the wine vintages are quite young.

There are also several informal dining spots as an alternative to the main dining room: a Lido Cafe, with four main serving lines; a poolside grill, and another indoor/outdoor grill located behind the aft swimming pool. The Lido Cafe has fine wood paneling and is much more elegant than the informal dining areas found aboard most ships, and has some seating in bay window areas with great ocean views.

In the center of the ship is Tastings, a delightful coffee/tea lounge; in one corner is a presentation of goodies made by COVA, the Milanese chocolatier – an exclusive to Celebrity Cruises (the original Cova Cafe di Milano is adjacent to the La Scala Opera House in Milan). This is the place to see and be seen. It is a delightful setting (as well as a good meeting place) for those who appreciate fine Italian coffees (espresso, espresso macchiato, cappuccino, and latte), pastries, and superb cakes.

Finally, for those who cannot live without them, freshly baked pizzas can be ordered and delivered to your cabin inside an insulated pouch.

ENTERTAINMENT. As aboard its identical sister *Galaxy*, there is a 1,000-seat showlounge, with side balconies, and no pillars to obstruct views (there are three high-tech "dazzle and sizzle" production shows per 7-night cruise.

Unfortunately, the production shows are not nearly as lavish as the showlounge they play in. In fact, compared to those mounted by some of the other major cruise lines, the shows are a letdown, and not in keeping with the elegant nature of the interior decor. Most consist mainly of running, jumping, smoke, colored laser lighting, very loud music and click tracks, and very little storyline. Bar service, supplied continuously during shows, can irritate.

While there are some good cabaret acts, they are the same ones seen aboard many ships of the major cruise lines. In other words, it is disappointing to note that there is absolutely nothing to distinguish Celebrity Cruises in the entertainment department. The ship does have a number of bands, although there is very little music for social dancing, other than disco and pop music.

SPA/FITNESS. The AquaSpa has 9,040 sq. ft (840 sq. meters) of space dedicated to well-being and body treatments, and includes a large fitness/exercise area, complete with all the latest high-tech muscle machines and video cycles, thalassotherapy pool, and seven treatment rooms.

The spa features some of the more unusual wellness treatments (including a steamy rasul room – for Mediterranean mud and gentle steam bathing). It is operated by Steiner, a specialist concession, whose enthusiastic staff will try to and sell you Steiner's own-brand Elemis beauty products. Personal training sessions in the gymnasium cost $83 for one hour.

Some fitness classes are free, while some, such as yoga, and kickboxing, cost $10 per class. However, being aboard will give you an opportunity to try some of the more exotic treatments (particularly some of the massages available). Massage (including exotic massages such as Aroma Stone massage, Chakra Balancing massage and other well-being massages), facials, pedicures, and beauty salon treatments are at extra cost.

Examples of treatment costs: massage at $109 (50 minutes), facial at $109, seaweed wrap (75 minutes) $190 – all plus a gratuity of 10 percent. Do make appointments as early as possible – aboard large ships, time slots go quickly, so the day you board is the best time to book treatments.

● **For more extensive general information about the Celebrity Cruises experience, see pages 131–5.**

WHERE NAUTICAL EXPRESSIONS COME FROM

If you've ever wondered where some terms or phrases came from, you have only to look to the sea, ships, and seamen.

In the doldrums

Doldrums is the name of a place in the ocean that is located either side of, and near, the equator. It is characterized by unstable trade winds or even lack of winds for days, if not weeks, at a time. A sailing ship caught in the Doldrums can be stranded due to lack of wind. If the situation was bad enough, or if danger threatened, the boats might be launched in order to tow the ship until the wind picked up. Today, if we are in the doldrums, we feel stagnated or even morose.

Mind your P's and Q's

Sailors would get credit at the waterfront taverns until they were paid. The innkeeper kept a record of their drinks, and he had to mind that no pints or quarts were left off of their accounts. Today, the term usually refers to manners.

Passed with flying colors

This comes from sailing ships that, when passing other ships at sea, would fly their colors (pennants, flags) if they wanted to be identified. Today we tend to mean by this phrase that a person has passed an exam or test or trial with great marks.

Pipe down

A boatswain's call denoting the completion of an all hands evolution, and that you can go below. This expression is now used to mean "keep quiet" or "quiet down."

Port and Starboard

Originally, the old sailing ships (like the Vikings), didn't have a rudder, and were steered by a board on the right side. This came to be the "steerboard" side or starboard. The other side was called "larboard" at first, but since the side with the board could not be against the dock, the left when facing forward, it became known as the "port" side.

Round robin

The term originated in the British nautical tradition. Sailors wishing to mutiny would sign their names in a circle so the leader could not be identified. Today the term is often used in sports and competitions to denote a series of games in which all members of a league play each other one time.

Celebrity Millennium
★★★★ +

Size: . . . . .Large Resort Ship	Passenger Decks: 11	Cabins (wheelchair accessible): 26
Tonnage: .90,228	Total Crew: 999	(17 with private balcony)
Lifestyle: . . . . .Premium	Passengers	Wheelchair accessibility . . . . .Best
Cruise Line: . . . . .Celebrity Cruises	(lower beds/all berths): 1,950/2,450	Cabin Current: . . . . .110 and 220 volts
Former Names: . . . . .Millennium	Passenger Space Ratio	Elevators: 10
Builder: . . . . .Chantiers de l'Atlantique	(lower beds/all berths): 46.2/36.8	Casino (gaming tables): . . . . .Yes
(France)	Crew/Passenger Ratio	Slot Machines: . . . . .Yes
Original Cost: . . . .$350 million	(lower beds/all berths): 1.9/2.4	Swimming Pools (outdoors): 2
Entered Service: . . . . .June 2000	Cabins (total): 975	Swimming Pools (indoors): 1
Registry: . . . . .Malta	Size Range (sq ft/m): 170.0–2,350.0/	(with magrodome)
Length (ft/m): 964.5/294.0	15.7–235.0	Whirlpools: 4
Beam (ft/m): 105.6/32.2	Cabins (outside view): 780	Self-Service Launderette: . . . . .No
Draft (ft/m): 26.2/8.0	Cabins (interior/no view): 195	Dedicated Cinema/Seats: Yes/368
Propulsion/Propellers: . . . .gas turbine/2	Cabins (for one person): 0	Library: . . . . .Yes
azimuthing pods (39,000 kW)	Cabins (with private balcony): 590	

OVERALL SCORE: 1,568 OUT OF A POSSIBLE 2,000 POINTS

OVERVIEW. This was the first Celebrity Cruises ship to be fitted with a "pod" propulsion system coupled with a gas turbine powerplant. Indeed, this is the first cruise ship in the world to be powered by quiet, smokeless, energy-efficient gas turbines (two GE gas turbines provide engine power while a single GE steam turbine drives the electricity generators). The ship was dogged by technical problems in its early days.

One delightful feature is a large conservatory located in a glasshouse environment and spreading across a whole foyer. It includes a botanical environment with flowers and plants. It is directly in front of the main funnel and a section of it has glass walls overlooking the ship's side. Facilities outdoors include two outdoor pools, one indoor/ outdoor pool, and six whirlpools.

Inside, the ship has an understated elegance, with the same high-class decor and materials (including lots of wood, glass and marble) and public rooms that have made other ships in the fleet so popular. The atrium (with separately enclosed room for shore excursions) is four decks high and houses the reception desk, tour operator's desk, and bank. Four glass-walled elevators travel through the ship's exterior (port) side, connecting the atrium with another seven decks, thus traveling through 10 passenger decks, including the tender stations – a nice ride.

Other facilities include a combination cinema/conference center, an expansive shopping arcade, with more than 14,450 sq. ft (1,300 sq. meters) of retail store space, a lavish four-decks-high showlounge with the latest in high-tech staging and lighting equipment, two-level library (one level for English-language books; a second level for books in other lan-

BERLITZ'S RATINGS

	Possible	Achieved
Ship	500	427
Accommodation	200	178
Food	400	291
Service	400	298
Entertainment	100	74
Cruise	400	300

guages); card room; CD listening room; art auction center with seating that makes it look more like a small chapel; Cosmos, a combination observation lounge/discotheque; an Internet Center containing 19 computer stations with wood-surround flat screens.

Gaming sports include the ship's overly large Fortunes Casino, with blackjack, roulette, and slot machines, and lots of bright lights and action. Michael's Club, originally a cigar smoker's haven, is now a piano lounge/bar.

Families cruising with children will appreciate the Fun Factory (for children) and The Tower (for teenagers). Children's counselors and youth activities staff are on hand.

Celebrity Millennium delivers a well-defined North American cruise experience at a very modest price. The "zero announcement policy" means there is little intrusion. My advice is to book a suite-category cabin for all the extra benefits it brings. The two-seating dining and two shows detract from an otherwise excellent product, and this ship (together with sisters *Celebrity Constellation*, *Celebrity Infinity* and *Celebrity Summit*) provide some of the best ships in the Premium segment of the marketplace.

There is, sadly, no walk-around wooden promenade deck outdoors. There are cushioned pads for poolside deck lounge chairs only, but not for chairs on other outside decks. Passenger participation activities are amateurish and should be upgraded. Although the officers have become more aloof lately, new management has done much to restore the art of hospitality. One thing is certain: cruising in a hassle-free, crime-free environment such as this is hard to beat, no matter how much or how little you pay.

ACCOMMODATION. There are 20 different grades. Almost half of the ship's accommodation has a "private" balcony. The accommodation is extremely comfortable. Suites, naturally, have more space, butler service, more and better amenities and more personal service than if you choose any of the standard cabin grades. There are several categories of suites, but those at the stern of the ship are in a prime location and have huge balconies that really are private and not overlooked from above.

All suites and cabins have wood cabinetry and accenting, interactive television and entertainment systems – you can go shopping, book shore excursions, play casino games, interactively, and even watch soft porn movies. Bathrooms have hairdryers, and 100% cotton towels.

Penthouse Suites: Two Penthouse Suites (on Penthouse Deck) are the largest accommodation aboard. Each occupies one half of the beam (width) of the ship, overlooking the ship's stern. Each measures a huge 2,530 sq. ft. (235 sq. meters): 1,432 sq. ft. (133 sq. meters) of living space, plus a huge wrap-around balcony measuring 1,098 sq. ft. (102 sq. meters) with 180° views, which occupies one half of the beam (width) of the ship, overlooking the ship's stern (it includes a wet bar, hot tub and whirlpool tub); however, note that much of this terrace can be overlooked by passengers on other decks above.

Features include a marble foyer, a separate living room (complete with ebony baby grand piano) and a formal dining room. The master bedroom has a large walk-in closet; personal exercise equipment; dressing room with vanity desk, exercise equipment; marble-clad master bathroom with twin washbasins; deep whirlpool bathtub; separate shower; toilet and bidet areas; flat-screen televisions (one in the bedroom and one in the lounge) and electronically controlled drapes. Butler service is standard, and a butler's pantry, with separate entry door, has a full-size refrigerator, temperature-controlled wine cabinet, microwave oven and good-sized food preparation and storage areas. For even more space, an interconnecting door can be opened into the adjacent suite.

Royal Suites: Eight Royal Suites, each measuring 733 sq. ft (68 sq. meters), are located towards the aft of the ship (four each on the port and starboard sides). The decor in each is different, and is in the style of a country (Africa, China, Mexico, France, India, Italy, Morocco and Portugal). Each features a separate living room with dining and lounge areas (with refrigerator, mini-bar and Bang & Olufsen CD sound system), and a separate bedroom. There are two entertainment centers with DVD players, and two flat-screen televisions (one in the living area, one in the bedroom), and a large walk-in closet with vanity desk. The marble-clad bathroom has a whirlpool bathtub with integral shower, and there is also a separate shower enclosure, two washbasins and toilet. The teakwood decked balcony is extensive (large enough for on-deck massage) and also has a whirlpool hot tub.

Celebrity Suites: Eight Celebrity Suites, each 467 sq ft (44 sq. meters), feature floor-to-ceiling windows, a separate living room with dining and lounge areas, two entertain-

ment centers with flat-screen televisions (one in the living room, one in the bedroom), and a walk-in closet with vanity desk. The marble-clad bathroom features a whirlpool tub with integral shower (a window with movable shade lets you look out of the bathroom through the lounge to the large ocean-view windows). Interconnecting doors allow two suites to be used as a family unit (as there is no balcony, these suites are ideal for families with small children).

These suites overhang the starboard side of the ship (they are located opposite a group of glass-walled lifts), and provide stunning ocean views from the glass-walled sitting/dining area, which extends out from the ship's side. A personal computer with wood-surround screen allows direct internet connectivity. Butler service is standard.

Sky Suites: There are 30 Sky Suites, each 308 sq ft (28.6 sq. meters), including the private balcony (some balconies may be larger than others, depending on location). Although these are designated as suites, they are really just larger cabins with a marble-clad bathroom with bathtub/shower combination. The suites also have a VCR player in addition to a television, and have a larger lounge area (than standard cabins) and sleeping area. Butler service is standard.

Butler Service: Butler service (in all accommodation designated as suites) includes full breakfast, in-suite lunch and dinner service (as required), afternoon tea service, evening hors d'oeuvres, free espresso and cappuccino, daily news delivery, shoeshine service, and other personal touches. Suite occupants in Penthouse, Royal, Celebrity and Sky suites also get welcome champagne; a full personal computer in each suite, including a printer and internet access (on request in the Sky Suites); choice of films from a video library; personalized stationery; tote bag; priority dining room seating preferences; private portrait sitting, and bathrobe; and in-suite massage service.

Concierge Class: In 2003, Celebrity Cruises added a third service "class" to some of the accommodation grades aboard this ship. Positioned between the top grade suite grades and standard cabin grades, Concierge Class offers added value to purchasers of these "middle-class" cabins.

Enhanced facilities include priority embarkation, disembarkation, tender tickets, alternative dining and spa reservations. Here's what you get in the Concierge Class cabins that others don't (except for the suites): European duvet; double bed overlay (no more falling "between the cracks" for couples); choice of four pillows (goose down pillow, isotonic pillow, body pillow, conformance pillow); eight-vial flower vase on vanity desk; throw pillows on sofa; fruit basket; binoculars; golf umbrella; leather telephone notepad; larger beach towels; hand-held hairdryer. The balcony gets better furniture. In the bathrooms: plusher Frette bathrobes; larger towels in sea green and pink (alternating days); flower in silver vase. It all adds up to excellent value for money.

Standard Outside-View/Interior (No View) Cabins: All other outside-view and interior (no view) cabins (those not designated as suites) have a lounge area with sofa or convertible sofa bed, sleeping area with twin beds that can convert to a double bed, a good amount of closet and drawer space, personal safe, mini-bar/refrigerator (all items are at extra cost), interactive television, and private bathroom. The cabins are nicely decorated with warm wood-finish furniture, and there is none of the boxy feel of cabins in so many ships, due to the angled placement of vanity and audio-video consoles. Even the smallest interior (no view) cabin has a good-sized bathroom and shower enclosure. **Wheelchair-Accessible Accommodation:** This is available in six Sky Suites, three premium outside-view cabins, eight deluxe ocean-view cabins, four standard ocean-view and five interior (no view) cabins measure 347 sq. ft to 362 sq. ft (32.2 to 33.6 sq. meters) and are located in the most practical parts of the ship and close to lifts for good accessibility (all have doorways and bathroom doorways and showers that are wheelchair-accessible.

CUISINE. The Metropolitan Dining Room, which seats 1,224 passengers, is the principal dining hall. Two decks high, it has a grand staircase connecting the two levels, a huge glass wall overlooking the sea, and a musician's gallery on the upper level, typically for a string quartet or quintet. There are two seatings for dinner (open seating for breakfast and lunch), at tables for two, four, six, eight or 10. The menu variety is good, the food has taste, and it is attractively presented. Full service in-cabin dining is also available for all meals, including dinner.

For casual meals, the self-serve buffet-style Ocean Cafe is an extensive area that can seat 754. At the after end of the Ocean Buffet, a separate pasta bar, sushi counter, grill/rotisserie and pizza servery provide freshly created items. Pizzas are made on board from pizza dough and do not come ready made for reheating, as with many cruise lines. On selected evenings, alternative dinners can be taken here (reservations needed). There is also an outdoors grill, for fast food items, adjacent to the swimming pool.

For champagne and caviar lovers, the Platinum Club has a platinum and silver *belle-époque* decor reminiscent of a 1930s gentleman's club.

Café al Bacio and Gelateria: Located on the third level of the atrium lobby and formerly called Cova Café, is the place to see and be seen, for coffees (espresso, cappuccino, latte), pastries, cakes, and gelato, in a trendy setting. **Alternative (Reservations-Only, Extra Cost) Dining:** Celebrity Cruises created its first true alternative restaurant aboard this ship. The Olympic Restaurant is named after White Star Line's transatlantic ocean liner (sister ship to *Titanic*). It is adjacent to the atrium lobby, and has a dining lounge that is rather like an ante-room that contains figured French walnut wood paneling from the à la carte dining room of the 1911 ship, which was decorated in Louis XVI splendor. When the panelling, sold by the scrapyard, was found in a house in Southport, northern England, Celebrity Cruises bought the house in order to obtain it.

A team of chefs prepares the cuisine exclusively for this restaurant. Fine tableside preparation is the feature of this alternative dining room, whose classic French cuisine and service are very good; this is, indeed, a room for a full dégustation, and not merely a dinner.

A wine cellar, in which it is possible to dine, is also a feature, as is a demonstration galley. The wine list is extremely extensive (with more than 400 labels represented). But the real treat for rare wine lovers is an additional list of rare vintage wines, including (when I was last aboard) a magnum of 1949 Château Petrus (at $12,400), a 1907 Heidsieck Monopole Champagne (a mere $7,000 and brought to the surface from a sunken German ship), and a Château Lafite-Rothschild Pouillac from 1890 (a snip at $2,160).

To enjoy classic French cuisine and service in this fine setting – it's rather like dining in a living museum – takes a minimum of three hours of culinary excellence and faultless service, and is among the very finest dining experiences at sea today. However, with just 134 seats, not all passengers will be able to experience it even once during a one-week cruise (reservations are needed, and a cover charge of $30 per person applies). A dine-in wine cellar is also provided, as is a demonstration galley, and tableside preparation is a feature of this alternative dining venue.

ENTERTAINMENT. The 900-seat Celebrity Theater is the three-deck-high venue for the ship's production shows and major cabaret acts. It is located in the forward part of the ship, with seating on main, and two balcony levels. The large stage is equipped with a full fly loft behind its traditional proscenium.

SPA/FITNESS. Wellness facilities include a large AquaSpa measuring 24,219 sq. ft (2,250 sq. meters). It has a large thalassotherapy pool under a huge solarium dome, complete with health bar for light breakfast and lunch items and fresh squeezed fruit and vegetable juices. There are 16 treatment rooms, plus eight treatment rooms with showers and one treatment room designed for wheelchair passengers, an aerobics room, gymnasium (with over 40 exercise machines), large men's and women's saunas, a unisex thermal suite for $20 a day (containing several steam and shower mist rooms with fragrances such as chamomile, eucalyptus and mint, and a glacial ice fountain), and beauty salon.

Sports facilities include a full-size basketball court, compact football, paddle tennis and volleyball, golf simulator, shuffleboard (on two different decks) and a jogging track. A 70-person capacity sports bar called Extreme (a first for a Celebrity Cruises' ship, although it just doesn't, somehow, belong) is located directly in front of the main funnel and has glass walls that overlook the ship's side.

● **For more extensive general information on what a Celebrity cruise is like, see pages 131–5.**

For more extensive general information on what a Celebrity cruise is like, see pages 131–5.

Celebrity Silhouette NOT YET RATED

Celebrity Silhouette is a sister ship to *Celebrity Eclipse* (2010), *Equinox* (2009) and *Celebrity Solstice* (2008). For details, see the pages for those ships. It is expected that *Celebrity Silhouette* will achieve a score similar to the other ships in the same series.

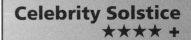

Celebrity Solstice
★★★★ +

Size: . . . . .Large Resort Ship	Passenger Decks: 14	Cabins (with private balcony): 1,216
Tonnage: 122,000	Total Crew: 1,253	Cabins (wheelchair accessible): 30
Lifestyle: . . . . .Premium	Passengers	Wheelchair accessibility . . . . .Best
Cruise Line: . . . . .Celebrity Cruises	(lower beds/all berths): 2,852/3,145	Cabin Voltage: . . . . .110/220 volts
Former Names: . . . . .none	Passenger Space Ratio	Elevators: 12
Builder: . . . . .Meyer Werft (Germany)	(lower beds/all berths): 42.7/38.7	Casino (gaming tables): . . . . .Yes
Original Cost: . . . .$641 million	Crew/Passenger Ratio	Slot Machines: . . . . .Yes
Entered Service: . . . . Nov 2008	(lower beds/all berths): 2.2/2.5	Swimming Pools (outdoors): 2
Registry: .Malta	Cabins (total): 1,426	Swimming Pools (indoors): 1
Length (ft/m): 1,033.4/315.0	Size Range (sq ft/m): 182.9–1,668.4/	Whirlpools: 6
Beam (ft/m): 120.7/36.8	17.0–155.0	Self-Service Launderette: . . . . .Yes
Draft (ft/m): 27.2/8.3	Cabins (outside view): 1,286	Dedicated Cinema/Seats: . . . . .No
Propulsion/Propellers: . . . . .diesel	Cabins (interior/no view): 140	Library: . . . . .Yes
(67,200kW)/2 pods	Cabins (for one person): 0	

OVERALL SCORE: 1,611 OUT OF A POSSIBLE 2,000 POINTS

OVERVIEW. The steeply sloping stern, which includes a mega-yacht-style ducktail platform above the propulsion pods, is very attractive, and nicely balances the ship's contemporary profile. Behind the two smallish funnels is a real grass outdoor area, the Lawn Club. This is the authentic stuff – not green Astroturf – so let's hope it likes the salty air. The club is open to all, so you can go putting, play croquet or bocce ball (like bowling or French boules), or picnic on the grass (picnic baskets not included), or perhaps sleep on it. In any event, it's delightful to walk barefoot on it. Several pool and water-play areas are positioned on Resort Deck: one in a glass-roofed solarium, a sports pool, a family pool, and a wet zone. But the deck space around the two pools isn't large enough for the number of passengers carried.

Inside, the decor is elegant, yet contemporary. There are several firmly established Celebrity "signature" rooms. One such is Michael's Club, an intimate, quiet lounge with classic English leather club chairs, a dramatic black glass chandelier, a grand Michelangelo marble fireplace and some contemporary artwork. Other features include a wine bar with a sommelier, a pre-dinner cocktail lounge that reflects the jazz age of the1930s and '40s; a bar with the look of an ocean-going yacht; Quasar, a bar with designs from the 1960s and '70s and large screens that create a nightly light show synchronized to music; and an observation lounge with a dance floor.

Celebrity's signature Martini Bar, which has a frosted bar – and more than 100 varieties of vodka as well as martinis – has a small alcove called Crush with an ice-filled table where you can participate in caviar and vodka tasting, or host a private party. It's very noisy and congested.

Fortunes Casino (non-smoking) has 16 gaming tables

BERLITZ'S RATINGS		
	Possible	Achieved
Ship	500	433
Accommodation	200	178
Food	400	302
Service	400	310
Entertainment	100	78
Cruise	400	310

and 200 slot machines. The ship also has a delightful two-deck library, but books on the higher of the 12 shelves are impossible to reach (still, it looks nice). The card room – located, unusually, in the center of the ship, with no ocean view windows to distract players – is unfortunately open, and attracts noise from adjacent areas, so it's almost useless as a serious card playing room.

An innovative Hot Glass Show, created in collaboration with Corning Museum of Glass, includes demonstrations and a narrated performance of glass-blowing, housed in an outdoor studio on the open deck as part of the Lawn Club. However, it's a novelty, and once you've seen it, you've seen it. Three resident glass-blowing artists host workshops.

Really good are elevator call buttons located in a floor-stand "pod" and, when the elevator arrives, a glass panel above it turns from blue to pink. Also good is the collection of designer chairs and sunloungers in various locations.

Passenger niggles include lack of usable drawer space in cabins; inadequate children's facilities and staff during school holiday periods; utter congestion caused by a bottleneck when you exit the showlounge; and noise in all areas of the lobby when the martini bar is busy. Also, it's best to forget looking for a deck chair after 8am.

Play areas include the Fun Factory (for 3–12 year-olds, featuring Leapfrog Schoolhouse's educational programs); and "X Club" – a high-tech teens-only chill-out room with a night-time dance club, and an integral coffee bar.

The onboard currency is the US dollar, and gratuities are automatically charged to your onboard account. *Celebrity Solstice* sails year-round from Fort Lauderdale (Port Everglades).

ACCOMMODATION. About 90% of the accommodation is in outside-view cabins. Of these, 85% have a balcony; indeed, this ship has more balcony cabins than any other cruise ship to date and, due to its slender width, there are very few interior (no-view) cabins. There are four suite-grade categories: Royal Suite, Celebrity Suite, Sky Suite, and Penthouse Suite. If you can afford it, book a suite-category cabin for the extra benefits it brings – it really is worth it. Note that most of the balcony cabins on Penthouse Deck and Sky Deck suffer from permanent shade because they are just under the wide deck overhang – the large suites surrounding the aft elevator foyers get much more sunlight.

Features in all grades of accommodation include: twin beds convertible to a queen-sized bed, sitting area, vanity desk with hairdryer, 32-inch flat-screen TV (larger screens in suites), but there's very little drawer space. The bathroom has a shower enclosure (with a useful foot-rail for leg-shaving), toilet, and tiny washbasin (but no soap dish, and the faucet gets in the way when washing your face or brushing your teeth). There's no retractable clothesline for hanging your washed small items; and the two hooks on the back of the bathroom door are tiny. Also standard in all cabins: wireless internet access (for a fee), premium bedding. However, although the closets have good hanging space, there is no shelving on which to place folded items, and drawers in the vanity desk cannot accommodate such items. Accommodations designated as suites have more space, larger balconies (with good quality sunloungers), and more personal amenities and goodies.

Like other cruise lines, Celebrity has added "Spa-Class" accommodation. Some 130 AquaSpa-class cabins share the relaxation room of the AquaSpa itself, incorporate select spa elements into the cabins, and allow for specialized access to the AquaSpa's Thermal Relaxation Room and a Persian Garden (with aromatherapy/steam rooms) on the same deck, and other spa amenities. Occupants also get assigned seating at the exclusive 130-seat Restaurant Blu. Features include: a choice of four pillows (conformance, body, goose, Isotonic); express luggage delivery; shoeshine; Frette bathrobes; dining and seating preferences in other alternative dining venues; and early embarkation and disembarkation. Bathrooms include a tub plus a separate shower enclosure.

Other accommodation grades are named Veranda-class; Sunset-Veranda-class; Concierge-class; Family oceanview with veranda; Deluxe Oceanview with veranda; Standard Oceanview; and Standard Interior (no view) cabins.

CUISINE. Grand Epernay, the ship's balconied principal dining room and included in the cruise price, is located towards the aft section of the ship close to the main lobby, and has ocean views on the port and starboard sides. The design is stunning and contemporary; the decor is brown and beige. However, the almost-backless tub-style chairs are not comfortable and lack a separate armrest. At the forward end, a two-deck high wine tower glistens (one hopes the wine is kept at the right temperature) and provides a stunning focal point. As for the food, it is a bit of a let-down; the decreased quality is all too obvious to repeat Celebrity passengers.

The following four dining venues are all located one deck above the main restaurant and galley (on Deck 5), and occupy the aft section of the ship:

● Murano is an extra-cost, reservations required venue ($30 for dinner) offering high-quality traditional dining with a French flair and exquisite table settings.

● Blu is a 130-seat specialty restaurant designated just for the occupants of AquaClass cabins. The room has pleasing (but rather cold) blue decor. The ambiance is cool.

● The Tuscan Grille, an extra-cost venue ($30 for dinner), serves Kobe beef and premium quality steaks, and has beautifully curved archways and great views.

● Silk Harvest is a Southeast Asian extra-cost dining venue ($20 for dinner) serving pan-Asian fusion cuisine that is unmemorable. It has wood-topped tables (no tablecloths).

For snacks and less ambitious meals, the options are:

● Bistro on Five (Deck 5, that is) is for coffee, cakes, crepes, pastries, and more. It gets busy at times and the serving counter is small, so it's a congested area.

● Café al Bacio & Gelateria is a coffeehouse featuring Lavazza Italian coffee and situated on one side of the main lobby, but it's small and lines quickly form at peak times.

● Oceanview Café and Grill is the expansive, tray-less, casual self-serve buffet venue. There are a number of food "islands" rather than those awful straight buffet counters, but the signage is reasonable. Condiments are hard to find.

● The AquaSpa Café is for light, healthier options (solarium fare), but the selections need improvement.

● The Mast Bar Grill and Bar is an outside venue that offers fast-food items.

ENTERTAINMENT. The 1,115-seat Solstice Theater, the main showlounge, stages three circus-themed production shows featuring in-your-face, formulaic acrobatics.

Colorful theme nights are held in the Observation Lounge (whose daytime bland and minimalist decor comes alive at night thanks to mood lighting effects). The 200-seat Celebrity Central hosts stand-up comedy, cooking demonstrations, enrichment lectures and feature films. Quasar is Celebrity's first nightclub, per se.

An Entertainment Court showcases street performers, psychics and caricaturists, and is in the center of the ship, linked to the adjacent Quasar nightclub, with its decor harking back to the 1960s and '70s. The Ensemble Lounge is a big-band era cocktail lounge with live jazz-styled music, set adjacent to the Murano, the specialty restaurant.

SPA/FITNESS. The AquaSpa, the largest spa aboard a Celebrity Cruises ship, is operated by Steiner Leisure. The fitness center includes kinesis (pulleys against gravity) workout equipment, plus familiar favorite muscle-pumping cardio-vascular machinery. There's also a relaxation area, AquaSpa station, and acupuncture center. Massages include fashionable things such as a Herbal Poultice massage and a Bamboo Massage using bamboo shoots and essential oils.

● **For more extensive general information on what a Celebrity cruise is like, see pages 131–5.**

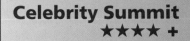

Celebrity Summit
★★★★ +

Size: ....Large Resort Ship	Passenger Decks: 11	Cabins (wheelchair accessible): 26	
Tonnage: 91,000	Total Crew: 999	(17 with private balcony)	
Lifestyle: ....Premium	Passengers	Wheelchair accessibility ....Best	
Cruise Line: ....Celebrity Cruises	(lower beds/all berths): 1,950/2,450	Cabin Current: ....110 and 220 volts	
Former Names: ....Summit	Passenger Space Ratio	Elevators: 10	
Builder: ....Chantiers de l'Atlantique	(lower beds/all berths): 46.6/37.1	Casino (gaming tables): ....Yes	
(France)	Crew/Passenger Ratio	Slot Machines: ....Yes	
Original Cost: ....$350 million	(lower beds/all berths): 1.9/2.4	Swimming Pools (outdoors): 2	
Entered Service: ....Nov 2001	Cabins (total): 975	Swimming Pools (indoors): 1	
Registry: ....Malta	Size Range (sq ft/m): 165.1–2,530.0/	(with magrodome)	
Length (ft/m): 964.5/294.0	15.34–235.0	Whirlpools: 4	
Beam (ft/m): 105.6/32.2	Cabins (outside view): 780	Self-Service Launderette: ....No	
Draft (ft/m): 26.2/8.0	Cabins (interior/no view): 195	Dedicated Cinema/Seats: Yes/368	
Propulsion/Propellers: .....gas turbine/2	Cabins (for one person): 0	Library: ....Yes	
azimuthing pods (39,000kW)	Cabins (with private balcony): 590		

OVERALL SCORE: 1,568 OUT OF A POSSIBLE 2,000 POINTS

OVERVIEW. *Celebrity Summit* is a sister ship to *Celebrity Constellation, Celebrity Infinity* and *Celebrity Millennium.* Jon Bannenberg (famous as a mega-yacht designer) designed the exterior that has a royal blue and white hull, although it has actually turned out to look extremely ungainly. This is the third Celebrity Cruises ship to be fitted with a "pod" propulsion system (and controllable pitch propellers) coupled with a quiet, smokeless gas turbine powerplant; two GE gas turbines provide engine power while a single GE steam turbine drives the electricity generators.

One neat feature is a conservatory which includes many seats set in a botanical environment of flowers, plants, trees, mini-gardens and fountains, designed by the award-winning floral designer Emilio Robba of Paris. It is located directly in front of the main funnel and has glass walls that overlook the ship's side.

Inside, the ship has the high-class decor and materials and public rooms that have made the other ships in the fleet so popular and user-friendly. The atrium (with separately enclosed room for shore excursions) is three decks high and houses the reception desk, tour operator's desk, and bank. Four dramatic glass-walled elevators travel through the ship's exterior (port) side, connecting the atrium with another seven decks, thus traveling through 10 passenger decks, including the tender stations – a nice ride.

Facilities include a combination Cinema/Conference Center, an expansive shopping arcade, with 14,500 sq. ft (1,300 sq. meters) of retail store space, a lavish four-decks-high showlounge with the excellent staging and lighting equip-

BERLITZ'S RATINGS		
	Possible	Achieved
Ship	500	427
Accommodation	200	178
Food	400	291
Service	400	298
Entertainment	100	74
Cruise	400	300

ment, a two-level library (one level for foreign/non-fiction books; a second level for fiction), a card room, a music room, and a combination observation lounge/discotheque. Michael's Club (originally a cigar smoker's haven), is now a piano lounge/bar. Gaming facilities include the ship's overly large Fortunes Casino, with blackjack, roulette, and slot machines, and lots of bright lights and action. Families will appreciate the Fun Factory (for children) and The Tower (for teenagers). Children's counselors and youth activities staff provide a wide range of supervised activities.

The ship's two-seating dining and two shows detract from an otherwise excellent product.

There is no walk-around promenade deck outdoors. There are cushioned pads for poolside sunloungers only, but not for chairs on other outside decks. Trying to reach Cabin Service or the Guest Relations Desk to answer the phone (to order breakfast, for example, if you don't want to do so via the interactive television) is a matter of luck, timing and patience. Elevators cannot handle the numbers at peak times.

ACCOMMODATION. There are 20 different grades, giving you a wide choice of size and location (the price you pay will depend on the grade, location and size chosen).

Almost half the accommodation has a "private" balcony; approximately 80 percent are outside-view suites and cabins, and 20 percent are interior (no view) cabins. The accommodation is extremely comfortable throughout this ship, regardless of which grade you choose. Suites, naturally, have more space, butler service (whether you want it or not), more and better amenities and more personal service than if you choose any of the standard cabin grades. There are several categories of suites, but those at the stern of the ship are in a prime location and have huge balconies that are really private and not overlooked from above.

All suites and cabins have wood cabinetry and accenting, interactive television and entertainment systems (you can go shopping, book shore excursions, play casino games, interactively, and even watch soft-porn movies). Bathrooms have hairdryers, and 100% cotton towels.

Penthouse Suites: Two Penthouse Suites (on Penthouse Deck) are the largest accommodation aboard. Each occupies one half of the beam (width) of the ship, overlooking the ship's stern. Each measures a huge 2,530 sq. ft (235 sq. meters) – 1,432 sq. ft (133 sq. meters) of living space, plus a huge wrap-around balcony measuring 1,098 sq. ft (102 sq. meters) with 180° views, which occupies one-half of the beam (width) of the ship, overlooking the ship's stern (it includes a wet bar, hot tub and whirlpool tub); however, note that much of this terrace can be overlooked by passengers on other decks above.

Features include a marble foyer, a separate living room (complete with ebony baby grand piano – bring your own pianist if you don't play yourself) and a formal dining room. The master bedroom has a large walk-in closet; personal exercise equipment; dressing room with vanity desk, exercise equipment; marble-clad master bathroom with twin washbasins; deep whirlpool bathtub; separate shower; toilet and bidet areas; flat-screen televisions (one in the bedroom and one in the lounge) and electronically controlled drapes. Butler service is standard, and a butler's pantry, with separate entry door, has a full-sized refrigerator, temperature-controlled wine cabinet, microwave oven and good-sized food preparation and storage areas. For even more space, an interconnecting door can be opened into the adjacent suite (ideal for multi-generation families).

Royal Suites: Eight Royal Suites, each measuring 733 sq. ft (68 sq. meters), are located towards the aft of the ship (four each on the port and starboard sides). Each has a separate living room with dining and lounge areas (with refrigerator, mini-bar and Bang & Olufsen CD sound system), and a separate bedroom. There are two entertainment centers with DVD players, and two flat-screen televisions (one in the living area, one in the bedroom), and a large walk-in closet with vanity desk. The marble-clad bathroom has a whirlpool bathtub with integral shower, and there is also a separate shower enclosure, two washbasins and toilet. The teakwood decked balcony is extensive (large enough for on-deck massage) and also has a whirlpool hot tub.

Celebrity Suites: Eight Celebrity Suites, each measuring 467 sq. ft (44 sq. meters), have floor-to-ceiling windows, a separate living room with dining and lounge areas, two entertainment centers with flat-screen televisions (one in the living room, one in the bedroom), and a walk-in closet with vanity desk. The marble-clad bathroom has a whirlpool bathtub with integral shower (a window with movable shade

lets you look out of the bathroom through the lounge to the large ocean-view windows). Interconnecting doors allow two suites to be used as a family unit (as there is no balcony, these suites are ideal for families with small children). These suites overhang the starboard side of the ship (they are located opposite a group of glass-walled elevators), and provide stunning ocean views from the glass-walled sitting/dining area, which extends out from the ship's side. A personal computer with wood-surround screen allows direct internet connectivity. Butler service is standard.

Sky Suites: There are 30 of these, each measuring 308 sq. ft (28.6 sq. meters), including the private balcony (some balconies may be larger than others, depending on the location). Although these are designated as suites, they are really just larger cabins that feature a marble-clad bathroom with bathtub/shower combination. The suites also have a VCR player in addition to a TV set, and have a larger lounge area (than standard cabins) and sleeping area. Butler service is standard.

Butler Service: Butler service (in all accommodation designated as suites) includes full breakfast, in-suite lunch and dinner service (as required), afternoon tea service, evening hors d'oeuvres, free espresso and cappuccino, daily news delivery, shoeshine service, and other personal touches.

Suite occupants in Penthouse, Royal, Celebrity and Sky suites also get welcome champagne; a full personal computer in each suite, including a printer and internet access (on request in Sky Suites); choice of films from a video library; personalized stationery; tote bag; priority dining room seating preferences; private portrait sitting, and bathrobe; and in-suite massage service.

Concierge Class: In 2003, Celebrity Cruises added a third service "class" to some of the accommodation grades aboard this ship. Positioned between the top grade suite grades and standard cabin grades, Concierge Class adds value to purchasers of these "middle-class" cabins.

Enhanced facilities include priority embarkation, disembarkation, tender tickets, alternative dining and spa reservations. Here's what you get in the Concierge Class cabins that others don't (except for the suites): European duvet; double bed overlay (no more falling "between the cracks" for couples); choice of four pillows (goose down pillow, isotonic pillow, body pillow, conformance pillow); eight-vial flower vase on vanity desk; throw pillows on sofa; fruit basket; binoculars; golf umbrella; leather telephone notepad; larger beach towels; hand-held hairdryer. The balcony gets better furniture. In the bathrooms: plusher Frette bathrobe; larger towels in sea green and pink (alternating days); flower in silver vase in bathroom. It all adds up to an excellent value for money, as well as better recognition from staff.

Standard Outside-View/Interior (No View) Cabins: All other outside-view and interior (no view) cabins have a lounge area with sofa or convertible sofa bed, sleeping area with twin beds that can convert to a double bed, a good amount of closet and drawer space, personal safe, mini-bar/refrigerator (extra cost), interactive television, and private bathroom. The cabins are nicely decorated with warm wood-finish furniture, and there is none of the boxy feel of cabins in so many ships, due to the angled placement of vanity and audio-video consoles. Even the smallest cabin has a good-sized bathroom and shower enclosure.

Wheelchair-Accessible Accommodation: This is available in six Sky Suites, three premium outside-view, eight deluxe ocean-view, four standard ocean-view and five interior (no view) cabins measuring from 347 to 362 sq. ft (32.2 to 33.6 sq. meters) and are located in the most practical parts of the ship and close to elevators for good accessibility. All have doorways and bathroom doorways and showers are wheelchair-accessible. Some cabins have extra berths for third or third and fourth occupants (note, however, that there is only one safe for personal belongings, which must be shared).

CUISINE. The 1,170-seat Cosmopolitan Restaurant, the ship's formal dining room. It is two decks high, has a grand staircase connecting the two levels, a huge glass wall overlooking the sea at the stern of the ship; electrically operated shades provide several different backdrops, and a musician's gallery on the upper level, typically for a string quartet/quintet. There are two seatings for dinner (open seating for breakfast and lunch), at tables for two, four, six, eight or 10. The dining room is a no-smoking area, and, you should note that, like all large dining halls, it can be extremely noisy.

The menu variety is good, the food has taste, and it is very attractively presented and served in a well-orchestrated operation that displays fine European traditions and training. Full service in-cabin dining is also available for all meals (including dinner). As a tribute to the French Line ship *Normandie*, a statue created by Leon-Georges Baudry, called "La Normandie", that once overlooked the ship's grand staircase and for the past 47 years graced the Fontainebleu Hotel in Miami, was purchased for $250,000 and can now be seen in this dining room.

For casual eating, the Waterfall Cafe is a self-serve buffet area, with six principal serving lines and 754 seats. There is also a grill and pizza bar.

For champagne and caviar lovers, the Champagne Bar has a platinum and silver art-deco decor that is reminiscent of a 1930s gentleman's club. It includes a diamond-pane reflective mirror wall. There's also a Martini Bar.

Alternative (Reservations-Only, Extra Cost) Dining Option: The Normandie Restaurant is an alternative dining room, adjacent to the conference center. It has gold lacquered paneling from the smoking room of the original French Line ship. Fine tableside preparation is the feature of this alternative dining room, whose classic French cuisine and service are very good indeed. This is haute cuisine at the height of professionalism. However, with just 134 seats, not all passengers can experience it even once during a one-week cruise (reservations are necessary, and a cover charge of $35 per person applies). There is a dine-in wine cellar (with more than 200 labels from around the world), and a demonstration galley. A team of 10 chefs prepares the cuisine exclusively for this restaurant. Tableside preparation is a feature of this alternative dining spot.

Café al Bacio and Gelateria: Located on the third level of the atrium lobby and formerly called Cova Café, is the place to see and be seen, for coffees (espresso, cappuccino, latte), pastries, cakes, and gelato, in a trendy setting.

ENTERTAINMENT. The 900-seat Celebrity Theater is the three-deck-high venue for the ship's production shows and major cabaret acts. It is located in the forward part of the ship, with seating on main, and two balcony levels. The large stage is equipped with a full fly loft behind its traditional proscenium.

SPA/FITNESS. Facilities include an AquaSpa (a multi-station thalassotherapy pool), 16 treatment rooms, plus eight treatment rooms with showers and one treatment room specifically designed for wheelchair passengers, aerobics room, gymnasium complete with more than 40 machines, large male and female saunas with large ocean-view porthole window, a unisex thermal suite for $20 a day (containing several steam and shower mist rooms with different fragrances such as chamomile, eucalyptus and mint, and a glacial ice fountain), and beauty salon.

Sports facilities include a full-size basketball court, compact football, paddle tennis and volleyball, golf simulator, shuffleboard (on two different decks) and a jogging track.

● **For more extensive general information on what a Celebrity cruise is like, see pages 131–5.**

Celebrity Xpedition
★★★★

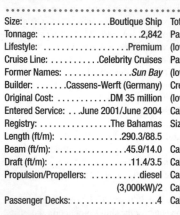

Size: . . . . .Boutique Ship	Total Crew: 64	Wheelchair accessibility . . . . .None
Tonnage: 2,842	Passengers	Cabin Voltage: .220
Lifestyle: . . . . .Premium	(lower beds/all berths): 94/98	Elevators: 0
Cruise Line: . . . . .Celebrity Cruises	Passenger Space Ratio	Casino (gaming tables): . . . . .No
Former Names: . . . . .Sun Bay	(lower beds/all berths): 30.2/29.0	Slot Machines: . . . . .No
Builder: . . . . . . .Cassens-Werft (Germany)	Crew/Passenger Ratio	Swimming Pools (outdoors): . . . . .No
Original Cost: . . . . .DM 35 million	(lower beds/all berths): 1.4/1.4	Swimming Pools (indoors): . . . . .No
Entered Service: . . .June 2001/June 2004	Cabins (total): 47	Whirlpools: 1
Registry: . . . . .The Bahamas	Size Range (sq ft/m): 156.0–460.0/	Fitness Center: . . . . .Yes
Length (ft/m): 290.3/88.5	14.5–42.7	Sauna/Steam Room: . . . . .Yes/No
Beam (ft/m): 45.9/14.0	Cabins (outside view): 47	Massage: . . . . .Yes
Draft (ft/m): 11.4/3.5	Cabins (interior/no view): 0	Self-Service Launderette: . . . . .No
Propulsion/Propellers: . . . . .diesel	Cabins (for one person): 0	Dedicated Cinema/Seats: . . . . .No
(3,000kW)/2	Cabins (with private balcony): 9	Library: . . . . .Yes
Passenger Decks: 4	Cabins (wheelchair accessible): 0	

OVERALL SCORE: 1,404 OUT OF A POSSIBLE 2,000 POINTS

OVERVIEW. This is the first specialist boutique ship for Celebrity Cruises and is like a small private club. The brochure rates may or may not include the Galápagos Islands visitor tax, which must be paid in cash at Guayaquil or Quito airports or in the islands.

There is a surprisingly good amount of open deck space – better, in proportion, than many larger ships, and much of it with teakwood decking, as well as teak sunloungers and patio furniture. Although there is no swimming pool – the ship's too small for one – there is a whirlpool tub on the uppermost open deck. Stabilizers were installed in 2004.

All accommodation is located forward half, with public rooms aft. The ambience is unhurried, yet subtly elegant. Except for the dining room, which can double as a conference room, there is only one public room: the main lounge, complete with bar, dance floor and bandstand.

This is ecotourism of the best kind. Shore excursions (by Zodiac inflatable boats) are in small groups led by Ecuadorian guides. On your return, waiters greet you with refreshing drinks and towels. Included in the fare: excursions, gratuities to shipboard staff, beverages including house wine, champagne, liquor, beer and soda.

SUITABLE FOR: *Celebrity Xpedition* is best suited to mature adults who want an intimate and casual cruise experience without the crowds, and would enjoy learning about the nature and wildlife of the Galápagos Islands.

ACCOMMODATION. There are four price categories in two cabin types: 9 Suites, measuring 247 sq. ft (23 sq. meters);

BERLITZ'S RATINGS		
	Possible	Achieved
Ship	500	336
Accommodation	200	139
Food	400	281
Service	400	302
Entertainment	n/a	n/a
Cruise	500	346

34 Comfort Cabins, 172 sq. ft (16 sq. meters); and 3 Comfort cabins, 156 sq. ft (14.5 sq. meters). All suites and cabins have twin beds (four comfort cabins have a double bed), TV, sofa, drinks table, vanity desk with hairdryer, mini-bar/refrigerator, and personal safe. Bathrooms all have a good-sized shower enclosure (there are no tubs) with soap/shampoo dispenser, black granite washbasin, and white marble-clad walls.

The largest accommodation is in nine suites, each with a private balcony. One suite is located forward, with forward-facing views, and has a sloping ceiling with character. Balcony partitions are almost private; the balcony deck is teak covered. Two of the suites can be joined together. One bedroom has two pull-down Murphy beds.

CUISINE. The Darwin Dining Room is an intimate room that operates on an open-seating basis. Nicely decorated, it has ocean-view windows along one side. A self-serve buffet offers salads, cold cuts and cheeses. House wines and beer are included in the fare; a few better wines can be bought. The cuisine depends on local suppliers; meat quality is poor, fish seafood and fruit good, vegetables inconsistent.

The casual, self-serve Seagull Buffet is just behind the main lounge on the open deck, with teak tables and chairs.

ENTERTAINMENT. Dinner and after-dinner conversation with fellow passengers is the main entertainment each evening.

SPA/FITNESS. There is a small fitness room, and adjacent unisex sauna located inside on the uppermost deck, while a small beauty salon is located on the lowest deck.

Clelia II
★★★★

Size: ....Boutique Ship	Propulsion/Propellors: ....diesel	Cabins (with private balcony): 16
Tonnage: 4,077	(3,514kW)/2 (CP)	Cabins (wheelchair accessible): 0
Lifestyle: ....Premium	Passenger Decks: 5	Wheelchair accessibility ....None
Cruise Line: ....Orion Expedition Cruises	Total Crew: 60	Cabin Current: ....110 volts
Former Names: ......*Renaissance Four*	Passengers	Elevators: 1
Builder: ....Cantieri Navale Ferrari	(lower beds/all berths): 100/100	Casino (gaming tables): ....No
(Italy)	Passenger Space Ratio	Slot Machines: ....No
Original Cost: .... $20 million	(lower beds/all berths): 40.7/40.7	Swimming Pools (outdoors): 0
Entered Service: ....Jan 1991/May 2011	Cabins: 50	Swimming Pools (indoors): 0
Registry: ....Malta	Size Range (sq ft/m): .215.0–258.3/20–24	Whirlpools: 1
Length (ft/m): 289.0/88.1	Cabins (outside view): 50	Self-Service Launderette: ....No
Beam (ft/m): 50.1/15.3	Cabins (interior/no view): 0	Dedicated Cinema/Seats: ....No
Draft (ft/m): 13.4/4.1	Cabins (for one person): 0	Library: ....Yes

BERLITZ'S OVERALL SCORE: 1,404 OUT OF A POSSIBLE 2,000 POINTS

OVERVIEW. Nicely refurbished in early 2009 and renamed after its former owner, Clelia Haji-Ioannou, *Clelia II* is a charming and very comfortable little ship that provides a destination-intensive, refined and relaxed cruise for those who don't like large ships and crowds.

It has the look and feel of a private yacht, with handsome interior styling, although the exterior profile isn't overly attractive. There are two teakwood walk-around promenade decks outdoors. A water jet-propelled shore tender hangs over the stern. A fleet of Zodiac inflatable craft for shore landings is carried. The open deck and sunbathing space is quite limited.

The accommodation is located forward, with public rooms aft. The pleasing colors and a refined and attractive interior decor reflect Greek design elements, and Greek artists are responsible for many pieces of art around the ship.

Public rooms include a small library, a lounge, and a comfortable lecture room that can accommodate all passengers (good for lectures), and a piano bar/lounge. Note that there is no lounge with a forward view, and thus the ship is not good for cruising in expedition regions such as Antarctica. Smoking is allowed only on open decks.

The onboard currency is the Australian dollar. Extensive pre-cruise documentation is provided.

SUITABLE FOR: *Clelia II* is best suited to mature adults who want a small ship environment that offers a high degree of comfort, but with excellent lecturers and decent cuisine.

ACCOMMODATION. The all-outside cabins, called "suites" in the brochure, combine highly polished imitation rosewood paneling with lots of mirrors, and fine, hand-crafted Italian furniture. All suites have twin beds that can convert to a

BERLITZ'S RATINGS

	Possible	Achieved
Ship	500	378
Accommodation	200	154
Food	400	245
Service	400	278
Entertainment	n/a	n/a
Cruise	500	349

queen-sized bed, a sitting area with three-person sofa, one chair, coffee table, minibar-refrigerator, a color TV/DVD player, and direct-dial satellite phone. Closet space is good, but space for stowing luggage is tight, and there is little drawer space. There are no music channels in the cabins, and there is no switch to turn off announcements.

The marble bathrooms are compact units that have reasonably sized showers (no bathrooms have a tub). There's a real teakwood floor, marble vanity, large mirror, recessed towel rail (good for storing toiletries), large oval washbasin, and built-in hairdryer. There is a high "lip" into the bathroom.

There are also 16 balcony suites with real teak wood balconies and polished railings, although the balcony is steel rather than glass. The suites provide a little more space that includes an office/large vanity desk.

CUISINE. The Restaurant, with single, open-seating dining, is bright (overly bright at night), and welcoming. It is on the lowest deck and has portholes rather than windows. There are tables for two, four, six, or eight. Dinners are normally sit-down affairs, although there could be an occasional self-serve buffet. Breakfast and lunch are usually buffets and can also be taken at an outdoor bar/café (weather permitting), in your suite, or in the restaurant. Continental dishes are complemented by local regional delicacies. The food quality, choice and presentation are all good, but not memorable.

ENTERTAINMENT. Lecturers and recaps provide the main after-dinner entertainment. Early nights are the norm.

SPA/FITNESS. There is a small aft-facing fitness room, and a beauty salon.

Clipper Adventurer
★★

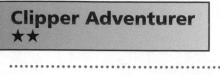

Size: . . . . .Boutique Ship	Passenger Decks: 5
Tonnage: .5,750	Total Crew: 72
Lifestyle: . . . . .Standard	Passengers
Cruise Line: . . . . .Quark Expeditions	(lower beds/all berths): 122/122
Former Names: . . . .*Alla Tarasova*	Passenger Space Ratio
Builder: . . . . .Brodgradiliste Uljanik	(lower beds/all berths): 47.1/47.1
(Yugoslavia)	Crew/Passenger Ratio
Original Cost: . . . . .n/a	(lower beds/all berths): 1.4/1.4
Entered Service: 1976/Apr 1998	Cabins (total): .61
Registry: . . . . .The Bahamas	Size Range (sq ft/m): 119.0–211.0/
Length (ft/m): 328.1/100.01	11.0–19.6
Beam (ft/m): 53.2/16.24	Cabins (outside view): 61
Draft (ft/m): 15.2/4.65	Cabins (interior/no view): 0
Propulsion/Propellers: diesel (3,884kW)/2	Cabins (for one person): 0

Cabins (with private balcony): 0
Cabins (wheelchair accessible): 0
Wheelchair accessibility . . . . .None
Cabin Current: . . . . .220 volts
Elevators: 0
Casino (gaming tables): . . . . .No
Slot Machines: .No
Swimming Pools (outdoors): . . . . .No
Swimming Pools (indoors): . . . . .No
Whirlpools: . . . . .No
Self-Service Launderette: . . . . .No
Dedicated Cinema/Seats: . . . . .No
Library: . . . . .Yes

OVERALL SCORE: 947 OUT OF A POSSIBLE 2,000 POINTS

OVERVIEW. *Clipper Adventurer* is asolidly built small ship. It has an ice-strengthened (A-1 ice classification), and a royal blue hull and white funnel, bow-thruster and stabilizers. But, even with an ice classification, it got stuck in an ice field in the Bellingshausen Sea in 2000. Fortunately, the Argentine Navy icebreaker *Almirante Irizar* freed it. The ship had a $15 million refit/conversion in 1997–98, and meets international safety codes and requirements. It specializes in operating close-in expedition-style cruising. There are 10 Zodiac rubber inflatable landing craft for in-depth excursions, and a covered promenade deck.

This cozy ship caters to travelers rather than mere passengers. The dress code is casual during the day, although at night many passengers wear jacket and tie. For trekking ashore, take long-sleeved garments. The public spaces are a little limited, with just one main lounge and bar. There is a small but decent library, with high wingback chairs.

There is no observation lounge with forward-facing views, although there is an outdoor observation area directly below the bridge. Quark Expeditions provides its own expedition staff, and experienced geologists and naturalist lecturers accompany all cruise expeditions. Smoking is permitted only on the outside decks. The onboard currency is the US dollar.

The passageways are narrow (it is difficult to pass housekeeping carts), and the stairs are steep on the outer decks.

SUITABLE FOR: *Clipper Adventurer* is best suited to couples and single travelers who enjoy nature and wildlife up close and personal, and who would wish to cruise in the

BERLITZ'S RATINGS		
	Possible	Achieved
Ship	500	219
Accommodation	200	99
Food	400	190
Service	400	211
Entertainment	100	40
Cruise	400	188

mainstream sense aboard large resort ships. This is for hardy, adventurous types who don't need vacuous entertainment or mindless parlor games.

ACCOMMODATION. All cabins (there are seven grades, including a dedicated price for single cabin occupancy) have outside views and twin lower beds, with private bathroom with shower, and toilet. The bathrooms are really tiny, although they are tiled, and have all the basics. Several double-occupancy cabins can be booked by single travelers, but special rates apply.

All cabins have a lockable drawer for valuables, telephone, and individual temperature control. Some have picture windows, while others have portholes. Two larger cabins (called suites in the brochure, which they really are not) are quite well equipped for the size of the vessel.

CUISINE. The dining room, with deep ocean-view windows, accommodates all passengers at a single seating. The food, a combination of American and Continental cuisine, is prepared freshly by chefs trained at some of America's finest culinary institutions. The food, however, is quite disappointing. There are limited menu choices, and far too much use of canned fruits and juices, particularly for breakfasts, which are repetitive. Gourmet it is not. Casual, self-service breakfast and luncheon buffets are taken in the main lounge.

ENTERTAINMENT. Dinner and after-dinner conversation in the ship's lounge/bar is the main entertainment.

SPA/FITNESS. There is a small sauna.

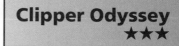

Clipper Odyssey
★★★

Boutique Ship: . . . . .5,218 tons	Passenger Decks: 5	Cabins (with private balcony): 8
Lifestyle: . . . . .Standard	Total Crew: 52	Cabins (wheelchair accessible): 1
Cruise Line: . . . . . .Zegrahm Expeditions	Passengers	Wheelchair accessibility . . . . .Fair
Former Names: . . . . . . .Oceanic Odyssey,	(lower beds/all berths): 128/128	Cabin Current: . . . . .115 volts
Oceanic Grace	Passenger Space Ratio	Elevators: 1
Builder: . . . . . . .NKK Tsu Shipyard (Japan)	(lower beds/all berths): 43.4/43.4	Casino (gaming tables): . . . . .No
Original Cost: . . . .$40 million	Crew/Passenger Ratio	Slot Machines: . . . . .No
Entered Service: . . . . .Apr 1989/Jun 2008	(lower beds/all berths): 2.4/2.4	Swimming Pools (outdoors): 1
Registry: . . . . .The Bahamas	Cabins (total): .64	Swimming Pools (indoors): 0
Length (ft/m): 337.5/102.9	Size Range (sq ft/m): . .182.9–258.3/17–24	Whirlpools: 1
Beam (ft/m): 50.5/15.4	Cabins (outside view): 64	Self-Service Launderette: . . . . .No
Draft (ft/m): 14.1/4.3	Cabins (interior/no view): 0	Dedicated Cinema/Seats: . . . . .No
Propulsion/Propellers: diesel (5,192kW)/2	Cabins (for one person): 0	Library: . . . . .Yes

OVERALL SCORE: 1,245 OUT OF A POSSIBLE 2,000 POINTS

OVERVIEW. *Clipper Odyssey* has a somewhat square, angular, but contemporary profile, with twin outboard funnels. The ship, designed in Holland and built in Japan, tried to copy the *Sea Goddess* (now *SeaDream*) small ship/ultra-yacht concept for the Japanese market. Operated by Japan's Showa Line, the ship was not really suited to Japan's often choppy seas. After 10 years, the company withdrew from passenger cruises, and Clipper Cruise Line (owned by Denmark's Clipper Group, but managed by International International Shipping Partners) bought the ship as an ideal addition to its small ship fleet. In June 2008 the ship began a five-year charter to Seattle-based Zegrahm Expeditions.

Considering the size of this ship, there are expansive areas outdoors, excellent for sunbathing or for viewing wildlife. The small swimming pool is just a "dip" pool, however. There is a wide teakwood outdoor jogging track. A decompression chamber for divers, originally included, is no longer used due to insurance requirements. But free snorkeling equipment is available, as is a small fleet of Zodiacs (inflatable landing craft for "soft" expedition use).

Inside, nothing jars the senses, as the interior design concept successfully balances East–West color combinations with some Indonesian accents. The ambiance is warm and intimate, and is for those who seek a small ship where entertainment and loud music isn't a priority. *Clipper Odyssey* will provide a pleasing antidote to cruising aboard large ships. The onboard currency is the US dollar.

There are lots of pillars in almost all public areas, which spoil the decor and sightlines.

SUITABLE FOR: *Clipper Odyssey* is best suited to couples and single travelers who enjoy nature and wildlife up close

BERLITZ'S RATINGS		
	Possible	Achieved
Ship	500	358
Accommodation	200	147
Food	400	219
Service	400	237
Entertainment	n/a	n/a
Cruise	500	284

and personal, and who would not dream of cruising in the mainstream sense aboard ships with large numbers of people. This is for hardy, adventurous types who don't need entertainment or games.

ACCOMMODATION. There are six cabin categories. The ship has all-outside cabins quite tastefully furnished and feature blond wood cabinetry, twin- or queen-sized beds, living area with sofa, personal safe, mini-bar/refrigerator, TV set and VCR, and three-sided mirror. All bathrooms have a deep, half-sized tub. Some cabins have private balconies; but these are very small, with awkward door handles. The bathroom toilet seats are extremely high. There is one suite, which is the size of two cabins. It provides more room, of course, with a lounge area, and more storage space.

CUISINE. The dining room has large ocean view picture windows. It is quite warm and inviting, and all passengers eat in a single seating. The unmemorable cuisine includes fresh foods from local ports, in a mix of regional and some Western cuisine, with open seating. There is much use of canned fruits and other cheap ingredients. A young, friendly American staff provides the service.

ENTERTAINMENT. There is no formal entertainment, although dinner and after-dinner conversation with fellow passengers in the ship's lounge/bar really becomes the entertainment each evening. Otherwise, it might be a good idea to bring a good book or two.

SPA/FITNESS. There is a tiny beauty salon, and an adjacent massage/body treatment room, while a small fitness room is located on a different deck.

Club Med 2
★★★★

Size: . . . . .Small Ship	Number of Masts: . . . . . . .5 (164 ft high)/	Size Range (sq ft/m): . . .193.8–322/18–30
Tonnage: .14,983	7 computer-controlled sails	Cabins (outside view): 197
Lifestyle: . . . . .Premium	Sail Area (sq ft/m2): 26,910/2,500	Cabins (interior/no view): 0
Cruise Line: . . . . .Club Med Cruises	Main Propulsion: . . . . .(a) engines (b) sails	Cabins (for one person): 0
Former Names: . . . . .none	Propulsion/Propellers: . . . . .diesel	Cabins (with private balcony): 0
Builder: . . . .Ateliers et Chantiers du Havre	(9,120kW)/2	Cabins (wheelchair accessible): 0
(France)	Passenger Decks: 8	Wheelchair accessibility . . . . .None
Original Cost: . . . .$125 million	Total Crew: 200	Cabin Current: . . . . .110 and 220 volts
Entered Service: . . . . Dec 1992	Passengers	Elevators: 2
Registry: . . . . .Wallis & Fortuna	(lower beds/all berths): 394/409	Casino (gaming tables): . . . . .No
Length (ft/m): 613.8/187.10	Passenger Space Ratio	Slot Machines: . . . . .No
Beam (ft/m): 65.6/20.00	(lower beds/all berths): 38.0/36.6	Swimming Pools (outdoors): 2
Draft (ft/m): 16.4/5.00	Crew/Passenger Ratio	Whirlpools: 0
Type of Vessel: . . . . .high-tech sail-cruiser	(lower beds/all berths): 1.9/2.0	Self-Service Launderette: . . . . .No
	Cabins (total): 197	Library: . . . . .Yes

OVERALL SCORE: 1,483 OUT OF A POSSIBLE 2,000 POINTS

OVERVIEW. *Club Med 2* is one of a pair of the world's largest high-tech sail-cruisers ever built (the other is *Wind Surf*, operated by Windstar Cruises), part-cruise ship, part-yacht. Five huge masts rise 221 ft (67.5 meters) above sea level; they carry seven triangular, self-furling Dacron sails with a total surface area of 26,881 sq. ft (2,497 sq. meters). No human hands touch the sails, as everything is controlled by computer from the bridge. The system computer also keeps the ship on an even keel (via the movement of a hydraulic ballast system, so there is no heeling (rolling) over 6 degrees. When the ship is not using the sails, four diesel-electric motors propel it at up to 12 knots.

The ship underwent an extensive refurbishment in October 2008, which saw the addition of 10 new 35m2 cabins, and the complete refit of all other cabins.

An extensive array of water sports facilities is provided (all except scuba gear are included in the cruise fare), and there's an aft marina platform (equipment includes 12 windsurfers, 3 sailboats, 2 water ski boats, several kayaks, 20 single scuba tanks, snorkels, and 4 motorized water sport boats. There are two small saltwater swimming pools (really dip pools). There is an open bridge policy.

Inside, facilities include a main lounge, meeting room and a golf simulator (extra charge) as well as a fitness and beauty center, and piano bar. No gratuities are expected or accepted. The onboard currency is the euro.

SUITABLE FOR: *Club Med 2* is best suited to youthful couples and singles who want contemporary facilities and some watersports in a very relaxed but quite chic and trendy set-

BERLITZ'S RATINGS

	Possible	Achieved
Ship	500	394
Accommodation	200	162
Food	400	282
Service	400	284
Entertainment	100	72
Cruise	400	289

ting that is different to "normal" cruise ships, with good food and service, but with little or no entertainment.

ACCOMMODATION. There are five suites and 192 standard cabins (all of equal size). All cabins are nicely equipped and very comfortable, and have an inviting decor that includes much blond wood cabinetry. They all feature a mini-bar/refrigerator, 24-hour room service (but you pay for food), a personal safe, color television, plenty of storage space, bathrobes, and a hairdryer. There are six, four-person cabins, and some 35 doubles are fitted with an extra Pullman berth – good for young families but cramped.

CUISINE. The two main dining rooms are Le Mediterannee and Le Magellen. Both have tables for two, for, six or eight. There is open seating, so you can sit with whom you wish. The Grand Bleu Restaurant has a delightful open terrace for informal meals. Complimentary wines and beers are available with lunch and dinner (there is also an à la carte wine list, at a price). Afternoon tea is a delight. The cuisine provides French, continental and Japanese specialties, and the creativity and presentation are good.

ENTERTAINMENT. This is limited to occasional cabaret acts. There is live music for dancing and listening each evening

SPA/FITNESS. The Health Spa has a unisex sauna, beauty salon, and treatment rooms for massage, facials and body wraps; there is also a decent fitness room, and a beauty salon. The spa facilities are split on three separate decks.

Coral
★★

Size:	Mid-Size Ship	Passenger Decks:	7	Cabins (with private balcony):	0
Tonnage:	14,155	Total Crew:	265	Cabins (wheelchair accessible):	2
Lifestyle:	Standard	Passengers		Wheelchair accessibility	None
Cruise Line:	Louis Cruises	(lower beds/all berths):	756/945	Cabin Current:	110 and 220 volts
Former Names:	Triton, Cunard Adventurer,	Passenger Space Ratio		Elevators:	2
	Sunward II	(lower beds/all berths):	18.7/14.9	Casino (gaming tables):	Yes
Builder:	Rotterdamsche Dry Dock (Holland)	Crew/Passenger Ratio		Slot Machines:	Yes
Original Cost:	n/a	(lower beds/all berths):	2.8/3.5	Swimming Pools (outdoors):	1
Entered Service:	Oct 1971/May 2005	Cabins (total):	378	Swimming Pools (indoors):	0
Registry:	Greece	Size Range (sq ft/m):	118.4–131.3/	Whirlpools:	0
Length (ft/m):	491.1/149.70		11.0–12.2	Self-Service Launderette:	No
Beam (ft/m):	70.5/21.50	Cabins (outside view):	142	Dedicated Cinema/Seats:	Yes/96
Draft (ft/m):	19.22/5.86	Cabins (interior/no view):	0	Library:	No
Propulsion/Propellers:	diesel (19,860kW)/2	Cabins (for one person):	0		

OVERALL SCORE: 944 OUT OF A POSSIBLE 2,000 POINTS

OVERVIEW. The all-white ship has a smart, but dated profile, a deep clipper bow, and twin funnels. It has been fairly well maintained, but is showing its age. There is a walk-around painted steel outdoors promenade deck, a decent amount of open deck space for sunbathing atop the ship, and small swimming pool on an aft deck. Some of the open space outdoors is covered by canvas awnings, providing shelter from the summer sun.

Inside, it's easy to find your way around. The few public rooms have cheerful, warm colors, although ceilings are low. Decor and artwork are eclectic, and deck names are Greek. There is no library, just some old paperbacks. Most public rooms have been refurbished in the past three years and are contemporary and comfortable. A couple of internet-access stations are provided in a small open area; connection charges are high, at €1 a minute.

Expect lines for buffets and shore excursions. Announcements are made in several languages. The onboard currency is the euro, and gratuities are charged to your onboard account (€8 per person, per day). The dress code is casual throughout – no formal nights.

SUITABLE FOR: *Coral* is best suited to first-time passengers who simply want to cruise the Greek Islands in a modicum of comfort, and at a modest price.

ACCOMMODATION. Cabins are in 15 price grades, depending on location and size. Most are very small, narrow, and basic. The closet and drawer space is minimal, and cabin soundproofing is very poor. There are 32 cabins (in the two highest grades) with a tub/shower; otherwise they have very small shower enclosures, and little space for toiletries.

BERLITZ'S RATINGS

	Possible	Achieved
Ship	500	231
Accommodation	200	91
Food	400	194
Service	400	216
Entertainment	100	40
Cruise	400	172

CUISINE. While the Dining Room is quite attractive and has contemporary colors and ambiance, it can be noisy. There are two seatings for dinner on most nights (typically an open seating for the first night), and open seating for breakfast and lunch, depending on the itinerary. Dining room seating and table assignments (except for the first night) are handled by the maître d' upon embarkation.

The cuisine is predominantly Continental, with some regional Greek specialties (much use of oil and salt). Vegetarian dishes are also available on lunch and dinner menus. Overall, the food is quite acceptable and varied. Service is hurried and indifferent.

Casual breakfast and lunch, with limited choices, can also be taken outside on deck poolside, or in the main lounge when the weather is not good. Additional light refreshments are available indoors at the Cafe Brazil.

ENTERTAINMENT. The Main Lounge is a single deck height, rectangular-shaped room (no sloping floor) designed mainly for small production shows and cabaret acts. Banquette and individual seating is set around a "thrust" stage, but six pillars obstruct sightlines.

SPA/FITNESS. A small gymnasium is located aft, close to the swimming pool – it's really just a "dip" pool; adjacent is a sauna and massage room. A beauty salon is located indoors on another deck – there is no natural light, which makes tinting and coloring difficult.

Massages, aromatherapy facials, manicures, pedicures, and hair beautifying treatments are available, but facilities are minimal – it's a compact ship.

Coral Princess
★★★★

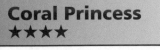

Size:	Large Resort Ship	Total Crew:	900	Cabins (wheelchair accessible):	20
Tonnage:	91,627	Passengers		Wheelchair accessibility	Good
Lifestyle:	Standard	(lower beds/all berths):	1,974/2,590	Cabin Current:	110 volts
Cruise Line:	Princess Cruises	Passenger Space Ratio		Elevators:	14
Former Names:	none	(lower beds/all berths):	46.4/35.3	Casino (gaming tables):	Yes
Builder:	Chantiers de l'Atlantique (France)	Crew/Passenger Ratio		Slot Machines:	Yes
Original Cost:	$360 million	(lower beds/all berths):	2.1/2.8	Swimming Pools (outdoors):	2
Entered Service:	Dec 2002	Cabins (total):	987		(+ 1 splash pool)
Registry:	Bermuda	Size Range (sq ft/m):	156–470.0/	Swimming Pools (indoors):	0
Length (ft/m):	964.5/294.0		14.4–43.6	Whirlpools:	5
Beam (ft/m):	105.6/32.2	Cabins (outside view):	879	Self-Service Launderette:	Yes
Draft (ft/m):	26/7.9	Cabins (interior/no view):	108	Dedicated Cinema/Seats:	No
Propulsion/Propellers:	gas turbine/2	Cabins (for one person):	0	Library:	Yes
Passenger Decks:	11	Cabins (with private balcony):	727		

OVERALL SCORE: 1,544 OUT OF A POSSIBLE 2,000 POINTS

OVERVIEW. *Coral Princess* has an instantly recognizable funnel due to two jet engine-like pods that sit high up on its structure but really are mainly for decoration. Four diesel engines provide the generating power. Electrical power is provided by a combination of four diesel and one gas turbine (CODAG) unit; the diesel engines are located in the engine room, while the gas turbine unit is located in the ship's funnel housing. The ship also has three bow thrusters and three stern thrusters.

The ship's interior layout is similar to that of the *Grand Princess*-class ships (but with two decks full of public rooms, lounges and bars instead of just one), and sensibly has three major stair towers for passengers (good from the safety and evacuation viewpoint), with plenty of lifts for easy access. For a large ship, the layout is quite user-friendly, and less disjointed than many ships of a similar size and, because of its slim beam, the ship is able to transit the Panama Canal, thus providing greater flexibility in deployment than the *Grand Princess*-class ships.

In a 2009 refit, an adults-only "Sanctuary" area was added to provide a quiet zone, comfortable, padded sun-loungers, and "serenity" steward service. Although there's a daily fee, it's worth it. Also added was a large "Movies Under the Stars" screen, in the second pool area just forward of the funnel. This ship has a walk-around open promenade deck, unlike many modern ships.

A flower shop allows you to order flowers and Godiva chocolates for cabin delivery – good for a birthday or anniversary – a cigar lounge (Churchill Lounge), and a martini bar (Crooners). The casino has a London theme. An AOL Internet Cafe is conveniently located on the top

BERLITZ'S RATINGS

	Possible	Achieved
Ship	500	436
Accommodation	200	154
Food	400	261
Service	400	294
Entertainment	100	85
Cruise	400	314

level of the four-deck-high lobby. The dreaded "fine arts" get their own room, so that paintings to be sold during the art auctions are not spread all over the ship. Adjacent is the Wedding Chapel (a live web-cam can relay ceremonies via the internet). The ship's captain can legally marry (American) couples, due to the ship's registry and a special dispensation (this should, however, be verified when in the planning stage, and may depend on where you live). Princess Cruises offers three wedding packages – Pearl, Emerald, Diamond; the fee includes registration and official marriage certificate. The Wedding Chapel can also host "renewal of vows" ceremonies (there is a fee).

ACCOMMODATION. With 33 price categories, in six types, there's a good choice: 16 Suites with balcony (470 sq. ft/43.6 sq. meters); 184 Mini-Suites with balcony (285–302 sq. ft/26.4–28.0 sq. meters); 8 Mini-Suites without balcony (300 sq. ft/27.8 sq. meters; 527 Outside-View Cabins with balcony (217–232 sq. ft/ 20.1–21.5 sq. meters); 144 Standard Outside-view Cabins (162 sq. ft/15 sq. meters); Interior (no view) Cabins (156 sq. ft/144.5 sq. meters). There are also 20 wheelchair-accessible cabins (217–374 sq. ft/20.1–34.7 sq. meters). All measurements are approximate. Almost all of the outside-view cabins have a private balcony. Some cabins can accommodate a third, or third and fourth person (good for families with children). Some cabins on Emerald Deck (Deck 8) have a view obstructed by lifeboats.

Suites: There are just 16 suites and, although none are really that large (when compared to such ships as *Norwegian Dawn* and *Norwegian Star*, where the largest suites measure a whopping 5,350 sq. ft/497 sq. meters, for example), each has a private balcony. All are named after islands (mostly coral-based islands in the Indian Ocean and Pacific Ocean). All suites are located on either Deck 9 or Deck 10. In a departure from many ships, *Coral Princess* does not have any suites or cabins with a view of the ship's stern. There are also four Premium Suites, located sensibly in the center of the ship, adjacent to a bank of six lifts. Six other suites (called Verandah Suites) are located further aft.

All Accommodation: All suites and cabins are equipped with a refrigerator, personal safe, television (with audio channels), hairdryer, satellite-dial telephone, and twin beds that convert to a queen-sized bed (there are a few exceptions). All accommodation has a bathroom with shower enclosure and toilet. Accommodation designated as suites and mini-suites (there are seven price categories) has a bathtub and separate shower enclosure, and two televisions.

All passengers receive turndown service and chocolates on pillows each night, bathrobes (on request) and toiletry amenity kits (larger, naturally, for suite/mini-suite occupants). There are no cabins for singles. Princess Cruises typically includes CNN, CNBC, ESPN and TNT on the in-cabin color television system (when available). There are no butlers – even for the top-grade suites. Cabin attendants have too many cabins to look after (typically 20), which does not translate to fine personal service.

CUISINE. The two main dining rooms, Bordeaux and Provence, are located in the forward section of the ship on the two lowest passenger decks, with the galley all the way forward so it doesn't intersect public spaces. Both are almost identical in design and layout (the ceilings are quite low and make the rooms appear more cramped than they are), and have plenty of intimate alcoves and cozy dining spots, with tables for two, four, six, or eight. There are two seatings for dinner, while breakfast and lunch are on an open-seating basis; you may have to stand in line at peak times, just as in almost any large restaurant ashore. Both dining rooms are non-smoking.

Horizon Court is the ship's casual 24-hour eatery, and is located in the forward section of Lido Deck, with superb ocean views. Several self-serve counters provide an array of food for breakfast and lunch buffets, and offer bistro-style casual dinners in the evening.

Alternative (Extra Charge) Eateries: There are two "alternative" dining rooms (Sabatini's and the Bayou Cafe), both enclosed (i.e. not open areas which passengers can walk through, as in some Princess Cruises ships). Both cost extra, and you must make a reservation.

Sabatini's is an Italian eatery, with colorful tiled Mediterranean-style decor; it is named after Trattoria Sabatini, the 200-year old institution in Florence (where there is no cover charge). It has Italian-style pizzas and pastas, with a variety of sauces, as well as Italian-style entrées (including tiger prawns and lobster tail – all provided with flair and entertainment by the waiters). The food is both creative and tasty (with seriously sized portions). Sabatini's is by reservation only, and there is a cover charge of $15 per person, for lunch or dinner (on sea days only).

The Bayou Cafe is open for lunch and dinner, and has a cover charge of $10 per person (including a free Hurricane cocktail), and evokes the charm of New Orleans' French Quarter, complete with wrought-iron decoration. The Bayou Cafe has Creole food (with platters such as Peel 'n' Eat Shrimp Piquante, Sausage Grillades, Oysters Sieur de Bienville and N'Awlins Crawfish "Mud Bug" Bisque delivered to the table when you arrive). Popular entrées include Seafood Gumbo, and Chorizo Jambalaya with fresh seafood and traditional dried spice mixes, as well as Cajun Grill items such as Smothered Alligator Ribs, Flambeaux Grilled Jumbo Prawns, Corn Meal Fried Catfish, Blackened Chicken Brochette, and Red Pepper Butter Broiled Lobster; desserts include sweet potato pie and banana whiskey pound cake. The room sports a small stage, with baby grand piano, and live jazz is also part of the dining scenario.

Other outlets include La Pâtisserie, in the ship's reception lobby coffee, cakes and pastries spot; a good place for informal meetings; there's also a Pizzeria, hamburger grill, and an ice cream bar (extra charge for the ice cream). Meanwhile, puffers and sippers should enjoy Churchill's, a neat cigar and cognac lounge, cleverly sited near a little hideaway bar called the Rat Pack Bar.

ENTERTAINMENT. The Princess Theatre is two decks high, and, unusually, there is much more seating in the upper level than on the main floor below. There are typically two production shows on a 7-day cruise, and three on a 10-day cruise. These are colorful, glamorous shows with well designed costumes and good lighting.

A second entertainment lounge (Universe Lounge) is designed more for cabaret-style features. It also has two levels (a first for a Princess Cruises ship), and three separate stages – so nonstop entertainment can be provided without constant set-ups. Some 50 of the room's seats are equipped with a built-in laptop computer. The room is also used for cooking demonstrations (it has a full kitchen set), and other life-enrichment participation activities. There is a good mix of music in the various bars and lounges.

For self-improvement, Princess Cruises' new "Scholar-Ship@Sea" program offers about 20 courses per cruise (six on any given day at sea). Although all introductory classes are free, if you want to continue any chosen subject in a smaller setting, charges apply. There are four core subjects: Culinary Arts, Visual/Creative Arts, Photography, and Computer Technology. There is a full culinary demonstration kitchen and a pottery studio complete with kiln.

SPA/FITNESS. The Lotus Spa is located aft on one of the ship's uppermost decks. It contains men's and women's saunas, steam rooms, changing rooms, relaxation area, beauty salon, aerobics exercise room and gymnasium with ocean-views packed with the latest high-tech muscle-pumping, cardio-vascular equipment. There are several large rooms for individual treatments.

● **For more extensive general information about a Princess Cruises cruise experience, see pages 148–51.**

Corinthian II
★★★★

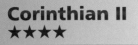

Size:	Boutique Ship	Passenger Decks:	.5	Cabins (with private balcony):	.4
Tonnage:	4,280	Total Crew:	.66	Cabins (wheelchair accessible):	.0
Lifestyle:	Standard	Passengers		Wheelchair accessibility	None
Cruise Line:	Travel Dynamics International	(lower beds/all berths):	.112/122	Cabin Current:	110 volts
Former Names:	Island Sun, Regina	Passenger Space Ratio		Elevators:	1
	Renaissance, Renaissance VIII	(lower beds/all berths):	.38.2/38.2	Casino (gaming tables):	No
Builder:	Nuovi Cantieri Appaunia (Italy)	Crew/Passenger Ratio		Slot Machines:	No
Original Cost:	$25 million	(lower beds/all berths):	.1.7/1.8	Swimming Pools (outdoors):	.0
Entered Service:	Dec 1991/May 2005	Cabins (total):	.61	Swimming Pools (indoors):	.0
Registry:	Mauritius	Size Range (sq ft/m):	.234.6–353.0/	Whirlpools:	1
Length (ft/m):	297.2/90.6		21.8–32.8	Self-Service Launderette:	No
Beam (ft/m):	50.1/15.3	Cabins (outside view):	.61	Dedicated Cinema/Seats:	No
Draft (ft/m):	12.9/2.95	Cabins (interior/no view):	.0	Library:	Yes
Propulsion/Propellers:	diesel (5000kW)/2	Cabins (for one person):	.0		

OVERALL SCORE: 1,546 OUT OF A POSSIBLE 2,000 POINTS

OVERVIEW. *Corinthian II* (originally built as one of a series of eight similar ships for the now-defunct Renaissance Cruises) has mega-yacht looks, a smart profile and handsome styling, with twin flared funnels and a "ducktail" (sponson) stern to provide good stability and seagoing comfort. This charming ship is operated by Travel Dynamics International year-round on "soft" destination-intensive" discovery cruises. The ship (upgraded in 2004) has a teak wrap-around promenade deck outdoors, and decent amount of open deck and sunbathing space.

A baby shore tender hangs off the aft deck and acts as ship-to-shore transportation. Some equipment for watersports is carried, and active types can enjoy wind surfing, scuba diving and snorkeling, deep sea fishing, mountain biking, golfing, and hiking.

Inside, you will find an elegant interior design, with polished wood-finish paneling throughout. There is also a very small book and video library.

This vessel is very comfortable and totally inviting, and features warm-weather cruising in regions devoid of large cruise ships. Although this intimate ship is not up to the standard of a Seabourn or Silversea ship, it will provide a good cruise experience at a moderate cost. Gratuities are appreciated but not required.

The onboard currency is the US dollar.

SUITABLE FOR: Mature adults who want to discover small ports, in a relaxed lifestyle combined with good food and service, and itineraries that enable you to "get away from it all, but in comfort."

BERLITZ'S RATINGS

	Possible	Achieved
Ship	500	392
Accommodation	200	159
Food	400	309
Service	400	306
Entertainment	n/a	n/a
Cruise	500	380

ACCOMMODATION. The spacious cabins combine highly polished imitation rosewood paneling with lots of mirrors and hand-crafted Italian furniture, lighted walk-in closets, vanity mirrors. In fact, there are a lot of mirrored surfaces in the decor, as well as just about everything you need, including a TV set and DVD player, a refrigerator, and free soft drinks and bottled water. However, the beds are fixed, so there's no underbed storage space.

The bathrooms are extremely compact units; they have real teakwood floors and marble vanities, and shower enclosures. None have tubs, not even the owner's suite. Cabins with balconies have glass panels topped with a polished wood railing.

CUISINE. The dining room operates with an open seating for all meals. It is small but quite smart, with tables for two, four, six, and eight. You simply sit where you like, with whom you like, and at what time you like.

The meals are self-service, buffet-style cold foods for breakfast and lunch, with hot foods chosen from a table menu and served properly, and sit down service for dinner. The food quality, choice, and presentation are all very good.

ENTERTAINMENT. There is no formal entertainment in the main lounge, the venue for all social activities (six pillars obstruct the sightlines to the small stage area anyway).

SPA/FITNESS. Water sports facilities include an aft platform, sailfish, snorkel equipment, and Zodiacs.

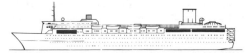

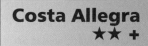

Costa Allegra
★★ +

Size: . . . . .Mid-Size Ship	Passenger Decks: 8	Cabins (with private balcony): 10
Tonnage: .28,430	Total Crew: 450	Cabins (wheelchair accessible): 8 (interior)
Lifestyle: . . . . .Standard	Passengers	Wheelchair accessibility . . . . .None
Cruise Line: . . . . .Costa Cruises	(lower beds/all berths): 820/1,072	Cabin Current: . . . . .110 and 220 volts
Former Names: . . . . .Annie Johnson	Passenger Space Ratio	Elevators: 4
Builder: . . . . . . .Mariotti Shipyards (Italy)	(lower beds/all berths): 34.7/26.5	Casino (gaming tables): . . . . Yes
Original Cost: . . . .$175 million	Crew/Passenger Ratio	Slot Machines: . . . . .Yes
Entered Service: . . . . .Dec 1992	(lower beds/all berths): 2.0/2.6	Swimming Pools (outdoors): 1
Registry: . . . . .Italy	Cabins (total): 410	Swimming Pools (indoors): 0
Length (ft/m): 616.1/187.8	Size Range (sq ft/m): 105.4–575.8/	Whirlpools: 2
Beam (ft/m): 83.9/25.6	9.8–53.5	Self-Service Launderette: . . . . .No
Draft (ft/m): 23.9/7.3	Cabins (outside view): 218	Dedicated Cinema/Seats: . . . . .No
Propulsion/Propellers: . . . . .diesel	Cabins (interior/no view): 192	Library: . . . . .Yes
(19,200kW)/2	Cabins (for one person): 0	

OVERALL SCORE: 1,092 (OUT OF A POSSIBLE 2,000 POINTS)

OVERVIEW. *Costa Allegra* originally began life as a container ship built for Sweden's Johnson Line, then underwent a skilful transformation into contemporary cruise ship, which resulted in a jazzy, angular-looking vessel with a low-slung appearance (fine when it debuted, but now it looks outdated). There are three bolt-upright yellow funnels that have become a signature item for almost all Costa Cruises' ships. Slightly longer and larger than its sister ship *Costa Marina* (after the addition of a 44ft/13.4-meter section), this vessel has a much better standard of interior fit and finish, and more outdoors space than its sister ship. It has an interesting glass-enclosed stern.

There is a high glass-to-steel ratio for the size of the ship, with numerous glass domes and walls admitting light, as well as Murano glass light fixtures in some places. There is a good amount of outdoor deck and sunbathing space, although there is no observation lounge with forward-facing views over the ship's bows. bows. No cushioned pads are provided for the sunloungers outdoors.

The decks are named after famous painters. The decor underwent a change in 2006 to provide more of an Asian ambiance, while still retaining a European feel; this was done before the ship was sent to China for local market cruising. There are few public restrooms.

The many loud and extended announcements (in several languages) quickly become tiresome. The opening hours for the small library are poor. Gratuities are added to your onboard account.

SUITABLE FOR: *Costa Allegra* provides a decent first cruise experience for young adults who enjoy European-style ser-

BERLITZ'S RATINGS		
	Possible	Achieved
Ship	500	275
Accommodation	200	120
Food	400	192
Service	400	226
Entertainment	100	57
Cruise	400	222

vice and a real upbeat, almost elegant atmosphere with an Italian accent and lots of noise.

ACCOMMODATION. There are several categories (the price will depend on grade, location and size). The standard cabins are quite light and airy, with splashes of fabric colors, and wood accenting, and are laid out in a practical manner. However, they are small, and there is little closet and drawer space, so take only casual clothing. There are many small interior (no view) cabins, and all cabins suffer from poor soundproofing. Many cabins also have pull-down (Pullman-style) berths for a third or fourth occupant. The bathrooms are compact, although they do have good shower enclosures, with sliding circular door instead of the usual limp curtain. The cabin service menu is extremely limited.

On Rousseau Deck there are three forward-facing suites (the largest accommodation on board), each of which has a living room, dinette and wet bar. A further 10 slightly smaller mini-suites feature a small, very narrow balcony, but it is really not private, as it can be seen from the walking track on the deck above.

CUISINE. The Montmartre Restaurant has 310 seats. It operates two seatings and has an international menu. It is fairly spacious (but noisy) and has expansive glass windows that look out over the stern, while the port side and starboard side have large portholes. It has tables for four, six, eight or 10 (there are no tables for two). Adjacent is the 134-seat Montemartre Verandah Restaurant is an à la carte, pay-to-eat venue with an Italo-Asian menu.

Four small dining venues were added in the 2006 refit.

These include Piazzetta Allegra, a pay-to-eat sushi and sashimi bar seating 110 with a karaoke area, and Almalfi, an Italian pay-to-eat à la carte restaurant with that seats 76 indoors and 52 outside, and has a dance floor. Excellent cappuccino and espresso coffees are always available in various bars around the ship, served in the right sized china cups.

ENTERTAINMENT. The Folies Bergères Showroom is a single level room. The sight lines are adequate, but could be better (14 pillars obstruct sight lines from several seats). Because it is only a single-level room, its poor ceiling height precludes jugglers and the like from working, and limits what can be achieved. In other words, don't expect much. The room is quite adequate, however, as a cabaret lounge.

For live dance music and listening music, head to the Flamenco Ballroom, located at the aft end of the ship. In addition, the Crystal Club Discotheque, one deck above the Flamenco Ballroom, is the place for the young at heart, late of night, and hard of hearing.

SPA/FITNESS. A new (Caracalla Spa) wellness center was created in 2006 from a 30-ton aluminum superstructure that houses a gymnasium, eight treatment rooms, two locker rooms, two saunas and a relaxation area.

The spa is operated by Steiner, a specialist concession, whose young staff will try to sell you Steiner's own-brand Elemis beauty products (spa girls have sales targets). fitness classes are free, while some cost extra. Do make appointments early as time slots can go quickly. There is also a jogging track outdoors.

● **For more extensive general information on what a Costa Cruises cruise is like, see pages 135–8.**

SHIP TALK

Abeam: off the side of the ship, at a right angle to its length.

Aft: near, toward, or in the rear of the ship.

Ahead: something that is ahead of the ship's bow.

Alleyway: a passageway or corridor.

Alongside: said of a ship when it is beside a pier or another vessel.

Amidships: in or toward the middle of the ship; the longitudinal center portion of the ship.

Anchor Ball: black ball hoisted above the bow to show that the vessel is anchored.

Astern: is the opposite of Ahead (i.e., meaning something behind the ship).

Backwash: motion in the water caused by the propeller(s) moving in a reverse (astern) direction.

Bar: sandbar, usually caused by tidal or current conditions near the shore.

Beam: width of the ship between its two sides at the widest point.

Bearing: compass direction, expressed in degrees, from the ship to a particular objective or destination.

Below: anything beneath the main deck.

Berth: dock, pier, or quay. Also means bed on board ship.

Bilge: lowermost spaces of the infrastructure of a ship.

Boat Stations: allotted space for each person during lifeboat drill or any other emergency when lifeboats are lowered.

Bow: the forward most part of the vessel.

Bridge: navigational and command control center.

Bulkhead: upright partition (wall) dividing the ship into compartments.

Bunkers: the space where fuel is stored; "bunkering" means taking on fuel.

Cable Length: a measured length equaling 100 fathoms or 600 feet.

Chart: a nautical map used for navigating.

Colors: refers to the national flag or emblem flown by the ship.

Companionway: interior stairway.

Course: direction in which the ship is headed, in degrees.

Davit: a device for raising and lowering lifeboats.

Deadlight: a ventilated porthole cover to prevent light from entering.

Disembark (also debark): to leave a ship.

Dock: berth, pier, or quay.

Draft (or draught): measurement in feet from the ship's waterline to the lowest point of its keel.

Embark: to join a ship.

Fantail: the rear or overhang of the ship.

Fathom: distance equal to 6 ft.

Flagstaff: a pole at the stern of a ship where the flag of its country of registry is flown.

Free Port: port or place free of customs duty and regulations.

Funnel: chimney from which the ship's combustion gases are propelled into the atmosphere.

Galley: the ship's kitchen.

Gangway: the stairway or ramp that provides the link between ship and shore.

● *More Ship Talk, page 330.*

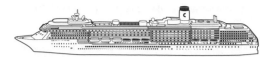

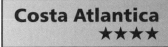

Costa Atlantica
★★★★

Size:	Large Resort Ship	Passenger Decks:	12	Cabins (wheelchair accessible):	8
Tonnage:	85,700	Total Crew:	920	Wheelchair accessibility	Good
Lifestyle:	Standard	Passengers		Cabin Current:	110 volts
Cruise Line:	Costa Cruises	(lower beds/all berths):	2,112/2,680	Elevators:	12
Former Names:	none	Passenger Space Ratio		Casino (gaming tables):	Yes
Builder:	Kverner Masa-Yards (Finland)	(lower beds/all berths):	40.5/31.9	Slot Machines:	Yes
Original Cost:	$335 million	Crew/Passenger Ratio		Swimming Pools (outdoors):	2
Entered Service:	July 2000	(lower beds/all berths):	2.3/2.9		(+1 indoor/outdoor)
Registry:	Italy	Cabins (total):	1,056	Swimming Pools (indoors):	No
Length (ft/m):	959.6/292.5	Size Range (sq ft/m):	161.4–387.5/	Whirlpools:	Yes
Beam (ft/m):	105.6/32.2		15.0–36.0	Self-Service Launderette:	No
Draft (ft/m):	25.5/7.8	Cabins (outside view):	843	Dedicated Cinema/Seats:	No
Propulsion/Propellers:	diesel-electric	Cabins (interior/no view):	213	Library:	Yes
	(34,000 kW)/2 azimuthing pods	Cabins (for one person):	0		
	(17.6 MW each)	Cabins (with private balcony):	742		

OVERALL SCORE: 1,436 OUT OF A POSSIBLE 2,000 POINTS

OVERVIEW. *Costa Atlantica* (sister: *Costa Mediterranea*) has basically the same exterior design and internal layout as that of parent company Carnival Cruise Lines' *Carnival Legend, Miracle, Pride* and *Spirit*. There are two centrally located swimming pools outdoors, one of which can be used in poor weather due to its retractable magrodome cover. A bar abridges two adjacent whirlpool tubs. There's a smaller pool for children, and a winding water slide that spans two decks in height – it starts on a platform bridge at the aft funnel. There is an additional whirlpool tub outdoors.

Inside, the layout is somewhat of an extension of that found in previous newbuilds for Costa Cruises – particularly that of *Costa Victoria*. The deck names are inspired by Federico Fellini movies (Roma Deck, Le Notte di Cabiria, La Voce della Luna, La Strada, La Luci del Varieta). There's even a deck named after a Fellini TV movie, Ginger and Fred. The interior design is, however, bold and brash – a mix of classical Italy and contemporary features. Good points include the fact that the interior design allows good passenger flow from one public space to another, and there are several floor spaces for dancing, and a range of bars and lounges for socializing.

You'll be struck by the immense size of the lobby space spanning eight decks. Take a drink from the lobby bar and look upwards – the surroundings are stunning. A small chapel is located forward of the uppermost level.

Other facilities include a winding shopping street with boutique stores (Fendi, Gianni Versace, Paul & Shark Yachting – as well as a shop dedicated to selling Caffe Flo-

BERLITZ'S RATINGS

	Possible	Achieved
Ship	500	427
Accommodation	200	152
Food	400	240
Service	400	273
Entertainment	100	64
Cruise	400	280

rian products), photo gallery, video games room, an observation balcony, a casino and library (with internet access).

Costa Cruises has updated its image, and is retraining its staff. With the debut of *Costa Atlantica* came many new, better, uniforms for many departments, as well as more choice in a ship that is designed to wow the hip and trendy as well as pay homage to many of Italy's great art and past masters.

Food and service levels have been raised to a better standard than that found aboard most other Costa Cruises ships to date. All printed materials (room service folio, menus, etc.) are in six languages (Italian, English, French, German, Portuguese, Spanish). The onboard currency is the US dollar or euro, depending on the region of operation.

Some tables in the Tiziano Dining Room have a less than comfortable view of the harsh lighting of the escalators between the galley and the two decks of the dining room.

Too many pillars obstruct passenger flow and sight lines throughout the ship. The many pillars in the dining room make it difficult for waiters to provide proper food service. The fit and finish of some interior decoration is quite poor. The hospitality levels and service are inconsistent, and below the standard of several other "major" cruise lines.

SUITABLE FOR: *Costa Atlantica* is best suited to young (and young at heart) couples and singles (plus families with children) that enjoy big city life, piazzas and outdoor cafes, constant activity accompanied by lots of noise (some call it ambiance), late nights, entertainment that is consistently loud, and an international mix of fellow passengers.

ACCOMMODATION. There are 14 categories. There is a healthy (78 percent) proportion of outside-view to interior (no view) cabins. All cabins have twin beds that convert into a queen-sized bed, individually controlled air-conditioning, television, and telephone. Many cabins have views obstructed by lifeboats on Deck 4 (Roma Deck), the lowest of the accommodation decks, as well as some cabins on Deck 5. Some cabins have pull-down (Pullman-style) berths that are fully hidden in the ceiling when not in use. There is too much use of fluorescent lighting in the suites and cabins, and the soundproofing could be much better. Some bathroom fixtures – bath and shower taps in particular – are frustrating to use until you get the hang of them.

Some of the most desirable suites and cabins are those with private balconies on five aft-facing decks (Decks 4, 5, 6, 7, and 8) with views overlooking the stern and ship's wash. Other cabins with private balconies will find the balconies not so private – the partition between one balcony and the next is not a full partition – so you might be able to hear your neighbors.

However, these balcony occupants all have good views through glass and wood-topped railings, and the deck is made of teak. The cabins are well laid out, typically with twin beds that convert to a queen-sized bed, vanity desk (with built-in hairdryer), large TV set, personal safe, and one closet that has moveable shelves – providing more space for luggage storage. However, the lighting is fluorescent, and much too harsh. The bathroom is a simple, modular unit that has shower enclosures with soap dispenser.

The largest suites are designated Penthouse Suites, although they are really quite small when compared with suites aboard other ships of a similar size. However, they do at least offer more space to move around in, and a slightly larger, better bathroom.

CUISINE. The large Tiziano Dining Room is located in the aft section of the ship on two levels, with a spiral stairway between them. There are two seatings, with tables for two, four, six or eight. Dinner on European cruises is typically scheduled at 7pm and 9pm to accommodate the later eating habits of Europeans. Themed evenings are a part of the Costa Cruises tradition, and three different window blinds help create a different feel. However, the artwork is placed at table height, so the room seems more closed-in than it should.

Alternative Dining: A reservations-only alternative for dinner, Ristorante Club Atlantica, with menus by Gualtiero Marchesi, is available six nights a week. There is a cover/service charge of €20 per person (passengers occupying suite-grade accommodation get a free pass for one evening). The food is decidedly better than in the main dining room, although it's nothing special.

Undoubtedly the place that most people will want to see and be seen is in the informal Caffe Florian – a replica of the famous indoor/outdoor cafe that opened in 1720 in St. Mark's Square, Venice. There are four separate salons (Sala delle Stagioni, Sala del Senato, Sala Liberty, and Sala degli Uomini Illustri), and the same fascinating mosaic, marble and wood floors, opulent ceiling art, and special lampshades. Even the espresso/cappuccino machine is a duplicate of that found in the real thing. The only problem is that the chairs are much too small.

Casual breakfast and luncheon self-serve buffet-style meals can be taken in the Botticelli Buffet Restaurant, adjacent to the swimming pools, with seating both indoors and outdoors. A grill (for hamburgers and hot dogs) and a pasta bar are conveniently adjacent to the second pool, while indoors is the Napoli Pizzeria.Excellent cappuccino and espresso coffees are always available in various bars around the ship, served in the right-sized china cups.

ENTERTAINMENT. A three-deck-high showlounge (the Caruso Theater) is an imposing room, with just over 1,000 seats. Spiral stairways at the back of the lounge connect all levels. Stage shows are best seen from the upper three levels, from where the sight lines are reasonably good. Directly underneath the showlounge is the Coral Lounge, a large lounge complete with its own bar. An onboard resident troupe of singers and dancers provides the cast members for colorful, high-energy production shows. However, the production shows are loud and quite poor. For nights when there are no production shows, the showlounge presents cabaret acts such as singers, comedy jugglers, magicians, ventriloquists, and so on. These are generally ho-hum, however.

A number of bands and small musical units provide a variety of live music in many of the ship's lounges and bars, and there is a discotheque.

SPA/FITNESS. The Ischia Spa is quite expansive, spanning two decks. Facilities include a solarium, eight treatment rooms, lecture rooms, sauna and steam rooms for men and women, a beauty parlor. A large gymnasium has floor-to-ceiling windows on three sides, including forward-facing ocean views, and an aerobics room with instructor-led classes. There is also a jogging track outdoors.

The spa is operated by Steiner, a specialist concession, whose young staff will try to sell you Steiner's own-brand Elemis beauty products. Some fitness classes are free, while some, such as yoga, and kick-boxing, cost $10 per class.

Massage (including exotic massages such as Aroma Stone massage, Chakra Balancing massage and other well-being massages), facials, pedicures, and beauty salon treatments are at extra cost (massage, for example, costs about $2 per minute, plus gratuity). Do make appointments as early as possible since time slots go quickly.

● **For more extensive general information on what a Costa Cruises cruise is like, see pages 135–8.**

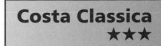

Costa Classica
★★★

Size: ....Mid-Size Ship	Passenger Decks: 10	Cabins (with private balcony): 10
Tonnage: ....52,950 tons	Total Crew: 650	Cabins (wheelchair accessible): 6
Lifestyle: ....Standard	Passengers	(interior)
Cruise Line: ....Costa Cruises	(lower beds/all berths): 1,308/1,766	Wheelchair accessibility ....Good
Former Names: ....none	Passenger Space Ratio	Cabin Current: ....110 and 220 volts
Builder: ....Fincantieri (Italy)	(lower beds/all berths): 40.4/29.9	Elevators: 8
Original Cost: ....$287 million	Crew/Passenger Ratio	Casino (gaming tables): ....Yes
Entered Service: ....Jan 1992	(lower beds/all berths): 2.0/2.7	Slot Machines: ....Yes
Registry:......................Italy	Cabins (total): 654	Swimming Pools (outdoors): 2
Length (ft/m): 718.5/220.61	Size Range (sq ft/m): 185.1–430.5/	Swimming Pools (indoors): 0
Beam (ft/m): 98.4/30.80	17.2–40.0	Whirlpools: 4
Draft (ft/m): 25.0/7.60	Cabins (outside view): 438	Self-Service Launderette: ....No
Propulsion/Propellers: ....diesel	Cabins (interior/no view): 216	Dedicated Cinema/Seats: ....No
(22,800kW)/2	Cabins (for one person): 0	Library: ....Yes

OVERALL SCORE: 1,245 OUT OF A POSSIBLE 2,000 POINTS

OVERVIEW. *Costa Classica* is an all-white ship, now almost 20 years old, with a straight slab-sided unflattering profile, which is topped by Costa Cruises' unmistakable trademark trio of tall yellow funnels. This was the ship that brought Costa into the mainstream of cruising, Italian-style, and was part of a multi-million plan to modernize the Costa Cruises (Costa Crociere) fleet.

Inside, the ship has contemporary, innovative Italian design and styling that is best described as befitting European tastes. The design incorporates much use of circles (large portholes instead of windows can be found in cabins on lower decks, and in the dining room, self-serve buffet area, coffee bar, and discotheque, for example). There is an excellent range of public rooms, lounges and bars. A number of specially designed business and meeting facilities can be found; the rooms provide multi-flexible configurations.

Some fascinating artwork includes six hermaphrodite statues in one lounge. There is a fine, if unconventional multi-tiered amphitheater-style showlounge, but the seats are bolt upright and downright uncomfortable for more than a few minutes. The multi-level atrium is stark, angular, and cold. The marble-covered staircases look pleasant, but are uncarpeted and a little dangerous if water or drinks are spilled on them while the ship is moving.

Perhaps the interior is best described as an innovative design project that almost works. A forward observation lounge/nightclub sits atop ship like a lump of cheese, and, unfortunately, fails to work well as a nightclub. Internet access is available from one of several computer terminals in the Internet Cafe.

In November 2002 the ship was scheduled to enter dry-

BERLITZ'S RATINGS

	Possible	Achieved
Ship	500	331
Accommodation	200	133
Food	400	214
Service	400	267
Entertainment	100	60
Cruise	400	240

dock for a $10 million "chop-and-stretch" operation to increase its tonnage to 78,000, its length to 870.7 ft (265.4 meters), and its passenger capacity to 2,516. However, this was shelved due to a dispute over the quality of workmanship of the mid-section that was produced by British shipyard Cammell Laird.

There is no wrap-around promenade deck outdoors. The ship's rather slow service speed (19.5 knots) means that itineraries have to be carefully chosen, as the ship cannot compete with the newer ships with faster service speeds.

The air-conditioning system in the Tivoli Dining Room is noisy. There are too many loud, repetitious and irritating announcements. Shore excursions are very expensive. Tipping envelopes provided in your cabin state the amount you are expected to give. The onboard currency is the euro.

SUITABLE FOR: *Costa Classica* is best suited to young (and young at heart) couples and singles (plus families with children) that enjoy big city life, piazzas and outdoor cafes, constant activity accompanied by lots of noise (some call it ambience), late nights, and entertainment that is consistently loud, and an international mix of fellow passengers.

ACCOMMODATION. There are 11 categories, the price depending on grade, size and location). These include 10 suites, while other cabins are fairly standard in size, shape, and facilities, a higher price being asked for cabins on the highest decks. All suites and cabins have twin lower beds, color television, and telephone.

Suites: The 10 suites, located in the center of Portofino Deck, each have a private rounded balcony, marble-clad bathrooms with Jacuzzi bathtub, and separate shower enclosure. There is plenty of space in the living and sleeping areas, and for the storage of luggage, as these really are very spacious suites.

Standard Outside-View/Interior (No View) Cabins: In general, the cabins are of a fairly generous size, and are laid out in a practical manner. They have cherry wood veneered cabinetry and accenting, and include a vanity desk unit with a large mirror. There are useful (unusual, for a cruise ship) sliding doors to the bathroom and closets, and the cabin soundproofing is poor. The soft furnishings are of good quality, but the room service menu is disappointing. The suites have more space (although they are not large by any means), and hand-woven bedspreads.

Some cabins have one or two extra pull-down (Pullman-style) berths – useful for families with small children.

CUISINE. The Tivoli Dining Room has a lovely indented clean white ceiling, although it is extremely noisy (there are two seatings, with dinner typically at 7pm and 9pm to accommodate the later eating habits of Europeans), and there are a good number of tables for two, as well as tables for four, six or eight.

Changeable wall panels help create a European Renaissance atmosphere, albeit at the expense of blocking off windows (but during dinner, it's dark outside anyway – unless you are in the far North). Romantic candlelight dining is provided on formal nights.

For casual outdoor eating, the Alfresco Cafe, with its teak deck and traditional canvas sailcloth awning, is moderately good, depending on what you expect. Unfortunately, breakfast and luncheon buffets are repetitious, quite poor and uncreative; there is little variety, and long lines are typical. The selection of bread rolls, fruits and cheeses is disappointing.

Excellent cappuccino and espresso coffees are always available in various bars around the ship, served in right-sized china cups.

ENTERTAINMENT. The Colosseo Theater, the ship's main showlounge, has an interesting amphitheatre-like design. However, the seats are bolt upright, and quite uncomfortable for any length of time. The Galileo discotheque, located atop the ship, for the young at heart, late of night, and hard of hearing.

SPA/FITNESS. The Caracalla Spa, located on one of the ship's uppermost decks, contains a gymnasium (with good forward-facing views over the ship's bows) with some high-tech muscle-pump machines, an aerobics exercise area, two hot tubs, Roman bath, health bar, sauna and steam rooms, and beauty salon.

The spa is operated by Steiner, a specialist concession, whose young staff will try to sell you Steiner's own-brand Elemis beauty products (spa girls have sales targets). Some fitness classes are free, while some, such as yoga and kick-boxing, cost extra. However, being aboard will give you an opportunity to try some of the more exotic treatments (particularly some of the massages available). Massage (including exotic massages such as Aroma Stone massage, Chakra Balancing massage and other well-being massages), facials, pedicures, and beauty salon treatments are at extra cost (massage, for example, costs about $2 per minute, plus gratuity). Do make appointments as early as possible as time slots can go quickly.

● **For more extensive general information on what a Costa Cruises cruise is like, see pages 135–8.**

THE BRIDGE

A ship's navigation bridge is manned at all times, both at sea and in port. Besides the captain, who is master of the vessel, other senior officers take "watch" turns for four- or eight-hour periods. In addition, junior officers are continually honing their skills as experienced navigators, waiting for the day when they will be promoted to master.

The captain is always in command at times of high risk, such as when the ship is entering or leaving a port, when the density of traffic is particularly high, or when visibility is severely restricted by poor weather.

Navigation has come a long way since the days of the ancient mariners, who used only the sun and the stars to calculate their course across the oceans. The space-age development of sophisticated navigation devices (using satellites) has enabled us to eliminate the guesswork of early navigation (the first global mobile satellite system came into being in 1979).

A ship's navigator today uses a variety of sophisticated instruments to pinpoint the ship's position at any time and establish its course.

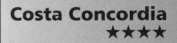

Costa Concordia
★★★★

Size:	Large Resort Ship	Passenger Decks:	14	Cabins (with private balcony):		.571
Tonnage:	112,000	Total Crew:	1,090	Cabins (wheelchair accessible):		.12
Lifestyle:	Standard	Passengers		Wheelchair accessibility		Good
Cruise Line:	Costa Cruises	(lower beds/all berths):	3,000/3,800	Cabin Current:		110 and 220 volts
Former Names:	none	Passenger Space Ratio		Elevators:		14
Builder:	Fincantieri (Italy)	(lower beds/all berths):	37.3/29.4	Casino (gaming tables):		Yes
Original Cost:	$565 million	Crew/Passenger Ratio		Slot Machines:		Yes
Entered Service:	July 2006	(lower beds/all berths):	2.7/3.4	Swimming Pools (outdoors):		.3
Registry:	Italy	Cabins (total):	1,500	Swimming Pools (indoors):		.0
Length (ft/m):	951.4/290.2	Size Range (sq ft/m):	482.2/179.7	Whirlpools:		.4
Beam (ft/m):	123.0/37.5		44.8/16.7	Self-Service Launderette:		No
Draft (ft/m):	26.4/8.05	Cabins (outside view):	.914	Dedicated Cinema/Seats:		No
Propulsion/Propellers:	diesel-electric	Cabins (interior/no view):	.586	Library:		Yes
(34,000kW)/2 azimuthing pods		Cabins (for one person):	.2			

OVERALL SCORE: 1,450 OUT OF A POSSIBLE 2,000 POINTS

OVERVIEW. This a slightly larger, extended version of *Costa Fortuna/Costa Magica*. One of the three pools can be covered by a sliding glass dome in case of poor weather – the ship operates Mediterranean cruises year-round – while one pool has a long water slide (great for kids). There is not a lot of open deck space, but *Costa Concordia* does absorb passengers well.

There are three decks full of bars and lounges plus lots of other public rooms. This ship has a nine-decks-high, glass-domed rotunda atrium lobby, with a lively bar on the lowest deck, adjacent to the reception and shore excursion desks. The Barcelona Casino is large and glitzy. There's also a chapel, and a small library that could be better, an internet center, card room, art gallery, and video game room. Most passengers are Italian.

SUITABLE FOR: *Costa Concordia* is best suited to those who enjoy entertainment that is consistently loud.

ACCOMMODATION. There are 20 price grades, from 2-bed interior (no view) cabins to 10 grand suites with private balcony, although in reality there are only three different sizes: Suites with balcony, 2- or 4-bed outside view cabins, and 2- or 4-bed interior (no-view) cabins, most of which measure about 160 sq.ft /15 sq.m. There are also two single cabins. The largest accommodation is provided in 8 Grand Suites (360 sq.ft/33.5 sq.m). They have a queen-sized bed; bathrooms have a tub and two washbasins. As suites go, they are not large.

CUISINE. There are two main dining rooms, allocated by accommodation grade and location. Both Milano and Roma restaurants have two seatings. Costa specializes in pasta – 50

BERLITZ'S RATINGS		
	Possible	Achieved
Ship	500	426
Accommodation	200	152
Food	400	251
Service	400	375
Entertainment	100	64
Cruise	400	282

types are typically provided. Almost all the wines – the majority Italian – are young. The two 100-seat Samsara dining spots are for those seeking spa food; this features food prepared with reduced calories, fat and salt.

Alternative (Reservations Required) Dining Option: The Club Concordia is an 80-seat upscale dining venue with seating under a large glass dome. There's a cover charge of €23 per person, and it's worth it. Molecular Gastronomy, interpreted by famed Italian chef Ettore Bocchia, is featured. Molecular cooking consists of using liquid nitrogen in order to make food produced with more taste.

Casual Eatery: The Parigi Buffet Restaurant is a self-serve eatery for breakfast, lunch, afternoon pizzas, and beverages (coffee and tea) at any time. Good cappuccino and espresso coffees are always available in various bars (at extra cost).

Additionally, Caffeteria Helsinki (which has Nordic decor) is the place to go for decent (extra cost) coffees.

ENTERTAINMENT. The Athena Theater, spanning three decks, is quite stunning, and has a revolving stage, hydraulic orchestra pit, superb sound, and seating on three levels.

SPA/FITNESS. The The ship's Samsara Spa has more than 22,600 sq. ft (2,100 sq. meters) of spa/wellness facilities, spread over two decks. It includes a large fitness room, separate saunas, steam rooms, UVB. Samsara cabin and suite occupants get unlimited access to the spa plus two treatments and fitness or meditation lessons.

● **For more extensive general information on what a Costa Cruises cruise is like, see pages 135–8.**

Costa Deliziosa
★★★★

Size: . . . . .Large Resort Ship	Passenger Decks: 13	Cabins (with private balcony): 772
Tonnage: .92,700	Total Crew: 1,050	Cabins (wheelchair accessible): 12
Lifestyle: . . . . .Standard	Passengers	Wheelchair accessibility . . . . .Good
Cruise Line: . . . . .Costa Cruises	(lower beds/all berths): 2,260/2,826	Cabin Voltage: . . . . .110 volts
Former Names: . . . . .none	Passenger Space Ratio	Elevators: 12
Builder: . . . . .Fincantieri (Italy)	(lower beds/all berths): 41.0/32.7	Casino (gaming tables): . . . . .Yes
Original Cost: . . . .€548 million	Crew/Passenger Ratio	Slot Machines: . . . . .Yes
Entered Service: . . . . .Mar 2010	(lower beds/all berths): 2.1/2.6	Swimming Pools (outdoors): 2
Registry: . . . . .Italy	Cabins (total): 1,130	Swimming Pools (indoors): 1
Length (ft/m): 958.0/292.0	Size Range (sq ft/m): 134.5–534.0/	(with retractable roof)
Beam (ft/m): 111.5/34.0	12.5–49.6	Whirlpools: 4
Draft (ft/m): 26.2/8.0	Cabins (outside view): 951	Self-Service Launderette: . . . . .No
Propulsion/Propellers: . . . . .diesel-electric	Cabins (interior/no view): 179	Dedicated Cinema/Seats: . . . . .No
(4.2 MW)/2 pods	Cabins (for one person): 0	Library: . . . . .Yes

BERLITZ'S OVERALL SCORE: 1,450 OUT OF A POSSIBLE 2,000 POINTS

OVERVIEW. *Costa Deliziosa*, sister to *Costa Luminosa* and the new flagship of Costa Cruises, was named in Dubai, the first new cruise ship to be named in an Arab city – so, instead of the traditional bottle of champagne, a bottle of fig juice was used to name it. It has a nicely balanced profile. A 4-D cinema features sound and lighting effects, with scent pumped in to heighten the experience. A two-deck midships Lido area swimming pool can be covered with a sliding glass roof in poor weather. There's a large 193.7-sq ft (18-sq meter) poolside movie screen.

The interior decor, which includes fine marble and gold, pays tribute to the senses, as you might expect from a ship called *Costa Deliziosa*. The public rooms include 11 bars, a large casino, and lots of lounges and entertainment venues. The focal point is the atrium lobby, with a large sculpture, *Sphere*, by Arnaldo Pomodoro.

Printed materials are in Italian, English, French, German, Portuguese, and Spanish. The onboard currency is the euro, and gratuities are charged to your onboard account.

ACCOMMODATION. About 68% of all accommodation suites and cabins have an ocean view; the 772 balcony cabins give this ship the distinction of having the largest number in the fleet to date. Four suites and 52 Samsara Spa cabins are located adjacent to (and considered part of) the designated wellness area. Samsara suite/cabin occupants get unlimited access to the spa plus two treatments and fitness or meditation lessons as part of their package, and dine in one of the two Samsara restaurants.

A pillow menu, with five choices, is available to suite-grade accommodation occupants, who also get bathrobes,

BERLITZ'S RATINGS

	Possible	Achieved
Ship	500	426
Accommodation	200	152
Food	400	251
Service	400	275
Entertainment	100	65
Cruise	400	281

better amenities than standard-grade cabin occupants, a shaving mirror, and walk-in closets – although the hangers are plastic. Background music is played 24 hours a day in all hallways and elevators, so you may well be aware of it if you are a light sleeper.

CUISINE. The Restaurant Albatros is the ship's large, main restaurant. It is located at the aft of the ship and there are two seatings for dinner. The Samsara Restaurant is for occupants of Samsara-grade accommodation, and is adjacent to the Taurus Restaurant.

The Club Restaurant is a reservations-only, intimate restaurant that features à la carte dining with a pristine show kitchen as part of the venue. The food is cooked à la minute and so it is fresher, looks better, and tastes better than food in the main dining room, and menus are under the direction of Italy's molecular cooking master, Ettore Bocchia (Costa's Consulting Chef). The Buffet Muscadins is the self-serve casual eatery. While there appears to be a decent choice of food, the layout of the venue invites congestion.

ENTERTAINMENT. The Theater Duse, with over 800 seats, spans three decks and is the ship's principal showlounge and features the latest computer-controlled lighting.

SPA/FITNESS. This area contains 37,674 sq ft (3,500 sq meters) of Samsara Spa space. Not far away, a Grand Prix Formula One simulator is housed in a glass enclosure. A golf simulator provides a choice of 37 18-hole courses.

● **For more extensive general information on what a Costa Cruises cruise is like, see pages 135–8.**

Costa Favolosa
NOT YET RATED

Size: . . . . .Large Resort Ship	Passenger Decks:. 13	Cabins (with private balcony): 579
Tonnage: .114,500	Total Crew: 1,110	Cabins (wheelchair accessible): 12
Lifestyle: . . . . .Standard	Passengers	Cabin Voltage: . . . . .110/220 volts
Cruise Line: . . . . .Costa Cruises	(lower beds/all berths): 3,012/3,780	Elevators: 14
Former Names: . . . . .none	Passenger Space Ratio	Casino (gaming tables): . . . . .Yes
Builder: . . . . .Fincantieri (Italy)	(lower beds/all berths): 38.0/30.2	Slot Machines: . . . . .Yes
Original Cost: . . . .€510 million	Crew/Passenger Ratio	Swimming Pools (outdoors): 2
Entered Service: . . . . .Jul 2011	(lower beds/all berths): 2.7/3.4	Swimming Pools (indoors): 2 (glass dome)
Registry:. . . . . .Italy	Cabins (total): 1,506	Whirlpools: 5
Length (ft/m): 952.0/290.0	Size Range (sq ft/m): 179.7–482.2/	Self-Service Launderette: . . . . .No
Beam (ft/m): 116.4/35.5	16.7–44.8	Dedicated Cinema/Seats: . . . . .No
Draft (ft/m): 27.2/8.3	Cabins (outside view): 926	Library: . . . . .Yes
Propulsion/Propellers: . . . . .diesel-electric	Cabins (interior/no view): 580	
(1.4mW)/2 azimuthing pods	Cabins (for one person): 0	

OVERALL SCORE: NYR OUT OF A POSSIBLE 2,000 POINTS

OVERVIEW. Displaying a single, large funnel, *Costa Favolosa* is a close sister to *Costa Serena*. Two pool areas can be covered with retractable glass domes – useful in case of bad weather, and one of the pools has a long water slide – great for kids. There is also a large poolside movie screen and, on one of the upper decks, a Grand Prix simulator. However, the open deck space can be pretty cramped when the ship is full, so the sunloungers, which don't have cushioned pads, will be crammed together

There are three decks full of bars and lounges plus many other public rooms. This ship has a glass-domed rotunda atrium lobby that is nine decks high, with great upward views from the lobby bar, as well as from its four glass panoramic elevators.

The Casino is large and glitzy, but always lively and entertaining – slot machines occupy a separate area to gaming tables, so serious gamers can concentrate. There's also a very small library, an internet-connection center, card room, art gallery, and video game room, together with a small chapel – a standard aboard all Costa Cruises' ships.

Although Costa Cruises is noted for its "Italian" style, ambience and spirit, there are few Italian crew members on board its ships. Although many officers are Italian, most of the crew members – particularly the dining room and housekeeping staff – are from the Philippines. The lifestyle on board is, however, perceived to be Italian – lively, noisy, with lots of love for life and a love of all things casual, even on so-called "formal" nights. Most passengers will be Italian, with a sprinkling of other European nationals.

Costa Cruises does a good job of providing first-time cruise passengers with a packaged seagoing vacation – par-

BERLITZ'S RATINGS		
	Possible	Achieved
Ship	500	NYR
Accommodation	200	NYR
Food	400	NYR
Service	400	NYR
Entertainment	100	NYR
Cruise	400	NYR

ticularly for families with children – that is a mix of sophistication and chaos, accompanied by loud music everywhere.

All of the printed materials – room service folio, menus, etc. – will typically be in six languages: Italian, English, French, German, Portuguese, and Spanish. During peak European school holiday periods, particularly Christmas and Easter, you can expect to be cruising with a lot of children of all ages.

Costa Cruises is a cruise line for those who like to enjoy life and party. As aboard other Costa ships, note that for embarkation, few staff members are on duty at the gangway when you arrive; they merely point you in the direction of your deck, or to the ship's elevators and do not escort you to your cabin.

ACCOMMODATION. There are 20 accommodation price grades, from 2-bed interior cabins to grand suites with private balcony although in reality there are only three different sizes: suites with "private" balcony – which are really not particularly large in comparison with some other large ships; 2- or 4-bed outside view cabins; and 2- or 4-bed interior (no-view) cabins. Fortunately, no cabins have views obstructed by lifeboats or other safety equipment views, and, in most cabins, twin beds can be changed to a double/queen-bed configuration.

Two Grand suites comprise the largest accommodation, and include a large balcony with hot tub. They have a queen-sized bed and larger living area with vanity desk; the bathrooms have a tub and two washbasins.

If you are into wellness treatments, there are 12 "Samsara Spa Suites" located just aft of the spa itself, although 99 cabins, including the 12 suites, are designated as Samsara-grade. Samsara suite/cabin occupants get unlimited access to the spa plus two treatments and fitness or meditation lessons as part of their package, and dine in one of the two Samsara restaurants. All Samsara-designated accommodation grades have an Oriental decorative theme, and special Samsara bathroom personal amenities.

A pillow menu, with five choices, has been introduced in all suite-grade accommodation. Note that only suite grades get bathrobes and better amenities, shaving mirror, and walk-in closets – although the hangers are plastic. Music is played 24 hours a day in all hallways and elevators, so you may well hear it if you are a light sleeper.

CUISINE. There are two main dining rooms, one located aft, te other in the ship's center, allocated according to your accommodation grade and location. There are two seatings.

Two 100-seat Samsara Restaurants (spa cuisine spots) are provided with separate entrances. These are for those seeking spa food (cuisine with reduced calories, fat and salt content, with menu creations under the direction of dietary consultant and Michelin-starred chef Ettore Boccia and his molecular Italian cuisine), while the two main restaurants offer traditional cruise fare. These dining venues are open for lunch and dinner to those in Samsara-grade suites and cabins, and to anyone else not in Samsara-grade accommodation – for dinner only – for an extra charge of €20 per day, or €120 for a 7-day cruise package.

Alternative (Reservations Required) Dining Option: The Club is a fairly elegant dining venue with seating under a huge glass dome, and Murano glass decorative elements. Fine table settings, china, silverware and leather-bound menus are provided. There's a cover charge of $20 per person, for service and gratuity.

Casual Eatery: A self-serve buffet restaurant offers breakfast, lunch, afternoon pizzas, and beverages (coffee and tea) at any time. A balcony level provides additional seating, but you'll need to carry your own food plates since there are no trays. Decent quality cappuccino and espresso coffees are always available in various bars, at extra cost.

Additionally, the Cafeteria will be the place to go for decent (extra cost) coffees and Italian pastries.

ENTERTAINMENT. The showlounge. which seats more than 800, utilizes the latest in LED technology. It is three decks high and is decorated in a Baroque style, with warm colors and a Murano glass chandelier. It is the venue for all production shows and large-scale cabaret acts, is quite stunningly glitzy, and has a revolving stage, hydraulic orchestra pit, superb sound, and seating on three levels – the upper levels are tiered through two decks.

Typically, revue-style shows are performed by a small troupe of resident onboard singers and dancers. Their fast-moving action, busy lighting and costume changes all add up to a high-energy performance.

SPA/FITNESS. The Samsara Spa is a large facility that occupies 23,186 sq.ft/2,154 sq. meters of space, spread over two decks. It includes a large fitness room, separate saunas, steam rooms, UVB solarium, changing rooms for men and women, and 10 body treatment rooms. Two VIP treatment rooms, available to couples for half-day rentals, are located on the upper level.

The Spa/fitness facilities are staffed and operated by Steiner Leisure, a specialist spa/beauty concession whose young staff will try to sell you Steiner's own-brand beauty products. Some fitness classes are free, while some, such as Pathway to Yoga, Pathway to Pilates, and Pathway to Meditation, cost €9 per class. Make appointments early as time slots can go quickly.

You can buy a day pass in order to use the sauna/steam rooms, thermal suite and relaxation area, at a cost of €35 per person. However, there is an additional no-charge sauna for men and women, but to access it you must walk through an active fitness area, maybe with your bathrobe on – not comfortable for everyone, especially women.

Treatment price examples: Samsara Aroma Stone Massage (75 mins, €146); Asian Stone Therapy (50 mins, €91); Swedish Massage (50 mins, €91); Samsara Frangipani Body Wrap (120 mins, including a full body massage, €199); Elemis Pro-Collagen Facial (50 mins, €108).

● **For more extensive general information on what a Costa Cruises cruise is like, see pages 135–8.**

Costa Fortuna
★★★★

Size: . . . . .Large Resort Ship	Passenger Decks: 13	Cabins (with private balcony): 522
Tonnage: 102,587	Total Crew: 1,068	Cabins (wheelchair accessible): 8
Lifestyle: . . . . .Standard	Passengers	Wheelchair accessibility . . . . .Good
Cruise Line: . . . . .Costa Cruises	(lower beds/all berths): 2,716/3,470	Cabin Current: . . . . .220 volts
Former Names: . . . . .none	Passenger Space Ratio	Elevators: 14
Builder: . . . . .Cantieri Sestri Navale (Italy)	(lower beds/all berths): 37.7/29.5	Casino (gaming tables): . . . . .Yes
Original Cost: . . . .$381 million	Crew/Passenger Ratio	Slot Machines: . . . . .Yes
Entered Service: . . . . . . .November 2003	(lower beds/all berths): 2.5/3.2	Swimming Pools (outdoors): 3
Registry: . . . . .Italy	Cabins (total): 1,358	Swimming Pools (indoors): 0
Length (ft/m): 892.3/272.0	Size Range (sq ft/m): 179.7–482.2/	Whirlpools: 5
Beam (ft/m): 124.6/38.0	16.7–44.8	Self-Service Launderette: . . . . .No
Draft (ft/m): 27.2/8.3	Cabins (outside view): 857	Dedicated Cinema/Seats: . . . . .No
Propulsion/Propellers: . . . .diesel-electric	Cabins (interior/no view): 501	Library: . . . . .Yes
34,000kW/2 azimuthing pods (17.6 MW each)	Cabins (for one person): 0	

OVERALL SCORE: 1,444 OUT OF A POSSIBLE 2,000 POINTS

OVERVIEW. The design of *Costa Fortuna* (together with sister ship *Costa Magica*, which made its debut in 2004) is based on the platform of *Carnival Triumph* and, although the bow is extremely short, the ship presents a well balanced profile. The name Fortuna is an interesting one: in Greek mythology, Fortuna is the daughter of Poseidon (it's also the name of the Temple Fortuna, located along one of the conserved streets of Pompeii).

The aft decks are tiered, with cut off quarters that make the ship look less square than it otherwise would. There are three pools, one of which can be covered by a sliding glass dome (magrodome) in case of inclement weather, while one pool has a long water slide. There is not a lot of open deck space for the number of passengers carried, so sunloungers tend to be crammed together – there are no cushioned pads.

Costa Fortuna is built to impress the trendy city-dweller at every turn, and the ship absorbs passengers quite well, with a good passenger space ratio. The interior decor focuses on the Italian passenger ships of yesteryear, so much of the finishing detail replicates the Art Deco interiors fitted aboard ocean liners such as the *Conte de Savoia*, *Michaelangelo*, *Neptunia*, *Rafaello*, *Rex*, etc., although in the kind of contemporary colors not associated with such ships (their interiors were rather subdued).

Deck names are those of major cities in Europe and South America (examples: Barcelona, Buenos Aires, Caracas, Lisbon, Genoa, Miami). Passenger flow is generally good, with few congestion points.

There are three decks full of lounges, and 11 bars. The interior focal point is a nine-deck high, glass-domed rotunda

BERLITZ'S RATINGS

	Possible	Achieved
Ship	500	426
Accommodation	200	146
Food	400	251
Service	400	275
Entertainment	100	64
Cruise	400	282

atrium lobby: it houses the Costa Bar on the lower level, a bank of four glass-walled elevators, and, in a tribute to ship buffs, some 26 models of Italian ships past and present, glued upside down on the ceiling – it's a weird feeling to look at them and then look at your feet. The lowest three decks connect the public rooms, the upper levels being mainly for accommodation decks. For those who like to gamble, the Neptunia 1932 Casino is the place to go. There's also a chapel – standard aboard all Costa ships – and a small library that's a bit of a token gesture, an internet center, card room, art gallery, and video game room.

The greater percentage of passengers are Italian, so the ship is lively, but quite noisy, with lots of children running around, particularly during school holiday periods. There are few Italians among the crew, however (except in key positions), as many are from the Philippines.

ACCOMMODATION. There are 15 price grades, from 2-bed interior cabins to grand suites with private balcony, although in reality there are only three different sizes: Suites with balcony, 2- or 4-bed outside view cabins (some 335 of which have portholes rather than windows), and 2- or 4-bed interior (no-view) cabins. There are also two single cabins – quite unusual for a large ship. In an example of good design, no cabins have lifeboat obstructed views – something not easy with large ships such as this.

The largest accommodation can be found in 8 Grand Suites, located in the center of the ship on one of the higher decks. They have a queen-sized bed; bathrooms have a bathtub and two washbasins.

Wheelchair-accessible cabins: Note that 12 of the most

desirable (outside-view) wheelchair-accessible cabins are rather idiotically located a long way from elevators, while 8 interior (no view) cabins are located close to elevators.

CUISINE. There are two dining rooms: the Michelangelo 1965 Restaurant (aft), whose ceiling features frescoes by the Great Masters, and the Rafaello 1965 Restaurant (mid-ships), are both two decks high and have two seatings. Dinner on European cruises is typically scheduled at 7pm and 9pm. Over 50 types of pasta are available during a typical one-week cruise. There is a wine list, although there are no wine waiters, and nearly all the wines (mostly Italian) are young.

Alternative (Reservations Required Dining Option: The Conte Grande 1927 Club is an upscale dining spot with seating for around 150 under a huge glass dome (if the lights were turned out, you might be able to see the stars). In its show kitchen, chefs can be seen preparing their masterpieces. Fine table settings, china, silverware and leather-bound menus are used. Reservations are required and there is a cover charge of $18.75 per person (for service and tip).

The Christoforo Columbus 1954 Buffet Restaurant is a self-serve eatery for breakfast, lunch, afternoon pizzas, and beverages at any time. Excellent cappuccino and espresso coffees are always available in the various bars aboard the ship.

ENTERTAINMENT. The Rex 1932 Theater spans three decks in the ship's forwardmost section. It is the setting for all production shows and large-scale cabaret acts, is quite stunning, and has a revolving stage, hydraulic orchestra pit, superb sound, and seating on three levels (the upper levels being tiered through two decks). Volume levels are high.

SPA/FITNESS. Facilities in the two-deck high Saturnia Spa (it measures about 14,424 sq. ft/1,340 sq. meters) include a large solarium, eight treatment rooms, sauna and steam rooms for men and women, and a beauty parlor. The gymnasium, full of techno-gym equipment for those into muscle-pumping and exertion, has floor-to-ceiling windows on three sides, including forward-facing ocean views, and there's an aerobics section with instructor-led classes (some, such as yoga, kick-boxing, cost extra). If you want to be near the spa, note that there are 18 two-bed cabins with ocean view windows, located adjacent (aft) of the spa.

● **For more extensive general information on what a Costa Cruises cruise is like, see pages 135–8.**

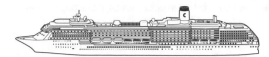

Costa Luminosa
★★★★

Size: . . . . .Large Resort Ship	Passenger Decks: 13	Cabins (with private balcony): 772
Tonnage: .92,700	Total Crew: 1,050	Cabins (wheelchair accessible): 12
Lifestyle: . . . . .Standard	Passengers	Wheelchair accessibility . . . . .Good
Cruise Line: . . . . .Costa Cruises	(lower beds/all berths): 2,260/2,826	Cabin Voltage: . . . . .110 volts
Former Names: . . . . .none	Passenger Space Ratio	Elevators: 12
Builder: . . . . .Fincantieri (Italy)	(lower beds/all berths): 41.0/32.7	Casino (gaming tables): . . . . .Yes
Original Cost: . . . .€420 million	Crew/Passenger Ratio	Slot Machines: . . . . .Yes
Entered Service: . . . . .June 2009	(lower beds/all berths): 2.1/2.6	Swimming Pools (outdoors): 2
Registry: . . . . .Italy	Cabins (total): 1,130	Swimming Pools (indoors): 1
Length (ft/m): 958.0/292.0	Size Range (sq ft/m): 134.5–534.0/	(with retractable roof)
Beam (ft/m): 111.5/34.0	12.5–49.6	Whirlpools: 4
Draft (ft/m): 26.2/8.0	Cabins (outside view): 951	Self-Service Launderette: . . . . .No
Propulsion/Propellers: . . . . .diesel-electric	Cabins (interior/no view): 179	Dedicated Cinema/Seats: . . . . .No
(42,000 kW)/2 pods	Cabins (for one person): 0	Library: . . . . .Yes

OVERALL SCORE: 1,445 OUT OF A POSSIBLE 2,000 POINTS

OVERVIEW. *Costa Luminosa*, a sister ship to Cunard Line's new *Queen Elizabeth*, is the Costa Cruises' new flagship, constructed as what is termed a *Vista*-class ship – although it is slightly larger than *Costa Atlantica* and *Costa Mediterranea*. A 4-D cinema features sound and lighting effects, with scent pumped in to heighten the experience.

Its two-deck midships Lido area swimming pool can be covered with a sliding glass roof. There's also a large 194-sq ft (18-sq meter) poolside movie screen. Other sporting features include a roller skating track.

The interior decor, which includes fine marble, wood and mother of pearl, pays tribute to light and lighting, as you might expect from a ship called *Costa Luminosa*, so it feels a little like cruising in a stunning special effects bubble – remember to take your sunglasses. The public rooms include 11 bars, a large Vega Casino, and lots of lounges and entertainment venues to play in.

One thing not to miss is a fascinating – and rather large, at 346 cm long (11.3-ft) – *Reclining Woman 2004* bronze sculpture by Fernando Bolero, in the Atria Supernova, the atrium lobby. Weighing 910kg (2,006 lbs), the suntanned, rather voluminous woman is depicted staring into the atrium space, with her legs in a dynamic position of movement.

Sony Playstation fans can enjoy "Play Station World," an area dedicated exclusively to PS3. Playstations are also available in cabins, on the pool-deck movie screen, and in the children's and teens' clubs.

Printed materials such as room service folio and menus are in six languages (Italian, English, French, German, Portuguese, Spanish). Onboard currency is the euro. Gratuities are not included in the fare.

BERLITZ'S RATINGS

	Possible	Achieved
Ship	500	427
Accommodation	200	153
Food	400	241
Service	400	275
Entertainment	100	66
Cruise	400	283

ACCOMMODATION. There are 14 price grades. About 68% of all accommodation suites and cabins have an ocean view; the 772 balcony cabins give this ship the distinction of having the largest number in the fleet to date. Four suites and 52 Samsara Spa cabins are located adjacent to (and considered part of) the designated wellness area. As part of their package, Samsara suite and cabin occupants get unlimited access to the spa plus two treatments and fitness or meditation lessons, and dine in one of the two Samsara restaurants. All Samsara-designated accommodation grades receive Samsara bathroom personal amenities and other goodies.

A pillow menu, with five choices, is available to suite-grade accommodation occupants, who also get bathrobes, better amenities than standard-grade cabin occupants, a shaving mirror, and walk-in closets – although the hangers are plastic. Note that background music is played 24 hours a day in all hallways and elevators, so you may well be aware of it if you are a light sleeper.

All of the cabins have twin beds that can be converted into a queen-sized bed, individually controlled air-conditioning, television, and telephone. Some many cabins have their views obstructed by lifeboats – on Deck 4 (Roma Deck), the lowest of the accommodation decks, as well as some cabins on Deck 5. Some cabins have pull-down Pullman berths that are fully hidden in the ceiling when not in use.

Some of the most desirable suites and cabins are those with private balconies on the five aft-facing decks (Decks 4, 5, 6, 7, and 8) with views overlooking the stern and ship's wash. The other cabins with private balconies will find the balconies not so private – the partition between one balcony and the next is not a full partition, so you will be able to hear your neighbors (or smell their smoke). However, these balcony occupants all have good views through glass and wood-topped railings, and the deck is made of teak. The cabins are well laid out, typically with twin beds that convert to a queen-sized bed, vanity desk with built-in hairdryer, large TV set, personal safe, and one closet that has moveable shelves – thus providing more space for luggage storage.

The largest suites are those designated as Penthouse Suites, although they are really quite small when compared with suites aboard other ships of a similar size. However, they do at least offer more space to move around in, and a slightly larger, better bathroom.

CUISINE. The Taurus Restaurant is the large, main restaurant. It is located at the aft of the ship and there are two seatings for dinner, which, on European cruises is typically at 7pm and 9pm. The Samsara Restaurant is for occupants of Samsara-grade accommodation, and is located adjacent to the Taurus Restaurant.

The Club Restaurant is a reservations-only, intimate restaurant that features à la carte dining with a pristine show kitchen as part of the venue. The food is cooked à la minute and so it is fresher, looks better, and tastes better than food in the main dining room, and menus are under the direction of Italy's molecular cooking master, Ettore Bocchia (Costa's Consulting Chef). It's a good idea to go for a meal in this venue, particularly to celebrate a special occasion, because it's different, and portions are small, and cooked to order rather than prepared en masse.

The Andromeda Buffet is the self-serve casual eatery. While there appears to be a decent choice of food, the layout of the venue invites congestion because of some narrow passageways between the indoor seating and the food dispensing areas.

ENTERTAINMENT. The Phoenix Theater, with over 800 seats, spans three decks (the actual space of the showlounge measures 1,300 sq meters/14,000 sq ft) and is the ship's main showlounge; it appears as if it is lit by a rainbow of lighting effects, using the latest computer-controlled lighting.

SPA/FITNESS. This area contains 3,500 sq meters (37,700 sq ft) of Samsara Spa space. Not far away, a Grand Prix Formula One simulator is housed in a glass enclosure. For tee-time, a golf simulator provides a choice of 37 18-hole courses.

● **For more extensive general information on what a Costa Cruises cruise is like, see pages 135–8.**

WHERE NAUTICAL EXPRESSIONS COME FROM

If you've ever wondered where some terms or phrases came from, you have only to look to the sea, ships, and seamen.

Booby Hatch

A booby hatch is a small, covered compartment under the deck, toward the bow. Sailors were punished by confinement in the booby hatch. The term has come to mean a mental institution.

Carry on

In the days of sail, the officer of the deck kept a weather eye constantly on the slightest change in the wind so sail could be reefed or added as necessary to ensure the fastest headway. Whenever a good breeze came along, the order to "carry on" would be given. It meant to hoist every bit of canvas the yards could carry. Pity the poor sailor whose weather eye failed him and the ship was caught partially reefed when a good breeze arrived. Through the centuries the term's connotation has changed somewhat usually meaning an order to resume work.

Clean Slate

It was the custom in sailing ships to record the vessel's courses, distances and tacks on a log slate. The new watch would start with a clean slate if things had been growing fine, disregarding what had gone before and starting anew. In a similar way, today, we refer to a new beginning or a second chance in life as starting with a "clean slate."

Davy Jones's Locker

This is seamen's slang for the bottom of the sea. There are several theories as to its origin: One is that Davy Jones was the owner of a sixteenth-century London pub where unwary sailors were drugged and put in lockers, and then awoke aboard ship to find they had been press-ganged into the Navy.

Devil to pay

Devil and the deep blue sea: In traditional wooden ships, the sailors had to caulk or pay the seams with hot tar between the planks of the deck to prevent leakage into the bilge. The devil seam was topmost on the hull next to the scuppers at the edge of the deck and the longest and most difficult seam to caulk. Hence, if there was the "devil to pay," then this was the most difficult and dangerous job since the sailor might be knocked down (scuppered) by a large wave and find himself between the "devil and the deep blue sea." The former phrase has come to mean that there will be a big price to pay for a particular action; the latter now refers to being on the horns of a dilemma.

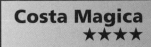

Costa Magica
★★★★

Size: . . . . .Large Resort Ship	Passenger Decks: 13	Cabins (wheelchair accessible): 8
Tonnage: 102,587	Total Crew: 1,068	Wheelchair accessibility . . . . .Good
Lifestyle: . . . . .Standard	Passengers	Cabin Current: . . . . .220 volts
Cruise Line: . . . . .Costa Cruises	(lower beds/all berths): 2,718/3,788	Elevators: 14
Former Names: . . . . .none	Passenger Space Ratio	Casino (gaming tables): . . . . .Yes
Builder: . . . . .Fincantieri (Italy)	(lower beds/all berths): 37.7/27.0	Slot Machines: . . . . .Yes
Original Cost: . . . .$418.5 million	Crew/Passenger Ratio	Swimming Pools (outdoors): 3
Entered Service: . . . . . . .November 2004	(lower beds/all berths): 2.5/3.2	Swimming Pools (indoors): 0
Registry: . . . . .Italy	Cabins (total): 1,359	Whirlpools: 5
Length (ft/m): 893.3/272.3	Size Range (sq ft/m): 179.7/482.2	Self-Service Launderette: . . . . .No
Beam (ft/m): 124.6/38	Cabins (outside view): 857	Dedicated Cinema/Seats: . . . . .No
Draft (ft/m): 27.2/8.3	Cabins (interior/no view): 501	Library: . . . . .Yes
Propulsion/Propellers: . . . .diesel-electric	Cabins (for one person): 0	
34,000kW/2 azimuthing pods (17.6 MW each)	Cabins (with private balcony): 522	

OVERALL SCORE: 1,445 OUT OF A POSSIBLE 2,000 POINTS

OVERVIEW. *Costa Magica* is built to impress at every turn. The ship absorbs passengers quite well, with a good passenger space ratio. Passenger flow is generally good. There is not a lot of open deck space for the number of passengers carried, so sunloungers tend to be crammed together. The interior decor is inspired by some of Italy's "magic" places (examples include Costa Smerelda, Isola Bella, Portofino, Spoleto).

There are three decks full of lounges (all named after Italian places), 11 bars, and lots of rooms to play in. The ship's life center features a nine-deck high, glass-domed rotunda atrium lobby which houses the Costa Bar on the lower level. The Sicily Casino (look out for the shiny armor, helmets and shields) is big, glitzy and noisy. There's also a chapel. The Bressanone Library is a nice room, although it is only open about an hour each day.

Most passengers are Italian, so the ship is lively (noisy), with lots of children running around (particularly during school holidays). There are few Italians among the crew, (except in key positions), as many are from the Philippines.

ACCOMMODATION. There are 15 price grades, from two-bed interior cabins to grand suites with private balcony. There are also two single cabins (unusual for a large ship). No cabins have lifeboat obstructed views. The largest accommodation can be found in 8 Grand Suites, located in the center of the ship on one of the higher decks. They have a queen-sized bed; bathrooms have a tub and two washbasins. **Wheelchair-accessible cabins:** Note that 12 of the most desirable (outside-view) wheelchair-accessible cabins are rather idiotically located a long way from elevators, while 8 interior (no view) cabins are located close to elevators.

BERLITZ'S RATINGS

	Possible	Achieved
Ship	500	427
Accommodation	200	146
Food	400	251
Service	400	275
Entertainment	100	64
Cruise	400	282

CUISINE. The two dining rooms, Costa Smeralda Restaurant (aft) and the Portofino Restaurant (midships), are both two decks high, and both have two seatings. Dinner on European cruises is typically scheduled at 7pm and 9pm. Almost all the wines are young.

Alternative (Reservations Required) Dining Option: The Vincenza Tavernetta Club is an upscale dining spot with seating for around 150 under a huge glass dome. Fine table settings, Versace china, woven cloth napkins, fine silverware and leather-bound menus are used. The recipes, from Belloni and Belloni, are excellent. There is a cover charge of $18.75 per person.

The Bellagio Buffet Restaurant is a self-serve eatery for breakfast, lunch, afternoon pizzas, and beverages at any time. The bars serve excellent cappuccino and espresso coffees.

ENTERTAINMENT. The Urbino Theater spans three decks in the forwardmost section of the ship. It is the setting for all production shows and large-scale cabaret acts, is quite stunning, and has a revolving stage, hydraulic orchestra pit, superb sound, and seating on three levels.

SPA/FITNESS. Facilities in the two-deck high Saturnia Spa include a large solarium, eight treatment rooms, sauna and steam rooms for men and women, and a beauty parlor. The gymnasium is full of techno-gym equipment. There's an aerobics section with instructor-led classes (some, such as yoga, kick-boxing, cost extra).

● **For more extensive general information on what a Costa Cruises cruise is like, see pages 135–8.**

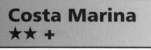

Costa Marina
★★ +

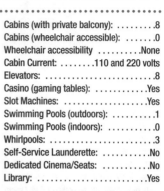

Size: . . . . .Mid-Size Ship	Passenger Decks: 8	Cabins (with private balcony): 8
Tonnage: .25,441	Total Crew: 400	Cabins (wheelchair accessible): 0
Lifestyle: . . . . .Standard	Passengers	Wheelchair accessibility . . . . .None
Cruise Line: . . . . .Costa Cruises	(lower beds/all berths): 772/1,005	Cabin Current: . . . . .110 and 220 volts
Former Names: . . . . .Axel Johnson	Passenger Space Ratio	Elevators: 8
Builder: . . . . .Mariotti Shipyards (Italy)	(lower beds/all berths): 32.9/25.3	Casino (gaming tables): . . . . .Yes
Original Cost: . . . .$130 million	Crew/Passenger Ratio	Slot Machines: . . . . .Yes
Entered Service: . . . . .July 1990	(lower beds/all berths): 1.9/2.5	Swimming Pools (outdoors): 1
Registry: . . . . .Italy	Cabins (total): .386	Swimming Pools (indoors): 0
Length (ft/m): 571.8/174.25	Size Range (sq ft/m):104.4–264.8/9.7–24.6	Whirlpools: 3
Beam (ft/m): 84.6/25.75	Cabins (outside view): 183	Self-Service Launderette: . . . . .No
Draft (ft/m): 26.1/8.20	Cabins (interior/no view): 205	Dedicated Cinema/Seats: . . . . .No
Propulsion/Propellers: diesel (19,152kW)/2	Cabins (for one person): 0	Library: . . . . .Yes

OVERALL SCORE: 1,090 OUT OF A POSSIBLE 2,000 POINTS

OVERVIEW. This angular-looking vessel, converted from a container carrier, has a contemporary, cutaway stern that is virtually replaced by a glass wall (in fact, the dining room windows), and a stark cluster of three yellow funnels. Today the design seems dated.

Most of the public rooms are above the accommodation decks and include several bars and lounges. There is generally good passenger flow throughout its public room spaces, although congestion occurs between first and second dinner seatings.

In 2002, *Costa Marina* underwent a considerable amount of interior redecoration and emerged as an Italian ship for German-speaking passengers ("La Deutsche Vita"). The onboard currency is the euro.

The fit and finish of this vessel, when it debuted as a cruise ship, were well below standard. There is a very limited amount of open deck and sunbathing space, and no observation lounge with forward-facing views. The swimming pool is very small. There are simply too many interior (no view) cabins. The library is really poor. Tipping envelopes in your cabin state the level of tip expected.

SUITABLE FOR: *Costa Marina* is best suited to young and young-at-heart German-speaking couples and singles (plus families with children) that enjoy European city life, plenty of activities, and entertainment that is consistently loud.

ACCOMMODATION. There are 12 categories, ranked by grade, size and location. Both the outside view and interior (no view) cabins are quite comfortable, but have plain, almost clinical, decor. Bathrooms are functional, but there is little space for toiletry items. The room service menu is poor.

BERLITZ'S RATINGS

	Possible	Achieved
Ship	500	275
Accommodation	200	120
Food	400	192
Service	400	226
Entertainment	100	58
Cruise	400	219

CUISINE. The 452-seat Cristal Restaurant is fairly spacious and has expansive glass windows overlooking the stern, while port and starboard sides have large portholes. There are two seatings but few tables for two, most of the tables being for four, six or eight. Romantic candlelight dining is typically featured on a formal night.

The cuisine is Continental in nature (with some German regional specialties). The quality of meats is good, although it is often disguised with gravies and rich sauces. Fish and seafood tend to be lacking in taste and are typically overcooked, and green vegetables are hard to come by. However, good pasta dishes are served each day (the pasta is made fresh on board daily), although quantity, not quality, is what appears from the galley. While the breads and rolls are typically good, the desserts are not. There is a wine list, although almost all wines are young – very young.

Excellent cappuccino and espresso coffees are always available in various bars, served in proper china cups.

ENTERTAINMENT. The Tropicana Showroom is a single level room; however, 14 pillars obstruct many sight lines from many seats. The room is adequate as a cabaret lounge.

SPA/FITNESS. The spa/fitness facilities are not large, but they include a solarium, several treatment rooms, sauna and steam rooms for men and women, beauty salon and gymnasium with floor-to-ceiling windows on three sides. There is also a jogging track outdoors.

● **For more extensive general information on what a Costa Cruises cruise is like, see pages 135–8.**

Costa Mediterranea
★★★★

Size: . . . . .Large Resort Ship	Passenger Decks: 11	Cabins (wheelchair accessible): 8
Tonnage: .85,700	Total Crew: 920	Wheelchair accessibility . . . . .Good
Lifestyle: . . . . .Standard	Passengers	Cabin Current: . . . . .110 volts
Cruise Line: . . . . .Costa Cruises	(lower beds/all berths): 2,112/2,680	Elevators: 12
Former Names: . . . . .none	Passenger Space Ratio	Casino (gaming tables): . . . . .Yes
Builder: . . .Kvaerner Masa-Yards (Finland)	(lower beds/all berths): 40.5/31.9	Slot Machines: . . . . .Yes
Original Cost: . . . .$335 million	Crew/Passenger Ratio	Swimming Pools (outdoors): 2
Entered Service: . . . . .May 2003	(lower beds/all berths): 2.2/2.9	(+1 indoor/outdoor)
Registry: . . . . .Italy	Cabins (total): 1,056	Swimming Pools (indoors): . . . . .No
Length (ft/m): 959.6/292.5	Size Range (sq ft/m): 161.4–387.5/	Whirlpools: . . . . .Yes
Beam (ft/m): 105.6/32.2	15.0–36.0	Self-Service Launderette: . . . . .No
Draft (ft/m): 25.5/7.8	Cabins (outside view): 843	Dedicated Cinema/Seats: . . . . .No
Propulsion/Propellers: . . . . .diesel-electric	Cabins (interior/no view): 213	Library: . . . . .Yes
(34,000 kW)/2 azimuthing pods	Cabins (for one person): 0	
(17.6 MW each)	Cabins (with private balcony): 742	

OVERALL SCORE: 1,437 OUT OF A POSSIBLE 2,000 POINTS

OVERVIEW. The first thing that regular passengers will notice is the length of this ship, which gives it an attractive sleekness. There are two centrally located swimming pools outdoors, one of which can be used in poor weather due to its retractable glass dome (magrodome) cover. A bar abridges two adjacent whirlpool tubs. Another smaller pool is for children; there is also a winding water slide that spans two decks in height (it starts on a platform bridge located at the aft funnel). There is also an additional whirlpool tub outdoors.

BERLITZ'S RATINGS

	Possible	Achieved
Ship	500	426
Accommodation	200	152
Food	400	240
Service	400	273
Entertainment	100	64
Cruise	400	282

Inside, the layout is just the same as in sister ship *Costa Atlantica*. The interior design is, however, bold and brash – a mix of classical Italy and contemporary features. There is good passenger flow from one public space to another, several floor spaces for dancing, and a range of bars and lounges for socializing. The dramatic eight-deck atrium lobby, with two grand stairways, presents a stunning wall decoration consisting of two huge paintings and 25-piece wall sculpture by Gigi Rigamonte (called *Danza*) that is best seen from any of the multiple viewing balconies on each deck above the main lobby-floor level (the squid-shaped wall lighting sconces are neat, too). But pillars throughout the ship obstruct passenger flow and pillars in the dining room provide an obstacle course for waiters.

The decor is said to be inspired by many Italian palaces (some known, many not) and by a profound live for art and architecture. It is extremely upbeat, bright, glitzy, and in-your-face wherever you go – I was amused by one of three larger-than-life digital faces of Dionisio in the Dionisio Lounge, with a door handle that sticks out of his mouth in a style that recalls Monty Python.

A small chapel is located forward of the uppermost level. Other facilities include a winding shopping street with boutique stores (typically including Fendi, Fossil, Paul & Shark Yachting), a photo gallery, video games room, observation balcony, a large Grand Canal Casino, and a library (with internet access but very few books). Food and service levels have been raised to a better standard than that found aboard most other Costa Cruises ships to date. But do expect irritating announcements (particularly for activities that bring in revenue, such as art auctions, bingo, horse racing), and much hustling for drinks. All printed materials (room service folio, menus, etc.) are in six languages (Italian, English, French, German, Portuguese, Spanish). The onboard currency is the euro or US dollar, depending on region of operation.

SUITABLE FOR: The vessel is best suited to young (and young at heart) couples and singles (plus families with children) that enjoy big city life, piazzas and outdoor cafes, constant activity accompanied by lots of noise, late nights, loud entertainment, and an international mix of passengers.

ACCOMMODATION. There are 14 price grades. There is a healthy (78 percent) proportion of outside-view to interior (no view) cabins. All of the cabins have twin beds that can be converted into a queen-sized bed, individually controlled air-conditioning, television, and telephone. Some many cabins have their views obstructed by lifeboats – on Deck 4 (Roma Deck), the lowest of the accommodation decks, as well as some cabins on Deck 5. Some cabins have pull-down Pullman berths that are fully hidden in the ceiling when not in use. There is too much use of fluorescent lighting in the suites and cabins, and the soundproofing could be much better. Some bathroom fixtures – bath and shower taps in particular – are frustrating to use until you get the hang of them.

Some of the most desirable suites and cabins are those with private balconies on the five aft-facing decks (Decks 4, 5, 6, 7, and 8) with views overlooking the stern and ship's wash. The other cabins with private balconies will find the balconies not so private – the partition between one balcony and the next is not a full partition, so you will be able to hear your neighbors (or smell their smoke).

However, these balcony occupants all have good views through glass and wood-topped railings, and the deck is made of teak. The cabins are well laid out, typically with twin beds that convert to a queen-sized bed, vanity desk (with built-in hairdryer), large television, personal safe, and one closet that has moveable shelves – thus providing more space for luggage storage. However, note that the lighting is fluorescent, and much too harsh (the bedside control is for a master switch only – other individual lights cannot be controlled). The bathroom is a simple, modular unit that has shower enclosures with soap dispenser; there is a good amount of stowage space for personal toiletry items.

The largest suites are those designated as Penthouse Suites, although they are really quite small when compared with suites aboard other ships of a similar size. However, they do at least offer more space to move around in, and a slightly larger, better bathroom.

CUISINE. The Ristorante degli Argentiere, the ship's main dining room, is extremely large and is located at the aft section of the ship on two levels with a spiral stairway between them. There are two seatings, with tables for two, four, six or eight. Dinner on European cruises is typically scheduled at 7pm and 9pm. Some tables in the dining room have a less than comfortable view of the harsh lighting of the escalators between the galley and the two decks of the dining room.

Alternative (Reservations-Only, Extra Cost) Dining: The Medusa Supper Club (with menu by Zeffirino – a famous restaurant in Genoa) is a more upscale dining spot located on two of the uppermost decks of the ship under a huge glass dome, with seating for approximately 150. It has an open kitchen where chefs can be seen preparing their masterpieces. Fine table settings, china and silverware are fea-

tured, as are leather-bound menus. Reservations are required and there is a cover charge of €20 per person (for service and tip). But you may think it's worth it in order to have dinner in a setting that is quieter and more refined than the main dining room.

The Perla del Lago Buffet is an extensive eatery that forms the aft third of Deck 9 (part of it also wraps around the upper section of the huge atrium). It includes a central area with several small buffet counters; there are salad counters, a dessert counter, and a 24-hour Posillipo Pizzeria counter, all forming a large eatery with indoor and outdoor seating. Movement around the buffet area is very slow, and requires you to stand in line for everything. Venture outdoors and you'll find a grill (for hamburgers and hot dogs) and a pasta bar, both conveniently located adjacent to the second of two swimming pools on the lido deck.

Other Venues: The place that most people will want to see and be seen is at the casual Oriental Cafe; there are four separate salons, which provide intimate spaces for drinks, conversation, and people-watching. Excellent cappuccino and espresso coffees are always available in various bars around the ship, served in the right-sized china cups.

ENTERTAINMENT. The Osiris Theater is the principal venue for all production shows and major cabaret acts. It spans three decks, and seating on all three levels. Sightlines to the stage are better from the second and third levels. Spiral stairways at the back of the lounge connect all three levels.

SPA/FITNESS. The expansive Ischia Spa spans two decks, is located directly above the navigation bridge in the forward part of the ship (accessed by the forward stairway elevators) and has approximately 13,700 sq. ft (1,272 sq. meters) of space. Facilities on the lower level include a solarium, eight treatment rooms, lecture rooms, sauna and steam rooms for men and women, a beauty parlor; the upper level consists of a large gymnasium with floor-to-ceiling windows on three sides, including forward-facing ocean views, and an aerobics room with instructor-led classes (the aerobics room and gymnasium together measure almost 6,000 sq. ft (557 sq. meters). There is also a jogging track outdoors, around the ship's mast and the forward third of the ship, as well as a multi-purpose court for basketball, volleyball and deck tennis.

● **For more extensive general information on what a Costa Cruises cruise is like, see pages 135–8.**

Costa Pacifica
★★★★

Size:.................. Large Resort Ship	Passenger Decks: 13	Cabins (wheelchair accessible): 12
Tonnage:...................... 114,500	Total Crew: 1,110	Wheelchair accessibility .... Good
Lifestyle: .... Standard	Passengers	Cabin Voltage: .... 110/220 volts
Cruise Line: .... Costa Cruises	(lower beds/all berths): 3,012/3,780	Elevators:............................ 14
Former Names: .... none	Passenger Space Ratio	Casino (gaming tables): .... Yes
Builder: .... Fincantieri (Italy)	(lower beds/all berths): 38.0/30.2	Slot Machines: .... Yes
Original Cost: .... €510 million	Crew/Passenger Ratio	Swimming Pools (outdoors): 2
Entered Service: .... Apr 2009	(lower beds/all berths): 2.7/3.4	Swimming Pools (indoors): .... 2 (glass dome)
Registry: .... Italy	Cabins (total): 1,506	Whirlpools:........................... 5
Length (ft/m): 952.0/290.0	Size Range (sq ft/m):.. 179.7–482.2/16.7–44.8	Self-Service Launderette: .... No
Beam (ft/m):................... 116.4/35.5	Cabins (outside view): 926	Dedicated Cinema/Seats: .... No
Draft (ft/m):..................... 27.2/8.3	Cabins (interior/no view):............. 580	Library:............................. Yes
Propulsion/Propellers: .... diesel-electric	Cabins (for one person):................ 0	
(34,000kW)/2 azimuthing pods	Cabins (with private balcony):.......... 579	

OVERALL SCORE: 1,454 OUT OF A POSSIBLE 2,000 POINTS

OVERVIEW. Sporting a single, large funnel, *Costa Pacifica* is a sister to the popular *Costa Concordia* and *Costa Serena*. Two pool areas can be covered with retractable glass domes – good in case of inclement weather – and one of the pools has a water slide (great for kids). There is also a huge screen for poolside movies. A Grand Prix simulator is positioned on one of the upper decks.

However, the open deck space is cramped when the ship is full, so sun-loungers tend to be crammed together, and they do not have cushioned pads.

This ship has a musical interior design theme featuring the "greatest hits." The lobby, for example, appears to be covered in musical symbols and instruments. The passenger flow inside is quite good, and the ship absorbs passengers reasonably well. It also provides a decent passenger space ratio, which means that it won't feel too crowded.

There are three decks full of bars and lounges plus many other public rooms. This ship has a glass-domed rotunda atrium lobby that is nine decks high, with great upward views from the lobby bar, as well as from its four glass panoramic elevators.

The casino is large and glitzy, but always lively and entertaining (slot machines occupy a separate area to gaming tables, so serious gamers can concentrate). There's also a very small library, an internet-connection center, card room, art gallery, and video game room, together with several other bars and lounges. A chapel is a standard aboard all Costa ships.

Although Costa Cruises is noted for its "Italian" style, ambience and spirit, there are few Italian crew members on board its ships. While many of the officers are Italian,

BERLITZ'S RATINGS		
	Possible	Achieved
Ship	500	427
Accommodation	200	152
Food	400	251
Service	400	275
Entertainment	100	67
Cruise	400	282

most of the crew members – particularly the dining room and housekeeping staff – are from the Philippines. The lifestyle on board is, however, perceived to be Italian – lively, noisy, with lots of love for life and a love of all things casual – even on so-called "formal" nights. Most passengers will be Italian, with a sprinkling of other European nationals. One night, at the end of each cruise, is typically reserved for a "Roman Bacchanal" – called a "Venetian Carnival" night on Europe/Mediterranean cruises – when it's fun to dress up toga-style for dinner and beyond.

Printed materials such as room service folio and menus will typically be in six languages (Italian, English, French, German, Portuguese, and Spanish). During peak European school holiday periods, particularly Christmas and Easter, expect to be cruising with a lot of children of all ages. Sony Play Station fans can enjoy "Play Station World," an area dedicated to PS3. Play Stations are also available in cabins, in the children's and teens' clubs, and can be used with the poolside movie screen.

Costa Cruises is a cruise line for those who like to enjoy life and party. As aboard other Costa ships, note that for embarkation, few staff members are on duty at the gangway when you arrive; they merely point you in the direction of your deck, or to the ship's elevators and do not escort you to your cabin.

SUITABLE FOR: Costa Cruises does a good job of providing first-time cruise passengers with a well-packaged holiday, particularly for families with children, that is a mix of sophistication and chaos, accompanied by loud music everywhere. This is a cruise line for those who like to party.

ACCOMMODATION. There are 20 price grades, from 2-bed interior cabins to grand suites with private balcony, although in reality there are only three different sizes: Suites with "private" balcony (which are really not particularly large in comparison with some other large ships), 2- or 4-bed outside view cabins, and 2- or 4-bed interior (no-view) cabins. Fortunately, no cabins have views obstructed by lifeboats or other safety equipment views, and, in all cabins, twin beds can be changed to a double/queen-bed configuration.

A total of eight Grand Suites comprise the largest accommodation. These are located in the center of the ship on one of the uppermost decks. They have a queen-sized bed and larger living area with vanity desk; the bathrooms have a tub and two washbasins.

If you like wellness treatments, there are 12 "Samsara Spa Suites" located just aft of the spa (although 99 cabins, including the 12 suites, are designated as Samsara-grade). Samsara suite/cabin occupants get unlimited access to the spa plus two treatments and fitness or meditation lessons as part of their package, and dine in one of the two Samsara restaurants. All Samsara-designated accommodation grades have an Oriental decorative theme, and special Samsara bathroom personal amenities.

A pillow menu, with five choices, is available in all suite accommodation grades. Note that only suite grades get bathrobes and better amenities, shaving mirror, and walk-in closets – although the hangars are plastic. Music is played 24 hours a day in all hallways and elevators, so you may well hear it if you are a light sleeper.

CUISINE. There are two main dining rooms (New York, New York, and My Way), allocated according to your accommodation grade and location. There are two seatings in each for dinner.

Two 100-seat Samsara Restaurants (spa cuisine spots) are provided with separate entrances, adjacent to the restaurant My Way. These two dining spots are for those seeking spa food (reduced calories, fat and salt, with menu creations under the direction of dietary consultant and Michelin-star chef Ettore Boccia and his molecular Italian cuisine), while the two main restaurants offer traditional cruise fare.

These dining venues are open for lunch and dinner to those in Samsara-grade suites and cabins, and to anyone else (for dinner only) for an extra charge of €20 per day, or €120 for a 7-day cruise package.

Alternative (Reservations Required) Dining Option: Club Blue Moon is an elegant dining venue with seating under a huge glass dome. Fine table settings, china, silverware and leather-bound menus are provided. There's a cover charge of $20 per person, for service and gratuity.

Casual Eatery: The La Paloma Buffet Restaurant is a self-serve eatery for breakfast, lunch, afternoon pizzas, and coffee and tea)at any time. A balcony level provides additional seating (you'll need to carry your own food plates – there are no trays). Decent quality cappuccino and espresso coffees are always available in various bars, at extra cost.

Additionally, the Caffeteria is the place to go for decent (extra cost) coffees and Italian pastries.

ENTERTAINMENT: The showlounge seats more than 800, and utilizes the latest in LED technology. It is three decks high and is decorated in a Baroque style, with warm colors and a Murano glass chandelier. It is the venue for all production shows and large-scale cabaret acts, is quite stunningly glitzy, and has a revolving stage, hydraulic orchestra pit, superb sound, and seating on three levels (the upper levels are tiered through two decks).

Typical fare consists of revue-style shows performed by a small troupe of resident onboard singers/dancers, with fast-moving action and busy lighting and costume changes that all add up to a high-energy performance.

SPA/FITNESS. The Samsara Spa is a large facility that occupies 23,186 sq.ft/2,154 sq. meters of space, spread over two decks. It includes a large fitness room, separate saunas, steam rooms, UVB solarium, and changing rooms for men and women, 10 body treatment rooms, and two VIP treatment rooms, which are available to couples for half-day rentals, are located on the upper level.

The spa/fitness facilities are staffed and operated by Steiner Leisure, a specialist spa/beauty concession, whose young staff will try to sell you Steiner's own-brand beauty products. Some fitness classes are free, while some, such as Pathway to Yoga, Pathway to Pilates, and Pathway to Meditation, cost €9 per class. Make appointments early as time slots can go quickly.

You can purchase a day pass in order to use the sauna/steam rooms, thermal suite and relaxation area, at a cost of €35 per person. However, there is an additional no-charge sauna for men and women, but to access it you must walk through an active fitness area – maybe with your bathrobe on (some women may not feel comfortable with this arrangement).

Treatment price examples: Samsara Aroma Stone Massage (75 mins, €146); Asian Stone Therapy (50 mins, €91); Swedish Massage (50 mins, €91); Samsara Frangipani Body Wrap (120 mins, including a full body massage, €199); Elemis Pro-Collagen Facial (50 mins, €108).

● **For more extensive general information on what a Costa Cruises cruise is like, see pages 135–8.**

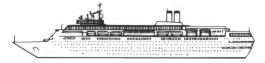

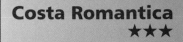

Costa Romantica
★★★

Size: . . . . .Mid-Size Ship	Total Crew: 610	Cabins (wheelchair accessible): .6 interior
Tonnage: .53,049	Passengers	Wheelchair accessibility . . . . .Good
Lifestyle: . . . . .Standard	(lower beds/all berths): 1,356/1,779	Cabin Current: . . . . .110 volts
Cruise Line: . . . . .Costa Crociere	Passenger Space Ratio	Elevators: 8
Former Names: . . . . .none	(lower beds/all berths): 39.1/29.8	Casino (gaming tables): . . . . .Yes
Builder: . . . . .Fincantieri (Italy)	Crew/Passenger Ratio	Slot Machines: . . . . .Yes
Original Cost: . . . .$325 million	(lower beds/all berths): 2.2/2.9	Swimming Pools (outdoors): 2
Entered Service: . . . . .Nov 1993	Cabins (total): .678	Swimming Pools (indoors): 0
Registry: . . . . .Italy	Size Range (sq ft/m): 185.1–430.5/	Whirlpools: 4
Length (ft/m): 718.5/220.61	17.2–40.0	Self-Service Launderette: . . . . .No
Beam (ft/m): 98.4/30.89	Cabins (outside view): 462	Dedicated Cinema/Seats: . . . . .No
Draft (ft/m): 25.0/7.60	Cabins (interior/no view): 216	Library: . . . . .Yes
Propulsion/Propellers: diesel (22,800kW)/2	Cabins (for one person): 0	
Passenger Decks: 10	Cabins (with private balcony): 10	

OVERALL SCORE: 1,247 OUT OF A POSSIBLE 2,000 POINTS

OVERVIEW. *Costa Romantica* is a bold, contemporary ship with an upright yellow funnel cluster of three typical of Italian styling today. Sadly, there is no wrap-around promenade deck outdoors, and so contact with the sea is minimal, although there is some good open space on several of the upper decks. Being Italian, the ship is chic and very tasteful, and will appeal to the sophisticated. The layout and flow are somewhat disjointed, however. The ship has a good number of business and conference facilities, with several flexible meeting rooms. The multi-level atrium is open and spacious, and has a revolving mobile sculpture. There is a small chapel and an internet café.

ACCOMMODATION. There are 11 price categories. These include 16 suites, 10 of which have a private semi-circular balcony, while six suites command views over the ship's bows. The other cabins are fairly standard in size, shape, and facilities; the ones on the highest decks cost more.

Suites/Mini-Suites: The 16 suites (with floor-to-ceiling windows) and 18 mini-suites are quite pleasant (except for the rounded balconies of the 10 suites on Madrid Deck, where a solid steel half-wall blocks the view). A sliding door separates the bedroom from the living room, and bathrooms are of a decent size. Cherry wood walls and cabinetry help make these suites warm and attractive.

The six suites at the forward section of Monte Carlo Deck are the largest, and have huge glass windows with commanding forward views, but no balconies.

Standard Outside-View/Interior (No View) Cabins: All other cabins are of a moderately generous size, and all have nicely finished cherry wood cabinetry and walls. However,

BERLITZ'S RATINGS

	Possible	Achieved
Ship	500	333
Accommodation	200	133
Food	400	214
Service	400	267
Entertainment	100	60
Cruise	400	240

the cabin bathrooms and shower enclosures are quite small. There are a good number of triple and quad cabins, ideal for families with children. The company's in-cabin food service menu is extremely basic.

CUISINE. The 728-seat Botticelli Restaurant is of a superior design. There are several tables for two, four, six or eight. There are two seatings (dinner on European cruises is typically at 7pm and 9pm), and there are both smoking and non-smoking sections. Romantic candlelight dining is typically featured on a formal night.

For casual meals and snacks, try the Giardino Buffet, but note that the buffet layout is extremely tight, and the buffet items are very much standard fare, with the exception of some good commercial pasta dishes. One would expect Italian waiters, but, sadly, this is not the case now, with most of the waiters coming from countries other than Italy.

ENTERTAINMENT. The L'Opéra Theater, the main show-lounge, is an interesting amphitheater-like design that spans two decks, with seating on both main and balcony levels. However, the seats are bolt upright, and quite uncomfortable and 10 large pillars obstruct many sightlines.

SPA/FITNESS. The Caracalla Spa contains a gymnasium with some high-tech muscle-pump machines, an aerobics exercise area, two hot tubs, Roman bath, health bar, sauna and steam rooms, and beauty salon.

● **For more extensive general information on what a Costa Cruises cruise is like, see pages 135–8.**

Costa Serena
★★★★

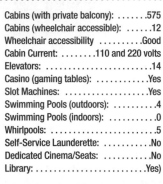

Size: . . . . .Large Resort Ship	Passenger Decks: 13	Cabins (with private balcony): 575
Tonnage: 114,147	Total Crew: .1,090	Cabins (wheelchair accessible): 12
Lifestyle: . . . . .Standard	Passengers	Wheelchair accessibility . . . . .Good
Cruise Line: Costa Crociere (Costa Cruises)	(lower beds/all berths): 3,000/3,780	Cabin Current: . . . . .110 and 220 volts
Former Names: . . . . .none	Passenger Space Ratio	Elevators: 14
Builder: . . . . .Fincantieri (Italy)	(lower beds/all berths): 38.0/30.1	Casino (gaming tables): . . . . .Yes
Original Cost: . . . .€475 million	Crew/Passenger Ratio	Slot Machines: . . . . .Yes
Entered Service: . . . . .May 2007	(lower beds/all berths): 2.7/3.4	Swimming Pools (outdoors): 4
Registry: . . . . .Italy	Cabins (total): 1,500	Swimming Pools (indoors): 0
Length (ft/m): 952.0/290.2	Size Range (sq ft/m): 482.2–179.7/	Whirlpools: 5
Beam (ft/m): 116.4/35.50	44.8–16.7	Self-Service Launderette: . . . . .No
Draft (ft/m): 27.2/8.3	Cabins (outside view): 914	Dedicated Cinema/Seats: . . . . .No
Propulsion/Propellers: . . . .diesel-electric	Cabins (interior/no view): 586	Library: . . . . .Yes)
34,000kW/2 azimuthing pods	Cabins (for one person): 0	

OVERALL SCORE: 1,449 OUT OF A POSSIBLE 2,000 POINTS

OVERVIEW. *Costa Serena* is the sister ship to *Costa Concordia* (debuted 2006), which is itself a slightly larger, extended version of *Costa Fortuna/ Costa Magica*, but with an additional 17 meters in length that allows for more cabins to accommodate another 300 passengers.

Two of the ship's four swimming pools can be covered by a sliding glass dome (magrodome) in case of poor weather, while one pool has a long water slide (great for kids), and there is a huge screen for poolside movies. There is not a lot of open deck space, so sunloungers tend to be crammed together (there are no cushioned pads). *Costa Serena* absorbs passengers reasonably well, and provides a decent passenger space ratio that means that it won't feel too crowded (except, perhaps, on the open decks).

There are three decks full of bars and lounges plus lots of other public rooms. This ship has a glass-domed rotunda atrium lobby (with four panoramic elevators providing great views) that is nine decks high, with great upward views from the lobby bar. Ride up in the glass elevators and you'll think you're cruising in the heavens – well, the clouds, anyway – due to the delightful interior design, which is themed around the heavens and astrology – even the ship's deck names are those of the Zodiac.

The Casino is large and glitzy, but always lively and entertaining (slot machines occupy a separate area to gaming tables, so serious gamers can concentrate). There's also a very small library, an internet-connection center, card room, art gallery, and video game room, together with several other bars and lounges to play in, plus a chapel – a standard aboard all Costa Cruises' ships.

Costa Cruises is noted for its "Italian" style, ambience

BERLITZ'S RATINGS

	Possible	Achieved
Ship	500	427
Accommodation	200	152
Food	400	252
Service	400	273
Entertainment	100	64
Cruise	400	281

and spirit. To be truthful, however, there are few Italian crew members on board its ships (while many of the officers are Italian, most of the crew members – particularly the dining room and housekeeping staff – are from the Philippines). The lifestyle on board is, however, perceived to be Italian – lively, noisy, with lots of love for life and a love of all things casual – even on so-called "formal" nights. Most passengers will be Italian, with a sprinkling of other European nationals. One night (at the end of each cruise) is typically reserved for a "Roman Bacchanal" (or Venetian Carnival night on Europe/Mediterranean cruises), when it's fun to dress up toga-style for dinner and beyond.

Costa Cruises does a good job of providing first-time cruise passengers with a well-packaged holiday – particularly for families with children – that is a mix of sophistication and basic fare, albeit accompanied by loud music everywhere.

All printed materials (room service folio, menus, etc.) will typically be in six languages (Italian, English, French, German, Portuguese, and Spanish). You can expect to be cruising with a lot of children of all ages during peak European holiday periods (such as Easter and Christmas). Costa Cruises is a cruise line for those who like to enjoy life and party. As aboard other Costa ships, note that for embarkation, few staff members are on duty at the gangway when you arrive; they merely point you in the direction of your deck, or to the ship's elevators and do not escort you to your cabin.

ACCOMMODATION. There are 20 price grades, from 2-bed interior cabins to grand suites with private balcony, although in reality there are only three different sizes: Suites with balcony (which are really not particularly large in comparison with some other large ships), 2- or 4-bed outside view cabins, and 2- or 4-bed interior (no-view) cabins. Fortunately, there are no cabins with lifeboat obstructed views, and, in most cabins, twin beds can be changed to a double/queen-bed configuration.

Eight Grand suites comprise the largest accommodation. These are located in the center of the ship on one of the uppermost decks. They have a queen-sized bed and larger living area with vanity desk; the bathrooms have a tub and two washbasins.

For anyone who likes to take wellness (spa) treatments, there are 12 "Samsara Spa Suites" located just aft of the spa itself (although 99 cabins, including the 12 suites, are designated as Samsara-grade. Samsara suite/cabin occupants get unlimited access to the spa plus two treatments and fitness or meditation lessons as part of their package, and dine in one of the two Samsara restaurants. All Samsara-designated accommodation grades have an Oriental decorative theme, and special Samsara bathroom personal amenities.

As this book was going to press, a five-choice pillow menu was being introduced in all suite-grade accommodation. Note that only suite-grades get bathrobes and better amenities, shaving mirror, and walk-in closets – although the hangars are plastic. Music is played 24 hours a day in all hallways (and elevators), so you may well hear it if you are a light sleeper (I receive many complaints and letters of frustration about this annoyance).

CUISINE. There are two main dining rooms (Ceres, located aft, and Vesta, in the ship's center), allocated according to your accommodation grade and location. There are two seatings.

Two 100-seat Samsara Restaurants (spa cuisine spots) are provided with separate entrances, adjacent to the Vesta Restaurant. These two dining spots are for those seeking spa food (reduced calories, fat and salt, with menu creations under the direction of dietary consultant and Michelin-star chef Ettore Boccia and his molecular Italian cuisine), while the two main restaurants offer traditional cruise fare. These dining venues are open for lunch and dinner to those in Samsara-grade suites and cabins, and to anyone else not in Samsara-grade accommodation (for dinner only) for an extra charge of €20 per day, or €120 for a 7-day cruise package.

Alternative (Reservations Required) Dining Option: Club Bacco is an upscale dining venue with seating under a huge glass dome. Fine table settings, china, silverware and leather-bound menus are provided. There's a cover charge of $20 per person (for service and gratuity). Ettore Boccia has also created the menus in this venue, with small portion dishes that present a delightful array and variety of new flavours (some traditional chefs call it "foam food").

Casual Eatery: The The Promotea Buffet Restaurant is a self-serve eatery for breakfast, lunch, afternoon pizzas, and beverages (coffee and tea) at any time. A balcony level provides additional seating (you'll need to carry your own food plates – there are no trays). Decent quality cappuccino and espresso coffees are always available in various bars (at extra cost).

Additionally, the Caffeteria will be the place to go for decent (extra cost) coffees and Italian pastries.

ENTERTAINMENT. The 1,287-seat Giove Theater spans three decks in the forward section of the ship. It is the venue for all production shows and large-scale cabaret acts, is quite stunningly glitzy, and has a revolving stage, hydraulic orchestra pit, superb sound, and seating on three levels (the upper levels are tiered through two decks).

Typically, revue-style shows (performed by a small troupe of resident onboard singers/dancers) are presented, with fast moving action and busy lighting and costume changes that all add up to a high-energy performance.

SPA/FITNESS. The ship's Samsara Spa (presently the largest spa at sea) has more than 23,186 sq. ft (2,154 sq. meters) of spa/wellness facilities, spread over two decks. It includes a large fitness room, separate saunas, steam rooms, UVB solarium, and changing rooms for men and women, 10 body treatment rooms, and two VIP treatment rooms, which are available to couples for half-day rentals, are located on the upper level.

The Spa/fitness facilities are staffed and operated by Steiner Leisure, a specialist spa/beauty concession, whose young staff will try to sell you Steiner's own-brand beauty products. Some fitness classes are free, while some, such as Pathway to Yoga, Pathway to Pilates, and Pathway to Meditation, cost €9 per class. Make appointments early as time slots can go quickly.

Note that to use the sauna/steam rooms, thermal suite and relaxation area, you'll need to purchase a day pass at a cost of €35 per person. However, there is an additional no-charge sauna for men and women, but to access it you'll need to walk through the active fitness area – maybe with your bathrobe on (not comfortable, especially for women).

Treatment price examples: Samsara Aroma Stone Massage (75 mins, €146); Asian Stone Therapy (50 mins, €91); Swedish Massage (50 mins, €91); Samsara Frangipani Body Wrap (120 mins, including a full body massage, €199); Elemis Pro-Collagen Facial (50 mins, €108).

● **For more extensive general information on what a Costa Cruises cruise is like, see pages 135–8.**

Costa Victoria
★★★+

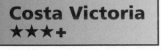

Size: . . . . .Large Resort Ship	Total Crew: 800	Cabins (wheelchair accessible): 6
Tonnage: .75,200	Passengers	Wheelchair accessibility . . . . .Good
Lifestyle: . . . . .Standard	(lower beds/all berths): 1,928/2,464	Cabin Current: . . . . . . .110 and 220 volts
Cruise Line: . . . . .Costa Cruises	Passenger Space Ratio	Elevators: 12
Former Names: . . . . .none	(lower beds/all berths): 39.0/30.5	Casino (gaming tables): . . . . .Yes
Builder: . . . . . . .Bremer Vulkan (Germany)	Crew/Passenger Ratio	Slot Machines: . . . . .Yes
Original Cost: . . . .$388 million	(lower beds/all berths): 2.4/3.0	Swimming Pools (outdoors): 2
Entered Service: . . . . .July 1996	Cabins (total): .964	Swimming Pools (indoors): 1
Registry: . . . . .Italy	Size Range (sq ft/m): 120.0–430.5/	Whirlpools: 4
Length (ft/m): 823.0/251.00	11.1–40.0	Self-Service Launderette: . . . . .Yes
Beam (ft/m): 105.5/32.25	Cabins (outside view): 573	Dedicated Cinema/Seats: . . . . .No
Draft (ft/m): 25.6/7.8	Cabins (interior/no view): 391	Library: . . . . .Yes
Propulsion/Propellers: diesel (30,000kW)/2	Cabins (for one person): 0	
Passenger Decks: 10	Cabins (with private balcony): 246	

OVERALL SCORE: 1,382 OUT OF A POSSIBLE 2,000 POINTS

OVERVIEW. *Costa Victoria* has an outdoor walk-around promenade deck (full of sunloungers) and a wrap-around jogging track. Inside is a lovely four-deck-high forward-facing observation lounge with a "beam-me-up" glass elevator; in the center is a cone-shaped waterfall. It is a stunning space, and has its own bar.

The seven-deck-high "planetarium" atrium has four glass lifts that travel up to a clear crystal dome. The uppermost level of the atrium is the deck where two outside swimming pools are located, together with four blocks of showers, and an ice cream bar and grill.

Unusual for a new ship is a pleasant (but tiny) indoor swimming pool and a sauna. Adjacent is a steam room, and gymnasium (limited assortment of equipment), as well as a covered walking/jogging track. There is also a tennis court.

Where this ship differs from most large ships is in its distinct European interior decor, with decidedly Italian styling. When inside, there is absolutely no feeling that this is a ship. Internet access is available from computer terminals in the Teens Center. The onboard currency is the euro or US dollar, depending on the region of operation.

ACCOMMODATION. There are 13 price categories. The six large Panorama suites (each with third/ fourth Pullman berths in tiny, train-like compartments) and 14 mini-suites have butler service; 65 percent of all other cabins have outside views, but they are small (for two). While the suites are not large, all other cabins are of rather mean dimensions. Only 16 of the interior (no view) cabins accommodate four people, while all other cabins are for two or three.

All cabins have wood cabinetry. There is a decent amount of closet and drawer space for two for a one-week

BERLITZ'S RATINGS

	Possible	Achieved
Ship	500	402
Accommodation	200	152
Food	400	220
Service	400	273
Entertainment	100	71
Cruise	400	264

cruise, excellent air-conditioning, mini-bar/refrigerator, and electric blackout window blind (no curtains). The ocean-view cabins have large picture windows. The cabin bathrooms are small but well appointed. There are six cabins for the disabled.

CUISINE. This ship has two main dining rooms: the 594-seat Minuetto Restaurant, and the 506-seat Fantasia Restaurant. There are two seatings, with smoking and no-smoking sections in both restaurants. They are expansive and feature marble and pine walls. The cuisine is good basic fare, and the presentation is adequate, but nothing special. Pasta is freshly made on board daily. **Alternative (reservations-only) dining:** Ristorante Magnifico by Zeffirino, is available six nights each week, with a service charge of €20 per person (passengers occupying suites will get a free pass for one evening).

The ship also has casual breakfast and lunch buffets with indoor/outdoor seating, although the buffet displays are very disappointing. There is also a pizzeria.

ENTERTAINMENT. The Festival Showlounge, spanning two decks, is the venue for production shows, major cabaret, and social functions.

SPA/FITNESS. The congested spa/fitness area, on a lower deck, is much too small for the size of the ship. It has a beauty salon, indoor swimming pool, treatment rooms, sauna and steam room, but cramped changing areas.

● **For more extensive general information on what a Costa Cruises cruise is like, see pages 135–8.**

Cristal
★★★

Size: . . . . .Mid-Size Ship	Propulsion/Propellers: diesel (19,120kW/2	Cabins (for one person): 0
Tonnage: .25,611	Passenger Decks: 7	Cabins (with private balcony): 10
Lifestyle: . . . . .Standard	Total Crew: 400	Cabins (wheelchair accessible): 6
Cruise Line: . . . . .Louis Cruises	Passengers	Wheelchair accessibility . . . . .None
Former Names: . . . . *Silja Opera,*	(lower beds/all berths): 966/1,278	Cabin Voltage: 110/220
SuperStar Taurus, Leeward,	Passenger Space Ratio	Elevators: 4
Sally Albatross, Viking Saga	(lower beds/all berths): 26.5/20.0	Casino (gaming tables): . . . . .Yes
Builder: . . . . .Wartsila (Finland)	Crew/Passenger Ratio	Slot Machines: . . . . .Yes
Original Cost: . . . . .n/a	(lower beds/all berths): 2.4/3.1	Swimming Pools (outdoors): 1
Entered Service: 1980/Jul 2007	Cabins (total): .483	Swimming Pools (indoors): 0
Registry: .Greece	Size Range (sq ft/m): 107.6–462.8/	Whirlpools: 1
Length (ft/m): 530.5/161.7	10.0–43.0	Self-Service Launderette: . . . . .No
Beam (ft/m): 100.0/30.5	Cabins (outside view): 318	Dedicated Cinema/Seats: . . . . .No
Draft (ft/m): 20.1/6.1	Cabins (interior/no view): 165	Library: . . . . .Yes

BERLITZ'S OVERALL SCORE: 1,236 OUT OF A POSSIBLE 2,000 POINTS

OVERVIEW. This ship has undergone a number of changes, modifications and mishaps during its busy life. Originally built as a Viking Line passenger ferry, it was extensively reconstructed in 1995 to the tune of $60 million, after which it was operated under charter to Norwegian Cruise Line (as *Leeward*). It was bought by Louis Cruises as a replacement for the ill-fated *Sea Diamond*, at a cost of almost $50 million.

Cristal has a smart wedge-shaped profile, with a squared-off stern and short, stubby bows, and the enclosed bridge looks like it's really one deck lower than it should be. The ship does, however, benefit from a good, walk-around teakwood promenade deck. The pool deck is very cramped, although the pool itself can be covered by a sliding glass dome roof (magrodome). There is no forward-facing observation lounge atop the ship, but there is a reasonable array of public rooms, lounges, bars and meeting places to choose from.

The onboard currency is the euro, and gratuities are not included in the fare. The dress code is casual throughout (no formal nights).

Note that, as this book was being completed, plans for the ship's refit/refurbishment had not been announced.

SUITABLE FOR: *Cristal* is best suited to first-time passengers who simply want to cruise the Greek Islands in a modicum of comfort, and at a bargain price.

ACCOMMODATION. There are three suite categories (Grand, Imperial, and Royal, plus an interior "suite"), and a mix of several outside-view cabins (some of which have bal-

BERLITZ'S RATINGS		
	Possible	Achieved
Ship	500	321
Accommodation	200	131
Food	400	230
Service	400	246
Entertainment	100	65
Cruise	400	243

conies) and interior (no view) cabins in 19 price grades.

The top-grade suites have neatly-angled private balconies and provide a decent amount of space for short cruises; the bathrooms feature a bathtub, separate shower, and good storage facilities for personal toiletry items.

Most of the standard cabins, however, are really quite small, but adequate enough for the 3- and 4-day Greek Isles cruises that this ship operates. The bathrooms, however, really are dimensionally-challenged (dancing with the shower curtain comes to mind). Also, note that some cabins have views obstructed by safety equipment.

CUISINE. There are two principal dining rooms, plus a number of other dining spots and casual eateries. There are two seatings for dinner on most nights (typically an open seating for the first night), and open seating for breakfast and lunch. Seating and table assignments are made by the maître d' during embarkation. The cuisine is predominantly Continental, with some regional (Greek) specialties (much use of oil and salt). Spa and vegetarian dishes are also available on lunch and dinner menus.

ENTERTAINMENT. The showlounge has tiered seating and decent sightlines.

SPA/FITNESS. Facilities include a beauty salon, fitness room, and sauna. Massages, aromatherapy facials, manicures, pedicures, and hair beautifying treatments are available.

Crown Princess
★★★★

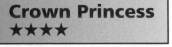

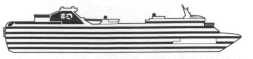

Ship:	Large Resort Ship	Passenger Decks:	15	Cabins (with private balcony):	881
Tonnage:	116,000	Total Crew:	1,163	Cabins (wheelchair accessible):	25
Lifestyle:	Standard	Passengers		Wheelchair accessibility	Best
Cruise Line:	Princess Cruises	(lower beds/all berths):	3,114/3,782	Cabin Current:	110 volts
Former Names:	none	Passenger Space Ratio		Elevators:	14
Builder:	Fincantieri (Italy)	(lower beds/all berths):	37.2/30.6	Casino (gaming tables):	Yes
Original Cost:	$500 million	Crew/Passenger Ratio		Slot Machines:	Yes
Entered Service:	May 2006	(lower beds/all berths):	2.6/3.2	Swimming Pools (outdoors):	4
Registry:	Bermuda	Cabins (total):	1,557	Swimming Pools (indoors):	0
Length (ft/m):	951.4/290.0	Size Range (sq ft/m):	163–1,279/	Whirlpools:	9
Beam (ft/m):	118.1/36.0		15.1–118.8	Self-Service Launderette:	Yes
Draft (ft/m):	26.2/8.0	Cabins (outside view):	1,105	Dedicated Cinema/Seats:	No
Propulsion/Propellers: gas turbine (25 MW)/2		Cabins (interior/no view):	452	Library:	Yes
azimuthing pods (21,000 kW each)		Cabins (for one person):	0		

OVERALL SCORE: 1,541 OUT OF A POSSIBLE 2,000 POINTS

OVERVIEW. *Crown Princess* has the same profile as half-sisters *Caribbean Princess, Golden Princess, Grand Princess, Ruby Princess* and *Star Princess*, but carries many more passengers than half-sisters (except *Caribbean Princess* and *Emerald Princess*) due to an extra deck (Riviera Deck) full of cabins, and the fact that two of the ship's 17 upper decks are made of aluminum (although lighter than steel, it does tend to "harden" over time).

Although the ship accommodates over 500 more passengers, the outdoor deck space remains the same, as do the number of elevators – so waiting time could increase during peak usage. The Passenger Space Ratio is also considerably reduced compared to that of its half-sisters.

One nice feature is The Sanctuary, an extra-cost adults-only retreat located forward on the uppermost deck. It provides a "private" place to relax and unwind and includes attendants to provide chilled face towels and deliver light bites; there are also two outdoor cabanas for massages. It's a plush, outdoor spa-inspired setting for relaxation with attentive service.

There is a good sheltered teakwood promenade deck, which almost wraps around (three times round is equal to one mile) and a walkway which goes to the (enclosed, protected) bow of the ship. The outdoor pools have various beach-like surroundings, and "Movies Under the Skies" and major sporting events are shown on a 300-sq-ft (28-sq-meter) movie screen located at the pool in front of the large funnel structure. Movies afloat in the open are a big hit with passengers – they remind many of drive-in movies, which have mostly disappeared from land-based venues.

Unlike the outside decks, there is plenty of space inside

BERLITZ'S RATINGS

	Possible	Achieved
Ship	500	433
Accommodation	200	168
Food	400	254
Service	400	291
Entertainment	100	82
Cruise	400	313

(but there are also plenty of passengers), and a wide array of public rooms, with many "intimate" (this being a relative word) spaces and places to play. The passenger flow has been well thought-out, and there is little congestion.

Atop the stern is a ship-wide glass-walled disco, Skywalkers. It's in a lower position than in sister ships, but still with spectacular views from the extreme port and starboard side windows (it would make a great penthouse).

The interior decor is attractive, with lots of earth tones (well suited to both American and European tastes). In fact, this is a culmination of the best of all that Princess Cruises has to offer from its many years of operating what is now a well-tuned, good-quality product. An extensive collection of artworks complements the interior design and colors well. If you see something you like, you will probably be able to purchase it on board – it's almost all for sale.

Crown Princess also includes a Wedding Chapel (a live web-cam can relay ceremonies via the internet). The ship's captain can legally marry American couples, thanks to the ship's Bermuda registry and a special dispensation (which should be verified when in the planning stage, according to where you reside). But to get married and take family and friends with you on your honeymoon may prove expensive. The "Hearts & Minds" chapel is also useful for "renewal of vows" ceremonies.

For children, there is a two-deck-high playroom, teen room, and a host of trained counsellors. Children have their own pools, hot tubs, and open deck area at the stern, thankfully away from adult areas. There are good netted-in areas; one section has a dip pool, while another has a mini-basketball court. There's a video games arcade, too.

Gamblers should enjoy the large casino, with more than 260 slot machines, and blackjack, craps and roulette tables, plus newer games such as Let It Ride Bonus, Spanish 21 and Caribbean Draw Progressive. A highlight may be the specially linked slot machines that provide a combined payout.

Other features include a decent library/computer room. Ship lovers should enjoy the wood-paneled Wheelhouse Bar, finely decorated with memorabilia and ship models tracing part of parent company P&O's history.

Crown Princess is a grand resort playground in which to roam when you are not ashore, and Princess Cruises delivers a consistently fine, well-packaged vacation product, always with a good degree of style, at an attractive, highly competitive price.

With many choices and "small" rooms (a relative term) to enjoy, the ship has been extremely well designed, and the odds are that you'll have an enjoyable cruise vacation. If you are not used to large ships, it will take you some time to find your way around this one, despite the company's claim that it offers passengers a "small ship feel, big ship choice."

ACCOMMODATION. There are six principal types of cabins and configurations: (a) grand suite, (b) suite, (c) mini-suite, (d) outside-view double cabins with balcony, (e) outside-view double cabins, and (f) interior (no view) double cabins. These come in 35 different brochure price categories (the choice is bewildering for both travel agents and passengers), and pricing depends on size and location.

Cabin bath towels are small, and drawer space is very limited. There are no butlers – even for the top-grade suites (which are not really large in comparison to similar suites aboard some other ships). Cabin attendants have too many cabins to look after (typically 20), which does not translate to fine personal service.

(a) The largest, most lavish suite is the Grand Suite. It has a large bedroom with queen-sized bed, huge walk-in (illuminated) closets, two bathrooms, a lounge (with fireplace and sofa bed) with wet bar and refrigerator, and a large private balcony on the port side (with hot tub that can be accessed from both balcony and bedroom).

(b/c) Suites (with a semi-private balcony) have a separate living room (with sofa bed) and bedroom (with a TV set in each). The bathroom is quite large and has both a tub and shower stall. The mini-suites also have a private balcony, and a separate living and sleeping area (with a television in each). The differences between the suites and mini-suites are basically in the size and appointments, the suite being more of a square shape while mini-suites are more rectangular, and have few drawers. Both suites and mini-suites have plush bathrobes, and fully tiled bathrooms with ample open shelf storage space. Suite and mini-suite passengers receive greater attention, including priority embarkation and disembarkation privileges. What is not good is that the most expensive accommodation has only semi-private balconies that can be seen from above and so there is little privacy.

(d/e/f). Both interior (no view) and outside-view (the out-sides come either with or without private balcony) cabins are of a functional, practical, design, although almost no drawers are provided. They are quite attractive, with warm, pleasing decor and fine soft furnishing fabrics; 80 percent of the outside-view cabins have a private balcony. Interior (no view) cabins measure 163 sq. ft (15.1 sq. meters).

The 28 wheelchair-accessible cabins measure 250–385 sq. ft (23.2–35.7 sq. meters); surprisingly, there is no mirror for dressing, and no full-length hanging space for long dresses (yes, some passengers in wheelchairs do also use mirrors and full-length clothing). Additionally, two family suites consist of two suites with an interconnecting door, plus a large balcony. These can sleep up to 10 (if at least four are children) or up to eight people (if all are adults).

All cabins receive turndown service and chocolates on pillows each night, bathrobes (on request) and toiletry amenity kits (larger, naturally, for suite/mini-suite occupants) that typically include soap, shampoo, conditioner, and hand/body lotion. A hairdryer is provided in all cabins, sensibly located at the vanity desk unit in the living area. All bathrooms have tiled floors, and there is a decent amount of open shelf storage space for personal toiletries, although the plain beige decor is very basic and unappealing.

Most outside-view cabins on Emerald Deck have views obstructed by the lifeboats. There are no cabins for singles. Your name is placed outside your suite or cabin in a documents holder – making it simple for delivery service personnel but also diminishing privacy. There is 24-hour room service (but some items on the room service menu are not available during early morning hours).

Some cabins can accommodate a third and fourth person in upper berths. However, in some cabins, the lower beds cannot then be pushed together to make queen-sized bed.

Almost all balcony suites and cabins can be overlooked both from the navigation bridge wing, as well as from the port and starboard sections of the ship's discotheque – high above the ship at the stern. Cabins with balconies on Dolphin, Caribe and Baja decks can be overlooked by passengers on balconies on the deck above. They are, therefore, not private.

However, perhaps the least desirable balcony cabins are eight balcony cabins located forward on Emerald Deck, as the balconies do not extend to the side of the ship and can be passed by walkers and gawkers on the adjacent Upper Promenade walkway (so occupants need to keep their curtains closed most of the time). Also, passengers occupying some the most expensive suites with balconies at the stern of the vessel may experience considerable vibration during certain ship maneuvers.

Note that most cabins on Emerald Deck 8 have a lifeboat-obstructed view.

CUISINE. As befits the size of the ship, there's a variety of options. There are three main dining rooms, plus Crown Grill, and Sabatini's. Of the three principal dining rooms for formal dining, one has traditional two seating dining, while the other two offer "anytime dining" (you choose when and with whom you want to eat). All are no-smoking and split into multi-tier sections in a non-symmetrical design that breaks what are quite large spaces into smaller sections for better ambiance. While six elevators go to Fiesta Deck, where two of the restaurants are located, only four go to Plaza Deck 5, where the Michelangelo Restaurant is located (this can cause waiting problems at peak times, particularly for anyone in a wheelchair).

Specially designed dinnerware, high-quality linens and silverware, Frette Egyptian cotton table linens, and silverware by Hepp of Germany are used in the main dining rooms. Note that 15% is added to all beverage bills, including wines.

Alternative (Extra Charge) Dining Options: There are two: Sabatini's, and Crown Grill. Both are open for dinner on days at sea. Sabatini's is an Italian eatery, with colorful tiled Mediterranean-style decor; it is named after Trattoria Sabatini, the 200-year old institution in Florence (where there is no cover charge). It has Italian-style pizzas and pastas, with a variety of sauces, as well as Italian-style entrées (including tiger prawns and lobster tail – all provided with flair and entertainment from by the staff of waiters (by reservation only, with a cover charge of $20 per person, for lunch or dinner). The 160-seat Crown Grill is located in a wide promenade area, to tempt you as you pass by. The cover charge is $25.

The cuisine in the alternative dining spots is decidedly better than in the three main dining rooms, with better quality ingredients and more attention to presentation and taste.

Casual eateries include a poolside hamburger grill and pizzeria (no additional charge), while extra charges do apply if you order some items at the International Café coffee bar/patisserie in the atrium lobby, opposite Vines (for no-extra-charge sushi and cheese, and extra-cost wine). Other casual meals can be taken in the Horizon Court, which is open 24 hours a day. It has large ocean-view on port and starboard sides and direct access to the two principal swimming pools and lido deck. There is no real finesse in presentation, however, as plastic plates are provided.

Ultimate Balcony Dinner/Breakfast: For something different, you could try a private dinner on your balcony, an all-inclusive evening featuring cocktails, fresh flowers, champagne and a deluxe four-course meal including Caribbean lobster tail – all served by a member of the dining staff on your private balcony; of course, it costs extra – $50 per person (or $25 per person for the Ultimate Balcony Breakfast).

ENTERTAINMENT. The Princess Theater (showlounge), the main entertainment venue, spans two decks and has comfortable seating on both main and balcony levels. It has $3 million worth of sound and light equipment, plus a 9-piece orchestra, and a scenery loading bay that connects directly from stage to a hull door for direct transfer to the dockside. The ship carries a resident troupe of almost 20 singers and dancers, plus and audio-visual support staff.

Club Fusion is a second entertainment lounge (located aft). It features cabaret acts (magicians, comedy jugglers, ventriloquists and others) at night, and lectures, bingo and horse racing during the day. Explorers, a third entertainment lounge, can also host cabaret acts and dance bands. A variety of other lounges and bars have live music, and Princess Cruises employs a number of male dance hosts as partners for women traveling alone.

SPA/FITNESS. The Lotus Spa is located forward on Sun Deck – one of the uppermost decks. Separate facilities for men and women include a sauna, steam room, and changing rooms; common facilities include a relaxation/waiting zone, body-pampering treatment rooms, and a gymnasium with packed with the latest high-tech muscle-pumping, cardio-vascular equipment, and great ocean views. Some fitness classes are free, while some cost extra.

Above the spa, The Sanctuary, an adults-only retreat, offers shade and solitude, although MP3 players are provided, pre-loaded with a variety of music, at a cost of $15 per person per half-day.

● **For more extensive general information on what a Princess Cruises cruise is like, see pages 148–51.**

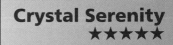

Crystal Serenity
★★★★★

Size: . . . . .Mid-Size Ship	Passenger Decks: 9	Cabins (with private balcony): 466
Tonnage: 68,870	Total Crew: 650	Cabins (wheelchair accessible): 8
Lifestyle: . . . . .Luxury/Premium	Passengers	Wheelchair accessibility . . . . .Best
Cruise Line: . . . . .Crystal Cruises	(lower beds/all berths): 1,100/1,100	Cabin Current: . . . . .110/220 volts
Former Names: . . . . .none	Passenger Space Ratio	Elevators: 8
Builder: Chantiers de l'Atlantique (France)	(lower beds/all berths): 62.6/62.6	Casino (gaming tables): . . . . .Yes
Original Cost: . . . .$350 million	Crew/Passenger Ratio	Slot Machines: . . . . .Yes
Entered Service: . . . . .June 2003	(lower beds/all berths): 1.7/1.7	Swimming Pools (outdoors): 1
Registry: . . . . .The Bahamas	Cabins (total): .550	Swimming Pools (indoors): 1
Length (ft/m): 820.2/250.0	Size Range (sq ft/m): 226–1,345.5/	(indoor/outdoor)
Beam (ft/m): 111.5/34.0	21–125	Whirlpools: 2
Draft (ft/m): 24.9/7.6	Cabins (outside view): 550	Self-Service Launderette: . . . . .Yes
Propulsion/Propellers: . . . . .2 pods/	Cabins (interior/no view): 0	Dedicated Cinema/Seats: Yes/202
diesel power	Cabins (for one person): 0	Library: . . . . .Yes

OVERALL SCORE: 1,702 OUT OF A POSSIBLE 2,000 POINTS

OVERVIEW. *Crystal Serenity* is the latest (slightly larger but still mid-size) close sister ship to the company's first ship, the former *Crystal Harmony* (now *Asuka II*) and to *Crystal Symphony*. This ship carries forward the same look, and profile. *Crystal Serenity* is a contemporary ship with a nicely raked clipper bow and well-balanced lines. While some might not like the "apartment block" look of the ship's exterior, it is the contemporary, "in" look, with balconies having become important standard features aboard almost all new cruise ships built today.

Pod propulsion is provided (*see page 45 for details*). Electrical power is provided by the latest generation of environmentally friendly diesel engines.

This ship has an excellent amount of open deck, sunbathing space, and sports facilities. The aft of two outdoor swimming pools can be covered by a magrodome (retractable glass dome) in poor weather. There is no sense of crowding in this superb example of comfort by design, high-quality construction and engineering. There is also a wide wrap-around teakwood deck for walking, pleasingly uncluttered by sunloungers.

With the exception of a gray, clinical photo gallery passageway, the decor in most areas is warm, inviting and contemporary. There is much use of rich wood paneling and detailing. The main lobby houses the reception desk (staffed 24 hours a day), concierge and shore excursion desks, and a lounge/bar (Crystal Cove) with baby grand piano. However, there are no passenger cabins forward of the lobby (they have instead become accommodation for officers and staff, a more sensible arrangement since this area really is considered to be "back of house").

BERLITZ'S RATINGS		
	Possible	Achieved
Ship	500	431
Accommodation	200	165
Food	400	341
Service	400	339
Entertainment	100	84
Cruise	400	342

Some of the most elegant public rooms include Palm Court (evoking images of Colonial-style grand hotel lounges); the Avenue Saloon (a favorite watering hole of the late-night crowd and a throwback to the gentlemen's clubs of yesteryear); the Connoisseur Club (for cigar and cognac enthusiasts); and the Stardust Club (cabaret entertainment lounge). Other new additions include a dedicated room for viewing art for auction, computer-learning center (24 terminals), an internet center, and Vintage Room (private dining room where 12 invited diners can enjoy exclusive vintage wines from around the world in special wine-tasting dinners).

The casino is centrally located, with no outside views to distract passengers who are intent on gaming. Instead, the location is adjacent to lifeboats on both sides (in this arrangement, the lifeboats do not obstruct either cabins or public rooms).

This ship has just about everything for the discerning, seasoned traveler who is prepared to pay for fine style, abundant space and the comfort and the facilities of a large vessel, including an excellent program of guest lecturers. The one thing that lets the product down is the fact that the dining room operation is in two seatings (however, many older passengers do want to eat early, while the line's younger passengers prefer to dine later, so there is some balance).

Your evenings will be necessarily rather structured due to the fact that there are two seatings for dinner (unless you eat in one of the alternative dining spots), and two shows (the showlounge cannot seat all passengers at once). This detracts from the otherwise luxurious setting of the ship and the fine professionalism of its staff. Many passengers feel that gratuities should really be included on a ship that is rated this highly (they can, however, be pre-paid).

The ship achieves a high rating because of its fine facilities, service and crew. It is the extra attention to detail that makes a cruise with this ship so special. The passenger mix is usually 85% North American (half from California) and 15% other nationalities. The ship should provide you with announcement-free cruising in a well-tuned, very professionally run, service-oriented ship, roughly the equivalent of a Four Seasons or Ritz Carlton hotel. All bottled water and (non-alcoholic) soft drinks are included in the price. The onboard currency is the US dollar, and gratuities are at your discretion (15% is added to bar accounts, however).

SUITABLE FOR: *Crystal Serenity* is best suited to sophisticated travelers (typically over 50) who seek contemporary ship surroundings, with fine quality fittings and furnishings, a wide range of public rooms and facilities, and excellent food and service from a well trained staff.

ACCOMMODATION. This consists of: four Crystal Penthouses with balcony; 32 Penthouse Suites with Balcony; 72 Penthouses with balcony; 78 superior outside-view cabins with balcony; 286 outside-view cabins with balcony; 84 outside-view cabins without balcony but with large picture windows. Two whole decks of accommodation are designated as suites (Deck 11, and Deck 10), while all other accommodation is located on Decks 9, 8 and 7.

Duvets and down pillows are provided, as are lots of other niceties, together with a data socket for connecting a laptop computer. All accommodation has a refrigerator and mini-bar, television, satellite-linked telephone, and hairdryer. There's a full range of Aveda personal toiletry amenities, a plush, full-length cotton bathrobe, and plenty of cotton towels (the largest of which measures a generous 70 by 34 inches/180 by 85cm). The in-cabin TV programming is excellent (although why it starts at Channel 53, and not Channel 1, is unclear), and close-captioned videos are provided for the hearing-impaired. The air-conditioning in bathrooms and walk-in closets is extremely loud. In suites/cabins with "private" balcony, the balcony partition is of the partial, not full, type, and so noisy neighbors (particularly if using mobile phones in ports of call) can prove intrusive. The balcony decking is teak, however.

Butlers provide excellent service in all the top category suites on Decks 10 and 11, where room service food arrives on silver trays. Afternoon tea trolley service and evening hors d'oeuvres are standard fare in "butler service" suites. **Crystal Penthouses (with balcony):** There are four Crystal Penthouses with private balcony (1,345 sq. ft/125 sq. meters). These are ideally located in the center of the ship on Penthouse Deck 11, each with outstanding views and large private balconies with outside lighting (they are a slightly different shape to those of the other ships in the fleet). There is a lounge with audio-visual entertainment center, separate master bedroom with king-sized bed and electric curtains, large walk-in closets, and large vanity desk.

The marble-clad bathrooms have ocean views; they are stunning and come with a whirlpool bathtub with integral shower, two washbasins, separate large shower enclosure, bidet and toilet, and plenty of storage space for toiletries.
Penthouse Suites (with balcony): There are 32 of these (538 sq. ft/50 sq. meters), all on Penthouse Deck 11. Each has a separate bedroom, walk-in closet and en-suite bathroom with full-size tub with integral shower, two washbasins, separate shower enclosure, bidet, toilet, and ample space for toiletries. The lounge has a large couch, coffee table and several armchairs, and there is a dining table and four chairs.
Penthouse Deck Cabin (with balcony): These are 66 of these, located on Penthouse Decks 10 and 11. They measure 403.6 sq. ft/37.5 sq. meters. All come with a private balcony, although eight that are located at the aft of Deck 11 have larger balconies. These units are really large cabins that have a sleeping area that can be curtained off from the lounge area, with its large, long vanity desk. The bathroom is large, and has a full-size bathtub (with integral shower), separate shower enclosure, and a bidet and toilet.
Superior Deluxe Outside-View Cabins (with balcony): This really is a standard outside-view cabin that is larger than any standard cabin aboard most other ships, and measures 269 sq. ft (25 sq. meters). The 78 cabins are longer than cabins that don't have a private balcony. They have a sleeping area with clothes closets, small couch, and drinks table, vanity desk with hairdryer. The bathroom has a bathtub with integral shower, two washbasins, and toilet. Large patio doors open onto a private balcony.
Deluxe Outside-View Cabins (with balcony): This is really a standard outside-view cabin that is larger than any standard cabin aboard most other ships, and measures 269 sq. ft (25 sq. meters). The 286 cabins, about the same size and shape as the "Deluxe" version but on a "superior" deck (Penthouse Deck 10), are longer than cabins that don't have a private balcony. They have a sleeping area with clothes closets, small couch, and drinks table, vanity desk with hairdryer. The bathroom has a tub with integral shower, two basins, and toilet. Patio doors open to a private balcony.
Deluxe Outside-View Cabins (no balcony): This is really a standard outside-view cabin (located on Deck 7, with the wrap-around promenade deck outside each cabin) that is larger than any standard cabin aboard most ships. The 84 cabins measure 226 sq. ft (21 sq. meters), and have a large window, sleeping area with clothes closets, small sofa and drinks table, vanity desk with hairdryer. The small bathroom has a bathtub with integral shower, two washbasins, and toilet.
Wheelchair Accessible Accommodation: This includes two penthouse grades, two cabins with balconies, and four cabins with large picture windows.

CUISINE. There is one main dining room (the Crystal Dining Room), two alternative dining rooms (reservations are required), and a sushi bar. The Crystal Dining Room is quite elegant, with a crisp, clean "California Modern" style that includes plenty of space around each table. It is well laid-out, and has a raised, circular central section, although it is noisy at times, and not conducive to a fine dining experience. There are tables for two (many positioned adjacent to large windows), four, six or eight. All restaurants are non-smoking areas. At dinner, a wandering trio serenades passengers at their tables, but this is tacky and not representative of fine dining.

The food is very attractively presented on large plates, and well served, using both plate service and silver service. It is of a very high standard with fine quality (high cost) ingredients. European dishes are predominantly featured (but in an American style). The menus are extremely varied, and feature a fine selection of meat, fish and vegetarian dishes. Special (off-menu) orders are available, as are caviar and other culinary niceties. Kosher meals are also available (frozen when brought on board); Kosher pots, pans and utensils are sterilized in salt water, and all plates used during service are hand-washed separately.

Overall, the food is really good for the size of ship, and, with the choice of the two alternative dining spots, receives high praise. Dinner in the main dining room is either in one of two seatings or, as of January 2011, open dining by reservation (by telephone before your cruise). While the early seating is simply too rushed for many, with two alternative restaurants, off-menu choices, a hand-picked European staff and excellent service, dining is often memorable. Fresh pasta and dessert flambeau specialties are made at the table each day by accommodating headwaiters.

Alternative Dining Spots (reservations required, no extra charge): There are two alternative restaurants (one Italian, the other Asian). Both are aft on Deck 7, and both have excellent views from large picture windows. Prego is for Italian food, Italian wines, and service with a flair. Silk Road has Asian-California "fusion" food. Although there is no extra charge, a "gratuity" is added to your account.

There is a separate sushi bar, with items selected by superb Los-Angeles-based Japanese super-chef Nobu Matsuhisa, and skillfully prepared on board by a Nobu-trained chef; the high-cost ingredients are flown regularly to the ship. The alternative dining spots provide an excellent standard of culinary fare – with food cooked to order at no extra charge, although many Crystal regulars feel the recommended $6 waiter gratuity per meal should be included in the cruise fare. To eat in one of Nobu's restaurants ashore costs a considerable amount; aboard the ship, not only is the food free, it is outstanding.

The Bistro: Located on the upper level of the two-deck-high lobby, this is a casual spot for coffees and pastries, served in the style and atmosphere of a European street cafe. The Bistro has unusual Crystal Cruises-logo china that can be bought in one of the ship's boutiques.

Casual Eateries: For casual meals, the Lido Cafe has an extensive self-serve buffet area. It's high up in the ship, with great views from its large picture windows. For casual poolside lunches, there is also the Trident Grill, as well as an ice cream/frozen yoghurt counter (no extra charge). Special themed luncheon buffets, with appropriate decor and service staff dressed accordingly, are provided at the Trident indoor/outdoor pool area. These include the popular Asian Buffet and Follow the Sun (Mediterranean) buffet.

ENTERTAINMENT. The Galaxy Lounge is the ship's principal showlounge. It is quite a large room with a high ceiling, but on one level (with a nicely sloping floor) for good visibility. Indeed, the sightlines are good from almost all seats. Both banquette and individual seating is provided. The stage, lighting, and sound equipment are all excellent.

The shows are elegant, with excellent costuming (though not much in the way of scenery), but some are seriously dated, too long, and Crystal Cruises' many repeat passengers know them all. In addition, many nights feature cabaret acts and classical artistes that are of a good caliber, and constantly changing. The bands and musical units are also, for the most part, of a high caliber, and there is plenty of music for social dancing. The ship also provides gentlemen hosts (called Ambassador Hosts) for the many single ladies that enjoy traveling with Crystal Cruises.

SPA/FITNESS. The Crystal Spa is located aft on Lido Deck 12, one of the ship's uppermost decks. Facilities include men's and women's changing rooms with sauna (which has a large porthole-shaped window) and steam rooms, gymnasium with high-tech muscle-pumping equipment, an aerobics exercise area, and reception/relaxation area.

Treatments are provided under the aegis of Steiner Platinum Service (Steiner being the concession). Facilities include one room dedicated to yoga and pilates classes (no extra charge), an aerobics/exercise room, plus separate sauna, steam rooms, and changing rooms for both men and women. There are seven treatment rooms (including one for couples, and one with a "dry float bed") for massage, facials, and other treatments, and a separate beauty salon.

Some staff will try to sell you Steiner's own-brand Elemis beauty products). Massage (including exotic massages such as Aroma Stone massage, Chakra Balancing massage and other well-being massages), facials, pedicures, and beauty salon treatments cost extra. Examples: Swedish Massage ($109 for 50 minutes); Deep Tissue Massage ($116 for 50 minutes).

There are also some excellent multi-therapy packages that provide you with hours of pampering. Example: Ceremony of Precious Metal (exotic lime and ginger salt glow, aroma spa ocean wrap, well-being massage) lasting 3 hours 30 minutes, for $323. A simple hair cut (for men) costs $25, while it is $57 for women with short hair for a shampoo, cut and blow-dry.

The ship has excellent open deck and sunbathing space, and sports facilities that include two full-size paddle tennis courts, electronic golf simulator, and golf driving range. One of two outdoor swimming pools has a magrodome (retractable glass dome) cover, while the one that is in the open is one of the longest aboard any ship today. Anyone trying to sunbathe quietly on the deck under and close to the paddle tennis courts will hear the noise of play (bat against ball) when the court is in use.

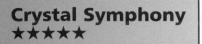

Crystal Symphony
★★★★★

Size:	Mid-Size Ship	Passenger Decks:	8	Cabins (with private balcony):	276
Tonnage:	51,044	Total Crew:	545	Cabins (wheelchair accessible):	7
Lifestyle:	Luxury/Premium	Passengers		Wheelchair accessibility	Best
Cruise Line:	Crystal Cruises	(lower beds/all berths):	960/1,010	Cabin Current:	110 and 220 volts
Former Names:	none	Passenger Space Ratio		Elevators:	8
Builder:	Masa-Yards (Finland)	(lower beds/all berths):	53.1/50.5	Casino (gaming tables):	Yes
Original Cost:	$300 million	Crew/Passenger Ratio		Slot Machines:	Yes
Entered Service:	Mar 1995	(lower beds/all berths):	1.7/1.8	Swimming Pools (outdoors):	2
Registry:	The Bahamas	Cabins (total):	480		(1 with magrodome)
Length (ft/m):	777.8/237.10	Size Range (sq ft/m):	201.2–981.7/	Swimming Pools (indoors):	0
Beam (ft/m):	98.0/30.20		18.7–91.2	Whirlpools:	2
Draft (ft/m):	24.9/7.60	Cabins (outside view):	480	Self-Service Launderette:	Yes
Propulsion/Propellers:	diesel-electric	Cabins (interior/no view):	0	Dedicated Cinema/Seats:	Yes/143
	(33,880kW)/2	Cabins (for one person):	0	Library:	Yes

OVERALL SCORE: 1,701 OUT OF A POSSIBLE 2,000 POINTS

OVERVIEW. *Crystal Symphony* is a contemporary ship with a nicely raked clipper bow and well-balanced lines. While some might not like the "apartment block" look of its exterior, it is the contemporary, "in" look, balconies having become standard aboard almost all new cruise ships. This ship has an excellent amount of open deck, sunbathing space, and sports facilities. The aft of two outdoor swimming pools can be covered by a magrodome in inclement weather.

BERLITZ'S RATINGS

	Possible	Achieved
Ship	500	430
Accommodation	200	163
Food	400	340
Service	400	342
Entertainment	100	84
Cruise	400	342

There is no sense of crowding anywhere – a fine example of comfort by design (form follows function) and high-quality construction. The ship combines large ship facilities with the intimacy of rooms found aboard many small vessels. There is a wide wrap-around teakwood deck for walking, uncluttered by lounge chairs.

The interior decor, much of which was refreshed in 2009, is restful, with color combinations that don't jar the senses. It has a good mixture of public entertainment lounges and small intimate rooms. Outstanding is the Palm Court, an observation lounge with forward-facing views over the ship's bows – it is tranquil, and one of the nicest rooms afloat (it is larger than aboard the sister ship).

There is an excellent book, video and CD-ROM library (combined with a Business Center). The theater has high-definition video projection and headsets for the hearing-impaired. Useful self-service launderettes are provided on each deck. Fine-quality fabrics and soft furnishings, china, flatware and silver are used. Excellent in-cabin television programming (including CNN) is transmitted, as well as close-captioned videos for the use of the hearing-impaired.

The Connoisseurs Club, adjacent to the Avenue Saloon, serves fine premium brands of liquor and cigars for those who appreciate them. The Computer Learning Center, with more than 20 stations, is a popular venue. Private lessons are available (but expensive).

This ship has just about everything for the discerning, seasoned traveler who wants to and is prepared to pay good money for fine style, abundant space and the comfort and the facilities of a large vessel capable of extended voyages, including an excellent program of guest lecturers.

The one thing that lets the product down is the fact that the dining room operation is in two seatings (however, having said that, there are many older passengers who want to eat early, while the line's younger passengers prefer to dine later, so there is some semblance of balance).

Crystal Cruises takes care of its ships, and its staff, and it is the staff that make the cruise experience special. They are a well-trained group that stress hospitality at all times. The ship achieves a high rating because of its fine facilities, service and crew. It is the extra attention to detail that really counts. The passenger mix is approximately 85 percent North American (typically half will be from California) and 15% other nationalities.

This is announcement-free cruising in a well-tuned, very professionally run, service oriented, ship, the approximate equivalent of a Four Seasons hotel. However, note that the score has gone downwards a little recently, the result of the fact that, in comparison to other ships available in the discounted marketplace, this is still a two-seating ship, which makes it more highly structured in terms of timing than it really should be. All bottled water and (non-alcoholic) soft drinks are included in the cost of your cruise (this feature was introduced with the debut of *Crystal Serenity*, but has now been applied fleet-wide). The onboard currency is the US dollar, and gratuities are at your discretion (15% is added to bar accounts, however).

In 2007, *Crystal Symphony* was given a $23 million refurbishment that included making the ship's main entertainment deck more contemporary. All suites/cabins received flat-screen televisions, new Murano bedside table lamps and Rubelli fabrics, and oval glass washbasins set in granite surrounds were introduced, together with a raft of other behind-the-scenes items that have helped bring the ship right up to date.

Your evenings will be necessarily rather structured due to the fact that there are two seatings for dinner (unless you eat in one of the alternative dining spots), and two shows (the showlounge cannot seat all passengers at once). This detracts from the otherwise luxurious setting of the ship and the fine professionalism of its staff. Many passengers feel that gratuities should really be included on a ship that is rated this highly (they can, however, be pre-paid).

Plastic patio furniture on suite and cabin balconies would be better replaced with the more elegant teak variety, to go with the teak decking.

SUITABLE FOR: *Crystal Symphony* is best suited to discerning adult travelers (typically over 50) that seek contemporary ship surroundings, with fine-quality fittings and furnishings, a wide range of public rooms and facilities, and excellent food and service from a well trained staff.

ACCOMMODATION. There are eight categories, with the most expensive suites located on the highest accommodation deck (Deck 10). There are two Crystal Penthouses with private balcony; 18 Penthouse Suites with private balcony; 44 Penthouse Cabins with balcony; 214 Cabins with balcony; 202 Cabins without balcony. Some cabins (grades G and I), have obstructed views. Except for the suites on Deck 10, most other cabin bathrooms are very compact units.

Regardless of the accommodation category you select, duvets and down pillows are provided, as are lots of other niceties, together with a data socket for connecting a personal laptop computer. All accommodation has a refrigerator and mini-bar, television, satellite-linked telephone, and hairdryer. A full range of Aveda personal toiletry amenities is provided, as is a plush cotton bathrobe, and plenty of cotton towels (the largest of which measures a generous 70 by 34 inches (180 by 85cm). The in-cabin television programming is excellent, and close-captioned videos are provided for the hearing-impaired.

Deck 10 Penthouses: Two delightful Crystal Penthouses measure 982 sq. ft (91 sq. meters) and have a huge private balcony (with outside light) and lounge with audio-visual entertainment center, separate master bedroom with king-sized bed and electric curtains, large walk-in closets, and stunning ocean-view marble bathrooms with a Philippe Stark whirlpool tub, bidet, two washbasins, and plenty of storage space for toiletry items. These really are among the best in fine, private, pampered living spaces at sea, and come with all the best priority perks, including laundry service.

Other Deck 10 Suites: All of the other suites on this deck have plenty of space (all feature a private balcony, with outside light), including a lounge with large sofa, coffee table and chairs, a sleeping area and walk-in closet. Rich wood cabinetry provides much of the warmth of the decor. The bathrooms are quite large, and are extremely well appointed, with full-sized bathtub and separate shower enclosure, two washbasins, bidet and toilet. In fact, any of the suites on this deck are equipped with everything necessary for refined, private living at sea.

Five butlers provide the best in personal service in all the top category suites on Deck 10 (with a total of 132 beds), where all room service food arrives on silver trays. Afternoon tea trolley service and evening hors d'oeuvres are standard fare in the "butler service" suites.

Decks 5/6/7/8/9: More than 50 percent of all cabins have private balconies. All are well equipped, and extremely comfortable, with excellent sound insulation. The balcony partitions, however, do not go from floor to ceiling, so you can hear your neighbors. Even in the lowest category of standard cabins, there is plenty of drawer space, but the closet hanging space may prove somewhat limited for long voyages. There are generously sized personal bathroom amenities, duvets and down pillows. European stewardesses provide excellent service and attention.

CUISINE. The Crystal Dining Room (totally non-smoking) is quite an elegant room, with crisp design, plenty of space around each table, and well-placed waiter service stations. It is well laid out, and has a raised, circular central section, although it is somewhat noisy at times, and not conducive to a fine dining experience. There are tables for two (many of them positioned adjacent to large windows), four, six or eight. Each evening at dinner, a wandering trio serenades passengers at their tables, but this is tacky and not representative of fine dining.

The food is very attractively presented on large plates, and well served (using both plate service as well as silver service in the best European traditions). It is of a very high standard with fine quality (high cost) ingredients. European dishes are predominantly featured (but in an American style). The menus are extremely varied, and feature a fine selection of meat, fish and vegetarian dishes. Special (off-menu) orders are available, as are caviar and other culinary niceties. Kosher meals are also available (frozen when brought on board). Kosher pots, pans and utensils are sterilized in salt water, and all plates used during service are hand-washed separately.

Overall, the food is really good for the size of ship, and, with the choice of the two alternative dining spots, receives high praise. Dinner in the main dining room is in two seatings with fixed table assignments, or you can choose open dining by reservation by telephone before your cruise. While the early seating is simply too rushed for many, with two alternative restaurants, off-menu choices, a hand-picked European staff and excellent service, dining is often memorable. The advantage of fixed table assignments is that your waiters get to know your personal preferences, likes and dislikes (unlike dining rooms with open seating, where you may be seated with different people each evening, and your waiter changes constantly). Fresh pasta and dessert flambeau specialties are made at the table daily by accommodating headwaiters.

The wine list is excellent (though pricey), with an outstanding collection of across-the-board wines, including a mouthwatering connoisseur selection.

Afternoon tea in the Palm Court is a civilized daily event. The Lido provides breakfast and luncheon buffets that are fairly standard fare.

Alternative Dining Spots (reservations required, no extra charge): Two alternative dining spots are the 75-seat Prego (featuring fine Italian cuisine, and specializing in good Italian wines), and the revamped 100-seat Silk Road Restaurant and Sushi Bar in keeping with sister ship *Crystal Serenity*. These rooms are located on Deck 6; each restaurant has a separate entrance and themed decor. Both provide an excellent standard of culinary fare, with food cooked to order at no extra charge – although many feel the recommended $6 waiter gratuity per meal should be included in the cruise fare.

The Bistro (on the upper level of the two-deck-high lobby) is a casual spot for coffees and pastries, served in the style and atmosphere of a European street cafe. The Bistro has unusual, Crystal Cruises-logo china that can also be purchased in one of the ship's boutiques.

For casual meals, the Lido Cafe has an extensive self-serve buffet area, located high up in the ship, and with great views from its large picture windows. For casual poolside lunches, there is also the Trident Grill, as well as an ice cream/frozen yoghurt counter (all at no extra charge). Several special themed luncheon buffets, with appropriate decor and service staff dressed accordingly, are provided at the Trident indoor/outdoor pool area. These include the popular Asian Buffet and Follow the Sun (Mediterranean) buffet.

ENTERTAINMENT. The Galaxy Lounge is the ship's principal showlounge. It is quite a large room with a high ceiling, but on one level (with a tiered floor) for good visibility. The sightlines are good from most seats, although there are a few pillars that obstruct sight lines from some seats. Both banquette and individual seating is provided. The stage, lighting, and sound equipment are all excellent.

The shows are elegant, with excellent costuming and scenery, but they are now seriously dated, too long, and Crystal Cruises' many repeat passengers know them all. In addition, many nights feature cabaret acts that are of a good caliber, and constantly changing. The bands and musical units are also, for the most part, of a high caliber, and there is plenty of music for social dancing. The ship also provides male hosts (called Ambassador Hosts) for the many single women who enjoy traveling with Crystal Cruises.

SPA/FITNESS. In 2000 an expanded range of Spa facilities and treatments was introduced, under the aegis of Steiner Platinum Service (Steiner being the concession). Facilities include one room dedicated to yoga and pilates classes (no extra charge), an aerobics/exercise room, plus separate sauna, steam rooms, and changing rooms for both men and women. There are seven treatment rooms (including one for couples, and one room featuring a "dry float bed") for various types of massage, facials, and other treatments, as well as a separate beauty salon.

Some staff will try to sell you Steiner's own-brand Elemis beauty products (spa girls have sales targets). Being aboard this ship will give you an opportunity to try some of the more exotic treatments (particularly some of the massages available). Massage (including exotic massages such as Aroma Stone massage, Chakra Balancing massage and other well-being massages), facials, pedicures, and beauty salon treatments are at extra cost. Examples: Swedish Massage ($109 for 50 minutes); Deep Tissue Massage ($116 for 50 minutes); Yin Yang Facial ($109 for 50 minutes).

There are also some excellent multi-therapy packages that provide you with hours of pampering. Some examples: Ceremony of Precious Metal (exotic lime and ginger salt glow, aroma spa ocean wrap, well-being massage) lasting 3 hours 30 minutes, for $323; Ceremony of Water (aroma stone therapy, Japanese silk booster facial, Japanese eye zone therapy) lasting 3 hours 30 minutes, for $365; Ceremony of Earth (frangipani body nourish ritual, absolute spa ritual, frangipani hair and scalp conditioning with style dry, exotic hand ritual with paraffin wax, sole delight foot treatment with paraffin wax) lasting 6 hours and 30 minutes, for $561. A simple hair cut (for men) costs $25, while it is $57 for women with short hair for a shampoo, cut and blow-dry.

The ship also has excellent open deck and sunbathing space, and sports facilities that include a full-sized paddle tennis court, electronic golf simulator, and golf driving range. One of two outdoor swimming pools has a magrodome (retractable glass dome) cover, while the one that is in the open is one of the longest aboard any ship today.

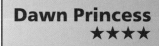

Dawn Princess
★★★★

Size:	Large Resort Ship	Passenger Decks:	10	Cabins (with private balcony):	446
Tonnage:	77,499	Total Crew:	900	Cabins (wheelchair accessible):	19
Lifestyle:	Standard	Passengers		Wheelchair accessibility	Good
Cruise Line:	Princess Cruises	(lower beds/all berths):	1,950/2,250	Cabin Current:	110 and 220 volts
Former Names:	none	Passenger Space Ratio		Elevators:	11
Builder:	Fincantieri (Italy)	(lower beds/all berths):	39.7/34.4	Casino (gaming tables):	Yes
Original Cost:	$300 million	Crew/Passenger Ratio		Slot Machines:	Yes
Entered Service:	May 1997	(lower beds/all berths):	2.1/2.5	Swimming Pools (outdoors):	4
Registry:	Great Britain	Cabins (total):	975	Swimming Pools (indoors):	0
Length (ft/m):	857.2/261.3	Size Range (sq ft/m):	135.0–635.0/	Whirlpools:	5
Beam (ft/m):	105.6/32.2		12.5–59.0	Self-Service Launderette:	Yes
Draft (ft/m):	26.5/8.1	Cabins (outside view):	603	Dedicated Cinema/Seats:	No
Propulsion/Propellers:	diesel-electric	Cabins (interior/no view):	372	Library:	Yes
	(46,080kW)/2	Cabins (for one person):	0		

OVERALL SCORE: 1,527 OUT OF A POSSIBLE 2,000 POINTS

OVERVIEW. *Dawn Princess* is an all-white ship with a decent contemporary profile, well balanced by a large funnel that contains a deck tennis/basketball/volleyball court in its sheltered aft base. There is a wide, teakwood walk-around promenade deck outdoors, some real teak steamer-style deck chairs (complete with royal blue cushioned pads), and 93,000 sq. ft (8,640 sq. meters) of space outdoors. A great amount of glass area on the upper decks provides plenty of light and connection with the outside world.

The ship absorbs passengers well, and has an almost intimate feel to it. A large poolside movie screen and an adults-only Sanctuary relaxation area were added in 2009.

The interiors are very pretty and warm, with attractive colors and welcoming decor that includes some very attractive wall murals and other artwork. The signage throughout the ship could be better, however. There are a number of dead ends in the interior layout, so it's not as user-friendly as a ship this size could be. The cabin numbering system is extremely illogical, with numbers going through several hundred series on the same deck.

There is a wide range of public rooms, with several intimate rooms and spaces so that you don't get the feel of being overwhelmed by large spaces. The interior focal point is a huge four-deck-high atrium lobby with winding, double stairways, and two panoramic glass-walled elevators.

There are two showlounges, one at each end of the ship; one is a 550-seat, theater-style showlounge (movies are also shown here) and the other is a 480-seat cabaret-style lounge, complete with bar.

The library, a very warm room, has six large butter-colored leather chairs for listening to compact audio discs,

BERLITZ'S RATINGS

	Possible	Achieved
Ship	500	422
Accommodation	200	161
Food	400	266
Service	400	291
Entertainment	100	86
Cruise	400	301

with ocean-view windows. There is a conference center for up to 300, as well as a business center with computers, copy and fax machines. The collection of artwork is good, particularly on the stairways, and helps make the ship feel smaller than it is, although in places it doesn't always seem coordinated. The casino, while large, is not really in the main passenger flow and so it does not generate the "walk-through" factor found aboard so many ships.

The most traditional room is the Wheelhouse Lounge/Bar, which is decorated in the style of a late 19th-century gentleman's club, with wood paneling and comfortable seating. The focal point is a large ship model from the P&O collection archives: aboard *Dawn Princess* it is *Kenya*.

One nice feature is the captain's cocktail party – it is typically held in the four-deck-high main atrium, so you can come and go as you pleasewithout having to stand in line to have your photograph taken with the captain. However, cruising aboard large ships such as this one has become increasingly an onboard revenue-based product. The in-your-face art auctions are overbearing, and the paintings, lithographs and faux, framed pictures strewn throughout the ship and clashing irritatingly with the ship's interior decor are an annoying intrusion into what should be a holiday, not a cruise inside a floating "art" emporium. There are no cushioned pads for the sunloungers on the open lido decks.

The swimming pools are small for so many passengers, and the pool deck is cluttered with white, plastic sunloungers, without cushioned pads. Waiting for tenders in anchor ports can prove irritating, but typical of large ship operations. Charging for use of the machines and washing powder in the self-service launderette is trifling.

As aboard most large ships, if you live in the top suites, you'll be well attended; if not, you'll just be one of a large number of passengers. *Dawn Princess* (like sister *Sun Princess*) is now dedicated to the Australian cruise region.

ACCOMMODATION. The brochure shows that there are 28 different cabin grades: 20 outside-view and 8 interior (no view) cabins. Although the standard outside-view and interior (no view) cabins are a little small, they are well designed and functional in layout, and have earth tone colors accentuated by splashes of color from the bedspreads. Proportionately, there are quite a lot of interior (no view) cabins. Many of the outside-view cabins have private balconies, and all seem to be quite well soundproofed, although the balcony partition is not the floor-to-ceiling type, so you can hear your neighbors clearly (or smell their smoke). Note that the balconies are very narrow, only just large enough for two small chairs, and there is no dedicated lighting.

A reasonable amount of closet and abundant drawer and other storage space is provided in all cabins – adequate for a 7-night cruise, as are a television and refrigerator. Each night a chocolate will appear on your pillow. The cabin bathrooms are practical, and come complete with most of the things needed, although they really are tight spaces, and are best described as one person at-a-time units. They do, however, have a decent shower enclosure, a small amount of shelving for your personal toiletries, real glasses, a hairdryer and a bathrobe.

The largest accommodation is in six suites, two on each of three decks located at the stern of the ship, with large private balcony (536–754 sq.ft/49.8–21.3 sq.meters, including balcony). These are well laid out, and have large bathrooms with two sinks, a Jacuzzi bathtub, and a separate shower enclosure. The bedroom has generous amounts of wood accenting and detailing, indented ceilings, and television sets in both bedroom and lounge areas. The suites also have a dining room table and four chairs.

The 32 mini-suites (374–536 sq.ft/34.7–49.7 sq.meters) typically have two lower beds that convert into a queen-sized bed. There is a separate bedroom/sleeping area with vanity desk, and a lounge with sofa and coffee table, indented ceilings with generous amounts of wood accenting and detailing, walk-in closet, and larger bathroom with Jacuzzi bathtub and separate shower enclosure.

There are 19 wheelchair-accessible cabins, which measure 213–305 sq. meters/19.7–28.2 sq.ft and are a mix of 7 outside view and 12 interior (no view) cabins.

Princess Cruises has CNN, CNBC, ESPN and TNT on the in-cabin TV system (when available, depending on area).

CUISINE. There are two main dining rooms of asymmetrical design, Florentine and Venetian – both non-smoking, as are all dining rooms aboard the ships of Princess Cruises, and each seating about 500. They are located adjacent to the two lower levels of the four-deck high atrium lobby. Each has its own galley and each is split into multi-tier sections, which help create a feeling of intimacy, although there is a lot of noise from the waiter stations, which are adjacent to many tables. Breakfast and lunch are provided in an open seating arrangement, while dinner is in two seatings.

On any given 7-day cruise, a typical menu cycle will include a Sailaway Dinner, Captain's Welcome Dinner, Chef's Dinner, Italian Dinner, French Dinner, Captain's Gala Dinner, and Landfall Dinner. The wine list is reasonable, but not good, and the company has, sadly, seen fit to eliminate all wine waiters. Note that 15% is added to all beverage bills, including wines.

For some really good meat, however, consider the Sterling Steakhouse; it's for those who want to taste four different cuts of Angus beef from the popular "Sterling Silver" brand of USDA prime meats – Filet Mignon, New York Strip, Porterhouse, and Rib-Eye – all presented on a silver tray.

There is also a barbecue chicken option, plus the usual baked potato or French fries as accompaniments. This is available as an alternative to the dining rooms, between 6.30pm and 9.30pm only, at an additional charge of $8 per person. However, it is not, as you might expect, a separate, intimate dining room, but is located in a section of the Horizon Buffet, with its own portable bar and some decorative touches to set it apart (from the regular Horizon Buffet).

The Horizon Buffet is open 24 hours a day, and, at night, has an informal dinner setting with sit-down waiter service; a small bistro menu is also available. The buffet displays are, for the most part, quite repetitious, but better than they have been in the past few years (there is no real finesse in presentation, however, as plastic plates are provided, instead of trays). The cabin service menu is very limited, and presentation of the food items featured is poor.

There is also a patisserie (for cappuccino/espresso coffees and pastries), a wine/caviar bar, and a pizzeria with cobblestone floors and wrought-iron decorative features, and excellent pizzas (there are six to choose from).

ENTERTAINMENT. There are two showlounges (both theatre and cabaret style). The main one, Princess Theater, has a sloping floor, with aisle-style seating (as found in shoreside movie theaters) that is well tiered, and with good sight lines to the raised stage from most of the 500 seats.

The second showlounge (Vista Lounge), located at the aft end of the ship, has cabaret entertainment, and also acts as a lecture and presentation room. Princess Cruises has a good stable of regular cabaret acts to draw from, so there should be something for almost all tastes.

SPA/FITNESS. A glass-walled health spa complex is located high atop the ship and includes a gymnasium with the latest high-tech machines. One swimming pool is "suspended" aft between two decks. There are two other pools, although they are not large for the size of the ship.

Sports facilities are located in an open-air sports deck positioned inside the ship's funnel and adaptable for basketball, volleyball, badminton or paddle tennis. Joggers can exercise on the wrap-around open Promenade Deck.

● **For more extensive general information about the Princess Cruises experience, see pages 148–51.**

Delphin
★★★

Size: ....Small Ship	Passengers	Cabin Voltage: ....220 volts
Tonnage: 16,214	(lower beds/all berths): 466/556	Elevators: 2
Lifestyle: ....Standard	Passenger Space Ratio	Casino (gaming tables): ....No
Cruise Line: Delphin Cruises/Hansa Cruises	(lower beds/all berths): 35.6/29.8	Slot Machines: ....No
Former Names: *Kazakhstan II/Belorussiya*	Crew/Passenger Ratio	Swimming Pools (outdoors): 1
Builder: ....Wartsila (Finland)	(lower beds/all berths): 1.9/2.3	Swimming Pools (indoors): 0
Original Cost: ....$25 million	Cabins (total): 233	Whirlpools: 0
Entered Service: .....Jan 1975/Dec 1993	Size Range (sq ft/m): 150.0–492.0/	Fitness Center: ....Yes
Registry: ....The Bahamas	14.0–45.7	Sauna/Steam Room: ....Yes/Yes
Length (ft/m): 512.5/156.24	Cabins (outside view): 128	Massage: ....Yes
Beam (ft/m): 71.8/21.90	Cabins (interior/no view): 105	Self-Service Launderette: ....Yes
Draft (ft/m): 20.3/6.20	Cabins (for one person): 0	Dedicated Cinema/Seats: ....No
Propulsion/Propellers: diesel (13,250kW)/2	Cabins (with private balcony): 0	Library: ....Yes
Passenger Decks: 8	Cabins (wheelchair accessible): 0	
Total Crew: 234	Wheelchair accessibility ....None	

OVERALL SCORE: 1,121 OUT OF A POSSIBLE 2,000 POINTS

OVERVIEW. *Delphin* is a reasonably smart-looking cruise ship (originally built as one of a series of five vessels in the same class), and is topped by a square funnel. It was refitted and refurbished throughout following a shipyard rollover incident (when it was known as *Belorussiya*). The ship's original car decks have long been converted into useful public rooms and additional cabins, and the former car loading ramps on the vessel's stern are now used for loading stores.

When the ship last underwent a major refurbishment, several new facilities were added; these improved almost all the public areas and added better health/fitness and spa facilities and an improved lido deck. But the circular "swimming" pool is small, and is best described as a "dip" pool. The promenade decks outdoors are teak-decked.

The interior decor is quite tasteful and warm, with colors that do not jar the senses. Flower bouquets and colorful artwork enhance the otherwise plain decor throughout.

Delphin will provide a very comfortable cruise experience for those German-speaking passengers looking for destination-intensive cruises, in comfortable, though not luxurious surroundings, at an extremely attractive price. It is not a luxury product, nor does it pretend to be. This is a good, basic product that represents very good value for money. The ship's interiors are always in excellent shape and spotlessly clean.

Hansa Cruises attracts many repeat passengers because of the destination-intensive itineraries and decent level of service. The company continues to spend money on little refinements throughout the ship, which are appreciated by

BERLITZ'S RATINGS

	Possible	Achieved
Ship	500	252
Accommodation	200	111
Food	400	233
Service	400	230
Entertainment	100	60
Cruise	400	235

those loyal repeat passengers. All port taxes and insurance are included. The currency on board is the euro.

A negative point is that there are many pillars throughout the public rooms, and these inhibit sight lines. The ceiling height is low in most public rooms, and the stairways are steep, with steps that are short and difficult to replace without major structural changes (a leftover from the ship's former life as a passenger ferry). The gangway is quite narrow. There is no walk-around promenade deck outdoors and no observation lounge/bar with forward-facing views over the ship's bows.

SUITABLE FOR: *Delphin* is best suited to German-speaking couples and single travelers of mature years who are seeking good value for money in a ship with traditional, quite comfortable (but not pretentious or luxurious) surroundings, at a modest price, with well planned itineraries.

ACCOMMODATION. There are several grades of accommodation to choose from. Typically, the higher the deck, the more expensive will be the accommodation.

The Boat Deck suites (located forward) are spacious and well equipped, with an abundance of drawers and good closet space, and all feature blond wood furniture, and a refrigerator. The bathrooms are very spacious, and come with full-sized bathtubs and large toiletries cabinet; bathrobes are also provided.

All the other outside-view and interior (no view) cabins are very compact units, yet adequate (but not for an around-the-world cruise), although there is little drawer space, and storage space is tight on the long cruises this ship often undertakes. All beds have European duvets, and all cabins receive fresh flowers each cruise. The bathrooms are small, but there is a decent amount of space for toiletries.

CUISINE. The single main dining room, the Pacific Restaurant, has 554 seats. It has a high ceiling, large ocean-view picture windows, pleasing decor, and seats all passengers in one seating – so there is no need to hurry over meals.

In general, the food is attractively presented – better now that the catering is actively managed in-house – and the variety of foods available is quite sound. The choice is good (with a heavy reliance on meat and game dishes), although selections for vegetarians are also available. There is a wine list with a good selection at moderate prices and sekt (sparkling wine) is provided at breakfast. The gala buffet is very good. Service comes with a smile from attractive German-speaking waitresses.

For casual meals, breakfast and lunch buffets can be taken in The Lido. The food provided is decent enough, with reasonable choice, although there is some repetition.

ENTERTAINMENT. The showlounge is a single level room that is really designed for cabaret-style entertainment. Sight lines are quite good from most seats, although it is obstructed in some seats by some pillars.

SPA/FITNESS. The spa facilities are located on the lowest deck of the ship, while a fitness room and beauty salon are located on different decks, so there is no cohesive spa as such. However, in the facility on the lowest deck is a sauna, steam room, solarium, and massage rooms. In addition, there is a dialysis station for up to 26 persons for special cruises when dialysis technicians are provided – they are not available on all cruises. Sports participants will find volleyball, basketball, and table tennis.

WHERE NAUTICAL EXPRESSIONS COME FROM

If you've ever wondered where some terms or phrases came from, you have only to look to the sea, ships, and seamen.

Scuttlebutt

A small drinking ladle with scuttles or holes in it to discourage sailors from idle chit chat (scuttlebutt) around the water barrel while their water ration dribbled back into the barrel. Today it usually refers to gossip or the latest news concerning a given situation or person.

Shape up

A helmsman working off a lee shore would point up and "shape up" to his course in order to avoid danger. In modern-day usage it is used similar

sense to mean "smarten up" or "pull yourself together."

Showing your true colors

Early warships often carried flags from many nations on board in order to elude or deceive the enemy. The rules of civilized warfare called for all ships to hoist their true national ensigns before firing a shot. Someone who finally "shows his true colors" is acting like a warship, which hails another ship flying one flag, but then hoisted its own flag when the vessel got within firing range.

Skyscraper

A small, triangular shaped sail that was set above the mains on the old

square-riggers to try to scrape (catch) more wind in areas of calm air. The term came ashore to represent anything that was tall enough to "scrape" the sky.

Slush fund

The fat obtained by "scraping the bottom of the barrel" by the ship's cook and secreted away in his "slush fund" for selling ashore to candle makers, tanneries, etc. Today the words describe a rainy-day fund or cash reserve. Another version of the term's derivation is that the grease (slush) from frying the salt pork on a voyage was kept and sold when the ship returned to port. The money raised was put into a "fund" for the crew.

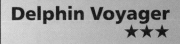

Delphin Voyager
★★★

Size: . . . . .Mid-Size Ship	Passenger Decks: 8	Cabins (with private balcony): 177
Tonnage: .21,884	Total Crew: 250	Cabins (wheelchair accessible): 2
Lifestyle: . . . . .Standard	Passengers	Wheelchair accessibility . . . . .Fair
Cruise Line: . . . . .Delphin Cruises	(lower beds/all berths): 650/650	Cabin Current: . . . . .110 volts
Former Names: . . . . .Orient Venus	Passenger Space Ratio	Elevators: 4
Builder: . . . . .Ishikawajima Heavy	(lower beds/all berths): 33.6/33.6	Casino (gaming tables): . . . . .No
Industries (Japan)	Crew/Passenger Ratio	Slot Machines: .No
Original Cost: . . . .$150 million	(lower beds/all berths): 2.6/2.6	Swimming Pools (outdoors): 1
Entered Service: . . . . .July 1990/Apr 2007	Cabins (total): 325	Swimming Pools (indoors): 0
Registry: . . . . .The Bahamas	Size Range (sq ft/m): 182.9–592.0/	Whirlpools: 0
Length (ft/m): 570.8/174.00	17.0–55.0	Self-Service Launderette: . . . . .Yes
Beam (ft/m): 78.7/24.00	Cabins (outside view): 269	Dedicated Cinema/Seats: . . . . .No
Draft (ft/m): 21.3/6.52	Cabins (interior/no view): 56	Library: . . . . .Yes
Propulsion/Propellers:diesel (13,830 kW)/2	Cabins (for one person): 0	

BERLITZ'S OVERALL SCORE: 1,243 OUT OF A POSSIBLE 2,000 POINTS

OVERVIEW. *Delphin Voyager* was the first cruise ship built (as *Orient Venus*) for its former Japanese owners, Venus Cruise. This is a conventional-shaped ship with a pleasant enough profile. There is a reasonable amount of open deck and sunbathing space, including an expansive amount of open deck space for sunbathing, aft of funnel.

Great views can be had from the Panorama Bar, a large observation lounge wrapped around the funnel housing – although there is no elevator access for disabled passengers, a chair-lift is provided. There is a good array of public rooms with tasteful, European decor, including a three-deck-high entrance lobby, the focal point of communication. Most public rooms arc set on one deck, providing good horizontal flow. The cruises provide good value for money, and drink prices are very reasonable. The onboard currency is the euro.

SUITABLE FOR: *Delphin Voyager* is best suited to German-speaking couples and single travelers of mature years who enjoy traveling in very comfortable surroundings, and who enjoy good food and service, all at a moderate cost. It offers a superb cruise and seminar/learning experience.

ACCOMMODATION. There are eight cabin grades, the three highest designated as "suite" grades. The standard cabins have decor best described as light, but plain, with a reasonable amount of closet space; however, the drawer space is quite limited.

The largest suites (there are three) have an expansive lounge area with large, plush armchairs, coffee table, and window-side chairs and drinks table, large windows, and a

BERLITZ'S RATINGS

	Possible	Achieved
Ship	500	331
Accommodation	200	128
Food	400	229
Service	400	241
Entertainment	100	61
Cruise	400	253

larger private balcony. There is a separate sleeping room (curtained off from the living room) with twin- or queen-sized bed, vanity/office desk, and larger bathroom.

All grades have a flat-screen color television set, telephone, hairdryer, and refrigerator. All cabins have a shower, with the exception of the three suites, which feature a bathtub and separate shower. 36 cabins have life-boat obstructed views.

New cabins were installed in a 2007 refit, but the original ones didn't receive much attention. So it's best to book one of the new cabins.

CUISINE/DINING. The main dining room – single seating with assigned tables – is quite attractive. It's actually split into two sections: the Atlantic Restaurant, located on the port side in a "railway carriage" format, and the Pacific Restaurant, located aft. There's plenty of space around the dining tables. The aft section of the Pacific Restaurant is perhaps the most desirable section, with its views over the stern. The table settings are standard, and the wine glasses are small. The food is average, and it certainly wouldn't win any awards – but everything is done to a tight budget.

ENTERTAINMENT. The horseshoe-shaped Show Lounge is a single level room, and has good sightlines to the platform stage. On most cruises, special featured entertainers are brought on board from ashore (singers, instrumentalists, storytellers, dance champions, and others).

SPA/FITNESS. There is a small spa, which consists of a gymnasium, saunas, and treatment rooms. There is also a special room with five fully-equipped dialysis stations for special cruises, when a dialysis technician is on board.

Deutschland
NOT RATED

Size:.....................Small Ship	Passenger Decks:...................7	Cabins (with private balcony):.........2
Tonnage: 22,400	Total Crew: 270	Cabins (wheelchair accessible): 1
Lifestyle: ....Premium	Passengers	Wheelchair accessibility ....Fair
Cruise Line: ....Peter Deilmann Reederei	(lower beds/all berths):........548/560	Cabin Current: ....230 volts
Former Names: ....none	Passenger Space Ratio	Elevators: 3
Builder: ...Howaldswerke Deutsche Werft	(lower beds/all berths):.......40.8/40.0	Casino (gaming tables): ....No
Original Cost: ....DM 212 million	Crew/Passenger Ratio	Slot Machines: ....No
Entered Service: ....May 1998	(lower beds/all berths):..........2.0/2.0	Swimming Pools (outdoors): 1
Registry:.....................Germany	Cabins (total): 294	Swimming Pools (indoors): 1
Length (ft/m): 574.1/175.0	Size Range (sq ft/m): 129.1–365.9/	Whirlpools: 0
Beam (ft/m): 75.4/23.0	12.0–34.0	Self-Service Launderette: ....No
Draft (ft/m): 19.0/5.8	Cabins (outside view): 220	Dedicated Cinema/Seats: Yes/83
Propulsion/Propellers: ....diesel	Cabins (interior/no view): 74	Library: ....Yes
(12,300 kW)/2	Cabins (for one person): 36	

OVERALL SCORE: NYR OUT OF A POSSIBLE 2,000 POINTS

OVERVIEW. *Deutschland,* now over 12 years old but in fine condition, is an important vessel for German-speaking passengers seeking a traditional ship. It has an angular, low-in-the-water profile that is not particularly handsome, and a large, single, squat, traditional funnel. The ship, built in sections by four shipyards, was assembled in Kiel, Germany. It is well maintained and kept very clean.

Although there is no wrap-around promenade deck outdoors as such (it's full of chairs around the central section where a swimming pool is located), you can walk along some of the open space (although there are windbreakers to negotiate). There are also port and starboard mid-ship walking decks under the inboard lifeboats. There is, in fact, a decent amount of open deck and sunbathing space for a ship of this size, including three aft decks for open-air lovers, and real teakwood deck chairs, with thick royal blue cushioned pads.

The Lido Deck has sides covered by canvas shading and white support pillars – like the ones you would find on seaside piers in England – as a setting for the outdoor swimming pool. The Lido Deck is a self-contained deck that has not only the pool, but also the casual Lido Buffet restaurant and Lido Terrasse Cafe. One could spend all day outdoors on this deck without having to dress to go indoors to eat. There is also a small waterfall aft of the pool.

The ship is laid out in a classic symmetrical pattern, and the interior decor has been successfully designed to re-create and reproduce the atmosphere of the ocean liners of the 1920s. The ship is beautifully decorated throughout (some might say overly decorated), with rich, dark woods and intricate brass and wrought-iron staircases that remind one of what were once called "gentlemen's clubs." There

BERLITZ'S RATINGS		
	Possible	Achieved
Ship	500	NYR
Accommodation	200	NYR
Food	400	NYR
Service	400	NYR
Entertainment	100	NYR
Cruise	400	NYR

is so much detail in the decoration work, and especially in the ornate ceilings, and cleaning it all is rather labor-intensive. There are quite a number of real statues, which don't seem to fit well aboard a cruise ship, but there are also many works of art on display.

There's a good range of public rooms and spaces, although these have been possible only by making the cabins smaller than one would expect of a ship of this size. The ship has an interesting, eclectic decor from different periods, as well as a wide assortment of cabin sizes, configurations and grades. The passenger mix is also somewhat varied.

There are two favorite drinking places: Zum Alten Fritz (Old Fritz) Bar, with dark wood interiors and Belle Epoque ambiance; and the Lili Marleen Salon (adjacent to the Berlin Restaurant), with mahogany channeled ceiling. Another nice public room is the Lido Terrace, which would have made a superb observation lounge had the designers extended it to the forward extremes of the deck. It is reminiscent of the winter gardens aboard the early transatlantic liners, and a delightful place to read or take afternoon tea.

The late Peter Deilmann's personal touch in the heavily detailed interiors is evident everywhere. *Deutschland* is registered under the German flag, but is actually placed under a second German register, which allows for the employment of many non-German staff. Thus, you will find Filipinos and other nationalities in the hotel service areas (the friendliness of the staff is good). The currency aboard is the euro, and the ship operates cashless cruising – charges must be settled on the last day of the cruise, when all purchases must, inconveniently, be made in cash.

Although the ship absorbs passengers well, the space

ratio could be better. The onboard product is generally sound, with attentive service, but the food and catering side of the operation could be improved. While the interiors are very attractive, the vessel does not come close to ships such as *Europa, Silver Shadow*, and *Silver Whisper*, with their much larger suites/cabins, open-seating dining (except *Europa*, which has open seating for breakfast and lunch, and assigned tables for dinner), and their abundance of cabins with private balconies. Smoking is permitted only on open decks. There is no internet center.

Just two suites have private balconies; most other cabins are very small when compared to other ships in the luxury and premium sectors of the international market. International passengers should note that the entertainment is almost totally in German; in fact, the whole ship is geared almost exclusively to German tastes.

SUITABLE FOR: *Deutschland* is best suited to German-speaking couples, and single travelers of mature years who seek a good value for money holiday in a very traditional cruise ship setting, with appealing itineraries and destinations, good food and attentive service. It could also appeal to English-speaking travelers used to being in European surroundings with a heavy German-speaking influence, and who can do without entertainment, onboard activities or shore excursions in English. I would not recommend the ship for children, due to the lack of facilities for them.

ACCOMMODATION. There are 10 categories (the higher the deck, the higher the cost). There are 18 outside view suites, 189 outside view doubles, 17 outside view single cabins; 12 interior (no view) doubles, 50 interior (no view) single cabins.

While many cabins are disappointingly small, all are furnished in fancy bird's-eye maple, and all the ceilings are fine, one-piece units, unlike the metal strip ceilings of most contemporary cruise vessels, and come with molded coving and ornamentation. The closet and drawer space is quite generous, and the attention to detail is very good. All beds have duvets and pillows. All cabins have a TV set, direct-dial satellite telephone, mini-bar/refrigerator, and real cabin keys (not plastic cards) are provided for all passengers. Many cabins have only one electrical outlet.

The bathrooms are also generously appointed, with a pink marble sink, gold anodized fittings, gilt-edged mirrors, hairdryer, and ample space for one's personal toiletry items. There is an electrical power outlet for shavers, with both 110 and 230 volts. Bathrobes are provided for all passengers.

Accommodations designated as suites (of which there are two grades) are reasonably large, with a living area that contains a couch, coffee table and two chairs; the bathroom has a full-size tub (all other cabins have showers only). Only the Executive Suites and Owner's Suites are (sensibly) located in the center of the ship, and each has a small private balcony. There is one wheelchair-accessible cabin (8042).

CUISINE. The main restaurant (Berlin), with 300 seats (and two seatings), is a very pleasant room, and all the chairs have armrests, although space for serving at window-side tables is limited, and the hard backs of the chairs are not really very comfortable.

There are tables for two, four, six or eight, and two seatings for dinner. Two cold buffet bars for cold cuts of meat, cheese and salad items (either your waiter can obtain the food for you or you can choose it yourself) are featured for breakfast and lunch. Overall, the cuisine is quite creative (with lots of courses, with small portions of nouvelle cuisine), with a wide variety of choice and good taste, although it is not really memorable (the desserts, however, are extremely good). The place settings are extensive.

The Restaurant Vierjahreszeiten (Four Seasons), with 104 seats, is an intimate dining room (principally for suite occupants and for à la carte dining, for which a reservation is necessary). There is much detailing and ornamentation in the decor, and the ornate ceiling lamps and indented ceiling coving create an elegant ambiance that is relatively intimate.

There are tables for two, four or six. There is also a small private dining room (the Chancellor Room) with a large oval table which seats 10–12 (ideal for those special occasions and celebrations).

The extensive wine list includes a fine selection of wines from Germany and Austria, although the choice of wines from other countries is very limited. Eating in this restaurant takes considerably longer than in the Berlin Restaurant, and is best for those seeking an evening of fine dining and conversation.

The Lido Restaurant is the ship's casual dining venue. It has large ocean-view windows on two sides and a centrally located, multi-section self-serve buffet station. Additionally, there is a Lido Terrasse, at the stern, with windows on three sides. It is set on two slightly different levels, houses the ship's library, and has statuary and a relaxing, garden conservatory-like setting. This room also has a bar, plus elegant tea (and coffee) service.

ENTERTAINMENT. The Kaisersaal (Emperor's Saloon) is the ship's showlounge. It is a galleried period room with red velveteen chairs and is more like a ballroom than showlounge. It is reminiscent of a small opera house, and has a beautiful, huge central chandelier.

However, sight lines are obstructed from some seats (on both upper and lower seating levels) by many large marble-effect pillars. The entertainment is geared to German tastes, and is mostly in German.

SPA/FITNESS. The main spa area is on Deck 3, and this includes a small indoor swimming pool (with a statue of a female diver at one end), sauna, solarium, thalassotherapy baths, and massage/body therapy rooms; there is also a dialysis station.

Deck 6 has a fitness/sport center (with a few exercise machines), a sauna with a sea view, and a steam room. A beauty salon is in yet another location, on Deck 7.

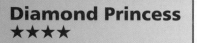

Diamond Princess
★★★★

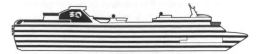

Size: ....Large Resort Ship	Passenger Decks: 13	Cabins (with private balcony): 750
Tonnage: 115,875	Total Crew: 1,238	Cabins (wheelchair accessible): 28
Lifestyle: ....Standard	Passengers	(18 outside/10 interior)
Cruise Line: ....Princess Cruises	(lower beds/all berths): 2,674/3,100	Wheelchair accessibility ....Good
Former Names: ....none	Passenger Space Ratio	Cabin Current: ....110 volts
Builder: Mitsubishi Heavy Industries (Japan)	(lower beds/all berths): 43.3/37.3	Elevators: 14
Original Cost: ....$400 million	Crew/Passenger Ratio	Casino (gaming tables): ....Yes
Entered Service: ....February 2004	(lower beds/all berths): 2.1/2.5	Slot Machines: ....Yes
Registry: ....Bermuda	Cabins (total): 1,337	Swimming Pools (outdoors): 4
Length (ft/m): 951.4/290.00	Size Range (sq ft/m): 168–1,329.3/	Swimming Pools (indoors): 0
Beam (ft/m): 123.0/37.50	15.6–123.5	Whirlpools: 9
Draft (ft/m): 26.4/8.05	Cabins (outside view): 1,000	Self-Service Launderette: ....Yes
Propulsion/Propellers: ....gas turbine (25	Cabins (interior/no view): 337	Dedicated Cinema/Seats: ....No
MW)/2 azimuthing pods (21,000 kW each)	Cabins (for one person): 0	Library: ....Yes

OVERALL SCORE: 1,544 OUT OF A POSSIBLE 2,000 POINTS

OVERVIEW. *Diamond Princess* has an instantly recognizable funnel due to two jet engine-like pods that sit high up on its structure but really are mainly for decoration. This is the first ship to be constructed by a Japanese shipyard for Princess Cruises (sister ship: *Sapphire Princess*). The ship is similar in size and internal layout to *Golden Princess, Grand Princess* and *Star Princess* (although of a slightly greater beam). Unlike its half-sister ships, however, all

BERLITZ'S RATINGS

	Possible	Achieved
Ship	500	431
Accommodation	200	168
Food	400	256
Service	400	293
Entertainment	100	82
Cruise	400	314

of which had a "spoiler" (containing a discotheque) located aft of the funnel, this has thankfully been removed from both *Diamond Princess* and *Sapphire Princess*, and has been replaced by a more sensible (and less weighty) aft-facing nightclub/discotheque structure (Skywalkers Nightclub) set around the base of the adjoining the funnel structure. The view from the nightclub overlooks aft-facing cascading decks and children's pool.

In December 2002, while the ship was under construction in the shipyard, a fire broke out on Deck 5. This lasted for 20 hours and burned some (548,980 sq ft (51,000 sq. meters) from Deck through Deck 13. The ship's hull was switched with that of identical sister *Sapphire Princess*, which was also under construction in the same yard at the same time. Consequently, the ship's debut was delayed from July 2003 to February 2004.

Diamond Princess is the first of the "Grand Class" ships to have a "pod" propulsion system installed *(for details, see page 29)*. Electrical power is provided by a combination of four diesel and one gas turbine (CODAG) unit; the diesel engines are located in the engine room, while the gas turbine unit is located in the ship's funnel housing, on each side of which is a cosmetic pod that resembles a jet aircraft

engine. Four areas focus on swimming pools; one of these is two decks high and is covered by a retractable glass dome, itself an extension of the funnel housing.

Unlike the outside decks, there is plenty of space inside the ship (but there are also plenty of passengers), and a wide array of public rooms, with many "intimate" (this being a relative word) spaces and places to play and enjoy. The passenger flow has been well thought out, and works with little congestion. The decor is attractive, with lots of earth tones. An extensive collection of art works has been chosen, and this complements the interior design and colors well.

Like half-sisters *Golden Princess, Grand Princess* and *Star Princess*, this ship also has a Wedding Chapel (a live web-cam can relay ceremonies via the internet). The ship's captain can legally marry (American) couples, due to the ship's Bermuda registry and a special dispensation (which should be verified when in the planning stage, according to where you reside). Princess Cruises offers three wedding packages – Pearl, Emerald, Diamond; the fee includes registration and official marriage certificate. The "Hearts & Minds" chapel is useful for "renewal of vows" ceremonies.

Gaming lovers should enjoy what is one of the largest casinos at sea (Grand Casino), with more than 260 slot machines; there are blackjack, craps and roulette tables, plus newer games such as Let It Ride Bonus, Spanish 21 and Caribbean Draw Progressive. But the highlight could well be the specially linked slot machines that provide a combined payout.

Other features include a library/CD-Rom computer room, and a separate card room. Ship lovers should enjoy the wood-paneled Wheelhouse Bar, finely decorated with memorabilia and ship models tracing part of parent company P&O's history. Aft of the International Dining Room is the Wake View Bar, with a spiral stairway that leads down to a great viewing spot for those who want to watch the ship's wake (like the one aboard the rivercruise stern paddle-wheeler *American Queen*); it is reached from the back of Club Fusion, on Promenade Deck. A high-tech hospital is provided, with live SeaMed tele-medicine link-ups with specialists at the Cedars-Sinai Medical Center in Los Angeles available for emergency help.

For youngsters and teenagers there is a two-deck-high playroom, teen room, and a host of specially trained counselors. Children have their own pools, hot tubs, and open deck area at the stern of the ship (away from adult areas).

If you are not used to large ships, it will take you some time to find your way around this one, despite the company's claim that this vessel offers passengers a "small ship feel, big ship choice."

The cabin bath towels are small, and drawer space is limited. There are no butlers – even for the top grade suites (which are not really large in comparison to similar suites aboard some other ships). Cabin attendants have too many cabins to look after (typically 20), which does not translate to fine personal service.

You'll have to live with the many extra charge items (such as for ice cream, and freshly squeezed orange juice) and activities (such as yoga, group exercise bicycling and kick boxing classes at $10 per session, not to mention $4 per hour for group babysitting services – at the time this book was completed). There's also a charge for using the washers and dryers in the self-service launderettes.

ACCOMMODATION. All passengers receive turndown service and chocolates on pillows each night, as well as bathrobes (on request) and toiletry amenity kits (larger for suite/mini-suite occupants). A hairdryer is provided in all cabins, sensibly located at the vanity desk unit in the living area. All bathrooms are tiled and have a decent amount of open shelf storage space for personal toiletries. Princess Cruises has BBC World, CNN, CNBC, ESPN and TNT on the in-cabin color TV system (when available, depending on cruise area).

The majority of the outside cabins on Emerald Deck have views obstructed by the lifeboats. Sadly, there are no cabins for singles. Your name is typically placed outside your suite or cabin – making it simple for delivery service personnel but also limiting your privacy. There is 24-hour room service (but some items on the room service menu are not available during early morning hours). Most balcony suites and cabins can be overlooked both from the navigation bridge wing. Cabins with balconies on Baja, Caribe, and Dolphin decks are also overlooked by passengers on balconies on the deck above.

CUISINE. All dining rooms are located on one of two decks. There are five principal dining rooms with themed decor and cuisine – smaller than the three dining rooms on the similarly sized *Golden Princess*, *Grand Princess* and *Star Princess*

because two dining rooms have been halved to become four; they are Sterling Steakhouse (for steak and grilled meats), Vivaldi (Italian fare), Santa Fe (southwestern USA cuisine), Pacific Moon (Asian cuisine) and International (the largest, located aft, with two seatings and "traditional" cuisine). These offer a mix of two seatings (with seating assigned according to the location of your cabin) and "anytime dining" (where you choose when and with whom you want to eat).

All dining rooms are non-smoking and are split into sections in a non-symmetrical design that breaks what are quite large spaces into many smaller sections, for better ambience and less noise pollution.

Specially designed dinnerware and good quality linens and silverware are featured: Dudson of England (dinnerware), Frette Egyptian cotton table linens, and silverware by Hepp of Germany.

Alternative dining options: Sabatini's is an informal eatery (reservations required; cover charge $20 per person). It features an eight-course meal, including Italian-style pizzas and pastas, with a variety of sauces, as well as Italian-style entrées (including tiger prawns and lobster tail – all provided with flair and entertainment by the waiters (by reservation only; the cover charge is $20 per person). The cuisine in this eatery is potentially better than in all the other dining rooms, with better quality ingredients and more attention to presentation, taste and delivery.

A poolside hamburger grill and pizza bar (no additional charge) are additional dining spots for casual bites, while extra charges will apply if you order items to eat at either the coffee bar/patisserie, or the caviar/champagne bar.

Other casual meals can be taken in the Horizon Court, open 24 hours a day, with large ocean-view on port and starboard sides and direct access to the two main swimming pools and lido deck (there is no finesse in presentation, however, and plastic plates, not trays, are provided).

ENTERTAINMENT. The Princess Theatre (showlounge) spans two decks and has comfortable seating on both main and balcony levels. It has $3 million in sound and light equipment, plus a 9-piece orchestra.

A second large entertainment lounge, Club Fusion, features cabaret acts acts at night, and lectures, bingo and horse racing during the day. A third entertainment lounge can also host cabaret acts and dance bands. Many other lounges and bars have live music, and a number of male dance hosts act as partners for women traveling alone.

SPA/FITNESS. The Lotus Spa complex, which has Japanese-style decor, surrounds one of the swimming pools (you can have a massage or other spa treatment in an ocean-view treatment room). Lotus Spa treatments include Chakra hot stone massage, Asian Lotus ritual (featuring massage with reflexology, reiki and shiatsu massage), deep-tissue sports therapy massage, lime and ginger salt glow, wild strawberry back cleanse, and seaweed mud wraps.

● **For more extensive general information about the Princess Cruises experience is like, see pages 148–51.**

Discovery
★★★

Size: . . . . .Mid-Size Ship	Passenger Decks: 8	Cabins (with private balcony): 0
Tonnage: .21,186	Total Crew: 350	Cabins (wheelchair accessible): 2
Lifestyle: . . . . .Standard	Passengers	Wheelchair accessibility . . . . .Fair
Cruise Line: . . . . . . .Voyages of Discovery	(lower beds/all berths): 710/796	Cabin Current: . . . . .110 and 220 volts
Former Names: .Platinum, Hyundai Pungak,	Passenger Space Ratio	Elevators: 4
Island Princess, Island Venture	(lower beds/all berths): 29.8/26.6	Casino (gaming tables): . . . . .Yes
Builder: Rheinstahl Nordseewerke (Germany)	Crew/Passenger Ratio	Slot Machines: . . . . .Yes
Original Cost: . . . .$25 million	(lower beds/all berths): 2.4/2.6	Swimming Pools (outdoors): 2
Entered Service: . . . . . .Feb 1972/May 2003	Cabins (total): 355	Swimming Pools (indoors): 0
Registry: . . . . .Bermuda	Size Range (sq ft/m): 125.9–441.3/	Whirlpools: 2
Length (ft/m): 553.6/168.74	11.7–41.0	Self-Service Launderette: . . . . .No
Beam (ft/m): 80.7/24.6	Cabins (outside view): 283	Dedicated Cinema/Seats: Yes/129
Draft (ft/m): 25.2/7.7	Cabins (interior/no view): 72	Library: . . . . .Yes
Propulsion/Propellers: diesel (13,400 kW)/2	Cabins (for one person): 0	

OVERALL SCORE: 1,111 OUT OF A POSSIBLE 2,000 POINTS

OVERVIEW. *Discovery*, formerly operated from 1972 to 1999 by Princess Cruises, has a very attractive traditional ship profile and well balanced, somewhat rounded exterior styling. As the former *Island Princess*, it was, together with sister ship *Pacific Princess* (presently *Pacific*), one of the pair of original "Love Boats" in the American television series *The Love Boat*. Hyundai Asan Cruises acquired the ship in 1999, and operated cruises from South Korea to North Korea.

In 2001, the entrepreneur Gerry Herrod, who formerly founded the long defunct Ocean Cruise Lines, and Orient Lines, bought the handsome ship and provided it under a lease-purchase scheme to Voyages of Discovery, part of the UK's All-Leisure Group. He then spent $10 million refurbishing and updating it for its present cruising role under the brand name of Voyages of Discovery, principally for the British market. For the winter season, the ship carries five Zodiac inflatable shore landing craft.

One of the ship's two outdoor swimming pools has a glass dome (magrodome) cover, which can be used in inclement weather conditions. There is no walk-around promenade deck outdoors, however.

Inside, the public areas are quite spacious considering the size of the ship, and there are numerous public rooms (some with high ceilings), with reasonably wide passageways. These include a lobby with mezzanine level and curved staircase (several shops and offices are on the upper level), and the Discovery Lounge, located aft, has a two-deck high glass wall overlooking the aft deck. There's an internet center, equipped with six computer workstations, a library with 5,000 books provided by the Marine Society,

BERLITZ'S RATINGS

	Possible	Achieved
Ship	500	232
Accommodation	200	102
Food	400	275
Service	400	253
Entertainment	100	44
Cruise	400	205

and bridge players will find tables in the Palm Court; there's a very small "casino." The decor throughout is tasteful, with pastel colors and artwork that is pleasing to the eye, if a little bland. The forward observation lounge also acts as an indoor dining area.

The ship, well maintained and quite elegant, provides comfortable surroundings for older passengers who want plenty of space but don't want to be part of larger, more impersonal ships. Specialist concessions run the hotel operations, dining, spa/beauty services, and shops. The onboard currency is the British pound. All gratuities are included.

Perhaps a self-serve launderette or ironing room (missed by many British passengers) would be a useful addition. Niggles include the tacky plastic flowers (particularly in the dining room), and the tired appearance of parts of the ship, which has probably passed its sell-by date.

SUITABLE FOR: *Discovery* is best suited to couples and single travelers of mature years who enjoy being transported to interesting destinations in the comfort of a ship that is now considered to be traditional in style, unpretentious and with a casual dress code, and without the trappings of much entertainment or organized parlor games.

ACCOMMODATION. There are as many as 15 price categories (rather a lot for a mid-sized ship). The price you pay will depend on the grade, location and size of the cabin.

There are five suites; these are of quite a decent size, and well designed, with plenty of space to move around in. Two of the suites are located forward, just under the navigation bridge, and command good views.

Most other cabins have ample room, are quite well appointed, and there is plenty of closet and drawer space. The top category cabins (on Bridge Deck and Promenade Deck) have a full bathtub, while all others have a shower enclosure (although many have obstructed views). None of the suites or cabins has a private balcony (the ship was built before private balconies came into vogue).

No matter what category of suites or cabin you choose, there is a television, telephone, personal safe and hairdryer in each. Some cabins have interconnecting doors, and some can accommodate a third/fourth person. But note that some cabins have an "L" bed configuration, and the beds are rather narrow, at 30 inches. Also, the small TV sets may be positioned too high for watching movies.

CUISINE. The Seven Continents Dining Room is a dated, 1970s-style dining room with a low ceiling and a slightly sunken center section. There are two seatings for dinner, but there are few tables for two, most being for four, six or eight people. Many chairs have very low backs. There are separate tables as well as banquette seating, but the banquette seating is hard and uncomfortable, canteen style, and waiters need to reach over to serve and clear dishes. The cuisine, upgraded from previous Voyages of Discovery ships, includes many classic British favorites, and the presentation and service are good. The wine list is adequate, and prices are reasonable, although the selection is small and consists mostly of younger wines. Casual breakfasts and lunches can be taken in the Yacht Club (an observation lounge), with fine ocean views on three sides or outdoors on the Lido Deck, adjacent to the swimming pool.

Alternative (Reservations Only) Dining Option: Alternative dinners can also be taken in the Yacht Club, with its observation lounge views on three sides, adjacent to the Lido; Continental and Italian specialties are featured, and there is no cover charge. A late-riser's breakfast is always popular; you can also opt for Continental Breakfast to be served in your cabin if you wish.

All dining venues are non-smoking.

ENTERTAINMENT. The "theater-in-the-round" Carousel Showlounge has banquette-style seating in several tiers, set around a "thrust" stage. The entertainment is low-key, which means only the occasional cabaret act is featured. There is live music throughout the ship for dancing.

SPA/FITNESS. The Spa Atlantis is positioned aft on two of the uppermost decks (a stairway connects the two). A beauty salon is on the upper deck, while a gymnasium (with aft-facing ocean-view windows), three treatment rooms, and male and female saunas are on the lower level. It is operated by a UK-based concession, Harding Brothers, and has products from Guinot and Thalgo. Staff often try to sell beauty products aggressively.

Sample prices include: full body massage, €45 (50 minutes); back, neck and shoulder massage, €30 (30 minutes); reflexology, €25; course of four yoga classes, €15; Pilates class, €5 (30 minutes); hairdressing services which include a shampoo, cut and finish for €15.

Disney Dream
NOT YET RATED

Size: . . . . Large Resort Ship	Passenger Decks: 14	Cabins (with private balcony): 901
Tonnage: 128,000	Total Crew: 1,458	Cabins (wheelchair accessible): 37
Lifestyle: . . . . Standard	Passengers	Wheelchair accessibility . . . . .Good
Cruise Line: . . . . Disney Cruise Line	(lower beds/all berths): 2,500/5,007	Cabin Current: . . . . 110 volts
Former Names: . . . . none	Passenger Space Ratio	Elevators: 14
Builder: . . . . Meyer Werft (Germany)	(lower beds/all berths): 51.2/25.5	Casino (gaming tables): . . . . No
Original Cost: . . . . n/a	Crew/Passenger Ratio	Slot Machines: . . . . No
Entered Service: . . . . Jan 2011	(lower beds/all berths): 1.7/3.4	Swimming Pools (outdoors): 3
Registry: . . . . The Bahamas	Cabins (total): 1,250	Swimming Pools (indoors): 0
Length (ft/m): 1,115.4/340.0	Size Range (sq ft/m): 169–1,781/	Whirlpools: 4
Beam (ft/m): 121.3/37.0	15.7–165.5	Self-Service Launderette: . . . . No
Draft (ft/m): 27.2/8.32	Cabins (outside view): 1,100	Dedicated Cinema/Seats: . . . . No
Propulsion/Propellers: . . . diesel-electric	Cabins (interior/no view): 150	Library: . . . . No
(72,000kW)/2	Cabins (for one person): 0	

OVERALL SCORE: NYR OUT OF A POSSIBLE 2,000 POINTS

OVERVIEW. Mickey's dream ship has grown up. Its construction began on 2 March 2009. Made of pieces of steel and pixie dust, the ship's exterior is about 40% larger than the first two Disney ships, *Disney Magic* and *Disney Wonder* and has two extra decks although the ship's design is similar – a tribute to the grand ocean liners of the 1930s. Like its sister ships, *Disney Dream* has two large funnels. The ship's bow has handsome gold scrollwork that more typically seen adorning the tall ships of yesteryear, and the exterior colors are also those of Mickey himself: red, yellow and black. Even the lifeboats are yellow, not orange, by special dispensation.

A 765-ft-long "Aqua-Duck" is a shipboard "watercoaster" spanning four decks in height – two-and-a-half times the length of a football field. It whisks you away on a high-speed flume ride that includes twists, drops, uphill acceleration at 20ft a second, and river rapids while moving along the ship's upper decks. It's pure Disney, really splashtastic and beyond anything aboard any other cruise ship dedicated to family cruising.

Disney whimsy and Art Deco style are the hallmarks of the interior decor. In the main three-deck-high lobby stands a bronze statue of none other than Admiral Donald (Duck). The decor is enhanced by original paintings, statues, and woodwork all bearing the Disney attention to detail.

Almost one entire deck is devoted to children and teens. It's a Small World Nursery is for the little ones. The Oceaneer Lab and Oceaneer Club both have an interactive play floor – a sort of down to earth Wii – where team actions translate to movement – a novel idea. "Edge" is for 11–13 year olds, a tween pad that's a chill-out zone including

BERLITZ'S RATINGS

	Possible	Achieved
Ship	500	NYR
Accommodation	200	NYR
Food	400	NYR
Service	400	NYR
Entertainment	100	NYR
Cruise	400	NYR

karaoke with green-screen technology. "Vibe" is for the real teens, an indoor/outdoor space for 14–17 year olds that is almost 9,000 sq. ft, accessed by a "teen-only" swipe card.

Grown-ups inhabit their own area of the ship, The District, which includes five different adults-only venues. There's also a centrally-located Concierge Lounge, for occupants of accommodation designated as Concierge Class, all on Deck 12.

Other venues include: Mickey's Mainsail, Sea Treasures, Whitecaps, and Whozits and Whatsits (retail shops); District Bar, Pink Champagne Bar, Skyline Bar, Waves Bar, Bon Voyage, Meridian Bar, 687 (sports bar), Currents Bar, Cove Café; and Arr-cade.

During the winter, *Disney Dream* sails on three- and four-day cruises to the Bahamas – as part of a seven-night vacation package that includes a three- or four-day stay at a Walt Disney World resort hotel in Orlando; the cruise then forms the second half of the vacation. It's all tied up in one well-controlled, seamless, crime-free environment that promises escape and adventure. You can also book just the cruise without the resort stay.

During the summer, the ship sails on four- and five-night cruises, with one or two calls at Castaway Bay – Disney's private beach island, whose facilities were enhanced in 2010. American Express cardholders get special treatment and extra goodies. Members of Disney's Vacation Club can exchange points for cruises.

At Port Canaveral, the Disney terminal was inspired by the original Ocean Terminal in Southampton, England, from which the famous ocean liners *Queen Elizabeth*, *Queen Mary*, and the ill-fated *Titanic* once sailed.

The onboard currency is the US dollar. Gratuities are extra, but 15% is added to all bar/drinks purchases.

Note that only a limited amount of information about the new ship was available when this book was completed. For other pertinent comments about the Disney Cruise Line experience, see the following entries for *Disney Magic* and *Disney Wonder*.

SUITABLE FOR: *Disney Dream* is really great for families with children or grandchildren. Couples and singles are also welcome, though there are few activities for couples in the daytime, but enough entertainment at night. You will, however, need to be a real Disney fan, as everything revolves around Disney and the family theme.

ACCOMMODATION. There are nine different types of suites and cabins, but many more price grades, depending on the size and location of the accommodation.

Interior cabins have a virtual porthole that gives you the feeling that you are in an outside cabin. It's done with high-definition cameras positioned on the outside decks to feed live video to each virtual porthole. You almost expect one or more Disney characters to "pop by" your porthole.

One new feature that's different to *Disney Magic* and *Disney Wonder*: all bathrooms have round tubs with a pull-down seat and hand-held shower hose – perfect for washing babies and small children. The bed frames have been elevated so that luggage can easily be stored underneath.

The largest accommodation can be found in the Concierge Royal Suite (1,781 sq. ft./165.5 sq. meters, including balcony), with hot tub. It can sleep five and has one master bedroom with a large walk-in closet, a living room (with one additional pull-down wall double bed and one pull-down single bed), two bathrooms (one has two washbasins), dining room, media library, pantry, and wet bar, plus a large balcony. These suites are located in the best possible position in the ship, with great ocean views.

If you opt for one of the 21 Concierge Class suites,

you'll get higher quality bed linen (Frette 300-thread count Egyptian cotton), feather and down duvets, cotton bathrobe, and H2O Plus bath and spa products.

CUISINE. There are three main dining rooms – Animator's Pallette, Royal Palace, and Enchanted Garden – each with a different decor. Passengers rotate through all three together with their waiter (server in Disney-speak).

Animator's Palate: expect to see the surfer-dude sea turtle (from *Finding Nemo*) swimming around the restaurant, making special appearances and interacting with passengers. Royal Palace has decor inspired by the classic Disney films *Cinderella, Snow White and the Seven Dwarfs, Beauty and the Beast,* and *Sleeping Beauty.* The Enchanted Garden is a whimsical main dining room inspired by the gardens of Versailles, and the lighting magically transforms from day to night.

Cabanas, is the casual eatery, open to all. At night, it becomes a restaurant where meals from the main dining room menu are available in an even more casual setting.

For something different, and as an escape to the big dining rooms, Palo is an Italian-cuisine themed adults-only restaurant. Additionally, there is a small coffee bar for those necessary espressos and cappuccinos.

ENTERTAINMENT. Live shows are presented at the Walt Disney Theater, the ship's 1,340-seat showlounge. It has a star-studded ceiling and proscenium arch stage.

Villains Tonight, which premiered in 2010 and features the villains in Disney's films, is one of the shows being presented, along with other Disney favorites.

The Buena Vista Theater – which is not to be confused with the Walt Disney Theater – is the ship's movie house, with 399 seats.

SPA/FITNESS. Senses Spa and Salon has 17 treatment rooms and private outdoor verandahs. Rainforest features steam heat, misty showers and hydrotherapy for relaxation.

Disney Magic
Disney Wonder
★★★★

Size: . . . . .Large Resort Ships	Propulsion/Propellers: . . . . .diesel-electric
Tonnage: . . . . .83,338 *(Disney Magic)*	(38,000kW)/2
85,000 *(Disney Wonder)*	Passenger Decks: 11
Lifestyle: . . . . .Standard	Total Crew: 945
Cruise Line: . . . . .Disney Cruise Line	Passengers
Former Names: . . . . .none	(lower beds/all berths): 1,750/3,325
Builder: . . . . .Fincantieri (Italy)	Passenger Space Ratio (lower beds/
Original Cost: . . . .$350 million each	all berths): . . . . .47.6/25.0 *(Disney Magic)*
Entered Service: July 1998 *(Disney Magic)*	48.5/25.5 *(Disney Wonder)*
Aug 1999 *(Disney Wonder)*	Crew/Passenger Ratio
Registry: . . . . .The Bahamas	(lower beds/all berths): 1.8/3.5
Length (ft/m): 964.5/294.00	Cabins (total): 875
Beam (ft/m): 105.7/32.22	Size Range (sq ft/m): 180.8–968.7/
Draft (ft/m): 26.2/8.0	16.8–90.0
	Cabins (outside view): 720

Cabins (interior/no view): 155
Family Cabins: 80
Cabins (with private balcony): 388
Cabins (wheelchair accessible): 12
Wheelchair accessibility . . . . .Good
Cabin Current: . . . . .110 volts
Elevators: 12
Casino (gaming tables): . . . . .No
Slot Machines: . . . . .No
Swimming Pools (outdoors): 3
Swimming Pools (indoors): 0
Whirlpools: 6
Self-Service Launderette: . . . . .Yes (3)
Dedicated Cinema/Seats: Yes/270
Library: . . . . .No

OVERALL SCORES: 1,490 (DISNEY MAGIC); 1,491 (DISNEY WONDER) **OUT OF 2,000 POINTS**

OVERVIEW. The first two ships in the Disney Cruise Line fleet are the identical 1998-built *Disney Magic* and the 1999-built *Disney Wonder.* Their profile is sleek, and combines streamlining with tradition and nostalgia, a black hull and two large red and black funnels designed to remind you of the ocean liners of the past (*Disney Magic* was the first cruise ship built with two funnels since the 1950s). One funnel is a dummy containing various public spaces, including a teen center, Aloft.

The ships were actually constructed in two halves, which were then joined together in the shipyard in Venice, Italy. The ships' whistles even play a sort of sickly version of "When You Wish Upon a Star." The bows have handsome gold scrollwork that more usually was seen adorning the tall sailing ships of yesteryear. There is a walk-around promenade deck outdoors for strolling – just as passengers did aboard the classic ocean liners.

Disney Cruise Line didn't add ostentatious decoration to the exterior. However, although Mickey Mouse's face and ears are painted on the funnels, there is also a special 85-ft (26-meter)-long paint stripe that cleverly incorporates Disney characters into the whimsical yellow paintwork along each side of the hull at the bow. Cute. The exterior colors are those of Mickey, too. Also of note is a 15-ft (4.5-meter) Goofy hanging upside down in a bosun's chair, painting the stern of *Disney Magic*; aboard *Disney Wonder*, Goofy is

BERLITZ'S RATINGS

DISNEY MAGIC

	Possible	Achieved
Ship	500	422
Accommodation	200	166
Food	400	205
Service	400	287
Entertainment	100	90
Cruise	400	320

DISNEY WONDER

	Possible	Achieved
Ship	500	423
Accommodation	200	166
Food	400	205
Service	400	287
Entertainment	100	90
Cruise	400	320

replaced by a similarly sized Donald Duck and Huey.

There are three outdoor pools: one pool for adults only (in theory), one for families, and one for children. One has a large poolside movie screen (guess which one has Mickey's face and ears painted into the bottom). However, there's music everywhere – four different types – and it's impossible to find a quiet spot; in fact, in many seats you get two types of music blaring at you at the same time. The children's pool has a long yellow water slide (available at specified times), held up by Mickey's giant hand, although the pool itself really is too small considering the number of small children usually aboard.

The ship is sectioned into main zones: one for adults only, one for families with children, and one for familes (or single parents) with toddlers. Each group has its own swimming pool and open deck/sunbathing areas – adults only at the front of the ship. A 24-by-14-ft Goofy Pool Jumbo Screen is positioned by the family pool area, just behind the forward funnel; it shows classic Disney animated and live-action movies, TV shows and sporting events.

Inside, the ship is quite stunning. Most public rooms have high ceilings, and the Art Deco theme of the old ocean liners or New York's Radio City Music Hall has been tastefully carried out. Have a look at the stainless steel/pewter Disney detailing on the handrails and balustrades in the three-deck-high lobby. The lobby provides a real photo opportunity, with a 6-ft (1.8-meter)-high bronze statue of Mickey Mouse in the role of a ship's helmsman *(Disney Magic)* or "The Little Mermaid" *(Disney Wonder)*. There's probably some pixie dust around somewhere, too. Mickey is also visible in many other areas of the lobby, albeit subtly – subtly for Disney, that is. All the artwork in public areas comes from Disney films or animation features, with many original drawings dating from the early 1930s. If you can't sleep, try counting the number of times Mickey's logo appears – it's an impossible task.

The children's entertainment areas measure 13,000 sq. ft (1,200 sq. meters), and more than 40 children's counselors run the extensive programmes. All registered children must wear an ID bracelet showing name, cabin number and muster station number, and parents are given pagers for emergencies. There are also separate teen clubs, "tween" clubs, and a video game arcade.

A child drop-off service is available in the evenings, and private babysitting services are available at around $11 an hour, as are character "tuck-ins" for children, and character breakfasts and lunches – all at extra cost. Free strollers are available, and parents can be provided with beepers in order to enjoy their time alone, away from their offspring for much of the day.

One Disney exclusive is the game show "Who Wants to be a Mouseketeer?" The prizes include free cruises and onboard credits of up to $1,000 and Tea with Wendy Darling from Disney's version of *Peter Pan*. Naturally, all the Disney characters are aboard for all cruises and there are lots of photo opportunities when they come out to play – typically when children's activities are scheduled.

Added in a 2005 refit were additional spaces for spa/fitness facilities, and Ocean Quest, *Disney Magic*'s fifth dedicated space for children; it contains a scale replica of the ship's bridge and LCD screen "windows" that let youngsters look out over the bridge via live video feed from the actual navigation bridge. Kids can sit in a captain's chair and play a simulation game where they steer into and out of various ports. Teens can go to Aloft, a teens-only dorm-like chill-out zone in the base of the dummy forward funnel; it has big-screen TV, MP3 players, computers with hi-tech games, and video games, and its decor is a cross between a college dorm and a coffee shop.

Two large shops sell an abundance of Disney-theme clothing, soft toys, collectibles and specialty items. Other public rooms include a superb, 977-seat Walt Disney Theater with tiered seating over four decks, piano bar, adults-only nightclub-cum-disco, a family lounge, and a dedicated cinema where classic Disney films are shown, as well as first-run movies.

Apart from the ports of call, the highlight for most is a day spent on Disney's private island, Castaway Cay. It is an outstanding private island – perhaps the benchmark for all private islands for families with children – with its own pier so that the ship can dock alongside – and is a cruise industry first. There is a post office with its own special Bahamas/Disney postage stamp, and a whole host of dedicated, well thought-out attractions and amenities for all ages. These include a large adults-only beach, complete with massage cabanas. Watersports equipment – floats, paddleboats, kayaks, hobie cats, aqua fins, aqua trikes, and snorkels – can be rented.

The ships really are like floating versions of Disney's incredibly popular theme parks – sea-going Never-Never Lands. In reality, they provide a highly programmed, well organized, strictly timed and regimented onboard experience, with tickets, lines and reservations necessary for almost everything. The onboard product has been fine-tuned since the ships first put to sea. Security is very good. Whether cruising with 1,000 or more children aboard will make for a relaxing holiday for those without kids will depend on how much noise they can absorb.

Take mainly casual clothing (casual with a capital "C"), although there *are* two "formal" nights on the 7-day cruise, and wish upon a star – that's really all you'll need to do to enjoy yourself aboard these stunning ships. The onboard currency is the US dollar. Members of Disney's Holiday Club can exchange points for cruises. It is expensive – but so is a stay at any Disney resort – gratuities are extra (suggested at about $10 per person, per day), and 15% is added to all bar/beverage/wine and spa accounts.

Lines at various outlets can prove irritating (some creative Disney Imagineering is needed), as can trying to get through to Guest Services by telephone. Gripes include: poky elevators; lines and signing up for activities; the food product and delivery falls short of less expensive cruise products; there is no proper library – something many adult passengers miss; and the early morning disembarkation and customs inspection is a definite turn-off for many.

For part of the year, *Disney Magic* operates 7-day cruises to the Eastern Caribbean and Castaway Cay in the Bahamas, offering three different itineraries. During the summer, it operates cruise in Europe and the Baltic. For part of the year, *Disney Wonder* operates 3- and 4-day cruises to the Bahamas as part of a 7-night vacation package that includes a 3- or 4-day stay at a Walt Disney World resort hotel in Orlando; the cruise then forms the second half of the vacation. It's all tied up in one encapsulated, well-controlled, seamless, and crime-free environment that promises escape and adventure. You can also book just the cruise without the resort stay. In 2011, *Disney Wonder* will sail on Alaska cruises in summer.

American Express cardholders get special treatment and extra goodies. Members of Disney's Vacation Club can exchange points for cruises.

SUITABLE FOR: *Disney Magic* and *Disney Wonder* are really great for families with children or grandchildren. Couples and singles are also welcome, though there are few activities for couples in the daytime, but enough entertainment at night). You will, however, need to be a real Disney fan, as everything revolves around Disney and the family theme; this means an emphasis on entertainment and good times, while food takes a back step into the world of "theme park" cuisine. For children of all ages (minimum 12 weeks old and above), it's hard to beat these two ships.

ACCOMMODATION. There are 12 accommodation grades, but only about six different cabin layouts; the price will depend on the grade, size and location chosen, and are linked to the resort accommodation for those taking a combined resort/cruise vacation. Spread over six decks, all suites and cabins have been designed for practicality and have space-efficient layouts.

Most cabins have common features such as a neat vertical steamer trunk for clothes storage, illuminated closets, a hairdryer located at a vanity desk or in the bathroom, and bathrobes for all passengers. Many cabins have third- and fourth pull-down berths that rise and are totally hidden in the ceiling when not in use, but the standard interior and outside cabins, while acceptable for two, are extremely tight with three or four. Some cabins can also accommodate a fifth person. The cabin decor is practical, creative, and colorful, with lots of neat styling touches. Cabins with refrigerators can have them stocked, at extra cost, with one of several drinks/soft drinks packages.

Bathrooms, although compact due to the fact that the toilet is separate, are really functional units, designed with split-use facilities so that more than one person can use them at the same time – good for families. Many have bathtubs, which are really shower tubs.

Accommodation designated as suites offers much more space, and extra goodies such as CD and DVD players, large-screen TVs, and extra beds (useful for larger families). Some suites are beneath the pool deck, teen lounge, or informal café, so there could be noise as the ceiling insulation is poor – although cabin-to-cabin insulation is good.

The two largest suites, the Walter E. Disney Suite and the Roy O. Disney Suite, are located beside the central bank of elevators. These are luxurious living spaces, each with two bedrooms, and all the Disney trimmings you'd expect.

THE LINKS WITH ORLANDO

Disney Cruise Lines' home port is Port Canaveral, where the company built a terminal costing $27 million. It is a copy of the original Ocean Terminal used by the transatlantic liners *Queen Elizabeth* and *Queen Mary* in Southampton, England. Transfers between Walt Disney World resorts in Orlando and the ship are included. Special buses feature vintage 1930s and1940s-style interior decor. Five of the 45 custom-made buses are outfitted to carry wheelchair passengers. Embarkation and disembarkation is a bit of an entertainment event rather than the hassle-laden affair that it has become for many cruise lines with large ships (if all the buses don't arrive together), and it's quite slick.

The cruise terminal's second floor has a neat 13,000 sq.ft. terazzo tile map of Florida's east coast and The Bahamas. If you drive to the port, parking for the duration of your cruise is available, at rates of around $10 per night set by the port authority.

Onboard airline check-in for post-cruise flights from Orlando is offered, with luggage transfer directly from ship to flight on any one of seven airlines: AirTran, Alaska, American, Continental, Delta, Northwest and United. You'll need to supply pre-registration information at Orlando Airport or at a hospitality desk at the Disney World Resort.

Wheelchair-bound passengers have a variety of cabin sizes and configurations, including suites with a private balcony – unfortunately you can't get a wheelchair through the balcony's sliding door – and extra-large bathrooms with excellent roll-in showers, and good closet and drawer space. Almost all the vessel is accessible. For the sight-impaired, cabin numbers and elevator buttons are braille-encoded. A 24-hour room service is available, and suites also get "concierge service." But the room service menu and cabin breakfast menu are limited. A 15% service charge applies to beverage deliveries, including tea and coffee.

CUISINE. Each ship has three main dining rooms, all non-smoking, each with over 400 seats, two seatings, and unique themes. Lumiere's (in the center of the ship on Deck 3) has Beauty and the Beast; Parrot Cay (Deck 4) has a tacky, pseudo-Caribbean theme; also on Deck 4 aft, with great ocean views over the stern, is Animator's Palate, the most visual of the three with food and electronic art that makes the evening decor change from black and white to full-color.

You will eat in all three dining rooms in rotation – twice per 7-day cruise – and move with your assigned waiter and assistant waiter to each dining room in turn, thus providing the variety of different decor and different menus. It's a great concept – and totally unlike any other cruise line. As you will have the same waiter in each of the three restaurants, any gratuities go only to "your" waiter. Parrot Cay and Lumiere's have open seating for breakfast and lunch, but the lunch menu is pitiful.

The noise level in all three dining rooms is extremely high. If the formal nights happen to fall on the evening you are due to eat in Parrot Cay, formal wear and the decor of Parrot Cay Restaurant just don't mix.

Alternative Dining Venue: Palo is a 140-seat reservations-only alternative restaurant (with a $5 cover/gratuity charge) serving Italian cuisine. It has a 270-degree view, and is for adults only (no "Munchkins" allowed); the à la carte cuisine is cooked to order, and the wine list is good, although prices are high. Make your reservations as soon as you board or you will miss out on the only decent food aboard this ship. Afternoon High Tea is also presented here, on days at sea.

Casual Dining Venue: Topsider's (incorporating Beach Blanket Buffet) is an indoor/outdoor café serving low-quality self-serve breakfast and lunch buffets with limited choice and presentation, and a buffet dinner, consisting mostly of fried foods, for children. However, the venue is often overcrowded at lunchtime, so it may be better to go to the Parrot Cay dining room, which offers breakfast and lunch buffet, too. A poolside Goofey's Galley has grilled panini sandwiches and wraps, and soft drinks are complimentary.

Scoops, an ice cream and frozen yogurt bar, opens infrequently; other fast-food outlets include Pluto's for hamburgers, hot dogs, and Pinocchio's, which is open all day but not in the evening, for basic pizza and sandwiches. On one night of the cruise, there is also an outdoor self-serve "Tropicalifragilisticexpialidocious" buffet.

A casual Outlook Café, installed in 2010, has fine views from Deck 10, just forward of the first funnel housing. Vegetarians and those looking for light cuisine will be underwhelmed by the lack of green vegetables. Guest chefs from Walt Disney World Resort prepare signature dishes each cruise, and also host cooking demonstrations.

ENTERTAINMENT. The entertainment and activities programs for families and children are extremely good. There are three large-scale stage shows in the stunning 977-seat showlounge, presenting original Disney musicals: *Disney Dreams, Hercules – The Muse-ical, The Golden Mickeys*, and the latest comedy production, *Villains Tonight*, bringing together a cast of Disney villains from many Disney films. Sadly, there is no live orchestra, although the lighting, staging and technical effects are excellent. There is also a Disney-themed Trivia Game Show.

For grown-ups, "Route 66" aboard *Disney Magic* and "Beal Street" aboard *Disney Wonder* are adult entertainments that include a wacky Hollywood-style "street," complete with three entertainment rooms. "Sessions" (*Disney Magic*) and "Cadillac" (*Disney Wonder*) are jazz piano lounges, with private headphones for listening to music of all types when no live music is scheduled. "Rockin' Bar D" (*Disney Magic*) and "Wavebands" (*Disney Wonder*) provide ear-splitting rock 'n' roll and country music. "Barrel of Laughs" offers improvisational comedy with audience participation. During the day, creative enrichment programs have been added.

Once each cruise, a late-night "Pirates In the Caribbean" poolside party includes fireworks. Special equipment installed in the Walt Disney Theatre and the Buena Vista Theatre allows participants to view Disney Digital 3-D movies.

SPA/FITNESS. Fancy a little pampering? The Vista Spa is a fitness/wellbeing complex that measures 10,700 sq ft/994 sq metres. The fitness/workout room, with high-tech Cybex muscle-toning equipment, has ocean-view windows overlooking the navigation bridge one deck below. There are 11 rooms for spa/beauty treatments – but note that the pounding from the basketball court on the sports deck directly overhead makes spa treatments less than relaxing. Three spa "villas" have indoor treatment suites connected to private outdoor verandahs with personal hot tub, open-air shower and chaise lounge. There's an area for spinning classes and a couple of private salons for Pilates instruction and one-on-one beauty and fitness consultations.

A Thermal Zone features a "tropical rain shower," sauna, mild steam room, aromatic steam room and a fog shower. Aromatic scents such as eucalyptus, lime, peppermint, rose and sage can be infused into the mild steam room, while chamomile is used in the aromatic steam room.

Exotic massages, aromatherapy facials, pedicures, and beauty salon treatments cost extra – massage, for example, costs about $2 per minute, plus gratuity. The Rasul mud and steam room is a must for couples, but make appointments early. For something extra special, consider booking a massage at Castaway Cay in a private beach hut on the beach that is open to the sea. It's magical.

A sports deck has a paddle tennis court, table tennis, basketball court, shuffleboard, and golf driving range.

easyCruise Life
★ +

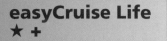

Size: ....Small Ship	Passenger Decks: 7	Cabins (wheelchair accessible): 1
Tonnage: 12,711	Total Crew: 79	Wheelchair accessibility ....None
Lifestyle: ....Standard	Passengers	Cabin Current: ......110 volts (European)
Cruise Line: ....easyCruise.com	(lower beds/all berths): 500/550	Elevators: 2
Former Names: .....Farah, The Jasmine,	Passenger Space Ratio	Casino (gaming tables): ....Yes
Palmira, Natasha, Lev Tolstoi	(lower beds/all berths): 25.4/23.1	Slot Machines: ....Yes
Builder: ......Szczesin Stocznia (Poland)	Crew/Passenger Ratio	Swimming Pools (outdoors): 1
Original Cost: ....n/a	(lower beds/all berths): 3.0/5.0	Swimming Pools (indoors): 0
Entered Service: 1981/May 2008	Cabins (total): 250	Whirlpools: 3
Registry: ....Malta	Size Range (sq ft/m): .129.1–247.5/12–23	Self-Service Launderette: ....No
Length (ft/m): 441.2/134.5	Cabins (outside view): 159	Dedicated Cinema/Seats: ....No
Beam (ft/m): 68.8/21.00	Cabins (interior/no view): 86	Library: ....No
Draft (ft/m): 19.0/5.8	Cabins (for one person): 3	
Propulsion/Propellers: diesel (12,800kW)/2	Cabins (with private balcony): 0	

BERLITZ'S OVERALL SCORE: 771 OUT OF A POSSIBLE 2,000 POINTS

OVERVIEW. *easyCruise Life,* originally built to carry up to 80 cars and many passengers on line voyages, has a square, angular profile with a stubby bow and a fat funnel amidships. It has a dark hull with a thick orange stripe along its length, together with its name. Outdoors facilities include a small swimming pool, volleyball court, and open sun decks with little space. It was extensively reconstructed for the easyCruise.com minimalist concept in 2008.

The public rooms are on one main deck, although the ceilings are mostly low and very plain. Included are a main lounge, large duty-free store, restaurant, bar and lounge, a chill-out café and bar, a casino with tables and slot machines, a very small children's playroom, and spa/beauty salon.

The no-frills ship delivers a 3- or 4-day cruise that is not a cruise at all in the traditional sense, but more like a water taxi. *easyCruise Life* provides budget travel in the Greek Isles, but the ship is extremely cramped, with a poor Passenger Space Ratio, not much soundproofing (think wood and tile floors), and few public rooms.

Still, because it's a small ship, it's easy to meet people, and easyCruise, the company, simply isn't trying to be like any other cruise line. If it appeals to you, book it on e-Bay, or through one of several tour operators. It provides transportation to get you around the Greek Islands – which is precisely what some people seek. Flights, meals, housekeeping services are all extra, and there's no room service.

Note that both the interior and exterior staircases are quite steep. There is no observation lounge with forward-facing views over the ship's bows. The ship has a limited amount of open deck and sunning space, and a tiny swimming pool; it's really just a "dip" pool.

BERLITZ'S RATINGS

	Possible	Achieved
Ship	500	220
Accommodation	200	98
Food	400	130
Service	400	163
Entertainment	100	25
Cruise	400	135

SUITABLE FOR: *easyCruise Life* is best suited to young and trendy passengers seeking a first taste of cruising aboard a ship of extremely modest facilities and features, but with good food.

ACCOMMODATION. Eight grades are spread over five decks. Although there are real beds, there's no carpet, no TV set, and no telephone in any cabin.

Standard Outside-view/Interior (No View) Cabins: All regular cabins are very small and utilitarian. There's little drawer space, and the under-bed storage space for luggage is tight. Most cabins have one or two beds and one or two upper Pullman berths. All suites/cabins have a private bathroom, with shower, and a small cabinet for toiletries (only soap is supplied).

Royal Suites/Presidential Suites: The two Royal Suites have a separate bedroom with a decent amount of closet and drawer space, and a large bathroom with tub and shower combination. The Presidential suites have a larger bathroom, with bathtub and shower combination, and each has a TV/VCR, and mini-bar; the ones with the best location are the two directly under the navigation bridge.

CUISINE. The fusiOn6 Restaurant/Bar, with tables for four, six or eight, is the main dining venue. It has large picture windows on three sides, although the ceiling is quite low and the noise level can be high. Wine glasses are small.

ENTERTAINMENT. The entertainment is strictly geared to the hearing-impaired market. A DJ is the salesman.

SPA/FITNESS. There is a wellness area, called the Aptiva Spa; it includes a sauna, and a small fitness room.

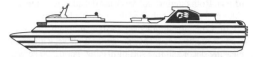

Emerald Princess
★★★★

Size:	.Large Resort Ship	Passenger Decks:	.15
Tonnage:	.113,561	Total Crew:	.1,200
Lifestyle:	.Standard	Passengers	
Cruise Line:	.Princess Cruises	(lower beds/all berths):	.3,114/3,782
Former Names:	.none-	Passenger Space Ratio	
Builder:	.Fincantieri (Italy)	(lower beds/all berths):	.36.2/29.8
Original Cost:	.$500 million	Crew/Passenger Ratio	
Entered Service:	.May 2007	(lower beds/all berths):	.2.5/3.1
Registry:	.Bermuda	Cabins (total):	.1,557
Length (ft/m):	.951.4/290.0	Size Range (sq ft/m):	.163–1,279/
Beam (ft/m):	.118.1/36.0		15.1–118.8
Draft (ft/m):	.26.2/8.0	Cabins (outside view):	.1,105
Propulsion/Propellers:	.diesel-electric	Cabins (interior/no view):	.452
	(42,000kW)/2	Cabins (for one person):	.0

Cabins (with private balcony):	.881
Cabins (wheelchair accessible):	.25
Wheelchair accessibility	.Good
Cabin Current:	.110 volts
Elevators:	.14
Casino (gaming tables):	.Yes
Slot Machines:	.Yes
Swimming Pools (outdoors):	.4
Swimming Pools (indoors):	.0
Whirlpools:	.9
Self-Service Launderette:	.Yes
Dedicated Cinema/Seats:	.No
Library:	.Yes

OVERALL SCORE: 1,546 OUT OF A POSSIBLE 2,000 POINTS

OVERVIEW. *Emerald Princess* has the same profile as sister *Crown Princess* (similar to half-sisters *Diamond Princess, Golden Princess, Grand Princess, Ruby Princess, Sapphire Princess* and *Star Princess*). Although the ship takes over 500 more passengers than the half-sisters, the outdoor deck space remains the same, as do the number of elevators – so waiting time will increase during peak periods. The Passenger Space Ratio is also considerably reduced.

One nice feature that's worth booking on days at sea is The Sanctuary, an extra-cost adults-only retreat located forward on the uppermost deck. It provides a "private" place to relax and unwind and includes attendants to provide chilled face towels and deliver light bites; there are also two outdoor cabanas for massages. It's well worth the $10 per half-day extra charge.

There is a good sheltered faux teak promenade deck – it's actually painted steel – which almost wraps around (three times round is equal to one mile) and a walkway which goes to the enclosed, protected bow of the ship. The outdoor pools have various beach-like surroundings, and "Movies Under the Skies" and major sporting events are shown on a 300-sq-ft (28-sq-meter) movie screen at the pool in front of the large funnel structure. Movies afloat in the open are a big hit with passengers – reminding many of drive-in movies, now virtually extinct in North America.

Unlike the outside decks, there is plenty of space inside (but there are also plenty of passengers), and a wide array of public rooms, with many "intimate" (this being a relative word) spaces and places to play. The passenger flow has been well thought-out, and there is little congestion.

Just aft of the funnel housing is a ship-wide glass-walled

BERLITZ'S RATINGS

	Possible	Achieved
Ship	500	435
Accommodation	200	168
Food	400	255
Service	400	292
Entertainment	100	82
Cruise	400	314

disco called Skywalkers. It's in a lower position than in the half-sister ships, but still has fine views from the port and starboard side windows – it would make a great penthouse.

The interior decor is attractive, with lots of earth tones, well suited to both American and European tastes. In fact, this is a culmination of the best of all that Princess Cruises has to offer from its many years of operating what is now a well-tuned, good-quality product.

An extensive collection of artworks has been chosen, and this complements the interior design and colors well. If you see something you like, you will probably be able to purchase it on board – it's almost all for sale.

Emerald Princess also has a wedding chapel, and a live web-cam can relay ceremonies via the internet. The captain can legally marry (American) couples, thanks to the ship's Bermuda registry and a special dispensation (which should be verified when in the planning stage, according to where you reside). But to get married and take your close family members and entourage with you on your honeymoon may prove expensive. The "Hearts & Minds" chapel is also useful for "renewal of vows" ceremonies.

For children, there is a two-deck-high playroom, teen room, and a host of trained counselors. Children have their own pools, hot tubs, open deck and sports court area at the stern of the ship, away from the adults.

Gamblers should enjoy the large Gatsby's Casino, with more than 260 slot machines, and blackjack, craps and roulette tables, plus games such as Let It Ride Bonus, Spanish 21 and Caribbean Draw Progressive. But the highlight could well be the linked slot machines that provide a combined payout.

Other features include a decent library/computer room, and a separate card room. Ship lovers should enjoy the wood-paneled Wheelhouse Bar, finely decorated with memorabilia and ship models tracing part of parent company P&O's history; while sports lovers should enjoy the sports bar, with its two billiard tables, and several television screens.

The ship is a fine, grand resort playground in which to roam when you are not ashore, and Princess Cruises delivers a consistently fine, well-packaged vacation product, always with a good degree of style, at an attractive, highly competitive price. Whether this really can be considered a relaxing holiday is a moot point, but with so many choices and "small" rooms to enjoy, the ship has been extremely well designed, and the odds are that you'll have an enjoyable cruise vacation.

If you are not used to large ships, it will take you some time to find your way around this one, despite the company's claim that it offers passengers a "small ship feel, big ship choice." And there are several points of congestion, particularly outside the shops when bazaar tables are set up outside on the upper level of the atrium lobby.

ACCOMMODATION. There are six principal types of cabins and configurations: (a) grand suite, (b) suite, (c) mini-suite, (d) outside-view double cabins with balcony, (e) outside-view double cabins, and (f) interior (no view) double cabins. These come in 35 different brochure price categories (the choice is bewildering for both travel agents and passengers), and pricing depends on size and location.

Cabin bath towels are small, and drawer space is very limited. There are no butlers – even for the top-grade suites (which are not really large in comparison to similar suites aboard some other ships). Cabin attendants have too many cabins to look after (typically 20), which does not translate to fine personal service.

(a). The largest, most lavish suite is the Grand Suite. It has a large bedroom with queen-sized bed, huge walk-in (illuminated) closets, two bathrooms, a lounge (with fireplace and sofa bed) with wet bar and refrigerator, and a large private balcony on the port side (with hot tub that can be accessed from both balcony and bedroom).

(b/c). Suites (with a semi-private balcony) have a separate living room (with sofa bed) and bedroom (with a TV set in each). The bathroom is quite large and has both a tub and shower stall. The mini-suites also have a private balcony, and a separate living and sleeping area (with a TV set in each). The differences between the suites and mini-suites are basically in the size and appointments, the suite being more of a square shape while mini-suites are more rectangular, and have few drawers. Both suites and mini-suites have plush bathrobes, and fully tiled bathrooms with ample open shelf storage space.

Suite and mini-suite passengers receive greater attention, including priority embarkation and disembarkation privileges. What is not good is that the most expensive accommodation has only semi-private balconies that can be seen from above and so there is little privacy.

(d/e/f). Both interior (no view) and outside-view (the outsides come either with or without private balcony) cabins are of a functional, practical, design, although almost no drawers are provided. They are quite attractive, with warm, pleasing decor and fine soft furnishing fabrics; 80 percent of the outside-view cabins have a private balcony. Interior (no view) cabins measure approximately 163 sq. ft (15.1 sq. meters).

The 28 wheelchair-accessible cabins measure 250–385 sq. ft (23.2–35.7 sq. meters); surprisingly, there is no mirror for dressing, and no full-length hanging space for long dresses (yes, some passengers in wheelchairs do also use mirrors and full-length clothing). Additionally, two family suites consist of two suites with an interconnecting door, plus a large balcony. These can sleep up to 10 (if at least four are children) or up to eight people (if all are adults).

All cabins receive turndown service and chocolates on pillows each night, bathrobes (on request) and toiletry amenity kits (larger, naturally, for suite/mini-suite occupants) that typically include soap, shampoo, conditioner, and hand/body lotion. A hairdryer is provided in all cabins, sensibly located at the vanity desk unit in the living area. All bathrooms have tiled floors, and there is a decent amount of open shelf storage space for personal toiletries, although the plain beige decor is very basic and unappealing.

Most outside-view cabins on Emerald Deck have views obstructed by the lifeboats. There are no cabins for singles. Your name is placed outside your suite or cabin in a documents holder – making it simple for delivery service personnel but also diminishing privacy. There is 24-hour room service – but some items on the room service menu are not available during early morning hours.

Some cabins can accommodate a third and fourth person in upper berths. However, in such cabins, the lower beds cannot then be pushed together to make queen-sized bed.

Almost all balcony suites and cabins can be overlooked both from the navigation bridge wing, as well as from the port and starboard sections of the ship's discotheque – high above the ship at the stern. Cabins with balconies on Dolphin, Caribe and Baja decks can be overlooked by passengers on balconies on the deck above. They are, therefore, not private. Also, passengers occupying some of the most expensive suites with balconies at the stern of the vessel may experience considerable vibration during certain ship maneuvers.

CUISINE. As befits the size of the ship, there's a variety of options. There are three main dining rooms (Botticelli, Da Vinci, and Michelangelo), plus Crown Steakhouse, and Sabatini's Trattoria. All are no-smoking.

Of the three principal dining rooms for formal dining, one has traditional two-seating dining, while the other two have "anytime dining" (you choose when and with whom you want to eat). All are split into multi-tier sections in a non-symmetrical design that breaks what are quite large spaces into smaller sections for better ambience.

While four elevators go to the deck where two of the restaurants are located, only two go to Plaza Deck 5, where the Palm Restaurant is located (this can cause waiting problems at peak times, particularly for anyone in a wheelchair).

Specially designed dinnerware, high-quality linens and silverware, Frette Egyptian cotton table linens, and silverware by Hepp of Germany are used in the main dining rooms. Note that 15% is added to all beverage bills, including wines.

Alternative (Extra Charge) Dining Options: There are two: Sabatini's, and Crown Grill. Both are open for lunch and dinner on days at sea. Sabatini's is an Italian eatery located on a high deck aft of the funnel housing, with colorful tiled Mediterranean-style decor; it is named after Trattoria Sabatini, the 200-year old institution in Florence (where there is no cover charge). It includes Italian-style multi-course antipasti and pastas, as well as Italian-style entrées, including tiger prawns and lobster tail. All are provided with flair and entertainment by the staff of waiters. It's by reservation only; cover charge $20 per person, for dinner.

The Crown Grill, located aft on Promenade Deck, is a reservation-only steakhouse, offering prime quality steaks and seafood. The cover charge is $25 (plus an additional charge for lobster).

The cuisine in these two dining spots is decidedly better than in the three main dining rooms, with better quality ingredients and more attention to presentation and taste.
Casual Eateries: These include a poolside hamburger grill and pizza bar (no additional charge), while extra charges do apply if you order items to eat either at the International Cafe (a coffee bar/ patisserie), or in Vines seafood/wine bar in the atrium lobby. Other casual meals can be taken in the Horizon Court (open 24 hours a day). It has large ocean-view on port and starboard sides and direct access to the two principal swimming pools and lido deck. Although there is a wide variety of food, there is no real finesse in presentation, however, as plastic plates are provided
Ultimate Balcony Dinner/Breakfast: For something dif-

ferent, you could try a private dinner on your balcony, an all-inclusive evening featuring cocktails, fresh flowers, champagne and a deluxe four-course meal including Caribbean lobster tail – all served by a member of the dining staff on your private balcony; of course, it costs extra – $50 per person (or $32 per couple for the Ultimate Balcony Breakfast).

ENTERTAINMENT. The 800-seat Princess Theater (show-lounge) is the main entertainment venue; it spans two decks and has comfortable seating on both main and balcony levels. It has $3 million worth of sound and light equipment, plus a nine-piece orchestra, and a scenery loading bay that connects directly from stage to a hull door for direct transfer to the dockside. The ship has its own resident troupe of almost 20 singers and dancers, plus and audio-visual support staff.

There is also a second entertainment lounge, Club Fusion, located aft. It features cabaret acts and karaoke contests at night, and lectures, bingo and horse racing during the day. Explorers Lounge, a third entertainment lounge, can also host cabaret acts and dance bands.

A variety of other lounges and bars have live music, including a string quartet, and street performers that appear in the main atrium lobby

SPA/FITNESS. The Lotus Spa is located forward on Sun Deck – one of the uppermost decks. Separate facilities for men and women include a sauna, steam room, and changing rooms; common facilities include a relaxation/waiting zone, body-pampering treatment rooms, and a gymnasium with packed with the latest high-tech muscle-pumping, cardio-vascular equipment, and great ocean views. Some fitness classes are free, while some cost extra.

● **For more extensive general information on what a Princess Cruises cruise is like, see pages 148–51.**

Empress
★★★

Size:	Large Resort Ship	Passenger Decks:	9	Cabins (with private balcony):	69
Tonnage:	48,563 tons	Total Crew:	685	Cabins (wheelchair accessible):	4
Lifestyle:	Standard	Passengers		Wheelchair accessibility	Fair
Cruise Line:	Pullmantur Cruises	(lower beds/all berths):	1,600/2,020	Cabin Current:	110 volts
Former Names:	Empress of the Seas,	Passenger Space Ratio		Elevators:	7
	Nordic Empress	(lower beds/all berths):	30.2/24.0	Casino (gaming tables):	Yes
Builder:	Chantiers de l'Atlantique (France)	Crew/Passenger Ratio		Slot Machines:	Yes – 220
Original Cost:	$170 million	(lower beds/all berths):	2.3/2.9	Swimming Pools (outdoors):	1
Entered Service:	June 1990/May 2008	Cabins (total):	800		(+1 wading pool)
Registry:	The Bahamas	Size Range (sq ft/m):	117.0–818/	Swimming Pools (indoors):	0
Length (ft/m):	692.2/211.00		10.8–76	Whirlpools:	4
Beam (ft/m):	100.7/30.70	Cabins (outside view):	471	Self-Service Launderette:	No
Draft (ft/m):	24.9/7.60	Cabins (interior/no view):	329	Dedicated Cinema/Seats:	No
Propulsion/Propellers: diesel (16,200 kW)/2		Cabins (for one person):	0	Library:	No

BERLITZ'S OVERALL SCORE: 1,226 OUT OF A POSSIBLE 2,000 POINTS

OVERVIEW. This all-white contemporary ship has a short bow and squared-off stern, and yet it manages to look reasonably well balanced with its bright red funnel. Originally known as *Nordic Empress*, it was designed specifically for the short-cruise market, for which the ship is quite well suited. In March 2008 the ship was transferred from the RCI fleet to Pullmantur Cruises, to operate as *Empress* for Spanish-speakers.

There is a polished wood walk-around promenade deck outdoors, and a dramatic use of glass-enclosed viewing spaces that provide good contact from the upper, open decks to the sea. Although the outdoor pool is decent enough (good at night for evenings under the stars), the two swimming pools provided are very small considering the number of passengers carried when the ship is full. In other words, there's not a lot of open deck space, and sunloungers are crammed together with little room to maneuver around them on sunny days at sea.

A nine-deck-high atrium is the focal point of the interior design, which tends to have many Scandinavian influences. Lots of crystal and brass were used to good effect to reflect light. Indeed, the clever use of lighting effects provides illuminating interiors that make it feel warm. Passenger flow is generally good, although, because two seatings and two show times are operated, some congestion is inevitable adjacent to the entrance foyer at show time. A small library was added a few years ago – a needed facility that was not included when the ship was built – and there are two areas around the atrium designated for card players.

A three-level casino has a sailcloth ceiling, but it is a noisy room. The Viking Crown Lounge, aft of the funnel, is a two-level nightclub-disco for the late-night set.

BERLITZ'S RATINGS

	Possible	Achieved
Ship	500	325
Accommodation	200	121
Food	400	218
Service	400	257
Entertainment	100	64
Cruise	400	241

Empress is a fairly smart ship with a high passenger density, and you won't be bored – there is an adequate array of activities for all ages. In the final analysis, you may be overwhelmed by the public spaces, and underwhelmed by the size of the cabins. However, this is basically a well-run, fine-tuned, highly structured cruise product geared particularly to those seeking an action-packed cruise vacation at a moderately good price, with lots of fellow passengers to keep you company. The onboard currency is the euro.

Standing in line for embarkation, disembarkation, shore tenders and for self-serve buffet meals is an inevitable aspect of cruising aboard all large ships.

SUITABLE FOR: *Empress* is best suited to young Spanish-speaking couples and singles seeking an all-inclusive cruise, and those who want a good basic getaway cruise aboard a ship that offers some good drinking places, lots of noise and good cheer, in fairly comfortable surroundings.

ACCOMMODATION. There are 15 different price categories. The largest accommodation is in the Royal Suite, located just under the navigation bridge on the port side. This has a queen-sized bed, walk-in closet, separate living area with bar, refrigerator and entertainment center; the bathroom has a whirlpool tub, and vanity dressing area. There is a private balcony.

Nine cabins have private balconies that overlook the ship's stern; these consist of two large owner's suites and seven "superior" ocean-view cabins. The other cabins with private balconies also have a decent amount of living space, and a small sofa, coffee table and chair, and vanity desk.

Almost all the other cabins are really dimensionally challenged, and only moderately comfortable. All grades of accommodation have twin beds that can convert to a queen-size configuration. The bathrooms (all refurbished in 2004) are nicely laid-out, and have a decent amount of space for personal toiletry items.

CUISINE. The Miramar Restaurant is non-smoking. It is two decks high, with both a main and balcony level, as well as large windows that overlook the stern of the ship, but it really is a noisy room. There are two seatings, at tables for four, six, eight or 10.

The cuisine is typical of mass banquet catering that offers standard fare comparable to that found in family-style restaurants ashore. While the menu descriptions provide a tempting read, the food, when it arrives, has little taste. **Alternative Dining Option:** There is one à la carte extra-charge restaurant (reservations are required). However, it's worth the extra money, as the food is so much better than in the dining room, and the room's intimacy makes it a nice, romantic place – it has a good number of tables for two. **Casual Dining Option:** For casual breakfasts and lunches,

the Panorama Buffet, with several buffet display stations, provides an alternative to the dining room, although there are often lines at peak times, and the selection is at best very average. There are no "active stations" – where items such as omelets could be made to order.

ENTERTAINMENT. The two-level Broadway Showroom has poor sight lines in the upper lateral balconies. It has a main floor level as well as a balcony level. However, the sight-lines from the balcony are almost useless as they are ruined by railings. Strong cabaret acts are also featured in the main showlounge.

The entertainment throughout is upbeat – in fact, it is difficult to get away from music and noise – but is typical of the kind of resort hotel found ashore in Las Vegas. There is even background music in all corridors and lifts, and constant music outdoors on the pool deck. If you want a quiet relaxing holiday, choose another ship.

SPA/FITNESS. A gymnasium has some good muscle-pumping equipment. Sports fans will like the climbing wall at the stern of the ship, behind the Starlight Discotheque.

RULES OF THE ROAD

Ships, the largest moving objects made by man, are subject to stringent international regulations. They must keep to the right in shipping lanes, and pass on the right (with certain exceptions). When circumstances raise some doubt, or shipping lanes are crowded, ships use their whistles in the same way an automobile driver uses directional signals to show which way he will turn. When one ship passes another and gives a single blast on its whistle, this means it is turning to starboard (right). Two blasts mean a turn to port (left).

The other ship acknowledges by repeating the same signal. Ships switch on navigational running lights at night — green for starboard, red for port, plus two white lights on the masts,

the forward one lower than the aft one.

Flags and pennants form another part of a ship's communication facilities and are displayed for identification purposes. Each time a country is visited, its national flag is shown. While entering and leaving a port, the ship flies a blue-and-white vertically striped flag to request a pilot, while a half-red, half-white flag (divided vertically) indicates that a pilot is on board. Cruise lines also display their own "house" flag from the mast.

A ship's funnel (smokestack) is one other means of identification, each line having its own design and color scheme. The size, height, and number of funnels were all points worth advertising at the turn of the

20th century. Most ocean liners of the time had four funnels and were called "four-stackers."

There are numerous customs at sea, many of them older than any maritime law. Superstition has always been an important element, as in the following example quoted from the British Admiralty Manual of Seamanship: "The custom of breaking a bottle of wine over the stem of a ship when it is being launched originates from the old practice of toasting prosperity to a ship with a silver goblet of wine, which was then cast into the sea in order to prevent a toast of ill intent being drunk from the same cup. This was a practice that proved too expensive, and it was replaced in 1690 by the breaking of a bottle of wine over the stem."

Enchantment of the Seas
★★★★

Size: . . . . .Large Resort Ship	Passenger Decks: 11	Cabins (wheelchair accessible): 20
Tonnage: 81,500	Total Crew: 840	Wheelchair accessibility . . . . .Good
Lifestyle: . . . . .Standard	Passengers	Cabin Current: . . . . .110 and 220 volts
Cruise Line: . . . . .Royal Caribbean	(lower beds/all berths): 2,252/2,730	Elevators: 9
International	Passenger Space Ratio	Casino (gaming tables): . . . . .Yes
Former Names: . . . . .none	(lower beds/all berths): 36.1/29.8	Slot Machines: . . . . .Yes
Builder: . . .Kvaerner Masa-Yards (Finland)	Crew/Passenger Ratio	Swimming Pools (outdoors): 2
Original Cost: . . . .$300 million	(lower beds/all berths): 2.6/3.2	Swimming Pools (indoors): 1
Entered Service: . . . . .July 1997	Cabins (total): 1,126	(indoor/outdoor w/sliding glass roof)
Registry: . . . . .The Bahamas	Size Range (sq ft/m): 158.2–1,267.0/	Whirlpools: 4
Length (ft/m): 990.1/301.8	14.7–117.7	Self-Service Launderette: . . . . .No
Beam (ft/m): 105.6/32.2	Cabins (outside view): 663	Dedicated Cinema/Seats: . . . . .No
Draft (ft/m): 25.5/7.6	Cabins (interior/no view): 463	Library: . . . . .Yes
Propulsion/Propellers: . . . . .diesel-electric	Cabins (for one person): 0	
(50,400kW)/2	Cabins (with private balcony): 248	

OVERALL SCORE: 1,407 OUT OF A POSSIBLE 2,000 POINTS

OVERVIEW. This is one of a pair of ships for this popular cruise line – sister to *Grandeur of the Seas*. It has a long profile, with a single funnel located well aft – almost a throwback to designs used during the 1950s. The stern is nicely rounded (rather like the older *Monarch of the Seas*-class ships), and a Viking Crown Lounge is set amidships. This, together with the forward mast, provides three distinct focal points in its exterior profile. There is a wrap-around promenade deck outdoors, but no cushioned pads for the tacky home patio-style plastic sunloungers.

A large Viking Crown Lounge (a trademark of all Royal Caribbean International ships) sits between funnel and mast at the top of the atrium lobby, and overlooks the forward section of the swimming pool deck, as aboard *Legend of the Seas* and *Splendour of the Seas*, with access provided from stairway off the central atrium.

The principal interior focal point is a seven-deck-high Centrum (atrium lobby), which provides a good meeting point (the Purser's Desk and Shore Excursion Desk are located on one of the lower levels). Many public entertainment rooms and facilities are located off the atrium.

This ship has good passenger flow inside. There is a good, varied collection of artworks (including several sculptures), principally by British artists, with classical music, ballet and theater themes. The casino is large and glitzy, and has a fascinating, theatrical glass-covered, but under-floor exhibit. The children's and teens' facilities are good, much expanded from previous ships in the fleet.

A delightful champagne terrace bar sits forward of the lower level of the two-deck-high dining room. There is a

BERLITZ'S RATINGS

	Possible	Achieved
Ship	500	411
Accommodation	200	152
Food	400	227
Service	400	260
Entertainment	100	77
Cruise	400	280

good use of tropical plants throughout the public rooms, which helps to counteract the rather plain and clinical pastel wall colors, while huge murals in opera scenes adorn several stairways.

Enchantment of the Seas has quite attractive interiors, and will provide a good cruise vacation, particularly for first-time passengers seeking comfortable surroundings similar to those in a Hyatt Hotel, with fabrics and soft furnishings that blend together to provide a contemporary resort environment. This company provides a well organized, but rather homogenous cruise experience, with the same old passenger participation activities and events that have been provided for more than 25 years. The onboard currency is the US dollar.

In 2005, the ship underwent a $60 million "chop-and-stretch" operation that added a 72.8-ft (22.2-meter) mid-section. It took six days to slice the ship in two before the mid-section was slotted in, increasing the ship's overall length to 990.1 ft (301.8 meters). The ship's tonnage was increased to 81,500 tons. The upgrade added another 151 passenger cabins (including two "family" cabins that can sleep six), and some public rooms were given a make-over at the same time. Sports facilities were augmented; these included two "ball zones," each with three basketball hoops of different heights to accommodate youth, teen and adult shooters. The pool deck was given more space plus soaring "suspension" bridges. Special handicap lifts were provided for the two pools, as was a new Splash Deck (children will love the 64 water jets) with a decorative night-time fiber-optic light show. "Bungee" trampolines were added to Deck 10 (above the Windjammer Café). The main dining room and Windjammer Café (casual eatery) were enlarged to handle the extra capacity, and so was the art auction gallery.

ACCOMMODATION. There are 16 price grades (the price depends on the grade, size and location, with location and grade perhaps more important, since so many of the cabins are of the same, or a very similar size).

All grades of suite/cabin are provided with a hairdryer. The room service menu has only the most basic selection.

There are five grades of suites: Royal Suite (1), Owner's Suite (5), Royal Family Suite (4), Grand Suite (12), and Superior Suite (44, including two superior suites for the disabled). All are well appointed and have pleasing decor (best described as Scandinavian Moderne), with good wood and color accenting (the largest has a baby grand piano).

Royal Suite. The largest accommodation can be found in the Royal Suite, located directly aft of the ship's navigation bridge on the starboard side. It has a separate bedroom with kind-size bed, walk-in closet and vanity dressing area, living room with queen-sized sofa bed, baby grand piano, refrigerator and wet bar, dining table, entertainment center, and large private balcony. The bathroom has a whirlpool tub, separate shower enclosure, two washbasins, and toilet.

Owner's Suite. The five owner's suites are at the forward end of the ship, just behind the navigation bridge, close to the Royal Suite. They have a queen-sized bed, separate living area with queen-size sofa bed, vanity dressing area, refrigerator and wet bar. The bathroom has a full-size tub, separate shower enclosure, toilet and two washbasins.

Royal Family Suite. These have two bedrooms with twin beds that convert to queen-size beds, living area with double sofa bed and Pullman bed, refrigerator, two bathrooms (one with tub), and private balcony. This suite can accommodate eight, and might suit families.

Grand Suite. Features include twin beds that can be convert to a queen-size bed, vanity dressing area, lounge area with sofa bed, refrigerator, and a bathroom with bathtub. There's also a private balcony.

Superior Suite. Features include twin beds that can be convert to a queen-size bed, vanity dressing area, lounge area with sofa bed, refrigerator, and a bathroom with tub. Private balcony. Note that although this is called a suite, it really is little more than a larger standard cabin with balcony.

Other Grades. All standard cabins have twin beds that convert to a queen-size bed, ample closet space for a one-week cruise, and a good amount of drawer space, although under-bed storage space is not good for large suitcases. The bathrooms have nine mirrors. Plastic buckets are provided for champagne/wine and are really tacky.

CUISINE. The 1,195-seat, no-smoking My Fair Lady Dining Room spreads over two decks, connected by a grand, sweeping staircase. Choose one of two seatings, or "My Time Dining" (eat when you want, during dining room hours) when you book.

Alternative dining option ($25 per person cover/gratuity charge): Chops Grill Steakhouse, added during the 2005 "stretch," is an à la carte steakhouse featuring steaks and veal chops; reservations are necessary – think big steaks, better service, an unhurried and more comfortable dining experience.

Casual, self-serve breakfasts and luncheons can be taken in the 790-seat informal Windjammer Marketplace. It has a great expanse of ocean-view glass windows, the decor is bright and cheerful, and buffet "islands" feature food from around the world. An intimate Champagne/Caviar Bar terrace is forward of the lower level of the two-deck-high dining room and just off the atrium for those who might like to taste something a little bit out of the ordinary, in a setting that is both bright and contemporary.

ENTERTAINMENT. The Orpheum Theater, the ship's principal showlounge, is a grand room located at the forward part of the ship, and has 875 seats. This is where the big production shows and major cabaret acts are staged.

A second showlounge, the 575-seat Carousel Lounge, is located aft, and is for smaller shows and adult cabarets, including late-night adult (blue) comedy. A variety of other lounges and bars feature almost constant live music; there's no real quiet (no music) bar to have a drink in.

There is even background music in all corridors and elevators, and constant music outdoors on the pool deck. If you want a quiet relaxing holiday, choose another ship.

SPA/FITNESS. The ShipShape Spa is aft of the funnel and spans two decks. Facilities include an expanded gymnasium (with all the latest machines), aerobics exercise room, sauna and steam rooms, a beauty salon, and 13 treatment rooms, including a couples massage room.

● **For more extensive general information about the Royal Caribbean cruise experience, see pages 151–6.**

Eurodam
★★★★

Size:	Large Resort Ship	Total Crew:	929
Tonnage:	86,700 tons	Passengers	
Lifestyle:	Standard	(lower beds/all berths):	2,104/2,671
Cruise Line:	Holland America Line	Passenger Space Ratio	
Former Names:	none	(lower beds/all berths):	41.2/32.4
Builder:	Fincantieri (Italy)	Crew/Passenger Ratio	
Original Cost:	$450 million	(lower beds/all berths):	2.2/2.8
Entered Service:	July 2008	Cabins (total):	1,052
Registry:	The Netherlands	Size Range (sq ft/m):	170.0–1,318.6/
Length (ft/m):	935.0/285.0		15.7–122.5
Beam (ft/m):	105.6/32.2	Cabins (outside view):	897
Draft (ft/m):	25.5/7.8	Cabins (interior/no view):	155
Propulsion/Propellers:	diesel-electric	Cabins (for one person):	0
	(34,000kW/2 pods (17.6 MW each)	Cabins (with private balcony):	708
Passenger Decks:	12	Cabins (wheelchair accessible):	30

Wheelchair accessibility	Good
Cabin Voltage:	110/220 volts
Elevators:	14
Casino (gaming tables):	Yes
Slot Machines:	Yes
Swimming Pools (outdoors):	2
	+ 1 children's pool
Swimming Pools (indoors):	1
	(indoor/outdoor with retractable dome)
Whirlpools:	5
Self-Service Launderette:	No
Dedicated Cinema/Seats:	Yes/170
Library:	Yes

BERLITZ'S OVERALL SCORE: 1,534 OUT OF A POSSIBLE 2,000 POINTS

OVERVIEW. *Eurodam* was the newest ship in the HAL fleet when it debuted in summer 2008. With one deck more than close sister *Noordam*, it has more cabins than *Noordam* (which itself had 35 more cabins than close sisters *Oosterdam, Westerdam* and *Zuiderdam*) but still the same number of elevators, and open deck space.

The ship has two funnels, positioned close together – one behind the other instead of side by side – the result of the machinery configuration. The ship has, in effect, two engine rooms – one with three diesels, and one with two diesels. A "pod" propulsion system is provided *(see page 45 for an explanation of the technicalities).*

One neat feature consists of 22 private (rent by the day) cabanas, with goodies such as champagne, chocolate strawberries, an iPod pre-stocked with music, bathrobes, fresh fruit and chilled towels (for two adults and two children, so they may not be the promised "quiet" spaces, after all). They are located in an area on observation deck and around the Lido Pool, with a daily charge for the 14 cabanas in The Retreat – $75 for sea days and $45 on port days; for the 8 Lido Deck cabanas it's $50 on sea days and $30 on port days. My recommendation: book a cabana in The Retreat – it will be less busy, and thus more relaxing.

The ship is designed to appeal to younger, more vibrant, multi-generational holidaymakers. There is a complete walk-around exterior teak promenade deck, and real teak "steamer" style sunloungers are provided. Additionally, there is a jogging track outdoors, located around the ship's mast and the forward third of the ship.

Exterior glass elevators, mounted midships on both port and starboard sides, provide fine ocean views from any one

BERLITZ'S RATINGS

	Possible	Achieved
Ship	500	427
Accommodation	200	168
Food	400	275
Service	400	279
Entertainment	100	77
Cruise	400	308

of the 11 passenger decks. There are two centrally located swimming pools outdoors, one of which can be used in inclement weather due to its retractable sliding glass roof.

Two whirlpool tubs, adjacent to the swimming pools, are abridged by a bar. A smaller (swimming) pool is available for children, and this incorporates a winding water slide that spans two decks in height. There is an additional whirlpool tub outdoors.

The intimate lobby (which has its own bar) spans three decks. Adjacent are interior elevators, and glass wall elevators with exterior views. The interior decor is bright in many areas, designed to attract a younger clientele). In keeping with the traditions of Holland America Line, a large collection of artwork is a standard feature, and pieces reflect the former Dutch East Indies.

There are two whole entertainment/ public room decks. Perhaps the most dramatic room aboard this ship is the showlounge, spanning four decks in the forward section of the ship. Other facilities include a winding shopping street with several boutique stores and logo shops, card room, an art gallery, photo gallery, and several small meetings rooms.

The casino is large (one has to walk through it to get from the restaurant to the showlounge on Lower Promenade Deck), and is equipped with all the necessary gaming paraphernalia and slot machines.

"Explorations" is a combination coffee bar (coffees and other drinks are at extra cost), lounge, an extensive library and internet-connect center, all in one attractive, open "lifestyle" environment adjacent to the Crows Nest Lounge.

For families with children, Club HAL's KidZone provides a whole area dedicated to children's facilities and extensive programming for different age groups (5–17), with one counselor for every 30 children. Free ice cream is provided at certain hours, plus hot hors d'oeuvres in all bars.

While this formula doesn't work so well for loyal repeat passengers used to the line's smaller ships, *Eurodam* offers a wide range of public rooms. Dutch artefacts and museum pieces from the 16th and 17th centuries are displayed.

The information desk in the lobby is small and somewhat removed from the main passenger flow on the two decks above it. Several pillars obstruct the passenger flow and lines of sight throughout the ship. There are no self-service launderettes – something that many families with children miss, even though special laundry packages are available.

ACCOMMODATION. Of the total 1,022 suites/cabins, 86% have an outside view, while 67 of these have a private balcony. Note that many cabins on Upper Promenade Deck have lifeboat-obstructed views. For an explanation of suites/cabins, see the entry for *Noordam*. A total of 37 cabins have inter-connecting doors. All balconies have solid steel railings instead of glass.

All suites/cabins feature Signature of Excellence premium amenities: plush Mariner's Dream beds, waffle/terry cloth robes, Egyptian cotton towels, flat panel TVs, DVD players, make-up mirrors with halo lighting, massage shower heads, large hair dryers, fresh flowers and complimentary fruit baskets.

Niggles include noisy air-conditioning (the flow can't be regulated or turned off in cabins or bathrooms; the only regulation is for temperature control), and lack of drawer space. Avoid cabins directly under the aft pool deck because deck chair dragging noises can be really irritating.

CUISINE. The two-deck-high Rembrandt main dining room is at the ship's aft, with seating at tables for two, four, six or eight on both main and upper levels (the galley is under the restaurant, accessed by port and starboard escalators). It provides a traditional HAL dining experience, with friendly service from smiling Indonesian and Filipino stewards.

Both open seating and fixed seatings (assigned tables and time) are available, plus an open-seating arrangement for breakfast and lunch; you'll be seated by restaurant staff when you enter. The dining room is a non-smoking venue. **Alternative themed dining spots** include the reservations-only Pinnacle Grill – the premium Sterling Silver steak and seafood restaurant and adjacent Pinnacle Bar; Tamarind, a 144-seat Pan-Asian restaurant (no charge for lunch; $15 for dinner); and the 72-seat Canaletto, an Italian eatery created nightly in a section of the Lido Cafe.

ENTERTAINMENT. Theatre-style seating in the ship's main showlounge.

SPA/FITNESS. The Greenhouse Spa is the largest yet for HAL, and includes a thermal suite (wet steam rooms with various herbal mists, plus dry saunas), and a large gymnasium. Sports enthusiasts can enjoy a basketball court, volleyball court, golf simulator.

● **For more extensive general information about Holland America Line, see pages 139–42.**

DID YOU KNOW...

● that motion pictures' most famous on-screen odd couple, Jack Lemmon and Walter Matthau, played gentlemen dance hosts intent on defrauding rich widows aboard a Caribbean cruise ship (*Westerdam*)? *Out to Sea*, a 1997 Martha Coolidge film, also starred Dyan Cannon, Gloria DeHaven, and Elaine Stritch. The "cruise ship" interior was filmed at Raleigh Studios in Hollywood.
● that Epirotiki Line's *Jupiter* was used to carry the 61 finalists of the 1976 Miss Universe contest (Epirotiki Line became part of the now defunct Royal Olympia Cruises)?
● that on Valentine's Day, 1998, some 5,000 couples renewed their vows aboard the ships of Princess Cruises?
● that a 15-ft-high model of Goofy hangs upside down over the stern of *Disney Magic*? He's painting the ship.
● that Carnival Cruise Lines and Mattel teamed up to produce a nautical-themed Barbie Doll? She can be found in the gift shops aboard all the company's ships.
● that the spa aboard the now withdrawn *Queen Elizabeth 2* was the first afloat to have a fully functional thalassotherapy pool; it was installed in 1994?
● that Steiner Leisure spa employees at sea massage over 30,000 bodies, deep cleanse 15,000 faces, blow dry 6,000 heads of hair, and manicure approximately 6,000 pairs of hands?
● that in 2002 Steiner Leisure purchased Mandara Spas and the Greenhouse Spas? Each brand continues to maintain its own identity.

Europa
★★★★★ +

Size: . . . . .Small Ship	Passenger Decks: 7	Cabins (wheelchair accessible): 2
Tonnage: .28,890	Total Crew: 280	Wheelchair accessibility . . . . .Good
Lifestyle: . . . . .Utterly Exclusive	Passengers	Cabin Current: . . . . .110 and 220 volts
Cruise Line: . . . . .Hapag-Lloyd Cruises	(lower beds/all berths): 408/450	Elevators: 4
Former Names: . . . . .none	Passenger Space Ratio	Casino (gaming tables): . . . . .No
Builder: . . .Kvaerner Masa-Yards (Finland)	(lower beds/all berths): 70.4/64.2	Slot Machines: .No
Original Cost: . . . . .DM260 million	Crew/Passenger Ratio	Swimming Pools (outdoors): 1
Entered Service: . . . . .Sept 1999	(lower beds/all berths): 1.4/1.6	Swimming Pools (indoors): 1
Registry: . . . . .The Bahamas	Cabins (total): .204	(indoor/outdoor with magrodome)
Length (ft/m): 651.5/198.6	Size Range (sq ft/m): 355.2–914.9/	Whirlpools: 1
Beam (ft/m): 78.7/24.0	33.0–85.0	Self-Service Launderette: . . . . .Yes
Draft (ft/m): 20.0/6.1	Cabins (outside view): 204	(ironing room)
Propulsion/Propellers: . . . . .diesel-electric	Cabins (interior/no view): 0	Dedicated Cinema/Seats: Yes/60
(21,600 kW)/2 azimuthing pods	Cabins (for one person): 0	Library: . . . . .Yes
(13.3 MW each)	Cabins (with private balcony): 168	

OVERALL SCORE: 1,853 OUT OF A POSSIBLE 2,000 POINTS

OVERVIEW. *Europa* has a sleek app-earance, with sweeping lines, a graceful profile, and Hapag-Lloyd's orange/ blue funnel. Look down from the aft Lido Deck fantail and you will see a rounded, graceful stern – unlike the box-like rears of so many contemporary ships.

This is a very stable ship in the open sea, with no vibration or noise – thanks partly to its "pod" propulsion system *(details, page 45).* It carries 14 Zodiac landing craft for use during close-up shore excursions; and boot-washing areas are also provided.

There is a walking/jogging area with rubberized deck (plus a wrap-around outdoors teak promenade deck out-doors), as well as a small FKK (FreiKörperKultur) deck for nude sunbathing. The sunloungers are aluminum with teak armrests, and have thick cushioned pads.

There is one swimming pool, in a long, rectangular in shape (modified from its original "bottle"-shaped design in December 2000), and, while not the widest, it is longer than the pools aboard many other cruise ships; it measures 56.7 by 16.8 ft (17.3 by 5.15 meters). Movies are shown poolside on a large screen on selected evenings, and themed social events are held here.

With this ship, Hapag-Lloyd has been able to reach and maintain the high standards that its passengers demand, due to the fact that most of Europa's hotel service crew are German-speaking nationals who understand the culture and can talk in depth about German/Swiss/Austrian life, unlike an international crew that can barely communicate.

The space per passenger is high, there is never a hint of a line, and both restaurant and show lounge seat a full comple-ment of passengers. *Europa* is one of the world's most spa-

BERLITZ'S RATINGS

	Possible	Achieved
Ship	500	474
Accommodation	200	183
Food	400	373
Service	400	359
Entertainment	100	91
Cruise	400	373

cious purpose-built cruise ships – an exquisite retreat. Step aboard and you'll find a world of relaxed, contemporary cruising that is intensely welcoming.

Europa is finely appointed, in the con-temporary style usually described as "minimalism" in hotel-speak. Only the very best quality soft furnishings have been chosen for the ship's interiors, subtly blending traditional with modern designs and materials. Most public rooms and hallways have extremely high ceilings, providing an enhanced sense of space and grandeur. The colors used in the ship's interior decor are light and con-temporary – there is no hint of glitz, garish colors, or neon.

Public rooms include the Club Belvedere (for afternoon tea and intimate music recitals), the Europa Lounge (the main showlounge), which has a U-shaped seating configu-ration and a proper stage, although there are several pillars. In addition, there is a Clipper Lounge/Bar (with high ceil-ings), an Atrium Piano Bar with Steinway baby grand piano. When the ship first debuted there was a casino, although this proved to be so little used that Hapag-Lloyd Cruises turned it into a multi-functional space for small cocktail parties, and as a high-class art gallery.

There is also a fine sidewalk Havana Bar cigar lounge. This clubby room is equipped with three large glass-fronted, fully temperature-controlled and conditioned humi-dor cabinets, and carries an extensive range of cigars from Cuba and other countries. Cigars stocked include a range (from 102mm to 232mm) of top brands. The bar also serves a fine range of armagnacs, calvados and cognacs, all poured tableside, as well as Cuban beer. Embedded in a wall adja-cent to the bar is a digital MP3 jukebox, with a push-button selection of 15,000 songs and instrumental music of every description, so you can choose what you want to hear.

What's really nice in this intimate spot – with its buttery soft leather chairs and sofas – is Irish Coffee, correctly presented (the glass should be rotated while the sugar is blended with the alcohol and heated gently over a candle flame, the liquor set alight before coffee and cream are added).

Other features include a business center, an electronic golf simulator room (there is also a golf driving range, and a shuffleboard court), and dedicated rooms for hobbies (arts and crafts), and for children. The nicely stocked library has an illuminated globe of the world, and is open 24 hours. There's also a small cinema/meeting/function room.

In 2004, an indoor/outdoor bar, Sansibar, was added above the Lido Café (with great aft-facing views), and is the "in" place for the late-night set. Adjacent to Sansibar is an electronic golf simulator, golf club, and teaching facility; a PGA golf pro is carried on all cruises.

There is a seven-deck-high central atrium, plus two glass-walled elevators (operated by "piccolos" on embarkation day), and a lobby on the lower level with a Steinway grand piano and lobby bar, reception desk, concierge desk, shore excursion desk and a future cruise sales desk.

Wheelchair passengers should note that a special ramp is provided from the swimming pool/outdoors deck down to where the lifeboats are located; only three other ships have them. Wheelchair access is good throughout this ship.

SUITABLE FOR: *Europa* should appeal to all those who desire to be aboard what is arguably the most luxurious and finest of all the smaller cruise ships. For the German-speaking market, nothing else comes close. The crew also speaks English for the few British and American passengers, and some cruises are designated as bi-lingual English/German language voyages. Combined with an enthusiastic and well-trained crew, whose aim is to serve and please passengers in the most sumptuous but unobtrusive manner, the tradition of luxury cruising in a contemporary setting is taken to its highest expression. with superb food and a wide range of creature comforts. Although a children's playroom is provided, *Europa* really is a ship for adults to cruise in a quiet, refined setting that mixes formality and informality well.

ACCOMMODATION. This is provided in five configurations and 10 price categories. It consists of all-outside-view suites: 2 Penthouse Grand Suites (Hapag, and Lloyd) and 10 Penthouse Deluxe Suites (Bach, Beethoven, Brahms, Handel, Lehar, Haydn, Mozart, Schubert, Strauss, Wagner, with each suite containing a large framed picture of the composer), 156 suites with private balcony, and 36 standard suites. There are two suites (with private balcony) for the disabled and 8 suites with interconnecting doors (good for families).

Almost all suites have a private balcony (with wide teakwood deck, and lighting), and come complete with a smoked glass screen topped by a teakwood rail. However, 12 suites that overlook the stern are among the most sought-after accommodation (six on each of two decks, each suite having private balconies with canvas "ceilings" for shade and privacy).

General Information: Each suite has a wood floor entry-way, and each has a sleeping area with twin beds that can convert to a queen-sized bed, and two bedside tables with lamps and two drawers. There is a separate lounge area (with curtain divider) and bird's-eye maple wood cabinetry and accenting (with rounded edges). Facilities include a refrigerator/mini-bar (beer and soft drinks are supplied at no extra charge), a writing/vanity desk and couch with large table in a separate lounge area. An illuminated walk-in closet provides ample hanging rail space, six drawers, personal safe (this can be opened with a credit card), umbrella, shoehorn, and clothes brush. European duvets are provided, and, in another cruise industry first, so is a full-color free daily newspaper (there's a wide choice). Almost all suites have totally unobstructed views and excellent soundproofing. All passengers receive a practical blue/beige shoulder travel bag, insulated lunch bag for shore excursions, leather keycard holder, and a generous supply of personal toiletries.

In what was a cruise industry first, a superb integrated color TV/computer monitor and "CIN" (Cruise Infotainment System) – 24 hours per day video and audio on-demand – is provided free, so you choose when you want to watch any one of up to 100 movies, or when you want to listen to any of the 1,000+ compact audio discs.

The infotainment system includes large flat screens and direct, 24 hours-a-day internet connection via a full wireless keyboard located in a drawer in an adjacent vanity unit (each passenger has an assigned email address), Restaurant seating plans, menus, ship's position and chart, deck plan, shore excursion video clips, plus other informational video clips and items are featured. Your private email address is provided with your tickets and other documentation (there is no charge for incoming or outgoing emails, only for attachments, and for internet access). A modem (data) socket is also provided should you decide to bring your own laptop computer (the ship can also provide a laptop for your use).

All suites have a 100% air-circulation system, illuminated walk-in closets and a generous amount of hanging and storage space. Western European butlers and cabin stewardesses are employed (butlers for the 12 premium suites on Deck 10, cabin stewardesses for all other suites).

The white/gray/sea green marble-tiled bathrooms are very well designed, have light decor, and include two good size cabinets for personal toiletries. All bathrooms have a full tub (plus an integral shower and a retractable clothesline) and separate glass-fronted shower enclosure. Thick, 100% cotton bathrobes are provided, as are slippers and an array of personal toiletries. Parents with babies get a video baby phone (camera via PDA with vibration alarm, and access via wireless LAN).

Penthouses (Deck 10): There are two Penthouse Grand suites, and 10 Penthouse Deluxe suites; all were totally refurbished in 2009, when electronically adjustable beds and Nespresso coffee machines were added. These have a teakwood entrance hall, spacious living room with full-size dining table and four chairs, fully stocked drinks cabinet with refrigerator butler service, complimentary bar set-up (replenished with whatever you need), laundry and ironing service included, priority spa reservations, caviar or other canapés daily before dinner, hand-made chocolates, petit-fours and other niceties at no extra charge. Balconies have teakwood decking, and white canvas ceiling shades. For the ultimate in exclusivity, the two Penthouse Grand suites also have even larger bathrooms (each with its own private sauna), and extensive forward views from their prime, supremely quiet location one deck above the navigation bridge; a very large wrap-around private balcony; larger walk-in closet (with its own window), and large flatscreen TVs. Well-trained butlers provide the highest level of unobtrusive service for these suites.

Spa suites: Newly created in 2007 are four delightful spa suites, located just forward to the Futuresse Spa on Deck 7. These are fine new suites, and incorporate a large private teak-decked balcony (good for massages); twin or queensized bed; walk-in closet; dark wood cabinetry housing a refrigerator (stocked with fruit juices and different mineral waters) and bar set-up, personal computer, flat-screen TV, and storage space including a jewelry drawer, with pullaround doors that can close off everything to view; writing/vanity desk, and floor-to-ceiling windows. The decor colors are warm reds, yellow and gold. There is a large window (with wooden blond) between the living/sleeping area and the bathroom. The bathroom itself has warm Asian decor, underwater lighted Jacuzzi bath, separate large

shower enclosure (with rain shower), toilet and gold, thick-glass washbasin, hand-held hairdryer, and plenty of storage space. A range of special toiletry amenities is provided, and special teas and other services are provided by spa personnel. And, for cruises longer than 10 days, a customized spa package (including treatments) is included in the price.

Suites for the Disabled (Deck 7): These spacious suites have one electronically operated bed with hydraulic elevator plus one regular bed, while a non-walk-in closet with drawers replaces the walk-in closet in all other suites. The bathroom has a roll-in shower area. All fittings are at the correct height, and there are several grab handles, plus an emergency call-for-help button. Wheelchair-accessible public toilets are provided on the main restaurant/entertainment deck.

CUISINE. With over 5,000 separate food ingredients carried at any one time, the executive chef can produce menus that don't repeat even for around-the-world and other long voyages for which this ship excels. The cuisine is outstanding, always full of surprises, and never boring. Seasonal and regional ingredients are featured, with much totally fresh fish and seafood as standard. This is as good as it gets. There are four restaurants to choose from.

The Europa Restaurant is a beautiful dining room that is two decks high, and can accommodate all passengers in one seating, with tables assigned for dinner only (breakfast and lunch are open seating). Passengers thus keep their favorite waiter throughout each cruise (for dinner). In common with most German ships, a small smoking sections is provided.

WHY DOES *EUROPA* SCORE SO HIGHLY?

The reason lies in the little details most cruise lines have long left behind in the age of discounts, the extras and the meticulous attention to personal comfort and service. If you are relaxing at the swimming pool in a hot climate, deck stewards will set your sunlounger and cover the mattress pad with a towel, serve you drinks, give you a cold herbal towel, and spray you with Evian water to keep you cool.

Naturally, only real glasses are used at the swimming pool and on the open decks – plastic glasses would not be considered. When drinks are served, they are placed on cotton doilies (not paper or cork – a touch of finesse not found aboard other ships). Real flowers, pot pourri and cloth towels (paper towels are not permissible at this rating level) are provided in all public restrooms. Indeed, fresh flowers are everywhere.

Details, details, details – that's what *Europa* cruising is all about, and what the ship's many repeat passengers expect. The prices for drinks and wines are also very reasonable (they are not included for the simple reason that ships that include drinks typically have a much more restricted selection, including young table

wines that may not be to all tastes); also, the ship provides many social functions and parties where drinks are provided free. Birthdays and anniversaries are quietly celebrated in one's suite – there are no singing waiters in the dining room to disturb other passengers.

Excellent port information is provided (both in written form and via the TV infotainment system). All port taxes and gratuities are included, although further tipping is not prohibited. The currency on board is the euro. The ship's voyage chart is auctioned each cruise, with the money collected going directly to charity.

When taking all things into account – the unhurried lifestyle of single seating dining, plenty of suites with private balconies, a fine array of classical music artists and lecturers, absolutely no vibration anywhere, and the outstanding cuisine and friendly, very attentive personal service from a staff dedicated to working aboard the world's finest cruise ship – it all adds up to the very best luxurious cruise ship and cruise experience available today (unless you have your own private motor yacht).

While most cruise lines have been

engaged in dressing down, Hapag-Lloyd has done the opposite: dining room staff have stunning uniforms for formal nights, consisting of tails and trousers.

Although there are ships with more grandiose penthouse suites, larger balconies, show lounges, health spas and other appointments – but aboard *Europa*, everything is in scale, and in relation to the requirements of its passengers. At present, while there are plenty of imitators, there are no equals.

There are few weak points, although perhaps an indoor swimming pool might be welcome. The balcony partitions are part-partitions, but would be more private if they were of the full (floor-to-ceiling) type – although this rarely presents a problem. Occupants of suites on Penthouse Deck 10 have private assisted concierge check-in aboard the ship, rather than in the cruise terminal, wherever possible.

While *Europa* is not for everyone, the ship, which provides a more formal cruise experience than some might seek, provides the setting for the highest expression of the art of unobtrusive service and hospitality.

There are tables for two (quite a few), four, six or eight. For superb service, there is a *chef de rang* and an assistant waiter system, so that the *chef de rang* is always at the station, with the assistant waiter acting as runner.

The cuisine is superb, and very varied. Plated presentation of food is provided for entrées with silver service for additional vegetables, as well as tableside flambeaux. The size of portions is sensible – never overwhelming. On days at sea, in addition to the regular, extensive breakfast, a Gourmet Breakfast menu includes such things as beef tartare, carpaccio of smoked tuna with wasabi cream, gooseliver tureen with orange confit, and other specialties rarely found aboard cruise ships today. In 2006 a new Cuisine Legeré menu was added (light, healthy, but very tasty spa cuisine).

Table settings include Dibbern china, 150-gram weight Robbe & Berking silverware and Riedel wine glasses. The cuisine is very international, but includes German favorites as well as regional dishes from around the world. The quality of food is extremely high. Although top-grade Iranian Ossetre caviar is found on dinner menus at least once each week, it is always available on request (at extra cost). Otherwise, most of the caviar comes from French farmed sturgeon – and is excellent. An extensive wine list includes a good selection of vintage French wines, as well as a well-balanced selection of Austrian, German and Swiss wines.

Alternative dining options: In a first for the cruise industry, chef Dieter Muller, who has three Michelin stars, has his first restaurant at sea – Two Stars, with a personally designed five-course menu (three courses for lunch). The menu changes three times during a world cruise, and seasonally during the rest of the year. He will participate in 15 cruises a year – about half of *Europa*'s program. Two Stars can be reserved once per cruise by all passengers. It is open for dinner nightly, and for lunch on sea days – and at no extra charge.

Venezia, a second alternative dining spot, is much loved for its fine Italian cuisine – and a wide variety of olive oils and grappa. It is open for lunch and dinner, and at no extra charge. Both venues are adjacent to and forward of the main restaurant, and provide the setting for a truly intimate dining experience, by reservation only.

For more casual dining, try the elegant Lido Café for serve-yourself breakfasts – the ship even makes its own preserves – luncheons and dinners, with both indoor and outdoor seating (under heat lamps when needed) and adjacent indoor/outdoor bar. Themed evening dining is also featured here, with full waiter service. There is a wide variety of food, and many special lunch buffets have a number of popular themes and regional specialties.

Europa is famous for its real German sausages, available in the Clipper Bar, and at a special Bavarian Fruschoppen featured once each cruise in the Lido Cafe. Late each night, "light bites", beautifully presented on silver trays, are taken around the various bars and lounges.

Afternoon tea is a sheer delight, with a selection of about 30 teas (loose tea, of course, never teabags). There are also several types of coffee and impeccably made liqueur coffees, heated in a hand-turned glass enclosure, and a superb selection of cakes (made fresh every day). Nautical tradition is kept up with bouillon service each morning at sea, and other daily niceties include fresh waffles and ice cream each afternoon around the pool.

ENTERTAINMENT. The Europa Lounge, whose decor is a rich red, is the main showlounge; it has a sloping floor, providing good sightlines from almost every seat. The ship excels in its fine, intellectual entertainment program (it is tailored more to the theme of the cruise), which includes a constant supply of high-quality classical and contemporary musical artistes, a variety of cabaret acts, as well as a programme of expert lecturers, poetry readers, and so on, together with an occasional colorful production show, and local shows brought on board in various ports.

The smaller, more intimate Clipper Lounge is the setting for late-night cabaret (vocalists, magicians, ballroom dance specialists, comedians). The ship carries a main showband, plus a number of small musical units to provide live music for listening or dancing. Classical concerts and recitals are provided in the Belvedere Lounge, with its dropped central circular floor and white Steinway grand piano. A summer Ocean Sun Festival has been an outstanding, successful and worthwhile addition to the classical music cruises.

SPA/FITNESS. The Ocean Spa has a wide range of beauty services and treatments, including hot stone massage, and an array of other rejuvenating treatments, including full-day spa packages. Shiseido cosmetics are the featured cosmetic/spa products for sale. The entire spa area was completely refitted and redecorated in May 2007 and is now a well integrated and very welcoming wellness and treatment area.

Facilities include a steam room and sauna (mixed), two shower enclosures and two foot-washing stations, relaxation room with 3 hot tiled beds, 3 wicker relax beds, and male and female changing/dressing rooms. There is also a separate gymnasium and a beauty salon. A Japanese Spa is featured (treatments include a cream body massage, gentle steam room and a two-tatami mat relaxation area), which is booked individually for a special 90-minute treatment.

Other treatments: Asian-style spa special (hot aroma body wrap with head, shiatsu and foot massages) (€90 for 60 minutes); Pacific style spa special – Lomi Lomi massage with warm aroma oils and body pack (€90 for 60 minutes); Classic Massage (€40 for 30 minutes); Shiatsu Massage (€60 for 30 minutes); Shiseido Intensive Facial (€110 for 90 minutes); Goddess of the Sea total indulgence program (€290 for three hours of pampering including a Lomi Lomi massage, body pack, and facial).

A nice touch is that the treatment rooms have music menus, so you can choose what music you wish to hear.

On cruises with more than four sea days, *Europa*'s shore-based wellness partner provides, at no extra charge, "Vital" specialists for lectures and wellness regimes, in addition to the ship's own fitness team.

Also newly introduced, on cruises with four or more sea days, is father and son (or daughter) fencing, with all equipment provided by *die fechtmeister*.

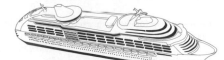

Explorer of the Seas
★★★★

Size: . . . . .Large Resort Ship	Passenger Decks: 14	Cabins (with private balcony): 757
Tonnage: .137,308	Total Crew: .1,181	Cabins (wheelchair accessible): 26
Lifestyle: . . . . .Standard	Passengers	Wheelchair accessibility . . . . .Best
Cruise Line: Royal Caribbean International	(lower beds/all berths): 3,114/3,840	Cabin Current: . . . . .110 volts
Former Names: . . . . .none	Passenger Space Ratio	Elevators: . . . . .14 (6 glass-enclosed)
Builder: . . .Kvaerner Masa-Yards (Finland)	(lower beds/all berths): 44.0/35.7	Casino (gaming tables): . . . . .Yes
Original Cost: . . . .$500 million	Crew/Passenger Ratio	Slot Machines: . . . . .Yes
Entered Service: . . . . .Oct 2000	(lower beds/all berths): 2.6/3.2	Swimming Pools (outdoors): 3
Registry: . . . . .The Bahamas	Cabins (total): 1,557	Swimming Pools (indoors): 0
Length (ft/m): 1,020.6/311.1	Size Range (sq ft/m): 151.0–1,358.0/	Whirlpools: 6
Beam (ft/m): 155.5/47.4	14.0–126.1	Self-Service Launderette: . . . . .No
Draft (ft/m): 28.8/8.8	Cabins (outside view): 939	Dedicated Cinema/Seats: . . . . .No
Propulsion/Propellers: . . . . .diesel-electric	Cabins (interior/no view): 618	Library: . . . . .Yes
(75,600kW)/3 pods	Cabins (for one person): 0	

OVERALL SCORE: 1,461 OUT OF A POSSIBLE 2,000 POINTS

OVERVIEW. This large, stunning, floating leisure resort is sister to *Adventure of the Seas, Mariner of the Seas, Navigator of the Seas* and *Voyager of the Seas*). The ship's propulsion is derived from three pod units, powered by electric motors – two azimuthing, and one fixed at the centerline– in the latest configuration of high-tech propulsion systems *(for details, see page 45)*.

With its large proportions, the ship provides more facilities and options, yet it has a healthy amount of space per passenger. It is too large to go through the Panama Canal, thus limiting itineraries almost exclusively to the Caribbean, where few islands can accept it, or for use as a floating resort. Spend the first few hours exploring the many facilities and public spaces and it will be time well spent.

Although *Explorer of the Seas* is large, the cabin hallways are warm and attractive, with artwork cabinets and wavy lines to lead you along and break up the monotony. There are plenty of colorful, even whimsical, decorative touches to prevent the environment being too clinical.

The four-decks-high Royal Promenade, which is 394 ft (120 meters) long, is the main interior focal point (it's a good place to hang out, to meet someone, or to arrange to meet someone). The length of two American football fields, it has two internal lobbies (atria) that rise as many as 11 decks high. Restaurants, shops and entertainment locations front this winding street and interior "with-view" cabins look into it from above. The Guest Reception and Shore Excursion counters are located at the aft end of the promenade, as is an ATM machine. Look up to see the large moving, asteroid-like sculpture (constantly growing and contracting), parades and street entertainers.

Arched across the promenade is a captain's balcony.

BERLITZ'S RATINGS

	Possible	Achieved
Ship	500	418
Accommodation	200	150
Food	400	222
Service	400	281
Entertainment	100	83
Cruise	400	307

Meanwhile, a stairway in the center of the promenade connects you to the deck below, where you'll find Schooner Bar (a piano lounge that is a feature of all RCI ships) and the colorful Casino Royale. Casino gaming includes blackjack, Caribbean stud poker, roulette, and craps, as well as 300 slot machines.

Aft of the casino is the Aquarium Bar; adjacent are some neat displays of oceanographic interest. Royal Caribbean International has teamed up with the University of Miami's Rosenstiel School of Marine and Atmospheric Science to study the ocean and the atmosphere. A small onboard laboratory is part of the project.

There is a regulation-size ice-skating rink (Studio B), with real ice, and stadium-style seating for up to 900, plus the latest in broadcast facilities. Ice Follies shows are also presented here. Slim pillars obstruct clear-view arena stage sightlines, however. If ice-skating in the Caribbean doesn't appeal, perhaps you'd like the stunning two-deck library (open 24 hours a day). A grand $12 million has been spent on permanent artwork.

Drinking places include a neat Aquarium Bar, which comes complete with 50 tons of glass and water in four large aquariums. Other drinking places include the intimate Champagne Bar, Crown & Anchor Pub, a Sidewalk Cafe (for continental breakfast, all-day pizzas, specialty coffees and desserts), Sprinkles (for round-the-clock ice cream and yoghurt), and Weekend Warrior (a sports bar), and a Connoisseur Club (for cigars and cognacs). Lovers of jazz might like Dizzy's, an intimate room for cool music within the Viking Crown Lounge, or the Schooner Bar piano lounge. Golfers might enjoy the 19th Hole, a golf bar, as they play the Explorer Links.

There are also several shops on the Royal Promenade,

including a jewelry shop, gift shop, and liquor store. At times, street entertainers appear, and parades happen.

A TV studio is adjacent to rooms useable for trade show exhibit space, with a 400-seat conference center and a multi-media screening room that seats 60. You can tie the knot in the Skylight Chapel, which even has wheelchair access via an electric stairlift. Outdoors, the pool and open deck areas provide a resort-like environment.

Families with children are also well catered to, as facilities for children and teenagers are quite extensive. "Aquanauts" is for 3–5 year olds; "Explorers" (6–8); "Voyagers" (9–12). Optix is a dedicated area for teenagers, including a daytime club (with computers), soda bar, disco with disc jockey and dance floor. Challenger's Arcade has the latest video games. Paint and Clay is an arts and crafts center for younger children. Adjacent to these indoor areas is Adventure Beach, an area for all the family to enjoy: it includes swimming pools, a water slide and game areas outdoors.

In terms of sheer size, this ship dwarfs most other ships in the cruise industry, but in terms of personal service, the reverse is the case, unless you have one of the top suites.

Passenger gripes: cabin bath towels and explosively noisy (vacuum) toilets; few quiet places to sit and read – almost everywhere there is intrusive background music. And if you have a cabin with a door that interconnecting door to another cabin, be aware that you'll be able to hear everything your next-door neighbours say and do.

ACCOMMODATION. There are 22 cabin categories, in four major groupings: Premium ocean-view suites and cabins, Promenade-view (interior-view) cabins, Ocean-view cabins, and Interior (no view) cabins. Many cabins are of a similar size – good for incentives and large groups, and 300 have interconnecting doors – good for families. Prices depend on grade, size and location.

Some 138 interior (no view) cabins have bay windows that look into a horizontal atrium, with interior cabins that look into a central shopping plaza. However, all cabins except for the Royal Suite and Owner's Suite have twin beds that convert to a queen-sized bed, TV set, radio and telephone, personal safe, vanity unit, mini-bar, hairdryer and private bathroom.

The largest accommodation includes luxurious penthouse suites, whose occupants have sole access to a concierge club. The grandest is the Royal Suite, on the port side of the ship, and measures 1,146 sq. ft (106.5 sq. meters). It has a king-sized bed in a separate, large bedroom, a living room with an additional queen-sized sofa bed, baby grand piano, refrigerator/wet bar, dining table, entertainment center, and large bathroom.

There are similar facilities in the slightly smaller, but still highly desirable Owner's Suites – there are 10, all in the center of the ship, on both port and starboard sides, each measuring 468 sq. ft (43 sq. meters) and four Royal Family suites (each measures 574 sq. ft (53 sq. meters). However, the four Royal Family suites, which have two bedrooms (including one with third/ fourth upper Pullman

berths) are located at the stern of the ship and have magnificent views over the ship's wake (and seagulls).

All cabins have a private bathroom with shower enclosure (towels are 100% cotton), plus interactive television and pay-per-view movies. Cabins with "private balconies" aren't so private, as the partitions are only partial.

CUISINE. The large main dining room is set on three levels, named after explorers (Christopher Columbus, Da Gama and Magellan). All three have exactly the same menus and are non-smoking. Choose one of two seatings, or "My Time Dining" (eat when you want, during dining room hours) when you book. Tables are for four, six, eight 10 or 12.

Alternative Dining Options: Alternative dining options for casual and informal meals at all hours (according to company releases) include:

● Cafe Promenade, for continental breakfast, all-day pizzas and speciality coffees (provided in paper cups).

● Windjammer Cafe, for casual buffet-style breakfast, lunch and light dinner (except on a cruise's last night).

● Island Grill (actually a section inside the Windjammer Cafe), for casual dinner (no reservations needed), with a grill and open kitchen.

● Portofino: the ship's "upscale" Italian restaurant, open for dinner only. Reservations are required, and there's a $6 gratuity per person. The food and its presentation are better than the food in the dining room. Choices include antipasti, soup, salad, pasta, main dish, dessert, cheese and coffee. The menu does not change throughout the cruise.

● Johnny Rockets, a retro 1950s all-day, all-night diner-style eatery, has hamburgers, malt shakes (at extra cost), and jukebox hits, with both indoor and outdoor seating.

● Sprinkles, for round-the-clock ice cream and yogurt, pastries and coffee.

ENTERTAINMENT. The 1,350-seat Palace Showlounge, a stunning room, is located at the forward end of the ship and spans the height of five decks (with only a few slim pillars and almost no disruption of sight lines). The room has a hydraulic orchestra pit and huge stage areas, together with sonic-boom loud sound, and superb lighting equipment.

The strongest cabaret acts perform in the main showlounge, while others play the Maharaja's Lounge.

SPA/FITNESS. The large ShipShape health spa measures 15,000 sq. ft (1,400 sq. meters). It includes a large aerobics room, fitness center (with the usual techno-gym equipment), several treatment rooms, men's and women's sauna/steam rooms. Another 10,000 sq. ft (930 sq. meters) is devoted to a Solarium (with magrodome sliding glass roof) for relaxation after you've exercised too much. A 32.8-ft (10-meter) rock-climbing wall has five climbing tracks. Other sports facilities include a roller-blading track, a dive-and-snorkel shop, a full-size basketball court and 9-hole, par 26 golf course.

● **For more extensive general information about the Royal Caribbean cruise experience, see pages 151–6.**

50 Years of Victory
NOT YET RATED

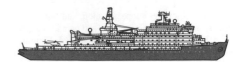

Size: ....Boutique	Passenger Decks: 6	Cabins (wheelchair accessible): 0
Tonnage: 23,439	Total Crew: 140	Wheelchair accessibility ....None
Lifestyle: ....Standard (Expedition)	Passengers	Cabin Voltage:...........................110 volts
Cruise Line: ....Quark Expeditions	(lower beds/all berths):.....................128	Elevators: 1
Former Names: ....none	Passenger Space Ratio	Casino (gaming tables): 0
Builder: ....Baltic Works, St. Petersburg	(lower beds/all berths):.........183.1/183.1	Slot Machines: 0
(Russia)	Crew/Passenger Ratio	Swimming Pools (outdoors): 1
Original Cost: ....n/a	(lower beds/all berths):................0.9/0.9	Swimming Pools (indoors): 0
Entered Service:...............................2009	Cabins (total):..50	Whirlpools:..0
Registry: ....Russia	Size Range (sq ft/m): 148.5–367.0/	Self-Service Launderette:.................Yes
Length (ft/m):.........................523.6/159.6	13.8–34.1	Dedicated Cinema/Seats: ....No
Beam (ft/m):...............................98.4/30.0	Cabins (outside view):............................50	Library: ....Yes
Draft (ft/m):................................36.3/11.08	Cabins (interior/no view):........................0	
Propulsion/Propellers: 2 x nuclear reactors,	Cabins (for one person):..........................0	
with 3 propulsion motors (75,000 hp)	Cabins (with private balcony):................0	

BERLITZ'S OVERALL SCORE: NYR OUT OF A POSSIBLE 2,000 POINTS

OVERVIEW. This dramatic, very impressive ship (*Let Pobedy*, or *50-Year Anniversary of Victory*), the world's largest icebreaker, is the first such ship with a spoon-shaped bow, the ideal shape for breaking through really stubborn ice up to 8 ft (2.5 meters) thick. The ship has a digital automated control system. Its building, originally started in October 1989, was not completed until the beginning of 2007, work having been halted in 1994 due to insufficient funds and started again in 2003. When the ship went through its sea trials in 2007 – actually after the 60th anniversary of the end of World War II, known to Russians as the Great Patriotic War – it was found to have exceptional maneuverability in thick ice, and a speed of over 21 knots.

An outstanding polar expedition cruise vessel, this ship is an advanced vessel of the *Arktika*-class of icebreaking ships. There are more crew members than passengers, giving a most impressive Passenger Space Ratio. The ship carries a fleet of Zodiac inflatable landing craft, and has a small "dip" pool at the stern, underneath the helicopter deck.

A number of thoroughly experienced lecturers are carried on each sailing. Each adventure/expedition voyage planned and operated by Quark Expeditions is something special in the world of adventure travel.

BERLITZ'S RATINGS

	Possible	Achieved
Ship	500	NYR
Accommodation	200	NYR
Food	400	NYR
Service	400	NYR
Entertainment	100	NYR
Cruise	400	NYR

The onboard currency is the US dollar. Gratuities to the staff are left to your discretion.

SUITABLE FOR: This type of cruising suits adventurous, hardy outdoors types of mature years who enjoy visiting some of the earth's most inhospitable places.

ACCOMMODATION. There are five price grades of accommodation (4 "suite" grades, 1 cabin grade). All have windows that actually *open*; all have outside views, and only two (46 and 48) have obstructed views. Each has private bathroom facilities.

CUISINE. There is one dining room, which operates in a single, open seating, so you sit with whomever you wish. The food is best described as carbohydrate-rich hearty fare – good for those energetic days of exploration.

ENTERTAINMENT. There isn't any as such, because this is real adventure cruising, with dinner and conversation among all participants being the main event each day.

SPA/FITNESS. Sauna, athletics (fitness) center, small swimming pool, and basketball court.

Freedom of the Seas
★★★★

Size: . . . . .Large Resort Ship	Passenger Decks: 15	Cabins (with private balcony): 842
Tonnage: 154,407	Total Crew: 1,397	Cabins (wheelchair accessible): 32
Lifestyle: . . . . .Standard	Passengers	Wheelchair accessibility . . . . .Best
Cruise Line: Royal Caribbean International	(lower beds/all berths): 3,634/4,375	Cabin Current: . . . . .110 volts
Former Names: . . . . .none	Passenger Space Ratio	Elevators: 14
Builder: . . .Kvaerner Masa-Yards (Finland)	(lower beds/all berths): 42.0/35.32	Casino (gaming tables): . . . . .Yes
Original Cost: . . . .$590 million	Crew/Passenger Ratio	Slot Machines: . . . . .Yes
Entered Service: . . . . .June 2006	(lower beds/all berths): 2.6/3.1	Swimming Pools (outdoors): 2
Registry: . . . . .The Bahamas	Cabins (total): 1,817	Swimming Pools (indoors): 0
Length (ft/m): 1,112.2/339.0	Size Range (sq ft/m): 153.0–2,025.0/	Whirlpools: 6
Beam (ft/m): 183.7/56.0	14.2–188.1	Self-Service Launderette: . . . . .No
Draft (ft/m): 27.8/8.5	Cabins (outside view): 1,084	Dedicated Cinema/Seats: . . . . .No
Propulsion/Propellers: . . . . .diesel-electric	Cabins (interior/no view): 733	Library: . . . . .Yes
(75,600 kW)/3 pods (42,000 kW)	Cabins (for one person): 0	

OVERALL SCORE: 1,510 OUT OF A POSSIBLE 2,000 POINTS

OVERVIEW. Bring your boxing gloves. Why? Because there's a full-sized boxing ring on board. Now read on... *Freedom of the Seas* (with sisters *Independence of the Seas* and *Liberty of the Seas*) is the largest purpose-built cruise ship ever constructed. An extension of the highly successful *Voyager*-class of ships, which Royal Caribbean International introduced in 1999 with *Voyager of the Seas*, this latest behemoth is at the cutting edge of contemporary resort ship design. The ship's length and beam were extended, enabling an increase in the number of cabins and passenger capacity, as well as a combined pool area 43 percent larger than the *Voyager*-class (but with 500 more passengers).

The extra length (at 1,112 ft/339 meters long, the ship is the length of 37 London double-decker buses; and with a beam of 185 ft/56 meters, it is wider than the Washington's White House, at 165 ft/50 meters) has enabled more innovative designs to be incorporated. These include two 16-person hot tubs cantilevered 12 ft (3.7 meters) over the sides of the ship in an adults-only Solarium area (although the Solarium's pool itself is small).

The ship's "pod" propulsion is powered by electric motors (two azimuthing, and one fixed at the centerline) instead of conventional rudders and propellers, in the latest configuration of high-tech systems that virtually eliminates vibration *(for further details, see page 45)*.

Perhaps the "wow" factor aboard this ship is its connection with water (of the seas), including a 40ft x 32ft (12.2 x 9.7 meters) "Flowrider" (wave simulator) surfing zone that is the ship's stern; a wall of water, flowing at 35,000 gallons per minute, provides the backdrop for board or body surfers – but no more than two at a time (don't

BERLITZ'S RATINGS

	Possible	Achieved
Ship	500	426
Accommodation	200	161
Food	400	235
Service	400	289
Entertainment	100	82
Cruise	400	317

worry if you get wiped out, the landing is soft). Then there's the H₂O Zone forward of the funnel, an interactive water-themed play area for families that includes a pool fed by a waterfall, and two hot tubs.

Also included are water cannons and spray fountains, water jets and ground gushers; by night the "water park" turns into a colorfully-lit "Sculpture Garden." Twin central pools consist of a main pool and a sports pool, with grandstand-style seating and competitive games including pole jousting.

Other active sports facilities include a rock-climbing wall, in-line skating area, an ice-skating rink, golf simulators, and that full-sized boxing ring (sparring partners included in the session) in the spa.

The same facilities (public rooms, bars and lounges) featured in the *Voyager*-class ships have been incorporated, but with the addition of substantial conference facilities, extensive wi-fi coverage and connectivity for cell phones. The four elements (earth, air, fire, and water) provide the decorative theme for the artwork aboard this ship.

Although this is one of the world's largest cruise ships (carry your GPS unit!), the cabin hallways have an extremely warm, attractive feel, with some neat whimsical interactive artwork cabinets and asymmetrical flow that leads you along and breaks up the monotony. In fact, there are plenty of colorful, whimsical, decorative touches typical of Scandinavian designers. Note that, if you meet someone somewhere, and want to meet them again, it's best to make an appointment and location, for this really is a large, Las Vegas-style American floating resort-city.

There are 16 bars and lounges. There's a whole promenade of shops, munching and drinking spots along an indoor mall-like environment called The Royal Promenade that is four decks high (some interior cabins have great views into the promenade-mall). The Royal Promenade is home to fashion, jewelry and perfume shops, a general store, logo shop, Promenade Cafe, Ben & Jerry's ice cream outlet, a Book Nook, a barber shop called A Close Shave (a razor shave "experience" costs $72), a pizzeria, and an English pub called The Bull and Bear (and do watch out for the stilt walkers and inflatable elephants when the circus is in town). Look at the ceiling in this large atrium and you'll see Vittoria Alata ("Winged Victory") flowing down towards you – an exact replica of the sculpture in the Piazza Venetia in Rome.

The forward section of this large space leads neatly into a large nightclub called Pharaoh's Palace (typically used for late-night adult comedy). One deck down from the Royal Promenade houses a large Casino Royale, The Crypt (discotheque), Schooner Bar (piano bar), Boleros (Latin hangout), and a photo gallery, while the forward section leads you into the three-decks high 1, 350-seat Arcadia Theatre. A whimsical piece of artwork on the forward starboard stairway includes a musical line whose tune is: "My Bonnie Lies Over the Ocean…"

There is also a regulation-size ice-skating rink (Studio B), featuring real, not fake, ice, with "bleacher" seating, and the latest in broadcast facilities. Superb "Ice Follies" shows are also presented here (but a number of slim pillars obstruct clear-view arena stage sight lines). Almost at the top of the ship is RCI's trademark Viking Crown Lounge, the cutely named Olive or Twist jazz lounge, and a wedding chapel.

Other facilities include a cigar smoker's lounge, conference center, a concierge lounge (for suite occupants only), and the comfortable 3,600-book Wilhemsen Library.

Children are also well catered to, with Adventure Ocean (for kids of 6 months to 17 years of age). In fact, children will love this ship and all the fun activities and sports.

Freedom of the Seas is fresh, exciting and very comfortable, with tasteful decor and many bars and lounges. It is certainly a great ship for young, active families with children, as long as you don't mind lines and signing up for popular activities like the "Flowrider" surf area (about a year ahead should do it), rock-climbing wall and boxing ring. Note also that there are only four banks of elevators (two forward and two aft) totaling 14, so if you have a cabin in the center of the ship, you'll need to walk forward or aft in order to travel vertically between decks; and there are only two major stairways – one forward, one aft – for such a large ship. On disembarkation day, you'll need to allow plenty of time to get an elevator, and, probably, for your luggage (there are no seats in the luggage hall in Maimi).

ACCOMMODATION. There is a wide range of suites and cabins in 14 categories and 21 price grades, from a Presidential Family Suite that can sleep up to 14 to twin-bed two person interior (no view) cabins, and interior cabins that look into an interior shopping/strolling atrium promenade. Price depends on grade. There are many family-friendly cabins, good for family reunions, but there are no single occupancy cabins. All outside-view cabins have even numbers; all interior (no view) cabins have odd numbers.

Some accommodation examples (from large to small): **Presidential Family Suite:** Located in the aft section, this suite (there is just one) comprises five rooms. These include two master bedrooms, each with twin beds that convert to a queen-size bed and ensuite bathroom with bathtub/shower (the toiletries cabinets are the same as in all other cabins); two other (very small) bedrooms that can sleep four; private balcony (sand-colored rubberized decking, not teak) with loungers, tables, chairs, a bar, and a decent view aft (although part of the balcony is overlooked by balconies on the decks above, and there is a lot of wasted space aft of the balcony because it doesn't extend to the very stern); lounge with two sofa beds, bar. The suite can accommodate eight to 14 (that's odd numbers breathing in, even numbers breathing out!), located aft (at the opposite end of the ship to the showlounge). Size: 1,215 sq. ft. (113 sq. meters), plus Balcony: 810 sq. ft (75 sq. meters). It's a pleasant enough apartment, but nothing special (it's really quite cramped and the ceilings are plain), but it could be good value for a large family (provided everyone gets on well in a confined space). **Owner's Suite:** Features include a queen-sized bed, private balcony, separate living area with queen-sized sofa bed, wet bar, vanity area, walk-in closet; bathroom with tub and shower. Sleeps up to five. Size: 506 sq. ft. (46 sq. meters) plus Balcony: 131 sq. ft. (12.1 sq. meters). **Royal Suite:** Perhaps the nicest decor of all the suites, the Royal Suite has a very spacious lounge (with black baby grand player piano, queen-sized sofa and entertainment center), wet bar, dining table. The bedroom is quite spacious and has a queen-sized bed; the bathroom has a jacuzzi bath, large walk-in shower, and two (rather gaudi gold) washbasins. Sleeps up to four. Size: 1,406 sq.ft. (130.6 sq. meters) plus 377 sq.ft. (35 sq. meters). **Grand Suite:** This has two twin beds convertible to queen-size, a private balcony, sitting area (some with sofa bed), vanity area; bathroom with tub and shower. Sleeps up to four. Size: 381 sq. ft. (35.3 sq. meters) plus Balcony: 89 sq. ft. (8.2 sq. meters). **Junior Suite:** Two twin beds convertible to queen-size, a private balcony, sitting area (some with sofa bed), vanity area; bathroom with tub and shower. Sleeps up to four. Size: 277 sq. ft. (25.7 sq. meters) plus Balcony: 65 sq. ft. (6.0 sq. meters). **Superior Oceanview Cabin:** Two twin beds convertible to queen-size, a private balcony, sitting area (some with sofa bed), vanity area; bathroom with shower. Sleeps 2 (some rooms sleep three or four). Size: 202 sq. ft. (18.7 sq. meters) + Balcony: 42 sq. ft. (3.9 sq. meters). **Deluxe Oceanview Cabin:** Two twin beds convertible to queen-size, a private balcony, sitting area (some with sofa bed), vanity area; bathroom with shower. Sleeps 2 (some rooms sleep three or four). Size: 173 sq. ft. (16.0 sq. meters) + Balcony: 46 sq. ft. (4.2 sq. meters). **Interior (promenade-view) Cabin:** These 172 cabins, on three decks, are interior cabins but with bay windows that allow occupants to look into the Royal Promenade. They have two twin beds convertible to queen-size; private bathroom with shower.

Interior (no view) Cabin: Two twin beds convertible to queen-size; private bathroom with shower. Sleeps two (some rooms sleep three or four). Size: 160 sq. ft. (14.8 sq.meters).

Family Ocean-view Cabin: Located at the front of the ship, it contains two twin beds (convertible to queen-size), sofa and/or Pullman beds, sitting area; bathroom, with shower. Accommodates six, and has 48-inch round windows. Size: 265 sq. ft. (24.6 sq. meters).

All grades of accommodation have a private bathroom (with tub and shower, or shower only, washbasin and toiletries cabinet – although they are disappointingly basic, modular and akin to bathrooms found in caravans/mobile homes), vanity desk with hairdryer, mini-bar, personal safe, flat-screen TV, radio, satellite-dial telephone, 9-inch thick mattresses and duvets. A room service menu is provided. Suite occupants have access to a Concierge Lounge, for more personal service (this saves going down to the reception desk and standing in line). Occupants of suite-grade accommodation have access to a Concierge Club lounge and its preferential services.

CUISINE. The extremely large main dining room is set on three levels (each has a theme and different name: Leonardo, Isaac, and Galileo). A dramatic staircase connects all three levels, but huge, fat support pillars obstruct the sight lines from many seats. All three have exactly the same menus and food. All dining venues are non-smoking. When you book, choose from one of two seatings – tables are for four, six, eight 10 or 12 – or "My Time Dining" (eat when you want, during dining room hours).

Alternative (extra-charge) Dining Options: These venues, all non-smoking, provide casual and informal meals at all hours (according to company statements):

● *Chops Grill*: for premium steaks, chops and special seafood, set in a great location. Open for dinner only, reservations required; cover charge $25.

● *Portofino*: this Euro-Italian restaurant is open for dinner only. Reservations required; cover charge $20. Choices include: antipasti, soup, salad, pasta, main dish, dessert, cheese and coffee (menu doesn't change during the cruise).

● *Promenade Café*: for continental breakfast, all-day pizzas, sandwiches and coffees (provided in paper cups).

● *Sprinkles*: for round-the-clock ice cream and yoghurt, pastries and coffee.

● *Windjammer Café*: self-serve casual buffet breakfast, lunch and dinner (except for the cruise's last night).

● *Jade Restaurant* (a section of the Windjammer Café): self-serve casual buffet breakfasts, lunch and dinner (no reservations necessary).

● *Johnny Rockets*, a retro 1950s all-day, all-night diner-style eatery that features hamburgers, hot dogs and other fast-food items, malt shakes and sodas (at extra cost) with indoor and outdoor seating (all indoor tables have a mini-jukebox; dimes are provided for you to make your selection of vintage records), and all-singing, all-dancing waitresses. Cover charge: $3.95.

You'll need to make reservations for Chops Grill or Portofino as early as you can in the cruise, because seating is limited and sells out quickly – not surprising when there are typically over 4,000 passengers on each cruise.

ENTERTAINMENT. The stunning Arcadia Theater is located on three decks at the forward end of the ship (actually five decks including orchestra pit and scenery storage space). It has only a few pillars and little disruption of sightlines. The room has a hydraulic orchestra pit and huge stage areas, together with sonic-boom loud sound, and some superb lighting equipment. A cast of 18 perform three production shows each cruise: "Marquee," a medley of performances, the musical "Now You See It!" magic show and "Once Upon a Time," a narrative based on the Brothers Grimm's fairytales.

Most of the cabaret acts are not what you would call headliners. The strongest acts perform in the main showlounge, while others are presented in the Nightclub, the venue for late-night adults-only comedy. The most entertaining shows, however, are the Ice Spectaculars. There is also a TV studio, adjacent to rooms that can also be used for trade show exhibit space (good for conventions at sea).

Royal Caribbean's production shows are colorful spectaculars that will remind you of Las Vegas casino hotels, fast-moving, razzle-dazzle shows that have little or no story line, and often poor linkage between themes and scenes, and choreography that is more stepping in place rather than dancing.

One "show" not to be missed is the "Greatest Show at Sea" Parade – a superbly executed 15-minute fun extravaganza that bumbles along the Royal Promenade at turtle speed; it replicates the parade of stars and animals at a circus of yesteryear (Barnum and Bailey's meets cruise ship). This is when it's really good to have one of those interior-view atrium cabins (sadly, the windows don't open, so you can't take photographs); otherwise, get a position early along the Royal Promenade.

SPA/FITNESS. The ShipShape health spa is large. It includes a large aerobics room, fitness center (with the usual stairmasters, treadmills, stationary bikes, weight machines and free weights), treatment rooms, and men's and women's sauna/steam rooms and relaxation areas. Sample prices: AromaStone Therapy massage, $195 (75 mins); Swedish Massage, $119 (50 mins); Couples massage, $260 (50 mins); facial, $119 (50 mins), plus tip.

The spa facility is operated by Steiner. Some (basic) exercise classes are free, but the good ones (examples: yoga, personal training) cost extra.

More active passengers can bodyboard, go boxing (in the full-size boxing ring in the middle of the spa; the cost is $83 for a personal session, or $10 as part of a Power-boxing class), climb (the rock-climbing wall at the back of the funnel housing), jog, putt, swim, skate, step, surf, workout and more (including play basketball and volleyball) in the sports area of the ship, located mostly aft of the funnel.

● **For more extensive general information on what a Royal Caribbean cruise is like, see pages 151–6.**

Fuji Maru
★★★

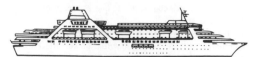

Size: . . . . .Small Ship	Passenger Decks: 8	Cabins (with private balcony): 0
Tonnage: 23,340	Total Crew: 190	Cabins (wheelchair accessible): 2
Lifestyle: . . . . .Standard	Passengers	Wheelchair accessibility . . . . .None
Cruise Line: . . .Mitsui OSK Passenger Line	(lower beds/all berths): 328/603	Cabin Current: . . . . .100 volts
Former Names: . . . . .none	Passenger Space Ratio	Elevators: 5
Builder: . . . . .Mitsubishi (Japan)	(lower beds/all berths): 71.1/38.7	Casino (gaming tables): . . . . .Yes
Original Cost: . . . .$63.5 million	Crew/Passenger Ratio	(gifts only, no cash prizes)
Entered Service: . . . . Apr 1989	(lower beds/all berths): 1.7/3.1	Slot Machines: .No
Registry: . . . . .Japan	Cabins (total): .164	Swimming Pools (outdoors): 1
Length (ft/m): 547.9/167.00	Size Range (sq ft/m): 182.9–376.7/	Swimming Pools (indoors): 0
Beam (ft/m): 78.7/24.00	17.0–35.0	Whirlpools: . . . . .0 (4 Japanese Baths)
Draft (ft/m): 21.4/6.55	Cabins (outside view): 164	Self-Service Launderette: . . . . .Yes
Propulsion/Propellers: . . . . .diesel	Cabins (interior/no view): 0	Dedicated Cinema/Seats: Yes/142
(15,740kW)/2	Cabins (for one person): 0	Library: . . . . .Yes

OVERALL SCORE: 1,186 OUT OF A POSSIBLE 2,000 POINTS

OVERVIEW. When *Fuji Maru* was completed in 1989, it was Japan's largest cruise ship. It has a well thought-out, and flexible, design for multifunctional uses, but its main use is for incentives, conventions, as a seminar and training ship, and only occasionally for individual passengers. The utilitarian outdoor decks are little used. The interiors are plain and a little clinical, although there is some good artwork throughout to brighten things up. There are extensive lecture and conference facilities. The largest lecture hall is two decks high, seats 600, and converts into a sports stadium or exhibition hall for industrial product introductions. The lobby is quite elegant and open and is part of a two-level atrium.

The ship has a classic, wood-paneled library. Other features include Japanese grand baths and a traditional Washitsu tatami mat room, and lecture room. A Hanaguruma owner's room is reasonably elegant for small formal functions. The Sakura Salon is soothing, with a blend of Western and traditional Japanese design. The media and TV systems include much high-tech equipment. However, there are many more modern ships in the international marketplace (some serving Japanese passengers), with better facilities, more dining choices, and a less utilitarian ambience, and so the score for this ship has been lowered slightly.

A specialist courier company will collect your luggage from your home before the cruise, and deliver it back after the cruise (this service available only in Japan). The onboard currency is the Japanese yen. As in any ship for Japanese passengers, tipping is not allowed.

There is a complete waste of open deck space, and maintenance of it is poor. The deck furniture is plastic. The lighting is too bright, which also increases the noise level.

BERLITZ'S RATINGS		
	Possible	Achieved
Ship	500	274
Accommodation	200	114
Food	400	249
Service	400	266
Entertainment	100	65
Cruise	400	218

SUITABLE FOR: Japanese-speaking couples and single travelers looking for modestly comfortable surroundings, decent food and service, all at low cost.

ACCOMMODATION. There are seven price grades. There are two suites that are quite lovely, with separate bedroom and living room. The deluxe cabins are also of a good standard, and come with a vanity/writing desk, mini-bar/refrigerator, and full-sized, deep bathtub. Almost all the other (standard) cabins are furnished very simply, but they are good for seminar and school cruises, with many accommodating three or four persons. The cabin insulation is reasonable, but could be better. The bathrooms are small and utilitarian. The folded blankets, a MOPAS (Mitsui OSK Passenger Line) tradition, are lovely.

CUISINE. The single, large dining room is quite attractive and has a high ceiling, but rather bright lighting. Both Japanese and Western cuisines are featured for all meals, in a single seating. The food itself is quite plain and simple, but with colorful presentation, and a good variety.

ENTERTAINMENT. The Pacific Lounge is the venue for entertainment events, social functions, and social dancing. It is a two deck high room, with seating on both main and balcony levels. On most cruises, special featured entertainers are brought on board from ashore.

SPA/FITNESS. There is no spa, but there are two Japanese Grand Baths (men's and women's) with ocean-view windows. These include washing stations and two small communal baths. There is a sauna, and massage is available.

Funchal
★★ +

Size: ....Small Ship	Passenger Decks: 6	Cabins (with private balcony): 0
Tonnage: 9,563	Total Crew: 155	Cabins (wheelchair accessible): 0
Lifestyle: ....Standard	Passengers	Wheelchair accessibility ....None
Cruise Line: Classic International Cruises	(lower beds/all berths): 430/524	Cabin Current: ....220 volts
Former Names: ....none	Passenger Space Ratio	Elevators: 3
Builder: ...Helsingor Skibsvog (Denmark)	(lower beds/all berths): 22.2/18.2	Casino (gaming tables): ....Yes
Original Cost: ....n/a	Crew/Passenger Ratio	Slot Machines: ....Yes
Entered Service: .....Oct 1961/May 1986	(lower beds/all berths): 2.7/3.3	Swimming Pools (outdoors): 1
Registry: ....Madeira	Cabins (total): 222	Swimming Pools (indoors): 0
Length (ft/m): 503.6/153.51	Size Range (sq ft/m): 102.2–252.9/	Whirlpools: 0
Beam (ft/m): 62.5/19.05	9.5–23.5	Self-Service Launderette: ....No
Draft (ft/m): 20.6/6.40	Cabins (outside view): 151	Dedicated Cinema/Seats: ....No
Propulsion/Propellers: ....diesel	Cabins (interior/no view): 71	Library: ....Yes
(7,356kW)/2	Cabins (for one person): 14	

OVERALL SCORE: 1,042 OUT OF A POSSIBLE 2,000 POINTS

OVERVIEW. *Funchal* has a classic 1960s small ship profile with well balanced, rounded lines, and pleasing real wooden decks, including one outdoor deck with two sheltered promenades, although they do not completely encircle the ship. Originally, the ship was built as the Portuguese Presidential Yacht, but was rebuilt as a one-class cruise ship in 1972–73 and has since undergone regular refurbishments. Its interior has lots of fine woodwork and heavy-duty fittings. One deck houses the main public rooms, the most appealing of which is the Porto Bar, reminiscent of a classy 19th-century drinking club. A highly polished wooden spiral stairway is a beautiful, classic piece of decoration not found in today's ships.

The mostly Portuguese staff is warm, friendly and quite attentive. This ship is popular with Europeans and Scandinavians during the summer and winter. It provides destination-intensive cruises in a pleasant, old-world atmosphere.

Funchal is like an old, well-worn shoe – comfortable, but in need of a little spit and polish, and so it hovers just a tad under the three-star level (a two-and-a-half star vessel with a three-star heart). The ship and overall product is actually quite good if you enjoy small, vintage vessels with all their accompanying eccentricities. While the ship cannot be compared to the latest brand new, larger ships, *Funchal* has a delightful character and charm. The feeling of camaraderie and friendliness from the loyal crew, some of whom have been aboard the ship for many years, offsets some of the hardware negatives.

The ship often operates under charter to various tour

BERLITZ'S RATINGS

	Possible	Achieved
Ship	500	201
Accommodation	200	101
Food	400	242
Service	400	240
Entertainment	100	55
Cruise	400	203

packagers and operators. The onboard currency, typically, is the euro.

SUITABLE FOR: *Funchal* is best suited to couples and single travelers seeking a first cruise aboard a small ship of vintage character and charm, with few facilities, but at a low price.

ACCOMMODATION. The cabins are extremely compact but tasteful, and come in both twin and double-bedded configurations. Each has a private bathroom, and there is just enough closet and drawer space. All bathrooms are typically provided with soap, shampoo, shower cap, shoeshine, sewing kit, and bathrobe (suites only).

CUISINE. There are two tastefully decorated dining rooms, Lisboa and the smaller Coimbra (which doubles as a video screening room after dinner). Both have ocean-view picture windows on port and starboard sides. There is just one seating, and tables are for four, six or eight (there are no tables for two). The food is European in style – it includes plenty of fresh fish – and is surprisingly good. The wine list includes Portuguese wines at modest prices.

ENTERTAINMENT. The Main Lounge is the showlounge, an H-shaped room that extends to the sides of the ship. The room has a flat floor, and the sight lines to the stage are poor from some seats. As this is a small and older vessel, entertainment is a low priority (and has a low budget).

SPA/FITNESS. There is a small beauty salon.

Galapagos Explorer II
★★★

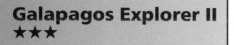

Size: . . . . .Boutique Ship	Passenger Decks: 5	Cabins (with private balcony): 4
Tonnage: 4,077	Total Crew: 72	Cabins (wheelchair accessible): 0
Lifestyle: . . . . .Standard	Passengers	Wheelchair accessibility . . . . .None
Cruise Line: . . . . .Canodros	(lower beds/all berths): 106/111	Cabin Current: . . . . .110 volts
Former Names: . . . . . .Renaissance Three	Passenger Space Ratio	Elevators: 1
Builder: . . . . .Cantieri Navale Ferrari (Italy)	(lower beds/all berths): 38.4/36.7	Casino (gaming tables): . . . . .Yes
Original Cost: . . . .$20 million	Crew/Passenger Ratio	Slot Machines: .Yes
Entered Service: . . . . .Aug 1990/Feb 1998	(lower beds/all berths): 1.4/1.5	Swimming Pools (outdoors): 1
Registry: .Liberia	Cabins (total): .53	Swimming Pools (indoors): 0
Length (ft/m): 293.1/89.35	Size Range (sq ft/m): 231.4–282.0/	Whirlpools: 1
Beam (ft/m): 50.1/15.30	21.5–26.2	Self-Service Launderette: . . . . .No
Draft (ft/m): 11.9/3.65	Cabins (outside view): 53	Dedicated Cinema/Seats: . . . . .No
Propulsion/Propellers: . . . . .diesel	Cabins (interior/no view): 0	Library: . . . . .No
(3,514kW)/2	Cabins (for one person): 0	

OVERALL SCORE: 1,244 OUT OF A POSSIBLE 2,000 POINTS

OVERVIEW. This is a comfortable and inviting ship (built as one of a series of eight similar small ships for the defunct Renaissance Cruises). While it is in good condition, the maintenance could be better. Its looks are quite contemporary in the style of a mega-yacht, with handsome styling. There is a wooden promenade deck outdoors. The limited number of public rooms have smart and restful, non-glitzy decor. The main lounge doubles as a lecture room, but perhaps it is the piano bar that provides the best place to relax after dinner in the evening. A doctor is carried at all times.

This ship provides a destination-intensive, refined, quiet and relaxed cruise for those who don't like crowds or dressing up. Naturalist guides trained at the Darwin Station lead the shore excursions (included in the fare), and the ship carries two glass-bottom boats. Take your passport, short and long-sleeve cotton shirts, good walking shoes, windbreaker, mosquito repellent, sunglasses with retaining strap, and personal medication. You will need to fly from Quito to San Cristobal (via Guayaquil) to join your cruise.

Galápagos Explorer II operates three-, four-, and seven night Galápagos cruises year-round from San Cristobal. Liquor, beer, cocktails, bottled water and soft drinks are included in the fare, but wine and champagne are not. Also included are guided visits to the islands. The brochure rates may or may not include the Galápagos Islands visitor tax (about $100), which must be paid in cash at Guayaquil or Quito airports or in the islands. Shore visits take place in "pangas" (local lingo for "dinghies").

Gratuities for shipboard staff are excessive, at a recommended $80 per person, per seven-night cruise. The onboard currency is the US dollar.

BERLITZ'S RATINGS

	Possible	Achieved
Ship	500	325
Accommodation	200	154
Food	400	209
Service	400	245
Entertainment	n/a	n/a
Cruise	500	311

The tiny "dip" pool is not a swimming pool. Sunbathing space is cramped. Plastic wood is everywhere (but looks good). The service is without finesse, but the crew is willing. The small library is attractive, but the book selection is poor. The ship does not sail well in inclement weather. It has not been cared for, and maintenance is poor.

SUITABLE FOR: The ship is best for couples and single travelers who want to cruise around the primitive Galápagos Islands, but want to do so in comfortable, stylish surroundings.

ACCOMMODATION. This is located forward, with public rooms aft. Pleasant, all-outside suites have a large picture window and combine gorgeous, highly polished imitation rosewood paneling with lots of mirrors, hand-crafted Italian furniture, and wet bar. All cabins have a queen-sized bed, a sitting area, a mini-bar/refrigerator, TV set, VCR and hairdryer. The small bathrooms have showers with a fold-down seat, real teakwood floors and marble vanities.

CUISINE. The small, elegant dining room has open seating, and tables for two, four, six, and eight. The meals are self-service buffet-style cold foods for breakfast and lunch (sometimes lunch will be on deck), with local delicacies. There is limited choice.

ENTERTAINMENT. Dinner and after-dinner conversation with fellow passengers forms the entertainment each evening.

SPA/FITNESS. There is a sauna. Water sports facilities include an aft platform, sailfish, snorkel gear, and Zodiacs.

Gemini
★★★ +

Size:	Mid-Size Ship	Passenger Decks:	.9	Cabins (wheelchair accessible):	.4
Tonnage:	.19,093	Total Crew:	.350	Wheelchair accessibility	.Fair
Lifestyle:	.Standard	Passengers		Cabin Current:	.220 volts
Cruise Line:	.Happy Cruises	(lower beds/all berths):	.800/940	Elevators:	.4
Former Names:	SuperStar Gemini,	Passenger Space Ratio		Casino (gaming tables):	.Yes
	Crown Jewel	(lower beds/all berths):	.23.8/21.2	Slot Machines:	.Yes
Builder:	.Union Navale de Levante (Spain)	Crew/Passenger Ratio		Swimming Pools (outdoors):	.1
Original Cost:	.$100 million	(lower beds/all berths):	.2.2/2.6	Swimming Pools (indoors):	.0
Entered Service:	.Aug 1992/Mar 2009	Cabins (total):	.400	Whirlpools:	.3 (2 outside/1 inside)
Registry:	.Bahamas	Size Range (sq ft/m):	.139.9–377.8/	Self-Service Launderette:	.No
Length (ft/m):	.537.4/163.81		13.0–35.1	Dedicated Cinema/Seats:	.No
Beam (ft/m):	.73.8/22.50	Cabins (outside view):	.241	Library:	.Yes
Draft (ft/m):	.17.7/5.40	Cabins (interior/no view):	.159		
Propulsion/Propellers:	.diesel	Cabins (for one person):	.0		
	(13,200kW)/2	Cabins (with private balcony):	.10		

BERLITZ'S OVERALL SCORE: 1,254 OUT OF A POSSIBLE 2,000 POINTS

OVERVIEW. *Gemini*, owned by the Clipper Group and chartered to Happy Cruises, part of Spain's Quail Travel Group, is a fairly smart-looking mid-sized contemporary cruise ship, with a white hull (with Happy Cruises emblazoned on the sides) and superstructure topped by a single dark blue funnel. When originally built for the long-defunct Crown Cruise Line, it was the largest cruise vessel constructed in Spain. Designed for informal cruising in warm weather waters, the ship has a sister in the (now stretched) *Braemar*, operated by Fred Olsen Cruise Lines.

There is a walk-around promenade deck outdoors, and passengers can also go to right to the bows of the ship for arrivals and departures (the mooring deck is underneath). There is a reasonable amount of open deck and sunbathing space for the size of the ship, and this includes a neat area high atop the ship in front of a glass windbreak area – good for those balmy evenings outdoors, away from the crowds inside. Cushioned pads are not provided for the plastic-webbed sunloungers, and the pool is small – very small.

Although the original interior fit and finish was poor, the décor presents a warm and upbeat look that is colourful and cheery. The ship has a traditional layout that provides reasonable horizontal passenger flow, although the passageways are quite narrow, and Deck 7, where most of the suites are located, is like a winding street. There are picture windows in almost all of the public rooms that connect passengers with the sea and the outside light. Many of the chairs and bar stools are of the low-back variety – made for people of small proportions.

Other features include a five-deck-high glass-walled

BERLITZ'S RATINGS

	Possible	Achieved
Ship	500	333
Accommodation	200	132
Food	400	234
Service	400	243
Entertainment	100	60
Cruise	400	252

atrium, which is set on the starboard side; it has clusters of green hanging over the balcony on each deck. Off-center stairways appear to add a sense of spaciousness to an interior design that surrounds passengers with light. The artwork is fairly plain and simple, although a colourful piece – *Georama* – by Ajis Mohamad of Malaysia, in three sections – adorns the main lobby. Public rooms include a discotheque/lounge (Starlight), small duty-free shop, casino, video arcade, children's center, card room, and a decent library with two internet-connect computer stations.

The dress code is totally casual. All in all, the company provides good value for money, cruising in a comfortable ship that is quite contemporary, and totally informal. The onboard currency is the euro, and the all-inclusive pricing means that (standard brand) drinks and gratuities are included. But shore excursions, use of medical facility, and spa treatments are not included, nor are room service items such as snacks or sandwiches.

There are many loud announcements. Music plays constantly in public spaces, hallways, and on open decks, making a relaxing cruise experience impossible. You can expect some crowding for the self-serve buffets, tenders, and the few elevators aboard this ship.

SUITABLE FOR: *Gemini* is suited to Spanish-speaking couples, singles, and families with children of all ages who want to cruise aboard a contemporary ship with decent facilities, at a reasonable price for an all-inclusive vacation.

ACCOMMODATION. There are 11 cabin categories, the price

depending on grade, location and size. These consist of suites (220.7–377.8 sq. ft/20.5–35.1 sq. meters), junior suites (225–258.3 sq. ft/20.9–24 sq. meters), ocean-view cabins with double bed (134.5–212 sq. ft/12.5–19.7 sq. meters), ocean-view cabins with twin beds (137.8 sq. ft/12.8 sq. meters), smaller ocean-view cabins with window (114.1–148.5 sq. ft/10.6–13.8 sq. meters), and very small interior (no-view) cabins (127–150.7 sq. ft/11.8–14 sq. meters). The cabin numbering system and signage is confusing, however, and contrary to nautical tradition.

Suites. The 10 Balcony Suites, each with a DVD/CD system, have a private balcony with lacquered wood floor, although the balcony partitions are not of the floor-to-ceiling type – so you can hear your neighbors clearly, or smell their smoke. The Premium and Deluxe Suites are really little larger than standard cabins, but come with more closet space. All suite category accommodation is nicely furnished, and, depending on the configuration, the sleeping area can be curtained off from the living area. Four cabins are adaptable for wheelchair users, although the ship's layout makes it quite awkward to get around.

Standard Cabins. The standard outside-view and interior (no-view) cabins, almost all of which are about the same size, are really quite small, although they are nicely furnished, and trimmed with blond wood cabinetry. Most have broad picture windows (some deluxe cabins on Deck 6 and Deck 7 have lifeboat-obstructed views), while cabins on the lowest deck have portholes instead of windows. They are practical and comfortable, with wood-trimmed accents and multi-colored soft furnishings, but there is very little drawer space, and the closet space is extremely small.

Each cabin has a private bathroom (of the "me first, you next" variety) with a tiled floor, small shower enclosure – even in accommodation designated as suites – two small toiletries cupboards, washbasin, and low-height toilet of the barking dog vacuum variety, and some under-basin storage space, and an electrical socket for shavers. Note that the cabin soundproofing is quite poor, however, and there is little room for luggage, so take only what is really necessary (casual clothing only). Some toiletry amenities are provided in all cabins. The towels are of 100% cotton. None of the cabin bathrooms has a bathtub – not even the so-called

"suites" – and hairdryers are not supplied for any cabin category (except suites), so take your own if you need to use one. The TV sets are of the old variety.

CUISINE. The Ocean Palace Restaurant is located aft; it is attractive, and has large picture windows on three sides – although accenting in the center of the ceiling makes the room appear almost circular. There are typically two seatings (dinner is 8pm and 10:15 pm), except when the ship is not full, when it may go to one open seating. It is not open for dinner each night; the schedule depends on the itinerary being operated.

The ambiance is friendly, but it can be noisy, depending on the passenger nationalities carried. There are few tables for two – most are for four, six or eight. Meals highlight continental European cuisine, with a Spanish flair, and there is open seating for all meals.

There is also a casual self-serve buffet-style restaurant, Mariners Buffet, with indoor and outdoor seating, for breakfast, lunch and dinner.

ENTERTAINMENT. The Galaxy Showlounge and Bar, which sits longitudinally along one side of the ship, with amphitheater-style seating in several tiers, is the venue for all main entertainment events. There is often congestion between first- and second-seating passengers at the single entrance to the room, which is poorly designed for passenger movement.

Fifteen pillars obstruct the sightlines to the stage, and the seating arrangement is quite poor. Don't expect much in the way of entertainment – it's loud, and rather like reality TV.

The Tropicana Lounge has a decent-size dance floor, with live music, and a large bar. Several other bars and lounges feature a mix of groups and entertaining musicians.

SPA/FITNESS. There is a health spa, although it is small, and has limited facilities. It includes a combined gymnasium/relaxation room, with separate rooms for men and women, a two-person sauna, steam room and small changing/locker area. There's also beauty salon. The day you board is the best time to book your desired treatments – which are not included in the "all-inclusive" cruise fare.

WHERE NAUTICAL EXPRESSIONS COME FROM

If you've ever wondered where some terms or phrases came from, you have only to look to the sea, ships, and seamen.

Square meal

This derives from the meals served on square wooden platters used on board ship. The platters could be easily stowed in racks between meals. Any substantial meal is now described as a "square meal."

Three Sheets to the Wind

A term said of a man under the influence of drink. A ship with three sheets in the wind would "stagger to and fro like a drunken man." Conversely, a drunken man behaves like a ship with three sheets in the wind.

To Know the ropes

There were miles and miles of cordage in the rigging of a square rigged ship. The only way of keeping

track of and knowing the function of all of these lines was to know their locations. It took an experienced seaman to know the ropes.

Under the weather

Refers to a sailor being in the uncomfortable position of having his station at the weather bow, subject to the pitching of the boat with spray constantly blown in his face. Used today to mean feeling unwell.

Golden Princess
★★★★

Size:	Large Resort Ship	Passenger Decks:	13	Cabins (with private balcony):	720
Tonnage:	108,865	Total Crew:	1,100	Cabins (wheelchair accessible):	28
Lifestyle:	Standard	Passengers			(18 outside/10 interior)
Cruise Line:	Princess Cruises	(lower beds/all berths):	2,624/3,124	Wheelchair accessibility	Best
Former Names:	none	Passenger Space Ratio		Cabin Current:	110 and 220 volts
Builder:	Fincantieri (Italy)	(lower beds/all berths):	41.4/34.8	Elevators:	14
Original Cost:	$450 million	Crew/Passenger Ratio		Casino (gaming tables):	Yes
Entered Service:	May 2001	(lower beds/all berths):	2.1/2.8	Slot Machines:	Yes
Registry:	Bermuda	Cabins (total):	1,312	Swimming Pools (outdoors):	4
Length (ft/m):	951.4/290.0	Size Range (sq ft/m):	161.4–764.2/	Swimming Pools (indoors):	0
Beam (ft/m):	118.1/36.0		15.0–71.0	Whirlpools:	9
Draft (ft/m):	26.2/8.0	Cabins (outside view):	940	Self-Service Launderette:	Yes
Propulsion/Propellers:	diesel-electric	Cabins (interior/no view):	372	Dedicated Cinema/Seats:	No
	(42,000kW)/2	Cabins (for one person):	0	Library:	Yes

OVERALL SCORE: 1,499 OUT OF A POSSIBLE 2,000 POINTS

OVERVIEW. *Golden Princess*, sister to *Grand Princess* and *Star Princess*, presents a bold, forthright profile, with a racy "spoiler" effect at the stern that I do not consider handsome (this acts as an observation lounge with aft-facing views by day, and a noisy discotheque by night). The ship has a flared snub-nosed bow and a galleon-like transom stern. At 118 ft/36 meters (but more than 43 ft/13 meters wider than the canal, including the navigation bridge wings) *Golden Princess* is too wide to transit the Panama Canal, with many balcony cabins overhanging the hull.

There is a good sheltered faux teak promenade deck – it's actually painted steel – which almost wraps around (three times round is equal to one mile) and a walkway that goes to the (enclosed, protected) bow of the ship. The outdoor pools have various beach-like surroundings. One lap pool has a pumped "current" to swim against. Four areas center on swimming pools, one of which is two decks high and is covered by a glass domed roof (magrodome), itself an extension of the funnel housing.

High atop the stern of the ship is a ship-wide glass-walled disco pod. Looking like an aerodynamic "spoiler," it is positioned high above the water, with spectacular views from the extreme port and starboard side windows; it's a good place to read a book in the daytime, but at night it's a discotheque. In a 2009 refit, a retreat, "The Sanctuary" (for which there is a charge) was added for adult passengers only; it has plush padded lounge chairs and the services of dedicated Serenity Stewards. The Sanctuary also has two private massage cabanas.

There is plenty of space inside the ship – but also plenty of passengers – and a wide array of public rooms,

BERLITZ'S RATINGS

	Possible	Achieved
Ship	500	414
Accommodation	200	163
Food	400	252
Service	400	289
Entertainment	100	80
Cruise	400	301

with many "intimate" (this being a relative word) spaces and places to play. The passenger flow has, however, been well thought-out, with little congestion, except at the photo gallery. The decor is attractive and warm, with lots of earth tones.

The main lobby has been opened up and transformed into La Piazza (in common with the newest ships in the fleet), with live street entertainment; an International café for coffees, fresh baked cookies, pastries, panini sandwiches and tapas; and Vines, a wine bar that also features seafood, artisan meats and cheeses. Also in the refit, the casino was relocated to Deck 7, and a new 300 sq ft (28 sq meter) poolside movie screen was added for "Movies Under the Stars."

An extensive collection of art works complement the elegant, non-glitzy interior design and colors. If you see something you like, you'll probably be able to buy it.

This ship also has a Wedding Chapel (a live web-cam can relay ceremonies via the internet). The ship's captain can legally marry (American) couples, due to the ship's Bermuda registry and a special dispensation (this should, however, be verified when in the planning stage, and may vary according to where you reside).

Princess Cruises offers three wedding packages: Pearl, Emerald, Diamond – the fee includes registration and official marriage certificate. However, to get married and take your close family members and entourage with you on your honeymoon could be heavy on the wallet. The "Hearts & Minds" chapel can also be used for "renewal of vows" ceremonies.

For youngsters there is a two-deck-high playroom and teen room located in the forward section of the ship (although the video games room is located at the opposite end of the ship), and a host of trained counselors.

Gamblers should enjoy the large casino, with more than 260 slot machines. There are blackjack, craps and roulette tables, plus games such as Let It Ride Bonus, Spanish 21 and Caribbean Draw Progressive.

Ship lovers should enjoy the wood-paneled Wheelhouse Bar, finely decorated with memorabilia and ship models tracing part of parent company P&O's history. There is an Internet Cafe, with a couple of dozen AOL-linked computer terminals ($7.50 per 15 minutes when this book was completed); but it should be called an Internet Center, as there is no cafe – not even any coffee.

A high-tech hospital is provided, with live SeaMed telemedicine link-up to specialists at the Cedars-Sinai Medical Center in Los Angeles available for emergency help – but this is hardly useful for international passengers who don't reside in the USA.

The automated telephone system is frustrating to use, and luggage delivery is inefficient. Lines can form at the Passenger Services Desk, and for open-seating breakfast and lunch. There are lots of many extra charge item (such as for ice cream, and freshly squeezed orange juice) and activities (such as yoga, group exercise bicycling and kick boxing classes at $10 per session, not to mention $4 per hour for group babysitting services). There is a charge for using the washers and dryers in the self-service launderettes (coins are needed).

Whether all this really can be considered a relaxing holiday is a moot point, but with many choices and "small" rooms to enjoy, the ship has been extremely well designed, and the odds are that you'll have a fine time, in a controlled, well packaged way.

ACCOMMODATION. There are six principal types of cabins and configurations: (a) grand suite, (b) suite, (c) mini-suite, (d) outside double with balcony, (e) outside double, and (f) interior (no view) double. There are, however, 35 different brochure price categories, making the choice bewildering for both travel agents and passengers. The price depends on grade, size and location. Many cabins have additional upper berths (there are 609), good for those with children.

(**a**) The largest, most lavish suite is the Grand Suite (B748, which is at the ship's stern – a different position to the two Grand Suites aboard sister ship *Grand Princess*). Although large for Princess Cruises, it does not compare with much larger suites (three times the size, in fact) aboard such ships as *Constellation, Infinity, Millennium, Norwegian Dawn, Norwegian Star, Summit*. It has a large bedroom with a queen-sized bed, huge walk-in (illuminated) closets, a large bathroom with full-size tub and separate shower enclosure, toilet, and washbasin, and a hot tub (accessed from the bedroom), a lounge (with sofa bed, dining table and chairs, wet bar and refrigerator, a guest bathroom (with toilet and washbasin), and a large private balcony.

(**b/c**) Suites (with a semi-private balcony) have a separate living room (with sofa bed) and bedroom (with a TV set in each). The bathroom is quite large and has both a tub and

shower stall. The mini-suites also have a semi-private balcony, and a separate living and sleeping area (with a television in each). The bathroom is also quite spacious, with both a bathtub and shower stall. The differences between the suites and mini-suites are basically in the size and appointments, the suite being more of a square shape while mini-suites are more rectangular, and have few drawers. Plush bathrobes and fully tiled bathrooms with ample open shelf storage space are provided. Passengers occupying the best suites receive greater attention, including priority embarkation and disembarkation privileges. What is not good is that some of the most expensive accommodation has only semi-private balconies that can be seen from above, so there is no privacy whatsoever (Suites C401, 402, 409, 410, 414, 415, 420, 421, 422, 423, 424 and 425 on Caribe Deck in particular). Also, the suites D105 and D106 (Dolphin Deck), which are extremely large, have balconies that can be seen from above.

(**d/e/f**) The standard interior and outside-view (the outsides come either with or without private balcony) cabins are of a functional, practical, design, although almost no drawers are provided. They are very attractive, with warm, pleasing decor and fine soft furnishing fabrics.

Additionally, two family suites consist of two suites with an interconnecting door, plus a large balcony. These can sleep up to 10 (if at least four are children), or up to eight people (if all are adults).

All passengers receive turndown service and chocolates on pillows each night, bathrobes (on request) and toiletry amenity kits (larger, naturally, for suite/mini-suite occupants) that typically include soap, shampoo, conditioner, and hand/body lotion. A hairdryer is provided in all cabins. All bathrooms are tiled and have a decent amount of open shelf storage space for personal toiletries. Princess Cruises receives BBC World, CNN, CNBC, ESPN and TNT on the in-cabin color television system (when available, depending on cruise area).

Most outside cabins on Emerald Deck have views obstructed by lifeboats. Your name is placed outside your suite or cabin – making it simple for delivery service personnel but also making it intrusive with regard to your privacy. Some cabins can accommodate a third and fourth person in upper berths. However, in such cabins, the lower beds cannot then be pushed together to make queen-sized bed. There are no cabins for singles.

Almost all balcony suites and cabins can be overlooked both from the navigation bridge wing, as well as from the port and starboard sections of the ship's discotheque – located high above the ship at the stern. Cabins with balconies on Dolphin, Caribe and Baja decks are also overlooked by passengers on balconies on the deck above; they are, therefore, not at all private.

However, perhaps the least desirable balcony cabins are the eight located forward on Emerald Deck, as the balconies do not extend to the side of the ship and can be passed by walkers and gawkers on the adjacent Upper Promenade walkway (so occupants need to keep their curtains closed most of the time). Also, passengers occupying some the most expensive suites with balconies at the stern of the vessel may experience considerable vibration during certain ship maneuvers.

Cabin bath towels are too small, and drawer space is limited. There are no butlers – even for the top-grade suites. Cabin attendants have too many cabins to look after (typically 20), which cannot translate to fine personal service.

CUISINE. There are a number of "Personal Choice" dining options. For formal meals there are three principal dining rooms (Bernini, Canaletto, and Donatello). There are two seatings in one restaurant, while "anytime dining" (where you choose when and with whom you want to eat) is featured in the other two. All three are non-smoking and split into multi-tier sections in a non-symmetrical design that breaks what are quite large spaces into many smaller sections, for better ambience. Each dining room has its own galley. While four elevators go to Fiesta Deck where the Canaletto and Donatello restaurants are located, only two go to Plaza Deck 5 where the Bernini Restaurant is located (this can cause long wait problems at peak times, particularly for anyone in a wheelchair). Note that 15% is added to beverage bills, including wines.

Alternative (Extra Charge) Dining: There are two alternative informal dining areas: Sabatini's and Crown Grill (added in a 2009 refit). Sabatini's is Italian, with colorful tiled Mediterranean-style decor; it is named after Trattoria Sabatini, the 200-year-old institution in Florence. It has Italian-style pizzas and pastas, with a variety of sauces, as well as Italian-style entrées (including tiger prawns and lobster tail). Sabatini's is by reservation only, and there is a cover charge of $15 per person, for lunch or dinner (on sea days only). Crown Grill, serving premium steaks and

seafood, is by reservation only. There is a $25 cover charge, and the venue has an open (show) galley. The cuisine in both of these spots is decidedly better than in the three main dining rooms.

A poolside hamburger grill and pizza bar (no extra charge) are additional dining spots for casual bites. Other casual meals can be taken in the Horizon Court – open 24 hours a day, with large ocean-view on port and starboard sides and direct access to the two principal swimming pools and lido deck. Plastic plates are used.

ENTERTAINMENT. The 748-seat Princess Theatre spans two decks and has comfortable seating on both main and balcony levels. It has a 9-piece orchestra, and a scenery loading bay that connects directly from stage to a hull door for direct transfer to the dockside). Princess Cruises prides itself on its glamorous all-American production shows (there are typically two or three shows each 7-day cruise).

The Vista Lounge is a second entertainment lounge. It presents cabaret acts at night, and lectures, bingo and horse racing during the day. Explorers, a third entertainment lounge, can host cabaret acts and dance bands. Many other lounges and bars have live music, and there are male dance hosts as partners for women traveling alone.

SPA/FITNESS. The Lotus Spa is a large complex that surrounds one of the swimming pools at the forward end of the ship. It comprises a large gymnasium with all the usual equipment, an aerobics room, sauna and steam rooms, beauty salon, treatment rooms, and a relaxation area.

● **For more extensive general information about the Princess Cruises experience, see pages 148–51.**

DID YOU KNOW...

● that the first vessel built exclusively for cruising was Hamburg-Amerika Line's two-funnel yacht, the 4,409-tonne *Princessin Victoria Luise*? This luxury ship even included a private suite reserved for the German kaiser.

● that the first ship to be fitted with real stabilizers (as opposed to an autogyro device) was the Peninsular & Oriental Steam Navigation Company's 24,215-tonne *Chusan*, built in 1949?

● that the first consecrated ocean-going Roman Catholic chapel aboard a passenger ship was in Compagnie Générale Transatlantique's *Ile de France* of 1928?

● that the latest life rafts called Hydrostatic Release Units (HRU), designed in Britain and approved by the Royal Navy, are now compulsory on all British-registered ships? Briefly, an HRU is capable of automatically releasing a life raft from its mountings when a ship sinks (even after it sinks) but can also be operated manually at the installation point, saving precious time in an emergency.

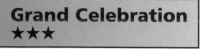

Grand Celebration
★★★

Size:...........................Large Resort Ship	Passenger Decks: 10	Cabins (with private balcony):.............10
Tonnage: 47,262	Total Crew: 620	Cabins (wheelchair accessible): 14
Lifestyle:.......................................Standard	Passengers	Wheelchair accessibility ....Fair
Cruise Line: ....Iberocruceros	(lower beds/all berths):.........1,494/1,896	Cabin Current: ....110/220 volts
Former Names: ....*Celebration*	Passenger Space Ratio	Elevators: 8
Builder:......................Kockums (Sweden)	(lower beds/all berths):.............31.6/24.9	Casino (gaming tables):......................Yes
Original Cost:........................$130 million	Crew/Passenger Ratio	Slot Machines:...................................Yes
Entered Service: ....Mar 1987/Jun 2008	(lower beds/all berths):.................2.4/3.0	Swimming Pools (outdoors):...................3
Registry:.......................................Panama	Cabins (total):......................................747	Swimming Pools (indoors): 0
Length (ft/m):.......................732.6/223.30	Size Range (sq ft/m): 184.0/17.1	Whirlpools:...2
Beam (ft/m):...........................92.5/28.20	Cabins (outside view):........................453	Self-Service Launderette:...................Yes
Draft (ft/m):...............................25.5/7.80	Cabins (interior/no view):...................296	Dedicated Cinema/Seats: ....No
Propulsion/Propellers:diesel (23,520kW)/2	Cabins (for one person):.........................0	Library:...Yes

BERLITZ'S OVERALL SCORE: 1,182 OUT OF A POSSIBLE 2,000 POINTS

OVERVIEW. First introduced as the fourth new ship for Carnival Cruise Lines, the ship has a rather angular exterior, typical of the space-conscious designs introduced in the early 1980s to try to maximize interior (revenue-generating) space. It is now operating for Iberocruceros, and the white hull is adorned with splashed of color, with the Iberocruceros, and the white hull is adorned with images of rather tall persons to hide the fact that there is no walk-around exterior promenade deck.

This all-white ship, now more than 20 years old, has extremely short bows, and a distinctive, large, swept-back wing-tipped blue funnel just aft of the center of the ship. The swimming pools are smaller than one would expect, and the open deck space can be extremely crowded

Inside, *Grand Celebration* has a double-width indoor promenade and a good selection of public rooms, including a large casino. The flamboyant interior decor in public rooms is bright, bold and stimulating, not relaxing, as is the colorful artwork. Facilities include a library and internet-connect center. Children are split into two age categories, with facilities for each: Club 5 (5–10 year olds), or Club 10 (10 years and older).

There's no escape from repetitious announcements – particularly for activities that bring revenue, such as bingo, or horse racing. Standing in line for embarkation, disembarkation, shore tenders and for self-serve buffet meals is inevitable when cruising aboard all large ships.

The onboard currency is the euro, and all gratuities to staff are included in this "mostly-inclusive" cruise. An optional drinks package (standard drink brands) can be bought at €16 per person, per day or €8 for a non-alcoholic drinks package for minors.

BERLITZ'S RATINGS

	Possible	Achieved
Ship	500	297
Accommodation	200	121
Food	400	216
Service	400	247
Entertainment	100	66
Cruise	400	235

SUITABLE FOR: This ship is a floating playground for young, Spanish-speaking active adults who enjoy constant stimulation, close contact with lots and lots of others. There is a wide range of entertainment and passenger participation activities from which to choose, and it should prove a good choice for families with children (there are several places for kids to explore).

ACCOMMODATION. The ship has a range of suites, outside-view cabins and interior (no view) cabins in four grades: suite with balcony; junior suite with balcony; outside-view: and interior (no-view) cabins, and 13 price grades. The cabins are quite standard and mostly identical in terms of layout and decor (which means they are good for large groups who want identical cabins for their participants), are of fairly generous proportions, except for the interior (no view) cabins, which are quite small. They are reasonably comfortable and well equipped, but nothing special. A 24-hour room service menu is also provided.

The best living spaces on board are in 10 suites, each of which has much more space, its own private balcony, a larger bathroom and more closet, drawer and storage space (good for families).

CUISINE/DINING. There are two dining rooms (Vista Hermoza, with 550 seats, and Riazor, with 450 seats). They are quite cramped when full, and extremely noisy (both are non-smoking), and they have low ceilings in the raised sections of their centers. There are tables for four, six or eight (none for two). The decor is bright and extremely colorful, to say the least. Dining is in two seatings: 8:30pm and 10:30pm. Meals for vegetarians and special children's menus are also available, as is a snack at midnight.

Presentation is simple, and few garnishes are used. Many meat and fowl dishes are disguised with gravies and sauces. There is much use of canned fruit and jellied desserts. This is all about banquet catering, with all its attendant standardization and production cooking.

Although there is a decent wine list, there are no wine waiters and so the regular waiters are expected to serve both food and wine. The service is highly programmed, although the waiters are willing and reasonably friendly.

Casual meals can be taken as self-serve buffets in the 280-seat Buffet Triana, although the meals provided are very basic, and quite disappointing, with much repetition (particularly for breakfast).

ENTERTAINMENT. The Astoria Showlounge is the main venue for large-scale production shows and major cabaret acts (although several pillars obstruct the views from some seats). Large-scale, high volume production shows are featured, together with a number of European cabaret acts.

Almost every lounge/bar has live bands and musical units, so there's always plenty of live music in the evening.

SPA/FITNESS. The Spa is located on the ship's uppermost deck, just aft of the mast, and accessed by the center stairway and lifts. It has a gymnasium (with some muscle-pumping cardiovascular machines) and views over the ship's main swimming pool, men's and women's changing rooms and saunas. The beauty salon is located in another spot.

Massage (including exotic massages such as Aroma Stone massage and Swedish Remedial Massage, facials, pedicures, and beauty salon treatments cost extra.

STEERING

Two different methods can be used to steer a ship:

Electrohydraulic steering uses automatic (telemotor-type) transmission from the wheel itself to the steering gear aft. This is generally used when traffic is heavy, during maneuvers into and out of ports, or when there is poor visibility. **Automatic steering** (gyropilot) is used only in the open sea. This system does not require anyone at the wheel because it is controlled by computer. However, aboard all ships, a quartermaster is always at the wheel, for extra safety, and just in case a need should arise to switch from one steering system to another.

Satellite Navigator

Using this latest high-tech piece of equipment, ship's officers can read, on a small television screen, the ship's position in the open ocean anywhere in the world, any time, and in any weather with pinpoint accuracy.

Satellite navigation systems use the information transmitted by a constellation of orbiting satellites. Each is in a normal circular polar orbit at an altitude of 450 to 700 nautical miles, and orbits the Earth in about 108 minutes.

Data from each gives the current orbital position every two minutes. Apart from telling the ship where it is, it continuously provides the distance from any given point, calculates the drift caused by currents and so on, and tells the ship when the next satellite will pass.

The basis of the satellite navigation is the US Navy Satellite System (NNSS). This first became operational in January 1964 as the precision guidance system for the Polaris submarine fleet and was made available for commercial use in 1967.

The latest (and more accurate) system is the GPS (Global Positioning System), which is now fitted to an increasing number of ships. This uses 24 satellites (18 of which are on-line at any given time) that provide accuracy in estimating a ship's position to plus or minus 6 ft. Another variation is the NACOS (Navigational Command System), which collects information from a variety of sources: satellites, radar, gyroscopic compass, speed log, and surface navigational systems as well as engines, thrusters, rudders, and human input. It then displays relevant computations and information on one screen, controlled by a single keyboard.

Grand Holiday
★★★

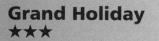

Size: . . . . .Mid-Size Ship	Passenger Decks: 9	Cabins (with private balcony): 10
Tonnage: .46,052	Total Crew: 660	Cabins (wheelchair accessible): 15
Lifestyle: . . . . .Standard	Passengers	Wheelchair accessibility . . . . .None
Cruise Line: . . . . .Iberocruceros	(lower beds/all berths): 1,452/1,800	Cabin Current: . . . . .110 volts
Former Names: . . . .*Holiday*	Passenger Space Ratio	Elevators: 8
Builder: . . . . . . .Aalborg Vaerft (Denmark)	(lower beds/all berths): 31.7/25.5	Casino (gaming tables): . . . . .Yes
Original Cost: . . . .$170 million	Crew/Passenger Ratio	Slot Machines: . . . . .Yes
Entered Service: . . . .July 1985/ May 2010	(lower beds/all berths): 2.2/2.7	Swimming Pools (outdoors): 3
Registry: . . . . .The Bahamas	Cabins (total): .726	Swimming Pools (indoors): 0
Length (ft/m): 726.9/221.57	Size Range (sq ft/m): 189.2–420.0/	Whirlpools: 2
Beam (ft/m): 92.4/28.17	17.0–39.0	Self-Service Launderette: . . . . .No
Draft (ft/m): 25.5/7.77	Cabins (outside view): 447	Dedicated Cinema/Seats: . . . . .No
Propulsion/Propellers: . . . . .diesel	Cabins (interior/no view): 279	Library: . . . . .Yes
(22,360kW)/2	Cabins (for one person): 0	

OVERALL SCORE: 1,160 OUT OF A POSSIBLE 2,000 POINTS

OVERVIEW. *Grand Holiday* was formerly *Holiday*, the second new ship ordered by parent company Carnival Cruise Lines. It is a bold, high-sided, all-white contemporary ship with a very short, rakish bow and stubby stern typical of so many vessels built in the 1980s. It has a distinctive swept-back wing-tipped funnel. Iberocruceros spent €55 million to refurbish the ship in 2010, when all cabins were completely refreshed.

The decks are named after cities and towns – Seville, Valencia, Lugo, Pamplona, Avila, Elche, Barcelona, Madrid, and Ronda. The passenger flow is good, although the ship does have a high density and always feels crowded. There are numerous public rooms on two entertainment decks to choose from, and these flow from a double-width indoor promenade. A real red-and-cream bus is located right in the middle of one of the two promenades, and this is used as a snack Cafe.

The bright interior decor has a distinct theme. There is plenty of music and entertainment, while junior cruisers have their own activity centers.

SUITABLE FOR: *Grand Holiday* is best suited to young Spanish-speaking couples seeking their first cruise experience, single passengers, tots, children and teens.

ACCOMMODATION. There are just four cabin categories: Suite with balcony; Junior Suite with balcony; exterior cabins, and interior (no view) cabins, in 13 different price grades. The price will depend on grade, size and location. The standard outside and interior (no view) cabins are plain but functional units that provide all the basics including a small vanity/writing desk. TV sets, however, are typically placed

BERLITZ'S RATINGS

	Possible	Achieved
Ship	500	293
Accommodation	200	122
Food	400	214
Service	400	241
Entertainment	100	64
Cruise	400	226

high in one corner and are not easy to see. The bathrooms are practical units, with decent-sized shower enclosures. Wall-mounted dispensers provide body soap and shampoo.

CUISINE. There are two main restaurants: Cantabrico and Alboran. Both are large, have low ceilings and raised center sections, and a cramped feeling.

The food is presented well, but few garnishes are used. Do remember that this really is banquet-style catering, with families and children in mind, so standardization and production cooking is the norm. Although there is a decent wine list, there are no wine waiters. The service is highly programmed, although the waiters are friendly.

The Ensenada Buffet is a self-serve buffet that provides all the basics (except service), although its layout is old in style and makes the venue seem more like a canteen than a restaurant. Still, it's good for that quick meal when the ship is in port and the family want to be out and about.

ENTERTAINMENT. The Grand Theater Bazan is the principal venue for large-scale production shows and major cabaret acts – although some pillars obstruct the views from several seats. It has a main and upper level.

Most lounges and bars have live music, so there's always plenty of life. There are two discos – one large, one small overlooking the ship's single swimming pool.

SPA/FITNESS. Some fitness classes are free, while some may cost extra. Do make appointments for any massages, facials or other beauty treatments (manicures/pedicures) as early as possible, because time slots do go quickly.

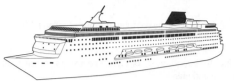

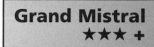

Grand Mistral
★★★ +

Size:	Mid-Size Ship	Passenger Decks:	.8	Cabins (with private balcony):	.80
Tonnage:	.48,200	Total Crew:	.470	Cabins (wheelchair accessible):	.2
Lifestyle:	.Standard	Passengers		Wheelchair accessibility	.Fair
Cruise Line:	.Iberocruceros	(lower beds/all berths):	.1,196/1,600	Cabin Current:	.110 and 220 volts
Former Names:	.Mistral	Passenger Space Ratio		Elevators:	.6
Builder:	.Chantiers de l'Atlantique (France)	(lower beds/all berths):	.39.5/30.1	Casino (gaming tables):	.Yes
Original Cost:	.$245 million	Crew/Passenger Ratio		Slot Machines:	.Yes
Entered Service:	July 1999/May 2005	(lower beds/all berths):	.2.4/3.4	Swimming Pools (outdoors):	.2
Registry:	.Marshall Islands	Cabins (total):	.598	Swimming Pools (indoors):	.0
Length (ft/m):	.709.9/216.4	Size Range (sq ft/m):	.139.9–236.8/	Whirlpools:	.2 (thalassotherapy)
Beam (ft/m):	.94.6/28.84		13.0–22.0	Self-Service Launderette:	.No
Draft (ft/m):	.22.4/6.85	Cabins (outside view):	.375	Dedicated Cinema/Seats:	.No
Propulsion/Propellers:	.diesel-electric	Cabins (interior/no view):	.223	Library:	.Yes
	(31,680 kW)/2	Cabins (for one person):	.0		

OVERALL SCORE: 1,315 OUT OF A POSSIBLE 2,000 POINTS

OVERVIEW. *Grand Mistral*, an all-white ship with a single blue funnel, was the first brand-new ship for the now defunct Festival Cruises (Mistral is the name of a famous desert wind; it's also the name of a violin concerto).

Grand Mistral is owned by a consortium of French investors and banks, and chartered to Iberocruceros, a vibrant tour operator (now 100% owned by the giant Carnival Corporation) for the Spanish-speaking family market. The ship's profile is similar to that of most new cruise ships, although the built-up stern makes it look bulky and less than handsome.

The lido deck surrounding the outdoor swimming pools (these are small, and regulated for use by various age groups in several time of day zones), has whirlpool tubs and a large bandstand is set in raised canvas-covered pods. Sunloungers have cushioned pads. There is no full walkaround promenade deck outdoors, although there is a partial walking deck on port and starboard sides under the lifeboats, plus an oval jogging track atop ship. The interior layout and passenger flow is good, as are the "you are here" deck signs, and the ship absorbs passengers quite well.

The interior layout and passenger flow is good, as are the "you are here" deck signs, and the ship absorbs passengers quite well. It is light and cheerful without being glitzy in any way (with not even a hint of colored neon), and there is much use of blonde/cherry wood paneling and rich, textured soft furnishings.

Public rooms, bars and lounges have names inspired by European places or establishments (examples: San Remo Casino, San Marco Lounge, Cafe Guon and Richlieu Library). There is a smoking room (Le Diplomate), with

BERLITZ'S RATINGS

	Possible	Achieved
Ship	500	369
Accommodation	200	135
Food	400	240
Service	400	252
Entertainment	100	58
Cruise	400	261

all the hallmarks of a gentleman's club of former times, a piano bar, and a library that has real writing desks (something many ships seem to omit).

Atop the ship is an observation lounge with a twist – it faces aft, instead of forward; it doubles as a discotheque for the late-night set. A conference center provides facilities that are useful for meetings.

There is also a decent-sized spa/beauty complex, set forward of the mast. This includes a fitness center with lots of muscle-toning equipment and lifecycles and life-rowing machines and a view over the bow of the ship through large floor-to-ceiling windows. There are six rooms for massage and other body treatments, as well as a sauna each for men and women, plus an aerobics exercise room. Adjacent to the spa is a video game room for teens, and a children's center.

Smokers are difficult to avoid, towels are small, and the square chairs in the Cafe Navona are uncomfortable and impractical. Standing in line for embarkation, disembarkation, shore tenders and for self-serve buffet meals is inevitable aboard all ships of this size. The onboard currency is the euro (except when the ship operates in Brazil during the Brazilian summer season, when the currency is the Brazilian Real). Gratuities are included. An optional drinks package (standard drink brands) can be bought for €16 per person, per day or €8 for a non-alcoholic drinks package for minors.

SUITABLE FOR: *Grand Mistral* is best suited to youthful Spanish-speaking couples and singles, and families with children that enjoy big city life and outdoor cafés, constant activity accompanied by lots of noise, late nights, entertainment that is loud, and food that focuses on quantity rather than quality.

ACCOMMODATION. There are three basic cabin types, in nine different price grades. There are 80 "suites" (each has a private balcony, although partitions are of the partial, and not the full type), ocean-view standard cabins and interior (no view) standard cabins. The price you pay will depend on grade, size and location.

The cabins on Deck 10 are subject to noise from the Lido Deck above. Good planning and layout means that no outside-view cabins have lifeboat-obstructed views. The cabin numbering system goes against maritime tradition, where even-numbered cabins are on the port side and odd-numbered cabins on the starboard; in *Grand Mistral*, the opposite is in effect.

All cabins have twin beds that convert to a queen-sized unit, bold, colorful bedspreads (with blankets and sheets, not duvets), a personal safe, a combination colour TV/VCR, telephone, a personal safe, and a good amount of closet and drawer space for a one-week cruise. The bathrooms, although not large, do have a good-sized shower enclosure, and there is a decent amount of stowage space for personal toiletries.

Accommodation designated as suites (these are really only larger cabins and not suites, as there is no separation of lounge and sleeping space), quite naturally, have more space, larger (walk-in) closets, more drawers and better storage space, plus a two-person sofa, coffee table and additional armchair, vanity desk, floor-to-ceiling mirrors and hairdryer; bathrooms have a bathtub/shower combination.

Six Grand Suites, added in 2007 at the ship's stern, are well-designed units that feature a separate bedroom (flat-screen TV), bedside tables, vanity desk, floor-to-ceiling windows, and door to balcony; the lounge has an audio-visual center, sofa, dining table, and lots of space, plus a balcony door. A large bathroom has contemporary styling, two Villeroy & Boch washbasins, dark hardwood storage cabinets, large Jacuzzi bathtub, separate shower enclosure (hand-held shower), and bathrobes.

In addition, there are two interior (no view) wheelchair accessible cabins for the handicapped, which provide more spacious interiors than standard cabins.

CUISINE. There are two dining rooms (and two seatings for meals), which can be configured in any of several different ways. Both have ocean-view windows. The principal dining room (Restaurant Mallorca, with 610 seats) has round tables for two, four, six or eight, and a small podium with baby grand piano.

A second dining venue – Restaurant Formentor, with 380 seats (chairs have no armrests), is on a different deck. Smaller and more intimate, it is for passengers occupying Deck 10 accommodation; it has tables for two, four or six, and ocean-view windows.

The food is quite sound, and, with varied menus and decent presentation, should prove a highlight for most passengers. The wine list features a good variety of standard wines at reasonable prices, but almost all are young.

There's also a casual Bahia de Palma cafeteria for al fresco self-serve buffet-style breakfasts and lunches, with ocean-view windows, but the flow is awkward and cramped. Additionally, there's also an outdoor pool bar; plus a pleasant little coffee bar (Café Navona, serving Brazilian coffee) on the upper level of the two-deck high lobby, with lifeboat-restricted ocean views.

ENTERTAINMENT. The Grand Theatre Ibiza, the showlounge, spans two decks, has a sloping floor, and good sight lines from most seats (there is banquette-style seating), and there is a small balcony level at the rear. Sadly, the designer forgot to include space for a live band, and the lighting facilities are less than high-tech. There's also a bar/lounge (Salon Formentera) on the lower (main) level at the entrance to the showlounge. Entertainment is, without doubt, the weak link in the chain of Iberocruceros.

SPA/FITNESS. The Santai Spa health/fitness facilities, located forward of the mast, are quite decent. Included is a gymnasium with high-tech muscle-pump equipment, lifecycles and life-rowing machines and a view over the bow of the ship through large floor-to-ceiling windows.

Other facilities include a thalassotherapy room, and beauty salon, six rooms for massage and other body treatments, as well as a sauna each for men and women, plus an aerobics exercise room. It's best to make appointments early, as the best time slots can go fairly quickly.

Sample prices: Balinese Massage or Shiatsu Massage, €74 for 45 minutes or €90 for 60 minutes; Cranial (head) Massage, €20.

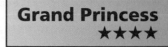

Grand Princess
★★★★

Size: ....Large Resort Ship	Passenger Decks: 13	Cabins (with private balcony): 710
Tonnage: 108,806	Total Crew: 1,100	Cabins (wheelchair accessible): 28
Lifestyle: ....Standard	Passengers	(18 outside/10 interior)
Cruise Line: ....Princess Cruises	(lower beds/all berths): 2,600/3,100	Wheelchair accessibility: ......Best
Former Names: ....none	Passenger Space Ratio	Cabin Current: ....110 and 220 volts
Builder: ....Fincantieri (Italy)	(lower beds/all berths): 41.8/35.0	Elevators: 14
Original Cost: ....$450 million	Crew/Passenger Ratio	Casino (gaming tables): ....Yes
Entered Service: ....May 1998	(lower beds/all berths): 2.3/2.8	Slot Machines: ....Yes
Registry: ....Bermuda	Cabins (total): 1,300	Swimming Pools (outdoors): 4
Length (ft/m): 951.4/290.0	Size Range (sq ft/m): 161.4–764.2/	Swimming Pools (indoors): 0
Beam (ft/m): 118.1/36.0	15.0–71.0	Whirlpools: 9
Draft (ft/m): 26.2/8.0	Cabins (outside view): 928	Self-Service Launderette: ....Yes
Propulsion/Propellers: .....diesel-electric	Cabins (interior/no view): 372	Dedicated Cinema/Seats: ....No
(42,000kW)/2	Cabins (for one person): 0	Library: ....Yes

OVERALL SCORE: 1,496 OUT OF A POSSIBLE 2,000 POINTS

OVERVIEW. *Grand Princess*, sister to *Golden Princess* and *Star Princess*, has a flared snub-nosed bow and a galleon-like transom stern. It is too wide to transit the Panama Canal, with many balcony cabins overhanging the hull.

There is a good sheltered faux teak promenade deck – it's actually painted steel – which almost wraps around, and a walkway that goes right to the enclosed, protected bow. The outdoor pools have various beach-like surroundings. One lap pool has a pumped "current" to swim against.

Unlike the outside decks, there is plenty of space inside the ship – but also plenty of passengers – and a wide array of public rooms, with many "intimate" (this being a relative word) spaces. The decor is very attractive and warm, with lots of earth tones.

Four areas center on swimming pools, one of which is two decks high and is covered by a magrodome. High atop the stern of the ship is a ship-wide glass-walled disco pod. It looks like an aerodynamic spoiler and is positioned 150 ft (45 meters) above the waterline, with spectacular views from the extreme port and starboard side windows (you can look along the ship's side and onto lots of "private" balconies).

An extensive collection of art works complements the interior design and colors well. If you see something you like, you'll probably be able to buy it on board.

This ship has a Wedding Chapel (a live web-cam can relay ceremonies via the internet). The ship's captain can marry (American) couples, due to the ship's Bermuda registry and a special dispensation – this should, however, be verified when in the planning stage, and may vary according to where you reside *(more details: page 149)*.

Another neat feature is the motion-based "virtual reality"

BERLITZ'S RATINGS		
	Possible	Achieved
Ship	500	413
Accommodation	200	163
Food	400	252
Service	400	287
Entertainment	100	80
Cruise	400	301

room with its enclosed motion-based rides, and a "blue screen" studio, where passengers can star in their own videos. There is an excellent library/computer room, and a separate card room. Youngsters have a two-deck-high playroom, teen's room, and trained counselors.

Gamblers should enjoy what is one of the largest casinos at sea, with more than 260 slot machines with dolphin-shaped handles; there are blackjack, craps and roulette tables, plus games such as Let It Ride Bonus, Spanish 21 and Caribbean Draw Progressive. A highlight is Neptune's Lair, a multimedia gaming extravaganza. Ship lovers should enjoy the wood-paneled Wheelhouse Bar, decorated with memorabilia and ship models tracing part of parent company P&O's history.

Princess Cays – Princess Cruises' own "private island" in the Caribbean – is "yours" (along with a couple of thousand other passengers) for a day; however, you will need to take a shore tender to get to and from it, and this can take some time. A high-tech hospital has live SeaMed telemedicine link-ups with specialists at the Cedars-Sinai Medical Center in Los Angeles for emergency help (hardly useful for passengers who don't reside in the USA).

This ship is full of revenue centers, designed to help you part with more money. The dress code has been simplified to formal or smart casual. Gratuities are automatically added to your account, at $10 per person, per day; gratuities for children are charged at the same rate. If you want to pay less, you'll have to line up at the reception desk. The onboard currency is the US dollar.

Whether this really can be considered a relaxing holiday is a moot point, but with so many choices and "small" rooms to enjoy, the ship has been extremely well designed;

the odds are that you'll have a fine time, in a controlled, well-packaged way. Niggles? The automated telephone system frustrates many passengers, and luggage delivery needs to be more efficient.

ACCOMMODATION. There are six types of cabins and configurations: (a) grand suite, (b) suite, (c) mini-suite, (d) outside double with balcony, (e) outside double, and (f) interior (no view) double. There are, however, 35 different brochure price categories; the choice is bewildering for both travel agents and passengers. Price depends on grade, size and location. Many cabins have additional upper berths (there are 609 of them), good for families with children.

(a) The plushest suite is the Grand Suite, which has a hot tub accessible from both the private balcony and from the bedroom, two bedrooms, lounge, two bathrooms, a huge walk-in closet, and plenty of drawer and storage space.

(b/c) Suites (with a semi-private balcony) have a separate living room (with sofa bed) and bedroom (with a TV set in each). The bathroom is quite large and has both a bathtub and shower stall. The mini-suites also have a private balcony, and feature a separate living and sleeping area (with a TV set in each). The differences between the suites and mini-suites are basically in the size and appointments. Passengers in both receive priority attention, including speedy embarkation and disembarkation privileges. What is unacceptable is that the most expensive accommodation has only semi-private balconies that can be seen from above and so there is absolutely no privacy (Suites C401, 402, 409, 410, 414, 415, 420, 421/422, 423, 424 and 425 on Caribe Deck). The suites D105 and D106 (Dolphin Deck) are extremely large, but their balconies can be seen from above.

(d/e/f) Both interior and outside-view (the outsides come either with or without private balcony) cabins are functional and practical, although almost no drawers are provided. They are attractive, with warm, pleasing decor and fine soft furnishing fabrics; 80% of the outside cabins have a private balcony. The tiled bathrooms have a good amount of open shelf storage space for personal toiletries.

There are also two family suites. These consist of two suites with an interconnecting door, plus a large balcony, and can sleep up to 10 (if at least four are children), or up to eight people (if all are adults).

Most outside cabins on Emerald Deck have views obstructed by lifeboats. Sadly, there are no cabins for singles. Your name is placed outside your suite or cabin – making it simple for delivery service personnel but compromising privacy. Some cabins can accommodate a third and fourth person in upper berths – but in such cabins, the lower beds cannot then be pushed together to make queen-sized bed.

Perhaps the least desirable balcony cabins are the eight located forward on Emerald Deck, as the balconies do not extend to the side of the ship and can be passed by walkers and gawkers on the adjacent Upper Promenade walkway. Also, passengers occupying some the most expensive suites with balconies at the stern of the vessel may experience considerable vibration during certain ship maneuvers.

The cabin bath towels are small, and drawer space is very limited. There are no butlers – even for the top grade suites. Cabin attendants have too many cabins to look after (typically 20), which cannot translate to fine personal service.

CUISINE. There is a variety of "Personal Choice" dining options. For formal meals, there are three main dining rooms, Botticelli, with 504 seats, Da Vinci (486), and Michelangelo (486). There are two seatings in one restaurant, while the other two have "anytime dining" where you choose when, and with whom, you want to eat. All three are non-smoking and split into multi-tier sections in a non-symmetrical design that breaks what are quite large spaces into many smaller sections. Each dining room has its own galley. While four elevators go to Fiesta Deck where the Botticelli and Da Vinci restaurants are located, only two go to Plaza Deck 5 where the Michaelangelo Restaurant is located (this can cause long waits at peak times, especially for wheelchair users).

Alternative (Extra Charge) Dining: There are two alternative informal dining areas: Sabatini's and Painted Desert. Both are open for lunch and dinner. Sabatini's is an Italian eatery, with colorful tiled Mediterranean-style decor. It has Italian-style pizzas and pastas, with a variety of sauces, as well as Italian-style entrées (including tiger prawns and lobster tail). Sabatini's is by reservation only, and there is a cover charge of $15 per person, for lunch or dinner (on sea days only). Painted Desert, a very open area, has "southwestern American food"; by reservation only, with a cover charge of $8 per person, for lunch or dinner on sea days only. The cuisine in both of these spots is decidedly better than in the three main dining rooms.

The poolside hamburger grill and pizza bar (no additional charge) are additional dining spots for casual bites, while extra charges will apply if you order items to eat at either the coffee bar/patisserie, or the caviar/champagne bar.

Other casual meals can be taken in the Horizon Court – open 24 hours a day, with large ocean-view on port and starboard sides and direct access to the two principal swimming pools and lido deck. Plastic plates are used.

ENTERTAINMENT. The 748-seat Princess Theater (showlounge) spans two decks and has comfortable seating on both main and balcony levels.

The Vista Lounge is a second entertainment lounge. It has cabaret acts at night, and lectures, bingo and horse racing during the day. Explorers, a third entertainment lounge, can also host cabaret acts and dance bands. Many lounges and bars have live music, and a number of gentlemen dance hosts act as partners for women traveling alone.

SPA/FITNESS. The Lotus Spa is a large complex that surrounds one of the swimming pools at the forward end. It comprises a large gymnasium with all the usual equipment, an aerobics room, sauna and steam rooms, beauty salon, ocean-view treatment rooms, and a relaxation area.

● **For more extensive general information about the Princess Cruises experience, see pages 148–51.**

Grand Voyager
★★★ +

Size: ....Mid-Size Ship	Passenger Decks: 8	Cabins (with private balcony): 12
Tonnage: 24,391	Total Crew: 360	Cabins (wheelchair accessible): 4
Lifestyle: ....Standard	Passengers	Wheelchair accessibility ....Good
Cruise Line: ....Iberocruceros	(lower beds/all berths): 840/920	Cabin Current: ....110 and 230 volts
Former Names: ....*Olympia Voyager,*	Passenger Space Ratio	Elevators: 4
Olympic Voyager	(lower beds/all berths): 29.0/26.5	Casino (gaming tables): ....Yes
Builder: ....Blohm & Voss (Germany)	Crew/Passenger Ratio	Slot Machines: ....Yes
Original Cost: ....$150.8 million	(lower beds/all berths): 2.3/2.5	Swimming Pools (outdoors): 1
Entered Service: ...July 2000 /June 2004	Cabins (total): 420	Swimming Pools (indoors): 0
Registry: ....The Bahamas	Size Range (sq ft/m): 140.0–375.0/	Whirlpools: 0
Length (ft/m): 590.5/180.0	13.0–34.8	Self-Service Launderette: ....No
Beam (ft/m): 83.6/25.5	Cabins (outside view): 294	Dedicated Cinema/Seats: ....No
Draft (ft/m): 23.2/7.1	Cabins (interior/no view): 126	Library: ....Yes
Propulsion/Propellers: diesel (37,800 kW)/2	Cabins (for one person): 0	

OVERALL SCORE: 1,314 OUT OF A POSSIBLE 2,000 POINTS

OVERVIEW. *Grand Voyager* (original name *Olympic Voyager*) was the first new ship ordered by Royal Olympia Cruises. However, the ship's high building cost was a problem, and it was put up for auction in March 2003. Having been bought by Horizon Navigation, it was placed under charter by Iberocruceros (100%-owned by the giant Carnival Corporation) and dedicated to the Spanish-speaking market.

The exterior hull design, called a "fast monohull," is similar to that of naval frigates, with a slender fore-body, and two engine rooms (forward and midships) that can provide a 28-knot speed – and even some additional power in reserve. The ship is well suited to destination-intensive (port-hopping) itineraries, allowing passengers more time in each port (or more ports per cruise). Its funnel is of a streamlined, swept-back design.

There is a limited amount of open deck space, although there are not many sunloungers. All exterior railings are made – unusually – of stainless steel (topped with thick, beautifully polished wood). The seawater swimming pool is located aft, and is quite small (most passengers will be enjoying the destinations served by this cruise line); adjacent are two shower enclosures.

The interior design combines contemporary touches with restrained decor, intended to remind one of the Mediterranean region the ship is designed for, with warm colors and an abundance of wood and opaque glass paneling. Perhaps the most striking, yet subtle, features in terms of design and decoration can be found in the artwork. Of particular note are two flowing poems etched in backlit opaque glass panels on the stairways (these poems are from Greece and Cyprus). However, to read the poems, you'll need to walk

BERLITZ'S RATINGS

	Possible	Achieved
Ship	500	389
Accommodation	200	135
Food	400	240
Service	400	252
Entertainment	100	58
Cruise	400	260

down the complete set of stairways. One poem, from 1911 (Ithaca) by the Greek poet Constantinos Petrou Kavafis, complements the other poem, Let's Say, by Cypriot poet Yannis Papadopoulos.

Most public rooms are located on one principal deck in a horizontal-flow layout that makes it easy to quickly find your way around, with a slightly winding open passageway that links several leisure lounges in one neat "street scene." There's a smoking room, adjacent to the main show lounge (Sala de Fiestas), for cigar and cognac devotees (with a black fireplace from the 1890s). In the popular Piano Bar, three ship models are cleverly displayed behind large glass wall panels. There's also a nightclub, a small library and a card room. Additionally, a casino (with its own bar) has table games, as well as slot machines.

There is no full walk-around promenade deck, although you can walk around parts of the vessel outdoors. There is considerable vibration when the ship is underway at high speed, and when maneuvering at slow speeds. There are no dedicated facilities or rooms for the large numbers of children or teens that are typically carried during the July/August summer holidays. None of the public toilets is accessible by wheelchair. There are not enough sunloungers considering the number of passengers carried, and not enough open deck space.

This is a "mostly-inclusive" product that is particularly suitable to families with children – although facilities for children are few. An optional drinks package (standard drink brands) can be bought for €16 per person, per day or €8 for a non-alcoholic drinks package for minors. The onboard currency is the euro, except when the ship operates in Brazil during the Brazilian summer season, when the currency is the Brazilian Real).

SUITABLE FOR: *Grand Voyager* is best suited to Spanish-speaking couples and single travelers who want to see as much as possible (in terms of destinations), in contemporary, comfortable, but not luxurious surroundings, and with food and service that are acceptable, but nothing special, all at a very modest cruise fare.

ACCOMMODATION. There are five categories (suite with balcony; suite with bay window; junior suite, window but no balcony; outside cabin; and interior (no-view cabin), in nine price grades, including one for wheelchair accessible cabins with spacious bathrooms and roll-in showers. The price will depend on grade, location and size.

Standard Cabins: The standard interior (no view) and outside-view cabins are quite compact, but practically laid-out, and the decor includes warm blond wood cabinetry, accents and facings, and pleasing soft furnishings. The bathrooms are small, but have a decent-sized shower enclosure, and good storage facilities for personal toiletry items. All cabins include TV set, hairdryer, mini-bar/refrigerator and personal safe. You should note that only one personal safe is provided in each cabin, although there could be as many as four persons sharing a cabin.

Outside-View Superior Cabins: These simply have a little more room than the standard interior (no view) and outside-view cabins (some have bay windows that extend over the side of the ship). The bathrooms are small, but have a decent-sized shower enclosure, and good storage facilities for personal toiletries.

Balcony Suites: The largest accommodation can be found in 12 Sky Suites located high atop the ship and in the forward-most section. They have large private balconies (some are more like large terraces), floor-to-ceiling windows, limited butler service, and 24-hour dining service.

Some suites have walk-in closets, while others have closets facing the entranceway, but all have an abundance of drawer and hanging space, and a chrome pullout shoe rack and tie rack. The bathroom has a combination tub/shower (although the bathtub is extremely small and is really only for sitting in) and retractable clothesline.

All suites have wood paneled walls with vanity desk, mini-bar/refrigerator, sofa, drinks table (it's fixed, and cannot be raised), and sleeping area partly separated from the lounge area by a wood/glass divider. Four of the suites have large structures above their balconies that are the port side and starboard side gangway lowering mechanisms; they

are noisy in ports of call and anchor ports, and thus the balconies cannot be considered very private.

Also, when the ship is traveling at speed, considerable wind sweeps across the balconies, and renders them almost useless. The balconies have (expensive) stainless steel railings instead of glass, topped with a thick wood railing. Outside-view and interior (no-view) cabins located aft on Deck 3 (Neptune Deck: Numbers 3120–3138 and 3121–3151) are subject to a substantial amount of throbbing noise from the diesel engines, and should be avoided (unless you like throbbing engine noise, that is).

CUISINE. The 470-seat Main Restaurant is located aft (one deck below the main "street" of public rooms and thus out of the main flow), and has picture windows on three sides. It has a semi-circular walkway, with minimalist decor, as its entrance.

The decor in the dining room itself is warm and welcoming, and quite tasteful, finished in what is best described as a "Greek Moderne" style; the chairs, however, do not have armrests. There are two seatings, and there are tables for two, four, six or eight. A few tables close to the entrance to the galley's escalators suffer from the service area, and, because of the single deck ceiling height and open waiter stations, the noise level can be considerable at times (depending on the nationalities of your fellow passengers).

For casual breakfast and lunch self-service buffets, the Garden Buffet is a pleasant but basic room, with large picture windows and an open feel. It has seating for 210 indoors and about 200 outdoors (where smokers congregate), and a bar outdoors is covered with a sailcloth-style cover. The two self-service buffet lines are small, and have a user-unfriendly layout that invites congestion – a victim of poor design.

Additional munching outlets include a pizza serving area/salad bar, and an ice cream bar.

ENTERTAINMENT. The Main Lounge is the venue for entertainment events. It is a single-level room with 420 seats although there are many pillars to obstruct the sight lines from many of those seats (about 40 per cent are almost useless). Entertainment is limited aboard this ship, whose show lounge is best for cabaret-style shows. There's a disco.

SPA/FITNESS. One of the nicest and most useful facilities aboard this ship can be found in the Spa. It includes a large fitness room, several massage/treatment rooms, sauna, steam room, and rest/changing area.

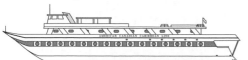

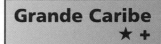

Grande Caribe
★ +

Size: ....Boutique Ship	Total Crew: 17	Cabins (wheelchair accessible): 0
Tonnage: 99	Passengers	Wheelchair accessibility ....None
Lifestyle: ....Standard	(lower beds/all berths): 100/100	Cabin Current: ....110 volts
Cruise Line: Blount Small Ship Adventures	Passenger Space Ratio	Elevators: 0
Former Names: ....none	(lower beds/all berths): 0.99/0.99	Casino (gaming tables): ....No
Builder: ....Blount Industries (USA)	Crew/Passenger Ratio	Slot Machines: ....No
Original Cost: ....$8 million	(lower beds/all berths): 5.8/5.8	Swimming Pools (outdoors): 0
Entered Service: ....June 1997	Cabins (total): 50	Swimming Pools (indoors): 0
Registry: ....USA	Size Range (sq ft/m): 72.0–96.0/	Whirlpools: 0
Length (ft/m): 183.0/55.7	6.6–8.9	Self-Service Launderette: ....No
Beam (ft/m): 40.0/12.1	Cabins (outside view): 41	Dedicated Cinema/Seats: ....No
Draft (ft/m): 6.5/1.9	Cabins (interior/no view): 9	Library: ....Yes
Propulsion/Propellers: diesel (1,044kW)/2	Cabins (for one person): 0	
Passenger Decks: 3	Cabins (with private balcony): 0	

OVERALL SCORE: 756 OUT OF A POSSIBLE 2,000 POINTS

OVERVIEW. *Grande Caribe* is the largest, most contemporary of the Blount-built vessels. During emergency drill, passengers are taught how to use fire extinguishers – a useful piece of training.

The ship's shallow draft enables it to cruise into off-the-beaten-path destinations well out of reach of larger ships. It also has a retractable navigation bridge – practical for those low bridges along inland waterways. *Grande Caribe*, together with sister vessel *Grande Mariner*, has stabilizers. An underwater video camera allows passengers, while seated in (dry) comfort in the lounge, to view on large-screen TV monitors what a scuba diver might see underneath the ship. Underwater lights, which attract fish and other marine life, are also fitted.

The style is casual – no jackets or ties – by day and night. There are two 24-passenger launches, one of which is a glass-bottomed boat, and snorkeling equipment.

There is one lounge/bar, located on a different deck to the dining room. Water sports facilities include a glass-bottom boat, sunfish sailboat and snorkeling equipment.

This basic, no-glitz vessel is good for anyone who does not want crowds, or a high standard of service. An electric stairway chair-lift is provided for those whose mobility is restricted. Gratuities given by passengers (high at the suggested $10–$15 per person, per day) are pooled and shared by all the staff. The onboard currency is the US dollar.

SUITABLE FOR: *Grande Caribe* is best suited to couples and single travelers who enjoy nature and wildlife up close and personal, and who would not dream of cruising in the mainstream sense aboard the large, warehouse-sized ships. This is for outdoors types who don't need entertainment or mind-

BERLITZ'S RATINGS

	Possible	Achieved
Ship	500	164
Accommodation	200	67
Food	400	155
Service	400	181
Entertainment	n/a	n/a
Cruise	500	189

less parlor games, but do want an all-American cruise experience, albeit at a high price. It's not for children.

ACCOMMODATION. The cabins are all extremely small, relatively utilitarian units, with very little closet space (but just enough drawers) and very small bathrooms, with new vacuum toilets. The twin beds convert to queen-sized beds, with good storage space under them. There is no room service menu, and only soap is supplied – bring your own shampoo and other toiletries. Each cabin has its own air conditioner, so passengers do not have to share air with the rest of the ship, or other passengers. Refreshingly, there are no cabin keys. Be prepared for noise from the generators.

CUISINE. The dining room seats all passengers in one open seating, so you dine with whomever you wish, making new friends and enjoying different conversation each day (it is also good for small groups). The tables convert to card tables for use between meals. Passengers are welcome to bring their own alcohol, as the company doesn't sell it aboard ship. Effervescent, young American waitresses provide the service, although there is no finesse. A hand-held Colonial bell is rung to summon passengers to the dining room.

ENTERTAINMENT. There is no formal entertainment, although dinner and after-dinner conversation with fellow passengers in the ship's lounge/bar really becomes the entertainment each evening. So, if you don't want to talk to your fellow passengers, take a good book.

SPA/FITNESS. No facilities.

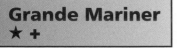

Grande Mariner
★ +

Size: . . . . .Boutique Ship	Passenger Decks: 3	Cabins (with private balcony): 0
Tonnage: 99	Total Crew: 17	Cabins (wheelchair accessible): 0
Lifestyle: . . . . .Standard	Passengers	Wheelchair accessibility . . . . .None
Cruise Line: Blount Small Ship Adventures	(lower beds/all berths): 100/100	Cabin Current: . . . . .110 volts
Former Names: . . . . .none	Passenger Space Ratio	Elevators: 0
Builder: . . . . .Blount Industries (USA)	(lower beds/all berths): 0.99/0.99	Casino (gaming tables): . . . . .No
Original Cost: . . . .$8 million	Crew/Passenger Ratio	Slot Machines: .No
Entered Service: . . . . .June 1998	(lower beds/all berths): 5.8/5.8	Swimming Pools (outdoors): 0
Registry: . . . . .USA	Cabins (total): .50	Swimming Pools (indoors): 0
Length (ft/m): 183.0/55.7	Size Range (sq ft/m): . .72.0–96.0/6.6–8.9	Whirlpools: 0
Beam (ft/m): 40.0/12.1	Cabins (outside view): 41	Self-Service Launderette: . . . . .No
Draft (ft/m): 6.5/1.9	Cabins (interior/no view): 9	Dedicated Cinema/Seats: . . . . .No
Propulsion/Propellers: .diesel (1,044kW)/2	Cabins (for one person): 0	Library: . . . . .Yes

OVERALL SCORE: 747 OUT OF A POSSIBLE 2,000 POINTS

OVERVIEW. *Grande Mariner* is the second of the two-ship Blount-built company. During passenger emergency drill, passengers are taught how to use fire extinguishers – useful training.

This vessel has a shallow draft, so it can cruise into off-the-beaten-path destinations well out of reach of larger ships, and also has a retractable navigation bridge – practical for those low bridges along the inland waterways. *Grande Mariner*, together with sister vessel *Grande Caribe*, has stabilizers. An underwater video camera allows passengers, while seated in (dry) comfort in the lounge, to view on large-screen TV monitors what a scuba diver might see underneath the ship. Underwater lights, which attract fish and other marine life, are also fitted.

The style is unpretentious and extremely casual (definitely no jackets or ties) both day and night. There are two 24-passenger launches (one of which is a glass bottom boat), sunfish sailboat, and some snorkeling equipment.

There is one lounge/bar, located on a different deck to the dining room – a departure for this company from its former vessels. An electric chair-lift is provided at all stairways for those who do not walk well. Water sports facilities include a glass-bottom boat, and sunfish sailboat.

All gratuities are pooled and shared by the staff (although the suggested daily rate is very high for the product delivered). The onboard currency is the US dollar.

SUITABLE FOR: *Grande Mariner* is best suited to couples and single travelers who enjoy nature and wildlife up close and would not dream of cruising in the mainstream sense aboard ships with large numbers of people. This is for outdoors types who don't need entertainment, but do want an

BERLITZ'S RATINGS

	Possible	Achieved
Ship	500	159
Accommodation	200	67
Food	400	155
Service	400	181
Entertainment	n/a	n/a
Cruise	500	185

all-American cruise experience, albeit at a high price. It's not for children.

ACCOMMODATION. The cabins are all extremely small, relatively utilitarian units, with very little closet space (but just enough drawers) and very small bathrooms. There are 50 cabins, each with twin beds that convert to queen-sized beds (there is good storage space under the beds). There is no room service menu, and only soap is supplied (bring your own shampoo and other toiletries). Each cabin has its own air conditioner, so passengers do not have to share air with the rest of the ship (and other passengers). Refreshingly, there are no cabin keys.

CUISINE. The dining room seats all passengers in a single, open seating, so you dine with whomever you wish. The advantage of this is that you can make new friends and enjoy different conversation each day (it is also good for small groups). The dining tables convert to card tables for use between meals. Passengers are welcome to bring their own alcohol, as the company does not sell it aboard ship. Effervescent, young American waitresses provide the service, although there is no finesse. A hand-held Colonial bell is rung to summon passengers to the dining room.

ENTERTAINMENT. There is no formal entertainment, although dinner and after-dinner conversation with fellow passengers in the ship's lounge/bar really provides the entertainment each evening. So, if you don't want to talk to your fellow passengers, take a good book.

SPA/FITNESS. No spa facilities.

Grandeur of the Seas
★★★★

Size: . . . . .Large Resort Ship	Passenger Decks: 11	Cabins (with private balcony): 212
Tonnage: .74,137	Total Crew: .760	Cabins (wheelchair accessible): 14
Lifestyle: . . . . .Standard	Passengers	Wheelchair accessibility . . . . .Good
Cruise Line: Royal Caribbean International	(lower beds/all berths): 1,950/2,446	Cabin Current: . . . . .110 and 220 volts
Former Names: . . . . .none	Passenger Space Ratio	Elevators: 9
Builder: . . .Kvaerner Masa-Yards (Finland)	(lower beds/all berths): 38.0/30.3	Casino (gaming tables): . . . . .Yes
Original Cost: . . . .$300 million	Crew/Passenger Ratio	Slot Machines: . . . . .Yes
Entered Service: . . . . .Dec 1996	(lower beds/all berths): 2.5/3.2	Swimming Pools (outdoors): 1
Registry: . . . . .The Bahamas	Cabins (total): 975	Swimming Pools (indoors): 1
Length (ft/m): 916.0/279.6	Size Range (sq ft/m): 158.2–1,267.0/	(indoor/outdoor w/sliding glass roof)
Beam (ft/m): 105.6/32.2	14.7–117.7	Whirlpools: 6
Draft (ft/m): 25.5/7.6	Cabins (outside view): 576	Self-Service Launderette: . . . . .No
Propulsion/Propellers: . . . . .diesel-electric	Cabins (interior/no view): 399	Dedicated Cinema/Seats: . . . . .No
(50,400kW)/2	Cabins (for one person): 0	Library: . . . . .Yes

OVERALL SCORE: 1,407 OUT OF A POSSIBLE 2,000 POINTS

OVERVIEW. This is one of a pair of ships for this popular cruise line (sister to *Enchantment of the Seas*). The vessel has an attractive contemporary profile, with a single funnel located well aft – almost a throwback to some ship designs used in the 1950s – and has a nicely rounded stern, rather like the older *Monarch of the Seas*-class ships. A Viking Crown Lounge is set amidships. This, together with the forward mast, provides three distinct focal points in its exterior profile. There is a walk-around promenade deck outdoors, but there are no cushioned pads for the tacky home patio-style plastic sunloungers.

A large Viking Crown Lounge, a trademark of all Royal Caribbean International ships, sits between funnel and mast at the top of the atrium lobby, and overlooks the forward section of the swimming pool deck, with access provided from stairway off the central atrium.

The principal interior focal point is a seven-deck-high Centrum (atrium lobby), which provides a good meeting point (the Purser's Desk and Shore Excursion Desk are located on one of the lower levels). Many public entertainment rooms and facilities can be located off the atrium.

This ship has good interior passenger flow. There is a good, varied collection of artworks (including several sculptures), principally by British artists, with classical music, ballet and theater themes. The casino is large and glitzy, and has a fascinating, somewhat theatrical glass-covered, but under-floor exhibit. The children's and teens' facilities are good, much expanded from previous ships in the fleet.

A neat champagne terrace bar sits forward of the lower level of the two-deck-high dining room. There is a good use of tropical plants throughout the public rooms, which

BERLITZ'S RATINGS

	Possible	Achieved
Ship	500	411
Accommodation	200	152
Food	400	227
Service	400	260
Entertainment	100	77
Cruise	400	280

helps counteract the rather plain and clinical pastel wall colors, while huge murals of opera scenes adorn several stairways. There are good children's and teens' facilities – larger than those of previous ships in the fleet. The onboard currency is the US dollar.

ACCOMMODATION. There are 16 price grades (the price depending on grade, size and location, with location and grade perhaps more important, since so many of the cabins are of the same, or a very similar size).

There are five grades of suites: Royal Suite (1), Owner's Suite (5), Royal Family Suite (4), Grand Suite (12), and Superior Suite (44, including two superior suites for the disabled). All are well appointed and have pleasing decor (best described as Scandinavian Moderne), with good wood and color accenting (the largest has a baby grand piano).

Royal Suite. The largest accommodation can be found in the Royal Suite, located directly aft of the ship's navigation bridge on the starboard side. It has a separate bedroom with king-sized bed, walk-in closet and vanity dressing area, living room with queen-sized sofa bed, baby grand piano, refrigerator and wet bar, dining table, entertainment center, and large private balcony. The bathroom has a whirlpool tub, separate shower enclosure, two washbasins, and toilet.

Owner's Suite. The five owner's suites are at the forward end of the ship, just behind the navigation bridge (close to the Royal Suite). They have a queen-sized bed, separate living area with queen-sized sofa bed, vanity dressing area, refrigerator and wet bar. The bathroom has a full-size bathtub, separate shower enclosure, toilet and two washbasins.

Royal Family Suite. Features include two bedrooms with twin beds that convert to queen-sized beds, living area with

double sofa bed and Pullman bed, refrigerator, two bathrooms (one with bathtub), and private balcony. This suite can accommodate eight, and might be suitable for families.
Grand Suite. Twin beds convert to a queen-sized bed. Vanity dressing area, lounge area with sofa bed, refrigerator, and a bathroom with bathtub, plus a private balcony.
Superior Suite. Twin beds that convert to a queen-sized bed. Vanity dressing area, lounge area with sofa bed, refrigerator, plus private balcony, and a bathroom with bathtub. Although this is called a suite, it really is little more than a larger standard cabin with balcony.
Other Grades. All standard cabins have twin beds that convert to a queen-sized bed, ample closet space for a one-week cruise, and a good amount of drawer space, although under-bed storage space is not good for large suitcases. The bathrooms have nine mirrors. Plastic buckets are provided for champagne/wine and are really tacky.

All grades of suite/cabin include a hairdryer. The room service menu is minimal, with only the most basic selection.

CUISINE. The 1,195-seat (non-smoking) Great Gatsby Dining Room is a large dining hall that is spread over two decks, with both levels connected by a grand, sweeping staircase. Choose one of two seatings, or "My Time Dining" (eat when you want, during dining room hours) when you book.

The cavernous, 790-seat informal Windjammer Cafe is the ship's casual eatery. It has a great expanse of ocean-view glass windows, and is where breakfast and lunch buffets are available as an alternative to the dining room.

An intimate terrace Champagne Bar is located forward of the lower level of the two-deck-high dining room and just off the atrium for those who might like to taste something a little out of the ordinary, in a setting that is bright and contemporary.

ENTERTAINMENT. The Palladium Theater is the ship's principal showlounge. It is located at the forward part of the ship (accessed by the forward stairway/lift bank), and is used for big production shows. It has excellent sightlines from 98 percent of the 875 seats. Another showlounge, the 575-seat South Pacific Lounge, is used for smaller shows and cabaret acts, including late-night adult (blue) comedy.

SPA/FITNESS. The ShipShape Spa is located aft of the funnel and spans two decks. Facilities include a gymnasium with all the latest muscle-pumping exercise machines, aerobics exercise room, sauna and steam rooms, a beauty salon, and a clutch of treatment rooms.

For the sporting, there is activity galore – including a rock-climbing wall, with several separate climbing tracks. It is located outdoors at the aft end of the funnel.

● **For more extensive general information about the Royal Caribbean experience, see pages 151–6.**

DID YOU KNOW...

● that Silvio Berlusconi, Italy's former premier, was once a cruise ship entertainer? He sang, and accompanying him, on piano, was Fedele Confalonieri, his oldest buddy, now president of Berlusconi's Mediaset empire.

● that the cruise ship used in the 1974 movie *Juggernaut*, in which seven bombs in oil drums were placed aboard, was *Maxim Gorkiy*? The film starred Richard Harris, Omar Sharif, David Hemmings, and Anthony Hopkins.

● that musical instruments of some of the stars of rock and pop can be found aboard Holland America Line's *Zaandam*? They were acquired from the "Pop and Guitars" auction at Christie's in London, and a Fender Squire Telecaster guitar signed by the Rolling Stones; A Conn Saxophone signed on the mouthpiece by former US President Bill Clinton; an Ariana acoustic guitar signed by David Bowie and Iggy Pop; a Fender Stratocaster guitar signed in silver ink by the members of the rock band Queen; a Bently "Les Paul" style guitar signed by various artists, including Carlos Santana, Eric Clapton, BB King, Robert Cray, Keith Richards and Les Paul.

● that the Cunard White Star Line's *Queen Mary* was the first ship to have a system of colored lights that varied according to music (chromosonics)?

● that Verdi wrote an opera to commemorate the opening of the Suez Canal? Its name is *Aîda*.

● that the 212-passenger *Seabourn Legend* was the star of the film *Speed 2: Cruise Control*, released in 1997 in the US? The film was shot on location in Marigot, the capital of the French side of the tiny two-nation Caribbean island of St. Martin/St. Maarten. The filming called for the building of almost a complete "town" at Marigot, into which the ship crashes.

● that *Titanic*, the stage musical, cost $10 million to mount in New York in 1997? That's $2.5 million more than it cost to build the original ship that debuted in 1912. The play debuted at the Lunt-Fontanne Theater in April 1997 (the ship sank on April 14, 1912).

● that the Hollywood film that made headlines by having the largest budget to date – but also made the most money – was based aboard a passenger liner? The film, of course, was *Titanic*, released in 1997.

Hanseatic
★★★★★

Size:	Boutique Ship	Passenger Decks:	7	Cabins (for one person):	0
Tonnage:	8,378	Total Crew:	122	Cabins (with private balcony):	0
Lifestyle:	Luxury	Passengers		Cabins (wheelchair accessible):	2
Cruise Line:	Hapag-Lloyd Cruises	(lower beds/all berths):	184/194	Wheelchair accessibility	None
Former Names:	Society Adventurer	Passenger Space Ratio		Cabin Current:	220 volts
Builder:	Rauma Yards (Finland)	(lower beds/all berths):	45.5/43.1	Elevators:	2
Original Cost:	$68 million	Crew/Passenger Ratio		Swimming Pools (outdoors):	1
Entered Service:	Mar 1993	(lower beds/all berths):	1.5/1.5	Whirlpools:	1
Registry:	The Bahamas	Cabins (total):	92	Self-Service Launderette:	No
Length (ft/m):	402.9/122.80	Size Range (sq ft/m):	231.4–470.3/	Lecture/Film Room:	Yes (seats 160)
Beam (ft/m):	59.1/18.00		21.5–43.7	Library:	Yes
Draft (ft/m):	16.1/4.91	Cabins (outside view):	92	Zodiacs:	14
Propulsion/Propellers:	diesel (5,880kW)/2	Cabins (interior/no view):	0	Helicopter Pad:	Yes

OVERALL SCORE: 1,746 OUT OF A POSSIBLE 2,000 POINTS

OVERVIEW. *Hanseatic,* under long-term charter to Hapag-Lloyd Cruises, was designed to operate worldwide expedition-style cruises in contemporary, but quite luxurious, surroundings. It is extremely environmentally friendly, and is one of the very few ships that will allow you to tour the engine room. It has a fully enclosed bridge and an ice-hardened hull with the highest passenger vessel ice classification, plus the very latest in high-tech navigation equipment.

A fleet of 14 Zodiac inflatable craft, each named after a famous explorer, is used for in-depth shore landings. These craft provide the ship with tremendous flexibility in itineraries, with excellent possibilities for up-close wildlife viewing in natural habitats. Rubber boots, parkas, boot-washing and storage rooms are provided – particularly useful for Arctic and Antarctic cruises. For warmer climes, a Bike Box, with 10 bicycles for passenger use at no charge, is offloaded in each port the ship is alongside (where possible). There's a Marine Lab, for examination of items.

Inside, the ship is equipped with fine-quality luxury fittings and soft furnishings. There is a choice of several public rooms (most located aft, with accommodation forward). All are well-furnished and decorated, and all have high ceilings which help make the ship feel much larger than its actual size. The library/observation lounge provides a good selection of hardback books in both English and German, including many geographical, travel, wildlife and archaeology books; it has a sunken bar, and a warm, inviting atmosphere, as well as two internet-access computer stations. Bouillon is also served at 11am each morning. A large lecture hall, with excellent audio-visual facilities, on a lower deck, can accommodate almost all passengers.

BERLITZ'S RATINGS

	Possible	Achieved
Ship	500	436
Accommodation	200	172
Food	400	346
Service	400	343
Entertainment	n/a	n/a
Cruise	500	449

Hanseatic provides destination-intensive, nature and life-enrichment cruises and expeditions in elegant, but unstuffy surroundings, to some of the world's most fascinating destinations, at a suitably handsome price. The passenger count is generally kept to about 150, which means plenty of comfort, no lines, and lots of space. In passageways and suites/cabins, 400 large, framed, black and white photographs depict wildlife and expedition experiences.

The ship is at its best when operating in the Arctic and Antarctic, but infirm passengers should be wary of the difficult conditions for shore landings in these areas. Safety is paramount, particularly in the Antarctic, and here the ship excels with professionalism, pride and skilled seamanship. Most of each day is taken up with being ashore, and evenings consist mainly of dinner and daily recaps. Lectures, briefings, and the amount of information provided about the itinerary and ports of call are excellent, and, for some cruises, include useful pocket-sized color port booklets. Well-qualified lecturers and naturalists accompany each cruise, and a discreet crew and service staff providing unobtrusive service are hallmarks of this ship. A full passenger list and an expedition cruise logbook is typically provided at the end of each voyage for all passengers – a fine reminder of the cruise.

Hanseatic operates in two languages, English and German (though many staff speak several languages) and caters well to both sets of passengers. All port taxes, insurance, staff gratuities, and Zodiac trips are included. A relaxed ambience and informal dress code prevail. The onboard currency is the euro.

There are just a few negatives about this ship. It is

mainly marketed to German-speaking and English-speaking passengers, so other nationalities may find it hard to integrate. Marine quality telescopes, mounted outdoors, would be a useful addition.

SUITABLE FOR: *Hanseatic* is best suited to well-traveled couples and solo travelers who are adventurous and enjoy learning about nature and the natural sciences, geography, history, gardening, art, and architecture, and want to be aboard a small ship with almost no entertainment or mindless parlor games, but with really good food and high-quality service. This ship is ideal for those who would never wish to set foot aboard one of the big "floating resort" ships on highly programmed cruises, and for those who want to experience destinations that are probably out of the ordinary (such as Antarctica) in style and a high degree of comfort.

ACCOMMODATION. There are no bad cabins, and accommodation is priced in seven grades. The price will depend on the grade, size and location you choose. The all-outside cabins, located in the forward section of the ship, are large and very well equipped, and include a separate lounge area next to a large picture window (which has a pull-down blackout blind as well as curtains), superb, high-intensity, moveable bedside reading lights, and refrigerator.

All furniture is in warm woods such as beech, and everything has rounded edges. Wood trim accents the ceiling perimeter, and acts as a divider between bed and lounge areas. Each cabin has a mini-bar, flat-screen interactive TV with internet access (when available) and wireless keyboard, and a complete infotainment system, including movies and audio tracks on demand at no extra charge, separate bedside 3-channel radio, , two locking drawers, a retro alarm clock, and plenty of closet and drawer space, as well as two separate cupboards and hooks for all-weather outerwear. One useful feature of all cabins is a blue, night/safety light, nicely hidden in each bathroom. A privacy curtain between the cabin door and the sleeping area of the cabin would be useful (you can be seen from the hallway when the cabin door is opened). Internet access and W-LAN for laptop computers was added in a 2009 refit.

All cabin bathrooms (superbly remodelled in 2009) have a large shower enclosure with curved glass wall, toiletries cabinets, wall-mounted hairdryer, and bathrobe. There are only two types of cabins; 34 have double beds, others have twin beds. Towels (the bath-sized towels are large), bed linens and pillowcases are 100% cotton, and individual cotton-filled duvet covers are provided. Laundry, dry cleaning and pressing are available.

Suites and cabins on Bridge Deck have impeccable butler service and in-cabin dining privileges, plus personalized stationery and a larger flat-screen TV. Free soft drinks in the refrigerator are replenished daily, but all liquor costs extra. Bulgari and Crabtree and Evelyn amenities are provided, as are anti-sunburn lotion and hair mist.

CUISINE. The 186-seat, no smoking Marco Polo restaurant

is elegant, warm and welcoming, with large picture windows on two sides as well as aft. There is one seating for dinner, and open seating for breakfast and lunch, although many passengers like to be seated at their "regular" table. On embarkation day, waiters introduce themselves after the meal, so hungry passengers won't be delayed by small talk.

The cuisine and service are absolutely first-rate, but are slightly more informal than, for example, aboard the larger *Europa*, which is at or close to the same price level. Top-quality ingredients are always used, and most items are purchased fresh when available. In some ports, passengers can go "shopping with the chef" to source local, regional ingredients and fresh fish.

The meals are very creative and nicely presented, each being appealing to the eye as well as to the palate. There is always an outstanding selection of breads, cheeses, desserts and pastry items. In the Arctic or Antarctic, table set-ups are often minimal, due to possible movement of the ship – stabilizers can't be used in much of the Antarctic – so cutlery is provided and changed for each course. Three types of sugar are presented when coffee or tea are ordered – it should never be placed on the table during meal service.

An alternative dining spot is the Columbus Lounge, with 74 seats indoors, as well as copious seating at outdoor tables. An informal, open seating, self-serve (or waiter service) buffet-style eatery by day, it changes into a second dining room night, suitably called Ethno, with themed dinners and barbeques featuring region-specific food. Reservations are required – you make them in the morning of the day you want to dine there – but there is no extra charge and no tipping at any time.

Also, each cruise includes a full Viennese teatime, as well as a daily teatime with a selection of cakes, pastries and finger sandwiches befitting a Viennese coffee house.

ENTERTAINMENT. There is no showlounge as such, although there is a lecture room. Entertainment is certainly not a priority aboard this ship, but the itinerary and destinations are the main show. There is no formal entertainment (except on some summer cruises, when a small classical music ensemble may be aboard), nor does the ship normally carry a band. Lectures, by some of the foremost authorities and experts in various fields associated with expeditions and nature are a principal attraction of any cruise aboard this ship – unless under charter for special theme cruises during the summer – as are after-dinner recaps of the day. Occasionally, the ship's crew may put on a little amateur dramatics event, or a seamen's choral presentation.

SPA/FITNESS. The spa facilities include a decently-sized gymnasium (with up-to-date cardio-vascular and muscle-toning equipment, treadmills and exercycles), and sauna, all located forward on the Sun Deck in an area that also includes a solarium and hot tub. There's also a cosmetics/make-up room. Massage is available, at €46 for 60 minutes, and €38 for 45 minutes, in a rather clinical room within the medical facility, on a lower deck.

Hebridean Princess
★★★★ +

Size:	Boutique Ship	Passenger Decks:	.5
Tonnage:	2,112	Total Crew:	.37
Lifestyle:	Luxury	Passengers	
Cruise Line:	Hebridean Island Cruises	(lower beds/all berths):	49/49
Former Names:	*Columbia*	Passenger Space Ratio	
Builder:	Hall Russell (Scotland)	(lower beds/all berths):	43.1/43.1
Original Cost:	n/a	Crew/Passenger Ratio	
Entered Service:	1964/Apr 1989	(lower beds/all berths):	1.3/1.3
Registry:	Great Britain	Cabins (total):	.30
Length (ft/m):	235.0/71.6	Size Range (sq ft/m):	144.0–340.0/
Beam (ft/m):	46.0/14.0		13.4–31.6
Draft (ft/m):	10.0/3.0	Cabins (outside view):	.24
Propulsion/Propellers:	diesel	Cabins (interior/no view):	.6
	(1,790kW)/2	Cabins (for one person):	.11

Cabins (with private balcony):	.4
Cabins (wheelchair accessible):	.0
Wheelchair accessibility	None
Cabin Current:	240 volts
Elevators:	.0
Casino (gaming tables):	No
Slot Machines:	No
Swimming Pools (outdoors):	.0
Swimming Pools (indoors):	.0
Whirlpools:	.0
Self-Service Launderette:	No
Dedicated Cinema/Seats:	No
Library:	Yes

OVERALL SCORE: 1,680 OUT OF A POSSIBLE 2,000 POINTS

OVERVIEW. Small and old can actually be chic and comfortable. *Hebridean Princess*, originally one of three Scottish ferries built for for David MacBayne Ltd – although actually owned by the British government – was skillfully converted into a gem of a cruise ship in order to operate island-hopping itineraries in Scotland, together with the occasional jaunt to Norway and an occasional sailing around the UK coast. It was renamed in 1989 by the Duchess of York. There is an outdoors deck for occasional sunbathing and al fresco meals, as well as a bar (occasionally, formal cocktail parties are held here when the weather conditions are right). There is no walk-around promenade deck, although there is an open deck atop ship. The ship carries a Zodiac inflatable runabout, as well as a rowing boat (for passenger use) and two Hardy shore tenders (*Scarba* and *Shona*).

Use of the ship's small boats, speedboat, bicycles (about a dozen), and fishing gear are included in the price, as are entrance fees to gardens, castles, other attractions, and the occasional coach tour (depending on the itinerary). The destination-intensive cruises have very creative itineraries and there really is plenty to do, despite the lack of big-ship features. Specialist guides, who give daily talks about the destinations to be visited and some fascinating history and the local folklore, accompany all cruises.

The principal public room inside the ship is the charming Tiree Lounge, which has a real brick-walled inglenook fireplace, as well as a very cozy bar with a wide variety of whiskies – the selection of single malts is excellent – and cognacs for connoisseurs. Naturally, the ship specializes in Scottish spirits.

This charming little ship has a warm, totally cosseted,

BERLITZ'S RATINGS

	Possible	Achieved
Ship	500	410
Accommodation	200	174
Food	400	350
Service	400	342
Entertainment	n/a	n/a
Cruise	500	404

traditional Scottish country house ambience and stately home service that is unobtrusive but always at hand when you need it. Agatha Christie's Inspector Hercule Poirot would be very much at home here, particularly in the Tiree Lounge – although he may be wary of the secret and intrigue that "Glen Etive" (a figure that dates from 1911– you'll need to go aboard to find it) holds. Who needs megaships when you can take a retro-cruise aboard this little gem of a ship? Direct bookings are accepted.

What is so appreciated by passengers is the fact that the ship does not have photographers or some of the trappings found aboard larger ships. Passengers also love the fact that there is no bingo, art auctions, or mindless parlor games. The onboard currency is the British pound.

Hebridean Princess has UK officers and an excellent Latvian service crew; all are discreet and provide unobtrusive service. This little ship remains one of the world's best-kept travel secrets (indeed, Queen Elizabeth II chartered the ship for a family-only celebration of her 80th birthday in 2006).

A roughly polished gem, it is especially popular with single passengers. More than half the passengers are repeaters. Children under nine are not accepted. Despite the shortcomings of the ship itself, it's the food that rates highly.

If you cruise from Oban, you can be met at Glasgow station (or airport) and taken to/from the ship by private motor coach. Passengers are "piped aboard" at embarkation by a Scottish bagpiper – a neat touch. All drinks (except premium brands, which incur a small extra charge), soft drinks and bottled (Scottish) mineral water are included in the fare, as are gratuities – the company requests that no additional gratuities be given.

Although this vessel is strong, it does have structural limitations and noisy engines that cause some vibration. However, the engines do not run at night because the ship anchors before bedtime, providing soul-renewing tranquility – except for the sound of a single generator. The ship does not have an elevator, so anyone with walking disabilities may find it challenging – and there may be several tender ports on each itinerary. It is often cold and very wet in the Scottish highlands and islands (flexible weather), so take plenty of warm clothing for layering.

SUITABLE FOR: *Hebridean Princess* is best suited to adult couples and single travelers of mature years who enjoy learning about nature and the natural sciences, geography, history, gardening, art, architecture, and want to be aboard a very small ship with almost no entertainment. This is ideal for those who would abhor big ship cruising.

ACCOMMODATION. The price will depend on the grade, size and location you choose. All cabins have different color schemes and names – there are no numbers, and, refreshingly, no door keys, although cabins can be locked from the inside. All are individually designed (no two cabins are identical) and created, with delightfully eclectic curtains, sweeping drapes over the beds, and lots of cushions. They really are quite delightful and quite different to almost all other cruise ships, and come in a wide range of configurations (some with single, some with double, some with twin beds), including four that have a private balcony (a delightfully private and self-indulgent bonus).

All except two cabins have a private bathroom with bath or shower (two cabins share a bathroom); all have a refrigerator, ironing board with iron, trouser press, brass clock, and tea/coffee making set. All towels and bathrobe are 100% cotton, as is the bed linen. Molton Brown personal toiletry items are provided.

All cabins come with Victorian-style bathroom fittings (many are gold-plated), and some have brass cabin portholes or windows that actually open. Three of the newest cabins added are outfitted in real Scottish Baronial style. Some cabins in the front of the ship are subject to the noise of the anchor being weighed each morning.

CUISINE. The Columba Restaurant is a non-smoking dining room with ocean-view windows, and tables that are laid with crisp white linen, and sometimes with lace overlays (note that, while days are casual, dinner means jackets and ties, and formal attire typically twice per cruise). Classic white Schonwald china is provided. There is a single seating, at assigned tables. Some chairs have armrests while some do not.

The cuisine is extremely creative, and at times outstanding – and about the same quality and presentation as *SeaDream I* and *SeaDream II*, although, typically, menus offer just one meat and one fish dish (a different fish each day), plus an alternative, casual option. Fresh, taste-filled ingredients are sourced and purchased locally, supporting Scottish suppliers such as H. D. Ferguson Butchers of Lochgilphead, Argyll – a welcome change from the mass catering of most ships. Although there are no flambeau items (the galley has electric, not gas, ranges), what is created is beautifully presented and of the highest standard. The desserts are also worth saving space for.

The breakfast menu is standard each day, although you can always ask for any favorites, and each day a speciality item is featured. Try the "porridge and a wee dram (Scotch whisky – single malt, of course)" – it's lovely on a cold morning, and it sets you up for the whole day.

Not to be missed is the exclusive theatrical treat "a tasting o' haggis wi' bashed neeps an champit tatties," accompanied by bagpipe music and an "address to the haggis" ceremony, traditionally given by the captain. Although there is waiter service for most things, there is also a good buffet table display during breakfast and luncheon. Wines are provided at lunch and dinner, although an additional connoisseur's list is available for those seeking fine vintage wines. Highly personal and attentive service from an attentive Latvian service staff completes the picture.

ENTERTAINMENT. The Tiree Lounge is the equivalent of a main lounge aboard this very small ship. Dinner is *the* entertainment of the evening. Occasionally, there might be after-dinner drinks, poetry readings, and an occasional storyteller, but little else (passengers neither expect nor need it).

SPA/FITNESS. There is no spa, as the ship is too small. The only concessions to fitness are an exercycle, treadmill, power stepper and slide (row) machine.

DID YOU KNOW...

Should staff name badges be on the left or right side of the body?

In the hospitality industry, name badges are worn on the *left* side of the body. There are two principal reasons for this:
● Typically 81 percent of humans are right-handed, and the human eye naturally goes towards the right (that is, the left side of the body of the person facing you).
● The right side of the body is considered reserved for the military, whose name badges are always worn on the right side of the body (medals being worn on the left, or most important, side).

You may also notice that when cameras pan in a documentary film made by painstaking professionals (such as in nature films), it is normal procedure to pan from right to left.

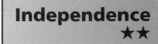

Independence
★★

Size:	.Boutique Ship	Total Crew:	27	Cabins (wheelchair accessible):	1
Tonnage:	.99	Passengers		Wheelchair accessibility	.None
Lifestyle:	.Standard	(lower beds/all berths):	.94/100	Cabin Current:	.110 volts
Cruise Line:	.American Cruise Lines	Passenger Space Ratio		Elevators:	1
Former Names:	.none	(lower beds/all berths):	.1.0/0.9	Casino (gaming tables):	.No
Builder:	.Chesapeake Shipbuilding (USA)	Crew/Passenger Ratio		Slot Machines:	.No
Original Cost:	.n/a	(lower beds/all berths):	.3.4/3.4	Swimming Pools (outdoors):	0
Entered Service:	.June 2010	Cabins (total):	.52	Swimming Pools (indoors):	0
Registry:	.USA	Size Range (sq ft/m):	.204.0–240.0/	Whirlpools:	0
Length (ft/m):	.223.0/67.9		18.9–22.2	Self-Service Launderette:	.No
Beam (ft/m):	.51.0/15.5	Cabins (outside view):	.51	Dedicated Cinema/Seats:	.No
Draft (ft/m):	.8.2/2.5	Cabins (interior/no view):	0	Library:	.Yes
Propulsion/Propellers:	.diesel/2	Cabins (for one person):	.5		
Passenger Decks:	.4	Cabins (with private balcony):	.23		

BERLITZ'S OVERALL SCORE: 962 OUT OF A POSSIBLE 2,000 POINTS

OVERVIEW. *Independence* is the fifth vessel in this cruise line's growing fleet (sister ships: *American Eagle, American Glory, American Spirit, American Star*). The company builds the ships in its own shipyard in Chesapeake, Maryland. *Independence* is built specifically for coastal and inland cruising, in a casual, unregimented setting, to destinations unreachable by large cruise ships.

The uppermost deck is open – good for views – behind a forward windbreaker; many plenty of sunloungers are provided, as is a small golf putting green.

The public rooms include an observation lounge, with views forward and to port and starboard side (complimentary cocktails and hors d'oeuvres are offered before dinner); a library/lounge; a small midships lounge, and an elevator that goes to all decks, including the outdoor sun deck.

Cruises are typically of 7–14 days' duration. The ship docks in the center, or within walking distance of most towns and ports. The dress code is "no ties casual." It is extremely expensive for what you get, compared to ships in the wider cruise industry – although this is a new ship and the cabins *are* larger and marginally better equipped than those of the slightly smaller sister ships. There are no additional costs, except for gratuities and port charges, because it's all included (quite different to big-ship cruising).

SUITABLE FOR: Couples and single travelers of mature years sharing a cabin and wishing to cruise in an all-American environment aboard a small ship where the destinations are more important than food, service or entertainment.

BERLITZ'S RATINGS

	Possible	Achieved
Ship	500	292
Accommodation	200	127
Food	400	210
Service	400	180
Entertainment	n/a	
Cruise	500	153

ACCOMMODATION. There are five cabin price grades (four are doubles, one is for singles). All cabins have twin beds (convertible to a king-size bed), a small desk with chair, flat-screen television, DVD player and internet access, and clothes hanging space. All cabins have internet access, a private (modular) bathroom with separate shower enclosure, washbasin and toilet (no cabin has a bathtub), windows that open, and satellite-feed TV sets.

Accommodations incorrectly designated as suites (23) also have a private balcony; although narrow, it does have two chairs and a small drinks table.

CUISINE. The dining salon, in the latter third of the vessel, has large, panoramic picture windows on three sides. Everyone eats in a single, open seating, at large tables, so you can get to know your fellow passengers; there are no assigned tables or places. The cuisine is Americana: simple, honest food highlighting regional specialties. The choice of entrées, appetizers, and soups is limited, however. There is no wine list, although basic white and red American table wines are included. On the last morning of each cruise, continental breakfast only is available.

ENTERTAINMENT. Dinner and after-dinner conversation with fellow passengers in the ship's lounge/bar *is* the entertainment each evening. Otherwise, take a good book.

SPA/FITNESS. There is a tiny fitness room with a few bicycles and other exercise machines.

Independence of the Seas
★★★★

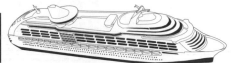

Size:	Large Resort Ship	Passenger Decks:	15	Cabins (with private balcony):	842
Tonnage:	154,407	Total Crew:	1,397	Cabins (wheelchair accessible):	32
Lifestyle:	Standard	Passengers		Wheelchair accessibility	Good
Cruise Line:	Royal Caribbean International	(lower beds/all berths):	3,634/4,376	Cabin Current:	110 volts
Former Names:	none	Passenger Space Ratio		Elevators:	14
Builder:	Kvaerner Masa-Yards (Finland)	(lower beds/all berths):	42.0/35.2	Casino (gaming tables):	Yes
Original Cost:	$590 million	Crew/Passenger Ratio		Slot Machines:	Yes
Entered Service:	May 2008	(lower beds/all berths):	2.6/3.1	Swimming Pools (outdoors):	2
Registry:	The Bahamas	Cabins (total):	1,817	Swimming Pools (indoors):	0
Length (ft/m):	1,112.2/339.0	Size Range (sq ft/m):	149.0–2,025.0/	Whirlpools:	6
Beam (ft/m):	184.0/56.0		13.8–188.1	Self-Service Launderette:	No
Draft (ft/m):	27.8/8.5	Cabins (outside view):	1,084	Dedicated Cinema/Seats:	No
Propulsion/Propellers:	diesel-electric	Cabins (interior/no view):	733	Library:	Yes
	(kW)/4 pods	Cabins (for one person):	0		

OVERALL SCORE: 1,510 OUT OF A POSSIBLE 2,000 POINTS

OVERVIEW. *Independence of the Seas* (together with sister ships *Freedom of the Seas* and *Liberty of the Seas*) is one of the largest-ever purpose-built cruise ship, although superseded in 2009 by RCI's first *Genesis*-class ship, *Oasis of the Seas*. It is an extension of the very successful *Voyager*-class of ships, which RCI introduced in 1999 with *Voyager of the Seas*.

The ship's length and beam were extended. This enabled an increase in the number of cabins and passenger capacity, as well as a combined pool area 43 percent larger than the *Voyager*-class (but with 500 more passengers). The extra length has enabled more innovative design elements to be incorporated, such as two 16-person hot tubs cantilevered 12 feet (3.7 meters) over the sides of the ship in an adults-only Solarium. The ship's pod propulsion virtually eliminates vibration *(for further details, see page 45).*

This *Freedom*-class ship is essentially split into three separate areas, rather like the Disney cruise ships: adults-only, family, or main.

The "wow" factor aboard the ship is its connection with water (of the seas) in the design of a dramatic water theme park afloat. By day, the H2O Zone (aft of the funnel) has an interactive water-themed play area for families that includes water cannons and spray fountains, water jets and ground gushers; by night the "water park" turns into a colourfully-lit sculpture garden. The ship's central pool has become a sports pool, with grandstand seating and competitive games that include pole jousting. Other active sports facilities include an Everlast boxing ring, rock-climbing wall (10 ft/3 meters taller than in the Voyager-class ships), in-line skating area, an ice-skating rink, and golf simulators.

BERLITZ'S RATINGS

	Possible	Achieved
Ship	500	426
Accommodation	200	161
Food	400	235
Service	400	289
Entertainment	100	82
Cruise	400	317

This ship has the same layout and facilities as *Freedom of the Seas* and *Liberty of the Seas*. It is now based year-round in the UK for cruises from Southampton, although the onboard currency remains the US dollar.

ACCOMMODATION. There is a wide range of suites and cabins in 14 categories and 21 price grades; the price you pay depends on the grade, from the 14-person Presidential Suite to twin-bed two person interior (no view) cabins, and interior cabins that look into an inside shopping/strolling atrium promenade. There are many family-friendly cabins, good for family reunions. For a detailed description of the accommodation, see *Freedom of the Seas (page 387).*

CUISINE. The main dining room is large and is set on three levels (each has a theme and different name: Galileo, Isaac, and Leonardo). A dramatic staircase connects all three levels, and huge, fat support pillars obstruct the sightlines from many seats. All three have the same menus and food.

Choose one of two seatings, or "My Time Dining" (eat when you want, during dining room hours) when you book (tables are for four, six, eight 10 or 12). All dining venues are non-smoking.

Alternative Dining Options: Alternative dining options for casual and informal meals at all hours (according to company statements) include:

● *Promenade Café*: for continental breakfast, all-day pizzas (Sorrento's), sandwiches and coffee in paper cups.

● *Windjammer Café*: for casual buffet-style breakfast, lunch and light dinner (except for the cruise's last night).

● *Island Grill* (a section of the Windjammer Café): for

casual dinner (no reservations necessary) featuring a grill and open kitchen.

● *Portofino:* this is the ship's "upscale" (non-smoking) Euro-Italian restaurant, open for dinner only. Reservations are required, and a there's a cover charge of $20 per person). Choices include: antipasti, soup, salad, pasta, main dish, dessert, cheese and coffee (the menu does not change during the cruise).

● *Chops Grill:* an intimate restaurant for steaks and seafood. A cover charge of $25 per person applies.

● *Johnny Rockets,* a retro 1950s all-day, all-night diner-style eatery that features hamburgers, hot dogs and other fast-food items, malt shakes, and jukebox hits, with both indoor and outdoor seating (all indoor tables have a mini-jukebox; dimes are provided for you to make your selection of vintage records), and all-singing, all-dancing waitresses that'll knock your socks off, if you can stand the volume. There is a cover charge.

● *Sprinkles:* for round-the-clock ice cream and yoghurt, pastries and coffee.

ENTERTAINMENT. The Showlounge is a stunning space, located at the forward end of the ship and spanning the height of five decks (with only a few slim pillars and almost no disruption of sightlines). The room has a hydraulic orchestra pit and huge stage area, together with sonic-boom loud sound, and superb lighting equipment.

In addition, the ship has an array of cabaret acts. The strongest are featured in the main showlounge, while others are presented in the Nightclub, the venue for late-night adults-only smutty comedy. The most entertaining shows, however, are the Spectaculars on ice. There is also a television studio (in case you thought you'd need one aboard a cruise ship), located adjacent to rooms that could be used, for example, for trade show exhibit space – good for conventions at sea.

SPA/FITNESS. The Independence Day Spa is large. It includes a large aerobics room, ShipShape fitness center (with the usual stairmasters, treadmills, stationary bikes, weight machines and free weights), treatment rooms, and men's and women's sauna/steam rooms and relaxation areas.

Sample prices: AromaStone Therapy massage, $195 (75 mins); Swedish Massage, $119 (50 mins); Couples massage, $269 (50 mins); facial, $119 (50 mins), plus tip. The spa facility is operated by Steiner, whose staff will try to hard-sell you Elemis products. Some (basic) exercise classes are free, but the good ones (examples: yoga, personal training) cost extra.

More active passengers can bodyboard, go boxing (in the full-size boxing ring in the middle of the spa; the cost is $83 for a personal session, or $10 as part of a Power-boxing class), climb (the rock-climbing wall at the back of the funnel housing), jog, putt, swim, skate, step, surf, workout and more (including play basketball and volleyball) in the sports area of the ship, located mostly aft of the funnel.

● **For more extensive general information on what a Royal Caribbean cruise is like, see pages 151–6.**

DID YOU KNOW...

● that the first regular steamship service across the North Atlantic was inaugurated on March 28, 1838, when the 703-ton steamer *Sirius* left London for New York via Cork, Ireland?

● that the winter of 1970–71 was the first time since 1838 that there was no regular passenger service on the North Atlantic?

● that the first scheduled transatlantic advertisement appeared in the *New York Evening Post* on October 27, 1817, for the 424-ton sailing packet *James Monroe* to sail from New York to Liverpool on January 5, 1818, and for *Couvier*

to sail from Liverpool to New York on January 1?

● that Cunard Line held the record from 1940 to 1996 for the largest passenger ship ever built (RMS *Queen Elizabeth*)?

● that the Dollar Steamship Line featured a round-the-world cruise that started October 15, 1910, from New York, aboard the ss *Cleveland?* The cruise was advertised as "one-class, no overcrowding" voyage. The cost was "$650 and up," according to an advertisement.

● that a round-the-world cruise was made in 1922–23 by Cunard's *Laconia* (19,680 grt), a three-class ship that sailed from New York? The itinerary included many ports of call that are still popular with world cruise passengers today. The vessel accommodated 350 persons in each of its first two classes, and 1,500 in third class, giving a total capacity of 2,200 passengers, more than many current ships.

● about the lady who went to her travel agent, who asked if she had enjoyed her cruise around the world? The lady replied, "Yes, but next year I want to go somewhere different."

Insignia
★★★★ +

Size: ....Mid-Size Ship	Total Crew: 386	Wheelchair accessibility ....Good
Tonnage: 30,277	Passengers	Cabin Voltage: ....110 and 220
Lifestyle: ....Premium	(lower beds/all berths): 684/824	Elevators: 4
Cruise Line: ....Oceania Cruises	Passenger Space Ratio	Casino (gaming tables): ....Yes
Former Names: ....*R One*	(lower beds/all berths): 44.2/36.7	Slot Machines: ....Yes
Builder: ....Chantiers de l'Atlantique	Crew/Passenger Ratio	Swimming Pools (outdoors): 1
Original Cost: ....$150 million	(lower beds/all berths): 1.7/2.1	Swimming Pools (indoors): 0
Entered Service: .....July 1998/Apr 2004	Cabins (total): 342	Whirlpools: ......2 (+ 1 thalassotherapy)
Registry: ....Marshall Islands	Size Range (sq ft/m): 145.3–968.7/	Fitness Centre: ....Yes
Length (ft/m): 593.7/181.0	13.5–90.0	Sauna/Steam Room: ....No/Yes
Beam (ft/m): 83.5/25.5	Cabins (outside view): 317	Massage: ....Yes
Draft (ft/m): 19.5/6.0	Cabins (interior/no view): 25	Self-Service Launderette: ....Yes
Propulsion/Propellers: ....diesel	Cabins (for one person): 0	Dedicated Cinema/Seats: ....No
(18,600 kW)/2	Cabins (with private balcony): 232	Library: ....Yes
Passenger Decks: 9	Cabins (wheelchair accessible): 3	

OVERALL SCORE: 1,574 OUT OF A POSSIBLE 2,000 POINTS

OVERVIEW. *Insignia* (sister ships: *Nautica* and *Regatta*) was one of a series of almost identical ships originally built for the now-defunct Renaissance Cruises. The exterior design balances the ship's high sides by painting the whole ship white (it previously had a dark blue hull), with a large, square white funnel. The addition of teak overlaid decking and teak lounge chairs has greatly improved what was a bland pool deck outdoors – but the front rows of double sunloungers are called cabanas, and it costs $100 a day to use them.

The interior decor is quite stunning, a throwback to ship decor of the ocean liners of the 1920s and '30s, with dark woods and warm colors, all carried out in fine taste (but a bit faux in places). This includes detailed ceiling cornices, both real and faux wrought-iron staircase railings, leather-paneled walls, trompe l'oeil ceilings, rich carpeting in hallways with an Oriental rug-look center section, and many other interesting (and expensive-looking) decorative touches. It feels like an old-world country club.

The public rooms are spread over three decks. The reception hall (lobby) has a staircase with intricate wrought-iron railings. A large observation lounge, the Horizon Bar, is located high atop ship. This has a long bar with forward views – for the barmen, that is.

There are plenty of bars – including one in each of the restaurant entrances. Perhaps the nicest is the casino bar/lounge, a beautiful room which is reminiscent of London's grand hotels and includes a martini bar. It has an inviting marble fireplace, comfortable sofas and individual chairs.

The Library is a grand Regency-style room, with a fireplace, a high, indented, trompe l'oeil ceiling, and an excel-

BERLITZ'S RATINGS		
	Possible	Achieved
Ship	500	417
Accommodation	200	160
Food	400	312
Service	400	295
Entertainment	100	77
Cruise	400	313

lent selection of books, plus very comfortable wingback chairs with footstools, and sofas you could sleep on. Oceania@Sea is the ship's internet connect center.

There may not be marble bathroom fittings, or caviar and other expensive niceties, but the value for money is good. The dress code is "smart casual." The onboard currency is the US dollar. Gratuities are added at $10.50 per person, per day (accommodation designated as suites have an extra $3 per person charge for the butler). A 15% gratuity is added to bar and spa accounts.

There is no wrap-around promenade deck outdoors (there is, however, a small jogging track around the perimeter of the swimming pool, and port and starboard side decks). Stairways, though carpeted, are tinny.

Oceania Cruises is a young company with a refreshing vision and desire to provide an extremely high level of food and service in an informal setting that is at once elegant yet comfortable, and that is exactly what it has achieved in a short space of time. Passenger niggles include all the "inventive" extra charges that can be incurred.

SUITABLE FOR: *Insignia* is best suited to couples who like good food and style, but want informality with no formal nights on board, and interesting itineraries, all at a very reasonable price well below what the luxury ships charge.

ACCOMMODATION. There are six cabin categories, and 10 price grades: 3 suite price grades; 5 outside-view cabin grades; 2 interior (no view) cabin grades. All of the standard interior (no view) and outside-view cabins (the lowest four grades) are extremely compact units, and extremely tight for two persons, particularly for cruises longer than five days. They have twin beds (or queen-sized bed), with good under-bed storage areas, personal safe, vanity desk with large mirror, good closet and drawer space (in rich, dark woods), 100% cotton bathrobe and towels, slippers, clothes brush and shoe horn. Color TVs carry a major news channel (where obtainable), plus a sports channel and round-the-clock movie channels.

About 100 cabins qualify as "Concierge Level" accommodation, and occupants get extra goodies such as enhanced bathroom amenities, complimentary shoeshine, tote bag, cashmere throw blanket, bottle of champagne on arrival, hand-held hairdryer, priority restaurant reservations, priority embarkation and dedicated check-in desk, **Owner's Suites**. The six Owner's Suites, measuring 962 sq.ft/89.3 sq.meters, provide the most spacious accommodation. They are fine, large living spaces located aft overlooking the stern on Decks 6, 7, and 8 (they are, however, subject to more movement and some vibration). They have extensive teak-floor private balconies that really are private and cannot be overlooked from the decks above. Each has an entrance foyer, living room, separate bedroom (the bed faces the sea, which can be seen through the floor-to-ceiling windows and sliding glass door), CD player (with selection of audio discs), fully tiled bathroom with Jacuzzi bathtub, and a small guest bathroom.

Vista Suites. There are four, each around 785.7 sq.ft/73 sq.meters, and located forward on Decks 5 and 6. They have extensive teak-floor private balconies that cannot be overlooked from the decks above. Each has an entrance foyer, living room, separate bedroom (the bed faces the sea, which can be seen through the floor-to-ceiling windows and sliding glass door), CD player (with selection of audio discs), and fully tiled bathroom with Jacuzzi bathtub.

Penthouse Suites. There are 52 of these (actually, they are not suites at all, but large cabins as the bedrooms aren't separate from the living areas). They do, however, measure around 322.9 sq.ft (30 sq. meters), and have a good-sized teak-floor balcony with sliding glass door (but with partial, and not full, balcony partitions) and teak deck furniture. The lounge area has a proper dining table and there is ample clothes storage space. The bathroom has a tub, shower enclosure, washbasin and toilet.

Cabins with Balcony. Cabins with private balconies (around 216 sq.ft/20 sq. meters), comprise about 66% of all cabins. They have partial, not full, balcony partitions and sliding glass doors, and 14 cabins on Deck 6 have lifeboat-obstructed views and no balcony. The living area has a refrigerated mini-bar, lounge area with breakfast table, and a balcony with teak floor, two teak chairs and a drinks table. The bathrooms, with tiled floors and plain walls, are compact, standard units, and include a shower stall with a strong, removable hand-held shower unit, hairdryer, toiletries storage shelves and retractable clothesline.

Outside View and Interior (No View) Cabins. These measure around 160–165 sq.ft (14.8–15.3 sq.meters), and have twin beds (convertible to a queen-sized bed), vanity desk, small sofa and coffee table, and bathroom with a shower enclosure with a strong, removable hand-held shower unit, hairdryer, toiletries storage shelves, retractable clothesline, washbasin, and toilet. Although they are not large, they are quite comfortable, with decent storage space.

All suites/cabins located at the stern may suffer from vibration and noise, particularly when the ship is proceeding at or close to full speed, or maneuvering in port.

CUISINE. Flexibility and choice are what the dining facilities aboard the Oceania ships are all about. There are four different restaurants:

● The **Grand Dining Room** has around 340 seats, and a raised central section, but the problem is the noise level: it's atrocious when the dining room is full – the effect of the low ceiling height. Being located at the ship's stern, there are large ocean-view windows on three sides (prime tables overlook the stern). The chairs are comfortable and have armrests. The menus change daily for lunch and dinner.

● The **Toscana Italian Restaurant** has 96 seats, windows along two sides, and a set menu (plus daily chef's specials).

● The cozy **Polo Grill** has 98 seats, windows along two sides and a set menu including prime steaks and seafood.

● The **Terrace Cafe** has seats for 154 indoors – not enough during cruises to cold-weather areas – and 186 outdoors. It is open for breakfast, lunch and casual dinners, when it has tapas (Tapas on the Terrace) and other Mediterranean food. As the ship's self-serve buffet restaurant, it incorporates a small pizzeria and grill. There are basic salads, a meat carving station, and a reasonable selection of cheeses.

All restaurants have open-seating dining, so you can dine when you want, with whom you wish. Reservations are needed in Toscana Restaurant and Polo Grill (but there's no extra charge), where there are mostly tables for four or six; there are few tables for two. There is a Poolside Grill Bar. All cappuccino and espresso coffees cost extra.

The food and service staff is provided by Apollo, a respected maritime catering company that has an interest in Oceania Cruises. The consultant chef is Jacques Pepin, well-known as a TV chef in America. Oceania Cruises' brochure reference to "cuisine so extraordinary it's unrivalled at sea" is hogwash – it's good, but not that good.

ENTERTAINMENT. The Regatta Lounge has entertainment, lectures and some social events. There is little entertainment due to the intensive nature of the itineraries. However, there is live music in several bars and lounges.

SPA/FITNESS/RECREATION. A lido deck has a swimming pool, and good sunbathing space, plus a thalassotherapy tub. A jogging track circles the swimming pool deck (but one deck above). The uppermost outdoors deck includes a golf driving net and shuffleboard court. The Oceania Spa consists of a beauty salon, three treatment rooms, men's and women's changing rooms, and steam room (there is no sauna). Canyon Ranch SpaClub operates the spa and beauty salon, and provides the staff. Note that 15% is added to your spa account, whether you like it or not.

Island Escape
★★★

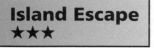

Size:	Mid-Size Ship	Passenger Decks:	10	Cabins (wheelchair accessible): 3
Tonnage	40,132	Total Crew:	540	Wheelchair accessibility .... None
Lifestyle:	Standard	Passengers		Cabin Current: 110 volts
Cruise Line:	Island/Thomson Cruises	(lower beds/all berths):	1,504/1,710	Elevators: 5
Former Names:	Viking Serenade,	Passenger Space Ratio		Casino (gaming tables): Yes
	Stardancer, Scandinavia	(lower beds/all berths):	26.6/23.4	Slot Machines: Yes
Builder:	Dubigeon-Normandie (France)	Crew/Passenger Ratio		Swimming Pools (outdoors): 1
Original Cost:	$100 million	(lower beds/all berths):	2.7/3.1	(magrodome)
Entered Service:	Oct 1982/Apr 2009	Cabins (total):	757	Swimming Pools (indoors): 0
Registry:	Bahamas	Size Range (sq ft/m):	143.1–398.2/	Whirlpools: 0
Length (ft/m):	623.0/189.89		13.3–37.0	Self-Service Launderette: No
Beam (ft/m):	88.6/27.01	Cabins (outside view):	462	Dedicated Cinema/Seats: No
Draft (ft/m):	23.6/7.20	Cabins (interior/no view):	295	Library: Yes
Propulsion/Propellers:	diesel	Cabins (for one person):	0	
	(19,800 kW)/2	Cabins (with private balcony):	5	

OVERALL SCORE: 1,109 OUT OF A POSSIBLE 2,000 POINTS

OVERVIEW. This ship, built for the long-defunct Scandinavian World Cruises to operate a cruise-ferry service between New York and Freeport, Bahamas, has been extensively reconstructed to operate as a full-fledged cruise ship. It has only a token bow, a fairly decent amount of open deck and sunbathing space, and a pool (more a "dip" pool) with a sliding glass dome that can be used in case of inclement weather.

The ship suffers from having an extremely boxy, angular shape with a short, stubby funnel, and has a "sponson" skirt that goes around the stern at the waterline – this is required for stability reasons. *Island Escape* underwent a $75 million reconstruction in 1991, when Royal Caribbean International (then Royal Caribbean Cruise Line) took over the ship. In 2001 it transferred to Island Cruises, a joint venture between the UK's First Choice Holidays and Royal Caribbean Cruises, and began cruising in 2002 under its current name. Today, Island Cruises is owned and operated by Thomson Cruises, part of the TUI group, and this is the company's most laid-back ship.

Inside, the accommodation is mostly located forward, while the public rooms are mostly in the aft third of the ship. There is a decent amount of public rooms and facilities, including six bars and a lounge/discotheque is cantilevered around the funnel with good ocean views. The decor employs tasteful colors and furnishings of decent quality, but some have seen better days. Other facilities include a cyber center for internet connection and email, and a coffee/pastry shop with three internet computer stations. The ceilings in many public areas and accommodation hallways are quite low – a legacy of the ship's original role as a cruise-ferry.

BERLITZ'S RATINGS

	Possible	Achieved
Ship	500	276
Accommodation	200	108
Food	400	203
Service	400	236
Entertainment	100	56
Cruise	400	230

The ship, now almost 30 years old, has a dual existence: in summer it operates specifically for the British family market, providing one-week cruises. In other words, this is cruising in utterly casual, comfortable, unpretentious surroundings that are quite upbeat, with a totally relaxed ambience that appeals to the young at heart. Children should enjoy themselves with "Palmy" a character they can even eat with, and there are lots of well-supervised activities.

Vacations can be extended with a "cruise-and-stay" package, with special pricing to make an extended break more affordable. If you book two cruises back-to-back, some entertainment may be repeated for the second week.

Background music is played almost everywhere inside the ship and on deck around the pool, making it difficult to find quiet spots to relax, chill out and simply read a book. Passenger participation events tend to be quite amateurish – although it depends on what you compare them to.

Standing in line for embarkation, disembarkation, shore tenders and for self-serve buffet meals can be an inevitable aspect of cruising aboard all ships carrying more than 1,000 passengers. The onboard currency is the British pound, and basic gratuities are included.

SUITABLE FOR: *Island Escape* is best suited to young and young-minded couples and singles of all ages, families with children and teenagers, who want a first cruise in a laid-back setting with plenty of life and entertainment for everyone, with food that is quantity rather than quality, and a low price.

ACCOMMODATION. There are just six categories, so choosing the right one for you shouldn't be difficult. The price will depend on grade, size and location. The cabins, however, are quite small, with little closet space, so take as few clothes as possible. They are moderately appointed with soft furnishings that are very cheerful, with upbeat colors. Almost all cabins have twin beds that can be pushed together to form a queen-sized bed; some cabins have an L-shaped arrangement, with immovable beds. All grades of accommodation have a TV set, telephone, and three-channel radio, dressing table and mirror. There are many interior (no view) cabins, and drawers and other storage space is extremely limited. If you'd like more space, it's best to go for one of the suite categories. Room service is available 24 hours a day, at extra cost.

The cabin bathrooms are really small, so you can expect to dance with the shower curtain, particularly if you are bigger than average – only some of the accommodation designated as suites have a bathtub. Eleven outside-view cabins have even numbers, and all interior (no view) cabins have odd numbers. Also, if you are cruising with young children, there's almost no space for baby strollers. If, after looking at the deck plans, you want to book a specific cabin number, it currently costs £35 per cabin extra. Some cabins have extra Pullman upper berths – good for families with young children. An in-cabin room service menu is available, but all items cost extra.

Island Suite: The "Island Suite," towards the aft on the port side, provides the largest accommodation. Although it doesn't have a balcony, it's relatively spacious. A tub and shower are provided in the bathroom, and there's a walk-in closet, and mini-bar/refrigerator.

Club Suites: Five other cabins (with balconies) at the stern are designated as suites. These have great views over the wash created by the ship's propellers, although they may be subject to a little vibration now and then. A tub and shower are provided in the marble-clad bathroom, and there's a walk-in closet in the sleeping area, and mini-bar/refrigerator and entertainment center in the living room. Additionally, another two suites (without balcony or bathtub) are located in the forward third of the ship one deck lower than the aft-facing suites, but with the same facilities.

CUISINE. The Island Restaurant, the main dining room, has ocean-view windows on two sides, and upbeat decor. There are tables for two, four, six or eight. It is open for breakfast, lunch and dinner; you can serve yourself from the buffets, or be served by a waiter. It's a very casual open-seating arrangement, and so waiters do not get to know your preferences. Although there is much repetition of salad items for lunch, there are plenty of main dish and dessert choices.

The menus contain a fair variety of British-style food items.

Oasis is a smaller, more intimate, exclusive and quieter restaurant, located one deck below the Island Restaurant. This à la carte (extra-cost) dining spot, with seats for two or four, is open only for dinner (reservations required), with full waiter service for all courses. The wine list is typical of a high street eatery, with European prices that provide decent value for money.

The ceiling is low in both venues, which provides a sense of intimacy, but the noise level is intense.

For breakfast, lunch and dinner – in fact, 24 hours a day – there is another place to go: the Beachcomber Cafe. This is really casual, and is ideal for grabbing a bite to eat while "taking the sun" on the open decks. Again, it's a self-serve buffet, with food constantly being refreshed. Tea and coffee are provided at a beverage station, with plastic cups and mugs. Additionally, there's the Café Brazil for pastries, extremely sinful cakes and pastries, and a range of espresso/cappuccino coffees, all at extra cost.

ENTERTAINMENT. The Ocean Theater is a single-level showlounge, with banquette and individual seating surrounding a "thrust" stage. Although it is a comfortable room, several pillars obstruct sight lines from some seats.

A resident troupe of young, enthusiastic singer/dancers provide the low-budget revue-style "shows" that are, at best, amateurish, with weak recorded tracks but lots of color. In addition, visiting cabaret acts – typically strong singers, magicians, and smutty comedians – are presented, both in their own shows and as the middle of a "pie" that includes the ship's resident troupe.

There is a ship's band, and several small musical units and pianists provide live music for dancing and listening in the bars and lounges. In addition, a throbbing discotheque is available for those who enjoy such things.

SPA/FITNESS. The Ship Shape Hair and Beauty Spa is surprisingly good for the size of the ship. There are treatment rooms for massage, separate saunas and changing rooms for men and women, and a large beauty salon. The gymnasium itself is quite large and contains lots of muscle-pumping, body toning equipment. It is located just aft of the main swimming pool on the port side of the ship.

Spa staff are provided by Harding Brothers, and treatments offered include massages, aromatherapy facials, manicures, pedicures, and hair beautifying treatments. Examples: Massage, £45 (50 minutes); Back, Neck and Shoulders Massage, £30 (20 minutes); Marine Algae Body Wrap, £40; Hydrodermie Facial, £45 (75 minutes). Do book appointments early, as time slots go quickly.

Island Princess
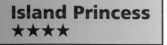
★★★★

Size: . . . . .Large Resort Ship	Total Crew: 900	Wheelchair accessibility . . . . .Good
Tonnage: 91,627	Passengers	Cabin Current: . . . . .110 volts
Lifestyle: . . . . .Standard	(lower beds/all berths): 1,974/2,590	Elevators: 14
Cruise Line: . . . . .Princess Cruises	Passenger Space Ratio	Casino (gaming tables): . . . . .Yes
Former Names: . . . . .none	(lower beds/all berths): 46.4/35.3	Slot Machines: . . . . .Yes
Builder: Chantiers de l'Atlantique (France)	Crew/Passenger Ratio	Swimming Pools (outdoors): 2
Original Cost: . . . .$360 million	(lower beds/all berths): 2.1/2.8	(+ 1 splash pool)
Entered Service: . . . . .June 2003	Cabins (total): 987	Swimming Pools (indoors): 0
Registry: . . . . .Bermuda	Size Range (sq ft/m): 156–470.0/14.4–43.6	Whirlpools: 5
Length (ft/m): 964.5/294.0	Cabins (outside view): 879	Self-Service Launderette: . . . . .Yes
Beam (ft/m): 105.6/32.2	Cabins (interior/no view): 108	Dedicated Cinema/Seats: . . . . .No
Draft (ft/m): 26/7.9	Cabins (for one person): 0	Library: . . . . .Yes
Propulsion/Propellers: . . . . .gas turbine/2	Cabins (with private balcony): 727	
Passenger Decks: 11	Cabins (wheelchair accessible): 20	

BERLITZ'S OVERALL SCORE: 1,542 OUT OF A POSSIBLE 2,000 POINTS

OVERVIEW. *Island Princess* (sister ship to *Coral Princess*) has an instantly recognizable funnel due to two jet engine-like pods that sit high up on its structure. Four diesel engines provide the generating power. Electrical power is provided by a combination of four diesel and one gas turbine (CODAG) unit; the diesel engines are located in the engine room, while the gas turbine unit is located in the ship's funnel housing. The ship also has three bow thrusters and three stern thrusters.

The ship's interior layout is similar to that of the *Grand Princess*-class ships (but with two decks full of public rooms, lounges and bars instead of just one), and sensibly features three major stair towers for passengers (good from the safety and evacuation viewpoint), with plenty of elevators for easy access. For a large ship, the layout is quite user-friendly, and less disjointed than many ships of a similar size. Because of its slim beam, the ship is able to transit the Panama Canal, thus providing greater flexibility in deployment than the *Grand Princess*-class ships.

New facilities for a Princess Cruises ship include a flower shop (where you can order flowers and Godiva chocolates for cabin delivery – good for a birthday or anniversary), cigar lounge (Churchill Lounge), martini bar (Crooners). Also different is a casino with a London theme.

What is very civilized is the fact that sunbathers who use the "quiet" deck forward of the mast have their own splash pool, so they won't have to go down two decks to get to the two main pools. Strollers will like the ship's full walk-around exterior promenade deck.

Surfers can find an AOL Internet Cafe conveniently located on the top level of the four-deck-high lobby.

BERLITZ'S RATINGS	Possible	Achieved
Ship	500	434
Accommodation	200	154
Food	400	261
Service	400	294
Entertainment	100	85
Cruise	400	314

Meanwhile, it's good to see that the dreaded "fine arts" get their own room, so that paintings to be sold during the art auctions are not spread all over the ship. Adjacent is the Wedding Chapel (a live web-cam can relay ceremonies via the internet). The ship's captain can legally marry (American) couples, due to the ship's registry and a special dispensation (this should, however, be verified when in the planning stage, and may depend on where you live). Princess Cruises offers three wedding packages – Pearl, Emerald, Diamond; the fee includes registration and official marriage certificate. The Wedding Chapel can host "renewal of vows" ceremonies (there is a charge for these).

ACCOMMODATION. There are 33 price categories, in six types: 16 Suites with balcony (470 sq. ft/43.6 sq. meters); 184 Mini-Suites with balcony (285–302 sq. ft/26.4–28.0 sq. meters; 8 Mini-Suites without balcony (300 sq. ft/27.8 sq. meters; 527 Outside-View Cabins with balcony (217–232 sq. ft/ 20.1–21.5 sq. meters); 144 Standard Outside-view Cabins (162 sq. ft/15 sq. meters); Interior (no view) Cabins (156 sq. ft/144.5 sq. meters). There are also 20 wheelchair-accessible cabins (217–374 sq. ft/20.1–34.7 sq. meters). The price you pay will depend on grade, size and location. Note that all measurements are approximate. Almost all of the outside-view cabins have a private balcony. Some cabins can accommodate a third, or third and fourth person (good for families with children). Some cabins on Emerald Deck (Deck 8) have a view obstructed by lifeboats.

Suites: There are just 16 suites and, although none are really that large (compared to such ships as *Norwegian Dawn* and *Norwegian Star*, where the largest measure a whopping 5,350 sq. ft/497 sq. meters, for example), each has a private balcony. All are named after islands (mostly coral-based islands in the Indian Ocean and Pacific Ocean). All suites are located on either Deck 9 or Deck 10. In a departure from many ships, *Island Princess* does not have any suites or cabins with a view of the ship's stern. There are also four Premium Suites, located sensibly in the center of the ship, adjacent to a bank of six lifts. Six other suites (called Verandah Suites) are located further aft.

All Accommodation: Suites and cabins have a refrigerator, personal safe, television (with audio channels), hairdryer, satellite-dial telephone, and twin beds that convert to a queen-sized bed (there are a few exceptions). All accommodation has a bathroom with shower enclosure and toilet. Accommodation designated as suites and mini-suites (there are seven price categories) have a bathtub and separate shower enclosure, and two TV sets.

All passengers receive turndown service and chocolates on pillows each night, bathrobes (on request) and toiletry kits. Most "outside-view" cabins on Emerald Deck have views obstructed by the lifeboats. There are no cabins for singles. Nor are there butlers – even for the top-grade suites. Cabin attendants have too many cabins to look after (typically 20), which does not translate to fine personal service. Princess Cruises typically includes CNN, CNBC, ESPN and TNT on the in-cabin color television system (when available).

CUISINE. There are two main dining rooms, named Bordeaux and Provence; they are located in the forward section of the ship on the two lowest passenger decks, with the galley all the way forward so it doesn't intersect public spaces (an example of good design). Both are almost identical in design and layout (the ceilings are quite low and make the rooms appear more cramped than they are), and have plenty of intimate alcoves and cozy dining spots, with tables for two, four, six, or eight. There are two seatings for dinner, while breakfast and lunch are on an open seating basis; you may have to stand in line at peak times. Both dining rooms are non-smoking.

Horizon Court is the ship's casual 24-hour eatery, and is located in the forward section of Lido Deck, with superb ocean views. Several self-serve counters provide an array of food for breakfast and lunch buffets, while each evening, bistro-style casual dinners are available.

Alternative (Extra Charge) Eateries: There are two "alternative" dining rooms, Sabatini's and the Bayou Cafe, both enclosed. They incur an extra charge, and you must make a reservation. Sabatini's is an Italian eatery, with colorful tiled Mediterranean-style decor; it has Italian-style pizzas and pastas, with a variety of sauces, as well as Italian-style entrées (including tiger prawns and lobster tail), all provided with flair and entertainment by the waiters. The food that is both creative and tasty (with seriously sized portions). There is a cover charge of $15 per person, for lunch or dinner (on sea days only).

The Bayou Cafe is open for lunch and dinner, and has a cover charge of $10 per person (including a free Hurricane cocktail), and evokes the charm of New Orleans' French

Quarter, complete with wrought-iron decoration. The Bayou Cafe serves Creole food (with platters such as Peel 'n' Eat Shrimp Piquante, Sausage Grillades, Oysters Sieur de Bienville and N'Awlins Crawfish "Mud Bug" Bisque delivered to the table when you arrive). Popular entrées include Seafood Gumbo, and Chorizo Jambalaya with fresh seafood and traditional dried spice mixes, as well as Cajun Grill items such as Smothered Alligator Ribs, Flambeaux Grilled Jumbo Prawns, Corn Meal Fried Catfish, Blackened Chicken Brochette, and Red Pepper Butter Broiled Lobster; desserts include sweet potato pie and banana whiskey pound cake. The room has a small stage, with baby grand piano, and live jazz is also part of the dining scenario.

Other outlets include La Pâtisserie, in the ship's reception lobby, a coffee, cakes and pastries spot and good for informal meetings. There's also a Pizzeria, hamburger grill, and an ice cream bar (extra charge for the ice cream). Meanwhile, puffers and sippers should enjoy Churchill's, a neat cigar and cognac lounge, cleverly sited near a neat little hideaway bar called the Rat Pack Bar.

ENTERTAINMENT. The Princess Theatre is two decks high, and, unusually, there is much more seating in the upper level than on the main floor below. A second entertainment lounge (Universe Lounge) is designed more for cabaret-style features. It also has two levels, and three separate stages – so non-stop entertainment can be provided without constant set-ups. Some 50 of the room's seats are equipped with a built-in laptop computer. The room is also used for cooking demonstrations (it has a full kitchen set), and other life enrichment participation activities.

Princess Cruises always provides plenty of live music in bars and lounges, with a wide mix of light classical, jazz, and dance music, from solo entertaining pianists to show-bands, and volume is normally kept to an acceptable level.

Feel in need of education? Now you can learn aboard ship, with "ScholarShip@Sea," a new Princess Cruises program, which debuted aboard this vessel. It includes about 20 courses per cruise (six on any given day at sea). Although all introductory classes are free, if you want to continue any chosen subject in a smaller setting, there are fees. There are four core subjects: Culinary Arts, Visual/ Creative Arts, Photography, and Computer Technology. A full culinary demonstration kitchen set has been built into the Universe Lounge (this can also play host to wine tasting), and a pottery studio complete with kiln has been built into the ship as part of the facilities.

SPA/FITNESS. The Lotus Spa is located aft on one of the ship's uppermost decks. It contains men's and women's saunas, steam rooms, changing rooms, relaxation area, beauty salon, aerobics exercise room and gymnasium with aft-facing ocean-views packed with the latest high-tech muscle-pumping, cardio-vascular equipment. There are several large rooms for individual treatments.

● **For more extensive general information about the Princess Cruises experience, see pages 148–51.**

Island Sky
★★★★ +

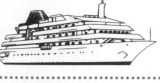

Size:	Boutique Ship
Tonnage:	4,280
Lifestyle:	Standard
Cruise Line:	Noble Caledonia
Former Names:	Regina Renaissance, Renaissance VIII
Builder:	Nuovi Cantieri Appaunia (Italy)
Original Cost:	$25 million
Entered Service:	Dec 1991/May 2004
Registry:	The Bahamas
Length (ft/m):	297.2/90.6
Beam (ft/m):	50.1/15.3
Draft (ft/m):	12.9/2.95
Propulsion/Propellers:	diesel (5000kW)/2
Passenger Decks:	5
Total Crew:	66
Passengers (lower beds/all berths):	116/116
Passenger Space Ratio (lower beds/all berths):	36.8/36.8
Crew/Passenger Ratio (lower beds/all berths):	1.7/1.7
Cabins (total):	59
Size Range (sq ft/m):	234.6 – 353.0/ 21.8 – 32.8
Cabins (outside view):	59
Cabins (interior/no view):	0
Cabins (for one person):	0
Cabins (with private balcony):	4
Cabins (wheelchair accessible):	0
Wheelchair accessibility	None
Cabin Voltage:	110
Elevators:	1
Casino (gaming tables):	No
Slot Machines:	No
Swimming Pools (outdoors):	0
Swimming Pools (indoors):	0
Whirlpools:	1
Self-Service Launderette:	No
Dedicated Cinema/Seats:	No
Library:	Yes

OVERALL SCORE: 1,562 OUT OF A POSSIBLE 2,000 POINTS

OVERVIEW. *Island Sky*, refurbished in 2004 before being chartered to Noble Caledonia, has contemporary mega-yacht looks and handsome styling, with twin flared funnels give this ship a smart profile, and a "ducktail" (sponson) stern provides good stability and seagoing comfort. This ship was originally built as one of a series of eight similar ships for the now-defunct Renaissance Cruises. Owned by a Bahamas-based company, it is operated year-round by Noble Caledonia, and was again completely refurbished in 2010.

There is one teak walk-around promenade deck outdoors, and a reasonable amount of open deck and sunbathing space. A "baby island" tender hangs off the aft deck and acts as ship-to-shore transportation. Some equipment for watersports is carried, together with a fleet of Zodiac inflatables for shore landings.

Inside, the interior design is elegant, with polished wood-finish paneling throughout. There is a very small library with two internet-connect computer workstations.

This vessel is very comfortable and totally inviting, and operates cruises in areas devoid of large cruise ships. Although this intimate ship is not quite up to the standard of a Seabourn or Silversea vessel, it will provide a good cruise experience at a moderate cost. Gratuities are included, as are house wine, beer and soft drinks during lunch and dinner. The onboard currency is the British pound.

SUITABLE FOR: Best suited to seasoned travelers who like a relaxed lifestyle combined with good food and service,

BERLITZ'S RATINGS

	Possible	Achieved
Ship	500	396
Accommodation	200	161
Food	400	312
Service	400	307
Entertainment	n/a	n/a
Cruise	500	386

and an itinerary that promises "get away from it all, but in comfort."

ACCOMMODATION. The spacious cabins combine highly polished imitation rosewood paneling with lots of mirrors and hand-crafted furniture, lighted walk-in closets, three-sided vanity mirrors – in fact, there are a lot of mirrored surfaces in the decor – and just about everything you need, including a refrigerator, a TV set and VCR, and wi-fi access. The bathrooms are extremely compact; they have real teakwood floors and marble vanities, and shower enclosures (none have tubs, not even the owner's suite). All were replaced in the 2010 refit.

CRUISE. The dining room operates with an open seating for all meals. It is small but quite smart, with tables for two, four, six, and eight. You simply sit where you like, with whom you like, and at what time you like. The meals are self-service, buffet-style foods for breakfast and lunch, with hot foods chosen from a table menu and served properly. The dining room operation works well. The food quality, choice, and presentation are all very decent.

ENTERTAINMENT. There is no formal entertainment in the main lounge, the venue for all social activities. Anyway, six pillars obstruct sightlines to the small stage area.

SPA/FITNESS. Water sports facilities include an aft platform, and Zodiacs.

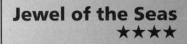

Jewel of the Seas
★★★★

Size: . . . . .Large Resort Ship
Tonnage: .90,090
Lifestyle: . . . . .Standard
Cruise Line: Royal Caribbean International
Former Names: . . . . .none
Builder: . . . . .Meyer Werft (Germany)
Original Cost: . . . .$350 million
Entered Service: . . . . .June 2004
Registry: . . . . .The Bahamas
Length (ft/m): 961.9/293.2
Beam (ft/m): 105.6/32.2
Draft (ft/m): 27.8/8.5
Propulsion/Propellers: . . . . .Gas turbine/2
azimuthing pods (20 MW each)

Passenger Decks: 12
Total Crew: .858
Passengers
(lower beds/all berths): 2,110/2,500
Passenger Space Ratio
(lower beds/all berths): 42.9/36.0
Crew/Passenger Ratio
(lower beds/all berths): 2.4/2.9
Cabins (total): 1,055
Size Range (sq ft/m): 165.8–1,216.3/
15.4–113.0
Cabins (outside view): 817
Cabins (interior/no view): 238
Cabins (for one person): 0

Cabins (with private balcony): 577
Cabins (wheelchair accessible): 14
(8 with private balcony)
Wheelchair accessibility . . . . .Good
Cabin Voltage: 110
Elevators: 9
Casino (gaming tables): . . . . .Yes
Slot Machines: . . . . .Yes
Swimming Pools (outdoors): 2
Swimming Pools (indoors): 0
Whirlpools: 3
Self-Service Launderette: . . . . .No
Dedicated Cinema/Seats: Yes/40
Library: . . . . .Yes

OVERALL SCORE: 1,520 OUT OF A POSSIBLE 2,000 POINTS

OVERVIEW. *Jewel of the Seas* is the fourth Royal Caribbean International ship to use gas and steam turbine power (sister ships: *Brilliance of the Seas, Radiance of the Seas* and *Serenade of the Seas*) instead of the conventional diesel or diesel-electric combination. Pod propulsion power *(see page 45 for description)* is also provided. As is common aboard almost all new cruise ships today, the navigation bridge is of the fully enclosed type. In the very front of the ship is a helipad, which also acts as a viewing platform.

Jewel of the Seas is a streamlined, contemporary ship, and has a two-deck-high wrap-around structure in the forward section of the funnel. Along the starboard side, a central glass wall protrudes, giving great views (cabins with balconies occupy the space directly opposite on the port side). The gently rounded stern has nicely tiered decks, which gives the ship an extremely well-balanced look.

Inside, the decor is contemporary, yet elegant, bright and cheerful, designed for young, active, hip types. The artwork is quite eclectic (so there should be something for all tastes), and provides a spectrum and a half of color works.

The ship's interior focal point is a nine-deck high atrium lobby that has glass-walled elevators (on the port side of the ship only) that travel through 12 decks, face the sea and provide a link with nature and the ocean. The Centrum (as the atrium is called) has several public rooms connected to it: the guest relations and shore excursions desks, a Lobby Bar, Champagne Bar, the Library, Royal Caribbean Online (an internet-connect center), the Concierge Club, and a Crown & Anchor Lounge. A great view can be had of the atrium by looking down through the flat glass dome high above it.

Other facilities include a delightful but very small library,

BERLITZ'S RATINGS		
	Possible	Achieved
Ship	500	428
Accommodation	200	158
Food	400	247
Service	400	297
Entertainment	100	81
Cruise	400	309

a Champagne Bar, and a large Schooner Bar that houses maritime art in an integral art gallery. Gambling devotees should enjoy the rather large, noisy and colorful Casino Royale. There's also a small dedicated screening room for movies (with space for two wheelchairs), as well as a 194-seat conference center, and a business center.

This ship also contains a Viking Crown Lounge (a Royal Caribbean International trademark), a large structure set around the base of the ship's funnel. It functions as an observation lounge during the daytime (with views forward over the swimming pool). In the evening, the space becomes a futuristic, high-energy dance club, as well as a more intimate and relaxed entertainment venue for softer mood music and "black box" theater.

Royal Caribbean Online is a dedicated computer center that has 12 PCs with high-speed internet access for sending and receiving email, located in a semi-private setting.

Youth facilities include Adventure Ocean, an "edu-tainment" area with four separate age-appropriate sections for junior passengers: Aquanaut Center (for ages 3–5); Explorer Center (6–8); Voyager Center (9–12); and the Optix Teen Center (13–17). There is also Adventure Beach, which includes a splash pool complete with waterslide; Surfside, with computer lab stations with entertaining software; and Ocean Arcade, a video games hangout.

The onboard product delivery is more casual and unstructured than RCI has previously been delivering. *Jewel of the Seas* offers more space and more comfortable public areas (and several more intimate spaces), slightly larger cabins and more dining options than most of the larger ships in the RCI fleet.

While the ship is quite delightful in many ways, the onboard operation is less spectacular, and suffers from a lack of service staff. There are no cushioned pads for the sunloungers, and the deck towels provided are quite thin and small. Spa treatments are extravagantly expensive (as they are aboard most ships today, in line with land-based spa prices in the U.S.). It is virtually impossible to escape background music anywhere. The onboard currency is the US dollar, and 15 percent is added to all bar and spa bills.

SUITABLE FOR: *Jewel of the Seas* is best suited to young-minded adult couples and singles of all ages, families with toddlers, tots, children, and teenagers who like to mingle in a large ship setting with plenty of life and high-energy entertainment for everyone, with food that is acceptable quantity rather than quality (unless you are prepared to pay extra for dining in the "alternative" restaurant), all delivered with friendly service that lacks polish.

ACCOMMODATION. There is a wide range of suites and standard outside-view and interior (no view) cabins to suit different tastes, requirements, and depth of wallet, in 10 different categories and 19 different price groups.

Apart from the largest suites (six owner's suites), which have king-sized beds, almost all other cabins have twin beds that convert to a queen-sized bed (all sheets are of 100% Egyptian cotton, although blankets are of nylon). All cabins have rich (but faux) wood cabinetry, including a vanity desk (with hairdryer), faux wood drawers that close silently (hooray), TV set, personal safe, and three-sided mirrors. Some cabins have ceiling-recessed, pull-down berths for third and fourth persons, although closet and drawer space would be extremely tight for four (even if two are children), and some have interconnecting doors (so families with children can cruise together, in adjacent cabins. Note that audio channels are available through the TV set, so you can't switch off its picture while listening. Data ports are provided in all cabins.

Many of the "private" balcony cabins are not very private, as they can be overlooked by anyone standing in the port and starboard wings of the Solarium, and from other locations.

Most cabin bathrooms have tiled accenting and a terrazzo-style tiled floor, and a shower enclosure in a half-moon shape (it is rather small, however, considering the size of some passengers), 100 % Egyptian cotton towels, a small cabinet for personal toiletries and a small shelf. There is little space to stow toiletries for two (or more).

The largest accommodation consists of a family suite with two bedrooms. One bedroom has twin beds (convertible to queen-sized bed), while a second has two lower beds and two upper Pullman berths, a combination that can sleep up to eight persons (this would be suitable for large families).

Occupants of accommodation designated as suites also get the use of a private Concierge Lounge (where priority dining room reservations, shore excursion bookings and beauty salon/spa appointments can be made).

CUISINE. Reflections, the principal dining room, spans two decks; the upper deck level has floor-to-ceiling windows, while the lower deck level has picture windows. It is a fine, but inevitably noisy dining hall, and eight huge, thick pillars obstruct the sightlines. Reflections seats 1,104, and its decor has a cascading water theme. There are tables for two, four, six, eight or 10 in two seatings. Two small private dining rooms (Illusions and Mirage) are located off the main dining room. No smoking is permitted in dining venues. There is an adequate wine list, with moderate prices.

Alternative Restaurants: Portofino, with 112 seats, offers Italian cuisine, and Chops Grille Steakhouse, with 95 seats and an open "show" kitchen, serves premium meats in the form of chops and steaks. Both have food that is of a much higher quality than in the main dining room and are typically open 6pm–11pm. There is an additional charge of $20 per person (including gratuities), and reservations are required. The dress code is smart casual.

Casual Eateries: Casual meals (for breakfast, lunch and dinner) can be taken in the self-serve, buffet-style Windjammer Cafe, which can be accessed directly from the pool deck. It has about 400 seats, and islands dedicated to specific foods, and indoors and outdoors seating. Additionally, there is the Seaview Cafe, open for lunch and dinner. Choose from the self-serve buffet, or from the menu for casual, fast-food seafood items including fish sandwiches, popcorn shrimp, fish 'n' chips, as well as non-seafood items such as hamburgers and hot dogs.

ENTERTAINMENT. Entertainment facilities include the three-level Coral Reef Theater, with 874 seats (including 24 wheelchair stations) and good sightlines from most seats due to steep tiers. A second entertainment venue is the Safari Club, which hosts cabaret shows, late-night adult (blue) comedy, and dancing to live music. All the ship's entertainment is upbeat – so much so that it's virtually impossible to get away from music and noise.

SPA/FITNESS. The ShipShape health, fitness and spa facilities have themed decor, and include a 10,176 sq.-ft (945 sq.-meter) solarium with whirlpool and counter current swimming under a retractable magrodome roof, a gymnasium (with 44 cardiovascular machines), 50-person aerobics room, sauna and steam rooms, and therapy treatment rooms.

For the more sporting, there is activity galore – including a rock-climbing wall that's 30 ft (9 meters) high, with five separate climbing tracks. It's free, and all safety gear is included, but you'll need to sign up.

Other sports facilities include a 9-hole miniature golf course, and an indoor/outdoor country club with golf simulator, a jogging track, and basketball court. Want to play pool? You can, thanks to two special tables whose technology adjusts automatically to the movement of the ship.

● **For more extensive general information about Royal Caribbean International cruises, see pages 151–6.**

Kapitan Khlebnikov
★★★

Size: ....Boutique Ship	Passenger Decks: 6	Cabins (wheelchair accessible): 0
Tonnage: 12,288	Total Crew: 60	Wheelchair accessibility ....None
Lifestyle: ....Standard	Passengers	Cabin Current: ....220 volts
Cruise Line: ......Murmansk Shipping/	(lower beds/all berths): 108/114	Elevators: 1
Quark Expeditions	Passenger Space Ratio	Casino (gaming tables): ....No
Former Names: ....none	(lower beds/all berths): 113.7/107.7	Slot Machines: ....No
Builder: ....Wartsila (Finland)	Crew/Passenger Ratio	Swimming Pools (outdoors): 0
Original Cost: ....n/a	(lower beds/all berths): 1.8/1.9	Swimming Pools (indoors): 1
Entered Service: 1981	Cabins (total): 54	Whirlpools: 0
Registry: ....Russia	Size Range (sq ft/m): 150.6–269/	Lecture/Film Room: ....No
Length (ft/m): 434.6/132.49	14.0–25.0	Library: ....Yes
Beam (ft/m): 87.7/26.75	Cabins (outside view): 54	Zodiacs: 4
Draft (ft/m): 27.8/8.50	Cabins (interior/no view): 0	Helicopter Pad: ....Yes (1 helicopter)
Propulsion/Propellers: .....diesel-electric	Cabins (for one person): 0	
(18,270 kW)/3	Cabins (with private balcony): 0	

OVERALL SCORE: 1,144 OUT OF A POSSIBLE 2,000 POINTS

OVERVIEW. *Kapitan Khlebnikov* is a real, working icebreaker, one of a fleet of 10 built in Finland to exacting Russian specifications. Converted to exclusive passenger use in 1994 (and since upgraded), it has an incredibly thick hull, forthright profile, a bow like an inverted whale head, and much technical equipment. In 1997, *Kapitan Khlebnikov* became the first vessel ever to circumnavigate Antarctica with passengers. "KK," as it is affectionately known, has also transited the Northwest Passage more times than any other expedition ship. An open bridge policy allows passengers to visit the bridge at almost any time. Strong diesel-electric engines (delivering 24,000 horsepower) allow it to plow through ice several feet thick. There is plenty of open deck and observation space, and a heated (but very small) indoor swimming pool.

There is always a team of excellent naturalists and lecturers aboard. A helicopter, when carried, can be used for sightseeing forays, as is a fleet of Zodiac rubber landing craft for in-your-face shore landings and wildlife spotting. *Kapitan Khlebnikov* is particularly good for tough expedition cruising, and will provide thoroughly practical surroundings, a friendly, experienced and dedicated group of crew members, and excellent value for the money. An expedition cruise logbook is typically provided at the end of each cruise for all passengers – a superb keepsake.

The ship offers only basic cruise amenities and very spartan, no-frills decor. Also, be prepared for some tremendous roaring noise when the ship breaks through pack ice.

SUITABLE FOR: This type of cruising suits adventurous,

BERLITZ'S RATINGS

	Possible	Achieved
Ship	500	263
Accommodation	200	113
Food	400	233
Service	400	224
Entertainment	n/a	n/a
Cruise	500	311

hardy outdoors types of mature years who enjoy being with nature in some of the earth's most inhospitable places. Suggested gratuities: $9–$12 per day.

ACCOMMODATION. The cabins, in four price categories, are spread over four decks in an accommodation block, and all have private facilities and plenty of storage space. Although nothing special, they are quite comfortable, with two lower beds (typically one is a fixed bed, the other being a convertible sofa bed, either in a twin or an L-shaped format), large closets, storage for outerwear and boots, and portholes that actually open. The bathrooms are practical units, although storage space for personal toiletries is tight. Four of the accommodation units are designated as "suites" that have more room, including a larger bathroom.

CUISINE. The one dining room is plain and unpretentious, yet quite comfortable. It is non-smoking; there is a single seating, with assigned tables. The food is hearty fare, with generous portions (and an emphasis on fish and potatoes). Fruits, vegetables and international cheeses tend to be in limited supply. Quark Expeditions has its own catering team. The wine list is pretty basic.

ENTERTAINMENT. Dinner is the main event of the evening, followed by discussion of what lies ahead for the next day. You might actually do a shore landing at night.

SPA/FITNESS. There is a gymnasium with some basic equipment, a small (heated) indoor swimming pool (really a "dip" pool), and a sauna.

Le Boreal
NOT YET RATED

Size: ....Small Ship	Passenger Decks: 6	Cabins (with private balcony): 125
Tonnage: 10,700	Total Crew: 140	Cabins (wheelchair accessible): 0
Lifestyle: ....Premium	Passengers	Wheelchair accessibility ....Fair
Cruise Line: ....Ponant Cruises	(lower beds/all berths): 224/264	Cabin Voltage: ....110 and 220 volts
Former Names: ....none	Passenger Space Ratio	Elevators: 2
Builder: ....Fincantieri (Italy)	(lower beds/all berths): 53.5/40.5	Casino (gaming tables): ....No
Original Cost: ....$100 million	Crew/Passenger Ratio	Slot Machines: ....Yes
Entered Service: ....May 2010	(lower beds/all berths): 1.5/1.8	Swimming Pools (outdoors): 2
Registry: ....Wallis & Fortuna	Cabins (total): 132	Swimming Pools (indoors): 0
Length (ft/m): 465.8/142.0	Size Range (sq ft/m): 215.2–301.3/	Whirlpools: 0
Beam (ft/m): 9.0/18.0	20.0–28.0	Self-Service Launderette: 0
Draft (ft/m): 15.4/4.7	Cabins (outside view): 132	Dedicated Cinema/Seats: ....No
Propulsion/Propellers: ....diesel-electric	Cabins (interior/no view): 0	Library: ....Yes
(4,600kW)/2	Cabins (for one person): 0	

BERLITZ'S OVERALL SCORE: NYR OUT OF A POSSIBLE 2,000 POINTS

OVERVIEW. One of two identical new ships catering to French-speakers, *Le Boreal* is a little gem of contemporary design – chic and uncluttered. The dark hull and sleek white superstructure look like a large private yacht, not a traditional cruise ship. The Passenger Space Ratio, a healthy 53.5, decreases if the 40 suites that convert into 20 are all occupied by two persons. The ship has a smart "sponson" skirt built-in at the stern for operational stability.

An outdoor sunbathing deck, forward of the funnel, has a small pool (with adjacent covered area), although there is no shower enclosure. Two staircases lead to an upper section, with an outdoor bar and grill. Another pool/sunbathing (and shaded area, covered with solar panels) is located aft.

Almost all public rooms are aft, with accommodation located forward. The decor is minimalist and super-yacht chic. The focal point is the main lobby, with a central, circular seating and tiled floor surround. The other flooring is wood, which can be noisy due to the lack of soft furnishings.

This is all-inclusive cruising (exception: spa treatments), with drinks, all port charges, gratuities, and shore excursions included in the fare. The crew is French-speaking, and the onboard currency is the euro.

SUITABLE FOR: *Le Boreal* is best suited to young-minded couples and singles who want sophisticated facilities in a relaxed but chic yacht-like environment quite different to most cruise ships, with very good food and decent service.

ACCOMMODATION. Of the 132 suites/ cabins, there are three Prestige Suites (301 sq.ft. plus 54 sq.ft. balcony); while 40 of the 94 deluxe cabins (200 sq.ft. plus 43 sq.ft. balcony) can be

BERLITZ'S RATINGS		
	Possible	Achieved
Ship	500	NYR
Accommodation	200	NYR
Food	400	NYR
Service	400	NYR
Entertainment	100	NYR
Cruise	400	NYR

combined into 20 larger suites, each with two bathrooms, and separate living area and bedroom.

Each deluxe and standard cabin has a large ocean-view window, two beds that convert to a queen-sized bed, and a long vanity desk, with good lighting. Features include a TV set, DVD player, refrigerator, and personal safe. The marble-appointed bathrooms have handheld shower hoses. Amenities include a minibar, personal safe, hairdryer, bathrobe, and French bathroom products. Wi-fi costs extra.

The cabin bathrooms have glass walls, enabling you to see through the cabin to the ocean.

CUISINE. The main restaurant, Restaurant Gastromique, is chic but not pretentious, seats all passengers in an open-seating arrangement, and has an integral wine room. The chairs are rather square and have very thin armrests and low backs – but they look good. An indoor/outdoor Grill provides a casual setting for up to 130.

ENTERTAINMENT. The showlounge has amphitheater-style seating for 260, and a raised stage suited to concerts and cabaret presentations. The venue is also used for expert specialist lecturers, and expedition-style recaps.

SPA/FITNESS. Spa facilities include a fitness room with ocean views, and a steam room.

L'Austral NOT YET RATED
L'Austral is an identical ship to Le Boreal and is set to debut in March 2011.

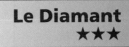

Le Diamant
★★★

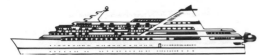

Size: ....Boutique Ship	Passenger Decks: 6	Cabins (wheelchair accessible): 0
Tonnage: 8,282	Total Crew: 140	Wheelchair accessibility ....None
Lifestyle: ....Premium	Passengers	Cabin Current: ....220 volts
Cruise Line: ....Ponant Cruises	(lower beds/all berths): 198/198	Elevators: 2
Former Names: ....*Song of Flower,*	Passenger Space Ratio	Casino (gaming tables): ....Yes
Explorer Starship	(lower beds/all berths): 41.8/41.8	Slot Machines: ....Yes
Builder: ....KMV (Norway)	Crew/Passenger Ratio	Swimming Pools (outdoors): 1
Original Cost: ....n/a	(lower beds/all berths): 1.4/1.4	Swimming Pools (indoors): 0
Entered Service: 1986/May 2004	Cabins (total): 99	Whirlpools: 1
Registry: ....Wallis and Fortuna	Size Range (sq ft/m): 183.0–398.0/	Self-Service Launderette: ....No
Length (ft/m): 407.4/124.2	17.0–37.0	Dedicated Cinema/Seats: ....No
Beam (ft/m): 52.4/16.0	Cabins (outside view): 99	Library: ....Yes
Draft (ft/m): 16.0/4.9	Cabins (interior/no view): 0	
Propulsion/Propellers: ....diesel	Cabins (for one person): 0	
(5,500kW)/2 (CP)	Cabins (with private balcony): 10	

OVERALL SCORE: 1,219 OUT OF A POSSIBLE 2,000 POINTS

OVERVIEW. *Le Diamant* is a charming boutique-sized cruise ship (originally built as the ro-ro vessel *Begonia* in 1974 and fully converted for cruising in 1986). Operated for many years by Radisson Seven Seas Cruises (now Regent Seven Seas Cruises), the ship was sold to the France's Compagnie des Isles du Ponant/Tapis Rouges, a joint venture. The ship has rather tall, twin funnels (with a platform between them) that give a somewhat squat profile. If only the foredeck and bow could be a little longer, it would provide a more sleek appearance. The ship has fairly been well maintained and is clean, although its interiors now look really tired. There's a good amount of sheltered open deck and sunbathing space. Water sports facilities include snorkel equipment.

The interior decor is warm, with pastel colors, accented by splashes of color are used throughout the public rooms, passageways, and stairways. Good quality soft furnishings and fabrics are provided, and make the ship feel chic and comfortable, though not luxurious.

The ship has a warm and caring crew that really tries hard to make you feel at home and comfortable and at home during your cruise vacation. Totally understated elegance and a warm, informal lifestyle are the hallmarks of a cruise aboard this nice ship. *Le Diamant* should provide you with a pleasing, destination-intensive, yet relaxing cruise experience, delivered with a decent amount of style and panache. The tender is in poor shape and needs replacing.

SUITABLE FOR: *Le Diamant* is for young-minded French-speaking couples and singles who want fairly contemporary

BERLITZ'S RATINGS

	Possible	Achieved
Ship	500	293
Accommodation	200	125
Food	400	248
Service	400	255
Entertainment	100	58
Cruise	400	240

facilities in a very relaxed but chic, yacht-like small ship setting that is different to "normal" cruise ships, with very good food and decent service.

ACCOMMODATION. There are 10 elegant suites; 10 cabins are strictly non-smoking. All others are well equipped, complete with bathrobes and slippers, refrigerator, and VCR. All come with excellent closet and drawer space.

Many have bathtubs, but they are tiny (shower tubs would be a better description). Disabled passengers should choose a cabin with a shower instead of a bath. There are no in-cabin dining facilities for dinner. When compared with the Seabourn and Silversea ships, the cabins are really rather plain.

CUISINE. The dining room is really most charming and has warm colors, a welcoming ambience, and one seating, with no assigned tables (tables are for two, four or six). Dining is in open seating. Free wines accompany lunch and dinner. The cuisine is, naturally, classic French, with small portions that are attractively presented. The personal service is good, from the warm, highly personable and attentive staff.

ENTERTAINMENT. The well-tiered show lounge is a good, comfortable room, and there are good sight lines from almost all the banquette-style seating.

SPA/FITNESS. The health spa facility is very compact and short on space, but is reasonably adequate, and includes a beauty salon and sauna.

Le Levant
★★★★

Size: . . . . .Boutique Ship	Passenger Decks: 5	Cabins (with private balcony): 0
Tonnage: 3,504	Total Crew: 50	Cabins (wheelchair accessible): 0
Lifestyle: . . . . .Premium	Passengers	Wheelchair accessibility . . . . .None
Cruise Line: . . . . .Ponant Cruises	(lower beds/all berths): 90/90	Cabin Current: . . . . .110 and 220 volts
Former Names: . . . . .none	Passenger Space Ratio	Elevators: 1
Builder: . . . . .Leroux & Lotz (France)	(lower beds/all berths): 38.9/38.9	Casino (gaming tables): . . . . .No
Original Cost: . . . .$35 million	Crew/Passenger Ratio	Slot Machines: . . . . .No
Entered Service: . . . . .Jan 1999	(lower beds/all berths): 1.8/1.8	Swimming Pools (outdoors): 1
Registry: . . . . .Wallis and Fortuna	Cabins (total): .45	Swimming Pools (indoors): 0
Length (ft/m): 328.0/100.00	Size Range (sq ft/m): 199.1/18.5	Whirlpools: 0
Beam (ft/m): 45.9/14.00	Cabins (outside view): 45	Self-Service Launderette: . . . . .No
Draft (ft/m): 11.4/3.50	Cabins (interior/no view): 0	Dedicated Cinema/Seats: . . . . .No
Propulsion/Propellers: diesel (3,000 kW)/2	Cabins (for one person): 0	Library: . . . . .Yes

OVERALL SCORE: 1,415 OUT OF A POSSIBLE 2,000 POINTS

OVERVIEW. *Le Levant* is a high-class vessel that has the looks of a stream-lined private mega-yacht. It has two slim funnels that extend over port and starboard sides to carry any soot away from the vessel. It was built in a specialist yacht-building yard in St Malo, France. There is an "open bridge" policy, so passengers may visit the bridge at any time, except when the ship is maneuvering in difficult conditions.

A stern "marina" platform is used for scuba diving, snorkeling or swimming. Two special landing craft are carried for shore visits, hidden in the stern, as well as six inflatable Zodiacs runabouts for landings in "soft" expedition areas such as the Amazon.

Inside, the vessel features contemporary, clean and uncluttered decor, and all the facilities of a private yacht. The public rooms are elegant and refined, with much use of wood trim and accenting. Particularly pleasing is the wood-paneled library. There is one grand salon, which accommodates all passengers, and is used by day as a lecture room, and by night as the main lounge/bar. A resident scuba dive master is aboard for all Caribbean sailings. Each cruise has life-enrichment lecturers aboard, as well as tour leaders.

This ship is often under charter to the New York-based Travel Dynamics International, which operates it in some offbeat destinations and cruise regions. In summer it may be in the Great Lakes, sailing between Toronto and Chicago (its pencil-slim beam allows it to navigate the locks). During the fall the ship heads to Canada/New England, and in the winter to the Caribbean and South America.

This is all-inclusive cruising, with all port charges, gratuities, and shore excursions included in the fare. The crew is almost entirely French. The onboard currency is the euro.

BERLITZ'S RATINGS

	Possible	Achieved
Ship	500	384
Accommodation	200	155
Food	400	272
Service	400	276
Entertainment	n/a	n/a
Cruise	500	328

SUITABLE FOR: *Le Levant* is best suited to young-minded couples and singles who want contemporary and sophisti-cated facilities in a very relaxed but chic, yacht-like small ship setting that is different to "normal" cruise ships, with very good food and decent service.

ACCOMMODATION. There are 45 ocean-view cabins (the brochure incorrectly calls them "suites") and all are midships and forward, in five price categories (a lot for such a small ship). Each cabin has a large ocean-view window, inlaid wood furniture and accenting, designer fabrics, two beds that will convert to a queen-sized bed, a television, VCR, refrigerator, personal safe, and personal amenity kits in the marble-appointed bathrooms, all of which feature a shower with a circular door – much better than a shower curtain; there are no bathtubs.

CUISINE. The Lafayette is a wood-panelled room that is warm and welcoming, with round and oval tables. The informal Veranda Restaurant has a panoramic view over-looking the stern (with both indoor and outdoor seating). Dining is in open seating. Free wines accompany lunch and dinner. The cuisine is, naturally, classic French.

ENTERTAINMENT. The Grand Salon, the main lounge, accom-modates all passengers. It is the only room where smoking is allowed, and there are built-in video screens for showing movies. The only other entertainment is a singer/pianist; the room has a small dance floor in its center.

SPA/FITNESS. There is a small fitness room, and a steam room (there is no sauna) and shower.

Boutique Ship: . . . . .1,489 tons	Main Propulsion: . . . . . .(a) engine (b) sails	Cabins (interior/no view): 0	
Lifestyle: . . . . .Premium	Propulsion/Propellers: . . . . .diesel/	Cabins (for one person): 0	
Cruise Line: . . . . .Ponant Cruises	sail power/1	Cabins (with private balcony): 0	
Former Names: . . . . .none	Passenger Decks: 3	Cabins (wheelchair accessible): 0	
Builder: . . . . .SFCN (France)	Total Crew: 30	Wheelchair accessibility . . . . .None	
Original Cost: .n/a	Passengers	Cabin Current: . . . . .220 volts	
Entered Service: 1991	(lower beds/all berths): 64/67	Elevators: . . . . .No	
Registry: .France	Passenger Space Ratio	Casino (gaming tables): . . . . .No	
Length (ft/m): 288.7/88.00	(lower beds/all berths): 23.2/22.2	Slot Machines: .No	
Beam (ft/m): 39.3/12.00	Crew/Passenger Ratio	Swimming Pools (outdoors): 0	
Draft (ft/m): 13.1/4.00	(lower beds/all berths): 2.1/2.2	Whirlpools: 0	
Type of Vessel: . . . . .high tech sail-cruiser	Cabins (total): .32	Self-Service Launderette: . . . . .No	
No. of Masts: 3	Size Range (sq ft/m): 139.9/13.0	Library: . . . . .Yes	
Sail Area (sq ft/sq m): 16,150/1,500	Cabins (outside view): 32		

OVERALL SCORE: 1,385 OUT OF A POSSIBLE 2,000 POINTS

OVERVIEW. Ultra sleek, and very efficiently designed, this contemporary sail-cruise ship has three masts that rise 54.7 ft (16.7 meters) above the water line, and features electronic winches that assist in the furling and unfurling of the sails. The total sail area measures approximately 1,500 sq. meters/16,140 sq. ft. This captivating ship has plenty of room on its open decks for sunbathing (although they have padded cushions, somehow the off-white plastic sunloungers are not at all elegant – teak would be so much more in keeping with the otherwise ultra-yacht look of the ship, although there probably is no room for them).

The very elegant, no-glitz interior design is clean, stylish, functional and ultra-high-tech. Three public lounges have pastel decor, soft colors and great European flair.

One price fits all. The ship is marketed mainly to young, sophisticated French-speaking passengers who love yachting and the sea. This is *très* French, and *très* chic and venturing off the beaten path is what cruising aboard *Le Ponant* is all about. The company also has a stunning mega-yacht cruise vessel, *Le Levant*. Gratuities are not "required", but they are expected. The onboard currency is the euro.

SUITABLE FOR: *Le Ponant* is best suited to young-minded couples and singles who want contemporary, sophisticated facilities in a very relaxed but chic setting that is different to "normal" cruise ships, with good food and service, no entertainment, and plenty of time for quiet relaxation.

ACCOMMODATION. There are five cabins on Antigua Deck (the open deck) and 27 on Marie Galante Deck (the lowest deck). Crisp, clean blond woods and pristine white cabins

BERLITZ'S RATINGS

	Possible	Achieved
Ship	500	382
Accommodation	200	143
Food	400	272
Service	400	288
Entertainment	n/a	n/a
Cruise	500	300

have twin beds that convert to a double. There's a mini-bar, personal safe, and a private bathroom. All cabins have portholes, crisp artwork, and a refrigerator. There is limited storage space, however, and few drawers (they are also very small). The cabin bathrooms are quite small, but efficiently designed.

CUISINE. The lovely Karukera dining room has an open seating policy, so you can sit where you wish and dine with anyone you want. There is fresh fish daily (when available), and dinner is always treated as a true *affaire gastonomique*. The chef goes out to buy fresh local food items, including fresh fish, produce and fruits.

Free wines are included for lunch and dinner, and the cuisine is, naturally, classic French. Being French, the selection of cheeses and bread (and breakfast croissants) are good. Free cappuccinos and espresso are available.

For casual breakfasts and luncheons, there is also the charming outdoor café under a canvas sailcloth awning.

ENTERTAINMENT. There is no professional entertainment as such (although occasionally the crew may put on a little soirée). Dinner is the main event each evening, and, being a French product, dinner can provide several hours' worth of entertainment in itself.

SPA/FITNESS. There is no spa, fitness room, sauna, or steam room aboard *Le Ponant*. However, for recreation, there are water sports facilities, and these include an aft marina platform (from which you can swim), windsurfers, water-ski boat, scuba and snorkel equipment. Scuba diving is an extra-cost item, per dive.

Legend of the Seas
★★★★

Size: ....Large Resort Ship	Passenger Decks: 11	Cabins (with private balcony): 231
Tonnage: 69,130	Total Crew: 720	Cabins (wheelchair accessible): 17
Lifestyle: ....Standard	Passengers	Wheelchair accessibility ....Good
Cruise Line: Royal Caribbean International	(lower beds/all berths): 1,800/2,076	Cabin Current: ....110 and 220 volts
Former Names: ....none	Passenger Space Ratio	Elevators: 11
Builder: Chantiers de l'Atlantique (France)	(lower beds/all berths): 38.3/33.2	Casino (gaming tables): ....Yes
Original Cost: ....$325 million	Crew/Passenger Ratio	Slot Machines: ....Yes
Entered Service: ....May 1995	(lower beds/all berths): 2.5/2.8	Swimming Pools (outdoors): 2
Registry: ....The Bahamas	Cabins (total): 900	(1 with sliding roof)
Length (ft/m): 867.0/264.2	Size Range (sq ft/m): 137.7–1,147.4/	Swimming Pools (indoors): 0
Beam (ft/m): 105.0/32.0	12.8–106.6	Whirlpools: 4
Draft (ft/m): 23.9/7.3	Cabins (outside view): 575	Self-Service Launderette: ....No
Propulsion/Propellers: ....diesel	Cabins (interior/no view): 325	Dedicated Cinema/Seats: ....No
(40,200 kW)/2	Cabins (for one person): 0	Library: ....Yes

OVERALL SCORE: 1,414 OUT OF A POSSIBLE 2,000 POINTS

OVERVIEW. This vessel, sister to *Splendour of the Seas*, has a contemporary profile and a nicely tiered stern. The pool deck amidships overhangs the hull to provide an extremely wide deck, while still allowing the ship to navigate the Panama Canal. With engines placed midships, there is little noise and no noticeable vibration, and the ship has an operating speed of up to 24 knots.

The interior decor is colorful, but rather glitzy for European tastes, although it makes a change from the bland interiors of many UK-based ships (the ship is based in Britain during the summer, and features Europe/Med cruising for both American and British passengers) The outside light is brought inside in many places, with over 2 acres (8,000 sq. meters) of glass providing contact with sea and air. There's an innovative single-level sliding glass roof (not a magrodome) over the more formal setting of one of two swimming pools, providing a multi-activity, all-weather indoor-outdoor area, called the Solarium. The glass roof provides shelter for the Roman-style pool and the health and fitness facilities (which are good) and slides aft to cover the miniature golf course when required (both cannot be covered at the same time, however).

Golfers might enjoy the 18-hole, 6,000-sq. ft (560 sq.-meter) miniature golf course. It has the topography of a real course, complete with trees, foliage, grass, bridges, water hazards, and lighting for play at night. The holes themselves are 155-230 sq. ft (14.3–21.3 sq. meters).

Inside, two full entertainment decks are sandwiched between five decks full of cabins, so there are plenty of public rooms to lounge and drink in. A multi-tiered seven-deck-high atrium lobby, complete with a huge stainless steel

BERLITZ'S RATINGS

	Possible	Achieved
Ship	500	399
Accommodation	200	153
Food	400	227
Service	400	275
Entertainment	100	76
Cruise	400	284

sculpture, connects with the impressive Viking Crown Lounge via glass-walled lifts. The casino is expansive, incredibly glitzy but usually packed. The library, outside of which is a bust of Shakespeare, is a nice facility, with almost 2,000 books.

There is, sadly, no separate cinema. The casino could be somewhat disorienting, with its mirrored walls and lights flashing everywhere, although it is no different to those found in Las Vegas gaming halls, and it can be difficult to find relaxation areas without music (except for the Viking Crown Lounge in the daytime).

ACCOMMODATION. There are 17 different grades – rather too many – but no cabins for singles. Royal Caribbean International has designed a ship with much larger standard cabins than in any of the company's previous vessels except *Splendour of the Seas*.

Some cabins on Deck 8 also have a larger door for wheelchair access in addition to the 17 cabins for the physically disabled, and the ship is very accessible, with ample ramped areas and sloping decks. All cabins have a sitting area and beds that convert to double configuration, and there is ample closet and drawer space. There is not much space around the bed, though, and the showers could have been better designed. Those cabins with balconies have glass railings rather than steel/wood to provide less intrusive sightlines.

The largest accommodation is the Royal Suite, which is beautifully designed, finely decorated, and features a baby grand piano, whirlpool bathtub, and other fine amenities. Several quiet sitting areas are located adjacent to the best cabins amidships.

CUISINE. The Romeo and Juliet Dining Room has dramatic two-deck-high glass side walls, so many passengers both upstairs and downstairs can see both the ocean and each other in reflection (it would, perhaps, have been even better located at the stern), but it is quite noisy when full. Choose one of two seatings, or "My Time Dining" (eat when you want, during dining room hours) when you book.

A cavernous indoor-outdoor Windjammer Café, located towards the bow and above the bridge, has good views on three sides from large ocean-view windows. A good-sized snack area provides even more informal eating options.

ENTERTAINMENT. The "That's Entertainment" Theatre seats 802 and is a single-level showlounge with tiered seating levels: sightlines are generally good from almost all seats.

Strong cabaret acts are also featured in the main showlounge. A second entertainment lounge, the Anchors Aweigh Lounge, is where cabaret acts, including late-night adult (blue) comedy are featured. Other lounges and bars have live music for listening and dancing.

The entertainment throughout is upbeat (in fact, it is difficult to get away from music and noise), but is typical of the kind of resort hotel found ashore in Las Vegas. There is even background music in all corridors and elevators, and constant music outdoors on the pool deck. If you want a quiet relaxing holiday, you should choose another ship.

SPA/FITNESS. The ShipShape Fitness Center has a gymnasium (it is located on the port side of the ship, aft of the funnel), and has a small selection of high-tech muscle-pumping equipment. There is also an aerobics studio (classes are offered in a variety of keep fit regimes), a beauty salon, and a sauna, as well as treatment rooms for such pampering things as massages, facials, etc. While the facilities are quite small when compared with those aboard the company's newer ships, they are adequate for the short cruises that this ship operates.

For more sporting passengers, there is activity galore – including a rock-climbing wall, with several separate climbing tracks. It is located outdoors at the aft end of the funnel.

● **For more extensive general information about the Royal Caribbean experience, see pages 151–6.**

FUN FACTS

● Cruise ship design is interesting. The beauty of design lies in curves, not in straight lines. Today's large resort ships, designed merely for cruising in warm weather regions and not for voyaging across the North Atlantic (heaven forbid, the delivery voyage was enough), are made of straight lines. They are boxy and cold in appearance, although they provide much more usable space inside the ship (some call it warehouse cruising). Take a look at *Saga Ruby* (the former *Vistafjord*) and you won't find a straight line anywhere. Then look at *Carnival Imagination* and compare the two.

● Beatrice Muller, in her early 80s, makes her permanent home at sea. She lives year-round aboard Cunard Line's *Queen Victoria*, paying a set amount to reside in her chosen cabin. She prefers being aboard the ship rather than sit around in a retirement home in Britain's damp climate, and proves that the world is her oyster. She loves it because she doesn't have to deal with the daily drudgery of shopping, doesn't need a car, or pay electric, gas or telephone bills. She communicates with her family by using the computer center's email service.

● Cruise lines and charity go hand in hand. Cunard donated 1,500 pieces of classic furniture from the 1994 refit of *QE2* to the Salvation Army for its adult rehabilitation program. Crew aboard the same ship donate money to buy guide dogs for the blind, or an ambulance for the St. John's Ambulance Brigade in the UK. Princess Cruises made a "sizeable" contribution to UNICEF following the death of Audrey Hepburn in 1993 (she named the company's *Star Princess*, now operating as *Sea Princess* for Princess Cruises). Passengers of Hapag-Lloyd's *Europa* have donated more than 1 million euros to children's homes in Vietnam. Both Holland America Line and Princess Cruises have contributed heavily to the Raptor Center in Juneau, Alaska.

● Someone forgot to "score" the champagne bottle when Dame Judi Dench named *Carnival Legend* in Harwich, England, on August 21, 2002. On the first two tries, the bottle didn't break. Then Dame Judi took the bottle in her own hands and smashed it against the side of the ship. It broke, and the foam and champagne went all over her. She was dubbed Dame Judi Drench.

● In the mid-1960s there were 12 "bell boys" ("piccolos" in hotels-peak) aboard the Cunard Line's RMS *Queen Elizabeth* and *Queen Mary*. They manned the elevators and opened the doors to the various restaurants. Each day, before they were allowed to work, they all lined up and their fingernails were inspected. Those were the days.

Liberty of the Seas
★★★★

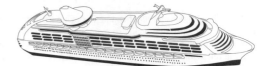

Size: . . . . .Large Resort Ship	Passenger Decks: 15	Cabins (with private balcony): 842
Tonnage: .154,407	Total Crew: 1,397	Cabins (wheelchair accessible): 32
Lifestyle: . . . . .Standard	Passengers	Wheelchair accessibility . . . . .Best
Cruise Line: Royal Caribbean International	(lower beds/all berths): 3,634/4,375	Cabin Current: . . . . .110 volts
Former Names: . . . . .none	Passenger Space Ratio	Elevators: 14
Builder: . . .Kvaerner Masa-Yards (Finland)	(lower beds/all berths): 42.0/35.3	Casino (gaming tables): . . . . .Yes
Original Cost: . . . .$590 million	Crew/Passenger Ratio	Slot Machines: . . . . .Yes
Entered Service: . . . . .Spring 2007	(lower beds/all berths): 2.6/3.1	Swimming Pools (outdoors): 2
Registry: . . . . .The Bahamas	Cabins (total): 1,817	Swimming Pools (indoors): 0
Length (ft/m): 1,112.2/339.0	Size Range (sq ft/m): 149.0–2,025.0/	Whirlpools: 6
Beam (ft/m): 184.0/56.0	13.8–188.1	Self-Service Launderette: . . . . .No
Draft (ft/m): 27.8/8/5	Cabins (outside view): 1,084	Dedicated Cinema/Seats: . . . . .No
Propulsion/Propellers: . . . . .diesel-electric	Cabins (interior/no view): 733	Library: . . . . .Yes
(kW)/4 azimuthing pods	Cabins (for one person): 0	

OVERALL SCORE: 1,510 OUT OF A POSSIBLE 2,000 POINTS

OVERVIEW. *Liberty of the Seas* (together with sister ships *Freedom of the Seas* and *Independence of the Seas*) is the largest ever purpose-built cruise ship. It is essentially split into three separate areas, rather like the Disney cruise ships – adults-only, family, or main.

The "wow" factor is its connection with water (of the seas) in the design of a dramatic water theme park afloat. By day, the H2O Zone (aft of the funnel) has an interactive water-themed play area for families that includes water cannons and spray fountains, water jets and ground gushers; by night the "water park" turns into a colourfully-lit sculpture garden. Meanwhile, the ship's central pool has become a sports pool, with grandstand seating and competitive games that include pole jousting. Other active sports facilities include an Everlast boxing ring, rock-climbing wall (10 ft taller than in the Voyager-class ships), in-line skating area, an ice-skating rink, and golf simulators.

The same facilities (public rooms, bars and lounges) featured in the Voyager-class ships have been incorporated, but with the addition of more conference and meetings facilities, extensive wi-fi capabilities and connectivity for cell phones. Other facilities include a large casino.

The cabin hallways have an extremely warm, attractive feel, with artwork cabinets and asymmetrical flow to lead you along and break up the monotony. In fact, there are plenty of colorful, even whimsical, decorative touches. Note that, if you meet someone you'd like to see again, you'll need to make an appointment and specify a location, for this really is a large, Las Vegas-style floating resort-city.

ACCOMMODATION. There is a wide range of cabins in 14

BERLITZ'S RATINGS

	Possible	Achieved
Ship	500	426
Accommodation	200	161
Food	400	235
Service	400	289
Entertainment	100	82
Cruise	400	317

categories and 21 price grades. The price depends on the grade, from the 14-person Presidential Suite to twin-bed two person interior (no view) cabins, and interior cabins that look into an inside shopping/strolling atrium promenade. There are many family-friendly cabins, good for family reunions.

Some accommodation examples (from large to small):

Presidential Family Suite: Two master bedrooms, each with twin beds (convertible to queen-size), private balcony, sofa bed, bar, private bathroom, bathtub, vanity, hair-dryer, closed-circuit flat screen TV and phone. Great views over the ship's fantail (stern). Occupants have access to the Concierge Club lounge and services. There is only one Presidential Family Suite on board (it can take up to 14, but this would be quite cramped). Size: 1,215 sq. ft. (112.8 sq. meters), plus balcony: 810 sq. ft (75.2 sq. meters), set with lounge area and dining table.

Royal Suite: Features a separate bedroom with king-size bed, private balcony, living room with queen-size sofa bed and private bathroom. Measures: 1,406 sq. ft.,(130.6 sq.meters); balcony 377 sq. ft. (35.0 sq.meters)

Royal Family Suite: Features two bedrooms with twin beds that convert to queen-size beds (one room has third and fourth Pullman beds), a private balcony, two bathrooms and living area with double sofa bed. Measures 588 sq. ft. (54.6 sq.meters); balcony 234 sq. ft. (21.7 sq.meters)

Owners Suite: Features include a queen-sized bed, private balcony, separate living area with queen-sized sofa bed, wet bar, vanity area, walk-in closet; bathroom with tub and shower, plus access to the Concierge Club lounge and attendant services. Sleeps up to five. Size: 506 sq. ft. (46 sq. meters) + Balcony: 131 sq. ft. (12.1 sq. meters).

Grand Suite: Two twin beds convertible to queen-size, a private balcony, sitting area (some with sofa bed), vanity area; bathroom with tub and shower. Access to the Concierge Club lounge and services. Sleeps up to four. Size: 381 sq. ft. (35.3 sq.meters) + Balcony: 89 sq. ft. (8.2 sq. meters).

Junior Suite: Two twin beds convertible to queen-size, private balcony, sitting area (some with sofa bed), vanity area; bathroom with tub and shower. Sleeps up to four. Size: 285.2 sq. ft. (26.5 sq.meters) + Balcony: 101 sq. ft. (9.3 sq.meters).

Superior Oceanview Cabin: Two twin beds convertible to queen-size, a private balcony, sitting area (some with sofa bed), vanity area; bathroom with shower. Sleeps 2 (some rooms sleep three or four). Size: 202 sq. ft. (18.7 sq. meters) + Balcony: 42 sq. ft. (3.9 sq. meters).

Deluxe Oceanview Cabin: Two twin beds convertible to queen-size, a private balcony, sitting area (some with sofa bed), vanity area; bathroom with shower. Sleeps 2 (some rooms sleep three or four). Size: 173 sq. ft. (16.0 sq. meters) + Balcony: 46 sq. ft. (4.2 sq. meters).

Promenade Cabin (interior, but overlooking the Royal Promenade): A view of the Royal Promenade with bay windows, two twin beds that can convert into queen-size, and private bathroom. Measures: 149 sq. ft. (13.8 sq.meters).

Promenade Family Cabin: Features two twin beds that can convert into queen-size, and private bathroom. Measures: 300 sq. ft. (27.8 sq.meters).

Interior (no view) Cabin: Two twin beds convertible to queen-size; private bathroom with shower. Sleeps two (some rooms sleep three or four). Size: 152sq. ft. (14.1 sq. meters).

Family Ocean-view Cabin: Located at the front of the ship, it contains two twin beds (convertible to queen-size), sofa and/or Pullman beds, sitting area; bathroom, with shower. Accommodates six, and features 48-inch round windows. Size: 265 sq. ft. (24.6 sq. meters).

All cabins have a private bathroom (with tub and shower, or shower only), vanity desk with hairdryer, mini-bar, personal safe, flat-screen TV, radio, and satellite telephone. A room service menu is provided. Suite occupants have access to a Concierge Lounge, for more personal service (this saves standing in line at the reception desk).

CUISINE. The main dining room is extremely large and is set on three levels (each has a theme and name: Galileo, Isaac, and Leonardo). A dramatic staircase connects all three levels, and huge, fat support pillars obstruct the sightlines from many seats. All three have the same menus and food. The dining venues are all non-smoking. Choose one of two seatings, or "My Time Dining" (eat when you want, during dining room hours) when you book. Tables are for four, six, eight 10 or 12.

Alternative Dining Options: Alternative dining options for casual and informal meals at all hours (according to company statements) include:

● *Promenade Café:* for continental breakfast, all-day pizzas (Sorento's), sandwiches and coffee (in paper cups).

● *Windjammer Café:* for casual buffet-style breakfast, lunch and light dinner (except for the cruise's last night).

● *Island Grill* (a section of the Windjammer Café): for casual dinner (no reservations necessary) featuring a grill and open kitchen.

● *Portofino:* this is an "upscale" (non-smoking) Euro-Italian restaurant, open for dinner only. Reservations are required, and a there's gratuity of $20 per person). Choices include: antipasti, soup, salad, pasta, main dish, dessert, cheese and coffee (the menu does not change during the cruise).

● *Chops Grill:* an intimate restaurant for steaks and seafood. A cover charge of $20 applies.

● *Johnny Rockets,* a retro 1950s all-day, all-night diner-style eatery that has hamburgers, hot dogs and other fast-food items, malt shakes, and jukebox hits, with both indoor and outdoor seating (indoor tables have a mini-jukebox), and all-singing, all-dancing waitresses that'll knock your socks off, if you can stand the volume. Cover charge: $3.95.

● *Sprinkles:* for round-the-clock ice cream and yoghurt, pastries and coffee.

ENTERTAINMENT. The Showlounge is a stunning space, located at the forward end of the ship and spanning the height of five decks (with only a few slim pillars and almost no disruption of sightlines). The room has a hydraulic orchestra pit and huge stage areas, together with sonic-boom loud sound, and superb lighting equipment. In addition, the ship has an array of cabaret acts. The strongest are featured in the main showlounge, while others are presented in the Nightclub, the venue for late-night adults-only comedy.

The most entertaining shows, however, are the Spectaculars on ice. There is also a television studio (in case you thought you'd need one aboard a cruise ship), located adjacent to rooms that could be used, for example, for trade show exhibit space (good for conventions at sea).

One performance not to be missed is the "Greatest Show at Sea" Parade – a superbly executed 15-minute fun extravaganza that bumbles along the Royal Promenade at turtle speed; it replicates the parade of stars and animals at a circus of yesteryear (Barnum and Bailey's meets cruise ship). This is when it's really good to have one of those interior-view atrium cabins (sadly, the windows don't open, so you can't take photographs); otherwise, get a position early along the Royal Promenade.

SPA/FITNESS. The ShipShape health spa is large. It includes a large aerobics room, fitness center, treatment rooms, and men's and women's sauna/steam rooms and relaxation areas. The spa facility is operated by Steiner. Some (basic) exercise classes are free, but the good ones (examples: yoga, personal training) cost extra. Sample prices: Swedish Massage $119 (50 mins); Couples massage $269 (50 mins); facial $119 (50 mins), plus tip.

More active passengers can bodyboard, go boxing (in the full-size boxing ring in the middle of the spa), climb (the rock-climbing wall at the back of the funnel housing), jog, putt, swim, skate, step, surf, workout and more (including play basketball and volleyball).

● **For more extensive general information on what a Royal Caribbean cruise is like, see pages 151–6.**

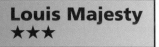

Louis Majesty
★★★

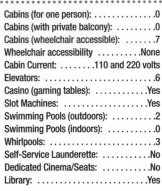

Size:	Mid-Size Ship	Passenger Decks:	.9	Cabins (for one person):	.0
Tonnage:	40,876	Total Crew:	.620	Cabins (with private balcony):	.0
Lifestyle:	Standard	Passengers		Cabins (wheelchair accessible):	.7
Cruise Line:	Louis Cruises	(lower beds/all berths):	1,462/1,792	Wheelchair accessibility	None
Former Names:	*Norwegian Majesty,*	Passenger Space Ratio		Cabin Current:	110 and 220 volts
	Royal Majesty	(lower beds/all berths):	27.9/22.8	Elevators:	.6
Builder:	Kvaerner Masa-Yards STX (Finland)	Crew/Passenger Ratio		Casino (gaming tables):	Yes
Original Cost:	$229 million	(lower beds/all berths):	.2.0/2.5	Slot Machines:	Yes
Entered Service:	Sept 1992/Dec 2009	Navigation Officers:	Norwegian	Swimming Pools (outdoors):	.2
Registry:	Malta	Cabins (total):	.731	Swimming Pools (indoors):	.0
Length (ft/m):	679.4/207.10	Size Range (sq ft/m):	118.4–374.5/	Whirlpools:	.3
Beam (ft/m):	90.5/27.60		11.0–34.8	Self-Service Launderette:	No
Draft (ft/m):	20.3/6.20	Cabins (outside view):	.481	Dedicated Cinema/Seats:	No
Propulsion/Propellers:diesel (21,120 kW)/2		Cabins (interior/no view):	.249	Library:	Yes

---

BERLITZ'S OVERALL SCORE: 1,242 OUT OF A POSSIBLE 2,000 POINTS

OVERVIEW. After many years as NCL's *Norwegian Majesty*, the all-white ship was transferred to Louis Cruises in 2009 and given a short refurbishment. Smart and modestly stylish, it is generally a well-designed vessel.

Inside, it is quite pretty, and is tastefully appointed, with lots of wood paneling and chrome/copper accents, reasonably discreet lighting, soothing colors, no glitz and almost no neon lighting. Wide passageways provide a feeling of inner spaciousness, and the ship has a nice touch of elegance. The circular lobby is bright and classical.

There are several public rooms, bars and lounges. There's also a small library, and card room. The Monte Carlo Casino is large and equipped with blackjack and roulette tables, and lots of slot machines. "Kids' Corner" has a full program of activities.

Louis Majesty will provide you with a comfortable cruise experience in warm, fairly elegant surroundings, with generally good food, and a decent helping of hospitality from a friendly crew. The onboard currency is the euro.

Passenger niggles include the fact that there are no cushioned pads for the plastic deck chairs. Also, the buffet area is simply too small for the number of passengers carried.

ACCOMMODATION. There are 17 different price grades. The suites have concierge service and extra goodies such as late afternoon snacks and hors d'oeuvre items. Although they cannot be considered large, they are quite well equipped, and come with DVDs and TV sets.

Almost all other outside-view and interior (no view) cabins are on the small side, but quite comfortable. The closets are really small, so suitcases have to be stored under

BERLITZ'S RATINGS		
	Possible	Achieved
Ship	500	321
Accommodation	200	137
Food	400	230
Service	400	246
Entertainment	100	65
Cruise	400	243

the bed to keep them out of the way. The bathrooms are a little tight, although there is a generous amount of room in the shower enclosures.

CUISINE. The main dining rooms are Seven Seas, with 636 seats, and the more intimate Four Seasons, with 266 seats. They can be rather noisy, because the tables are very close together. The food, menu, creativity and service are basically quite sound, with a good selection of breads and bread rolls. There is also a 56-seat Le Bistro Restaurant, which serves Italian- and Continental-style cuisine for alternative dinners in an intimate environment (no reservations needed).

For self-serve meals in casual surroundings, Café Royale is a small buffet venue with 112 seats. It is open for breakfast, lunch and snacks. An outdoor grill serves fast food items, including pizza. A small coffee bar/lounge serves a variety of coffees. The wine list is quite decent and moderately priced, though you won't find any vintage wines, and the glasses are small. All dining spots are non-smoking.

ENTERTAINMENT. The Palace Showlounge, located aft, is shaped like an amphitheater, with banquette and individual tub chairs. Some 14 pillars obstruct the sightlines. The ship carries a number of bands and solo entertaining musicians.

SPA/FITNESS. Bodywaves, the spa/fitness center, is adjacent to the disco at the aft of Promenade Deck, and contains a small gymnasium with muscle-toning equipment, an aerobics exercise area, men's and women's saunas and cramped changing rooms, and Vanity Fair beauty salon. The spa/fitness center is operated by a concession.

Maasdam
★★★★

Size: . . . . .Mid-Size Ship	Passenger Decks: 10	Cabins (with private balcony): 150
Tonnage: 55,451	Total Crew: 557	Cabins (wheelchair accessible): 6
Lifestyle: . . . . .Premium	Passengers	Wheelchair accessibility . . . . .Good
Cruise Line: . . . . . .Holland America Line	(lower beds/all berths): 1,266/1,627	Cabin Current: . . . . .110 and 220 volts
Former Names: . . . . .none	Passenger Space Ratio	Elevators: 8
Builder: . . . . .Fincantieri (Italy)	(lower beds/all berths): 43.8/34.0	Casino (gaming tables): . . . . .Yes
Original Cost: . . . .$215 million	Crew/Passenger Ratio	Slot Machines: . . . . .Yes
Entered Service: . . . . .Dec 1993	(lower beds/all berths): 2.2/2.9	Swimming Pools (outdoors): 1
Registry: . . . . .The Netherlands	Cabins (total): 632	Swimming Pools (indoors): 1
Length (ft/m): 719.3/219.30	Size Range (sq ft/m): 186.2–1,124.8/	(magrodome)
Beam (ft/m): 101.0/30.80	17.3–104.5	Whirlpools: 2
Draft (ft/m): 24.6/7.50	Cabins (outside view): 502	Self-Service Launderette: . . . . .Yes
Propulsion/Propellers: . . . . .diesel-electric	Cabins (interior/no view): 131	Dedicated Cinema/Seats: Yes/249
(34,560 kW)/2	Cabins (for one person): 0	Library: . . . . .Yes

OVERALL SCORE: 1,412 OUT OF A POSSIBLE 2,000 POINTS

OVERVIEW. *Maasdam* is one of a series of four almost identical ships in the same series – the others are *Statendam, Ryndam* and *Veendam*. Although the exterior styling is rather angular (some would say boxy – the funnel certainly is), it is softened and balanced somewhat by the fact that the hull is painted black. There is a full wrap-around teak promenade deck outdoors – excellent for strolling, and, thankfully, no sign of synthetic turf anywhere. The sun-loungers on the exterior promenade deck are wood, and have comfortable cushioned pads, while those at the swimming pool on Lido Deck are of white plastic. Holland America Line keeps its ships clean and tidy, and there is good passenger flow throughout the public areas.

In the interiors of this "S" -class ship, an asymmetrical layout helps to reduce bottlenecks and congestion. Most of the public rooms are concentrated on two decks, Promenade Deck, and Upper Promenade Deck, which creates a spacious feel to the ship's interiors. In general, a restrained approach to interior styling is taken, using a mixture of contemporary materials combined with traditional woods and ceramics. There is, fortunately, little "glitz" anywhere.

What is noticeable is the array of artworks throughout the ship (costing about $2 million), assembled and nicely displayed to represent the fine Dutch heritage of Holland America Line and to present a balance between standard itineraries and onboard creature comforts. Several oil paintings of former Holland America Line ships by Stephen Card (an ex-captain) adorn stairway landings. Also noticeable are the fine flower arrangements throughout the public areas and foyers – used to good effect to brighten up what to some is dull decor.

BERLITZ'S RATINGS

	Possible	Achieved
Ship	500	372
Accommodation	200	150
Food	400	248
Service	400	287
Entertainment	100	72
Cruise	400	283

Atop the ship, with forward facing views that wrap around the sides, is the Crow's Nest Lounge. By day it makes a fine observation lounge, with large ocean-view windows, while by night it turns into a nightclub with extremely variable lighting.

The atrium foyer is three decks high, although its light-catching green glass sculpted centerpiece (*Totem* by Luciano Vistosi, composed of almost 2,000 pieces of glass) makes it look a little crowded, and leaves little room in front of the purser's office (called the Front Office). A hydraulic glass roof covers the reasonably-sized swimming pool/whirlpools and central Lido area, whose focal point is a large dolphin sculpture, so that this can be used in either fine or poor weather.

Maasdam, a well-built ship, has fairly decent interior decor. Holland America Line is constantly fine-tuning its performance and its regular passengers (almost all of whom are North American – there are few international passengers) find the company's ships comfortable and well-run. The company continues its strong maritime traditions, although the food and service components still let the rest of the cruise experience down. Perhaps the ship's best asset is its friendly and personable Filipino and Indonesian crew, although communication can prove frustrating and service is inconsistent. The onboard currency is the US dollar.

This ship has a large, relaxing Leyden Library; a card-room, an Explorer's Lounge (good for afternoon tea and after-dinner coffee), a Crows Nest (the ship's observation lounge that doubles as a late-night spot and discotheque), an intimate Piano Bar, and, of course, a casino.

Holland America Line's many repeat passengers always seem to enjoy the fact that social dancing is always on the menu. In the final analysis, however, the score for this ship ends up just a disappointing tad under what it could be if the food and food service staff were more memorable (more professional training might help).

An escalator travels between two of the lower decks (one of which was originally planned to be the embarkation point), but it is almost pointless. The charge to use the washing machines and dryers in the self-service launderette is petty, particularly for suite occupants, as they pay high prices for their cruises. The men's urinals in public restrooms are unusually high.

ACCOMMODATION. The accommodation ranges from small interior (no view) cabins to a large penthouse suite, in 17 price categories. The price you pay will depend on the grade, size and location you choose. All cabin televisions receive CNN and TNT.

The interior (no view) and outside (with a view) standard cabins feature twin beds that convert to a queen-size bed, and there is a separate living space with sofa and coffee table. However, although the drawer space is generally good, the closet space is actually very tight, particularly for long cruises (although more than adequate for a 7-night cruise). Bathrobes are also provided for all suites/cabins, as are hairdryers, and a small range of personal toiletries (soap, conditioning shampoo, body lotion, shower cap, vanity kit). The bathrooms are quite well laid out, but the bathtubs are small units better described as shower tubs.

On Navigation Deck, 28 suites have accommodation for up to four. These suites also have in-suite dining as an alternative to the dining room, for private, reclusive meals. These are very spacious, tastefully decorated and well laid-out suites, and have a separate, good-sized living room, bedroom with two lower beds (convertible to a king-size bed), dressing room, plenty of closet and drawer space (walk-in closet), marble bathroom with Jacuzzi tub and separate toilet/washroom with bidet.

The largest accommodation of all is a penthouse suite. There is only one, on the starboard side of Navigation Deck at the forward staircase. It has a king-sized bed (TV and video player) and vanity desk; large walk-in closet with superb drawer space, oversize whirlpool bath (it could seat four) and separate shower enclosure, separate washroom with toilet, bidet and washbasin; living room with writing desk, large television and full set of audio equipment; dressing room, large private balcony (with teak lounge chairs and drinks tables, dining table and four chairs), pantry (with large refrigerator, toaster unit, and full coffee/tea making facilities and food preparation area, and a separate entrance from the hallway), mini-bar/refrigerator, a guest toilet and floor-to-ceiling windows. There is no bell push.

CUISINE. The Rotterdam Dining Room, which is a non-smoking venue, spans two decks. It is located at the stern of the ship, is quite dramatic, and has a grand staircase, panoramic views on three sides, and a music balcony. Both open seating and fixed (assigned tables and times) seating are available, while breakfast and lunch are open-seating (you'll be seated by restaurant staff when you enter). The waiter stations in the dining room are very noisy for anyone seated adjacent to them.

Alternative dining option: Added in 2003, the Pinnacle Grill is located just forward of the balcony level of the main dining room on the starboard side. The 66-seat dining spot features Pacific Northwest cuisine (Dungeness crab, Alaska salmon, halibut and other regional specialties). The new venue (reservations are necessary, and a cover/service charge of $20 applies) was created out of the former private dining wing of the main dining room, plus a slice of the Explorer's Lounge. A Bulgari show plate, Rosenthal china, Reidel wine glasses, and Frette table linen are used. The Pinnacle Grill is a much better dining experience than the main dining room and worth it for that special celebration.

For more casual evening eating, the Lido Buffet is open for casual dinners on all except the last night of each cruise, in an open-seating arrangement. Tables are set with crisp linens, flatware and stemware. A set menu is featured, and this includes a choice of four entreés.

The dual-line, self-serve Lido Buffet (one side is for smokers, the other side for non-smokers) is also the place for casual breakfasts and lunches. Again there is much use of canned fruits (good for older passengers with few teeth) and packeted items, although there are several commercial low-calorie salad dressings. The beverage station also lets it down, for it is no better than those found in family outlets ashore in the United States. In addition, a poolside grill provides basic American hamburgers and hot dogs.

Passengers will need to eat in the Lido Cafe on any days when the dining room is closed for lunch (this is typically once or twice per cruise, depending on the itinerary).

ENTERTAINMENT. The Showroom at Sea, located at the forward part of the ship, spans two decks, with banquette seating on both main and upper levels. It is basically a well-designed room, but the ceiling is low and the sight lines from the balcony level are quite poor.

SPA/FITNESS. The Ocean Spa is located one deck below the navigation bridge at the very forward part of the ship. It includes a gymnasium (with all the latest muscle-pumping exercise machines, including an abundance of treadmills) with ocean views, an aerobics exercise area, large beauty salon with ocean-view windows to the port side, several treatment rooms, and men's and women's sauna, steam room and changing areas.

● **For more extensive general information on what a Holland America Line cruise is like, see pages 139–42.**

Majesty of the Seas
★★★

Size:	Large Resort Ship	Passenger Decks:	11	Cabins (with private balcony):	62
Tonnage:	73,941	Total Crew:	827	Cabins (wheelchair accessible):	4
Lifestyle:	Standard	Passengers		Wheelchair accessibility	Fair
Cruise Line: Royal Caribbean International		(lower beds/all berths):	2,380/2,774	Cabin Current:	110 volts
Former Names:	none	Passenger Space Ratio		Elevators:	11
Builder: .Chantiers de l'Atlantique (France)		(lower beds/all berths):	30.8/26.3	Casino (gaming tables):	Yes
Original Cost:	$300 million	Crew/Passenger Ratio		Slot Machines:	Yes
Entered Service:	Apr 1992	(lower beds/all berths):	2.8/3.3	Swimming Pools (outdoors):	2
Registry:	The Bahamas	Cabins (total):	1,190	Swimming Pools (indoors):	0
Length (ft/m):	879.9/268.2	Size Range (sq ft/m):	118.4–670.0/	Whirlpools:	2
Beam (ft/m):	105.9/32.3		11.0–62.2	Self-Service Launderette:	No
Draft (ft/m):	24.9/7.6	Cabins (outside view):	732	Dedicated Cinema/Seats:	No
Propulsion/Propellers:	diesel	Cabins (interior/no view):	458	Library:	Yes
	(21,844 kW)/2	Cabins (for one person):	0		

OVERALL SCORE: 1,246 OUT OF A POSSIBLE 2,000 POINTS

OVERVIEW. When first introduced, this ship (together with its two sisters, *Monarch of the Seas* and *Sovereign of the Seas*) was an innovative vessel. Royal Caribbean International's trademark Viking Crown lounge and bar surrounds the funnel and provides a stunning view, but it has no soul and looks dated. The open deck space is very cramped when full, as aboard any large ship, although there seems to be plenty of it. There is a basketball court.

The interior layout is a little awkward, as it is designed in a vertical stack, with most of the public rooms located aft, and the accommodation located forward (this ensures quiet areas) There is, however, an impressive array of spacious and elegant public rooms, although the decor calls to mind the IKEA school of interior design, despite a re-vitalization in 2007 when all cabins were refreshed and more casual eating options introduced. A stunning five-deck-high Centrum lobby has cascading stairways and two glass-walled elevators.

There is a decent two-level showlounge and a selection of shops, albeit with lots of tacky merchandise, and an "All items at $10" store – good for souvenirs. Casino gamers will find blackjack, craps, Caribbean stud poker and roulette tables, plus an array of slot machines in Casino Royale.

Among the public rooms, the library is a nice feature for quite relaxation, and there is a decent selection of books. An internet-connect center has 10 workstations, but the cost if quite high; the ship is also wi-fi enabled – but there is a cost, of course. The entertainment program is quite sound, and there is a decent range of children's and teens' programs (teens have their own chill-out room – adults not allowed) and cheerful youth counselors.

BERLITZ'S RATINGS

	Possible	Achieved
Ship	500	333
Accommodation	200	119
Food	400	221
Service	400	260
Entertainment	100	66
Cruise	400	247

This fairly smart-looking resort ship provides a well tuned, yet impersonal, short cruise experience (3- and 4-day Bahamas cruises year-round from Miami) for a lot of passengers. The dress code is very casual. In the final analysis, you will probably be overwhelmed by the public spaces, and under whelmed by the size of the cabins. Because the public rooms are mostly located aft (accommodation is located in the forward section of the ship), there is often a long wait for elevators, particularly at peak times (after dinner, shows, and talks). But at least the restrooms are quite welcoming.

ACCOMMODATION. There are 17 price categories. The price will depend on the grade, size and location you choose. **Suites:** Thirteen suites on Bridge Deck are reasonably large and nicely furnished (the largest is the Royal Suite), with separate living and sleeping spaces. They provide more space, with better service and more perks than standard-grade accommodation.

Standard Cabins: The standard outside-view and interior (no view) cabins are incredibly small, however, although an arched window treatment and colorful soft furnishings do give the illusion of more space. Almost all cabins have twin beds that can be converted to a queen-sized or double bed configuration, together with moveable bedside tables, and flat-screen TV sets. All of the standard cabins have very little closet and drawer space (you will need some luggage engineering to stow your cases). You should, therefore, think of packing only minimal clothing, which is all you really need for a short cruise.

All cabins have a private bathroom, with shower enclosure, toilet and washbasin. All are provided with good mattresses, and duvets.

CUISINE. There are two main dining rooms: Moonlight, located on the lowest level of the atrium lobby, and Starlight, one deck higher. Choose one of two seatings, or "My Time Dining" (eat when you want, during dining room hours) when you book (tables for two to eight). The dining operation is well orchestrated, with emphasis on highly programmed (insensitive), extremely hurried service that many find intrusive.

For casual breakfasts and lunches, the Windjammer Marketplace is the place to go. It is split into various specialty areas including American, Asian, Latin, and Mediterranean fare. Compass Deli is a bar in which you can make up your own sandwich. Also added in the 2007 refit is a Johnny Rockets 1950s retro diner for fast foods such as hamburgers and hot dogs, sodas and shakes, (a $3.95 cover charge applies); it is located on the new upper deck section of the Windjammer Marketplace. Additionally and at no extra cost, there is Sorrento's for American-Italian pizzas. All dining venues are non-smoking.

For coffee fans, Café Latte-tudes serves Seattle's Best Coffee brand (extra cost) in paper cups. And for ice cream lovers, there's Freeze Ice Cream.

ENTERTAINMENT. A Chorus Line is the ship's principal show lounge; it has both main and balcony levels, with banquette seating, but many pillars supporting the balcony level provide less than good sightlines from the side seats on the lower level.

Royal Caribbean's large-scale production shows are extremely colorful spectaculars that will remind you of Las Vegas casino hotel shows, with their high-energy hype, presentation and glitz. They are fast-moving, razzle-dazzle shows that rely a lot on lighting and special effects, but have little or no storyline, often poor linkage between themes and scenes, and choreography that is more stepping in place rather than dancing. Strong cabaret acts are also featured in the main showlounge.

The entertainment throughout is upbeat (in fact, it is difficult to get away from music and noise), but is typical of the kind of resort hotel found ashore in Las Vegas. There is even background music in all corridors and lifts, and constant music outdoors on the pool deck.

SPA/FITNESS. The Majesty Day Spa – much improved in the 2007 refit – has a gymnasium with aft-facing views (it is located at the aft of the ship, and a selection of high-tech muscle-pumping equipment. There is also an aerobics studio, and classes are offered in a variety of keep-fit regimes. There is also a beauty salon, and a sauna, and 10 treatment rooms for pampering massages, facials, etc. While the facilities are not as extensive as those aboard the company's newer ships, they are adequate for the short cruises that this ship operates.

For the more sporting, there is activity galore – including a rock-climbing wall, with several separate climbing tracks. It is located outdoors at the aft end of the funnel.

● **For more extensive general information about the Royal Caribbean cruise experience, see pages 151–6.**

EXPEDITIONS: DID YOU KNOW...

● that Quark Expeditions made maritime history in July/ August 1991, when its chartered Russian icebreaker, *Sovetskiy Soyuz*, made a spectacular 21-day voyage to negotiate a passage from Murmansk, Russia, to Nome, Alaska, across the North Pole? Although the polar ice cap had been navigated by the US nuclear submarines *Skate* and *Nautilus*, as well as by dirigible and airplane, this was the first passenger ship to make the hazardous crossing.

● that in 1984, Salen Lindblad Cruising made maritime history by negotiating a westbound voyage through the Northwest Passage, a 41-day epic that started from St. John's, Newfoundland, in Canada, and ended at Yokohama, Japan? The search for a Northwest Passage to the Orient attracted brave explorers for more than four centuries. Despite numerous attempts and loss of life, including Henry Hudson in 1610, a "white passage" to the East remained an elusive dream. Amundsen's 47-ton ship *Gjoa* eventually navigated the route in 1906, taking three years to do so. It was not until 1943 that a Canadian ship, *St. Roch*, became the first vessel in history to make the passage in a single season. *Lindblad Explorer*

became the 34th vessel, and the first cruise vessel, to complete the Northwest Passage.

● that the most expensive expedition cruise excursion was a cruise/dive to visit the resting place of RMS *Titanic* aboard the two deep-ocean submersibles *Mir I* and *Mir II* used in James Cameron's Hollywood blockbuster. Just 60 participants went as observers in 1998, and another 60 were taken in 1999.

● that a passenger once asked the operations director of a well-known expedition cruise ship where the best shops were in Antarctica? His reply: "On board, madam!"

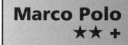

Size:	Mid-Size Ship	Passenger Decks:	8	Cabins (with private balcony):	0
Tonnage:	22,080	Total Crew:	356	Cabins (wheelchair accessible):	2
Lifestyle:	Standard	Passengers		Wheelchair accessibility	Fair
Cruise Line:	Transocean Tours	(lower beds/all berths):	848/915	Cabin Current:	110 and 220 volts
Former Names:	*Aleksandr Pushkin*	Passenger Space Ratio		Elevators:	4
Builder:	VEB Mathias Thesen Werft	(lower beds/all berths):	26.0/24.1	Casino (gaming tables):	No
	(Germany)	Crew/Passenger Ratio		Slot Machines:	No
Original Cost:	n/a	(lower beds/all berths):	2.3/2.5	Swimming Pools (outdoors):	1
Entered Service:	Apr 1966/Apr 2008	Cabins (total):	425	Swimming Pools (indoors):	0
Registry:	The Bahamas	Size Range (sq ft/m):	93.0–484.0/8.6–44.9	Whirlpools:	3
Length (ft/m):	578.4/176.28	Cabins (outside view):	292	Self-Service Launderette:	No
Beam (ft/m):	77.4/23.60	Cabins (interior/no view):	133	Dedicated Cinema/Seats:	No
Draft (ft/m):	26.8/8.17	Cabins (for one person):	(many doubles	Library:	Yes
Propulsion/Propellers:	diesel(14,444 kW)/2		sold for single occupancy)		

OVERALL SCORE: 1,082 OUT OF A POSSIBLE 2,000 POINTS

OVERVIEW. This ship was built as one of five almost identical sister ships for the Russian/Ukrainian fleet; the others were *Ivan Franko, Mikhail Lermontov, Shota Rustaveli,* and *Taras Shevchenko* – all named after Russian and Ukrainian writers. It was originally constructed to re-open the Leningrad to Montreal transatlantic route in 1966, after a long absence since 1949. The vessel has a traditional "real-ship" profile, an extremely strong ice-strengthened hull, and huge storage spaces for long voyages.

The now-defunct Orient Lines and its single ship, *Marco Polo,* was bought by Norwegian Cruise Line in 1998, the ship having undergone a $20 million transformation in 1992–4, including the fitting of stabilizers. In 2007 NCL sold Orient Lines and *Marco Polo* passed sold to Greek owners Global Maritime. In 2008, it began a charter operation for Germany's Transocean Tours – who, as it happens, had chartered the same ship some 20 years previously. Although the plan was to operate it until 2012, Transocean Tours sub-chartered the ship to Cruise & Maritime Voyages, the UK's newest cruise line. Having had a £3 million refit/refurbishment in 2009, it now operates child-free cruises exclusively from the UK with Tilbury (London International Cruise Terminal) as the ship's home port.

Marco Polo is fitted with the latest navigational aids and biological waste treatment center, and carries 10 Zodiac landing craft for in-depth shore trips in eco-sensitive areas.

This is a comfortable vessel throughout and, because it has a deep draft, rides well in unkind sea conditions. There are two large, forward-facing open-deck viewing areas. There is also a helicopter-landing pad. The teakwood-decked aft swimming pool/lido deck area is kept in good

BERLITZ'S RATINGS

	Possible	Achieved
Ship	500	273
Accommodation	200	120
Food	400	198
Service	400	219
Entertainment	100	56
Cruise	400	216

condition. Joggers and walkers can circle around the ship – not on the promenade deck, but one deck above, although this goes past vast air intakes that are noisy, and the walkway is narrow.

As soon as you walk aboard, you feel a warm, welcoming, homely ambiance. There is a wide range of public rooms, most of which are arranged on one horizontal deck. A sense of spaciousness pervades, as most have high ceilings. The interior decor is quite tasteful, with careful use of mirrored surfaces, as well as colors that do not clash and are relaxing but not boring; the subdued lighting helps maintain an air of calmness and relaxation.

Although this ship is more than 40 years old, it is in remarkably fine shape. Indeed, it's in better shape than many ships only 10 years old, and its interiors are constantly being refurbished and refreshed.

All in all, *Marco Polo* operates well-planned destination-intensive cruises, and offers really good value for money in very comfortable, unpretentious but tasteful surroundings, while a friendly and accommodating crew helps to make a cruise a pleasant, no-hassle experience.

The onboard currency is the British pound. Gratuities are automatically applied to your onboard account (£5 per person, per night; £4 for cruises longer than 16 nights).

Passenger niggles: There is no observation lounge with forward-facing views over the ship's bows. There are many "lips" or raised thresholds, so you need to be on your guard when walking through the ship, and particularly when negotiating the exterior stairways, which could prove difficult for mobility-limited passengers.

SUITABLE FOR: *Marco Polo* is best suited to couples and single travelers of mature years who enjoy visiting interesting destinations in the comfort of a ship that is traditional in style, unpretentious yet pleasing, and without the trappings of much entertainment or organized parlor games.

ACCOMMODATION. The cabins, which come in 15 price grades, depending on location and size, are a profusion of different sizes and configurations. All are pleasingly decorated, practical units with good, solid, rich wood cabinetry, wood and mirror-fronted closets, adequate drawer and storage space, TV set, thin cotton bathrobe (upper grades only), and bathroom-mounted hairdryer and non-vacuum, non-noisy toilets. Carpets, curtains and bedspreads are all nicely color-coordinated. Weak points include extremely poor sound insulation between cabins – you can probably hear you neighbours brushing their hair – and the fact that the bathrooms are small, with little storage space for toiletries, which is a particular concern during long cruises.

The largest accommodation is found in two suites: Dynasty and Mandarin, on Columbus Deck. These have a separate living room, and marble bathroom with tub/shower, walk-in closet, refrigerator, and a TV set/DVD unit. Slightly smaller are two Junior Suites, on Pacific Deck. All suites have superior locations on port and starboard sides for forward-facing views over the ship's bow.

Also quite comfortable are the Superior Deluxe oceanview cabins that have two lower beds (some can be converted to a queen-sized bed), marble bathroom with tub/shower, and refrigerator.

Some cabins on Upper Deck and Sky Deck have lifeboat-obstructed views. It would be advisable to avoid cabins 310/312 as these are located close to the engine room doorway and the noise level is considerable. No cabins have a balcony because the ship was built for long-distance ocean/sea crossings before they became popular.

CUISINE/DINING. The Waldorf, located in the center of the ship, is nicely decorated in soft pastel colors, practical in design, and functions well, but it has a low ceiling, is noisy, and the tables are very close together. There are two seatings, with tables for two to 10, and good place settings/china. The food itself is of a modest standard, but presentation, quality and taste could certainly be improved. The wine and prices are reasonable, although most wines are young.

Marco's Restaurant is the place to head for informal self-serve breakfasts and lunches – there is seating inside as well as outdoors around the ship's single, aft swimming pool. On some evenings during each cruise, it also becomes an alternative dining spot for about 75 people. Reservations are required, but there is no extra charge.

A 15% gratuity is added to all bar and wine accounts. The onboard currency is the euro.

ENTERTAINMENT. The Ambassador Lounge is the principal venue for shows, cabaret acts, and lectures. A single-level room, it has banquette seating and fairly decent sightlines, although there are several pillars to obstruct the view from several seats. Entertainment is low-key and low-budget, and consists of a few cabaret acts (singers, magicians, comedians and others).

There's live music for social dancing and listening in several of the ship's bars and cocktail lounges.

SPA/FITNESS. This is an older ship that was built when spa and wellbeing facilities were not really thought about. A Health Spa was added in a later refit. It is located aft on Upper Deck, and contains a small gymnasium (it's not large, but there are a few treadmills, exercycles, and some muscle-toning equipment), a beauty salon, a sauna, changing facilities, and treatment rooms (for massages, facials, and other body pampering treatments).

The spa is operated by Mandara Spa, and treatments have a Far Eastern flavor (Indonesian facials, coconut body polish, aromatherapy massages).

WASTE DISPOSAL

Environmental concerns are taken very seriously by the cruise industry. Cruise ships must be capable of efficient handling of garbage and waste materials, as trash generated by passengers and crew must be managed, stored, and disposed of efficiently and economically. The larger the ship, the more waste is created, and the greater the need for reliable disposal systems.

The sheer magnitude of waste materials can be highly problematic, especially on long cruises. If solid waste is not burnable, or cannot be disposed of overboard (this must be biodegradable), it must be stored for later off-loading and disposal on land.

The latest cruise ships have "zero-discharge" facilities. These include incinerators and food waste handling systems that include vacuum transportation from feeding stations in all galleys and food preparation areas, recycling and storage systems for ash, glass, metal and paper. But many older cruise ships have outdated garbage handling equipment.

Food waste is typically sent to a pulping machine that has been partially filled with water. Cutting mechanisms reduce the waste and allow it to pass through a special sizing ring to be pumped directly overboard or into a holding tank or an incinerator when the ship is within three-mile limits.

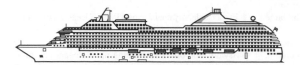

Marina
NOT YET RATED

Size: ....Mid-Size Ship	Total Crew: 800	Cabins (wheelchair accessible): 6
Tonnage: 65,000	Passengers	Wheelchair accessibility ....Good
Lifestyle: ....Premium	(lower beds/all berths): 1,258/1,258	Cabin Current: ....110, 220 volts
Cruise Line: ....Oceania Cruises	Passenger Space Ratio	Elevators: 6
Former Names: ....none	(lower beds/all berths):........51.6/51.6	Casino (gaming tables): ....Yes
Builder: ....Fincantieri (Italy)	Crew/Passenger Ratio	Slot Machines: ....Yes
Original Cost: ....$530 million	(lower beds/all berths): 1.5/1.5	Swimming Pools (outdoors): 1
Entered Service: ....Jan 2011	Cabins (total): 629	Swimming Pools (indoors): 0
Registry: ....Marshall Islands	Size Range (sq ft/m): 172.2–2,000/	Whirlpools: 3
Length (ft/m): 776.5/236.7	16.0–185.0	Self-Service Launderette:...........Yes
Beam (ft/m): 105.3/32.1	Cabins (outside view): 608	Dedicated Cinema/Seats: ....No
Draft (ft/m): 24.2/7.4	Cabins (interior/no view): 18	Library: ....Yes
Propulsion/Propellers: .....diesel-electric	Cabins (for one person): 0	
Passenger Decks:..................11	Cabins (with private balcony): 593	

OVERALL SCORE: NYR OUT OF A POSSIBLE 2,000 POINTS

OVERVIEW. Built in 55 blocks, *Marina* is the first newbuild for this popular, and growing, small cruise line. The ship's profile is quite handsome, with a nicely rounded front, it is topped by a swept-back funnel. Able to cruise at a speed 25% faster than the three existing ships in the Oceania Cruises fleet (*Insignia, Nautica, Regatta*), it can therefore operate more longer-distance cruises.

Oceania Cruises has been careful to try to keep the warm and tasteful "country house" decor style for which it has become known – the smaller ships were designed by the Scottish designer John McNeece – together with an uncomplicated layout that makes it easy for you to find your way around.

The signature design of the main foyer staircase aboard the smaller Oceania ships, a scaled-down copy of the one aboard the ill-fated *Titanic*, has been retained, and enhanced by real Lalique glass – this one is simply stunning. Public rooms include nine bars and lounges. There is a 2,000-book library, set on the port side of the funnel housing, which also containsthe staffed Oceania @ Sea computer center, and Barista's coffee bar/lounge. A Monte Carlo Casino is located between two bars – the Grand Bar and Martinis. There are also three boutiques, and several dining venues, plus something new for Oceania Cruises, a Culinary Center – a cooking demonstration kitchen, run in conjunction with the US-based *Bon Appétit* magazine, as well as an Artist's Loft with constantly changing artists – bring your paintbrushes. However, in keeping essentially the same format, there are actually not many different lounges – because most are drinking venues.

Does the ship exude the intimacy that the smaller trio of ships in the fleet, *Insignia, Nautica,* and *Regatta*? In a

BERLITZ'S RATINGS		
	Possible	Achieved
Ship	500	NYR
Accommodation	200	NYR
Food	400	NYR
Service	400	NYR
Entertainment	100	NYR
Cruise	400	NYR

word – yes, it's really homey and comfortable, although it means that you will need to walk a little more. The dress code is "country club casual" – no pyjamas or track suits, but no ties either. In other words, perfect for the Aventura, Palm Springs or Scottsdale fraternity, but not Monte Carlo.

The onboard currency is the US dollar. Gratuities are added at $10.50 per person, per day, and accommodations designated as suites have an extra $3 per person charge for the butler, applied. A 15% gratuity is added to bar and spa accounts.

ACCOMMODATION. There are 17 different price categories, with four suite grades: Owner's suite; Oceania suite; Vista suite; Penthouse suite – and 4 cabin grades: Concierge-Level Verandah cabin; Verandah cabin; De-Luxe Ocean-View cabin; and Interior (no-view) cabin. Price depends on size and location. Most cabins are spread over five decks, plus half a deck for some of the largest suites.

Around 96% of all accommodations have teak-decked balconies. All suites/cabins have a bathtub and shower, large vanity with drawers for personal toiletries. There's no tie rack in the closets because the dress code is "country club (no tie) casual." The decor include lots of grays and browns – the sort of earthy colors that don't jar the senses.

Standard veranda cabins measure 282 sq. ft (26 sq. meters). Veranda and Concierge-level cabins have a sitting area and teak balcony with a chaise lounge, armchair and table. Personal toiletries are included. Concierge-level accommodation grades get L'Occitane personal toiletries.

Penthouse Suites measure 420 sq. ft (39 sq. meters) with living/dining room separate from the sleeping area, walk-in closet and bathroom with a double vanity. The large veranda has a hot tub.

Oceania Suites measure about 1,030 sq.ft (96 sq. metres) and have a living room, dining room, separate bedroom, walk-in closet, teak-decked balcony with Jacuzzi tub, main bathroom, and a second bathroom for guests.

Vista Suites range from 1,200 sq. ft to 1,500 sq. ft (111–139 sq. meters) and offer the same features as Oceania Suites but add floor-to-ceiling windows overlooking the bow.

The Owner's Suite, at more than 2,000 sq. ft (186 sq. meters), spans the entire beam of the ship (about 105 ft/32 meters). It is decked out in furniture, fabrics, lighting and bedding from the Ralph Lauren Home collection with design by New York-based Tocar, Inc. It is outfitted with a Yamaha baby grand piano, private fitness room, laptop computers, Bose audio system, and a teak-decked balcony with Jacuzzi tub.

Suite-category occupants get niceties like champagne upon arrival, 1,000-thread-count linens, 42-inch plasma TV set, Hermès and Clarins bath amenities, butler service and ensuite delivery from any of the ship's restaurants. Amenities include the line's signature Tranquility beds, wi-fi laptop computer, refrigerated mini bar with unlimited free soft drinks and bottled water replenished daily, personal safe, writing desk, cotton bathrobes, slippers and marble and granite bathroom. Priority check-in and early embarkation and priority luggage delivery are extra perks. Occupants of Owner's, Vista, Oceania and Penthouse suites can have in-suite course-by-course dining from any restaurant menu, making private dining possible as a change to being in the restaurants – a nice alternative on longer voyages.

CUISINE. The six main open-seating dining venues (Grand Dining Room, Jacques, Polo Grill, Toscana, Privée, La Réserve) provide plenty of choice, enough even for long cruises. However, the banquette seating in some venues does not evoke the image of premium dining as much as individual seating does.

The Grand Dining Room has 566 seats, and a domed, or raised, central ceiling. Versace bone china, Christofle silver, fine linens are featured.

French celebrity chef Jacques Pépin, Oceania's executive culinary director, has his first sea-going restaurant, Jacques, with 124 seats. It deploys antique flatware and Lalique glassware, and offers fine dining in an elegant but informal setting, with roast free-range meats, nine classic French dessert items and a choice of 12 AOC cheeses.

Polo Grill, with 134 seats, serves steaks and seafood, including Oceania's signature 32-ounce bone-in King's Cut prime rib. The setting is classic traditional steakhouse, with dark wood paneling and classic white tablecloths.

The 124-seat Toscana features Italian-style cuisine, served on Versace china.

Privée, with seating for up to 10 in a private setting, invites exclusivity for its seven-course dégustation menu.

La Réserve is the venue for wine and food pairings, and, with just 24 seats, it's also really intimate.

The Terrace Café is the ship's casual self-serve buffet-style venue; outdoors, as an extension of the café is Tapas on the Terrace – good for light bites.

Red Ginger is a specialty restaurant which offers "classic and contemporary" Asian cuisine; the setting is visually refined, with ebony and dark wood finishes, but the banquette-style seating lets the venue down.

The poolside Waves Grill, shaded from the sun, is for burgers, seafood and other fast food items, cooked to order.

Baristas is a coffee bar that overlooks the pool deck.

And if you like to cook, or learn about cooking, a Bon Appétit Culinary Center provides 24 workstations, with one-off or multiple lessons.

ENTERTAINMENT. The 600-seat Marina Lounge, the show-lounge, spans two decks, with tiered amphitheater-style seating. It's more cabaret-style entertainment than big production shows, in keeping with the cruise line's traditions.

SPA/FITNESS. The Canyon Ranch Spa Club provides wellness and personal spa treatments. The facility includes a fitness center, beauty salon, several treatment rooms (including a couples room), sauna and steam rooms, thalassotherapy pool (hot tub). A fitness (jogging) track is located aft of the funnel, above two of the specialty restaurants, and, sensibly, away from all accommodation decks.

Mariner of the Seas
★★★★

Size: . . . . .Large Resort Ship	Passenger Decks: 14	Cabins (with private balcony): 765
Tonnage: .137,276	Total Crew: .1,185	Cabins (wheelchair accessible): 26
Lifestyle: . . . . .Standard	Passengers	Wheelchair accessibility . . . . .Best
Cruise Line: Royal Caribbean International	(lower beds/all berths): 3,114/3,840	Cabin Current: . . . . .110 volts
Former Names: . . . . .none	Passenger Space Ratio	Elevators: . . . . .14 (6 glass-enclosed)
Builder: . . .Kvaerner Masa-Yards (Finland)	(lower beds/all berths): 44.0/35.7	Casino (gaming tables): . . . . .Yes
Original Cost: . . . .$500 million	Crew/Passenger Ratio	Slot Machines: . . . . .Yes
Entered Service: . . . . .Spring 2004	(lower beds/all berths): 2.6/3.2	Swimming Pools (outdoors): 3
Registry: . . . . .The Bahamas	Cabins (total): 1,557	Swimming Pools (indoors): 0
Length (ft/m): 1,020.6/311.1	Size Range (sq ft/m): 151.0–1,358.0/	Whirlpools: 6
Beam (ft/m): 155.5/47.4	14.0–126.1	Self-Service Launderette: . . . . .No
Draft (ft/m): 28.8/8.8	Cabins (outside view): 939	Dedicated Cinema/Seats: . . . . .No
Propulsion/Propellers: . . . . .diesel-electric	Cabins (interior/no view): 618	Library: . . . . .Yes
(75,600kW)/3 azimuthing pods	Cabins (for one person): 0	

BERLITZ'S OVERALL SCORE: 1,457 OUT OF A POSSIBLE 2,000 POINTS

OVERVIEW. *Mariner of the Seas* is a stunning, large, floating leisure resort, sister to *Adventure of the Seas, Explorer of the Seas, Navigator of the Seas* and *Voyager of the Seas*, which debuted between 1999 and 2003, respectively. The exterior design is not unlike an enlarged version of the company's Vision-class ships.

The ship's propulsion is derived from three pod units, powered by electric motors (two azimuthing, and one fixed at the centerline) instead of conventional rudders and propellers.

With large proportions, the ship provides more facilities and options, yet the ship manages to have a healthy passenger space ratio (the amount of space per passenger). Being a "non-Panamax" ship, it is simply too large to go through the Panama Canal, thus limiting its itineraries almost exclusively to the Caribbean (where only a few islands can accept it), or for use as a floating island resort. Spend the first few hours exploring all the many facilities and public spaces aboard this vessel and it will be time well spent.

Although *Mariner of the Seas* is a large ship, the cabin hallways are warm and attractive, with artwork cabinets and wavy lines to lead you along and break up the monotony. In fact, there are plenty of colorful, even whimsical, decorative touches to help you avoid what would be a very clinical environment.

Embarkation and disembarkation take place through two stations/access points, designed to minimize lines (that's more than 1,500 people for each access point). Once inside the ship, you'll need good walking shoes, particularly when you need to go from one end to the other – it really is quite a long way.

BERLITZ'S RATINGS

	Possible	Achieved
Ship	500	418
Accommodation	200	150
Food	400	222
Service	400	277
Entertainment	100	83
Cruise	400	307

The four-decks-high Royal Promenade, which is 393.7 ft (120 meters) long, is the main interior focal point (it's a good place to hang out, to meet someone, or to arrange to meet someone). The length of two football fields (American football, that is), it has two internal lobbies (atria) that rise to as many as 11 decks high. Restaurants, shops and entertainment locations front this winding street and interior "with-view" cabins look into it from above. It is designed loosely in the image of London's fashionable Burlington Arcade – although there's not a real brick in sight, and I wonder if the designers have ever visited the real thing. It is, however, an imaginative piece of design work, and most passengers (particularly those who enjoy shopping malls) enjoy it immensely.

The super-atrium houses a "traditional" pub (the Wig & Gavel), with draft beer and plenty of "street-front" seating (North American passengers always seem to sit down, while British passengers prefer to stand at the bar). There is also a Champagne Bar, a Sidewalk Cafe (for continental breakfast, all-day pizzas, specialty coffees and desserts), Sprinkles (for round-the-clock ice cream and yoghurt), and a sports bar. There are also several shops – jewelry shop, gift shop, logo souvenir shop, and a Tommy Hilfiger signature store. Altogether, the Royal promenade is a nice place to see and be seen, and it sees action throughout the day and night. Comedy art has its place here, too, for example in the *trompe l'oeil* painter climbing up the walls. The Guest Reception and Shore Excursion counters are located at the aft end of the promenade, as is an ATM machine. Things to watch for: look up to see the large moving, asteroid-like sculpture (constantly growing and contracting). At times, street entertainers appear, and parades happen, while at other (carefully orchestrated) times it's difficult to walk through the area as it is filled to the brim with shopping items – like a cheap bazaar.

Arched across the promenade is a captain's balcony. Meanwhile, in the center of the promenade is a stairway that connects you to the deck below, where you'll find the Schooner Bar (a piano lounge that is a feature of all RCI ships) and the colorful Casino Royale. This is naturally large and full of flashing lights and noises. Gaming includes blackjack, Caribbean stud poker, roulette, and craps, as well as 300 slot machines. Aft of the casino is Bolero's Bar.

There's also a regulation-size ice-skating rink (Studio B), featuring real, not fake, ice, with "bleacher" seating for up to 900, and the latest in broadcast facilities. Ice Follies shows are presented here. Slim pillars obstruct clear-view arena stage sight lines, however. If ice-skating in the Caribbean doesn't appeal, you may enjoy the stunning two-deck library (open 24 hours a day). A grand $12 million was spent on permanent artwork.

Drinking places include a neat Aquarium Bar, complete with 50 tons of glass and water in four large aquariums (whose combined value is over $1 million).

Drinking places include the small and intimate Champagne Bar, and a Connoisseur Club – for cigars and cognacs. Lovers of jazz might appreciate Ellington's, an intimate room for cool music atop the ship in the Viking Crown Lounge, or the Schooner Bar piano lounge. Golfers might enjoy the golf bar, as they play the Mariner Dunes.

There is a large television studio, adjacent to rooms that can be used for trade show exhibit space, with conference center that seats 400 and a multi-media screening room that seats 60. Lovers could tie the knot in a wedding chapel in the sky, the Skylight Chapel (it's located on the upper level of the Viking Crown Lounge, and even has wheelchair access via an electric stairway lift). Outdoors, the pool and open deck areas provide a resort-like environment.

Families with children are also well catered to, as facilities for children and teenagers are quite extensive. "Aquanauts" is for 3–5 year-olds; "Explorers" is for 6–8 year-olds; "Voyagers" is for 9–12 year-olds. Optix is a dedicated area for teenagers, including a daytime club (with several computers), soda bar, and dance floor. "Challenger's Arcade" features an array of the latest video games. Paint and Clay is an arts and crafts center for younger children. Adjacent is Adventure Beach, an area for all the family; it includes swimming pools, a water slide and game areas outdoors.

In terms of sheer size, this ship dwarfs almost all other ships in the cruise industry, but in terms of personal service, the reverse tends to be the case, unless you happen to reside in one of the top suites. Royal Caribbean International does, however, try hard to provide a good standard of programmed service from its hotel service staff. Remember to take lots of extra pennies – you'll need them to pay for all the additional-cost items.

ACCOMMODATION. There is an extensive range of 22 cabin categories in four major groupings: Premium ocean-view suites and cabins, Promenade-view (interior-view) cabins, Ocean-view cabins, and Interior (no view) cabins. Many cabins are of a similar size – good for incentives and large groups, and 300 have interconnecting doors – good for families. If you do have a cabin with an interconnecting door to another cabin, be aware that you'll probably be able to hear everything your next-door neighbors say and do. Bathroom toilets are explosively noisy – like a barking dog.

A total of 138 interior (no view) cabins have bay windows that look into a horizontal atrium – first used to good effect aboard the Baltic passenger ferries *Silja Serenade* (1990) and *Silja Symphony* (1991) with interior cabins that look into a central shopping plaza. Regardless of what cabin grade you choose, however, all except for the Royal Suite and Owner's Suite have twin beds that convert to a queen-sized unit, television, radio and telephone, personal safe, vanity unit, mini-bar (called an Automatic Refreshment Center) hairdryer and private bathroom.

The largest cabins includes luxuriously appointed penthouse suites (whose occupants, sadly, must share the rest of the ship with everyone else, except for their own exclusive, and private, concierge club). The grandest is the Royal Suite, which is positioned on the port side of the ship, and measures 106.5 sq. meters/ 1,146 sq. ft). It features a king-sized bed in a separate, large bedroom, a living room with an additional queen-sized sofa bed, baby grand piano (no pianist is included, however), refrigerator/wet bar, dining table, entertainment center, and large bathroom.

Slightly smaller, but still highly desirable are the Owner's Suites (there are 10, all located in the center of the ship, on both port and starboard sides, each measuring 43 sq. meters/ 468 sq. ft) and four Royal Family suites (each 53 sq. meters/574 sq. ft), all of which feature similar items. However, the four Royal Family suites, which have two bedrooms (including one with third/fourth upper Pullman berths) are at the stern of the ship and have magnificent views over the ship's wake (and seagulls).

All cabins feature twin beds that convert to a queen-sized bed, a private bathroom with shower enclosure (towels are 100% cotton), as well as interactive, closed-circuit and satellite television, and pay-per-view movies. Cabins with "private balconies" are not so private, as the partitions are only partial, not full. The balcony decking is made of Bolidt – a sort of rubberized sand – and not wood, while the balcony rail is of wood.

CUISINE. The main dining room has a total seating capacity of 1,919); it is massive, and is set on three levels. A dramatic staircase connects all three levels, and huge, fat support pillars obstruct the sight lines. All three levels (Rhapsody in Blue, Top Hat and Tails, and Sound of Music) have exactly the same menus and food. There are also two small private wings for private groups, each seating 58 persons. When you book, choose one of two seatings, or "My Time Dining" (eat when you want, during dining room hours). Tables are for four, six, eight 10 or 12. The place settings, china and cutlery are of good quality.

Alternative Dining Options: These are for casual and informal meals at all hours and include:

● **Cafe Promenade:** for continental breakfast, all-day pizzas, pastries, desserts and specialty coffees (sadly provided in paper cups).

● **Windjammer Cafe:** for casual buffet-style breakfast, lunch and light dinner (except the last night of the cruise).

● **Island Grill:** (this is actually a section inside the Windjammer Cafe), for casual dinner (no reservations necessary) featuring a grill and open kitchen.

● **Portofino:** this is the ship's "upscale" Euro-Italian restaurant, open for dinner only. Reservations are required, and a $20 gratuity per person applies. The food and its presentation are better than the food in the dining room, although the restaurant is not large enough for all passengers to try even once during a cruise. Choices include antipasti, soup, salad, pasta, main dish, dessert, cheese and coffee. The menu does not change throughout the cruise.

● **Johnny Rockets**, a retro 1950s all-day, all-night diner-style eatery that features hamburgers, malt shakes (at extra cost), and jukebox hits, with both indoor and outdoor seating seating (all indoor tables feature a mini-jukebox; dimes are provided for you to make your selection of vintage records), and all-singing, all-dancing waitresses who'll knock your socks off, if you can stand the volume.

● **Sprinkles:** for round-the-clock ice cream and yoghurt.

ENTERTAINMENT. The 1,350-seat Savoy showlounge is a stunning room that could well be the equal of many such rooms on land. It is located at the forward end of the ship and spans the height of five decks (with only a few slim pillars and almost no disruption of sight lines from almost any seat in the house). The room features a hydraulic orchestra pit and huge stage areas, together with sonic-boom loud sound, and some superb lighting equipment.

In addition, the ship has a whole array of cabaret acts. Although many of the cabaret acts are not what you would call headliners (the strongest cabaret acts are featured in the main showlounge, while lesser acts are presented in the Lotus Lounge, which is also the venue for late-night adults-only comedy), they regularly travel the cruise ship circuit.

The entertainment throughout is really upbeat, but is typical of the kind of resort hotel found ashore in Las Vegas. There is even background music in all corridors and lifts, and constant music outdoors on the pool deck. If you want a quiet relaxing holiday, this isn't the right ship for you.

There is also a television studio (in case you thought you'd need one aboard a cruise ship), located adjacent to rooms that could be used, for example, for trade show exhibit space (good for conventions at sea).

SPA/FITNESS. The ShipShape health and fitness spa is large, and measures 15,000 sq. ft (1,400 sq. meters). It includes a large aerobics room, fitness center (with the usual stairmasters, treadmills, stationary bikes, weight machines and free weights), treatment rooms, men's and women's sauna/steam rooms, while another 10,000 sq. ft (930 sq. meters) is devoted to a Solarium (with magrodome sliding glass roof) for relaxation after you've exercised too much.

For the more sporting, there is activity galore – including a rock-climbing wall that's 32.8 ft high (10 meters), with five separate climbing tracks. It is located outdoors at the aft end of the funnel. You'll get a great "buzz" being 200 ft (60 meters) above the ocean while the ship is moving. Other sports facilities include a roller-blading track, a dive-and-snorkel shop.

● **For more extensive general information about the Royal Caribbean experience, see pages 151–6.**

DID YOU KNOW...

● that most of the major cruise lines have replaced champagne with sparkling wine for the captain's welcome aboard cocktail party?

● that the liner *Amerika* in 1938 was the first ship to have an alternative restaurant open separately from the dining saloons? It was named the Ritz Carlton.

● that the first à la carte restaurant aboard a passenger ship was in the German ship *Amerika* of 1905?

● that TUI Cruises' *Mein Schiff* is the only ship with an espresso coffee machine in every cabin?

● that a whole county in Iowa raises all its beef cattle for sale to Carnival Cruise Lines?

● that the first "en suite" rooms (with private bathroom) were on board Cunard Line's *Campania* of 1893?

● that the first single-berth cabins built as such were also aboard the *Campania*?

● that the first liner to offer private terraces with their first-class suites was *Normandie* in 1935 (the Trouville Suite had four bedrooms as well as a private terrace)?

● that the first ships to feature private balconies were the *Saturnia* and *Vulcania* in the early 1900s?

● that the first ship to be fitted with interior plumbing was the 6,283-ton *Normandie* of 1883?

● that the first ship fitted with an internal electric lighting system was the Inman liner *City of Berlin* in 1879?

● that Carnival Cruise Lines places more than 10 million chocolates on passenger pillows each year?

● that the whole disc of the sun is visible for 24 hours a day at some points north of the Arctic Circle? North Cape (May 14–July 29); Hammerfest (May 16–July 27); Tromso (May 20–July 22); Harstad (May 26–July 19); Bodo (June 4–July 8).

Mein Schiff
★★★★

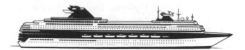

Size: . . . . .Large Resort Ship	Passenger Decks: 10	Cabins (with private balcony): 430
Tonnage: 77,713	Total Crew: 780	Cabins (wheelchair accessible): 8
Lifestyle: . . . . .Standard	Passengers	Wheelchair accessibility . . . . .Good
Cruise Line: . . . . TUI Cruises	(lower beds/all berths): 1,948/2,725	Cabin Current: . . . . .110 and 220 volts
Former Names: . .Celebrity Galaxy, Galaxy	Passenger Space Ratio	Elevators: 10
Builder: . . . . .Meyer Werft (Germany)	(lower beds/all berths): 39.8/28.5	Casino (gaming tables): . . . . .Yes
Original Cost: . . . .$320 million	Crew/Passenger Ratio	Slot Machines: . . . . .Yes
Entered Service: . . . .Dec 1996/May 2009	(lower beds/all berths): 2.0/3.4	Swimming Pools (outdoors): 2
Registry: . . . . .Malta	Cabins (total): .974	Swimming Pools (indoors): 0
Length (ft/m): 865.8/263.9	Size Range (sq ft/m): 169.0–1,219.0/	Whirlpools: 4
Beam (ft/m): 105.6/32.20	15.7–113.2	Self-Service Launderette: . . . . .No
Draft (ft/m): 25.2/7.70	Cabins (outside view): 665	Dedicated Cinema/Seats: Yes/200
Propulsion/Propellers: . . . . .diesel	Cabins (interior/no view): 309	Library: . . . . .Yes
(31.5 MW)/2	Cabins (for one person): 0	

BERLITZ'S OVERALL SCORE: 1,546 OUT OF A POSSIBLE 2,000 POINTS

OVERVIEW. *Mein Schiff*, originally built for Celebrity Cruises as *Galaxy*, was transferred in 2009 to newcomer TUI Cruises (part of TUI Travel – Europe's largest tour operator) specifically for German-speaking passengers, in a joint venture with Royal Caribbean Cruises, parent of Royal Caribbean International. The ship underwent a major conversion at that time. Its name ("My Ship") was suggested by several entrants to a magazine competition; the winner, whose name was drawn from a hat, was Oliver Krimmel, a Stuttgart designer. A sister ship, *Mein Schiff II*, will be introduced in May 2011.

The ship has good tender loading platforms. But, although there are more than 4.5 acres (1.8 hectares) of space on the open decks, it does seem a little small and crowded when the ship is full. Some 10 charming two-person cabanas can be rented on an upper, outside deck, with great ocean views, but insulated from the life that goes on around the ship.

Inside, there is a four-deck-high main foyer, which houses the reception desk and shore excursion station. The ship benefits from having a small, dedicated cinema, which doubles as a conference and meeting center with all the latest audio-visual technology, including simultaneous translation and headsets for the hearing-impaired.

There are still one or two pieces of the whimsical works of art originally chosen by Christina Chandris, whose family founded Celebrity Cruises. The interior decor is at once contemporary in style, but with many restful colors and combinations throughout.

Relaxation is a key element of the product, and *Mein Schiff* is equipped with individual hammocks in various locations, including on cabin balconies as well as in public areas. Additionally, "Meditation Islands" are installed on

BERLITZ'S RATINGS

	Possible	Achieved
Ship	500	414
Accommodation	200	165
Food	400	282
Service	400	308
Entertainment	100	71
Cruise	400	306

deck: the ship's rail is fitted with mini-balconies, equipped with special blinds. Here, passengers are able to enjoy a private space for relaxation.

This large, all-inclusive resort ship has just about all you need to have an enjoyable and rewarding cruise experience, and will provide competition for well-known AIDA Cruises, whose ships, by comparison, do not have a traditional dining room, and have few service staff.

There are 10 bars, four restaurants and six bistros, and good facilities for families with children.

The ship delivers a fine product worth much more than the cruise fare charged when compared to several other large-ship cruise lines. TUI Cruises has got the onboard product just about right for contemporary German-speaking passengers, with many more dining and eating choices and more class and style than AIDA's ships, and with far better food and plenty of snappily-dressed service personnel. Indeed, *Mein Schiff* is on track to become the benchmark for a high-value cruise vacation in Germany.

Making it even more user-friendly for families is the all-inclusive pricing introduced in October 2010, though this excludes the extra-cost restaurants Richard's Fines Essen, Blaue Welt Sushi Bar and the Surf 'n' Turf steakhouse and also excursions and spa treatments.

The dress code is smart casual, and the onboard currency is the euro.

SUITABLE FOR: *Mein Schiff* is for German-speaking families with children who want to cruise aboard a large ship with a contemporary environment, good itineraries, decent food and good European-style service from a well-trained crew that delivers a product that's fresh and surprisingly good.

ACCOMMODATION. There are 10 price grades, depending on

your preference for the size and location of your living space, but the accommodation is very comfortable throughout. Every cabin has its own Nespresso coffee machine, which takes pre-portioned packets of espresso coffee. The first two are included, but any additional packets cost €1 each. All accommodation grades are designated no-smoking.

Most suites with private balconies have floor-to-ceiling windows and sliding doors to balconies, and a few have outward opening doors. Suite-grade accommodation gets European duvets on the beds, instead of sheets and blankets. A balcony massage service is also available (it's worth it). Suite occupants get special cards to open their doors, plus priority service throughout the ship and for embarkation and disembarkation, free cappuccino/espresso coffees served by a butler, welcome champagne, flowers, video recorder, and picnic baskets as required. Suite occupants also get a private, 100-seat concierge lounge/bar and social venue (the "X" Lounge) atop the ship, with great ocean views – a good place for reading a book during the day.

Penthouse Suites: These two suites, located amidships, are the largest. Each is 1,173 sq. ft (108.9 sq. meters), and has its own butler's pantry. There is an inter-connecting door so that it can link to the suite next door to become an impressive 1,515-sq. ft (141-sq. meter) apartment.

Most of the Deck 10 suites and cabins are of generous proportions, are beautifully equipped, and have balconies with full floor-to-ceiling partitions, and large flat-screen TV sets. The Sky Deck suites are also excellent, and most of them have huge balconies; unfortunately, the partitions are not quite of the floor-to-ceiling type, so you can hear your neighbors. Also included are wall clock, large floor-to-ceiling mirrors, marble-topped vanity/writing desk, excellent closet and drawer space, and even dimmer-controlled ceiling lights.

Standard Outside-view/Interior (No-View) Cabins: All of the standard interior and outside cabins are of a good size (larger than those aboard the ships of AIDA Cruises, for example), and come nicely furnished with twin beds that convert to a queen-sized unit. The bathrooms are spacious and well equipped, and have generous-size showers, hairdryers, and space for personal toiletry items. Baby-monitoring telephones are provided in all cabins. There are no cabins for single occupancy.

CUISINE. Restaurants and bistros range from self-serve buffet style to service, with a focus on healthy eating. All dining venues are non-smoking, and there is no pre-defined seating, so you can dine when you want, and with whomever you want – good for multi-generational families. The emphasis is on healthy food, including power food, brain food, soul food, erotic food, new food (quinoa, soya and tofu dishes), including fresh fish.

The Atlantik Restaurant is a stunning, two-level dining hall – somewhat reminiscent of the dining halls aboard the ocean liners of the 1930s – with a grand staircase that flows between both levels and perimeter alcoves that provide more intimate dining spaces. However, there's one big difference, in that this restaurant has 2-meter-wide trapeze bars built into its center (talk about swinging food – or is that food for swingers?). Tables are for two, four, six, eight or 10.

Alternative dining venue: Richard's Gourmet Restaurant is an à la carte, reservations-only venue, with a calming, restful wood-laden interior where high-quality fine dining and service can be found.

Other dining venues: Surf 'n' Turf Steakhouse, for premium steaks and grilled seafood, with aged beef commanding different price points.

In a venue that is covered by a retractable glass dome, in the aft section of the ship, three eateries, combined with a communal bar provide completely different food experiences: Bistro La Vela (Italian cuisine, including an "active" pasta cooking station, and pizza); Gosch Sylt, for fresh fish and seafood; Tapas Y Mas, for tapas-tasting dishes. This venue is a most popular place to meet the "in" set.

Other dining spots around the ship include: La Vida Sana: for wellness cuisine; Blaue Welt (Blue World) Sushi Bar, on the upper level of the atrium; Vino, a wine tasting bar; and a coffee lounge set around the atrium lobby, for specialty coffees and pastries.

For informal breakfasts and lunches, the two-level self-serve Anckelmannsplatz Buffet – the name comes from the road on which the TUI Cruises offices are located in Hamburg – is the place to go. There are several serving counters and "active" food islands; the venue has warm wood-accented decor, and eight bay windows provide some prime seating spots. There are also two poolside grills – one located adjacent to the midships pools, the other wedged into an area aft of the swimming pool/hot tub cluster.

ENTERTAINMENT. The Theater is a 927-seat showlounge spanning two decks, with seating on both main and cantilevered balcony levels. There are excellent sightlines from all seats. The large-scale production shows are excellent. It has a revolving stage, "hard" curtain and large fly tower.

SPA/FITNESS. The Spa and More, located at the front of the ship one deck above the navigation bridge, has 18,299 sq. ft (1,700 sq. meters) of space. It includes a large fitness/exercise area with all the latest muscle machines and video cycles; beauty salon; thalassotherapy pool; seven treatment rooms; a Rasul room, for Mediterranean mud and gentle steam bathing; and private "spa suites." Private "spa suites," with fine, relaxing views are located above the ship's navigation bridge and can be rented for the morning, afternoon, or the whole day. Atop the ship at the front is a healthy FKK *(freikorperkulture)* deck for the naked sunbathing set.

Minerva
★★★ +

Size: ....Small Ship	Propulsion/Propellers: diesel/2 (3,480 kW)/2	Cabins (for one person): 4
Tonnage: 12,500	Passenger Decks: 6	Cabins (with private balcony): 12
Lifestyle: ....Standard	Total Crew: 157	Cabins (wheelchair accessible): 2
Cruise Line: ....Swan Hellenic	Passengers	Wheelchair accessibility ....Fair
Discovery Cruises	(lower beds/all berths): 352/474	Cabin Current: ....220 Volts
Former Names: *Explorer II, Alexander von*	Passenger Space Ratio	Elevators: 2
Humboldt, Saga Pearl, Minerva, Okean	(lower beds/all berths): 35.5/26.3	Casino (gaming tables): ....No
Builder: ....Mariotti (Italy)	Crew/Passenger Ratio	Slot Machines: ....No
Original Cost: ....n/a	(lower beds/all berths): 2.1/3.0	Swimming Pools (outdoors): 1
Entered Service: ....Apr 1996/May 2008	Cabins (total): 178	Swimming Pools (indoors): 0
Registry: ....The Bahamas	Size Range (sq ft/m): 139.9–360.6/	Whirlpools: 0
Length (ft/m): 436.3/133.0	13.0–33.5	Self-Service Launderette: ....Yes
Beam (ft/m): 65.6/20.0	Cabins (outside view): 126	Dedicated Cinema/Seats: Yes/96
Draft (ft/m): 19.6/6.0	Cabins (interior/no view): 52	Library: ....Yes

OVERALL SCORE: 1,324 OUT OF A POSSIBLE 2,000 POINT

OVERVIEW. Originally intended as a spy ship (*Okean*) for the Soviet navy, the strong, 1989-built ice-strengthened hull was constructed at Nikolajev on the River Ingul in Ukraine; it had a stern ramp for launching submersibles for submarine tracking. The hull was bought by Monaco-based V-Ships, the present owners, who towed it to Italy for conversion into a "soft expedition" cruising vessel. The ship, under charter for six years, now operates for Swan Hellenic Discovery Cruises, part of the UK's All Leisure Group's Voyages of Discovery.

It's déja-vu for Swanners, as Swan Hellenic passengers are affectionately known. The ship has quite an angular profile, with a single, central funnel, and a slightly rounded stern. It does not handle unkind seas well, and the navigation bridge looks as if it should have been located one deck higher. There's ample open and shaded deck space for this size of ship, particularly in the aft section, and there is also a teak walk-around promenade deck. The uppermost passenger deck is artificial turf – awful when wet.

A fleet of rubber inflatable Zodiacs is carried for excursions ashore, ideal for inhospitable locations such as in Antarctica without landing piers or formal docking arrangements. The interior decor is homely and restrained, like a country house hotel, not in the slightest bit glitzy, for passengers with good taste, although cushions would be a welcome addition to the many sofas. Lectures and briefings are set in the Auditorium, the ship's main lounge. Fine wool carpets inhabit the passageways and public rooms.

Perhaps the most appreciated and used public room is the excellent library, with its great range of reference books (many of university-standard), with its classical decor and

BERLITZ'S RATINGS		
	Possible	Achieved
Ship	500	311
Accommodation	200	114
Food	400	287
Service	400	288
Entertainment	n/a	n/a
Cruise	500	324

motifs, while Shackleton's Lounge, exuding a country-house atmosphere, is a fine place for a relaxing drink. Cigar smokers should appreciate the special smoking room and humidor service and high back leather chairs that provide a sense of well-being and privacy.

Despite the small cabins and tiny bathrooms, it's really the excellent food and very friendly service throughout the ship, plus a fine library, that makes a cruise aboard *Minerva* a rather special soft expedition vacation experience. The onboard currency is the pound sterling. All gratuities are included, although port charges are extra.

SUITABLE FOR: *Minerva* is mainly aimed at the so-called Swanners – couples and single travelers of a mature age who seek to cruise off the beaten track in comfortable surroundings, and who don't need the entertainment and organized parlor games found aboard larger ships. This ship is not recommended for children.

ACCOMMODATION. There are five different grades of cabins, in 16 price categories: Owner's Suite, Suite, Deluxe, Superior, and Standard. The price depends on the grade and location chosen rather than any great difference in the size of the accommodation. Most of the standard cabins really are quite small, particularly when compared to the "standard" cabin size on the latest ships today. There are few cabins with private balcony.

Owner's Suites (2): These Bridge Deck measure 360 sq. ft (33.5 sq. meters). Facilities include a queen-sized bed, an extra-large double closet and ample drawer space; separate lounge area with sofa, table and chair, and vanity table/writing desk, television/DVD player combo, refrigerator, hairdryer and binoculars; floor to ceiling patio doors leading to private balcony; bathroom with bath/ shower combination and toilet.

Suites (10): These suites on Bridge Deck measure 290 sq. ft (27 sq. meters). Facilities include twin beds or queen-sized bed, two double closets and ample drawer space; separate lounge area with sofa, table and chair, and vanity table/writing desk (poor lighting), small television/DVD player combo, refrigerator, hairdryer and binoculars; floor to ceiling patio doors leading to private (Astroturf-covered) balcony; bathroom with tub/shower and toilet.

Deluxe: These measure 226 sq. ft (21 sq. meters). Facilities include twin beds or queen-sized bed, two double closets and ample drawer space; separate lounge area with sofa, table and chair, and vanity table/writing desk, television and VCR, refrigerator, hairdryer and binoculars; large picture window; bathroom with bath/shower and toilet.

Superior: These measure 162 sq. ft (15 sq. meters). Facilities include twin beds or queen-sized bed, two double closets and ample drawer space; separate lounge area with sofa, table and chair, and vanity table/writing desk, television and VCR, refrigerator, hairdryer and binoculars; large picture window; bathroom with bath/shower and toilet.

Standard Outside-View or Interior (No View) Cabins: These "standard" cabins are small (140 sq. ft/13 sq. meters) when compared to the size of standard cabins aboard today's newest ships, which is around 182 sq. ft (17 sq. meters). Facilities include twin beds or queen-sized bed, two double closets and ample drawer space; separate lounge area with sofa, table and chair, and vanity table/writing desk, television and VCR, refrigerator, hairdryer and binoculars; large picture window (outside-view cabins only; or porthole, depending on deck and price category); bathroom with shower enclosure (small) and toilet.

The bathrooms have a raised "lip" to step over, are totally white, and have very small showers (except for the suites, which have bathtubs and green/black marble floors), although plumbing fixtures were poorly installed. No matter what grade of accommodation you book, all grades have a hairdryer, 100% cotton bathrobe, TV with music channels, and a direct-dial telephone. However, there is little space for hanging outerwear parkas and other gear for expedition cruises, and some cabins on B Deck are subject to noise and vibration from the ship's engines/generators.

Because the insulation is quite poor, Bridge Deck suites suffer from noise that bleeds through from the Darwin lounge under them. This typically happens on itineraries where there is evening entertainment rather than when the ship is operating in the Antarctic region when fewer passengers are carried.

CUISINE. The Dining Room has open-seating dining, allowing you to dine with whomever you wish, in both the main restaurant and the informal indoor/outdoor café. The menus are very good, and the food itself is of a really high quality. It's also very creative, attractively presented, and has plenty of taste. In fact, it's far superior to the food aboard the previous ship of the same name. The wine list is really good, and so is the rather special champagne. The service staff really provide fine service, and they are very pleasant, friendly and willing.

Coffees and teas are available 24 hours a day from a beverage station in the self-serve Bridge Café, in which you can have casual breakfasts, luncheons, and dinners in an open-seating arrangement; for dinner, the menu is the same as in the main dining room.

ENTERTAINMENT. Although there is a main lounge, this is used principally for lectures, and occasionally for cabaret acts and classical music ensembles. The ship has a small band and solo entertaining musicians to provide live music for dancing and listening.

SPA/FITNESS. There is a small gymnasium on Funnel Deck (with side-facing views), while a beauty salon is located near the restaurant. Massages and aromatherapy facials, manicures, pedicures and hair beautifying treatments are available, and there is also a small sauna and adjacent shower, but no changing facilities.

DID YOU KNOW...

● that on the earliest cruise ships there was little entertainment, and passengers were expected to clean their own cabins? Orders enforced on all ships sailing from Great Britain in 1849, for example, instructed all passengers to be in their beds by 10pm.

● that the first "en suite" rooms (with private bathroom) were on board Cunard Line's *Campania*, which made its debut in 1893?

● that the first single-berth cabins built as such were also aboard the *Campania*?

● that the first ships to incorporate private balconies were the *Saturnia* and *Vulcania* in the early 1900s?

● that the first ship to be fitted with interior plumbing was the 6,283-ton *Normandie*, which introduced it in 1883?

● that the first liner to offer private terraces with their first-class suites was *Normandie* in 1935 – the Trouville Suite had no fewer than four bedrooms as well as a private terrace?

● that the first ship fitted with an internal electric lighting system was the Inman liner *City of Berlin* in 1879?

● that Carnival Cruise Lines places more than 10 million chocolates on passenger pillows each year?

Monarch of the Seas
★★★

Size: . . . . .Large Resort Ship
Tonnage: .73,937
Lifestyle: . . . . .Standard
Cruise Line: Royal Caribbean International
Former Names: . . . . .none
Builder: .Chantiers de l'Atlantique (France)
Original Cost: . . . .$300 million
Entered Service: . . . . .Nov 1991
Registry: . . . . .The Bahamas
Length (ft/m): 879.9/268.2
Beam (ft/m): 105.9/32.3
Draft (ft/m): 24.9/7.6
Propulsion/Propellers: . . . . .diesel
(21,844 kW)/2

Passenger Decks: 11
Total Crew: 858
Passengers
(lower beds/all berths): 2,384/2,774
Passenger Space Ratio
(lower beds/all berths): 31.0/26.6
Crew/Passenger Ratio
(lower beds/all berths): 2.8/3.3
Cabins (total): 1,192
Size Range (sq ft/m): 118.4–670.0/
11.0–62.2
Cabins (outside view): 732
Cabins (interior/no view): 460
Cabins (for one person): 0

Cabins (with private balcony): 62
Cabins (wheelchair accessible): 4
Wheelchair accessibility . . . . .Fair
Cabin Current: . . . . .110 volts
Elevators: 11
Casino (gaming tables): . . . . .Yes
Slot Machines: . . . . .Yes
Swimming Pools (outdoors): 2
Swimming Pools (indoors): 0
Whirlpools: 2
Self-Service Launderette: . . . . .No
Dedicated Cinema/Seats: . . . . .No
Library: . . . . .Yes

OVERALL SCORE: 1,248 OUT OF A POSSIBLE 2,000 POINTS

OVERVIEW. The ship is almost identical in size and appearance to sister ships *Majesty of the Seas* and *Sovereign of the Seas* but with an improved internal layout, better public room features, passenger flow and signage. Royal Caribbean International's trademark Viking Crown lounge and bar surrounds the funnel and provides a stunning view, although the original Scandinavian tub chairs are extremely small and have no back support. The open deck space is very cramped when full, as aboard any large ship, although there seems to be plenty of it. There is a basketball court for sports lovers.

Following a grounding just before Christmas 1998, the ship underwent the replacement of 460 tons of bottom shell plating. At the same time, a new facility for toddlers was created. The children's and teens' programs are good, overseen by enthusiastic youth counselors, and there is a busy but sound activities program for adults.

The interior layout is a little awkward, as it is designed in a vertical stack, with most public rooms located aft, and the accommodation forward. There is, however, an impressive array of spacious and elegant public rooms, although the decor definitely brings to mind the IKEA school of interior design. A stunning five-deck-high Centrum lobby has cascading stairways and two glass-walled elevators.

There is a decent two-level showlounge and decent shops, albeit with lots of tacky merchandise. Casino gamers will find blackjack, craps, Caribbean stud poker and roulette tables, plus an array of slot machines.

This floating resort provides a well-tuned, yet very impersonal, short cruise experience for a lot of passengers. The dress code is very casual. There are many public rooms

BERLITZ'S RATINGS		
	Possible	Achieved
Ship	500	334
Accommodation	200	119
Food	400	221
Service	400	260
Entertainment	100	66
Cruise	400	248

and spaces to play in, including a five-deck-high atrium, which really is the interior focal point of the ship, and has glass lifts. Among the public rooms, the library offers space for relaxation and has a decent selection of books.

The ship provides a decent enough range of facilities with consistently sound, but highly programmed service from a reasonably attentive young staff. In the final analysis, you will probably be overwhelmed by the public spaces, and underwhelmed by the size of the cabins. The ship underwent an extensive internal refurbishment in 2003 and still looks fresher for it.

ACCOMMODATION. There are 17 categories. The price you pay will depend on the grade, size and location you choose. Note that there are no cabins with private balconies.
Suites: Thirteen suites on Bridge Deck are reasonably large and nicely furnished (the largest is the Royal Suite), with separate living and sleeping spaces. They provide more space, with better service and more perks than standard-grade accommodation.
Standard Cabins: The standard outside-view and interior (no view) cabins are very small, although an arched window treatment and colorful soft furnishings do give the illusion of more space.

Almost all cabins have twin beds that can be converted to a queen-sized or double bed configuration, together with moveable bedside tables. However, when in a queen-bed configuration, the bed is typically flush against the wall, and access is from one side only. All of the standard cabins have very little closet and drawer space (you will need some luggage engineering to stow your cases). You should, therefore, think of packing only minimal clothing, which is all you really need for a short cruise.

All cabins have a private bathroom, with a shower enclosure, toilet and washbasin.

CUISINE. The two large, no-smoking dining rooms, Claude's and Vincent's, are located off the Centrum lobby (Claude's is one deck above Vincent's). There are tables for four, six or eight, but no tables for two. When you book, choose one of two seatings, or "My Time Dining" (eat when you want, during dining room hours). The dining operation is well-orchestrated, with emphasis on highly programmed service.

The cuisine is typical of mass banquet catering that offers standard fare comparable to that found in American family-style restaurants ashore. While menu descriptions are tempting, the actual food may be somewhat disappointing and unmemorable (many items are pre-prepared ashore to keep costs down).

However, a decent selection of light meals is provided, and a vegetarian menu is available. The selection of breads, rolls, fruit and cheese is quite poor, however, and could do with improvement. Caviar (once a standard menu item) now incurs a hefty extra charge. Menus typically include a Welcome Aboard Dinner, French Dinner, Italian Dinner, International Dinner, and Captain's Gala Dinner.

The wine list is not extensive, but the prices are moderate. The waiters, many from Caribbean countries, eastern Europe and Goa, are perhaps overly friendly for some tastes – particularly on the last night of the cruise, when tips are expected.

For casual breakfasts and lunches, the Windjammer Café is the place to go, although there are often long lines at peak times. Although the selection is just average, several themes, such as Mexican and Indian, are featured. On the aft of the upper level of the venue is Sorrento's Pizzeria.

ENTERTAINMENT. The Sound of Music is the name of the principal showlounge; it has both main and balcony levels, with banquette seating, although sight lines from many of the balcony seats are poor.

A smaller entertainment lounge, the April in Paris Lounge, is where cabaret acts, including late-night adult (blue) comedy are featured, as well as music for dancing.

The entertainment throughout is upbeat (in fact, it is difficult to get away from music and noise). There is even background music in all corridors and elevators, and constant music outdoors on the pool deck. If you want a quiet relaxing holiday, choose another ship.

SPA/FITNESS. The ShipShape Fitness Center has a gymnasium with aft-facing views (it is located at the aft of the ship) and a selection of high-tech muscle-pumping equipment. There is also an aerobics studio, and classes are offered in a variety of keep fit regimes. There is also a beauty salon, and a sauna, as well as treatment rooms for pampering massages, facials, etc. While the facilities are not as extensive as those aboard RCI's newer ships, they are adequate for the short cruises that this ship operates.

For the more sporting, there is activity galore – including a rock-climbing wall, with several separate climbing tracks. It is located outdoors aft of the funnel and wraparound Viking Crown Lounge.

● **For more extensive general information about the Royal Caribbean experience, see pages 151–6.**

For more extensive general information about the Royal Caribbean experience, see pages 151–6.

QUOTABLE QUOTES

These are some of the questions I have been asked by newcomers to cruising:

"Does the crew sleep on board?"

"How far above sea level are we?"

"Is the island surrounded by water?"

"Are all Caribbean islands the same size?"

"How many fjords to the dollar?"

"How does the captain know which port to go to?"

"Can we get off in the Panama Canal?"

"Does the ship generate its own electricity?"

"Does this elevator go up as well as down?"

"Will this elevator take me to my cabin?"

"What time's the midnight buffet?"

"Are there two seatings at the midnight buffet?"

"Does the chef cook himself?"

"What happens to the ice sculptures after they melt?"

"What time's the 2 o'clock tour?"

"Where's the bus for the walking tour?"

"Can you see the Equator from the deck?"

"Why is the sauna so hot?"

MSC Armonia
★★★★

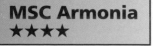

Size:	.Large Resort Ship	Passenger Decks:	.10
Tonnage:	.58,625	Total Crew:	.710

Size: . . . . .Large Resort Ship
Tonnage: 58,625
Lifestyle: . . . . .Standard
Cruise Line: . . . . .MSC Cruises
Former Names: . . . .*European Vision*
Builder: .Chantiers de l'Atlantique (France)
Original Cost: . . . .$245 million
Entered Service: . . .June 2001/May 2004
Registry: . . . . .Italy
Length (ft/m): 823.4/251.0
Beam (ft/m): 94.4/28.8
Draft (ft/m): 22.4/6.85
Propulsion/Propellers: . . . . .diesel-electric
(31,680kW)/2 azimuthing pods

Passenger Decks: 10
Total Crew: .710
Passengers
(lower beds/all berths): 1,566/2,223
Passenger Space Ratio
(lower beds/all berths): 37.4/26.3
Crew/Passenger Ratio
(lower beds/all berths): 2.2/3.1
Cabins (total): 783
Size Range (sq ft/m): 139.9–236.8/
13.0–22.0
Cabins (outside view): 511
Cabins (interior/no view): 272
Cabins (for one person): 0

Cabins (with private balcony): 132
Cabins (wheelchair accessible): 2
Wheelchair accessibility . . . . .Good
Cabin Current: . . . . .110 and 220 volts
Elevators: 9
Casino (gaming tables): . . . . .Yes
Slot Machines: . . . . .Yes
Swimming Pools (outdoors): 2
Swimming Pools (indoors): 0
Whirlpools: . . . . .1 (thalassotherapy)
Self-Service Launderette: . . . . .No
Dedicated Cinema/Seats: . . . . .No
Library: . . . . .Yes

OVERALL SCORE: 1,431 OUT OF A POSSIBLE 2,000 POINTS

OVERVIEW. Built originally for the now defunct Festival Cruises, the ship was a cousin to Festival's first new ship *Mistral*, but with an additional deck that allowed for the addition of more suites with private balconies in what is more like a premium real estate area. The additional deck also provided a better balance to the ship's overall profile. A 115-ft (35-meter) mid-section was added to increase the ship's length and provide more cabins and public rooms.

The ship is fitted with a high-tech azimuthing "pod" propulsion system *(see page 45 for a definition)*. As *European Vision*, the ship began its working life auspiciously, having been selected to be a floating hotel to accommodate the leaders and staff of the G8 summit in 2001. In 2004, Festival Cruises ceased operations. The ship was bought by MSC Cruises for €215 million and renamed *MSC Armonia*.

The exterior deck space is barely adequate for the number of passengers carried, no more. The lido deck surrounding the outdoor swimming pool also has whirlpool tubs and a large bandstand is set in raised canvas-covered pods (all sunloungers have cushioned pads).

Inside, the layout and passenger flow is good, as are the "you are here" deck signs. The decks are named after European cities – e.g. Oxford Deck (with British public room names), Venice Deck (with Italian public room names), and Biarritz Deck (with French public room names). The decor is "European Moderne" – whatever that means – but it does include crisp, clean lines, minimalism in furniture designs (including some chairs that look interesting but are totally impractical). However, the interior colors are good; nothing jars the senses, but rather calms them, unlike many ships.

BERLITZ'S RATINGS	Possible	Achieved
Ship	500	403
Accommodation	200	155
Food	400	235
Service	400	298
Entertainment	100	55
Cruise	400	285

Facilities include Amadeus, the ship's nightclub, and La Gondola Theater, for production shows and cabaret, plays and other theatrical presentations. There's a cigar smoking room (called Ambassador), which has all the hallmarks of a gentleman's club; as well as Vivaldi, a piano lounge. The Goethe Library/Card Room has real writing desks (something many ships seem to omit). There is an extensive internet cafe, as well an English pub called the White Lion. Gamblers will find solace in the Lido Casino, with blackjack, poker and roulette games, plus an array of slot machines.

The onboard currency is the euro, and 15% is added to all drinks/beverage orders.

Standing in line for embarkation, disembarkation, shore tenders and for self-serve buffet meals is an inevitable aspect of cruising aboard all large ships. Heavy smokers are everywhere, and are virtually impossible to avoid (in typical European fashion, ashtrays are simply moved – if used at all – to wherever smokers happen to be sitting or standing). Announcements are in several languages.

The staff is more focused on Italian passengers than those who speak any other European language. If you are considering two back-to-back 7-day cruises, note that some ports may be duplicated, and menus and entertainment are based on a 7-day cycle, so there is much product repetition (including the cruise director's jokes). Regular passenger complaints include poor ports of call information.

The wheelchair-bound should note that there is no access to the uppermost forward and aft decks, although access throughout most of the interior is very good. The passenger hallways are a little narrow on some accommodation decks to pass when housekeeping carts are in place, however.

The company keeps prices low by providing air transportation that may be at inconvenient times, or that involves long journeys by bus. In other words, be prepared for a little discomfort in getting to and from your cruise in exchange for low cruise rates.

SUITABLE FOR: *MSC Armonia* is best suited to adult couples and singles (plus families with children) who enjoy big city life, piazzas and outdoor cafes, constant activity accompanied by lots of noise (some call it ambiance), late nights, entertainment that is loud and of questionable quality, and food that is quantity rather than quality. It is for those who are comfortable hearing several (European) languages everywhere around them.

ACCOMMODATION. There are 11 categories, the price depending on grade, size and location. These include 132 suites with private balcony (the partitions are only of the partial and not the full type), outside-view cabins and interior (no view) cabins.

Suite grade accommodation (they are not true suites, as there is no separate bedroom and lounge) also has more room, a larger lounge area, walk-in closet, wall-to-wall vanity counter, a bathroom with combination tub and shower, toilet, and private balcony (with light). Bathrobes are provided. In general, the "suites" are well laid out and nicely furnished. However, except for the very highest category, the suite bathrooms are very plain, with white plastic washbasins and white walls, and mirrors that steam up.

Even the smallest interior (no- view) cabins are quite spacious, with plenty of space between the two lower beds. All grades of accommodation have sheets and blankets as bed linen (no duvets), and are equipped with a TV set, hairdryer, mini-bar/refrigerator, personal safe (cleverly positioned behind a vanity desk mirror), bathroom with shower and toilet, and 100% cotton towels. However, the standard grade cabins are quite small when compared to many other ships, at a modest 140 sq. ft (13 sq. meters).

CUISINE. The four dining spots are no-smoking. The principal dining room, the 610-seat Marco Polo Restaurant, typically has two seatings for dinner, and open seating for breakfast and lunch. However, for breakfast and lunch, you may well be seated with others with whom you may not be able to communicate very satisfactorily, given the mixture of languages on board.

In general, the cuisine is acceptable, if unmemorable. The menus are varied and the presentation is generally sound, and should prove a highlight for most passengers. The wine list has a wide variety of wines at fairly reasonable prices, although most of the wines are very young.

La Pergola, the most formal restaurant, has stylish Italian cuisine. It is assigned to all passengers occupying accommodation designated as suites, although other passengers can dine in it too, on a reservations-only basis.

Chez Claude, on the starboard side aft, adjacent to the ship's funnel, is a grill area for fast-food items. La Brasserie is a casual, self-serve buffet eatery, open 24 hours a day. The selections are very standardized (minimal). Cafe San Marco, on the upper, second level of the main lobby, is available for coffee and pastry items.

ENTERTAINMENT. La Gondola Theater is two decks high, and is the main venue for production shows, cabaret acts, plays and other theatrical presentations. It is a well designed room (except for the fact that no space was allocated for a live showband), with good sight lines from most seats, and four entrances that allow easy access and exit.

Entertainment is weak, although it could improve somewhat as more ships are brought into service by MSC Cruises. Other shows consist of unknown cabaret acts (typically singers, magicians, mime artistes, comedy jugglers, and others) doing the cruise ship circuit. The ship carries a number of bands and small musical units that provide live music for dancing or listening.

SPA/FITNESS. The Atlantica Spa has numerous body-pampering treatments, a gymnasium with ocean views, and an array of high-tech, muscle-toning and strengthening equipment. There's also a thermal suite (with different kinds of steam rooms combined with aromatherapy infusions such as chamomile and eucalyptus) and a rasul chamber (a combination of two or three different kinds of special application mud, and gentle steam shower).

The spa, operated by the Italian concession OceanView, offers a wide range of well-being treatments.

For the sports-minded, there's a simulated climbing wall outdoors, while other sports and fitness facilities include volleyball/basketball court, and mini-golf.

● **For more extensive general information about the MSC Cruises experience, see pages 143–4.**

MSC Fantasia
★★★★ to ★★★★ +

Size: ....Large Resort Ship	Passenger Decks: 1	Cabins (with private balcony): 1,260
Tonnage: 133,500	Total Crew: 1,325	Cabins (wheelchair accessible): 43
Lifestyle: ....Standard	Passengers	Wheelchair accessibility ....Best
Cruise Line: ....MSC Cruises	(lower beds/all berths): 3,274/3,959	Cabin Voltage: ....110 volts
Former Names: ....none	Passenger Space Ratio	Elevators: 14
Builder: ....STX Europe (France)	(lower beds/all berths): 40.7/33.7	Casino (gaming tables): ....Yes
Original Cost: ....$550 million	Crew/Passenger Ratio	Slot Machines: ....Yes
Entered Service: ....Dec 2008	(lower beds/all berths): 2.5/3.0	Swimming Pools (outdoors): 3
Registry: ....Panama	Cabins (total): 1,637	Swimming Pools (indoors): 1
Length (ft/m): 1,093.5/333.3	Size Range (sq ft/m): 161.4–699.6/	(with glass dome)
Beam (ft/m): 124.3/37.9	15.0–65.0	Whirlpools: 13
Draft: 27.72/8.45	Cabins (outside view): 1,354	Self-Service Launderette: ....No
Propulsion/Propellers: .....diesel-electric	Cabins (interior/no view): 283	Dedicated Cinema/Seats: ....No
(40mW)/2	Cabins (for one person): 0	Library: ....Yes

---

BERLITZ'S OVERALL SCORE: 1,528/1,570 (YACHT CLUB) OUT OF A POSSIBLE 2,000 POINTS

OVERVIEW. Built in 67 blocks (some of which exceed 600 tons), *MSC Fantasia* is the latest generation of large ships for this growing family-owned company – and the largest ship ever built for a European cruise company. It is 10 meters longer than the Eiffel Tower is high, and the propulsion power is the equivalent of 120 Ferraris. There are four swimming pools, one of which can be covered by a glass dome. You can drive an F1 Ferrari race car in the simulator, as well as experience several different hair-raising, seat-of-your pants rides in the adjacent 4-D theater.

The interior design is really an enlargement and extension of the smaller *MSC Musica* and *MSC Orchestra*-class ships, but with some superb new additions – including an exclusive area called the MSC Yacht Club – for occupants of the ship's 99 suites. The Yacht Club includes a Top-Sail Lounge (a private observation lounge), private sunbathing with integral dip pool, two hot tubs, and concierge services such as making dining reservations, and booking excursions and spa treatments.

Facilities include a really large three-deck high theater-style showlounge, a nightclub/discotheque, numerous lounges and bars, library, card room, an internet center, virtual reality center, shopping gallery (the shops are integrated with many bars, lounges and entertainment areas so that shopping becomes a city-like environment). Gamers will like the Monte Carlo Casino, featuring blackjack, poker and roulette games, plus an array of slot machines.

Drinking places include a pub-like venue and several comfortable lounges with live music. A neat mini-golf course is located on the port side of the funnel, while a walking

BERLITZ'S RATINGS			
	Possible	Achieved	Yacht Club
Ship	500	425	426
Accommodation	200	162	162
Food	400	260	283
Service	400	300	313
Entertainment	100	77	76
Cruise	400	304	310

and jogging track encircles the two swimming pools. The ship is designed to accommodate families with children, who have their own play centers (a children's club and jungle adventure playground), youth counselors, and programs. The onboard currency is the euro, and 15% is added to all drinks/beverage orders.

SUITABLE FOR: Best suited to young adult couples, singles, and families with tots, children and teens who enjoy big-ships, a city-style life, with all its attendant noise and different nationalities and languages (mostly European).

ACCOMMODATION. Eighty percent of cabins have an outside view, and 95% of these have a balcony (a standard balcony cabin will measure almost 172 sq. ft (16 sq. meters), plus bathroom and balcony). There are 99 suites in a "MSC Yacht Club" VIP section; each measures 29 sq. meters and comes with full butler service. The private area, on two decks, consists of a pool (with skydome) and sun deck with access via private elevators, an observation lounge/bar, direct access to the spa, a private galley for room service, and a private concierge lounge with an integral library.

A black marble floor leads to a magnificent Swarovski glass staircase which connects the concierge facilities between Deck 15 and 16 under a glass-domed ceiling.

CUISINE. There are four dining venues. The two-deck-high Il Cherchio d'Oro (Main Restaurant) is in the aft section. It has a ship-wide balcony level, with a stairway to connect its two levels. As well as its Mediterranean cuisine, light "always available" choices are provided.

Red Velvet is a specialty restaurant, with a different menu each evening devoted to a different region of Italy. The Murano chandeliers are special.

L'Etoile is a classic French restaurant, with decor reminiscent of the Belle Epoque era. Menus focus on one of three themes: the sea, the countryside, and the kitchen garden, and change seasonally. There's also an extra-charge Tex-Mex restaurant, El Sombrero, which serves burritos, fajitas, enchiladas, tacos, tortillas and more, with a choice of several Mexican beers.

Casual breakfasts and lunches can be taken in a large self-serve buffet-style eatery. Another casual spot in which to watch your fellow passengers is the Il Cappuccino Coffee Bar. Located two decks above the main reception area, it serves all types of coffees and teas, as well as fine chocolate delicacies.

Tasting Venues: Optiions include La Cantina Toscana, a wine bar that offers wine tasting paired with food from several regions of Italy, in a setting which includes alcove seating and L'Africana, with a decor of dark African hardwoods.

ENTERTAINMENT. L'Avanguardia, the main showlounge, has 1,603 seats, and facilities rival almost any found on land.

SPA/FITNESS. The Aurea Wellbeing Center has a beauty salon, several treatment rooms, a gymnasium with great ocean views. There's also a thermal suite, containing different kinds of steam rooms combined with herbal aromatherapy infusions, in a calming Asia-themed environment. The spa is operated by OceanView, a specialist spa provider.

Sports facilities include deck quoits, shuffleboard courts, large tennis/basketball court, minigolf, and a jogging track.

● **For more extensive general information about the MSC Cruises experience, see pages 143–4.**

SAFETY MEASURES

Fire Control
If anyone sounds the fire alarm, an alarm is automatically set off on the bridge. A red panel light will be illuminated on a large plan, indicating the section of the ship that has to be checked so that the crew can take immediate action.

Ships are sectioned into several zones, each of which can be tightly closed off. In addition, almost all ships have a water-fed sprinkler system that can be activated at the touch of a button, or automatically activated when sprinkler vials are broken by fire-generated heat. New electronic fire detection systems are being installed aboard ships in order to increase safety further.

Emergency Ventilation Control
This automatic fire damper system also has a manual switch that is activated to stop or control the flow of air to all areas of the ship, in this way reducing the fanning effect on flame and smoke via air-conditioning and fan systems.

Watertight Doors Control
Watertight doors throughout the ship can be closed off, in order to contain the movement of water flooding the ship. A master switch activates all the doors in a matter of seconds. All watertight doors can be operated electrically and manually, which means that nobody can be trapped in a watertight compartment.

Stabilizers Control
The ship's two stabilizing fins can be extended, housed, or controlled. They normally operate automatically under the command of a gyroscope located in the engine control room.

MSC Lirica
★★★★

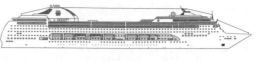

Size: . . . . .Large Resort Ship	Passenger Decks: 10	Cabins (with private balcony): 132
Tonnage: .59,058	Total Crew: 701	Cabins (wheelchair accessible): 4
Lifestyle: . . . . .Standard	Passengers	Wheelchair accessibility . . . . .Good
Cruise Line: . . . . .MSC Cruises	(lower beds/all berths): 1,560/2,065	Cabin Current: . . . . .110/220 volts
Former Names: . . . . .none	Passenger Space Ratio	Elevators: 9
Builder: .Chantiers de l'Atlantique (France)	(lower beds/all berths): 37.5/28.3	Casino (gaming tables): . . . . .Yes
Original Cost: . . . .$266 million	Crew/Passenger Ratio	Slot Machines: . . . . .Yes
Entered Service: . . . . .Mar 2003	(lower beds/all berths): 2.2/2.9	Swimming Pools (outdoors): 2
Registry: .Panama	Cabins (total): .780	Swimming Pools (indoors): 0
Length (ft/m): 830.7/253.25	Size Range (sq ft/m): 139.9–302.0/	Whirlpools: 2
Beam (ft/m): 94.4/28.8	. . . . .13.0–28.0	Self-Service Launderette: . . . . .No
Draft (ft/m): 22.4/6.85	Cabins (outside view): 504	Dedicated Cinema/Seats: . . . . .No
Propulsion/Propellers: . . . . .diesel	Cabins (interior/no view): 276	Library: . . . . .Yes
(31,680kW)/2 azimuthing pods	Cabins (for one person): 0	

OVERALL SCORE: 1,439 OUT OF A POSSIBLE 2,000 POINTS

OVERVIEW. *MSC Lirica*, sister to *MSC Opera*, was the first of a pair of new-builds for Mediterranean Shipping Cruises (MSC), Italy's largest privately owned cruise line (its former name was Star Lauro Cruises).

The blue funnel is quite sleek, with a swept-back design, and carries the MSC logo. The ship is fitted with an azimuthing pod propulsion system *(for details, see page 45)*.

Inside, the layout and passenger flow is quite good with the exception of a couple of points of congestion (typically when the first seating comes out of the dining room and passengers on second seating are waiting to go in. The decor has many Italian influences, and this includes clean lines, minimalism in furniture design, and an eclectic collection of colors and soft furnishings that somehow work well together, and without any hint of garishness.

Real wood and marble have been used extensively in the interiors, and the high quality reflects MSC's commitment to the vessel's future. The "fit and finish" of the interior decor, and most carpeting, is very good.

Facilities include the ship's main showlounge, a nightclub/discotheque, several lounges and bars, an internet center (Cyber Cafe, with 10 terminals), a virtual reality center, a shopping gallery named Rodeo Drive (with shops that have an integrated bar and entertainment area so that shopping becomes a city-like environment where you can shop, drink, and be entertained all in one convenient area), and a children's club. Gamblers may find solace in the Las Vegas Casino, with blackjack, poker and roulette games, together with an array of slot machines. There is also a card room, but the integral library is small and disappointing, and there are no hardback books.

BERLITZ'S RATINGS

	Possible	Achieved
Ship	500	407
Accommodation	200	156
Food	400	236
Service	400	299
Entertainment	100	55
Cruise	400	286

The ship is designed to accommodate families with children, who have their own play center, youth counselors, and programming. Anyone who is wheelchair-bound should note that there is no access to the uppermost forward and aft decks, although access throughout most of the interior of the ship is very good (there are also several wheelchair-accessible public restrooms). The passenger hallways are a little narrow on some decks for you to pass when housekeeping carts are in place, however.

Some things that passengers find irritating: the ship's photographers always seem to be in your face; the telephone numbering system to reach such places as the information bureau (2224) and hospital (2360) are not easy to remember (single digit numbers would be better).

Standing in line for embarkation, disembarkation, shore tenders and for self-serve buffet meals is an inevitable aspect of cruising aboard all large ships.

The onboard currency is the euro, and gratuities are extra even though bar drinks already include the 15% seervice charge added to all drinks/beverage orders.

SUITABLE FOR: *MSC Lirica* is best suited to young adult couples, singles, and families with tots, children and teens who enjoy big ship surroundings, a big city life, with all its attendant noise (some call it ambience), and passengers of different nationalities and languages (mostly European).

ACCOMMODATION. There are 11 different price levels for accommodation, depending on the grade and location you choose: one suite category, five outside-view cabin grades, and five interior (no view) cabin grades. Included are 132 "suites" with private balcony (note that the partitions between each balcony are of the partial and not the full wall type), outside-view cabins and interior (no view) cabins.

No matter what grade of cabin you choose, all have a mini-bar and personal safe, satellite-linked television, several audio channels, and 24-hour room service (note that while tea and coffee are complimentary, snacks for room service carry a delivery charge of €2.50 each time).

Accommodation designated as Suites (they are not true suites, as there is no separate bedroom and lounge – in other words, it is not a "suite" of rooms) also has more room, a larger lounge area, walk-in closet, wall-to-wall vanity counter, a bathroom with combination bathtub and shower, toilet, and semi-private balcony with light (the partitions are of the partial, not full, type). The bathrobes are 100% cotton. However, except for the very highest category, the suite bathrooms are very plain, with white plastic wash-basins and white walls, and mirrors that steam up.

According to the rules of feng shui, it is bad luck to place any mirror in such a position that it can be seen by anyone lying in bed (there are two floor-to-ceiling mirrors opposite the bed).

Some cabins on Scarlatti Deck have views obstructed by lifeboats, while those on Deck 10 aft (10105–10159) can be subject to late night noise from the discotheque on the deck above.

CUISINE. There are two dining rooms (La Bussola Restaurant, and the smaller, slightly more intimate L'Ippocampo Restaurant, located one deck above), both of which have large ocean-view picture windows at the aft end of the ship. There are two seatings for meals, in keeping with all other ships in the MSC fleet, and tables are for two, four, six or eight.

La Pergola is the most formal restaurant, offering stylish Italian cuisine. It is assigned to all passengers occupying accommodation designated as suites, although other passengers can dine in it too, on a reservations-only basis. As you might expect, the food and service are superior to that in the main dining room.

Casual, self-serve buffets (for breakfast and lunch) can be taken in Le Bistrot Cafeteria (there are serving lines on both port and starboard sides). For fast foods, there is also a grill and a pizzeria (both are located outside, adjacent to the swimming pool and ship's funnel).

The Coffee Corner, located on the upper, second level of the main lobby, is the place for coffees and pastry items – as well for people-watching throughout the day. Although there are windows, the view is not of the ocean, but of the stowed gangways and associated equipment.

ENTERTAINMENT. The Broadway Theater is the ship's main showlounge, located in the forward section of the ship. It has tiered seating set in a sloping floor, and sightlines are good from most seats. The room can also serve as a venue for large social functions. There is no separate bandstand, and the shows work with recorded music; hence there is little consistency in orchestration and sound balance.

High-quality entertainment has not, to date, been part of MSC's mindset. Hence, production shows and variety acts tend to be adequate at best. The Lirica Lounge (located one deck above the showlounge) is the place for social dancing, with live music provided by a band. Meanwhile, for the young and lively set, there is The Blue Club (the ship's throbbing, ear-melting discotheque).

SPA/FITNESS. The Lirica Health Center is located one deck above the navigation bridge at the forward end of the ship. The complex features a beauty salon, several treatment rooms offering massage and other body-pampering treatments, as well as a gymnasium with ocean views and an array of high-tech, muscle-toning and strengthening equipment. There's also a thermal suite, containing different kinds of steam rooms combined with aromatherapy infusions, at €12 per session, or six sessions for €60.

The health center is run as a concession by the Italian company OceanView, with European hairstylists and Balinese massage and body treatment staff. Examples of treatment prices: full body massage, shiatsu massage, both at €90 for 50 minutes; cranial massage, €20 for 20 minutes; facial, €65; shampoo and finish, €32. Gratuities are not included, and are not charged to your account.

● **For more extensive general information about the MSC Cruises experience, see pages 143–4.**

MSC Magnifica
★★★★

Size:	Large (Resort) Ship	Total Crew:	987	Cabins (wheelchair accessible):	17
Tonnage:	92,409	Passengers		Wheelchair accessibility	Good
Lifestyle:	Standard	(lower beds/all berths):	2,518/3,013	Cabin Voltage:	110 volts
Cruise Line:	MSC Cruises	Passenger Space Ratio		Elevators:	13
Former Names:	none	(lower beds/all berths):	37.0/30.9	Casino (gaming tables):	Yes
Builder:	Aker Yards (France)	Crew/Passenger Ratio		Slot Machines:	Yes
Original Cost:	n/a	(lower beds/all berths):	2.5/3.0	Swimming Pools (outdoors):	2
Entered Service:	Mar 2010	Cabins (total):	1,259	Swimming Pools (indoors):	0
Registry:	Panama	Size Range (sq ft/m):	150.6–301.3/	Whirlpools:	4
Length (ft/m):	963.9/293.8		14.0–28.0	Self-Service Launderette:	No
Beam (ft/m):	105.6/32.2	Cabins (outside view):	1,000	Dedicated Cinema/Seats:	No
Draft (ft/m):	25.2/7.7	Cabins (interior/no view):	275	Library:	Yes
Propulsion/Propellers:	diesel/2	Cabins (for one person):	0		
Passenger Decks:	13	Cabins (with private balcony):	827		

BERLITZ'S OVERALL SCORE: 1,467 OUT OF A POSSIBLE 2,000 POINTS

OVERVIEW. *MSC Magnifica* is one of a quartet of the same class (the others: *MSC Musica, MSC Poesia, MSC Orchestra*). The ship has a blue funnel with a swept-back design that balances an otherwise large-ship profile. The hull contains large circular porthole-style windows instead of square or rectangular ones. From a technical viewpoint, the ship is powered by diesel motors driving electric generators to provide power to two conventional propellers.

The interior layout and passenger flow is quite good, and decks are named after Mediterranean destinations, such as Capri, Positano, Porto Venere, Ischia. The decor has plenty of Italian and Mediterranean influences, including clean lines, minimalism in furniture design, and a collection of colors, soft furnishings and fabrics that work well together. Real wood and marble have been used extensively in the Italianate interiors, and the high quality reflects the commitment that MSC Cruises has in the vessel's future. Some of the artwork is quite whimsical, but in keeping with the ship's contemporary design features.

The focal point of the ship is the main three-deck high lobby, with a water-feature backdrop and a crystal piano on a small stage that appears to float on a pond. Other facilities include a large main show lounge, a nightclub, discotheque (which also houses two bowling lanes), numerous lounges and bars (including L'Olimpiade sports/wine/food bar), library, card room, an internet center, 4-D virtual reality center, children's club, and dedicated cigar lounge.

One of the nicest venues is the Tiger Lounge, with its animal-themed decor and sumptuous but heavy chairs and long curvy bar. A shopping area, which includes an electronics store, has an integrated bar and entertainment area

BERLITZ'S RATINGS

	Possible	Achieved
Ship	500	414
Accommodation	200	156
Food	400	243
Service	400	298
Entertainment	100	62
Cruise	400	294

that flows through the main lobby so that shopping becomes a city-like environment where you can shop, drink, and be entertained all in one convenient area. Cigar smokers will find a cigar lounge with specialized smoke extraction and stocking a selection of Cuban (including Cohiba, Monte Cristo, Romeo e Juliet, Partagas), Dominican (Davidoff), and Italian (Toscana) smokes.

Drinking places include a pub-like venue as well as several comfortable lounges with live music. A mini-golf course is on the port side of the funnel, while a walking/jogging track encircles an upper level above the two swimming pools. The ship is designed to accommodate families with children, who have their own play center, video games room, youth counselors, and activity programs.

Although access throughout most of the interior of the ship is very good, anyone who is wheelchair-bound should note that the passenger hallways are narrow on some decks for you to pass when housekeeping carts are in place. Sadly, there is no walk-around open promenade deck.

The on-board currency is the euro, and 15% is added to all bar drink prices.

ACCOMMODATION. There are 12 price levels, depending on grade and location: suites, outside-view cabins, and interior (no view) cabins. Included are 18 "suites" with private balcony, mini-suites, outside-view cabins and interior (no view) cabins. Contrary to nautical convention, the cabin numbering system has even numbered cabins on the starboard side, and odd numbered cabins on the port side.

All cabins have very high-quality Italian bed linen (400-count cotton for suites, 300-count cotton for all other cabins), a mini-bar, personal safe, satellite flat-screen TV set, several audio channels, and 24-hour room service. Note that, while continental breakfast is complimentary from 7:30am to 10am, room service snacks are available at extra cost at any other time.

Accommodation designated as "suites" – they are not true suites, as there is no separate bedroom and lounge – also has more space, although they are small compared to suites on some of the major cruise lines. They have a larger lounge area, walk-in closet, and vanity desk with drawer-mounted hairdryer; a bathroom with combination tub and shower, toilet, and semi-private balcony with light. The partitions between each balcony are of the partial, not full, type. The bathrobes and towels are 100% cotton, and a pillow menu with a choice of five pillows is available.

Many cabins on Camogli Deck have views obstructed by lifeboats. Some of the most popular cabins are those at the aft section of the ship, with views over the stern from the balcony cabins. The 17 cabins for the disabled are spacious and well-equipped.

Cuisine. There are two principal dining rooms: L'Edera and Quattro Venti. They are located aft, with large ocean-view picture windows. There are two seatings for meals, in keeping with other ships in the MSC Cruises fleet, and tables are for two, four, six or eight; seating is both banquette-style and in individual chairs – although the chairs are slim and do not have armrests. All dining venues are managed and supervised by experienced Italians.

Casual, self-serve buffets for breakfast and lunch are set out in the Sahara Cafeteria, or at a pool deck outside fast-food eatery. Coffee/tea and pastries can be taken in several bars adjacent to the midships atrium lobby.

Alternative Dining Spots: Enclosed in the ship's center, on Amalfi Deck, Shanghai is a Chinese à la carte extra-cost restaurant. L'Oesi is a reservation-required, extra charge, à la carte dining spot that, by day, forms the aft section of the Sahara Cafeteria, with its Moroccan decor. Dinners are cooked to order from the adjacent galley.

The Sports Bar is a venue for lite-bite snack foods (examples: chicken breast and rocket salad; eggs stuffed with salmon roe; smoked salmon rosettes; assorted sole rolls – all at a small additional cost).

Silver trays full of late-night snacks are taken throughout the ship by waiters, and on some days, special late-night desserts, such as flambé items, are showcased in various lounges. The ship makes its own ice cream.

All sorts of coffees are available in the many bars and lounges – €1.10 for an espresso and €1.50 for a cappuccino, both plus 15% gratuity, is extremely good value.

Entertainment. The Royal Theater is the large, principal show lounge, and its tiered seating spans three decks in the forward section of the ship, with good sightlines from most of the plush, comfortable seats. The room can also serve as a venue for large groups or social functions. All the large-scale production shows are performed to prerecorded music – there is no showband.

The L'Amethista Lounge is the place for social dancing and functions such as cooking demonstrations, with live music provided by a band. And, for the young and lively crowd, there's the ear-melting T32 discotheque. With its floor-to-ceiling windows, it is a quiet, pleasant place to relax and read during sea days.

Additionally, big-screen movies are shown on a mega-screen above the forward pool, just behind the ship's mast.

Spa/Fitness. The Aurea Spa is one deck above the navigation bridge at the forward end of the ship. The complex has a beauty salon, several treatment rooms offering massage and other body-pampering treatments, and a gymnasium with forward ocean views and an array of muscle-toning and strengthening equipment. There's also a Middle East-themed thermal suite, containing steam rooms and saunas with aromatherapy infusions, and a relaxation/hot tub room; to use these facilities costs €30 per day, or €150 per cruise. Sports facilities include table tennis, a tennis court mini golf course, golf practice net, two shuffleboard courts, and a jogging track.

● **For more extensive general information about the MSC Cruises experience, see pages 143–4.**

MSC Melody
★★★

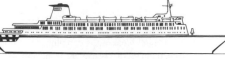

Size: ....Mid-Size Ship	Passenger Decks: 9	Cabins (with private balcony): 0
Tonnage: 36,500	Total Crew: 535	Cabins (wheelchair accessible): ......Yes
Lifestyle: ....Standard	Passengers	Wheelchair accessibility ....Fair
Cruise Line: ....MSC Cruises	(lower beds/all berths): 1,098/1,600	Cabin Current: ....110 volts
Former Names: .Star/ShipAtlantic, Atlantic	Passenger Space Ratio	Elevators: 4
Builder: ............C.N.I.M. (France)	(lower beds/all berths): 33.2/22.8	Casino (gaming tables): ....Yes
Original Cost: ....$100 million	Crew/Passenger Ratio	Slot Machines: ....Yes
Entered Service: ....Apr 1982/June 1997	(lower beds/all berths): 2.0/2.9	Swimming Pools (outdoors): 1
Registry: ....Panama	Cabins (total): 549	Swimming Pools (indoors): 1
Length (ft/m): 671.9/204.8	Size Range (sq ft/m): 137.0–427.0/	Whirlpools: 3
Beam (ft/m): 89.7/27.4	12.7–39.5	Self-Service Launderette: ....No
Draft (ft/m): 25.5/7.8	Cabins (outside view): 392	Dedicated Cinema/Seats: Yes/227
Propulsion/Propellers: ....diesel	Cabins (interior/no view): 157	Library: ....Yes (2 book racks)
(22,070 kW)/2	Cabins (for one person): 0	

BERLITZ'S OVERALL SCORE: 1,175 OUT OF A POSSIBLE 2,000 POINTS

OVERVIEW. The ship has a short, stubby, foreshortened bow and squat funnel, and an all-white hull and superstructure. There is a good amount of outdoor deck space, but noise levels can be high when the ship is full (particularly in summer). The interior is quite spacious, with plenty of public rooms, mostly high-ceilinged. The decor is somber in places, and the lighting is quite subdued. There is a generous amount of stainless steel and teakwood trim. A large observation lounge (with good views from large picture windows) is rather wasted as an informal eating area.

There is a fairly good indoor-outdoor pool area (which can be covered in bad weather). There is a fairly good children's program at peak periods, and several children's and teens' counselors. About 60% of passengers will be Italian. Expect lots of extra charges. The onboard currency is the euro, and 15% is added to all drinks/beverage orders. There may be a charge for shuttle buses in some ports of call.

The almost constant loud announcements are intrusive. There is no walk-around promenade deck outdoors, and cushioned pads are not provided for the sunloungers. The ship has only four elevators – not nearly enough, and they are not linked. Standing in line for embarkation, disembarkation, and buffet meals is inevitable aboard large ships. There is often extreme congestion in the foyer adjacent to the showlounge, particularly on gala evenings when show audiences and the captain's cocktail party crowd merge.

SUITABLE FOR: Best suited to couples, singles, and families with children and teens who enjoy big ship surroundings, a big city life, with all its attendant noise, and passengers of different nationalities and languages.

BERLITZ'S RATINGS		
	Possible	Achieved
Ship	500	297
Accommodation	200	126
Food	400	220
Service	400	240
Entertainment	100	58
Cruise	400	234

ACCOMMODATION. There are 12 categories and price grades. Six suites have plenty of space for families of four, and have a decent walk-in closet. The bathroom is large and has a full-size tub, oversize basin, and an uncomfortable square toilet. Other outside-view and interior (no view) cabins are of a good size, and have ample closet and drawer space. Many cabins have upper berths – good for families, although with four persons there is very little space for luggage. The cabin soundproofing is extremely poor, and the room service menu is quite basic.

CUISINE. The Galaxy Restaurant, on a lower deck (Restaurant Deck), is large and quite attractive even though the decor is from the 1980s, but the tables are very close together and the noise level is extremely high. There are two seatings, and many Italian dishes. The food quality generally is adequate for the price, but doesn't live up to menu descriptions. Each cruise usually includes two gala evenings. There is a limited wine list.

ENTERTAINMENT. The Club Universe is just forward of midships on Lounge Deck. Although the ceiling is high, it is a single-level room with banquette seating. The ship has a showband and several small musical units.

SPA/FITNESS. The SeaSport Health and Fitness Center has a gymnasium (with treadmills, exercycles, and muscle-pumping equipment), beauty salon, and massage room.

● **For more extensive general information about the MSC Cruises experience, see pages 143–4.**

MSC Musica
★★★★

Size:	Large Resort Ship	Passenger Decks:	13
Tonnage:	92,409	Total Crew:	987
Lifestyle:	Standard	Passengers	
Cruise Line:	MSC Cruises	(lower beds/all berths):	2,550/3,013
Former Names:	none	Passenger Space Ratio	
Builder:	Aker Yards (France)	(lower beds/all berths):	36.2/30.6
Original Cost:	$360 million	Crew/Passenger Ratio	
Entered Service:	July 2006	(lower beds/all berths):	2.6/3.0
Registry:	Panama	Cabins (total):	1,275
Length (ft/m):	963.9/293.8	Size Range (sq ft/m):	150.6–301.3/
Beam (ft/m):	105.6/32.2		14.0–28.0
Draft (ft/m):	25.2/7.7	Cabins (outside view):	1,000
Propulsion/Propellers:	diesel	Cabins (interior/no view):	275
	(31,680kW)/2	Cabins (for one person):	0

Cabins (with private balcony): 827
Cabins (wheelchair accessible): 17
Wheelchair accessibility ....Good
Cabin Voltage: ....110/220 volts
Elevators: 13
Casino (gaming tables): ....Yes
Slot Machines: ....Yes
Swimming Pools (outdoors): 2
Swimming Pools (indoors): 0
Whirlpools: 4
Self-Service Launderette: ....No
Dedicated Cinema/Seats: ....No
Library: ....Yes

OVERALL SCORE: 1,462 OUT OF A POSSIBLE 2,000 POINTS

OVERVIEW. *MSC Musica* is an extension and evolution of the slightly smaller *MSC Lirica* and *MSC Opera*. The blue funnel is quite sleek, with a swept-back design and carries the MSC logo in gold lettering, and forward of the mast, additional decks provide a more balanced profile. The hull features large circular porthole-style windows instead of square or rectangular windows. From a technical viewpoint, the ship is powered by diesel motors driving electric generators to provide power to two conventional propellers.

BERLITZ'S RATINGS

	Possible	Achieved
Ship	500	412
Accommodation	200	156
Food	400	243
Service	400	298
Entertainment	100	62
Cruise	400	291

The interior layout and passenger flow is quite good with the exception of a couple of points of congestion, typically when the first seating exits the two main dining rooms and passengers on the second seating are waiting to enter. The musically-themed decor has many Italian influences, including clean lines, minimalism in furniture design, and a collection of colors, soft furnishings and fabrics that work well together, although it's a little more garish than one would expect.

Real wood and marble have been used extensively in the interiors, and the high quality reflects the commitment that MSC Cruises has in the vessel's future.

The focal point of the ship is the main three-deck high lobby, with a water-feature backdrop and a crystal piano on a small stage that appears to float on a pond. Other facilities include a large main show lounge, a nightclub, discotheque, numerous lounges and bars (including a wine bar), library, card room, an internet center, virtual reality center, children's club, and cigar lounge with specialized smoke extraction and a selection of Cuban (including Cohiba, Monte Cristo, Romeo e Juliet, Partagas), Dominican (Davidoff), and Italian (Toscana) smokes.

A shopping gallery, which includes an electronics store, has an integrated bar and entertainment area that flows through the main lobby so that shopping becomes a city-like environment where you can shop, drink, and be entertained all in one convenient area. Gamblers will like the expansive San Remo Casino (with blackjack, poker and roulette games, together with an array of slot machines).

Drinking places include a pub-like venue as well as several comfortable lounges with live music. A mini-golf course is on the port side of the funnel, while a walking/jogging track encircles an upper level above the two swimming pools. The ship is designed to accommodate families with children, who have their own play center, video games room, youth counselors, and activity programs.

Some of the artwork is whimsical, but fishermen will appreciate the stuffed head from a blue marlin caught by Pierfrancesco Vago, president of MSC Cruises in 2004 – weighing 588 pounds (266.7 kg), it stands at the Blue Marlin Bar on the pool deck. And do check out the "restroom with a view" – the men's/ladies toilets adjacent to the Blue Marlin pool deck bar have a great ocean view (you can even watch the passing scenery while sitting on the toilet if you leave the door open).

The on-board currency is the euro, and 15% is added to all drinks/beverage orders.

Although access throughout most of the interior of the ship is very good, anyone who is wheelchair-bound should note that the passenger hallways are a little narrow on some decks for you to pass when housekeeping carts are in place. Sadly, there is no walk-around open promenade deck.

SUITABLE FOR: *MSC Musica* is best suited to young adult couples, singles, and families with tots, children and teens who enjoy big ship surroundings, a big city life, with all its attendant noise (some call it ambience), and passengers of different nationalities and languages (mostly European).

ACCOMMODATION. There are 12 price levels, depending on grade and location: suites, outside-view cabins, and interior (no view) cabins. Included are 18 "suites" with private balcony, mini-suites, outside-view cabins and interior (no view) cabins. Contrary to nautical convention, the cabin numbering system has even numbered cabins on the starboard side, and odd numbered cabins on the port side.

All cabins have a mini-bar and personal safe, satellite flat-screen TV, several audio channels, and 24-hour room service. Note that, while continental breakfast is complimentary from 7:30 to 10am, room service snacks are available at extra cost at any other time.

Accommodation designated as "suites" (they are not true suites, as there is no separate bedroom and lounge) also has more room (although they are small compared to suites on some of the major cruise lines), a larger lounge area, walk-in closet, and vanity desk with drawer-mounted hairdryer; a bathroom with combination bathtub and shower, toilet, and semi-private balcony with light (the partitions between each balcony are of the partial, not full, type). The bathrobes and towels are 100% cotton. The suite bathrooms are plain, with white plastic washbasins and white walls, and mirrors that steam up.

Many cabins on Forte Deck have views obstructed by lifeboats. Also, cabins on the uppermost accommodation deck (Cantata Deck) may be subject to sunloungers being dragged across the deck above when it is set up or cleaned early in the morning. Some of the most popular cabins are those at the aft end of the ship, with views over the ship's stern from the balcony cabins (on Virtuoso, Adagio, Intermezzo and Forte decks).

The 17 cabins for the disabled are spacious and well equipped.

CUISINE. There are two main dining rooms (L'Oleandro and Le Maxim's), both located aft, with large ocean-view picture windows. There are two seatings for meals, and tables are for two, four, six or eight; seating is both banquette-style and in individual chairs; the chairs, however, are slim and lack armrests. All dining venues are managed by Italians.

Passengers occupying accommodation designated as suites and deluxe grades are typically assigned the best tables in the quietest sections of Le Maxim's restaurant, which itself is quieter than L'Oleandro, the main dining room.

Casual, self-serve buffets (for breakfast and lunch) can be taken in the Gli Archi Cafeteria (one section of which forms the reservations-only Il Giardino; or at a pool deck outside fast-food eatery. Coffee/tea and pastries can be taken in several bars adjacent to the midships atrium lobby.
Alternative Dining Spots:
● *Il Giardino* is an à la carte dining spot; the cost is Euro18 per person for dinner.

● *Kaito* is a Japanese sushi bar with counter and table seating and a menu that has a fine array of à la carte sashimi pieces, nigiri and temaki sushi and maki rolls, tempura and teriyaki items, and a choice of several types of cold or hot sake, and Japanese beer.
● *Enoteca Wine Bar* is a very creative wine bar, and provides a selection of famous regional cheeses, hams and wine in a relaxing and entertaining bistro-style setting.

In other words, there are more dining choices than aboard other previous MSC Cruises ships, if you are willing to pay extra.

Silver trays full of late-night snacks are taken throughout the ship by waiters, and on some days, special late-night desserts, such as flambé items, are showcased in various lounges like the Il Tucana Lounge. The ship makes its own ice cream.

ENTERTAINMENT. The Theatro La Scala, the large, principal show lounge, is in the forward section of the ship. It has tiered seating on two levels (the sightlines are good from most of the plush, comfortable seats). The room can also serve as a venue for large groups or social functions.

High-quality entertainment has not, to date, been a priority for MSC Cruises. Production shows and variety acts tend to be amateurish (particularly when compared to some other major cruise lines). There is no showband, and all shows are performed to recorded music "click" tracks.

The Il Tucano (Tucan) Lounge (aft of the show lounge) is the place for social dancing and functions such as cooking demonstrations, with live music provided by a band. Another nightclub, the Crystal Lounge, provides music for the social dance set. Meanwhile, for the young and lively crowd, the ship's ear-melting G32 discotheque is the place to head for; with its floor-to-ceiling windows, it is a quiet, pleasant place to relax and read during sea days.

Additionally, big-screen movies are shown on a large screen above the forward pool, just behind the ship's mast.

SPA/FITNESS. The Aloha Beauty Farm (spa center) is one deck above the navigation bridge at the forward end of the ship. The complex has a beauty salon, several treatment rooms offering massage and other body-pampering treatments, and a gymnasium with forward ocean views and an array of high-tech, muscle-toning and strengthening equipment. There's also a Middle East-themed thermal suite, containing steam rooms and saunas with aromatherapy infusions, and a relaxation/hot tub room; to use these facilities costs €30 per day, or €150 per cruise. Examples of treatment prices: Aromaspa Massage, €158 (90 minutes); shiatsu massage, €99 (50 minutes); facial, €99 (50 minutes).

The spa is run as a concession by Steiner Leisure, with European hairstylists and massage/body treatment staff.

Sports facilities include table tennis, a tennis court mini golf course, golf practice net, two shuffleboard courts, and a jogging track.

● **For more extensive general information about the MSC Cruises experience, see pages 143–4.**

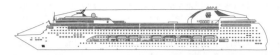

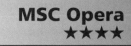

MSC Opera
★★★★

Size: . . . . .Large Resort Ship	Passenger Decks: 10	Cabins (with private balcony): 200
Tonnage: 59,058	Total Crew: .701	Cabins (wheelchair accessible): 4
Lifestyle: . . . . .Standard	Passengers	Wheelchair accessibility . . . . .Good
Cruise Line: . . . . .MSC Cruises	(lower beds/all berths): 1,756/2,200	Cabin Voltage: . . . . .110 and 220
Former Names: . . . . .none	Passenger Space Ratio	Elevators: 9
Builder: .Chantiers de l'Atlantique (France)	(lower beds/all berths): 33.6/26.8	Casino (gaming tables): . . . . .Yes
Original Cost: . . . .$266 million	Crew/Passenger Ratio	Slot Machines: . . . . .Yes
Entered Service: . . . . .Mar 2004	(lower beds/all berths): 2.5/3.1	Swimming Pools (outdoors): 2
Registry: . . . . .Italy	Cabins (total): 878	Swimming Pools (indoors): 0
Length (ft/m): 830.7/256.25	Size Range (sq ft/m): 139.9–302.0/	Whirlpools: 2
Beam (ft/m): 94.4/28.8	13.0–28.0	Self-Service Launderette: . . . . .No
Draft (ft/m): 22.4/6.85	Cabins (outside view): 504	Dedicated Cinema/Seats: . . . . .No
Propulsion/Propellers: . . . . .diesel	Cabins (interior/no view): 276	Library: . . . . .Yes
(31,680kW)/2 azimuthing pods	Cabins (for one person): 0	

OVERALL SCORE: 1,445 OUT OF A POSSIBLE 2,000 POINTS

OVERVIEW. *MSC Opera* was the second of the new ships built for MSC Cruises, Italy's largest privately owned cruise line. The first was *MSC Lirica*. However, *MSC Opera* has almost 100 cabins more than *MSC Lirica*. The blue funnel is quite sleek, with a swept-back design and carries the MSC logo in gold lettering. Although similar in size and structure to *MSC Lirica,* there are many modifications, mostly in technical spaces, and improvements in the layout of public rooms. More cabins have a private balcony.

All decks are named after operas. The interior layout and passenger flow is quite good with the exception of a couple of points of congestion, typically when the first seating exits the dining room and passengers on second seating are waiting to enter. The decor has many Italian influences, including clean lines, minimalism in furniture design, and a collection of colors, soft furnishings and fabrics that work well together, and without any hint of garishness. Real wood and marble have been used extensively in the interiors, and the high quality reflects the commitment that MSC Cruises has in the vessel's future. The "fit and finish" of the interior decor, and most carpeting, is very good.

Facilities include the ship's main show lounge, a nightclub/discotheque, several lounges and bars, an internet center with 10 terminals, a virtual reality center, a children's club, a shopping gallery named Via Conditti (with shops that have an integrated bar and entertainment area so that shopping becomes a city-like environment where you can shop, drink, and be entertained all in one convenient area). Gamblers will find pleasure in the Monte Carlo Casino, with blackjack, poker and roulette games, together with an array of slot machines. There is also a card room, but the integral

BERLITZ'S RATINGS

	Possible	Achieved
Ship	500	410
Accommodation	200	156
Food	400	234
Service	400	298
Entertainment	100	62
Cruise	400	285

library is small and disappointing, and there are no hardback books.

Possible drinking places include the Sotto Vento Pub (under the show lounge), or the La Cabala lounge. Outside on deck, a neat 8-hole mini-golf course wraps around the funnel, while a walking/jogging track encircles the ship's two swimming pools. The ship is designed to accommodate families with children, who have their own play center, youth counselors, and programming.

Anyone who is wheelchair-bound should note that there is no access to the uppermost forward and aft decks, although access throughout most of the interior of the ship is very good (there are also several wheelchair-accessible public restrooms). The passenger hallways are a little narrow on some decks for you to pass when housekeeping carts are in place, however.

Minor niggles include the "in your face" photographers; constant music in every lounge; and the fact that standing in line for embarkation, disembarkation, shore tenders and for self-serve buffet meals is an inevitable aspect of cruising aboard all large ships (although lines are minimal when the ship operates from Port Everglades). Smokers are everywhere, and are virtually impossible to avoid (in typical European fashion, ashtrays are simply moved – if used at all – to wherever smokers happen to be sitting). Sadly, there is no forward observation lounge.

The onboard currency is the euro, and 15% is added to all drinks/beverage orders

SUITABLE FOR: *MSC Opera* is best suited to young adult couples, singles, and families with tots, children and teens who enjoy big ship surroundings, a big city life, with all its attendant noise (some call it ambience), and passengers of different nationalities and languages (mostly European).

ACCOMMODATION. There are 11 price levels, depending on grade and location: one suite category, five outside-view cabin grades, and five interior (no view) cabin grades. Included are 172 "suites" with private balcony, outside-view cabins and interior (no view) cabins. The cabin numbering system has even numbered cabins on the starboard side, and odd numbered cabins on the port side – contrary to nautical convention.

All cabins have a mini-bar and personal safe, satellite TV, several audio channels, and 24-hour room service (note that while tea and coffee are complimentary, snacks for room service carry a delivery charge of €2.50 each time).

Accommodation designated as Suites (they are not true suites, as there is no separate bedroom and lounge) also has more room, a larger lounge area, walk-in closet, wall-to-wall vanity counter, a bathroom with combination bathtub and shower, toilet, and semi-private balcony with light (the partitions betwen each balcony are of the partial, not full, type). 100 percent cotton bathrobes are provided. However, except for the very highest category, the suite bathrooms are very plain, with white plastic washbasins and white walls, and mirrors that steam up.

Some cabins on Othello Deck and Rigoletto Deck have views obstructed by lifeboats, while those on Turandot Deck aft (10192–10241) may be subject to late-night and early morning noise from the cafeteria on the deck above. Also, cabins on the uppermost accommodation deck are subject to deck chairs and tables being dragged across the deck when it is set up or cleaned early in the morning.

CUISINE. There is one principal dining room (La Caravella Restaurant), with large ocean view picture windows in the aft third of the ship. There are two seatings for meals, in keeping with other ships in the MSC Cruises fleet, and tables are for two, four, six or eight.

L'Approdo Restaurant is assigned to all passengers occupying accommodation designated as suites, although other passengers can dine in it too, on a reservations-only basis. As you might expect, the food and service are superior to that in the main dining room.

Casual, self-serve buffets (for breakfast and lunch) can be taken in Le Vele Cafeteria (the serving lines on both port and starboard sides are quite cramped, and the food is quite basic); or at the pool deck outside the fast food eatery, with grill and pizzeria. Coffee/tea and pastries can be taken in the Aroma Café set around the upper level of the two-deck-high atrium lobby, but annoying videos constantly play on TVsets in the forward sections.

ENTERTAINMENT. The 713-seat Theatre dell Opera is the ship's main show lounge, located in the forward section of the ship. It has tiered seating set in a sloping floor, and the sightlines are good from most seats, which are plush and comfortable. The room can also serve as a venue for large social functions. There is no separate bandstand, and the shows work with recorded music; hence there is little consistency in orchestration and sound balance.

High-quality entertainment has not, to date, been a priority for MSC Cruises. Hence, production shows and variety acts tend to be amateurish at best (when compared to some other major cruise lines).

The Opera Lounge (one deck above the show lounge) is for social dancing, with a live band. Meanwhile, for the young and lively set, there is the Byblos Discotheque (the ship's throbbing, ear-melting discotheque).

SPA/FITNESS. The Opera Health Center is located one deck above the navigation bridge at the forward end of the ship. The complex features a beauty salon, several treatment rooms offering massage and other body-pampering treatments, as well as a gymnasium with ocean views and an array of high-tech, muscle-toning and strengthening equipment. There's also a thermal suite, containing different kinds of steam rooms combined with aromatherapy infusions, at €12 per session, or six sessions for €60.

The health center is run as a concession by the Italian company OceanView, with European hairstylists and Balinese massage and body treatment staff. Examples of treatment prices: Balinese massage, €93 (45 minutes); shiatsu massage, €90 (45 minutes); hot stone therapy, €100 (45 minutes); facial, €65; pedicure, €40. Gratuities are not included, and are not charged to your account.

● **For more extensive general information about the MSC Cruises experience, see pages 143–4.**

MSC Orchestra
★★★★

Size:	Large Resort Ship	Passenger Decks:	13
Tonnage:	92,409	Total Crew:	987
Lifestyle:	Standard	Passengers	
Cruise Line:	MSC Cruises	(lower beds/all berths):	2,550/3,013
Former Names:	none	Passenger Space Ratio	
Builder:	Aker Yards (France)	(lower beds/all berths):	36.2/30.6
Original Cost:	$360 million	Crew/Passenger Ratio	
Entered Service:	May 2007	(lower beds/all berths):	2.6/3.0
Registry:	Italy	Cabins (total):	1,275
Length (ft/m):	963.9/293.8	Size Range (sq ft/m):	150.6–301.3/
Beam (ft/m):	105.6/32.2		14.0–28.0
Draft (ft/m):	25.2/7.7	Cabins (outside view):	1,000
Propulsion/Propellers:	diesel electric	Cabins (interior/no view):	275
	(40.4MW)/2	Cabins (for one person):	0

Cabins (with private balcony):	827
Cabins (wheelchair accessible):	17
Wheelchair accessibility	Good
Cabin Voltage:	110/220 volts
Elevators:	13
Casino (gaming tables):	Yes
Slot Machines:	Yes
Swimming Pools (outdoors):	2
Swimming Pools (indoors):	0
Whirlpools:	4
Self-Service Launderette:	No
Dedicated Cinema/Seats:	No
Library:	Yes

BERLITZ'S OVERALL SCORE: 1,465 OUT OF A POSSIBLE 2,000 POINTS

OVERVIEW. *MSC Orchestra* is a sister to *MSC Musica*, which entered service in 2006. The ship has a balanced profile. The blue funnel is of a sleek, swept-back design and carries the MSC logo in gold lettering. From a technical viewpoint, the ship is powered by diesel motors driving electric generators to provide power to two conventional propellers.

The interior layout and passenger flow is quite good with the exception of a couple of points of congestion – typically when the first seating exits the two main dining rooms and passengers on the second seating are waiting to enter. The decor is decidedly European, with many Italian influences, including clean lines, minimalism in furniture design, and a collection of high-quality soft furnishings and fabrics in warm colors that work beautifully together, and with no hint of garishness at all (arguably much nicer and softer than sister ship *MSC Musica*). Real wood and marble have been used extensively in the interiors, and the high quality reflects the commitment that MSC Cruises has in its product and the vessel's future.

Facilities include a large main show lounge, a nightclub/discotheque, numerous lounges and bars (including the stunning "Out of Africa" Savannah Lounge, library, card room, an internet center, virtual reality center, shopping gallery (the shops are integrated with many bars, lounges and entertainment areas so that shopping becomes a city-like environment where you can shop, drink, and be entertained all in one convenient area).

Cigar lovers will find a peaceful cigar lounge with specialized smoke extraction and a selection of Cuban (including Cohiba, Monte Cristo, Romeo e Juliet, Partagas), Dominican (Davidoff), and Italian (Toscana) smokes. Gam-

BERLITZ'S RATINGS		
	Possible	Achieved
Ship	500	413
Accommodation	200	156
Food	400	243
Service	400	298
Entertainment	100	62
Cruise	400	293

blers will find pleasure in the Monte Carlo Casino, featuring blackjack, poker and roulette games, plus an array of slot machines, and a couple of gilt female nude reclining sculptures.

Drinking places include a pub-like venue as well as several comfortable lounges that have live music. Outside on deck a neat mini-golf course is locate don the port side of the funnel, while a walking/jogging track encircles the ship's two swimming pools. The ship is really designed to accommodate families with children, who have their own play centers (a children's club and jungle adventure playground), youth counselors, and programs. Although access throughout most of the interior is very good, anyone who is wheelchair-bound should note that the passenger hallways are a little narrow on some decks for you to pass when housekeeping carts are in place.

The onboard currency is the euro, and 15% is added to all drinks/beverage orders.

SUITABLE FOR: *MSC Orchestra* is best suited to young adult couples, singles, and families with tots, children and teens who enjoy big-ship surroundings, a city-style life, with all its attendant noise (some call it ambience), and passengers of different nationalities and languages (mostly European)

ACCOMMODATION. There are 12 price levels, depending on grade and location. Included are suites with private balcony, outside-view cabins, and interior (no view) cabins with private balcony; outside-view cabins)no balcony) and interior (no view) cabins. Contrary to nautical convention, the cabin numbering system has even numbered cabins on the starboard side, and odd numbered cabins on the port side.

All cabins have a mini-bar and personal safe, satellite TV, several audio channels, and 24-hour room service (note that, while tea and coffee are complimentary, snacks for room service incur a delivery charge).

Accommodation designated as "suites" (they are not true suites, as there is no separate bedroom and lounge) also has more room, a larger lounge area, walk-in closet, wall-to-wall vanity counter, a bathroom with combination bathtub and shower, toilet, and semi-private balcony with light (the partitions between each balcony are of the partial, not full, type). Bathrobes (100% cotton) are provided. However, except for the very highest category, the suite bathrooms are very plain, with white plastic washbasins and white walls, and mirrors that steam up.

Some cabins have views obstructed by lifeboats. Also, cabins on the uppermost accommodation deck may be subject to deck chairs and tables being dragged across the deck when it is set up or cleaned early in the morning.

CUISINE. There are two principal dining rooms, Villa Borghese Restaurant and L'Ibiscus. They are located in the aft section of the ship, and have large ocean-view picture windows. There are two seatings for dinner, and open seating for breakfast and lunch, in keeping with other ships in the MSC Cruises fleet. Tables are for two, four, six or eight, and some alcove banquette seating.

Anyone occupying upper-grade accommodation typically gets better tables in quieter areas.

Alternative (extra-cost) Dining Venues:
● The *Shanghai Chinese Restaurant* provides an alternative dining spot for a change from the main restaurants. This is the first real Chinese restaurant aboard any cruise ship (mainly because of the challenges of providing high-temperature wok and deep fryer preparation). Dim sum steamed dishes are also featured (typically for lunch). Food from four main cuisines is featured (Beijing, Cantonese, Shanghai and Szechzuan), as is Tsing Tao beer.
● The *Four Seasons Restaurant* is another alternative dining spot which offers à la carte Italian cuisine in a garden-like setting (cover charge: €18 per person), and fine china.

Casual, self-serve buffets (for breakfast and lunch) can be taken in the lido café-style Four Seasons Restaurant; or at a pool deck outside fast-food grill and pizzeria (La Piazzetta). Coffee/tea (at extra cost) and pastries can be taken in several bars (all fitted with coffee machines) set around the first and second levels of the atrium lobby, in which a delightful four-piece classical ensemble regularly performs.

ENTERTAINMENT. Covent Garden is the ship's stunning large show lounge. Located in the forward section of the ship, it has tiered seating set in a sloping floor, and the sightlines are good from most seats, which are plush and comfortable. The room can also serve as a venue for large social functions. High-quality entertainment has not, to date, been a priority for MSC Cruises. But providing production shows and variety acts that appeal to a multinational audience is a challenge.

The Opera Lounge (located one deck above the show lounge) is the place for social dancing, with live music provided by a band. Meanwhile, for the young and lively set, the ship's G32 discotheque is the hot place to head for.

Additionally, a large poolside movie screen provides movie-goers with more choices. Activities are provided by a team of multi-lingual animators.

SPA/FITNESS. The Orchestra Health Center (Body and Mind spa) is located one deck above the navigation bridge at the forward end of the ship. The complex has a beauty salon, several treatment rooms offering massage and other body-pampering treatments, as well as a gymnasium with ocean views and an array of high-tech, muscle-toning and strengthening equipment.

There's also a thermal suite, containing different kinds of steam rooms combined with aromatherapy infusions, at €12 per session, or six sessions for €60; there's also a neat juice/smoothie bar opposite the reception desk.

The health center is run as a concession by the Italian company OceanView, with European hairstylists and fine Balinese massage and body treatment staff. Examples of treatment prices: Balinese massage, €93 (45 minutes); shiatsu massage, €90 (45 minutes); hot stone therapy, €100 (45 minutes); facial, €65; pedicure, €40. Gratuities are not included, and are not charged to your account.

Sports facilities include deck quoits, two shuffleboard courts, large tennis and basketball court, minigolf, and a jogging track.

● **For more extensive general information about the MSC Cruises experience, see pages 143–4.**

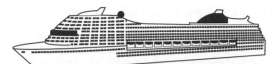

MSC Poesia
★★★★

Size:	Large Resort Ship	Total Crew:	987	Cabins (wheelchair accessible):	.17
Tonnage:	92,490	Passengers		Wheelchair accessibility	Good
Lifestyle:	Standard	(lower beds/all berths):	2,550/3,013	Cabin Voltage:	110/220 volts
Cruise Line:	MSC Cruises	Passenger Space Ratio		Elevators:	13
Former Names:	none	(lower beds/all berths):	36.2/30.6	Casino (gaming tables):	Yes
Builder:	Fincantieri (Italy)	Crew/Passenger Ratio		Slot Machines:	Yes
Original Cost:	$360 million	(lower beds/all berths):	2.6/3.0	Swimming Pools (outdoors):	2
Entered Service:	Oct 2008	Cabins (total):	1,275	Swimming Pools (indoors):	0
Registry:	Panama	Size Range (sq ft/m):	150.6–301.3/	Whirlpools:	4
Length (ft/m):	963.9/293.8		14.0–28.0	Self-Service Launderette:	No
Beam (ft/m):	105.6/32.2	Cabins (outside view):	1,000	Dedicated Cinema/Seats:	No
Draft (ft/m):	26.2/8.0	Cabins (interior/no view):	275	Library:	Yes
Propulsion/Propellers: diesel (58,000kW)/2		Cabins (for one person):	0		
Passenger Decks:	13	Cabins (with private balcony):	827		

BERLITZ'S OVERALL SCORE: 1,467 OUT OF A POSSIBLE 2,000 POINTS

OVERVIEW. *MSC Poesia* is a sister ship to *MSC Musica* and *MSC Orchestra*. The ship's blue funnel has a sleek, swept-back design and carries the MSC logo in gold lettering, and a balanced profile. The hull has large circular porthole-style windows instead of square or rectangular ones. From a technical viewpoint, the ship has a conventional rudders and propellers propulsion system, while a new anti-foul paint was applied to the ship's underwater hull – the first newly built ship to have this new sleek paint applied.

The interior layout and passenger flow is quite good with the exception of a couple of points of congestion, typically when the first seating exits the two main dining rooms and passengers on the second seating are waiting to enter. The musically-themed decor has many Italian influences, including clean lines, minimalism in furniture design, and a collection of colors, soft furnishings and fabrics that work well together, although it's a little more garish than one would expect.

Real wood and marble have been used extensively in the interiors, and the high quality reflects the commitment that MSC Cruises has in the vessel's future.

The focal point of the ship is the main three-deck high lobby, with a water-feature backdrop and a crystal piano on a small stage that appears to float on a pond. Other facilities include a large main show lounge, a nightclub, discotheque, numerous lounges and bars (including a wine bar), library, card room, an internet center, virtual reality center, children's club, and cigar lounge with specialized smoke extraction and a selection of Cuban (including Cohiba, Monte Cristo, Romeo e Juliet, Partagas), Dominican (Davidoff), and Italian (Toscana) smokes.

BERLITZ'S RATINGS

	Possible	Achieved
Ship	500	414
Accommodation	200	156
Food	400	243
Service	400	298
Entertainment	100	62
Cruise	400	294

A shopping gallery, which includes an electronics store, has an integrated bar and entertainment area that flows through the main lobby so that shopping becomes a city-like environment where you can shop, drink, and be entertained all in one convenient area. Gamblers can find entertainment pleasure in the expansive Casino (with blackjack, poker and roulette games, together with an array of slot machines).

Drinking places include a pub-like venue as well as several comfortable lounges that have live music. On deck, a mini-golf course is on the port side of the funnel, while a walking/jogging track encircles an upper level above the ship's two swimming pools. The ship is designed to accommodate families with children, who have their own play center, video games room, youth counselors, and activity programs.

Some of the artwork is quite whimsical. And do check out the "restroom with a view" – the men's/ladies' toilets adjacent to the Blue Marlin pool deck bar have a great ocean view – you can even watch the passing scenery while sitting on the toilet if you leave the door open.

Although access throughout most of the interior of the ship is very good, anyone who is wheelchair-bound should note that the passenger hallways are a little narrow on some decks for you to pass when housekeeping carts are in place. There is no walk-around open promenade deck.

The onboard currency is the euro, and 15% is added to all drinks/beverage orders.

SUITABLE FOR: Best suited to young adult couples, singles, and families with tots, children and teens who enjoy big ship surroundings, a big city life, with its attendant buzz, and caters to passengers of different nationalities and languages (mostly European). The on-board currency is the euro. Gratuities are charged to your onboard account, at €6 per person, per day, but bar drink prices include a service charge.

ACCOMMODATION. There are 12 price levels, depending on grade and location: suites, outside-view cabins, and interior (no view) cabins. Included are 18 "suites" with private balcony, mini-suites, outside-view cabins and interior (no view) cabins. Contrary to nautical convention, the cabin numbering system has even numbered cabins on the starboard side, and odd numbered cabins on the port side.

All cabins have a mini-bar and personal safe, satellite flat-screen TV, several audio channels, and 24-hour room service. Note that, while continental breakfast is complimentary from 7:30 to 10am, room service snacks are available at extra cost at any other time.

Accommodation designated as "suites" – they are not true suites, as there is no separate bedroom and lounge – also has more room (although they are small compared to suites on some of the major cruise lines), a larger lounge area, walk-in closet, and vanity desk with drawer-mounted hairdryer; a bathroom with combination bathtub and shower, toilet, and semi-private balcony with light (the partitions between each balcony are of the partial, not full, type). The bathrobes and towels are 100% cotton. The suite bathrooms are plain, with white plastic washbasins and white walls, and mirrors that steam up.

Some of the most popular cabins are at the aft end of the ship, with views over the stern from the balconies. The 17 cabins for the disabled are spacious and well equipped.

CUISINE. There are two principal dining rooms, both aft with large ocean-view picture windows. There are two seatings for meals, as aboard other ships in the MSC Cruises fleet, and tables are for two, four, six or eight; seating is both banquette-style and in individual chairs; the chairs, however, are slim and do not have armrests.

All dining venues are managed by Italian nationals.

Alternative Dining Spots:
● A *Tex-Mex Restaurant* is the ship's featured à la carte dining spot; reservations are necessary, and there is an extra cost.
● *Kaito* is a Japanese restaurant, incorporating a sushi bar. It has a very extensive menu.
● The *Wine Bar* provides a selection of famous regional

cheeses, hams and wine in a bistro-style setting that is relaxing and entertaining.

Casual, self-serve buffets (for breakfast and lunch) can be taken in the Cafeteria, or at a pool deck outside fast-food eatery. Coffee/tea and pastries can be taken in several bars adjacent to the midships atrium lobby.

Additionally, silver trays full of late-night snacks are taken throughout the ship by waiters, and on some days, special late-night desserts, such as flambé items, are showcased in various lounges.

ENTERTAINMENT. There is one large, principal showlounge, located in the forward section of the ship. It has tiered seating on two levels – the sightlines are good from most of the plush, comfortable seats. The room can also be a venue for large groups or social functions. There is no showband, and all shows are performed to pre-recorded music tracks. Another large lounge, aft of the showlounge, is the place for social dancing and functions such as cooking demonstrations, with live music provided by a band.

Additionally, big-screen movies are shown on a large screen above the forward pool, just behind the ship's mast.

SPA/FITNESS. The Poesia Health Center (Body and Mind spa) is located one deck above the navigation bridge at the forward end of the ship.

The facility includes a beauty salon, several treatment rooms offering massage and other body-pampering treatments, as well as a gymnasium with ocean views and an array of high-tech, muscle-toning and strengthening equipment. There's also a thermal suite, containing different kinds of steam rooms combined with aromatherapy infusions, at €12 per session, or six sessions for €60, and a juice/smoothie bar.

The health center is run as a concession by the Italian company OceanView, with European hairstylists and fine Balinese massage and body treatment staff. Examples of treatment prices: Balinese massage, €93 (45 minutes); shiatsu massage, €90 (45 minutes); hot stone therapy, €100 (45 minutes); facial, €65; pedicure, €40. Gratuities are not included, and are not charged to your account.

Sports facilities include deck quoites, two shuffleboard courts, a large tennis and basketball court, minigolf, and a jogging track.

● **For more extensive general information about the MSC Cruises experience, see pages 143–4.**

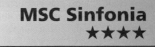

MSC Sinfonia
★★★★

Size:	Large Resort Ship	Passenger Decks:	10	Cabins (wheelchair accessible):	2
Tonnage:	58,600 tons	Total Crew:	710	Wheelchair accessibility	Good
Lifestyle:	Standard	Passengers		Cabin Current:	110 and 220 volts
Cruise Line:	MSC Cruises	(lower beds/all berths):	1,566/2,223	Elevators:	9
Former Names:	European Stars	Passenger Space Ratio		Casino (gaming tables):	Yes
Builder: Chantiers de l'Atlantique (France)		(lower beds/all berths):	37.4/27.6	Slot Machines:	Yes
Original Cost:	$245 million	Crew/Passenger Ratio		Swimming Pools (outdoors):	1
Entered Service:	Apr 2002/Mar 2005	(lower beds/all berths):	2.2/3.1	Swimming Pools (indoors):	0
Registry:	Italy	Cabins (total):	783	Whirlpools:	1 (thalassotherapy)
Length (ft/m):	823.4/251.0	Size Range (sq ft/m):	139.9–236.8/13–22	Self-Service Launderette:	No
Beam (ft/m):	94.4/28.8	Cabins (outside view):	511	Dedicated Cinema/Seats:	No
Draft (ft/m):	22.4/6.85	Cabins (interior/no view):	272	Library:	Yes
Propulsion/Propellers:	diesel	Cabins (for one person):	0		
	(31,680 kW)/2 pods	Cabins (with private balcony):	132		

BERLITZ'S OVERALL SCORE: 1,431 OUT OF A POSSIBLE 2,000 POINTS

OVERVIEW. *MSC Sinfonia* was originally built and operated by the now-defunct Festival Cruises. Like sister ship *MSC Armonia*, it was built on the platform of the *Mistral*, with an 114.8-ft long (35-meter) mid-section added to increase the ship's length and provide more space per passenger than *Mistral*. *MSC Sinfonia* has an azimuthing pod propulsion system, instead of conventional rudders and propellers *(for explanation, see page 45)*. The lido deck surrounding the outdoor swimming pool also has whirlpool tubs and a large bandstand is set in raised canvas-covered pods.

The interior layout is stylish. Passenger flow is good, as are the "you are here" deck signs. The decor is decidedly "European Moderne" and includes clean lines, minimalism in furniture designs (including some chairs that look interesting but are totally impractical unless you are prepared to face reconstructive surgery).

Facilities include Amadeus, the ship's show lounge, and La Gondola Theater, for plays and other theatrical presentations. There's a cigar smoking room (Ambassador), with the hallmarks of a gentleman's club of former times, as well as a piano bar. The Goethe Library/Card Room has real writing desks (something many ships seem to omit), and this ship has an internet cafe, as well an English pub called the White Lion. Those who enjoy gambling may find excitement in the Lido Casino, with blackjack, poker and roulette games, plus the usual one-armed slot machines. The onboard currency is the euro.

Standing in line for embarkation, disembarkation, shore tenders and for self-serve buffet meals is an inevitable aspect of cruising aboard all large ships. The heavy smokers are virtually impossible to avoid (in typical European fashion,

BERLITZ'S RATINGS

	Possible	Achieved
Ship	500	395
Accommodation	200	155
Food	400	254
Service	400	295
Entertainment	100	54
Cruise	400	278

ashtrays are simply moved – if used at all – to wherever smokers happen to be sitting). All announcements are in several languages, although these are thankfully fewer than in the past. The entertainment is of a low standard, with intrusive animateurs that mean well, but who perform as one would expect to find in a holiday camp – with great energy and enthusiasm but little else.

The cruise line keeps prices low by providing air transportation that may be at inconvenient times, or transportation involving long journeys by bus, depending on itinerary. So be prepared for a little discomfort in getting to and from your cruise in exchange for low cruise rates. The constant push for onboard revenue is also very irritating – you have to pay extra even for a visit to the ship's navigation bridge. Regular passenger complaints include poor ports of call information.

The onboard currency is the euro, and 15% is added to all drinks/beverage orders.

SUITABLE FOR: *MSC Sinfonia* is best suited to young adult couples, singles, and families with tots, children and teens who enjoy big ship surroundings, a big city life, with all its attendant noise (some call it ambience), and passengers of different nationalities and languages (mostly European). The international mix of passengers adds to the overall ambiance of the cruise experience.

ACCOMMODATION. There are 11 price categories, the price depending on the grade, size and location. These include 132 suites with private balcony (note that the partitions are only of the partial and not the full type), outside-view cabins and interior (no view) cabins.

Suite grade accommodation has more room, a larger lounge area, walk-in closet, wall-to-wall vanity counter, a bathroom with combination tub and shower, toilet, and private balcony (with light). But they are not true suites, as there is no separate bedroom and lounge – in other words, these are not "suites" of rooms. Bathrobes are provided.

In general, the "suites" are well laid out and nicely furnished. However, except for the very highest category, the suite bathrooms are very plain, with white plastic washbasins and white walls, and mirrors that steam up. According to the rules of feng shui, however, it is bad luck to place any mirror in such a position that it can be seen by anyone lying in bed.

Even the smallest interior cabins are sensibly spacious and well designed, with plenty of space between lower beds. All grades of accommodation have sheets and blankets as bed linen (no duvets), and are equipped with a TV set, hairdryer, mini-bar/refrigerator, personal safe (cleverly positioned behind a vanity desk mirror), bathroom with shower and toilet, and 100% cotton towels (except for hand towels, which, when I last sailed, were 86% cotton and 14% polyester).

However, the standard grade cabins are quite small when compared to many other new ships, at a modest 140 sq. ft (13 sq. meters). Note that cabins located under the aft self-service buffet can be noisy.

CUISINE. All dining spots are non-smoking venues. There are two main dining rooms, the 610-seat Il Galeone Restaurant and the Il Covo Restaurant; both have two seatings and share the same menu. The cuisine is reasonably sound, and, with varied menus and good presentation, should prove a highlight for most passengers. The wine list has a wide variety of wines at fairly reasonable prices, although almost all are very young.

La Terrazza is the ship's casual, self-serve buffet eatery, open 24 hours a day. The selections are very standardized, however, and could be better. Café del Mare, adjacent to one of two swimming pools and to the ship's funnel, is a grill area for fast food.

Meanwhile, coffee/tea and pastries can be taken in Le Baroque Café, which is set around the upper level of the two-deck high atrium lobby. It's a good location for people-watching, but annoying music videos are constantly played on TV sets in the forward sections.

ENTERTAINMENT. The Gondola Theater is two decks high, and is the main show lounge, for production shows, cabaret acts, plays and other theatrical presentations. It is a well designed room (except for the fact that no space was allocated for a live showband), with good sightlines from most seats, and four entrances that allow easy access.

Entertainment is a weak area for MSC Cruises, although this could improve as more ships are brought into service and more money is assigned to this important aspect of the company's cruise product. Other shows consist of unknown cabaret acts (typically singers, magicians, mime artistes, comedy jugglers, and others) doing the cruise ship circuit. The principal difficulty aboard this ship is that the ship operates year-round in five or six languages, making any entertainment (other than visual acts such as mime, magic or juggling) virtually impossible.

The ship carries a number of bands and small musical units that provide live music for dancing or listening in various lounges and bars throughout the ship.

SPA/FITNESS. The Atlantica Spa, one deck above the navigation bridge at the forward end of the ship, has numerous body-pampering treatments, as well as a gymnasium with ocean views and an array of high-tech, muscle-toning and strengthening equipment.

There's also a thermal suite (this contains different kinds of steam rooms combined with aromatherapy infusions such as camomile and eucalyptus) and a rasul chamber (a combination of two or three different kinds of special application mud, and gentle steam shower – highly recommended for couples).

The spa is run as a concession by the Italian company OceanView, with European hairstylists and Balinese massage and body treatment staff. Examples of treatment prices: Balinese massage, €93 (45 minutes); shiatsu massage, €90 (45 minutes); hot stone therapy, €100 (45 minutes); facial, €65; pedicure, €40. Gratuities are not included, and are not charged to your account.

For the sports-minded, there is a simulated climbing wall outdoors, while other sports and fitness facilities include volleyball/basketball court, and mini-golf.

● **For more extensive general information about the MSC Cruises experience, see pages 143–4.**

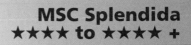

MSC Splendida
★★★★ to ★★★★ +

Size: ....Large Resort Ship	Passenger Decks: 13	Cabins (with private balcony): 1,260
Tonnage: 133,500	Total Crew: 1,313	Cabins (wheelchair accessible): 43
Lifestyle: ....Standard	Passengers	Wheelchair accessibility ....Good
Cruise Line: ....MSC Cruises	(lower beds/all berths):.........3,300/3,900	Cabin Voltage:...........................110 volts
Former Names: ....none	Passenger Space Ratio	Elevators: 14
Builder: ....Aker Yards (France)	(lower beds/all berths):.............40.4/34.2	Casino (gaming tables):.....................Yes
Original Cost:.........................$550 million	Crew/Passenger Ratio	Slot Machines:....................................Yes
Entered Service: ....July 2009	(lower beds/all berths):.................2.5/3.0	Swimming Pools (outdoors):...................3
Registry:....................................Panama	Cabins (total):...................................1,650	Swimming Pools (indoors): 1 (glass dome)
Length (ft/m):......................1,093.5/333.3	Size Range (sq ft/m): 161.4–699.6/	Whirlpools:...13
Beam (ft/m):............................124.6/38.0	15–65	Self-Service Launderette:....................No
Draft:......................................27.2/8.45	Cabins (outside view):....................1,354	Dedicated Cinema/Seats: ....No
Propulsion/Propellers: ....diesel	Cabins (interior/no view):...................283	Library: ....Yes
(40,000 kW)/2	Cabins (for one person):........................0	

OVERVIEW. This is a sister ship to *MSC Fantasia*. The public rooms include a large showlounge, a nightclub/disco, many lounges and bars (most with live music), library, card room, an internet center, a virtual reality center (with 4-D racing thrills experience), and an extensive shopping gallery. It all feels rather like a European city-center.

The ship is well designed to accommodate families with children, who have their own play centers (a club and jungle adventure playground), youth counselors, and programs. Many head for Virtual World to try one of five white-knuckle 4-D rides in a 10-seat thrill room.

The onboard currency is the euro, and 15% is added to all drinks/beverage orders.

ACCOMMODATION. Eighty percent of the cabins are outsides, of which 95% have a balcony – the standard balcony cabin is almost 172 sq ft (16 sq meters), plus bathroom and balcony. It's worth paying extra to stay in one of the 99 "suites" (each 312 sq ft (29 sq. meters) in the Yacht Club area, at the top, front end of the ship. Here, you'll get silver-tray room service, a reserved section of the Villa Verde restaurant, plus access to a "members only" sundeck sanctuary area that includes its own bar and food counters, small dip pool, two hot tubs, and open lounging deck. It's a world away from the hustle and bustle of the main pool decks.

The Yacht Club has its own serene concierge lounge at the front of the ship. Just aft of the lounge is a small library and concierge reception desk, Svarovski glass stairway that to the Yacht Club accommodation suites, and a private elevator to access the Aurea Spa one deck below. The lounge has its own galley and dedicated chef. Each day, he pre-

BERLITZ'S RATINGS

	Possible	Achieved	Yacht Club
Ship	500	425	426
Accommodation	200	162	162
Food	400	260	283
Service	400	300	313
Entertainment	100	77	76
Cruise	400	304	310

pares items only available to "members." These are all small plate dishes, artfully prepared and presented, using fresh, locally sourced ingredients.

CUISINE. There are four dining venues: the main restaurant (Villa Verde), an Italian/Mediterranean specialty à la carte restaurant (L'Olivo), a Tex-Mex restaurant (Santa Fe), a section of the main restaurant for Yacht Club suite passengers only, and a large casual self-serve lido buffet-style eatery (Bora Bora Cafeteria). Coffee/tea (at extra cost) and pastries are served in several bars. Villa Verde has two seatings for dinner, and open seating for breakfast and lunch, like other MSC Cruises ships. Tables are for two, four, six or eight, and there's some alcove banquette seating.

ENTERTAINMENT. The Strand Theater has plush seating in tiers for as many as 1,700, and good sightlines. Because the passengers are multilingual, the shows concentrate on visual entertainment such as mime, magic, dancing, and acrobatics, and are performed with recorded music.

SPA/FITNESS. The Aurea Spa (16,000 sq ft/1,485 sq meters) and has a beauty salon, well-equipped treatment rooms, and a large gymnasium with ocean views. Included is a large thermal suite, and saunas. The decor is welcoming and restful. The spa is run as a concession by the Italian company OceanView. Sports facilities include deck quoits, large tennis/basketball court, minigolf, and a jogging track.

● **For more extensive general information about the MSC Cruises experience, see pages 143–4.**

National Geographic Endeavour
★★

Size:	Boutique Ship
Tonnage:	3,132
Lifestyle:	Standard
Cruise Line:	Lindblad Expeditions
Former Names:	Caledonian Star, North Star, Lindmar, Marburg
Builder:	A.G. Weser Seebeckwerft (Germany)
Original Cost:	n/a
Entered Service:	1966/1984
Registry:	The Bahamas
Length (ft/m):	292.6/89.20
Beam (ft/m):	45.9/14.00
Draft (ft/m):	20.3/6.20
Propulsion/Propellers:	diesel (3,236kW)/1

Passenger Decks:	6
Total Crew:	64
Passengers (lower beds/all berths):	113/124
Passenger Space Ratio (lower beds/all berths):	27.7/25.2
Crew/Passenger Ratio (lower beds/all berths):	1.7/1.9
Cabins (total):	62
Size Range (sq ft/m):	191.6–269.1/ 17.8–25.0
Cabins (outside view):	62
Cabins (interior/no view):	0
Cabins (for one person):	14

Cabins (with private balcony):	0
Cabins (wheelchair accessible):	0
Wheelchair accessibility	None
Cabin Current:	110/220 volts
Elevators:	0
Casino (gaming tables):	No
Slot Machines:	No
Swimming Pools (outdoors):	1
Whirlpools:	0
Self-Service Launderette:	No
Lecture/Film Rooms:	Yes
Library:	Yes
Zodiacs:	10
Helicopter Pad:	No

BERLITZ'S OVERALL SCORE: 945 OUT OF A POSSIBLE 2,000 POINTS

OVERVIEW. Renamed in 2005, the former *Endeavour* was originally built as a stern factory fishing trawler for North Sea service, before being morphed into a passenger ship. Today, it is tidy and well cared for as an expedition cruise vessel operating "soft" expedition cruises. There is an open bridge policy for all passengers. The vessel carries Zodiac landing craft for in-depth excursions, and there is an enclosed shore tender. An aft stairway (it is steep) leads down to the landing craft platform. The ship has a warm, intimate ambiance, and a casual dress code.

This small ship has a reasonable number of public rooms and facilities, including a lecture room/lounge/bar/library, where videos are also stocked for in-cabin use. Specialized lecturers accompanying each cruise make this a real life-enrichment experience for a clientele wanting to travel and learn, while enveloped in comfortable, unpretentious surroundings. There's a good book selection.

This likeable, homey little ship runs well-organized destination-intensive, soft expedition-style cruises, at a very reasonable price. It attracts loyal repeat passengers who don't want to sail aboard ships that look like apartment blocks. The itineraries include Antarctica, where this ship started operating in 1998. The onboard currency is the US dollar.

The interior stairways are a little steep, as is the exterior stairway to the Zodiac embarkation points. Noise from the diesel engines can be irksome, particularly on the lower decks.

Recommended gratuities are $10 per person, per day.

SUITABLE FOR: This ship and its type of soft adventure/exploration cruising are best suited to adventurous, hardy

BERLITZ'S RATINGS

	Possible	Achieved
Ship	500	198
Accommodation	200	86
Food	400	193
Service	400	217
Entertainment	n/a	n/a
Cruise	500	251

types who enjoy being with nature and wildlife in some of the most interesting (sometimes inhospitable) places on earth, but cosseted aboard a small, modestly comfortable ship.

ACCOMMODATION. There are five categories of cabins: 1 suite category and 4 non-suite categories. The all-outside-view cabins (all above the waterline) are very compact, but reasonably comfortable, and they are decorated in warm, muted tones. All cabins have a mini-bar/refrigerator, VCR, a decent amount of closet and drawer space (but tight for long voyages), and a clock.

The bathrooms are tight, with little space for the storage of personal toiletries.

Four "suites" are basically double the size of a standard cabin, and have a wood partition separating the bedroom and lounge area. The bathroom is still small, however.

CUISINE. The dining room is small and charming, but the low-back chairs are not very comfortable. Open seating is operated in this non-smoking room. The cuisine is European in style with reasonably high quality, fresh ingredients, but not a lot of menu choice. Salad items, in particular, are rather scarce on variety, as are international cheeses. Service is attentive and friendly.

ENTERTAINMENT. The main lounge is the venue for lectures, slide shows and occasional film presentations. There are no shows (none are needed), and no facilities for them.

SPA/FITNESS. There is a small fitness room (about three people and it is full) and tiny sauna.

National Geographic Polaris
★★

Size: ....Boutique Ship	Passenger Decks: 4	Cabins (with private balcony): 0
Tonnage: 2,214	Total Crew: 44	Cabins (wheelchair accessible): 0
Lifestyle: ....Standard	Passengers	Wheelchair accessibility ....None
Cruise Line: ....Lindblad Expeditions	(lower beds/all berths): 82/84	Cabin Current: ....220 volts
Former Names: .Polaris, Lindblad Polaris,	Passenger Space Ratio	Elevators: 0
Oresund	(lower beds/all berths): 27.0/26.3	Casino (gaming tables): ....No
Builder: ......Aalborg Vaerft (Denmark)	Crew/Passenger Ratio	Slot Machines: ....No
Original Cost: ....n/a	(lower beds/all berths): 1.8/1.8	Swimming Pools (outdoors): 0
Entered Service: 1960/May 1987	Cabins (total): 41	Whirlpools: 0
Registry: ....Ecuador	Size Range (sq ft/m): 99.0–229.2/	Self-Service Launderette: ....No
Length (ft/m): 236.6/72.12	9.2–21.3	Lecture/Film Room: ....No
Beam (ft/m): 42.7/13.03	Cabins (outside view): 41	Library: ....Yes
Draft (ft/m): 13.7/4.30	Cabins (interior/no view): 0	Zodiacs: 8
Propulsion/Propellers: diesel (2,354 kW)/2	Cabins (for one person): 0	Helicopter Pad: ....No

BERLITZ'S OVERALL SCORE: 943 OUT OF A POSSIBLE 2,000 POINTS

OVERVIEW. This is what is often termed a "soft" expedition cruise vessel. It is of modest proportions, and has a dark blue hull and white superstructure. A "cute" vessel, it has been well maintained and operated, having been skillfully converted from a Scandinavian ferry. It sports a fantail and an aft lounge area outdoors. The ship carries several Zodiac inflatable rubber landing craft, as well as a glass-bottom boat.

Inside, there are few public rooms, although the Scandinavian-style interior furnishings and decor are very tidy and welcoming (if dated), accented by lots of wood trim. Has a friendly, very intimate atmosphere on board, with Filipino service staff. There is a good team of lecturers and nature observers, whose daily recaps are a vital part of the experience. A restful, well-stocked library helps passengers learn more about the region and the natural world.

If you are going on a Galápagos cruise, it is important to take with you: passport, short and long-sleeve cotton shirts, good walking shoes, windbreaker, mosquito repellent (mosquitoes are at their worst between December and July, particularly in Bartolome), sunglasses with retaining strap, and any personal medication. You will need to take a flight from Quito to San Cristobal (via Guayaquil) to join your cruise.

This is a decent enough small vessel, operating year-round nature-intensive "soft" expedition cruises based in and around the Galápagos Islands. It's an area to which the ship is well suited because only 90 passengers from any one ship are allowed at any one time in the islands, where tourism is managed well by the local Equadorians. In fact, this ship is among the best suited to this region.

Bottled water is provided at no extra charge. All port

BERLITZ'S RATINGS

	Possible	Achieved
Ship	500	189
Accommodation	200	85
Food	400	186
Service	400	216
Entertainment	n/a	n/a
Cruise	500	267

charges are included in this product, which is marketed by Lindblad Expeditions and Noble Caledonia. The onboard currencies are the US dollar and Ecuadorian sucre.

SUITABLE FOR: This type of cruising is best suited to adventurous, hardy outdoors types who enjoy being with nature and wildlife in one of the most interesting places on earth.

ACCOMMODATION. There are five price grades. The cabins, all above the waterline (while most have windows, a few have portholes), are fairly roomy and nicely appointed, but there is little drawer space. Some have been refurbished, and have large (lower) beds. Each cabin has either a double bed or two single beds, a small writing desk, and hairdryer. Some of the larger cabins also have a third (upper) berth. The cabin bathrooms are tiny (the towels are small, too).

CUISINE. The Dining Room has big picture windows and a wrap-around view. Seating is now at individual tables (formerly family style) in a leisurely single seating.

The ship's cuisine is basically sound, with emphasis on local fish and seafood, and other Ecuadorian regional specialties (meats are poor). Breakfast and lunch are self-serve buffet-style. The wine selection is very limited.

ENTERTAINMENT. Lectures, briefings and recaps are the main onboard entertainment events, together with dinner and after-dinner conversation.

SPA/FITNESS. There is a small fitness room (large enough for two). Beauty isn't a big concern on such cruises.

National Geographic Sea Bird
★ +

Size: ....Boutique Ship	Propulsion/Propellers: diesel/2	Cabins (for one person): 2
Tonnage: 99.7	Passenger Decks: 4	Cabins (with private balcony): 0
Lifestyle: ....Standard	Total Crew: 22	Cabins (wheelchair accessible): 0
Cruise Line: ......Lindblad Expeditions/	Passengers	Wheelchair accessibility ....None
National Geographic	(lower beds/all berths): 70/70	Cabin Current: ....110 volts
Former Names: ....Sea Bird,	Passenger Space Ratio	Elevators: 0
Majestic Explorer	(lower beds/all berths): 1.4/1.4	Casino (gaming tables): ....No
Builder: ....Whidbey Island (USA)	Crew/Passenger Ratio	Slot Machines: ....No
Original Cost: ....n/a	(lower beds/all berths): 3.1/3.1	Swimming Pools (outdoors): 0
Entered Service: 1981	Cabins (total): 36	Swimming Pools (indoors): 0
Registry: ....The Bahamas	Size Range (sq ft/m): 73.0–202.0/	Whirlpools: 0
Length (ft/m): 151.9/46.3	6.7–18.7	Self-Service Launderette: ....No
Beam (ft/m): 30.8/9.4	Cabins (outside view): 36	Dedicated Cinema/Seats: ....No
Draft (ft/m): 8.0/2.4	Cabins (interior/no view): 0	Library: ....No

BERLITZ'S OVERALL SCORE: 743 OUT OF A POSSIBLE 2,000 POINTS

OVERVIEW. This ship carries a fleet of motorized Zodiac landing craft for use as shore tenders and for up-close shore exploration. A number of sea kayaks are also carried. An open-bridge policy means you can go to the navigation bridge at any time. The vessel is small enough to operate in ports and narrow inlets inaccessible to larger ships. Lecturers and recap sessions are held daily.

This small craft (and sister ship *National Geographic Sea Lion*) is adequate for looking at nature and wildlife close-up, in modest but comfortable surroundings that provide an alternative to big-ship cruising. Cruises visit Alaska, Baja California and the Sea of Cortes. Tipping is suggested at about $7 per person per day. The onboard currency is the US dollar.

In the cabins, the mattresses are enclosed in a wood frame with sharp corners, which you bang into constantly.

SUITABLE FOR: *National Geographic Sea Bird* is best suited to older couples and single travelers who enjoy learning about nature, geography, history and other life sciences in casual, non-dressy surroundings without a hint of pretension. They are likely to be hardy, outdoors types who don't need entertainment or silly parlor games.

ACCOMMODATION. All cabins have rudimentary furniture, but all have an outside view through picture windows, except for those on the lowest deck, which have portholes

BERLITZ'S RATINGS		
	Possible	Achieved
Ship	500	141
Accommodation	200	71
Food	400	149
Service	400	185
Entertainment	n/a	n/a
Cruise	500	197

but no view. Some cabins have double beds, some have twin beds (they can be pushed together to form a queen-sized bed), and some are for singles, at a surcharge of 150%. There is just enough room to stow your luggage.

All cabins have a private bathroom, although it really is tiny. There is no room service for food or beverages.

CUISINE. The dining room (non-smoking), which has ocean-view picture windows, is large enough to accommodate all passengers in a single seating. The tables are not assigned, and so you can sit with whom you like. The food is unpretentious, good and wholesome, although its presentation is very plain, with no frills, and features regional specialties. The wine list is very limited, and is comprised mostly of wines from California.

ENTERTAINMENT. There is no formal entertainment, although dinner and after-dinner conversation with fellow passengers in the ship's lounge/bar really becomes the entertainment. So, if you're not in the mood to talk to your fellow passengers, retire with a good book, or go outside, where you'll usually find that nature provides varied entertainment.

SPA/FITNESS. There are no spa or fitness facilities aboard this very small cruise vessel.

National Geographic Sea Lion
★ +

Size: . . . . .Boutique Ship	Propulsion/Propellers: diesel/2	Cabins (for one person): 2
Tonnage: 99.7	Passenger Decks: 4	Cabins (with private balcony): 0
Lifestyle: . . . . .Standard	Total Crew: 22	Cabins (wheelchair accessible): 0
Cruise Line: . . . . . . .Lindblad Expeditions/	Passengers	Wheelchair accessibility . . . . .None
National Geographic	(lower beds/all berths): 72/76	Cabin Current: . . . . .110 volts
Former Names: . . . . .Sea Lion,	Passenger Space Ratio	Elevators: 0
Great Rivers Explorer	(lower beds/all berths): 1.3/1.3	Casino (gaming tables): . . . . .No
Builder: . . . . .Whidbey Island (USA)	Crew/Passenger Ratio	Slot Machines: .No
Original Cost: .n/a	(lower beds/all berths): 3.2/3.4	Swimming Pools (outdoors): 0
Entered Service: 1982	Cabins (total): .37	Swimming Pools (indoors): 0
Registry: . . . . .The Bahamas	Size Range (sq ft/m): 73.0–202.0/	Whirlpools: 0
Length (ft/m): 151.9/46.3	6.7–18.7	Self-Service Launderette: . . . . .No
Beam (ft/m): 30.8/9.4	Cabins (outside view): 37	Dedicated Cinema/Seats: . . . . .No
Draft (ft/m): 8.0/2.4	Cabins (interior/no view): 0	Library: . . . . .No

OVERALL SCORE: 743 OUT OF A POSSIBLE 2,000 POINTS

OVERVIEW. This ship carries a fleet of motorized Zodiac landing craft for use as shore tenders and for up-close shore exploration. A number of sea kayaks are also carried. An open-bridge policy means that you are allowed to go to the navigation bridge at any time.

This small craft is adequate for looking at nature and wildlife close up, in modest but comfortable surroundings that provide an alternative to big-ship cruising. It is small enough to operate in ports and narrow inlets inaccessible to larger ships. Lectures and recap sessions are held each day.

Cruises visit Alaska, Baja California and the Sea of Cortes. Tipping is suggested at about $7 per person per day. The onboard currency is the US dollar.

Note that in the cabins, the mattresses are enclosed in a wood frame with sharp corners, which you can all too easily bang into constantly.

SUITABLE FOR: *National Geographic Sea Lion* is best suited to older couples and single travelers who enjoy learning about nature, geography, history and other life sciences, in casual, non-dressy surroundings without a hint of pretension. They are likely to be hardy, outdoors types who don't need entertainment or silly parlor games.

ACCOMMODATION. All the cabins aboard this little ship have an outside view through picture windows, except for those

BERLITZ'S RATINGS

	Possible	Achieved
Ship	500	141
Accommodation	200	71
Food	400	149
Service	400	185
Entertainment	n/a	n/a
Cruise	500	197

on the lowest deck, which have portholes. Some cabins have double beds, some have twin beds (they can be pushed together to form a queen-sized bed), and some are for singles, at a surcharge of 15%. There is plenty of room to stow your luggage.

All cabins have a private bathroom, although it really is tiny. There is no room service for food or beverages.

CUISINE. The dining room (non-smoking), which has ocean-view picture windows, is large enough to accommodate all passengers in a single seating. The tables are not assigned, and so you can sit with whom you like. The food is unpretentious, good and wholesome, although its presentation is very plain, with no frills, and features regional specialties.

The wine list is very limited, and is comprised mostly of wines from California.

ENTERTAINMENT. There is no formal entertainment, although dinner and after-dinner conversation with fellow passengers in the ship's lounge/bar really becomes the entertainment each evening. So, if you don't want to talk to your fellow passengers, take a good book, or go outside, where you'll find nature provides the rest of the entertainment.

SPA/FITNESS. There are no spa or fitness facilities aboard this very small cruise vessel.

Nautica
★★★★ +

Size:...................... Mid-Size Ship	Passenger Decks:....................9	Cabins (with private balcony):.......232
Tonnage:.........................30,277	Total Crew:.....................386	Cabins (wheelchair accessible):.......3
Lifestyle:...................Premium	Passengers	Wheelchair accessibility..........Good
Cruise Line:.............Oceania Cruises	(lower beds/all berths):........684/824	Cabin Current:.........110/220 volts
Former Names:.................R Five	Passenger Space Ratio	Elevators:........................4
Builder:.........Chantiers de l'Atlantique	(lower beds/all berths):.......44.2/36.7	Casino (gaming tables):.............Yes
Original Cost:.............£150 million	Crew/Passenger Ratio	Slot Machines:...................Yes
Entered Service:.......Dec1998/Nov 2005	(lower beds/all berths):.........1.7/2.1	Swimming Pools (outdoors):..........1
Registry:.............Marshall Islands	Cabins (total):.....................342	Swimming Pools (indoors):..........0
Length (ft/m):.............593.7/181.0	Size Range (sq ft/m): 145.3–968.7/13.5–90.0	Whirlpools:........2 (+1 thalassotherapy)
Beam (ft/m):.................83.5/25.5	Cabins (outside view):............317	Self-Service Launderette:..........Yes
Draft (ft/m):..................19.5/6.0	Cabins (interior/no view):...........25	Dedicated Cinema/Seats:..........No
Propulsion/Propellers: .diesel (18,600 kW)/2	Cabins (for one person):.............0	Library:........................Yes

OVERALL SCORE: 1,575 OUT OF A POSSIBLE 2,000 POINTS

OVERVIEW. *Nautica* was formerly one of a series of eight almost identical ships, originally built for the now-defunct Renaissance Cruises, the cruise industry's first totally non-smoking cruise line. The exterior design manages to balance the ship's high sides by painting the whole ship white (it previously had a dark blue hull), with a large, square white funnel.

The addition of teak overlaid decking and teak lounge chairs greatly improved what was formerly a bland pool deck outdoors – but the front rows of double sunloungers are called cabanas, and it costs $100 per day to use them. Its sister ships are *Insignia* (formerly Renaissance Cruises' *R One*) and *Regatta* (formerly *R Two*).

While there is no wrap-around promenade deck outdoors, there is a small jogging track around the perimeter of the swimming pool, and port and starboard side decks.

The interior decor is stunning and elegant, a throwback to ship decor of the ocean liners of the 1920s and '30s, with dark woods and warm colors, all carried out in fine taste (but a bit *faux* in places). This includes detailed ceiling cornices, both real and *faux* wrought-iron staircase railings, leather-paneled walls, *trompe l'oeil* ceilings, rich carpeting in hallways with an Oriental rug-look center section, and many other interesting (and expensive-looking) decorative touches. It feels like an old-world country club.

The public rooms are spread over three decks. The reception hall (lobby) has a staircase with intricate wrought-iron railings. A large observation lounge, called the Horizon Bar, is located high atop ship.

There are plenty of bars – including one in each of the restaurant entrances. Perhaps the nicest is the casino bar/lounge, a beautiful room reminiscent of London's grand

BERLITZ'S RATINGS

	Possible	Achieved
Ship	500	418
Accommodation	200	160
Food	400	312
Service	400	295
Entertainment	100	77
Cruise	400	313

hotels and includes a martini bar. It has an inviting marble fireplace, comfortable sofas and individual chairs.

The Library is a grand Regency-style room, with a fireplace, a high, indented, *trompe l'oeil* ceiling, and excellent selection of books, plus very comfortable wingback chairs with footstools, and sofas you could sleep on. Oceania@Sea is the ship's internet connect center.

The dress code is "smart casual." The onboard currency is the US dollar. Gratuities are added at $10.50 per person, per day (accommodation designated as suites have an extra $3 per person charge for the butler). A 15% gratuity is added to bar and spa accounts.

The stairways, though carpeted, are tinny. Oceania Cruises is a young company with a refreshing vision and desire to provide an extremely high level of food and service in an informal setting that is at once elegant yet comfortable, and that is exactly what it has achieved. Passenger niggles include all the "inventive" and highly irritating extra charges that can be incurred.

SUITABLE FOR: *Nautica* is best suited to couples who like good food and style, but want informality with no formal nights on board, and interesting itineraries, all at a very reasonable price well below what the luxury ships charge.

ACCOMMODATION. There are six cabin categories, and 10 price grades (3 suite price grades; 5 outside-view cabin grades; 2 interior (no view) cabin grades).

All of the standard interior (no view) and outside-view cabins (the lowest four grades) are extremely compact units, and extremely tight for two persons (particularly for cruises longer than five days). They have twin beds (or queen-sized bed), with good under-bed storage areas, personal safe, vanity desk with large mirror, good closet and drawer space (in rich, dark woods), 100% cotton bathrobe and towels, slippers, clothes brush and shoe horn. Color TVs carry a major news channel (where obtainable), plus a sports channel and round-the-clock movie channels.

Certain cabin categories (about 100 of them) qualify as "Concierge Level" accommodation, and occupants get extra goodies such as enhanced bathroom amenities, complimentary shoeshine, tote bag, cashmere throw blanket, bottle of champagne on arrival, hand-held hairdryer, priority restaurant reservations, and priority embarkation.

Owner's Suites. The six Owner's Suites, measuring around 962 sq.ft/89.3 sq.meters, provide the most spacious accommodation. They are fine, large living spaces located aft overlooking the stern on Decks 6, 7, and 8 (they are, however, subject to more movement and some vibration). They have extensive teak-floor private balconies that really are private and cannot be overlooked from the decks above. Each has an entrance foyer, living room, separate bedroom (the bed faces the sea, which can be seen through the floor-to-ceiling windows and sliding glass door), CD player (with selection of audio discs), fully tiled bathroom with Jacuzzi bathtub, and a small guest bathroom.

Vista Suites. There are four, each measuring around 785.7 sq.ft/73 sq.meters, and located forward on Decks 5 and 6. They have extensive teak-floor private balconies that cannot be overlooked by anyone from the decks above. Each has an entrance foyer, living room, separate bedroom (the bed faces the sea, which can be seen through the floor-to-ceiling windows and sliding glass door), CD player (with audio discs), and fully tiled bathroom with Jacuzzi tub.

Penthouse Suites. There are 52 of these (actually, they are not suites at all, but large cabins as the bedrooms aren't separate from the living areas). They do, however, measure around 322.9 sq.ft (30 sq. meters), and have a good-sized teak-floor balcony with sliding glass door (but with partial, and not full, balcony partitions) and teak deck furniture. The lounge area has a proper dining table and there is ample clothes storage space. The bathroom has a tub, shower enclosure, washbasin and toilet.

Cabins with Balcony. Cabins with private balconies (around 216 sq.ft/20 sq. meters), comprise about 66% of all cabins. They have partial, not full, balcony partitions, and sliding glass doors. On Deck 6, 14 cabins have lifeboat-obstructed views and no balcony. The living area has a refrigerated mini-bar, lounge area with breakfast table, and a balcony with teak floor, two teak chairs and a drinks table. The bathrooms, with tiled floors and plain walls, are compact, standard units, and include a shower stall with a strong, removable hand-held shower unit, hairdryer, toiletries storage shelves and retractable clothesline.

Outside View and Interior (No View) Cabins. These measure around 160–165 sq.ft (14.8–15.3 sq.meters), and have twin beds (convertible to a queen-sized bed), vanity desk, small sofa and coffee table, and bathroom with a shower enclosure with a strong, removable hand-held shower unit, hairdryer, toiletries storage shelves,

retractable clothesline, washbasin, and toilet. Although they are not large, they are quite comfortable, with a decent amount of storage space.

Suites/cabins located at the stern of the ship may suffer from vibration and noise, particularly when the ship is proceeding at or close to full speed, or maneuvering in port.

CUISINE. Flexibility and choice are what the dining facilities aboard the Oceania ships are all about. There are four different restaurants:

● The **Grand Dining Room** has around 340 seats, and a raised central section, but the problem is the noise level – because of the low ceiling height, it's atrocious when the dining room is full. Being located at the stern, there are large ocean-view windows on three sides (prime tables overlook the stern). The chairs are comfortable and have armrests. The menus change daily for lunch and dinner.

● **Toscana Italian Restaurant** has 96 seats, windows along two sides, and a set menu (plus chef's daily specials).

● The cozy **Polo Grill** has 98 seats, windows along two sides and a set menu including prime steaks and seafood.

● The **Terrace Café** has seats for 154 indoors – not enough during cruises to cold-weather areas – and 186 outdoors. It is open for breakfast, lunch and casual dinners, when it offers tapas and other Mediterranean food. As the ship's self-serve buffet restaurant, it incorporates a small pizzeria and grill. There are basic salads, a meat carving station, and a reasonable selection of cheeses.

All restaurants have open-seating dining, so you can dine when you want, with whom you wish. Reservations are needed in Toscana Restaurant and Polo Grill (but there's no extra charge), where there are mostly tables for four or six; there are few tables for two. There is a Poolside Grill Bar. All cappuccino and espresso coffees cost extra.

The food and service staff is provided by Apollo, a well-known and respected maritime catering company that also has an interest in Oceania Cruises. The consultant chef is Jacques Pepin (well-known as a television chef in America), who oversees the cuisine.

ENTERTAINMENT. The Nautica Lounge has entertainment, lectures and some social events. There is little entertainment due to the intensive nature of the itineraries. However, there is live music in several bars and lounges.

SPA/FITNESS. A lido deck has a swimming pool, and good sunbathing space, plus a thalassotherapy tub. A jogging track circles the swimming pool deck (but one deck above). The uppermost outdoors deck includes a golf driving net and shuffleboard court. The Oceania Spa consists of a beauty salon, three treatment rooms, men's and women's changing rooms, and steam room (there is no sauna). Canyon Ranch SpaClub operates the spa and beauty salon, and provides the staff. Examples of pricing include: full body massage $99 (50 minutes); body contour wrap, $159 (75 minutes); personal training session $75 (75 minutes); shampoo, style and dry $29 (short hair); manicure $29; pedicure $39. Note that 15% is added to your spa account.

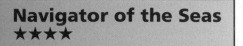

Navigator of the Seas
★★★★

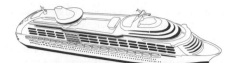

Size: . . . . .Large Resort Ship	Passenger Decks: 14	Cabins (with private balcony): 765
Tonnage: 137,276	Total Crew: 1,185	Cabins (wheelchair accessible): 26
Lifestyle: . . . . .Standard	Passengers	Wheelchair accessibility . . . . .Best
Cruise Line: Royal Caribbean International	(lower beds/all berths): 3,114/3,835	Cabin Current: . . . . .110 volts
Former Names: . . . . .none	Passenger Space Ratio	Elevators: . . . . .14 (6 glass-enclosed)
Builder: . . .Kvaerner Masa-Yards (Finland)	(lower beds/all berths): 44.0/35.7	Casino (gaming tables): . . . . .Yes
Original Cost: . . . .$500 million	Crew/Passenger Ratio	Slot Machines: . . . . .Yes
Entered Service: . . . . .Spring 2003	(lower beds/all berths): 2.6/3.2	Swimming Pools (outdoors): 3
Registry: . . . . .The Bahamas	Cabins (total): 1,557	Swimming Pools (indoors): 0
Length (ft/m): 1,020.6/311.1	Size Range (sq ft/m): 151.0–1,358.0/	Whirlpools: 6
Beam (ft/m): 155.5/47.4	14.0–126.1	Self-Service Launderette: . . . . .No
Draft (ft/m): 28.8/8.8	Cabins (outside view): 939	Dedicated Cinema/Seats: . . . . .No
Propulsion/Propellers: . . . . .diesel-electric	Cabins (interior/no view): 618	Library: . . . . .Yes
(75,600 kW)/3 pods	Cabins (for one person): 0	

OVERALL SCORE: 1,456 OUT OF A POSSIBLE 2,000 POINTS

OVERVIEW. *Navigator of the Seas* is a stunning, large, floating leisure resort (sister to *Adventure of the Seas, Explorer of the Seas*, and *Voyager of the Seas*).

The ship's propulsion is derived from three pod units, powered by electric motors (two azimuthing, and one fixed at the centerline) instead of conventional rudders and propellers, in the latest configuration of high-tech propulsion systems. With its large proportions, the ship provides more facilities and options, yet the ship manages to have a healthy passenger space ratio (the amount of space per passenger).

Being a "non-Panamax" ship, it is simply too large to go through the Panama Canal, thus limiting its itineraries almost exclusively to the Caribbean – where few islands can accept it – or for use as a floating island resort. Spend the first few hours exploring all the many facilities and public spaces aboard this vessel and it will be time well spent.

Although *Navigator of the Seas* really is a large ship, the cabin hallways are warm and attractive, with artwork cabinets and wavy lines to lead you along and break up the monotony. In fact, there are plenty of colorful, even whimsical, decorative touches to help you avoid what would otherwise be a very clinical environment.

Embarkation and disembarkation take place through two stations/access points, designed to minimize the inevitable lines at the start and end of the cruise (that's more than 1,500 people for each access point). Once inside the ship, you'll need good walking shoes, particularly when you need to go from one end to the other – it really is quite a long way.

The four-decks-high Royal Promenade, which is 394 ft (120 meters) long, is the main interior focal point of the

BERLITZ'S RATINGS		
	Possible	Achieved
Ship	500	418
Accommodation	200	150
Food	400	222
Service	400	276
Entertainment	100	83
Cruise	400	307

ship (it's also a good place to hang out, or to meet someone). The length of two football fields (American football, that is), it has two internal lobbies (atria) that rise to as many as 11 decks high. Restaurants, shops and entertainment locations front this winding street and interior "with-view" cabins look into it from above. It is designed loosely in the image of London's fashionable Burlington Arcade – although there's not a real brick in sight. It is, however, an imaginative piece of design work, and most passengers (particularly those who like shopping malls) enjoy it immensely.

The super-atrium houses a "traditional" English-style pub (Two Poets Pub), with draft beer and plenty of "streetfront" seating (it's funny, but North American passengers sit down, while British passengers prefer to stand at the bar). There is also a Champagne Bar, a Sidewalk Cafe (for continental breakfast, all-day pizzas, specialty coffees and desserts), Sprinkles (for round-the-clock ice cream and yoghurt). There are also several shops – for jewelry, gifts, liquor and logo souvenirs.

Altogether, the Royal promenade is a nice place to see and be seen, and there is action throughout the day and night. The Guest Reception and Shore Excursion counters are located at the aft end of the promenade, as is an ATM, while opposite is the cozy Champagne Bar. Watch for the parades and street entertainers.

Arched across the promenade is a Captain's Balcony. Meanwhile, in the center of the promenade is a stairway that connects you to the deck below, where you'll find the Schooner Bar (a piano lounge that is a feature found aboard all RCI ships) and the colorful Casino Royale. This is naturally large and full of flashing lights and noises. Gaming includes blackjack, Caribbean stud poker, roulette, and craps, as well as 300 slot machines.

There is also a regulation-size ice-skating rink (Studio B), featuring real, not fake, ice, with "bleacher" seating for up to 900, and the latest in broadcast facilities. Ice Follies shows are also presented here. A number of slim pillars obstruct clear-view arena stage sight lines, however. If ice-skating in the Caribbean doesn't appeal, perhaps you'd like the stunning two-deck library (it's the first aboard any ship, and it is open 24 hours a day). A grand amount of money was spent on permanent artwork.

Drinking places include a neat Aquarium Bar, which comes complete with 50 tons of glass and water in four large aquariums (whose combined value is over $1 million). Other drinking places include the aforementioned Champagne Bar, the Crown & Anchor Pub, and a Connoisseur Club – for cigars and cognacs.

Lovers of jazz might appreciate the Cosmopolitan Club, an intimate room for cool music atop the ship within the Viking Crown Lounge, or the Schooner Bar piano lounge. Golfers might enjoy the 19th Hole, a golf bar, as they play the Navigator Links.

There is a large TV studio, adjacent to rooms that can be used for trade show exhibit space, with conference center that seats 400 and a multi-media screening room that seats 60. Lovers could tie the knot in a wedding chapel in the sky, the Skylight Chapel (it's located on the upper level of the Viking Crown Lounge, and even has wheelchair access via an electric stairway lift). Meanwhile, outdoors, the pool and open deck areas provide a resort-like environment.

Families with children are also well catered to, as facilities for children and teenagers are extensive (they are much larger than aboard sister ships *Adventure of the Seas, Explorer of the Seas and Voyager of the Seas*). An area called Adventure Ocean is split into age-related areas: "Aquanauts" is for 3–5 year-olds; "Explorers" is for 6–8 year-olds; "Voyagers" is for 9–12 year-olds. The Living Room and Fuel are dedicated areas for teenagers, that include a daytime club (with several computers), soda bar, and disco; there's also an array of the latest video games. Paint and Clay is an arts and crafts center for younger children. Adjacent to these indoor areas is Adventure Beach, an area for all the family; this includes swimming pools, a water slide and game areas outdoors.

In terms of sheer size, this ship dwarfs all others in the cruise industry, but in terms of personal service, the reverse is the case, unless you happen to reside in one of the top suites. Royal Caribbean International does, however, try hard to provide a good standard of programmed service from its hotel staff. This is impersonal city life at sea, millennium-style, and a superb, well-designed alternative to a land-based resort, which is what the company wanted to build. Welcome to the escapist world of highly programmed resort living aboard ship.

Remember to take plenty of extra funds – you'll need them to pay for all the additional-cost items. The onboard currency is the US dollar.

The ship is large, so remember that if you meet someone somewhere, and want to meet them again you'll need to make an appointment – for this really is a large, Las Vegas-style floating resort-city for the lively of heart and fleet of foot. The best advice I can give you is to arrange to meet somewhere along the Royal Promenade.

SUITABLE FOR: *Navigator of the Seas* is best suited to young-minded adults and couples of all ages, families with toddlers, tots, children, and teenagers who like to mingle in a large ship setting with plenty of entertainment for everyone, with food that focuses on quantity rather than quality (unless you are prepared to pay extra in the "alternative" restaurant), all delivered with friendly but unpolished service.

ACCOMMODATION. There is an extensive range of 22 cabin categories, in four major groupings: Premium ocean-view suites and cabins, Promenade-view (interior-view) cabins, Ocean-view cabins, and Interior (no view) cabins. Note that many cabins are of a similar size (good for incentives and large groups), and 300 have interconnecting doors (good for families).

Suites and cabins with private balcony have Bolidt floors (a substance that looks like rubberized sand) instead of wood. If you have a cabin with an interconnecting door to another cabin, you should be aware that noise can filter through from the adjoining room. Also, the bathroom toilets are quite noisy. The price you pay will depend on the grade, size and location you choose.

A total of 138 interior (no view) cabins have bay windows that look into a horizontal atrium – first used to good effect aboard the Baltic passenger ferries *Silja Serenade* (1990) and *Silja Symphony* (1991) with interior cabins that look into a central shopping plaza. These cabins measure 157 sq. ft (15 sq. meters). Regardless of which cabin grade you choose, all except for the Royal Suite and Owner's Suite have twin beds that convert to a queen-sized unit, a TV set, radio and telephone, personal safe, vanity unit, mini-bar (called an Automatic Refreshment Center) hairdryer and private bathroom.

The largest accommodation includes luxuriously appointed penthouse suites (whose occupants, sadly, must share the rest of the ship with everyone else, except for their own exclusive, and private, concierge club). The grandest is the Royal Suite, which is positioned on the port side of the ship, and measures 1,146 sq. ft/106.5 sq. meters). It has a king-sized bed in a separate, large bedroom, a living room with an additional queen-sized sofa bed, baby grand piano (no pianist is included, however), refrigerator/wet bar, dining table, entertainment center, and large bathroom.

The slightly smaller, but still highly desirable, Owner's Suites (there are 10 of these, all located in the center of the ship, on both port and starboard sides, each measuring 468 sq. ft/43 sq. meters) and four Royal Family suites (each 574 sq. ft/53 sq. meters), all featuring similar items. However, the four Royal Family suites, which have two bedrooms (including one with third/fourth upper Pullman berths) are at the stern of the ship and have magnificent views over the ship's wake (and seagulls).

All cabins have a private bathroom with shower enclosure (towels are 100% cotton), as well as interactive, closed-circuit and satellite TV, and pay-per-view movies. Cabins with "private balconies" aren't so private, as the partitions are only partial, not full. The balcony decking is made of Bolidt and not wood, while the balcony rail is of wood.

CUISINE. The main dining room, with a capacity of almost 2,000, is large and noisy. It is set on three levels, with a dramatic staircase connecting all three levels. All three have exactly the same menus and food. There are also two small private wings for private groups, each seating about 58 persons. All dining venues are non-smoking. When you book, choose one of two seatings, or "My Time Dining" (eat when you want, during dining room hours). Tables are for four, six, eight 10 or 12. The china and cutlery are good-quality.

Alternative (Extra Cost) Dining
Alternative dining options for casual and informal meals at all hours (according to company releases) include:

● **Cafe Promenade:** for continental breakfast, all-day pizzas and specialty coffees (provided in paper cups).

● **Windjammer Cafe:** for casual buffet-style breakfast, lunch and light dinner (except for the cruise's last night).

● **Chops Grille** (a steakhouse that is actually a little section inside the Windjammer Cafe): for casual dinner (no reservations necessary) featuring a grill and open kitchen. A cover charge of $25 per person applies. Premium meats and steaks served include Veal Chop, New York Striploin Steak, Filet Mignon, and Prime Rib of Beef.

● **Portofino:** this is the ship's "upscale" (non-smoking) Euro-Italian restaurant, open for dinner only. Reservations are required; a $20 cover charge/gratuity per person applies. The food and its presentation are better than the food in the dining room, although the restaurant is not large enough for all passengers to try even once during a cruise. Choices include: antipasti, soup, salad, pasta, main dish, dessert, cheese and coffee.

● **Johnny Rockets:** a retro 1950s all-day, all-night American diner-style eatery that features hamburgers, malt shakes (at extra cost), and jukebox hits, with both indoor and outdoor seating (all indoor tables have a mini-jukebox; dimes are provided for you to make your selection of vintage records), and all-singing, all-dancing waitresses that'll knock your socks off, if you can stand the volume.

● **Sprinkles:** for round-the-clock ice cream and yoghurt (in the Royal Promenade).

ENTERTAINMENT. The 1,350-seat Metropolis Showlounge is a really stunning room that could well be the equal of many such rooms on land. It is located at the forward end of the ship and spans the height of five decks (with only a few slim pillars and almost no disruption of sight lines from almost any seat in the house). The room has a hydraulic orchestra pit and huge stage areas, together with sonic-boom loud sound, and some superb lighting equipment.

In addition, the ship has a whole array of cabaret acts. Although many of these are not what you would call headliners, they regularly travel the cruise ship circuit. The strongest cabaret acts perform in the main showlounge, while others are presented in the Ixtapa Lounge, which is also the venue for late-night adults-only comedy.

There is also a television studio, located adjacent to rooms that could be used, for example, for trade show exhibition space – good for conventions at sea.

SPA/FITNESS. The ShipShape Spa is large, and measures 15,000 sq. ft (1,400 sq. meters). It includes a large aerobics exercise room, fitness center (with the usual stairmasters, treadmills, stationary bikes, weight machines and free weights), treatment rooms, men's and women's sauna/steam rooms, while another 10,000 sq. ft (930 sq. meters) is devoted to a Solarium (with magrodome sliding glass roof) for relaxation after you've exercised too much.

For the more sporting, there is activity galore – including a rock-climbing wall that's 32.8 ft high (10 meters), with five separate climbing tracks. It is located outdoors at the aft end of the funnel. You'll get a great "buzz" being 200 ft (60 meters) above the ocean while the ship is moving.

Other sports facilities include a roller-blading track, a dive-and-snorkel shop, a full-size basketball court and 9-hole, par 26 golf course.

● **For more extensive general information about the Royal Caribbean experience, see pages 151–6.**

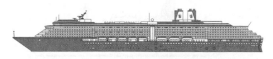

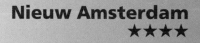

Nieuw Amsterdam
★★★★

Size: . . . . .Large Resort Ship	Total Crew: 929	Wheelchair accessibility . . . . .Good
Tonnage: .86,700	Passengers	Cabin Current: . . . . .110/220 volts
Lifestyle: . . . . .Premium	(lower beds/all berths): 2,106/2,671	Elevators: 14
Cruise Line: . . . . . . .Holland America Line	Passenger Space Ratio	Casino (gaming tables): . . . . .Yes
Former Names: . . . . .none	(lower beds/all berths): 41.2/32.4	Slot Machines: .Yes
Builder: . . . . .Fincantieri (Italy)	Crew/Passenger Ratio	Swimming Pools (outdoors): . . . . . . .2 + 1
Original Cost: .n/a	(lower beds/all berths): 2.2/2.8	children's pool
Entered Service: . . . . .Jul 2010	Cabins (total): 1,053	Swimming Pools (indoors): 1
Registry: . . . . .The Netherlands	Size Range (sq ft/m): 170.0–1,318.6/	(indoor/outdoor with retractable dome)
Length (ft/m): 935.0/285.0	15.7–122.5	Whirlpools: 5
Beam (ft/m): 105.6/32.2	Cabins (outside view): 897	Self-Service Launderette: . . . . .No
Draft (ft/m): 25.5/7.8	Cabins (interior/no view): 156	Dedicated Cinema/Seats: Yes/170
Propulsion/Propellers: . . . . .diesel-electric	Cabins (for one person): 0	Library: . . . . .Yes
(34,000 kW/2 pods (17.6 mW each)	Cabins (with private balcony): 708	
Passenger Decks: 12	Cabins (wheelchair accessible): 30	

OVERALL SCORE: 1,535 OUT OF A POSSIBLE 2,000 POINTS

OVERVIEW. A "Vista"-class ship – sister to *Eurodam, Noordam, Oosterdam, Westerdam* and *Zuiderdam* – *Nieuw Amsterdam* is named after the Dutch name for New York City and the interior design reflects the great city. The ship, the latest in a line of HAL ships to carry this name, has two upright "dustbin lid" funnels in a close-knit configuration – one in front of the other. There's a "pod" propulsion system *(see page 45 for an explanation)*.

BERLITZ'S RATINGS

	Possible	Achieved
Ship	500	428
Accommodation	200	168
Food	400	274
Service	400	278
Entertainment	100	77
Cruise	400	310

As aboard the other *Vista*-class HAL ships, the main pool deck can be covered with a glass dome roof for use in cooler regions. There is a complete walk-around exterior teak promenade deck, and real teak "steamer" style sun-loungers are provided.

What's neat are the little tented cabanas on the aft deck, providing private shaded space in an open-air environment. They are filled with goodies such as champagne, chocolate strawberries, an iPod pre-stocked with music, bathrobes, fresh fruit and chilled towels for two adults and two children. Naturally, there's an extra cost for these canvas havens.

There are two whole entertainment/ public room decks. Perhaps the most dramatic room aboard this ship is the showlounge, spanning four decks in the forward section of the ship. Other facilities include a winding shopping street with boutique stores and logo shops, card room, an art gallery, large casino, photo gallery, and small meeting rooms.

The ship is designed to appeal to younger, more vibrant, multi-generational holidaymakers. The onboard currency is the US dollar, and gratuities are automatically added to your onboard account.

Passenger niggles include noisy cabin air-conditioning – the flow can't be regulated or turned off, the only regulation being for temperature control.

● **For more extensive comments about the facilities, dining venues, entertainment and spa/fitness facilities, see the entry for *Eurodam* on page 378–9.**

Nippon Maru
★★★★

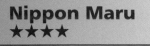

Size: ....Small Ship	Passenger Decks: 7	Cabins (with private balcony): 27
Tonnage: 22,472	Total Crew: 230	Cabins (wheelchair accessible): 2
Lifestyle: ....Standard	Passengers	Wheelchair accessibility ....Fair
Cruise Line: ...Mitsui OSK Passenger Line	(lower beds/all berths): 408/607	Cabin Current: ....100 volts
Former Names: ....none	Passenger Space Ratio	Elevators: 5
Builder: .....Mitsubishi Heavy Industries	(lower beds/all berths): 55.0/37.0	Casino (gaming tables): ....Yes
(Japan)	Crew/Passenger Ratio	(gifts only, no cash prizes)
Original Cost: ....$59.4 million	(lower beds/all berths): 2.5/3.7	Slot Machines: ....No
Entered Service: ....Sept 1990	Cabins (total): 204	Swimming Pools (outdoors): 1
Registry: ....Japan	Size Range (sq ft/m): 150.6–430.5/	Swimming Pools (indoors): 0
Length (ft/m): 546.7/166.65	14.0–40.0	Whirlpools: ....4 Japanese baths
Beam (ft/m): 78.7/24.00	Cabins (outside view): 184	Self-Service Launderette: ....Yes
Draft (ft/m): 21.4/6.55	Cabins (interior/no view): 18	Dedicated Cinema/Seats: ....Yes
Propulsion/Propellers: diesel (15,740 kW)/2	Cabins (for one person): 6	Library: ....Yes

OVERALL SCORE: 1,503 OUT OF A POSSIBLE 2,000 POINTS

OVERVIEW. *Nippon Maru* has a nicely-shaped stern, and a single, large, blood-orange color, swept-back funnel almost at the stern, with an exterior styling that is very traditional, with a conventional twin rudder/propeller combination. There is a decent amount of open outdoors space. The ship had a four-month refit in 2009–10, when a new hydraulic tender loading platform was created.

Deck extensions created space for more public rooms, a new dining room for suite-class and deluxe-grade passengers, a piano lounge, and a new health/fitness facility. New suites and balcony cabins were added; balconies were added to 26 cabins, and public rooms and hallways were given a facelift.

The interior's focal point is an atrium lobby that spans six decks. The ship has a lot of public rooms for its size, and some have high ceilings, giving a good sense of spaciousness. Public rooms include a showlounge, piano lounge, a 54-seat screening room/lecture room (Mermaid Theatre), a gaming corner (no cash prizes, but give-aways), and a washitsu tatami room within the Horizon Lounge. Organized children's activities are provided on certain cruises.

The service staff and crew provide really warm, friendly service with a smile, The onboard currency is the Japanese yen, and tipping is not allowed.

SUITABLE FOR: *Nippon Maru* is best suited to Japanese-speaking couples and single travelers who want very comfortable surroundings, and who enjoy decent food and Japanese "Omotenashi" service, all at a decent cost.

ACCOMMODATION. The new suites, on Deck 6, are large, and have a separate sleeping and living areas. A sofa, two

BERLITZ'S RATINGS

	Possible	Achieved
Ship	500	377
Accommodation	200	147
Food	400	307
Service	400	301
Entertainment	100	81
Cruise	400	290

chairs, and coffee table occupy one section of the lounge; there is also a vanity/writing desk with espresso machine and tea-making facilities. The sleeping area's two beds can be pushed together. The bathroom includes a "washlet." Slippers and bathrobes are provided, plus an excellent variety of personal grooming items. The nine new suites, added in the refit, include two suites with huge balconies, on the starboard side. The deluxe-grade cabins are nicely decorated, and the living area has a table and two chairs, and two beds. The standard cabins have blond wood cabinetry and good drawer space. Many have a third (or third and fourth) pull-down upper Pullman berth.

CUISINE. The Mizuho dining room, which seats around 320, serves both traditional Japanese cuisine and Western dishes. There is one open seating. A new, premium dining room, Kasuga, has been added for suite- and deluxe-grade occupants; it includes the excellent Shiosai sushi bar.

ENTERTAINMENT. The Dolphin Hall has a proscenium-arched stage, wooden dance floor, and seating on both the lower (main) level and the upper (balcony) level of this two-deck high room. There's social dancing, and a program of culturally rich lecturers and classical music artistes (including traditional Japanese instruments).

SPA/FITNESS. A new Terraké Spa includes beauty and nail treatment rooms, three body treatment rooms, and a small fitness room. There's a traditional Japanese Grand Bath (one for women, one for men, open until 1am), with washing stations and a sauna. Adjacent is a sports massage room.

Noordam
★★★★

Size: ....Large Resort Ship	Passenger Decks: 11	Cabins (with private balcony): 641
Tonnage: 82,300	Total Crew: 820	Cabins (wheelchair accessible): 28
Lifestyle: ....Premium	Passengers	Wheelchair accessibility ....Good
Cruise Line: ....Holland America Line	(lower beds/all berths): 1,918/2,457	Cabin Current: ....110 volts
Former Names: ....none	Passenger Space Ratio	Elevators: 14
Builder: ....Fincantieri (Italy)	(lower beds/all berths): 42.9/33.4	Casino (gaming tables): ....Yes
Original Cost: ....$400 million	Crew/Passenger Ratio	Slot Machines: ....Yes
Entered Service: ....Feb 2006	(lower beds/all berths): 2.3/2.9	Swimming Pools (outdoors): 2
Registry: ....The Netherlands	Cabins (total): 959	+ children's pool
Length (ft/m): 935.0/285.0	Size Range (sq ft/m): 170.0–1,318.6/	Swimming Pools (indoors):1 (indoor/outdoor)
Beam (ft/m): 105.6/32.25	15.7–122.5	Whirlpools: 5
Draft (ft/m): 25.5/7.8	Cabins (outside view): 806	Self-Service Launderette: ....No
Propulsion/Propellers: ......diesel-electric	Cabins (interior/no view): 153	Dedicated Cinema/Seats: Yes/170
(34,000 kW)/2 pods (17.6 MW each)	Cabins (for one person): 0	Library: ....Yes

OVERALL SCORE: 1,519 OUT OF A POSSIBLE 2,000 POINTS

OVERVIEW. *Noordam* (with 35 cabins more than close sisters *Oosterdam, Westerdam, Zuiderdam*) is one of the Vista-class of ships in the Holland America Line fleet, designed to appeal to multi-generational holidaymakers.

The twin working funnels are the result of the slightly unusual machinery configuration; the ship has, in effect, two engine rooms – one with three diesels, and one with two diesels and a gas turbine. A pod propulsion system is provided *(see page 45 for explanation)*, powered by a diesel-electric system, with a small gas turbine located in the funnel for the reduction of emissions.

There is a complete walk-around exterior teak promenade deck, and teak "steamer" style sunloungers are provided. Additionally, there is a jogging track outdoors, located around the ship's mast and the forward funnel of the ship. Exterior glass elevators, mounted midships on both port and starboard sides, provide fine ocean views from any one of 10 decks. There are two centrally located swimming pools outdoors, and one can be used in inclement weather due to its retractable sliding glass roof. Two whirlpool tubs, adjacent to the swimming pools, are abridged by a bar. A smaller (swimming) pool is available for children, and this incorporates a winding water slide that spans two decks in height. There is an additional whirlpool tub outdoors.

The intimate lobby spans three decks, and is topped by a beautiful, rotating, Waterford Crystal globe of the world. Adjacent are interior and glass wall elevators with exterior views. The interior decor is bright in many areas (in order to attract a younger clientele), and the ceilings are particularly noticeable. A large collection of artwork is a standard feature, and pieces reflect the former Dutch East Indies.

BERLITZ'S RATINGS

	Possible	Achieved
Ship	500	427
Accommodation	200	162
Food	400	269
Service	400	275
Entertainment	100	77
Cruise	400	309

There are two whole entertainment/public room decks. Perhaps the most dramatic room aboard this ship is the showlounge, spanning four decks in the forward section of the ship. Other facilities include a winding shopping street with several boutique stores and logo shops, card room, an art gallery, photo gallery, and several small meetings rooms. The casino is large (one has to walk through it to get from the restaurant to the showlounge on one of the entertainments decks), and is equipped with all the gaming paraphernalia and slot machines you can think of.

Sports enthusiasts can enjoy a basketball court, volleyball court, golf simulator. "Explorations" is a combination coffee bar (coffees and other drinks are at extra cost), lounge, an extensive library and internet-connect center, all contained in one attractive, open "lifestyle" environment – it's a popular area for relaxation and reading, although noise from the coffee machine can interrupt concentration.

For families with children, Club HAL's KidZone provides a whole area dedicated to children's facilities and extensive programming for different age groups (5–17), with one counselor for every 30 children. Free ice cream is provided at certain hours, plus hot hors d'oeuvres in all bars.

While this formula may not work well for the loyal repeat passengers used to the line's smaller ships, Noordam offers a wide range of public rooms with a reasonably intimate atmosphere and the overall feel of the ship is quite homely and comforting, with fresh flowers everywhere, as well as some nicely showcased Dutch artifacts and museum pieces from the 16th and 17th centuries. Perhaps the ship's best asset is its friendly and personable crew (most are from Indonesia and the Philippines).

The information desk in the lobby is small and somewhat removed from the main passenger flow on the two decks above it. Many pillars obstruct the passenger flow and lines of sight throughout the ship. There are no self-service launderettes (something families with children miss – although special laundry packages are available).

ACCOMMODATION. There are 24 price categories: 16 outside-view/8 interior (no view). Some cabins on the lowest accommodation deck (Main Deck) have views obstructed by lifeboats. Some cabins that can accommodate a third and fourth person have very little closet space, and only one personal safe. Some cabins have interconnecting doors – good for families with children. Occupants of suites also get exclusive use of the Neptune Lounge and concierge service, priority embarkation and disembarkation, and other benefits. In many of the suites/cabins with private balconies the balconies are not so private, and can be overlooked from various public locations.

Penthouse Verandah Suites: Two suites offer the largest accommodation (1,318 sq. ft/122.5 sq. meters, including balcony). These have a separate bedroom with a king-sized bed; there's also a walk-in closet, dressing room, living room, dining room, butler's pantry, mini-bar and refrigerator, and private balcony (verandah). The main bathroom has a large whirlpool bathtub, two washbasins, toilet, and plenty of storage space for personal toiletry items. Personalized stationery and free dry cleaning are included, as are hot hors d'oeuvres and other goodies daily.

DeLuxe Verandah Suites: Next in size are 60 of these suites (563 sq. ft/52.3 sq. meters). These have twin beds that convert to a king-sized bed, vanity desk, lounge area, walk-in closet, mini-bar and refrigerator, and bathroom with full-size bathtub, washbasin and toilet. Personalized stationery and complimentary dry cleaning are included, as are hot hors d'oeuvres and other goodies.

Verandah Suites: There are 100 of these (actually they are cabins, not suites, and measure (284 sq. ft/26.3 sq. meters). Twin beds can convert to a queen-sized bed; there is also a lounge area, mini-bar and refrigerator, while the bathroom has a tub, washbasin and toilet. Floor to ceiling windows open onto a private balcony (verandah).

Outside-view Cabins: Standard outside cabins (197 sq. ft/18.3 sq. meters) have twin beds that can convert to a queen-size bed. There's a small sitting area, while the bathroom has a tub/ shower combination. The interior (no view) cabins are slightly smaller (182.9 sq. ft/ 17 sq. meters).

Niggles include noisy cabin air-conditioning – the flow can't be regulated or turned off; the only regulation is for temperature control.

CUISINE. The 1,045-seat Vista (main) Dining Room is two decks high, with seating (at tables for two, four, six or eight) on both main and balcony levels (the galley is underneath the restaurant, accessed by port and starboard escalators), and is at the stern. It provides a traditional Holland America Line dining experience, with friendly service from smiling Indonesian and Filipino stewards. Both open seating and fixed (assigned tables and times) seating are available, while breakfast and lunch are open-seating (you'll be seated by restaurant staff when you enter). The dining room is a non-smoking venue.

Holland America Line can provide Kosher meals, although these are prepared ashore, frozen, and brought to your table sealed in their original containers.

Alternative Dining Option: The 148-seat Pinnacle Grill is a more upscale dining spot (with higher quality ingredients, and better presentation than in the larger main dining room). On Lower Promenade Deck, it fronts onto the second level of the atrium lobby (note that tables along the outer section of the restaurant are open to it and can suffer from noise from the Atrium Bar one deck below – but the tables are good for those who like to see and be seen). "Pacific Northwest" cuisine is featured (with items such as sesame-crusted halibut with ginger-miso; and an array of premium quality steaks). Formal table settings, china and silverware are featured, as are leather-bound menus. The wine menu (expanded in 2006) features some fine wines from around the world, including many gorgeous Bordeaux reds. Reservations are required and there is a cover charge of $30 per person for service and gratuity.

Informal Eateries: For casual eating, there is an extensive Lido Café, an eatery that wraps around the funnel, with indoor-outdoor seating and ocean views. It includes several sections including a salad bar, Asian stir-fry and sushi section, deli sandwiches, and a separate dessert buffet, although lines can form for made-to-order items (omelets for breakfast, pasta for lunch, etc.).

There's also an outdoor grill bar (adjacent to the Lido pool) with fast-food items such as hamburgers, veggie burgers, hot dogs, chicken and fries. On certain days, barbecues and other culinary specialties are available poolside.

ENTERTAINMENT. The 867-seat Vista Lounge is the principal venue for Las Vegas-style revues and major cabaret shows. The main floor level has a bar in its starboard aft section. Spiral stairways at the back of the lounge connect all levels. Stage shows are best seen from the upper levels, from where the sightlines are quite good.

SPA/FITNESS. The Greenhouse Spa is a large, two-decks-high health spa, and is located directly above the navigation bridge. Facilities include a solarium, hydrotherapy pool, unisex thermal suite – a unisex area incorporating a Laconium (gentle sauna), Hammam (mild steam), and Chamomile Grotto (small aromatic steam room).

There is also a beauty salon, 11 massage/therapy rooms (including one for couples), and a large gymnasium with floor-to-ceiling windows on three sides and forward-facing ocean views, and the latest high-tech muscle-toning equipment.

● **For more extensive general information on what a Holland America Line cruise is like, see pages 139–42.**

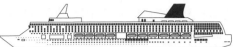

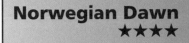

Norwegian Dawn
★★★★

Size: . . . . .Large Resort Ship	Passenger Decks: 11	Cabins (wheelchair accessible); 20
Tonnage: 91,740	Total Crew: 1,318	Wheelchair accessibility . . . . .Best
Lifestyle: . . . . .Standard	Passengers	Cabin Current: . . . . .110 AC
Cruise Line: . . . . .Norwegian Cruise Lines	(lower beds/all berths): 2,244/2,840	Elevators: 12
Former Names: . . . . .none	Passenger Space Ratio	Casino (gaming tables): . . . . .Yes
Gross Tonnage: 91,000	(lower beds/all berths): 40.8/32.0	Slot Machines: . . . . .Yes
Builder: . . . . .Meyer Werft (Germany)	Crew/Passenger Ratio	Swimming Pools (outdoors): 2
Original Cost: . . . .$400 million	(lower beds/all berths): 1.7/3.0	Swimming Pools (indoors): 1
Entered Service: . . . . .Oct 2002	Cabins (total): 1,122	Whirlpools: . . .4 (+ 1 children's whirlpool)
Registry: . . . . .Bahamas	Size Range (sq ft/m): 142.0–5,350.0/	Self-Service Launderette: . . . . .No
Length (ft/m): 964.9/294.13	13.2–497.0	Dedicated Cinema/Seats: Yes/151
Beam (ft/m): 105.6/32.2	Cabins (outside view): 787	Library: . . . . .Yes
Draft (ft/m): 26.9/8.2	Cabins (interior/no view): 335	
Propulsion/Propellers: . . . .diesel-electric/	Cabins (for one person): 0	
2 azimuthing pods (19.5MW each)	Cabins (with private balcony): 511	

OVERALL SCORE: 1,487 OUT OF A POSSIBLE 2,000 POINTS

OVERVIEW. *Norwegian Dawn* (sister to *Norwegian Star*, which debuted in 2001) was constructed in 64 sections, ("blocks"). It is a state-of-the-art vessel for Norwegian Cruise Line, and features a "pod" propulsion system *(see page 45 for a detailed explanation).*

The hull displays interesting logos on top of its white paint, depicting the ship's itineraries: the port side features the cruise itinerary from New York to the Bahamas and Florida, while the starboard side features the winter itinerary from Miami to the Caribbean. Dolphins, the Statue of Liberty, and representations of the four original paintings displayed on board (the Impressionists Matisse, Renoir, Van Gogh, and the pop artist Andy Warhol). It is a colorful concept, and makes the ship easy to spot in a sea of similar-sized ships in port.

Facilities include a large Dawn Club Casino gaming area, an Internet Cafe (with 24 computer stations and internet connection), a 1,150-seat showlounge with main floor and balcony level, a 3,000-book library, a card room, a writing and study room, a business center, conference and meeting rooms, and a retail shopping complex measuring 20,000 sq. ft (1,800 sq. meters).

As in sister ship *Norwegian Star*, a good deal of space is devoted to children's facilities (the T-Rex Kids' Center and Teen Club) – all tucked well away from adult recreation areas, at the aft end of the ship. Children of all ages will get to play in a superb wet 'n' wild space-themed water park (complete with large pool, water slide, and paddle pool). There's a room full of cots for toddlers to use for sleepovers, and even the toilets are at a special low height. Teens,

BERLITZ'S RATINGS		
	Possible	Achieved
Ship	500	418
Accommodation	200	156
Food	400	267
Service	400	285
Entertainment	100	67
Cruise	400	294

too, are well catered for, and get their own cinema (with DVD movies), discotheque with dance floor, and their own whirlpool (hot) tub.

With so many dining choices (some of which cost extra), your final cruise and dining experience will be determined by how much you are prepared to spend. You will need to plan where you want to eat well in advance, and make the necessary reservations, or you may be disappointed.

More choices, including more dining options, add up to a very attractive holiday package, particularly suitable for families with children, in a very contemporary floating leisure center that really does provide ample facilities for you to have an enjoyable time. The dress code is casual – very casual (no jacket and tie needed, although you are welcome to dress formally if you so wish). There is no suggested dress code on the daily programme.

While the initial cruise fare seems very reasonable, the extra costs and charges soon mount up if you want to sample more than the basics. Although service levels and finesse are sometimes inconsistent, the level of hospitality is very good – made so much better and brighter by the addition of a great number of Asian female staff rather than the surly and inconsistent Caribbean Basin staff still found aboard some NCL ships.

Despite the company's name, Norwegian Cruise Line, there's almost nothing Norwegian about this product, except for some senior officers. The staff, incidentally, includes many Southeast Asians who already have service experience aboard parent company Star Cruises' big ships.

Cruising aboard large ships such as this has become

increasingly an onboard revenue-based product. The ship is full of revenue centers designed to help you part with even more money than what is paid for in the price of your cruise ticket. You can expect to be subjected to a stream of flyers advertising daily art auctions, "designer" watches, "inch of gold/silver" and other promotions.

Gratuities for staff – cabin attendants, dining room waiters, etc. – are automatically added to your onboard account at $12 per person, per day (or you can pre-pay on-line); you can, however, reduce or otherwise amend these if necessary before you disembark, but in May 2005 the gratuity became a non-adjustable "service charge." In addition, a 15% gratuity is added to all bar bar purchases, and 18% for spa treatments. The onboard currency is the US dollar.

Although the suites and junior suites are quite spacious, the standard interior (no view) and outside-view cabins are very small when compared to those of other major cruise lines such as Carnival or Celebrity, particularly when occupied by three or four persons; the bathrooms, however, are of quite a decent size, and have large shower enclosures. Music played in some areas bleeds through into others; for example, Latin music played in Salsas (on the second level of the lobby) is heard throughout the lobby and the internet café on the third level of the lobby and is most disconcerting. Communication (particularly between some of the Asian staff and passengers) is weak. Standing in line for embarkation, disembarkation, shore tenders and for self-serve buffet meals is an inevitable aspect of cruising aboard all large ships – even those designated as "Freestyle".

ACCOMMODATION. There are 29 price/grades (the price will depend on the grade, location and size). Regardless of the accommodation you choose, all cabins have tea and coffee making sets (note that only "coffee creamer" is provided, so tea drinkers who want fresh milk need to arrange this with their steward, or call room service), rich cherry wood cabinetry, bathroom with sliding door and separate toilet, shower enclosure and washbasin compartments, and European duvets. The private balconies of the top suites have teak decks, while most other cabins with balconies feature a "Bolidt" (rubberized sand-like) deck, and smoked glass/wood rail panels that provide good sightlines. Audio channels can be found on the in-cabin television system, but you cannot turn off the picture. Elemis personal amenities are provided in the bathroom.

Garden Villas. The largest living spaces are two huge Garden Villas (Vista and Horizon), high atop the ship in a pod located forward of the ship's funnel, and overlooking the main swimming pool and recreation deck. These villas have huge glass walls and landscaped private roof gardens for outdoor dining (with whirlpool tubs, naturally), and huge private sunbathing areas completely shielded from anyone. Each has three bedrooms and bathrooms, and a large living room overlooking the lido/pool deck. These units have their own private elevator access and private stairway. Each measures 5,350 sq ft. (497 sq meters) and can be combined to create a huge, double-sized "house" measuring 10,700 sq ft

(994-sq-meters), including a private outdoor Italian garden. Butler service is provided, naturally.

Owner's Suites. Four Owner's Suites (each measures 750 sq.ft./69.6 sq. meters) are located in the very front of the ship. Two of these are nestled under the enclosed navigation bridge wings on Deck 11 (the other two are located in the equivalent space on the deck below). They have an entrance (with wooden door front), large lounge/dining room, and separate bedroom (with king-sized bed beneath a mirrored ceiling, and television with integral DVD player. The bathroom (almost as large as a standard cabin) has a full-sized tub with shower and TV; separate shower enclosure, separate toilet, and a dressing area with his-and-hers walk-in closets. There are forward facing (open) and side facing (enclosed) private balconies. Butler service is provided. If you don't need the entertaining space of the Garden Villas, these owner's suites are delightful living spaces. However, they do suffer occasionally from noise generated in Spinnaker's (a nightclub/disco) on the deck above. Each Owner's Suite can also be interconnected to a Penthouse Suite and balcony cabin (very useful for large families when parents want their privacy).

Penthouse Suites. There are 30 Penthouse Suites; each measures 366 sq.ft./34 sq. meters. Features include a bedroom with queen sized bed, walk-in closet, living room with dining table, and bathroom with separate shower enclosure and bathtub. Penthouse Suites on Deck 11 can be interconnected to children's cabin with double sofa bed and a pull-down Pullman-style) bed with separate bathroom and shower enclosure. These suites also have a private balcony, and butler service.

Romance Suites. There are four Romance Suites, each measuring 288 sq.ft./26.7 sq. meters. They include a separate bedroom with queen-sized bed, a sitting area with double sofa bed, and living and dining areas. The bathroom has a full-sized tub and shower. These suites also have a private balcony.

Mini Suites. There are 107 mini suites (measuring 229 sq. ft/21.2 sq. meters), each with two lower beds that convert into a queen-sized bed, and a sitting area with double sofa bed. The bathroom has a full-sized tub and shower. Floor-to-ceiling windows open onto a private balcony.

All suites are lavishly furnished (most in rich cherry wood), although closet space in some of the smaller units is tight. Some suites have extras like a trouser press, and a full range of toiletries by L'Occidentale. Suites also get butlers, who can serve all meals en-suite from the menus of a number of restaurants.

Although they are nicely furnished and quite well equipped, the standard outside-view and interior (no view) cabins are quite small, particularly when occupied by three or four persons. Some cabins have interconnecting doors (good for families with children). Many cabins have third- and fourth-person pull-down berths or trundle beds.

A small room service menu is available (non-food items cost extra, and a 15% service charge and a gratuity are added to your account). Bottled water is placed in each cabin (but a charge will be made to your account if you open the bottle).

CUISINE. With "Freestyle Dining", you can choose which restaurant to eat in, at what time, and with whom (there are no assigned dining rooms, tables or seats). While this is fine in theory, in practice it means that you have to make reservations (including the time that you want to eat), so "freestyle dining" actually turns out to be programmed dining. All restaurants and eateries are non-smoking.

Although there are three principal dining rooms, there are also a number of other themed eating establishments, giving a wide range of choice – though some cost extra, and require advance reservations (particularly for dinner). There are two entire decks of restaurants to choose from, involving 10 different restaurants and eateries. Note that NCLs dress code states that: "jeans, T-shirts, tank tops and bare feet are not permitted in restaurants."

● **Venetian**: the first main dining room (seats 472) offers traditional six-course dining (open 5.30pm–midnight). The dining room is located aft, and has good views over the ship's stern (at least in the daytime), although the sight-lines from some seats are obstructed by 14 pillars. The room has a baby grand piano in the center of the forward part of the room. If you want a quieter table, I recommend being seated in one of two wings in the forward section (near the entrance/steps).

● **Aqua**: the second main dining room (seats 344) offers traditional six-courses (open 5.30pm–midnight).

● **Impressions**: the third main dining room (seats 236) offers lighter cuisine (open 5.30pm–midnight). The waiter stations are too close to the tables and are very noisy.

● **Bamboo (a Taste of Asia)**: a Japanese/Thai/Chinese restaurant, with 140 seats, features a sit-up conveyor-belt style sushi/sashimi bar, sake bar, show galley, and separate room with a teppanyaki grill. In the evenings, music from Gatsby's lounge/bar (on the deck below) completely fill the restaurant (through an open lobby-like well), and a quiet meal is almost impossible. All items are at extra cost (there is an "all you can eat" sushi charge of $10).

● **Le Bistro**: a French restaurant with 72 seats, featuring Le Bistro's nouvelle cuisine (the decor includes four Impressionist paintings on loan from the private collection of the chairman of Star Cruises, parent company of NCL), although they don't really match the room's decor. A cover charge of $12.50 applies (there's also a line for you to add an *extra* gratuity – very cheeky). Best food on board and worth the extra cost.

● **Blue Lagoon**: a food court-style eatery; 68 seats; serving hamburgers, fish & chips, pot pies and wok fast dishes.

● **Garden Cafe**: an indoor/outdoor self-serve buffet eatery (seats 490). It includes "action stations" featuring made-to-order omelets, waffles, fruit, soups, ethnic specialities and pasta dishes.

● **Salsa**: a Spanish tapas eatery and bar (seats 112) with a selection of hot and cold tapas dishes and authentic entertainment, located on the second level of the atrium lobby.

● **La Trattoria**; located inside the indoor/outdoor buffet (seats 162), this eatery serves pasta, pizza and other popular Italian fare.

● **Cagney's Steak House**: arranged atop the ship (seats 112), incorporates a show kitchen, and serves US prime steaks and seafood. Be prepared for large portions, and a cover charge of $17.50.

Other eating/drinking spots include the Pearly Kings (an English pub for draft beer and perhaps a game of darts); Havanas, a cigar and cognac lounge; Java, an atrium lobby Cafe and bar (hot and frozen coffees, teas and pastries); a Beer Garden (grilled foods); a Gelato Bar (ice cream); and a Gym and Spa Bar (health food snacks and drinks).

ENTERTAINMENT. The Stardust Theatre seats 1,037, and is the venue for colorful Las-Vegas-style production shows and major cabaret acts. It is designed in the style of an opera house, spans three decks, and has a steeply tiered main floor and port and starboard balconies.

There are three production shows in a typical 7-day cruise (all ably performed by the Jean Ann Ryan Company): Bollywood, Music of the Night, and South Beach Rave. These are all very colorful, high-energy, razzle-dazzle shows (with much use of pyrotechnics, laser and color-mover lighting), with so much happening on stage that by the end of the evening, if you are a typical passenger, you will be tired and unable to remember much about the shows, which are, however, very entertaining.

The ship carries a number of bands and solo entertaining musicians, which provide live music for listening and dancing in several of the lounges and bars. Throughout the ship, loud Latin music prevails. In Spinnakers Lounge, the ship's nightclub, a Pachanga Party (a Miami South Beach rave) is held each cruise.

SPA/FITNESS. Wellness devotees should enjoy the two-deck-high El Dorado health spa complex (operated by the Hawaii-based Mandara Spa, owned by Steiner), located at the stern of the ship (with large ocean-view windows on three sides). There are many facilities and services (almost all at extra charge), including Thai massage (in the spa, outdoors on deck, in your cabin or on your private balcony).

In addition, there is an indoor lap pool (measuring 37 ft/11.2 meters), hydrotherapy pool, two sit-in deep tubs, aromatherapy and wellness centers, and mud treatment room treatment rooms (there are 15 treatment rooms in all, including one specifically designed for couples). The fitness and exercise rooms, with the latest Cybex muscle-pumping equipment, are located not within the spa, but at the top of the glass-domed atrium lobby. Included is a room for exercycle classes. Some classes, such Pathway to Yoga, Body Cycling Class and Body Beat Class (cardio kick-boxing), cost extra.

Recreational sports facilities include a jogging track, golf driving range, basketball and volleyball courts, as well as four levels of sunbathing decks.

● **For more extensive general information on what an NCL cruise is like, see pages 144–7.**

Norwegian Epic
★★★★

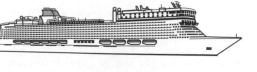

Size: . . . . .Large Resort Ship	Passenger Decks: 15	Cabins (wheelchair accessible): 42
Tonnage: 153,000	Total Crew: 1,730	Wheelchair accessibility . . . . .Good
Lifestyle: . . . . .Standard	Passengers	Cabin Current: . . . . .110 volts
Cruise Line: . . . . . .Norwegian Cruise Line	(lower beds/all berths): 4,200/5,400	Elevators: 16
Former Names: . . . . .none	Passenger Space Ratio	Casino (gaming tables): . . . . .Yes
Builder: . . . . .STX Europe (France)	(lower beds/all berths): 36.4/28.3	Slot Machines: . . . . .Yes
Original Cost: . . . .$735 million	Crew/Passenger Ratio	Swimming Pools (outdoors): 4
Entered Service: . . . . .June 2010	(lower beds/all berths): 2.4/3.1	Swimming Pools (indoors): 1
Registry: . . . . .Panama	Cabins (total): 2,100	Whirlpools: 9
Length (ft/m): 1,066.2/325.0	Size Range (sq ft/m): . . . . .n/a	Self-Service Launderette: . . . . .No
Beam (ft/m): 133.0/40.5	Cabins (outside view): 1,415	Dedicated Cinema/Seats: . . . . .No
Draft: 28.5/8.6	Cabins (interior/no view): 685	Library: . . . . .Yes
Propulsion/Propellers: . . . . diesel-electric	Cabins (for one person): 0	
(79.8 MW)/2	Cabins (with private balcony): 1,415	

BERLITZ'S OVERALL SCORE: 1,543 (OUT OF A POSSIBLE 2,000 POINTS)

OVERVIEW. *Norwegian Epic* is a blast, and all about lifestyle – bistro eateries, lots of color and noise, and perceived über-chic South Beach life at sea. But if you want to be part of it all, it could cost you an arm and a leg above the price of your cruise. This is perhaps the most extreme example of "all exclusive" cruising, and is a throwback to the days when First Class, Cabin Class, and Tourist Class meant passengers could not access certain areas of the ship – the familiar "pay more, get more" philosophy. This is a ship for the "effortlessly casual." Overall, it is perhaps the best example of a contemporary uber-ship, for cruising with attitude – and volume.

The largest ship ever constructed in STX Europe's French shipyard, in St Nazaire, *Norwegian Epic* is just a tad larger than *Queen Mary 2*, and operates year-round cruises in the Caribbean. Its profile isn't very handsome, because several decks above the navigation bridge make it look really top heavy, like a square lump of cheese, but the two side-by-side funnels – between which is a 60-ft wide rock climbing wall – bring some semblance of balance. The ship is about 30% wider than the Norwegian *Jewel*-class ships, and is a prototype for NCL.

The pool deck has an Aqua Park, with three major water slides – one involves inner tubes that give you a spin spitting you out into a big bowl, reminiscent of a washing machine – and a large rock-climbing wall and rappelling wall. Aft is a large movie screen with amphitheatre-style seating, and a nightclub within an area called Spice H2O, which also includes a sun deck.

The three lowest passenger decks contain the main entertainment venues, restaurants and other dining venues, show

BERLITZ'S RATINGS		
	Possible	Achieved
Ship	500	432
Accommodation	200	158
Food	400	277
Service	400	287
Entertainment	100	85
Cruise	400	304

lounges and a large casino. Some spaces open to two or three decks in height to create an illusion of space – like mini-atriums. The main lobby is three decks high, and the ship's dramatic three-deck-high chandelier is the largest at sea.

Two escalators help avoid congestion – perhaps even gridlock at peak times. Sandwiched between these three lower entertainment decks and the upper entertainment decks are seven decks mainly comprised of accommodation units. Something new for NCL is a bridge viewing room, located just behind the ship's navigation bridge.

In an attempt to extract more money from passengers, a number of "exclusive" experiences have been created, including a members-only POSH Beach Club, above the more exclusive Courtyard area atop the ship. This has a Miami South Beach vibe and includes four pay-extra experiences: (1) POSH Vive, 6–9am, when you can participate in yoga classes and treatments in private cabanas. (2) POSH Rehab till noon, so you can recover from a hard night, with Bloody Marys and chill-out music. (3) POSH Sol, noon–6pm, when you can can lounge on day beds and enjoy a beach-themed atmosphere. (4) Pure POSH, echoing Caesar's Palace in Las Vegas, where you can drink and dance under the stars. It's all just a little bit decadent – shades of the Savoy without the finesse.

Other ship features include a novel Ice Bar, a chill-out, chat-up venue inspired by the original ice bars and ice hotels of Scandinavia. In this frozen chamber of iced vodka, the centrepiece is a giant ice cube that glows and changes color. The Ice Bar accommodates 25 passengers who are given fur coats, gloves and hats because the room's temperature does not rise above –8°C (around 17°F). Naturally, there's a cover charge (ice charge!).

Then there's Halo, an über bar, where garden and courtyard villa occupants, who pay a premium for much better accommodation, have exclusive access, although others can use it by paying a cover charge. This bar sits at the top of the ship on Deck 16 and showcases art and jewelry, "modelled" by shop staff, Everything's available for purchase, of course.

Facilities, lounges and bars include the hedonistic Bliss Ultra Lounge and Nightclub – it's a bit like Saturday night on Ocean Drive on Miami's South Beach, although boa constrictors are not permitted on board. Already popular on *Norwegian Gem* and *Norwegian Pearl*, this bowling alley by day and hot bed club by night is a popular venue for late-night owls.

Spice H2O is a tiered pool complex for adults only, set at the stern of the ship. Like the POSH club, Spice H2O is a nightclub venue, which also interacts with a poolside screen over the pool. This provides a smaller version of the AquaTheatre aboard RCI's *Oasis of the Seas*, with its amphitheatre-style seating.

With all-day-long music and a huge screen, different themes prevail: (1) Sunny Spice 8am–11am, including spicy drinks and breakfast; (2) Daytime Aqua Spice with sun and water and Chinese take-away food items; (3) Evening Sunset Spice, with a perfect sunset every day; (4) All Spice at night, offering a show of aqua ballet and dancing. A "Beyond the Velvet Rope" package for all clubs is available at extra cost.

Despite the marketing hype about this exceptionally trendy ship, few major public rooms, except the main showlounge and aft restaurant, are more than one deck high.

Family-friendly cabins are within easy access to the Kid's Crew facilities, in two zones: for Kids 2–9, and tweens of 10–12 years of age. Nickleodeon is the family entertainment brand on all cruises, as part of NCL's children's programming. Activities include: Slime Time Live, an interactive game; Nick Live, with poolside entertainment; Character breakfast, at extra charge; and meet and greet. There's also a Nickleodean in-cabin TV channel. So expect to see Sponge Bob, Dora the Explorer, Patrick Star, Diego as part of the family-themed entertainment. Preschoolers can be kept amused year-round.

This is a big ship, but the elevators are forward and aft – there are none in the middle of the ship, which is tough for mobility-limited passengers. Yet *Norwegian Epic* has more elevators than the much larger *Oasis of the Seas*.

A "ship within a ship" two-deck complex provides a private courtyard/pool area, male and female steam rooms, concierge lounge, and private dining rooms and lounge for those willing to pay for exclusivity.

The ship sails on alternating seven-day eastern and western Caribbean itineraries during the winter season, and operates Mediterranean cruises in summer. If you have time and enjoy days at sea, you might try a repositioning voyage.

The onboard currency is the US dollar, and gratuities are automatically charged to your onboard account ($12 per person, per day), or you can pre-pay on-line. Bar purchases incur a 15% gratuity; spa treatments a severe 18%.

ACCOMMODATION. There are an astonishing 38 different accommodation price levels in 13 accommodation grades, including the first Loft Suites at sea – although upstairs/downstairs suites have been available for years aboard ships such as *Saga Ruby* and the now withdrawn *QE2*. In true nautical tradition, even-numbered cabins are on the port side, with odd-numbered cabins on the starboard side.

The Courtyard Suites (Decks 16, 17) are located in the "block of cheese" in the forward section, above the ship's navigation bridge. There are six courtyard "villas" – two face forward, while six overlook the central pool section of the ship, although none has a private balcony. Occupants, however, have access to a four-deck gated-community style grouping of facilities, including a concierge lounge, private courtyard and pool, his and hers steam rooms, and private sunbathing areas – so no need to go to the rest of the ship underneath you, except to disembark or go out to the entertainment decks to play, or escape.

All outside-view suites/cabins have a "private" balcony. In a "New Wave" concept, the designers have introduced curved walls in a wave shape that provides a contemporary look and feel to cabins. LED lighting, backlit domed ceiling, comfortable sofa seating (except Standard Cabins), vanity desk, and minibar. A palette of soft, warm colors in each cabin melds beautifully with walnut and rosewood colored veneers and stark white surfaces. Bathrooms have a separate toilet; tub or tub/shower combination, and separate vanity washbasin.

Although they are approximately the same size as current standard industry cabins, there is an efficient use of space, achieved by separating the toilet and shower unit to either side of the entryway, and by curving the bulkheads and furniture to give the cabins a more open, wavy, and contemporary feel – a sort of Uri Geller effect.

Eight Spa Suites have private key-card entry to the adjacent Mandara Spa, and complimentary 24-hour access to the Thermal Spa. These have more space and larger balconies, so of course they're more expensive – but more exclusive, too.

Solo travellers can take one of the 128 Studio (non-sharing) cabins, many of which are inter-connecting. A window looks out into the passageway. On Decks 11 and 12, these are priced for single occupancy – although they can be occupied by two since there is a double bed. They measure 100 sq. ft (9.3 sq. meters), and occupants have access to a common lounge. In the Interior Cabins and Studio "Stateroom" categories, the bed faces the cabin door, so there's absolutely no privacy – and many are really tiny.

CUISINE. There are certainly plenty of dining venues to choose from. With 21 restaurants, dining venues and casual eateries, it will take some planning in order to eat where you want, when you want, despite NCL's claim to "Freestyle Dining." Actually, there is no "main" dining room as such. In other words, just like in a city or town, you choose where to eat – unless, of course, there are no tables available, which is possible at peak times when everyone wants to see a show simultaneously, and you'll have to wait for a table. There is also no Lido self-service buffet as aboard almost all other large resort ships. Instead, different food outlets have been created in numerous locations – 11 are included in the cruise fare, while the others have a cover charge of between $5 and $25 a person. Because gratuities are automatically added to your onboard account, if you change dining venues every time you eat, you don't need to think about tips.

● Cagney's Steakhouse & Churrascaria, with 276 seats, expands the New York-style favorite of earlier NCL ships to include Argentine churrasco offerings of skewered meats presented by tableside passadors. The spot adds a large self-help salad bar in its center.

● Taste, in the atrium on Deck 5, is touted as a European retro-chic restaurant with brick details and floor to ceiling velvet curtains. The menu includes traditional and contemporary cuisine and the venue is open for breakfast, lunch and dinner.

● The Manhattan Room, located aft, is a two-deck-high restaurant reminiscent of an elegant Art Deco supper club, and has a dance floor for live music. It's the closest thing to a main dining room, and has a spectacular glass window wall at the ship's stern.

● La Cucina is for – what else but Italian-style dishes, from Tuscany, of course. It's at the front of the ship, providing great ocean views, one deck above the navigation bridge.

● The 124-seat Le Bistro serves French cuisine; there has been a Le Bistro aboard all NCL ships since the first one was installed aboard the now scrapped *Norway*.

● Multiple Asian-themed venues include Shanghai's for Chinese dishes and noodle bar specialties with an open kitchen and 133 seats; the 20-seat Wasabi for sushi and sakes; and a showy, food-chopping venue, the adjacent Teppanyaki Grill, with 115 seats.

● The Epic Club and Courtyard Grill, in the Courtyard Villas complex, are exclusive to suite and villa occupants and split between an elegant, private club-style restaurant with a large wine display and a casual outdoor area for breakfast and lunch. It can accommodate 127.

● O'Sheehan's is a neighborhood-style sports bar and grill, open 24 hours. It is adjacent to a bowling alley.

● Café Jardin (Garden Café) is a large self-serve buffet venue, with 728 seats, and is modeled on an English country garden conservatory (but with a French name and excel-

lent ocean views). The casual venue includes "action" stations where chefs prepare pasta and other items, made to order (join the line). The outdoor seating area, the Great Outdoors, looks over the Aqua Park. A special section for children, the Kids Café, has child-friendly (low height) tables and seats.

ENTERTAINMENT. The Epic Theater, at the front of the ship, spans two decks. Major production shows are presented here, together with mainline cabaret acts. The other principal entertainment venue is the Bliss Ultra Lounge, the decadent venue which contains a bowling alley – there's another one in Sheehan's on the deck above. This is where late-night comedy and some cabaret acts are presented.

A series of celebrity look-alike shows featuring Elvis, Madonna, and Tina Turner, is part of the entertainment offering. They are produced by Legends in Concert, the Las Vegas company that provided shows for "The Strip" for over 25 years.

The "Spiegel Tent" is a two-deck-high Cirque-like space, and combines a show with dinner. It's a mix of in-your-face street theatre, acrobatics, Berlin-style "foodertainment," with lots of clowning and satire during the two-hour dining/show experience. There's a canvas cover charge.

As part of NCL's creative "Check In, Rock Out" program, guitar enthusiasts can rent a real Gibson guitar and a set of headphones to play in the comfort of their cabin, at a cost of $10 a day.

SPA/FITNESS. The Smile Spa and Pulse Fitness Center complex is possibly the largest at sea (31,000 sq.ft/2,880 sq. meters). Operated by the Steiner-owned Mandara Spa, it is in the center of the ship, and some of the 24 treatment rooms have no view. The Fitness Center has port side ocean views; the aerobics room has no view. Numerous facilities and services are offered, almost all at extra charge.

Sports facilities include six bowling lanes in two venues (O'Sheehans Neighborhood Bar & Grill, and Bliss Ultra Lounge). There's also a full-size basketball court, volleyball, soccer, dodge ball, a batting cage, bungee trampoline, and a 24-ft (7.3-meter) tall climbing cage called the spider web, and an abseiling wall. Walkers should note that only 2.2 laps around the walking track equals 1 mile.

● **For more extensive general information on what an NCL cruise is like, see pages 144–7.**

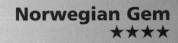

Norwegian Gem
★★★★

Size: . . . . .Large Resort Ship	Passenger Decks: 12	Cabins (with private balcony): 540
Tonnage: .93,530	Total Crew: 1,100	Cabins (wheelchair accessible): 27
Lifestyle: . . . . .Standard	Passengers	Wheelchair accessibility . . . . .Good
Cruise Line: . . . . . .Norwegian Cruise Line	(lower beds/all berths): 2,394/2,846	Cabin Current: . . . . .110 volts
Former Names: . . . . .none	Passenger Space Ratio	Elevators: 12
Builder: . . . . .Meyer Werft (Germany)	(lower beds/all berths): 39.0/32.8	Casino (gaming tables): . . . . .Yes
Original Cost: . . . .$390 million	Crew/Passenger Ratio	Slot Machines: . . . . .Yes
Entered Service: . . . . .Oct 2007	(lower beds/all berths): 2.1/2.5	Swimming Pools (outdoors): 2
Registry: . . . . .Panama	Cabins (total): 1,197	Swimming Pools (indoors): 0
Length (ft/m): 964.8/294.1	Size Range (sq ft/m): 142.0–4,390.0/	Whirlpools: 6
Beam (ft/m): 105.6/32.2	13.2–407.8	Self-Service Launderette: . . . . .Yes
Draft (ft/m): 26.9/8.2	Cabins (outside view): 792	Dedicated Cinema/Seats: . . . . .No
Propulsion/Propellers: . . . .diesel-electric/	Cabins (interior/no view): 405	Library: . . . . .Yes
2 pods (19.5MW each)	Cabins (for one person): 0	

BERLITZ'S OVERALL SCORE: 1,487 OUT OF A POSSIBLE 2,000 POINTS

OVERVIEW. This ship's design and layout is similar to that of *Norwegian Pearl*, and has a "pod" propulsion system for vibration-free cruising *(details: page 45)*. The ship's white hull has a colourful, funky string of gems along its sides as a design. There are plenty of deck lounge chairs – in fact, more than the total of passengers. Water slides are included for the adult swimming pools (children have their own pools at the ship's stern – out of sight of the adult areas).

BERLITZ'S RATINGS		
	Possible	Achieved
Ship	500	410
Accommodation	200	156
Food	400	267
Service	400	285
Entertainment	100	67
Cruise	400	294

Inside the ship is an entertaining mix of bright, funky, but warm colors and decor that you probably wouldn't have in your home, and yet somehow they all work extremely well in this large resort ship setting designed to attract the young, active, and trendy.

There are 11 bars and lounges, including "Bar Central," four specialty bars: martini bar, champagne and wine bar, beer and whiskey bar, and a cigar lounge; these interconnect with the lobby, yet have distinct personalities. The lobby houses a Java Bar, plus a two-deck-high movie screen, typically used to show sports events and Wii activities. One neat room is the "Bliss Ultra Lounge & Night Club," located at the aft end of the ship; rather like a South Beach club, it houses a 24-hours a day V-shaped sports bar and lounge complex, including a bowling alley with four real bowling lanes – the cost is $5 per person, including special playing shoes, and it is limited to six persons per lane. The lounge doesn't have many seats, but does have a couple of beds.

The casino is typical of larger resort ship casinos, with plenty of gaming tables, slot machines, noise, and smoke. So, if you walk through the casino to get from the showlounge to other public rooms, you'll be subject to cigarette smoke. A new twist in the onboard casino scene has

appeared, however, with poolside black-jack now established in its own "open-air casino" on the pool deck.

Because NCL is all about cruising with families of all ages, much space is devoted to children's facilities, all of which are thoughtfully tucked well away from adult recreation areas, at the aft end of the ship. Children of all ages will get to play in a superb wet 'n' wild space-themed water park (the Aqua Kid's Club), complete with large pool, water slide, and paddle pool; there's also 30-ft by 19-ft climbing wall at the ship's funnel. There's a room full of cots for toddlers to use for sleepovers. Teens, too, are well catered for, and have their own cinema, discotheque with dance floor, and hot tub.

Plenty of choices, including many dining options, add up to a very attractive holiday package, highly suitable for families with children, in a floating leisure center that really does provide ample facilities for enjoyment.

The dress code is very casual: no jacket and tie needed, although you are welcome to dress formally – but jeans are probably essential. Although service levels and finesse may be inconsistent, the level of hospitality aboard NCL ships is good – made better and brighter by the addition of a good number of Asian staff. Despite the company's name (Norwegian Cruise Line), there's little that's Norwegian about this product, except for some senior officers. There's plenty of lively music, constant activity, entertainment, and food that is mainstream and acceptable but nothing more (even when you pay extra to eat in the "alternative" dining spots).

While the initial cruise fare is reasonable, extra costs and charges soon mount up if you want to sample more than the basics. The ship is full of revenue centers which are designed to help you part with even more money than what is paid for in the price of your cruise ticket. You can expect to be subjected to a stream of flyers advertising daily art auctions, "designer" watches, gold and silver chain by the inch, and other promotions, and long programme announcements three times daily by the cruise director.

The onboard currency is the US dollar. Gratuities are automatically added to your onboard account at $10 per person, per day; you can, however, reduce or otherwise amend these if necessary before you disembark. Alternatively, you can pre-pay online. In addition, a 15% gratuity is added to all bar purchases, and 18% for spa treatments.

ACCOMMODATION. There are 32 different price grades, so there's something for all tastes, from small interior (no view) cabins to lavish suites in a private courtyard setting.

Although they are nicely furnished and quite well equipped, the standard outside-view and interior (no view) cabins are quite small, particularly when occupied by three or four persons. Over 250 cabins have interconnecting doors (good for families with children). So, interior (no-view) cabins can connect; outside view cabins can connect; and outside view and balcony cabins can connect, providing families with much choice. Also for families, many cabins also have third- and fourth-person pull-down berths or trundle beds, and about 280 cabins have interconnecting doors – ideal for family cruising.

A small room service menu is available (all non-food items are at extra cost, and a 15% service charge is automatically added to your account). Bottled water is placed in each cabin, but you will be charged if you open the bottle.

The following suites are available:

Courtyard Villas/Garden Villas: The two Garden Villa Suites, each of which measures 4,390 sq.ft. (407.8 sq.m), and 10 Courtyard Villas share a private courtyard with its own small pool, hot tub, and small fitness room, and have butler service. These units enjoy exclusivity – rather like accommodation in a gated community – where others cannot live unless they pay the asking price.

Deluxe Owner's Suites: These two suites, named Black Pearl and Golden Pearl, are set high atop all other accommodation, have stunning ocean views, and consist of a master bedroom with king-size bed, a dining/lounge area, a decent-sized balcony, and access to the private courtyard.

Penthouse Suites: Located at the front of the ship, they have a (partly) private balcony directly under the navigation bridge.

CUISINE. There are two main dining rooms: the 304-seat Grand Palace, with its minimalist decor; and the 558-seat Magenta Restaurant. There are several other themed eating spots, giving a wide range of choice; some cost extra, and require advance reservations, particularly for dinner; all are part of NCL's "Freestyle Dining" (there are no assigned dining rooms, tables or seats, so you'll need to plan your meals and times accordingly).

With 17 video screens located around the ship, you can check how busy each dining spot is and make a booking and find out if, or how long, you'll need to wait for a table (pagers are also available, so you can go bar-hopping while you wait for a table in your chosen venue). The system generally works well (with colored bars to indicate whether a restaurant is "full," "moderately busy," or "empty;" this has cut down the frustration of waiting a long time for a table, although on "formal" nights (when you may want to see the production shows), congestion certainly does occur. Note that NCL's dress code states that: "jeans, T-shirts, tank tops and bare feet are not permitted in restaurants," and all dining venues are non-smoking.

Alternative Restaurants/Eateries include *Cagney's Steak House* (serving steaks from 5oz to 48oz); *Blue Lagoon* (for trendy fast-food street snacks); *Le Bistro* for classic French cuisine; *Orchid Garden*, an Asian eatery complete with sushi bar and Teppanyaki grill (where the chef puts on a display in front of you); *La Cucina*, serving Italian cuisine; *Latin Restaurant*; the *Garden Café*, a large self-serve buffet-style restaurant, for casual meals; *Kids' Café*; and a *Java Café*, which serves Lavazza coffee, in the lobby.

ENTERTAINMENT. The Stardust Theater seats 1,042, and is the venue for colorful Las-Vegas-style production shows and major cabaret acts. It is designed in the style of an opera house, spans three decks, and has a steeply tiered main floor and port and starboard balconies.

There are three production shows in a typical 7-day cruise (all ably performed by the Jean Ann Ryan Company). They are colorful, high-energy, razzle-dazzle shows (with much use of pyrotechnics, laser and color-mover lighting.

The ship has a number of bands and solo entertaining musicians, which provide live music for listening and dancing in several lounges and bars. Throughout the ship, loud Latin music prevails. In the nightclub, a Pachanga Party (a Miami South Beach rave) is featured each cruise.

SPA/FITNESS. Wellness devotees should enjoy the two-deck-high Yin-Yang Health Spa complex (operated by the Hawaii-based Mandara Spa, owned by Steiner). It is located in the front of the ship, with large ocean-view windows on three sides. There are many facilities and services to pamper you – almost all at extra charge – including Thai massage (in the spa, outdoors on deck, in your cabin or on your private balcony), and 18 treatment rooms. There's also a 37-ft (11.2-meter) indoor lap pool, hydrotherapy pool, two sit-in deep tubs, aromatherapy and wellness centers, and mud treatment room.

The Body Waves fitness and exercise rooms are within the spa and feature the latest Cybex muscle-pumping equipment. Some classes, such as Pathway to Yoga, Body Cycling Class and Body Beat Class (cardio kick-boxing) cost extra.

Recreational sports facilities include a jogging track, golf driving range, basketball and volleyball courts, as well as several levels of sunbathing decks, plus the four bowling lanes, and a funnel-mounted rock-climbing wall.

● **For more extensive general information on what an NCL cruise is like, see pages 144–7.**

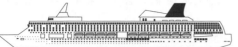

Norwegian Jade
★★★★

Size: . . . . .Large Resort Ship	Passenger Decks: 12	Cabins (with private balcony): 763
Tonnage: 93,558	Total Crew: .1,000	Cabins (wheelchair accessible): 27
Lifestyle: . . . . .Standard	Passengers	Wheelchair accessibility . . . . .Good
Cruise Line: . . . . . .Norwegian Cruise Line	(lower beds/all berths): 2,466/2,890	Cabin Current: . . . . .110 volts
Former Names: . . . .*Pride of Hawaii*	Passenger Space Ratio	Elevators: 12
Builder: . . . . .Meyer Werft (Germany)	(lower beds/all berths): 37.9/32.3	Casino (gaming tables): . . . . .Yes
Original Cost: . . . .$390 million	Crew/Passenger Ratio	Slot Machines: . . . . .Yes
Entered Service: . . . .May 2006/Mar 2008	(lower beds/all berths): 2.4/2.8	Swimming Pools (outdoors): 2
Registry: . . . . .The Bahamas	Cabins (total): 1,233	Swimming Pools (indoors): 0
Length (ft/m): 964.8/294.1	Size Range (sq ft/m): 142.0–4,390.0/	Whirlpools: 6
Beam (ft/m): 105.6/32.2	13.2–407.8	Self-Service Launderette: . . . . .No
Draft (ft/m): 26.9/8.2	Cabins (outside view): 834	Dedicated Cinema/Seats: . . . . .No
Propulsion/Propellers: . . . .diesel-electric/	Cabins (interior/no view): 425	Library: . . . . .Yes
2 azimuthing pods (20.0MW each)	Cabins (for one person): 0	

BERLITZ'S OVERALL SCORE: 1,481 OUT OF A POSSIBLE 2,000 POINTS

OVERVIEW. Built from 67 blocks, this is a sister ship to *Norwegian Jewel*. After service as *Pride of Hawaii*, it underwent a small transformation, including the addition of a casino, to become *Norwegian Jade*, for cruising in Europe and the Caribbean; some interior decor elements from the ship's former life in Hawaii remain. The ship features a "pod" propulsion system *(see page 45 for a detailed explanation)*. The interior decor is decidedly bright and cheerful.

Norwegian Jade's interior focal gathering place is "Bar Central" – three specialty bars (Magnum's Champagne/ Wine Bar, Mixers' Martini/ Cocktail Bar, and Tankard's Beer/Whiskey Bar) that are connected but have distinct personalities. They are located on the deck above the reception lobby. All told, there are a dozen bars and lounges on board. Other facilities include a casino, three meeting rooms, a chapel, card room, bridge viewing room, and the *SS United States* Library (with original photography and material about America's last ocean liner).

The dress code is casual – very casual; no jacket and tie needed, although you are welcome to dress formally if you wish. In fact, there is no suggested dress code in the daily program. Children are well provided for, and have their own facilities, including a Kids' Club; teens have their own disco, the Wipe-Out Club.

While the initial cruise fare seems very reasonable, the extra costs and charges soon mount up if you want to sample more than the basics. This ship has an all-American crew and service. It is full of revenue centers designed to help you part with more of your money. You can expect to be subjected to a stream of flyers advertising daily art auctions, "designer" watches, and many other promotions (including

BERLITZ'S RATINGS

	Possible	Achieved
Ship	500	416
Accommodation	200	155
Food	400	267
Service	400	283
Entertainment	100	67
Cruise	400	293

poolside "Inch of Gold" sales outlets).

A non-changeable service charge – this is, not a gratuity – for staff is automatically added to your onboard account at $12 per person per day, or you can pre-pay online. The onboard currency is the US dollar.

Passenger niggles include waiting to use the interactive dining reservation screens in the public areas; lines for breakfast in the main dining spots (particularly before the shore excursions start); and poor service and hospitality in some areas.

SUITABLE FOR: *Norwegian Jade* is best suited to youthful adult couples, single passengers, and families with children and teenagers who want contemporary, upbeat surroundings, good facilities, plenty of entertainment lounges and bars and high-tech sophistication – all in a neat, highly programmed, well packaged cruise in an Americana setting.

ACCOMMODATION. There are 33 price grades, determined by size and location. Although they are nicely furnished and quite well equipped, the standard outside-view and interior (no view) cabins are quite small, particularly when occupied by three or four persons. Over 250 cabins have interconnecting doors (good for families with children). So, interior (no-view) cabins can connect; outside view cabins can connect; and outside view and balcony cabins can connect, providing families with much choice. Also for families, many cabins also have third- and fourth-person pull-down berths or trundle beds.

A small room service menu is available (all non-food items cost extra, and a 15% service charge/gratuity is added to your account). Bottled water is placed in each cabin, but a charge is made to your account if you open the bottle.

Garden Villas: Two multi-room villas have great views over the pool deck (and ocean). Each has a roof terrace and private garden, with open-air dining, hot tub, and private sunning and relaxation areas. They are, perhaps, the most extravagant suites at sea today. Each has a living room with Bose audio-visual equipment (including a CD/DVD library), grand piano, wet bar, and refrigerator. Each has three bedrooms (king- or queen-sized bed) with ensuite bathroom, walk-in closet. Each Garden Villa measures approximately 4,390 sq ft./407.8 sq meters – the ultimate in living space, exclusivity and privacy.

Courtyard Villas: 10 Courtyard Villas (up to 660 sq.ft./61 sq.m.) share a private courtyard with its own (small) pool, hot tub, massage bed, and fitness room – all in a setting that is distinctly Asian. They also share a private concierge lounge with the two largest villas, as well as butler and concierge service. These units enjoy exclusivity – rather like accommodation in a gated community. The two Garden Villas each have three bedrooms (with ensuite bathroom), living room, dining room, and stunning views.

Owner's Suites: Each of these five units (approximately 1,195 sq.ft/111 sq.meters) has a large bedroom with king-size bed and audio-visual entertainment center, and a living room with dining area. The bathroom has a tub, separate shower enclosure and powder room. Some Owner's suites can interconnect with Penthouse Suites.

Penthouse Suites: There are 24 of these, measuring up to 600 sq.ft. (55.5 sq.meters), featuring a bedroom with queen-sized bed, living room with dining area; the bathroom has a bathtub/shower or separate shower enclosure. Some can be interconnect to a kid's room with double sofa bed and a Pullman bed with separate bathroom with shower.

All villas and suites have a private balcony, walk-in closet, rich cherry wood cabinetry, tea/coffee/espresso/cappuccino makers, plus butler and concierge service.

CUISINE. With "Freestyle Dining", you can choose which restaurant to eat in, at what time, and with whom (there are no assigned dining rooms, tables or seats). In practice, it means that you have to make reservations (including the time that you want to eat), so "freestyle dining" actually turns out to be programmed dining. There are two entire decks of restaurants, all non-smoking and totaling 10 restaurants and eateries. Some are included in the cruise fare, others cost extra.

The two main restaurants (included in the cruise fare) are Alizar (310 seats) and Grand Pacific (486 seats). Cagney's Steak House (176 seats), and Blue Lagoon (a casual eatery serving American food and seating 94), and Le Bistro (a classic French restaurant, with 129 seats – check out the beautiful, and real, Van Gogh painting) are favorite NCL alternative dining venues. Paniola (100 seats) offers trendy tapas and salsa fare. Jade Garden (including a sushi counter, sake bar, and a 32-seat Teppanyaki Grill), has Southeast Asian cuisine. The 70-seat Papa's Italian Kitchen has a long wooden table that creates a farmhouse ambiance. Self-serve buffet-style meals can be taken in the Garden Café, and its outdoor section. Lavazza (Italian) coffees can be found in the Aloha Café.

You can make reservations through the Freestyle Dining information system; plasma screens showing waiting times for the various venues are located in high-traffic areas.

ENTERTAINMENT. The 1,042-seat Stardust Theatre is the venue for colorful Las-Vegas-style production shows and major cabaret acts. It is designed in the style of an opera house, spans three decks, and has a steeply tiered main floor and port and starboard balconies. Colorful, high-energy, razzle-dazzle production shows are ably performed by the Jean Ann Ryan Company.

Bands and solo entertaining musicians provide live music for listening and dancing in several lounges and bars. Throughout the ship, loud music prevails. In Spinnakers Lounge (the ship's nightclub located high atop the ship with great ocean views on three sides), a Pachanga Party (a Miami South Beach rave) is held during each cruise.

SPA/FITNESS. The two-deck-high Yin and Yang health spa complex, operated by the Steiner-owned Mandara Spa, is at the stern (with large ocean-view windows on three sides). There are many facilities and services, almost all at extra charge. In addition, there is an indoor lap pool (measuring 37 ft/ 11.2 meters), hydrotherapy pool, two sit-in deep tubs, aromatherapy and wellness centers, and mud treatment room treatment rooms, including one for couples. Spa treatments incur an 18% gratuity.

The fitness and exercise rooms are located not within the spa, but at the top of the glass-domed atrium lobby (they have the latest Cybex muscle-pumping equipment). Included is a room for exercycle classes.

Recreational sports facilities include a jogging track, two golf driving nets (there's a golf pro shop, too), basketball and volleyball courts, paddle tennis, mini-golf, oversized chess, and several sunbathing decks.

● **For more extensive general information on what an NCL cruise is like, see pages 144–7.**

Norwegian Jewel
★★★★

Size:	Large Resort Ship	Passenger Decks:	12	Cabins (with private balcony):	540
Tonnage:	93,000	Total Crew:	1,000	Cabins (wheelchair accessible):	27
Lifestyle:	Standard	Passengers		Wheelchair accessibility	Good
Cruise Line:	Norwegian Cruise Line	(lower beds/all berths):	2,376/2,846	Cabin Current:	110 volts
Former Names:	none	Passenger Space Ratio		Elevators:	12
Builder:	Meyer Werft (Germany)	(lower beds/all berths):	39.1/32.6	Casino (gaming tables):	Yes
Original Cost:	$390 million	Crew/Passenger Ratio		Slot Machines:	Yes
Entered Service:	Aug 2005	(lower beds/all berths):	2.3/2.8	Swimming Pools (outdoors):	2
Registry:	Panama	Cabins (total):	1,188	Swimming Pools (indoors):	0
Length (ft/m):	964.8/294.1	Size Range (sq ft/m):	142.0–4,390.0/	Whirlpools:	6
Beam (ft/m):	105.6/32.2		13.2–407.8	Self-Service Launderette:	No
Draft (ft/m):	26.9/8.2	Cabins (outside view):	783	Dedicated Cinema/Seats:	No
Propulsion/Propellers:	diesel-electric/2	Cabins (interior/no view):	405	Library:	Yes
	azimuthing pods (20.0MW each)	Cabins (for one person):	0		

OVERALL SCORE: 1,486 OUT OF A POSSIBLE 2,000 POINTS

OVERVIEW. The ship, assembled from 67 blocks, and whose basic design and layout is similar to that of *Norwegian Gem* and *Norwegian Pearl*, features a "pod" propulsion system (*see page 45 for explanation*). The white hull has a colourful, funky design on its sides featuring sparkling jewels. There are plenty of sunloungers (in fact, the number is greater than the number of passengers carried). Water slides are included for the adult swimming pools (children have their own pools at the ship's stern – out of sight of the adult areas).

Inside the ship, you'll be met by an eclectic mix of colors and decor that you probably wouldn't have in your home, and yet somehow it works extremely well in this large resort ship setting designed to attract the young, active, and trendy.

There are 13 bars and lounges to enjoy, including "Bar Central," three specialty bars that are connected but have distinct personalities. Shakers Martini and Cocktail Bar is a 1960s-inspired lounge; Magnum's Champagne and Wine Bar recalls Paris of the 1920s and the liner Normandie; and Maltings Beer and Whiskey Pub is a contemporary bar with artwork themed around whiskey and beer production.

A good deal of space is devoted to children's facilities, which are all tucked well away from adult recreation areas, at the aft end of the ship. Children of all ages will get to play in a superb wet 'n' wild space-themed water park (complete with large pool, water slide, and paddle pool). There's a room full of cots for toddlers to use for sleepovers, and even the toilets are at a special low height. Teens, too, are well catered for, and have their own cinema, discotheque with dance floor, and hot tub.

Plenty of choices, including many dining options, add up

BERLITZ'S RATINGS

	Possible	Achieved
Ship	500	417
Accommodation	200	156
Food	400	267
Service	400	285
Entertainment	100	67
Cruise	400	294

to a very attractive vacation package, particularly suitable for families with children, in a contemporary floating leisure center that really does provide ample facilities for you to have an enjoyable time. The dress code is very casual (no jacket and tie needed, although you are welcome to dress formally if you wish).

The level of hospitality aboard NCL ships is good – made so much better and brighter by the addition of a great number of Asian female staff. Despite the company's name (Norwegian Cruise Line), there's little that's Norwegian about this product, except for some senior officers. There's plenty of lively music, constant activity, entertainment, and food that is mainstream and acceptable but nothing more (unless you pay extra to eat in the "alternative" dining spots). All this is delivered by a smiling, friendly service staff that lacks polish but is willing.

While the initial cruise fare is reasonable, extra costs and charges soon mount up if you want to sample more than the basics. The ship is full of revenue centers which are designed to help you part with even more money than what is paid for in the price of your cruise ticket. You can expect to be subjected to a stream of flyers advertising daily art auctions, "designer" watches, "inch of gold/silver" and so on.

Gratuities for staff (cabin attendants, dining room waiters, etc.) are automatically added to your onboard account at $10 per person, per day; you can, however, reduce or otherwise amend these if necessary before you disembark. Alternatively, you can pre-pay online. In addition, a 15% gratuity is added to all bar purchases, and 18% for spa accounts. The onboard currency is the US dollar.

ACCOMMODATION. There are 26 price grades, so there's

something for all tastes, from small interior (no view) cabins to lavish penthouse suites in a private courtyard setting.

Although they are nicely furnished and quite well equipped, the standard outside-view and interior (no view) cabins are quite small, particularly when occupied by three or four persons. Over 250 cabins have interconnecting doors (good for families with children). So, interior (no-view) cabins can connect; outside view cabins can connect; and outside view and balcony cabins can connect, providing families with much choice. Also for families, many cabins also have third- and fourth-person pull-down berths or trundle beds.

A small room service menu is available (all non-food items are at extra cost, and a 15% service charge/gratuity are automatically added to your account). Bottled water is placed in each cabin, but a charge will be made to your account if you open the bottle.

Courtyard Penthouses/Suites: Two Garden Villas (each measures 4,390 sq ft./407.8 sq meters), and 10 Courtyard Villas share a private courtyard with its own (small) pool, hot tub, massage bed, and fitness room – all in a setting that is distinctly Asian. They also share a private concierge lounge with the two largest villas, as well as butler and concierge service. These units enjoy exclusivity – rather like accommodation in a gated community – where others cannot live unless they pay the asking price. The two largest are duplex apartments, with a spiral stairway between the upper and lower quarters.

CUISINE. There are two main dining rooms: the 552-seat Tsar's Palace, designed to look like the interior of Catherine the Great's palace in St. Petersburg (Russia), and the 310-seat Azura. There are also a number of other themed eating establishments, giving a wide range of choice – though some cost extra, and require advance reservations (particularly for dinner). There are 10 different restaurants and eateries (some are included in the cruise fare, while others incur an extra charge) that represent NCL's "Freestyle Dining," allowing you to choose which restaurant to eat in, at what time, and with whom (there are no assigned dining rooms, tables or seats).

The 17 video screens located around the ship enable you to check how long you'll have to wait for a table at each dining spot. Pagers are also available, so you can go bar-hopping while you wait for a table. The system works well, although on "formal" nights (when you may want to see the show), congestion can occur. NCL's dress code states that: "jeans, T-shirts, tank tops and bare feet are not permitted in restaurants," and all dining venues are non-smoking.

Alternative Restaurants/Eateries: Cagney's House (for fine steaks and seafood), Blue Lagoon (Asian street food), and Le Bistro (French cuisine) are NCL favorites. Tango's a contemporary spot with bright colors and Latin/tapas fare. Chin Chin is an Asian eatery (with a Teppanyaki Grill and sushi counter). Mama's Italian Kitchen is novel in that it features a long wooden table running through the room to create the ambiance of a Tuscan farmhouse. For really casual (self-serve) buffet-style eating, there's the light, airy Great Outdoors. Finally, the Garden Café incorporates an ice cream bar, and Kid's Café (wisely located opposite the children's play areas, with its own kid-height counter). For coffee, head to the Java Café in the lobby – it's a great place for people watching. Three of the "alternative" restaurants incur a cover charge, while others are free.

ENTERTAINMENT. The Stardust Theatre seats 1,037, and is the venue for colorful Las-Vegas-style production shows and major cabaret acts. It is designed in the style of an opera house, spans three decks, and has a steeply tiered main floor and port and starboard balconies.

There are two or three production shows in a typical 7-day cruise (all ably performed by the Jean Ann Ryan Company). These are all very colorful, high-energy, razzle-dazzle shows (with much use of pyrotechnics, laser and color-mover lighting), with so much happening on stage that by the end of the evening, if you are a typical passenger, you will be tired and unable to remember much about the shows, which are, however, very entertaining.

The ship carries a number of bands and solo entertaining musicians, which provide live music for listening and dancing in several of the lounges and bars. Throughout the ship, loud Latin music prevails. In Spinnakers Lounge (the ship's nightclub), a Pachanga Party is featured each cruise (a Miami South Beach rave).

SPA/FITNESS. Wellness devotees should enjoy the two-deck-high Bora Bora health spa complex (operated by the Hawaii-based Mandara Spa, owned by Steiner), located in the front of the ship (with large ocean-view windows on three sides). There are many facilities and services to pamper you (almost all at extra charge), including Thai massage in the spa, outdoors on deck, in your cabin or on your private balcony.

In addition, there is a 37 ft (11.2 meters) indoor lap pool, hydrotherapy pool, two sit-in deep tubs, aromatherapy and wellness centers, and mud treatment room treatment rooms (there are 15 treatment rooms in all, including one specifically designed for couples), and heated tile loungers in a relaxation area.

The fitness and exercise rooms are located not within the spa, but at the top of the glass-domed atrium lobby (they feature the latest Cybex muscle-pumping equipment). Included is a room for exercycle classes. Some classes, such as Pathway to Yoga, Body Cycling Class and Body Beat Class (cardio kick-boxing) cost extra.

Recreational sports facilities include a jogging track, golf driving range, basketball and volleyball courts, as well as four levels of sunbathing decks.

● **For more extensive general information on what an NCL cruise is like, see Page 144–7.**

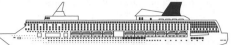

Norwegian Pearl
★★★★

Size:	Large Resort Ship	Passenger Decks:	12	Cabins (with private balcony):	540
Tonnage:	93,530	Total Crew:	1,100	Cabins (wheelchair accessible):	27
Lifestyle:	Standard	Passengers		Wheelchair accessibility	Good
Cruise Line:	Norwegian Cruise Line	(lower beds/all berths):	2,394/2,846	Cabin Current:	110 volts
Former Names:	none	Passenger Space Ratio		Elevators:	12
Builder:	Meyer Werft (Germany)	(lower beds/all berths):	39.0/32.8	Casino (gaming tables):	Yes
Original Cost:	$390 million	Crew/Passenger Ratio		Slot Machines:	Yes
Entered Service:	Dec 2006	(lower beds/all berths):	2.1/2.5	Swimming Pools (outdoors):	2
Registry:	Panama	Cabins (total):	1,197	Swimming Pools (indoors):	0
Length (ft/m):	964.8/294.1	Size Range (sq ft/m):	142.0–4,390.0/	Whirlpools:	6
Beam (ft/m):	105.6/32.2		13.2–407.8	Self-Service Launderette:	Yes
Draft (ft/m):	26.9/8.2	Cabins (outside view):	792	Dedicated Cinema/Seats:	No
Propulsion/Propellers:	diesel-electric/	Cabins (interior/no view):	405	Library:	Yes
	2 pods (19.5MW each)	Cabins (for one person):	0		

OVERALL SCORE: 1,485 OUT OF A POSSIBLE 2,000 POINTS

OVERVIEW. This ship, built from 67 pre-assembled blocks, and whose basic design and layout is similar to that of *Norwegian Jewel*, has a "pod" propulsion system *(see page 45 for explanation)* for vibration-free cruising. The ship's white hull has a colourful, funky string of pearl design along its sides. There are plenty of deck lounge chairs; in fact, the number is greater than the number of passengers carried. Water slides are included for the adult swimming pools (children have their own pools at the ship's stern).

Inside the ship, you'll be met by an entertaining, eclectic mix of colors and decor that you probably wouldn't have in your home, and yet somehow they all work extremely well in this large resort ship setting designed to attract the young, active, and trendy.

There are 13 bars and lounges, including "Bar Central," four specialty bars: martini bar, champagne and wine bar, beer and whiskey bar, and a cigar bar; these interconnect with the lobby, yet feature distinct personalities. The lobby houses a Java Bar, plus a large movie screen, typically used to show sports events. One neat room is the "Bliss Ultra Lounge & Night Club," at the aft end of the ship; rather like a South Beach club, it houses a 24-hours a day sports bar and lounge complex. This includes a bowling alley with four real bowling lanes – the first aboard any cruise ship (it costs $5 per person, including special playing shoes, and is limited to six persons per lane). The lounge doesn't actually have many seats, but does have a couple of beds, as well as arcade games that include a Mad Wave Motion Theater, with its wild, moving seats.

Because NCL is all about cruising with families of all ages, much space is devoted to children's facilities, all

BERLITZ'S RATINGS	Possible	Achieved
Ship	500	418
Accommodation	200	156
Food	400	267
Service	400	284
Entertainment	100	67
Cruise	400	293

thoughtfully tucked well away from adult recreation areas, at the aft end of the ship. Children of all ages will get to play in a superb wet 'n' wild space-themed water park (the Aqua Kid's Club), complete with large pool, water slide, and paddle pool; there's also 30-ft x 19-ft climbing wall at the funnel. There's a room full of cots for toddlers to use for sleepovers. Teens, too, are well catered for, and have their own cinema, discotheque with dance floor, and hot tub.

Plenty of choices, including many dining options, add up to a very attractive holiday package, highly suitable for families with children, in a contemporary floating leisure center that really does provide ample facilities for enjoyment. The dress code is very casual – no jacket and tie needed.

Although service levels and finesse may be inconsistent, the level of hospitality aboard NCL ships is good – made better and brighter by the addition of a good number of Asian female staff. Despite the company's name (Norwegian Cruise Line), there's little that's Norwegian about this product, except for some senior officers. There's plenty of lively music, constant activity, entertainment, and food that is mainstream and acceptable but nothing more (even when you pay extra to eat in the "alternative" dining spots).

While the initial cruise fare is reasonable, extra costs and charges soon mount up if you want to sample more than the basics. The ship is full of revenue centers designed to help you part with your money. You can expect to be subjected to a stream of flyers advertising daily art auctions, "designer" watches, "inch of gold/silver" and other promotions, and long program announcements three times daily by the cruise director.

The onboard currency is the US dollar. Gratuities for

staff (cabin attendants, dining room waiters, etc.) are automatically added to your onboard account at $12 per person, per day; you can, however, reduce or otherwise amend these if necessary before you disembark. Alternatively, you can pre-pay online. In addition, a 15% gratuity is added for all bar purchases, and 18% for spa treatments.

ACCOMMODATION. There are 32 different price grades, so there's something for all tastes, from small interior (no view) cabins to lavish suites in a private courtyard setting.

Although they are nicely furnished and quite well equipped, the standard outside-view and interior (no view) cabins are quite small, particularly when occupied by three or four persons. Over 250 cabins have interconnecting doors (good for families with children). So, interior (no-view) cabins can connect; outside view cabins can connect; and outside view and balcony cabins can connect, providing families with much choice. Also for families, many cabins also have third- and fourth-person pull-down berths or trundle beds, and about 280 cabins have interconnecting doors – ideal for family cruising.

A small room service menu is available (all non-food items cost extra, and a 15% service charge/gratuity are automatically added to your account). Bottled water is placed in each cabin, but a charge will be made to your account if you open the bottle.

The following suites are available:

Courtyard Villas/Garden Villas: The two Garden Villa Suites, each 4,390 sq.ft. (407.8 sq.m), and 10 Courtyard Villas share a private courtyard with its own small pool, hot tub, and small fitness room, and have butler service. These units enjoy exclusivity – rather like accommodation in a gated community, where others cannot live unless they pay the asking price.

Deluxe Owner's Suites: These two suites, Black Pearl and Golden Pearl, are set high atop all other accommodation, have stunning ocean views, and consist of a master bedroom with king-size bed, a dining/lounge area, a decent-sized balcony, and access to the private courtyard.

CUISINE. The two principal dining rooms are the 304-seat Indigo, with its minimalist decor; and the 558-seat Summer Palace, slightly reminiscent of a Russian tsar's palace. There are eight other themed eating spots, giving a wide range of choice; some cost extra, and require advance reservations, particularly for dinner; all are part of NCL's "Freestyle Dining." With "Freestyle Dining", you can choose which restaurant to eat in, at what time, and with whom (there are no assigned dining rooms, tables or seats).

With 17 video screens located around the ship, you can check how busy each dining spot is and make a booking and find out if, or how long, you'll need to wait for a table (pagers are also available, so you can go bar-hopping while you wait for a table in your chosen venue). The system generally works well (with colored bars to indicate whether a restaurant is "full," "moderately busy," or "empty;" this has cut down the frustration of waiting a long time for a table, although on "formal" nights (when you may want to

see the production shows), there's always congestion. NCL's dress code states that "jeans, T-shirts, tank tops and bare feet are not permitted in restaurants" – but this rule is not enforced. All dining venues are non-smoking.

Alternative Restaurants/Eateries: Cagney's Steak House (featuring steaks from 5oz–24oz), Blue Lagoon (for trendy fast-food street snacks), and Le Bistro are NCL favorites; others include a tapas bar, and Lotus Garden, an Asian eatery complete with sushi bar and Teppanyaki grill (where the chef puts on a display in front of you).

There's also the Garden Café, a large self-serve buffet-style restaurant, for casual (mob-scene) meals. It incorporates several active service stations with very repetitive food, and finding a table can be an exercise in frustration.

ENTERTAINMENT. The showlounge, seating 1,042, is the venue for colorful Las-Vegas-style production shows and major cabaret acts. It is designed in the style of an opera house, spans three decks, and has a steeply tiered main floor and port and starboard balconies.

There are three production shows in a typical 7-day cruise, all ably performed by the Jean Ann Ryan Company. All are colorful, high-energy, razzle-dazzle shows (there is much use of pyrotechnics, laser and color-mover lighting), with so much happening on stage that by the end of the evening, if you are a typical passenger, you may be tired and unable to remember much about the shows, which are, however, very entertaining.

The ship carries a number of bands and solo entertaining musicians, which provide live music for listening and dancing in several of the lounges and bars. There's loud Latin music throughout the ship. In the nightclub, a Pachanga Party (a Miami South Beach rave) is held each cruise.

SPA/FITNESS. Wellness devotees should enjoy the two-deck-high South Pacific Health Spa complex (operated by the Hawaii-based Mandara Spa, owned by Steiner). It is located in the front of the ship, with large ocean-view windows on three sides. There are many facilities and services to pamper you (almost all at extra charge), including Thai massage (in the spa, outdoors on deck, in your cabin or on your private balcony). There's also a 37-ft (11.2-meter) indoor lap pool, hydrotherapy pool, two sit-in deep tubs, aromatherapy and wellness centers, and mud treatment room treatment rooms. There are 15 treatment rooms in all, including one specifically designed for couples.

The Body Waves fitness and exercise rooms are located within the spa and have the latest Cybex muscle-pumping equipment. Some classes, such as Pathway to Yoga, Body Cycling Class and Body Beat Class (cardio kick-boxing) cost extra.

Recreational sports facilities include a jogging track, golf driving range, basketball and volleyball courts, as well as several levels of sunbathing decks, plus the four bowling lanes, and a funnel-mounted rock-climbing wall.

● **For more extensive general information on what an NCL cruise is like, see Page 144–7.**

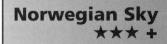

Norwegian Sky
★★★ +

Size: ....Large Resort Ship	Passenger Decks: 12	Cabins (wheelchair accessible): 6
Tonnage: 77,104	Total Crew: 950	Wheelchair accessibility ....Good
Lifestyle: ....Standard	Passengers	Cabin Current: ....110 volts
Cruise Line: ......Norwegian Cruise Line	(lower beds/all berths): 2,002/2,450	Elevators: 12
Former Names: ....*Pride of Aloha,*	Passenger Space Ratio	Casino (gaming tables): ....Yes
Norwegian Sky	(lower beds/all berths): 38.5/31.4	Slot Machines: ....Yes
Builder: ....Lloyd Werft (Germany)	Crew/Passenger Ratio	Swimming Pools (outdoors): 2
Original Cost: ....$332 million	(lower beds/all berths): 2.6/3.2	Swimming Pools (indoors): 0
Entered Service: .....Aug 1999/Jun 2008	Cabins (total): 1,001	Whirlpools: 5
Registry: ....The Bahamas	Size Range (sq ft/m): 120.5–488.6/	Self-Service Launderette: ....No
Length (ft/m): 853.0/260.00	11.2–45.4	Dedicated Cinema/Seats: ....No
Beam (ft/m): 105.8/32.25	Cabins (outside view): 574	Library: ....Yes
Draft (ft/m): 26.2/8.00	Cabins (interior/no view): 427	
Propulsion/Propellers: .....diesel-electric	Cabins (for one person): 0	
(50,000 kW)/2	Cabins (with private balcony): 252	

OVERALL SCORE: 1,388 OUT OF A POSSIBLE 2,000 POINTS

OVERVIEW. In 2004 *Norwegian Sky* was "Hawaiianized" and morphed into *Pride of Aloha* for NCL's Hawaii cruise operation. It withdrew from that market in May 2008 and was transferred to NCL for short cruises in the Caribbean. The outdoor space is quite generous, with an extra wide pool deck – created from port and starboard "overhangs" that resulted from balconies added to cabins on two decks beneath it – with two swimming pools and four hot tubs.

The interior decor reflects the ship's operating area, and the focal point is the ship's eight-deck high atrium lobby, with spiral sculptures and rainbow-colored sails. Public rooms include a shopping arcade, children's playroom (there is also a splash pool in a prime open deck area forward atop ship), internet center with 14 terminals and coffee available from an adjacent bar, several lounges and bars, small conference room, the Mark Twain library; Captain Cook's for cigars and cognac. Those with a black belt in shopping should know the Black Pearl Gem Shop is a joint venture.

Norwegian Sky is a resort at sea, and caters well to a multi-generational clientele, with lots of choices for dining and entertainment. It provides a fine, comfortable base from which to explore. The onboard currency is the US dollar.

The hustling for passengers to attend art auctions is aggressive and annoying, as is the constant bombardment for revenue activities and the daily junk mail that arrives at one's cabin door. There are many announcements – particularly annoying are those that state what is already written in the daily program. There is little connection to the sea from many public rooms. Passenger hallways are quite plain.

BERLITZ'S RATINGS

	Possible	Achieved
Ship	500	395
Accommodation	200	149
Food	400	258
Service	400	232
Entertainment	100	74
Cruise	400	280

ACCOMMODATION. There are 19 price categories: 13 for outside-view suites and cabins, and six for interior (no view) cabins. All the standard outside-view and interior (no view) cabins have two lower beds that can convert to a queen-sized bed, a small lounge area with sofa and table, and a decent amount of closet space, but very little drawer space, and the cabins themselves are disappointingly small. However, each is decorated in colorful Hawaiian style, with an explosion of floral themes and vibrant colors.

More than 200 outside-view cabins have their own private balcony. Each cabin has a small vanity/writing desk, color TV set, personal safe, climate control, and a laptop computer connection socket. Audio can be obtained only through the TV set. Bottled water is placed in each cabin – but your account will be charged if you open it.

The largest accommodation is four Owner's Suites. Each has a hot tub, large teak table, two chairs and two sun-loungers outside on a huge, very private, forward-?facing teakwood floor balcony just under the ship's navigation bridge, with large floor-to-ceiling windows. Each suite has a separate lounge and bedroom. The lounge has a large dining table and four chairs, two two-person sofas, large television, DVD/CD player, coffee table, queen-sized pull-down Murphy's bed, guest closet, writing desk, wet bar with two bar stools, refrigerator and sink, several cupboards for glasses, and several drawers and other cupboards for storage. The bedroom, which has sliding wood half-doors that look into the lounge, has a queen-sized bed (with European duvet) under a leaf-glass chandelier, vanity desk, TV, walk-in closet with plenty of hanging rail space, five open shelves and large personal safe. The white-tiled bathroom, although not large, has a full-sized tub with retractable clothesline above, separate shower enclosure with glass doors, deep washbasin, and toiletries cabinets.

There are 10 Junior Suites, each with a private teak decked balcony; these suites face aft in a secluded position and overlook the ship's wash. They have almost the same facilities as those in the owner's suites, except for the outdoor hot tub, and the fact that there is less space.

CUISINE. You can choose which restaurant you would like to eat in, at what time, and with whom.

The main dining rooms – Palace Restaurant, with 510 seats, and Crossings Restaurant, with 556 seats – have tables for four, six or eight and an open-seating arrangement. The cuisine in both includes regional specialties However, it's best to have dinner in one of the specialty restaurants, as the food in these two large dining rooms is just so-so.

A smaller eatery, the 83-seat Plantation Club Restaurant, is an à la carte, light-eating option serving "healthy" spa dishes and tapas. It has half-moon shaped alcoves and several tables for two. The wine list is quite decent and well arranged, with moderate prices, although you won't find many good vintage wines. The cutlery is very ordinary and there are no fish knives.

For classic and nouvelle French cuisine, the 102-seat Bistro has an à la carte menu. The decor is inspired by royal and aristocratic gardens. For premium steaks and lamb chops, there's Cagneys Restaurant, with 84 seats, intimate seating alcoves and good food (at extra cost).

Other eateries include Pacific Heights, a casual Pacific Rim/Asian Fusion eatery that has steaks plus local fish and seafood. Casual, self-serve buffet-style meals can be taken in the Garden Café.

ENTERTAINMENT. The 1,000-seat two-decks-high (main and balcony levels) Stardust Theater is the venue for production shows and major cabaret acts, although the sightlines are quite poor from some seats.

The ship has a number of bands and solo entertaining musicians, providing live music for listening and dancing in several lounges and bars.

SPA/FITNESS. Body Waves is a large health/fitness spa – including an aerobics room and a separate gymnasium, and several treatment rooms. Mandara Spa – headquartered in Honolulu, but owned by Steiner Leisure – is the operator of the spa/fitness center, and provides all staff and treatments as the concession. A whopping 18% gratuity is added to spa treatments.

Sports fans will appreciate the large basketball/volleyball court, baseball-batting cage, golf-driving net, platform tennis, shuffleboard and table tennis facilities, and sports bar (with baseball and surfing themes) with live satellite television coverage of sports events and major games on several TV screens. Joggers will find a wrap-around indoor/outdoor jogging track.

● **For more extensive general information on what an NCL cruise is like, see pages 144–7.**

QUOTABLE QUOTES

These are some of the questions I have been asked by newcomers to cruising:

"How many knots does the ship go to the gallon?"

"How does the captain know which port to go to?"

"Does the island float?"

"Do you send the laundry ashore?"

"Do these stairs go up as well as down?"

"Why is it that my 3-year old can wear shorts to dinner but I can't?"

"Do we have to eat dinner at both seatings?"

"I know that ships often serve smoked salmon, but I am a non-smoker"

"Can the iced tea be served hot?"

"Can you please change this spoon for a fork? I've already got five spoons"

"Why can't the late-night show be in the morning?"

"Do we have to leave the ship to go on tour?"

Overheard in Livorno: "Can we book a tour to Pizza from here?"

Overheard aboard an Alaska cruise: "Does the helicopter tour leave from the upper deck?"

Overheard on an around-the-world cruise: "Why did we stop so often?"

Norwegian Spirit
★★★★

Size: . . . . .Large Resort Ship	Passenger Decks: 10	Cabins (with private balcony): 374
Tonnage: 75,338	Total Crew: 1,300	Cabins (wheelchair accessible): 4
Lifestyle: . . . . .Standard	Passengers	Wheelchair accessibility . . . . .Good
Cruise Line: . . . . . .Norwegian Cruise Line	(lower beds/all berths): 1,966/2,475	Cabin Current: . . . . .240 volts
Former Names: . . . .*SuperStar Leo*	Passenger Space Ratio	Elevators: 9
Builder: . . . . .Meyer Werft (Germany)	(lower beds/all berths): 38.1/30.4	Casino (gaming tables): . . . . .Yes
Original Cost: . . . .$350 million	Crew/Passenger Ratio	Slot Machines: . . . . .Yes
Entered Service: . . . . .Oct 1998/May 2004	(lower beds/all berths): 1.5/2.1	Swimming Pools (outdoors): 2
Registry: . . . . .Panama	Cabins (total): 983	Swimming Pools (indoors): 0
Length (ft/m): 879.2/268.0	Size Range (sq ft/m): 150.6–638.3/	Whirlpools: 4
Beam (ft/m): 105.6/32.2	14.0–59.3	Self-Service Launderette: . . . . .No
Draft (ft/m): 25.9/7.9	Cabins (outside view): 609	Dedicated Cinema/Seats: . . . . .No
Propulsion/Propellers: . . . . .2 diesels	Cabins (interior/no view): 379	Library: . . . . .Yes
(50,400kW)/2	Cabins (for one person): 0	

OVERALL SCORE: 1,485 OUT OF A POSSIBLE 2,000 POINTS

OVERVIEW. *Norwegian Spirit* (ex-*Super-Star Leo*), was the first brand new ship ordered by parent company Star Cruises specifically for the Southeast Asia market. It was moved to NCL in 2004 in a fleet redeployment. There is a full wrap-around promenade deck outdoors, good for strolling, and lots of outdoor space, including a whole area devoted to children's outdoor activities and pool.

Inside, there are two indoor boulevards, and a large, stunning, two-deck-high central atrium lobby, with three glass-walled lifts and ample space to peruse the shops and cafes that line its inner sanctum. The lobby itself is modeled after the lobby of the Hyatt Hotel in Hong Kong, with little clutter from the usual run of desks found aboard other cruise ships.

The interior design theme revolves around art, architecture, history and literature. The ship has a mix of both eastern and western design and decor details. Three stairways are each carpeted in a different color, which helps new cruise passengers find their way around easily.

A 450-seat room atop the ship functions as an observation lounge during the day and a nightclub at night, with live music. From it, a spiral stairway takes you down to a navigation bridge viewing area, where you can see the captain and bridge officers at work.

There is a business center (complete with conference center – good for small groups) and writing room, and a smoking room, for those who enjoy cigars and cognac. A shopping concourse is set around the second level of the lobby.

Want the casino? The casino complex is at the forward end of the atrium boulevard on Deck 7 (not between showlounge and restaurant as in most western ships). This includes a large general purpose, brightly lit casino,

BERLITZ'S RATINGS

	Possible	Achieved
Ship	500	418
Accommodation	200	156
Food	400	267
Service	400	284
Entertainment	100	67
Cruise	400	293

Maharajah's, with gaming tables and slot machines.

Families with children should note that teens have their own huge video arcade, while younger children get to play in a wet 'n' wild aft pool (complete with pirate ship and caves) and two whirlpool tubs. Plus there's all the fun and facilities of Charlie's childcare center, which includes a painting room, computer learning center, and small cinema. Even the toilets are at a special low height, and there's a room full of cots for toddlers. Over 15,000 sq. ft (1,400 sq. meters) is devoted to children's facilities – all tucked well away from adult recreation areas.

The dress code is extremely casual (no jacket and tie needed). Watch out for the extra costs and charges to mount up if you order more than the basics. With many dining choices (some of which cost extra) to accommodate different tastes and styles, your cruise and dining experience will largely depend on how much you are prepared to spend. Gratuities for staff are added to your onboard account, or you can pre-pay online, and 15 percent is added to all bar purchases, while 18% is added for spa treatments. The onboard currency is the US dollar.

Because this is quite a stunning ship and offers a wide choice of dining venues, keeping consistency of product delivery will depend on the quality of the service and supervisory staff. There are many extra-cost items (in addition to the à la carte/extra charge dining spots), and there is constant intrusion into your cruise experience with announcements for things such as art auctions, bingo and horse racing. Note that standing in line for embarkation, disembarkation, shore tenders and for self-serve buffet meals is an inevitable aspect of cruising aboard all large ships.

ACCOMMODATION. Three whole decks of cabins have private balconies, while two-thirds of all cabins have an outside view. Both the standard outside-view and interior (no view) cabins really are very small (particularly given that all cabins have extra berths for a third/fourth person), although the bathrooms have a good-sized shower enclosure. So, take only the smallest amount of clothing you can get away with. All cabins have a personal safe, 100% cotton towels and 100% cotton duvets or sheets. Note that, in cabins with balconies, the balconies are extremely narrow, and the cabins themselves are very small (the ship was originally constructed for 3- and 4-day cruises).

Choose one of the six largest Executive Suites (named Hong Kong, Malaysia, Shanghai, Singapore, Thailand and Tokyo) and you'll have an excellent amount of private living space, with separate lounge, and bedroom. Each has a large en-suite bathroom that is part of the bedroom and opens onto it. It has a gorgeous mosaic tiled floor, kidney bean-shaped whirlpool bathtub, two sinks, separate shower enclosure (with floor-to-ceiling ocean-view window) and separate toilet (with glass door). There are TV sets in the lounge, bedroom and bathroom. The Singapore and Hong Kong suites and the Malaysia and Thai suites can be combined to form a double suite (good for families with children). Butler service and concierge come with the territory.

Choose one of the 12 Zodiac suites (each is named after a sign of the Zodiac) and you will get the second largest accommodation aboard the ship. Each suite has a separate lounge, bedroom, and bathroom, and an interconnecting door to an ocean-view cabin with private balcony (good for families). All cabinetry features richly lacquered woods, large (stocked) wet bar with refrigerator, dining table (with a top that flips over to reveal a card table) and four chairs, sofa and drinks table, and trouser press. The bedrooms are small, but have a queen-sized bed; there is a decent amount of drawer space, although the closet space is rather tight (it contains two personal safes). The large en-suite bathrooms are similarly designed to those in the Executive Suites.

A small room service menu is available (all non-food items cost extra, and both a 15% service charge as well as a gratuity are added to your account). Butler service and concierge come with the territory.

CUISINE. There is certainly plenty of choice when it comes to formal dining and casual eateries. There are, in all, eight places to eat (all are non-smoking), of which two are at extra charge. You will, therefore, need to plan where you want to eat well in advance, or you may be disappointed.

Windows Restaurant: The equivalent of a main dining room, it seats 632 (in two seatings), is two decks high at the aft-most section, and has huge cathedral-style windows set in three sections overlooking the ship's stern and wake.

Waiter stations are tucked neatly away in side wings, which help to keep down noise levels.

Garden Room Restaurant: This has 268 seats.

Raffles Terrace Cafe: a large self-serve buffet restaurant with indoor/outdoor seating for 400 and pseudo-Raffles Hotel-like decor, with rattan chairs, overhead fans, etc.

Taipan: a Chinese Restaurant, with traditional Hong Kong-themed decor and items such as dim sum made from fresh, not frozen, ingredients (cover charge applicable, reservations necessary).

Shogun Asian Restaurant: a Japanese restaurant and sushi bar, for sashimi, sushi, and tempura. A section can be closed off to make the Samurai Room, with 22 seats, while a traditional Tatami Room has seats for eight. There's also a teppanyaki grill, with 10 seats, where the chef cooks in front of you.

Maxim's: a small à la carte restaurant with ocean-view windows; fine cuisine in the classic French style (cover charge applicable, reservations necessary).

Blue Lagoon Café: a small, casual street cafe with about 24 seats, featuring noodle dishes, fried rice and other Southeast Asian cuisine (adjacent is a street bar called The Bund).

The Café: a casual pâtisserie serving several types of coffees, teas, cakes and pastries (at extra cost), in the atrium lobby.

ENTERTAINMENT. The Moulin Rouge Showlounge, with 973 seats, is the main venue. It is two decks high, with a main and balcony levels. The room has almost no support columns to obstruct the sightlines, and a revolving stage for Broadway-style reviews and other production shows (typically to recorded music), although there's little space for an orchestra. The show lounge is also used as a large-screen cinema, and has excellent surround sound.

SPA/FITNESS. The Roman Spa and Fitness Center is located on one of the uppermost decks, just forward of the Tivoli Pool. It has a gymnasium full of high-tech muscle-toning equipment, and aerobics exercise room, hair and beauty salon, and saunas, steam rooms, and changing rooms for men and women, as well as several treatment rooms, and aqua-swim pools that provide counter-flow jets (swimming against the current). The spa facility is operated by the Hawaii-based Mandara Spa, owned by Steiner Leisure.

The fitness and exercise rooms are located not within the spa, but at the top of the glass-domed atrium lobby (they feature the latest Cybex muscle-pumping equipment). Included is a room for exercycle classes. Sports facilities include a jogging track, golf driving range, basketball and tennis courts, and there are four levels of sunbathing decks.

● **For more extensive general information on what an NCL cruise is like, see pages 144–7.**

Norwegian Star
★★★★

Size:	.Large Resort Ship	Passenger Decks:	.12

Size: . . . . .Large Resort Ship
Tonnage: .91,740
Lifestyle: . . . . .Standard
Cruise Line: . . . . . .Norwegian Cruise Line
Former Names: . . . . .none
Builder: . . . . .Meyer Werft (Germany)
Original Cost: . . . .$400 million
Entered Service: . . . . .Dec 2001
Registry: . . . . .Panama
Length (ft/m): 964.9/294.13
Beam (ft/m): 105.6/32.2
Draft (ft/m): 26.9/8.2
Propulsion/Propellers: . . .diesel-electric/2
   azimuthing pods (19.5 MW each)

Passenger Decks: 12
Total Crew: 1,100
Passengers
(lower beds/all berths): 2,244/2,846
Passenger Space Ratio
(lower beds/all berths): 40.8/32.0
Crew/Passenger Ratio
(lower beds/all berths): 2.0/3.7
Cabins (total): 1,122
Size Range (sq ft/m): 142.0–5,350.0/
   13.2–497.0
Cabins (outside view): 787
Cabins (interior/no view): 363
Cabins (for one person): 0

Cabins (with private balcony): 509
Cabins (wheelchair accessible): 20
Wheelchair accessibility . . . . .Best
Cabin Current: . . . . .110 AC
Elevators: 12
Casino (gaming tables): . . . . .Yes
Slot Machines: . . . . .Yes
Swimming Pools (outdoors): 2
Swimming Pools (indoors): 1
Whirlpools: . . .4 (+ 1 children's whirlpool)
Self-Service Launderette: . . . . .No
Dedicated Cinema/Seats: Yes/151
Library: . . . . .Yes

OVERALL SCORE: 1,485 OUT OF A POSSIBLE 2,000 POINTS

OVERVIEW. *Norwegian Star* is a sister ship to *Norwegian Dawn*, which debuted in 2002. It has a "pod" propulsion system *(see page 45 for explanation).* A large structure located forward of the funnel houses a children's center, and, one deck above, the two outstanding "villa" suites described in the accommodation section above. The ship's hull is adorned with a decal consisting of a burst of colorful stars and streamers.

There are plenty of sunloungers – in fact, the number is greater than the number of passengers carried. Water slides are included for the adult swimming pools. Children have their own pools at the ship's stern – out of sight of the adult areas.

Inside the ship, you'll be met by a truly eclectic mix of bright colors and decor that you probably wouldn't have in your home (unless you were color-blind) – and yet somehow it works extremely well in this large ship setting that is meant to attract young, active types.

Facilities include an Internet Cafe with 17 computer stations, a 1,150-seat showlounge with main floor and two balcony levels, 3,000-book library, card room, writing and study room, business center, karaoke lounge, conference and meeting rooms and associated facilities, and a retail shopping complex of 20,000 sq. ft (1,800 sq. meters). In 2004, a 929-sq. meter (10,000-sq. ft) casino was added.

Children of all ages will get to play in a superb wet 'n' wild space-themed water park (complete with large pool, water slide, and paddle pool). They also get their own dedicated cinema (DVD movies are featured all day long), a jungle gym, painting area, and computer center. Even the toilets are at a special low height. Teens, too, are well

BERLITZ'S RATINGS

	Possible	Achieved
Ship	500	417
Accommodation	200	155
Food	400	269
Service	400	280
Entertainment	100	67
Cruise	400	297

catered for, and get their own cinema (with DVD movies), discotheque with dance floor, and whirlpool (hot) tub.

With so many dining choices (some costing extra) to accommodate the tastes of an eclectic mix of nationalities, the amount you are prepared to spend will determine what your final cruise and dining experience will be like. To make the most of your vacation, you will need to plan where you want to eat well in advance, and make the necessary reservations, or you may be disappointed. More choices, including more dining options, add up to a very attractive package, particularly suitable for families with children, in a very contemporary floating leisure center that really does provide ample facilities for enjoyment, as well as provide you with the opportunity to immerse yourself in all things Hawaiian. The dress code is very casual – no jacket and tie needed, although you are welcome to dress formally if you wish.

While the initial cruise fare seems very reasonable, the extra costs and charges soon mount up if you want more than the basics. Although service levels and finesse are sometimes inconsistent, the level of hospitality is very good – made so much better and brighter by the addition of a great number of Asian female staff rather than the surly and inconsistent Caribbean staff still found on some of the smaller NCL ships.

Despite the company's name (Norwegian Cruise Line), there's almost nothing Norwegian about this product, except for some of the ship's senior officers. The staff, incidentally, includes many Southeast Asians who have service experience aboard parent company Star Cruises' big ships.

Gratuities for staff (cabin attendants, dining room waiters, etc) are added to your onboard account at $12 per person, per day; you can reduce or otherwise amend these if necessary before you disembark or you can pre-pay online. In addition, a 15% gratuity is added for all bar purchases, and 18% for spa treatments. The onboard currency is the US dollar.

The hustling for passengers to attend art auctions is both aggressive and annoying. Standing in line for embarkation, disembarkation, shore tenders and for self-serve buffet meals is an inevitable aspect of cruising aboard all large ships – even those designated as "Freestyle".

Reaching room service tends to be an exercise in frustration. Communication, particularly between the many new Asian staff and passengers, remains weak.

ACCOMMODATION. With 29 price grades, this is a mix that includes something for everyone. There are 36 suites (including two of the largest aboard any cruise ship); 372 "balcony-class" standard cabins with private balconies, 415 outside-view cabins (no balcony); 363 interior (no view) cabins; 36 suites with balconies, and 20 wheelchair-accessible cabins. Suites and cabins with private balconies have easy-to-use sliding glass doors.

Regardless of the accommodation (and thus the price you pay for your cruise), all have a powerful hairdryer (located in the cabin itself, and not, thankfully, in the bathroom), and a tea and coffee making sets, rich cherry wood cabinetry, and a bathroom with a sliding door and a separate toilet, shower enclosure and washbasin compartments. There is plenty of wood accenting in all accommodation, including wood frames surrounding balcony doors – a nice touch that will be subliminally appreciated by passengers.

The largest accommodation is in two huge Garden Villas (Vista and Horizon), located high atop the ship in a pod that is located forward of the ship's funnel, and overlooks the main swimming pool. Each measures 5,350 sq ft. (497 sq meters) and can be combined to create a huge, double-sized "house" measuring 10,700 sq ft (994-sq-meters). These villas have huge glass walls and landscaped private roof gardens (one has a Japanese-style garden, the other a Thai-style garden) for outdoor dining (with whirlpool tubs, naturally), and huge private sunbathing areas that are completely shielded from anyone; the garden itself extends to 1,720 sq. ft (160 sq. meters).

Each suite has three bedrooms (one with a sliding glass door that leads to the garden) and bathrooms (one bathroom has a large corner tub, and two washbasins set in front of large glass walls that overlook the side of the ship as well as the swimming pool, although most of the view is of the overlarge waterslide), and a large living room (with Yamaha baby grand piano) with glass dining table and eight chairs, overlooking the lido/pool deck. These units have their own private elevator and private stairway, and can be combined to create a large, 10,700 sq.-ft (994 sq.-meter) "house" (the garden is included in the measurements)

There are many suites (the smallest measures 290 sq.

ft/27 sq. meters) in several different configurations. Some overlook the stern, while others are in the forward part of the ship. All are lavishly furnished, although closet space in some of the smaller units is tight.

Although the suites and junior suites are quite spacious, the standard interior (no view) and outside-view cabins are very small when compared to those of other major cruise lines such as Carnival or Celebrity, particularly when occupied by three or four persons (the bathrooms, however, are of quite a decent size, and have large shower enclosures). Some cabins have interconnecting doors (good for families with children), and many cabins have third- and fourth-person pull-down berths or trundle beds.

A small room service menu is available (all non-food items cost extra, and a 15% service charge and a gratuity are automatically added to your account). Bottled water is placed in each cabin, but a charge will be made to your account if you open the bottle.

CUISINE. NCL features "Freestyle Dining", so you can choose which restaurant to eat in, at what time, and with whom. You can eat in a different restaurant every night – just like going out on the town ashore – or you can eat in the same restaurant every day, even having the same waiter, as in traditional cruising. Freestyle Dining also appears to work far better for individuals rather than large groups.

All restaurants and eateries are non-smoking. The dress code states that: "jeans, T-shirts, tank tops and bare feet are not permitted in restaurants", although this is not followed in practice, particularly when families with young children are aboard at peak holiday times. On Formal Nights, many passengers want to eat in the two large main dining rooms, and this can create a logjam.

Although there are two main dining rooms (come when you want), there are several other themed eating establishments, giving a wide range of choice. It would be wise to plan in advance, particularly for dinner. In fact, there are two entire decks of dining establishments, involving 10 restaurants and eateries, and 11 different menus nightly.

● **Versailles**, the ornate 375-seat first main dining room, is decorated in brilliant red and gold. This offers the traditional six-course dining experience (open 5.30pm–midnight). This is located aft and has excellent views through windows that span two decks.

● **Aqua:** a contemporary-styled 374-seat second main dining room, offering lighter cuisine (open 5.30pm–midnight), and an open galley where you can view the preparation of pastries and dessert items.

● **Soho:** Pacific Rim cuisine is where East meets West (California and Asian cuisine) in culinary terms. Has a live lobster tank (the first aboard a ship outside Southeast Asia). A main dining area that can seat 132, plus private dining rooms (each seats 10). A collection of pop art (including Andy Warhol prints) adorns the walls.

● **Ginza:** a Japanese restaurant, with 193 seats, a sit-up sushi bar, tempura bar, show galley, and separate "teppanyaki grill" room.

● **Le Bistro:** a French restaurant, with 66 seats, serving nouvelle cuisine and six courses.

● **Blue Lagoon:** a funky food court-style eatery with 88 seats (both indoors and outdoors on the Promenade Deck), with hamburgers, fish and chips, potpies and fast (wok stir-fried) dishes.

● **Market Cafe:** a large indoor/outdoor self-serve buffet eatery, with almost 400 ft (120 meters) of buffet counter space. "Action Stations" has made-to-order omelets, waffles, fruit, soups, ethnic specialities and pasta dishes.

● **La Trattoria**, an Italian (evening only) dining spot located within the indoor/outdoor buffet area, has pasta, pizza and other popular Italian fare.

● **Steakhouse:** this serves prime USDA beef steaks and lamb chops.

● **Endless Summer:** a Hawaiian themed restaurant – arranged around the second level of the central atrium and incorporating a performance stage and a large movie screen.

Other eating/drinking spots include the Red Lion (an English pub for draft beer and perhaps a game of darts); Havana Club, a cigar and cognac lounge; Java Cafe, an atrium lobby Cafe and bar (for hot and frozen coffees, teas and pastries); a Beer Garden (for grilled foods); a Spinkles (an ice cream bar); a Gym and Spa Bar (for health food snacks and drinks); and Gatsby's wine bar (at the entrance to Soho).

Overall, the food provided is adequate, but lacks taste and presentation quality, although the menus make the dishes sound good. There's a reasonably decent selection of breads, rolls, cheeses and fruits. The wine list is quite decent and well arranged, together with moderate prices, although you won't find any good vintage wines (and the wine glasses are small). The cutlery is very ordinary (there are no fish knives). There is no formal afternoon tea, although you can make your own from various beverage stations. Overall service is just so-so. Breakfast and lunch buffets tend to have unimaginative presentation (more variety and better ingredients would be useful).

A lavish "chocoholics" buffet is available once each cruise – a firm favorite among regular passengers.

ENTERTAINMENT. The Stardust Theatre seats 1,037, and is the venue for colorful Las-Vegas-style production shows and major cabaret acts. It is designed in the style of an opera house, spans three decks, and has a steeply tiered main floor and port and starboard balconies.

Two or three production shows are presented in a typical 7-day cruise (all ably performed by the Jean Ann Ryan Company). These are all very colorful, high-energy, high-volume razzle-dazzle shows (with much use of pyrotechnics, laser and color-mover lighting). There's so much happening that by the end of the evening you'll be tired and may not remember a great deal about the shows – even though they're very entertaining.

The ship has a number of bands and solo entertaining musicians, which provide live music for listening and dancing in several of the ship's lounges and bars.

SPA/FITNESS. Wellness devotees should enjoy the two-deck-high Barong health spa complex (operated by the Hawaii-based Mandara Spa, owned by Steiner), located at the stern of the ship (with large ocean-view windows on three sides).

There are many facilities and services to pamper you (almost all at extra charge), including Thai massage (in the spa, outdoors on deck, in your cabin or on your private balcony). In addition, there is an indoor lap pool (measuring 37 ft/11.2 meters), hydrotherapy pool, aromatherapy and wellness centers, and mud treatment room treatment rooms (there are 15 treatment rooms in all, including one specifically designed for couples).

Mandara Spa (headquartered in Honolulu, but owned by Steiner Leisure) is the operator of the spa/fitness center, and provides all staff and treatments as the concession.

The fitness and exercise rooms are not within the spa, but at the top of the atrium lobby, and have the latest Cybex muscle-pumping equipment. Included is a room for exercycle classes. Recreational sports facilities include a jogging track, golf driving range, basketball and volleyball courts, as well as four levels of sunbathing decks.

● **For more extensive general information on what an NCL cruise is like, see pages 144–7.**

Norwegian Sun
★★★ +

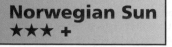

Size: . . . . .Large Resort Ship	Passenger Decks: 12	Cabins (with private balcony): 252
Tonnage: .78,309	Total Crew: 980	Cabins (wheelchair accessible): 6
Lifestyle: . . . . .Standard	Passengers	Wheelchair accessibility . . . . .Good
Cruise Line: . . . . . .Norwegian Cruise Line	(lower beds/all berths): 2,002/2,400	Cabin Current: . . . . .110 volts
Former Names: . . . . .none	Passenger Space Ratio	Elevators: 12
Builder: . . . . .Lloyd Werft (Germany)	(lower beds/all berths): 39.1/32.6	Casino (gaming tables): . . . . .Yes
Original Cost: . . . .$332 million	Crew/Passenger Ratio	Slot Machines: . . . . .Yes
Entered Service: . . . . .Nov 2001	(lower beds/all berths): 2.0/2.4	Swimming Pools (outdoors): 2
Registry: . . . . .The Bahamas	Cabins (total): 1,001	Swimming Pools (indoors): 0
Length (ft/m): 853.0/260.0	Size Range (sq ft/m): 120.5–488.6/	Whirlpools: 4
Beam (ft/m): 105.8/32.25	11.2–45.4	Self-Service Launderette: . . . . .No
Draft (ft/m): 26.2/8.00	Cabins (outside view): 675	Dedicated Cinema/Seats: . . . . .No
Propulsion/Propellers: . . . . .diesel-electric	Cabins (interior/no view): 326	Library: . . . . .Yes
(50,000 kW)/2	Cabins (for one person): 0	

OVERALL SCORE: 1,393 OUT OF A POSSIBLE 2,000 POINTS

OVERVIEW. *Norwegian Sun* is a close sister ship to *Norwegian Sky,* but with better outfitting and finishing detail, plus one additional deck of balcony cabins, and crew cabins were added to accommodate an extra 200 crew, needed for the Freestyle dining concept. The amount of outdoor space is quite good, especially the ultra-wide pool deck, with its two swimming pools and four Jacuzzi tubs, and plenty of sunloungers, albeit arranged in rows, camp-style.

A separate cabaret venue, Dazzles Lounge, has an extremely long bar. Other features include a large casino (this will operate 24 hours a day, with special facilities and rooms for high-rollers and "club" members), a shopping arcade, children's playroom (there is also a splash pool in a prime open deck area), and a video arcade.

Other facilities include a small conference room, library and beauty salon, a lounge for smoking cigars and drinking cognac, and an internet cafe, located on the Promenade Deck within the ship's atrium lobby, with 20 computer stations. Numerous shops showcase a wide range of goods, from inexpensive to very expensive.

Young passengers will find an array of facilities, which include a children's playroom called Kid's Corner (for "junior sailors" ages 3–5; (First Mates (ages 6–9); Navigators (ages 10–12); and Teens (ages 13–17).

With this ship, Norwegian Cruise Line has made an effort to provide more and better public rooms and more entertainment facilities than aboard its smaller ships. There are certainly plenty of options for eating. But the ship is full of revenue centers, designed to help you part you from your money. You can expect to be subjected to a stream of flyers advertising daily art auctions, "designer" watches, and

BERLITZ'S RATINGS		
	Possible	Achieved
Ship	500	400
Accommodation	200	149
Food	400	258
Service	400	232
Entertainment	100	74
Cruise	400	280

other promotions, while "artworks" for auction are strewn throughout the ship.

Gratuities for staff are added to your onboard account at $12 per person, per day; you can, however, reduce or otherwise amend these before you disembark. Alternatively, you can pre-pay online. In addition, a 15% gratuity is added for bar purchases, and a substantial 18% for spa treatments. The onboard currency is the US dollar.

The standard interior (no view) and outside-view cabins are very small when compared to those of other major cruise lines. The food in the large dining rooms is a weak point. There are many plastic plates, Styrofoam and plastic cups and plastic stirrers in use in the casual eateries.

ACCOMMODATION. There are 30 different categories, including 6 grades of suites, 15 grades of outside-view cabins and nine grades of interior (no view) cabins, so choosing the right accommodation requires some thought.

All of the standard outside-view and interior (no view) cabins have common facilities, such as: two lower beds that can convert to a queen-sized bed, a small lounge area with sofa and table, and a decent amount of closet and drawer space, although the cabins themselves are disappointingly small. Over 200 outside-view cabins have a private balcony. Each cabin has a small vanity/ writing desk, color TV set, personal safe, refrigerator, climate control, and laptop computer connection socket. Bottled water is placed in each cabin (but a charge will be made to your account if you open the bottle).

There are two Honeymoon/Anniversary Suites, located at the front of the ship, with forward facing and side views.

Each suite has a separate lounge and bedroom. The lounge has a large dining table and chairs, two sofas, large television, DVD/CD player, coffee table, queen-sized pull-down Murphy's bed, guest closet, writing desk, wet bar with two bar stools, refrigerator and sink, several cupboards for glasses, and several drawers and other cupboards for storage. The sleeping area has twin beds that convert to a queen-sized bed, and walk-in closet with a good amount of hanging space. The tiled bathroom, although not large, has a full-size whirlpool tub and shower, retractable clothesline, deep washbasin, and personal toiletries cabinets.

The largest accommodation is in two Owner's Suites – each with a hot tub, large teak table, two chairs and two sun-loungers outside on a huge, private, forward-facing teak floor balcony just under the ship's navigation bridge, with large floor-to-ceiling windows. Each suite has a separate lounge and bedroom. The lounge has a large dining table and chairs, two sofas, large TV set, DVD/CD player, coffee table, queen-sized pull-down Murphy's bed, guest closet, writing desk, wet bar with two bar stools, refrigerator and sink, several cupboards for glasses, and several drawers and other cupboards for storage.

The bedroom, with sliding wood half-doors that look into the lounge, has a queen-sized bed (with European duvet) under a leaf-glass chandelier, vanity desk, TV set, walk-in closet with plenty of hanging rail space, several open shelves and large personal safe. The tiled bathroom, although not large, has a full-size tub with retractable clothesline above, separate shower enclosure with glass doors, deep washbasin, and personal toiletries cabinets.

There are also a number of other suites – each with a private teakwood balcony; these suites face aft in a secluded position and overlook the ship's wash. They have some of the same facilities as found in the owner's suites, except for the outdoor hot tub, and the fact that there is less space. All cabins have tea/coffee making sets, personal safe, satellite-linked telephone, and private bathroom with bath or shower.

CUISINE. NCL has "Freestyle Dining", so you can choose which restaurant you would like to eat in, at what time, and with whom. Although there are two large dining rooms, there are also a number of other themed eating establishments – although it would be wise to plan in advance, particularly for dinner. All are non-smoking, and some incur an extra charge. The dress code states that: "jeans, T-shirts, tank tops and bare feet are not permitted in restaurants."

The two main dining rooms – the 564-seat Four Seasons Dining Room, and the 604-seat Seven Seas Dining Room, have tables for two, four, six or eight. Sandwiched between the two (rather like a train carriage) is a third, 84-seat Italian Restaurant, Il Adagio, available as an à la carte dining option (for which there is an extra charge), with window-side tables for two or four persons. Reservations are necessary.

There are also several other dining options, most located on one of the upper-most decks of the ship, with great views from large picture windows. These include:
● **Le Bistro:** a 90-seat alternative dining spot for some

fine French-style meals, including tableside cooking. Reservations are necessary for dinner.
● **Las Ramblas:** a Spanish/Mexican style eatery serving tapas (light snack items).
● **Ginza:** a Japanese Restaurant, with a sushi bar (all you can eat for $10) and a teppanyaki grill (show cooking in a U-shaped setting where you sit around the chef). Reservations are needed for dinner.
● **East Meets West:** a Pacific Rim Fusion Restaurant, featuring à la carte California/Hawaii/Asian cuisine. Reservations are necessary for dinner.
● **Pacific Heights:** a Healthy Living Restaurant (with 80 seats), featuring spa cuisine and Cooking Light menus. Reservations are necessary for dinner.
● **Garden Cafe:** a busy 24-hour restaurant indoor/outdoor self-serve buffet-style eatery with fast foods and salads.

Although the menus make meals sound appetizing, overall the food is rather unmemorable, lacking taste and mostly overcooked. However, the presentation is generally quite good. There is a reasonable selection of breads, rolls, and pastry items, but the selection of cheeses is very poor.

The wine list is well balanced, and there is also a connoisseur list of premium wines, although the vintages tend to be young. There are many types of beer (including some on draught in the popular Sports Bar & Grill).

There is no formal afternoon tea, although you can make your own at beverage stations (but it's difficult to get fresh milk as non-dairy "creamers" are typically supplied). The service is, on the whole, adequate, nothing more.

A lavish "chocoholics" buffet is featured once each cruise – a firm favorite among NCL passengers.

ENTERTAINMENT. The Stardust Theater is a two-level show lounge with more than 1,000 seats and a large proscenium stage. However, the sightlines are obstructed in a number of seats by several slim pillars. Two or three production shows are presented in a typical 7-day cruise (all ably performed by the Jean Ann Ryan Company). These are all very colorful, high-energy, high-volume razzle-dazzle shows (with much use of pyrotechnics, laser and color-mover lighting). The ship carries a number of bands and solo entertaining musicians. These provide live music for listening and dancing in several of the lounges and bars, including the loud Dazzles, home to musical groups.

SPA/FITNESS. Bodywaves, at the top of the atrium, is a large health/fitness spa (including an aerobics room and separate gymnasium), several treatment rooms, and men's and women's saunas/steam rooms and changing rooms.

There is a wrap-around indoor-outdoor jogging track. a large basketball/volleyball court, baseball-batting cage, golf-driving range, platform tennis, shuffleboard and table tennis facilities, and sports bar with 24-hour live satellite TV coverage of sports events and major games.

● **For more extensive general information on what an NCL cruise is like, see pages 144–7.**

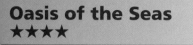

Oasis of the Seas
★★★★

Size: . . . . .Large Resort Ship	Passenger Decks: 16	Cabins (with private balcony): 1,956
Tonnage: 222,900	Total Crew: 2,164	Cabins (wheelchair accessible): 46
Lifestyle: . . . . .Standard	Passengers	Wheelchair accessibility . . . . .Good
Cruise Line: Royal Caribbean International	(lower beds/all berths): 5,408/6,360	Cabin Voltage: . . . . .110 volts
Builder: . . . . .Aker Yards (Finland)	Passenger Space Ratio	Elevators: 24
Original Cost: . . . .$1.5 billion	(lower beds/all berths): 41.6/35.4	Casino (gaming tables): . . . . .Yes
Entered Service: . . . . .Dec 2009	Crew/Passenger Ratio	Slot Machines: . . . . .Yes
Registry: . . . . .The Bahamas	(lower beds/all berths): 2.4/2.9	Swimming Pools (outdoors): 6
Length (ft/m): 1181.1/360.0	Cabins (total): 2,704	Swimming Pools (indoors): 0
Beam (ft/m): 216.5/66.0	Size Range (sq ft/m): . . . . .n/a	Whirlpools: 10
Draft (ft/m): 30.0/9.15	Cabins (outside view): 2,210	Self-Service Launderette: . . . . .No
Propulsion/Propellers: . . . . .diesel-electric	Cabins (interior/no view): 496	Dedicated Cinema/Seats: . . . . .No
(97.2MW)/3 pods	Cabins (for one person): 0	Library: . . . . .Yes

BERLITZ'S OVERALL SCORE: 1,524 OUT OF A POSSIBLE 2,000 POINTS

OVERVIEW. The world's largest cruise ship yet is, like its sister *Allure of the Seas,* a record-breaker. *Oasis of the Seas,* Finland's largest-ever export, and the first cruise ship to cost more than $1 billion, is the ultimate "moveable resort vacation." RCI has done a good job of creating what appears to be a lot of outdoor and indoor/outdoor space for relaxation, aqua-bathing and sports. There are several swimming pools, three of which ("main," "beach" and "sports") are positioned high on Deck 15 (Pool and Sports Zone) of the 16 passenger decks, as is an H$_2$O Zone. Two large hot tubs are cantilevered over the ship's side. The water for the swimming pools alone weighs 2,300 tons. Yet the carbon footprint of *Oasis* is lower than that of its predecessors (RCI's *Freedom-* and *Voyager*-class ships), and it has a much improved energy efficiency.

The ship is packed with innovative design elements – none more so than the dramatic Central Park, the first real park at sea – making it the new benchmark for large, floating self-contained resorts. It is the first RCI ship to have twin (side by side) funnels; the exhaust tubes are also partly retractable so that the ship can pass under bridges.

The sides of the ship's superstructure have been built out, and overhang the hull to create the spacious beam needed by the interior design. The stern also has some overhang, to accommodate an outdoor aqua-stage and arena (the "Aquatheater"). The name of the ship is positioned high up, so it's clearly visible to any ship following in its wake. While the ship's design from the front aspect is quite handsome, if bulky, the aft end looks as if it's been chopped off and unfinished when viewed from the side profile. Perhaps a more rounded stern would have made the profile better – although when you're on board, it looks well rounded. It is, after all,

BERLITZ'S RATINGS

	Possible	Achieved
Ship	500	430
Accommodation	200	160
Food	400	234
Service	400	294
Entertainment	100	86
Cruise	400	320

a large block of apartments sitting on a white hull. The open stern makes it look like a ship with a huge aft aircraft hangar. Overall, though, it's stunning.

Public spaces are arranged as seven neighborhoods: Central Park, the Boardwalk, the Royal Promenade, the Pool and Sports Zone, Vitality at Sea Spa/Fitness Center, Entertainment Place and Youth Zone. The most popular are the Boardwalk and Central Park, both open to the air, and the indoor Royal Promenade.

The Boardwalk. An echo of Coney Island, the Boardwalk, which is open to the skies, contains shops (naturally) and an art gallery for those peculiar people who go on a cruise to peruse or buy "artwork." At least, there are no art auctions as such. Instead, art displayed in Central Park's Art Actually, where artists who contributed to the ship's $10.5 million dollar collection can sell additional works to passengers. There's also a hand-crafted carousel for children, with beautifully made white horses. *Oasis* isn't the first passenger ship to have a carousel – there was one aboard the *SS Ile de France,* the ship used in the 1960 movie *The Last Voyage.* Kids will also love the carousel, donut shop, ice cream parlour and candy store.

Dining/nibble spots include the Boardwalk Donut Shop; Johnny Rockets, a burger/milk shake diner; and the covered Seafood Shack for fish and seafood. If you are in a Central Park cabin, you need to take the elevator to get to the closest pool – it's like going to the top of your building to take a dip. Let's hope the pool volleyball game doesn't end up with the ball being tossed into the park – or onto someone's balcony while they're having coffee.

Central Park. This space is 328 ft/100 meters long. The vegetation is real, with 27 trees and almost 12,000 plants, including a vertical "living" plant wall. But, unlike its New

York inspiration, it includes, at its lower level, a "town center." At night, it's just about the only quiet and serene area, and is best for couples. Vintages wine bar is a great place to chill out, and there are several reservations-required, extra-charge dining venues; the poshest is 150 Central Park, while Chops Grille and Giovanni's Table are favourites for South Beach types. There's also Vintages wine and tapas bar, a nice place to relax in the late afternoon.

The Royal Promenade. This is a development of the Royal Promenade theme aboard the *Voyager*- and *Freedom*-class ships, but with more eating and entertainment venues. Interior-view promenade cabins have balconies that look down onto the action in Central Park. An oval-shaped Rising Tide Bar moves through three floors and links the double-width Royal Promenade with Central Park.

ACCOMMODATION. Remarkably, there are 37 price grades, reflecting the choice of location and size. Suite occupants get access to a concierge lounge and associated services. There are many family-friendly cabins, good for family reunions, but there are no single-occupancy cabins. The cabin numbering system is a bit awkward to get used to. In a first for RCI, cabin doors open *outwards* (towards you), as in most European and Scandinavian hotels. In many of the lower grade accommodation, access to the closet is awkward – often with small sofas in the way. Most cabins feel extremely small, given the size of the ship.

There are 475 cabins with views into either Central Park or Royal Promenade, the two horizontal atriums, from their curved interior balconies (four of which are wheelchair-accessible). This includes 80 Central Park-view cabins with windows (not balconies) and fine views. But you'll need to keep your curtains closed for privacy, which rather defeats the object. Noise could be generated along the inner promenades, particularly late at night with street parades and non-stop music. So, your balcony experience could be like a continuous street party.

Although a few ships such as *Saga Ruby* have upstairs/downstairs suites, RCI has brought bi-level loft suites to large resort ships. These offer spectacular ocean views, with floor-to-ceiling, double-height windows. Each has a lower living area plus a private balcony with sun chairs, and a stairway that connects to the sleeping area which overlooks the living area and has extended ocean views. Modern designs are dotted with abstract, modern art pieces.

There are 28 Loft Suites, with 25 Crown Loft suites measuring 545 sq ft (51 sq meters). In addition there are three more spacious Loft Suites: the 1,524-sq. ft (141-sq meter) Royal Loft Suites, sleeping six, which each has its own baby grand piano, indoor and outdoor dining areas, private wet bar, a library and extended 843-sq ft (78.3-sq meter) balcony with a flat-screen TV set, entertainment area and Jacuzzi. Two large Sky Loft Suites measure 722 sq. ft (67 sq meters) and 770 sq ft (71 sq meters), and a 737 sq ft (68 sq meters) Crown Accessible Loft Suite includes an elevator to aid disabled passengers.

Standard Cabins (balcony and non-balcony class): Electrical sockets are located below the vanity desk unit in a user-unfriendly position (perhaps this will be corrected aboard *Allure of the Seas*). This is particularly poor for anyone trying to use the hairdryer in the 50% of cabins where the sockets are positioned on the right side. Also, it's difficult to watch television from the bed.

The washbasins in non-suite grade cabins are very small and low, at just 30½ inches (77.5cm) above floor level. Be careful – it's easy to hit your head on the mirror above. Small soap bars are provided, while shampoo is provided in a dispenser in the shower enclosure. Unfortunately, the shower head is fixed – so it is difficult to spray yourself thoroughly. Although there is no soap dish, or indentation in the washbasin surround for soap, useful touches include a blue ceiling nightlight in each bathroom.

Cabins are exposed to noise and whatever is happening on the Boardwalk itself, including rehearsals and sports activities in the Aqua Theater aft, bells from the Carousel, rowdy revelers on the Boardwalk late at night, plus screaming ziplining participants high above during the day, not to mention loud music from live bands playing at one of the pools, and exceedingly loud announcements by the cruise director repeating what's already printed in the daily program.

Boardwalk-view balcony cabin occupants will need to close their curtains for privacy at times. However, the curved balconies – good for storing luggage to free up space inside the cabin – provide a sense of connectivity with the open air and a community feeling, as you look across at balconies on the opposite side of the Boardwalk. All have a sea view aft; those close to the aft Aqua Theater can stay on their balconies for a great view of any shows or events. The lowest deck of Boardwalk-view cabins, have windows but no balcony – and actually the view is mainly of the top of things such as the carousel or beach hut-like structures. The best Boardwalk balcony cabins are, in my view, located on decks 8–12. For more privacy, however, it might be best to book an ocean-view balcony cabin, not one that overlooks the Boardwalk. Cabins in the forward-most section of the ship may be subject to noises from the marine decks (winches, anchor, ropes, and so on).

Many suite-grade cabins have bathrooms with faux granite washbasin counter tops, and two washbasins. Some have bidets, Jacuzzi tubs and a separate shower enclosure. Some Family Suite grades have a separate, small room with bunk beds; some have curtains to separate them, some don't.

CUISINE. Because *Oasis of the Seas* is a large resort ship, the main meals in Opus, main dining room, which is spread over three decks, are all about well-timed production cooking and fast delivery – essentially a banquet catering operation. Almost inevitably, the food is tasteless (except for salt) and utterly underwhelming. When you book, choose one of two seatings, or "My Time Dining" (eat when you want, during dining room hours). There are tables of all sizes, including large ones for family reunions.

Alternative Dining Venues: Dining spots in Central Park include: *Antonio's Table* (Italian cuisine); *Park Café* (coffee, pastry items and salads); *150 Central Park*; the *Rising Tide Bar* (drinks that move); and *Vintages* wine bar.

OASIS OF THE SEAS: WHAT'S GOOD AND WHAT'S NOT

THE POSITIVES

The Passenger Space Ratio is good for such a large vessel. The design concept is a continuum of the Freedom-class ships, themselves an extension of the Voyager-class ships – and then some. However, the increase in size has meant that RCI has been able to incorporate more of the facilities that young families seek for action-packed cruise vacations, including 37 bars and more than 20 places to eat or snack. And the latest technology means that *Oasis* is 30% more energy-efficient than even the Freedom-class ships.

The ship has been designed remarkably well, with large public spaces made possible by the split superstructure design – the idea of Harri Kulovaara, who first achieved this with Silja Serenade in 1986. This gives the ship the interior space needed to provide The Boardwalk, Central Park, and the Royal Promenade (all parts of the "seven neighbourhoods" concept). Excellent, large touch-screen ship information screens provide electronic maps at each stairway, and elevators are color-coordinated in either pink or blue for the fore and aft sections of the ship. There are no elevators in the center of the ship; all are in forward and aft locations, but there are enough of them, and they are speedy.

It's all rather novel, and should appeal to families with children. The only reminder that you're aboard a ship is the presence of the other 5,400 or so passengers – in a ship that could swallow 6,295. Because Central Park and the Boardwalk are open to the elements – so you could hide under a tree – but better take an umbrella just in case it rains in the sunny Caribbean.

Although not as stunning as the Aquaventure experience at Dubai's Atlantis Resort Hotel, where you can slide 27 meters down a ziggurat through shark infested waters or sleep underwater, the Pool and Sports Zone forward of the twin funnels is a real adventurous fun place for families. An adults-only open-air solarium and rentable cabanas are part of the outdoor scene today, and Oasis provides several. Two Flow-Riders are part of the sports line-up; these are located atop the ship around the aft exhaust mast, together with basketball courts and golf. The ship also has the largest jogging track at sea.

The Solarium is the most welcoming large, light-filled and restful (despite the background music) space. High atop ship, it is frequented by few children – so adults can "escape" the Las Vegas-like atmosphere of most other parts of the ship. On the subject of casinos, the roulette tables are stunning – all electronic and touch-buttony (no need to place chips on the table – simply touch a screen with your finger). There's also blackjack, craps, Caribbean Stud Poker, and 450 slot machines, plus a player's club and poker room – but this really can be a smoke-filled place, even in the "no-smoking" area. The casino entrance is dedicated to the history of gaming.

The Caribbean itinerary for this ship includes a "private" beach day at Labadee, the company's leased island, whose facilities were upgraded in 2009. RCI has built its own 800-ft pier, making it a logistically simple matter for anyone to access the ship and beach several times during the day-long stay. Do try the zipline – it's one of the world's longest, and a real blast. Other new additions: an alpine coaster, a beach club with 20 private cabanas, new dining facilities, a larger artisans' market and a Haitian Cultural Center.

A cruise aboard *Oasis of the Seas* commands a premium over other ships in the RCI fleet, but it should provide a fine family cruise experience, with a wide range of choices (many at extra cost). This means you'll need to plan how you will spend your time, and where you would like to eat, well in advance of your cruise. Overall, if you are in suite-grade accommodation, you'll be treated well, while those in anything else receive second-class service, and will hear the word "no" a lot. But that's part and parcel of a large resort ship with its "metropolitan"-style cruise experience.

THE NEGATIVES

If all 5,400 passengers want a sunlounger at the same time, forget it – and those who secure one will find them so tightly packed together that there's little space to put their belongings. It's sad to see that exterior wooden railings have mostly been replaced by fibreglass railings – this is particularly noticeable on balconies.

Live or recorded music is everywhere, 24 hours a day, whether inside or outside the ship, including elevators and accommodation hallways. Ordering room service is complicated – you can't do it by phone, only by using the interactive touch-screen television in your suite/cabin. Standing in line to make reservations for the main shows can be time-consuming and frustrating (the reservation booth is in the middle of the Royal Promenade). You could make them online before your cruise – good for families that like to plan their vacations together – but who knows what you may want to do on which day of your cruise? Getting reservations in one of the specialty restaurants takes a bit of effort, unless you are occupying suite-grade accommodation. Smoking is permitted in several bars and lounges aboard this ship and the smell of stale smoke permeates several areas. Cigar smokers will probably be underwhelmed by the cigar lounge.

The sense of being aboard a cruise ship is somewhat lost in all the large spaces to play in, but what this ship offers is a moveable resort full of facilities. There are few quiet nooks and crannies – except for a small, cramped library, with oversized leather chairs, and perhaps the Solarium. Passengers complain constantly about the retail shop staff and their uncaring attitude. Other niggles include waiting for elevators; that the ship is simply too large to meet friends unless you are very specific about place and time); that the Windjammer Café is always busy; about the wine packages for purchase, which can be served only in certain venues; and the fact that bars do not have any snacks such as nuts. While RCI has programming and passenger flow down to a fine art, a few bottlenecks do occur – but then, they do also at baseball stadiums and airports, both of which are as impersonal as this ship.

Oasis of the Seas operates from the purpose-built $75 million Terminal 18 in Port Everglades (Ft. Lauderdale), whose restroom facilities are minimal. Getting to the terminal is where people experience delays and frustration. Disembarkation notes: If the two "flybridge" gangways are working, disembarkation is relatively speedy. However, when only one is working, a line forms in the Royal Promenade, in which case it's better to sit for a while in the Café Promenade until the line goes down. Disembarkation for non-US citizens can be appallingly slow.

150 Central Park: The most exclusive restaurant aboard the ship, it combines cutting-edge cuisine with interesting design. An observation window into the kitchen gives passers-by the opportunity to watch the chefs and staff in action. KeriAnn Van Raesfeld offers a multi-course tasting menu. It's open for dinner only. Reservations are required and there's an extra charge – perhaps worth it to celebrate something special.

Chops Grille: Royal Caribbean's popular "signature" steak-house, open for dinner only, offers premium cut meats. The cover charge is $25 per person.

Chef's Table, on the upper level of the Concierge lounge, is available to all passengers, at $70 per person for dinner, and offers a six-course meal with wine. It is hosted by the executive chef, but, with just 14 seats, trying to get a reservation could be difficult.

Giovanni's Table ($10 for lunch; $15 for dinner): This casual Italian dining spot has a rustic feel, yet modern flair. It offers toasted herb breads, pizzas, salads, pastas, sandwiches, braised meat dishes and stews.

Central Park Café, a casual dining spot with a high level of variety and flexibility, is an indoor/outdoor food market with walk-up (line-up) counters and limited waiter service. The menu includes freshly prepared salads, made-to-order sandwiche, paninis, crêpes and hearty soups. Guests order directly from the chefs behind the food stations.

Seafood Shack, on the Boardwalk, is noisy. It offers mediocre seafood items, and most passengers find it extremely disappointing for its $8.95 cover charge, and often a wait to get a tablecloth-less table. But then it *is* a bit of a shack – so it lives up to its name.

Vintages is a wine bar with a robust selection of fine wines, accompanied by cheese and tapas (à la carte item charge). Price examples: a glass of Caymus is $23, Stags Leap $19, Francis Coppola Reserve $12–$25, Beringer Private Reserve $15, and Silverado $8.75.

Other dining and snacking spots on the Boardwalk include: *Boardwalk Donut Shop* and *Johnny Rockets*, a burger/milk shake diner, with a $3.95 charge for breakfast and $4.95 for lunch and "dinner."

Elsewhere, dining venues/eateries include *Izumi*, offering Japanese-style cuisine, at an à la carte price; *Sorrento's Pizzeria*; *Park Café* (for salads and light bites); and *Wipe Out Café*. For those with a sweet tooth, there's a 1940s-style *Cupcake Shop*. Naturally, if you're thinking of getting married, you could have a cupcake wedding cake. For lighter, more health-conscious fare, there's a self-serve section in the *Solarium Bistro* for breakfast and lunch – it's usually the quietest place, too.

The *Windjammer Café* is the (free) casual self-serve eatery common to all RCI ships. However, note that no trays are provided, only oval plates, so if you are disabled or have mobility difficulties you may need to ask for help. Also, because they're plastic, it's impossible to get a hot plate. The venue is simply too small to handle the number of people that can invade it at peak times – in the morning before an excursion, or at lunchtime following the return of excursions. Sadly, it ends up as a bit of a frustration zone;

my advice is to try some of the other venues to avoid the overcrowding. The food varies from acceptable to less than acceptable – fresh fruit tends to be hard and unripe – and it's best to arrive early, when things have just been cooked and set up. Although there's a decent enough variety, the quality of some of the meat its is poor and overcooked.

Regular coffee is available free in many venues, but espresso and cappuccinos (in paper cups) cost extra.

The longest waiting lines are for Johnny Rockets and the Seafood Shack. Note that the cover charges quoted above are subject to change – check with RCI's website or your travel provider for the latest prices.

ENTERTAINMENT. The 1,380-seat Opal Theatre, spread over three decks, is the main showlounge, which stages the popular musical *Hairspray*. It's a brilliant, 90-minute-long production, just like a Broadway show, and is performed four times during each cruise. There's also an aerial acrobatic show, *Come Fly With Me*.

The 750-seat AquaTheater, located outside at the ship's stern with a 6,000 sq. ft stage, is a combination show theatre, sound stage and events space, which, among other things, features the comedy dive show *Splish Splash*, a sort of take-off of *Le Rêve* in at the Wynn in Las Vegas. Some great viewing places can be had high in the wings on both port and starboard sides. Computer-controlled colored fountains are played at various times, using chromosonics to make colors change according to the music.

Studio "B": Online bookings for the ice shows guarantees entry to the venue (but not an assigned seat) is on a first-come, first-serve basis. *Frozen in Time* is a stunning, must-see ice show.

There's no charge for any of the shows, and bookings – including the times you want to see the shows – can be madeat www.royalcaribbean.com up to three months before your cruise, although reservations are not required. It is extremely difficult to change any reservations. None of this is helpful if you simply want to get away from it all on vacation and postpone any decisions until you are on board.

SPA/FITNESS. The Vitality at Sea Spa (Vass) includes a Vitality Café for extra-cost health drinks and snacks. The fitness center includes 158 cardio and resistance machines. An extra-cost thermal suite includes saunas, steam rooms, and heated tiled loungers. You can't just take a sauna for 10 minutes without paying for a one-day pass, at $30 per person. Steiner Leisure provides the staff and treatments. Gratuities are at your discretion and not automatically added.

However, the facility really is not that large, given the number of passengers carried. It's best not to book a massage when the ship is due to arrive or leave an anchor port because some treatment rooms experience immense vibration when the anchor chain is in use. Sports facilities include two surfboard pools, golf putting course, ziplining, and an ice-skating rink.

● **For more extensive general information on what an RCI cruise is like, see pages 151–6.**

Ocean Countess
★★★

Size: ....Mid-Size Ship	Propulsion/Propellers: ....diesel	Cabins (for one person): 20
Tonnage: 17,593	(15,670 kW)/2	Cabins (with private balcony): 0
Lifestyle: ....Standard	Passenger Decks:...................8	Cabins (wheelchair accessible): 0
Cruise Line: Cruise and Maritime Voyages	Total Crew: 350	Wheelchair accessibility ....None
Former Names: ......*Olympia Countess,*	Passengers	Cabin Current: ....110 and 220 volts
Olympic Countess, Awani Dream I,	(lower beds/all berths): 780/898	Elevators: 2
Cunard Countess	Passenger Space Ratio	Casino (gaming tables): ....Yes
Builder: ....Burmeister & Wein (Denmark)	(lower beds/all berths): 22.5/19.5	Slot Machines: ....Yes
Original Cost: ....£12 million	Crew/Passenger Ratio	Swimming Pools (outdoors): 1
Entered Service: .....Aug 1976/Apr 2010	(lower beds/all berths): 2.2/2.5	Swimming Pools (indoors): 0
Registry: ....Madeira	Cabins (total): 400	Whirlpools: 2
Length (ft/m): 536.6/163.56	Size Range (sq ft/m): 87.1–322.9/8.1–30.0	Self-Service Launderette: ....No
Beam (ft/m): 74.9/22.84	Cabins (outside view): 265	Dedicated Cinema/Seats: Yes/126
Draft (ft/m): 19.0/5.82	Cabins (interior/no view): 135	Library: ....Yes

OVERALL SCORE: 1,178 OUT OF A POSSIBLE 2,000 POINTS

OVERVIEW. *Ocean Countess* has had an eventful history. It was originally completed for Cunard Line as an informal Caribbean cruise vessel – although the ship, one of a pair, was actually ordered for a US airline, Overseas National Airways, which went bankrupt, after which Cunard took over the contract. It was bought in 1997 by Royal Olympic Cruises from its former operators, the long defunct Awani Dream Cruises, of Indonesia, which purchased the vessel from Cunard. In 2004 Royal Olympia Cruises ceased operating, and the ship was sold to Piraeus-based Majestic International Cruises at auction aboard the ship in Durban (price $6.1 million), and renamed *Ocean Countess*. Look closely and you'll still find some Cunard items on board.

The ship had a $6 million refit in 2009 and was then placed on charter to UK operator Cruise & Maritime Voyages, which explains the intitials CM on the funnel.

Ocean Countess still displays a fairly smart, modern profile with crisp, clean lines, blue hull and a distinctive blue swept-back funnel. Its almost identical twin presently operates as *Golden Iris* for Israel's Mano Cruise.

Inside, there is a good selection of public rooms, most with attractive, light colors and cheerful decor, and most located on one deck, making access easy. The showlounge is a single-level room with raised seating on its port and starboard sides – eight pillars obstruct the sightlines, however, and the ceiling is low. Aft of the showlounge is The Hamptons, an indoor-outdoor entertainment lounge/nightclub that incorporates a large aft open deck area and is pleasant during warm-weather cruises.

Anyone seeking a casual, child-free, destination-intensive cruise will probably like this comfortable vessel,

BERLITZ'S RATINGS

	Possible	Achieved
Ship	500	307
Accommodation	200	114
Food	400	221
Service	400	239
Entertainment	100	61
Cruise	400	236

which is a change from the newer, larger ships of today, and is well suited to cruising in the Aegean/Mediterranean region. The onboard currency is the British pound. Gratuities, which are pooled are pooled among the crew, are automatically applied to your onboard account (£5 per person, per night; £4 for cruises longer than 16 nights). Note that this is a very high-density ship, with small cabins.

SUITABLE FOR: Good for British adult couples and solo travelers seeking a more traditional, standard ship, with decent facilities, with food that is quite basic and service that is well-meaning and friendly.

ACCOMMODATION. There are 14 price grades: three for suites, five with outside view windows or portholes, and four for interior (no view) cabins. Prices depend on grade, location and size. Note that 20 cabins in two price categories have been assigned as single occupancy units – they were originally for two persons – which gives solo travelers a little more space.

Deluxe/Standard Outside View/Interior No View Cabins: These are mostly of a standard, very compact size, and come in light colors and plain, but pleasant decor. It is adequate for short cruises. They are best described as space-efficient units with metal fixtures and poor insulation – you can talk to your neighbors without having to use the telephone! All standard cabins have two lower beds; some are in a twin shape, while others are in an L shape, but they are fixed and cannot be moved together. Many cabins also have a third upper berth. The cabins on the lowest deck (Admiral Deck 3) suffer from vibration and the odor of diesel fuel, and have portholes, as do cabins on the deck above, Main Deck 4. All other cabins on the upper decks have windows. The cabin bathrooms are small modular units – good for one, but quite impossible for two people to use at the same time. They contain a shower enclosure, toilet and washbasin, but little storage space for toiletries.

The largest accommodation is in the "suites" on Promenade Deck 7 and Upper Deck 6 (in four price grades). These all have a double bed, a good amount of closet space, lounge area with sofa or chairs, TV, and a larger bathroom with tub and shower, toilet and washbasin. If you are seeking more space, these are the rooms to go for.

Two Owner's Suites, each of which can accommodate a third person on a sofa bed, were added immediately forward and adjacent to the Kensington Restaurant. Both of these (almost) L-shaped suites measure 322.9 sq.ft (30 sq. meters), have a layout that allows lots of light through large picture windows (but no balconies), and provide the most space of any accommodation aboard this ship. Each has a queen-sized bed, vanity/writing desk, and lounge area with minibar. The bathroom has a tub and shower.

CUISINE. The Kensington Restaurant is located in the middle of the ship; it is one deck high, and seats 487. It has large ocean-view picture windows on two sides, and seating is mostly at tables for four, six or eight, in two seatings. Banquet-style catering is standard, tailored for international passengers. There is a limited selection of fresh fruits and cheeses, but cheerful service from an attentive, friendly staff.

Additionally, a casual self-serve open-air area, the Boat House, is located at the stern of the ship on Upper Deck 6 is for breakfast, lunches and sometimes, depending on the itinerary, buffet dinners. However, the choice of food is limited, and lacks creativity, variety and presentation – think British school canteens and overcooked food and you'll get the general idea.

ENTERTAINMENT. The 400-seat Holyrood Show Lounge is the venue for shows and entertainment events. It is a single-level, rectangular-shaped room with a black granite dance floor, designed for cabaret acts, and not production-style shows. Although the sides of the room are raised, several pillars obstruct the sightlines.

The ship has a main showband, together with small musical units and solo pianists to provide live music for dancing and listening in the various lounges and bars. These include the Tower Piano Bar, situated in what is a very nice observation lounge that includes a small library and card playing area.

SPA/FITNESS. There is a small gymnasium, the 20 Twelves Gym, located on one side of the funnel housing, on the pool deck. A jogging track provided on the deck above is difficult to use because it is narrow and passengers tend to place their deck chairs there for sunbathing. Limited massage facilities and a small changing area are provided on the opposite side to the gymnasium, while a beauty salon is located indoors on another deck (Upper Deck 6), aft of the restaurant.

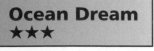

Ocean Dream
★★★

Size: ....Mid-Size Ship	Passenger Decks: 10	Cabins (wheelchair accessible): 11
Tonnage: 35,190	Total Crew: 550	Wheelchair accessibility ....Fair
Lifestyle: ....Standard	Passengers	Cabin Current: ....110/220 volts
Cruise Line: ....Pullmantur Cruises	(lower beds/all berths): 1,022/1,350	Elevators: 8
Former Names: ....*Pacific Star,*	Passenger Space Ratio	Casino (gaming tables): ....Yes
Costa Tropicale, Tropicale	(lower beds/all berths): 34.4/26.0	Slot Machines: ....Yes
Builder: ......Aalborg Vaerft (Denmark)	Crew/Passenger Ratio	Swimming Pools (outdoors): 3
Original Cost: ....$100 million	(lower beds/all berths): 1.8/2.5	Swimming Pools (indoors): 0
Entered Service: .....Jun 1982/Mar 2008	Cabins (total): 511	Whirlpools: 0
Registry: ....The Bahamas	Size Range (sq ft/m): 180.0–398.2/16.7–37.0	Self-Service Launderette: ....Yes
Length (ft/m): 671.7/204.76	Cabins (outside view): 324	Dedicated Cinema/Seats: ....No
Beam (ft/m): 86.7/26.45	Cabins (interior/no view): 187	Library: ....Yes
Draft (ft/m): 23.3/7.11	Cabins (for one person): 0	
Propulsion/Propellers: diesel (19,566kW)/2	Cabins (with private balcony): 12	

BERLITZ'S OVERALL SCORE: 1,110 OUT OF A POSSIBLE 2,000 POINTS

OVERVIEW. This was the first new ship ordered by Carnival Cruise Lines. It was sent to Costa Cruises in 2001, and in 2008 Pullmantur Cruises acquired and refurbished it. It has a fairly distinctive, though boxy look and profile. Open deck space is very limited, and there is no walk-around promenade deck outdoors.

The interior layout and passenger flow is generally good. The public rooms are bright and cheerful, with many bold, bright color splashes. Rooms include a card room, internet-connect center, piano bar, and several bars and lounges. Pullmantur Cruises caters to young cruisers as well as their parents, particularly during school vacation periods.

This is a very standard product, with banquet catering. But families should have fun in the sun; there are plenty of opportunities for gaming and partying. The onboard currency is the euro, and all drinks and gratuities are included, so it's really a good-value vacation.

SUITABLE FOR: *Ocean Dream* is best suited to Spanish-speaking families, young couples, and singles seeking a standard cruise in modestly contemporary surroundings.

ACCOMMODATION. There are nine cabin price categories. Most of the "standard" interior (no view) and outside-view cabins are all of the usual cookie-cutter variety (but of a decent size), with an imaginative European-style decor, and just enough closet and drawer space for a week's cruise. A number of cabins have third and fourth person upper berths – useful for families with small children. The bathrooms are plain, but adequate for short cruises, although there's little

BERLITZ'S RATINGS		
	Possible	Achieved
Ship	500	271
Accommodation	200	113
Food	400	209
Service	400	246
Entertainment	100	58
Cruise	400	213

storage space for personal toiletry items.

The largest accommodation is in 12 "suites" – each with a small (narrow) semi-private balcony. Naturally, there is more space, with the living and sleeping areas divided. The bathrooms are marginally larger, too. But all these suites have their views largely blocked by the positioning of lifeboats. The cabin soundproofing could be better, and the room service menu is quite basic.

CUISINE. The Restaurant Principal is on the ship's lowest deck. It is colorful, very cheerful, brightly lit, but noisy and rather cramped, making proper service quite difficult. There are tables for four, six or eight (none for two), and dining is in two seatings (dinner on European cruises is typically at 7pm and 9pm).

The Buffet Panorama is a self-service buffet facility, with European selections that are quite basic, as is the selection of breads, rolls, fruit and cheeses. At night, as the Lido Café, it becomes a bistro and provides a casual (dress-down) alternative to eating in the main dining room. There's also a pizzeria. Good cappuccino and espresso coffees are available in the various bars.

ENTERTAINMENT. The Salon de Espectaculos (showlounge) is a single-level room that has bright, cheerful decor, although sightlines to the stage are obstructed from several seats. A mix of banquette and individual seating is provided, together with small drinks tables.

SPA/FITNESS. The spa/fitness area is located just behind the ship's mast, and is small. It contains a gymnasium, sauna and changing rooms for men and women.

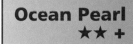

Ocean Pearl
★ ★ +

Size: . . . . .Mid-Size Ship	Propulsion/Propellers: diesel (13,400kW)/2	Cabins (for one person): 0
Tonnage: .22,945	Passenger Decks: 8	Cabins (with private balcony): 0
Lifestyle: . . . . .Standard	Total Crew: 450	Cabins (wheelchair accessible): 0
Cruise Line: . . . . .Happy Cruises/ISP	Passengers	Wheelchair accessibility . . . . .None
Former Names: . . . . *Clipper Pacific,*	(lower beds/all berths): 1,076/1,257	Cabin Current: . . . . .110 volts
Clipper Pearl, Dream, Dream Princess,	Passenger Space Ratio	Elevators: 4
Sundream, Song of Norway	(lower beds/all berths): 21.3/18.2	Casino (gaming tables): . . . . .Yes
Builder: . . . . .Wartsila (Finland)	Crew/Passenger Ratio	Slot Machines: . . . . .Yes
Original Cost: . . . .$13.5 million	(lower beds/all berths): 2.3/2.7	Swimming Pools (outdoors): 1
Entered Service: . . . . .Nov 1970/Mar 2010	Cabins (total): 538	Swimming Pools (indoors): 0
Registry: . . . . .The Bahamas	Size Range (sq ft/m): 118.4–265.8/	Whirlpools: 0
Length (ft/m): 637.5/194.32	11.0–24.7	Self-Service Launderette: . . . . .No
Beam (ft/m): 78.8/24.03	Cabins (outside view): 346	Dedicated Cinema/Seats: . . . . .No
Draft (ft/m): 21.9/6.70	Cabins (interior/no view): 192	Library: . . . . .Yes

OVERALL SCORE: 1,080 OUT OF A POSSIBLE 2,000 POINTS

OVERVIEW. This ship, originally built more than 40 years ago as one of the first three ships for Royal Caribbean Cruise Line, still looks fairly smart, and has a sharply raked bow and a single funnel, aft of which is a large amount of open deck space for sports. There is a polished walk-around wooden deck outdoors – good for strolling, but make sure you wear shoes with non-slip soles. There is a reasonable amount of open deck space, but it really feels crowded when the ship is full, particularly around the small swimming pool in the center of the ship, where everyone wants to be on a sunny day.

This is the sister ship to *Aquamarine* (Louis Cruises), and was "stretched" with the insertion of a mid-section in 1978 when operated by Royal Caribbean Cruise Line (today called Royal Caribbean International).

Inside the ship, the layout is quite logical, making it easy to find one's way around. The decor has fairly bright, crisp colors. The accommodation passageways are narrow, but they do contain artwork and some wood trim. In fact, there is a fair amount of artwork throughout this ship. There are several lounges and bars, including a casino, piano bar, discotheque, internet-connect center, and video games room. Most of these are located on one deck. Children have their own Club Pelicanos to play in.

There are many loud announcements. The space per passenger is poor. The cabin TV sets are small, except for those in the "suites". Couples who travel without children will be surrounded by large number of children during the summer months – and, thus, increased noise levels. The food is of cost-control quality, and the presentation is so-so. There are no cushioned pads for the deck lounge chairs.

BERLITZ'S RATINGS		
	Possible	Achieved
Ship	500	252
Accommodation	200	104
Food	400	217
Service	400	238
Entertainment	100	58
Cruise	400	211

Happy Cruises (formerly Quail cruises) is part of Spain's Quail Travel group. The onboard currency is the euro, and all-inclusive pricing means that standard-brand drinks and gratuities are included. Shore excursions, use of medical facility, and spa treatments are not included, nor are room service items such as snacks or sandwiches.

SUITABLE FOR: *Ocean Dream* is best suited to young Spanish-speaking families who are used to package holidays, tight budgets, and the inclusive aspects they offer.

ACCOMMODATION. The cabins are split into just four price grades (Standard, Superior, Promenade and Deluxe) and six types, making it an easy matter to select the type of accommodation you want. The price will depend on the cabin grade, location, and size.

Most cabins are of a similar size (most are dimensionally challenged, I would say) and the insulation between them is quite poor. But do remember that this ship is now more than 40 years old. The cabins also have mediocre closets and very little storage space, perhaps because the ship was built originally for Caribbean cruising, yet somehow passengers seem to manage. They are adequate for a one-week cruise, as you will need only casual clothes, and, with these destination-intensive cruises, you won't need many clothes anyway – shoes can always go under the bed.

The bathrooms are very small – functional rather than attractive – and the showers have a curtain you will probably need to dance with. Larger-than-average persons may well become frustrated quickly.

The largest cabins are named after famous explorers.

Only the owner's suite has a refrigerator. The cabin voltage is 110 volts; American-style two-flat-pin sockets are provided, so you may need adapters for electrical appliances such as a hairdryer.

CUISINE. The main dining room is reasonably attractive, but noisy, and there are two seatings. The food is unmemorable. It's basic, no-frills cuisine – acceptable for those who don't expect much in the way of presentation or quality. There is plenty of it, however; indeed, it is quantity that prevails, but remember that it is all provided at a low cost – as is a cruise aboard this ship, compared to more expensive cruise products. Table wines are included in the fare, but almost all are very young – typical of those you might find in your local supermarket. The same sized glasses are used for both red and white wines, and they are small.

Casual meals can be taken in the Lido Café, the ship's self-serve buffet; but note that breakfast items are really repetitious. The Ocean Café, which is located on the starboard side, is for coffees.

ENTERTAINMENT. The Salon Espectaculo (showlounge) has a "thrust" stage and hardwood dance floor. It is a single-level room that wasn't designed for large-scale production shows but more for cabaret acts. Many seats have poor sightlines, obstructed by several pillars.

The revue-style shows are typically of the end-of-pier variety type, with an energetic, well-meaning cast of young people who also double as cruise staff during the day, together with professional cabaret acts such as vocalists, magicians, multi-instrumentalists, ventriloquists, comedians, and others. Another, smaller lounge, located aft, is the Salon Tropicana, with a stage and dance floor; it is used mainly as a nightclub

SPA/FITNESS. There is a beauty salon located on Main Deck, and a small fitness room and sauna (in a different location), but little else – when this ship was built there was little demand for spa facilities. Hairdressing services are available, as are manicures, pedicures, and massage. Sports facilities include basketball.

A PASSENGER'S PRAYER

"Heavenly Father, look down on us, Your humble, obedient passengers who are doomed to travel the seas and waterways of this earth, taking photographs, mailing postcards, buying useless souvenirs, and walking around in ill-fitting swimwear.

"We beseech You, oh Lord, to see that our plane is not hijacked, our luggage is not lost, and that our oversized carry-ons go unnoticed.

"Protect us from surly and unscrupulous taxi drivers, avaricious porters, and unlicensed, English-speaking guides in foreign places.

"Give us this day Divine guidance in the selection of our cruise ships and our travel agents — so that we may find our bookings and dining room reservations honored, our cabins of generous proportions, that our luggage arrives before the first evening meal, and that our beds are made up.

"We humbly ask that our shower curtains and personal safes do not provoke us into meaningless frustration and destructive thoughts.

"We pray for art auction-free cruise ships, duty-free-free zones, and mobile phone-free restaurants and open decks.

"We pray that our cabin telephones work, the operator (human or electrical) speaks our tongue, and that there are no phone calls from our children forcing us to abandon our cruise early.

"Lead us, dear Lord, to good, affordable restaurants in the world ashore, where the food is superb, the waiters friendly, and the wine included in the price of a meal.

"Please grant us a cruise director who does not "cream" excessively from the spoils of bingo or horse racing, or does not stress only those jewelry stores from which he accepts an offering.

"Grant us the strength to take shore excursions – to visit the museums, cathedrals, spice stalls, and gift shops listed in Berlitz Pocket Guides.

"And if on our return journey by non-air-conditioned buses we slip into slumber, have mercy on us for our flesh is weak, hot, and tired.

"Give us the wisdom to tip correctly at the end of our voyage. Forgive us for under-tipping out of ignorance, and over-tipping out of fear. Please make the chief purser and ship's staff loves us for what we are and not for what we can contribute to their worldly goods or company comment forms.

"Dear God, keep our wives from shopping sprees and protect them from bargains they do not need or cannot afford. Lead them not into temptation in St. Thomas or Hong Kong for they know not what they do.

"Almighty Father, keep our husbands from looking at foreign women and comparing them to us. Save them from making fools of themselves in cafés and nightclubs. Above all, please do not forgive them their trespasses for they know exactly what they do.

"And when our voyage is over and we return home to our loved ones, grant us the favor of finding someone who will look at our home videos and listen to our stories, so our lives as tourists will not have been in vain. This we ask you in the name of our chosen cruise line, and in the name of American Express, Visa, MasterCard, and our banks. Amen."

Ocean Princess
★★★★

Size: . . . . .Mid-Size Ship	Passenger Decks: 9	Cabins (with private balcony): 232
Tonnage: .30,277	Total Crew: 373	Cabins (wheelchair accessible): 3
Lifestyle: . . . . .Standard	Passengers	Wheelchair accessibility . . . . .Good
Cruise Line: . . . . .Princess Cruises	(lower beds/all berths): 688/826	Cabin Current: . . . . .110 and 220 volts
Former Names: .Tahitian Princess, R Four	Passenger Space Ratio	Elevators: 4
Builder: Chantiers de l'Atlantique (France)	(lower beds/all berths): 44.1/36.6	Casino (gaming tables): . . . . .Yes
Original Cost: . . . .$150 million	Crew/Passenger Ratio	Slot Machines: . . . . .Yes
Entered Service: . . . . .Nov 1999/Dec 2002	(lower beds/all berths): 1.8/2.2	Swimming Pools (outdoors): 1
Registry: .Gibraltar	Cabins (total): 344	Swimming Pools (indoors): 0
Length (ft/m): 593.7/181.0	Size Range (sq ft/m): 145.3–968.7/	Whirlpools: . . . . . .2 (+ 1 thalassotherapy)
Beam (ft/m): 83.5/25.5	13.5–90.0	Self-Service Launderette: . . . . .Yes
Draft (ft/m): 19.5/6.0	Cabins (outside view): 317	Dedicated Cinema/Seats: . . . . .No
Propulsion/Propellers: . . . . .diesel-electric	Cabins (interior/no view): 27	Library: . . . . .Yes
(18,600kW)/2	Cabins (for one person): 0	

OVERALL SCORE: 1,487 OUT OF A POSSIBLE 2,000 POINTS

OVERVIEW. *Ocean Princess* (formerly *Tahitian Princess*, but renamed in 2009) and its sister ship *Pacific Princess* are an ideal size for smaller ports. *Ocean Princess* now has an all-white hull, which makes the ship appear larger – when owned by the now defunct Renaissance cruises, it had a blue hull with white superstructure. It has a large, square-ish white funnel.

The interior decor is stunning and elegant, a throwback to ship decor of the ocean liners of the 1920s and '30s. This includes detailed ceiling cornices, both real and faux wrought-iron staircase railings, leather- and cherry wood paneled walls, *trompe l'oeil* ceilings, rich carpeting in hallways with an Oriental rug-look center section, and many other interesting (and expensive-looking) decorative touches. The overall feel is of an old-world country club. The staircase in the main, two-deck-high foyer may remind you of the one in the 1998 blockbuster movie *Titanic*.

The public rooms are basically spread over three decks. The reception hall (lobby) has a staircase with intricate wrought-iron railings. The Nightclub, with forward-facing views, sits high in the ship and has Polynesian-inspired decor and furniture.

There are plenty of bars – including one in the entrance to each of the restaurants. Perhaps the nicest can be found in the casino bar/lounge, a beautiful room reminiscent of London's grand hotels and understated gaming clubs. It has an inviting marble fireplace and comfortable sofas and individual chairs. There is also a large Card Room, which incorporates an Internet Center, with eight stations.

The Library, a grand room, is designed in the Regency style by the Scottish interior designer John McNeece, and

BERLITZ'S RATINGS

	Possible	Achieved
Ship	500	406
Accommodation	200	155
Food	400	265
Service	400	287
Entertainment	100	72
Cruise	400	302

has a fireplace, a high, indented, *trompe l'oeil* ceiling, and an excellent selection of books, plus some comfortable wing-back chairs with footstools, and sofas you can easily fall asleep on – it's the most relaxing room aboard.

The value for money is extremely good, and gives you with a chance to cruise in comfort aboard a mid-sized ship with some interesting dining choices. There's very little entertainment, but it is certainly not needed in these cruise areas. *Ocean Princess* is much more about relaxation than the larger ships in the fleet, and would make a good child-free vessel.

In common with all ships in the Princess Cruises fleet, 15% is added to all bar and spa accounts (drink prices are moderate, while beer prices are high), and a standard gratuity (about $10 per person, per day) is automatically added to your onboard account. If you think this is too much and want to reduce the amount, you'll need to go to the reception desk to do so.

There is no walk-around promenade deck outdoors (there is, however, a small jogging track around the perimeter of the swimming pool, and port and starboard side decks), and no wooden decks outdoors (instead, they are covered by Bolidt, a sand-colored rubberized material). There is no sauna. Stairways, although carpeted, are tinny. In order to keep the prices low, often the air routing to get to and from your ship is often not the most direct. There is a charge for using machines in the self-service launderette and you have to obtain tokens from the reception desk – a change machine in the launderette itself would be better.

SUITABLE FOR: *Ocean Princess* is best suited to couples (young and not so young), families with children and teenagers, and older singles who like to mingle in a mid-size ship setting with pleasing, sophisticated surroundings and lifestyle, reasonably good entertainment and fairly decent food and service, all at an affordable price.

ACCOMMODATION. There is a variety of about eight different cabin types. All of the standard interior (no view) and outside-view cabins (the lowest four grades) are extremely compact units, and extremely tight for two persons, particularly for cruises longer than seven days. Cabins have twin beds (or queen-size bed), with good under-bed storage areas, personal safe, vanity desk with large mirror, good closet and drawer space (in rich, dark woods), and bathrobe. Color TVs carry a major news channel (where obtainable), plus a sports channel and several round-the-clock movie channels. The bathrooms, which have tiled floors and plain walls, are compact, standard units, and include a shower enclosure with a removable, strong hand-held shower unit, hairdryer, 100% cotton towels, toiletries storage shelves and a retractable clothesline.

The suites/cabins that have private balconies (66 percent of all suites/cabins, or 73 percent of all outside view suites/ cabins) have partial, and not full, balcony partitions, sliding glass doors, and, due to good design and layout, only 14 cabins on Deck 6 have lifeboat-obstructed views. The balcony floor is covered in thick plastic matting (teak would be nicer), and some awful plastic furniture.

Mini-Suites: The 52 accommodation units designated as mini-suites are in reality simply larger cabins than the standard varieties, as the sleeping and lounge areas are not divided. While not overly large, the bathrooms have a good-sized bathtub and ample space for storing personal toiletry items. The living area has a refrigerated mini-bar, lounge area with breakfast table, and a balcony with two plastic chairs and a table.

Owner's Suites: The 10 Owner's Suites are the most spacious accommodation, and are fine, large living spaces located in the forward-most and aft-most sections of the accommodation decks – particularly nice are those that overlook the stern, on Deck 6, 7 and 8. They have more extensive balconies that really are private and cannot be overlooked by anyone from the decks above. There is an entrance foyer, living room, bedroom (the bed faces the sea, which can be seen through the floor-to-ceiling windows and sliding glass door), CD player, bathroom with Jacuzzi bathtub, as well as a small guest bathroom.

Be aware that all suites/cabins located at the stern of the ship may suffer from vibration and noise, particularly when the ship is close to full speed, or maneuvering in port.

CUISINE. Flexibility and choice are what this mid-sized ship's dining facilities are all about. There is a choice of four different dining spots (one is a casual self-serve buffet):

● **The Club Restaurant** has 338 seats (all chairs have armrests), and includes a large raised central section.

There are large ocean-view windows on three sides, several prime tables overlooking the stern, and a small band-stand for occasional live dinner music. The noise level in this dining room can be high, due to its single deck height ceiling. This restaurant is operated in two seatings (the others have an open dining hours); dinner is typically 6pm and 8.15pm.

● **Sabatini's Trattoria** is an Italian restaurant, with 96 seats (all chairs have armrests), windows along two sides, and a set "Bellissima" three-hour degustation menu. The cover charge is $15 per person.

● **The Sterling Steakhouse** is an "American steak house", has 98 seats (all chairs have armrests), and windows along two sides. There's a set menu, together with added daily chef's specials. The cover charge is $8 per person.

● **The Lido Cafe** has seating for 154 indoors and 186 outdoors (with white plastic patio furniture). It is open for breakfast, lunch and casual dinners. It is the ship's self-serve buffet restaurant (24 hours a day), and incorporates a small pizzeria and grill. Basic salads, a meat carving station, and a reasonable selection of cheeses are served daily.

All restaurants have open-seating dining, although reservations are necessary in Sabatini's Trattoria and Sterling Steakhouse, where there are mostly tables for four or six (there are few tables for two). There is a Poolside Grill and Bar for fast food items.

ENTERTAINMENT. The 345-seat Cabaret Lounge has a stage, and circular hardwood dance floor with banquette and individual tub chair seating, and raised sections on port and starboard sides. It is not large, and not really designed for production shows, so cabaret acts form the main focus, with mini-revue style shows presented by a troupe of resident singer/dancers in a potted version of what you might experience aboard the large ships of Princess Cruises.

Inevitably, art auctions and bingo are pushed almost daily. The entertainment highlight for many, however, is a song and dance show put on by locals of all ages, so you become immersed in the art and culture of the islands.

A band, small musical units, and solo entertaining pianists provide live music for shows and dancing in the various lounges and bars before and after dinner.

SPA/FITNESS. There is a gymnasium with ocean-view windows. It has some high-tech muscle-toning equipment and treadmills, steam rooms (no sauna), changing areas for men and women, and a beauty salon with ocean views. The spa is operated by Steiner, a specialist concession.

A lido deck has a swimming pool, and good sunbathing space, while one of the aft decks has a thalassaotherapy pool. A jogging track circles the swimming pool deck, but one deck above. The uppermost outdoors deck includes a golf driving net and shuffleboard court.

● **For more extensive general information about the Princess Cruises experience, see pages 148–51.**

Oceana
★★★★

Size: . . . . .Large Resort Ship	Passenger Decks: 10	Cabins (with private balcony): 410
Tonnage: 77,499	Total Crew: 850	Cabins (wheelchair accessible): 19
Lifestyle: . . . . .Standard	Passengers	Wheelchair accessibility . . . . .Good
Cruise Line: . . . . .P&O Cruises	(lower beds/all berths): 1,950/2,272	Cabin Current: . . . . .110 and 220 volts
Former Names: . . . . .Ocean Princess	Passenger Space Ratio	Elevators: 11
Builder: . . . . .Fincantieri (Italy)	(lower beds/all berths): 39.7/34.1	Casino (gaming tables): . . . . .Yes
Original Cost: . . . .$300 million	Crew/Passenger Ratio	Slot Machines: . . . . .Yes
Entered Service: . . . . .Feb 2000/Nov 2002	(lower beds/all berths): 2.2/2.5	Swimming Pools (outdoors): 4
Registry: . . . . .Bermuda	Cabins (total): 975	Swimming Pools (indoors): 0
Length (ft/m): 857.2/261.30	Size Range (sq ft/m): 158.2–610.3/	Whirlpools: 5
Beam (ft/m): 105.6/32.20	14.7–56.7	Self-Service Launderette: . . . . .Yes
Draft (ft/m): 25.9/7.9	Cabins (outside view): 603	Dedicated Cinema/Seats: . . . . .No
Propulsion/Propellers: . . . . .diesel-electric	Cabins (interior/no view): 372	Library: . . . . .Yes
(28,000 kW)/2	Cabins (for one person): 0	

OVERALL SCORE: 1,494 OUT OF A POSSIBLE 2,000 POINTS

OVERVIEW. The all-white *Oceana* has a pleasing profile for a large ship, and is well balanced by its large funnel, which contains a deck tennis/basketball/ volleyball court in its sheltered aft base. There is 93,000 sq. ft (8,600 sq. meters) of space and a wide, teakwood wrap-around promenade deck outdoors. A great amount of glass area on the upper decks provides plenty of light and connection with the outside world. The ship underwent a few changes to make it more user-friendly for British (as distinct from American) passengers.

The ship, while large, absorbs passengers well, although its open lounge architecture means bleed-through music and little sense of intimacy. Its interiors are pretty and warm, with attractive colors and welcoming decor that includes some attractive wall murals and other artwork.

There is a wide range of public rooms, with several intimate rooms and spaces, so that you don't feel overwhelmed by large spaces. The interior focal point is a large four-deck-high atrium lobby with winding, double stairways and two panoramic glass-walled lifts.

There is plenty of space throughout the public areas, and the traffic flow is quite good. The library is a warm room and has six large buttery leather chairs for listening to compact audio discs, with ocean-view windows.

The collection of artwork is decent, particularly on the stairways, and this helps make the ship feel smaller than it really is. The Monte Carlo Club Casino, while large, is not really in the main passenger flow and so it does not generate the "walk-through" factor found aboard so many ships. Without question, the most traditional room aboard is the Yacht and Compass Bar, decorated in the style of a turn-of-

BERLITZ'S RATINGS

	Possible	Achieved
Ship	500	416
Accommodation	200	159
Food	400	254
Service	400	286
Entertainment	100	81
Cruise	400	298

the-century gentleman's club, with wood paneling and comfortable seating.

Ballroom dance fans will be pleased to note that there are several good-sized wooden dance floors. The ship usually carries a professional dance couple as hosts and teachers, and there is plenty of dancing time included in the entertainment programming.

Children have their own Treasure Chest (for ages 2–5), The Hideout (6–9 year-olds), and for older children (aged 10–13) there is The Buzz Zone. P&O Cruises provides an abundance of staff to look after the children, as well as many activities to keep them out of adult areas. A night nursery is available from 6pm to 2am (there is a per child charge after midnight). While many children don't like organized clubs, they will probably find they make new friends quickly during a cruise.

As is the case aboard most large ships, if you live in the best accommodation (a suite), you will be well attended; if you do not, you will merely be one of a very large number of passengers aboard a ship that caters to families with children (lots of them in peak vacation periods). One nice feature is the Captain's cocktail party – it is held in the four-deck-high main atrium so you can come and go as you please, with no standing in line to have your photograph taken with the captain if you don't want to.

This ship is all about British-ness and will be comfortingly familiar for families with children who want to go abroad but take their British traditions and food with them. Most cabin stewards and dining room personnel are from India, and provide service with a well-balanced smile and warmth that many other nationals find difficult to equal.

However, note that in the quest for increased onboard

revenue (and shareholder value), even birthday cakes are an extra-cost item, as are espressos and cappuccinos (fake ones, made from instant coffee, are available in the dining rooms). Also at extra cost are ice cream, and bottled water (these can add up to a considerable amount). You can expect to be subjected to a stream of flyers advertising daily art auctions, "designer" watches and other promotions. For gratuities (which are optional), you should typically allow £3.50 (about $5.50) per person, per day. The onboard currency is the British pound.

A fine British brass band send-off accompanies all sailings from Southampton. Other touches include church bells that sound throughout the ship for the interdenominational Sunday church service. A coach service for any passengers embarking or disembarking in Southampton covers much of the UK. Car parking is also available – there is one rate for undercover parking, and another rate for parking in an open compound.

There are a number of dead ends in the interior layout, so it's not as user-friendly as it should be. Standing in line for disembarkation, shore tenders and for self-serve buffet meals is an inevitable aspect of cruising aboard all large ships. You may be subjected to announcements for revenue-producing activities such as art auctions, bingo, horse racing that intrude constantly into your cruise.

The swimming pools are actually rather small and will be crowded when the ship is full; also the pool deck is cluttered with white, plastic deck lounge chairs, which don't have cushioned pads (the rule about not leaving sunloungers unattended for more than half an hour is flouted by most British passengers, who are keen to keep their favored position).

While the ship's interior space is a non-smoking environment, smoking is permitted on cabin balconies and in designated spots on the open decks.

SUITABLE FOR: *Oceana* is best suited to adults of all ages (couples and single travelers, young and not so young), and families with children of all ages. The ship is particularly suitable as an excellent value for money cruise for first-time tabloid-reading passengers.

ACCOMMODATION. There are 19 different cabin grades, designated as: suites (with private balcony), mini-suites (with private balcony), outside-view twin-bedded cabin with balcony, outside-view twin bedded cabin, and interior (no view) twin-bedded cabins. The price you pay will depend on the grade, location and size you choose. Although the standard outside-view and interior (no view) cabins are a little small, they are well designed and functional in layout, and have earth tone colors accentuated by splashes of color from the bedspreads. Proportionately, there are quite a lot of interior (no view) cabins.

The cabin numbering system is illogical, with numbers going through several hundred series on the same deck. The walls of the passenger accommodation decks are very plain – some artwork would be an improvement.

Many of the outside-view cabins have private balconies, and all seem to be quite well soundproofed, although the balcony partition is not of the floor to ceiling type, so you can hear your neighbors clearly (or smell their smoke). The balconies are very narrow, and only just large enough for two small chairs, and there is no dedicated outdoor balcony lighting. Many cabins have third- and fourth-person upper bunk beds – these are good for families with children. Tea and coffee-making facilities are provided in all cabins – a comforting addition.

There is a reasonable amount of closet and abundant drawer and other storage space in all cabins; although this is adequate for a 7-night cruise, it could prove to be quite tight for longer. Also provided are a color television, and refrigerator, and each night a chocolate will appear on your pillow. The cabin bathrooms are practical units, and come complete with all the details one needs, although again, they really are tight spaces, best described as one person at-a-time units. Fortunately, they have a shower enclosure of a decent size, a small amount of shelving for your personal toiletries, real glasses, and a hairdryer.

High-quality personal toiletries are by Temple Spa; suite occupants get larger bottles and a wider selection.

Also standard in all cabins are Slumberland 8-inch sprung mattresses, 10.5 tog duvets (blankets and pillows if you prefer), Egyptian cotton towels, improved tea/coffee making facilities with speciality teas (long-life is provided) and a Nick Munro-designed bespoke tray.

Suites: The largest accommodation is in six suites, two on each of three decks at the aft of the ship (with a private balcony giving great views over the stern). Each of these suites – Oronsay, Orcades, Orion, Orissa, Orsova, Orontes, all P&O ships of yesteryear – has a large private balcony. They are well laid out, and have large, marble-clad bathrooms with two washbasins, a Jacuzzi bathtub, and a separate shower enclosure. The bedroom has generous amounts of wood accenting and detailing, indented ceilings, and TV sets in both bedroom and lounge areas, which also have a dining room table and four chairs.

Mini-Suites: Mini-suites typically have two lower beds that convert to a queen-sized bed. There is a separate bedroom/sleeping area with vanity desk, and a lounge with sofa and coffee table, indented ceilings with generous amounts of wood accenting and detailing, walk-in closet, and a larger, marble-clad bathroom with Jacuzzi bathtub and a separate shower enclosure. There is also a private balcony.

Standard Outside-view/Interior (No View) Cabins: A reasonable amount of closet and abundant drawer and other storage space is provided in all cabins (adequate for 7 nights but a little tight for longer cruises), as are a TV set and refrigerator. Each night a chocolate will appear on your pillow. The cabin bathrooms are practical, and come with all the details one needs, although they really are tight spaces, best as one-person at-a-time units. They do, however, have a decent shower enclosure, a small amount of shelving for personal toiletries, real glasses, and a hairdryer.

You can receive BBC World channel on the in-cabin color television system (when available, depending on cruise area), as well as movies (there is no dedicated theater aboard this ship). The cabin service menu is rather limited, and presentation of the food items could be better.

CUISINE. There are two principal asymmetrically designed dining rooms, Adriatic and Ligurian (each seats about 500), located adjacent to the two lower levels of the four-deck high atrium lobby. Which dining room you are assigned to will depend on the location of your accommodation. Each has its own galley and each is split into multi-tier sections, which help create a feeling of intimacy, although there is a lot of noise from the waiter stations adjacent to many tables. Breakfast and lunch are provided in an open-seating arrangement, while dinner is in two seatings.

The cuisine is decidedly British – a little adventurous at times, but always with plenty of curry dishes and other standard British items. Don't expect exquisite dining – this is British hotel catering that doesn't pretend to offer caviar and other gourmet foods. But what it does present is attractive and tasty, with some excellent gravies and sauces to accompany meals.

In keeping with the Britishness of P&O Cruises, the desserts are always good. A statement in the onboard cruise folder states that P&O Cruises does not knowingly purchase genetically modified foods, though it makes no mention of all those commercial American cereals.

The service is provided by a team of friendly stewards – most from India, with which P&O has had a long relationship. The wine list is quite reasonable.

The Plaza, a self-serve buffet, is located above the navigation bridge, with some commanding views. At night, this large room (there are two food lines – one each on both port and starboard sides) is transformed into an informal dinner setting with sit-down waiter service. For an extra £9.50 you can experience the "Tasting Menu" – a selection of small cosmopolitan dishes, with three different menus per cruise.

Outdoors on deck, with a sheltered view over the Riviera Pool, the Horizon Grill has fast-food items for those who don't want to change from their sunbathing attire.

For other informal eats, there is also Café Jardin, with a Frankie's Bar & Grill-style menu serving Italian inspired dishes such as antipasti, glazed belly pork Marco Polo and rib-eye steak alla rosmarino. Upgraded in a March 2008 refit, it is on the uppermost level of the four-deck high atrium lobby.

In addition, there is Explorer's (for cappuccino, espressos and pastries), and Magnums (a champagne/ caviar bar).

ENTERTAINMENT. There are two showlounges (Footlights Theatre, and Starlights), one at each end of the ship. The Footlights, located at the forward end of the ship, is a superb 550-seat, theater-style showlounge, for production shows and theater events (movies can also be shown here), while Starlights is a 480-seat cabaret-style lounge with bar.

P&O Cruises places a big emphasis on a decent quality of entertainment. To this end, there's a resident group of actors, singers and dancers who provide theater-style presentations such as cut-down versions of well-known musicals. In addition, the ship features a whole array of cabaret acts. Although many of the cabaret acts are not what you would call headliners, they do regularly travel the cruise ship circuit. Classical concerts are scheduled for many of the cruises throughout the year.

Ballroom dance aficionados will be pleased to note that there are several good-sized wooden dance floors aboard this ship. P&O Cruises carries a professional dance couple as hosts and teachers, and there's plenty of dancing time included in the entertainment programming.

SPA/FITNESS. The Ocean Spa has facilities that are contained in a glass-walled complex located on one of the highest decks at the aft part of the ship. It includes a gymnasium, with all the associated high-tech muscle-pumping equipment, a combination aerobics/exercise class room, sauna, steam room, and several treatment rooms. If you want to book spa treatments (massage, facial, hair beautification), it is wise to do so as soon after you embark as possible, as time slots do fill up quickly aboard large ships such as this.

The spa is operated by Harding Brothers, a UK concession that provides the staff and range of beauty and wellness treatments. Examples of treatments include: Body Toning (detox for the body); Body Bien Etre (body scrub and massage); Seaweed Wrap; Collagen Velvet Facial Mask.

One swimming pool is "suspended" aft between two decks and forms part of the spa complex (two other pools are located in the center of the ship), although they are not large for the size of the vessel. Sports facilities are located in an open-air sports deck positioned inside the ship's funnel structure and can be adapted to basketball, volleyball, badminton or paddle tennis. Joggers can exercise on the wrap-around open Promenade Deck. There's an electronic golf simulator, so no need to bring your own clubs.

● **For more extensive general information about the P&O Cruises experience, see pages 147–8.**

Oosterdam
★★★★

- Size: . . . . .Large Resort Ship
- Tonnage: .81,769
- Lifestyle: . . . . .Premium
- Cruise Line: . . . . . . .Holland America Line
- Former Names: . . . . .none
- Builder: . . . . .Fincantieri (Italy)
- Original Cost: . . . .$400 million
- Entered Service: . . . . .August 2003
- Registry: . . . . .The Netherlands
- Length (ft/m): 935.0/285.0
- Beam (ft/m): 105.6/32.25
- Draft (ft/m): 25.5/7.80
- Propulsion/Propellers: . . . . .diesel-electric
- (34,000 kW)/2 azimuthing pods
- (17.6 MW each)

- Passenger Decks: 11
- Total Crew: .800
- Passengers
- (lower beds/all berths): 1,918/2,387
- Passenger Space Ratio
- (lower beds/all berths): 43.6/34.2
- Crew/Passenger Ratio
- (lower beds/all berths): 2.3/2.9
- Cabins (total): 924
- Size Range (sq ft/m): 185.0–1,318.6/
- 17.1–122.5
- Cabins (outside view): 788
- Cabins (interior/no view): 136
- Cabins (for one person): 0
- Cabins (with private balcony): 623

- Cabins (wheelchair accessible): 28
- Wheelchair accessibility . . . . .Good
- Cabin Current: . . . . .110 volts
- Elevators: 14
- Casino (gaming tables): . . . . .Yes
- Slot Machines: . . . . .Yes
- Swimming Pools (outdoors): 2
- +1 children's pool
- Swimming Pools (indoors): 1
- (indoor/outdoor)
- Whirlpools: 5
- Self-Service Launderette: . . . . .No
- Dedicated Cinema/Seats: Yes/170
- Library: . . . . .Yes

OVERALL SCORE: 1,520 OUT OF A POSSIBLE 2,000 POINTS

OVERVIEW. *Oosterdam* (sister ships: *Eurodam, Nieuw Amsterdam, Noordam, Westerdam* and *Zuiderdam*) is one of the latest generation of "Vista"-class ships for Holland America Line, designed to appeal to younger, more vibrant, multi-generational, family-oriented holidaymakers.

The twin working funnels are the result of the slightly unusual machinery configuration; the ship has, in effect, two engine rooms – one with three diesels, and one with two diesels and a gas turbine. A pod propulsion system is provided *(see page 45)*, powered by a diesel-electric system, with a small gas turbine located in the funnel for the reduction of emissions.

There is a complete walk-around exterior teak promenade deck, and teak "steamer" style sunloungers are provided. Additionally, there is a jogging track outdoors, located around the ship's mast and the forward third of the ship. Exterior glass elevators, mounted midships on both port and starboard sides, provide fine ocean views from any one of 10 decks. There are two centrally located swimming pools outdoors, and one can be used in inclement weather due to its retractable sliding glass roof. Two whirlpool tubs, adjacent to the swimming pools, are abridged by a bar. Another smaller pool is available for children; it incorporates a winding water slide that spans two decks in height. There is an additional whirlpool tub outdoors.

The intimate lobby spans three decks, and is topped by a beautiful, rotating, Waterford crystal globe of the world. Adjacent are interior and glass wall elevators with exterior views. The interior decor, is bright, yet comfortable – designed to attract a younger clientele. The ceilings are particularly noticeable in the public rooms. In keeping with the

BERLITZ'S RATINGS

	Possible	Achieved
Ship	500	428
Accommodation	200	162
Food	400	269
Service	400	277
Entertainment	100	76
Cruise	400	308

traditions of Holland America Line, a large collection of artwork is a standard feature. Included are some superb paintings of former Holland America Line ships on the mid-ship stairwells by maritime artist Captain Stephen Card.

Also notable are many pieces reflecting the former Dutch East Indies. The cast-aluminum elevator doors are also interesting – the design being inspired by the deco designs from New York's Chrysler Building.

There are two whole entertainment/public room decks. Without doubt, the most dramatic room aboard this ship is the showlounge, spanning four decks in the forward section of the ship. Other facilities include a winding shopping street with several boutique stores and logo shops, an internet center, library, card room, an art gallery, photo gallery, and several small meetings rooms. The casino is large (one has to walk through it to get from the restaurant to the showlounge on one of the entertainments decks), and is equipped with all the gaming paraphernalia and slot machines you can think of. Sports enthusiasts can enjoy a basketball court, volleyball court, golf simulator. For families with children, Club HAL's KidZone provides a whole area dedicated to children's facilities and extensive programming for different age groups (5–17), with one counselor for every 30 children. The company provides free coffee at the Java Bar, and free ice cream at certain hours, as well as hot hors d'oeuvres in all bars.

This formula may not work well for those loyal repeat passengers used to the line's smaller ships. However, *Oosterdam* does offer a range of public rooms with a reasonably intimate atmosphere and the overall feel of the ship is quite homely and comforting. Perhaps the ship's best asset is its friendly and personable Filipino and Indonesian crew, although communication (in English) can be frustrating.

The information desk in the lobby is small and somewhat removed from the main passenger flow on the two decks above it. Many pillars obstruct the passenger flow and lines of sight throughout the ship. There are no self-service launderettes – something families with children might miss, although special laundry packages are available.

ACCOMMODATION. There are 24 price categories: 16 outside-view/8 interior (no view). Some cabins on the lowest accommodation deck (Main Deck) have views obstructed by lifeboats. Some cabins that can accommodate a third and fourth person have very little closet space, and only one personal safe. Some cabins have interconnecting doors – good for families with children. Occupants of suites also get exclusive use of the Neptune Lounge and concierge service, priority embarkation and disembarkation, and other benefits. In many of the suites/cabins with private balconies the balconies are not so private, and can be overlooked from various public locations.

Penthouse Verandah Suites: Two suites offer the largest accommodation (1,318 sq. ft/122.5 sq. meters, including balcony). These have a separate bedroom with a king-sized bed; there's also a walk-in closet, dressing room, living room, dining room, butler's pantry, mini-bar and refrigerator, and private balcony (verandah). The main bathroom has a large whirlpool bathtub, two washbasins, toilet, and plenty of storage space for personal toiletry items. Personalized stationery and free dry cleaning are included, as are hot hors d'oeuvres and other goodies daily.

DeLuxe Verandah Suites: Next in size are 60 of these suites (563 sq. ft/52.3 sq. meters). These have twin beds that convert to a king-sized bed, vanity desk, lounge area, walk-in closet, mini-bar and refrigerator, and bathroom with full-size bathtub, washbasin and toilet. Personalized stationery and complimentary dry cleaning are included, as are hot hors d'oeuvres and other goodies.

Verandah Suites: There are 100 of these Verandah Suites (actually they are cabins, not suites, and measure (284 sq. ft/26.3 sq. meters). Twin beds can convert to a queen-sized bed; there is also a lounge area, mini-bar and refrigerator, while the bathroom has a tub, washbasin and toilet. Floor to ceiling windows open onto a private balcony (verandah).

Outside-view Cabins: Standard outside cabins (197 sq. ft/18.3 sq. meters) have twin beds that can convert to a queen-size bed. There's a small sitting area, while the bathroom has a tub/ shower combination. The interior (no view) cabins are slightly smaller (182.9 sq. ft/ 17 sq. meters).

Niggles include noisy air-conditioning – the flow in cabins and bathrooms can't be turned off and the only regulation is for temperature control.

CUISINE. The 1,045-seat Vista (main) Dining Room is two decks high, with seating at tables for two, four, six or eight on both main and balcony levels – the galley is underneath the restaurant, accessed by port and starboard escalators – and is at the stern. It provides a traditional Holland America Line dining experience, with friendly service from smiling Indonesian and Filipino stewards. Both open seating and fixed (assigned tables and times) seating are available, while breakfast and lunch are open-seating (you'll be seated by restaurant staff on entry). The dining room is a non-smoking venue.

Holland America Line can provide Kosher meals, although these are prepared ashore, frozen, and brought to your table sealed in their original containers.

Alternative Dining Option: The 130-seat Pinnacle Grill is a slightly more upscale dining spot (with higher quality ingredients, and better presentation than in the larger main dining room). It is on Lower Promenade Deck, and fronts onto the second level of the atrium lobby. Pacific Northwest cuisine is featured (with items such as sesame-crusted halibut with ginger-miso, Peking duck breast with blackberry sauce, and an array of premium quality steaks). Fine table settings, china and silverware are featured, as are leather-bound menus. The wine bar offers mostly American wines. Reservations are required and there is a cover charge of $30 per person for service and gratuity.

Informal Eateries: For casual eating, there is an extensive Lido Cafe, an eatery that wraps around the funnel housing and extends aft; there are also some fine views over the ship's central multi-deck atrium. It includes a pizzeria/Italian specialties counter, a salad bar, Asian stir-fry counter, deli sandwiches, and a separate dessert buffet, although movement around the buffet area can be very slow.

There is an outdoor self-serve buffet (adjacent to the fantail pool), which serves fast-food items such as hamburgers and hot dogs, chicken and fries, as well as two smaller buffets adjacent to the midships swimming pool area, and a Windsurf Cafe in the atrium lobby (open 20 hours a day), for coffee, pastries, snack foods, deli sandwiches and liqueur coffees (evenings only) – all at extra cost.

ENTERTAINMENT. The 867-seat Vista Lounge is the ship's principal venue for Las Vegas-style revues and major cabaret shows. The main floor level has a bar in its starboard aft section. Spiral stairways at the back of the lounge connect all levels. Stage shows are best seen from the upper levels, from where the sightlines are quite good.

SPA/FITNESS. The Greenhouse Spa is a large, two-decks-high health spa, and is located directly above the navigation bridge. Facilities include a solarium, hydrotherapy pool, unisex thermal suite – a unisex area incorporating a Laconium (gentle sauna), Hammam (mild steam), and Camomile Grotto (small aromatic steam room). There is also a beauty parlor, 11 massage/therapy rooms (including one for couples), and a large gymnasium with floor-to-ceiling windows on three sides and forward-facing ocean views, and the latest high-tech muscle-toning equipment.

● **For more extensive general information on what a Holland America Line cruise is like, see pages 139–42.**

Oriana
★★★★

Size: . . . . .Large Resort Ship	Passenger Decks: 10	Cabins (with private balcony): 118
Tonnage: .69,153	Total Crew: 760	Cabins (wheelchair accessible): 8
Lifestyle: . . . . .Standard	Passengers	Wheelchair accessibility . . . . .Good
Cruise Line: . . . . .P&O Cruises	(lower beds/all berths): 1,818/2,179	Cabin Current: . . . . . . .110 and 220 volts
Former Names: . . . . .none	Passenger Space Ratio	Elevators: 10
Builder: . . . . .Meyer Werft (Germany)	(lower beds/all berths): 38.0/31.7	Casino (gaming tables): . . . . .Yes
Original Cost: . . . .£200 million	Crew/Passenger Ratio	Slot Machines: . . . . .Yes
Entered Service: . . . . .Apr 1995	(lower beds/all berths): 2.3/2.5	Swimming Pools (outdoors): 3
Registry: . . . . .Bermuda	Cabins (total): 909	Swimming Pools (indoors): 0
Length (ft/m): 853.0/260.0	Size Range (sq ft/m): 150.6–500.5/	Whirlpools: 5
Beam (ft/m): 105.6/32.2	14.0–46.5	Self-Service Launderette: . . . . .Yes
Draft (ft/m): 25.9/7.9	Cabins (outside view): 592	Dedicated Cinema/Seats: Yes/189
Propulsion/Propellers: . . . . .diesel	Cabins (interior/no view): 317	Library: . . . . .Yes
(47,750 kW)/2	Cabins (for one person): 0	

OVERALL SCORE: 1,497 OUT OF A POSSIBLE 2,000 POINTS

OVERVIEW. Although more than 15 years old, this ship has a feeling of timeless elegance. It has a good amount of outdoor space, and enough sunloungers for all passengers. The interiors are gentle, welcoming and restrained, and a 2006 revamp refreshed some of the interior spaces and cabins, and added more children's facilities. There is a good amount of open deck and sunbathing space – an important plus for its outdoors-loving British passengers. It has an extra-wide walk-around promenade deck outdoors. The stern superstructure is nicely rounded and has several tiers that overlook the pool and children's outdoor facilities.

BERLITZ'S RATINGS		
	Possible	Achieved
Ship	500	415
Accommodation	200	157
Food	400	246
Service	400	308
Entertainment	100	82
Cruise	400	289

Inside, the well laid-out design provides good horizontal passenger flow, and wide passageways. Very noticeable are the fine, detailed ceiling treatments. As it is a ship for all types of people, specific areas have been designed to attract different age groups and lifestyles.

There is a four-deck-high atrium with a soft waterfall. It is elegant but not glitzy, and is topped by a dome of Tiffany glass. The many public rooms provide plenty of choice, with lots of nooks and crannies in which to sit and read.

The L-shaped Anderson's Lounge (named after Arthur Anderson, founder of the Peninsular Steam Navigation Company in the 1830s) contains an attractive series of 19th-century marine paintings, and is decorated in the manner of a fine British gentleman's club.

Atop the ship and forward is the Crow's Nest, a U-shaped room with one small wing that can be closed off for small groups. A long bar includes a ship model (former P&O ship *Ranpura*) in a glass case. Two small stages are set into the forward port and starboard sections, and there is a wooden dance floor. Smoking is permitted only on cabin balconies and in designated spots on the open decks.

The library is a fine room, with a good range of hardback books (and a librarian), inlaid wood tables and bookcases crafted by Lord Linley's company, and some comfortable chairs. On the second day of almost any cruise, however, the library will have been almost stripped of books by word-hungry passengers. Adjacent is Thackeray's, a writing room named after the novelist William Makepeace Thackeray, a P&O passenger in 1844. Lord's Tavern is the most sporting place to pitch a beverage or two, or take part in a singalong. It is decorated with cricket memorabilia. There's also a small casino, with table games and slot machines.

The carpeting throughout is of a high quality, much of it custom designed and made from 100% wool. There arè some fine pieces of sculpture that add the feeling of a floating museum, and original artworks by all-British artists that include several tapestries and sculptures.

Children and teens have "Club Oriana", their own rooms (Peter Pan and Decibels), their own daily programming and activities, Play Station 2 units, and their own outdoor pool. Children can be entertained until 10pm, which gives parents time to have dinner and go dancing. The cabins also have a baby-listening device. A special night nursery for small children (ages 2–5) is available (6pm–midnight, no charge; from midnight to 2am there is a charge).

There is a wide variety of mainly British entertainment. There is also a program of theme cruises (antiques, art appreciation, classical music, comedy, cricket, gardening, jazz, motoring, popular fiction, Scottish dance).

Oriana, a sort of Benidorm at sea, provides a decent, well organized, "traditional" cruise experience. It's all about Britishness and will be comfortably familiar for families with children who want to go abroad but take their British values and food preferences with them, and sail from a UK port. Most cabin stewards and dining room personnel are from India, and provide service with a warm smile. However, in the quest for increased onboard revenue, even birthday cakes cost extra, as do real espressos and cappuccinos (fake ones, made from instant coffee, are available in the dining rooms). Ice cream and bottled water also cost extra.

Passenger gripes include ear-splitting announcements, poorly trained reception desk staff, and poor hospitality from many of the crew. Beware the many smokers.

A British brass band send-off usually accompanies sailings from Southampton. Other touches include church bells sounded for the interdenominational Sunday service. The onboard currency is the British pound. For gratuities (optional), allow £3 (around US$4.50) per person, per day.

SUITABLE FOR: *Oriana* is best for adults of all ages (although most cruises attract passengers over 50), and families with children of all ages who want a cruise that starts and ends in the UK, aboard a large ship with all the facilities of a small resort, with food and service that are acceptable, though not as good as aboard some other cruise ships.

ACCOMMODATION. The wide range of cabin configurations and categories (in 18 grades) includes family cabins with extra beds (110 cabins can accommodate up to four persons). In a 2006 make-over, all received new 8-inch Slumberland mattresses, duvets and high-quality bedlinen.

Standard interior (no view) cabins and outside-view cabins are well equipped, but compact. There is much use of rich, warm limed oak or cherry wood in all cabins, which makes even the least expensive four-berth cabin seem inviting. All cabins have good closet and drawer space, small refrigerator, full-length mirror, and blackout curtains (essential for North Cape cruises). Satellite television provided typically includes BBC World, although reception may not be good in all areas. Cabin soundproofing could be better.

A number of cabins are provided for passengers traveling singly. Singles who share a cabin should note that only one personal safe is provided in most twin-bedded cabins. Although the cabins for four persons (family cabins) do have four small personal safes, there are no privacy curtains.

The standard cabin bathrooms are modestly sized, and have mirror-fronted cabinets, although the lighting is quite soft; all have a wall-mounted hairdryer. High-quality personal toiletries are by Temple Spa; suite occupants get larger bottles and more of a choice.

There are eight suites, each measuring 500 sq. ft (46 sq. meters), with butler service. Features include a separate bedroom with two lower beds convertible to a queen-sized bed, walk-in dressing area, two double closets, plenty of drawer space. The lounge area has a sofa, armchairs and table, writing desk, binoculars, umbrella, trouser press, iron and ironing board, two TV sets, VCR, personal safe, hairdryer and refrigerator. The bathroom has a whirlpool bath, shower and toilet, and there is also a guest bathroom. All in all, the suites, and particularly the bathrooms, are very disappointing when compared with similarly sized suites in other ships. The private balcony has two sunloungers, tables and chairs. Suite occupants get priority embarkation, and their own lounge in the Southampton cruise terminal.

Other balcony cabins (called outside deluxe) measure 210 sq. ft (19 sq. meters). There is plenty of closet and drawer space. The bathrooms are somewhat disappointing and dated, and have a very small, plain washbasin. One would expect marble or granite units in these grades.

CUISINE. There are two restaurants, both with two seatings: Peninsula (located amidships), and Oriental (aft). The galley is between the two restaurants. Both are moderately handsome (each has tables for two, four, six or eight), but in the aft dining room the noise level can be high at many tables, due to the room's position above the propellors.

The meals are mostly of the unmemorable "Middle-England" variety, and the presentation generally lacks creativity. Curries are heavily featured, particularly on luncheon menus. Afternoon tea is disappointing. Note that the typical menu cycle is 14 days; anyone on a long voyage may find it quite repetitive. The former Curzon Room is now a 96-seat Oriana Rhodes (a Gary Rhodes at sea) restaurant (revenue comes before classical concerts, but provides an additional dining choice – good for special occasions). Two principal menus are rotated every few days, and there are special menus for the Christmas/New Year's cruise; the extra cost is £15 per person. The adjacent Tiffany's Bar serves as a pre-dinner ante-room.

The Conservatory is for casual self-serve breakfast and luncheon buffets, and 24-hour self-serve beverage stands, although the selection of teas is poor. On some evenings, it becomes a reservation-only alternative restaurant, Le Bistro, with sit-down service and French Bistro, Indian or Southeast Asian cuisine. An Al Fresco Pizzeria serves pizza slices, bread-based and not made from pizza dough.

ENTERTAINMENT. The Theatre Royal is a well designed room, located at the forward end of Promenade Deck. It has a sloping floor, and good sightlines from most seats. The fare is mainly British, from production shows staged by a resident company to top British "names" and lesser artists.

A second, smaller Pacific Lounge is a multi-function entertainment venue, for cabaret acts (including late-night comedy), and can also be used as a lecture room. However, pillars obstruct the stage view from a number of seats.

Ballroom dance fans will be pleased to make use of the four good-sized wooden dance floors. The ship always carries a professional dance couple as hosts and teachers.

SPA/FITNESS. The Oasis Spa is reasonably large, and provides the latest alternative treatment therapies. A gymnasium features high-tech muscle toning equipment. The unisex sauna is a large facility; there is also a steam room and several treatment rooms. The spa is operated by Harding Brothers, a UK concession.

● **For more extensive general information on the P&O Cruise experience, see pages 147–8.**

Orient Queen
★★★

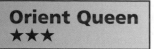

Size:	Mid-Size Ship	Passenger Decks:	7
Tonnage:	16,916	Total Crew:	400
Lifestyle:	Standard	Passengers	
Cruise Line:	Louis Cruises	(lower beds/all berths):	828/910
Former Names:	Orient Queen, Bolero, Starward	Passenger Space Ratio	
		(lower beds/all berths):	26.3/18.5
Builder:	A.G. Weser (Germany)	Crew/Passenger Ratio	
Original Cost:	n/a	(lower beds/all berths):	2.4/2.9
Entered Service:	Dec 1968/Aug 2006	Cabins (total):	414
Registry:	Greece	Size Range (sq ft/m):	111.9–324.0/
Length (ft/m):	525.9/160.30		10.4–30.1
Beam (ft/m):	74.9/22.84	Cabins (outside view):	192
Draft (ft/m):	22.5/6.86	Cabins (interior/no view):	200
Propulsion/Propellers: diesel (12,950kW)/2		Cabins (for one person):	0

Cabins (with private balcony):	0
Cabins (wheelchair accessible):	2
Wheelchair accessibility	None
Cabin Current:	110/220 volts
Elevators:	4
Casino (gaming tables):	Yes
Slot Machines:	Yes
Swimming Pools (outdoors):	2
Swimming Pools (indoors):	0
Whirlpools:	0
Self-Service Launderette:	No
Dedicated Cinema/Seats:	Yes/210
Library:	Yes

BERLITZ'S OVERALL SCORE: 1,103 OUT OF A POSSIBLE 2,000 POINTS

OVERVIEW. The open deck and sunbathing space is very limited (some of the decks are of plain, painted steel), and cluttered with (wood) sunloungers and sun shade umbrellas on the aft decks. Just forward of the twin funnels is an enclosed sports facility while aft of the mast is a large solarium-style shielded housing, with multi-level lounge/bar/disco that is adjacent to one of the ship's small swimming pools.

There is a decent choice of public rooms, including six bars, all of which have clean, contemporary furnishings and upbeat, cheerful fabric colors and a mix of traditional and contemporary decor. The Greek staff is friendly and welcoming. The dress code is casual and the onboard currency is the euro.

The diesel engines are noisy and tend to "throb" in some parts of the vessel (particularly when the ship is going full speed), including in many cabins on the lower decks.

SUITABLE FOR: *Orient Queen* is best suited to adult couples and single travelers who want to visit the Greek Isles in some degree of comfort. The ship provides a good basic cruise experience in rather crowded, but moderately comfortable surroundings, at a modest price.

ACCOMMODATION. There are four Royal Suites, and 54 "suites." Otherwise the cabins are very compact units that are moderately comfortable, and are decorated in soft colors. They are, however, adequate for a short cruise experience, particularly as the ship is in port each day. While the closet space is very limited, there are plenty of drawers, although they are metal and tinny.

The bathrooms are small and tight, and the towels are

BERLITZ'S RATINGS

	Possible	Achieved
Ship	500	279
Accommodation	200	94
Food	400	221
Service	400	245
Entertainment	100	56
Cruise	400	208

not large. The toilets are of the "gentle flush" (non-vacuum) variety. Soundproofing between cabins is poor, and the air-conditioning is quite noisy.

The four Royal suites are of a decent size (for the size of the ship). There is ample floor space to walk in these suites, which have a king-sized bed, vanity desk, curtained-off closet, plenty of drawer and storage space for luggage, a lounge with a sofa that converts into an additional bed, drinks table and two chairs. A large pillar obstructs the room's flow. The bathroom has a small but deep Jacuzzi tub with integral hand-held shower. All suites/cabins have flat-screen televisions, refrigerator and telephone.

CUISINE. There are four eateries. The 444-seat Mermaid (main) Restaurant is cheerful, even almost charming, and has some prime tables that overlook the stern. Seating is at tables for four, six or eight. There are two seatings, and smoking is permitted at any table. The cuisine is Mediterranean, with some Greek specialties, while the wine list features mainly young wines. Breakfast and lunch buffets are provided indoors at the casual self-serve Horizon Café with seating provided outdoors at tables set around the aft swimming pool, but space is tight.

ENTERTAINMENT. The 420-seat El Cabaret showlounge, a single-level room, provides "low budget, low quality" entertainment. There's also a nightclub/discotheque. A casino operates during cruises from Beirut.

SPA/FITNESS. There is a beauty salon, and a massage/body treatment room – on two different decks.

Orion
★★★★ +

Size:	Boutique Ship	Passenger Decks:	5	Cabins (for one person):	0
Tonnage:	4,050	Total Crew:	75	Cabins (with private balcony):	9
Lifestyle:	Premium	Passengers		Cabins (wheelchair accessible):	0
Cruise Line:	Orion Expedition Cruises	(lower beds/all berths):	106/125	Wheelchair accessibility	None
Former Names:	none	Passenger Space Ratio		Elevators:	1
Builder:	Cassens-Werft (Germany)	(lower beds/all berths):	38.2/32.4	Casino (gaming tables):	No
Original Cost:	n/a	Crew/Passenger Ratio		Slot Machines:	No
Entered Service:	Nov 2003/Mar 2006	(lower beds/all berths):	1.4/1.6	Swimming Pools (outdoors):	0
Registry:	The Bahamas	Cabins (total):	53	Swimming Pools (indoors):	0
Length (ft/m):	337.0/102.7	Size Range (sq ft/m):	175.0–345.0/	Whirlpools:	1
Beam (ft/m):	46.0/14.00		16.3–32.1	Self-Service Launderette:	No
Draft (ft/m):	12.6/3.8	Cabins (outside view):	53	Lecture/Film Room/Seats:	Yes/98
Propulsion/Propellers:	diesel/1	Cabins (interior/no view):	0	Library:	Yes (open 24 hours)

BERLITZ'S OVERALL SCORE: 1,612 OUT OF A POSSIBLE 2,000 POINTS

OVERVIEW. This small ship, an enlargement and refinement of two previous cruise ships built at the same shipyard, *Sun Bay* and *Sun Bay II*, is a beauty, and the latest in the quest to build the ideal expedition cruise ship. It has all the comforts of home, and then some – as well as specialist equipment for expedition cruising. Although a small ship, *Orion* has stabilizers, bow and stern thrusters for maximum maneuverability, and a fleet of 10 heavy-duty Zodiac inflatable landing craft and a fishing boat (named *BeeKay*).

There is also an aft marina platform for swimming off. Orion Expedition Cruises, owned by KSL Capital Partners in Denver, Colorado, has a long-term charter of this fine boutique expedition vessel. There is no swimming pool, nor is one needed, but there is a hot tub, set amid an open deck, which also houses a bar, and a small rock garden/water feature. All outdoor tables, chairs, and steamer-style sunloungers are made of hardwood.

The interior decor is really warm and inviting, and provides a cozy, cosseting atmosphere that is far removed from the majority of (larger) expedition-style cruise ships today. Public rooms include an observation lounge (Galaxy Lounge), which opens onto a wrap-around open promenade deck; it also connects with the small Vega Health Spa.

Other public rooms include Leda Lounge (main lounge), a boutique, and a dedicated Cosmos Lecture Hall with surround sound system for lectures and movies. Typically, five expedition, culture, history and marine biology lecturers are carried on each expedition voyage.

The reception desk is open 24 hours a day, and there's also an internet-connect computer in the library (with its green leather seating); the cost is A$50 for two hours.

Some rooms are clustered around a glass-walled atrium

BERLITZ'S RATINGS

	Possible	Achieved
Ship	500	422
Accommodation	200	163
Food	400	309
Service	400	300
Entertainment	n/a	n/a
Cruise	400	418

and the ship's single elevator. A special "mud room" is provided (complete with boot washing stations), and this is adjacent to a Zodiac/tender loading platform on the port side. The artwork features one theme, exploration, and myth associated with exploration – according to one myth, Neptune was Orion's father, for example, while Queen Eurayle of the Amazon was his mother.

This is about as far away from big cruise ships as you can get, with well-planned itineraries to some of the most remote regions of the southern hemisphere, including the islands of Papua New Guinea, the Kimberly region of Australia, "Wild" Tasmania, and Antarctica's McMurdo Sound and Ross Sea regions. If you want magic moments in soft adventure travel, wrapped in the comfort of fine surroundings and good food, then it would be hard to beat *Orion*.

But make sure you can walk well, because some of the expeditions are quite demanding. Talk about exclusive cruising – this is it. Actually, cruising is the wrong word for this type of eco-travel; it's more like having a magic carpet whisk to you to destinations that most people have never heard of – particularly on the spectacular Papua New Guinea itineraries.

Most yachting types tend to want to sell their own boats after being pampered aboard an *Orion* expedition voyage. Incidentally, all cabins display black and white photographs of yachts, by Beken of Cowes.

The onboard currency is the Australian dollar (A$). Note that when the ship operates in Australian waters (on Kimberly itineraries, for example), an Australian sales tax is added to all wine and beverage accounts. Drinks really should be included with this kind of product. Bottled water is provided for all passengers at no charge.

SUITABLE FOR: *Orion* is best suited to mature couples and single travelers who like learning about nature and wildlife up close, who enjoy quietly exploring the world around them, and who would not dream of cruising in the mainstream sense aboard ships with large numbers of people and a big city environment around them. This ship is for those in search of life enrichment in high-class surroundings and the company of well-educated and well-traveled people.

ACCOMMODATION. There are four grades of suites, and two grades of cabins. No matter what grade of accommodation you book (the size and location will dictate the price you pay), the facilities are top rate. All suites/cabins feature twin beds that can be converted to a queen-sized bed, a TV set, a DVD/CD player, a mini-refrigerator, ample closet space, a small personal safe.

The marble-clad bathroom houses a small toiletries cabinet, single washbasin, and a large shower enclosure, with a retractable clothes line. Personal toiletry items (shampoo, conditioner, body lotion, shower gel, and two sizes of soap) are by Escada. All the cabinetry was custom-made, and the bathrooms were fitted individually, which is rare in today's modular-fit world.

There are 13 suites, nine of which have a small "French" balcony (meaning you can just about step out onto it), four owner's suites, six balcony suites, two Deluxe suites, and one rather odd-shaped but delightful Junior suite. These have more space, and some share a narrow communal balcony (meaning there is no partition between them), sofa, glass drinks table, and good-sized vanity desk. Only the four owners' suites have a bathtub; all other suites/cabins have large shower enclosures.

CUISINE. The Constellation Restaurant has ocean-view picture windows, artwork based on the astrological signs, and serves all passengers in one open seating. However, because of its low ceiling, it can be a rather noisy. The cuisine is extremely good and varied, and, in addition to an à la carte menu, each dinner features a four-course signature menu by one of Australia's new breed of high-profile chefs, Serge Dansereau of "The Bathers' Pavilion" in Sydney.

The portions are not large but they are colourful and cre-ative. Expect to find Tasmanian oysters, crocodile, emu, and kangaroo among the offerings. Place settings include Bauscher china and Hepp silverware.

The ship carries a decent range of mostly Australian wines, including outstanding reds such as Wolf Blass Black Label, and Yalumba's The Octavius Old Vine Shiraz; and whites such as Leeuwin Estate's Art Series Chardonnay, and Devil's Lair 5th Leg Chardonnay-Sauvignon. There are also some nice, less-pricey alternatives whites such as the Bunnamagoo Estate Chardonnay, and the Chain of Ponds Unwooded Chardonnay; and reds such as the Penfolds Bin 389, and the perfectly acceptable Bunnamagoo Merlot. If you want champagne, several French champagnes are available, such as the top of the range Krug Grande Cuvee, or the tasty Veuve Cliqout. Note that there is no sommelier on board, but the wines are well served by the waiters or maître d' hotel.

Delphinus Outdoor Café, an open deck aft of the Leda Lounge, serves as an al fresco dining spot for casual breakfasts, lunches, and occasional barbecue dinners.

Continental breakfast and afternoon tea are also served in the Galaxy Lounge, and espresso/cappuccinos are available (at no extra charge) in two lounges/bars and restaurant, but do watch out for the delicious brownies on the bar counter!

The service staff is Filipino; they are warm, and communicate well with passengers.

ENTERTAINMENT. There is no formal entertainment (although the ship typically carries an entertaining duo), while lecturers provide daily recaps and fascinating, in-depth talks on marine or plant biology each evening.

SPA/FITNESS. The Vega Health Spa consists of a fitness center, sauna, shower enclosure, and a private treatment room (for massages). A beauty salon is located two decks below. Spa treatments include deep tissue massage (at A$ 90 for 60 minutes); facial (A$ 60 for 30 minutes, A$90 for 60 minutes). Four top-to-toe massage experiences: each lasts 90 minutes and costs A$130); they are called Top End, Island and Reef, Tasmania, and Antarctica, and include an aromatherapy massages. The ship carries a range of personal beauty products used on board and also for sale; creams, oils and other ingredients are also mixed by the therapist and tailored to your own needs and requirements.

Size:	.Mid-Size Ship	Total Crew:	.350	Cabins (wheelchair accessible):	.2

Size: ....Mid-Size Ship
Tonnage: 20,636
Lifestyle: ....Standard
Cruise Line: ....
Former Names: *Pacific Princess, Sea Venture*
Builder: .Rheinstahl Nordseewerke (Germany)
Original Cost: ....$25 million
Entered Service: ......Feb 1972/May 2005
Registry: ....The Bahamas
Length (ft/m): 553.6/168.74
Beam (ft/m): 80.7/24.6
Draft (ft/m): 25.2/7.7
Propulsion/Propellers: .diesel (13,400 kW)/2
Passenger Decks: 8

Total Crew: 350
Passengers
(lower beds/all berths): 640/750
Passenger Space Ratio
(lower beds/all berths): 32.2/27.5
Crew/Passenger Ratio
(lower beds/all berths): 1.8/2.1
Cabins (total): 320
Size Range (sq ft/m): 125.9–441.3/
11.7–41.0
Cabins (outside view): 250
Cabins (interior/no view): 70
Cabins (for one person): 0
Cabins (with private balcony): 0

Cabins (wheelchair accessible): 2
Wheelchair accessibility ....Fair
Cabin Current: ....110 and 220 volts
Elevators: 4
Casino (gaming tables): ....Yes
Slot Machines: ....Yes
Swimming Pools (outdoors): 2
Swimming Pools (indoors): 0
Whirlpools: 0
Self-Service Launderette: ....No
Dedicated Cinema/Seats: Yes/170
Library: ....Yes

OVERALL SCORE: 1,013 OUT OF A POSSIBLE 2,000 POINTS

OVERVIEW. As the former *Pacific Princess*, this mid-size ship was one of the pair of original "Love Boats" in the American TV series *The Love Boat*. It is quite handsome, with a relatively high superstructure and well-balanced lines, but it now needs better maintenance. There is a decent amount of open deck space and several sunbathing areas, but no walk-around promenade deck outdoors. One swimming pool has a moveable glass roof for use in inclement weather.

Inside, the public areas are quite spacious, for the size of the ship, and there are numerous public rooms, with reasonably wide passageways. These include a movie theater, and an aft lounge with a two-deck high glass wall overlooking the aft pool deck. A forward observation lounge also acts as an indoor buffet dining area. The casino and the Cova da Pirate karaoke bar are popular. There's also a boutique, small library and internet-connect center.

The ship provides comfort for passengers who dislike large resort ships. Concessions run the dining, spa/beauty services, and shops. The ship is operated for the Spanish-speaking market under Quail Cruises. The onboard currency is the euro, and drinks and all gratuities are included.

SUITABLE FOR: *Pacific* is best suited to Spanish-speaking couples, singles, and families with children of all ages who want a first cruise experience in a traditional ship, with plenty of public rooms and a lively party atmosphere, food that is quantity rather than quality, at low cost.

ACCOMMODATION. There are eight price grades. The five suites are of quite a decent size, and well designed, with

BERLITZ'S RATINGS

	Possible	Achieved
Ship	500	239
Accommodation	200	104
Food	400	209
Service	400	220
Entertainment	100	45
Cruise	400	196

plenty of space to move around in (two are located forward, just under the navigation bridge, and command good views). Most other cabins have ample room, are quite well appointed, and there is plenty of closet and drawer space. The top category cabins have a full bathtub, while all others have a shower enclosure. None of the suites or cabins has a private balcony.

All suites and cabins will provide you with a TV set, telephone, personal safe and hairdryer. Some cabins have interconnecting doors, and some can accommodate a third/fourth person.

CUISINE. The main restaurant is a reasonably comfortable room, and is operated in two seatings. The wine list is adequate, and prices are reasonable, although the selection is small and consists mostly of younger wines. Casual breakfasts and lunches can be taken in the observation lounge, with fine ocean views on three sides or outdoors on the Lido Deck, adjacent to the swimming pool.

ENTERTAINMENT. The "theater-in-the-round" showlounge has banquette-style seating in several tiers, set around a "thrust" stage. The entertainment is low-key, which means only the occasional cabaret act is featured. There is live music throughout the ship for dancing.

SPA/FITNESS. The Health Spa is positioned aft on two of the uppermost decks (a stairway connects the two). A beauty salon is on the upper deck, while a gymnasium with aft-facing ocean-view windows, three treatment rooms, and separate male and female saunas are on the lower level.

Pacific Dawn
★★★

Size:	Large Resort Ship	Total Crew:	710	Cabins (wheelchair accessible): 13
Tonnage:	70,285	Passengers		Wheelchair accessibility ....Fair
Lifestyle:	Standard	(lower beds/all berths): 1,596/2,020		Cabin Current: ....110 and 220 volts
Cruise Line:	P&O Cruises (Australia)	Passenger Space Ratio		Elevators: 12
Former Names:	*Regal Princess*	(lower beds/all berths): 44.0/34.7		Casino (gaming tables): ....Yes
Builder:	Fincantieri Navali (Italy)	Crew/Passenger Ratio		Slot Machines: ....Yes
Original Cost:	$276.8 million	(lower beds/all berths): 2.2/2.8		Swimming Pools (outdoors): 2
Entered Service:	Aug 1991/Nov 2007	Cabins (total): 798		Swimming Pools (indoors): 0
Registry:	Great Britain	Size Range (sq ft/m): 189.4–586.6/		Whirlpools: 4
Length (ft/m):	811.0/247.2	17.6–54.5		Self-Service Launderette: ....Yes
Beam (ft/m):	105.6/32.2	Cabins (outside view): 620		Dedicated Cinema/Seats: ....No
Draft (ft/m):	25.5/7.8	Cabins (interior/no view): 178		Library: ....Yes
Propulsion/Propellers: diesel (24,000kW)/2		Cabins (for one person): 0		
Passenger Decks:	11	Cabins (with private balcony): 148		

BERLITZ'S OVERALL SCORE: 1,181 OUT OF A POSSIBLE 2,000 POINTS

OVERVIEW. In October 2007, *Regal Princess* was withdrawn from the Princess Cruises fleet and transferred to P&O Cruises (Australia) for cruises down under, as *Pacific Dawn*. As *Regal Princess*, this was the second ship in the 70,000-ton range for Princess Cruises, and as such foreshadowed the even larger ships this successful company went on to build. The ship underwent an extensive refit and refurbishment in 2007 to better suit it to its new role.

The ship has rather a jumbo-jet look to it when viewed from the front, with a dolphin-like upper structure (made of lightweight aluminum alloy), and a large upright "dust-bin-like" funnel (also made from aluminum alloy) placed aft. Inside, the contemporary styling of the period is mixed with traditional features and a spacious interior layout. The interior spaces are well designed, although the layout itself is quite disjointed. The understated decor of soft pastel shades is highlighted by some colorful artwork.

An observation dome, set high atop the ship like the head of a dolphin, houses a multi-purpose lounge/comedy club. The ship has decent health and fitness facilities. A striking, elegant three-deck-high atrium has a grand staircase with fountain sculpture; stand-up cocktail parties are held here. Characters Bar, located adjacent to the pizzeria on the open deck forward, has wonderful drink concoctions and some unusual glasses.

This ship provides a very pleasant cruise in elegant and comfortable surroundings, and an attentive staff will make you feel welcome. However, the open deck space is extremely limited for the size of the ship and the number of passengers carried, and, sadly, there is no forward observation viewpoint outdoors. There is no walk-around prom-

BERLITZ'S RATINGS		
	Possible	Achieved
Ship	500	295
Accommodation	200	132
Food	400	213
Service	400	244
Entertainment	100	60
Cruise	400	237

enade deck outdoors (the only walking space being along the sides of the ship). In fact, there is little contact with the outdoors at all. The sunbathing space is really limited when the ship is full, although as many passengers are often over 50 years old, perhaps this is not quite so crucial.

The interior layout is reasonable, but a little disjointed. Galley fumes often waft over the aft open decks.

Regular passenger gripes include the automated telephone system and luggage delivery. Lines often form, particularly for the purser's office, and for open-seating breakfast and lunch in the dining room. P&O Australia scrapped automatic tipping from October 2010.

ACCOMMODATION. There are many different price grades; the price will depend on the location and size you choose. In general, the cabins are well designed and have large bathrooms as well as good soundproofing. Walk-in closets, refrigerator, personal safe, color television and an interactive video system are provided in all cabins, as are chocolates on your pillow each night.

Twin beds convert to queen-size beds in standard cabins. Bathrobes and personal toiletry amenities are provided. The outside-view cabins for disabled passengers have their views obstructed by lifeboats.

The 14 most expensive suites (each with a large private balcony) are very well equipped, with a practical design that positions most things in just the right place. They have the following names (in alphabetical order): Amalfi, Antibes, Cannes, Capri, Corfu, La Palma, Madeira, Majorca, Malaga, Marbella, Monaco, Portofino, St. Tropez, and Sorrento.

The bedroom is separated from the living room by a

heavy wooden door, and there are television sets in both rooms. The closet and drawer space is very generous, and there is enough of it even for long cruises.

CUISINE. The Palm Court Dining Room is a no-smoking room, and is large, although the galley divides it into a U-shape. Some of the most desirable tables overlook the stern, but it's a pity there are no tables for two. There are two seatings.

Despite the fact that the portions are generous, the food and its presentation are somewhat disappointing, and tastes bland. The quality of fish is poor (often disguised by crumb or batter coatings), the selection of fresh green vegetables is limited, and few garnishes are used. However, do remember that this is big-ship banquet catering, with all its attendant standardization and production cooking.

Meats are of a decent quality, although often disguised by gravy-based sauces. Pasta dishes are large, served by the section headwaiters. If you like desserts, order a sundae at dinner, as most other desserts are just so-so.

While ice cream ordered in the dining room is included in the price, if you order one anywhere else, you'll have to pay extra for it.

There is a good pizzeria for informal meals; this is particularly popular at lunchtime and in the afternoons. Themed late-night buffets are provided, but afternoon teas are poor. For sweet snacks during the day, a patisserie (items cost extra) is located in the spacious lobby.

ENTERTAINMENT. The International Showlounge spans two decks (with seating on both main and balcony levels). It is located at the forward most part of the ship, and accessed by the forward stairway and elevators. The lower level has seating clustered around the stage, as you would find in a true variety theatre ashore.

P&O Cruises Australia provides plenty of live music for the various bars and lounges, with a wide mix of light classical, jazz, and dance music, from solo entertaining pianists to large show bands, and volume is normally kept to an acceptable level. Three times during each cruise, a stunning laser light and sound show take place in the atrium.

SPA/FITNESS. The spa/fitness center is located low down in the ship (accessible by elevator and stairs), and contains a gymnasium, aerobics exercise room, steam room, sauna and changing areas, and Images, the beauty salon. It is operated by Steiner, a specialist concession, whose young staff will try to sell you its own-brand Elemis beauty products.

QUOTABLE QUOTES

Overheard in Alaska:
"Are the glaciers always here?"

Overheard in the cigar smoking room: "I'm looking for a no-smoking seat"

Overheard in the dining room in the Caribbean:
"Is all the salmon smoked? I am a non-smoker"
"Waiter, this vichyssoise is cold."
"Was the fish caught this morning by the crew?"

Overheard on an Antarctic cruise:
"Where is the good shopping in Antarctica?"

Overheard on a cruise taking in the British Isles:
"Windsor Castle is terrific. But why did they build it so close to the airport?"

Overheard on an Athens tour:
"Why did the Greeks build so many ruins?"

Overheard in the dining room:
Passenger: "Waiter: What is caviar?"
Waiter: "Fish eggs, sir."
Passenger: "In that case, I'll have two, over-easy!"

Overheard on a QE2 round-the-world cruise, in Kagoshima, with Mount Suribaya in the background:
"Can you tell me what time the volcano will erupt? I want to be sure to take a photograph."

Pacific Dream
★★★ +

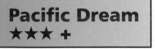

Size: . . . . .Mid-Size Ship	Passenger Decks: 10	Cabins (with private balcony): 68
Tonnage: .46,811	Total Crew: 620	Cabins (wheelchair accessible): 5
Lifestyle: . . . . .Standard	Passengers	Wheelchair accessibility . . . . .Good
Cruise Line: . . . . Pullmantur Cruises	(lower beds/all berths): 1,506/1,875	Cabin Current: . . . . .110 volts
Former Names: . . . . . .*Island Star, Horizon*	Passenger Space Ratio	Elevators: 7
Builder: . . . . .Meyer Werft (Germany)	(lower beds/all berths): 31.0/24.9	Casino (gaming tables): . . . . .Yes
Original Cost: . . . .$185 million	Crew/Passenger Ratio	Slot Machines: . . . . .Yes
Entered Service: . . . .May 1990/Mar 2010	(lower beds/all berths): 2.6/3.2	Swimming Pools (outdoors): 2
Registry: . . . . .The Bahamas	Cabins (total): .753	Swimming Pools (indoors): 0
Length (ft/m): 681.1/207.6	Size Range (sq ft/m): 114.1–383.2/	Whirlpools: 0
Beam (ft/m): 95.1/29.0	10.6/35.6	Self-Service Launderette: . . . . .No
Draft (ft/m): 23.6/7.2	Cabins (outside view): 587	Dedicated Cinema/Seats: . . . . .No
Propulsion/Propellers: . . . . .diesel	Cabins (interior/no view): 165	Library: . . . . .Yes
(19,960kW)/2	Cabins (for one person): 0	

BERLITZ'S OVERALL SCORE: 1,344 (OUT OF A POSSIBLE 2,000 POINTS)

OVERVIEW. *Pacific Dream,* the first brand-new ship ordered by original owners Celebrity Cruises, is a fairly contemporary ship, with sharp angles that are softened by an all-white exterior and large logo. There is a good amount of open deck space – although most of it is crammed with sunloungers – and one good-sized swimming pool for adults, plus a splash pool for children. The ship had an extensive $23 million refit in 2005, when more cabins and balconies were added, and was refurbished further in 2009 when it was transferred from Island Cruises to Pullmantur Cruises.

Inside, the ship has good passenger flow. The public rooms, including several lounges and bars, are quite spacious and many have high ceilings. There is a good-sized Monte Carlo casino, and duty-free shops for jewelry, liquor, and perfumes. The decor is fresh and upbeat, with plenty of color, and wood paneling creates a warm ambiance. A two-deck-high lobby, where the reception desk is located, has a contemporary yet "retro" feel to it. Other rooms include three internet-connect centers – located on both upper and lower levels of the showlounge – card game room, meeting room, and an enclosed photo gallery.

Doors to public restrooms and the outdoor decks are heavy, and the plain public restrooms need brighter decor. Background music is played almost everywhere inside the ship and on deck around the pool, making it difficult to find quiet spots to relax, chill out and simply read a book.

The onboard currency is the euro. This is all-inclusive cruising, so no further tipping is needed.

SUITABLE FOR: *Pacific Dream* is best suited to Spanish-

BERLITZ'S RATINGS

	Possible	Achieved
Ship	500	371
Accommodation	200	147
Food	400	234
Service	400	264
Entertainment	100	63
Cruise	400	265

speaking adult couples, singles and families with children seeking a large contemporary ship, with decent food and service from a well-trained crew.

ACCOMMODATION. There are 15 different price grades, including outside-view suites and cabins, and interior (no view) cabins, but even the smallest cabin is quite spacious and well appointed. The price will depend on the grade, size and location – the higher the deck, the higher the cost. Several outside view cabins have lifeboat-obstructed views. Strangely, cabin numbers are the opposite of normal maritime tradition which dictates that even-numbered cabins are on the port, or left side of the ship – but here they are on the starboard, or right side.

Standard Cabins: All standard outside-view and interior (no view) cabins have good-quality fittings with wood accenting, are tastefully decorated and of an above-average size, with an excellent amount of closet and drawer space, and reasonable insulation between cabin, depending on the location. All have twin beds that convert to a queen-sized bed, and a good amount of closet and drawer space. The bathrooms have a generous shower area, although the bathroom towels are a little small, as is storage space for personal toiletries. The lowest-grade outside-view cabins have a porthole, but all others have picture windows.

Suites: Located on Platinum Deck (Deck 11), these two suites have a private balcony. The suites have a separate bedroom with European duvet, lounge with sofa bed and audio-visual control center. The bathroom is large and comes with a whirlpool tub and an integral shower.

Junior Suites: Although tastefully furnished, these are, in reality, little larger than standard outside-view cabins. They do, however, have a generous amount of drawer and other storage space, separate sleeping area plus a lounge area, and large bathrooms.

CUISINE. The Condesa Restaurant, the main dining room, is set on a single level, but its central section, which houses the self-serve buffet counters and food islands, is raised. It is large, yet there is also a sense of intimacy; there are tables for two, four, six or eight, and open seatings. The chairs do not have armrests, due to space limitations.

The wine list is decent enough, and includes many Spanish and South American wines, with prices that provide quite good value for money.

The Buffet Panorama is the place for al fresco, bistro-like eating, and is open 24 hours a day – although, as in most buffets, hot food items are seldom hot. The eatery extends outdoors alfresco-style with The Grill, for fast-food items. The stone-white Plaza Café, which may remind you of a Greek plaza, is the place for informal coffees and pastries and is a great place to see and be seen – although, with few soft furnishings, it can be pretty noisy at times.

ENTERTAINMENT. The two-level Broadway Showlounge is a two-deck high room that can double as a movie theater; it has side balconies on the upper level, and good sightlines from most seats. The room has a large stage (for this size of ship), decent lighting and sound equipment, and shows are aimed at a general family audience.

A resident troupe of young, enthusiastic singer/dancers provide the low-budget revue-style amateurish "shows", with weak prerecorded tracks but lots of color. Cabaret acts are also presented.

There is a main ship's band and several small musical units and pianists to provide live music for dancing and listening in the bars and lounges. In addition, a throbbing Zoom Discotheque is provided for the hearing-impaired disco set.

SPA/FITNESS. A Fitness Center is located aft of the funnel. The facilities include a gymnasium with ocean views and the high-tech muscle-pump equipment, an exercise area, several therapy treatment rooms, and men's/women's sauna.

Pacific Pearl
★★★ +

Size:	.Large Resort Ship	Passenger Decks:	.12	Cabins (wheelchair accessible):	.8
Tonnage:	.63,524	Total Crew:	.514	Wheelchair accessibility	.Good
Lifestyle:	.Standard	Passengers		Cabin Current:	.220 volts
Cruise Line:	.P&O Cruises (Australia)	(lower beds/all berths):	.1,624/1,692	Elevators:	.9
Former Names:	.Ocean Village, Arcadia,	Passenger Space Ratio		Casino (gaming tables):	.Yes
	Star Princess, FairMajesty	(lower beds/all berths):	.39.1/37.5	Slot Machines:	.Yes
Builder:	Chantiers de L'Atlantique (France)	Crew/Passenger Ratio		Swimming Pools (outdoors):	.3
Original Cost:	.$200 million	(lower beds/all berths):	.3.1/3.2	Swimming Pools (indoors):	.0
Entered Service:	.Mar 1987/May 2010	Cabins (total):	.812	Whirlpools:	.4
Registry:	.Great Britain	Size Range (sq ft/m):	.148.0–538.2/	Self-Service Launderette:	.Yes
Length (ft/m):	.810.3/247.00		13.7–50.0	Dedicated Cinema/Seats:	.Yes/205
Beam (ft/m):	.105.6/32.20	Cabins (outside view):	.622	Library:	.No
Draft (ft/m):	.26.9/8.20	Cabins (interior/no view):	.190		
Propulsion/Propellers:	.diesel-electric	Cabins (for one person):	.0		
	(39,000kW)/2	Cabins (with private balcony):	.64		

BERLITZ'S OVERALL SCORE: 1,364 OUT OF A POSSIBLE 2,000 POINTS

OVERVIEW. *Pacific Pearl* was originally designed and built for Sitmar Cruises, a company absorbed into Princess Cruises in 1988 before the ship was completed.

After a refurbishment that brightened the interior passageways, public rooms and dining spots, the former *Arcadia* morphed into *Ocean Village* in 2003, and became a trendy ship designed for younger couples and families who wanted to take a cruise, but didn't want the sedentary "eat when we tell you to and relax" image typical of traditional cruise ships. During that 2003 refit, several new cabins were added, although the overall number of crew was reduced because not so many were needed for this more casual style of cruising, particularly in the food service areas. The casino was also relocated, displacing the library, and the former casino became an internet center/bar. In 2010, the ship was transferred to P&O Cruises (Australia), to become *Pacific Pearl* for Australasian passengers.

Pacific Pearl is a well proportioned ship, with a decent amount of open deck and sunbathing space. On the open leisure deck are two pools, one with sloping steps, the other with vertical steps, and one has a sit-in bar. The aft pool will probably be used by families with children. Four hot tubs sit on a raised platform, and two shower cubicles stand adjacent to a poolside Splash Bar.

The ship's interiors are upbeat and trendy in a high-street sort of fashion with decor by the designers who did a great job with the ships of AIDA Cruises, which also belongs to the Carnival Corporation. But they also include a few items that have a link with the past, such as the art deco stainless steel balustrades and the soulless stainless steel elevators.

BERLITZ'S RATINGS		
	Possible	Achieved
Ship	500	356
Accommodation	200	138
Food	400	249
Service	400	273
Entertainment	100	74
Cruise	400	274

There aren't a lot of public rooms to play in, although one nice feature is the fact that the public rooms do have ceilings that are higher than average for contemporary cruise ships.

The focal point of the interior is a three-deck-high foyer, highlighted by a large blue and yellow painted (it's actually stainless steel underneath) kinetic sculpture resembling a Swiss Army knife (its blades move slowly) that brings one's attention to a multi-deck horseshoe-shaped staircase. A domed observation lounge, the Dome, sits atop the ship, forward of the mast. It is a restful spot for cocktails; at night it turns into a night-spot/discotheque with a sunken dance floor.

For retail therapy, several shops are clustered around the second and third levels of the three-deck high atrium lobby, plus a dedicated cinema. Other facilities include a casino, aft of the upper level of the two-deck high showlounge, The Oval lounge/bar (good for sports fans), Connexions Bar (for adult-only comedy, and karaoke), and the Blue Bar, a more traditional drinking lounge.

Families should enjoy the children's facilities, which are extensive. There is an indoor play area (Turtle Cove for 3–6 year olds, and Shark Shack for 7–10 years olds) located at the aft end of the ship, while the exterior aft deck has a paddling pool and games area. Teenagers have their own area, the Gaming Room.

The vacation includes a variety of active sports such as mountain biking, abseiling, jet skiing, jeep safaris, quad biking, parasailing, helicopter flight-seeing, and snorkeling, all at extra cost. The ship carries a "fleet" of mountain bikes. Both active and passive cruising, therefore, are on offer. In marketing terms, this ship and dress-down onboard product is designed for informal cruising.

It's a pity there is no full walk-around promenade deck outdoors – open port and starboard walking areas stretch only partly along the sides. There is no library. The elevators have a "London Underground" voice that intones "mind the doors." The onboard currency is the Australian dollar. Note that duty- and tax-free shopping is not available on Australian coastal cruises, except Queensland cruises that take in Willis Island.

SUITABLE FOR: *Pacific Pearl* is best suited to young couples and singles of all ages, families with children and teenagers, who like to mingle in a large ship setting with plenty of life, music and entertainment for everyone, with food that is quantity rather than quality, delivered with friendly service that lacks polish, at an attractive price.

ACCOMMODATION. There are four basic types, in 14 different price grades, the price depending on grade, location and size. These include two grades of suites: 36 suites with private balcony and bathtub, plus separate shower enclosure, two suites with shower, but no balcony. There are also 28 suites with private balcony, and shower. All other accommodation consists of standard outside-view and interior (no view) grade cabins, which are of a decent size. If you like to fall asleep with soft music playing, however, note that because music is available only through the TV set, you can't access any of the music channels without having a TV picture on.

Standard Outside-view/Interior (No View) Cabins: All are equipped with twin beds that can, in most cases, be placed together to form a queen-sized bed. All have a good amount of storage space, including wooden drawer units, plus some under-bed space for luggage, and a walk-in (open) closet. A direct dial telephone is provided. However, the sound insulation between cabins is quite poor – TV sound late at night can be particularly irritating, as can loud children, or fellow passengers banging drawers. A number of cabins also have third- and fourth person berths – good for families with children, but the drawer and storage space becomes tight, and there is only one personal safe.

The bathrooms are of a modular design, and are of quite a decent size, with good shower enclosures, and a retractable clothesline. None have tubs, except in one of the grades designated as suites, as the ship was originally built for American passengers, who prefer showers to baths. Soap is provided, and a soap/ shampoo dispenser is fitted into the shower enclosure, although there is no conditioner. Coffee and tea making facilities are provided in all cabins.

CUISINE. The dining concept is simple: meals are taken in a self-serve buffet style setting, so you can dress as casually as you like. To this end, there are several dining spots, including two large self-serve buffet restaurants (Plantation, and Waterfront), a bistro, La Luna pizzeria on deck for lunch or dinner (there is a cover charge at night, when reservations are needed). All dining venues are non-smoking.

Plantation, located high up in the ship, has great ocean views. The Waterfront also has large ocean-view windows and self-serve buffet display counters. There are plenty of tables, most of which are for four, six or eight persons. Plantation is open 24 hours a day, while the blandly decorated Waterfront has set opening hours, detailed in the daily program. At night, Plantation serves Asian and Oriental themed buffets.

In general, the food is typical of what you would find in a couples-only or family-style holiday village – modern British with a Mediterranean touch – with plenty of choices for families with children. It is straightforward, unfussy and unpretentious, with little use of garnishes. Vegetarian dishes are included daily. The service is warm and light-hearted. Note that if you want bar snacks such as peanuts or crisps, you have to pay extra.

For better quality, freshly prepared food, try Salt Grill, located in one corner on the port side of the Waterfront Restaurant. This dining spot features fine New World cuisine created by celebrity chef Luke Mangan. There's a cover charge, and reservations are needed.

ENTERTAINMENT. The Marquee Theatre is the venue for all of the principal entertainment events. It is a horseshoe-shaped room, with main and balcony levels, and there are adequate sightlines from most of the banquette-style seating, although the sightlines from the front row seats on the upper level are obstructed by the required balcony railing.

There is a wide variety of entertainment, from production shows to cabaret-style acts that may or may not be well-known "names" – lesser artistes, and comedians. There is also live music throughout the many lounges and bars – in fact, there is no bar without music, so sitting down for a quiet drink or two is not an option.

SPA/FITNESS. Facilities include a beauty salon, gymnasium, and the Aqua Wellness/Fitness Center, with a sauna/steam room complex. It is located on the lowest passenger deck, and is not particularly attractive or inviting.

It is wise to book treatments (massages, facials, etc) as soon as possible after you embark, as time slots do fill up quickly aboard large ships such as this. Some exercise classes are free, but most incur a charge.

Pacific Princess
★★★★

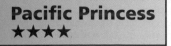 

Size: ....Mid-Size Ship	Passenger Decks: 9	Cabins (wheelchair accessible): 3
Tonnage: 30,277	Total Crew: 373	Wheelchair accessibility ....Good
Lifestyle: ....Standard	Passengers	Cabin Current: ....110 and 220 volts
Cruise Line: ......P&O Cruises Australia/	(lower beds/all berths): 688/826	Elevators: 4
Princess Cruises	Passenger Space Ratio	Casino (gaming tables): ....Yes
Former Names: ....R Three	(lower beds/all berths): 44.1/36.6	Slot Machines: ....Yes
Builder: Chantiers de l'Atlantique (France)	Crew/Passenger Ratio	Swimming Pools (outdoors): 1
Original Cost: ....$150 million	(lower beds/all berths): 1.8/2.2	Swimming Pools (indoors): 0
Entered Service: .....Aug 1999/Nov 2002	Cabins (total): 344	Whirlpools: ......2 (+ 1 thalassotherapy)
Registry: ....Gibraltar	Size Range (sq ft/m): 145.3–968.7/	Self-Service Launderette: ....Yes
Length (ft/m): 593.7/181.0	13.5–90.0	Dedicated Cinema/Seats: ....No
Beam (ft/m): 83.5/25.5	Cabins (outside view): 317	Library: ....Yes
Draft (ft/m): 19.5/6.0	Cabins (interior/no view): 27	
Propulsion/Propellers: .....diesel-electric	Cabins (for one person): 0	
(18,600kW)/2	Cabins (with private balcony): 232	

BERLITZ'S OVERALL SCORE: 1,487 OUT OF A POSSIBLE 2,000 POINTS

OVERVIEW. *Pacific Princess* was originally one of eight almost identical ships ordered and operated by the defunct Renaissance Cruises. It now has an all-white hull instead of black, which makes the ship appear larger, and a large, square-ish funnel. It cruises for part of the year under the Princess Cruises banner in French Polynesia, and six months from Sydney, Australia, under the P&O Cruises brand name.

BERLITZ'S RATINGS		
	Possible	Achieved
Ship	500	406
Accommodation	200	155
Food	400	265
Service	400	287
Entertainment	100	72
Cruise	400	302

A lido deck has a swimming pool, and good sunbathing space, while one of the aft decks has a thalassotherapy pool. A jogging track circles the swimming pool deck (but one deck above). The uppermost outdoors deck includes a golf driving net and shuffleboard court.

The interior decor is quite stunning and elegant, a throwback to ship decor of the ocean liners of the 1920s and '30s, executed in fine taste. This includes detailed ceiling cornices, both real and faux wrought-iron staircase railings, leather- and cherry wood-paneled walls, *trompe l'oeil* ceilings, and rich carpeting in hallways with an Oriental rug-look center section. The overall feel is of an old-world country club. The staircase in the main, two-deck-high foyer recalls the staircase in the 1997 movie *Titanic*.

The public rooms are spread over three decks. The reception hall (lobby) has a staircase with intricate wrought-iron railings. The Nightclub, with forward-facing views, sits high in the ship and has Polynesian-inspired decor and furniture.

There are plenty of bars – including one in the entrance to each restaurant. Perhaps the nicest of all bars and lounges are in the casino bar/lounge that is a beautiful room reminiscent of London's grand hotels and understated gaming clubs. It has an inviting marble fireplace (in fact, there are three such fireplaces aboard) and comfortable sofas and individual chairs. There is also a large Card Room, which incorporates an internet center with eight stations.

The Library is a beautiful, grand Regency-style room, with a fireplace, a high, indented, *trompe l'oeil* ceiling, and an excellent selection of books, plus very comfortable wingback chairs with footstools, and sofas you could sleep on (it's the most relaxing room aboard).

Although there may not be marble bathroom fittings, or caviar and other expensive niceties, the value for money is extremely good, and you have the opportunity to cruise in comfort aboard a mid-sized ship with plenty of dining choices. There's very little entertainment, but it is certainly not needed in the cruise areas featured. *Pacific Princess* and sister ships *Royal Princess* and *Tahitian Princess* are much more about relaxation than the larger ships in the Princess Cruises fleet, and would make good child-free vessels.

As with all Princess Cruises ships, 15% is added to all bar and spa accounts (drink prices are moderate, but beer prices are high), and a standard gratuity (about $10 per person, per day) is automatically added to onboard accounts – if you think this is too much and want to reduce the amount, you'll need to go to the reception desk to do so.

There is no walk-around promenade deck outdoors (there is, however, a small jogging track around the perimeter of the swimming pool, and port and starboard side decks), and no wooden decks outdoors (instead, they are covered by Bollidt, a sand-colored rubberized material). There is no sauna. The room service menu is extremely limited. Stairways, although carpeted, are tinny. In order to keep the prices low, often the air routing to get to/from your ship is not the most direct.

There is a charge – tokens must be obtained from the reception desk – for using the machines in the self-service launderette. A change machine in the launderette itself would be more user-friendly.

ACCOMMODATION. There is a variety of about eight different cabin types to choose from. The price will depend on the grade, location and size you choose.

All of the standard interior (no view) and outside-view cabins are extremely compact units, and extremely tight for two persons – especially for cruises longer than seven days. Cabins have twin beds (or queen-size bed), with good under-bed storage areas, personal safe, vanity desk with large mirror, good closet and drawer space (in rich, dark woods), and bathrobe. Color TVs carry a major news channel (where obtainable), plus a sports channel and several round-the-clock movie channels. The bathrooms, which have tiled floors and plain walls, are compact, standard units, and include a shower enclosure with a removable, strong hand-held shower unit, hairdryer, 100% cotton towels, toiletries storage shelves and a retractable clothesline.

The suites/cabins that have private balconies (66 percent of all suites/cabins, or 73 percent of all outside view suites/cabins) have partial, and not full, balcony partitions, sliding glass doors, and, due to good design and layout, only 14 cabins on Deck 6 have lifeboat-obstructed views. The balcony floor is covered in thick plastic matting – teak would be nicer – and some awful plastic furniture.

Mini-Suites: The 52 accommodation units designated as mini-suites, are in reality simply larger cabins than the standard varieties, as the sleeping and lounge areas are not divided. While not overly large, the bathrooms have a good-sized bathtub and ample space for storing personal toiletry items. The living area has a refrigerated mini-bar, lounge area with breakfast table, and a balcony with two plastic chairs and a table.

Owner's Suites: The 10 Owner's Suites are the most spacious accommodation, and are fine, large living spaces located in the forward-most and aft-most sections of the accommodation decks (particularly nice are those that overlook the stern, on Deck 6, 7 and 8). They have more extensive balconies that really are private and cannot be overlooked by anyone from the decks above. There is an entrance foyer, living room, bedroom (the bed faces the sea, which can be seen through the floor-to-ceiling windows and sliding glass door), CD player, bathroom with Jacuzzi bathtub, as well as a small guest bathroom.

CUISINE. There are four different dining spots: three restaurants and one casual self-serve buffet:

● **The Club Restaurant** has 338 seats (all chairs have armrests), and includes a large raised central section. There are large ocean-view windows on three sides, and some prime tables that overlook the stern, as well as a small bandstand for occasional live dinner music. However, the noise level can be high, owing to the single-deck-height ceiling.

● **Sabatini's Trattoria** is an Italian restaurant, with 96 seats (all chairs have armrests), windows along two sides,

and a set *bellissima* three-hour "degustation" menu. The cover charge is $15 per person.

● **The Sterling Steakhouse** is an "American steak house" which has a good selection of large, prime steaks and other meats. It has 98 comfortable seats (all chairs have armrests), and windows along two sides. There's a set menu, together with added daily chef's specials. The cover charge is $8 per person.

● **The Lido Cafe** has seating for 154 indoors and 186 outdoors (with white plastic patio furniture). It is open for breakfast, lunch and casual dinners. It is the ship's self-serve buffet restaurant (open 24 hours a day), and has a small pizzeria and grill.

All restaurants have open-seating dining, so you dine when you want, although reservations are necessary for Sabatini's Trattoria and Sterling Steakhouse, where there are mostly tables for four or six (there are few tables for two). In addition, there is a Poolside Grill and Bar for those fast-food items provided for on-deck munching.

All suites/cabins located at the stern of the ship may suffer from vibration and noise, particularly when the ship is proceeding at or close to full speed, or maneuvering in port.

ENTERTAINMENT. The 345-seat Cabaret Lounge, located in the forward part of the ship on Deck 5, is the main venue for entertainment events and some social functions. The single-level room has a stage, and circular hardwood dance floor with adjacent banquette and individual tub chair seating, and raised sections on port and starboard sides. It is not a large room, and not really designed for production shows, so cabaret acts and local entertainment form the main focus, with mini-revue style shows with colorful costumes, presented by a troupe of resident singer/dancers in a potted version of what you might experience aboard the large ships of Princess Cruises. Inevitably, art auctions and bingo are pushed almost daily.

The ship carries a band, small musical units, and solo entertaining pianists to provide live music for shows and dancing in the lounges and bars before and after dinner.

SPA/FITNESS. Facilities, which are located in the forward part of the ship on a high deck (Deck 9) consist of a gymnasium (with ocean view windows) with some high-tech muscle-toning equipment and treadmills, steam rooms (no sauna) and changing areas for men and women, and a beauty salon with ocean view windows.

The spa is operated by Steiner, a specialist concession whose retail products will be pushed. Some fitness classes are free (Stepexpress, Power Walk, Total Body Conditioning, Xpress Circuit are examples), while some, such as yoga and kick-boxing, cost extra. Massage (including exotic massages such as Aroma Stone massage, Chakra Balancing massage and other well-being massages), facials, pedicures, and beauty salon treatments cost extra – massage, for example, is about $2 per minute, plus gratuity.

● **For more extensive general information about the Princess Cruises experience, see pages 148–51.**

Pacific Sun
★★★

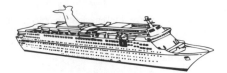

Size:	Mid-Size Ship	Passenger Decks:	.9	Cabins (with private balcony):	.10
Tonnage:	.47,262	Total Crew:	.670	Cabins (wheelchair accessible):	.14
Lifestyle:	.Standard	Passengers		Wheelchair accessibility	.Fair
Cruise Line:	.P&O Cruises (Australia)	(lower beds/all berths):	.1,486/1,896	Cabin Current:	.110 volts
Former Names:	.Jubilee	Passenger Space Ratio		Elevators:	.8
Builder:	.Kockums (Sweden)	(lower beds/all berths):	.31.8/24.9	Casino (gaming tables):	.Yes
Original Cost:	.$134 million	Crew/Passenger Ratio		Slot Machines:	.Yes
Entered Service:	.July 1986/Nov 2004	(lower beds/all berths):	.2.2/2.8	Swimming Pools (outdoors):	.3
Registry:	.The Bahamas	Cabins (total):	.743	Swimming Pools (indoors):	.0
Length (ft/m):	.733.0/223.4	Size Range (sq ft/m):	.182.9–419.8/	Whirlpools:	.2
Beam (ft/m):	.92.5/28.2		17.0–39.0	Self-Service Launderette:	.Yes
Draft (ft/m):	.24.7/7.5	Cabins (outside view):	.453	Dedicated Cinema/Seats:	.No
Propulsion/Propellers:	.diesel	Cabins (interior/no view):	.290	Library:	.Yes
	(23,520 kW)/2	Cabins (for one person):	.0		

BERLITZ'S OVERALL SCORE: 1,172 OUT OF A POSSIBLE 2,000 POINTS

OVERVIEW. Formerly *Jubilee*, the third new-build ordered by Carnival Cruise Lines, this ship has a bold, forthright, angular all-white profile, short bows, and a slim funnel. In 2004, it was transferred to P&O Cruises (Australia), and refurbished to provide passenger facilities for year-round cruises from Australia and New Zealand. The ship was renamed *Pacific Sun* by the Australian swimming star Lisa Curry-Kenny.

The ship has a youthful, sporty image. There is a decent amount of sunbathing space outdoors, and one of the two swimming pools has a twisting, two-deck high controlled water slide that empties you into it. The top deck is now an adults-only sanctuary area.

Inside the ship, most of the public rooms are arranged on one deck (Atlantic Deck), making for easy-access passenger flow. A double-wide indoor promenade, Park Lane, acts as a boulevard, off which a variety of bars and lounges and other public rooms are located. The decor consists of contemporary colors in all the public rooms (the rooms themselves were not changed that much during the recent refurbishment) except for the rather more elegant Churchill's Library, a decent place to sit and read, or connect to the internet (watch out for the knights in suits of armor). A large Sporting Club Casino (with gaming tables for blackjack, roulette, pokies, and lots of slot machines) provides almost round-the-clock action.

This ship lays on constant entertainment and activities designed for passenger participation in a party-like setting, and is a floating playground for young, active adults who enjoy constant stimulation, close contact with lots and lots of others, as well as glitz, glamour and gambling. There's plenty for kids to do, too, and facilities (including a chil-

BERLITZ'S RATINGS

	Possible	Achieved
Ship	500	297
Accommodation	200	119
Food	400	233
Service	400	232
Entertainment	100	62
Cruise	400	228

dren's club and activity center) to cater to up to 300 of them.

Pacific Sun, based in Freemantle, is now more than 20 years old, but will provide novice Aussie and Kiwi cruise-goers with a good first-cruise experience in comfortable, but visually busy surroundings. Note that standing in line for embarkation, disembarkation, shore tenders and for self-serve buffet meals is an inevitable aspect of cruising aboard all large ships; this one is no exception. There is no walk-around promenade deck outdoors. Oh, and it's a pity about those ridiculous art auctions – and the same tacky, useless "art" seen aboard so many other cruise ships, particularly those in the Carnival Corporation. But it's all part of "Funship Cruising" in the down-under world.

The onboard currency is the Australian dollar. P&O Australia scrapped automatic tipping from October 2010.

SUITABLE FOR: *Pacific Sun* is best suited to young, and young-at-heart couples, singles and families with children for a first cruise, Australian style, who want a good basic getaway cruise aboard a ship that offers some good drinking places, lots of noise, good cheer, in upbeat surroundings, with friendly service that lacks polish.

ACCOMMODATION. There are several different price categories for ocean-view and interior (no view) cabins (most of which are of the same approximate size), and two categories for suites. The price you pay depends on the deck and location of the accommodation chosen (typically, the higher the deck, the more you pay).

Especially nice are 10 large suites on Verandah Deck (although there are obstructed views from four of them), each of which has a private balcony. Almost all other cabins are relatively spacious units that are neatly appointed, and have attractive, though rather spartan, decor.

The ocean-view cabins have large picture windows. There are many, many interior (no view) cabins, although they are actually quite spacious, and good for anyone on a low budget (however, if this is your first cruise, try to book one of the ocean-view cabins), with two lower beds, small vanity unit, and a reasonable-sized bathroom. Some cabins have additional upper berths, and even rollaway beds – good for families with small children, although space will be extremely limited unless the kids are very, very small.

CUISINE/DINING. There are two no-smoking dining rooms: Burgundy, located midships, and Bordeaux, located aft, with the galley between them. They are quite cramped when full, and extremely noisy – particularly at those tables adjacent to the large waiter stations – and they have low ceilings in their raised center sections. There are tables for four, six or eight (there are no tables for two), and many banquette seats (individual chairs do not have armrests). Window-side tables are for six and are typically also the quietest tables. The decor is bright and extremely colorful and jolly. At night, the elegant setting of Churchill's Library becomes a steakhouse.

The Lido Deck poolside self-serve Outback Bar & Grill offers casual meals. At night, it provides a casual (dress down) alternative to eating in the main dining rooms, serving pasta, steaks, salads and desserts. For casual food there's also a sushi bar and a poolside pizzeria; and New Zealand natural ice cream is served at a counter close by.

ENTERTAINMENT. The Atlantis Showlounge, the principal venue for production shows and major cabaret acts, is two decks high, decorated in high glitz, and has seating on both main and balcony levels. However, pillars obstruct the sight lines on the main level, and railings obstruct sight lines from many seats on the balcony level. In a typical cruise, there will be several production shows, typically with a cast of two lead singers and a clutch of dancers, backed by a live orchestra. The room also doubles as a cinema for big-screen movies. Almost every lounge/bar has live bands and musical units, so there is always plenty of live music happening, mostly in the evenings.

SPA/FITNESS. The Lotus Spa is on the ship's uppermost deck, just aft of the mast, and accessed by the center stairway and lifts. The facility is small by today's standards, but a former gymnasium is now a relaxation area, while a new gymnasium with some high-tech muscle-pumping cardio-vascular machines has views over the ship's stern. There are also changing rooms and saunas for men and women. The beauty salon is located in another spot, just aft of the Showlounge.

Spa/beauty treatments and fitness facilities are operated by Steiner Leisure, a concession, whose young staff will try to sell you Steiner's own-brand beauty products. Some fitness classes are free (Stepexpress, Power Walk, Total Body Conditioning, Xpress Circuit are examples), while some, such as yoga and kick-boxing, cost extra. However, being aboard will give you an opportunity to try some of the more exotic treatments.

Massage, including Aromatherapy massage, Hot Stone massage, Chakra Balancing massage, Asian Lotus ritual (featuring massage with reflexology, reiki and shiatsu massage), deep-tissue sports therapy massage, and other well-being massages, lime and ginger salt glow, wild strawberry back cleanse, and seaweed mud wraps, among others devised to make you feel good (and leave you poorer), facials, pedicures, and beauty salon treatments cost extra.

If you want to book spa and beauty treatments, it is wise to do so as soon after you embark as possible, as the limited number of time slots do fill up quickly. Note that there are few treatments compared to, say the Caribbean ships, because many Australians consider wellbeing treatments rather "namby pamby."

Pacific Venus
★★★★

Size: . . . . .Mid-Size Ship	Passenger Decks: 7	Cabins (wheelchair accessible): 1
Tonnage: .26,518	Total Crew: 220	Wheelchair accessibility . . . . .Fair
Lifestyle: . . . . .Standard	Passengers	Cabin Current: . . . . .110 volts
Cruise Line: . . . . .Venus Cruise	(lower beds/all berths): 476/620	Elevators: 4
Former Names: . . . . .none	Passenger Space Ratio	Casino (gaming tables): . . . . .Yes
Builder: . . . . .Ishikawajima Heavy	(lower beds/all berths): 55.7/42.7	Slot Machines: .3
Industries (Japan)	Crew/Passenger Ratio	Swimming Pools (outdoors): 1
Original Cost: . . . .$114 million	(lower beds/all berths): 2.1/2.8	(+ 1 for children)
(Yen13 billion)	Cabins (total): 238	Swimming Pools (indoors): 0
Entered Service: . . . . .Apr 1998	Size Range (sq ft/m): 164.6–699.6/	Whirlpools: 1
Registry: . . . . .Japan	15.3–65.0	Self-Service Launderette: . . . . .Yes (5)
Length (ft/m): 601.7/183.4	Cabins (outside view): 238	Dedicated Cinema/Seats: Yes/94
Beam (ft/m): 82.0/25.0	Cabins (interior/no view): 0	Library: . . . . .Yes
Draft (ft/m): 21.3/6.5	Cabins (for one person): 0	
Propulsion/Propellers: diesel (13,636 kW)/2	Cabins (with private balcony): 20	

OVERALL SCORE: 1,548 OUT OF A POSSIBLE 2,000 POINTS

OVERVIEW. Venus Cruise is part of Japan Cruise Line, which is itself part of SHK Line Group, a joint venture between the Shin Nohonkai, Hankyu and Kanpu ferry companies (operating more than 20 ferries). There is a decent amount of open deck space aft of the funnel – good for deck sports – while protected sunbathing space is provided around the small swimming poo. All sunloungers have cushioned pads.

The base of the funnel itself is the site of a day/night lounge, which overlooks the swimming pool – it is slightly reminiscent of Royal Caribbean International's funnel-wrapped Viking Crown lounges aboard its first ships. There is plenty of space per passenger. The decor is clean and fresh, with much use of pastel colors and blond woods, giving the interiors a feeling of warmth.

One deck (Deck 7) has a double-width indoor promenade, with high ceiling height, off which are located the dining rooms. The atrium, three decks high, has a crystal chandelier as its focal point, and a white baby grand piano on its lower level, where the Reception Desk is located.

There are special rooms for meetings and conference organizers, for times when the ship is chartered. There is a piano salon with colorful low-back chairs, a large main hall which has a finely sculptured high ceiling and 720 moveable seats and hosts production shows, a 350-seat main lounge for cabaret shows and ballroom dancing, a small movie theater, and a library/writing room and card room. A casino gaming area is located as part of the Top Lounge set at the front of the funnel. There's also a smoking room, Chashitsu (tatami mat) room, karaoke room (for rent) and card room/mah jong room, self-service launderettes on each accommodation deck

BERLITZ'S RATINGS

	Possible	Achieved
Ship	500	395
Accommodation	200	147
Food	400	309
Service	400	316
Entertainment	100	76
Cruise	400	305

(no charge), and two (credit card/coin) public telephone booths.

Overall, this company provides a well-packaged cruise in a ship that has a very comfortable, serene environment. The dress code is relaxed, the onboard currency is the Japanese yen, and no tipping is allowed.

The ship actually features two classes: Salon Class and Standard Class. Salon Class passengers pay more, but get suite-grade accommodation, eat in the Grand Siecle private dining room (it used to be an à la carte restaurant when the ship debuted), and lots of extra goodies and services, including a welcome embarkation basket, more personal toiletries, and priority tickets for shows and shore tenders.

There are few cabins with private balcony. The open walking promenade decks are rubber-coated steel – teak would be more desirable. The ship is often operated under charter to various travel organizations, so drinks may or may not be included in the cruise price; when operated by Venus Cruise, alcoholic beverages are not included.

SUITABLE FOR: *Pacific Venus* is best suited to Japanese-speaking couples and single travelers of mature years who enjoy traveling in very comfortable surroundings, and who enjoy good food and service, all at a moderate cost.

ACCOMMODATION. There are four different types: royal suites, suites, deluxe cabins, state cabins (in four different price grades), and standard cabins. All are located from the uppermost to lowermost decks, respectively. All suites and cabins have an outside view.

The four Royal Suites (named Archaic, Elegant, Modern, and Noble) are decorated in two different styles – one contemporary, one more traditional Japanese style. Each has a private balcony, with sliding door (balcony table and two chairs), an expansive lounge area with large sofa and plush armchairs, coffee table, window-side chairs and drinks table, floor-to-ceiling windows, and a large flat-screen TV set, with separate VCR/DVD unit. There is a separate bedroom, with twin- or queen-sized bed, vanity/writing desk, large walk-in closet with personal safe. Also provided are high-quality binoculars, camera tripod, humidifier, coffee/tea making set, and free minibar set-up. The large bathroom has ocean-view windows, Jacuzzi bathtub, a separate shower enclosure, and his/hers washbasins.

Sixteen other suites also have private balconies (with teak table and two chairs), a good-sized living area with vanity/writing desk, dining table, chair and curved sofa, separate sleeping area, and bathroom with deep tub slightly larger than the Royal suites, and single large sink. There is ample lighted closet and drawer space (two locking drawers instead of a personal safe), and a VCR/DVD unit.

The 20 Deluxe cabins have large picture windows fronted by a large, curtained arch, sleeping area with twin or queen beds, plus a daytime sofa that converts into a third bed.

The "state" cabins, many of which have upper berths for third passengers, are in three price levels, have decor that is best described as basic, with reasonable closet space, but very little drawer space.

The standard cabins are really plain, but can accommodate three persons – useful for families – although the drawer and storage space is a bit tight.

All accommodation grades have a tea drinking set with electric hot water kettle, color TV, telephone, stocked minibar/refrigerator – all items included in the cruise price. Bathrooms have a hairdryer, and lots of Shiseido personal toiletries (particularly in the suites, which include aftershave, hair liquid, hair tonic, skin lotion, body lotion, shampoo, rinse, razor, toothbrush, toothpaste, sewing kit, shower cap, hairbrush, clothes brush and shoe horn). All room service menu items cost extra – this is typical of all Japanese cruise ships – except for Salon-class suite-grade accommodation. All passengers receive a yukata (Japanese-style light cotton robe); suite occupants also get a plush bathrobe, and all accommodation grades have electric, automatic toilets (washlets) with heated seats.

CUISINE. The Primavera Restaurant, the ship's main dining venue, is located aft, with ocean views on three sides, and has a high ceiling. Passengers dine in one seating, and tables are for six, 10 or 12. The food consists of both Japanese and Western items; the menu is varied and the food is attractively presented. For breakfast and lunch it includes a self-serve buffet display, while dinner is typically a fully-served set meal.

A separate intimate 42-seat restaurant, Grand Siècle, is reserved for occupants of suite-grade (Salon Class) accommodation ; it is tastefully decorated in Regency-style, with fine wood-paneling and a detailed, indented ceiling. It has mostly tables for two (with plenty of space for correct service), better quality chopsticks, nori seaweed, and better quality and variety of fine china. Cold and hot towels are provided, and the whole dining experienced is far better than in the Primavera.

ENTERTAINMENT. Le Pacific Main Lounge is the venue for all shipboard entertainment (it also functions as a lecture and activities room during the day). It is a single-level room with seating clustered around a "thrust" stage so that entertainers are in the very midst of their audience.

On most cruises, special featured entertainers are brought on board from ashore (singers, instrumentalists, storytellers, dance champions, and others).

SPA/FITNESS. Spa facilities include male and female Grand Baths, which include two bathing pools and health/cleansing stations, ocean-view windows, a steam room, a gymnasium with ocean-view windows (in a different location just aft of the funnel); and a sauna.

Japanese massage is available, as are hairdressing and barber services in the small salon, located on the lowest passenger-accessible deck of the ship.

Paul Gauguin
★★★★

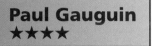

Size:	Small Ship	Passenger Decks:	7	Cabins (with private balcony):	89
Tonnage:	19,200	Total Crew:	215	Cabins (wheelchair accessible):	1
Lifestyle:	Premium	Passengers		Wheelchair accessibility	Fair
Cruise Line:	Paul Gauguin Cruises	(lower beds/all berths):	332/332	Cabin Current:	110 volts
Former Names:	none	Passenger Space Ratio		Elevators:	4
Builder: Chantiers de l'Atlantique (France)		(lower beds/all berths):	57.8/57.8	Casino (gaming tables):	Yes
Original Cost:	$150 million	Crew/Passenger Ratio		Slot Machines:	Yes
Entered Service:	Jan 1998/Jan 2010	(lower beds/all berths):	1.5/1.5	Swimming Pools (outdoors):	1
Registry:	The Bahamas	Cabins (total):	166	Swimming Pools (indoors):	0
Length (ft/m):	513.4/156.50	Size Range (sq ft/m):	200.0–588.0/	Whirlpools:	0
Beam (ft/m):	72.1/22.00		18.5–54.6	Self-Service Launderette:	No
Draft (ft/m):	16.8/5.15	Cabins (outside view):	165	Dedicated Cinema/Seats:	No
Propulsion/Propellers:	diesel-electric	Cabins (interior/no view):	0	Library:	Yes
	(9,000 kW/2	Cabins (for one person):	0		

OVERALL SCORE: 1,547 OUT OF A POSSIBLE 2,000 POINTS

OVERVIEW. Built by a French company specifically to operate in shallow waters, *Paul Gauguin* is now owned (actually under long-term charter) by Pacific Beachcombers of Tahiti, which also own the Intercontinental Tahiti, Intercontinental Bora Bora Le Moana, Intercontinental Bora Bor and Intercontinental Moorea. The ship cruises around French Polynesia and the South Pacific and, while it could carry many more passengers, it is forbidden to do so by French law. It benefited from a $9 million refurbishment in 2009, has a well-balanced, all-white profile, and is topped by a single funnel.

This smart ship also has a retractable aft marina platform, and carries two water skiing boats and two inflatable craft for water sports. Windsurfers, kayaks, plus scuba and snorkeling gear are available for your use; all except scuba gear, are included in the cruise fare.

Inside, there is a pleasant array of public rooms, and both the artwork and the decor have a real French Polynesia look and feel. The interior colors are quite restful, although a trifle bland.

Expert lecturers on Tahiti and Gauguin accompany each cruise, and a Fare (pronounced *foray*) Tahiti Gallery offers books, videos, and other materials on the unique art, history, and culture of the islands. Three original Gauguin sketches are displayed under glass.

Le Casino is where the casino action runs high, the major attraction being the roulette and blackjack gaming tables. The library is pleasant enough, although it could be larger.

The dress code is very relaxed – every day. The standard itinerary means that the ship docks only in Papeete and shore tenders are used in all other ports. There is little

BERLITZ'S RATINGS		
	Possible	Achieved
Ship	500	397
Accommodation	200	169
Food	400	304
Service	400	320
Entertainment	100	71
Cruise	400	286

entertainment, as the ship stays overnight in several ports (so little is needed). The ship's high crew-to-passenger ratio translates to a high level of personalized service. The ship has become a favorite of travelers to these climes, and the quiet, refined atmosphere on board makes it sort of clubby, with passengers getting to know each other easily. Wi-fi spots are provided.

Where the ship really shines is in the provision of a lot of water sports equipment, and its shallow draft allows it to navigate and anchor in lovely little places that larger ships couldn't possibly get to. All in all, it's a delightful cruise and product, and all gratuities to staff are included. The euro is the currency in Tahiti and its islands, as Tahiti is a French territory.

Islands, beaches and watersports are what this ship is good at. Perhaps the best island experience is in Bora Bora. *Paul Gauguin*'s shallow draft means there could be some movement, as the ship is a little high-sided for its size. The spa is very small, and the fitness room is windowless.

SUITABLE FOR: *Paul Gauguin* is best suited to couples and single travelers (typically over 50) who seek specialized itineraries, good regional cuisine and service, with almost no entertainment, all wrapped up in a contemporary ship which can best be described as elegant and quiet in its appointments and comfort levels.

ACCOMMODATION. There are eight suite/cabin grades, priced according to location and size. The outside-view cabins, half of which have private balconies, are nicely equipped, although they are strictly rectangular (and none have more interesting shapes). Most have large windows, except those on the lowest accommodation deck, which have portholes. Each has queen- or twin-sized beds (convertible to queen), and wood-accented cabinetry with rounded edges. A mini-bar/refrigerator (stocked with complimentary soft drinks) DVD player, personal safe, hairdryer and umbrellas are standard.

The marble-look bathrooms are large and pleasing and have a tub as well as a separate shower enclosure. All passengers are provided with 100% cotton bathrobes, and soft drinks and mineral water are included in the cruise price.

The two largest suites have a private balcony at the front and side of the vessel. Although there is a decent amount of in-cabin space, with a beautiful long vanity unit (and plenty of drawer space), the bathrooms are disappointingly small and plain, and too similar to all other standard cabin bathrooms.

Butler service is provided in all accommodation designated as Owners Suite, Grand Suites, Ocean-view "A" and "B" category suites.

CUISINE/DINING. L'Etoile is the name of the main dining room for lunch and dinner, while La Veranda, an alternative dining spot, is open for breakfast, lunch and dinner. Both dining rooms feature "open seating" which means that passengers can choose when they want to dine and with whom. This provides a good opportunity to meet new people for dinner each evening. The chairs have armrests, making it more comfortable for a leisurely mealtime. La Veranda provides dinner by reservation, with alternating French and Italian menus; the French menus are provided by Jean-Pierre Vigato, a two-star Michelin chef with his own restaurant ("Apicius") in Paris.

The dining operation is well orchestrated, with cuisine and service of a high standard. All non-alcoholic beverages, plus select wines and liquor, are included in the fare, while premium wines are available at extra cost.

An outdoor bistro provides informal cafe fare on deck aft of the pool, while the Connoisseur Club offers a luxurious retreat for cigars, cognacs, and wine tasting.

ENTERTAINMENT. Le Grand Salon is the venue for shows and cabaret acts. It is a single-level room, and seating is in banquette and individual tub chairs. Sightlines are quite good from most seats, although there are some obstructions. Don't expect lavish production shows (there aren't any), as the main entertainment consists of local Polynesian shows brought on board from ashore, plus the odd cabaret act. A new piano lounge was added in the 2006 refit.

SPA/FITNESS. The Spa, on Deck 6 in the ship's center, is the name of the spa/wellbeing space. It includes a fitness centre with muscle-pumping and body toning equipment, a steam room, several treatment rooms, changing area (very small), and beauty salon. The Spa/beauty services and staff are provided by Algotherm. There is no sauna, but use of the steam room is complimentary. Body pampering treatments include various massages, aromatherapy facials, manicures, pedicures, and hairdressing services.

THE TRUTH ABOUT TONNAGE

The International Convention of Tonnage Measurement of Ships, was introduced in 1969, implemented in 1982, and actually came into force on July 18, 1994. It required ship owners to re-measure the (former) gross register tonnage of their vessels (1 grt = 100 cubic ft of enclosed space/2.8 cubic meters).

The Convention states: "The gross tonnage (GT) of a ship shall be determined by the following formula: GT-K1V where V = Total volume of all enclosed spaces of the ship in cubic meters; and K1 = 0.2+0.02 log 10 V..." Actually, measurements of gross and net tonnage are really dimensionless numbers. So the word "ton" is no longer used in maritime terminology.

Tonnage (gt) was originally a key measure of the carrying capacity of a ship was *not* how much it weighed,

but how much space it had available for cargo. A common cargo was wine, which was shipped in large casks called "tuns." A tun held 8 barrels of wine or about 242 gallons. Soon they started measuring the cargo area based on how many of these boxes or tuns could be fit in. Thus, a ship that could transport 8,000 barrels of wine was known as a 1,000 tun ship. "Tun" evolved into "ton" and then into "Gross Registered Ton." The clipper (tall) ships in the mid-1800s ranged in size from 400 grt to 4,000 grt.

The advent of steel hulled ships and steam engines allowed the building of larger vessels, with, for example, the *Titanic* measuring what was then a large 48,000 gt.

What is "displacement tonnage?"

Displacement tonnage is an estimate of the weight of a merchant vessel's structure to the nearest 100 long tons or metric tons (they are not quite the same); or volumetric tonnage (measured by volume).

How does a giant ship stay afloat?

As the Greek scientist Archimedes (c.287–212BC) discovered, an object will float provided its weight is equal to or less than the amount of water it displaces.

Large resort ships such as *Oasis of the Seas*, which has a tonnage of 222,900, displace a lot of water, although they are essentially hollow, because most of the internal weight, such as engines and propulsion machinery, is placed at the bottom of the hull. This allows the ship to remain upright, even though many decks tower above the waterline.

Pearl Mist
NOT YET RATED

Size:.................... Small Ship	Total Crew: 60	Cabins (wheelchair accessible):...... 4
Tonnage:................. 8,700 tons	Passengers	Wheelchair accessibility ....None
Lifestyle:................. Standard	(lower beds/all berths): 214/214	Cabin Voltage:.............. 110 volts
Cruise Line:........ Pearl Seas Cruises	Passenger Space Ratio	Elevators: 1
Former Names:................. none	(lower beds/all berths): 40.6/40.6	Casino (gaming tables): .... No
Builder:..... Irving Shipyards (Canada)	Crew/Passenger Ratio	Slot Machines: .... No
Original Cost:............ $50 million	(lower beds/all berths): 3.5/3.5	Swimming Pools (outdoors):......... 0
Entered Service:........... Jan 2011	Cabins (total): 105	Swimming Pools (indoors):.......... 0
Registry:........... Marshall Islands	Size Range (sq ft/m):..... 302.0–580.0/	Whirlpools: 1
Length (ft/m):........... 330.0/100.5	28.0–53.8	Self-Service Launderette:.......... No
Beam (ft/m):............... 55.7/17.0	Cabins (outside view):............ 108	Dedicated Cinema/Seats:.......... No
Draft (ft/m): 10.0/3.1	Cabins (interior/no view): 0	Library: .... Yes
Propulsion/Propellers: diesel (6,300hp)/2	Cabins (for one person): 0	
Passenger Decks:................. 6	Cabins (with private balcony):...... 108	

OVERALL SCORE: NYR OUT OF A POSSIBLE 2,000 POINTS

OVERVIEW. This is Pearl Seas Cruises' first ship (delivered over a year late by Canada's Irving Shipyards), designed and built for international ocean-going cruises. Pearl Seas Cruises is an offshore outgrowth of the all-American company, American Cruise Lines, based in Connecticut, and the onboard product is expected to be an extension of the ACL onboard product. But don't confuse the USA's Pearl Seas Cruises with Australia's Pearl Sea Cruises.

Pearl Mist is designed to be a much more comfortable and upscale vessel than the ships belonging to American Cruise Lines. It has greater speed, the latest navigational technology, and better onboard facilities and service. It is meant to appeal to passengers who enjoy discovering ports in the company of like-minded people, away from the hunting grounds of crowded large resort ships.

Public rooms include two principal lounges, the Pacific Lounge, and the Atlantic Lounge; one is above, and the other is below the navigation bridge.

Other public rooms include a small Coral Lounge located just behind the mast; a library, and two small midship lounges – one named Caribbean lounge. A single elevator goes to all decks, including the outdoor sun deck.

The ship cruises in the east coast waters of the USA and Canada during the summer season and in the Caribbean during the winter season, from St. Martin. The onboard currency is the US dollar. Gratuities are extra.

BERLITZ'S RATINGS

	Possible	Achieved
Ship	500	NYR
Accommodation	200	NYR
Food	400	NYR
Service	400	NYR
Entertainment	100	NYR
Cruise	400	NYR

SUITABLE FOR: *Pearl Mist* is best suited to couples and single travelers of mature years sharing a cabin and wishing to cruise in an all-American environment aboard a small ship where the destinations are a more important consideration than food, service, or entertainment.

ACCOMMODATION. There are seven cabin price grades, but all accommodation grades are outside view suites/cabins with private balcony, although the balcony is not exactly what you would call large. All feature twin beds that convert to a king-sized bed, with high-quality bed linens; bathrooms have a walk-in shower. Some cabins can be interconnected, so a couple can have a bathroom each.

CUISINE. The single dining room, at the stern of the ship, accommodates all passengers in a single, open seating, so you can sit where and with whom you want. Complimentary cocktails and hors d'oeuvres are offered before dinner in the lounges.

ENTERTAINMENT. The Main Lounge is the venue for evening entertainment, lectures, and recaps. Any entertainment will be brought on board from ashore in the ports of call.

SPA/FITNESS. The small spa has a beauty salon. There is also one hot tub (Jacuzzi) on deck.

Pride of America
★★★ +

Size: . . . . .Large Resort Ship	Passenger Decks: 11	Cabins (wheelchair accessible): 22
Tonnage: .81,000	Total Crew: .1,000	Wheelchair accessibility . . . . .Good
Lifestyle: . . . . .Standard	Passengers	Cabin Current: . . . . .110 volts
Cruise Line: . . . . . .Norwegian Cruise Line	(lower beds/all berths): 2,144/2,440	Elevators: 10
Former Names: . . . . .none	Passenger Space Ratio	Casino (gaming tables): . . . . .Yes
Builder: . . . . . .Ingalls Shipbuilding (USA)/	(lower beds/all berths): 37.7/33.1	Slot Machines: . . . . .Yes
Lloyd Werft (Germany)	Crew/Passenger Ratio	Swimming Pools (outdoors): 2
Original Cost: . . . .$450 million	(lower beds/all berths): 2.1/2.4	Swimming Pools (indoors): 0
Entered Service: . . . . .July 2005	Cabins (total): 1,072	Whirlpools: . . . . .n/a
Registry: . . . . .USA	Size Range (sq ft/m): 129.1–1,377.8/	Self-Service Launderette: . . . . .No
Length (ft/m): 921.9/281.0	12.0–128.0	Dedicated Cinema/Seats: . . . . .No
Beam (ft/m): 106.6/32.2	Cabins (outside view): 843	Library: . . . . .Yes
Draft (ft/m): 26.25/8.0	Cabins (interior/no view): 229	
Propulsion/Propellers: . . . .diesel-electric/	Cabins (for one person): 0	
2 pods (17MW each)	Cabins (with private balcony): 665	

BERLITZ'S OVERALL SCORE: 1,268 OUT OF A POSSIBLE 2,000 POINTS

OVERVIEW. *Pride of America,* which sank during its dockside during construction at Germany's Lloyd Werft, sails on inter-island cruises, focusing on the islands of Hawaii. The 85,850 sq.-ft./7,975 sq.-meter open deck space includes a sunning/ pool deck inspired by Miami's South Beach (think Ocean Drive/Lincoln Mall) and Art Deco area.

The stunning interior design of the ship is modeled after a "Best of America" theme (all the public rooms are named after famous Americans). Facilities include the Capitol Atrium (a lobby spanning eight decks and said to be inspired by the Capitol Building and White House), a large casino, a conservatory complete with tropical landscaped garden and live exotic birds, Soho Art Gallery (holding art auctions), Washington Library, and Newbury Shopping Center. The Rascal's Kids Center and Kids' Pool is a supervised facility designed around a theme of America's native animals.

There are extensive meeting and conference facilities (US corporations qualify for tax-deductible meetings expenses as the ship sails under the US flag, at least until January 2012), with six dedicated meetings rooms ranging in size from boardrooms for 10 people to an auditorium for up to 250. The ship has a mainly Hawaiian crew, and you can expect lots of Americana.

The on-board currency is the US dollar. A (non-changeable) service charge (this is not a gratuity) for staff is automatically added to your onboard account at $10 per person ($5 for children aged 3–12) per day; this is pooled for all crew and provides payment when they are on vacation. You will also be expected to also provide gratuities. In addition, a 15% gratuity, plus Hawaii sales tax (this is a US

BERLITZ'S RATINGS

	Possible	Achieved
Ship	500	383
Accommodation	200	149
Food	400	219
Service	400	205
Entertainment	100	74
Cruise	400	238

flag ship) is added to all bar and spa treatment accounts.

Don't expect good service – the majority of the crew simply don't cut it. Although the islands are pleasant, a cruise aboard this ship is an exercise in patience testing, and frustration. *Pride of America* is a good example of how not to run a cruise ship, and cabin cleanliness, in particular, is poor.

SUITABLE FOR: The ship will suit first-time young couples, single passengers, children and teenagers who enjoy big city nightlife, who want contemporary, upbeat surroundings, and the latest in facilities, plenty of entertainment lounges and bars and high-tech sophistication – all in one neat, well packaged cruise vacation, with plenty of music, constant activity and entertainment.

ACCOMMODATION. Of the 950 cabins, 77% have outside views, while 64% of these have private balconies, and there are also a large number of family-friendly interconnecting cabins. Many cabins have third/fourth upper berths, some family-special cabins can accommodate as many as six. Some suites have king-sized beds, while most cabins have twin beds that can be placed together to make a queen-sized bed. A number of cabins are wheelchair-accessible, while some cabins are equipped for the hearing-impaired.

Grand Suite: The largest accommodation is in the Grand Suite, with approximately 1,400 sq. ft./130 sq. meters of living space. The suite is located high atop the ship forward of the sun deck and offers sweeping views from its wrap-around outdoor terrace. It has a large living room with Bang & Olufsen entertainment center (television, DVD/CD player with library), computer internet-connect access, and wet bar, separate dining room with dining table and six chairs (butler included). The master bedroom includes a king-sized bed, large bathroom, with whirlpool tub and separate shower enclosure; dressing area with flat-screen TV, and walk-in closet. At the entrance to the suite is a guest powder room. There is a wrap-around verandah, and facilities include open-air dining and a hot tub), plus a private sunbathing and entertainment area.

Owner's Suite: There are five, each approximately 870 sq.ft./80 sq. meters and named after indigenous flowers in Hawaii (Bird of Paradise, Gardenia, Orchid, Plumeria). Each has a bedroom with king-sized bed, walk-in closet, dressing area, separate living room with Bang & Olufsen entertainment center, and computer internet-connect access. The bathroom has a whirlpool tub and separate shower enclosure. There is also a large private balcony with hot tub, outdoor dining facilities and sun beds.

Deluxe Penthouse Suites: There are six units, each measuring approximately 735 sq.ft./68 sq. meters. They have a separate bedroom with king-size bed and walk-in closet; the bathroom has a whirlpool tub, separate shower enclosure, two washbasins, dressing area; living room with Bang & Olufsen entertainment center, wet bar, and private balcony.

Penthouse Suites: There are 28, each measuring 504–585 sq.ft/47–54.5 sq. meters. These have a separate bedroom with king-size bed and walk-in closet; the bathroom has a whirlpool tub, separate shower enclosure, two washbasins, dressing area; living room with Bang & Olufsen entertainment center, wet bar, and private balcony.

Family Suites: There are eight, each measuring approximately 360 sq.ft./33.5 sq. meters. Each has a main bedroom with two twin beds that can be converted to a queen-sized bed, a living room with double sofa bed and entertainment center, separate den with single sofa bed. Another four family "suites" have an interconnecting door between two cabins (thus there are two bathrooms). These four measure 330–380 sq.ft./30.5–35 sq. meters.

Standard Outside View and Interior (No View) Cabins: Outside view cabins have either a window or porthole, depending on location. All cabins have twin beds that can convert into a queen-sized bed, TV, satellite-dial telephone, and personal safe; the bathrooms have a built-in hairdryer.

CUISINE. NCL's ships operate "Freestyle Cruising," which means that there are several restaurants and informal dining spots. You can choose from two main dining rooms, and six other à la carte, informal and casual spots, some of which incur a cover (or portion) charge ($12.50–$17.50 per person). Smoking is banned in all restaurants and food outlets.

Traditional Dining Rooms:
● The 628-seat Skyline Restaurant is the main restaurant, and the decor is inspired by the skyscrapers of the 1930s.
● The 496-seat Liberty Dining Room is the second main restaurant, with two seatings.

Alternative Dining Options:
● The Lone Star Steak House seats 106. This is a contemporary steak house with Texan decor (the artwork includes Houston Space Center, Texas Rangers and Dallas Cowboys).
● China Town is a Pacific Rim/Asian Fusion restaurant that has a sushi/sashimi bar and a Teppanyaki grill room with two tables (food is prepared in front of you with a bit of showmanship) that can accommodate up to 32.
● Jefferson's Bistro, which accommodates 104, is the ship's "signature" restaurant, and features an à la carte menu of classic and nouvelle French cuisine. The decor is inspired by that of Thomas Jefferson's home in Monticello (Thomas Jefferson was the US ambassador to France from 1785 to 1789 before becoming America's third president).
● Little Italy is a casual Italian eatery that serves pasta, pizza and other popular light Italian fare. It has 116 seats.
● Cadillac Diner accommodates 106 (70 indoors, 36 outdoors) and is open 24 hours a day. It has Cadillac seats and a video juke box. There's fast food galore, with hamburgers and hot dogs, fish and chips, potpies and wok dishes.
● Aloha Cafe/Kids Cafe is an indoor/outdoor self-serve buffet-style eatery with a Hawaii theme; there are 322 indoor and 310 outdoor seats. A special section for children has counter tops just the right height, as well as chairs and tables that have been shrunk from adult to a kid-friendly size.

Other indoor eateries and bars include the Napa Wine Bar (wines by the glass), Pink's Champagne and Cigar Bar (inspired by Hawaii's "Pink Palace" Hotel on Waikiki Beach), the Gold Rush pub (karaoke is practiced here; there's also a darts board and bar billiards), and the John Adams Coffee Bar; while outdoor eateries and drinking places include the Key West Bar and Grill, and the Waikiki Bar.

ENTERTAINMENT. The Hollywood Theater, the ship's principal showlounge, seats 840. Large-scale production shows will be featured, together with local Hawaiian shows. There is also a 590-seat cabaret lounge, named the Mardi Gras Lounge, which will typically feature cabaret entertainment (including late-night comedy).

SPA/FITNESS. The Santa Fe Spa and Fitness Center is decorated with artifacts from New Mexico and designed to be a tranquil center for mind and body. The spa is staffed and operated by Mandara Spa (originating in Bali, now headquartered in Hawaii, but owned by Steiner Leisure), and includes Ayurvedic-style treatments. While some fitness classes are free, some – such as yoga, and kick-boxing – typically cost $10 per class.

Massage (including exotic massages such as Hot Stone, Lomi Lomi, and other well-being massages), facials, pedicures, and beauty salon treatments cost extra (massage, for example, costs about $2 per minute, plus gratuity).

● **For more extensive general information on what an NCL cruise is like, see pages 144–7.**

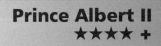

Prince Albert II
★★★★ +

Size:	Boutique Ship	Propulsion/Propellers:	diesel (4,500kw)/2
Tonnage:	6,072	Passenger Decks:	5
Lifestyle:	Premium	Total Crew:	111
Cruise Line:	Silversea Cruises	Passengers:	
Former Names:	World Discoverer, Dream 21,	(lower beds/all berths):	132/158
Baltic Clipper, Sally Clipper, Delfin Star, Delfin		Passenger Space Ratio	
Clipper, World Adventurer, Delfin Clipper		(lower beds/all berths):	46.0/38.4
Builder:	Rauma-Repola (Finland)	Crew/Passenger Ratio:	
Original Cost:	$50 million	(lower beds/all berths):	1.1/1.4
Entered Service:	July 1989/June 2008	Cabins (total):	66
Registry:	The Bahamas	Size Range (sq.ft./m.):	172.2–785.7/16.0–73.0
Length (ft/m):	354.9/108.20	Cabins (outside view):	66
Beam (ft/m):	51.1/15.60	Cabins (interior/no view):	0
Draft (ft/m):	13.1/4.00	Cabins (for one person):	0

Cabins (with private balcony):	6
	+ 14 French balconies
Cabins (wheelchair accessible):	0
Wheelchair accessibility	None
Cabin Current:	110/220 volts
Elevators:	2
Casino (gaming tables):	No
Slot Machines:	No
Swimming Pools (outdoors):	0
Swimming Pools (indoors):	0
Whirlpools:	2
Self-Service Launderette:	No
Movie Theater/Seats:	No
Library:	No

BERLITZ'S OVERALL SCORE: 1,684 OUT OF A POSSIBLE 2,000 POINTS

OVERVIEW. Twin swept-back outboard funnels highlight the semi-smart exterior design of this small specialist 20-year-old expedition cruise ship. It has a dark ice-hardened hull, carries a fleet of eight Zodiac inflatable landing craft for shore landings and exploration, and has one boot washing station (called the "Mud Room," it has six bays).

Silversea Cruises bought the ship in 2007, towed it to Italy from Singapore, where it had been laid up for four years, and had it completely refitted it at the Mariotti shipyard in Genoa. The idea behind the conversion is to take Silversea Cruises passengers to more remote regions of the world, but in style.

The accommodation is located forward, with all public rooms aft, an arrangement that helps keep noise to a minimum in accommodation areas. The interior has many European design elements, including warm color combinations. Public rooms include an observation lounge, large lecture room/cinema with bar, and library/internet center.

This small expedition cruise vessel has many of the creature comforts of much larger vessels. It will provide a very comfortable expedition-style cruise experience in tasteful and elegant surroundings. All passengers receive a pre-cruise amenities package that typically includes a field guide, backpack, carry-on travel bag, and luggage tags.

The ship will specialize in Polar itineraries. An expedition leader, plus other lecturers provide specialized in-depth education about wildlife, geography and other interesting subjects that enrich the expedition cruise experience. The onboard currencies are both the US dollar and the euro.

There is no walk-around promenade deck outdoors – the ship is too small for one.

BERLITZ'S RATINGS		
	Possible	Achieved
Ship	500	411
Accommodation	200	174
Food	400	334
Service	400	334
Entertainment	n/a	n/a
Cruise	500	431

SUITABLE FOR: *Prince Albert II* is best suited to adventurous couples and single travelers of mature years who enjoy nature and wildlife at close range.

ACCOMMODATION. There are six types of accommodation, and 11 price grades. The cabins – quite large for such a small ship – are fitted out to a fairly high standard, with ample closet and drawer space. All cabins have outside views and have twin beds that can convert to a queen-sized bed, TV/DVD unit, telephone, hairdryer, refrigerator, and lockable drawer for valuables.

Although only six suites have a large private balcony (they really are not needed in cold-weather regions), another 14 cabins have glass doors that open onto a few inches of space outdoors. The suites have whirlpool bathtubs. The owner's suite has two rooms, linked by an interconnecting door, to provide a separate lounge, bedroom, and two bathrooms.

The sizes are: Owners Suites (538 sq.ft./50 sq.meters); Medallion Suites (358 sq.ft./33.2 sq.meters); Grand Suites (650 sq.ft./60.3 sq.meters); Silver Suites (430.5 sq.ft./40 sq.meters); Veranda Suites (215 sq.ft./20 sq.meters); Explorer Class (190 sq.ft./27.5 sq.meters); Expedition Suites (430.5 sq.ft./40 sq.meters).

CUISINE. The spacious dining room has pastel-colored decor, and accommodates all passengers in one seating. Casual alfresco bites can be had at the outdoor grill.

ENTERTAINMENT. Daily recaps; after-dinner conversation.

SPA/FITNESS. Facilities include a small gymnasium, sauna, and treatment room (for massage).

Princess Danae
★★★

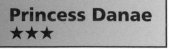

Size:	Small Ship	Propulsion/Propellers:	diesel	Cabins (for one person):	6
Tonnage:	16,531		(9,850 kW)/2	Cabins (with private balcony):	6
Lifestyle:	Standard	Passenger Decks:	7	Cabins (wheelchair accessible):	0
Cruise Line:	Classic International Cruises	Total Crew:	240	Wheelchair accessibility	None
		Passengers		Cabin Current:	220 volts
Former Names:	Baltica, Starlight Express, Danae, Therisos Express, Port Melbourne	(lower beds/all berths):	568/707	Elevators:	2
		Passenger Space Ratio		Casino (gaming tables):	Yes
Builder:	Swan, Hunter (UK)	(lower beds/all berths):	29.5/23.9	Slot Machines:	Yes
Original Cost:	n/a	Crew/Passenger Ratio		Swimming Pools (outdoors):	1
Entered Service:	July 1955/1996	(lower beds/all berths):	2.3/2.7	Swimming Pools (indoors):	0
Registry:	Panama	Cabins (total):	283	Whirlpools:	2
Length (ft/m):	532.4/162.30	Size Range (sq ft/m):	183.0–270.0/17.25	Self-Service Launderette:	No
Beam (ft/m):	70.0/21.34	Cabins (outside view):	217	Dedicated Cinema/Seats:	Yes/130
Draft (ft/m):	25.2/7.69	Cabins (interior/no view):	66	Library:	Yes

OVERALL SCORE: 1,112 OUT OF A POSSIBLE 2,000 POINTS

OVERVIEW. *Princess Danae* began as a cargo-passenger liner, was turned into a cruise ship in 1972, and was almost destroyed by fire in Genoa in 1991. Well-built with a deep draught, it is a good sea ship, and quite stable in all sea conditions. There is a decent amount of open deck space for sunbathing.

Princess Danae provides a moderately comfortable cruise experience in unpretentious surroundings. It was refurbished in 2005–6, and some public rooms were revamped. The interior decor is pleasing, but quite traditional, in keeping with the ship's character. The thick, real wood railings are constantly being maintained to perfection, as are the brass fittings in the navigation bridge. The ship has a traditional ambiance, with some contemporary features. Public rooms include a cinema – unusual for a ship of this size – a shop, small casino, piano bar, and a club room/library with integral bar.

The ship typically operates Caribbean cruises in winter, and European cruises in summer. It is often chartered to tour operators of various nationalities, and so its character changes, as does the level of food and service. Use the rating only as a guide, as the actual product can be inconsistent. However, the officers and crew are very friendly, and the service is warm and heartfelt. In fact, it's the warm ambiance and unpretentious, unstuffy environment that passengers really like about this ship. The onboard currency is the euro, and gratuities are not included.

Passenger niggles include the fact that there is no observation lounge with forward-facing views over the bows; much of the open deck area is covered with Astroturf; the white plastic sunloungers (wood or stainless would be better) look tacky and spoil the traditional feel of the ship.

BERLITZ'S RATINGS		
	Possible	Achieved
Ship	500	292
Accommodation	200	116
Food	400	234
Service	400	230
Entertainment	100	42
Cruise	400	198

ACCOMMODATION. There are 11 price grades. Most cabins are of good size, are quite comfortable, and have rather heavy-duty furniture and fittings with a decent amount of storage space. The lower-grade cabins are really plain, but adequate, although the bathrooms are minimal and functional, but uninviting. While 210 cabin bathrooms have a tub and shower, 70 have only a shower. Accommodation designated as suites (six with a private balcony) and junior suites also have a writing/ vanity desk, minibar, hairdryer, and satellite-link telephone. The towels are small.

CUISINE. The 394-seat Mimosa Restaurant is decorated quite nicely and has a high ceiling. It has open seating, and tables are for four, six or eight (the chairs do not have armrests). The cuisine is Continental/European, with some regional specialties. Typically, a self-serve buffet table is set up in the center of the restaurant for breakfast items, salads and cheeses for lunch, dinner and late-night snacks.

Casual, self-serve buffet meals are available in the Lido Bar, with its indoor-outdoor bamboo seating. The ship's former disco has been turned into a charming little Garden Café (with bamboo furniture).

ENTERTAINMENT. The Main Lounge is a single-level room with 380 seats, and a thrust stage best used for cabaret acts. Stage lighting is minimal, and could be better. The ship carries a main band, and several small musical units, and solo pianists to provide live music for dancing or listening.

SPA/FITNESS. There is a gymnasium and sauna, and a windowless beauty salon.

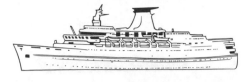

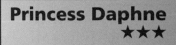

Princess Daphne
★★★

Size:	.....Small Ship	Propulsion/Propellers: diesel (9,850 kW)/2	Cabins (for one person): 0
Tonnage:	15,833	Passenger Decks: 7	Cabins (with private balcony): 6
Lifestyle:	.....Standard	Total Crew: 240	Cabins (wheelchair accessible): 0
Cruise Line:	.Classic International Cruises	Passengers	Wheelchair accessibility .....None
Former Names:	Ocean Monarch,	(lower beds/all berths): 479/594	Cabin Current: 220
	Switzerland, Daphne,	Passenger Space Ratio	Elevators: 2
	Akrotiri Express, Port Sydney	(lower beds/all berths): 33.0/26.6	Casino (gaming tables): .....Yes
Builder:	.....Swan, Hunter (UK)	Crew/Passenger Ratio	Slot Machines: .....Yes
Original Cost:	.....n/a	(lower beds/all berths): 1.9/2.4	Swimming Pools (outdoors): 1
Entered Service:	.....Mar 1955/2008	Cabins (total): 241	Swimming Pools (indoors): 0
Registry:	.....Madeira	Size Range (sq ft/m): 200.0–270.0/	Whirlpools: 2
Length (ft/m):	.....532.7/162.39	18.5–25.0	Self-Service Launderette: .....No
Beam (ft/m):	.....70.0/21.34	Cabins (outside view): 188	Dedicated Cinema/Seats: .....No
Draft (ft/m):	.....41.9/12.80	Cabins (interior/no view): 53	Library: .....Yes

OVERALL SCORE: 1,131 OUT OF A POSSIBLE 2,000 POINTS

OVERVIEW. *Princess Daphne*, sister to *Princess Danae*, is a solid ship built over half a century ago as a cargo-passenger liner for voyages between the UK and Australia, and converted in 1972 to a full-time cruise ship. Now, several owners later, it is operated by Lisbon-based Classic International Cruises and also operates under charter to various other companies. Refurbished in 2008, it provides a very comfortable cruise experience.

It has a pleasing, traditional profile, and the interior decor and furnishings combine the classic and contemporary. There are four bars, an internet-connect center, a library and card room, photo shop, boutique, fitness center, and a really good amount of outdoors space for sunbathing. The Portuguese crew are always polite and provide warm, friendly service.

There is, sadly, no forward observation lounge. The onboard currency is the euro, and gratuities are not included. Drink prices are very reasonable.

SUITABLE FOR: *Princess Daphne* is best suited to adult couples and solo travelers of mature years who seek to cruise aboard a traditional style of ship that is of a handy size, with moderate facilities that are unpretentious yet quite comfortable, and at a modest cruise price.

ACCOMMODATION. There are 13 cabin price grades. All suites/cabins have a bathroom either with a full-size tub/shower combination or shower only, personal safe, multichannel audio, TV set, and satellite-linked telephone. All cabins have good solid fittings, heavy-duty doors and plain decor. There really is plenty of closet and drawer space, but the cabin insulation is poor.

BERLITZ'S RATINGS

	Possible	Achieved
Ship	500	292
Accommodation	200	110
Food	400	225
Service	400	235
Entertainment	100	51
Cruise	400	218

Suites: The largest accommodation is in six of the 27 suites. Each has a separate bedroom, with double bed. The living room has a sofa, large glass topped coffee table, writing desk, TV set, radio channels, hairdryer and personal safe. The bathroom has a full-size tub/shower, washbasin and toilet. Each suite has a private balcony.

Standard Exterior View or Interior (no view) Cabins: Some grades have double beds, while others have an L-shaped two lower bed configuration.

CUISINE. The Restaurant has 476 seats, large picture windows, and an uncluttered seating arrangement, with several tables for two located by large picture windows; other tables are for four, six or eight. Breakfast, lunch, and dinner are served in a single seating. Casual self-serve buffet lunches can also be taken in the Neptune Bar, with its views aft over the ship's swimming pool and hot tubs.

ENTERTAINMENT. The Main Lounge, seating 350, is designed for cabaret acts. There is a wooden dance floor, and a marginally raised "stage", but it's not a showlounge – just a lounge with a small stage. There are several slim pillars, and seating is in tub chairs. Sightlines from seats not close to the stage are quite poor. However, entertainment is a low-key affair aboard this ship. The room is better as a lecture hall, and for dancing.

SPA/FITNESS. There is a decent-sized health spa, built in what was formerly a cinema. It houses a gymnasium, with a reasonable array of muscle-toning equipment, changing area, sauna, and several massage/treatment rooms.

Prinsendam
★★★★ +

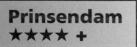

Size:	Mid-Size Ship	Passenger Decks:	9	Cabins (with private balcony):	168
Tonnage:	37,983	Total Crew:	443	Cabins (wheelchair accessible):	6
Lifestyle:	Premium	Passengers		Wheelchair accessibility	Best
Cruise Line:	Holland America Line	(lower beds/all berths):	837/837	Cabin Current:	110 volts
Former Names:	Seabourn Sun,	Passenger Space Ratio		Elevators:	4
	Royal Viking Sun	(lower beds/all berths):	45.3/45.3	Casino (gaming tables):	Yes
Builder:	Wartsila (Finland)	Crew/Passenger Ratio		Slot Machines:	Yes
Original Cost:	$125 million	(lower beds/all berths):	1.8/1.8	Swimming Pools (outdoors):	2
Entered Service:	Dec 1988/May 2002	Cabins (total):	395	Swimming Pools (indoors):	0
Registry:	The Netherlands	Size Range (sq ft/m):	137.7–723.3/	Whirlpools:	4
Length (ft/m):	674.2/205.5		12.8–67.2	Self-Service Launderette:	Yes
Beam (ft/m):	91.8/28.0	Cabins (outside view):	371	Dedicated Cinema/Seats:	Yes/101
Draft (ft/m):	23.6/7.2	Cabins (interior/no view):	24	Library:	Yes
Propulsion/Propellers: diesel (21,120 kW)/2		Cabins (for one person):	3		

OVERALL SCORE: 1,642 OUT OF A POSSIBLE 2,000 POINTS

OVERVIEW. *Prinsendam* is a contemporary, well-designed ship with sleek, flowing lines, a sharply raked bow, and a well-rounded profile, with lots of floor-to-ceiling glass. Originally ordered and operated by the long defunct Royal Viking Line as *Royal Viking Sun*, it was bought by Seabourn Cruise Line in 1998. Following an extensive refit and refurbishment programme, the ship was renamed *Seabourn Sun* in 1999.

In 2002, it was transferred to Holland America Line as *Prinsendam*, and the hull color was changed from all-white to a dark blue hull with white superstructure. In 2009 an aft deck, including 21 new cabins, was added. The shore tenders are thoughtfully air-conditioned.

Wide teak wood decks provide excellent walking areas including a decent wrap-around promenade deck outdoors. The swimming pool (outdoors on Lido Deck) is not large, but it is quite adequate, while the deck above has a croquet court and golf driving range. The interior layout is very spacious – it is even more ideal when no more than 600 passengers are aboard. Impressive public rooms and tasteful decor now reign. Two handrails – one of wood, one of chrome – are provided on all stairways, a thoughtful touch.

The Crow's Nest, the ship's forward observation lounge, is an elegant, contemporary (at least in decor), lounge. Pebble Beach is the name of the electronic golf simulator room, complete with wet bar, with play possible on 11 virtual courses. An Explorations Café was installed at the end of 2007 in a refit that also saw an expansion of the shopping arcade and surrounding areas.

The Erasmus Library (formerly the Ibsen Library) is well organized, although it is simply not large enough for long-distance cruising. The former Compass Rose room

BERLITZ'S RATINGS		
	Possible	Achieved
Ship	500	416
Accommodation	200	174
Food	400	315
Service	400	326
Entertainment	100	82
Cruise	400	329

has now become the Explorer's Lounge.

The Oak Room is the ship's cigar/pipe smoker's lounge; it has a marble fireplace, which sadly cannot be used due to United States Coast Guard regulations. I have always thought it would make a fine library, although it is also excellent as a cigar smoking room. There is a computer-learning center, with several workstations.

Whether by intention or not, the ship has a two-class feeling, with passengers in "upstairs" penthouse suites and "A" grade staterooms gravitating to the quieter Crow's Nest lounge (particularly at night), while other passengers (the participants) go to the main entertainment deck. Male "dance hosts" act as partners for women traveling alone.

The ship's wide range of facilities includes a concierge, self-service launderettes (useful on long voyages), a varied guest lecture program, 24-hour information office, and true 24-hour cabin service, for the discriminating passenger who demands spacious personal surroundings, and good food and service, regardless of price. This ship operates mainly long-distance cruises in great comfort, and free shuttle buses are provided in almost all ports of call.

While *Prinsendam* isn't perfect, the few design flaws (for example: poorly designed bar service counters) are minor points. It is an extremely comfortable ship – smaller than other Holland America Line ships, and more refined. The elegant decorative features include Dutch artwork and memorabilia.

Added benefits include a fine health spa facility, spacious, wide teakwood decks and many teak sunloungers. However, the good points are marred by the bland quality of the dining room food and service, and the lack of understanding of what it takes to make a "luxury" cruise experience, despite what is stated in the company's brochures.

There are only four elevators, so anyone with walking disabilities may have to wait for some time during periods of peak usage (e.g. before meals). This spacious ship shows signs of wear and tear in some areas (particularly in the accommodation passageways), despite recent refurbishments. The library is too small (particularly for some of the long cruises operated) and difficult to enter for anyone confined to a wheelchair.

SUITABLE FOR: *Prinsendam* is best suited to older adult couples and singles who like to mingle in a mid-size ship operating longer cruises, in an unhurried setting with fine quality surroundings, with some eclectic, antique artwork, good food and service from a smiling Indonesian and Filipino crew who like to serve but who lack finesse.

ACCOMMODATION. There are 15 grades, ranging from Penthouse Verandah Suites to standard interior (no view) cabins. All suites and cabins have undergone some degree of refurbishment since the ship was taken over by Holland America Line in 2002.

Penthouse Verandah Suite: The Penthouse Verandah Suite (723 sq. ft/67 sq. meters), is a most desirable living space, although not as large as other penthouse suites aboard some other ships. It is light and airy, and has two bathrooms, one of which has a large whirlpool bathtub with ocean views, and anodized gold bathroom fittings. The living room contains a large dining table and chairs, and large sofas. There is also a substantial private balcony, and butler service.

Deluxe Verandah Suites: There are 18 of these (8 on Sports Deck/10 on Lido Deck). Located in the forward section of the ship, they have large balconies, two sofas, large bar/ entertainment center, (mini-bar/refrigerator, color television, VCR and CD player); bathrooms have separate toilet, sink and toiletries cabinets, connecting sliding door into the bedroom, large mirror, two toiletries cabinets, plenty of storage space, full bathtub, and anodized gold fittings. Each evening the butler brings different goodies – hot and cold hors d'oeuvres and other niceties. If you do choose one of these suites, it might be best on the starboard side where they are located in a private hallway, while those on the port side (including the Penthouse Verandah Suite) are positioned along a public hallway. The 10 suites on Lido Deck are positioned along private port and starboard side hallways.

Passengers in Penthouse and Deluxe Verandah Suites are provided with a private concierge lounge, high tea served in the suite each afternoon, hors d'oeuvres before dinner each evening (on request), complimentary laundry pressing and dry cleaning, private cocktail parties with captain, priority disembarkation, and more.

Other Cabin Grades: Most of the other cabins (spread over six other decks) are of generous proportions and have just about everything you would need (including a VCR).

Many (about 38 percent) have a small, private balcony. All cabins have walk-in closets, lockable drawers, full-length mirrors, hairdryers, and ample cotton towels. A few cabins have third berths, while some have interconnecting doors (good for couples who want two bathrooms and more space or for families with children).

In all grades of accommodation, passengers receive a basket of fresh fruit, fluffy cotton bathrobes, evening turn-down service, and a Holland America Line signature tote bag. Filipino and Indonesian cabin stewards and stewardesses provide unobtrusive personal service.

Four well-equipped, L-shaped cabins for the disabled are quite well designed, fairly large, and equipped with special wheel-in bathrooms with shower facilities and closets.

CUISINE. The La Fontaine Dining Room wraps around the aft end of Lower Promenade Deck and has extensive ocean-view windows; there's a second, smaller (quieter) section along the starboard side. There is plenty of space around tables. A good number of window-side tables are for two persons, although there are also tables for four, six or eight. Crystal glasses, and Rosenthal china and fine cutlery are provided.

There are two seatings for dinner, at assigned tables, and an open-seating arrangement for breakfast and lunch (you'll be seated by restaurant staff when you enter). The dining room is a non-smoking venue.

Alternative Dining Option: A small, quiet dining spot is the Pinnacle Dining Room, with 48 seats, wood-paneled decor that increases the feeling of intimacy and privacy, and great ocean views, is set on the port side. Table settings include Bulgari china, Reidel glassware, and Frette table linens. The venue specializes in fine steaks and seafood. Seating preference is given to suite occupants. Reservations are required, and there is a cover charge.

There is a well-chosen wine list, although there is a great deal of emphasis on California wines, the prices of which are quite high.

There is also an enlarged Lido Restaurant, for decent casual dining and self-serve buffet-style meals. This eatery has both indoor and outdoor seating.

ENTERTAINMENT. The Queens showlounge is an amphitheater-style layout, with a well tiered floor, and both banquette and individual seating. While Holland America Line isn't known for fine entertainment, what it does offer is a consistently good, tried and tested array of cabaret acts.

SPA/FITNESS. The extensive Greenhouse Health Spa includes six treatment rooms (with integral showers), a rasul chamber (for mud and gentle steam heat treatments, combined with gentle steam), a gymnasium with views over the stern, and separate sauna, steam room, and changing rooms for men and women. The spa is operated by Steiner.

● **For more extensive general information on what a Holland America Line cruise is like, see pages 139–42.**

Professor Multanovskiy
★★

Size: . . . . .Boutique Ship	Passenger Decks: 3	Cabins (with private balcony): 0
Tonnage: 1,753	Total Crew: 25	Cabins (wheelchair accessible): 0
Lifestyle: . . . . .Standard	Passengers	Wheelchair accessibility . . . . .None
Cruise Line: . . . . . .Oceanwide Expeditions	(lower beds/all berths): 49/49	Cabin Current: . . . . .220 volts
Former Names: . . . . .none	Passenger Space Ratio	Elevators: 0
Builder: . . . . .Wartsila (Finland)	(lower beds/all berths): 35.7/35.7	Casino (gaming tables): . . . . .No
Original Cost: .n/a	Crew/Passenger Ratio	Slot Machines: .No
Entered Service: 1983	(lower beds/all berths): 1.9/1.9	Swimming Pools (outdoors): 0
Registry: . . . . .Russia	Cabins (total): .29	Swimming Pools (indoors): 0
Length (ft/m): 213.2/65.0	Size Range (sq ft/m): . . . . .n/a	Whirlpools: 0
Beam (ft/m): 42/12.8	Cabins (outside view): 29	Self-Service Launderette: . . . . .No
Draft (ft/m): 15.0/4.6	Cabins (interior/no view): 0	Dedicated Cinema/Seats: . . . . .No
Propulsion/Propellers: diesel (2,327 kW)/2	Cabins (for one person): 9	Library: . . . . .Yes

OVERALL SCORE: 947 OUT OF A POSSIBLE 2,000 POINTS

OVERVIEW. *Professor Multanovskiy*, which has a dark hull and white superstructure, was originally built in Finland for the former Soviet Union's polar and oceanographic research programme run by the Russian Academy of Science. It should not be taken as a cruise ship, although it was converted in the early 1990s to carry passengers, and then fitted out specifically for expedition cruising when refurbished in 1996. Other ships in the series are *Akademik Boris Petrov, Akademik Golitsyn, Akademik M.A. Laurentiev, Akademik Nikolaj Strakhov, Akademik Shokalskiy, Livonia, Professor Khromov* and *Professor Molchanov*.

This ship is typically operated under charter to various "expedition" cruise companies. It has an ice-hardened, steel hull, which is good for cruising in both the Arctic and Antarctic, and strong Russian diesel engines. All passengers have access to the navigation bridge. There are several inflatable Zodiac landing craft for close-in shore excursions and nature observation trips. Inside, the limited public rooms consist of a library and lounge/bar. The dining rooms are also used for lectures. Medical facilities are good.

This is expedition-style cruising, in a very small ship with limited facilities. However, it provides a somewhat primitive, but genuine adventure experience, taking you "up-close and personal" to places others only dream about. The bigger ships cannot get this close to Antarctica or the Arctic, but this little vessel will sail you right to the face of the ice continent.

Quark Expeditions charters this ship for the Antarctic (winter) season, and has its own staff and lecturers on board. It also oversees the food, to make sure that everything is up to its usual high standard.

BERLITZ'S RATINGS

	Possible	Achieved
Ship	500	227
Accommodation	200	87
Food	400	203
Service	400	188
Entertainment	n/a	n/a
Cruise	500	242

SUITABLE FOR: *Professor Multanovskiy* is best suited to couples and single travelers who enjoy viewing nature and wildlife at close quarters, and who would not dream of cruising in the mainstream sense aboard ships with large numbers of people. This is for hardy, adventurous types who don't feel the need for onboard entertainment.

ACCOMMODATION. There are five grades, the price depending on the grade and location you choose. With the exception of one "suite," almost all other cabins are very small, Spartan, and rather clinical. There are two-berth cabins with shower and toilet, or there are two-bed cabins on the lowest deck, whose occupants must share a bathroom.

CUISINE. There are two dining rooms (the ship's galley is actually located between them), and all passengers are accommodated in a single seating. The meals are hearty international fare, with no frills. When the ship is under charter to Quark Expeditions, Western rather than Russian chefs oversee the food operation, and the quality of meals and variety of foods is much better.

ENTERTAINMENT. There is no formal entertainment, although dinner and after-dinner conversation with fellow passengers in the ship's lounge/bar really becomes the entertainment each evening. So, if you don't want to talk to your fellow passengers, take a good book, or go outside, where you'll find nature is nothing less than diverting.

SPA/FITNESS. There are no spa or fitness facilities, although there is a sauna.

Queen Elizabeth
NOT YET RATED

Size: . . . . .Large Resort Ship	Passenger Decks: 12	Cabins (with private balcony): . . . . . . .n/a
Tonnage: .92,000	Total Crew: 1,003	Cabins (wheelchair accessible): 20
Lifestyle: . . . . .Standard	Passengers	Wheelchair accessibility . . . . .Good
Cruise Line: . . . . .Cunard Line	(lower beds/all berths): 2,092/2,172	Cabin Current: . . . . .110/220 volts
Former Names: . . . . .none	Passenger Space Ratio	Elevators: 12
Builder: . . . . .Fincantieri (Italy)	(lower beds/all berths): 43.9/41.6	Casino (gaming tables): . . . . .Yes
Original Cost: . . . .€500 million	Crew/Passenger Ratio	Slot Machines: . . . . .Yes
Entered Service: . . . . .Oct 2010	(lower beds/all berths): 2.0/2.1	Swimming Pools (outdoors): 2
Registry: . . . . .Great Britain	Cabins (total): 1,046	Swimming Pools (indoors): 0
Length (ft/m): 964.5/294.0	Size Range (sq ft/m): . .152.0–1,493 sq.ft/	Whirlpools: 5
Beam (ft/m): 105.9/32.3	14.0–138.5	Self-Service Launderette: . . . . .Yes
Draft (ft/m): 26.2/8.0	Cabins (outside view): 892	Dedicated Cinema/Seats: . . . . .No
Propulsion/Propellers: . . . . diesel-electric	Cabins (interior/no view): 154	Library: . . . . .Yes
(64.0 MW)/pod propulsion (2)	Cabins (for one person): 820	

BERLITZ'S OVERALL SCORE: NYR OUT OF A POSSIBLE 2,000 POINTS

OVERVIEW. The red ensign continues! *Queen Elizabeth* is the second largest Cunarder ever ordered in the company's long history. The first section of the keel, weighing 364 tons, was laid on 2 July 2009 in Fincantieri's Monfalcone shipyard. However, the ship is a pretend ocean liner, and is susceptible to rolling and pitching, just like sister ship *Queen Victoria*, due to its "Vista"-class hull design. Anyone comparing this ship with the former *Queen Elizabeth 2* can't fail to notice the difference in the design of the ship's stern – *QE2*'s was beautifully rounded, while the new ship's is flat and unromantic. And the foredeck is, in a word, disappointing.

The ship is aimed at the North American and British markets, but really is for anyone who is an Anglophile, because Cunard is a resolutely British experience – although it's not like it used to be. Unlike *Queen Mary 2*, it can transit the Panama Canal – useful for long voyages. The rating and score are expected to be similar to that of sister ship *Queen Victoria*.

The ship sports a few more cabins, and therefore more passengers, than *Queen Victoria*, but the dimensions and number of elevators remain the same. Outdoors facilities include a promenade deck; it's not teak, but a rubberized deck covering made to look like wooden planking, which gets hot and stays hot in warm weather areas. You can almost walk around – the forward section is for marine use only – with several deck lounge chairs with comfortable Cunard-logo cushioned pads; it's a good place to read a book. One open deck atop the ship has a life-sized chess board.

Other features include a majestic three-deck high Grand Lobby with a sweeping staircase, sculpted balconies and other elegant decorative touches, and a Cunardia floating

BERLITZ'S RATINGS

	Possible	Achieved
Ship	500	NYR
Accommodation	200	NYR
Food	400	NYR
Service	400	NYR
Entertainment	100	NYR
Cruise	400	NYR

museum whose glass cabinets display models of former Cunard ships, old menus and daily programs.

One "wow" factor is a beautiful 18½-ft (5.6-meter) high David Linley marquetry panel "sculpture" that spans two-and-a-half decks and adorns the three-deck grand stairway. Crafted from nine natural woods sourced from several countries, it depicts the port bow of the original *Queen Elizabeth* as seen from sea level.

Several public rooms are two decks high; these include the gold-beige Queen's Room, with a large, wooden ballroom dance floor measuring about 1,000 sq.ft/93 sq. meters; above are two huge ceiling-mounted chandeliers. The bandstand is fronted by a large proscenium arch, while cantilevered balconies line the room's starboard side. Traditional British afternoon tea is served in this art deco-style grand room – though the tea itself is pretty basic.

The Royal Arcade is a cluster of seven shops, including Harrods, selling goods connected with modern-day Britain, all set in an arcade-like environment. The Library is a really stunning two-deck-high wood-paneled 6,000-book facility serviced by two full-time librarians, although there are few chairs in which to sit in and read. There's also a bookshop (in another location, on the same deck as the upper level of the library) selling maritime-related books, memorabilia, maps and stationery. The Library is a great place to meet people, quietly.

The layout is a little disjointed on the uppermost decks, although the general flow is reasonably good. Note that access between the aft deck and the pool area and winter gardens can be gained only by going through the expansive buffet area. This makes for congestion at the self-serve buffet as people are constantly passing through, as in a railway carriage.

The key point is that *Queen Elizabeth* is a *cruise ship* posing as an *ocean liner*. It does, however, provide a traditional setting for those who enjoy dressing for dinner, either formally or semi-formally. Passengers get cocktail parties, and enjoy the lecturers and speakers who sail on each voyage – Cunard wisely calls them voyages, not cruises.

There's no doubting Cunard's British heritage, but trying to find British service staff is challenging. Cunard claims to be British, but that's really a bit of marketing hype. Still, nice touches like destination-themed sail-away music, the afternoon tea experience, a wide variety of entertainment, and semi-decent service, albeit lacking in finesse, help Cunard to stand out from the crowd.

The onboard currency is the US dollar. Gratuities (called a Hotel and Dining charge, of $11–$13, depending on your accommodation grade) are automatically added to your onboard account daily.

ACCOMMODATION. There are three class categories of accommodation: Queens Grill, 7 price grades; Princess Grill, 4 price grades; Britannia Accommodation, 21 price grades. That's 32 different price grades! Still, it's all about location, location, location. But however much or little you pay, passengers all embark and disembark via the same gangway. In keeping with maritime tradition, even-numbered cabins are on the port side, with odd-numbered cabins on the starboard side. The six top suites are named after former Cunard commodores, all of whom have been knighted by the Queen.

The amount of drawer space in the standard cabins is less than one would expect, and there is little room for luggage storage. Note that the air conditioning cannot be turned off in cabins or bathrooms.

Grand Suites: 4, measuring 1,918–2,131 sq.ft. Named Bisset, Charles, Illingworth and Rostron, they are located aft, with great ocean views from their private wrap-around balconies, which contain a complete wet bar. The suites have two bedrooms with walk-in closets; bathroom with bathtub and separate shower enclosure; lounge; and dining room with seating for six. In-suite dining from the Queens Grill menus is also available.

Master Suites: 2, measuring 1,100 sq.ft. Named Britten and Thomson, both are located in the center of the ship.

Penthouse Suites, measuring 520–707 sq.ft.

Queens Suites, measuring 508–771 sq.ft.

Princess Suites, measuring 342–513 sq.ft.

Balcony Cabins, measuring 242–472 sq.ft.

Outside-View Cabins, measuring 180–201 sq.ft.

Interior (no-view) Cabins, measuring 151–243 sq.ft.

All accommodation grades have both British three-pin (240-volt) sockets and American and European-style two-pin (110-volt) sockets. Gilchrist & Soames personal toiletries (bath/shampoo gel, shampoo, conditioner, shower cap, cotton buds) are supplied to all passengers, and a hairdryer is stored in the vanity desk units. Some cabins have nicely indented ceilings with suffused lighting.

The regular cabins (Grades C/D) are small, but functional. However, the cabinetry resembles that in an Ibis hotel – a bit austere and lacking in character. There is a distinct lack of drawer space in a cabin supposedly designed for two persons – it's very noticeable on long voyages, and the additional drawers located under the bed may prove challenging for some to use. The premium mattresses are excellent – as is the bed linen (European duvets are standard).

The bathrooms, also, are stunningly bland, similar to those found aboard the ships of Princess Cruises, with small washbasins, and little storage space for personal toiletries. The fixed-head shower doesn't permit the thorough wash that hand-held flexible hoses do. Overall, the standard (lower grade) cabins are a little underwhelming – so, for more space and quality, consider booking one of the higher grade cabins, or, better still, go for Grill-class accommodation – the perks and increased attention and service are really worth it. The walls in most accommodation passageways are rather plain, and could do with a little artwork to dress them up.

CUISINE. Cunard Line is respected for its cuisine and service, with a wide variety of well-prepared and presented dishes made from good ingredients. The 878-seat Britannia Restaurant – the name is taken from a former Cunard ocean liner of 1914–50 – is located in the aft section. It is two decks high, with seating on both main and balcony levels – the balcony level houses what are known as Britannia Club passengers, with single seat dining, while those on the lower level have two seatings for dinner. Spiral stairways link both levels. Waterford Wedgwood china is provided.

Exclusive Dining (Queens Grill, Princess Grill): As with its sister ships, there are two special Grill-Class-only restaurants. These have a single-seating arrangement, providing a more intimate and exclusive dining experience than can be found in the two-seating main Britannia Restaurant.

The 142-seat Queens Grill (on the port side), with its single-seating dining, is for passengers in suites and the top grades of accommodation, and provides the best cuisine and service aboard the ship. The beloved Cunard Grill experience also includes alfresco dining in The Courtyard, a seldom-used courtyard terrace suitably protected from the wind, and access for Grill-class passengers only to an exclusive lounge and bar to their own upper terrace deck, with dedicated staff.

The 132-seat Princess Grill (on the starboard side), with single-seating dining, is for passengers in middle-class accommodation grades.

The Verandah Restaurant, an "alternative" eating place available to all passengers, is located on the second level of the three-deck high lobby. Reservations are required, and there is a cover charge for lunch or dinner.

Casual Eatery: The Lido Café (on Deck 11) has panoramic views, indoor/outdoor seating for approximately 470, and features a fairly standard multi-line self-serve buffet arrangement. It's a bit downmarket for what is supposed to be a stylish ship – the original *Queen Elizabeth* didn't have such a facility – but then, these are different times. At night, the venue is transformed into three distinct flavours: Asado (South American Grill); Aztec (Mexican cuisine); Jasmine (Asian cuisine), each with a small cover charge.

For excellent Lavazza coffee and light bites, there's the Parisian-style Café Carinthia, located one deck above the Purser's Desk and adjacent to the popular Veuve Clicquot champagne bar.

For traditional British pub food, the Golden Lion Pub features fish 'n' chips, steak and mushroom pie, a plough-man's lunch, and, of course, bangers (sausages) and mash.

ENTERTAINMENT. The 830-seat, three-deck-high Royal Court Theatre is designed in the style of a classic opera house. It features 20 private "royal boxes," which can be reserved by any passengers for special nights, and a special package includes champagne and chocolates, ticket printed with name and box number – in the tradition of a real London West End theatre. There's a lounge for pre-show drinks.

A "Victoriana" show is all about good old British tradition, while other production shows and a good variety of cabaret entertainment are presented here. The Royal Court Theatre is also used to show large-screen movies. The ship has a number of bands, small combos and solo entertainers.

A Big Band night is sometimes held in the Queens Room, where afternoon tea is served and live music is provided. Some bars and lounges have live jazz.

SPA/FITNESS. The Cunard Royal Health Club and Spa consists of a beauty salon, large gymnasium with high-tech muscle-pumping equipment and great ocean views; aerobics area; separate changing rooms for men and women, each with its own ocean-view sauna; a Thermal Area with sauna and steam rooms (extra-cost day passes are available if you don't book a treatment, at $35 per day, or at less per day cost for a multi-use pass); several body treatment rooms; a rasul chamber for private Hammam-style mud/steam bathing; and a relaxation area.

Sample prices (check on board for the latest prices): Swedish Massage $119 (55 mins); Deep Tissue Massage $129 (55 mins); Hot Stones Massage $149 (75 mins); Monticelli Mud Treatment $119 (60 mins); Rasul Chamber for couples ($75).

Sports include paddle tennis, croquet, and British bowls.

● **For more extensive general information on what a Cunard Line cruise is like, see pages 138–9.**

Queen Mary 2
★★★★★ to ★★★★

Size: ....Large Ocean Liner	Passenger Decks: 12	Cabins (wheelchair accessible): 30
Tonnage: 148,528	Total Crew: 1,254	Wheelchair accessibility ....Best
Lifestyle: .....Luxury/Premium/Standard	Passengers	Cabin Current: ....110 and 220 volts
Cruise Line: ....Cunard Line	(lower beds/all berths): 2,620/3,090	Elevators: 22
Former Names: ....none	Passenger Space Ratio	Casino (gaming tables): ....Yes
Builder: Chantiers de l'Atlantique (France)	(lower beds/all berths): 56.6/48.0	Slot Machines: ....Yes
Original Cost: ....$800 million	Crew/Passenger Ratio	Swimming Pools (outdoors): 3
Entered Service: ....Jan 2004	(lower beds/all berths): 2.0/2.4	Swimming Pools (indoors): 2
Registry: ....Great Britain	Cabins (total): 1,310	Whirlpools: 8
Length (ft/m): 1,131.9/345.03	Size Range (sq ft/m): 194.0–2,249.7/	Fitness Center: ....Yes
Beam (ft/m): 134.5/41.00	18.0–209	Sauna/Steam Room: ....Yes/Yes
Draft (ft/m): 32.6/9.95	Cabins (outside view): 1,017	Massage: ....Yes
Propulsion/Propellers: ....gas turbine	Cabins (interior/no view): 293	Self-Service Launderette: ....Yes
(103,000kW) and diesel-electric/4 pods	Cabins (for one person): 0	Dedicated Cinema/Seats: ....Yes
(2 azimuthing, 2 fixed/21.5 MW each)	Cabins (with private balcony): 953	Library: ....Yes

OVERALL SCORE: OUT OF A POSSIBLE 2,000 POINTS: GRILL CLASS 1,702; BRITANNIA CLASS 1,541

OVERVIEW. RMS *Queen Mary 2*, designated a Royal Mail Ship by the British Post Office, offers the pleasures of crossing the North Atlantic comfortably on a regular schedule, with the latest high-tech facilities and conveniences.

A ship of superlatives, *Queen Mary 2* is the largest passenger ship ever built – in terms of gross tonnage, length, and beam, though not passengers carried – and is five times the length of Cunard Line's first ship, *Britannia*, which plied the North Atlantic from 1840. Taller than the Empire State Building, it is the first new ship to be built for Cunard Line since 1969, when *QE2* first sailed from Southampton to New York. *QM2* operates regularly scheduled transatlantic crossings for much of the year, and an annual round-the-world cruise from 2007.

Queen Mary 2's exterior design resembles that of the now retired *QE2*, and for good reason: it was designed by naval architect Stephen Payne, an ocean liner specialist. This superbly designed ship is able to weather any unkind conditions on the North Atlantic, or anywhere else – hence her long foredeck, extra-thick plating and hull, designed to maintain a high speed and battle against unkind sea conditions. It has a large, contemporary funnel and beautifully tiered stern, but it is too wide of beam to transit the Panama Canal.

The power and propulsion system comprises an environmentally friendly General Electric marine gas turbine and diesel-electric power plant developing 157,000 horsepower (117.2 MW) – enough to provide power to the 200,000 inhabitants of its home port, Southampton. The ship is propelled by the world's first four-pod propulsion system (Rolls-Royce), which can power through the waters of the North Atlantic at up to 30 knots (the contracted top speed is 29.3 knots, although the ship can easily exceed this). Each pod weighs 270 tons – more than an empty Boeing 747 jumbo jet – and they are powered by a diesel-electric system. Indeed, this ship can go backwards faster than many cruise ships can go forwards.

QM2 was built at the Chantiers de l'Atlantique shipyard in France, in a dry dock measuring 1,360 by 207 ft (415 by 63 meters). The first steel was cut on January 16, 2002, while the keel laying took place on July 4, 2002 – 162 years to the day that the first Cunard steamship, *Britannia*, made its first crossing. The huge ship, constructed in 98 large blocks, each weighing up to 600 tons, was completed an incredibly short 24 months later (964 days, to be exact).

One of the many delightful features is the ship's Tyfon whistle: (there are two: one is new, and the other a copy of the whistle from the original *Queen Mary*, carried to Europe by *QE 2* prior to being fitted to *QM2* in the shipyard). Manufactured by Kockums in Sweden, the replica was inspected, cleaned and converted from steam power to air power. It is 7 ft long and 3 ft high (2.1 meters by 0.9 meters), and weighs 1,400 pounds (635 kg). Both whistles are tuned so that they do not disturb passengers on deck, yet they can be heard 10 miles away.

Almost everything about the liner is British in style, but with some American decor input and accents, and even the four tender stations have London names: Belgravia, Chelsea, Kensington and Knightsbridge. There is a wide walk-around

BERLITZ'S RATINGS

	Possible	Achieved
Grill Class		
Ship	500	440
Accommodation	200	175
Food	400	325
Service	400	335
Entertainment	100	84
Cruise	400	343
Britannia Class		
Ship	500	408
Accommodation	200	147
Food	400	280
Service	400	295
Entertainment	100	83
Cruise	400	328

promenade deck outdoors (with the forward section under cover from the weather or wind). Three times around is 6,102 ft (1,860 meters), or 1.1 miles (1.6 km). Inside are several other walking promenades – good if the weather is poor (for instance, it's almost 300 steps, or three minutes, from fore to aft along Deck 9). A full line of teak "steamer" chairs are provided on the open walk around promenade deck, but still leaves plenty of room for walkers to pass. However, plastic sunloungers are provided on some other open decks – particularly at the aft of the ship. An exterior, winged observation platform, directly under the navigation bridge, offers great sightlines along the ship's length, as well as forward.

Robert Tillberg, the interior designer, produced a stylish, elegant interior design, with towering public spaces, sweeping staircases and grand public rooms that exude a feeling of timelessness. High ceilings – typically two decks of *QM2* are the equivalent of three decks in height of a regular cruise vessel – provide a great sense of space and grandeur. While many ships are designed inward with a central atrium, *QM2* is different. You enter the public rooms from a central location and will always be looking out, with the sea in the background. What's good is the fact that just four staircases traverse all decks (unlike *QE2*, which has 10, having been built as a three-class ship, then changed before introduction to a two-class liner). Deck signage is good, and it's quite easy to find one's way around the ship for the most part, although more fore and aft signs would be useful.

There are, however, a few ostentatious gold pillars and tacky decorative elements, including some awful "bas-reliefs" in the accommodation passageways – perhaps the "Miami Beach" view of what a transatlantic liner looks like. But, for the most part, the ship's interiors are quite stunning, and subtly so. The use of wood laminate paneling may abhor ship buffs, as did the plastic laminates when *QE2* debuted in 1968–69, but is the result of stringent SOLAS regulations.

The spacious atrium lobby, spanning six decks, has an elegant staircase and exclusive works of art. In the main elevator lobby attached to the central atrium, a wall mural of Samuel Cunard welcomes you aboard; it looks like an enlarged photograph, although it is made from almost 700 postage stamp-sized digital images of previous Cunard ships.

Here's a deck-by-deck look at the facilities and public rooms aboard what is undoubtedly the most superlative ocean liner ever (starting at the lowest deck and working our way upward, forward to aft):
● Deck 2 has Illuminations (with planetarium), and the Royal Court Theatre, the lower level of the six-deck high atrium lobby, the Purser's Desk, Video Arcade, Empire Casino, Golden Lion Pub, and the lower level of the two-deck high Britannia Restaurant.
● Deck 3 has the upper level of Illuminations and the Royal Court Theatre, the second level of the six-deck high atrium lobby, Mayfair Shops, Sir Samuel's, The Chart Room, Champagne Bar (Veuve Clicquot is the "house" champagne), the upper level of the Britannia Restaurant, the Queens Room, and the G32 Nightclub.

● Decks 4/Deck 5/Deck 6 have accommodation and the third, fourth and fifth levels of the six-deck high atrium lobby; at the aft end of Deck 6 are the facilities for children, including an outdoor pool (Minnows Pool).
● Deck 7 has the Canyon Ranch Spa, the Winter Garden, the sixth and uppermost level of the six-deck high atrium lobby, expansive Kings Court Buffet, Queens Grill Lounge, Queens Grill and Princess Grill dining salons.
● Deck 8 (forward) has the upper level of the Canyon Ranch Spa, and the Library and Bookshop. The center section has accommodation. In the aft section are the alternative restaurant Todd English, Terrace Bar, and swimming pool outdoors.
● Deck 9 (forward) has the Commodore Club, Boardroom and the Cigar Club (Churchills). The rest of the deck has accommodation and a Concierge Club for suite occupants.
● Deck 10 has accommodation only.
● Deck 11 (forward) has an outdoors observation area. The rest of the deck has accommodation. The aft section outdoors has a whirlpool tub and sunbathing deck.
● Deck 12 (forward) has accommodation. The mid-section has an indoor/outdoor pool (with sliding glass roof), and golf areas (Fairways), located just aft of the public restrooms. The aft section has the Boardwalk Café, dog kennels, and shuffleboard courts.
● Deck 13 has the Sports Centre, Regatta Bar, a splash pool, and extensive outdoor sunbathing space.

There are 14 lounges, clubs and bars. An observation lounge, the delightful Commodore Club, has commanding views forward over the bows; light jazz is played in this bar, which is connected to the Boardroom and Cigar Lounge. Other drinking places include a Golden Lion Pub, a wine bar (Sir Samuel's), a nautically-themed cocktail bar (The Chart Room), and Champagne/Coffee Bar. Bars outdoors include the Regatta Bar and Terrace Bar. The G32 nightclub, which has a main and mezzanine level, is located at the aft end of the ship, away from passenger cabins; it is named after the number designated to the ship by its French builder. The Empire Casino has a bar, as well as the latest high-tech slot machines, and traditional gaming tables.

The Queens Room is a grand ballroom, and, with the largest dance floor at sea, is a stunning, gloriously proportioned room, with a Hollywood-Bowl-style bandstand canopy. It has a dramatic high ceiling, two huge crystal chandeliers, highly comfortable armchairs, and is used for dancing, cocktail parties, and afternoon teas.

Illuminations, the first full-scale planetarium at sea, is a stunning multi-purpose show lounge space that also func-

COMPARING *QM2* AND *QE2*

Cunard Line's many repeat passengers who loved *QE2* will inevitably make comparisons between the two ships. *QM2* has two classes and only four staircases; *QE2* had three classes and 10 staircases. *QE2* had many cabins for single occupancy; *QM2* has none, and single-occupancy premiums are extremely high. *QE2* had a Baggage Master; *QM2* does not. *QE2*'s Queens Grill and Princess Grill restaurants were far more intimate, and had nicer decor than those of *QM2*. Aboard *QM2* there is no private lounge for Princess Grill passengers; but they do share the Queens Grill Lounge.

tions as a 473-seat grand cinema and a broadcast studio. As a planetarium, it has tiered seating rows, with 150 very comfortable reclining seats and plush fabrics, allowing you to sit in a special area under a dome, which is 38 ft/11.5 meters in diameter and almost 20 ft/6 meters deep that forms the setting for the night sky. It's worth reserving a seat for at least one of the five outstanding 20-minute programs, when the dome is lowered and 13 computers take you out of this world.

A Maritime Quest Exhibit provides a beautifully constructed Cunard history plus shipbuilding milestones throughout history, including John Brown's shipyard that built the original *Queen Mary* in the 1930s.

Just aft of the Canyon Ranch Spa is a colonial-style Winter Garden reminiscent of London's Kew Gardens, where flowers bloom year-round (which means they are artificial – some are downright tacky). This peaceful garden setting is for relaxation; a string quartet could well be playing for afternoon tea, which is also served in the much larger, elegant Queen's Room.

There are five swimming pools, including one that can be enclosed under a retractable sliding glass roof; this is useful in bad weather. A large area (21,100 sq. ft/1,960 sq. meters) of open sunning space includes a sports bar at one end. Sports facilities include an electronic golf simulator, putting green, giant chess board and a paddle tennis court.

The ship's Library and Bookshop, the world's largest floating bookshop, is a fine facility that's very popular on transatlantic crossings. Located forward and staffed by full-time librarians from Ocean Books, it has a superb display of 8,000 books in several languages. The area includes leather sofas and armchairs, six internet-connect computers, and a large selection of magazines. It is a delightful facility, but there are few chairs, and the adjacent bookshop is quite small.

ConneXions, an education center, includes seven sophisticated classrooms for Oxford University's "Oxford Discovery" programs. Classes in such things as computer learning, seamanship and navigation, art and wine appreciation, history, languages and photography are taught. Meanwhile, fast-access internet connectivity and a multitude of computer terminals can be found in the Internet Center (several connection packages are provided). Full wi-fi service for your own laptop is available round the clock in the Chart Room, Commodore Club, Golden Lion Pub, Grand Lobby, Library, Queens Grill Lounge, Sir Samuels Wine Bar and the Winter Garden.

Children have their own space, with a dedicated play area, the Play Zone. English nannies supervise toddlers, while older children use The Zone.

You *can* take your dog with you on transatlantic crossings – but not on cruises – and 12 kennels are overseen by a kennel master. Dogs and cats receive a complimentary gift pack containing a *QM2*-logo coat, frisbee, name tag, food dish and scoop; a portrait with pet owners; a crossing certificate and personalized cruise card. Other pet perks include an assortment of toys, cat posts and scratchers, and a selection of top-brand premium pet foods. You can make kennel reservations when you book. The cost: $300–$500. Dogs must be fitted with a microchip, issued with a PETS certificate or official PET passport, and vaccinated against rabies.

SUITABLE FOR: *Queen Mary 2* is best suited to a wide range of couples and single travelers who enjoy the cosmopolitan setting of a floating city at sea that has a maritime heritage and background unequaled by any other ship and cruise line today, with its extensive array of facilities, public rooms, and dining rooms.

THE NEGATIVE ASPECTS OF THE *QM2* EXPERIENCE

Queen Mary 2 really is a floating city – with an elite Grill-class section – and, like any city, there are several parts of town. Some are elegant, some not so elegant, and some are slightly tacky.

The framed, animated cartoons on display, and for sale, in The Gallery don't quite go with the *QM2*'s ocean liner image; neither do art auctions or bazaar stalls selling gold chains, tee-shirts and other tacky items found aboard many cruise ships today. Gratuities are charged to your onboard account at $11–$13 per person, per day, according to the grade of accommodation chosen. A 15% gratuity is included in all beverage and wine orders. As for extra charges, drinks prices are quite reasonable, but a 10-inch by 8-inch embarkation photo can cost close to $30.

A crossing or voyage aboard *QM2* can be considered luxurious only if you travel in Queens Grill accommodation. Otherwise, the experience ranges from "standard" to

"premium" in the other accommodation grades (and little different to regular cruise ships in these market segments). While there are a few delightful wooden sunloungers with green padded cushions, the majority of sunloungers, particularly on the open decks aft, are plastic. To the disappointment of many regular transatlantic passengers, there are no single cabins.

QM2, unlike *QE2*, has no dedicated cinema – a shame since the ship is specifically built for the North Atlantic crossings, when a cinema is much appreciated by frequent passengers (films are, however, shown daily in Illuminations or the Royal Theatre). The grill rooms are too large to be intimate, and are more akin to the kind of steakhouses one finds in large North American cities.

QM2 passengers are a mixed bunch. Most are well dressed, although numerous "tracksuiters'" inhabit the ship, particularly in the Kings Court. Overall, some may feel overwhelmed by the decor's understated

look, or by the bold carpets, but, whatever you may think, the ship absorbs passengers well. While not as ornate as some would like, *QM2* is decidedly spacious and comforting, once you find your way around, although it'll take a week to discover all the out-of-the-way nooks and crannies.

Where several tender ports are included in itineraries, spending time obtaining tender tickets to go ashore detracts from the overall experience – although itineraries have been planned to include as many "alongside" ports as possible.

The passenger flow is generally sound, although there are difficulties in accessing some of the public rooms due to the rather disjointed interior design, and the ship absorbs passengers extremely well with no sense of crowding.

Sadly, there is nowhere to have breakfast outdoors if you don't have a balcony cabin, and lunch at the outdoors Boardwalk Café consists mainly of fast-food items.

ACCOMMODATION. Although there are now four separate categories – Queens Grill, Princess Grill, Britannia Club, and Britannia – *Queen Mary 2* really operates as a two-class ship (Grill Class and Britannia Class), and the restaurant to which you are assigned depends on the accommodation grade you choose.

There are 10 categories, in 25 different price grades. The price you pay will depend on grade, location and size. From standard outside-view cabins to the most opulent suites afloat, there is something for every taste and pocketbook – a choice unrivaled aboard any other cruise vessel.

Perhaps the most noticeable difference between this ship and *QE2* is the addition of a large number of cabins with private balconies – 75 percent of all cabins have them, although they are really of little use when crossing the North Atlantic. When *QE2* debuted in 1969, there was not one single balcony cabin. However, the balconies have steel bulkheads that obscure ocean views when you are seated. Some 12 cabins look inwards to the atrium lobby, which spans six decks.

All grades have a 20-inch (or larger) color television with concealed interactive keyboard, internet connectivity (via a data port for your laptop). All beds have fluffy European duvets, mini-fridge, personal safe, hand-held hairdryer, and all bathrooms have toiletry amenities supplied by Canyon Ranch (the spa/fitness concession).

Other features include digital video on demand (English-, French- and German-language movies are available), music on demand with 3,000 titles, audio books on demand, and email and digital photographs preview and purchase – the system can be blocked so that children cannot access it. One channel is devoted to the eventful history of Cunard Line since 1840.

A number of cabins can accommodate a third or fourth person, although they are so small as to be useful only for contortionists. They are, however, the most inexpensive way of experiencing this fine ship. Note that you get a different cabin breakfast menu depending on whether you travel in Grill Class or Britannia Class accommodation.

For the largest accommodation in the cruise industry, two combinations offer the equivalent of a large house at sea. At the front of the ship, you can combine the Queen Elizabeth and Queen Mary suites with the Queen Anne and Queen Victoria suites to produce one huge suite measuring 5,016 sq. ft (466 sq. meters). Even this can be eclipsed at the other end of the ship, by joining Grand Duplex apartments at the lower level to the adjacent penthouses to produce an unprecedented 8,288 sq. ft (770 sq. meters).

Balmoral/Sandringham Duplexes (Grade Q1): The largest stand-alone accommodation can be found in the Balmoral and Sandringham Duplexes (2,249 sq. ft/209 sq. meters). These are located aft in prime real estate territory, with superb views along the entire length of the ship. Upstairs is a bedroom with wood-framed king-sized bed, and large (but not so private) balcony; downstairs is a living room with sofa, coffee table, dining table, and writing desk. There are two marble-clad bathrooms with whirlpool

bath and separate shower enclosure, toilet and bidet, and two washbasins.

Queen Elizabeth/Queen Mary Suites (Grade Q2): The Queen Elizabeth Suite and Queen Mary Suite (1,194 sq. ft/111 sq. meters) are both located just under the navigation bridge, with good views over the ship's long bows. There are living and dining areas, with a large private balcony (but not as large as the Balmoral/ Sandringham duplex balconies). The master, marble-clad bathroom has a whirlpool bathtub and shower enclosure, and a second bathroom with a shower enclosure (no bathtub). Each suite has the convenience of private elevator access.

Queen Anne/Queen Victoria Suites (Grade Q3): These two suites (796.5 sq. ft/74 sq. meters) have the most commanding views over the ship's long bows. They consist of a bedroom with master, marble-clad bathroom with whirlpool bathtub and separate shower enclosure; separate living/dining area, and a second bathroom with a shower enclosure (no tub).

Duplex Apartments (Grade Q2): There are three duplex apartments: Buckingham and Windsor (each 1,291 sq. ft/120 sq. meters), and Hollyrood (1,566 sq. ft/145 sq. meters). Each has a gymnasium, balcony, butler and concierge service, and superb views over the ship's stern.

Penthouse Suites (Grade Q4): There are six penthouse suites (758 sq. ft/70 sq. meters). These have a living and dining area, large private balcony, bedroom and dressing room with master, marble-clad bathroom with whirlpool bathtub and separate shower enclosure.

Suites (506 sq ft (Grade Q5/Q6): These 82 suites (506 sq. ft/47 sq. meters) have a large private balcony, living area, dressing room, marble-clad bathroom with whirlpool tub/shower. Beds can be arranged in a king-size or twin-bed configuration.

Junior Suites (Grade P1/P2): There are 76 Junior Suites (381 sq. ft/35 sq. meters). Each has a lounge area, large private balcony, and marble-clad bathroom with whirlpool tub and separate shower enclosure. Beds can be arranged in a king-sized or twin-bed configuration.

Deluxe/Premium Balcony Cabins: These 782 cabins (248 sq. ft/23 sq. meters) include a sitting area with sofa, and bathroom with shower enclosure. Beds can be arranged in a king-sized or twin-bed configuration.

Standard Outside-View/Interior (No View) Cabins: There are 62 outside-view cabins and 281 interior (no view) cabins measuring 194 sq. ft/18 sq. meters). Beds can be arranged in a king-sized or twin-bed configuration.

Atrium View Cabins: Each of these 12 interior cabins (194 sq. ft/18 sq. meters) has an unusual view – into the six-deck high atrium lobby. Beds can be arranged in a king-sized or twin-bed configuration. An en-suite bathroom has a shower enclosure, washbasin, toilet, and toiletries cabinet.

Wheelchair Accessible Cabins: There are 30 suites and cabins (in various categories) specially designed for wheelchair users. All have pull-down closet hanging rails, above-bed emergency pull-cord, and large, well-equipped bathrooms with roll-in showers and handrails. Facilities for blind passengers include Braille signs and tactile room signs. Eight special wheelchair-accessible elevators are provided to service the dining areas. Additionally, some 36 cabins have been designated to accommodate deaf or hearing-impaired passengers. There are headsets in the Royal Theatre and Planetarium, and closed-caption television.

CUISINE. Naturally, you should expect lavish dining, and accept nothing less. In all there are 14 bars, and 7 galleys serving 10 dining rooms and eateries. All dining rooms and eateries have ocean-view windows.

An fine selection of wines and champagnes is available (selections and recommendations were made by Michael Broadbent, one of the world's top wine experts), with per bottle prices varying between $20 and $315 (white wines), $20 and $2,650 (red wines), and $35 and $875 (champagne), all plus a 15% gratuity.

Britannia Restaurant: This main dining room seats 1,347, and spans the full beam of the ship. A lavish room almost three decks high, it has two grand sweeping staircases which enable you to make your entry in style. Above the staircase is a huge light well (reminiscent of the great oceanliners of yesteryear) and large, classic columns, while the centerpiece backdrop to the staircase is a huge tapestry of *QM2* against the New York skyline. Breakfast

and lunch are now in an open-seating arrangement, while dinner is in two seatings, all with crisp linen and fine china, of course. Vegetarian options are provided on all lunch and dinner menus. One downside of open seating for breakfast or lunch is that you will probably have a different waiter each time, who will not know your preferences. Another is that if you are seated on the lower level underneath the balcony formed along the port and starboard sides of the upper level, you'll get the feeling of being enclosed in an inferior space. And that is exactly what it is – an inferior space. It's better to get a table in the central well or on the upper level.

In 2007, 46 staterooms were re-graded (category AA) and occupants of these cabins are now served somewhat upgraded cuisine in an exclusive private dining area within the Britannia Restaurant (Britannia Club Class). This single-seating club-like restaurant will offer the Britannia Restaurant menu, plus various à la carte options and tableside flambé service.

Queens Grill/Princess Grill: There are two Grill Rooms (Queens Grill and Princess Grill), which I call small dining salons. Which restaurant you dine in depends on your accommodation grade and the price paid. Both the 200-seat Queens Grill and 178-seat Princess Grill are located aft and have, in theory, fine ocean-view windows – although walkers passing by on the exterior promenade deck can be disturbing in the daytime, so window blinds have to be kept down, which rather negates the outside view. They were modified and given a more intimate feel during a dry-dock in 2005, and both feature an ungainly black marble contemporary statue I have named the "Black Widow" in their entrances. Passengers in the most spacious and luxurious suites, therefore, may feel less special, being mixed, as they are, among all others in Grill Class accommodation. Canyon Ranch Spaclub recommendations are provided on all lunch and dinner menus, as are vegetarian options.

The Queens Grill is decorated in gold, and passengers who dine in this exclusive establishment have their own Queens Grill Bar and Terrace. Unfortunately, Cunard chose not to dispense with waiter stations, which can be noisy at times. The chairs are comfortable, and many have armrests, and the dining table height is just right. An impressive à la carte menu is provided in addition to the regular menu (Queens Grill regulars also know they can order specials at any time). The dining experience in the Queen Grill is, in a word, excellent and includes free caviar, an extra-cost item in the Princess Grill.

Todd English Restaurant: This alternative 216-seat reservations-only restaurant (cover charge: $20 for lunch and $30 for dinner) is named after Todd English, the chef whose restaurant in Boston (Olives) has become one of the best-known in high gastronomic circles

---

TRANSATLANTIC CROSSINGS ON *QM2*

The ship is supremely quiet in operation, with almost no vibration, even when traveling at top speed in poor weather. The large amount of personal luggage allowed is especially useful for anyone relocating, or for extended holidays. When you arrive in New York or Southampton, after six days of not having to lift a finger, it often proves to be a bittersweet anti-climax after the calming effects of *QM2* on one's inner being. I can think of little that is more pleasing to the soul or more civilized than a transatlantic crossing, of being cosseted in the finery of dining in any of the three grill restaurants with their fine cuisine and presentation (Grill Class accommodations only).

As a transatlantic ocean liner, this ship has no equal; it rides extremely well, and displays superb sea-keeping characteristics, with virtually no vibration from its pod propulsion system. If you can afford to travel in Grill Class accommodation, you will be cosseted in high comfort, and experience the very best service available in the grand transatlantic ocean liner traditions of today (including reserved open deck sunning space). If you travel in Britannia Class accommodation, the ship will provide you with a way to cross the North Atlantic, but with dining arrangements that are more akin to many of the large resort ships of today – although this

equates to a dumbing down of food quality and presentation.

Note that if you travel in accommodation with a balcony and you want sunshine on the crossing from Southampton to New York (westbound), book a suite/cabin on the port side. Eastbound, book on the starboard side. Going westbound, the Statue of Liberty will normally be on the port side, and, on leaving New York, on the starboard side.

QM2 now berths not in Manhattan but at the Red Hook Pier 12 passenger terminal in Brooklyn. In Southampton, England, the ship docks at the Queen Elizabeth II Ocean Terminal. Four special transatlantic packages are named The Queens, The Princess, The Buckingham and The Windsor. Each provides a combination of a one-way crossing with hotels and flights of differing classes and standards, according to the fare paid. Tailor-made programs are also available.

A few niggling items dent the premium image. One example is wooden stirrers (instead of real spoons) in the Kings Court – an indication of the "Carnivalization" of Cunard Line, although, to be honest, without the Carnival Corporation, Cunard Line would not have survived in today's harsh economic climate.

Another regret is the removal of an old transatlantic favorite, mid-morning bouillon service on deck.

in the US. It represents the American television chef's first venture at sea. The restaurant, with its Moorish decor, features his noted Mediterranean cuisine. The room has been designed with intimate detailing and architecture and overlooks the Pool Terrace, allowing for al fresco dining. Food presentation is excellent, although overly fussy at times, but the venue is disappointing.

Kings Court: This nondescript, informal eatery has 478 seats and obnoxious daytime lighting, and is reminiscent of such eateries found in land-based shopping malls. It offers self-serve breakfast and lunch. Breakfast is basically the same every day and includes British traditional standards: eggs, bacon, kippers and fried tomatoes. The lunch menu changes daily, and includes several Indian dishes (such as curried rice and chicken). Pizza, however, cannot be recommended (think cardboard with toppings). However, go to the beverage station and you'll find wooden stirrers – this is not acceptable for an ocean liner.

At night, decorated screens transform Kings Court into four different dining venues: an Italian Trattoria (La Piazza), Asian cuisine (Lotus), a British eatery (The Carvery) for roast meats, and a Chef's Galley; all have full sit-down tablecloth service. The 36-seat Chef's Galley has a live demonstration of the meal preparation that you then enjoy – at no extra charge. Cooking demonstrations can be broadcast via close circuit TV onto a large screen. Colorful "street entertainment" is performed in the Kings Court on some evenings.

Fast Foodies can find comfort foods in the outdoors Boardwalk café (weather permitting), while pub lovers can find traditional British fare in the always-popular Golden Lion Pub (including steak & mushroom pie, bangers and mash, and fish and chips). If you are shy and retiring and want complete privacy, or if you are recuperating from a busy working life, you can also order from the restaurant menus and have breakfast, lunch and dinner served in your own suite or cabin.

ENTERTAINMENT. The Royal Court Theatre, a lovely venue, has tiered seating for 1,094, though some sightlines are less than ideal, and is the main venue for evening entertainment, with lavish West End-style productions as well as featured headline entertainers and cabaret acts such as illusionists, comedians, comedy jugglers, acrobats, vocalists, and others. The Royal Academy of Dramatic Art (RADA) supplies a company of actors/actresses to perform and lead acting workshops in both the Royal Court Theatre and Illuminations (incorporating the Planetarium).

The ship carries a number of high-class bands, small musical units, duos and solo entertainers who provide live music in most of the 14 lounges and bars. Under a partnership with Oxford University, the ship's enrichment program features specialist lecturers such as authors, artists, historians, scientists and other celebrated intellectuals. Also, under a partnership with New York's Juilliard School of Music, selected jazz musicians join spring, summer and fall transatlantic crossings for special jazz performances in the Royal Court Theatre.

SPA/FITNESS. Health Spa and Beauty Services are provided in a 20,000 sq. ft (1,850 sq. meters) Canyon Ranch Spa Club arranged on two decks. Wellbeing treatments include many variations on the theme of massage and skin treatments, including Ayurvedic massage, aromatherapy and seaweed treatments, facials and masks, conditioning body scrubs and therapeutic body cocoons.

A thalassotherapy pool (with airbed recliner loungers, neck fountains, a deluge waterfall, airtub and body massage jet benches), whirlpool, and thermal suite (with saunas and aromatic steam rooms, and a Rasul treatment chamber) are part of the facilities of the extensive spa. There is a daily charge for using the facilities ($25 on sea days, $19 for port days), although this is waived if you purchase a treatment. In all, there are 24 wellbeing (body and skincare) treatment rooms.

Treatment price examples: Standard Massage $119 for 50 minutes; Hot Stone Massage $189 for 80 minutes; Aromatherapy Massage $129 for 50 minutes, $189 for 80 minutes; Facial $129 for 50 minutes; Shampoo/Set/Dry $39–$59 depending on hair length; Manicure $39 for 30 minutes; Pedicure $69-$119 for 60–80 minutes. You could also have a "Euphoria" treatment, which is a bath, facial and scalp massage followed by a body massage, for "just" $239. Prices include a gratuity. Treatment prices are for sea days (prices slightly less on port days).

A gymnasium has the latest equipment, as well as free weights. In addition, a beauty salon offers a full menu of services for hair and skin, and Canyon Ranch's own range of natural skincare products (Living Essentials) is available for sale. As there are only six hairdressing chairs, appointments should be booked as early as possible. The spa is staffed by 51 Canyon Ranch employees and operated as a concession.

● **For more extensive general information on what a Cunard Line cruise is like, see pages 138–9.**

Queen Victoria
★★★ + to ★★★★

Size:	Large Resort Ship	Passenger Decks:	12	Cabins (with private balcony):	718
Tonnage:	90,049	Total Crew:	1,001	Cabins (wheelchair accessible):	20
Lifestyle:	Premium	Passengers		Wheelchair accessibility	Good
Cruise Line:	Cunard Line	(lower beds/all berths):	2,014/2,172	Cabin Current:	110/220 volts
Former Names:	none	Passenger Space Ratio		Elevators:	12
Builder:	Fincantieri (Italy)	(lower beds/all berths):	44.7/41.4	Casino (gaming tables):	Yes
Original Cost:	$390 million	Crew/Passenger Ratio		Slot Machines:	Yes
Entered Service:	Dec 2007	(lower beds/all berths):	2.2/2.4	Swimming Pools (outdoors):	2
Registry:	Great Britain	Cabins (total):	1,007	Swimming Pools (indoors):	0
Length (ft/m):	964.5/294.0	Size Range (sq ft/m):	143.0–2,131.3/	Whirlpools:	5
Beam (ft/m):	105.9/32.3		13.2–198.0	Self-Service Launderette:	Yes
Draft (ft/m):	26.2/8.0	Cabins (outside view):	864	Dedicated Cinema/Seats:	No
Propulsion/Propellers:	diesel-electric	Cabins (interior/no view):	143	Library:	Yes
	(63.4mW)/pod propulsion (2)	Cabins (for one person):	0		

OVERALL SCORE: OUT OF A POSSIBLE 2,000 POINTS: GRILL CLASS 1,672; BRITANNIA CLASS 1,483

OVERVIEW. *Queen Victoria* flies the British Red Ensign for the ship's UK registry, and is aimed at the North American and British markets, but really is for anyone who is an Anglophile, because Cunard is still a resolutely British experience. Basically a stretched, modified platform and layout as the "Vista" series of ships (examples: *Arcadia, Carnival Legend, Costa Atlantica, Costa Luminosa, Costa Mediterranea, Oosterdam*), and of almost the same length as the now retired *QE2*, the Cunard version has an additional passenger deck, a specially strengthened hull lengthened by 36 ft (11 meters), giving the ship more of an "ocean liner" feel – and a modified, more traditional interior layout also reminiscent of yesteryear's ocean liners.

Outdoors facilities include a promenade deck; it's not teak, but a rubberized deck covering made to look like wooden planking, which gets hot and stays hot in warm weather areas. You can almost walk around – the forward section is for marine use only – and several deck lounge chairs with comfortable Cunard-logo cushioned pads make it a good place to read a book. One open deck atop the ship has a life-sized chess board.

Queen Victoria also has a rather classy interior layout that takes the best and most favourite public rooms, bars and lounges aboard *QM2* and from the now retired *QE2* and sets them into a high-tech ship designed to offer both trans-Atlantic and trans-Pacific crossings (but with a maximum speed of 23.7 knots), as well as squeeze through the Panama Canal and offer a mix of short and long voyages.

BERLITZ'S RATINGS

Grill Class	Possible	Achieved
Ship	500	428
Accommodation	200	166
Food	400	328
Service	400	329
Entertainment	100	82
Cruise	400	339
Britannia Class		
Ship	500	397
Accommodation	200	125
Food	400	274
Service	400	292
Entertainment	100	83
Cruise	400	312

The interior decor is best termed "traditional" in Cunard-speak, with many of the public rooms finely decorated in Edwardian/Victoria styles, with delightful wrought-iron balustrading on the staircases and in some of the bars. Most rooms have fine wood (veneer) paneling and decorative accents like wrought-iron horseshoe-shaped stairways, scrolled woodwork and etched glass panels.

Other features include a majestic three-deck high Grand Lobby with a sweeping staircase, sculpted balconies and other elegant decorative touches, and a Cunardia floating museum whose glass cabinets display models of former Cunard Line ships, old menus and daily programs.

Several public rooms are two decks high; these include the gold-beige Queen's Room, with a large, proper wooden ballroom dance floor (it measures about 1,000 sq.ft/93 sq. meters); above are two huge ceiling-mounted chandeliers. The bandstand is fronted by a large proscenium arch, while cantilevered balconies line the room's starboard side. Traditional British afternoon tea is served in this art deco-style grand room – although the tea itself is pretty basic.

The Royal Arcade is a cluster of seven shops, including Harrods, Royal Doulton and Wedgwood, set in an arcade-like environment.

At the forward end is a horseshoe-shaped staircase, above which is a magnificent British-made chiming pillar clock made by Dent of London – the company that created Big Ben at the Houses of Parliament and the official clock-maker to Queen Victoria herself, since 1841.

Some other venues worth noting:

● The **Library** is a really stunning two-deck-high wood-panelled 6,000-book facility with two full-time librarians. But there are few chairs on which to sit in and read. A bookshop in another location sells maritime-related books, memorabilia, maps and stationery. The Library is a great place to meet people, quietly, and the carpet is rather special, with the names of great authors scattered throughout.

● **Golden Lion Pub** – a must aboard a Cunarder. This one lies along the starboard side, and is a good gathering place for karaoke, sing-along, and quiz enthusiasts – plus, it has good pub food.

● The **Commodore Club** acts as a large observation lounge, with its ocean views on three sides, and late-night room for low-volume interactive entertainment.

● The adjacent **Churchill's Cigar Lounge**, on the starboard side, is a haven for smokers.

● **Chart Room Bar**, adjacent to the Britannia Restaurant – a place for a quiet drink before dinner.

● **Hemispheres**, positioned aft of the mast and adjacent to the Commodore Club, overlooks the wood-decked Pavilion Pool; this is the high-volume disco and themed nightclub.

● There's also a fairly large **casino** (no smoking) on the port side of the lower level of the Royal Court.

A grand conservatory (Winter Gardens), with central fountain and retractable glass roof, has a moveable glass wall to an open-air swimming pool. Rattan furniture and ceiling fans help to conjure up the area's colonial theme.

Art works worth more than $2 million, including original etchings by the liner's namesake and her husband Prince Albert, adorn various walls. An Internet Center is located adjacent to the Reception Desk on Deck 1.

The layout is a little disjointed on the uppermost decks, although the general flow is reasonably good. Note that access between the aft deck and the pool area and Winter Gardens can be gained only by going through the expansive buffet area. This makes for congestion at the self-serve buffet as people are constantly passing through, as in a railway carriage; but it's a very popular area and provides a wide choice of food items and special themed buffet food.

The pitiful amount of drawer space in the standard cabins is disappointing, even though new under-bed drawers were added at the end of 2008, leaving almost no space left for luggage storage.

*Queen Victoria*a very comfortable, likeable cruise ship posing as an ocean liner and it provides a suitable setting for passengers who enjoy dressing properly for dinner, either in formal or semi-formal attire. Passengers get cocktail party invitations, and enjoy the intellectual lecturers and specialist speakers who sail on each voyage – Cunard wisely calls them voyages, not cruises.

There's no doubting Cunard's British heritage, but trying to find British staff aboard this ship is like looking for a needle in a haystack – the proclaimed "Britishness" is really just marketing hype. Still, nice touches such as destination-themed sail-away music, the afternoon tea experience – but made with tea bags, not loose tea, so it's difficult to get the strength you like – a wide variety of entertainment, and

semi-decent service, albeit lacking in smiles or finesse, are some of the things that make Cunard stand out from the crowd. Note that the air conditioning that cannot be turned off in cabins or bathrooms.

The onboard currency is the US dollar – another reason to take the Britishness claims with a pinch of salt. A per person, per day gratuity is charged to your onboard account, and a 15% gratuity is added to all bar and wine accounts. Gratuities – called a Hotel and Dining charge – of $11–$13, depending on accommodation grade, are automatically added to your onboard account daily.

SUITABLE FOR: *Queen Victoria* is best suited to a couples and single travelers who enjoy the cosmopolitan setting of a ship that features traditional British ocean liner-style decor, world-wide itineraries, and dressing for dinner.

ACCOMMODATION. There are 31 different price grades (but just eight types of accommodation, which ranges from "ample" to opulent (note: balconies are included in measurements, which are approximate); 7 Queens Grill, 8 Princess Grill, and 20 Britannia grades. In the accommodation hallways, cabins on the port side (left side of the ship, facing forward) will find a red carpet, while those on the starboard (right) side will find a blue carpet.

Grand Suites (4, measuring 1,918–2,131 sq.ft). They are located aft, with great ocean views from their private wrap-around balconies, which contain a complete wet bar. The suites have two bedrooms with walk-in closets; bathroom with bathtub and separate shower enclosure; lounge; dining room (with seating for six). In-suite dining from the Queens Grill menus is also available.

Master Suites (2, measuring 1,100 sq.ft.), both located in the center of the ship (Deck 7).

Penthouse Suites (25, measuring 520–707 sq.ft).

Queens Suites (35, measuring 508–771 sq.ft).

Princess Suites (61, measuring 342–513 sq.ft).

Balcony Cabins (581, measuring 242–472 sq.ft).

Outside-View Cabins (146, measuring 180–201 sq.ft).

Interior (no-view) Cabins (143, measuring 151–243 sq.ft).

All accommodation grades have both British three-pin (240-volt) sockets and American and European-style two-pin (110-volt) sockets. Gilchrist & Soames personal toiletries (bath/shampoo gel, shampoo, conditioner, shower cap, cotton buds) are supplied to all passengers, and a hairdryer is stored in the vanity desk units. Some cabins have nicely indented ceilings with suffused lighting. However, the in-cabin flat-screen TV sets are small – not good for bedtime movie watching.

The regular cabins (Grades C/D) are small, but functional, although completely lacking in "wow" factor. The cabinetry resembles that in an Ibis hotel – a bit austere and lacking character. There is a distinct lack of drawer space in a cabin supposedly designed for two persons – it's very noticeable on long voyages, and the additional drawers located under the bed may prove challenging for some to use (it could be said that, when first introduced, *Queen Victoria* sailed without her drawers). The premium mattresses are, however, excellent, as is the bed linen; European duvets are standard.

The bathrooms, also, are stunningly bland, similar to those found aboard the ships of Princess Cruises, with small washbasins and little storage space for toiletries, and cold, tiled floors. The fixed-head shower doesn't permit the thorough wash that hand-held flexible hoses do. Overall, the standard (lower grade) cabins are a little underwhelming – so, for more space and quality, consider booking one of the higher grade cabins, or, better still, go for Grill-class accommodation – the perks and increased attention and service are really worth it. The walls in most accommodation passageways are rather plain, and could do with a little artwork.

CUISINE. Cunard is respected for its cuisine and service, with a wide variety of well-prepared and presented dishes made from good ingredients. The Britannia Restaurant – the name is taken from a former Cunard ocean liner of 1914–50 – is located in the ship's aft section. It is two decks high, with seating on both the main level (two seatings for dinner, but open seating for breakfast and lunch) and balcony level (which houses what are known as Britannia Club passengers – with single seat dining). A horseshoe-shaped stairway links both levels. While the lower level diners have a good sea view through large picture windows, balcony diners get a promenade view. Waterford Wedgwood china is used, and there's a wide range of wines (and prices).
Exclusive Dining (Queens Grill, Princess Grill)
There are two special Grill-Class only restaurants. These have a single-seating arrangement, providing a much more intimate and exclusive dining experience than can be found in the two-seating main Britannia Restaurant.

On the port side, the 142-seat Queens Grill, with its single-seating dining, is for passengers in suites and top category accommodation grades, and provides the best cuisine and service aboard the ship. The famous Cunard Grill experience also includes alfresco dining in a seldom used courtyard terrace (The Courtyard), suitably protected from the wind, and exclusive access for Grill-class passengers to their own upper terrace deck, with dedicated staff as well as the Grills' lounge and bar.

On the starboard side, the 132-seat **Princess Grill**, with single-seating dining, is for passengers in middle-class accommodation grades.
Alternative Dining Venue: The 87-seat Todd English Restaurant has the look and feel of a classic English dining salon, with fussy Mediterranean cuisine based on Todd English's chain of Olive-brand restaurants in the USA and presented on creative china. The restaurant is on the second level of the three-deck high lobby. Reservations are required, and there is a cover charge of $20 for lunch and $30 for dinner.
Casual Eatery: The Lido Café (on Deck 11) has good panoramic views, indoor/outdoor seating for 468, and offers a fairly standard multi-line self-serve buffet arrangement. For excellent Lavazza coffees from Maria (the coffee machine), and light bites, there's the Parisian-style Café Carinthia, located one deck above the Purser's Desk and adjacent to the popular Veuve Clicquot champagne bar.

For traditional British pub food, the Golden Lion Pub serves fish 'n' chips, steak and mushroom pie, ploughman's lunch, and, of course, bangers (sausages) and mash – particularly good at lunchtime – with a nice draft pint of bitter, naturally.

Cabin service is available 24 hours a day, so you can always have extra items when you are feeling peckish.

ENTERTAINMENT. The 830-seat, three-deck-high Royal Court Theatre is designed in the style of a classic opera house. In the tradition of a real London West End theatre, it provides 20 private "royal boxes" which can be reserved by any passengers for special nights. A special package includes champagne and chocolates, and ticket printed with name and box number. There's also a lounge for pre-show drinks.

A "Victoriana" show is all about good old British tradition. Other production shows include Celtic Heartbeat and Stroke of Genius, and a good variety of cabaret entertainment is presented. The Royal Court Theatre is also used to show large-screen movies. The ship has a number of bands, small combos and solo entertainers. A Big Band night is sometimes a feature in the Queens Room, and live jazz can be heard in several bars and lounges.

SPA/FITNESS. The Cunard Royal Health Club and Spa consists of a beauty salon, large gymnasium with high-tech muscle-pumping equipment and great ocean views; aerobics area; changing rooms for men and women (each with its own ocean-view sauna); a Thermal Area with sauna and steam rooms (extra-cost day passes are available if you don't book a treatment, at $35 per day, or at less per day cost for a multi-use pass); several body treatment rooms; a rasul chamber for private Hammam-style mud/steam bathing; and a relaxation area.

Sample prices: Swedish Massage $119 (55 mins); Deep Tissue Massage $129 (55 mins); Hot Stones Massage $149 (75 mins); Monticelli Mud Treatment $119 (60 mins); Rasul Chamber for couples ($75).

● **For more extensive general information on what a Cunard Line cruise is like, see pages 138–9.**

Radiance of the Seas
★★★★

Size: ....Large Resort Ship	Passenger Decks: 12	Cabins (with private balcony): 577
Tonnage: 90,090	Total Crew: 858	Cabins (wheelchair accessible): 14
Lifestyle: ....Standard	Passengers	(8 with private balcony)
Cruise Line: Royal Caribbean International	(lower beds/all berths): 2,112/2,500	Wheelchair accessibility ....Good
Former Names: ....none	Passenger Space Ratio	Cabin Current: ....110/220 volts
Builder: ....Meyer Werft (Germany)	(lower beds/all berths): 42.6/36.0	Elevators: 9
Original Cost: ....$350 million	Crew/Passenger Ratio	Casino (gaming tables): ....Yes
Entered Service: ....Apr 2001	(lower beds/all berths): 2.4/2.9	Slot Machines: ....Yes
Registry: ....The Bahamas	Cabins (total): 1,056	Swimming Pools (outdoors): 2
Length (ft/m): 961.9/293.2	Size Range (sq ft/m): 165.8–1,216.3/	Swimming Pools (indoors): 0
Beam (ft/m): 105.6/32.2	15.4–113.0	Whirlpools: 3
Draft (ft/m): 27.8/8.5	Cabins (outside view): 813	Self-Service Launderette: ....No
Propulsion/Propellers: .....Gas turbine/2	Cabins (interior/no view): 237	Dedicated Cinema/Seats: Yes/40
azimuthing pods (20 MW each)	Cabins (for one person): 0	Library: ....Yes

OVERALL SCORE: 1,446 OUT OF A POSSIBLE 2,000 POINTS

OVERVIEW. *Radiance of the Seas* was the first Royal Caribbean International ship to use gas and steam turbine power instead of the more conventional diesel or diesel-electric combination. Pod propulsion is provided *(see page 45 for a detailed explanation).*

As aboard all RCI vessels, the navigation bridge is of the fully enclosed type (good for cruising in cold-weather areas such as Alaska). In the very front of the ship is a helipad, which also acts as a viewing platform for passengers.

Radiance of the Seas is a streamlined contemporary ship, and has a two-deck-high wrap-around structure in the forward section of the funnel. Along the ship's starboard side, a central glass wall protrudes, giving great views (cabins with balconies occupy the space directly opposite on the port side). The gently rounded stern has nicely tiered decks. One of two swimming pools can be covered by a large glass dome for use as an indoor/outdoor pool.

Inside, the decor is contemporary, yet elegant, bright and cheerful. A nine-deck high atrium lobby has glass-walled elevators (on the port side of the ship) that travel through 12 decks, face the sea and provide a link with nature and the ocean. The Centrum (as the atrium is called), has several public rooms connected to it: the guest relations (the contemporary term for purser's office) and shore excursions desks, a Lobby Bar, Champagne Bar, the Library, Royal Caribbean Online, the Concierge Club, and a Crown & Anchor Lounge. A great view can be had of the atrium by looking down through the flat glass dome high above it.

Other facilities include a delightful, but very small library. There's also a Champagne Bar, and a large Schooner Bar that houses maritime art in an integral art gallery. Gamblers

BERLITZ'S RATINGS		
	Possible	Achieved
Ship	500	415
Accommodation	200	154
Food	400	238
Service	400	262
Entertainment	100	78
Cruise	400	299

should enjoy Casino Royale, with its French Art Nouveau decorative theme and 11 crystal chandeliers. There's also a small dedicated screening room for movies (with space for two wheelchairs), as well as a 194-seat conference center, and a business center.

The Viking Crown Lounge is a large structure set around the base of the ship's funnel. It functions as an observation lounge during the daytime (with views forward over the swimming pool). In the evening, the space features Starquest – a futuristic, high-energy dance club, and Hollywood Odyssey – a more intimate and relaxed entertainment venue for softer mood music and "black box" theater.

For those who wish to go online, Royal Caribbean Online is a dedicated computer center with 12 computers, located in a semi-private setting (in addition, data ports are provided in all cabins). Four more internet-access terminals are located in Books 'n' Coffee, a bookshop with coffee and pastries, located in an extensive area of shops.

Youth facilities include Adventure Ocean, an "edutainment" area with four separate age-appropriate sections for junior passengers: Aquanaut Center (for ages 3–5); Explorer Center (6–8); Voyager Center (9–12); and the Optix Teen Center (13–17). There is also Adventure Beach, which includes a splash pool complete with waterslide; Surfside, with computer lab stations with entertaining software; and Ocean Arcade, a video games hangout.

The artwork aboard this ship is really eclectic (so there should be something for all tastes), and provides a spectrum and a half of color works. It ranges from Jenny M. Hansen's *A Vulnerable Moment* glass sculpture to David Buckland's "Industrial and Russian Constructionism

1920s" in photographic images on glass and painted canvas, to a huge multi-deck high contemporary bicycle-cum-paddlewheel sculpture design suspended in the atrium.

Radiance of the Seas offers more space and more comfortable public areas (and several more intimate spaces), slightly larger cabins and more dining options – for the younger, active, hip and trendy set – than most RCI ships. The grand amount of glass provides more contact with the ocean around you. In the final analysis, however, while the ship is quite delightful in many ways, the onboard operation is less so, and suffers from a lack of trained service staff.

ACCOMMODATION. There is a wide range of suites and standard outside-view and interior (no view) cabins in 10 different categories and 19 different price groups.

Apart from the largest suites (six owner's suites), which have king-sized beds, almost all other cabins have twin beds that convert to a queen-sized bed (all sheets are of 100% Egyptian cotton, although the blankets are synthetic). All cabins have rich (but faux) wood cabinetry, including a vanity desk (with hairdryer), faux wood drawers that close silently (hooray), television, personal safe, and three-sided mirrors. Some cabins have ceiling recessed, pull-down berths for third and fourth persons, although closet and drawer space would be extremely tight for four persons (even if two of them are children), and some have interconnecting doors (so families with children can cruise together, in separate, but adjacent cabins. Audio channels are available through the TV set, whose picture cannot be turned off while listening to an audio channel.

Most bathrooms have tiled accenting a terrazzo-style tiled floor, and a small shower enclosure in a half-moon shape, 100% Egyptian cotton towels, a small cabinet for personal toiletries and a small shelf. In reality, there is little space to stow personal toiletries for two (or more).

The largest accommodation consists of a family suite with two bedrooms. One bedroom has twin beds (convertible to queen-sized bed), while a second has two lower beds and two upper Pullman berths, a combination that can sleep up to eight persons (this would be suitable for large families).

Occupants of accommodation designated as suites also get the use of a private Concierge Lounge (where priority dining room reservations, shore excursion bookings and beauty salon/spa appointments can be made). Many of the "private" balcony cabins are not very private, as they can be overlooked from various locations.

CUISINE. Cascades, the main dining room, spans two decks (the upper deck level has floor-to-ceiling windows, while the lower deck level has picture windows), and is a lovely, but noisy, dining hall – reminiscent of those aboard the transatlantic liners in their heyday (however, eight huge, thick pillars do obstruct the sight lines). It seats 1,104, and has cascading water themed decor. There are tables for two, four, six, eight or 10 Two small private dining rooms (Breakers, with 94 seats and Tides, with 30 seats) are located off the main dining room. When you book, choose one of two seatings, or "My Time Dining" (eat when you want, during dining room hours). No smoking is permitted in the dining venues.

Alternative dining options: Portofino, with 112 seats (and a magnificent "cloud" ceiling), has Italian cuisine (choices include: antipasti, soup, salad, pasta, main dish, dessert, cheese and coffee). Chops Grill Steakhouse, with 95 seats and an open (show) kitchen, serves premium meats in the form of veal chops and steaks (New York Striploin Steak, Filet Mignon, and Prime Rib of Beef). The food in these venues is of a much higher quality than in the main dining room, though the menus do not change during the cruise. There is an additional charge of $20 per person for Portofino, and $25 per person for Chops Grille (including gratuities), and reservations are required for both dining spots, which are generally open 6pm –11pm. The dress code is smart casual.

Casual meals can be taken for breakfast, lunch and dinner in the self-serve, buffet-style Windjammer Cafe, accessible directly from the pool deck. It has islands dedicated to specific foods, and indoors and outdoors seating.

Additionally, there is the Seaview Café, open for lunch and dinner. The self-serve buffet and the menu offer fast-food seafood items, plus hamburgers and hot dogs.

ENTERTAINMENT. The three-level Aurora Theater has 874 seats (including 24 stations for wheelchairs) and good sightlines from most seats. The Colony Club hosts casual cabaret shows, including late-night adult (blue) comedy, and provides live music for dancing. The entertainment throughout is upbeat. There is even background music in all corridors and elevators, and constant music outdoors on the pool deck. If you want a quiet, relaxing holiday, choose another ship.

SPA/FITNESS. The ShipShape Spa's health, fitness and spa facilities have themed decor, and include a 10,176 sq.-ft (945 sq.-meter) solarium with whirlpool and counter current swimming under a retractable magrodome roof, a gymnasium (with 44 cardiovascular machines), 50-person aerobics room, sauna and steam rooms, and therapy treatment rooms. All are located on two of the uppermost decks, forward of the mast, with access from the forward stairway.

A climate-controlled 10,176 sq. ft (945 sq. meter) indoor/outdoor Solarium (with sliding glass roof that can be closed in cool or inclement weather) provides facilities for relaxation. It has a fascinating African themed decor, and includes a whirlpool and counter current swimming.

For more sporting passengers, there is activity galore – including a rock-climbing wall that's 30 ft (9 meters) high, with five separate climbing tracks. It is located outdoors at the aft end of the funnel. There is also an exterior jogging track.

Other sports facilities include a 9-hole miniature golf course with novel 17th-century decorative ornaments, and an indoor/outdoor country club with golf simulator, a jogging track, and basketball court. Want to play pool? Well, you can, thanks to two specially stabilized tables.

● **For more extensive general information about the Royal Caribbean experience, see pages 151–6.**

Regatta
★★★★ +

Size: . . . . .Mid-Size Ship	Passenger Decks: 9	Cabins (with private balcony): 232
Tonnage: .30,277	Total Crew: 386	Cabins (wheelchair accessible): 3
Lifestyle: . . . . .Premium	Passengers	Wheelchair accessibility . . . . .Good
Cruise Line: . . . . .Oceania Cruises	(lower beds/all berths): 684/824	Cabin Current: . . . . .110 and 220 volts
Former Names: . . . . .R Two	Passenger Space Ratio	Elevators: 4
Builder: . . . . . . .Chantiers de l'Atlantique	(lower beds/all berths): 44.2/36.7	Casino (gaming tables): . . . . .Yes
Original Cost: . . . .£150 million	Crew/Passenger Ratio	Slot Machines: . . . . .Yes
Entered Service: Dec1998/Dec 2003	(lower beds/all berths): 1.7/2.1	Swimming Pools (outdoors): 1
Registry: . . . . .Marshall Islands	Cabins (total): 342	Swimming Pools (indoors): 0
Length (ft/m): 593.7/181.0	Size Range (sq ft/m): 145.3–968.7/	Whirlpools: . . . . . . .2 (+1 thalassotherapy)
Beam (ft/m): 83.5/25.5	13.5–90.0	Self-Service Launderette: . . . . .Yes
Draft (ft/m): 19.5/6.0	Cabins (outside view): 317	Dedicated Cinema/Seats: . . . . .No
Propulsion/Propellers: . . . . .diesel	Cabins (interior/no view): 25	Library: . . . . .Yes
. . . .(18,600 kW)/2	Cabins (for one person): 0	

OVERALL SCORE: 1,572 (OUT OF A POSSIBLE 2,000 POINTS)

OVERVIEW. *Regatta* was formerly one of a series of eight almost identical ships, originally built for the now-defunct Renaissance Cruises, the cruise industry's first totally non-smoking cruise line. The ship's present owners, Cruise Invest, have chartered the ship to Oceania Cruises. The exterior design manages to balance the ship's high sides by painting the whole ship white (it previously had a dark blue hull), with a large, square white funnel. The addition of teak overlaid decking and teak lounge chairs have greatly improved what was formerly a bland pool deck outdoors – but the front rows of double sunloungers are called cabanas, and it costs $100 per day to use them.

The interior decor is stunning and elegant, a throwback to the ocean liners of the 1920s and '30s, with dark woods and warm colors, all carried out in fine taste (but a bit *faux* in places). It feels like an old-world country club.

The public rooms are spread over three decks. The reception hall (lobby) has a staircase with intricate wrought-iron railings. A large observation lounge, called the Horizon Bar, is located high atop ship.

There are plenty of bars – including one in each of the restaurant entrances. Perhaps the nicest is the casino bar/lounge, a beautiful room reminiscent of London's grand hotels and includes a martini bar. It has an inviting marble fireplace, comfortable sofas and individual chairs.

The Library is a grand Regency-style room, with a fireplace, a high, indented, *trompe l'oeil* ceiling, and excellent selection of books, plus very comfortable wingback chairs with footstools, and sofas you could sleep on. Oceania @Sea is the internet connect center.

The dress code is "smart casual." Gratuities are added at

BERLITZ'S RATINGS

	Possible	Achieved
Ship	500	416
Accommodation	200	160
Food	400	312
Service	400	295
Entertainment	100	76
Cruise	400	313

$10.50 per person, per day (accommodation designated as suites have an extra $3 per person charge for the butler). A 15% gratuity is added to bar and spa accounts. Onboard currency: the US dollar.

There is no walk-around promenade deck outdoors (there is, however, a small jogging track around the perimeter of the swimming pool, and port and starboard side decks). Stairways, though carpeted, are tinny. Oceania Cruises is a young company with a refreshing vision and desire to provide a high level of food and service in an informal setting that is elegant yet comfortable, and that is exactly what it has achieved. Passenger niggles include all the "inventive" extra charges that can be incurred.

SUITABLE FOR: *Regatta* is best suited to couples who like good food and style, but want informality with no formal nights on board, and interesting itineraries, all at a very reasonable price well below what the luxury ships charge.

ACCOMMODATION. There are six cabin categories, and 10 price grades (3 suite price grades; 5 outside-view cabin grades; 2 interior (no view) cabin grades. All of the standard interior (no view) and outside-view cabins (the lowest four grades) are extremely compact units, and extremely tight for two persons (particularly for cruises longer than five days). They have twin beds (or queen-sized bed), with good under-bed storage areas, personal safe, vanity desk with large mirror, good closet and drawer space (in rich, dark woods), 100% cotton bathrobe and towels, slippers, clothes brush and shoe horn. Color TVs carry a major news channel (where obtainable), plus a sports channel and round-the-clock movie channels.

Certain cabin categories (about 100 of them) qualify as "Concierge Level" accommodation, and occupants get extra goodies such as enhanced bathroom amenities, complimentary shoeshine, tote bag, cashmere throw blanket, bottle of champagne on arrival, hand-held hairdryer, priority restaurant reservations, and priority embarkation.

Owner's Suites. The six Owner's Suites, measuring around 962 sq.ft/89.3 sq.meters, provide the most spacious accommodation. They are fine, large living spaces located aft overlooking the stern on Decks 6, 7, and 8 (they are, however, subject to more movement and some vibration). They have extensive teak-floor private balconies that really are private and cannot be overlooked from the decks above. Each has an entrance foyer, living room, separate bedroom (the bed faces the sea, which can be seen through the floor-to-ceiling windows and sliding glass door), CD player (with selection of audio discs), fully tiled bathroom with Jacuzzi bathtub, and a small guest bathroom.

Vista Suites. There are four, each measuring around 785.7 sq.ft/73 sq.meters, and located forward on Decks 5 and 6. They have extensive teak-floor private balconies that cannot be overlooked by anyone from the decks above. Each has an entrance foyer, living room, separate bedroom (the bed faces the sea, which can be seen through the floor-to-ceiling windows and sliding glass door), CD player (with selection of audio discs), and fully tiled bathroom with Jacuzzi bathtub.

Penthouse Suites. There are 52 of these (actually, they are not suites at all, but large cabins as the bedrooms aren't separate from the living areas). They do, however, measure around 322.9 sq.ft (30 sq. meters), and have a good-sized teak-floor balcony with sliding glass door (but with partial, and not full, balcony partitions) and teak deck furniture. The lounge area has a proper dining table and there is ample clothes storage space. The bathroom has a tub, shower enclosure, washbasin and toilet.

Cabins with Balcony. Cabins with private balconies (around 216 sq.ft/20 sq. meters), comprise about 66% of all cabins. They have partial, not full, balcony partitions, sliding glass doors, and only 14 cabins on Deck 6 have lifeboat-obstructed views. The living area has a refrigerated mini-bar, lounge area with breakfast table, and a balcony with teak floor, two teak chairs and a drinks table. The bathrooms, with tiled floors and plain walls, are compact, standard units, and include a shower stall with a strong, removable hand-held shower unit, hairdryer, toiletries storage shelves and retractable clothesline.

Outside View and Interior (No View) Cabins. These measure around 160–165 sq.ft (14.8–15.3 sq.meters), and have twin beds (convertible to a queen-sized bed), vanity desk, small sofa and coffee table, and bathroom with a shower enclosure with a strong, removable hand-held shower unit, hairdryer, toiletries storage shelves, retractable clothesline, washbasin, and toilet. Although they are not large, they are quite comfortable, with a decent amount of storage space.

All suites/cabins located at the stern of the ship may suffer from vibration and noise, particularly when the ship is proceeding at or close to full speed, or maneuvering in port.

CUISINE. Flexibility and choice are what the dining facilities aboard the Oceania ships are all about. There are four different restaurants:

● The **Grand Dining Room** has around 340 seats, and a raised central section, but the problem is the noise level – because of the low ceiling height, it's atrocious when the dining room is full. Being located at the stern, there are large ocean-view windows on three sides (prime tables overlook the stern). The chairs are comfortable and have armrests. The menus change daily for lunch and dinner.

● The **Toscana Italian Restaurant** has 96 seats, windows along two sides, and a set menu (plus daily chef's specials).

● The cozy **Polo Grill** has 98 seats, windows along two sides and a set menu including prime steaks and seafood.

● The **Terrace Cafe** has seats for 154 indoors – not enough during cruises to cold-weather areas – and 186 outdoors. It is open for breakfast, lunch and casual dinners, when it has tapas (Tapas on the Terrace) and other Mediterranean food. As the ship's self-serve buffet restaurant, it incorporates a small pizzeria and grill. There are basic salads, a meat carving station, and a reasonable selection of cheeses.

All restaurants have open-seating dining, so you can dine when you want, with whom you wish. Reservations are needed in Toscana Restaurant and Polo Grill (but there's no extra charge), where there are mostly tables for four or six; there are few tables for two. There is a Poolside Grill Bar. All cappuccino and espresso coffees cost extra.

The food and service staff is provided by Apollo, a respected maritime catering company that also has an interest in Oceania Cruises. The consultant chef is American TV chef Jacques Pepin. Oceania Cruises' brochure claims "Cuisine so extraordinary it's unrivalled at sea" is hogwash – it's good, but not that good.

ENTERTAINMENT. The Regatta Lounge has entertainment, lectures and some social events. There is little entertainment due to the intensive nature of the itineraries. However, there is live music in several bars and lounges.

SPA/FITNESS. A lido deck has a swimming pool, and good sunbathing space, plus a thalassotherapy tub. A jogging track circles the swimming pool deck (but one deck above). The uppermost outdoors deck includes a golf driving net and shuffleboard court. The Oceania Spa consists of a beauty salon, three treatment rooms, men's and women's changing rooms, and steam room (there is no sauna). Canyon Ranch SpaClub operates the spa and beauty salon, and provides the staff.

Examples of pricing include: full body massage $99 (50 minutes); foot and ankle massage $39 (20 minutes); body contour wrap, $159 (75 minutes); botanical therapy facial, $99 (75 minutes); personal training session $75 (75 minutes); shampoo, style and dry $29 (short hair); manicure $29; pedicure $39. Note that 15% is added to your spa account, whether you like it or not.

Rhapsody of the Seas
★★★★

Size: ....Large Resort Ship	Passenger Decks: 11	Cabins (with private balcony): 229
Tonnage: 78,491	Total Crew: 765	Cabins (wheelchair accessible): 14
Lifestyle: ....Standard	Passengers	Wheelchair accessibility ....Good
Cruise Line: Royal Caribbean International	(lower beds/all berths): 2,000/2,435	Cabin Current: ....110 and 220 volts
Former Names: ....none	Passenger Space Ratio	Elevators: 9
Builder: Chantiers de l'Atlantique (France)	(lower beds/all berths): 39.2/32.2	Casino (gaming tables): ....Yes
Original Cost: ....$275 million	Crew/Passenger Ratio	Slot Machines: ....Yes
Entered Service: ....May 1997	(lower beds/all berths): 2.6/3.1	Swimming Pools (outdoors): 1
Registry: ....The Bahamas	Cabins (total): 1,000	Swimming Pools (indoors): 1
Length (ft/m): 915.3/279.0	Size Range (sq ft/m): 135.0–1,270.1/	(inside/outside)
Beam (ft/m): 105.6/32.2	12.5–118.0	Whirlpools: 6
Draft (ft/m): 24.9/7.6	Cabins (outside view): 593	Self-Service Launderette: ....No
Propulsion/Propellers: .....diesel-electric	Cabins (interior/no view): 407	Dedicated Cinema/Seats: ....No
(50,400kW)/2	Cabins (for one person): 0	Library: ....Yes

OVERALL SCORE: 1,490 OUT OF A POSSIBLE 2,000 POINTS

OVERVIEW. This striking all-white ship, sister to *Vision of the Seas*, shares design features that make many (but not all) of the Royal Caribbean International ships identifiable, including a Viking Crown Lounge and a terrific multi-level nightspot – the music can be loud and overbearing, however.

The Viking Crown Lounge (which is also the ship's disco) aboard this sister ship is positioned just aft of the center of the ship, above the central atrium lobby. The funnel is well aft – a departure from all other RCI ships to date – which positions the Viking Crown lounge around the funnel or at its base. The ship's stern is beautifully rounded.

There is a reasonable amount of open-air walking space, although this tends to become cluttered with sun-loungers. There's also a wide range of interesting public rooms, lounges and bars, and the interiors have been cleverly designed to avoid congestion and aid passenger flow into revenue areas. Speaking of which, for those who enjoy gambling, the astrologically-themed casino is large and rather glitzy (although not as bold as aboard some of the company's other ships), again typical of most of the new large ships; a couple of pieces of "electrostatic" art in globe form provide fascinating relief.

The atrium lobby is the ship's interior focal point – this is always a good place to arrange to meet anyone – and has a large kinetic sculpture, called *Diadem*. It is a multi-material construction that spans six decks, and features an astrological theme, as do many of the decorative elements throughout the ship. The interior decor throughout is imaginative, and provides a connection between sea and stars.

There is, predictably, a large shopping area, although the

BERLITZ'S RATINGS

	Possible	Achieved
Ship	500	425
Accommodation	200	166
Food	400	240
Service	400	286
Entertainment	100	81
Cruise	400	292

merchandise is consistently tacky. The artwork throughout the ship is really upbeat and colorful, and has a musical theme: classical, jazz, popular and rock 'n' roll. Much improved over previous new ships in the fleet is the theater, with more entrances and fewer bottlenecks; there are still pillars obstructing sight-lines from many seats. Also improved are the facilities for children and teens.

Ship enthusiasts will like the chair fabric in the Shall We Dance lounge, with its large aft-facing windows, and the glass case-enclosed mechanical sculptures. What, in particular, makes this ship feel warm and cozy are the use of fine, light wood surfaces throughout its public rooms, as well as the large array of potted plants everywhere.

ACCOMMODATION. There are 18 grades, prices depending on grade, size and location. The standard interior (no view) and exterior view cabins are of an adequate size, and have just enough functional facilities to make them comfortable for a one-week cruise, but longer might prove confining. The decor is bright and cheerful, although the ceilings are plain; the soft furnishings make this home away from home look like the inside of a modern Scandinavian hotel – with minimalist tones, and splashes of color. Twin lower beds convert to queen-sized beds, and there is a reasonable amount of closet and drawer space, but there is little room to maneuver between the bed and desk/television unit.

The bathrooms are small but functional, although the shower units themselves are small, and there is no cabinet for one's personal toiletries. The towels should be larger and thicker. In the passageways, upbeat artwork depicts musical themes, from classical to jazz and popular.

Choose a "C" grade suite if you want spacious accommodation that includes a separate (curtained-off) sleeping area, a good-sized outside balcony (with part, not full, partition), lounge with sofa, two chairs and coffee table, three closets, plenty of drawer and storage space, television and VCR. The bathroom is large and has a full-size bathtub, integral shower, and two washbasins/two toiletries cabinets.

For the best accommodation aboard this ship, choose the Royal Suite, which resembles a Palm Beach apartment, and comes complete with a white baby grand (player) piano. It has a separate bedroom with king-size bed, living room with queen-sized sofa bed, refrigerator/mini-bar, dining table, entertainment center, and vanity dressing area.

The decor is simple and elegant, with pastel colors, and wood-accented ceiling treatments. Located just under the starboard side navigation bridge wing, it has its own private balcony.

CUISINE. The two-level Edelweiss Dining Room is attractive and works well, although the noise level can be high. When you book, choose one of two seatings, or "My Time Dining" (eat when you want, during dining room hours).

The Windjammer Cafe is the casual dining spot for self-serve buffets. The area is well designed, with contemporary decor and colors, but the food is basic fare and disappointing; the self-service buffet area is small for the number of passengers using it. More money needs to be spent for better ingredients and more variety. Each evening, the room offers an alternative to the more formal dining room. The evening buffets have a different theme, something this company has been doing for more than 25 years – perhaps the time has come for more creativity.

There is a hamburger/hot dog grill counter in the Solarium, but typically you don't get a choice of how well done or not so well done you get your hamburgers – everything appears to be well done. The company has introduced a drinks package (available at all bars, in the form of cards or stickers) that enables you to pre-pay for a selection of standard soft drinks and alcoholic drinks. The packages are not exactly easy to understand.

ENTERTAINMENT. The Broadway Melodies Theater is the ship's principal showlounge. It is a large, but well-designed room with main and balcony levels, and good sight lines from most of the banquette seats.

Other cabaret acts are featured in the Shall We Dance Lounge, located aft, and these include late-night adult (blue) comedy, as well as live music for dancing. A number of other bars and lounges have live music of differing types.

The entertainment throughout is upbeat. There is even background music in all passenger hallways and elevators, and constant music outdoors on the pool deck. If you want a quiet relaxing holiday, choose another ship.

SPA/FITNESS. There are good health spa facilities, set in a spacious environment on one of the uppermost decks. The decor has Egypt as its theme, with pharaohs lining the pool. The spa is operated by Steiner, a specialist concession

For the more sporting, there is activity galore – including a rock-climbing wall, with several separate climbing tracks. It is located outdoors at the aft end of the funnel.

● **For more extensive general information on what a Royal Caribbean cruise is like, see pages 151–6.**

QUOTABLE QUOTES

These are some of the questions I have been asked over the years by newcomers to cruising:

"Will we have time to take the shore excursion?"

"Are the entertainers paid?"

"Why don't we have a Late Night Comedy Spot in the afternoon?"

"Is the mail brought in by plane?"

"Why aren't the dancers fully dressed?"

"How do we know which photos are ours?"

"Will the ship wait for the tour buses to get back?"

"Will I get wet if I go snorkeling?"

"Do the Chinese do the laundry by hand?"

"Does the ship dock in the middle of town?"

"Is the doctor qualified?"

"Who's driving the ship if the captain is at the cocktail party?"

"Does the sun always rise on the left side of the ship?"

"Is trapshooting held outside?"

"I'm married, but can I come to the Singles Party?"

"Should I put my luggage outside the cabin before or after I go to sleep?"

"Does an outside cabin mean it's outside the ship?"

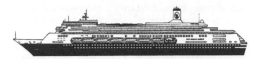

Rotterdam
★★★★

Size:	.Mid-Size Ship	Passenger Decks:	.12	Cabins (with private balcony):	.160
Tonnage:	.59,652	Total Crew:	.593	Cabins (wheelchair accessible):	.20
Lifestyle:	.Premium	Passengers		Wheelchair accessibility	.Best
Cruise Line:	.Holland America Line	(lower beds/all berths):	.1,320/1,668	Cabin Current:	.110 and 220 volts
Former Names:	.none	Passenger Space Ratio		Elevators:	.12
Builder:	.Fincantieri (Italy)	(lower beds/all berths):	.45.1/35.7	Casino (gaming tables):	.Yes
Original Cost:	.$250 million	Crew/Passenger Ratio		Slot Machines:	.Yes
Entered Service:	.Dec 1997	(lower beds/all berths):	.2.2/2.8	Swimming Pools (outdoors):	.1
Registry:	.The Netherlands	Cabins (total):	.660	Swimming Pools (indoors):	.1
Length (ft/m):	.777.5/237.00	Size Range (sq ft/m):	.184.0–1,124.8/		(magrodome cover)
Beam (ft/m):	.105.8/32.25		17.1–104.5	Whirlpools:	.2
Draft (ft/m):	.25.5/7.80	Cabins (outside view):	.542	Self-Service Launderette:	.Yes
Propulsion/Propellers:	.diesel-electric	Cabins (interior/no view):	.118	Dedicated Cinema/Seats:	.Yes/235
	(37,500kW)/2	Cabins (for one person):	.0	Library:	.Yes

OVERALL SCORE: 1,539 OUT OF A POSSIBLE 2,000 POINTS

OVERVIEW. This latest *Rotterdam* has been constructed to look like a slightly larger (longer and beamier), but certainly a much sleeker version of the *"S" class* ships, while retaining the graceful lines of the former *Rotterdam*, including a nicely raked bow and a more rounded exterior, as well as the familiar interior flow and design style. Also retained is the twin-funnel feature well recognized by former Holland America Line passengers, though it has been somewhat more streamlined. This *Rotterdam* (the sixth Holland America Line ship to bear the name) is capable of 25 knots (some call it the *Fastdam*), which is useful for longer itineraries.

Two decks (Promenade Deck and Upper Promenade Deck) house most of the public rooms, and these are sandwiched between several accommodation decks. The layout is quite easy to learn, and the signage is good.

The interior decor is best described as restrained, with much use of wood accenting. As a whole, the decor of this ship is extremely refined, with much of the traditional ocean liner detailing so loved by frequent Holland America Line passengers. The focal interior point is a three-deck high atrium, in an oval, instead of circular, shape. The atrium's focal point is a huge "one-of-a-kind" custom-made clock, which includes an astrolabe, an astrological clock and 14 other clocks in a structure that takes up three decks (the clock's design is based on an antique Flemish original).

One room has a glass ceiling similar to that aboard a former *Statendam*. The Ambassador's Lounge has an interesting brass dance floor, similar to the dance floor that adorned the Ritz-Carlton room aboard the previous *Rotterdam*.

Instead of just two staircases aboard the "S"-class ships,

BERLITZ'S RATINGS

	Possible	Achieved
Ship	500	428
Accommodation	200	165
Food	400	281
Service	400	279
Entertainment	100	76
Cruise	400	310

Rotterdam has three (better from the viewpoint of safety, passenger accessibility and evacuation). There is a pool, covered by a glass dome, on the Lido Deck between the mast and the ship's twin funnels, as aboard the company's "S"-class ships, which have only one large, very square funnel.

The ship has allotted more space to children's and teens' play areas, although these really are token gestures by a company that traditionally does not cater well to children. However, grandparents do take their grandchildren with them (to the delight of parents, who get a well-deserved break). Enhanced children's programming is brought into play according to the number of children carried.

Popcorn is available at the Wajang Theatre for moviegoers, while adjacent is the popular Java Cafe. The casino, which is located in the middle of a major passenger flow, has blackjack, roulette, poker and dice tables alongside the requisite rows of slot machines.

Holland America Line has a long legacy in Dutch maritime history. The artwork aboard this ship (it cost $2 million) consists of a collection of 17th-century Dutch and Japanese artifacts together with contemporary works specially created for the ship, although there seems little linkage between some of the items.

As part of its "Signature of Excellence" (refreshing the ships) program, the ships have received a "Mix," a new open area. The trendy, upbeat space combines three specialty theme bars: Champagne (serving champagne and sparkling wines) from around the world, Martinis (in individual shakers), and Spirits & Ales (a sports bar – beer and baseball/basketball for the boys). Additionally, Microsoft

Surface touch-screen technology is available for playing checkers and chess, air hockey, and other sports games.

Holland America Line's flagship replaced the former ship of the same name when it was retired in 1997 – just in time for the start of the company's 125th anniversary in 1998. It is a most contemporary ship for Holland America Line, with lighter, brighter decor. It is an extremely comfortable vessel in which to cruise, with some fine, elegant and luxurious decorative features. However, these are marred somewhat by the poor quality of dining room food and service and the lack of understanding of what it takes to make a so-called "luxury" cruise experience, despite what is touted in the company's brochures.

With one whole deck of suites (and a dedicated, private concierge lounge, and preferential passenger treatment), the company has in effect created a two-class ship. Passenger niggles include the charge to use the washing machines and dryers in the self-service launderette – petty and irritating, particularly for the occupants of suites, as they pay high prices for their cruises; inadequate room service, and poor staff communication. Non-smokers should avoid this ship, as smokers seem to be everywhere.

In a 2009 refit, 23 Verandah Deck cabins were converted into "Spa Cabins," while new Lancei-style cabins were created on Lower Promenade Deck.

ACCOMMODATION. There are 17 categories, prices depending on grade, size and location. Accommodation is spread over five decks (some cabins have full or partially obstructed views). Interestingly, no cabin is more than 144 ft (44 meters) from a stairway, which makes it easier to get from cabins to public rooms. All cabin doors have a bird's-eye maple look, and hallways have framed fabric panels to make them less clinical. Cabin televisions carry CNN and TNT.

All standard inside and outside cabins are tastefully furnished, and have twin beds that convert to a queen-sized bed (space is tight for walking between beds and vanity unit). There is a decent amount of closet and drawer space, although this will prove tight for the longer voyages featured.

The bathrooms, which are fully tiled, are disappointingly small (particularly for long cruises) and have small shower tubs, utilitarian personal toiletries cupboards, and exposed under-sink plumbing. There is no detailing to distinguish them significantly from bathrooms aboard the "S"-class ships.

There are 36 full verandah suites (Navigation Deck), including four penthouse suites, which share a private Concierge Lounge with a concierge to handle such things as special dining arrangements, shore excursions and special requests – although strangely there are no butlers for these suites, as aboard ships with similar facilities. Each suite has a separate steward's entrance and separate bedroom, dressing and living areas. Suite passengers get personal stationery, complimentary laundry and ironing, cocktail-hour hors d'oeuvres and other goodies, as well as priority embarkation and disembarkation. The concierge lounge, with its latticework teak detailing and private library is accessible only by private key-card.

Disabled passengers have a choice of 20 cabins, including two of the large "penthouse" suites (which include concierge services). However, there are different cabin configurations, and it is wise to check with your booking agent.

CUISINE. The La Fontaine Dining Room seats 747, spans two decks, and has are tables for four, six or eight, but only nine tables for two. Both open seating and fixed (assigned tables and times) seating are available, while breakfast and lunch are open-seating (you'll be seated by restaurant staff when you enter). Fine Rosenthal china and good cutlery are provided. It is a non-smoking venue.

Alternative (Reservations Required) Dining Option: There is also an 88-seat Odyssey Italian alternative restaurant, decorated in the manner of an opulent 17th-century baroque Italian villa, and available to all passengers. The room, whose basic color is black with gold accenting, is divided into three sections. Cuisines from the Perugia, Tuscany and Umbria regions of Italy are featured.

ENTERTAINMENT. The 577-seat Showlounge at Sea is the venue for all production shows, strong cabaret, and other entertainment features. It is two decks high (with main and balcony level seating). The decor includes umbrella-shaped gold ceiling lamps of Murano glass, and the stage features hydraulic lifts and three video screens, as well as closed-loop system for the hearing-impaired.

SPA/FITNESS. The Ocean Spa is located one deck above the navigation bridge at the very forward part of the ship. It includes a gymnasium (with all the latest muscle-pumping exercise machines, including an abundance of treadmills) with forward views over the ship's bows, an aerobics exercise area, large beauty salon with ocean-view windows to the port side, several treatment rooms, and men's and women's sauna, steam room and changing areas.

● **For more extensive general information on what a Holland America Line cruise is like, see pages 139–42.**

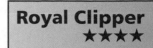

Royal Clipper
★★★★

Size: ....Small Ship	Sail Area (sq ft/m2): 56,000/5,204.5
Tonnage: 5,061	Main Propulsion: ....42 sails
Lifestyle: ....Premium	Propulsion/Propellers: diesel (3,700kW)/1
Cruise Line: ....Star Clippers	Passenger Decks: 5
Former Names: ....none	Total Crew: 100
Builder: ......De Merwede (Holland)	Passengers
Original Cost: ....\$75 million	(lower beds/all berths): 228/255
Entered Service: ....Oct 2000	Passenger Space Ratio
Registry: ....Luxembourg	(lower beds/all berths): 22.1/19.8
Length (ft/m): 439.6/134.0	Crew/Passenger Ratio
Beam (ft/m): 54.1/16.5	(lower beds/all berths): 2.2/2.5
Draft (ft/m): 18.5/5.6	Cabins (total): 114
Type of Vessel: sail-cruise (square rigger)	Size Range (sq ft/m): 100.0–320.0/
Number of Masts: 5	9.3–29.7

Cabins (outside view): 108
Cabins (interior/no view): 6
Cabins (for one person): 0
Cabins (with private balcony): 14
Cabins (wheelchair accessible): 0
Wheelchair accessibility ....None
Cabin Current: ....220 volts
Elevators: 0
Casino (gaming tables): ....No
Slot Machines: ....No
Swimming Pools (outdoors): 3
Whirlpools: 0
Self-Service Launderette: ....No
Library: ....Yes

OVERALL SCORE: 1,540 (OUT OF A POSSIBLE 2,000 POINTS)

OVERVIEW. The culmination of an owner's childhood dream, *Royal Clipper* is a stunning sight under sail. Being marketed as the world's largest true fully rigged sailing ship, this is a logical addition to the company's two other, smaller, 4-masted tall ships (*Star Clipper* and *Star Flyer*). *Royal Clipper*'s 5-masted design is based on the only other 5-masted sailing ship to be built, the 1902-built German tall ship *Preussen*, and has approximately the same dimensions, albeit 46 ft (14 meters) shorter (it is much larger than the famous *Cutty Sark*, for example). It is almost 40 ft (12.1 meters) longer than the largest sailing ship presently in commission – the four-mast Russian barkentine *Sedov*. To keep things in perspective, *Royal Clipper* is the same length overall as *Wind Spirit* and *Wind Star* – the computer-controlled cruise-sail vessels of Windstar Cruises.

The construction time for this ship was remarkably short, owing to the fact that its hull had been almost completed (at Gdansk shipyard, Poland) for another owner (the ship was to be named *Gwarek*) but became available to Star Clippers for completion and fitting out. The ship is instantly recognizable due to its geometric blue and white hull markings. Power winches, as well as hand winches, are employed in deck fittings, as well as a mix of horizontal furling for the square sails and hydraulic power assist to roll the square sails along the yardarm. The sail handling system, which was designed by the ship's owner, Mikael Krafft, is such that it can be converted from a full rigger to a schooner in an incredibly short time.

Its masts reach as high as 197 ft (60 meters) above the waterline, and the top 19 ft (5.8 meters) can be hinged over 90° to clear bridges, cable lines and other port-based

BERLITZ'S RATINGS

	Possible	Achieved
Ship	500	406
Accommodation	200	157
Food	400	288
Service	400	296
Entertainment	n/a	n/a
Cruise	500	393

obstacles. Up to 42 sails can be used: 26 square sails (fore upper topgallant, fore lower topgallant, fore upper topsail, fore lower topsail, foresail, main royal, main upper topgallant, main lower topgallant, main upper topsail, main lower topsail, mainsail, middle royal, middle upper topgallant, middle lower topgallant, middle upper topsail, middle lower topsail, middle course, mizzen upper topgallant, mizzen lower topgallant, mizzen upper topsail, mizzen lower topsail, mizzen course, jigger topgallant, jigger upper topsail, jigger lower topsail, crossjack), 11 staysails (main royal staysail, main topgallant staysail, main topmast staysail, middle royal staysail, middle topgallant staysail, middle topmast staysail, mizzen royal staysail, mizzen topgallant staysail, mizzen topmast staysail, jigger topgallant staysail, jigger topmast staysail); 4 jibs (flying jib, outer jib, inner jib, fore topmast staysail) and 1 gaff-rigged spanker, it looks quite magnificent when under full sail – an area of some 54,360 sq. ft (5,050 sq. meters). Also, watching the sailors manipulate ropes, rigging and sails is like watching a ballet – the precision and cohesion of a group of men who make it all look so simple.

As a passenger, you are allowed to climb to special lookout points aloft – maybe even for a glass of champagne. Passengers are also allowed on the bridge at any time (but not in the galley or engine room).

There is a large amount of open deck space and sunning space aboard this ship – something most tall ships lack, although, naturally, this is laid with ropes for the rigging. A marina platform can be lowered at the stern of the vessel, from where you can use the surfboards, sailing dinghies, take a ride on the ship's own banana boat, or go water-skiing or swimming. Snorkeling gear is available free, but there is a charge for scuba diving gear. You will be asked to sign a waiver if you wish to use the water sports equipment.

Inside, a midships atrium three decks high sits under one of the ship's three swimming pools, and sunlight streams down through a piano lounge on the uppermost level inside the ship and down into the dining room, which is on the lower level. A forward observation lounge is a real plus, and this is connected to the piano lounge via a central corridor. An Edwardian library/card room is decorated with a *belle époque* fireplace. A lounge, the Captain Nemo Club, is where passengers can observe fish and sea life when the ship is at anchor, through thick glass portholes (floodlit from underneath at night to attract the fish).

This delightful, quite spectacular tall ship for tourists operates 7-night and 14-day cruises in the Grenadines and Lower Windward Islands of the Caribbean during the winter and 7-night and 14-night cruises in the Mediterranean during the summer. It is good to note that the officers navigate using both traditional (sextant) and contemporary methods (advanced electronic positioning system).

Being a tall ship with true sailing traditions, there is, naturally, a parrot (sometimes kept in a large, gilded cage, but often seen around the ship on someone's shoulder), which is part of the crew, as aboard all Star Clippers' ships. The general ambiance is extremely relaxed, friendly and casual – completely unpretentious. The passenger mix is international (often consisting of a good cross-section of yachting types) and the dress code is casual at all times (shorts and casual tops are the order of the day – yachting wear), with no ties needed at any time.

There is no doubt that *Royal Clipper* is a superb vessel for the actual experience of sailing – a tall ship probably without equal, as much more time is spent actually under sail than aboard almost any other tall ship, including the smaller *Sea Cloud* and *Sea Cloud II*. However, apart from the sailing experience, it is in the cuisine and service that the lack of professionalism and poor standards of delivery shows. The result is a score that could be higher if the cuisine and service were better.

The suites and cabins are larger than those aboard the tall ships of the Windjammer Barefoot Cruises fleet, while, in general, smaller than aboard *Sea Cloud* and *Sea Cloud II*. While the food and service are far superior to the Windjammers, both are well below the standard found aboard *Sea Cloud* and *Sea Cloud II*. I do not include the Windstar Cruises ships (*Wind Spirit, Wind Star, Wind Surf*), because they cannot, in any sense of the word, be considered tall ships. *Royal Clipper*, however, is exactly that – a real, working, wind-and-sails-in-your-face tall ship with a highly personable captain and crew that welcome you as if you were part of the team. What also gives the ship a little extra in the scoring department is the fact that many water sports are included in the price of your cruise.

This vessel is not for the physically impaired, or for children. The steps of the internal stairs are steep, as in most sailing vessels. The tipping system, where all tips are pooled – the suggested amount is around $8 per pas-

senger, per day – causes concern for many passengers. The onboard currency is the euro.

SUITABLE FOR: *Royal Clipper* is best suited to couples and singles who would probably never even consider a "normal" cruise ship, but who enjoy sailing and the thrill of ocean and wind, but want these things wrapped in a package that includes accommodation, food, like-minded companions, interesting destinations, and don't want the bother of owning or chartering their own yacht.

ACCOMMODATION. There are eight accommodation grades (the price you pay will depend on the grade, size and location you choose): Owner's Suite (2), Deluxe Suite (14), and Categories 1–6. No matter what grade you choose (price will depend on location and size), all have polished wood-trimmed cabinetry and wall-to-wall carpeting, personal safe, full-length mirror, small television with audio channels and 24-hour text-based news, and private bathroom. All feature twin beds (86 of which convert into a queen-sized bed, while 28 are fixed queen-sized beds that cannot be separated), hairdryer and satellite-linked telephone. The six interior (no view) cabins and a handful of other cabins have a permanently fixed double bed.

Most cabins have a privacy curtain, so that you cannot be seen from the hallway when the cabin attendant opens the door (useful if you are not wearing any clothes). In addition, 27 cabins sleep three.

The two owner's suites, located at the very aft of the ship, provide the most lavish accommodation, and have one queen-sized bed and one double bed, a separate living area with semi-circular sofa, large vanity desk, wet bar/refrigerator, marble-clad bathroom with whirlpool bathtub, plus one guest bathroom, and butler service. The two suites have an interconnecting door, so that the combined super-suite can sleep eight persons. However, there is no private balcony.

The 14 "Deck Suites" have interesting names: Ariel, Cutty Sark, Doriana, Eagle Wing, Flying Cloud, France, Golden Gate, Gloria, Great Republic, Passat, Pommern, Preussen, and Thermopylae. However, they are not actually suites, as the sleeping area cannot be separated from the lounge – they are simply larger cabins with a more luxurious interior, more storage space and a larger bathroom. Each has two lower beds convertible to a queen-sized, small lounge area, mini-bar/ refrigerator, writing desk, small private balcony, and marble-clad bathroom with combination whirlpool tub/shower, washbasin and toilet, and butler service. The door to the balcony can be opened so that fresh air floods the room; note that there is a 12-inch (30-cm) threshold to step over.

There are no curtains, only roll-down shades for the windows and balcony door. The balcony itself typically has two white plastic chairs and drinks table; however, teak chairs and table would be more in keeping with the nature of the ship. The 14 balconies are not particularly private, and most have ship's tenders or zodiacs overhanging them, or some rigging obscuring the views.

Two other name cabins (Lord Nelson and Marco Polo – designated as Category 1 cabins) are located aft, but do not have private balconies, although the facilities are similar.

The interior (no view) cabins and the lowest grades of outside-view cabins are extremely small and tight, with very little room to move around the beds. Therefore, take only the minimum amount of clothing and luggage. When in cabins where beds are linked together to form a double bed, you will have to clamber up over the front of the bed, as both sides have built-in storm barriers (this applies in inclement weather conditions only).

There is a small room service menu (all items cost extra).

CUISINE. The Dining Room is constructed on several connecting levels (getting used to the steps is not easy), and seats all passengers at one seating under a three-deck-high atrium dome. You can sit with whom you wish at tables for four, six, eight or 10. However, it is a noisy dining room, due to the positioning of the many waiter stations, and the waiting staff are poorly trained, making mealtimes less enjoyable than one would wish. Some tables are badly positioned so that correct waiter service is impossible, and much reaching over has to be done in order to serve everyone.

One corner can be closed off for private parties. Breakfasts and lunches are self-serve buffets, while dinner is a sitdown affair with table service, although the ambiance is always friendly and lighthearted. The wine list consists of very young wines, and prices are quite high.

The cuisine is certainly nothing to write home about.

Although perfectly acceptable, it certainly cannot be considered in the same class as that found aboard ships such as *Sea Cloud* or *Sea Cloud II*.

ENTERTAINMENT. There are no entertainment shows, nor are any expected by passengers aboard a tall ship such as this, where sailing is the main purpose of a cruise. There is, however, live music, which is provided by a single lounge pianist/singer. Otherwise, dinner is the main evening event, as well as "Captain's Storytime", recaps of the day's interesting events, and conversation with fellow passengers in the lounge or on deck (under the stars) provides engaging entertainment.

During the daytime, when the ship is sailing, passengers can learn about the sails, and the captain or chief officer will give briefings as the sails are being furled and unfurled. The closest this tall ship comes to any kind of "show" is when, one evening towards the end of each cruise, a "sailor's choir", comprised of the ship's crew, presents a nautical performance of sea songs, sea shanties, and other light diversions.

SPA/FITNESS. The Royal Spa is located on the lowest passenger deck and, although not large, incorporates a beauty salon, Moroccan steam room (for which there is a charge), and a small gymnasium with porthole views, several muscle-pump machines body toning equipment, treadmills, rowing machines, and exercycles. Thai massage as well as traditional massage, aromatherapy facials, and other beauty treatments, are available.

Ruby Princess
★★★★

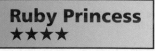
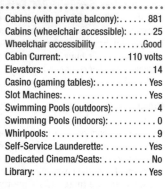

Size:	Large Resort Ship	Passenger Decks:	15
Tonnage:	113,561	Total Crew:	1,200
Lifestyle:	Standard	Passengers	
Cruise Line:	Princess Cruises	(lower beds/all berths):	3,114/3,782
Former Names:	none	Passenger Space Ratio	
Builder:	Fincantieri (Italy)	(lower beds/all berths):	36.4/30.0
Original Cost:	$500 million	Crew/Passenger Ratio	
Entered Service:	Sept 2008	(lower beds/all berths):	2.5/3.1
Registry:	Bermuda	Cabins (total):	1,557
Length (ft/m):	951.4/290.0	Size Range (sq ft/m):	163–1,279/
Beam (ft/m):	118.1/36.0		15.1–118.8
Draft (ft/m):	26.2/8.0	Cabins (outside view):	1,105
Propulsion/Propellers:	diesel-electric	Cabins (interior/no view):	452
	(42,000kW)/2)	Cabins (for one person):	0

Cabins (with private balcony):	881
Cabins (wheelchair accessible):	25
Wheelchair accessibility	Good
Cabin Current:	110 volts
Elevators:	14
Casino (gaming tables):	Yes
Slot Machines:	Yes
Swimming Pools (outdoors):	4
Swimming Pools (indoors):	0
Whirlpools:	9
Self-Service Launderette:	Yes
Dedicated Cinema/Seats:	No
Library:	Yes

BERLITZ'S OVERALL SCORE: 1,547 OUT OF A POSSIBLE 2,000 POINTS

OVERVIEW. *Ruby Princess*, among the best ships in the standard family market, has the same profile, interior layout and public rooms as sister ships *Crown Princess* (2006) and *Emerald Princess* (2007). Although it accommodates over 500 more passengers than earlier half-sisters such as *Diamond Princess*, the outdoor deck space remains the same, as do the number of elevators – so waiting time can be frustrating during peak usage. The Passenger Space Ratio is also considerably reduced.

The Sanctuary, an extra-cost adults-only retreat, is a feature worth paying extra for if you are cruising in a warm-weather area. It is located forward on the uppermost deck, it provides a "private" place to relax and unwind and includes attendants to provide chilled face towels and deliver water and light bites; there are also two outdoor cabanas for private couples massage.

While The Sanctuary, which also has two massage cabanas, takes space away from what was formerly a communal passenger area, it is worth the extra cost of $10 per half-day if you are seeking some quiet time, in or out of the sun. However, the ship's flags flap incessantly on the mast structure within the venue, which reduces the tranquility.

There's a good sheltered faux wood promenade strolling deck – it's actually painted steel – which almost wraps around the front and aft sections of the ship; three times round is equal to one mile. The outdoor pools have various beach-like surroundings, and "Movies Under the Skies" and major sporting events are shown on a 300-sq-ft (28-sq-meter) movie screen located at the pool in front of the large funnel structure. Movies afloat in the open are a big hit with passengers.

BERLITZ'S RATINGS

	Possible	Achieved
Ship	500	435
Accommodation	200	168
Food	400	256
Service	400	292
Entertainment	100	82
Cruise	400	314

With the interior layout and flow similar to that of the sister ships, the main public bars and lounges are located off one double-wide promenade deck. The main lobby is the focal meeting point. Called La Piazza, it's like a town square; it houses a 44-seat International Café with a patisserie/deli and lots of nice cakes and pastries; and Vines, a wine, cheese and corner combined with a sushi/tapas counter.

Although on several *Grand*-class ships the library is also located in this area, the library aboard this ship has been moved to a little corner adjacent to the Wheelhouse Bar. There are pleasant bars and lounges. One intimate lounge is Crooners, a New York-style piano bar, with around 70 seats on the upper level of the lobby. Perhaps the nicest of all is Adagio's, a gem of a room, adjacent to Sabatini's. The passenger flow is well thought-out, and, despite the high passenger carry, there is little congestion.

High atop the stern is a ship-wide glass-walled disco pod. It looks like an aerodynamic "spoiler" and is positioned high above the water, with spectacular views. It would make a great penthouse, but is a good place to read a book during the daytime. The interior decor is attractive, with lots of earth tones well suited to both American and European tastes, with nothing too glitzy.

Ruby Princess also includes a wedding chapel called Hearts and Minds, also good for renewal of vows ceremonies; a live web-cam can relay ceremonies via the internet. The ship's captain can legally marry American couples, thanks to the ship's Bermuda registry and a special dispensation – which should be verified when in the planning stage, according to where you reside. But to get married and take your close family members and entourage with you on your honeymoon is going to cost a lot.

For children, there are several playrooms, a teen room, and a host of trained counselors. Children have their own pools, hot tubs, and open deck area at the stern, away from adult areas. There are good netted-in areas; one section has a dip pool, while another has a mini-basketball court. The Wizard's Academy is an enrichment program from the California Science Center.

Gamblers should enjoy Gatsby's, with more than 260 slot machines, and blackjack, craps and roulette tables, plus newer games such as Let It Ride Bonus, Spanish 21 and Caribbean Draw Progressive. A highlight might be the linked slot machines that provide a combined payout.

Ship lovers should enjoy the wood-paneled Wheelhouse Bar, finely decorated with memorabilia and ship models. A high-tech hospital has SeaMed tele-medicine link-ups to specialists at the Cedars-Sinai Medical Center in Los Angeles, who are available for emergency help.

The ship is a veritable resort playground in which to roam when you are not ashore. Princess Cruises delivers a consistently fine, well-packaged vacation product, always with a good degree of style, at an attractive, highly competitive price. Whether it's a relaxing vacation is a moot point, but with so many choices and "small" rooms to enjoy, the ship has been extremely well designed, and the odds are that you'll enjoy it. If you are not used to large ships, it will take you some time to find your way around this one, despite the company's claim that it offers passengers a "small ship feel, big ship choice."

ACCOMMODATION. There are six main types of cabins and configurations: (a) grand suite, (b) suite, (c) mini-suite, (d) outside-view double cabins with balcony, (e) outside-view double cabins, and (f) interior (no view) double cabins. These come in 35 different brochure price categories. The choice is quite bewildering for both travel agents and passengers, but pricing will depend on two things: size and location. By comparison, the largest suite is slightly smaller, and the smallest interior (no-view) cabin is slightly larger than the equivalent suite/cabins aboard *Golden, Grand* and *Star Princess.*

Cabin bath towels are small, and drawer space is very limited. There are no butlers – even for the top-grade suites, which are not large in comparison to similar suites aboard some other similarly-sized ships. Cabin attendants have too many cabins to look after – typically 20 – which does not translate to fine personal service.

(a) The largest, most lavish suite is the Grand Suite: A750, located at the stern. It has a large bedroom with queen-sized bed, huge walk-in (illuminated) closets, two bathrooms, a lounge with fireplace, sofa bed, wet bar and refrigerator, and a large private balcony on the port side, with a hot tub accessible from both balcony and bedroom.

(b/c) Suites (with a semi-private balcony) have a separate living room with sofa bed, and bedroom, with a TV set in each. The bathroom is quite large and has both a tub and shower stall. The mini-suites also have a private balcony,

and a separate living and sleeping area, with a TV set in each. The differences between the suites and mini-suites are basically in the size and appointments, the suite being more of a square shape while mini-suites are more rectangular and have few drawers. Both suites and mini-suites have plush bathrobes, and fully tiled bathrooms with ample open shelf storage space. Suite and mini-suite passengers receive greater attention, including priority embarkation and disembarkation privileges. What is not good is that the most expensive accommodation has only semi-private balconies that can be seen from above and so there is little privacy – Suites C401, 402, 404, 406, 408, 410, 412, 401, 405, 411, 415 and 417 on Riviera Deck 14. Also, the suites D105 and D106 (Dolphin Deck 9), which are extremely large, have balconies that are overlooked from above.

(d/e/f). Both interior (no-view) and outside-view cabins (the outsides come either with or without private balcony) are of a functional, practical, design, although almost no drawers are provided. They are quite attractive, with warm, pleasing decor and fine soft furnishing fabrics; 80 percent of the outside-view cabins have a private balcony. Interior (no view) cabins measure 163 sq. ft (15.1 sq. meters).

The 28 wheelchair-accessible cabins measure 250–385 sq. ft (23.2–35.7 sq. meters); surprisingly, there is no mirror for dressing, and no full-length hanging space for long dresses – some passengers in wheelchairs *do* use mirrors and full-length clothing. Additionally, two family suites consist of two suites with an interconnecting door, plus a large balcony. These can sleep up to 10 if at least four are children, or up to eight people if all are adults.

All cabins receive turndown service and heart-shaped chocolates on pillows each night, bathrobes (on request unless you are in suite-grade accommodation) and toiletry amenity kits (larger, naturally, for suite/mini-suite occupants) that typically include soap, shampoo, conditioner, and hand/body lotion. A hairdryer is provided in all cabins, sensibly located at the vanity desk unit in the living area. All bathrooms have tiled floors, and there is a decent amount of open shelf storage space for toiletries, although the plain beige decor is basic and unappealing.

Most outside-view cabins on Emerald Deck have views obstructed by lifeboats. There are no cabins for singles. Your name is placed outside your suite or cabin in a documents holder, making it simple for delivery service personnel but also reducing privacy. There is 24-hour room service, but some items on the room service menu are not available during early morning hours.

Some cabins can accommodate a third and fourth person in upper berths. However, in such cabins, the lower beds can't then be pushed together to make queen-sized bed.

Almost all balcony suites and cabins can be overlooked both from the navigation bridge wing, as well as from the port and starboard sections of the ship's discotheque – high above the ship at the stern. Cabins with balconies on Dolphin, Caribe and Baja decks can be overlooked by passengers on balconies on the decks above; they are, therefore, not at all private. Also, passengers occupying some the most expensive suites with balconies at the stern of the vessel may experience some vibration during certain ship maneuvers. Note that many cabins on Emerald Deck 8 have a lifeboat-obstructed view.

CUISINE. As befits the size of the ship, there's a lot of dining options. There are three main dining rooms, plus Sterling Steakhouse, and Sabatini's Trattoria.

The three rooms for formal dining are Botticelli, Da Vinci, and Michelangelo. The Botticelli Dining Room has traditional two seating dining (typically 6pm and 8:15pm for dinner), while "anytime dining" – where you choose when and with whom you want to eat – is offered in Da Vinci and Michelango. All are no-smoking venues and split into various sections in a non-symmetrical design that breaks the large spaces into smaller parts for better ambiance; each restaurant has its own galley.

Dinnerware by Dudson of England, high-quality linens and silverware, Frette Egyptian cotton table linens, and silverware by Hepp of Germany are used in the main dining rooms. Note that 15% is added to all beverage bills, including wines.

Alternative (Extra Charge) Dining Options: Sabatini's, and Crown Grill. Both are open for lunch and dinner on days at sea (reservations are required). Sabatini's is a 132-seat Italian eatery with some painted scenes of Tuscan villas and gardens and colorful tiled Mediterranean-style decor; it is named after Trattoria Sabatini, the 200-year old institution in Florence – where there is no cover charge. It has Italian-style pizzas and pastas, with a variety of sauces, as well as Italian-style entrées, including tiger prawns and lobster tail, all provided with flair and entertainment by the staff of waiters. A cover charge of $20 per person applies for lunch or dinner. It is also open for breakfast for suite/mini-suite occupants only – when it really is a quiet haven.

The 138-seat-seat Crown Grill is the place to go for an excellent array of steaks, chops and sizzled seafood items. It is located off the main indoor Deck 7 promenade. Seating is mainly in semi-private alcoves, and the venue incorporates a show kitchen for those who like to watch the action. The cover charge is $25 per person, and reservations are required.

The cuisine in the alternative dining venues is deservedly better than in the three main dining rooms (it is cooked à la minute), with better quality ingredients and more attention to presentation and taste.

Casual eateries include a poolside hamburger grill and pizza bar (no additional charge), while extra charges do apply if you order items to eat at the coffee bar/patisserie, or the caviar/champagne bar.

Other casual meals can be taken in the 312-seat Horizon Court, with its indoor-outdoor seating, open 24 hours a day. It has large ocean-view windows on port and starboard sides and direct access to the principal swimming pools and lido deck forward, and a more secluded aft pool deck and several terraces.

There is no real finesse in presentation, however, as plastic plates are provided and the central display sections are really crowded. An aft section, Café Caribe, provides themed menus (Italian, French, Bavarian, for example) each evening, and may be provide welcome change from the busy main dining venues.

A "Pub Lunch" is offered on sea days in the Wheelhouse Bar. It includes bangers (sausages) and mash, cottage pie, fish and chips, and ploughman's lunch – at no extra cost.

The International Cafe, on Deck 5 in The Piazza, is the place for coffees and specialty coffees, pastries, light lunches, and delightful afternoon cakes, most at no extra cost.

Ultimate Balcony Dinner/Breakfast: For something different, you could try a private dinner on your balcony, an all-inclusive evening featuring cocktails, fresh flowers, champagne and a deluxe multi-course meal – all served by a member of the dining staff. It costs extra – $50 per person for dinner, or $32 per couple for the Ultimate Balcony Breakfast – which really is superb value for money.

Chef's Dinner: For a $75 per person charge, this exclusive dining experience showcases the talents of the executive chef in a mini-dégustation that includes an array of appetizers in the galley. It really is a fine dining experience that includes good wines paired with dishes that include high-quality meat and seafood dishes, and extremely creative presentation. It's worth taking the three hours needed to enjoy this special evening dining experience, with food that is lovingly prepared over many hours; the slow-cooked roast veal shank is outstanding.

ENTERTAINMENT. The Princess Theater (showlounge) is the main entertainment venue; it spans two decks and has comfortable seating on both main and balcony levels. It has $3 million worth of sound and light equipment, plus a nine-piece orchestra, and a scenery loading bay that connects directly from stage to a hull door for direct transfer to the dockside. The ship has a resident troupe of 19 singers and dancers, plus an army of audio-visual support staff.

Club Fusion is a second entertainment lounge, located aft. It features cabaret acts at night, and lectures, bingo and horse racing during the day. Explorers, a third entertainment lounge, can also host cabaret acts and dance bands. A variety of other lounges and bars have live music, and Princess Cruises employs a number of male dance hosts as partners for women traveling alone.

SPA/FITNESS. The Lotus Spa is located forward on Sun Deck – one of the uppermost decks. Separate facilities for men and women include a sauna, steam room, and changing rooms; common facilities include a relaxation/waiting zone, body-pampering treatment rooms, and a gymnasium with packed with the latest high-tech muscle-pumping, cardio-vascular equipment, and great ocean views. Some fitness classes are free, while some cost extra.

A 50-minute facial costs $169; a 50-minute massage costs $159; a 50-minute couples' cabana massage in The Sanctuary costs $269 for two.

● **For more extensive general information on what the Princess Cruises experience is like, see pages 148–51.**

Ryndam
★★★★

Size: . . . . .Mid-Size Ship	Passenger Decks: 10	Cabins (with private balcony): 150
Tonnage: .55,451	Total Crew: 557	Cabins (wheelchair accessible): 6
Lifestyle: . . . . .Premium	Passengers	Wheelchair accessibility . . . . .Fair
Cruise Line: . . . . . .Holland America Line	(lower beds/all berths): 1,266/1,627	Cabin Current: . . . . .110 and 220 volts
Former Names: . . . . .none	Passenger Space Ratio	Elevators: 8
Builder: . . . . .Fincantieri (Italy)	(lower beds/all berths): 43.8/34.0	Casino (gaming tables): . . . . .Yes
Original Cost: . . . .$215 million	Crew/Passenger Ratio	Slot Machines: . . . . .Yes
Entered Service: . . . . .Nov 1994	(lower beds/all berths): 2.2/2.9	Swimming Pools (outdoors): 1
Registry: . . . . .The Netherlands	Cabins (total): .633	Swimming Pools (indoors): 1
Length (ft/m): 719.3/219.3	Size Range (sq ft/m): 186.2–1,124.8/	(magrodome)
Beam (ft/m): 101.0/30.8	17.3–104.5	Whirlpools: 2
Draft (ft/m): 24.6/7.5	Cabins (outside view): 502	Self-Service Launderette: . . . . .Yes
Propulsion/Propellers: . . . . .diesel-electric	Cabins (interior/no view): 131	Dedicated Cinema/Seats: Yes/249
(34,560kW)/2	Cabins (for one person): 0	Library: . . . . .Yes

OVERALL SCORE: 1,420 OUT OF A POSSIBLE 2,000 POINTS

OVERVIEW. *Ryndam* is one of a series of four almost identical ships – the others being *Maasdam, Statendam,* and *Veendam.* The exterior styling is rather angular (some would say boxy), although it is softened and balanced by the black hull. There is a full walk-around teakwood promenade deck outdoors – excellent for strolling, and, thankfully, no sign of synthetic turf. The sunloungers on the exterior promenade deck are wood, and come with comfortable cushioned pads, while those at the swimming pool on Lido Deck are of white plastic. Holland America Line keeps its ships clean and tidy, and there is good passenger flow throughout the public areas. A 2010 refurbishment created "Mix," which combines library, lounge, interenet center, and coffec bar; and 16 cabins near the spa were transformed into "spa" cabins.

In the interiors of this "S" -class ship, an asymmetrical layout helps to reduce bottlenecks and congestion. Most of the public rooms are concentrated on two decks, Promenade Deck, and Upper Promenade Deck, which creates a spacious feel. In general, a restrained approach to interior styling is taken, using a mixture of contemporary materials combined with traditional woods and ceramics. There is, fortunately, little "glitz" anywhere.

What is outstanding is the array of artworks throughout the ship (costing about $2 million), assembled and nicely displayed to represent the fine Dutch heritage of Holland America Line. Also noticeable are the fine flower arrangements throughout the public areas and foyers – used to good effect to brighten up what some consider dull decor.

Atop the ship, with forward facing views that wrap around the sides is the Crow's Nest Lounge. By day it makes a fine observation lounge, with large ocean-view

BERLITZ'S RATINGS		
	Possible	Achieved
Ship	500	372
Accommodation	200	150
Food	400	254
Service	400	287
Entertainment	100	72
Cruise	400	285

windows, while by night it turns into a nightclub with extremely variable lighting. The three-deck high atrium foyer is attractive, although its sculptured centerpiece makes it look a little crowded, and leaves little room in front of the purser's office. A hydraulic glass roof covers the reasonably sized swimming pool/whirlpools and central Lido area (whose focal point is a large dolphin sculpture) so that this can be used in fine or inclement weather. There is a large and quite lovely and relaxing reference library.

Ryndam is a well-built ship, and has fairly decent interior fit and finish. Holland America Line constantly fine-tunes its performance as a cruise operator and its regular passengers (almost all of whom are North American) find the company's ships very comfortable and well-run, even though the present food and service components let down the rest of the cruise experience.

Perhaps the ship's best asset is its personable Filipino and Indonesian crew, although communication can prove frustrating. The onboard currency is the US dollar.

Holland America Line's many repeat passengers always seem to enjoy the fact that social dancing is on the menu. The company provides complimentary cappuccino and espresso coffees, and free ice cream during certain hours of the day aboard its ships, as well as hot hors d'oeuvres in all bars – something other major lines seem to have dropped, or charge extra for. However, the score for this ship ends up a tad under what it could be if the food and waiting staff were better (more professional training might help). This ship is now deployed year-round in the Caribbean, where its rather dark interior decor contrasts with the strong sunlight.

An escalator travels between two of the lower decks

(one of which was originally planned to be the embarkation point), but it is almost pointless. The charge to use the washing machines and dryers in the self-service launderette is petty, particularly for suite occupants, as they pay steep prices for their cruises. The men's urinals in public restrooms are unusually high.

ACCOMMODATION. This ranges from small interior (no view) cabins to a large penthouse suite, in 7 types and almost 30 price categories. All cabin televisions carry CNN.

The interior (no view) and outside (with a view) standard cabins have twin beds that convert to a queen-sized bed, and there is a separate living space with sofa and coffee table. However, although the drawer space is generally good, the closet space is actually very tight, particularly for long cruises (although more than adequate for a 7-night cruise). Bathrobes are also provided for all suites/cabins, as are hairdryers, and a small range of personal amenities. The bathrooms are quite well laid out, but the bathtubs are small units better described as shower tubs. Some cabins have interconnecting doors.

On Navigation Deck, 28 suites have accommodation for up to four. These suites also have in-suite dining as an alternative to the dining room, for private, reclusive meals. These are very spacious, tastefully decorated and well laid-out, and have a separate living room, bedroom with two lower beds (convertible to a king-sized bed), a good sized living area, dressing room, plenty of closet and drawer space, marble bathroom with Jacuzzi tub.

The largest accommodation of all is a penthouse suite. There is only one, located on the starboard side of Navigation Deck at the forward staircase. It has a king-sized bed, a TV set and video player, and a vanity desk, a large walk-in closet with superb drawer space, oversize whirlpool bath (it could seat four) and separate shower enclosure, and a separate washroom with toilet, bidet and washbasin. The living room has a writing desk, a large television and a full set of audio equipment. There's a dressing room, a large private balcony (with teak lounge chairs and drinks tables, dining table and four chairs), a pantry (with large refrigerator, toaster unit, and full coffee/tea making facilities and food preparation area, and a separate entrance from the hallway), mini-bar/refrigerator, a guest toilet and floor to ceiling windows. Note that there is no bell push.

CUISINE. The Rotterdam Dining Room spans two decks. It is located at the stern, is quite dramatic, and has two grand staircases to connect the two levels, panoramic views on three sides, and a music balcony. Both open seating and fixed (assigned tables and times) seating are available, while breakfast and lunch are open-seating (you'll be seated by restaurant staff when you enter). There are tables for two, four, six or eight.

The dining room is a non-smoking venue. The waiter stations in the dining room are very noisy for anyone seated adjacent to them. Fine Rosenthal china and cutlery are used (although there are no fish knives). Live music is provided for dinner each evening; once each cruise, a

Dutch Dinner is featured (hats are provided), as is an Indonesian Lunch. "Lighter option" meals are always available for the health-conscious.

Alternative Dining Option: An intimate restaurant, the Pinnacle Grill, was added in 2002. It is located just forward of the balcony level of the main dining room on the starboard side. The 66-seat dining spot (reservations are necessary, and a cover/service charge of $20 applies) features Pacific Northwest cuisine (fresh Alaskan salmon and halibut, and other regional specialties, plus a selection of premium steaks such as filet mignon from Black Angus beef). The Pinnacle Grill is a much better dining experience than the main dining room and enhances that special celebration.

For more casual evening eating, the Lido Buffet is open for dinners on all except the last night of each cruise, in an open-seating arrangement; part of it is designated as Canaletto for dinner, featuring Italian fare. Tables are set with crisp linens, flatware and stemware. The set menu includes a choice of four entrées. The dual-line, self-serve Lido Buffet (one side is for smokers, the other side for non-smokers) is also the place for casual breakfasts and lunches. Again there is much use of canned fruits and packeted items, although there are several commercial low-calorie salad dressings. The choice of cheeses (and accompanying crackers) is very poor. The beverage stations are poor – no better than those found in the average family outlet ashore in the United States. In addition, a poolside grill provides basic American hamburgers and hot dogs.

Passengers will need to eat in the Lido Cafe on days when the dining room is closed for lunch – typically once or twice per cruise, depending on the ship's itinerary.

ENTERTAINMENT. The Showroom at Sea spans two decks, with banquette seating on both main and upper levels. It is basically a well designed room, but the ceiling is low and the sightlines from the balcony level are poor.

While Holland America Line is not known for its fine entertainment, what the line does offer is a consistently good, tried and tested array of cabaret acts that constantly rove the cruise ship circuit. The production shows, however, while a good attempt, fall short on storyline, choreography and performance, with colorful costuming and lighting hiding the weak spots.

A number of bands, a string ensemble and solo musicians present live music in many lounges and bars. There's dancing in the Crow's Nest (by day an observation lounge), and serenading string music in the Explorer's Lounge and dining room.

SPA/FITNESS. The Greenhouse Spa is one deck below the navigation bridge at the very forward part of the ship. It includes a gymnasium with ocean views, an aerobics exercise area, large beauty salon with ocean-view windows to the port side, several treatment rooms, and men's and women's sauna, steam room and changing areas. The spa is operated by Steiner, a specialist concession.

● **For more extensive general information on what a Holland America Line cruise is like, see pages 139–42.**

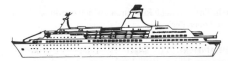

Saga Pearl II
NOT YET RATED

Size:	.Small Ship	Passenger Decks:	.8	Cabins (with private balcony):	.20
Tonnage:	.18,591	Total Crew:	.252	Cabins (wheelchair accessible):	.0
Lifestyle:	.Standard	Passengers		Wheelchair accessibility	.Fair
Cruise Line:	.Saga Cruises	(lower beds/all berths):	.446/446	Cabin Current:	.220 volts
Former Names:	.Astoria, Arkona, Astor	Passenger Space Ratio		Elevators:	.3
Builder:	.Howaldtswerke Deutsche Werft	(lower beds/all berths):	.41.6/41.6	Casino (gaming tables):	.No
	(Germany)	Crew/Passenger Ratio		Slot Machines:	.No
Original Cost:	.$55 million	(lower beds/all berths):	.1.9/1.9	Swimming Pools (outdoors):	.1
Entered Service:	.Dec 1981/Oct 2009	Cabins (total):	.258	Swimming Pools (indoors):	.1
Registry:	.The Bahamas	Size Range (sq ft/m):	.150.0–725.0/	Whirlpools:	.0
Length (ft/m):	.539.2/164.35		13.4–65.3	Self-Service Launderette:	.No
Beam (ft/m):	.74.1/22.60	Cabins (outside view):	.178	Dedicated Cinema/Seats:	.No
Draft (ft/m):	.20.0/6.11	Cabins (interior/no view):	.82	Library:	.Yes
Propulsion/Propellers: diesel (13,200kW)/2		Cabins (for one person):	.0		

BERLITZ'S OVERALL SCORE: NYR OUT OF A POSSIBLE 2,000 POINTS

OVERVIEW. *Saga Pearl II* – formerly *Astoria*, operated by Transocean Tours – is a traditional-looking cruise ship originally built for the long-defunct Astor Cruises. It was given a multi-million pound refit in 2009 that added a superb new 3,000-book library, an array of balcony cabins, and new galleys.

There is a good amount of open deck and sunbathing space for its size, with some good teakwood decks, polished wood railings, and cushioned pads for sunloungers. However, there is no walk-around promenade deck outdoors – just a small walking area under the lifeboats on both sides. Unusually for a ship of this size, there is an indoor swimming pool and wellness center, which its half-sister *Saga Ruby* has, too.

The ship's interior fittings and decor are pleasing, and include a great deal of rosewood paneling, and wood accenting throughout. The ship has been maintained extremely well. Subdued lighting and soothing ambiance, highlighted by fine artwork, make for a relaxing, non-glitzy cruise experience. The well-stocked library is a good meeting and relaxation venue.

The ship has British navigation and engineering officers and traditional European-style hotel service, with and a mostly Filipino hotel service staff. The reception desk is open 24 hours daily.

Saga Pearl II provides good value for money cruising in comfort, and is best recommended for passengers who appreciate quality, fine surroundings, and excellent destination-intensive itineraries, all packaged neatly in an informal ambiance. Many cruises have special themes. Saga Cruises staff, available aboard every cruise, go out of their way to ensure you have an excellent cruise experience in

BERLITZ'S RATINGS

	Possible	Achieved
Ship	500	NYR
Accommodation	200	NYR
Food	400	NYR
Service	400	NYR
Entertainment	100	NYR
Cruise	400	NYR

very comfortable surroundings. The currency aboard *Saga Pearl II* is the British pound. Port taxes, insurance and gratuities to staff are all included in the cruise fare.

SUITABLE FOR: *Saga Pearl II* is best suited to English-speaking couples, and single travelers of mature years who seek a good value for money holiday in a traditional cruise ship setting, with appealing itineraries and destinations, good food and friendly service.

ACCOMMODATION. The accommodation consists of 24 price categories. including 10 grades for single-occupancy cabins, and is spread over four accommodation decks. Some 40 "French" balconies were added in the 2009 refit, which means occupants can open the doors for fresh air, but there is no balcony to step out onto.

Grand Suites: Two Boat Deck suites (725 sq. ft/65.3 sq. meters) provide really large spaces, and have just about everything needed for refined, private living aboard this ship. There is a separate bedroom with double bed, living room with sofa, dining table and chairs. The tiled bathroom has a large tub, separate shower enclosure, and plenty of storage space for personal toiletries.

Suites: 34 Suites (269.1 sq. ft/25 sq. meters) have a separate bedroom with twin beds, living room with sofa, dining table and chairs. The tiled bathroom has a large tub, separate shower enclosure, and plenty of storage space for personal toiletry items.

Outside-view Cabins/Interior (No View) Cabins: The standard cabins (139.9 sq. ft/13 sq. meters) are quite well appointed and decorated, and all feature crisp, clean colors

– some might find them plain. The bathrooms are quite compact units, although there is a decent-sized shower enclosure. They are fully tiled, however, and have a decent cabinet for storing toiletries. Passengers in all grades get 100% cotton towels, and bathrobe. The cabin service menu is very limited and could be better.

CUISINE. The Dining Room is a no-smoking venue. Located fairly high in the ship, it has big, ocean-view picture windows and is reasonably attractive, with dark wood paneling and restful decor. There is a single, open seating, at tables for four, six or eight. Two small wings, each with one 12-seat table, can be used for small groups. The wine list contains a decent selection of wines from many regions, and all at inexpensive to moderate price levels.

Self-serve buffets, for breakfast and lunch, and as a casual alternative to dinner in the Dining Room, can be taken in The Verandah Restaurant, which overlooks the aft pool and open deck area.

ENTERTAINMENT. The Discovery Lounge is the main showlounge. It is a single-level room, although there are 14 pillars that obstruct the sight lines from many of the seats. The stage also acts as the dance floor and cannot be raised for shows. The entertainment, therefore, consists of cabaret-style shows typically with singers, magicians and other visual acts.

SPA/FITNESS. The spa is located on the lowest passenger deck, and contains a sauna (but no steam room), solarium, indoor swimming pool, treatment rooms and changing areas. Massage, facials, manicures and pedicures are some of the services offered, although the beauty salon itself is located on the deck above the spa.

KNOTS AND LOGS

A knot is a unit of speed measuring one nautical mile. (A nautical mile is equal to one-60th of a degree of the earth's circumference and measures exactly 6,080.2 ft (1,852 km). It is about 800 ft (243 meters) longer than a land mile. Thus, when a ship is traveling at a speed of 20 knots (note: this is never referred to as 20 knots per hour), it is traveling at 20 nautical miles per hour (1 knot equals 1.151 land miles).

This unit of measurement has its origin in the days prior to the advent of modern aids, when sailors used a log and a length of rope to measure the distance that their boat had covered, as well as the speed at which it was advancing. In 1574, a tract by William Bourne, entitled A Regiment for the Sea, records the method by which this was done. The log was weighted down at one end while the other end was affixed to a rope. The weighted end, when thrown over the stern, had the effect of making the log stand upright, thus being visible. Sailors believed that the log remained stationary at the spot where it had been cast into the water, while the rope unraveled. By measuring the length of rope used, they could ascertain how far the ship had traveled, and were thus able to calculate its speed.

Sailors first tied knots at regular intervals, eventually fixed at 47 ft 3 inches (14.4 meters) along a rope, then counted how many knots had passed through their hands in a specified time (later established as 28 seconds), and measured by the amount of sand that had run out of an hourglass. They then used simple multiplication to calculate the number of knots their ship was traveling at over the period of an hour.

The data gathered in this way were put into a record, called a logbook. Today, a logbook is used to record the day-to-day details of the life of a ship and its crew as well as other pertinent information.

Conversion Chart

10 knots = 11.5 mph (18.50 km)	18 knots = 20.7 mph (33.31 km)
11 knots = 12.65 mph (20.35 km)	19 knots = 21.85 mph (35.16 km)
12 knots = 13.8 mph (22.20 km)	20 knots = 23.00 mph (37.01 km)
13 knots = 14.95 mph (24.05 km)	21 knots = 24.15 mph (38.86 km)
14 knots = 16.1 mph (25.90 km)	22 knots = 25.3 mph (40.71 km)
15 knots = 17.25 mph (27.76 km)	23 knots = 26.45 mph (42.56 km)
16 knots = 18.4 mph (29.61 km)	24 knots = 27.6 mph (44.41 km)
17 knots = 19.55 mph (31.46 km)	25 knots = 28.75 mph (46.26 km)

Saga Ruby
★★★★

Size: ....Mid-Size Ship	Passenger Decks: 9	Cabins (with private balcony): 25
Tonnage: 24,492	Total Crew: 380	Cabins (wheelchair accessible): 4
Lifestyle: ....Premium	Passengers	Wheelchair accessibility ....Fair
Cruise Line: ....Saga Cruises	(lower beds/all berths): 655/655	Cabin Current: ....110 volts
Former Names: ....Caronia, Vistafjord	Passenger Space Ratio	Elevators: 6
Builder: ....Swan, Hunter (UK)	(lower beds/all berths): ....37.3/37..3	Casino (gaming tables): ....No
Original Cost: ....$35 million	Crew/Passenger Ratio	Slot Machines: ....No
Entered Service: ....May 1973/	(lower beds/all berths): 1.7/1.7	Swimming Pools (outdoors): 1
March 2005	Cabins (total): 376	Swimming Pools (indoors): 1
Registry: ....Great Britain	Size Range (sq ft/m): 66.7–871.9/	Whirlpools: 2
Length (ft/m): 626.9/191.09	6.2–81.0	Self-Service Launderette: ....Yes
Beam (ft/m): 82.1/25.05	Cabins (outside view): 324	Dedicated Cinema/Seats: Yes/190
Draft (ft/m): 27.0/8.23	Cabins (interior/no view): 52	Library: ....Yes
Propulsion/Propellers: diesel (17,900kW)/2	Cabins (for one person): 70	

OVERALL SCORE: 1,421 OUT OF A POSSIBLE 2,000 POINTS

OVERVIEW. *Saga Ruby* has classic liner styling and profile, and really does look like a traditional ship. It was built for long-distance, low-density cruising – the original capacity was just 500 passengers. The ship was built with excellent quality materials, has been well maintained, is smooth and quiet in operation, and is stable at sea due to its deep draft. Each day, the ship's bell is sounded at noon in accordance with maritime tradition. Previously Cunard Line's *Caronia,* the ship was taken over by Saga Cruises and given a £17 million refit in 2004–5.

The open decks and sunbathing space are expansive. There is a wide teak walk-around promenade deck outdoors, and sunloungers have cushioned pads – ideal for resting, relaxation, and for reading a good book. Bouillon is served on sea days.

Inside, the spacious and elegant public rooms – mostly located on one deck (Veranda Deck) – have high ceilings and tasteful decor, and wide interior stairwells are subtly illuminated. The ship's interior decor and soft furnishings are of soft, earth-toned colors that provide a calm, soothing and non-threatening environment for the longer cruises that Saga passengers enjoy. The Britannia Lounge is at the front of this deck; behind it the Theater (dedicated cinema), Card Room, Ballroom (show lounge) and the Lido Cafe. There's also an expansive and well-used library, a computer learning center, and separate internet-connect center. Few ships of this size can match the relaxing ambience and gracious service from a well-organized, friendly and happy mix of European and Filipino service staff. There are refreshingly few announcements and interruptions.

This ship provides a refined, user-friendly environment

BERLITZ'S RATINGS

	Possible	Achieved
Ship	500	362
Accommodation	200	151
Food	400	280
Service	400	274
Entertainment	100	80
Cruise	400	274

with a wide range of public rooms for adults (the ship is child-free). Male dance hosts are provided for the many single women who travel.

Saga Cruises includes many things that other UK-based cruise operators charge extra for: transfers to the ship, all gratuities, shuttle buses in ports of call (where possible), and newspapers in the library in each port of call (subject to availability). The onboard currency is the British pound.

SUITABLE FOR: *Saga Ruby* is best suited to couples and single travelers who must be over 50 (although spouses and partners can be as young as 45) and who seek a holiday afloat in a classic ship setting that is unpretentious, yet provides a decent standard of accommodation, good food and friendly service, as well as interesting itineraries and destinations, with fellow passengers likely to be almost all English, in a setting that doesn't try to compete with today's warehouse-sized new ships.

ACCOMMODATION. The brochure lists 21 cabin categories (seven of which are for single travelers wanting a cabin to themselves), from duplex penthouse suites with huge private balconies, to small interior (no view) cabins, in a wide range of different configurations. The cabins are smaller than those aboard former sister ship *Saga Rose* but all are well appointed, with good-sized bathrooms Some cabins have a full-sized bathtub, while others have a shower enclosure only; hand-held shower hoses are standard (better and more hygienic than fixed showers).

The grandest living spaces are the two duplex suites (Concerto and Symphony). They are superb living spaces and occupy two levels. The lower level has a large bedroom and marble-clad bathroom with Jacuzzi bathtub. The upper level has an expansive living room with floor-to-ceiling windows with unobstructed front and side views, a Bang & Olufsen sound system, treadmill, private bar, and a large bathroom (with Jacuzzi bathtub) and separate private sauna. There is a huge, private balcony outdoors on deck, complete with a two-person hot tub, a teak deck, and great views. A private internal stairway connects the upper and lower levels.

Most other cabins designated as suites (on Bridge Deck lower level, and Sun Deck) have private balconies, are nicely equipped, and have ample closet and drawer space (some also have a large walk-in closet), vanity desk, large beds, and bookshelves filled with suitable destination books or novels. The marble-clad bathrooms are large and have a full-sized Jacuzzi bathtub, two washbasins, toilet and bidet.

All other cabins are tastefully decorated, and all have a refrigerator, mini-bar, personal safe, European duvets (in two thicknesses), a range of Molton Brown toiletries (Temple Spa amenities in suite accommodation, and thick 100% cotton bathrobes. The wooden cabinetry has nicely rounded edges. Bathrooms have a whisper-quiet (gentle, non-vacuum) toilet.

This ship has an excellent range of cabins for single travelers (unlike almost all new cruise ships). Some Sun Deck and Promenade Deck suites have obstructed views. All suites and cabins have a flat-screen TV with integral DVD player.

CUISINE. Although it lacks the grandeur, high ceiling or grand stairway of sister ship *Saga Rose*, the Saga Dining Room is elegant, and single-seating dining at assigned tables is featured (this is refreshing, when so many of today's cruise ships have two seatings). There are tables for two, four, six or eight (there are more tables for two than aboard many other cruise ships). Senior officers often host tables for dinner (and always do so on formal nights). Single-waiter service is provided, as in the European tradition, by Filipino waiters. Some tables are a little close together, however, making it hard for waiters to serve properly in some areas.

A wide range of menu items is provided (including many British favorites), with a reasonably high standard of quality and variety. A cold table is set for such things as breads and cheeses at lunchtime, and passengers can help themselves or be served. Salad items, many salad dressings, juices, and a selection of international cheeses) are always available. Plate service (where vegetables and entrées are set on the main course plate) is provided, and extra vegetables are available on request. This is service in the classic seagoing tradition, in unhurried style.

There is a good selection of cakes and pastry items (and scones, of course) for afternoon tea. Vegetarian items and diabetic desserts are always available and other special dietary items can be provided with sufficient notice. The wine list has a good selection, with prices that reflect excellent value for money.

Alternative (Reservations Required) Dining: View is a delightful à la carte restaurant (an alternative no-smoking dining spot located above the nightclub) that is elegant and very intimate (with only 12 tables), with excellent cuisine from a varied menu. It has the feel of a small, exclusive bistro. Reservations are required, but there is no extra charge.

Casual Eatery: The Lido Café, greatly expanded in the 2004–5 refit, is a well laid out casual dining area with a range of self-service buffets for breakfast, lunch and dinner. While there is some repetition of breakfast items, other meals offer a wide variety of hot and cold food items. A self-serve tea/coffee/beverage station is available 24 hours a day; a machine provides espresso and cappuccino at no extra cost, and ice cream is free, too – most ships now charge extra for these items.

Bar drinks (and wine) prices are extremely reasonable, and include gratuities. Once each cruise, there is a champagne breakfast.

ENTERTAINMENT. The Ballroom is the main venue for entertainment, revue shows, cabaret acts, lectures, and social functions such as the Captain's Cocktail Party. It is among the nicest such rooms afloat for proper cocktail parties (where you stand and mingle, rather than sit), with furniture that can be moved for almost any configuration, and a large real wood dance floor. The port and starboard side seating sections are raised, and sight lines are generally good from most seats. The ship has conservative, reasonably sophisticated, classically oriented entertainment. A resident troupe of singers and dancers presents mini-revue shows.

Most of the other entertainment consists of cabaret acts (such as vocalists, magicians, ventriloquists, comedy jugglers and others), and there is a large floor for social dancing, an important feature for many passengers. A number of bands and musical units provide ample live music for dancing or listening throughout the various lounges and bars. Each evening, the Preview Club, which overlooks the ship's outdoor swimming pool at the aft end of the ship, becomes the late-night spot.

SPA/FITNESS. The Spa Aquarius is located low down in the ship, on "C" Deck, where there is also a rather nice indoor pool, gymnasium, men's and women's sauna and changing rooms with adjacent shower enclosures, plus a unisex steam room. A gymnasium, with elevator access, is located high up on Bridge Deck; it has high-tech equipment and great port and starboard ocean views.

The spa treatments and beauty services are staffed and operated by Harding Brothers, a concession whose staff also run the fitness and aerobics classes. Spa treatments offered include several types of massage, aromatherapy facials, seaweed body wraps, and hair beautifying services.

Sapphire
★ ★ +

Size: .Small Ship	Propulsion/Propellers: diesel (11,050kW)/2	Cabins (for one person): 0
Tonnage: 12,263	Passenger Decks: 8	Cabins (with private balcony): 0
Lifestyle: . . . . .Standard	Total Crew: 250	Cabins (wheelchair accessible): 0
Cruise Line: . . . . .Louis Cruises	Passengers	Wheelchair accessibility . . . . .None
Former Names: . . . . . .*Princesa Oceanica,*	(lower beds/all berths): 576/650	Cabin Current: . . . . .110 volts
Sea Prince V, Sea Prince, Ocean	Passenger Space Ratio	Elevators: 5
Princess, Princess Italia, Italia	(lower beds/all berths): 21.1/18.7	Casino (gaming tables): . . . . .Yes
Builder: . . .Cantieri Navale Felszegi (Italy)	Crew/Passenger Ratio	Slot Machines: . . . . .Yes
Original Cost: . . . . .n/a	(lower beds/all berths): 2.3/2.6	Swimming Pools (outdoors): 1
Entered Service: . . . . .Aug 1967/Apr 1996	Cabins (total): .288	Swimming Pools (indoors): 0
Registry: . . . . .Marshall Islands	Size Range (sq ft/m): 75.3–226.0/	Whirlpools: 0
Length (ft/m): 491.7/149.8	7.0–21.0	Self-Service Launderette: . . . . .No
Beam (ft/m): 70.9/21.5	Cabins (outside view): 157	Dedicated Cinema/Seats: Yes/170
Draft (ft/m): 22.3/6.8	Cabins (interior/no view): 131	Library: . . . . .Yes

OVERALL SCORE: 1,030 OUT OF A POSSIBLE 2,000 POINTS

OVERVIEW. *Sapphire* has had many previous names and owners, and an interesting life. In 1993, the ship sank in the Amazon River before being bought by its present owners and refitted. It has long, low-slung, handsome lines and a swept-back aft-placed funnel – all of which combine to provide a very attractive profile for this small ship. Louis Cruises purchased the ship in 1995 and, following an extensive refurbishment, placed it into service in 1996. Since it took over the ship, the company has lavished much care and attention in keeping it in good condition.

There is a good amount of open deck and sunbathing space, but the heated swimming pool is very small, and is really only a "dip" pool.

Inside, the contemporary interior decor is fairly smart. There is a mix of attractive colors, together with much use of mirrored surfaces, which help to give the public rooms a feeling of spaciousness and warmth. Most public rooms do have a low ceiling height, however. Harry's Bar is the most popular gathering place, although there are few seats – the gaming tables are adjacent. Other public rooms include the Marco Polo Lounge for evening shows, the Monte Carlo Casino, the Starlight Theater (a cinema with comfortable seating), and a card room and token library.

This ship will take you to some decent destinations (for most of the year it operates 7-day Greek Island and Egypt cruises from Cyprus) in reasonably contemporary surroundings, and in a relaxed, casual, yet comfortable style. The realistic, inexpensive price of this product is a bonus for first-time passengers seeking a cruise aboard a mid-sized ship that is still considered very much a "traditional" cruise ship rather than one of the floating mega-resorts

BERLITZ'S RATINGS

	Possible	Achieved
Ship	500	242
Accommodation	200	105
Food	400	206
Service	400	225
Entertainment	100	48
Cruise	400	204

operated by the major cruise lines. Your fellow travelers are likely to be English-speaking British and Cypriot passengers. Gratuities are added to your onboard account at the rate of £2 per person per day.

The ceilings are quite low throughout the ship, with the exception of a couple of the public rooms. Some cabins are subject to noise from the engines and generators.

SUITABLE FOR: *Sapphire* is best suited to couples and single travelers (not recommended for children) for a first cruise in a comfortable, clubby setting that provides a decent array of public rooms and facilities, and a destination-intensive cruise that provides decent value for money.

ACCOMMODATION. There are five price grades: Premier Outside (the largest), Superior Outside, Standard Outside, Superior Interior (no view), and Standard Interior (no view). The price you pay will depend on the grade, size and location you choose; generally, the higher the deck, the more expensive the accommodation.

The outside-view and interior (no view) cabins are of a reasonable size, and have pleasing, though plain, decor, soft furnishings, and fittings. In almost all cases, the cabin closet and drawer space is very limited. Some cabins (but not many) have a double bed, while most have two beds and many cabins have a third or third and fourth upper berth – good for families with young children.

All cabins have tiled bathrooms, with a shower enclosure, toilet and washbasin, but they are small, and there is little storage space for personal toiletries. There is a 24-hour cabin service menu, although there is only a limited choice of items (and these come at extra cost).

The Premier Outside cabins are the largest, and have two beds, plus a sofa bed, and the bathroom has either a shower or bathtub. Nine out of the 15 Premier Outside grade cabins have a lifeboat-obstructed view, as do two of the Super Outside grade cabins.

CUISINE. The 330-seat Four Seasons Restaurant is quite a charming room that has an art deco feel to it, a raised center ceiling, and glass dividers, although the noise level from the waiter stations can be high. There are two seatings. The cuisine is international, but do remember that this is a low-cost cruise, and so you shouldn't expect high-class cuisine. What is provided, however, is surprisingly decent fare that is tasty and well presented. The service from a willing, friendly staff is reasonably attentive. Low-cost vegetarian lunch boxes are available upon request for anyone going ashore on shore excursions. The price of drinks is extremely reasonable, as are wines – but don't expect good vintages, as almost all the wine stock is very young.

For casual breakfasts and luncheons, the Cafe de Paris, located indoors but looking out onto the pool deck, is the place (it also has a bar) to head for, although the self-serve breakfast buffets are a little repetitive.

ENTERTAINMENT. The Marco Polo Lounge is the venue for all entertainment events and most social functions. It is a single-level room that was designed for cabaret acts rather than "production" shows. The sight lines are fair from the majority of seats, but best from the first few rows closest to the stage. The room also has a hardwood dance floor and social dancing typically takes place after any shows. A resident troupe of dancers provides "openers and closers" for the revue-style shows, where a cabaret act (such as a singer, magician, comedian, or musical specialist) is inserted into the middle "star" spot. This is, however, a small ship operating low-budget cruises, so you should not expect much in the way of quality entertainment.

The ship has a band and a couple of small musical units for live dancing and listening music.

SPA/FITNESS. There are no facilities, with the exception of a small beauty salon, where basic hairdressing and hair beautifying treatments are available.

PET PEEVES: 30 THINGS THAT EXASPERATE PASSENGERS

❶ Long lines and waiting periods for disembarkation.

❷ The appalling number of merchandising flyers put under the cabin door.

❸ Tiny tub chairs (for size-challenged passengers).

❹ Superfluous language (example: "sleep system" instead of "bed").

❺ Cruise brochures that use models, and provide the anticipation of an on-board product that a ship cannot deliver; the result is a big disappointment for passengers.

❻ Cruise brochures that state that their ship has a "small ship feel, big ship choice" when it really caters to more than 3,000 passengers.

❼ Aboard large resort ships, getting Cabin Services, or the "Guest Relations Desk," or an Operator to answer the telephone can be an exercise in frustration, patience, and gross irritation.

❽ Constant, irritating, and repetitive announcements for bingo, horse racing, art auctions, and the latest gizmos for sale in the shops.

❾ "Elevator" music playing non-stop in passageways and on open decks (even worse: rock and rap music).

❿ Any announcement that is repeated. Any announcement that is repeated.

⓫ In-cabin announcements at any time, except for emergencies; they are completely unnecessary for programmed events and shore excursions.

⓬ Flowers in one's cabin that are not watered by the steward(ess).

⓭ Bathrobes provided but never changed during the cruise.

⓮ Mini-bar/refrigerators that lack limes and lemons for drink mixes.

⓯ Skimpy towels.

⓰ Garnishes, when "parsley with everything" seems to be the rule of the seagoing entrée experience.

⓱ Baked Alaska parades.

⓲ Paper, plastic, or polystyrene plastic cups for drinks of any kind.

⓳ Paper napkins for meals or buffets; they should be linen or cotton.

⓴ Plastic plates, often too small, for buffets.

㉑ Buffets where only cold plates are available, even for hot food items.

㉒ Artwork placed aboard ships, but with the cruise line not caring or knowing enough about it to place the name of the artist and the year of creation alongside, whether it is a painting or a sculpture.

㉓ Repetitious breakfast and luncheon buffets and uncreative displays.

㉔ Shopping lecturers, shopping videos, art auctions, carpet auctions.

㉕ Shore-side porters who take your bags when you get off the bus, or out of your car, then stand there until tipped (worst ports: Fort Lauderdale and Miami).

㉖ Cabin stewards/stewardesses who place small folded pieces of paper in cabin door frames to show when their passengers have left their cabins.

㉗ Audiovisual technicians who think that the volume level of the show should equal that for a major rock concert.

㉘ Private island days, when the tender ride to get to the island is longer than the flight to get to the ship.

㉙ Ships that ask you to settle your shipboard account before the morning of disembarkation.

㉚ The use of cellphones in ships' public rooms.

More Pet Peeves: page 591

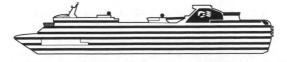

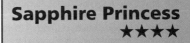

Sapphire Princess
★★★★

Size: ....Large Resort Ship	Passenger Decks: 13	Cabins (with private balcony): 750
Tonnage: ....115,875 tons	Total Crew: 1,238	Cabins (wheelchair accessible): 28
Lifestyle: ....Standard	Passengers	(18 outside/10 interior)
Cruise Line: ....Princess Cruises	(lower beds/all berths): 2,674/3,100	Wheelchair accessibility ....Good
Former Names: ....none	Passenger Space Ratio	Cabin Current: ....110 volts
Builder: Mitsubishi Heavy Industries (Japan)	(lower beds/all berths): 43.3/37.3	Elevators: 14
Original Cost: ....$400 million	Crew/Passenger Ratio	Casino (gaming tables): ....Yes
Entered Service: ....May 2004	(lower beds/all berths): 2.1/2.5	Slot Machines: ....Yes
Registry: ....Bermuda	Cabins (total): 1,337	Swimming Pools (outdoors): 4
Length (ft/m): 951.4/290.00	Size Range (sq ft/m): 168–1,329.3/	Swimming Pools (indoors): 0
Beam (ft/m): 123.0/37.50	15.6–123.5	Whirlpools: 9
Draft (ft/m): 26.4/8.05	Cabins (outside view): 1,000	Self-Service Launderette: ....Yes
Propulsion/Propellers: ......gas turbine	Cabins (interior/no view): 337	Dedicated Cinema/Seats: ....No
(25 MW)/2	Cabins (for one person): 0	Library: ....Yes

OVERALL SCORE: 1,544 OUT OF A POSSIBLE 2,000 POINTS

OVERVIEW. *Sapphire Princess* has an instantly recognizable funnel due to two jet engine-like pods that sit high up on its structure, but really are mainly for decoration. This is the second ship to be constructed by a Japanese shipyard for Princess Cruises (sister ship *Diamond Princess* debuted in 2004). The ship is similar in size and internal layout to *Golden Princess, Grand Princess* and *Star Princess*, although of a slightly greater beam. Unlike its half-sister ships, however, all of which had a "spoiler" (containing a discotheque) located aft of the funnel, this has thankfully been removed from both *Diamond Princess* and *Sapphire Princess*, and has been replaced by a more sensible (and less weighty) aft-facing nightclub/discotheque structure (Skywalkers Nightclub) set around the base of the adjoining the funnel structure. The view from the nightclub overlooks aft-facing cascading decks and children's pool.

In December 2002, while the ship was under construction in the shipyard (as *Diamond Princess*), a fire broke out on Deck 5 and did much damage. The ship's hull was switched with that of identical sister *Sapphire Princess*, which was being built in the same yard at the same time.

The actual hull form in *Sapphire Princess* (and sister *Diamond Princess*) is slightly different to that of other "Grand Class" ships, and is slightly wider. Electrical power is provided by a combination of four diesel and one gas turbine (CODAG) unit; the diesel engines are located in the engine room, while the gas turbine unit is located in the ship's funnel housing, on each side of which is a cosmetic pod that resembles a jet aircraft engine.

Four areas focus on swimming pools, one of which is two decks high and is covered by a magrodome (retractable

BERLITZ'S RATINGS

	Possible	Achieved
Ship	500	431
Accommodation	200	168
Food	400	256
Service	400	293
Entertainment	100	82
Cruise	400	314

glass dome), itself an extension of the funnel housing.

The interiors of the ship are overseen and outfitted by the Okura Group, whose Okura Hotel is one of the best in Tokyo. Fit and finish quality is superior that of the Italian-built *Golden Princess, Grand Princess* and *Star Princess*. Unlike the outside decks, there is plenty of space inside the ship (but there are also plenty of passengers), and a wide array of public rooms to choose from, with many "intimate" (this being a relative word) spaces and places to enjoy. The passenger flow has been well thought out, and works with little congestion. The decor is attractive, with lots of earth tones, well suited to both American and European tastes. In fact, this ship is perhaps the culmination of the best of all that Princess Cruises has to offer from its many years of operating what is now a well-tuned, good-quality product. An extensive collection of art works has been chosen, and this complements the interior design and colors well.

This ship also has a Wedding Chapel. The ship's captain can legally marry American couples (a live web-cam can relay ceremonies via the internet), due to the ship's Bermuda registry and a special dispensation (which should be verified when in the planning stage, according to where you reside). Princess Cruises offers three wedding packages – Pearl, Emerald, Diamond. The "Hearts & Minds" chapel is also useful for "renewal of vows" ceremonies.

Gaming lovers should enjoy what is presently one of the largest casinos at sea (Grand Casino), with more than 260 slot machines; there are blackjack, craps and roulette tables, plus newer games such as Let It Ride Bonus, Spanish 21 and Caribbean Draw Progressive. But the highlight could well be the specially linked slot machines that provide a combined payout.

Other features include a library/CD-Rom computer room, and a separate card room. Ship lovers should enjoy the wood-paneled Wheelhouse Bar, finely decorated with memorabilia and ship models tracing part of parent company P&O's history. Aft of the International Dining Room is the Wake View Bar, with a spiral stairway that leads down to a great viewing spot for those who want to watch the ship's wake; it is reached from the back of Club Fusion, on Promenade Deck.

A high-tech hospital is provided, with live SeaMed telemedicine link-ups with specialists at the Cedars-Sinai Medical Center in Los Angeles available for emergency help.

For youngsters and teenagers there is a two-deck-high playroom, teen room, and a host of specially trained counselors. Children have their own pools, hot tubs, and open deck area at the stern of the ship (away from adult areas). *Sapphire Princess* is a grand playground in which to roam and play when you are not ashore. Princess Cruises delivers a fine, well-packaged holiday product, with some sense of style, at an attractive, highly competitive price, and this ship will appeal to those that really enjoy big city life, with all the trimmings and lots of fellow passengers. The ship is full of revenue centers, however, which are designed to help you part with even more money than you paid for in the price of your cruise ticket (cruise lines have become increasingly shrewd). Expect to be subjected to a stream of flyers advertising daily art auctions, "designer" watches and the like, while "artworks" for auction are strewn throughout the ship.

Whether a cruise aboard this ship really can be considered a relaxing holiday is a moot point, but with so many choices and "small" rooms to enjoy, the ship has been extremely well designed, and the odds are that you'll have a fine cruise holiday, as long as you plan your movements and timing carefully.

The dress code is formal or smart casual – interpreted by many as jeans and trainers. Gratuities to staff are automatically added to your account, at $10 per person, per day, with gratuities for children charged at the same rate. If you want to pay less, you'll need to go to the reception desk to have these charges adjusted (that could mean lining up with many other passengers wanting to do the same). The onboard currency is the US dollar.

If you are not used to large ships, it will take you some time to find your way around this one, despite the company's claim that this vessel offers passengers a "small ship feel, big ship choice."

Lines form for many things aboard large ships, but particularly so for the purser's (information) office, and for open-seating breakfast and lunch in the four main dining rooms. Long lines for shore excursions and shore tenders are also a fact of life aboard such large ships, as is waiting for elevators at peak times, embarkation (an "express check-in" option is available by completing certain documentation 40 days before your cruise) and disembarkation. You'll have to live with the many extra-charge items

such as for ice cream, freshly squeezed orange juice, and activities such as yoga, group exercise bicycling and kick boxing classes (at $10 per session), and $4 per hour for group babysitting services (at the time this book was completed). There's also a charge for using the washers and dryers in the self-service launderettes.

ACCOMMODATION. All passengers receive turndown service and chocolates on pillows each night, bathrobes (on request) and toiletry amenity kits (larger, naturally, for suite/mini-suite occupants) that typically include soap, shampoo, conditioner, and hand/body lotion. A hairdryer is provided in all cabins, sensibly located at the vanity desk unit in the living area. All bathrooms are tiled and have a decent amount of open shelf storage space for toiletries.

You should note that the majority of the outside cabins on Emerald Deck have views obstructed by the lifeboats. Sadly, there are no cabins for singles. Your name is typically placed outside your suite or cabin – making it simple for delivery service personnel but also eroding your privacy. There is 24-hour room service (some items on the room service menu are not, however, available during early morning hours). Most of the balcony suites and cabins can be overlooked both from the navigation bridge wing.

Cabins with balconies on Baja, Caribe, and Dolphin decks are also overlooked by passengers on balconies on the deck above; they are, therefore, not at all private. Cabin bath towels are small, and drawer space is limited. There are no butlers – even for the top grade suites (which are not really large in comparison to similar suites aboard some other ships). Cabin attendants have too many cabins to look after (typically 20), which does not translate to fine personal service.

CUISINE. There are several "personal choice" dining options, but all dining rooms are located on one of two decks in the ship's center. There are five principal dining rooms with themed decor and cuisine – smaller than the three dining rooms in the similarly sized *Golden Princess, Grand Princess* and *Star Princess* (actually two dining rooms were halved in size to become four). They are: Sterling Steakhouse (for steak and grilled meats), Vivaldi (Italian fare), Santa Fe (southwestern USA cuisine) and Pacific Moon (Asian cuisine) and International (the largest, located aft with two seatings and "traditional" cuisine). These offer a mix of two seatings (seating is assigned according to the location of your cabin) and "anytime dining" (where you choose when and with whom you want to eat).

All dining rooms are non-smoking and are split into sections in a non-symmetrical design that breaks what are quite large spaces into many smaller sections, for better ambience and less noise pollution.

Specially designed dinnerware and good quality linens and silverware are used: Dudson of England (dinnerware), Frette Egyptian cotton table linens, and silverware by Hepp of Germany. Note that 15% is added to all beverage bills, including wines.

Alternative Dining Option: Sabatini's is an informal eatery (reservations required; cover charge $20 per person). It offers an eight-course meal, including Italian-style pizzas and pastas, with a variety of sauces, as well as Italian-style entrées including tiger prawns and lobster tail. The cuisine in this eatery is potentially better than in all the other dining rooms – better quality ingredients and more attention to presentation and taste, all delivered with more flair.

A poolside hamburger grill and pizza bar (no additional charge) are additional dining spots for casual bites, while extra charges will apply if you order items to eat at either the coffee bar/patisserie, or the caviar/champagne bar. Other casual meals can be taken in the Horizon Court, which is open 24 hours a day, with large ocean-view on port and starboard sides and direct access to the two principal swimming pools and lido deck (there is no finesse in presentation, however, as plastic plates are provided).

ENTERTAINMENT. The Princess Theatre (show lounge) spans two decks and has comfortable seating on both main and balcony levels. It has $3 million in sound and light equipment, plus a 9-piece orchestra, and a scenery loading bay that connects directly from stage to a hull door for direct transfer to the dockside.

Princess Cruises prides itself on its glamorous all-American production shows, and the shows aboard this ship should not disappoint (there are typically two or three shows each 7-day cruise). The ship carries its own resident troupe of singers/dancers and audio-visual support staff.

There is also a second large entertainment lounge, Club Fusion. It features cabaret acts (magicians, comedy jugglers, ventriloquists and others) at night, and lectures, bingo and horse racing during the day. A third entertainment lounge can also host cabaret acts and dance bands. A host of other lounges and bars have live music, and Princess Cruises will have a number of male dance hosts as partners for women traveling alone.

SPA/FITNESS. The Lotus Spa is located forward on Sun Deck – one of the uppermost decks. Separate facilities for men and women include a sauna, steam room, and changing rooms; common facilities include a relaxation/waiting zone, body-pampering treatment rooms, and a gymnasium with packed with the latest high-tech muscle-pumping, cardio-vascular equipment, and great ocean views. Some fitness classes are free, while some incur an extra charge.

The Lotus Spa is operated by Steiner Leisure. You can make online reservations for any spa treatments before your cruise – so you can obtain the time you want, instead of all that frustration often encountered when aboard a ship.

● **For more extensive general information on what the Princess Cruises experience is like, see pages 148–51.**

PET PEEVES: 30 MORE THINGS THAT EXASPERATE PASSENGERS

Continued from page 588
㉛ Sunbed hoggers.
㉜ Cabin air-conditioning that cannot be turned off.
㉝ Obscenely overcrowded casual self-serve stuff-your-face buffet venues.
㉞ No small "clutch purse" shelves in women's public restrooms.
㉟ Hairdryers with "on" buttons that must be kept pressed.
㊱ Personal safes located at floor level, or so high that you can't reach.
㊲ Overuse by staff of the word "excellent" (as in "how are you today?").
㊳ Aboard most ships, 15 percent is automatically added to wine bills. For doing the same job for a $125 wine as for one costing $15 he makes a lot more. You should insist on adding your own gratuity.
㊴ Daily programs printed in blue ink (hard to read).
㊵ Tacky trinket tables set up as tourist traps outside the onboard shops.

㊶ Overly bright shopping malls (RCI's Royal Arcades aboard Oasis-, Freedom, and Voyager-class ships).
㊷ User-unfriendly automated telephone answering systems that provide number options to connect you to various services – you start to wonder whether the answering service is located in a call center in India.
㊸ Fluorescent lighting in bathrooms.
㊹ Bathroom mirrors that steam up.
㊺ Toilet tissue paper that is too thin (2-ply) so you need twice as much.
㊻ Toilet paper folded to a point, then sealed with a gummed label.
㊼ Soap bars that are not large enough to wash the hands of a leprechaun.
㊽ Pool towels provided in passenger cabins. This is user-unfriendly for anyone on the lowest accommodation decks, who are expected to carry them up to exterior decks, and down again, when they may be wet and heavy.
㊾ If you want to reduce, or otherwise

change, the "automatic gratuities" charged to your cabin aboard the large resort ships, you may have to provide the reason, in writing, to present to the reception desk.
㊿ Mechanically obtuse bath plugs.
51 Cost of bottled mineral water.
52 Cabin air conditioning that can't be turned off.
53 Frequent and annoying onboard revenue announcements.
54 Outrageously high Alaska excursion prices.
55 Intrusive bazaar stalls and sales tables everywhere.
56 Pushy spa sales people.
57 Overcrowded buffet venues.
58 Poorly trained food service staff.
59 Announcements giving details of items that were already printed in the daily program.
60 Lack of port information for independent passengers not wishing to take organized excursions.

Sea Cloud
★★★★★

Size: . . . . .Boutique Ship	Number of Masts: 4 (17.7 meters)/30 sails	Cabins (outside view): 34
Tonnage: 2,532	Sail Area (sq ft/m2): 32,292/3,000	Cabins (interior/no view): 0
Lifestyle: .Luxury	Main Propulsion: . . . . .sail power	Cabins (for one person): 0
Cruise Line: . . . . .Sea Cloud Cruises	Propulsion/Propellers: diesel (4,476kW)/2	Cabins (with private balcony): 0
Former Names: . . . . . .*Sea Cloud of Grand*	Passenger Decks: 3	Cabins (wheelchair accessible): 0
Cayman, IX-99, Antama, Patria,	Total Crew: 60	Wheelchair accessibility . . . . .None
Angelita, Sea Cloud, Hussar	Passengers	Cabin Current: . . . . .220 volts
Builder: . . . . .Krupp Werft (Germany)	(lower beds/all berths): 68/69	Elevators: 0
Entered Service: . . . . Aug 1931/1979	Passenger Space Ratio	Casino (gaming tables): . . . . .No
(restored)	(lower beds/all berths): 37.2/36.6	Slot Machines: .No
Registry: . . . . .Malta	Crew/Passenger Ratio	Swimming Pools (outdoors): 0
Length (ft/m): 359.2/109.5	(lower beds/all berths): 1.1/1.1	Whirlpools: 0
Beam (ft/m): 48.2814.9	Cabins (total): .34	Self-Service Launderette: . . . . .No
Draft (ft/m): 16.8/5.13	Size Range (sq ft/m): 102.2–409.0/	Library: . . . . .Yes
Type of Vessel: . . . . .barque	9.5–38.0	

OVERALL SCORE: 1,704 OUT OF A POSSIBLE 2,000 POINTS

OVERVIEW. If you want the most romantic, exhilarating, inspiring, soul-refreshing time of your life, take a cruise aboard *Sea Cloud*, the oldest and most beautiful sailing ship in the world – its 75th birthday was celebrated in style in 2006. It is the largest private yacht ever built – three times the size of Captain Cook's *Endeavour* – and a stunningly beautiful ship when under sail.

Sea Cloud is a completely authentic 1930s barque whose three masts are almost as high as a 20-story building – the main mast is 178 ft/ 54 meters above the main deck. This was the largest private yacht ever built when completed in 1931 by E.F. Hutton for his wife, Marjorie Merriweather Post, the American cereal heiress. Originally constructed for $1 million as *Hussar* in the Krupp shipyard in Kiel, Germany, this steel-hulled yacht is immensely impressive when in port, but exhilarating when under full sail.

During World War II, the vessel saw action as a weather observation ship, under the code name *IX-99*. You can still see five chevrons on the bridge, one for each half-year of duty, serving as a reminder of those important years.

There is plenty of deck space, even under the vast expanse of white sail, and the promenade deck outdoors still has wonderful varnished sea chests. The decks themselves are made of mahogany and teak, and wooden "steamer"-style sunloungers are provided.

One of the most beautiful aspects of sailing aboard this ship is its "Blue Lagoon," which is located at the very stern of the vessel. Weather permitting, you can lie down on the thick blue padding and gaze up at the stars and night sky – it's one of the great pleasures – particu-

BERLITZ'S RATINGS

	Possible	Achieved
Ship	500	423
Accommodation	200	173
Food	400	348
Service	400	335
Entertainment	n/a	n/a
Cruise	500	425

larly when the ship is under sail, with engines turned off.

The original engine room, with diesel engines, is still in operation for the rare occasions when sail power can't be used. An open-bridge policy is the norm (except during times of poor weather or navigational maneuvers).

In addition to its retained and refurbished original suites and cabins, some newer, smaller cabins were added in 1979 when a consortium of German yachtsmen and businessmen purchased the ship. The owners spent $7.5 million refurbishing it. The interiors exude warmth, and are finely hand crafted. There is much antique mahogany furniture, fine original oil paintings, gorgeous carved oak paneling, parquet flooring and burnished brass everywhere, as well as some finely detailed ceilings. There is no doubt that Marjorie Merryweather Post was accustomed only to the very finest things in life.

Sea Cloud is the most romantic sailing ship afloat. It operates under charter for much of the year, and sails in both the Caribbean and European/Mediterranean waters.

A cruise aboard *Sea Cloud* is, in summary, a really exhilarating experience. This is a ship like no other, for the discerning few to relish the uncompromising comfort and elegance of a bygone era. A kind of stately home afloat, *Sea Cloud* remains one of the finest and nicest travel experiences in the world. The activities are few, and so relaxation is the key, in a setting that provides fine service and style, but in an unpretentious way. Note that some staircases are steep, as they are aboard almost all sailing vessels.

The only "dress-up" night is the Captain's Welcome Aboard Dinner, but otherwise, smart casual clothing is all that is needed (no tuxedo). Note that mini-skirts would be impractical due to the steep staircases in some places – trousers are more practical. Also note that a big sailing vessel such as this can heel to one side occasionally (so take flat shoes rather than high heels).

The crew is of mixed nationality, and the sailors who climb the rigging and set the sails include females as well as males. On the last night of the cruise, the sailors' choir sings seafaring songs. Gratuities are suggested at $15 per person, per day, although these can be charged to your account. The US dollar is the onboard currency.

The German owner, Sea Cloud Cruises, also operates the rivercruise vessels *River Cloud* and *River Cloud II* for cruising along the rivers of Europe, and, in 2001 introduced a brand new companion sailing ship, *Sea Cloud II*.

Sea Cloud sails, for part of each year, under charter to Hapag-Lloyd Cruises. On those occasions, white and red wines and beer are included for lunch and dinner; soft drinks, espresso and cappuccino coffees are also included at any time; shore excursions are an optional extra, as are gratuities. Details may be different for other charter operators (such as Abercrombie & Kent).

Passengers are not permitted to climb the rigging, as may be possible aboard some other tall ships. This is because the mast rigging on this vintage sailing ship is of a very different type to the more modern sailing vessels (such as *Royal Clipper, Star Clipper, Star Flyer,* and *Sea Cloud II*). However, passengers may be able participate occasionally in the furling and unfurling of the sails.

Although now 75 years young, *Sea Cloud* is so lovingly maintained and operated that anyone who sails aboard it cannot fail to be impressed and totally absorbed by the character of this beautiful tall ship. If you seek entertainment, casinos, bingo, horse racing and flashy resort cruising, this is not the ship for you.

The food and service are good, as is the interaction between passengers and crew, many of whom have worked aboard the ship for many, many years. One bonus is the fact that the doctor on board is available at no charge for medical emergencies or seasickness medication.

In 2001, the ship suffered a fire while in Rijeka, which put it out of commission for many months. However, all necessary repairs were painstakingly made and it is now in a beautiful original condition.

Rigging: For the sailors among you, the sails are (in order, from fore to aft mast, top to bottom):
Fore Mast: flying jib, outer jib, inner jib, fore topmast staysail, fore royal, fore topgallant, fore upper-top sail, fore lower-top sail, foresail.
Main Mast: main royal staysail, main topgallant staysail, main topmast staysail, skysail, main royal, main topgallant, main upper topsail, main lower topsail, main sail.
Mizzen Mast: mizzen royal staysail, mizzen topgallant staysail, mizzen topmast staysail, mizzen royal topsail, mizzen topgallant, mizzen upper topsail, mizzen lower topsail, mizzen course.
Spanker Mast: spanker top mast staysail, spanker staysail, spanker-gaff topsail, spanker.

SUITABLE FOR: *Sea Cloud* is best suited to couples and singles (not children) who would probably never consider a "normal" cruise ship, but who enjoy sailing aboard a real tall ship but want the experience wrapped in a package that includes accommodation, good food, like-minded companions, interesting destinations, and don't want the bother of owning or chartering their own mega-yacht.

ACCOMMODATION. Because *Sea Cloud* was built as a private yacht, there is a wide variation in cabin sizes and configurations. Some cabins have double beds, while some have twin beds (side by side or in an L-shaped configuration) that are fixed and cannot be placed together. Many of the original cabins have a fireplace, now with an electric fire, and some of the fittings in some bathrooms remind me of those found in similar bathrooms in the lovely Hotel Abtei in Hamburg.

All the cabins are very comfortable, but those on Main Deck (Cabins 1–8) were part of the original accommodation aboard this ship. Of these, the two owner's suites (Cabins 1 and 2) are really opulent, and feature real, original Chippendale furniture, fine gilt detailing, a real fireplace, French canopy bed, and large Italian Carrara marble bathrooms with gold fittings.

Owner's Cabin Number 1 is decorated in white throughout, and has a French double bed, a marble fireplace and Louis Phillippe chairs; the bathroom is appointed in Carrara marble, with cut-glass mirrors, and faucets (taps) in the shape of swans. Owner's Cabin Number 2, completely paneled in rich woods, retains the mahogany secretary used 60 years ago by Edward F. Hutton (Marjorie's husband), its dark wood decor reminiscent of the 1930s.

Other cabins (both the original ones, and some newer additions) are beautifully furnished (all were refurbished in 1993) and are surprisingly large for the size of the ship. There is a good amount of closet and drawer space and all cabins have a personal safe and telephone. The cabin bathrooms, too, are quite luxurious, and equipped with everything you will need, including bathrobes and hairdryer, and an assortment of toiletries (there is a 110-volt AC shaver socket in each bathroom). The "new" cabins are rather small for two persons, so it's best to take minimal luggage.

There is no cabin food or beverage service. Also, if you occupy one of the original cabins on Main Deck you may be subjected to some noise when the motorized capstans are used to raise and lower or trim the sails. On one day each cruise, an "open-house" cocktail party is held on the Main Deck, with all cabins available for passengers to see.

CUISINE. The dining room, created from the original owner's living room/saloon, is located in the center of the vessel. It is exquisite and elegant in every detail (it also houses the ship's library) has beautiful wood paneled walls and a wood beam ceiling. There is ample space at each table, so there is never a crowded feeling, and meals are taken in an open-seating arrangement. German chefs are in charge, and the cuisine is very international, with a good balance of nouvelle cuisine and regional dishes featured (depending on which region the ship is sailing in). High quality food and cuisine are featured throughout, although there is little choice, due to the size of the galley. Place settings for dinner (often by candlelight) are navy blue, white and gold Bauscher china.

There is always excellent seafood and fish (this is purchased fresh, locally, when available, as are most other ingredients). For breakfast and lunch, there are self-serve buffets. These are really good, and beautifully presented (usually indoors for breakfast and outdoors on the Promenade Deck for lunch). Meal times are announced by the ship's bell. European wines are provided for lunch and dinner (vintages tend to be young, however). Soft drinks and bottled water are included in the price, while alcoholic drinks cost extra. On the last day of each cruise, homemade ice cream is produced.

ENTERTAINMENT. There is a keyboard player/singer for the occasional soirée, but nothing else (nothing else needed – the thrill of sailing is the entertainment). Dinner and after-dinner conversation with fellow passengers really becomes the entertainment each evening. So, if you are feeling anti-social and don't want to talk to your fellow passengers, take a good book (or two).

SPA/FITNESS. There are no spa or fitness facilities. However, for recreation (particularly at night), there is the Blue Lagoon, an area of seating (with blue cushioned pads) at the very aft of the ship, where you can lie down and watch the heavens.

ENVIRONMENTAL ISSUES

There are three types of waste water: bilge water, black water (or sewage) and grey water.

Bilge water is oily engine run-off and condensation that collects in the bilge, a compartment at the bottom of a vessel's hull where water is collected and later pumped out. Grey water comes from showers and sinks. Black water, perhaps the most damaging to the environment, comes from the toilets and from the drains and sinks of the medical center. When water is treated to reduce its oil content below 15 parts of oil per million parts of water, international law allows it to be discharged virtually anywhere.

Few accidents have happened, and most cruise ships' environmental standards meet or surpass all international laws; the cruise industry represents only 0.2 percent of all ocean-going vessels worldwide.

Cruise ship owners are working towards stricter emission limits for particulate matter and sulfur oxides, and reducing nitrogen oxide levels (compared to existing emissions levels) that will probably be imposed within the next few years. Older engines (those built before January 1, 2000) will be required to achieve a 20% reduction in nitrogen oxides starting in 2010.

The latest generation of propulsion machinery (engines) is, however, much more fuel efficient than older ships. For example, RCI's *Freedom*-class ships are 10% more fuel efficient than the *Voyager*-class ships, and the company's *Oasis*-class ships, introduced in 2009, are 15% more fuel efficient than the *Freedom*-class ships.

In the past 10 years, cruise ships have spent huge sums of money in new technology; the result is that waste and garbage has been almost cut in half, while sustaining cruise capacity growth just approaching around eight percent annually. The latest hull coatings increase fuel efficiency; the coating, which reduces surface resistance in the water, is completely non-toxic. Many large resort ships now have environmental officers on board to oversee compliance with environmental regulations and requirements.

Cruise lines reduce the solid waste they generate by purchasing in bulk, encouraging suppliers to use more efficient packaging, reusing packaging when possible and packaging more environmentally friendly materials. Other examples:

● Advanced purification systems treat all onboard wastewater.

● Ships actively recycle glass, met-als, wood, cardboard and paper.

● Excess heat generated in the ships' engine boilers is rerouted to power evaporators used in the process of turning sea water into potable water.

● Special high-tech compacters process garbage (the one aboard *Queen Mary 2*, for example, is four decks high).

● Dry cleaning machines now use non-hazardous detergents formulated with soy, banana and orange extracts.

● Materials printed on board can now be produced using soy-based inks.

● Some ships "plug in" to clean, local hydroelectric when they dock in ports cities such as Seattle and Juneau.

● The only solid waste discharged to sea is food waste, considered safe because, either fish consume it or natural elements break it down in the water. And some use only seafood farmed from sustainable sources. NCL and NCL America ships offload their used cooking oil for recycling to bio-diesel.

What you can do to help

Specially marked garbage containers are scattered throughout each ship for you to use.

Sea Cloud Hussar
NOT YET RATED

Size: ....Boutique Ship	Passenger Decks: 4	Cabins (wheelchair accessible): 0
Tonnage: 4,200	Total Crew: 90	Wheelchair accessibility ....None
Lifestyle: ....Standard	Passengers	Cabin Voltage: ....110 volts
Cruise Line: ....Sea Cloud Cruises	(lower beds/all berths): 136/136	Elevators: 1
Former Names: ....none	Passenger Space Ratio	Casino (gaming tables): ....No
Builder: ..Factoria de Naval Marin (Spain)	(lower beds/all berths): 30.8/30.8	Slot Machines: ....No
Original Cost: ....€69 million	Crew/Passenger Ratio	Swimming Pools (outdoors): 0
Entered Service: ....Jan 2011	(lower beds/all berths): 1.5/1.5	Swimming Pools (indoors): 0
Registry: ....Malta	Cabins (total): 69	Whirlpools: 1
Length (ft/m): 445.2/135.7	Size Range (sq ft/m): 215.2–430.5/	Self-Service Launderette: ....No
Beam (ft/m): 56.4/17.2	20–40	Dedicated Cinema/Seats: ....No
Draft (ft/m): 18.5/5.65	Cabins (outside view): 69	Library: ....Yes
Propulsion/Propellers: .....diesel-electric	Cabins (interior/no view): 0	
(4,920kW)/1	Cabins (for one person): 0	
3,975 sq.m (42,771 sq.ft) of sail	Cabins (with private balcony): 26	

BERLITZ'S OVERALL SCORE: NYR OUT OF A POSSIBLE 2,000 POINTS

OVERVIEW. *Hussar* was the name of the largest private yacht ever built when completed in 1931 by E.F. Hutton for his wife, Marjorie Merriweather Post, the American cereal heiress. After several owners, *Hussar* eventually became *Sea Cloud*, for Hamburg-based Sea Cloud Cruises. In tribute, the company has named its newest tall ship *Sea Cloud Hussar*. The figurehead on the ship's bows is a classic gold eagle.

Sea Cloud Hussar is the largest three-mast tall ship ever constructed to carry passengers. It's a real tall ship, and all the sails are rigged by hand (no electric winches to help). There are 3,975 sq. meters (42,771 sq. ft) of sail (in 27 sails), and the main mast towers 190 ft above the waterline (157.5 ft above the deck). The ship also has one environmentally-friendly diesel-electric engine for help in getting into and out of ports – and when there is no wind. Weather permitting, you can lie down on thick padding and gaze up at the stars and night sky – it's one of the great pleasures – particularly when the ship is under sail, with the engine off. All deck furniture is teak, and comes with padded cushions.

Although there is no swimming pool, there is a large hot tub and teak surround on the open deck. There is also a swimming platform at the stern of the ship, which operates in Europe, Northern Europe, the Middle East, and in the Indian Ocean. The onboard currency is the euro.

ACCOMMODATION. There are five cabin grades, equipped with twin beds convertible to a queen-sized bed, minibar, vanity desk, walk-in closet or enclosed closet (wardrobe), infotainment system, personal safe, hairdryer, and e-mail

BERLITZ'S RATINGS

	Possible	Achieved
Ship	500	NYR
Accommodation	200	NYR
Food	400	NYR
Service	400	NYR
Entertainment	100	NYR
Cruise	400	NYR

access. Bathrooms have a marble floor and wooden cabinetry. Two sets of two cabins have interconnecting doors.

There are three Owner's Suites, each with a veranda, a full-sized bathtub, and separate shower enclosure; 23 Junior Suites; and 43 Deluxe Cabins.

SUITABLE FOR: *Sea Cloud* is best suited to couples and singles (not children) who would avoid a "normal" cruise ship, but enjoy sailing in comfort aboard a real tall ship with like-minded companions.

CUISINE. The wood-paneled main dining room seats all passengers in one seating. There is ample space at each table, so there is never a crowded feeling, and meals are taken in an open-seating arrangement. German chefs provide cuisine that is very international, with a good balance of high-quality nouvelle cuisine and regional dishes, depending on which region the ship is sailing in. Table settings are elegant, and meal times are announced by the ship's bell. The place settings for dinner, often by candlelight, are navy blue, white and gold Bauscher china.

Soft drinks and bottled mineral water are included in the price; alcoholic drinks cost extra. European wines are provided for lunch and dinner.

A Lido Bistro/Bar provides casual fare in the open air.

ENTERTAINMENT. It's all about after-dinner conversation with newfound friends.

SPA/FITNESS. Sauna, steam room, hairdresser, fitness room, and relaxation area.

Sea Cloud II
★★★★★

Size: ....Boutique Ship	Sail Area (sq ft/m2): 32,292/3,000	Cabins (outside view): 48
Tonnage: 3,849	Main Propulsion: ....sail power	Cabins (interior/no view): 0
Lifestyle: ....Luxury	Propulsion/Propellers: diesel (2,500kW)/2	Cabins (for one person): 0
Cruise Line: ....Sea Cloud Cruises	Passenger Decks: 4	Cabins (with private balcony): 0
Former Names: ....none	Total Crew: 60	Cabins (wheelchair accessible): 0
Builder: Astilleros Gondan, Figueras (Spain)	Passengers	Wheelchair accessibility ....None
Original Cost: ....DM 50 million	(lower beds/all berths): 96/96	Cabin Current: ....110 and 220 volts
Entered Service: ....Feb 2001	Passenger Space Ratio	Elevators: 0
Registry: ....Malta	(lower beds/all berths): 40.0/40.0	Swimming Pools (outdoors): 0
Length (ft/m): 383.8/117.0	Crew/Passenger Ratio	Whirlpools: 0
Beam (ft/m): 52.9/16.15	(lower beds/all berths): 1.6/1.6	Self-Service Launderette: ....No
Draft (ft/m): 17.7/5.4	Cabins (total): 48	Library: ....Yes
Type of Vessel: ....barque	Size Range (sq ft/m): 215.2–322.9/	
Number of Masts: ....3 (24 sails)	20.0–30.0	

BERLITZ'S OVERALL SCORE: 1,702 OUT OF A POSSIBLE 2,000 POINTS

OVERVIEW. This new, three-mast tall ship is slightly longer (and beamier) than the original *Sea Cloud*, and has the look, ambience and feel of a 1930s sailing vessel, but with all the latest high-tech navigational aids. The ship complements the company's beautiful, original, 1931-built *Sea Cloud* in almost every way, including its external appearance – except for a very rounded stern in place of the counter stern of the original ship.

Despite some appallingly low standards in the original fitting out of its interiors and carpeting by a shipyard that needs to learn the meaning of the word "quality", Sea Cloud Cruises quickly acted to correct the irritating items, and can now satisfy those seeking the very best of luxurious comfort and surroundings inside a wonderful sailing vessel.

A small water sports platform is built into the aft quarter of the starboard side (with adjacent shower), and the ship carries four inflatable craft for close-in shore landings, as well as snorkeling equipment.

The interior designers have managed to continue the same beautiful traditional look and design as that of *Sea Cloud*. These design details and special decorative touches will make those who have been on the sister ship feel instantly at home. Whether the modern materials used will stand up to 70 years of use like those of the original *Sea Cloud* remains to be seen, although they are of a high quality. In any event, passengers who have sailed aboard the original ship will compare the original with the new.

The main lounge is truly elegant, with sofa and large individual tub chair seating around oval drinks tables. The ceiling is ornate, with an abundance of wood detailing, and an oval centerpiece is set around skylights to the open deck

BERLITZ'S RATINGS		
	Possible	Achieved
Ship	500	435
Accommodation	200	173
Food	400	337
Service	400	333
Entertainment	n/a	n/a
Cruise	500	424

above. A bar is set into the aft port side of the room, which has audio-visual aids built in – for lectures and presentations.

A treasured aspect of sailing aboard this ship is its "Blue Lagoon", at the very stern of the vessel – part of the outdoor bar and casual dining area. Weather permitting, you can lie on thick blue padding and gaze up at the stars and warm night sky – it's a huge pleasure, particularly when the ship is under sail, with the engines turned off.

Overall, *Sea Cloud II* is one of the most luxurious true sailing ships in the world, although it is not the largest – that distinction goes to competitor Star Clippers' *Royal Clipper*. However, in terms of interior design, degree of luxury in appointments, the passenger flow, fabrics, food and service, the ceiling height of public rooms, larger cabins, great open deck space, better passenger space ratio and crew to passenger ratio, there is none better than *Sea Cloud II*. I have sailed aboard both vessels and I can promise you a memorable sail-cruise experience.

Your personal experience will depend on which company is operating the ship under charter when you sail, and exactly what is to be included in the package. This is, however, as exclusive as it gets – sailing in the lap of luxury.

Rigging: This consists of up to 24 sails: flying jib, outer jib, inner jib; fore royal, fore topgallant, fore upper topsail, fore lower topsail, fore course; main royal staysail, main topgallant staysail, main topmast staysail; sky sail, main royal, main topgallant, main upper topsail, main lower topsail, main sail; mizzen topgallant staysail, mizzen topmast staysail; mizzen gaff topsail, mizzen upper gaff sail, mizzen lower gaff sail, middle gaff, upper gaff.

If you have sailed aboard the original *Sea Cloud*, you

will probably be disappointed with the more limited space and decoration of the equivalent cabins aboard this ship.

SUITABLE FOR: *Sea Cloud II* is best suited to couples and singles (not children) who would probably never consider a "normal" cruise ship, but who enjoy sailing aboard a real tall ship and want this experience wrapped in a package that includes accommodation, good food, like-minded companions, interesting destinations, and don't want the bother of owning or chartering their own mega-yacht.

ACCOMMODATION. The decor in the cabins is very tasteful 1920s retro, with lots of bird's-eye maple wood paneling, brass accenting, and beautiful molded white ceilings. All cabins have a vanity desk, hairdryer, refrigerator (typically stocked with soft drinks and bottled water), and a combination TV/video player.

All cabins have a private bathroom with shower enclosure (or tub/shower combination), and plenty of storage space for your personal toiletries. Note that the cabin electrical current is 220 volts, although all bathrooms also include a 110-volt socket for shavers.

There are two suites. Naturally, these have more space – but not as much space as the two owner's suites aboard *Sea Cloud* – and comprise a completely separate bedroom, with four-poster bed, and living room, while the marble-clad bathroom has a full-sized tub.

There are 16 junior suites. These provide a living area and sleeping area with twin beds that convert to a queen-sized bed. The marble-clad bathroom is quite opulent, and has a small tub/shower combination, with lots of little cubbyholes to store personal toiletry items.

CUISINE. The one-seating dining room operates an open-seating policy, so you can dine with whom you wish, when you wish. It is decorated in a light, modern maritime style, with wood and carpeted flooring, comfortable chairs with armrests, and circular light fixtures. The gold-rimmed plates used for the captain's dinner – typically a candlelit affair – have the ship's crest embedded in the white porcelain; they are extremely elegant and highly collectible. The place settings for dinner, also often by candlelight, are navy blue, white and gold Bauscher china.

There is always excellent seafood and fish (this is purchased fresh, locally, when available, as are most other ingredients). For breakfast and lunch, there are self-serve buffets. These are really good, and beautifully presented (usually indoors for breakfast and outdoors on the Promenade Deck for lunch). Meal times are announced by the ship's bell.

European wines are typically provided for lunch and dinner – vintages tend to be young, however. Soft drinks and bottled water are included in the price, while alcoholic drinks cost extra. On the last day of each cruise, homemade ice cream is produced.

ENTERTAINMENT. There is a keyboard player/singer for the occasional soirée, but nothing else (nothing else needed – the thrill of sailing is the entertainment). Dinner and after-dinner conversation with fellow passengers really becomes the entertainment each evening. So, if you are feeling anti-social and don't want to talk to your fellow passengers, take a good book or two.

SPA/FITNESS. There is a health/fitness area, with a small gymnasium, and sauna. Massage is available.

Sea Princess
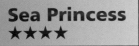
★★★★

Size:	Large Resort Ship	Passenger Decks:	10
Tonnage:	77,690	Total Crew:	850
Lifestyle:	Standard	Passengers	
Cruise Line:	Princess Cruises	(lower beds/all berths):	2,016/2,272
Former Names:	Adonia, Sea Princess	Passenger Space Ratio	
Builder:	Fincantieri (Italy)	(lower beds/all berths):	39.3/34.1
Original Cost:	$300 million	Crew/Passenger Ratio	
Entered Service:	Dec 1998/Apr 2005	(lower beds/all berths):	2.2/2.5
Registry:	Great Britain	Cabins (total):	1,008
Length (ft/m):	857.2/261.3	Size Range (sq ft/m):	158.2–610.3/
Beam (ft/m):	105.6/32.2		14.7–56.7
Draft (ft/m):	26.5/8.1	Cabins (outside view):	603
Propulsion/Propellers:	diesel-electric	Cabins (interior/no view):	405
	(46,080kW)/2	Cabins (for one person):	0

Cabins (with private balcony):	411
Cabins (wheelchair accessible):	19
Wheelchair accessibility	Good
Cabin Current:	110 and 220 volts
Elevators:	11
Casino (gaming tables):	Yes
Slot Machines:	Yes
Swimming Pools (outdoors):	4
Swimming Pools (indoors):	0
Whirlpools:	5
Self-Service Launderette:	Yes
Dedicated Cinema/Seats:	No
Library:	Yes

OVERALL SCORE: 1,487 OUT OF A POSSIBLE 2,000 POINTS

OVERVIEW. This all-white ship (sister ships: *Dawn Princess, Sun Princess*) has a profile balanced by a large, swept-back funnel which contains a deck tennis/basketball/volleyball court in its sheltered aft base. There is a wide, teak wrap-around promenade deck outdoors, some real teak steamer-style deck chairs (with cushioned pads), and 93,000 sq. ft (8,640 sq. meters) of outdoors space. A large glazed area on the upper decks provides plenty of light and connection with the outside world.

Sea Princess absorbs passengers well and has a decent passenger space ratio for a large ship; some areas even have an intimate feel to them, which is what the interior designers intended. The interiors are attractive and welcoming with pastel colors and decor that includes countless wall murals and other artwork.

There is a wide range of public rooms to choose from (including 13 bars), with several intimate rooms and spaces so that you aren't overwhelmed by large spaces. A large, four-deck-high atrium lobby has winding, double stairways and two panoramic glass-walled elevators.

There is a library, a warm room that has large buttery leather chairs for listening to CDs and audio books, with ocean-view windows; a card room and reading room. The artwork collection is good, particularly on the stairways, and helps make the ship feel smaller than it is. The Grand Casino is slightly out of the main passenger flow and so it does not generate the "walk-through" factor found aboard so many ships. Internet connectivity can be found in Cyberspace, a lounge/internet connect room close to the pools on Riviera Deck.

Perhaps the most popular drinking venue is the Wheel-

BERLITZ'S RATINGS

	Possible	Achieved
Ship	500	413
Accommodation	200	159
Food	400	255
Service	400	283
Entertainment	100	78
Cruise	400	299

house Bar, with decor that is a pleasing mix of traditional and modern (it's like a gentleman's club, with its wood paneling and comfortable seating), a bandstand and dance floor. For families with children, plenty of space is provided in The Fun Zone children's center, on the starboard side of the Riviera (pool) Deck.

One nice feature is the fact that the captain's cocktail party – normally held in the four-deck-high main atrium, so you can come and go as you please. However, note that in the quest for increased onboard revenue, even birthday cakes are now an extra-cost item, as are espressos and cappuccinos (fake ones, made from instant coffee, are available in the dining rooms). Also at extra cost are ice cream, except in the restaurant, and bottled water; these can add up to a considerable amount on a long cruise.

Sea Princess, transferred from the UK-based P&O Cruises to Princess Cruises in 2005 and now marketed to both British and North American passengers, operates cruises from the UK in summer and in the Caribbean in winter. The onboard currency is the US dollar.

Note that there are a number of dead ends in the interior layout, so it's not as user-friendly as it could be. The swimming pools are quite small considering the number of passengers carried, and the pool deck is cluttered with plastic sunloungers. The digital voice announcing lift deck stops is annoying for many. At the end of the day – as is the case aboard most large ships – you will be well attended if you live in the top-grade cabins; if you do not, you will merely be one of a very large number of passengers.

ACCOMMODATION. There are 19 different cabin price grades, designated as: suites (with private balcony), mini-suites (with private balcony), outside-view twin-bedded cabins with balcony, outside-view twin-bedded cabins, and interior (no view) twin-bedded cabins. Although the standard outside-view and interior (no view) cabins are a little small, they are functional, and have earth tone colors accentuated by splashes of color from the bedspreads. Proportionately, there are quite a lot of interior (no view) cabins.

Many outside-view cabins have private balconies, and all seem to be quite well soundproofed, although the balcony partition is not of the floor to ceiling type, so you can hear your neighbors – or smell their smoke. The balconies are very narrow – just large enough for two small chairs – and there is no outdoor balcony light. Some cabins have third- and fourth-person upper bunk beds – good for families with children.

There is a reasonable amount of closet space and abundant drawer and other storage space in the cabins; although adequate for a 7-night cruise, it can prove challenging for longer cruises. Also provided are a color television, and refrigerator, and each night a chocolate will appear on your pillow. The cabin bathrooms are practical units, and come complete with all the facilities one needs, although again, they really are tight spaces. Fortunately, they have a shower enclosure of a decent size, a small amount of shelving for your toiletries, real glasses, and a hairdryer.
Suites: The largest cabins are six suites (two on each of three decks at the stern), each with its own large private balcony. These suites are well laid out, and the large bathrooms have two washbasins, a Jacuzzi tub and separate shower enclosure. The bedroom has generous amounts of wood accenting and detailing, indented ceilings, TV sets in the bedroom and lounge areas, and a dining table and four chairs.
Mini-Suites: These typically have two lower beds convertible into a queen-sized bed. There is a separate bedroom/sleeping area with vanity desk, and a lounge with sofa and coffee table, indented ceilings, generous amounts of wood accenting and detailing, walk-in closet; the bathroom has a Jacuzzi bathtub and separate shower enclosure.
Standard Outside-view/Interior (No View) Cabins: The cabin bathrooms are practical, but compact. They do, however, have a decent shower enclosure, a small amount of shelving for toiletries, real glasses, and a hairdryer.

The cabin numbering system is quite illogical, however, with numbers going through several hundred series on the same deck. The room service menu is very limited.

CUISINE. There are two main, asymmetrically designed dining rooms (each seating about 500), Rigoletto and Traviata, located adjacent to the two lower levels of the four-deck high atrium lobby. They are non-smoking, and the one you are assigned to depends on your cabin location. Each has its own galley and each is split into multi-tier sections, which help create a feeling of intimacy, although there is a lot of noise from the waiter stations. Breakfast and lunch are provided in an open seating arrangement; dinner is in two seatings. The wine list is quite reasonable; 15% is added to all beverage bills, including wines.

Horizon Court is the ship's 24-hour casual, self-serve buffet. At night, this large room, which resembles a food court, can be transformed into an informal bistro dinner setting with waiter service. Reservations are necessary and there may be a cover charge.

Outdoors on deck, with a sheltered view over the Riviera Pool, the Terrace Grill features fast-food items for those who don't want to change from sunbathing attire. In the evening, the grill offers steaks, seafood, and a "white sisters" mixed grill. A cover charge applies for dining under the stars.

For informal eats, Verdi's, on the uppermost level of the atrium lobby, serves steaks and seafood (at extra cost). In addition, there's a patisserie (for cappuccino/espresso coffees and pastries) opposite the reception desk on the lowest deck of the atrium, and a wine/caviar bar called Rendezvous (on Promenade Deck). Note that coffee or tea from any of the ship's bars costs extra.

ENTERTAINMENT. There are two showlounges (Princess Theater, and the Vista Lounge), one forward, one aft. The Princess Theater, located forward, is a 550-seat, theater-style showlounge, where the main production shows and theater events are staged and movies can also be shown. The Vista Lounge is a 480-seat lounge and bar for cabaret entertainment and lectures.

In addition, the ship has an array of cabaret acts. Although many are not what you would call headliners, they regularly travel the cruise ship circuit. Classical concerts are scheduled for many cruises throughout the year.

SPA/FITNESS. The Lotus Spa has facilities that are contained in a glass-walled complex located on Lido Deck – one of the highest decks, at the aft section of the ship. It includes a gymnasium with ocean views aft and to port, with all the associated high-tech muscle-pumping and body toning equipment, a combination aerobics/exercise room, sauna and steam room, and several well-being treatment rooms. Some fitness and exercise classes may cost extra.

Forming part of the outside area of the spa complex, one swimming pool is "suspended" aft between two decks (two other pools are located in another area in the center of the ship), although they are not large for the size of the ship. Sports facilities are located in an open-air sports deck positioned inside the ship's funnel and adaptable for basketball, volleyball, badminton, or paddle tennis. Joggers can exercise on the wrap-around open Promenade Deck. There's also an electronic golf simulator – no need to bring your own clubs.

● **For more extensive general information about the Princess Cruises experience, see pages 148–51.**

Seabourn Legend
★★★★★

Size: ....Small Ship	Propulsion/Propellers: diesel (7,280kW)/2	Cabins (for one person): 0
Tonnage: 9,961	Passenger Decks: 6	Cabins (with private balcony): 6
Lifestyle: ....Luxury	Total Crew: 160	Cabins (wheelchair accessible): 4
Cruise Line: .....The Yachts of Seabourn	Passengers	Wheelchair accessibility ....None
Former Names: ....*Queen Odyssey,*	(lower beds/all berths): 212/212	Cabin Current: ....110 and 220 volts
Royal Viking Queen	Passenger Space Ratio	Elevators: 3
Builder: ....Schichau Seebeckwerft	(lower beds/all berths): 46.9/46.9	Casino (gaming tables): ....Yes
(Germany)	Crew/Passenger Ratio	Slot Machines: ....Yes
Original Cost: ....$87 million	(lower beds/all berths): 1.3/1.3	Swimming Pools (outdoors): 1
Entered Service: ....Mar 1992/July 1996	Cabins (total): 106	Swimming Pools (indoors): 0
Registry: ....Bahamas	Size Range (sq ft/m): 277.0–575.8/	Whirlpools: 3
Length (ft/m): 442.9/135.0	25.7–53.5	Self-Service Launderette: ....Yes
Beam (ft/m): 62.9/19.20	Cabins (outside view): 106	Dedicated Cinema/Seats: ....No
Draft (ft/m): 16.4/5.0	Cabins (interior/no view): 0	Library: ....Yes

OVERALL SCORE: 1,774 OUT OF A POSSIBLE 2,000 POINTS

OVERVIEW. *Seabourn Legend* is a contemporary ship with a handsome profile, almost identical in looks and size to *Seabourn Pride* and *Seabourn Spirit*, but younger, and built to a much higher standard, with streamline "decorator" bars (made by Mercedes Benz) located along the side of the upper superstructure and a slightly different swept-over funnel design.

The ship has two fine mahogany water taxis for use as shore tenders. There is also an aft water sports platform and marina, which can be used in suitably calm warm-water areas. Water sports facilities include a small, enclosed "dip" pool, sea kayaks, snorkel equipment, windsurfers, water ski boat, and Zodiac inflatable boats.

Inside, a wide central passageway divides port and starboard side accommodation. The finest quality interior fixtures, fittings, and fabrics have been combined in its sumptuous public areas to present an outstanding, elegant decor, with warm color combinations (there is no glitz anywhere) and some fine artwork. The dress code, relaxed by day, is more formal at night.

There have been many recent complaints about falling standards aboard the Seabourn ships, particularly in regard to maintenance (the ships are more than 10 years old). Food, presentation and service, passengers said, wasn't what it used to be. However, I am happy to report that the product delivered now is extremely good, and more consistent (particularly in food and service) than, say, the Silversea Cruises ships, which are larger and carry more passengers.

Seabourn Legend provides discerning passengers with an outstanding level of personal service and a very civilized cruise experience. For a grand, small-ship cruise experience

BERLITZ'S RATINGS		
	Possible	Achieved
Ship	500	449
Accommodation	200	186
Food	400	347
Service	400	353
Entertainment	100	86
Cruise	400	353

in fine surroundings, with only just over 100 other couples as neighbors, this ship is difficult to beat. All drinks (except premium brands and connoisseur wines) are included, as are gratuities, fine aromatherapy Molton Brown bath products and large soaps by Bronnley, Chanel and Hermès, short massages (called "massage moments") on deck, open-seating dining, use of watersports equipment, one included Exclusively Seabourn shore excursion per cruise, and movies under the stars. *Seabourn Legend* can cruise to places where large cruise ships can't, thanks to its ocean-yacht size. DHL can provide luggage pick-up and delivery service. Port charges and insurance are not included. The onboard currency is the US dollar.

The three Seabourn ships, which provide an excellent hotel service product, are superior to other upscale ships such as *Seven Seas Mariner* and *Seven Seas Voyager*, but still not up to the standard of *Europa*'s fine product delivery and hospitality.

The sunloungers have now thankfully been changed to a steel-mesh design, although they are hard-surfaced and need pads to make them comfortable for more than a few minutes. There is no walk-around promenade deck outdoors. The range of cigars offered is limited. The Club suffers from over-amplified music. Non-American passengers should note that almost all entertainment and activities are geared towards American tastes, despite the increasingly international passenger mix.

SUITABLE FOR: *Seabourn Legend* is best suited to sophisticated, well traveled couples (typically over 50, but possibly younger) who seek a small ship setting – they wouldn't be seen dead aboard today's huge standard resort cruise ships – with excellent food that approaches gourmet standards, and fine European-style service in chic surroundings that border on the elegant and luxurious.

ACCOMMODATION. This is spread over three decks, and there are nine price categories, the price depending on size, grade and location. All suites are comfortably large and very nicely equipped with everything one might need. They are, for example, larger than those aboard the smaller *Sea-Dream I* and *SeaDream II*, but then the ship is also larger, and carries almost twice as many passengers.

All suites have a sleeping area with European duvets and Frette linens (but there is a vanity mirror opposite the bed, which won't please *feng shui* practitioners) and separate lounge area with Bose wave radio/CD unit, DVD player and flat-screen TV, vanity desk (with hairdryer) and personalized stationery, world atlas, mini-bar and refrigerator stocked with soft drinks and two bottles of your favorite liquor at embarkation, a large walk-in closet (illuminated automatically when you open the door), digital personal safe, and wall-mounted clock and barometer. A full passenger list is also provided – a rarity today – as are a fresh fruit basket, replenished daily, and flowers..

Marble-clad bathrooms have one or two washbasins, depending on accommodation grade, a decent (but not full-sized) tub (four suites have a shower enclosure only – no bathtub), plenty of storage areas, 100% thick cotton towels, plush terrycloth bathrobe, designer soaps and Molton Brown toiletries. A selection of five aromatherapy bath preparations by Molton Brown can be ordered from your stewardess, who will prepare your bath for you.

Course-by-course in-cabin dining is available during dinner hours (the cocktail table raises to form a dining table); there is 24-hour room service. Also provided are: personalized stationery, and fancy ticket wallet, suitably boxed and nicely packaged before your cruise. Non-smoking cabins are available. Menus for each dinner are delivered to your suite during the day.

In 2001, Seabourn Cruise Line added 36 French balconies to suites on two out of three accommodation decks. These are not balconies in the true sense, but have two doors that open wide onto a tiny teakwood balcony that is just 27 cm (about 10.6 inches) wide. The balconies do allow you to have fresh sea air, however, together with some salt spray.

Four Owner's suites (Ibsen/Grieg, each measuring 530 sq. ft/49 sq. meters and Eriksson/Heyerdahl, each 575 sq. ft/53 sq. meters), and two Classic Suites (Queen Maud/Queen Sonja, each 400 sq. ft/37 sq. meters) offer superb, private living spaces. Each has a walk-in closet, second closet, full bathroom plus a guest toilet with washbasin. There is a fully secluded forward- or side-facing balcony, with sun lounge chairs and wooden drinks table (Ibsen/Grieg do not have balconies).

The living area has ample bookshelf space, including a complete edition of *Encyclopaedia Britannica*, large refrigerator/drinks cabinet, television and DVD player (plus a second TV set in the bedroom). All windows, as well as

the door to the balcony, have manually operated blackout blinds, and a complete blackout is possible in both bedroom and living room.

CUISINE. The Restaurant is a part-marble, part-carpeted dining room that has portholes and elegant decor but it is not as warm and intimate as that found aboard the smaller SeaDream ships, with their wood paneling. The silverware (150 gram weight – the best available) is by Robbe & Berking. Open-seating dining means that you can dine when you want, with whom you wish. Course-by-course meals can also be served in your cabin.

Dining is memorable. The menus, overseen by celebrity chef Charlie Palmer, are creative and well-balanced, with a wide selection of foods, including regional dishes. Seabourn Cruise Line's cuisine is artfully presented, with many items cooked to order. Special orders are available, as is caviar (sevruga). Flambeaus and flaming desserts can be cooked at your table. The selection of exotic fruits and cheeses is good.

Each day, basic table wine is included for lunch and dinner, but all others (the decent ones) cost extra. The wine list is quite extensive, with prices ranging from moderate to high; many of the wines come from the smaller, more exclusive vineyards. The European dining room staff is hand picked and provides excellent, unhurried service.

Relaxed breakfasts (until 11am), lunch buffets and casual (themed) candlelight dinners (including a new "2" tasting menu) can be taken in the popular Veranda Cafe, adjacent to the swimming pool, instead of in the dining room. Additionally, the Sky Grill provides an above-poolside setting complete with candlelit dining and specializing in steaks and seafood. All dining venues are non-smoking.

ENTERTAINMENT. The King Olaf Lounge is the venue for all entertainment events, including shows, cabaret acts, lectures, and most social functions. It has a sloping floor that provides good sightlines from just about every seat. Because this is a small, upscale ship, the typically four-person "production" shows are of limited scope, as dinner is almost always the main event. You can, however, expect to see the occasional cabaret act. Singers also tend to do mini-cabaret performances in The Club, one deck above the showlounge, the gathering place for late-night drinkers.

SPA/FITNESS. A small, well equipped health spa/fitness center, The Spa at Seabourn, is located just aft of the navigation bridge. It provides sauna and steam rooms (with separate facilities for men and women) and integral changing room; and a separate exercise room with video tapes for private, individual aerobics workouts; and a beauty salon.

The Spa at Seabourn is staffed and operated by concession Elemis by Steiner. Treatment prices are equal to those in an expensive land-based spa (examples: Elemis Aroma Stone Therapy $178 for 75 mins, Facial $111). The beauty salon offers hair beautifying treatments and conditioning, while in the gymnasium, personal training sessions, yoga classes, mat Pilates and body composition analysis are available at extra cost.

Seabourn Odyssey
★★★★★

Size:.................... Small Ship	Total Crew:................... 330	Cabins (wheelchair accessible):...... 7
Tonnage:.................. 32,000	Passengers	Wheelchair accessibility .... .Good
Lifestyle:.................... Luxury	(lower beds/all berths):....... 450/462	Cabin Voltage:.............. 110 volts
Cruise Line:.... The Yachts of Seabourn	Passenger Space Ratio	Elevators:....................... 3
Former Names:................ none	(lower beds/all berths):...... 71.1/69.2	Casino (gaming tables):........... Yes
Builder:.............. Mariotti (Italy)	Crew/Passenger Ratio	Slot Machines:.................. Yes
Original Cost:........... $250 million	(lower beds/all berths):........ 1.3/1.4	Swimming Pools (outdoors):......... 2
Entered Service:........... Jun 2009	Cabins (total):.................. 225	Swimming Pools (indoors):......... 0
Registry:................. Bahamas	Size Range (sq ft/m):..... 295.0–438.1/	Whirlpools:...................... 6
Length (ft/m):........... 649.6/198.0	27.5–133.6	Self-Service Launderette:......... Yes
Beam (ft/m):.............. 83.9/25.6	Cabins (outside view):............ 225	Dedicated Cinema/Seats:.......... No
Draft (ft/m):................ 21.3/6.5	Cabins (interior/no view):.......... 0	Library:....................... Yes
Propulsion/Propellers:. . diesel-electric/2	Cabins (for one person):........... 0	
Passenger Decks:................ 8	Cabins (with private balcony):...... 199	

BERLITZ'S OVERALL SCORE: 1,787 OUT OF A POSSIBLE 2,000 POINTS

OVERVIEW. This, the first of three new, larger ships for Seabourn, looks like an up-sized version of its three smaller "yachts" (*Seabourn Legend, Seabourn Pride, Seabourn Spirit*). However, *Seabourn Odyssey* (and sister ships *Seabourn Quest* and *Seabourn Sojourn*) has the second highest passenger space ratio in the cruise industry – only the passenger space ratio of the expedition ship *50 Years of Victory* is greater – so passengers will never feel crowded. Also, unlike the smaller ships, *Seabourn Odyssey, Seabourn Quest* and *Seabourn Sojourn* are full of balcony cabins.

In reality, this is a ship with a yacht-like ambiance – well, a big yacht, sort of like Roman Abramovich's yacht *Eclipse*. There are two outdoor swimming pools (midships and aft); the aft pool is in a more secluded area, although there's not a lot of sunbathing space and the sunloungers are of the steel mesh variety, not comfortable without a pad.

One of the most pleasing outdoor areas is the Sky Bar – good for those balmy evenings in the right cruise areas. But for stargazing, the hot tub located by the ship's bow is a delight, and it's dimly lit and peaceful. While real teak is used in most outdoor areas, Flexteak (faux teak) is used in some locations.

All accommodation areas are in the forward section, with most public rooms located aft – so accommodation is quiet, but you'll need to pass through several decks to get to some public rooms. However, there is an Observation Lounge, which has great views, and is a well laid out, very comfortable room. The Marina, at the stern, has a staging area from which watersports are organized in weather-suitable areas.

The interior decor uses light woods, tame colors and suitably rich soft furnishings to create a contemporary, restrained

BERLITZ'S RATINGS

	Possible	Achieved
Ship	500	457
Accommodation	200	186
Food	400	348
Service	400	354
Entertainment	100	87
Cruise	400	355

and relaxing environment, which is good considering the low ceiling height in most public rooms.

Seabourn Square, a "concierge lounge," has a relaxed and club-like ambiance designed to encourage sociability. The area – although considered the "town square," it's not in the center of the ship – includes a library, internet-connect computer stations, an outdoor terrace and a coffee bar that's particularly good for late-riser coffees and pastries. Its "concierges" can provide in-port shopping tips, set up shore excursions, get dinner reservations in ports of call, and so on. Wi-fi is available throughout the ship. There's also a "private" diamond showroom, called The Collection.

The onboard currency is the US dollar, and drinks, wines with meals, and all gratuities are included, though premium brands and high-quality wines cost extra.

What's really good: The staff, high service levels, attention to detail, and the Spa (fitness/wellness) facilities.

What's not so good: The high charge for internet-connectivity ($39 per day). The "vertical stacking" layout is not really user-friendly. The cabin doors are rather narrow, and doors within the cabins are of varying heights and sizes, and feel utilitarian rather than luxurious. A second washbasin is pretty pointless, really, unless you wash at the same time as your spouse or partner. Most public rooms are of a single deck height, which doesn't create a good feeling of spaciousness, and support pillars are everywhere (Mariotti should look at *Europa* and learn that it's not necessary to have so many pillars – or fire doors that protrude outside bulkheads instead of being integral to them).

Seabourn Odyssey operated a 108-day around-the-world cruise in 2010 – Seabourn's first such cruise.

ACCOMMODATION. There are 13 different grades of suites in 18 price categories, although the smaller units are really large cabins. Fully 90 percent of cabins have a private balcony. Even the smallest cabin is a generous 269 sq.ft. All cabins have a separate bathtub and shower enclosure in a granite bathroom setting, twin beds convertible to a queen-sized bed, flat-screen TV plus CD and DVD, minibar , vanity desk with hairdryer, world atlas, personalized stationery, and large walk-in closet with personal safe.

The ship's interior designers have done a good job of creating a very homely, contemporary living space in the suites/cabins, although the walls are rather plain and unimaginative. It's good to see that the beds are high enough off the floor to enable even the largest suitcases to be stowed underneath. All drawers are fitted with soft gel, which means they are quiet – no more "slamming" contests with your next-door neighbor.

The cabins are bathed in soft earthy tones, although a splash of color wouldn't go amiss. The cabinetry has many seams and strips covering joints which make me feel some joinery courses are needed among the ship's outfitters. One neat feature is a leather-clad vanity stool/table that converts into a backgammon table. The design of a "cube table" that can be "inserted" under a glass-topped table when not being used as a footrest is a smart, practical idea for making more space.

Seabourn Suites and Veranda Suites are quite narrow, and feel cramped, with little space in the passageway between the bed and the opposite wall. However, the bathrooms are generously proportioned, with grey and choco-late-brown decor; there are two washbasins, a bathtub, and a separate shower enclosure.

Some size examples (excluding balcony): Grand Suites (1,135 sq.ft), including two-bedrooms; Signature Suites (819 sq. ft); Wintergarden Suites (914 sq.ft). Rather neat suites within a glass-enclosed solarium, set in front of the funnel, with a side balcony; Owners Suites 611-675 sq.ft); Penthouse Suite 436-611 sq.ft); Veranda Suite (269-298 sq.ft); Seabourn Suite (295 sq.ft).

DINING. There are three dining venues plus a poolside grill:
● The Restaurant has open-seating dining at tables for two, four, six or eight, with menus designed by American celebrity chef Charlie Palmer. It is a large venue that actu-ally feels a bit "clinical" rather than "classical" with its white-on-white decor and double-height ceiling in its central section. The most sought-after seats are in the center rather than along the port and starboard sides, which have a window, but low ceiling height.
● Restaurant 2, with around 50 seats, has regional, seasonal cuisine and tasting menus, perhaps for a mini-dégustation; however, the ceiling height is rather low, which makes the feeling cramped. The cuisine is contemporary, with a flirta-tion with fusion, where taste and flavours are what the expe-rience is all about. This venue shares the same galley as the adjacent The Colonnade.
● The Colonnade, located aft, has indoor/outdoor seating and is nicely decorated, although its "free-flow" design could be better; there's too little outdoor seating for the demand in warm-weather areas, when many passengers like to eat outdoors. During dinner, passengers who are dressed formally on designated formal nights have to co-inhabit the space with those who are more casually dressed. The venue is also adjacent to one of the fine dining restaurants.
● The Patio Grill is in a casual poolside setting outdoors – and most enjoyable on a balmy evening, as a change to the air-conditioned interior dining venues.

In addition, a 24-hour, in-suite menu offers the à la carte items served in the main dining room during dinner hours.

ENTERTAINMENT. The Grand Salon is a nicely configured main entertainment venue for cabaret performances, social dancing, and for use as a cinema. However, the stage is small – large enough for a live band, but performers need to use the dance floor area – and the room has so many pillars that it's awkward to see anything, and a decorative steel ceiling grating in the central section is cold and unappealing. Small production shows are performed well to pre-recorded tracks. However, the audio equipment and sound dispersion in the room is excellent.

The Club is a cool, trendy nightclub/disco with mini-malist design. Located beneath the Grand salon, it incorpo-rates a comfortable casino.

SPA/FITNESS. The Spa at Seabourn, operated by Elemis, occupies the aft section of two decks, and is quite large, at 11,500 sq.ft (1,068 sq. meters). It offers full services in a very pleasant setting that includes a two-deck-high waterfall at the entrance and seven indoor/outdoor treatment rooms, as well as a thalassotherapy pool, thermal suite (for which a pass will cost you $30 per day) and complete salon facilities, while a hot tub and relaxation area on the deck above is accessed by a spiral staircase. Separate saunas and steam rooms (for males and females) are provided, but they are extremely small. In the gymnasium, personal training ses-sions, yoga classes, mat Pilates and body composition analy-sis are available at extra cost, but some basic exercise programs are free. Sample treatment costs: Thai Massage, $213; Swedish Remedial Massage, $132; Deep Tissue Mas-sage, $141; Regenerating Facial, $135.

Seabourn Pride
★★★★★

Size:	.Small Ship	Passenger Decks:	.6	Cabins (with private balcony):
Tonnage:	.9,975	Total Crew:	.160	Cabins (wheelchair accessible):
Lifestyle:	.Luxury	Passengers		Wheelchair accessibility
Cruise Line:	.The Yachts at Seabourn	(lower beds/all berths):	.212/212	Cabin Current:

Size: ....Small Ship
Tonnage: 9,975
Lifestyle: ....Luxury
Cruise Line: .....The Yachts at Seabourn
Former Names: ....none
Builder: ....Seebeckwerft (Germany)
Original Cost: ....$50 million
Entered Service: ....Dec 1988
Registry: ....Bahamas
Length (ft/m): 439.9/134.10
Beam (ft/m): 62.9/19.20
Draft (ft/m): 16.8/5.15
Propulsion/Propellers: ....diesel
(5,355kW)/2

Passenger Decks: 6
Total Crew: 160
Passengers
(lower beds/all berths): 212/212
Passenger Space Ratio
(lower beds/all berths): 47.09/47.09
Crew/Passenger Ratio
(lower beds/all berths): 1.3/1.3
Cabins (total): 106
Size Range (sq ft/m): 277.0–575.0/
25.7–53.4
Cabins (outside view): 106
Cabins (interior/no view): 0
Cabins (for one person): 0

Cabins (with private balcony): 6
Cabins (wheelchair accessible): 4
Wheelchair accessibility ....None
Cabin Current: ....110 and 220 volts
Elevators: 3
Casino (gaming tables): ....Yes
Slot Machines: ....Yes
Swimming Pools (outdoors): 1
(plus 1 aft marina-pool)
Swimming Pools (indoors): 0
Whirlpools: 3
Self-Service Launderette: ....Yes
Dedicated Cinema/Seats: ....No
Library: ....Yes

OVERALL SCORE: 1,769 OUT OF A POSSIBLE 2,000 POINTS

OVERVIEW. This pleasantly appointed cruise vessel has sleek exterior styling, handsome profile with swept-back, rounded lines, and is an identical sister vessel to *Seabourn Spirit*. It has two fine mahogany water taxis for use as shore tenders. An aft water sports platform and marina can be used in suitably calm warm-water areas. Water sports facilities include a small, enclosed "dip" pool, sea kayaks, snorkel equipment, windsurfers, water ski boat, and Zodiac inflatable boats.

BERLITZ'S RATINGS		
	Possible	Achieved
Ship	500	452
Accommodation	200	186
Food	400	347
Service	400	348
Entertainment	100	86
Cruise	400	350

A wide central passageway divides port and starboard side accommodation. Inviting, sumptuous public areas have warm colors. Fine quality interior fixtures, fittings, artwork and fabric combine to present an outstanding, elegant decor. For a small ship, there is wide range of public rooms. These include a main lounge (staging small cabaret shows), nightclub, an observation lounge with bar, large, deep armchairs, and a cigar smoking area complete with cabinet, cigar humidor and small selection of good cigars. There is a small business center, small meeting room, and a small casino with roulette and blackjack tables, plus a few slot machines tucked away.

Not for the budget-minded, this ship is for those desiring supremely elegant, stylish, small-ship surroundings, but is perhaps rather small for long voyages in open waters.

During the past two years, there have been many complaints about falling standards aboard the Seabourn ships, particularly with regard to maintenance – they are now over 10 years old – and that food, presentation and service had deteriorated. However, the company has now turned things around, and the product delivered is extremely good.

Seabourn Pride provides discerning passengers with an outstanding level of personal service and an utterly civi-

lized cruise experience. For a grand, small ship cruise experience in fine surroundings, with only just over 100 other couples as neighbors, this ship is difficult to beat. All drinks (except premium brands and connoisseur wines) are included, as are gratuities, fine aromatherapy bath selections from Molton Brown and large soaps by Bronnley, Chanel and Hermès, short massages on deck (called "massage moments"), open-seating dining, use of watersports equipment, one free Exclusively Seabourn shore excursion per cruise, and movies under the stars. *Seabourn Pride* is able to cruise to places where large cruise ships can't, due to its ocean-yacht size. DHL provides luggage pick-up and delivery service.

Port charges and insurance are not included. The onboard currency is the US dollar.

In the final analysis, the three Seabourn ships provide an excellent product, and are superior to other upscale ships such as *Seven Seas Mariner* and *Seven Seas Voyager*, but still not up to the standard of *Europa*'s fine product delivery and hospitality.

The sunloungers have now thankfully been changed from plastic to a steel mesh design. There is no walk-around promenade deck outdoors. There is only one dryer in the self-service launderette. Non-American passengers should note that almost all entertainment and activities are geared towards American tastes, despite the increasingly international passenger mix.

SUITABLE FOR: *Seabourn Pride* is best to sophisticated, well traveled couples (typically over 50, but possible younger) who seek a small ship setting with excellent food that approaches gourmet standards, and fine European-style service in surroundings that can best be described as bordering on the elegant and luxurious.

ACCOMMODATION. This is spread over three decks, and there are nine price categories, the price depending on size, grade and location you choose. The all-outside cabins (called suites in brochure-speak) are comfortably large and beautifully equipped with everything one could reasonably need. Electric blackout blinds are provided for the large windows in addition to curtains. All cabinetry is made of blond woods, with softly rounded edges, and cabin doors are neatly angled away from the passageway.

All the suites have a sleeping area (European duvets are standard, as are Frette linens) and separate lounge area with Bose Wave Radio/CD unit, DVD player and flat-screen TV, vanity desk (with hairdryer) and personalized stationery, world atlas, mini-bar and refrigerator (stocked with soft drinks, and two bottles of your favorite liquor when you embark), a large walk-in closet (illuminated automatically when you open the door) and wooden hangers, electronic personal safe, umbrella, and wall-mounted clock and barometer.

A full passenger list is also provided – a rarity these days – as are a fresh fruit basket, replenished daily, and flowers.

Marble-clad bathrooms have one or two washbasins, depending on the accommodation grade, a decent (but not full-sized) tub (four suites have a shower enclosure only – no tub), plenty of storage areas, 100% thick cotton towels, plush terrycloth bathrobe, designer soaps and Molton Brown personal amenity items. A selection of five Molton Brown aromatherapy bath preparations can be ordered from your stewardess, who will prepare your bath.

In 2001, Seabourn Cruise Line added 36 French balconies to suites on two out of three accommodation decks. These are not balconies in the true sense of the word, but they do have two doors that open wide, onto a tiny teakwood balcony that is just 27 cm (about 10.6 inches) wide. The balconies allow you to have fresh sea air, however, together with some salt spray.

Course-by-course in-cabin dining is available during dinner hours (the cocktail table can be raised to form a dining table); there is 24-hour room service. Also provided are: personalized stationery, and fancy ticket wallet. Non-smoking cabins are available. Menus for each dinner are delivered to your suite during the day.

Four Owner's suites (King Haakon/King Magnus, each measuring 530 sq. ft/49 sq. meters, and Amundsen/Nansen, each 575 sq. ft/53 sq. meters), and two Classic Suites (King Harald/King Olav, each 400 sq. ft/ 37 sq. meters) offer superb, private living spaces. Each has a walk-in closet, second closet, full bathroom plus a guest toilet with washbasin. There is a fully secluded forward- or side-facing balcony, with sunloungers and wooden drinks table. The living area has ample bookshelf space (including a complete edition of

Encyclopedia Britannica), large refrigerator/drinks cabinet, television and DVD player (plus a second TV set in the bedroom). All windows, as well as the door to the balcony, have manually operated blackout blinds, and a complete blackout is possible in both bedroom and living room.

CUISINE. The Restaurant is a part-marble, part-carpeted dining room that has portholes and elegant decor. The silverware (150 gram weight – the best available) is by Robbe & Berking. Open-seating dining means that you can dine when you want, with whom you wish.

The menus, overseen by celebrity chef Charlie Palmer, are creative and well-balanced, with a wide selection of foods and regional cuisine. Seabourn Cruise Line's fine, creative cuisine is artfully presented, with many items cooked to order. Special orders are available, and caviar is always available on request. Tableside flambeaus and flaming desserts can be presented at your table. There is always a good selection of exotic fruits and cheeses.

Each day, basic table wine is included for lunch and dinner, but all others (the decent ones) cost extra. The wine list is quite extensive, with prices ranging from moderate to high; many of the wines come from the smaller, more exclusive vineyards. The hand-picked European dining room staff provide excellent, unhurried service.

In addition, relaxed breakfasts (available until 11am) and lunch buffets and casual (themed) candlelight dinners, including a new "2" tasting menu, can be taken in the popular Veranda Cafe adjacent to the swimming pool.

Additionally, the Sky Grill provides an above-poolside setting featuring candlelit dining and specializing in steaks and seafood. All dining venues are non-smoking.

ENTERTAINMENT. The Magellan Lounge is the venue for all entertainment events. It is a room with a sloping floor that provides good sight lines from just about every seat. "Production" shows are of limited scope, as dinner is usually the main event. You can, however, expect to see the occasional cabaret act. Singers also tend to do mini-cabaret performances in The Club (one deck above the show-lounge), the gathering place for late-night drinkers.

SPA/FITNESS. There's a small but well equipped health spa/fitness center, The Spa at Seabourn. It has sauna and steam rooms (separate facilities for men and women), an equipment-packed gymnasium (but the ceiling height is low), and a beauty salon.

The spa is staffed and operated by concession Elemis by Steiner. Treatment prices equal those in an expensive land-based spa (examples: Elemis Aroma Stone Therapy $178 for 75 mins; Reflexology $111 for 45 mins; Facial $111). The beauty salon has hair beautifying treatments and conditioning, while in the gymnasium, personal training sessions, yoga classes, mat Pilates and body composition analysis are available at extra cost.

Seabourn Quest
NOT YET RATED

Size:	Small Ship	Total Crew:	330	Cabins (wheelchair accessible):	7
Tonnage:	32,000	Passengers		Wheelchair accessibility	Good
Lifestyle:	Luxury	(lower beds/all berths):	450/462	Cabin Current:	110 volts
Cruise Line:	The Yachts of Seabourn	Passenger Space Ratio		Elevators:	3
Former Names:	none	(lower beds/all berths):	71.1/69.2	Casino (gaming tables):	Yes
Builder:	Mariotti (Italy)	Crew/Passenger Ratio		Slot Machines:	Yes
Original Cost:	$250 million	(lower beds/all berths):	1.3/1.4	Swimming Pools (outdoors):	2
Entered Service:	Jun 2011	Cabins (total):	225	Swimming Pools (indoors):	0
Registry:	Bahamas	Size Range (sq ft/m):	295.0–438.1/	Whirlpools:	6
Length (ft/m):	649.6/198.0		27.5–133.6	Self-Service Launderette:	Yes
Beam (ft/m):	83.9/25.6	Cabins (outside view):	225	Dedicated Cinema/Seats:	No
Draft (ft/m):	21.3/6.5	Cabins (interior/no view):	0	Library:	Yes
Propulsion/Propellers:	diesel-electric/2	Cabins (for one person):	0		
Passenger Decks:	8	Cabins (with private balcony):	199		

BERLITZ'S OVERALL SCORE: NYR (OUT OF A POSSIBLE 2,000 POINTS)

OVERVIEW. This, the last of three new (larger) ships for Seabourn, looks like a ship-sized version of its three smaller "yachts" *(Seabourn Legend, Seabourn Pride, Seabourn Spirit)*. However, *Seabourn Quest* (together with sisters *Seabourn Odyssey* and *Seabourn Sojourn)* does have the highest passenger space ratio in the cruise industry, so passengers will never feel crowded.

BERLITZ'S RATINGS		
	Possible	Achieved
Ship	500	NYR
Accommodation	200	NYR
Food	400	NYR
Service	400	NYR
Entertainment	100	NYR
Cruise	400	NYR

There are two outdoor swimming pools, midships and aft; the aft pool is in a delightful area, although there's not a lot of sunbathing space. One of the most pleasing outdoor areas is the Sky Bar – good for those balmy evenings in the right cruise areas. But for stargazing, the hot tub located by the ship's bow is a delight, and it's dimly lit and peaceful.

All the accommodation areas are in the forward section, with most public rooms located aft, so accommodation is quiet, but you'll need to traverse through several decks to get to some of the public rooms. The Marina, at the stern, has a staging area from which watersports are organized.

Seabourn Square, a "concierge lounge," has a relaxed, club-like ambiance designed to encourage sociability. The area includes a library, shops, eight internet-connect computer stations, an outdoor terrace and a coffee bar. Its "concierges" can provide in-port shopping tips, set up shore excursions, get dinner reservations in ports of call, etc. Wi-fi is available throughout the ship. There's a private diamond showroom, called The Collection. The onboard currency is the US dollar, and drinks, wines with meals, and all gratuities are included, though premium brands and high-quality wines cost extra.

What's really good? The staff and service levels, and the wellness facilities.

What's not so good? The "vertical stacking" layout is not really user-friendly. While real teak is used in most outdoor areas, Flexteak (faux teak) is used in other areas. The cabin doors are rather narrow, and doors within the cabins are of varying heights and sizes, and feel utilitarian rather than luxurious. A second washbasin is pretty pointless unless you and your partner usually wash at the same time. Most public rooms are of a single deck height, so there's not such a good feeling of spaciousness, and support pillars are everywhere – Mariotti, the builders, should look at *Europa* to see it's not necessary to have so many pillars. Expect the ship to receive a similar score and rating to that of sister ships *Seabourn Odyssey* and *Seabourn Sojourn*.

ACCOMMODATION. There are 13 different grades of suites in 18 price categories, although the smaller units are really large cabins. Fully 90 percent of cabins have a private balcony. Even the smallest cabin is a generous 269 sq.ft (25 sq. meters). All cabins have a separate tub and shower enclosure in a granite bathroom setting, twin beds convertible to a queen-sized bed, flat-screen TV plus CD and DVD, mini-bar, vanity desk with hairdryer, world atlas, personalized stationery, and large walk-in closet with personal safe. One neat feature is a vanity stool/table that converts into a backgammon table. The cabins are bathed in soft earthtones, although a splash of color wouldn't go amiss. The cabinetry has many seams and strips covering joints that I feel the ship's outfitters would benefit from a joinery course.

Some size examples, excluding balcony: Grand Suites 1,135 sq.ft (105 sq. meters), including two-bedrooms; Signature Suites 819 sq. ft (76 sq. meters); Wintergarden Suites

914 sq.ft (85 sq. meters). Rather neat suites within a glass-enclosed solarium, set in front of the funnel, with a side balcony: Owners Suites 611–675 sq.ft (57–63 sq. meters), Penthouse Suite 436–611 sq.ft (41–57 sq. meters), Veranda Suite 269–298 sq.ft (25–28 sq. meters), and Seabourn Suite 295 sq.ft (27 sq. meters).

CUISINE. There are three venues, plus a poolside grill:
● The Restaurant has open-seating dining at tables for two, four, six or eight, with menus designed by American celebrity chef Charlie Palmer. It is a large venue, all dressed in white, with a double-height ceiling in its central section. The most sought-after seats are here rather than along the port and starboard sides, which have a window, but low ceiling height.
● Restaurant 2, with around 50 seats, has regional, seasonal cuisine and tasting menus, perhaps for a mini-dégustation. However, the ceiling height is rather low and the feeling is cramped.
● The Colonnade, located aft, has indoor/outdoor seating and is nicely decorated, although its "free-flow" design could be better; there's too little outdoor seating for the increased demand in warm-weather areas.
● The Patio Grill is in a casual poolside setting outdoors. In addition, a 24-hour, in-suite menu offers the à la carte items served in the main dining room during dinner hours.

ENTERTAINMENT. The Grand Salon is nicely configured. It is the main entertainment venue, for cabaret performances, social dancing, and for use as a cinema. However, there are so many pillars, which make it awkward to see anything – poor design and ill-judged shipbuilding techniques – and a decorative steel ceiling grating in the central section is cold and unappealing.

The Club is a cool, trendy nightclub/disco with minimalist design. Located beneath the Grand salon, it incorporates a comfortable casino.

SPA/FITNESS. The Spa at Seabourn, operated by Elemis, occupies the aft section of two decks, and is the largest aboard any luxury ship, at 11,500 sq.ft (1,068 sq.meters). It offers full services in a very pleasant setting that includes a two-deck-high waterfall at the entrance and seven appealing indoor/outdoor treatment rooms, as well as a thalassotherapy pool and complete salon facilities, while a hot tub and relaxation area on the deck above is accessed by a spiral staircase.

In the gymnasium, personal training sessions, yoga classes, mat Pilates and body composition analysis are available at extra cost, but some basic exercise programs are free. Sample treatment costs: Thai Massage, $213; Swedish Remedial Massage, $132; Deep Tissue Massage, $141; Regenerating Facial, $135.

WORLD CRUISES: DID YOU KNOW...

● that the longest around-the-world cruise took place in 2010? It was aboard the little cruise ship *Spirit of Oceanus* and lasted 333 days, from March 5, 2010 to January 19, 2011, from Singapore to Singapore.
● that the first regular steamship service across the North Atlantic was inaugurated on March 28, 1838, when the 703-ton steamer *Sirius* left London for New York via Cork, Ireland?
● that the winter of 1970–71 was the first time since 1838 that there was no regular passenger service on the North Atlantic?
● that the first scheduled trans-atlantic advertisement appeared in

the *New York Evening Post* on October 27, 1817, for the 424-ton sailing packet *James Monroe* to sail from New York to Liverpool on January 5, 1818, and for *Couvier* to sail from Liverpool to New York on January 1?
● that Cunard Line held the record from 1940 to 1996 for the largest passenger ship ever built (RMS *Queen Elizabeth*)?
● that the Dollar Steamship Line featured a round-the-world cruise that started October 15, 1910, from New York, aboard the SS *Cleveland*? The cruise was advertised as "one-class, no overcrowding" voyage. The cost was "$650 and up," according

to an advertisement.
● that a round-the-world cruise was made in 1922–23 by Cunard's *Laconia* (19,680 grt), a three-class ship that sailed from New York? The itinerary included many ports of call that are still popular with world cruise passengers today. The vessel accommodated 350 persons in each of its first two classes, and 1,500 in third class, giving a total capacity of 2,200 passengers, more than many current ships.
● about the lady who went to her travel agent, who asked if she had enjoyed her cruise around the world? The lady replied, "Yes, but next year I want to go somewhere different."

Seabourn Sojourn
★★★★★

Size:	.Small Ship	
Tonnage:	.32,000	
Lifestyle:	.Luxury	
Cruise Line:	.The Yachts of Seabourn	
Former Names:	.none	
Builder:	.Mariotti (Italy)	
Original Cost:	.$250 million	
Entered Service:	.Jun 2010	
Registry:	.Bahamas	
Length (ft/m):	.649.6/198.0	
Beam (ft/m):	.83.9/25.6	
Draft (ft/m):	.21.3/6.5	
Propulsion/Propellers:	.diesel-electric/2	
Passenger Decks:	.8	

Total Crew: .330
Passengers
(lower beds/all berths): .450/462
Passenger Space Ratio
(lower beds/all berths): .71.1/69.2
Crew/Passenger Ratio
(lower beds/all berths): .1.3/1.4
Cabins (total): .225
Size Range (sq ft/m): .295.0–438.1/ 27.5–133.6
Cabins (outside view): .225
Cabins (interior/no view): .0
Cabins (for one person): .0
Cabins (with private balcony): .199

Cabins (wheelchair accessible): .7
Wheelchair accessibility .Good
Cabin Current: .110 volts
Elevators: .3
Casino (gaming tables): .Yes
Slot Machines: .Yes
Swimming Pools (outdoors): .2
Swimming Pools (indoors): .0
Whirlpools: .6
Self-Service Launderette: .Yes
Dedicated Cinema/Seats: .No
Library: .Yes

OVERALL SCORE: 1,787 OUT OF A POSSIBLE 2,000 POINTS

OVERVIEW. This, the second of three new (larger) ships for Seabourn, looks like a ship-sized version of its three smaller "yachts" (*Seabourn Legend, Seabourn Pride, Seabourn Spirit*). However, *Seabourn Sojourn* does have the highest passenger space ratio in the cruise industry, so passengers will never feel crowded. There are two outdoor swimming pools, midships and aft; the aft pool is in a delightful area, although there's not a lot of sunbathing space.

BERLITZ'S RATINGS		
	Possible	Achieved
Ship	500	457
Accommodation	200	186
Food	400	348
Service	400	354
Entertainment	100	87
Cruise	400	355

One of the most pleasing outdoor areas is the Sky Bar – good for those balmy evenings in the right cruise areas. But for stargazing, the hot tub located by the ship's bow is a delight, and it's dimly lit and peaceful.

All the accommodation areas are located in the forward section, with most public rooms located aft – so accommodation is quiet, but you'll need to traverse through several decks to get to some of the public rooms. The Marina, at the stern, has a staging area from which water sports are organized; this can be crowded when the ship is operating short cruises and the Marina is used only once.

Seabourn Square, a "concierge lounge," has a relaxed, club-like ambiance designed to encourage sociability. The area includes a library, shops, eight internet-connect computer stations, an outdoor terrace and a coffee bar. Its "concierges" can provide in-port shopping tips, set up shore excursions, get dinner reservations in ports of call, etc. Wi-fi is available throughout the ship. There's a private diamond showroom, called The Collection. The onboard currency is the US dollar, and drinks, wines with meals, and all gratuities are included, though "premium" brands and high-quality, vintage wines cost extra.

What's really good? The staff and service levels – which,

together with cuisine, are perhaps the most important elements of the Seabourn cruise experience, and the fitness/wellness facilities.

What's not so good? Seabourn Sojourn is not a yacht, despite the company's marketing name. The "vertical stacking" layout is not really user-friendly. While real teak is used in most outdoor areas, Flexteak (faux teak) is used in other areas, and looks cheap.

The cabin doors are quite narrow, and doors within the cabins are also of varying heights and sizes, and feel utilitarian rather than luxurious. A second washbasin is pretty pointless unless you and your partner usually wash at the same time. Most public rooms are of a single deck height, so there's not such a good feeling of spaciousness, and support pillars are everywhere – Mariotti, the builders, should look at *Europa* to see it's not necessary to have so many pillars.

ACCOMMODATION. There are 13 different grades of suites in 18 price categories, although the smaller units are really large cabins. Fully 90 percent of cabins have a private balcony. Even the smallest cabin is a generous 269 sq.ft (25 sq. meters). All cabins have a separate tub and shower enclosure in a granite bathroom setting, twin beds convertible to a queen-sized bed, flat-screen TV plus CD and DVD, mini-bar, vanity desk with hairdryer, world atlas, personalized stationery, and large walk-in closet with personal safe.

One neat feature is a vanity stool/table that converts into a backgammon table. The cabins are bathed in soft earth-tones, although a splash of color wouldn't go amiss. The cabinetry has many seams and strips covering joints that I feel the ship's outfitters would benefit from a joinery course.

The flat-screen TV sets are small in the standard Seabourn and Verandah suites. You can play iPods through the TV system, but its sound quality is really quite poor.

Some size examples, excluding balcony: Grand Suites 1,135 sq.ft (105 sq. meters), including two-bedrooms; Signature Suites 819 sq. ft (76 sq. meters); Wintergarden Suites 914 sq.ft (85 sq. meters). Rather neat suites within a glass-enclosed solarium, set in front of the funnel, with a side balcony: Owners Suites 611–675 sq.ft (57–63 sq. meters), Penthouse Suite 436–611 sq.ft (41–57 sq. meters), Veranda Suite 269–298 sq.ft (25–28 sq. meters), and Seabourn Suite 295 sq.ft (27 sq. meters).

CUISINE. There are three dining venues plus a poolside grill:
● The Restaurant has open-seating dining at tables for two, four, six or eight, with menus designed by American celebrity chef Charlie Palmer. It is a large venue, all dressed in white, with a double-height ceiling in its central section (the most sought-after seats are here rather than along the port and starboard sides, which have a window, but low ceiling height).
● Restaurant 2, with around 50 seats, has regional, seasonal cuisine and tasting menus, perhaps for a mini-dégustation; however, the ceiling height is rather low and the feeling is cramped.
● The Colonnade, located aft, has indoor/outdoor seating and is nicely decorated, although its "free-flow" design could be better, there's too little outdoor seating for the increased demand in warm-weather areas.

● The Patio Grill is in a casual poolside setting outdoors. In addition, a 24-hour, in-suite menu offers the à la carte items served in the main dining room during dinner hours.

ENTERTAINMENT. The Grand Salon is nicely configured. It is the main entertainment venue, for cabaret performances, social dancing, and for use as a cinema. However, there are so many pillars, which make it awkward to see anything – poor design and ill-judged shipbuilding techniques – and a decorative steel ceiling grating in the central section is cold and unappealing.

The Club is a cool, trendy nightclub/disco with minimalist design. Located beneath the Grand salon, it incorporates a comfortable casino.

SPA/FITNESS. The Spa at Seabourn, operated by Elemis, occupies the aft section of two decks, and is the largest aboard any luxury ship, at 11,500 sq.ft (1,068 sq.meters). It offers full services in a very pleasant setting that includes a two-deck-high waterfall at the entrance and seven appealing indoor/outdoor treatment rooms, as well as a thalasso-therapy pool and complete salon facilities, while a hot tub and relaxation area on the deck above is accessed by a spiral staircase. In the gymnasium, personal training sessions, yoga classes, mat Pilates and body composition analysis are available at extra cost, but some basic exercise programs are free. Sample treatment costs: Thai Massage, $213; Swedish Remedial Massage, $132; Deep Tissue Massage, $141; Regenerating Facial, $135.

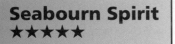

Seabourn Spirit
★★★★★

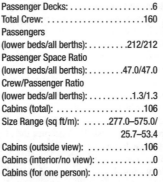

Size: ....Small Ship	Passenger Decks: 6	Cabins (with private balcony): 6
Tonnage: 9,975	Total Crew: 160	Cabins (wheelchair accessible): 4
Lifestyle: ....Luxury	Passengers	Wheelchair accessibility ....None
Cruise Line: .....The Yachts at Seabourn	(lower beds/all berths): 212/212	Cabin Current: ....110 and 220 volts
Former Names: ....none	Passenger Space Ratio	Elevators: 3
Builder: ....Seebeckwerft (Germany)	(lower beds/all berths): 47.0/47.0	Casino (gaming tables): ....Yes
Original Cost: ....$50 million	Crew/Passenger Ratio	Slot Machines: ....Yes
Entered Service: ....Nov 1989	(lower beds/all berths): 1.3/1.3	Swimming Pools (outdoors): 1
Registry: ....Bahamas	Cabins (total): 106	(plus aft marina-pool)
Length (ft/m): 439.9/134.10	Size Range (sq ft/m): 277.0–575.0/	Swimming Pools (indoors): 0
Beam (ft/m): 62.9/19.20	25.7–53.4	Whirlpools: 3
Draft (ft/m): 16.8/5.15	Cabins (outside view): 106	Self-Service Launderette: ....Yes
Propulsion/Propellers: ....diesel	Cabins (interior/no view): 0	Dedicated Cinema/Seats: ....No
(5,355kW)/2	Cabins (for one person): 0	Library: ....Yes

OVERALL SCORE: 1,770 OUT OF A POSSIBLE 2,000 POINTS

OVERVIEW. This finely appointed cruise vessel has sleek exterior styling, handsome profile with swept-back, rounded lines, and is an identical sister vessel to *Seabourn Pride*. It has two fine mahogany water taxis for use as shore tenders. An aft water sports platform and marina can be used in suitably calm warm-water areas. Water sports facilities include a small, enclosed "dip" pool, sea kayaks, snorkel equipment, windsurfers, water ski boat, and Zodiac inflatable boats.

Inside, a wide central passageway divides port and starboard side accommodation. Inviting, sumptuous public areas have warm colors. Fine quality interior fixtures, fittings, fabric and artwork combine to present an outstanding, elegant (but minimalist) decor. For a small ship, there is wide range of public rooms. These include a main lounge (staging small cabaret shows), nightclub, an observation lounge with bar, large, deep armchairs, and a cigar smoking area with cabinet, cigar humidor and small selection of good cigars.

There is also a small business center, small meeting room, even a small casino with roulette and blackjack tables, with a few slot machines tucked away.

During the past two years, there have been many complaints about falling standards aboard the Seabourn ships, particularly in regard to maintenance (they are now over 10 years old). Food, presentation and service, passengers said, had deteriorated. However, the company has now turned things around, and the product is extremely good.

Seabourn Spirit provides discerning passengers with an outstanding level of service and an utterly civilized cruise. For a grand, small ship cruise experience in fine surroundings, with only just over 100 other couples as neighbors,

BERLITZ'S RATINGS

	Possible	Achieved
Ship	500	453
Accommodation	200	186
Food	400	347
Service	400	348
Entertainment	100	86
Cruise	400	350

this ship is hard to beat. All drinks (except for premium brands and connoisseur wines) are included, as are gratuities, Molton Brown aromatherapy bath products and large soaps by names such as Bijan, Chanel and Hermès, short massages on deck ("massage moments") , open-seating dining, use of watersports equipment, one free Exclusively Seabourn shore excursion per cruise, and movies under the stars. *Seabourn Spirit* is able to cruise to places where large cruise ships can't, due to its ocean-yacht size. Port charges and insurance are not included. The onboard currency is the US dollar.

The three Seabourn ships provide an excellent product, superior to other upscale ships such as *Seven Seas Mariner* and *Seven Seas Voyager*, but still not up to the standard of *Europa*'s fine product delivery and hospitality. DHL can provide luggage pick-up and delivery service.

The sunloungers have now thankfully been changed from plastic to a steel mesh design. There is no walk-around promenade deck outdoors. There is only one dryer in the self-service launderette. Non-American passengers should note that almost all entertainment and activities are geared towards American tastes, despite the increasingly international passenger mix.

SUITABLE FOR: *Seabourn Spirit* best suits sophisticated couples (mostly over 50, but possibly younger) who seek a small-ship setting with excellent food approaching gourmet standards, and fine European-style service in surroundings best described as bordering on the elegant and luxurious.

ACCOMMODATION. This is spread over three decks, and

there are nine price categories, the price depending on size, grade and location you choose. The all-outside cabins (called suites in brochure-speak) are comfortably large and beautifully equipped with everything one could reasonably need. Electric blackout blinds are provided for the large windows in addition to curtains. All cabinetry is made of blond woods, with softly rounded edges, and cabin doors are neatly angled away from the passageway.

The suites are larger than those aboard the smaller *Sea-Dream I* and *SeaDream II*, but then the ship is also larger, and carries almost twice as many passengers.

All suites have a sleeping area (European duvets are standard, as are Frette linens) and separate lounge area with Bose Wave Radio/CD unit, DVD player and flat-screen TV, vanity desk (with hairdryer) and personalized stationery, world atlas, mini-bar and refrigerator (stocked with soft drinks, and two bottles of your favorite liquor when you embark), a large walk-in closet (illuminated automatically when you open the door) and wooden hangers, electronic personal safe, umbrella, and wall-mounted clock and barometer. A full passenger list is also provided – a rarity these days – as are a fresh fruit basket, replenished daily, and flowers.

Marble-clad bathrooms feature one or two washbasins (depending on the accommodation grade), a decent (but not full-sized) tub (four suites have a shower enclosure only – no tub), plenty of storage areas, 100% thick cotton towels, plush terrycloth bathrobe, designer soaps and Molton Brown personal amenity items. A selection of five special bath preparations by Molton Brown can be ordered from your stewardess, who will prepare your bath.

Course-by-course in-cabin dining is available during dinner hours (the cocktail table can be raised to form a dining table); there is 24-hour room service. Also provided are: personalized stationery, and fancy ticket wallet, suitably boxed and nicely packaged before your cruise. Non-smoking cabins are available. Menus for each dinner are delivered to your suite during the day.

In 2001, Seabourn Cruise Line added 36 French balconies to suites on two out of three accommodation decks. These are not balconies in the true sense of the word, but they do feature two doors that open wide, onto a tiny teakwood balcony that is just 27 cm (about 10.6 inches) wide. The balconies do allow you to have fresh sea air, however, together with some salt spray.

Four Owner's suites (Bergen/Oslo, each measuring 530 sq. ft/49 sq. meters and Copenhagen/Stockholm, each 575 sq. ft/53 sq. meters), and two Classic Suites (Helsinki/Reykjavik, each 400 sq. ft/37 sq. meters) offer superb, private living spaces. Each has a walk-in closet, second closet, full bathroom plus a guest toilet with washbasin. There is a fully secluded forward- or side-facing balcony, with sun lounge chairs and wooden drinks table.

The living area has ample bookshelf space, including a complete edition of *Encyclopaedia Britannica*, a large

refrigerator/drinks cabinet, television and DVD player, plus a second TV set in the bedroom. All windows, as well as the door to the balcony, have manually operated blackout blinds, and a complete blackout is possible in both bedroom and living room.

CUISINE. The Restaurant is a part-marble, part-carpeted dining room that has portholes and elegant decor. The silverware (150 gram weight – the best available) is by Robbe & Berking. Open-seating dining means that you can dine when you want, with whom you wish.

The menus, overseen by celebrity chef Charlie Palmer, are nicely balanced, with a wide selection of foods and regional cuisine. Seabourn Cruise Line's fine, creative cuisine is artfully presented, with many items cooked to order. Special orders are available, and caviar is always available on request. Tableside flambeaus and flaming desserts are possible. There is a good selection of exotic fruits and cheeses.

Basic table wine is included for lunch and dinner, but all others (the decent ones) cost extra. The wine list is quite extensive, with prices ranging from moderate to high; many of the wines come from the smaller, more exclusive vineyards. The hand-picked European dining room staff provides excellent, unhurried service.

In addition, relaxed breakfasts (available until 11am), lunch buffets and casual (themed) candlelit dinners, including a new "2" tasting menu, can be taken in the popular Veranda Cafe adjacent to the swimming pool, instead of in the dining room.

Additionally, the Sky Grill provides an above-poolside setting featuring candlelit dining and specializing in steaks and seafood. All dining venues are non-smoking.

ENTERTAINMENT. The Amundsen Lounge is the venue for all entertainment events. It is a room with a sloping floor that provides good sightlines from just about every seat. "Production" shows are of limited scope, as dinner is usually the main event. You can, however, expect to see the occasional cabaret act. Singers also tend to do mini-cabaret performances in The Club (one deck above the show-lounge), the gathering place for late-night drinkers.

SPA/FITNESS. A small but well-equipped health spa/fitness center, called The Spa at Seabourn, has sauna and steam rooms (with separate facilities for men and women), and a separate exercise room, with video tapes for private, individual aerobics workouts, and a beauty salon.

The Spa at Seabourn is staffed and operated by concession Elemis by Steiner. Treatment prices are equal to those in an expensive land-based spa (examples: Elemis Aroma Stone Therapy $178 for 75 mins; Reflexology $111 for 45 mins; Facial $111). The beauty salon has hair beautifying treatments and conditioning, while in the gymnasium, personal training sessions, yoga classes, mat Pilates and body composition analysis are available at extra cost.

SeaDream I
★★★★★

Size:	.Boutique Ship
Tonnage:	.4,253
Lifestyle:	.Exclusive
Cruise Line:	.Seadream Yacht Club
Former Names:	.Seabourn Goddess I, Sea Goddess I
Builder:	.Wartsila (Finland)
Entered Service:	.Apr 1984/May 2002
Registry:	.The Bahamas
Length (ft/m):	.343.8/104.81
Beam (ft/m):	.47.9/14.60
Draft (ft/m):	.13.6/4.17
Propulsion/Propellers:	.diesel (3,540kW)/2
Passenger Decks:	.5
Total Crew:	.89
Passengers (lower beds/all berths):	.110/110
Passenger Space Ratio (lower beds/all berths):	.38.6/38.6
Crew/Passenger Ratio (lower beds/all berths):	.1.2/1.2
Cabins (total):	.54
Size Range (sq ft/m):	.195.0–490.0/ 18.1–45.5
Cabins (outside view):	.55
Cabins (interior/no view):	.0
Cabins (for one person):	.0
Cabins (with private balcony):	.0
Cabins (wheelchair accessible):	.0
Wheelchair accessibility	.None
Cabin Current:	.110 and 220 volts
Elevators:	.1
Casino (gaming tables):	.Yes
Slot Machines:	.Yes
Swimming Pools (outdoors):	.1
Swimming Pools (indoors):	.0
Whirlpools:	.1
Self-Service Launderette:	.No
Dedicated Cinema/Seats:	.No
Library:	.Yes

OVERALL SCORE: 1,786

BERLITZ'S RATINGS

	Possible	Achieved
Ship	500	439
Accommodation	200	173
Food	400	371
Service	400	370
Entertainment	n/a	n/a
Cruise	500	433

OVERVIEW. *Sea Dream I* and *Sea Dream II*, reviewed here together, were originally funded by about 800 investors, and operated under the Norske Cruise banner. They have an ultra-sleek profile, with deep blue hull and white superstructure, and the ambiance of a private club. After the ships were bought by SeaDream Yacht Club in 2001, they were completely refurbished, with many changes to public rooms and outdoor areas, and several new features added to create what are contemporary, chic, and desirable, if aging, vessels.

A "Top of the Yacht" bar, crafted in warm wood, was added to both ships in 2001. So were eight special alcoves set to the port and starboard sides of the funnel, equipped with two-person sun loungers with thick pads (and two equipped for one person); however, there is quite a bit of noise from the adjacent funnel. You are encouraged to sleep under the stars if you wish, and cotton sleep suits are provided.

At the front part of the deck there are more sun loungers and a couple of large hammocks, as well as a golf simulator (with a choice of 30 courses).

Inside, there is a feeling of unabashed but discreet sophistication. Elegant, chic public rooms have flowers and pot pourri everywhere. The main social gathering places are the lounge, a delightful library/living room with a selection of about 1,000 books, a piano bar (which can be more like a karaoke bar at times), and a small casino (two blackjack tables and five slot machines).

The two SeaDream ships really are the ultimate exclusive boutique vessels – like having your own private yacht in which hospitality, anticipation and personal recognition are art forms practiced to a high level. The staff is delightful and accommodating ("no" is not in their vocabulary). The dress code is resort casual. Fine-quality furnishings and fabrics are used throughout, with marble and blond wood accents.

So what type of persons will enjoy the SeaDream Yacht Club experience? This is for experienced, independent travelers who don't like regular cruise ships, large ships, glitzy lounges, a platoon of people and kids running around, or dressing up – no tuxedos or gowns are allowed, and ties are not needed. The *SeaDreams* provide the setting for personal indulgence and refined, unstructured and langorous private living at sea, in a casual, private setting akin to that on a mega-yacht. One delightful feature of each cruise in warm weather areas is a "caviar in the surf" beach barbecue.

Life could hardly be better at sea – so, as many regular SeaDream Yacht Club passengers say, why bother with ports of call at all? Embarkation never starts before 3pm, in case you are eager to get aboard.

All drinks (with the exception of premium brands and connoisseur wines), American farmed sevruga caviar, and gratuities are included, but port charges and insurance are not. The price of a cruise is just that: the price of a cruise. Air and/or other travel arrangements can be made on your own, or through your own travel agent, or you can use the excellent services of Total Travel Marine, whose offices in London and Miami specialize in first, business or coach air arrangements as partner to SeaDream Yacht Club, with 24-hour, 365-day service. The onboard currency is the US dollar.

These were the first of the mega-yacht-style ships when built, and none of the cabins has a private balcony – ships with private balconies made their debut just a couple of years later, and, anyway, yachts don't have balconies. One not so positive item is the fact that the reception desk is now called the Concierge, although it is doubtful whether the staff has the kind of in-depth knowledge that is expected of a concierge.

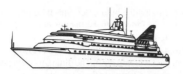

SeaDream II
★★★★★

Size:	.Boutique Ship
Tonnage:	.4,333
Lifestyle:	.Exclusive
Cruise Line:	.SeaDream Yacht Club
Former Names:	.Seabourn Goddess II, Sea Goddess II
Builder:	.Wartsila (Finland)
Original Cost:	.$34 million
Entered Service:	.May 1985/Jan 2002
Registry:	.The Bahamas
Length (ft/m):	.343.8/104.81
Beam (ft/m):	.47.9/14.60
Draft (ft/m):	.13.6/4.17
Propulsion/Propellers:	diesel (3,540kW)/2
Passenger Decks:	.5
Total Crew:	.89
Passengers (lower beds/all berths):	.110/110
Passenger Space Ratio (lower beds/all berths):	.39.3/39.3
Crew/Passenger Ratio (lower beds/all berths):	.1.2/1.2
Cabins (total):	.54
Size Range (sq ft/m):	.195.0–490.0/ 18.1–45.5
Cabins (outside view):	.54
Cabins (interior/no view):	.0
Cabins (for one person):	.0
Cabins (with private balcony):	.0
Cabins (wheelchair accessible):	.0
Wheelchair accessibility	.None
Cabin Current:	.110 and 220 volts
Elevators:	.1
Casino (gaming tables):	.Yes
Slot Machines:	.Yes
Swimming Pools (outdoors):	.1
Swimming Pools (indoors):	.0
Whirlpools:	.1
Self-Service Launderette:	.No
Dedicated Cinema/Seats:	.No
Library:	.Yes

SUITABLE FOR: *The SeaDreams are* best suited to sophisticated, independent and well-traveled couples who are typically over 40, but possible younger - who seek a small ship setting (they wouldn't be seen dead aboard today's huge standard resort cruise ships), with excellent food that is approaching gourmet standards, and fine European-style service in surroundings that borders on the elegant and refined while remaining trendy. However, because they are popular for small company charters, you may find that the date and itinerary you want will not be available, so you may be asked to change to the sister ship and a different itinerary.

ACCOMMODATION. There are three types, and six price categories (depending on location, size and grade): Yacht Club (standard) Cabin, Commodore Club Suite, Admiral Suite and Owner's Suite.

Yacht Club Cabins: Incorrectly called "suites" in the brochure, the standard cabins are, more correctly, fully equipped "mini-suites" with an outside view through windows or portholes (depending on deck and price category). Each measures 195 sq. ft (18.1 sq. meters), which isn't large by today's cruise ship standards; however, it is large compared to cabins aboard many private motor yachts, and extremely large when compared to ocean-going racing yachts. The sleeping area has twin beds that can be put together to form a queen-sized configuration; beds are positioned next to the window (or porthole) so that you can entertain in the living area without going past the sleeping area, as you must aboard the slightly larger Seabourn or Silversea ships, for example; a curtain separates the sleeping and lounge areas. All cabinetry and furniture is of thick blond wood, with nicely rounded edges.

A long vanity desk in the sleeping area has a large mirror above it (however, there is no three-sided mirror for women to check the back of their hair) and two small drawers for cosmetic items; there is also a brass clock located on one wall. A mirror is placed opposite the bed, which won't please those who follow feng shui principles.

In the lounge area, a long desk has six drawers, plus a vertical cupboard unit that houses a sensible safe, refrigerator and drinks cabinet stocked with your choice of drinks. There is also a 20-inch (51.5-mm) flat-screen television, CD and DVD player, and an MP3 audio player with a choice of more than 100 selections. The beds have the finest linens, including thick cotton duvets, and non-allergenic pillows are also available. There's little room under the beds for luggage, although this can be taken away and stored.

One drawback is the fact that the insulation between cabins is not particularly good, although rarely does this present a problem, as most passengers aboard the SeaDreams are generally extremely quiet, considerate types who are allergic to noise. Incidentally, a sleep suit is supplied in case you want to sleep out on deck under the stars in one of the on-deck two-person beds – but more of those later.

When the ships became *SeaDreams I* and *II* all the bathrooms were totally refurbished. The old tiling was discarded and replaced by new cheerful decor that is more hip and trendy, with softer colors and larger (beige) marble tiles. The former tiny sit-in bathtubs have been taken out – these will be missed by many regular European passengers – and replaced by a multi-jet power glassed-in shower enclosure. A new washbasin set in a marble-look surround and two glass shelves make up the facilities, while an under-sink cupboard provides further space for larger personal toiletry items. Bulgari personal toi-

OVERALL SCORE: 1,788

BERLITZ'S RATINGS

	Possible	Achieved
Ship	500	440
Accommodation	200	173
Food	400	371
Service	400	370
Entertainment	n/a	n/a
Cruise	500	434

letries are provided. Gorgeously thick, plush, 100% cotton SeaDream-logo bathrobes and towels are also supplied.

However, the bathrooms really are small, particularly for those who are of larger than average build, despite their having been completely rebuilt. Also, the doors still open inward, so space inside is at a premium. The toilet is located in a rather awkward position, and, unless you close the door, you can see yourself in the mirror facing of the closets, opposite the bathroom door.

Commodore Club Suites: For larger accommodation, choose one of 16 Commodore Club Suites. These consist of two standard cabins with an interconnecting door, thus providing you with a healthy 380 sq. ft (36 sq. meters) of living space. One cabin is made into a lounge and dining room, with table and up to four chairs, while the other becomes your sleeping area. The advantage is that you get two bathrooms (his and hers). One disadvantage is that the soundproofing between cabins could be better.

Admiral Suite: Added in 2008–09, this suite occupies space previously devoted to the ship's boutique, and adjacent to the piano bar/library. It's a little smaller than the Owner's Suite, but is well laid out and extremely comfortable.

Owner's Suite: For the largest living space, go for the Owner's Suite. This measures a grand 490 sq. ft (45.5 sq. meters). It's the only accommodation with a bathroom that incorporates a real full-sized tub; there's also a separate shower enclosure and lots of space for personal toiletries.

In all grades of accommodation, passengers receive personalized stationery, a personal email address, a 100% cotton sleep suit, Bulgari personal toiletries, 24-hour room service, and "sweet dreams" chocolates.

CUISINE. The dining salon, called The Restaurant, is elegant and inviting, and has bird's-eye maple wood paneled walls and alcoves showcasing beautiful hand-made glass creations. It is cozy, yet with plenty of space around each table for fine service, and the ship provides a floating culinary celebration in an open-seating arrangement, so you can dine whenever, and with whomever, you want. Course-by-course meals can also be served out on deck.

Tables can be configured for two, four, six, or eight. They are laid with a classic setting of a real glass base (show) plate, Porsgrund china, pristine white monogrammed table linen, and fresh flowers.

Candlelit dinners are part of the inviting setting. There is even a box of spare spectacles for menu reading in case you forget your own. You get leather-bound menus, and close to impeccable personalized European service.

The SeaDream Yacht Club experience really is all about dining. The ships will not disappoint, and culinary excellence prevails. Only the very freshest and finest quality ingredients are used in the best culinary artistry. Fine, unhurried European service is provided. Additionally, caviar (American farmed Hacklefish malossol caviar, sadly, and not Russian caviar, whose purchase and supply today is challenging) and good quality champagne are available whenever you want them. The ice cream, made on board, is excellent.

The ships provide extremely creative cuisine, and every-thing is prepared individually to order. Special orders are possible, although the former popular flaming desserts have almost disappeared. You can also dine, course by course in your suite for any meal, at any time – you can also eat à la carte 24 hours a day if you wish. The dining room is not open for lunch, which disappoints those who do not want to eat outside, particularly in hot climates.

Good-quality table wines are included in the cruise fare for lunch and dinner. Real wine connoisseurs, however, will appreciate the availability of an extra wine list, full of special vintages and premier crus at extra cost. If you want to do something different with a loved one, you can also arrange to dine one evening on the open (but covered) deck, overlooking the swimming pool and stern – it can be a magical and very romantic setting.

The Topside Restaurant is the informal open-air dining venue that was created from what used to be the outdoor cafe. Now it has glass sides and a glass ceiling. Informal dining is its theme, whether for breakfast, lunch or the occasional dinner. Teak tables and chairs add a touch of class.

ENTERTAINMENT. There is no evening entertainment as such, other than a duo or solo musician to provide music for listening and dancing in the lounge. Dinner is the main event, and videos are available to take to your cabin.

SPA/FITNESS. The holistic approach to wellbeing plays a big part in relaxation and body pampering aboard the *Sea-Dreams*. To this end, when you enter the Asian Spa/Wellness Centre you enter another world, housed together with a good sized gymnasium, and a small beauty salon. There are three massage rooms, a small sauna, and steam shower enclosure.

The spa, located in a private area forward on Deck 4, is staffed and operated as a concession, by Universal Maritime Services. SeaDream's Traditional Thai Massage ($115 for 50 minutes, or $145 for 75 minutes including herbal compresses). Massage on the beach is available when the ship operates its famous beach party.

Other types of massages offered include Shiatsu ($115 for 50 minutes), and Swedish Body Massage ($115 for 50 minutes). Body scrubs such as Body Glow, Javanese Lulur (Javanese body scrub, at $55 for 30 minutes). For the ultimate in "pampership", there's Perfect Bliss (3 hours 20 minutes of body pampering, for $320).

Meanwhile, golfers should enjoy the electronic golf simulator, with a choice of several golf courses to play. For more recreational facilities, note that at the stern is a small, retractable, water sports platform. Equipment carried for sporting types include a water-ski boat, sailboat, wave runners (jet skis), kayaks, wake boards, snorkeling equipment and two Zodiacs. The use of all this equipment is included in the price of a cruise.

The sea conditions have to be just right (minimal swell) for these items to be used, which, on average is once or twice during a typical 7-night cruise. You may also be allowed to swim off the stern platform if conditions permit. Ten mountain bikes are also carried, so you can pedal away when ashore.

Serenade of the Seas
★★★★

Size: ....Large Resort Ship	Passenger Decks: 12	Cabins (with private balcony): 577
Tonnage: 90,090	Total Crew: 858	Cabins (wheelchair accessible): 14
Lifestyle: ....Standard	Passengers	(8 with private balcony)
Cruise Line: Royal Caribbean International	(lower beds/all berths): 2,100/2,500	Wheelchair accessibility ....Best
Former Names: ....none	Passenger Space Ratio	Cabin Current: ....110/220 volts
Builder: ....Meyer Werft (Germany)	(lower beds/all berths): 42.9/36.0	Elevators: 9
Original Cost: ....$350 million	Crew/Passenger Ratio	Casino (gaming tables): ....Yes
Entered Service: ....August 2003	(lower beds/all berths): 2.4/2.9	Slot Machines: ....Yes
Registry: ....The Bahamas	Cabins (total): 1,050	Swimming Pools (outdoors): 2
Length (ft/m): 961.9/293.2	Size Range (sq ft/m): 165.8–1,216.3/	Swimming Pools (indoors): 0
Beam (ft/m): 105.6/32.2	15.4–113.0	Whirlpools: 3
Draft (ft/m): 27.8/8.5	Cabins (outside view): 813	Self-Service Launderette: ....No
Propulsion/Propellers: .....gas turbine/2	Cabins (interior/no view): 237	Dedicated Cinema/Seats: Yes/40
azimuthing pods (20 MW each)	Cabins (for one person): 0	Library: ....Yes

OVERALL SCORE: 1,491 OUT OF A POSSIBLE 2,000 POINTS

OVERVIEW. This is the third Royal Caribbean International ship to use gas and steam turbine power (the others are sister ships *Brilliance of the Seas* and *Radiance of the Seas*) instead of the formerly conventional diesel or diesel-electric combination.

Podded propulsion power is also provided. Briefly, two pods, which resemble huge outboard motors, replace internal electric propulsion motors, shaft lines, rudders and their machinery, and are compact, self-contained units that typically weigh about 170 tons each. Although they are at the stern, pod units pull, rather than push, a ship through the water. As is common aboard all RCI vessels, the navigation bridge is of the fully enclosed type – good for cruising in cold-weather areas such as Alaska. In the very front of the ship is a helipad, which also acts as a viewing platform for passengers – good for up-close-and-personal cruising in Alaska. One of two swimming pools can be covered by a large glass dome for use as an indoor/outdoor pool.

Serenade of the Seas is a streamlined contemporary ship, and has a two-deck-high wrap-around structure in the forward section of the funnel. Along the starboard side, a central glass wall protrudes, giving great views (cabins with balconies occupy the space directly opposite on the port side). The gently rounded stern has nicely tiered decks, which gives the ship an extremely well-balanced look.

Inside the ship, the decor is contemporary, yet elegant, bright and cheerful, designed for young, active, hip and trendy types. The artwork is quite eclectic (so there should be something for all tastes), and provides a spectrum and a half of color works.

The interior focal point is a nine-deck high atrium lobby

BERLITZ'S RATINGS

	Possible	Achieved
Ship	500	424
Accommodation	200	158
Food	400	242
Service	400	291
Entertainment	100	78
Cruise	400	298

with glass-walled elevators (on the port side of the ship only) that travel through 12 decks, face the sea and provide a link with nature and the ocean. The Centrum (as the atrium is called), has several public rooms connected to it: the guest relations (the contemporary term for purser's office) and shore excursions desks, a Lobby Bar, Champagne Bar, the Library, Royal Caribbean Online (an internet-connect center), the Concierge Club, and a Crown & Anchor Lounge. A great view of the atrium can be had by looking down through the flat glass dome high above it.

Other facilities include a delightful, but very small library and, in the atrium lobby, a Coffee Shop that also sells pastries and cakes – it's rather like a small Seattle coffee house. There's a Champagne Bar, and a large Schooner Bar (a popular favorite aboard RCI ships, with nautical riggings, ship replicas, maritime art and other nautically-themed ephemera). Gambling devotees should enjoy the rather large, noisy and very colorful Casino Royale. There's also a small dedicated screening room for movies (with space for two wheelchairs), as well as a 194-seat conference center, and a business center.

This ship has a Viking Crown Lounge, a Royal Caribbean International trademark, is a large structure set around the base of the ship's funnel. It is an observation lounge during the daytime (with views forward over the swimming pool). In the evening, the space transforms itself into a futuristic, high-energy dance club, as well as a more intimate and relaxed entertainment venue for softer mood music and "black box" theater.

For those who wish to go online, Royal Caribbean Online, located in a semi-private setting, is a dedicated computer center with 12 stations providing high-speed internet access for sending and receiving email. Four more internet-access computer terminals are located in Books 'n' Coffee, a bookshop with coffee and pastries, located in an extensive area of shops.

Youth facilities include Adventure Ocean, an "edutainment" area with four separate age-appropriate sections for junior passengers: Aquanaut Center (for ages 3–5); Explorer Center (6–8); Voyager Center (9–12); and the Optix Teen Center (13–17). There is also Adventure Beach, which includes a splash pool complete with waterslide; Surfside, with computer lab stations with entertaining software; and Ocean Arcade, a video games hangout.

The onboard product delivery is more casual and unstructured than RCI has previously been delivering. *Serenade of the Seas* offers more space and more comfortable public areas (and several more intimate spaces), slightly larger cabins and more dining options than most of the larger ships in the RCI fleet.

There is also a grand amount of glass that provides more contact with the ocean around you; of course, more glass means more cleaning of glass. However, at the end of the day, the overall product is similar to that delivered aboard other ships in the fleet. In the final analysis, while the ship is quite delightful in many ways, the onboard operation is less spectacular, and suffers from a lack of service staff. The onboard currency is the US dollar, and 15% is added to all bar and spa bills.

Many of the "private" balcony cabins are not very private, as they can be overlooked by anyone standing in the port and starboard wings of the Solarium, and from other locations. There are no cushioned pads for the sunloungers, and the deck towels provided are quite thin and small. Spa treatments are extravagantly expensive – as they are aboard most ships today, in line with land-based spa prices in the United States. It is virtually impossible to escape background music anywhere aboard this ship. Standing in lines for embarkation, the reception desk, disembarkation, for port visits, shore tenders and for the self-serve buffet stations in the Windjammer Cafe is an inevitable aspect of cruising aboard this large ship.

ACCOMMODATION. There is a wide range of suites and standard outside-view and interior (no view) cabins to suit different tastes, requirements, and depth of wallet, in 10 different categories and 19 different price groups. The price will depend on the grade, size and location you choose.

Apart from the largest suites (six owner's suites), which have king-sized beds, almost all other cabins have twin beds that convert to a queen-sized bed (all sheets are of 100% Egyptian cotton, although blankets are of synthetic fabric). All cabins have rich (but faux) wood cabinetry, including a vanity desk (with hairdryer), faux wood drawers that close silently (hooray), television, personal safe, and three-sided mirrors. Some cabins have a recessed ceiling, pull-down berths for third and fourth persons, although closet and drawer space would be extremely tight for four persons (even if two of them are children), and some have

interconnecting doors (so families with children can cruise together, in separate, but adjacent cabins).

Audio channels are available through the television; however, if you want to go to sleep with soft music playing in the background you'll need to put a towel over the television screen, as it is impossible to turn the picture off. Data ports are provided in all cabins.

Most cabin bathrooms have tiled accenting and a terrazzo-style tiled floor, and a shower enclosure in a half-moon shape (it is rather small, however), 100% Egyptian cotton towels, a small cabinet for personal toiletries and a small shelf. In reality, there is little space to stow personal toiletries for two (or more).

The largest accommodation consists of a family suite with two bedrooms. One bedroom has twin beds (convertible to queen-sized bed), while a second has two lower beds and two upper Pullman berths, a combination that can sleep up to eight persons – this would suit large families.

Occupants of accommodation designated as suites also get the use of a private Concierge Lounge, where priority dining room reservations, shore excursion bookings and beauty salon/spa appointments can be made.

CUISINE. "Reflections" is the ship's principal dining room. It spans two decks; the upper deck level has floor-to-ceiling windows, while the lower deck level has picture windows. It is a pleasant, but inevitably noisy dining hall – reminiscent of those aboard the transatlantic liners in their heyday (however, eight huge, thick pillars obstruct the sightlines – the dining room would be much nicer without them).

Reflections seats 1,104 hungry persons, and its decor features a cascading water theme. There are tables for two, four, six, eight or 10. Two small private dining rooms (Illusions with 94 seats and Mirage with 30 seats) are located off the main dining room. Choose one of two seatings, or "My Time Dining" (eat when you want, during dining room hours). No smoking is permitted in the dining venues.

The cuisine is typical of mass banquet catering that offers standard fare comparable to that found in American family-style restaurants ashore. The menu descriptions make the food sound better than it is – the ship uses many mixes and pre-prepared items. However, a decent selection of light meals is provided, and a vegetarian menu is available. The selection of breads, rolls, fruit and cheese is quite poor, however, and could do with improvement. Caviar, once a standard menu item, now incurs a hefty extra charge. Menus typically include a "Welcome Aboard" Dinner, French Dinner, Italian Dinner, International Dinner, Captain's Gala Dinner.

One thing this company does once each cruise is to put on a "Galley Buffet" whereby passengers go through a section of the galley picking up food for a midnight buffet. There is an adequate wine list, moderately priced.

Alternative Restaurants. There are two: Portofino, with 112 seats, featuring Italian cuisine (choices include: antipasti, soup, salad, pasta, main dish, dessert, cheese and coffee); and Chops Grill Steakhouse, with 95 seats and an open "show" kitchen, serving premium meats in the form of veal chops and steaks (New York Striploin Steak, Filet Mignon, and Prime Rib of Beef).

Both alternative dining spots have food that is of a much higher quality than in the main dining room, with extremely good presentation and experienced service. The menus do not change throughout the cruise. There is an additional charge of $20 per person (this includes gratuities to staff), and reservations are required for both dining spots, which are typically open 6pm–11pm. Be prepared to eat a lot of food and so do justice to the cover charge. The dress code in the alternative dining spots is smart casual.

Casual Eateries: Also, casual meals (for breakfast, lunch and dinner) can be taken in the self-serve, buffet-style Windjammer Cafe, which can be accessed directly from the pool deck. It has islands dedicated to specific foods, and indoors and outdoors seating, but it gets seriously crowded at peak times. Additionally, there is the Seaview Cafe, open for lunch and dinner. Choose from the self-serve buffet, or from the menu for casual, fast-food seafood items including fish sandwiches, popcorn shrimp, fish 'n' chips, as well as non-seafood items such as hamburgers and hot dogs. The decor, naturally, is marine- and ocean-related.

ENTERTAINMENT. Facilities include the three-level Tropical Theater, with 874 seats (including 24 stations for wheelchairs) and good sight lines from most seats. Strong cabaret acts are also featured in the main showlounge.

A second entertainment venue is the Safari Club. This is where more casual cabaret shows, including late-night adult (blue) comedy, and live music for dancing are featured.

All of the entertainment throughout this ship is upbeat – in fact, it is virtually impossible to get away from music and noise – but is typical of the kind of resort hotel found in Las Vegas. There is even background music in all corridors and elevators, and constant music on the pool deck. If you want a quiet holiday, choose another cruise line.

SPA/FITNESS. The ShipShape Spa's health, fitness and spa facilities have themed decor, and include a 10,176 sq.-ft (945 sq.-meter) solarium, a gymnasium (with 44 cardiovascular machines), 50-person aerobics room, sauna and steam rooms, and therapy treatment rooms. All are located on two of the uppermost decks of the ship, forward of the mast, with access from the forward stairway.

The climate-controlled 10,176 sq. ft (945 sq. meters) indoor/outdoor Solarium (with magrodome sliding glass roof that can be closed in cool or inclement weather conditions) provides facilities for relaxation. It has fascinating Balinese-themed decor, and includes a whirlpool and counter current swimming under a retractable magrodome roof. One neat feature is the Temple Gate Falls, a carved wooden gateway with water cascading down its sides.

For the more sporting passengers, there is activity galore – including a rock-climbing wall that's 30-ft (9 meters) high, with five separate climbing tracks. It is located outdoors at the aft end of the funnel.

Other sports facilities include a 9-hole miniature golf course, and an indoor/outdoor country club with golf simulator, a jogging track, and basketball court. Want to play pool? Well, you can, thanks to two special tables (called STables), whose technology adjusts to the movement of the ship automatically; you can find the tables in the Bombay Billiard Room, part of the Colony Club.

● **For more extensive general information about the Royal Caribbean experience, see pages 151–6.**

Seven Seas Mariner
★★★★ +

Size: ....Mid-Size ship	Passenger Decks: 9	Cabins (with private balcony): 354
Tonnage: 48,015	Total Crew: 445	Cabins (wheelchair accessible): 6
Lifestyle: ....Luxury/Premium	Passengers	Wheelchair accessibility ....Best
Cruise Line: ..Regent Seven Seas Cruises	(lower beds/all berths): 708/752	Cabin Current: ....110 volts
Former Names: ....none	Passenger Space Ratio	Elevators: 6
Builder: Chantiers de l'Atlantique (France)	(lower beds/all berths): 67.8/63.8	Casino (gaming tables): ....Yes
Original Cost: ....$240 million	Crew/Passenger Ratio	Slot Machines: ....Yes
Entered Service: ....Mar 2001	(lower beds/all berths): 1.6/1.7	Swimming Pools (outdoors): 1
Registry: ....The Bahamas	Cabins (total): 354	Swimming Pools (indoors): 0
Length (ft/m): 713/217.3	Size Range (sq ft/m): 301.3–2,002.0/	Whirlpools: 3
Beam (ft/m): 95.1/29.0	28.0–186.0	Self-Service Launderette: ....Yes (3)
Draft (ft/m): 21.4/6.5	Cabins (outside view): 354	Dedicated Cinema/Seats: ....No
Propulsion/Propellers: ...diesel-electric/2	Cabins (interior/no view): 0	Library: ....Yes
azimuthing pods (8.5 MW each)	Cabins (for one person): 0	

OVERALL SCORE: 1,651 OUT OF A POSSIBLE 2,000 POINTS

OVERVIEW. This is the largest ship in the Regent Seven Seas Cruises fleet, and the first to receive a "pod" propulsion system, replacing the traditional shaft and rudder system. The pods have forward-facing propellers that can turn through 360° *(see page 45)*.

For the technically minded, the ship was built in 32 blocks, using the same hull design as for what is presently *Grand Mistral* (Iberocruceros), but originally the defunct Festival Cruises' *Mistral*, although the interior design is totally different. In the fitting out stage, for example, many changes were made to accommodate Regent Seven Seas Cruises' need for all-outside-view suites. Its passenger space ratio is now the highest in the cruise industry, just a fraction above that for *Europa*.

Seven Seas Mariner is operated by Regent Seven Seas Cruises, which is owned by Prestige Cruise Holdings, a division of finance company Apollo Management. The ship was extensively refurbished in 2009.

There is a wide range of public rooms to play in, almost all of which are located under the accommodation decks. Three sets of stairways (forward, center, aft) mean it is easy to find your way around the vessel. An atrium lobby spans nine decks, with the lowest level opening directly onto the tender landing stage.

Facilities include a delightful observation lounge, a casino, a shopping concourse (conveniently located opposite the casino) – complete with open market area, a garden lounge/promenade arcade, a large library with internet-connect computers, business center, card room and a conference room, a, cigar-smoking lounge (called the Connoisseur Club, for cigars, cognacs and other assorted niceties), and a photo gallery.

BERLITZ'S RATINGS

	Possible	Achieved
Ship	500	438
Accommodation	200	177
Food	400	318
Service	400	310
Entertainment	100	83
Cruise	400	325

With the introduction of *Seven Seas Mariner*, Seven Seas Cruises moved into a new breed of larger ships that are more economical to operate, and provide more choices for passengers. However, the downside of a larger ship such as this is that there is a loss of sense of intimacy that the company's smaller ships used to have. Thus, some of the former personal service of the smaller ships has been absorbed into a larger structure.

Another downside is the fact that this ship is simply too large to enter the small harbors and berths that the company's smaller ships could access, and so loses some of the benefits of small upscale ship cruising.

So, it's swings and roundabouts when it comes to scoring the ship. At present, it scores very highly in terms of hardware and software, but operationally may lose a few points if it is deemed that it can enter only mid-size ship ports. By comparison, this ship is a more upscale version of the eight ships in the former Renaissance Cruises fleet – with better food, more choices, and a staff that are more hospitality-conscious and generally better trained. *Seven Seas Mariner* has ended up just a tad under the score base needed for it to join the "Berlitz Five Star" Club.

Basic gratuities are included, as are all alcoholic and non-alcoholic beverages and complimentary table wines for lunch and dinner – although premium and connoisseur selections are also available at extra cost. The onboard currency is the US dollar.

Service and hospitality are mostly sound. The same carpeting is used throughout the public areas, with no relief or change of color or pattern on the stairwells. The decor is more restrained, but with a contemporary look and feel.

Much of the intimacy and close-knit ambience of smaller vessels is missing, and, because of all those cabins with balconies, the feeling of privacy and relaxation can also translate into less passengers and ambience in public rooms and for entertainment events, depending on the passenger mix.

SUITABLE FOR: *Seven Seas Mariner* is best suited to well traveled couples and single travelers (typically over 50) who seek excellent itineraries, fine food and good service, with some entertainment, all wrapped up in a contemporary ship which can best be described as elegant and quiet in its appointments and comfort levels.

ACCOMMODATION. There are 13 categories of cabins. The price you pay will depend on the grade, location and size you choose. *Seven Seas Mariner* was the cruise industry's first "all-suite, all-balcony" ship (terminology that marketing departments enjoy, although it is not actually correct, as not all accommodation has sleeping areas completely separated from living areas).

All grades of accommodation have private, marble-clad bathrooms with bathtub, and all suite entrances are neatly recessed away from the passenger hallways, to provide an extra modicum of quietness. In comparison with *Seven Seas Navigator*, the bathrooms aboard this ship are not as large in the lower grade of accommodation.

Master Suite: The largest accommodation (1,580 sq. ft/147 sq. meters), in two Master Suites, has two separate bedrooms, living room with TV/VCR and CD player, walk-in closet, dining area, large, two marble-clad bathrooms with bathtub and separate shower enclosure, and two private teakwood-decked balconies. These suites are located on the deck under the ship's navigation bridge, one balcony providing delightful forward-facing views, while a second balcony provides port or starboard views. Butler service is provided, as is a Nespresso coffee machine. To keep things in perspective, these two Master Suites are nowhere near as large as the two Penthouse Suites aboard the much larger Celebrity Cruises ships *Constellation, Infinity, Millennium* and *Summit* (which measure 2,350 sq. ft/218 sq. meters).

Mariner Suite: Six Mariner Suites (739 sq. ft/69 sq. meters), located on port and starboard sides of the atrium on three separate decks, have a separate bedroom, living room with TV/VCR and CD player, walk-in closet, dining area, large, marble-clad bathroom with tub and separate shower enclosure, and a good sized private balcony with either port or starboard views. Butler service is provided, as is a Nespresso coffee machine.

Grand Suites: Two Grand Suites (707 sq. ft/66 sq. meters) are located one deck above the ship's navigation bridge, and have a separate bedroom, living room with TV/VCR and CD player, walk-in closet, dining area, two marble-clad bathrooms with tub and separate shower enclosure, and a good sized private balcony with port or starboard views. Butler service is provided, as is a Nespresso coffee machine.

Seven Seas Suites: Six spacious suites (697 sq. ft/65 sq. meters) overlook the ship's stern (two suites are located on each of four decks) and have very generous private balcony space and good wrap-around views over the ship's stern and to port or starboard. However, the balconies are only semi-private and can be partly overlooked by neighbors in Horizon Suites as well as from above. Another two Seven Seas Suites are located just aft of the ship's navigation bridge and measure a slightly smaller 600 sq ft (56 sq. meters) and have balconies with either port or starboard views. These suites have a separate bedroom, living room with TV/VCR and CD player, walk-in closet, dining area, large, and marble-clad bathroom with a combination tub/shower.

Horizon Suites: There are 12 Horizon Suites (522 sq. ft/48 sq. meters) overlooking the ship's stern (three suites are located on each of four decks, sandwiched between the Seven Seas Suites) and have a good-sized balcony (though not as large as the Seven Seas Suites) and good views. These suites have a separate bedroom, living room with TV/VCR, walk-in closet, dining area, large, marble-clad bathroom with a combination tub/shower.

All Other Cabins: All other cabins (Categories A–H in the brochure, listed as Deluxe Suites and Penthouse Suites) measure 300 sq. ft (28 sq. meters) and have twin beds that can convert to a queen-sized bed (European duvets are standard), small walk-in closet, marble-lined bathroom with combination tub/shower, 100% cotton Anichini bathrobe and towels, vanity desk, hairdryer, TV/VCR, refrigerator (stocked with soft drinks and bar set-up on embarkation), personal safe. In these suites, the sleeping area is separated from the living area only by partial room dividers, and therefore is a cabin (albeit a good-sized one), and not a suite.

Six wheelchair-accessible suites are located as close to an elevator as one could possibly get, and provide ample living space, together with a large roll-in shower and all bathroom fittings located at the correct height.

CUISINE. There are four different dining venues, all operated on an open-seating basis, so that you can sit with whom you want, when you wish. In reality, this means that dining aboard ship is like dining on land – you can go to a different dining spot each night. The downside of this is that waiters don't get to know and remember your preferences. Reservations are required in two of the four dining spots. In general, the cuisine is good to very good, with creative presentation and a wide variety of food choices.

The main dining room is the 570-seat Compass Rose Restaurant, located in the center of the ship. It has a light, fresh decor, and seating at tables for two, four, six or eight – although, with a majority of seating at tables for six or eight, it's not that intimate. A large pre-dinner drinks bar is conveniently located adjacent on the starboard side. For a mid-sized ship, the downside is that, with a single-deck height, the restaurant has a rather cramped feeling. Fine Dudson china is used.

The 80-seat Prime Seven Steakhouse, located adjacent to the Compass Rose Restaurant and added during the ship's latest refit/refurbishment, is the smallest of the specialty alternative dining spots. It serves USDA prime, dry-aged steaks (from 32-ounce Porterhouse, carved tableside, to prime rib, filet mignon, and Surf & Turf. New Zealand double-cut lamb chops, double-cut Kurobata pork chops, veal chop, oven-roasted half chicken, Alaskan king crab legs and Maine lobster. It's the most intimate dining spot – though, again, the single-deck ceiling height makes it feel cramped. There is seating for two, four or six, and reservations are required.

A 120-seat "supper club", called Signatures, with its own dedicated galley, is located one deck above the main galley (for convenient vertical supply and staff access), and has ocean views along the room's port side. It is directed and staffed by chefs wearing the white toque and blue riband of Le Cordon Bleu, the world's most prestigious culinary society, and the cuisine is classic French. Doors open onto a covered area outdoors, complete with small stage and dance floor. Porsgrund china is used, as are silver show plates and the very finest silverware. Seating is at tables of two, four, or six, and reservations are required. However, the single-deck ceiling height robs the room of the feeling of grandeur that would better suit fine classic French cuisine.

For more casual meals, La Veranda is a large self-serve indoor/outdoor cafe with seats for 450 (the teakwood-decked outdoor seating is particularly pleasant), and the decor is fresh and light. This eatery has several food islands and substantial counter display space. There is also an outdoor grill, adjacent to the swimming pool.

As another variation on the dining theme, you can also choose to dine in your cabin – most passengers do so for breakfast, for example, and some do for dinner instead of "going out" to the "public" restaurants. There is a 24-hour room service menu, and, during regular dinner hours, the full dining room menu is available.

ENTERTAINMENT. The Constellation Theater is the ship's main showlounge. It spans two decks and is quite stunning, and the sight lines are very good from almost all seats on both main and balcony levels. The proscenium stage is large enough to provide space for scenery changes and includes a "thrust" stage that is good for presenting more intimate cabaret acts. Seven Seas Cruises has an eclectic entertainment program that is tailored to each individual ship.

Aboard *Seven Seas Mariner*, both production shows and cabaret acts are featured. The ship carries its own production show troupe of eight singers/dancers who perform the colorful shows – the cast is, however, small for the size of the stage. Cabaret acts tend to feature vocalists, magicians and comedy jugglers, among others.

There is also Stars nightclub, with an oval-shaped dance floor, and a Horizon Lounge – both rooms could be used for intimate late-night cabaret. A number of bands and small musical units and solo pianist entertainers can be found providing live music in several lounges and bars.

SPA/FITNESS. Health and fitness facilities include an extensive health spa with gymnasium and aerobics room, beauty parlor, and separate changing, sauna and steam rooms for men and women. The spa is located not at the top of the ship, as is common with many other ships today, but just off the atrium in the center of the ship.

Canyon Ranch SpaClub operates the spa and beauty services as a concession, and provides the staff. Here are some sample prices for treatments: European aromatherapy massage, $120 (50 minutes); four hand massage, $220 (50 minutes); reflexology session, $60 (25 minutes); rejuvenation facial, $155 (60 minutes); mini facial, $70 (30 minutes); neck-to-toe seaweed body wrap, $75 (50 minutes); micro-sea body scrub, $40 (30 minutes). There's a range of beauty products for the body and wellbeing books for sale.

Sports devotees can play in the paddle tennis court, golf driving and practice cages.

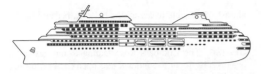

Seven Seas Navigator
★★★★ +

Size: . . . . .Small Ship	Passenger Decks: 8	Cabins (with private balcony): 196
Tonnage: 28,550	Total Crew: 325	Cabins (wheelchair accessible): 4
Lifestyle: . . . . .Luxury/Premium	Passengers	Wheelchair accessibility . . . . .Good
Cruise Line: . .Regent Seven Seas Cruises	(lower beds/all berths): 490/530	Cabin Current: . . . . .110 and 220 volts
Former Names: . . . . .none	Passenger Space Ratio	Elevators: 5
Builder: . . . . .T. Mariotti (Italy)	(lower beds/all berths): 58.2/53.8	Casino (gaming tables): . . . . .Yes
Original Cost: . . . .$200 million	Crew/Passenger Ratio	Slot Machines: . . . . .Yes
Entered Service: . . . . .Aug 1999	(lower beds/all berths): 1.5/1.6	Swimming Pools (outdoors): 1
Registry: . . . . .Bermuda	Cabins (total): 245	Swimming Pools (indoors): 0
Length (ft/m): 559.7/170.6	Size Range (sq ft/m): 301.3–1,173.3/	Whirlpools: 2
Beam (ft/m): 71.5/21.8	28.0–109.0	Self-Service Launderette: . . . . .Yes
Draft (ft/m): 21.3.0/6.5	Cabins (outside view): 245	Dedicated Cinema/Seats: . . . . .No
Propulsion/Propellers: . . . . .diesel	Cabins (interior/no view): 0	Library: . . . . .Yes
(13,000kW/2	Cabins (for one person): 0	

OVERALL SCORE: 1,595 OUT OF A POSSIBLE 2,000 POINTS

OVERVIEW. *Seven Seas Navigator* was built using a hull that was already constructed in St. Petersburg, Russia, as the research vessel *Akademik Nikolay Pilyugin*. After launching the hull, the name *Blue Sea* was used for a short time. The superstructure was incorporated into the hull in an Italian shipyard – the result being that for all intents and purposes a new ship was delivered in record time. However, the result is less than handsome – particularly at the ship's stern. It is, however, large enough to be stable over long stretches of water, and there is an excellent amount of space per passenger. In 2009, the ship recived a "ducktail" stern to aid stability and buoyancy.

The interiors have a mix of classical and contemporary Italian styling and decor throughout, with warm, soft colors and fine quality soft furnishings and fabrics. At the opposite end of the ship is Galileo's, a large piano lounge with good views over the stern.

A Navigator's Lounge has warm mahogany and cherry wood paneling and large, comfortable, mid-back tub chairs. Meanwhile, next door, cigars and cognac (and other niceties) can be taken in the delightful Connoisseur's Club – the first aboard a Regent Seven Seas Cruises vessel. The extensive library also has several computers with direct email/internet access (for a fee).

The ship is designed for worldwide cruise itineraries, and is one of the upscale ships in the diverse Regent Seven Seas Cruises fleet. As with all ships in the fleet, all gratuities are included. The onboard currency is the US dollar.

There is no walk-around promenade deck outdoors, although there is a jogging track high atop the aft section of the ship around the funnel housing. Two of the upper, outer

BERLITZ'S RATINGS

	Possible	Achieved
Ship	500	414
Accommodation	200	180
Food	400	307
Service	400	304
Entertainment	100	78
Cruise	400	312

decks are laid with green Astroturf, which cheapens the look of the ship – these decks would be better in teak. The ceilings in several public rooms (including the main restaurant) are quite low, which makes the ship feel smaller and more closed in than it is. The ship suffers from a considerable amount of vibration, which detracts from the comfort level when compared with other vessels of the same size.

Basic gratuities are included, as are all alcoholic and non-alcoholic beverages, starting in 2007, plus complimentary table wines for lunch and dinner.

SUITABLE FOR: *Seven Seas Navigator* is best suited to well-traveled couples and single travelers (typically over 50) who seek excellent itineraries, fine food and good service, with some entertainment, all wrapped up in a contemporary ship which can best be described as elegant and quiet in its appointments and comfort levels.

ACCOMMODATION. There are 11 price grades (priced by grade, location and size). The company markets this as an "all-suite" ship. Even the smallest suite is quite large, and all have outside views. Almost 90 percent of all suites have a private balcony, with floor-to-ceiling sliding glass doors, while 10 suites are interconnecting, and 38 suites have an extra bed for a third occupant. By comparison, even the smallest suite aboard this ship is more than twice the size of the smallest cabin aboard the world's largest cruise ships, Royal Caribbean International's Voyager-class ships.

All grades of accommodation have a walk-in closet, European king-sized bed or twin beds, wooden cabinetry with nicely rounded edges, plenty of drawer space, mini-bar/refrigerator (stocked with complimentary soft drinks and bar set-up on embarkation), TV/DVD, personal safe and other accoutrements of fine living at sea in the latest design format. The marble-appointed bathroom has a full-size bathtub, as well as a separate shower enclosure, 100% cotton bathrobe and towels, and hairdryer.

The largest living spaces can be found in four master suites, with forward-facing views – all have double-length side balconies. Each suite has a completely separate bedroom with dressing table; the living room has a full dining room table and chairs for up to six persons, wet bar, counter and bar stools, large 3-person sofa and six armchairs, and an audio-visual console/entertainment center, and a Nespresso coffee machine. Each suite has a large main, marble-clad, fully tiled bathroom with full-sized bathtub and separate shower enclosure, a separate room with bidet, toilet and washbasin, with plenty of shelf and other storage space for personal toiletries. There is a separate guest bathroom.

Next in size are the superb Navigator Suites, which have a completely separate bedroom, walk-in closet, large lounge with mini-bar/refrigerator (stocked with complimentary soft drinks and bar set-up on embarkation), personal safe, compact disc player, large TV/DVD player, and dining area with large table and four chairs. The marble-clad, fully tiled bathroom has a full-sized bathtub with hand-held shower, plus a separate shower enclosure (the door to which is only 18 inches/45 cm, however), large washbasin, toilet and bidet, and ample shelf space for personal toiletries.

It is unfortunate that the Navigator Suites are located in the center of the ship, as they are directly underneath the swimming pool deck. They are, thus, subject to noise attacks at 6am daily, when deck cleaning is carried out, and chairs are dragged across the deck directly over the suites. They are further subjected to noise attacks whenever pool deck stewards drag and drop sunloungers into place. Despite these disadvantages, the Navigator Suites are delightful living spaces.

Four suites for the physically challenged have private balconies, and are ideally located adjacent to the elevators (correcting a mistake made when the company's former *Radisson Diamond* was constructed, when they were located as far from any elevators as they possibly could be). However, while the suites are very practical, it is almost impossible to access the balcony, because of the "lip" or "threshold" at the bottom of the sliding glass door.

CUISINE. The Compass Rose Dining Room has large ocean-view picture windows and open-seating dining, which means that you may be seated when and with whom you wish. There are a few tables for two, but most are for four, six, or eight persons. Also, with a low ceiling height and noisy waiter stations, the overall feeling is cramped and unbecoming in terms of the lack of space and grace. Complimentary wines are served during dinner, although a connoisseur wine list is available for those who prefer to choose a vintage wine (at extra cost). The company also features "heart healthy" cuisine.

An alternative dining spot, La Veranda, for informal dining, serves dinners with an emphasis on regional cuisine, with reservations required. Prime 7, for steaks and seafood, is in an elegant new setting. For fast-food, there is also a small indoor/outdoor Grill, adjacent to the swimming pool.

You can also dine in your cabin. There is a 24-hour room service menu; also, during regular dinner hours, you can make your choice from the full dining room menu.

ENTERTAINMENT. The Seven Seas Lounge, a two-deck-high showlounge, has reasonable sightlines from most seats on both main and balcony levels (although pillars obstruct the views from some side balcony seats). Seven Seas Cruises has an eclectic entertainment program tailored to each ship. *Seven Seas Navigator* puts on both production shows and cabaret acts. Bands and small musical units and solo pianist entertainers provide live music in several lounges and bars.

SPA/FITNESS. The redesigned spa (comprising the original health center space plus the former observation lounge), fitness center and beauty salon are now located in the most forward part of the ship's top deck. Canyon Ranch SpaClub operates the spa and beauty services as a concession, and provides the staff. Here are some sample prices for treatments: European aromatherapy massage, $120 (50 minutes); four hand massage, $220 (50 minutes) and $310 (80 minutes); reflexology session, $60 (25 minutes); mini-facial, $70 (30 minutes); "anti-aging" facial, $185 (75 minutes). Canyon Ranch also sells its own beauty products.

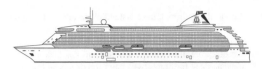

Seven Seas Voyager
★★★★+

Size: . . . . .Mid-Size Ship	Passenger Decks: 9	Cabins (with private balcony): 354
Tonnage: 41,827	Total Crew: 445	Cabins (wheelchair accessible): 4
Lifestyle: . . . . .Luxury/Premium	Passengers	Wheelchair accessibility . . . . .Best
Cruise Line: . .Regent Seven Seas Cruises	(lower beds/all berths): 708/752	Cabin Current: . . . . .110 volts
Former Names: . . . . .none	Passenger Space Ratio	Elevators: 6
Builder: . . . . .T. Mariotti (Italy)	(lower beds/all berths): 59.0/55.6	Casino (gaming tables): . . . . .Yes
Original Cost: . . . .$240 million	Crew/Passenger Ratio	Slot Machines: . . . . .Yes
Entered Service: . . . . .Mar 2003	(lower beds/all berths): 1.65/1.6	Swimming Pools (outdoors): 1
Registry: . . . . .The Bahamas	Cabins (total): 354	Swimming Pools (indoors): 0
Length (ft/m): 669.2/204.0	Size Range (sq ft/m): 356.0/1,399.3/	Whirlpools: 3
Beam (ft/m): 94.5/28.8	33.0–130.0	Self-Service Launderette: . . . . .Yes (3)
Draft (ft/m): 23.0/7.0	Cabins (outside view): 354	Dedicated Cinema/Seats: . . . . .No
Propulsion/Propellers: . . .diesel-electric/2	Cabins (interior/no view): 0	Library: . . . . .Yes
azimuthing pods (8.5MW each)	Cabins (for one person): 0	

OVERALL SCORE: 1,654 OUT OF A POSSIBLE 2,000 POINTS

OVERVIEW. Slightly narrower and smaller than *Seven Seas Mariner*, *Seven Seas Voyager* has a central corridor for accommodation designated as suites (sister ship *Seven Seas Mariner* has two corridors – port and starboard). This is presently the second ship in the Regent Seven Seas Cruises fleet to receive a "pod" propulsion system (the first being *Seven Seas Mariner*), replacing the traditional shaft and rudder system. The pods have forward-facing propellers that can be turned through 360° *(details: page 45)*.

For the technically minded, the ship was built in 32 blocks (with the same basic hull design as *Seven Seas Mariner*), with a few modifications. The passenger space ratio is among the highest in the cruise industry, at about the same as the smaller, but better-built *Europa*.

Seven Seas Voyager is operated by Regent Seven Seas Cruises, under the umbrella of Prestige Cruise Holdings, which is owned by the financial company Apollo Management. The ship was extensively refurbished in 2009.

There is a decent range of public rooms in which to play, almost all of which are located under the accommodation decks. Three sets of stairways (forward, center, aft) mean it is easy to find your way around the vessel. An atrium lobby spans nine decks, with the lowest level opening directly onto the tender landing stage.

Facilities include a showlounge that spans two decks, an observation lounge (it's the only place aboard this ship where you can see the bows, a casino, a shopping concourse (conveniently located opposite the casino) – complete with an open "market" area, a large library, internet-connect center and business center (Club.com, and Coffee.com), card room and a small conference room.

BERLITZ'S RATINGS

	Possible	Achieved
Ship	500	437
Accommodation	200	177
Food	400	324
Service	400	306
Entertainment	100	83
Cruise	400	327

There is also a nightclub (Voyager) with an oval-shaped dance floor, a cigar-smoking lounge (the Connoisseur Club, for cigars, cognacs and other assorted nicotics), and the usual photo gallery.

Regent Seven Seas Cruises has clearly moved into a new breed of larger ships that are more economical to operate, provide better economies of scale, as well as more choices for passengers. However, the downside of a larger ship such as this is that there is a loss of the sense of intimacy that the company's smaller ships used to have. Thus, some of the former personal service of the smaller ships has been absorbed into a larger structure, although this does not always translate well.

Another downside is the fact that this ship is too large to enter the small harbors and berths that smaller ships can, and so loses some of the benefits of the smaller upscale ships such as those of the more stylish Hapag-Lloyd, Sea-Dream, Seabourn and Silversea. Also, much of the intimacy and close-knit ambiance of the smaller vessels is missing. So it's swings and roundabouts when it comes to scoring the ship.

At present, the ship scores well in terms of hardware – a combination of all the best of *Seven Seas Mariner* and *Seven Seas Navigator* – and software, but operationally may lose a few points if it is deemed that the ship can only enter mid-size ship ports.

Basic gratuities are included, as are all drinks, including complimentary table wines for lunch and dinner (premium and connoisseur selections are available at extra cost). The onboard currency is the US dollar. *Seven Seas Voyager* has ended up just a tad under the score base needed for it to join the "Berlitz Five Star" Club.

Service and hospitality levels have decreased in the past 24 months, and the drinks-inclusive policy doesn't help matters much. So the overall delivery of a quality onboard experience is on the downward slope. The decor is a little glitzy in places, plain in others.

Passenger gripes: there is no walk-around outdoor promenade deck (and the promenade on Deck is only partially covered in teak), and no forward-viewing exterior deck with views over the ship's bows.

SUITABLE FOR: *Seven Seas Voyager* is best suited to well-traveled couples and single travelers (typically over 50) who seek excellent itineraries, fine food and good service, with some entertainment, all wrapped up in a contemporary ship which can best be described as elegant and quiet in its appointments and comfort levels.

ACCOMMODATION. There are 12 accommodation price grades. The price you pay will depend on the grade, size and location you choose. As the ship was built with a central corridor design, this has allowed for larger suites (and much larger bathrooms) than aboard *Seven Seas Mariner*, with which many repeat passengers will no doubt compare it. This is Regent Seven Seas Cruises' second "all-suite all-balcony" ship – terminology that marketing departments thoroughly enjoy, although not actually correct, as not all accommodation has sleeping areas that are completely separated from living areas.

However, all grades of accommodation have private, marble-clad bathrooms with tub – although marble floors can be very cold on bare feet – walk-in closet with personal safe, and most suite entrances are neatly recessed away from passenger hallways (a central corridor), so as to provide an extra modicum of quietness. All have a "private" balcony, although all measure only 50 sq. ft (4.6 sq. meters) with the exception of those in the Master Suites and Grand Suites; however, they do have pleasing teak decking. All partitions are of the partial type, except for the Master Suites and Grand Suites, which have full floor-to-ceiling partitions, and are completely private.

Master Suites (1,162 sq. ft/108 sq. meters). The largest accommodation can be found in two Master Suites (1100 and 1001 each measure 1,403 sq. ft/130.3 sq. meters when added with one Grand Suite via an interconnecting door,) while (700 and 701 measure 1,335 sq. ft (124 sq. meters). Each has two separate bedrooms, living room with TV/DVD player, walk-in closet with personal safe, dining area, large, two marble-clad bathrooms with bathtub and separate shower enclosure, and private teakwood-decked balconies. These suites are located on the deck under the ship's navigation bridge, one balcony providing delightful forward-facing views, while a second balcony provides port or starboard views. Butler service is provided, as is a Nespresso coffee machine. To keep things in perspective, these two Master Suites are nowhere near as large as the two Penthouse Suites aboard the much larger Celebrity Cruises ships *Constellation, Infinity, Millennium* and *Summit* (which measure 2,350 sq. ft/235 sq. meters). The bathrooms, which are

open to the bedroom, have a stand-alone tub with integral shower, separate shower enclosure, toilet, bidet and washbasin. The private balcony (the partitions are floor-to-ceiling, and, therefore, completely private) has teak decking and teak deck furniture (two chairs and drinks table).

Grand Suites (876 sq. ft/81.3 sq. meters). Two Grand Suites (1104, 1005) are located one deck above the ship's navigation bridge. They are very pleasant living spaces, and feature a separate bedroom, living room with TV/DVD player, walk-in closet, dining area, and two marble-clad bathing areas. One bathing area, which is open to the bedroom (a curtain can be used to close it off), has a large five-sided sit-in bathtub placed in a glass walled enclosure on the balcony (but with no access door to the balcony, which can only be accessed from the lounge/dining area). The second is a bathroom with separate shower enclosure, bidet, toilet and washbasin. The suites have a private balcony with port or starboard views. There is also an additional (guest) toilet. Butler service is provided, as is a Nespresso coffee machine. The private balcony (the partitions are floor-to-ceiling, and, therefore, completely private) has teak decking and teak deck furniture (two chairs and drinks table).

Voyager Suites (603 sq. ft/56 sq. meters). Eight Voyager Suites, located on port and starboard sides of the atrium on three separate decks, have a separate bedroom, living room with TV/DVD player, walk-in closet, dining area, large, marble-clad bathroom with bathtub and separate shower enclosure, and a good sized private balcony with either port or starboard views. Butler service is provided. The balcony has teakwood deck, part partitions, and white plastic deck furniture.

Seven Seas Suites (657 sq. ft/61 sq. meters) Aft. Six spacious suites overlook the ship's stern (two suites are located on each of four decks), and have a generous wrap-around balcony, and good views over the ship's stern and to port or starboard. However, the balconies are only semi-private and can be partly overlooked by neighbors in other suites as well as from above – they do have teak decking, but white plastic deck furniture. Butler service is provided.

Another four Seven Seas Suites are located amidships and measure a slightly smaller 545 sq. ft (50.6 sq. meters), and have small balconies with either port or starboard views. These suites have a separate bedroom, living room with TV/DVD player, walk-in closet, dining area, large, and marble-clad bathroom with a combination tub/shower. Butler service is provided.

Penthouse Suites (370 sq. ft/34.3 sq. meters). There are 32 Category "A" Penthouse Suites and 32 Category "B" Penthouse Suites (Category "A" Suites have the better location, but the size is the same). These have a sleeping area with dressing table and adjacent lounge area, walk-in closet, and bathroom with tub, washbasin, separate shower enclosure, and toilet. The balcony is accessed from the lounge. The balcony has teakwood deck, part partitions, and white plastic deck furniture. Butler service is provided.

Horizon Suites (522 sq. ft/48.4 sq. meters). There are 29 Horizon Suites overlooking the ship's stern (some are sandwiched between the larger Seven Seas Suites) and have a good-sized balcony (though not as large as those of the Seven Seas Suites) and delightful aft-facing views. These suites have a separate bedroom, living room with TV/DVD player, walk-in closet, dining area, large, marble-clad bathroom with a combination tub/shower. The balcony has teakwood deck, part partitions, and white plastic deck furniture.

All Other Cabins (356 sq. ft/33 sq. meters). All other cabins (Categories C–H in the brochure, listed as Deluxe Suites) are larger than those of the same grade aboard *Seven Seas Mariner*. They have twin beds that can convert to a queen-sized bed (European duvets are standard), small walk-in closet, marble-lined bathroom with combination tub/shower, 100% cotton bathrobe 100% cotton towels, vanity desk, hairdryer, TV/DVD player, refrigerator (stocked with soft drinks and bar set-up on embarkation), personal safe. In these suites, the sleeping area is separated from the living area only by partial room dividers, and therefore is a cabin (albeit a good-sized one), and not a suite.

Four wheelchair-accessible suites (761, 762, 859, and 860) are all located as close to an elevator as one could possibly get, and provide ample living space, together with a large roll-in shower and all bathroom fittings located at the correct height.

CUISINE. There are four different dining venues, all of which are operated on an open-seating basis, so that you can sit with whom you want, when you wish. In reality, this means that dining aboard ship is like dining on land – you can go to a different dining spot each night. The downside of this is that waiters do not get to know and remember your preferences.

Reservations are required in two of the four dining spots. In general, the cuisine is very good, with creative presentation and a wide variety of food choices.

The main dining room is the 570-seat Compass Rose Restaurant, which is located in the center of the ship, has a light, fresh decor, and seating at tables for two, four, six or eight (with more tables for two or four than *Seven Seas Mariner*). A large pre-dinner drinks bar (actually the Voyager Lounge) is conveniently located close by on the port side. Dudson china, from England, is used.

A 120-seat supper club, Signatures – which shares a galley with Latitudes – is located one deck above the Compass Rose Restaurant galley (for convenient vertical supply and staff access), and has ocean views along the room's port side. It is directed and staffed by chefs wearing the white toque and Blue Riband of Le Cordon Bleu in Paris, the most prestigious culinary authority in the world; hence the cuisine is classic French. Doors open onto a covered area outdoors, complete with stage and dance floor. Porsgrund china is used, as are custom-made silver show plates and the fine silverware. Seating is at tables of two, four, or six, and reservations are required.

For food entertainment, make a reservation in Latitudes. It has real show business flair and an open "show" kitchen (also used for Le Cordon Bleu cooking demos). Dinner is at a set time (typically 7.30pm) and consists of a set menu (the only choice being the main course, which is fish or meat). Seating is in alcoves or at open tables. This restaurant provides an entertaining meal.

Prime 7 is a classic American steakhouse added during the ship's latest, extensive refit/refurbishment. It offers USDA prime, dry-aged steaks from 32-ounce Porterhouse, carved tableside, to prime rib, filet mignon, and Surf & Turf. There's also New Zealand double-cut lamb chops, double-cut Kurobata pork chops, veal chop, oven-roasted half chicken, Alaskan king crab legs and Maine lobster.

For more casual meals, La Veranda is a large self-serve indoor/outdoor café with seats for 450 (the teakwood-decked outdoor seating is particularly pleasant), and the decor is fresh and light. This eatery has a substantial amount of counter display space. There is also an outdoor grill, adjacent to the swimming pool, for fast food items, and Coffee Connection for coffees and pastries.

For another variation on the dining theme, you can also choose to dine in your cabin. There is a comprehensive 24-hour room service menu, and, during regular dinner hours, you can choose from the full (Compass Rose) dining room menu, and be served course by course.

ENTERTAINMENT. The Constellation Showlounge spans two decks and is quite a stunning room; the sightlines are very good from almost all seats in both main and balcony levels.

A troupe of 10 singers/dancers provides colorful mini-Las Vegas-style revues and production shows that are entertaining. Additionally, cabaret acts (vocalists, illusionists, ventriloquists, comedians, and others) provide stand-alone evening shows. The ship carries a main showband, and several small musical units and soloists (such as a singer/harpist and singer/pianist).

SPA/FITNESS. The Canyon Ranch SpaClub include a reasonably extensive (though not quite as large as one might expect) health spa with gymnasium (plenty of cardio-vascular equipment) and aerobics room, beauty salon, and separate changing, sauna and steam rooms (small) for men and women.

Specialist Canyon Ranch SpaClub provides the staff and spa and beauty services, which are located not at the top of the ship, as is common with many other ships today, but in the forward section of the ship, above the showlounge.

Here are some sample prices for treatments: European aromatherapy massage, $120 (50 minutes); four hand massage, $220 (50 minutes) and $310 (80 minutes); reflexology session, $60 (25 minutes); mini-facial, $70 (30 minutes); "anti-aging" facial, $185 (75 minutes). Canyon Ranch also sells its own range of beauty products.

Sports devotees can play in the paddle tennis court, golf driving and practice cages.

Silver Cloud
★★★★+

Size: . . . . .Small Ship	Passenger Decks: 6	Cabins (with private balcony): 110
Tonnage: 16,927	Total Crew: 210	Cabins (wheelchair accessible): 2
Lifestyle: .Luxury	Passengers	Wheelchair accessibility . . . . .Fair
Cruise Line: . . . . .Silversea Cruises	(lower beds/all berths): 296/315	Cabin Current: . . . . . . .110 and 220 volts
Former Names: . . . . .none	Passenger Space Ratio	Elevators: 4
Builder: . . . . .Visentini/Mariotti (Italy)	(lower beds/all berths): 57.1/53.7	Casino (gaming tables): . . . . .Yes
Original Cost: . . . .$125 million	Crew/Passenger Ratio	Slot Machines: . . . . .Yes
Entered Service: . . . . .Apr 1994	(lower beds/all berths): 1.4/1.5	Swimming Pools (outdoors): 1
Registry: . . . . .The Bahamas	Cabins (total): 148	Swimming Pools (indoors): 0
Length (ft/m): 514.4/155.8	Size Range (sq ft/m): 240.0–1,314.0/	Whirlpools: 2
Beam (ft/m): 70.62/21.4	22.2–122.0	Self-Service Launderette: . . . . .Yes
Draft (ft/m): 17.3/5.3	Cabins (outside view): 148	Dedicated Cinema/Seats: Yes/306
Propulsion/Propellers: . . . . .diesel	Cabins (interior/no view): 0	Library: . . . . .Yes
(11,700kW)/2	Cabins (for one person): 0	

OVERALL SCORE: 1,664 OUT OF A POSSIBLE 2,000 POINTS

OVERVIEW. *Silver Cloud* has quite a handsome profile, with a sloping stern reminiscent of an "Airstream" trailer. The size is just about ideal for highly personalized cruising in an elegant environment. The vertical cake-layer stacking of public rooms aft and the location of accommodation units forward ensures quiet cabins. There is a synthetic turf-covered walk-around promenade deck outdoors, and a spacious swimming pool deck with teak/aluminum deck furniture (little "Silversea" touches such as cold towels, water sprays and fresh fruit provide poolside pampering on hot days).

The spacious interior is well planned, with elegant decor and fine quality soft furnishings throughout, accented by the gentle use of brass fittings (some of sub-standard quality and now showing blotchy patches in several places), fine woods and creative ceilings. The ship was given a multi-million dollar makeover in 2003, and in 2009 an extensive refit saw the addition of a proper observation lounge, with covered passageway to access it – so passengers do not have to go outside to do so. All suites were also refreshed.

There is a business center as well as a CD-ROM and hardback book library, open 24 hours a day. There is an excellent amount of space per passenger and there is no hint of a line anywhere in this unhurried environment. Good documentation is provided before your cruise, all of which comes in a high-quality document wallet.

An elegant, announcement-free onboard ambience prevails, and there is no pressure, no hype, and an enthusiastic staff to pamper you, with a high ratio of Europeans. Insurance is now extra (it was included when Silversea Cruises first started). All drinks, gratuities and port taxes are included, and no further tipping anywhere on board is nec-

BERLITZ'S RATINGS

	Possible	Achieved
Ship	500	411
Accommodation	200	177
Food	400	333
Service	400	335
Entertainment	100	74
Cruise	400	334

essary – though it is not prohibited. This ship is perhaps ideal for those who enjoy spacious surroundings, excellent food, and some entertainment. It would be difficult not to have a good cruise holiday aboard this ship, albeit at a fairly high price.

Silversea Cruises has come a long way since it began in 1994 and has re-invented itself, with a more defined and refined product, and its Italian Heritage theme. Its many international passengers react well to the ambience, food, service and the staff, most of whom will go out of their way to please.

Silversea Cruises has "all-inclusive" fares, including gratuities. They do not, however, include vintage wines, or massage, or other personal services, but they do include many things that cost extra aboard the ships of many other cruise lines. The passenger mix includes many nationalities, which makes for a more interesting experience, although the majority of passengers are North American. Children are sometimes seen aboard, although they are not really welcomed by most passengers, who enjoy cruising without them. The onboard currency is the US dollar.

In 2002, Silversea Cruises introduced "Personalized Voyages" whereby you choose the port of embarkation and disembarkation and the length of cruise you want (minimum is five days). While this is a flexible feature, the onboard programming is already set, so you may be joining and leaving in the middle of a "normal" cruise.

Although the ship is showing signs of wear, it will undergo a big refurbishment in 2009. The actual onboard product delivered is very good, particularly with regard to the cuisine and its presentation. Shuttle buses are provided in most ports of call, and all the little extras that passengers receive aboard this ship makes it an extremely pleasant cruise experience, in surroundings that are very comfortable and contemporary without being extravagant, with open seating dining and drinks included, cold canapés and hot hors d'oeuvres served in the bars in the pre-dinner cocktail hour, a captain's welcome aboard and farewell cocktail party and other niceties.

Some vibration is evident when bow thrusters or the anchors are used, particularly in the forward-most cabins. The self-service launderette is not large enough for longer cruises. Crew facilities are minimal, leading to a high crew turnover which undermines service.

SUITABLE FOR: *Silver Cloud* is best suited to discerning, well-traveled couples (typically over 50) who seek a small ship setting (they wouldn't be seen dead aboard today's huge standard resort cruise ships), with excellent food that is approaching gourmet standards, and fine European-style service in surroundings that can best be described as bordering on the elegant and luxurious.

ACCOMMODATION. There are seven price grades in this "all-suite" ship. The all-outside-view suites (75 percent of which have fine private teakwood balconies) have convertible queen-to-twin beds and are beautifully fitted out. They have large floor-to-ceiling windows, large walk-in closets, dressing table, writing desk, stocked mini-bar/refrigerator (no charge), and fresh flowers.

The marble floor bathrooms have a tub, fixed shower-head (this is not as hygienic as a hand-held unit), single washbasin, and plenty of high-quality towels. Personalized stationery, an eight-pillow menu (from soft down to memory foam), bathrobes, and a range of Acqua di Parma bathroom amenities are provided in all suites.

All suites have televisions and VCR or DVD players (top grade suites also have CD-players). However, the walk-in closets do not actually provide much hanging space (particularly for such items as full-length dresses), and it would be better for the door to open outward instead of inward. The drawers themselves are poorly positioned, but several other drawers and storage areas are provided in the living area.

Although the cabin insulation above and below each cabin is good, the insulation between cabins is not – a privacy curtain installed between entry door and sleeping area would be most useful – and light from the passageway leaks into the cabin, making it hard to achieve a dark room.

The top-grade suites feature teak balcony furniture, while other suites do not – but all balconies have teak floors. Suites with balconies on the lowest deck can suffer from sticky salt spray when the ship is moving, so the balconies require lots of cleaning. Each evening, the stewardesses bring plates of canapés to your suite – just right for a light bite with cocktails. Stay in the Grand, Royal, Rossellini or Owner's Suite and you get unobtrusive butler service from butlers certified by the Guild of Professional Butlers, London.

CUISINE. The main dining room (called, simply, "The Restaurant") provides open-seating dining in elegant surroundings. It has an attractive arched gazebo center and a wavy ceiling design as its focal point, and is set with fine Eschenbach china and well-balanced Christofle silverware. Meals are served in an open seating, which means you can eat when you like (within the given dining room opening times), and with whom you like.

The dining is good throughout the ship, with a choice of three dining salons, and both the cuisine and its presentation have been improved substantially since the beginning of 2004. Standard table wines are included for lunch and dinner, but there is also a "connoisseur list" of premium wines at extra charge. All meals are prepared as à la carte items, with almost none of the pre-preparation that existed previously.

An alternative, intimate 24-seat dining salon, La Saletta (adjacent to the main dining room) and degustation menus include dishes designed by Relais Châteaux Gourmands chefs for Silversea Cruises (the cuisine-oriented division of Relais & Châteaux) paired with selected wines. Reservations are required, and the per person cost is $30.

For more informal dining, there's La Terrazza for self-serve breakfast and lunch buffets and informal eveningdining with different regional Italian dishes nightly. Both indoor and outdoor seating is at teakwood tables and chairs.

The ship also provides 24-hour in-cabin dining service. Full course-by-course dinners are available, although the balcony tables in the standard suites are rather low for dining outdoors.

ENTERTAINMENT. The Showlounge hosts all entertainment events and some social functions. The room spans two decks and has a sloping floor; both banquette and individual seating are provided, with good sightlines.

Although Silversea Cruises places more emphasis on food than entertainment, what is provided is quite tasteful and not overbearing, as aboard some larger ships. A decent array of cabaret acts does the Silversea circuit and small colorful production shows have been reintroduced.

Most of the cabaret acts provide intelligent entertainment that is generally appreciated by the ship's well-traveled international clientele. Also, more emphasis is now placed on classical music ensembles. There is also a band, as well as several small musical units for live music in the evenings in The Bar, and Panorama Lounge.

SPA/FITNESS. Although "The Spa at Silversea" facility is not large, it underwent a sea change in 2007, with redesigned, more welcoming decor, and an updated range of treatments and spa packages for both men and women. Massage and other body pampering treatments, facials, pedicures, and beauty salon treatments cost extra.

Facilities include a separate sauna for men and women, several treatment rooms, and a beauty salon. A separate gymnasium (formerly an observation lounge), located atop the ship, provides sea views.

Silver Shadow
★★★★★

Size: ....Small Ship	Passenger Decks: 7	Cabins (with private balcony): 157
Tonnage: 28,258	Total Crew: 295	Cabins (wheelchair accessible): 2
Lifestyle: ....Luxury	Passengers	Wheelchair accessibility ....Good
Cruise Line: ....Silversea Cruises	(lower beds/all berths): 388/400	Cabin Current: ....110 and 220 volts
Former Names: ....none	Passenger Space Ratio	Elevators: 5
Builder: ....Visentini/Mariotti	(lower beds/all berths): 72.8/70.6	Casino (gaming tables): ....Yes
(Italy)	Crew/Passenger Ratio	Slot Machines: ....Yes
Original Cost: ....$150 million	(lower beds/all berths): 1.3/1.3	Swimming Pools (outdoors): 1
Entered Service: ....Sept 2000	Cabins (total): 194	Swimming Pools (indoors): 0
Registry: ....The Bahamas	Size Range (sq ft/m): 287.0–1,435.0/	Whirlpools: 2
Length (ft/m): 610.2/186.0	26.6–133.3	Self-Service Launderette: ....Yes
Beam (ft/m): 81.8/24.8	Cabins (outside view): 194	Dedicated Cinema/Seats: ....No
Draft (ft/m): 19.6/6.0	Cabins (interior/no view): 0	Library: ....Yes
Propulsion/Propellers: diesel/2	Cabins (for one person): 0	

OVERALL SCORE: 1,750 OUT OF A POSSIBLE 2,000 POINTS

OVERVIEW. *Silver Shadow* is one of the second generation of vessels in the four-ship Silversea Cruises fleet. It is slightly larger than the first two ships, *Silver Cloud* and *Silver Wind*, with a more streamlined forward profile and large, sleek single funnel. However, the stern section is not particularly handsome. There is a generous amount of open deck and sunbathing space, and aluminum/teak deck furniture is provided.

Silversea Cruises has come a long way since it began in 1994, and is re-inventing itself, with a more defined and refined product, and its Italian Heritage theme. The company's many international passengers react well to the ambience, food, service and the helpful staff. The cruise line has "all-inclusive" fares, including gratuities (they do not, however, include vintage wines, or massage, or other personal services), but they do include many things that are at extra cost compared aboard the ships of many other cruise lines. The passenger mix includes many nationalities, which makes for a more interesting experience although the majority of passengers are North American (children are sometimes seen aboard, although they are not really welcomed by most passengers, who enjoy cruising without them). The onboard currency is the US dollar.

Few ships make it to a five-star Berlitz rating, but Silversea Cruises has earned an enviable reputation for high quality, and, although the ship is showing signs of wear, the onboard product is very good, particularly the cuisine and its presentation. Shuttle buses are provided in most ports of call, and all the little extras that passengers receive make this an extremely pleasant cruise experience, in surroundings that are comfortable and contemporary without being extravagant, with open seating dining and drinks included,

BERLITZ'S RATINGS		
	Possible	Achieved
Ship	500	452
Accommodation	200	181
Food	400	341
Service	400	347
Entertainment	100	85
Cruise	400	344

cold canapés and hot hors d'oeuvres served in the bars in the pre-dinner cocktail hour, a captain's welcome aboard and farewell cocktail party. The swimming pool is surprisingly small, as is the fitness room, although it was expanded in 2007.

In 2002, Silversea Cruises introduced "Personalized Voyages" whereby you choose the port of embarkation and disembarkation and the length of cruise (minimum five days). While this is flexible, the onboard programming is already set, so you may be joining and leaving in the middle of a "normal" cruise.

"The Humidor, by Davidoff," the cigar smoking lounge; has 25 seats and the style of an English smoking club. Other additions include a champagne bar and a computer-learning center, with four computer terminals (wi-fi costs extra).

SUITABLE FOR: *Silver Shadow* is best suited to discerning, well-traveled couples (typically over 50) who seek a small ship setting, with excellent food that is approaching gourmet standards, and fine European-style service in surroundings bordering on the elegant and luxurious.

ACCOMMODATION. There are eight price grades in this all-suite ship. All suites have double vanities in the marble-floored bathrooms, which also have a bathtub and separate shower enclosure. Silversea-monogrammed Frette bed linen is provided in all grades, as are an eight-pillow menu (from soft down to memory foam), 100% cotton bathrobes, a range of Acqua di Parma bathroom amenities, and personalized stationery. Stay in the Grand, Royal, Rossellini or Owner's Suite and you get unobtrusive butler service (butlers are certified by the Guild of Professional Butlers, London).

Vista Suites: These suites (287 sq. ft/27 sq. meters) do not have a private balcony. Instead there is a large window, twin beds that convert to a queen-sized bed, sitting area, television and VCR, refrigerator, writing desk, personal safe, cocktail cabinet, dressing table with hairdryer, and walk-in closet. The bathroom is marble-clad in gentle colors, and has two (his 'n' hers) washbasins, full-sized bathtub, separate shower enclosure, and toilet.

Veranda Suites: Each of the Veranda Suites (really a Vista Suite plus a veranda) measures 345 sq. ft (33 sq. meters) and have convertible twin-to-queen beds. They are well fitted out with just about everything you would need, including large floor-to-ceiling windows, large walk-in closet, dressing table, writing desk, stocked mini-bar/refrigerator (all drinks are included in the price of your cruise), and fresh flowers. The marble-clad bathrooms have two washbasins, full-sized tub, separate shower enclosure, and toilet.

Silver Suites: These measure 701 sq. ft (65 sq. meters). These are much wider than the Vista Suites or Veranda Suites and have a separate bedroom, an entertainment center with CD player, TV/VCR unit (in both bedroom and living room) and much more living space that includes a large dining area with table and four chairs. The marble-clad bathrooms have two washbasins, full sized tub, separate shower enclosure, and toilet.

Owner's Suites: The two Owner's Suites, each of which measures 1,208 sq. ft (112 sq. meters), are much larger units and includes an extra powder room/toilet for guests, as well as more living space. There is a 200 sq.-ft (18 sq.-meter) veranda, two bedrooms (with queen-sized beds), two walk-in closets, two living rooms, two sitting areas, separate dining area, an entertainment center with flat-screen plasma television in the living room and TV/VCR player in each bedroom, telephones, refrigerators, cocktail cabinet, writing desk, dressing tables with hairdryers. There are two marble-clad bathrooms, one with a full sized whirlpool tub and two washbasins, separate toilet, and separate shower, as well as a powder room for guests. Owner's Suites can be configured as one or two bedrooms.

Royal Suites: Stately accommodation can be found in two Royal Suites, which measure either 1,312 sq. ft (122 sq. meters) or 1,352 sq. ft (126 sq. meters). These are two-bedroom suites, with two teakwood verandas, two living rooms, sitting areas, dining area, queen-size beds, an entertainment center with flat-screen plasma television in the living room and TV/VCR player in each bedroom, telephones, refrigerators, cocktail cabinet, writing desk, two closets, dressing tables with hairdryers. There are two marble-clad bathrooms, one with a full-sized whirlpool tub and two washbasins, separate toilet, and separate shower, as well as a powder room for guests. Royal Suites can be either a one- or two-bedroom configuration.

Grand Suites: There are two of these, one measuring 1,286 sq. ft (119 sq. meters), and the other (including an adjoining suite with interconnecting door) 1,435 sq. ft (133 sq. meters). These have two bedrooms, two large walk-in closets, two living rooms, Bang & Olufsen entertainment centers, and large, forward-facing, private verandas that face

forwards. These really are sumptuous apartments that have all the comforts of home, and then some.

Disabled Suites: There are two suites for the physically disabled (535 and 537), both adjacent to a lift and next to each other. Measuring a generous 398 sq. ft (37 sq. meters), they are well equipped with an accessible hanging rail, and roll-in bathroom with roll-in shower unit.

CUISINE. The main dining room, "The Restaurant," provides open-seating dining in elegant surroundings. Three grand chandeliers provide an upward focal point, while you can dine when you want, and with whom you wish. Meals can also be served, course-by-course, in your suite, although the balcony tables are rather low for dining outdoors. The cuisine is very good, with a choice of formal and informal areas. Standard table wines are included for lunch and dinner, with a "connoisseur list" of premium wines at extra cost. Once each cruise, there's a "Galley Brunch" when the galley is transformed into a large "chef's kitchen." There's dinner dancing with a live band on some nights.

As an alternative to the main restaurant, Le Champagne, at an extra cost of $30 per person, offers a more intimate, reservation-only dining spot that enables diners to dine from highly specialized dégustation menus that marries international cuisine together with vintage wines selection by Relais et Châteaux sommeliers (although the wines cost extra).

For more informal meals, La Terrazza is for self-serve breakfast and lunch buffets; outdoor seating is at teakwood tables and chairs. The buffet design and set-up presents flow problems during breakfast, however, and "active" stations for cooking eggs or pasta to order would help. In the evening, La Terrazza features regional Italian cuisine, and softer lighting to create a more intimate atmosphere and experience.

Adjacent to La Terazza is a wine bar and a cigar smoking room. A poolside grill provides a casual alternative daytime bistro-style eatery, for grilled and fast food items.

ENTERTAINMENT. The Showlounge is the venue for all entertainment events and some social functions. The room spans two decks and has a sloping floor; both banquette and individual seating are provided, with good sightlines from almost all seats.

Although Silversea Cruises places more emphasis on food than entertainment, what is provided is quite tasteful. A decent array of cabaret acts does the Silversea circuit, and small, colorful production shows have been reintroduced. More emphasis is now placed on classical music ensembles. There is a band, and several small musical units for live music in the evenings in The Bar, and the Panorama Lounge.

SPA/FITNESS. "The Spa at Silversea" health/fitness facility, just behind the Observation Lounge, high atop the ship. had a complete make-over in 2007. It includes a gymnasium, beauty salon, and separate saunas and steam rooms for men and women, plus several personal treatment rooms. A new range of body-pampering services was introduced for men and women (massage and other treatments, facials, pedicures, and beauty salon treatments cost extra).

Silver Spirit
★★★★★

Size: . . . . .Small Ship	Passenger Decks: 8	Cabins (with private balcony): 258
Tonnage: .36,009	Total Crew: 370	Cabins (wheelchair accessible): 4
Lifestyle: . . . . .Luxury	Passengers	Wheelchair accessibility . . . . .Best
Cruise Line: . . . . .Silversea Cruises	(lower beds/all berths): 540/608	Cabin Voltage: . . . . .110 volts
Former Names: . . . . .none	Passenger Space Ratio	Elevators: 6
Builder: . . . . .Fincantieri (Italy)	(lower beds/all berths): 66.6/59.2	Casino (gaming tables): . . . . .Yes
Original Cost: . . . .$250 million	Crew/Passenger Ratio	Slot Machines: . . . . .Yes
Entered Service: . . . . .Dec 2009	(lower beds/all berths): 1.4/1.6	Swimming Pools (outdoors): 1
Registry: . . . . .The Bahamas	Cabins (total): .270	Swimming Pools (indoors): 0
Length (ft/m): 642.3/195.8	Size Range (sq ft/m): 312.1–1,614.6/	Whirlpools: 4
Beam (ft/m): 86.9/26.5	29–150	Self-Service Launderette: . . . . .Yes
Draft (ft/m): 20.9/6.4	Cabins (outside view): 270	Dedicated Cinema/Seats: . . . . .No
Propulsion/Propellers: . . . .diesel-electric/	Cabins (interior/no view): 0	Library: . . . . .Yes
(26,100kW)/2	Cabins (for one person): 0	

BERLITZ'S OVERALL SCORE: 1.772 OUT OF A POSSIBLE 2,000 POINTS

OVERVIEW. *Silver Spirit*, larger than *Silver Shadow* and *Silver Whisper,* is the newest, latest, "all-inclusive" (not really, because two alternative dining venues cost extra) addition to the Silversea Cruises fleet. It represents a substantial investment in new tonnage.

Silver Spirit, also the name of a famous Rolls-Royce motor car, has a similar profile to the smaller *Silver Shadow* and *Silver Whisper,* with a nicely shaped stern with tiered aft decks, but exudes more style and provides more choice than Silversea Cruises' other ships. Although there's a main pool and hot tub deck, there's little shade, and no hot tubs on any other deck, away from the pool deck.

Also, because there are so many balcony suites/cabins,, there's no walk-around outdoor promenade deck.

The ship's layout has a cake-layer stacking of almost all the public rooms in the aft section, and the accommodation located forward, so there is minimal noise in passenger accommodation, although it means there is more "vertical" walking (stairs) for passengers and no "flow-through" horizontal deck where passengers can parade. However, regular Silversea Cruises passengers are used to this arrangement with other ships, and it's good exercise.

The ship's interior decor is elegant and understated, but bland (muted colors), a mix of art deco and modern, but not contemporary.

The Observation Lounge, located at the front of the ship with access from a central passageway, has fine ocean views, and it's a very comfortable place to relax and read. A Panorama Lounge is located at the ship's stern and is a comfortable multi-function room. Non-smokers should note that smoking is allowed on the port side. A cigar lounge,

BERLITZ'S RATINGS

	Possible	Achieved
Ship	500	458
Accommodation	200	182
Food	400	343
Service	400	349
Entertainment	100	87
Cruise	400	353

with doors that open in to the casino, has a pleasing list of cigars (including, for example: Cohiba Corona Especiales, at $49; Robusto, at $49; Monte Cristo, at $30, and Roeo and Juliet, at $35). The casino itself features five blackjack tables, American Roulette table, and 52 slot machines.

Silversea Cruises features "all-inclusive" fares, which include gratuities (but not vintage wines, or massage, or other personal services), but they do include many things that cost extra compared to the ships of some other cruise lines. The passenger mix includes many nationalities, which makes for a more interesting experience although most passengers are North American. Children are sometimes seen aboard, although they are not really welcome by most passengers. The onboard currency is the US dollar.

Shuttle buses are provided in most ports of call, and all the little extras that passengers receive aboard this ship makes it an extremely pleasant cruise experience, in surroundings that are very comfortable and contemporary without being extravagant. Among these are open-seating dining and drinks included, cold canapés and hot hors d'oeuvres served in the bars in the pre-dinner cocktail hour, a captain's welcome aboard and farewell cocktail party and other niceties.

Passenger niggles include the lack of electrical sockets in the cabins; there are almost no shaded outdoor areas; the "butler" service is sometimes poor, not least because each has butler about 15 cabins to look after.

SUITABLE FOR: *Silver Spirit* is for discerning, well-traveled couples, typically over 50, who are looking for a smaller ship setting with fine food and European-style service in surroundings bordering on the elegant and luxurious.

ACCOMMODATION. *Silver Spirit* features "all-suite" accommodation – a standard aboard all the ships of Silversea Cruises. Regular passengers will understand the names and attributes of each of them. Some suites can accommodate a third person. Eight of the suites have interconnecting doors, so families and friends can be adjacent.

Accommodation consists of: two Owner's suites (approx. 1,291.7 sq. ft/ 120 sq. meters for one bedroom and 1,614 sq.ft/ 150 sq. meters for two bedrooms); six Grand suites in the front of the ship (990 sq.ft/ 92 sq. meters for one bedroom and 1,302 sq.ft/ 117 sq. meters for two bedrooms); 26 Silver suites (742 sq.ft/ 69 sq. meters); Midship Veranda suites (376 sq.ft/ 35 sq. meters); 222 Verandah suites (376 sq.ft/ 35 sq. meters); and 14 Vista suites (312 sq.ft/ 29 sq. meters).

No matter which suite you choose, you'll get personalized stationery, a menu that provides a choice of eight pillows (from soft down to memory foam), bathrobes, and an array of Bulgari bathroom amenities. All have walk-in closets with personal safe, TV set, DVD unit, and vanity desk with hairdryer. Suite bathrooms are marble-clad, with marble and wood floors, and contain one washbasin the smaller ships have two (even though two people seldom use the washbasins at the same time), full-sized tub, separate shower enclosure (with a fixed "rainshower" and a separate hand-held hose), and toilet.

Occupants of the Owner's Suites or Grand Suites receive unobtrusive butler service, from 21 butlers, who are certified by the Guild of Professional Butlers in London.

The suites/cabins have recessed lighting in the ceiling – a nice touch that allows a little diffused mood lighting when needed. Balconies have sliding doors that can move if not securely locked when not in use. Non-smokers should be aware that Silversea Cruises allows smoking in cabins.

CUISINE. There are certainly plenty of dining choices. *The Restaurant* is the name of the ship's main dining room – a light, airy venue, although its design is quite disappointing – in particular because of its low ceiling height. It seats up to 456, and has an integral dance floor. This is all about open-seating dining in elegant surroundings, with unhurried, unobtrusive service. It is open for breakfast, lunch and dinner; tables are set with fine china, silverware, and Reidel wine glasses. For complete privacy, meals can also be served, course-by-course, in your suite.

● *Le Champagne*, located adjacent to The Restaurant, is an extra-cost, reservations-required, dinner-only venue offering a six-course mini-dégustation menu, based on Relais & Château menus. Sadly, the banquette seating along the outer walls detracts from the otherwise very comfortable, uncluttered, intimate dining spot, which has a small walk-in wine room as its central, focal point. The extra cost is $30 per person ($200 if wine pairing is included).

● *Seishin* Restaurant, also located adjacent to The Restaurant, is an extra-cost reservations-required venue, with just 24 seats, for Asian cuisine. It serves Kobe beef, sushi items, and Asian seafood, and an octagonal display counter is the focal point to the venue. It is open for dinner only, and the extra cost is $40 per person for an 11-item menu ($80 if sake is included, but $20 if only four items are chosen).

● *La Terrazza* is the venue for self-serve buffet-style items for breakfast and lunch. Each evening, it turns into an Italian-themed dining spot, with waiter service and regional Italian cuisine cooked to order. Reservations are required for dinner (not open for lunch).

● *Stars Supper Club,* with 58 seats and a dance floor, is designed in the manner of an English supper club of the 1920s, to provide an intimate, club-like ambiance and all-night entertainment – which means volume-intrusive. Reservations are required for dinner (not open for lunch).

● *The Pool Grill* is a casual outside eatery serving steaks, seafood, and pizza – which cannot possibly be considered a luxury food item, but then, this *is* a ship with Italian connections. Meals are served on hot stones, which act as plates, so you can't touch them, but this is more a casual eating novelty than proper dining.

Additionally, a lobby bar serves Lavazza Italian coffees, wines, spirits, and pastries.

ENTERTAINMENT. The Showlounge, in the ship's aft section, has a main stage and two ancillary side stages. It seats about 320 passengers, and there are good sightlines from all seats but no beverage service. It's a lovely room, and seating consists of two-person love seats, and each has a small table for personal items, such as ladies' clutch purses for formal evenings. Production shows have been re-introduced, and these, together with cabaret acts, provide a balanced entertainment program.

SPA/FITNESS. The Spa at Silversea, with 8,300 sq.ft (770 sq. meters) of space, is quite large for this size of ship, and includes a sanctuary for total relaxation and detox. Located at the stern of the ship, above La Terrazza, it is a haven for me-time and personal treatments.

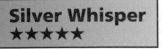

Silver Whisper
★★★★★

Size: ....Small Ship	Passengers	Cabin Current: ....110 and 220 volts
Tonnage: 28,258	(lower beds/all berths): 388/400	Elevators: 5
Lifestyle: ....Luxury	Passenger Space Ratio	Casino (gaming tables): ....Yes
Cruise Line: ....Silversea Cruises	(lower beds/all berths): 72.8/70.6	Slot Machines: ....Yes
Former Names: ....none	Crew/Passenger Ratio	Swimming Pools (outdoors): 1
Builder: ....Visentini/Mariotti(Italy)	(lower beds/all berths): 1.3/1.3	Swimming Pools (indoors): 0
Original Cost: ....$150 million	Cabins (total): 194	Whirlpools: 2
Entered Service: ....July 2001	Size Range (sq ft/m): 287.0–1,435.0/	Fitness Center: ....Yes
Registry: ....The Bahamas	26.6–133.3	Sauna/Steam Room: ....Yes/Yes
Length (ft/m): 610.2/186.0	Cabins (outside view): 194	Massage: ....Yes
Beam (ft/m): 81.8/24.8	Cabins (interior/no view): 0	Self-Service Launderette: ....Yes
Draft (ft/m): 19.6/6.0	Cabins (for one person): 0	Dedicated Cinema/Seats: ....No
Propulsion/Propellers: diesel/2	Cabins (with private balcony): 157	Library: ....Yes
Passenger Decks: 7	Cabins (wheelchair accessible): 2	
Total Crew: 295	Wheelchair accessibility ....Good	

OVERALL SCORE: 1,753 OUT OF A POSSIBLE 2,000 POINTS

OVERVIEW. *Silver Whisper*, which Russia's Vladimir Putin chartered in 2003 to host guests for the three-day celebrations of St. Petersburg's 300th anniversary, is the second generation of vessels in the Silversea Cruises fleet (its sister is *Silver Shadow*), and is slightly larger than the line's first two ships, *Silver Cloud* and *Silver Wind*, but with a more streamlined profile and large, sleek single funnel.

Silversea Cruises has come a long way since it began in 1994, and has re-invented itself with a more defined and refined product, and its Italian Heritage theme. The company's many international passengers react well to the ambience, food, service and the staff, most of whom go out of their way to please. The cruise line has "all-inclusive" fares, including gratuities (although additional grauities are not expected, they are not prohibited). The fares do not include vintage wines, or massage, or other personal services, but they do include many things that are at extra cost compared aboard the ships of many other cruise lines. The passenger mix includes many nationalities, which makes for a more interesting experience, although the majority of passengers are North American. Children are sometimes seen aboard, although they are not really welcomed by most passengers. The onboard currency is the US dollar.

Few ships make it to a five-star Berlitz rating today, but Silversea Cruises emphasis on quality has earned it an enviable reputation, particularly for cuisine. Shuttle buses are provided in most ports of call, and all the little extras that passengers receive makes this ship an extremely pleasant cruise experience, in surroundings that are very comfortable and contemporary without being extravagant, with open seat-

BERLITZ'S RATINGS

	Possible	Achieved
Ship	500	452
Accommodation	200	181
Food	400	341
Service	400	349
Entertainment	100	85
Cruise	400	345

ing dining and drinks included, cold canapés and hot hors d'oeuvres served in the bars in the pre-dinner cocktail hour, a captain's welcome aboard and farewell cocktail party and other niceties.

In 2002, Silversea Cruises introduced "Personalized Voyages" whereby you choose the port of embarkation and disembarkation and the length of cruise (minimum is five days). But the onboard programming is set, so you may be joining and leaving in the middle of a cruise.

Aluminum/teak deck furniture is provided around the ship's swimming pool, although the pool itself is quite small. "The Humidor, by Davidoff," a 25-seat cigar smoking lounge, has been styled like an English smoking club. There's a wine bar and computer learning center.

SUITABLE FOR: *Silver Whisper* is best suited to discerning, well-traveled couples (typically over 50) who are looking for a small-ship setting with excellent food approaching gourmet standards, and fine European-style service in surroundings bordering on the elegant and luxurious.

ACCOMMODATION. There are eight cabin price categories in this "all-suite" ship. All grades have double vanities in the marble-floored bathrooms, plus tub and separate shower enclosure. Silversea-monogrammed Frette bed linen is provided in all grades, as is an eight-pillow menu (from soft down to memory foam), 100% cotton bathrobes, a fine array of Acqua di Parma bathroom amenities, and personalized stationery. Stay in the Grand, Royal, Rossellini or Owner's Suite and you get unobtrusive butler service from butlers certified by the Guild of Professional Butlers in London.

Vista Suites: These suites measure 287 sq. ft (27 sq. metes), and do not have a private balcony. Instead there is a large window, twin beds that convert to a queen-sized bed, sitting area, TV and VCR player, refrigerator, writing desk, personal safe, cocktail cabinet, dressing table with hairdryer, and walk-in closet. The bathroom is marble-clad in gentle colors, and has two (his 'n' hers) washbasins, full-sized tub, separate shower enclosure, and toilet.

Veranda Suites: Each of the Veranda Suites (really a Vista Suite plus a veranda) measures 345 sq. ft (32 sq. meters) and has convertible twin-to-queen beds. They are well fitted-out, and have large floor-to-ceiling windows, large walk-in closet, dressing table, writing desk, stocked mini-bar/refrigerator (drinks included in the cruise price), and fresh flowers. The marble-clad bathrooms have two washbasins, full-sized bathtub, separate shower enclosure, and toilet.

Silver Suites: The Silver Suites measure 701 sq. ft. (65 sq. meters). These are much wider than the Vista Suites or Veranda Suites and have a separate bedroom, an entertainment center with CD player, TV/VCR unit (in both bedroom and living room) and much more living space that includes a large dining area with table and four chairs. The marble-clad bathrooms have two washbasins, full-sized tub, separate shower enclosure, and toilet.

Owner's Suites: The two Owner's Suites, each 1,208 sq. ft (112 sq. meters), are much larger units and includes an extra bathroom for guests, as well as more living space. There is a 200 sq. ft (18 sq. meter) veranda, two bedrooms (with queen-sized beds), two walk-in closets, two living rooms, two sitting areas, separate dining area, an entertainment center with flat-screen plasma television in the living room and TV/VCR player in each bedroom, telephones, refrigerators, cocktail cabinet, writing desk, dressing tables with hairdryers. There are two marble-clad bathrooms, one with a full-sized whirlpool tub and two washbasins, separate toilet, and separate shower, plus a powder room for guests. Owner's Suites can be a one- or two-bedroom configuration.

Royal Suites: Stately accommodation can be found in two Royal Suites, which measure either 1,312 sq. ft (122 sq. meters) or 1,352 sq. ft (126 sq. meters). These are two-bedroom suites, with two teakwood verandas, two living rooms, sitting areas, dining area, queen-size beds, an entertainment center with flat-screen plasma television in the living room and TV/VCR player in each bedroom, telephones, refrigerators, cocktail cabinet, writing desk, two closets, dressing tables with hairdryers. There are two marble-clad bathrooms, one with a full-sized whirlpool tub and two washbasins, separate toilet, and separate shower, as well as a powder room for guests. Royal Suites can be either a one- or two-bedroom configuration.

Grand Suites: There are two Grand Suites, one 1,286 sq. ft (119 sq. meters), and the other (including an adjoining suite with interconnecting door) 1,435 sq. ft (133 sq. meters). These have two bedrooms, two large walk-in closets, two living rooms, Bang & Olufsen entertainment centers, and large, forward-facing, private verandas that face forwards. These really are sumptuous apartments that have all the comforts of home, and then some.

Disabled Suites: There are two suites for the physically disabled (535 and 537), both adjacent to an elevator, and next to each other. They measure a generous 398 sq. ft (37 sq. meters). The suites are well-equipped with an accessible hanging rail, and roll-in bathroom with roll-in shower unit.

CUISINE. The main dining room ("The Restaurant") provides open-seating dining in elegant surroundings. Three grand chandeliers provide an upward focal point, while you can dine when you want, and with whom you wish (within the given opening times). Meals can also be served, course-by-course, in your suite, although the balcony tables are rather low for dining outdoors. The dining is good throughout the ship, with a choice of formal and informal areas, although the cuisine and presentation doesn't quite match up to that of products such as the smaller Seabourn Cruise Line ships. Cristofle silverware is provided. Standard table wines are included for lunch and dinner, but there is also a "connoisseur list" of premium wines at extra charge.

Once each cruise, there's a "Galley Brunch" when the galley is transformed into a large "chef's kitchen."

As an alternative to the main restaurant, Le Champagne, at an extra-cost of $30 per person, offers a more intimate, reservation-only dining spot that enables diners to dine from highly specialized dégustation menus that marries international cuisine together with vintage wines selection by Relais et Châteaux sommeliers (and Reidel wine glasses).

La Terrazza has self-serve breakfast and lunch buffets. The buffet design and set-up presents flow problems during breakfast, however, and "active" stations for cooking eggs or pasta to order would help. In the evening this room La Terrazza serves regional Italian cuisine, and softer lighting to create a more intimate atmosphere and experience.

Adjacent to the café is a wine bar and a cigar smoking room. A poolside grill provides a casual alternative daytime dining spot.

ENTERTAINMENT. The Showlounge spans two decks and has a sloping floor; both banquette and individual seating are provided, with good sightlines from almost all seats.

A decent array of cabaret acts does the Silversea circuit, most providing intelligent entertainment, and colorful production shows are back. More emphasis is placed on classical music ensembles. A band and small musical units provide music in the evenings in The Bar and the Panorama Lounge.

SPA/FITNESS. "The Spa at Silversea" health/fitness facility, just behind the Observation Lounge, high atop the ship, had a complete make-over in 2007. It includes a gymnasium, beauty salon, and separate saunas and steam rooms for men and women, plus several personal treatment rooms. A new range of body-pampering services was introduced for men and women (massage and other treatments, facials, pedicures, and beauty salon treatments cost extra). Treatment examples: Deep Tissue Massage, $116 for 50 minutes; Hot Stones Massage, $210 for 75 minutes; In-Suite Couples Massage, $320 for 50 minutes, or $385 for 80 minutes; Elemis Aromapure Facial, $115 for 50 minutes.

Silver Wind
★★★★+

Size ....Small Ship	Total Crew: 197	Cabins (wheelchair accessible): 2
Tonnage: 16,927	Passengers	Wheelchair accessibility ....Fair
Lifestyle: ....Luxury	(lower beds/all berths): 296/315	Cabin Current: ....110 and 220 volts
Cruise Line: ....Silversea Cruises	Passenger Space Ratio	Elevators: 4
Former Names: ....none	(lower beds/all berths): 57.1/53.7	Casino (gaming tables): ....Yes
Builder: ....Visentini/Mariotti (Italy)	Crew/Passenger Ratio	Slot Machines: ....Yes
Original Cost: ....$125 million	(lower beds/all berths): 1.5/1.5	Swimming Pools (outdoors): 1
Entered Service: ....Jan 1995	Cabins (total): 148	Swimming Pools (indoors): 0
Registry: ....Italy	Size Range (sq ft/m): 240.0–1,314.0/	Whirlpools: 2
Length (ft/m): 514.4/155.8	22.2–122.0	Self-Service Launderette: ....Yes
Beam (ft/m): 70.62/21.4	Cabins (outside view): 148	Dedicated Cinema/Seats: Yes/306
Draft (ft/m): 17.3/5.3	Cabins (interior/no view): 0	Library: ....Yes
Propulsion/Propellers: diesel (11,700kW)/2	Cabins (for one person): 0	
Passenger Decks: 6	Cabins (with private balcony): 110	

OVERALL SCORE: 1,669 OUT OF A POSSIBLE 2,000 POINTS

OVERVIEW. *Silver Wind* has a quite handsome profile, with a sloping stern reminiscent of an "Airstream" trailer. The size is just about ideal for personalized cruising in an elegant environment. The vertical cake-layer stacking of public rooms aft and the location of accommodation units forward ensures quiet cabins. There is a synthetic turf-covered walk-around promenade deck outdoors (this should be upgraded to teak or Bolidt), and a fairly spacious swimming pool and sunbathing deck, with teak/aluminum deck furniture (little "Silversea" touches such as cold towels, water sprays and fresh fruit provide poolside pampering on hot days).

Although the ship had a multi-million dollar makeover in 2003, another makeover in 2009 made it more user-friendly by adding a proper observation lounge and covered walkway to access it. The spacious interior is well-planned, with elegant decor and fine-quality soft furnishings throughout, accented by brass fittings (some of which is of sub-standard quality and shows blotchy patches in several places), fine woods and creative ceilings.

There is an excellent amount of space per passenger and there is no hint of a line anywhere in this unhurried environment. Before your cruise, good documentation is provided in a high-quality document wallet and presentation box. There is a useful internet center, a 24-hour library with hardback books, CD-ROMs and DVDs, and a cigar lounge.

An elegant, announcement-free onboard ambiance prevails, and there is no pressure, no hype, and an enthusiastic staff to pamper you, with a high ratio of Europeans. Insurance, included when Silversea Cruises first started, now costs extra. All drinks, gratuities and port taxes are included, and no further tipping anywhere on board is nec-

BERLITZ'S RATINGS		
	Possible	Achieved
Ship	500	413
Accommodation	200	177
Food	400	333
Service	400	335
Entertainment	100	74
Cruise	400	337

essary (though it is not prohibited). This ship is ideal for those who enjoy spacious surroundings, excellent food, and some entertainment. It would be difficult not to have good cruise holiday aboard this ship, albeit at a fairly high price. The company's many international passengers like the ambience, food, service and the staff, most of whom go out of their way to please.

Silversea Cruises has "all-inclusive" fares, including gratuities (they do not, however, include vintage wines, or massage, or other personal services), but they do include many things that are at extra cost compared aboard the ships of many other cruise lines. The passenger mix includes many nationalities, which makes for a more interesting experience, although most passengers are North American. Children are sometimes seen aboard, although they are not really welcomed by most passengers. The onboard currency is the US dollar.

After 10 years, Silversea Cruises re-invented itself, with a more defined and refined product and an Italian Heritage theme. The past few years saw the delivery of a tarnished Silver(sea) service; however, I am pleased that this has been recognized and that Silversea Cruises is now polishing the silver again). Shuttle buses are provided in most ports of call, and all the little extras that passengers receive aboard this ship makes it an extremely pleasant cruise experience, in surroundings that are very comfortable and contemporary without being extravagant, with open seating dining and drinks included, cold canapés and hot hors d'oeuvres served in the bars in the pre-dinner cocktail hour, a captain's welcome aboard and farewell cocktail party and other niceties.

In 2002, Silversea Cruises introduced "Personalized Voyages" whereby you choose the port of embarkation and disembarkation and the length of cruise you want (minimum is five days). While this is a flexible feature, the onboard programming is already set, so you may be joining and leaving in the middle of a "normal" cruise.

Passenger niggles include the fact that some vibration is evident when bow thrusters or the anchors are used, particularly in the forward-most suites. The self-service launderette is poor and not large enough for longer cruises, when passengers like to wash their own small items.

Crew facilities are minimal, and so keeping consistency is difficult, because the crew turnover is quite high.

SUITABLE FOR: *Silver Wind* is best suited to discerning, well-traveled couples (typically over 50) who seek a small ship setting, with food approaching gourmet standards, and fine European-style service in surroundings that can best be described as bordering on the elegant and luxurious.

ACCOMMODATION. There are seven price grades. The all-outside suites (75 percent of which have fine private teak-wood-floor balconies) have convertible queen-to-twin beds and are nicely fitted out with just about everything one needs, including large floor-to-ceiling windows, large walk-in closets, dressing table, writing desk, stocked mini-bar/refrigerator (no charge), and fresh flowers. The marble floor bathrooms have a tub, fixed shower head (this is not as hygienic as a hand-held unit), single washbasin, and plenty of high-quality towels. Personalized stationery, an eight-pillow menu (from soft down to memory foam), bathrobes, and an array of Acqua di Parma bathroom amenities are provided in all suites.

Stay in the Grand, Royal, Rossellini or Owner's Suite and you get unobtrusive butler service from butlers certified by the Guild of Professional Butlers in London.

All suites have TV and VCR or DVD players (top-grade suites also have CD players). However, the walk-in closets don't actually provide much hanging space (particularly for such items as full-length dresses), and it would be better for the door to open outward instead of inward. The drawers themselves are poorly positioned, although several other drawers and storage areas are provided in the living area. Although the cabin insulation above and below each suite is good, the insulation between them is not – a privacy curtain installed between entry door and sleeping area would be useful – and light from the passageway leaks into the suite, making it hard to achieve a dark room.

The top grades of suites have teak balcony furniture, while others don't – but all balconies have teak floors. Suites with balconies on the lowest deck can suffer from sticky salt spray when the ship is moving, so the balconies need lots of cleaning. Each evening, the stewardesses bring plates of canapés to your suite – just right for a light bite with cocktails.

CUISINE. The main dining room (called, simply, "The Restaurant") provides open-seating dining in elegant surroundings. It has an attractive arched gazebo center and a wavy ceiling design as its focal point, and is set with fine Limoges china and well-balanced Christofle silverware. Meals are served in an open seating, which means you can eat when you like (within the given dining room opening times), and with whom you like.

The cuisine/dining experience is good, with a choice of three dining salons. Standard table wines are included for lunch and dinner, but there is also a "connoisseur list" of premium wines at extra charge. All meals are now prepared as à la carte items, with almost none of the pre-preparation that existed previously (special orders are also possible).

An alternative dining salon, the intimate 24-seat La Saletta, adjacent to the main dining room, has dégustation menus that include dishes designed by Relais & Châteaux Gourmands chefs for Silversea Cruises (the cuisine-oriented division of Relais & Châteaux) paired with selected wines. Reservations are required, and the per person extra cost is $30.

For more informal dining, La Terrazza offers self-serve breakfast and lunch buffets. In the evening it serves Italian regional dishes and has softer lighting, with both indoor and outdoors seating at teakwood tables and chairs.

There is a 24-hour in-cabin dining service; full course-by-course dinners are available, although the balcony tables in the standard suites are rather low for dining outdoors.

ENTERTAINMENT. The Showlounge is the venue for all entertainment events and some social functions. The room spans two decks and has a sloping floor; both banquette and individual seating are provided, with good sightlines from almost all seats.

Although Silversea Cruises places more emphasis on food than entertainment, what is provided is quite tasteful and not overbearing, as aboard some larger ships. A decent array of cabaret acts does the Silversea circuit, and small, colorful production shows have been reintroduced. Most of the cabaret acts provide intelligent entertainment.

Also, more emphasis is now placed on classical music ensembles. There is also a band, as well as several small musical units for live music in the evenings in The Bar, and the Panorama Lounge.

SPA/FITNESS. Although "The Spa at Silversea" facility is not large, it underwent a sea change in 2007, with redesigned, more welcoming decor, and an updated range of treatments and spa packages for both men and women. Massage and other body pampering treatments, facials, pedicures, and beauty salon treatments cost extra.

Facilities include a separate sauna for men and women, several treatment rooms, and a beauty salon. A separate gymnasium (formerly an observation lounge), located atop the ship, provides sea views.

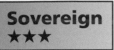

Sovereign
★★★

Size: . . . . .Large Resort Ship	Passenger Decks: 11	Cabins (with private balcony): 62
Tonnage: .73,192	Total Crew: 825	Cabins (wheelchair accessible): 6
Lifestyle: . . . . .Standard	Passengers	Wheelchair accessibility . . . . .Fair
Cruise Line: . . . . .Pullmantur Cruises	(lower beds/all berths): 2,306/2,882	Cabin Current: . . . . .110 volts
Former Names: . . . .Sovereign of the Seas	Passenger Space Ratio	Elevators: 13
Builder: Chantiers de l'Atlantique (France)	(lower beds/all berths): 31.7/25.3	Casino (gaming tables): . . . . .Yes
Original Cost: . . . .$183.5 million	Crew/Passenger Ratio	Slot Machines: . . . . .Yes
Entered Service: . . . . . . .Jan 1988/2008	(lower beds/all berths): 2.7/3.4	Swimming Pools (outdoors): 2
Registry: . . . . .The Bahamas	Cabins (total): 1,153	Swimming Pools (indoors): 0
Length (ft/m): 879.9/268.2	Size Range (sq ft/m): 118.4–670.0/	Whirlpools: 2
Beam (ft/m): 105.9/32.3	11.0–62.2	Self-Service Launderette: . . . . .No
Draft (ft/m): 24.9/7.6	Cabins (outside view): 722	Dedicated Cinema/Seats: . . . . .No
Propulsion/Propellers: . . . . .diesel	Cabins (interior/no view): 431	Library: . . . . .Yes
(21,844kW)/2	Cabins (for one person): 0	

OVERALL SCORE: 1,242 OUT OF A POSSIBLE 2,000 POINTS

OVERVIEW. Pullmantur Cruises bought *Sovereign* (ex-*Sovereign of the Seas*) from Royal Caribbean International in 2008 and, after extensive refurbishment, it is now Pullmantur's flagship. It has a balanced, smart, contemporary profile and nicely rounded lines. Open deck space is not generous, although the ship benefits from a wide walk-around outdoors polished wood promenade deck.

The interior layout is unusual for a large resort ship in that most of the public rooms are located aft (in a sort of cake-layer stacking), with the accommodation located forward, as this helps to keep the noise level down in cabins.

There is a good array of spacious, fairly smart public rooms, with lots of wood paneling and fairly elegant decor that also has some bright color splashes. The ship has a range of rooms for children and teens, including a chill-out lounge and an open aft sundeck with open-air dance floor.

The dress code is very casual. This is a high-density ship that is well-run, highly programmed, and geared to families with children. The onboard currency is the euro, and gratuities are included.

SUITABLE FOR: *Sovereign* is best suited to Spanish-speaking families, young couples, and singles seeking a standard cruise at an all-inclusive price (drinks included).

ACCOMMODATION. There are 16 cabin price grades. Some cabins have interconnecting doors – useful for families.
Suites: Thirteen suites on Bridge Deck (the largest of which is the Royal Suite) are reasonably large and nicely furnished, with separate living and sleeping spaces.
Standard Cabins: The standard outside-view and interior

BERLITZ'S RATINGS

	Possible	Achieved
Ship	500	327
Accommodation	200	119
Food	400	229
Service	400	254
Entertainment	100	63
Cruise	400	250

(no-view) cabins are very small, although an arched window treatment and colorful soft furnishings give the illusion of more space. Almost all cabins have twin beds that can be converted to a queen-sized or double-bed configuration. There is little closet and drawer space. All cabins have a private bathroom, with shower enclosure, toilet and washbasin.

CUISINE/DINING. Two dining rooms, El Guardiana and El Duero, are off the Centrum (lobby) and have tables for four, six, or eight persons (no tables for two). There are two seatings in each venue, and table wines are included in the fare. An à la carte restaurant is an extra-cost venue offering menus at €20 and €24. For casual meals and snacks, the two-level Buffet Panorama is the place to go, although It is usually congested at peak times, but it's open almost 24 hours a day. Several food islands provide pasta and deli sections and a carving station. Asian fusion and Asian tapas are available on the venue's upper level.

ENTERTAINMENT. The Follies Lounge has both main and balcony levels, with banquette seating. On the stage is a video wall with 50 screens. A smaller venue, Finian's Rainbow Lounge, is where cabaret acts, including late-night adult comedy, are featured, as well as music for dancing.

SPA/FITNESS. There is a gymnasium with fine ocean views, full of muscle-pumping cardio-vascular equipment. There's also an aerobics studio, a hair and nails salon, and a sauna, as well as 11 treatment rooms, including one for couples' massages – all of which form The Spa. An outdoors rock-climbing wall has several climbing tracks.

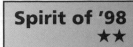

Spirit of '98
★★

Size: ....Boutique Ship	Passenger Decks: 4	Cabins (with private balcony): 0
Tonnage: 1,472	Total Crew: 30	Cabins (wheelchair accessible): 1
Lifestyle: ....Standard	Passengers	Wheelchair accessibility ....None
Cruise Line: ....Cruise West	(lower beds/all berths): 96/99	Cabin Current: ....110 volts
Former Names: ....*Pilgrim Belle,*	Passenger Space Ratio	Elevators: 1
Colonial Explorer, Victorian Empress	(lower beds/all berths): 15.3/14.8	Casino (gaming tables): ....No
Builder: ......Bender Shipbuilding (USA)	Crew/Passenger Ratio	Slot Machines: ....No
Original Cost: ....n/a	(lower beds/all berths): 3.2/3.2	Swimming Pools (outdoors): 0
Entered Service: 1984/1993	Cabins (total): 49	Swimming Pools (indoors): 0
Registry: ....USA	Size Range (sq ft/m): 80.0–510.0/	Whirlpools: 0
Length (ft/m): 192.0/58.2	7.4–47.3	Self-Service Launderette: ....No
Beam (ft/m): 40.0/12.1	Cabins (outside view): 49	Dedicated Cinema/Seats: ....No
Draft (ft/m): 9.3/2.8	Cabins (interior/no view): 0	Library: ....Some bookshelves
Propulsion/Propellers: diesel/2	Cabins (for one person): 0	

OVERALL SCORE: 946 OUT OF A POSSIBLE 2,000 POINTS

OVERVIEW. *Spirit of '98* is a distinctive-looking vessel built to resemble a late 1800s coastal cruising vessel. It is particularly suited to in-depth glacier spotting, and for close-in cruising along the coastline of Alaska. There is only one public room – the Grand Salon, although it is large. You are much closer to nature aboard a small cruise vessel such as this. There are no lines, no loud rap and rock music, no shows, no casino. There is a viewing area outdoors right at the ship's bow. There is an "open bridge" policy, and the company is concerned about protecting the natural environment.

The dress code is absolutely casual – not even a jacket for men, and no ties, please. However, do take comfortable walking shoes, as well as photographic materials for wildlife spotting. Smoking is permitted only on the outside decks. All tips are pooled by all staff, using the amounts recommended in the cruise line's brochure of $10 per passenger, per day (this is high for the services offered). The cruising areas are Alaska, the Pacific Northwest, and California's wine country. The onboard currency is the US dollar.

This ship is very small. There is an almost constant throbbing from the diesel engines/generator. There is no doctor on board, except for cruises in the Sea of Cortes. There are no cushioned pads for the sunloungers.

SUITABLE FOR: *Spirit of '98* is best suited to couples and single travelers (mostly over 60) who enjoy nature and wildlife up close and personal. It would particularly suit those seeking an all-American crew and cruise experience, and those who don't need the kind of entertainment or vapid parlor games that some large ships provide.

BERLITZ'S RATINGS

	Possible	Achieved
Ship	500	196
Accommodation	200	118
Food	400	189
Service	400	212
Entertainment	n/a	n/a
Cruise	500	231

ACCOMMODATION. There are six grades of cabin. The Owner's Suite is the largest accommodation in the Cruise West fleet, and has large picture windows on both sides. It consists of two rooms; a lounge/living room with game table, TV/VCR, refrigerator and fully stocked complimentary bar. There is a separate bedroom with a king-sized bed, and large bathroom with Jacuzzi tub.

There are also four irregular-shaped deluxe cabins at the front of the vessel, with decent closet space, a queen-sized bed (or twin beds that convert to a double bed), and a bathroom with a separate shower enclosure. Two of the cabins also have an extra sofa bed. The other cabins are quite small, but are reasonably comfortable, and have a large picture window. While a few cabins have queen-sized or double beds, most have single beds that cannot be moved together. Each cabin has its own private bathroom, although these really are tiny, and have a wall-mounted shower. There is no room service for food or snack items.

CUISINE. The Klondyke Dining Room, decorated in the style of 100 years ago, is elegant. The cuisine is decidedly plain and simple (though tasty) American fare. Expect lots of seafood. The ingredients are mostly fresh, and local. Wine and full bar services are provided.

ENTERTAINMENT. There is no formal entertainment, although dinner and after-dinner conversation with fellow passengers in the ship's lounge/bar really constitutes the entertainment each evening.

SPA/FITNESS. There are no spa or fitness facilities.

Spirit of Adventure
★★★

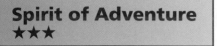

Size:	.Small Ship	Propulsion/Propellers:	..diesel (7,060kW)/2
Tonnage:	.9,570	Passenger Decks:	.8
Lifestyle:	.Standard	Total Crew:	.168
Cruise Line:	.Spirit of Adventure/ Saga Cruises	Passengers (lower beds/all berths):	.352/352
Former Names:Berlin, Princess Mahsuri, Berlin		Passenger Space Ratio	
Builder:	.Howaldtswerke Deutsche Werft (Germany)	(lower beds/all berths):	.27.1/27.1
		Crew/Passenger Ratio	
Original Cost:	.n/a	(lower beds/all berths):	.2.0/2.0
Entered Service:	.June 1980/Mar 2006	Cabins (total):	.206
Registry:	.The Bahamas	Size Range (sq ft/m):	.92.5–191.6/8.6–17.8
Length (ft/m):	.457.0/139.3	Cabins (outside view):	.174
Beam (ft/m):	.57.5/17.52	Cabins (interior/no view):	.32
Draft (ft/m):	.15.7/4.8	Cabins (for one person):	.60

Cabins (with private balcony):	.0
Cabins (wheelchair accessible):	.1
Wheelchair accessibility	.None
Cabin Current:	.220 volts
Elevators:	.1
Casino (gaming tables):	.No
Slot Machines:	.No
Swimming Pools (outdoors):	.1
Swimming Pools (indoors):	.1
Whirlpools:	.0
Self-Service Launderette:	.Yes
Dedicated Cinema/Seats:	.No
Library:	.Yes

OVERALL SCORE: 1,249 OUT OF A POSSIBLE 2,000 POINTS

OVERVIEW. *Spirit of Adventure,* a somewhat angular ship, has an all-white hull (with blue line between hull and superstructure), a balanced profile with buff-colored funnel and black top, and an ice-strengthened hull. As *Berlin,* the ship was featured for many years in the long running German TV show *Traumschiff* (Dream Ship).

In 1986 the ship was "chopped and stretched" and a 20-meter mid-section was added. Saga Holidays purchased it in April 2005, refurbished it for warm-weather cruising, and assigned it to sister company, Spirit of Adventure. Despite its small size, it is a good sea ship and rides well.

The interiors are crisp, contemporary and well-appointed, with tasteful European decor and furnishings. The Library is a fine room, with a 3,000-book library/DVD collection (open 24 hours), plus internet access at four computer stations.

The swimming pool, located aft, is tiny (it's really just a "dip" pool). The surrounding open-deck and sunbathing space is cramped, because it's in the same area as the outdoor seating for The Verandah dining venue. However, a reasonable amount of open-deck sunbathing space can be found on the uppermost deck, forward of the mast.

This well-run, soft-adventure ship provides a destination-intensive fly-cruise experience in a comfortable, well maintained, intimate ship for those who seek to explore and learn about less visited places, and who do not need constant entertainment. Itineraries include Europe, the Aegean Sea and Black Sea, Indian Ocean, Southeast Asia, and Antarctica.

The value for money is good. Insurance and staff gratuities are included in the cruise fare, as are scheduled or

BERLITZ'S RATINGS		
	Possible	Achieved
Ship	500	275
Accommodation	200	109
Food	400	276
Service	400	251
Entertainment	n/a	n/a
Cruise	500	338

charter flights (plus all airport fees and taxes), visas (for full UK-resident British citizens), port taxes, luggage handling, some shore excursions (others are available at extra cost), and lectures. Additionally, mountain bikes are available for anyone wanting to explore independently (or on escorted rides). The onboard currency is the British pound.

While the ship is not the latest, and doesn't have any cabins with balconies, its attention to passenger care, and the company's meet-and-greet and transfer services are extremely good. Shuttle buses are also provided in many ports of call. Onboard wines and drinks prices are very low in comparison with almost all other cruise lines.

Note that there is only one elevator – it doesn't go to the two topmost decks or to the Spa Aquarius on the lowermost deck – and the passenger accommodation hallways are rather narrow. However, it's the Filippino hotel crew that makes this ship so popular with passengers. It's also the manner in which Saga's meet-and-greet and passenger handling systems work, supplying the kind of care and attention many cruise lines seem to have forgotten about.

SUITABLE FOR: *Spirit of Adventure* is best suited to couples and single travelers over 21 who seek a holiday in a traditional ship setting that is unpretentious, yet provides a decent standard of accommodation, food and friendly service, as well as some interesting itineraries, destinations, and shore programs (many of which are included).

ACCOMMODATION. There are four types: Superior Suite, Junior Suite, Standard outside-view and interior (no view) cabins, in 20 price categories (12 for double occupancy and eight for single occupancy – a wide range). Most of the cabins are small by today's standards, but they are comfortable enough for short cruises. There are no balcony cabins. While most cabins have fixed twin beds that cannot be moved together (over 60 cabins do have a double bed), there are also many cabins for single occupancy (unlike most large ships today). The bathrooms have showers but no tubs, and storage space for toiletries is quite limited. All cabins have a refrigerator, TV/DVD player and a pair of binoculars. A range of Molton Brown personal toiletry items is provided for all accommodation grades. Note that cabins nearest the engine room do suffer from more noise, otherwise the cabins are quiet, although the insulation is actually rather poor.

The largest accommodation can be found in two Owner's Suites (Rhapsody and Sonata); both have a double bed, lounge area, more closet and drawer space, and larger bathroom.

Regardless of which accommodation is chosen, an extensive 24-hour room service menu is available.

The ships's 220-volt electricity system uses European-style two-pin round sockets, so UK passengers will need to bring converters.

CUISINE. The charming dining room has large, ocean-view picture windows and dark wood accents. There are tables for four, six, and dining is in an open seating arrangement. Regional specialties are featured, plus an international cuisine that includes many traditional British favorites. The chef often goes ashore in ports of call to buy fresh local fish and produce when possible.

Casual meals (breakfast, lunch and dinner) can be taken in The Verandah, a self-serve buffet-style venue with both indoor and outdoor seating areas; a self-help beverage station is open 24 hours a day. A good variety of well prepared and presented items is the norm. There's also 24-hour room service.

ENTERTAINMENT. The Sirocco Lounge is a single-level venue designed for cabaret performances, but used principally for musical concerts, destination and specialist subject lectures and guest speakers, and other social gatherings. The Yacht Club Lounge/Bar is the evening/late-night gathering place for pub-style entertainment and passenger participation events.

SPA/FITNESS. Spa Aquarius is an indoor health spa, including a shallow swimming pool, small fitness area, massage room, sauna and relaxation room – deep inside the ship on a lower deck (there is no elevator access). A beauty salon is in a separate location, adjacent to the Library. Some fitness classes are free, while others (such as Pilates/Yoga) incur a £5 charge. Sample treatment prices: Hot Stones Massage (£60 for 75 minutes); Combination Seaweed Wrap and Body Massage (£65 for 90 minutes); Well-Being Full Body Massage (£45 for 50 minutes); Facials (£42–£68).

Spirit of Alaska
★★

Size: . . . . .Boutique Ship
Tonnage: 529
Lifestyle: . . . . .Standard
Cruise Line: . . . . .Cruise West
Former Names: . . . .*Pacific Northwest Explorer*
Builder: . . . . .Blount Marine (USA)
Original Cost: .n/a
Entered Service: 1980/1991
Registry: . . . . .USA
Length (ft/m): 143.0/43.5
Beam (ft/m): 28.5/8.6
Draft (ft/m): 7.5/2.2
Propulsion/Propellers: diesel/1
Passenger Decks: 4
Total Crew: 21
Passengers
(lower beds/all berths): 78/82
Passenger Space Ratio
(lower beds/all berths): 6.7/6.4
Crew/Passenger Ratio
(lower beds/all berths): 3.9
abins (total): .39
Size Range (sq ft/m): . . .80–128/7.4–11.6
Cabins (outside view): 27
Cabins (interior/no view): 12
Cabins (for one person): 0
Cabins (with private balcony): 0
Cabins (wheelchair accessible): 0
Wheelchair accessibility . . . . .None
Cabin Current: . . . . .110 volts
Elevators: 0
Casino (gaming tables): . . . . .No
Slot Machines: . . . . .No
Swimming Pools (outdoors): 0
Swimming Pools (indoors): 0
Whirlpools: 0
Self-Service Launderette: 0
Dedicated Cinema/Seats: . . . . .No
Library: . . . . .Some bookshelves

OVERALL SCORE: 920

BERLITZ'S RATINGS

	Possible	Achieved
Ship	500	173
Accommodation	200	83
Food	400	199
Service	400	210
Entertainment	n/a	n/a
Cruise	500	255

Four of the ships operated by Cruise West *(Spirit of Alaska, Spirit of Columbia, Spirit of Discovery, Spirit of Endeavour)* **all are similar in terms of size, facilities, and the onboard dining and cruise experience, and so we have combined our assessment.**

OVERVIEW. These little ships are all about eco-tourism, and can take you close to nature and wildlife for an up-close experience. Cruising aboard these ships is all about simple pleasures and being with nature, especially as they're not allowed out into the big seas and oceans of the world.

Public rooms consist of a lounge that is a multi-functional space for meetings (plus a couple of bookcases with books about nature and wildlife), and a dining room. There are no cruise directors; instead, naturalists and other specialists give talks and act as leaders on shore excursions.

The staff aboard these small ships have to be multi-flexible, doing a little of this and a little of that. So, although service comes with a smile, it rarely comes with finesse or correctness. Small ship service can be compared to that provided by B&B establishments ashore – homely but not perfect. The captains have the flexibility to deviate to take in particular areas of interest.

The dress code is absolutely casual (not even a jacket for men, and no ties, please). However, do take comfortable walking shoes, as well as photographic materials for wildlife spotting. Smoking is permitted only on the outside decks. All tips are pooled by all staff, using the amounts recommended in the cruise line's brochure of $10 per passenger, per day (this is high for the services offered). The cruising areas are Alaska, the Pacific Northwest, and California's wine country. The onboard currency is the US dollar.

Passenger gripes: Because the ships are small, there is an almost constant throbbing from the diesel engines/generator. There is no doctor on board (except for cruises in the Sea of Cortes), and there are no cushioned pads for the deck lounge chairs.

SUITABLE FOR: These small ships are best suited to couples and single travelers (mostly over 60) who enjoy nature and wildlife up close and personal. It would particularly suit those seeking an all-American crew and cruise experience, and those who don't need the kind of entertainment large ships provide.

DINING. All meals are taken in the dining room at a set time (except for Continental breakfast, which is typically provided in the lounge), which tends to be early, which means it's regimented and not at all flexible. Don't expect outstanding cuisine (the galley is small, and the range of food items very limited, except for fresh local fish and seafood, which is normally very good); it's really simple Americana fare. As for wines, well, the choice is extremely limited (as in family restaurants on land).

ACCOMMODATION. There are several cabin categories, depending on the ship. All are small when compared to most cruise ships, but they are basically comfortable, and each cabin has a large picture window (a few cabins have portholes) and a (very) small clothes closet. A few cabins have double beds, but most have single beds that cannot be moved together (a few cabins may also have upper/lower berths instead of beds). Each has its own little bathroom, with a wall-mounted shower. Each cabin also has a small washbasin. There is no room service for food or snack items.

Bulky clothing for the outdoors is necessary in Alaska, but there's almost no storage space for it in the tiny, utilitarian cabins aboard these small ships.

ENTERTAINMENT. Dinner and after-dinner conversation with fellow passengers in the ship's lounge/bar constitutes the entertainment each evening.

SPA/FITNESS. There are no spa or fitness facilities

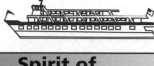

Spirit of Columbia
★★

Size: ....Boutique Ship
Tonnage: 514
Lifestyle: ....Standard
Cruise Line: ....Cruise West
Former Names: ....*New Shoreham II*
Builder: ....Blount Marine (USA)
Original Cost: ....n/a
Entered Service: 1979/1995
Registry: ....USA
Length (ft/m): 143.0/43.5
Beam (ft/m): 28.0/8.5
Draft (ft/m): 6.5/1.9
Propulsion/Propellers: diesel/2
Passenger Decks: 4
Total Crew: 20
Passengers
(lower beds/all berths): 78/80
Passenger Space Ratio
(lower beds/all berths): 6.5/6.4
Crew/Passenger Ratio
(lower beds/all berths): 3.9/4.0
Cabins (total): 39
Size Range (sq ft/m): .80–121.0/7.4–11.2
Cabins (outside view): 27
Cabins (interior/no view): 12
Cabins (for one person): 0
Cabins (with private balcony): 0
Cabins (wheelchair accessible): 0
Wheelchair accessibility ....None
Cabin Current: ....110 volts
Elevators: 0
Casino (gaming tables): ....No
Slot Machines: ....No
Swimming Pools (outdoors): 0
Swimming Pools (indoors): 0
Whirlpools: 0
Self-Service Launderette: 0
Dedicated Cinema/Seats: ....No
Library: ....Some bookshelves

OVERALL SCORE: 919

BERLITZ'S RATINGS

	Possible	Achieved
Ship	500	174
Accommodation	200	82
Food	400	199
Service	400	209
Entertainment	n/a	n/a
Cruise	500	255

Spirit of Discovery
★★

Size: ....Boutique Ship
Tonnage: 730
Lifestyle: ....Standard
Cruise Line: ....Cruise West
Former Names: .*Independence, Columbia*
Builder: ....Eastern Shipping (USA)
Original Cost: ....n/a
Entered Service: 1982/1992
Registry: ....USA
Length (ft/m): 166.0/50.5
Beam (ft/m): 37.0/11.2
Draft (ft/m): 7.5/2.2
Propulsion/Propellers: diesel/2
Passenger Decks: 3
Total Crew: 20
Passengers
(lower beds/all berths): 84/84
Passenger Space Ratio
(lower beds/all berths): 10.8/10.8
Crew/Passenger Ratio
(lower beds/all berths): 4.2/4.2
Cabins (total): 43
Size Range (sq ft/m): ..64–126.0/5.9–11.7
Cabins (outside view): 43
Cabins (interior/no view): 0
Cabins (for one person): 2
Cabins (with private balcony): 0
Cabins (wheelchair accessible): 0
Wheelchair accessibility ....None
Cabin Current: ....110 volts
Elevators: 0
Casino (gaming tables): ....No
Slot Machines: ....No
Swimming Pools (outdoors): 0
Swimming Pools (indoors): 0
Whirlpools: 0
Self-Service Launderette: ....No
Dedicated Cinema/Seats: ....No
Library: ....Some bookshelves

OVERALL SCORE: 920

BERLITZ'S RATINGS

	Possible	Achieved
Ship	500	175
Accommodation	200	82
Food	400	199
Service	400	209
Entertainment	n/a	n/a
Cruise	500	255

Spirit of Endeavour
★★

Size: ....Boutique Ship
Tonnage: 1,425
Lifestyle: ....Standard
Cruise Line: ....Cruise West
Former Names: ....*Newport Clipper*
Builder: ....Blount Marine (USA)
Original Cost: ....n/a
Entered Service: 1983/1996
Registry: ....USA
Length (ft/m): 207.0/63.0
Beam (ft/m): 37.0/11.2
Draft (ft/m): 8.0/2.4
Propulsion/Propellers: diesel/2
Passenger Decks: 4
Total Crew: 32
Passengers
(lower beds/all berths): 102/107
Passenger Space Ratio
(lower beds/all berths): 13.9/13.3
Crew/Passenger Ratio
(lower beds/all berths): 3.1/3.3
Cabins (total): 51
Size Range (sq ft/m): ...80–128/7.4–11.6
Cabins (outside view): 51
Cabins (interior/no view): 0
Cabins (for one person): 0
Cabins (with private balcony): 0
Cabins (wheelchair accessible): 0
Wheelchair accessibility ....None
Cabin Current: ....110 volts
Elevators: 0
Casino (gaming tables): ....No
Slot Machines: ....No
Swimming Pools (outdoors): 0
Swimming Pools (indoors): 0
Whirlpools: 0
Self-Service Launderette: 0
Dedicated Cinema/Seats: ....No
Library: ....Some bookshelves

OVERALL SCORE: 920

BERLITZ'S RATINGS

	Possible	Achieved
Ship	500	175
Accommodation	200	82
Food	400	199
Service	400	209
Entertainment	n/a	n/a
Cruise	500	255

Spirit of America
★★

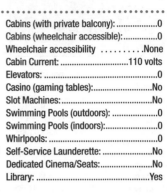

Size:	Boutique Ship	Passenger Decks:	4	Cabins (with private balcony):	0
Tonnage:	1,471	Total Crew:	29	Cabins (wheelchair accessible):	0
Lifestyle:	Standard	Passengers		Wheelchair accessibility	None
Cruise Line:	Cruise West	(lower beds/all berths):	102/111	Cabin Current:	110 volts
Former Names:	Spirit of Glacier Bay,	Passenger Space Ratio		Elevators:	0
	Spirit of Nantucket, Nantucket Clipper	(lower beds/all berths):	14.4/13.2	Casino (gaming tables):	No
Builder:	Jeffboat (USA)	Crew/Passenger Ratio		Slot Machines:	No
Original Cost:	$9 million	(lower beds/all berths):	3.5/3.8	Swimming Pools (outdoors):	0
Entered Service:	Dec 1984/May 2008	Cabins (total):	51	Swimming Pools (indoors):	0
Registry:	USA	Size Range (sq ft/m):	120.5–137.7/	Whirlpools:	0
Length (ft/m):	207.0/63.00		11.2–12.8	Self-Service Launderette:	No
Beam (ft/m):	37.0/11.20	Cabins (outside view):	51	Dedicated Cinema/Seats:	No
Draft (ft/m):	8.0/2.40	Cabins (interior/no view):	0	Library:	Yes
Propulsion/Propellers:	diesel (700 kW)/2	Cabins (for one person):	0		

OVERALL SCORE: 948 OUT OF A POSSIBLE 2,000 POINTS

OVERVIEW. This small, shallow draft, American-registered ship, renamed in 2008, was built for coastal and inland cruises and is very maneuverable. It has been quite well maintained, although it is now showing signs of aging, and some serious attention is needed. There is a wrap-around teakwood walking deck outdoors.

The extremely high-density ship has only two public rooms: the dining room, and an observation lounge. Passengers can visit the bridge at any time. This ship is not recommended for night owls. Although passengers are typically over 60, there is no elevator.

The service is provided by young, friendly all-American college-age types. This is most definitely an "Americana" experience for those seeking particularly to learn more about the coastal ports around the USA, including Alaska. The ship has a casual, unstructured lifestyle, rather like a small (but certainly not luxurious) country club afloat. This should not be compared with big-ship ocean cruising.

Specialist lecturers are part of every cruise. These highlight the learning experience that is an essential part of cruising with Cruise West. As the ship is often in coastal destinations, a few bicycles would be a welcome addition for many passengers. There is a no-smoking policy for all interior areas. The onboard currency is the US dollar.

The engine noise level is high when the ship is underway. The per diem price is steep for what you get, and the air fare is extra.

SUITABLE FOR: *Spirit of America* is best suited to couples and single travelers who enjoy nature and wildlife up close and personal, and who would not dream of cruising in the

BERLITZ'S RATINGS		
	Possible	Achieved
Ship	500	199
Accommodation	200	76
Food	400	209
Service	400	231
Entertainment	n/a	n/a
Cruise	500	233

mainstream sense, aboard ships with large numbers of people. This is for outdoors types who don't need entertainment or mindless parlor games, but do want an all-American cruise experience.

ACCOMMODATION. There are four grades of all-outside cabins. All are extremely small and equipped in a very basic manner (think mobile home rather than cruise ships or hotels). They are fairly tastefully furnished, with wood-accented trim and good sound insulation. The windows are fixed and cannot be opened.

Honeymooners and lovers should note that beds are of the twin variety, and are bolted to the deck and wall.

Bathrooms are cramped and the shower head is fixed, but, thoughtfully, a night-light is provided. There's little space for personal toiletries. No cabins have personal balconies.

CUISINE. The dining room is warm and inviting, and has large picture windows. There is one seating, and you can sit with whomever you wish. There are no tables for two. The ship has simple and plain American cuisine that is quite tasty, although the menu choice is limited and the portions are small. The chefs are trained by the Culinary Institute of America, and all ingredients are fresh. The chocolate chip cookies are popular and are served at various times, typically in the lounge.

ENTERTAINMENT. The main entertainment is dinner and after-dinner conversation with fellow passengers.

SPA/FITNESS. No facilities aboard this very small vessel.

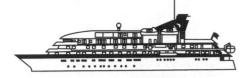

Spirit of Oceanus
★★★

Size: ....Boutique Ship	Passenger Decks: 5	Cabins (with private balcony): 12
Tonnage: 4,200	Total Crew: 64	Cabins (wheelchair accessible): 0
Lifestyle: ....Standard	Passengers	Wheelchair accessibility ....None
Cruise Line: ....Cruise West	(lower beds/all berths): 120/127	Cabin Current: ....110 volts
Former Names: ....*MegaStar Sagittarius,*	Passenger Space Ratio	Dining Rooms: 1
Sun Viva, Renaissance Five	(lower beds/all berths): 35.0/33.0	Elevators: 1
Builder: ....Nuovi Cantieri Apuania	Crew/Passenger Ratio	Casino (gaming tables): ....No
(Italy)	(lower beds/all berths): 1.8/4.7	Slot Machines: ....No
Entered Service: 1991/2001	Cabins (total): 60	Swimming Pools (outdoors): 1
Registry: ....The Bahamas	Size Range (sq ft/m): 215.0–353.0/	Swimming Pools (indoors): 0
Length (ft/m): 294.5/89.7	20.0–32.7	Whirlpools: 1
Beam (ft/m): 50.1/15.30	Cabins (outside view): 60	Self-Service Launderette: ....No
Draft (ft/m): 13.2/4.05	Cabins (interior/no view): 0	Dedicated Cinema/Seats: ....No
Propulsion/Propellers: .diesel (5,000kW)/2	Cabins (for one person): 0	Library: ....Yes

OVERALL SCORE: 1,222 OUT OF A POSSIBLE 2,000 POINTS

OVERVIEW. *Spirit of Oceanus* has a contemporary exterior, a private yacht-like look and handsome styling with twin, flared funnels. The navigation bridge is a well-rounded half-moon design. There is a teakwood promenade deck outdoors, and a reasonable amount of open deck and sunbathing space. The deck furniture is teak and the sunloungers have thick cushioned pads. There is a teakwood water sports platform at the stern of the ship (not used in Alaska), plus a number of Zodiac inflatable rubber landing craft. Snorkeling gear is provided (not used in Alaska).

The main lounge, the focal point for social activities, has six pillars that destroy sightlines to the small stage area. There is a very small book and video library.

The ship was acquired by Cruise West in 2001 and is the only ocean-going vessel in its fleet. It cruises Alaska and British Columbia in summer, and sails to Tahiti, the Fijian Islands and other Pacific Ocean itineraries in winter. In 2010 it will undertake a 335-day world cruise. The onboard currency is the US dollar.

SUITABLE FOR: *Spirit of Oceanus* is best suited to couples and single travelers who enjoy nature and wildlife up close in a contemporary small-ship setting, and who would not dream of cruising in the mainstream sense aboard ships with large numbers of people.

ACCOMMODATION. There are six price categories. Fine all-outside-view cabins (called "suites" in the brochure) combine highly polished imitation rosewood paneling with lots of mirrors, and fine, hand-crafted Italian furniture. All suites have twin beds that can convert to a queen-sized bed, a sit-

BERLITZ'S RATINGS

	Possible	Achieved
Ship	500	339
Accommodation	200	150
Food	400	215
Service	400	237
Entertainment	n/a	n/a
Cruise	500	281

ting area with three-person sofa, one individual chair, coffee table, mini-bar/refrigerator (stocked with juices and bottled water), TV/VCR, direct-dial satellite telephone, and a bowl of fresh fruit on embarkation day. While closet space is good, space for stowing luggage is tight, and there is little drawer space. There are no music channels in the cabins, and there is no switch to turn off announcements in your cabin.

The marble bathrooms are compact units that have showers (no bathrooms have a tub) with fold-down (plastic) seat, real teakwood floor, marble vanity, large mirror, recessed towel rail , and built-in hairdryer. There is a high "lip" into the bathroom.

CUISINE. The Restaurant, which has an open-seating policy, is bright, elegant, welcoming, and non-smoking. It is on the lowest deck and has portholes rather than windows, due to international maritime construction and insurance regulations. There are tables for two, four, six, or eight. Dinners are normally sit-down affairs, although, depending on the itinerary and length of cruise, there could be an occasional buffet.

Breakfast and lunch are typically self-serve buffets and can be taken at the poolside (weather permitting), in your cabin, or in the restaurant.

ENTERTAINMENT. There is no formal entertainment, so dinner and after-dinner conversation with fellow passengers in the ship's lounge/bar really constitutes the entertainment each evening.

SPA/FITNESS. Small fitness center. Massage is available.

Spirit of Yorktown
★★

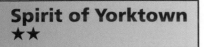

Size: . . . . .Boutique Ship	Total Crew: 33	Cabins (wheelchair accessible): 0
Tonnage: 2,354	Passengers	Wheelchair accessibility . . . . .None
Lifestyle: . . . . .Standard	(lower beds/all berths): 138/138	Cabin Current: . . . . .110 volts
Cruise Line: . . . . .Cruise West	Passenger Space Ratio	Elevators: 0
Former Names: . . . . .Yorktown Clipper	(lower beds/all berths): 17.0/17.0	Casino (gaming tables): . . . . .No
Builder: . . . .First Coast Shipbuilding (USA)	Crew/Passenger Ratio	Slot Machines: . . . . .No
Original Cost: . . . .$12 million	(lower beds/all berths): 3.4/3.4	Swimming Pools (outdoors): 0
Entered Service: . . . . .Apr 1988	Cabins (total): 69	Swimming Pools (indoors): 0
Registry: . . . . .USA	Size Range (sq ft/m): 121.0–138.0/	Whirlpools: 0
Length (ft/m): 257.0/78.30	11.2–12.8	Self-Service Launderette: . . . . .No
Beam (ft/m): 43.0/13.10	Cabins (outside view): 69	Dedicated Cinema/Seats: . . . . .No
Draft (ft/m): 8.0/2.43	Cabins (interior/no view): 0	Library: . . . . .Yes
Propulsion/Propellers: .diesel (1,044kW)/2	Cabins (for one person): 0	
Passenger Decks: 4	Cabins (with private balcony): 0	

BERLITZ'S OVERALL SCORE: 949 OUT OF A POSSIBLE 2,000 POINTS

OVERVIEW. *Yorktown Clipper* was built specifically to operate coastal and inland waterway cruises. The draft is small, and the ship has good maneuverability, and has been quite well maintained since new, although it is showing signs of wear and tear. There is a teakwood outdoor sun deck. Inflatable rubber Zodiac craft are used for close-in shore excursions.

Inside, there is a glass-walled observation lounge, the ship's principal public room. This ship offers a decidedly American experience for those seeking to learn more about the coastal ports around the USA during the summer months, while Caribbean cruises are operated in winter.

The lifestyle is casual and unregimented – rather like a small, congenial country club. There are always one or two lecturers aboard, which enhances the learning experience. The price, however, is very high for what you get when compared to many other ships, and the air fare is extra. There is a no-smoking policy throughout all interior areas.

This is a high-density ship, with only two public rooms: a dining room and a lounge. The engine noise level is high when the ship is underway. Although there is a wrap-around teakwood walking deck outdoors, it is quite narrow. The per diem price is steep, and the air fare is extra. There is no elevator, which can be a disadvantage for older passengers.

SUITABLE FOR: The vessel is best suited to couples and single travelers who enjoy nature and wildlife at close range. This is for outdoors types who don't need constant entertainment, but do want an all-American cruise experience. The onboard currency is the US dollar.

BERLITZ'S RATINGS

	Possible	Achieved
Ship	500	200
Accommodation	200	76
Food	400	209
Service	400	231
Entertainment	n/a	n/a
Cruise	500	233

ACCOMMODATION. The all-outside cabins are really quite small (think mobile home, not cruise ship), but, with lots of wood-accented trim and restful colors, they are marginally comfortable and tastefully furnished. There are no cabins with private balconies, and the fixed windows cannot be opened. The bathrooms, too, are small, with little space for toiletries, but a night-light is provided, so you don't have to turn on bright lights in the middle of the night – a thoughtful touch. Fixed shower heads are provided, making it difficult to wash thoroughly. There is no room service for food and beverage items, as found aboard larger ships.

CUISINE. The dining room is warm and fairly inviting and has large picture windows, although there are no tables for two. There is one open seating, so you can dine with whom you wish. The service is provided by a young, all-American, mid-western team, whose friendly approach makes up for a lack of finesse.

The cuisine is generally of a good quality, made from locally purchased fresh ingredients. There is little menu choice, but the food provided is nicely presented. There is an adequate but very limited selection of breads and fruits, and the wine list is generally limited to American wines.

ENTERTAINMENT. There is no formal entertainment. Dinner and after-dinner conversation with fellow passengers in the ship's lounge/bar really constitute the main diversion each evening.

SPA/FITNESS. No facilities are provided.

Splendour of the Seas
★★★★

Size: . . . . .Large Resort Ship	Passenger Decks: 11	Cabins (with private balcony): 231
Tonnage: 69,130	Total Crew: 720	Cabins (wheelchair accessible): 17
Lifestyle: . . . . .Standard	Passengers	Wheelchair accessibility . . . . .Good
Cruise Line: Royal Caribbean International	(lower beds/all berths): 1,804/2,064	Cabin Current: . . . . .110 and 220 volts
Former Names: . . . . .none	Passenger Space Ratio	Elevators: 11
Builder: . . . . .Chantiers de l'Atlantique	(lower beds/all berths): 38.3/33.4	Casino (gaming tables): . . . . .Yes
(France)	Crew/Passenger Ratio	Slot Machines: . . . . .Yes
Original Cost: . . . .$325 million	(lower beds/all berths): 2.5/2.8	Swimming Pools (outdoors): 2
Entered Service: . . . . .Mar 1996	Cabins (total): 902	(1 with sliding roof)
Registry: . . . . .The Bahamas	Size Range (sq ft/m): 137.7–1,147.4/	Swimming Pools (indoors): 0
Length (ft/m): 867.0/264.2	12.8–106.6	Whirlpools: 4
Beam (ft/m): 105.0/32.0	Cabins (outside view): 575	Self-Service Launderette: . . . . .No
Draft (ft/m): 24.5/7.3	Cabins (interior/no view): 327	Dedicated Cinema/Seats: . . . . .No
Propulsion/Propellers: diesel(40,200kW)/2	Cabins (for one person): 0	Library: . . . . .Yes

OVERALL SCORE: 1,415 OUT OF A POSSIBLE 2,000 POINTS

OVERVIEW. *Splendour of the Seas,* sister to *Legend of the Seas,* has a contemporary profile that looks somewhat unbalanced (although it grows on you), and does have a nicely tiered stern. The pool deck amidships overhangs the hull to provide an extremely wide deck, while still allowing the ship to navigate the Panama Canal. With engines placed amidships, there is little noise and no noticeable vibration, and the ship has an operating speed of up to 24 knots.

The interior decor is very colorful, but perhaps a little too glitzy for European tastes. The outside light is brought inside in many places, with an extensive amount of glass area that provides contact with sea and air (more than 2 acres/8,000 sq. meters of glass). There's an innovative single-level sliding glass roof (not a magrodome) over the more formal setting of one of two swimming pools, providing a large, multi-activity, all-weather indoor/outdoor area, called the Solarium. The glass roof provides shelter for the Roman-style pool and adjacent health and fitness facilities (which are superb) and slides aft to cover the miniature golf course when required – both cannot be covered at the same time, however.

Golfers might enjoy the 18-hole, 6,000 sq.-ft (557 sq.-meter) miniature golf course, with the topography of a real golf course, complete with trees, foliage, grass, bridges, water hazards, and lighting for play at night. The holes are 155–230 sq. ft. (14–21 sq. meters).

Inside, two full entertainment decks are sandwiched between five decks full of cabins. The tiered and balconied showlounge, which covers two decks, is expansive and has excellent sightlines, and very comfortable seats. Several large-scale production shows are provided here, and the orchestra

BERLITZ'S RATINGS

	Possible	Achieved
Ship	500	401
Accommodation	200	153
Food	400	227
Service	400	274
Entertainment	100	76
Cruise	400	284

pit can be raised or lowered as required. A multi-tiered seven-deck-high atrium lobby, complete with a huge stainless steel sculpture, connects with the impressive Viking Crown Lounge via glass-walled elevators. The casino is really expansive, overly glitzy and absolutely packed. The library, outside of which is a bust of Shakespeare, is a fine facility, and has more than 2,000 books.

The casino could be somewhat disorienting, with its mirrored walls and lights flashing everywhere, although it is no different to those found in Las Vegas gaming halls. There is, sadly, no separate cinema. As with any large ship, you can expect to find yourself standing in lines for embarkation, disembarkation, buffets and shore excursions, although the company does its best to minimize such lines.

ACCOMMODATION. There are 17 cabin price grades, which is far too many. The price you pay will depend on the grade, location and size you choose.

Royal Caribbean International has realized that small cabins do not please passengers. The company therefore set about designing a ship with much larger standard cabins than in any of the company's previous vessels – except for sister ship *Legend of the Seas.*

Some cabins on Deck 8 also have a larger door for wheelchair access in addition to the 17 cabins for the disabled, and the ship is very accessible, with ample ramped areas and sloping decks.

All cabins have a sitting area and beds that convert to double configuration, and there is ample closet and drawer space, although there is not much space around the bed – and the showers could have been better designed.

Cabins with balconies have glass railings rather than steel/wood to provide less intrusive sightlines.

The largest accommodation, the Royal Suite, is a superb living space for those who can afford the best. It is beautifully designed, finely decorated, and has a baby grand piano and whirlpool bathtub. Quiet sitting areas are located adjacent to the best cabins amidships. There are no cabins for singles.

CUISINE. The two-deck-high King and I dining room has dramatic two-deck-high glass side walls, so many passengers both upstairs and downstairs can see both the ocean and each other in reflection (it would, perhaps, have been even better located at the stern), but it is quite noisy when full (call it atmosphere). When you book, choose one of two seatings, or "My Time Dining" (eat when you want, during dining room hours).

For casual meals, there are two informal options: a cavernous indoor-outdoor cafe, located towards the bow and above the bridge, and a good-sized snack area.

ENTERTAINMENT. The 42nd Street Theater seats 802 and is a single-level showlounge with tiered seating levels. The sightlines are generally good from almost all seats. Strong cabaret acts are also featured in the main show lounge.

Other cabaret acts are featured in the Top Hat Lounge, and these include late-night adult (blue) comedy, as well as live music for dancing. A number of other bars and lounges have live music of differing types.

SPA/FITNESS. The ShipShape Fitness Center has a gymnasium (it is located on the port side of the ship, aft of the funnel), and has a small selection of high-tech muscle-pumping equipment. There is also an aerobics studio (classes are offered in a variety of keep-fit regimes), a beauty salon, and a sauna, as well as rooms for such pampering treatments as massages, facials, etc. While the facilities are quite small when compared with those aboard the company's newer ships, they are adequate for the short cruises that this ship operates. The spa is operated by Steiner, a specialist concession.

For the more sporting, there is activity galore – including a rock-climbing wall, with several separate climbing tracks. It is outdoors at the aft end of the funnel.

● **For more extensive general information about the Royal Caribbean cruise experience, see pages 151–6.**

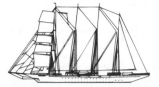

Star Clipper
★★★★

Size: . . . . .Boutique Ship	Sail Area (sq. ft/sq.m): 36,221/3,365/	Cabins (outside view): 79
Tonnage: 2,298	16 manually furled sails	Cabins (interior/no view): 6
Lifestyle: . . . . .Standard	Main Propulsion: . . . . .sail power	Cabins (for one person): 0
Cruise Line: . . . . .Star Clippers	Propulsion/Propellers: . . . . .diesel	Cabins (with private balcony): 0
Former Names: . . . . .none	(1,030kW)/1	Cabins (wheelchair accessible): 0
Builder: . . . . .Scheepswerven van	Passenger Decks: 4	Wheelchair accessibility . . . . .None
Langerbrugge (Belgium)	Total Crew: 72	Cabin Current: . . . . .110 volts
Original Cost: . . . .$30 million	Passengers	Elevators: 0
Entered Service: . . . . .May 1992	(lower beds/all berths): 170/180	Casino (gaming tables): . . . . .No
Registry: . . . . .Luxembourg	Passenger Space Ratio	Slot Machines: .No
Length (ft/m): 378.9/115.5	(lower beds/all berths): 13.5/12.7	Swimming Pools (outdoors): 2
Beam (ft/m): 49.2/15.0	Crew/Passenger Ratio	Whirlpools: 0
Draft (ft/m): 17.7/5.6	(lower beds/all berths): 2.3/2.5	Self-Service Launderette: . . . . .No
Type of Vessel: . . . . .barkentine schooner	Cabins (total): .85	Library: . . . . .Yes
Number of Masts: . . . . .4 (208 ft)	Size Range (sq ft/m): .95.0–225.0/8.8–21.0	

OVERALL SCORE: 1,402 OUT OF A POSSIBLE 2,000 POINTS

OVERVIEW. *Star Clipper* is one of a pair of almost identical tall ships – its sister ship is *Star Flyer*, which was the first clipper sailing ship to be built for 140 years, became the first commercial sailing vessel to cross the North Atlantic in 90 years. It is, first and foremost a sailing vessel with cruise accommodation that evokes memories of the 19th-century clipper sailing ships. This is an accurate four-mast, barkentine-rigged vessel with graceful lines, a finely shaped hull and masts that are 206 ft (63 meters) tall.

Breathtaking when under full sail, the ship displays excellent sea manners (healing is kept to a very comfortable 6%). This working sailing ship relies on the wind about 80 percent of the time. For the nautically-minded, the sailing rig consists of 16 sails. These include: fore staysail, inner jib, outer jib, flying jib, fore course, lower topsail, upper topsail, lower topgallant, upper topgallant, main staysail, upper main staysail, mizzen staysail, main fisherman, jigger staysail, mizzen fisherman, and spanker. The square sails are furled electronically by custom-made winches.

During a typical cruise, you'll be able to climb the main mast to a platform 75 ft/25 meters above the sea and help with the ropes and sails at appropriate times – this could be an unnerving experience if you're not used to heights, but it is an exhilarating experience when the ship is moving, under sail. However, one really neat chill-out pleasure is to lie in the netting at the front of the ship's bows, watching the bow wake as it streams along the ship's sides.

A diesel engine is used as the main propulsion engine when the ship is not under sail (in poor wind conditions), and two generators are provided for supplying electrical

BERLITZ'S RATINGS		
	Possible	Achieved
Ship	500	382
Accommodation	200	134
Food	400	249
Service	400	271
Entertainment	n/a	n/a
Cruise	500	366

power and for desalinating the approximately 40 tons of seawater each day for shipboard needs – engine room visits are offered. The crew performs almost every task, including hoisting, trimming, winching and repairing the sails (helped by electric winches). Water sports facilities include a water ski boat, sunfish, scuba and snorkel equipment, and eight Zodiac inflatable craft. Sports directors provide basic dive instruction for a fee.

Some of the amenities of large modern cruise vessels are provided, such as air conditioning, cashless cruising, occasional live music, a small shop, and two pools to "dip" in. Inside the vessel, classic Edwardian nautical decor throughout is clean, warm, intimate, and inviting. The paneled library has a fireplace, and chairs that are comfortable. A cruise aboard it means no lines, no hassle, and "Sailing a Square Rigger" and other nautical classes are a part of every cruise, as is stargazing at night.

Depending on the itinerary and region, passengers may gather for "captain's story time," normally held on an open deck area adjacent to the bridge, or bar – which, incidentally, has a collection of single malt whiskies. The captain may explain sailing maneuvers when changing the rigging or directing the ship as it sails into port, and notes the important events of the day.

The vessel promotes total informality and provides a carefree sailing cruise experience in a totally unstructured and relaxed setting at a reasonable price. Take minimal clothing: short sleeved shirts and shorts for the men, shorts and tops for the women are the order of the day (smart casual at night). No jackets, ties, high-heeled shoes, cocktail dresses, or formal wear are needed. In fact, you should take only casual clothes, and flat shoes (there are lots of ropes and sailing rig to negotiate on deck, not to mention the high thresholds to climb over and steps to negotiate – this is, after all a tall ship, not a cruise ship). The deck crew consists of real sailors, brought up with yachts and tall ships – most wouldn't set foot aboard a "normal" cruise ship.

It is no exaggeration to say that to be sailing aboard either *Star Clipper* or *Star Flyer* is to seem to have died and gone to yachtsman's heaven, as there is plenty of sailing during the course of a typical one-week cruise. The whole experience evokes the feeling of sailing aboard some famous private yacht, and even the most jaded passenger should enjoy the feel of the wind and sea close at hand. Just don't expect fine food to go with what is decidedly a fine sailing experience – which is what Star Clipper is all about. Note that 12.5% is added to all beverage purchases. The onboard currency is the euro, wherever the ship operates. Tips are pooled – the suggested amount is 8 euros per passenger, per day.

Note that the type of the internal stairways are short and steep, as in all sailing vessels, and so this ship cannot be recommended for anyone with walking disabilities. Also, there is no doctor on board, although there is a nurse.

SUITABLE FOR: *Star Clipper* is best suited to couples and singles who would probably never even consider a "normal" cruise ship, but who enjoy sailing and the thrill of ocean and wind, but want these things wrapped in a package that includes accommodation, decent food, like-minded companions, interesting destinations, an almost unstructured lifestyle, and for those who don't want the bother of owning or chartering their own yacht.

ACCOMMODATION. There are six cabin price grades plus one owner's suite. The price will depend on grade, location and size; generally, the higher the deck, the more expensive a cabin. The cabins are quite well equipped and comfortable; they have rosewood-trimmed cabinetry and wall-to-wall carpeting, two-channel audio, color TV and individual DVD player, lockable personal safe and full-length mirrors. The bathrooms are very compact but practical units, and have gray marble tiling, glazed rosewood toiletries cabinet and paneling, some under-shelf storage space, washbasin, shower stall and toilet. There is no "lip" to prevent water from the shower from moving over the bathroom floor.

Individual European 100% individual cotton duvets are provided. There is no cabin food or beverage service.

The deluxe cabins (called "deck cabins") are larger, and additional features include a full-sized Jacuzzi tub (or corner tub), flat-screen television and individual DVD player, and mini-bar/refrigerator (note, however, that these cabins are subject to noise pollution from the same-deck Tropical Bar's music at night (typically until midnight), from the electric winches during sail maneuvers, and from noisy walkabout exercisers in the early morning.

The cabins in the lowest price grade are interior cabins with upper and lower berths, and not two lower beds – so someone will need to be agile to climb up to the upper berth

(a ladder is provided, of course). A handful of cabins have a third, upper Pullman-style berth (good for families with children, but note that closet and drawer space will be at a premium with three persons in a cabin, so do take only the minimal amount of clothing). Luggage can be stored under the bed, where extra large drawers are also provided.

CUISINE. The dining room is quite attractive, and has lots of wood and brass accenting and nautical decor. There are self-serve buffet breakfasts and lunches, together with a mix of buffet and à la carte dinners (generally with a choice of three entrées) in a one (open) seating environment.

The seating arrangement, mostly at tables of six, adjacent to a porthole or inboard, makes it difficult for waiters to serve properly – food is passed along the tables that occupy a porthole position. However, you can dine with whomever you wish, and this is supposed to be a casual experience, after all.

While cuisine aboard the Star Clippers ships is perhaps less than the advertised "gourmet" excellence (as far as presentation and choice are concerned), it is fairly creative – and there's plenty of it. Also, one has to take into account the small galley provided – changed to a better layout in a recent refurbishment. Passenger niggles include repetitious breakfasts and lunchtime salad items (lack of space prevents more choices), although most passengers are happy with the dinners, which tend to be good, although there is a lack of green vegetables.

Perhaps fewer passenger cabins and more room in the galley would have enabled the chefs to provide a better dining experience than the present arrangement. There is a good choice of bread rolls, pastry items, and fruit.

Tea and coffee is available 24 hours a day (mugs, tea cups and saucers are provided), in the lounge (in view of the fact that there is no cabin food service. Drinks prices include a service charge, currently 12.5%.

ENTERTAINMENT. There are no entertainment shows as such, except for an occasional local folklore show from ashore, nor are any expected by passengers aboard a tall ship such as this. There is, however, live music, which is typically provided by a solo lounge pianist/singer. Otherwise, dinner is the main evening event, as well as "captain's story-time" recapping the day's events, and conversation with fellow passengers.

During the day, when the ship is sailing, passengers can learn about the sails (or their repair), and the captain or chief officer will give briefings as the sails are being furled and unfurled. The closest this tall ship comes to any kind of "show" is perhaps on provided by members of the crew, plus a few traditional sea shanties.

SPA/FITNESS. There are no fitness facilities, or beauty salon, although a masseuse provides Oriental massage. However, for recreation, the ship does have a water sports program. Facilities include kayaks, a water ski boat, sunfish, scuba and snorkel equipment, and eight Zodiac inflatable craft. Use of scuba facilities costs extra.

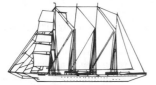

Star Flyer
★★★★

Size: ....Boutique Ship	Sail Area (sq. ft/sq.m): 36,221/3,365/	Cabins (outside view): 79
Tonnage: 2,298	16 manually furled sails	Cabins (interior/no view): 6
Lifestyle: ....Standard	Main Propulsion: ....sail power	Cabins (for one person): 0
Cruise Line: ....Star Clippers	Propulsion/Propellers: ....diesel	Cabins (with private balcony): 0
Former Names: ....none	(1,030kW)/1	Cabins (wheelchair accessible): 0
Builder: ....Sheepswerven van	Passenger Decks:...................4	Wheelchair accessibility ....None
Langerbrugge (Belgium)	Total Crew: 72	Cabin Current: ....110 volts
Original Cost: ....$25 million	Passengers	Elevators: 0
Entered Service: ....July 1991	(lower beds/all berths): 170/180	Casino (gaming tables): ....No
Registry: ....Luxembourg	Passenger Space Ratio	Slot Machines: ....No
Length (ft/m): 378.9/115.5	(lower beds/all berths): 13.5/12.7	Swimming Pools (outdoors): 2
Beam (ft/m): 49.2/15.0	Crew/Passenger Ratio	Whirlpools: 0
Draft (ft/m): 17.7/5.6	(lower beds/all berths): 2.3/2.5	Self-Service Launderette: ....No
Type of Vessel: .....barkentine schooner	Cabins (total): 85	Library: ....Yes
No. of Masts: ....4 (208 ft)	Size Range (sq ft/m): .95.0–225.9/8.8–21.0	

OVERALL SCORE: 1,402 OUT OF A POSSIBLE 2,000 POINTS

OVERVIEW. *Star Flyer* is one of a pair of almost identical tall ships (its sister ship is *Star Clipper*). It is, first and foremost, a sailing vessel with cruise accommodation that evokes memories of the 19th-century clipper sailing ships. This is an accurate four-mast, barkentine-rigged vessel with graceful lines, a finely shaped hull and masts that are 206 ft (63 meters) tall. The ship now sails year-round from Papeete, Tahiti.

Breathtaking when under full sail, the ship displays excellent sea manners. This working sailing ship relies on the wind about 80 percent of the time. A diesel engine is used as backup in emergencies, for generating electrical power and for desalinating the approximately 40 tons of seawater each day for shipboard needs. The crew performs almost every task, including hoisting, trimming, winching and repairing the sails (helped by electric winches).

The whole cruise experience evokes the feeling of sailing aboard some famous private yacht a century ago. *Star Flyer*, the first clipper sailing ship to be built for 140 years, became the first commercial sailing vessel to cross the North Atlantic in 90 years.

Some of the amenities of large modern cruise vessels are provided, such as air-conditioning, cashless cruising, occasional live music, a small shop, and two pools to "dip" in. Inside the vessel, classic Edwardian nautical decor throughout is clean, warm, intimate, and inviting. The paneled library has a fireplace, and chairs that are comfortable. A cruise aboard it means no lines, no hassle, and "Sailing a Square Rigger" classes are a part of every cruise.

Each morning, passengers typically gather for "captain's

BERLITZ'S RATINGS

	Possible	Achieved
Ship	500	382
Accommodation	200	134
Food	400	249
Service	400	271
Entertainment	n/a	n/a
Cruise	500	366

story-time" – normally held on an open deck area adjacent to the bar – which, incidentally, has a fine collection of single malt whiskies. The captain also explains sailing maneuvers when changing the rigging or directing the ship as it sails into port, and notes the important events of the day. Passengers are encouraged to lend a hand, pulling on thick ropes to haul up the main sail. And they love it.

The vessel promotes total informality and provides a carefree sailing cruise experience in a totally unstructured setting at a modest price. Take minimal clothing: short-sleeved shirts and shorts for the men, shorts and tops for the women are the order of the day (and night). No jackets, ties, high-heeled shoes, cocktail dresses, or the slightest hint of formal wear is needed. The deck crew consists of real sailors, brought up with yachts and tall ships – and most would not set foot aboard a cruise ship.

It is no exaggeration to say that to be sailing aboard either *Star Clipper* or *Star Flyer* is to seem to have died and gone to yachtsman's heaven, as there is plenty of sailing during the course of a typical one-week cruise. Even the most jaded passenger should enjoy the feel of the wind and sea close at hand – just don't expect fine food to go with what is decidedly a fine sailing experience. The food, its quality, variety, presentation and service are sound, but there's room for improvement.

The steps of the internal stairs are steep, as in most sailing vessels.

Tips are pooled (the suggested amount is $8 per passenger, per day) and 12.5% is added to all beverage purchases. The onboard currency is the euro.

SUITABLE FOR: *Star Flyer* is best suited to couples and singles who would probably never even consider a "normal" cruise ship, but who enjoy sailing and the thrill of ocean and wind, but want these things wrapped in a package that includes accommodation, food, like-minded companions, interesting destinations, and don't want the bother of owning or chartering their own yacht.

ACCOMMODATION. There are six cabin price grades (plus one owner's suite). The price will depend on the grade, location and size chosen (generally, the higher the deck, the more expensive your cabin will be). The cabins are quite well equipped and comfortable; they have rosewood-trimmed cabinetry and wall-to-wall carpeting, two-channel audio, color TV and individual DVD player, lockable personal safe and full-length mirrors.

The bathrooms are very compact but practical units, and have gray marble tiling, glazed rosewood toiletries cabinet and paneling, some under-shelf storage space, washbasin, shower stall and toilet. There is no "lip" to stop water from the shower from moving over the bathroom floor.

Individual European 100% individual cotton duvets are provided. Note that a cabin food or beverage service is not available.

The deluxe cabins (called "deck cabins") are larger, and additional features include a full-sized Jacuzzi tub (or corner tub), flat-screen television and individual DVD player, and mini-bar/refrigerator. But these cabins are subject to noise pollution from the same-deck Tropical Bar's music at night (typically until midnight), from the electric winches during sail maneuvers, and from noisy walkabout exercisers in the early morning.

The cabins in the lowest price grade are interior cabins with upper and lower berths, and not two lower beds – so someone will need to be agile to climb up to the upper berth (a ladder is provided, of course). A handful of cabins have a third, upper Pullman-style berth – good for families with children, but note that closet and drawer space will be at a premium with three persons in a cabin, so do take only the minimal amount of clothing. Luggage can be stored under the bed, where extra large drawers are also provided.

CUISINE. The dining room is quite attractive, and has lots of wood and brass accenting and nautical decor. There are self-serve buffet breakfasts and lunches, together with a mix of buffet and à la carte dinners (generally with a choice of two entrées). There is one (open) seating. The seating arrangement (mostly with tables of six, adjacent to a porthole) makes it difficult for waiters to serve properly. However, you can dine with whomever you wish, and this is supposed to be a casual experience. While cuisine aboard Star Clippers' ships is perhaps less than the advertised "gourmet" excellence (as far as presentation and choice are concerned), it is fairly creative, and one has to take into account the small galley provided (changed to a better layout in a recent refurbishment).

Perhaps fewer passenger cabins and more room in the galley would have enabled the chefs to provide a better dining experience than the present arrangement. There is a limited choice of bread rolls, pastry items, and fruit.

Tea and coffee should be, but is not, available 24 hours a day (now provided in china mugs), particularly in view of the fact that there is no cabin food service. Note that drinks prices include a service charge, currently 12.5%.

ENTERTAINMENT. There are no entertainment shows, nor are any expected by passengers aboard a tall ship such as this, where sailing is the main purpose of a cruise aboard *Star Flyer*. There is, however, live music, which is provided by a single lounge pianist/singer. Otherwise, dinner is the main evening event, as well as talks by the captain. Conversation with fellow passengers in the lounge or on deck (under the stars) provides engaging entertainment.

During the daytime, when the ship is sailing, passengers can learn about the sails, and the captain or chief officer will give briefings as the sails are being furled and unfurled. The closest this tall ship comes to any kind of "show" is when, one evening towards the end of each cruise, a "sailor's choir", comprised of the ship's crew, presents a nautical performance of sea songs, sea shanties, and other light diversions.

SPA/FITNESS. There are no fitness facilities, or beauty salon, or anything related to spa services aboard this tall ship. However, for recreation, the ship does have a water sports programme. Facilities include a water ski boat, sunfish, scuba and snorkel equipment, and eight Zodiac inflatable craft. Water sports directors provide basic dive instruction, for a fee.

Size:	Large Resort Ship	Passenger Decks:	13	Cabins (with private balcony):	711
Tonnage:	108,977	Total Crew:	1,200	Cabins (wheelchair accessible):	28
Lifestyle:	Standard	Passengers			(18 outside/10 interior)
Cruise Line:	Princess Cruises	(lower beds/all berths):	2,602/3,102	Wheelchair accessibility	Best
Former Names:	none	Passenger Space Ratio		Cabin Current:	110 volts
Builder:	Fincantieri (Italy)	(lower beds/all berths):	41.8/35.1	Elevators:	14
Original Cost:	$460 million	Crew/Passenger Ratio		Casino (gaming tables):	Yes
Entered Service:	Feb 2002	(lower beds/all berths):	2.3/2.8	Slot Machines:	Yes
Registry:	Bermuda	Cabins (total):	1,301	Swimming Pools (outdoors):	4
Length (ft/m):	951.4/290.0	Size Range (sq ft/m):	161.4–1,314.0/	Swimming Pools (indoors):	0
Beam (ft/m):	118.1/36.0		15.0–122.0	Whirlpools:	9
Draft (ft/m):	26.2/8.0	Cabins (outside view):	935	Self-Service Launderette:	Yes
Propulsion/Propellers:	diesel-electric	Cabins (interior/no view):	366	Dedicated Cinema/Seats:	No
	(42,000kW)/2	Cabins (for one person):	0	Library:	Yes

OVERALL SCORE: 1,496 OUT OF A POSSIBLE 2,000 POINTS

OVERVIEW. The design for this large cruise ship, whose sister ships are *Golden Princess* and *Grand Princess* (and slightly larger half-sister *Caribbean Princess*), presents a bold, forthright profile, with a racy "spoiler" effect at its galleon-like transom stern that I (and others) do not consider handsome (the "spoiler" acts as a stern observation lounge by day, and a stunning discotheque by night). *Star Princess* is quite a ship. With a beam of 118 ft/36 meters, including the navigation bridge wings and with many balcony cabins overhanging the ship's hull, it is too wide – by more than 13 ft/3.9 meters – to transit the Panama Canal. When the ship was delivered by the shipyard in Italy, *Star Princess* went through the Suez Canal (the largest passenger ship ever to do so), then sailed to Singapore for its maiden voyage, before going to Los Angeles; thus the ship did half an around-the-world sailing before commencing service on the US west coast.

A few changes – compared with *Golden Princess* and *Grand Princess* – have been incorporated, including a substantially enlarged and much improved children's area (the Fun Zone) at the stern of the vessel. Also different, and improved, is the layout of the Lotus Spa, particularly the placement of the saunas/changing rooms.

There is a good sheltered faux teak promenade deck – it's actually painted steel – which almost wraps around (three times round is equal to one mile) and a walkway which goes right to the (enclosed, protected) bow of the ship. The outdoor pools have various beach-like surroundings. One lap pool has a pumped "current" to swim against.

Unlike the outside decks, there is plenty of space inside the ship – but there are also plenty of passengers – and a

BERLITZ'S RATINGS

	Possible	Achieved
Ship	500	414
Accommodation	200	163
Food	400	252
Service	400	289
Entertainment	100	79
Cruise	400	299

wide array of public rooms to choose from, with many "intimate" (this being a relative word) spaces and places to play. The passenger flow has been well thought-out, and works with little congestion. The decor is attractive, with lots of earth tones, well suited to both American and European tastes. In fact, this is a culmination of the best of all that Princess Cruises has to offer from its many years of operating what is now a well-tuned, good-quality product.

Four areas center on swimming pools, one of which is two decks high and is covered by a magrodome, itself an extension of the funnel housing. High atop the stern of the ship is a ship-wide glass-walled disco pod. It looks like an aerodynamic "spoiler" and is positioned high above the water, with spectacular views from the extreme port and starboard side windows.

An extensive collection of art works complements the interior design and colors well. If you see something you like, you can buy it on board – it's almost all for sale.

Like its sisters *Golden Princess* and *Grand Princess*, *Star Princess* also has a Wedding Chapel; a live web-cam can relay ceremonies via the internet. The ship's captain can legally marry American couples, thanks to the ship's Bermuda registry and a special dispensation – which should be verified when in the planning stage, according to where you reside. Princess Cruises offers three wedding packages – Pearl, Emerald, Diamond. The fee includes registration and official marriage certificate. However, to get married and take your close family members and entourage with you on your honeymoon is going to cost a lot of money. The "Hearts & Minds" chapel is also useful for "renewal of vows" ceremonies.

For children, there is a two-deck-high playroom, teen room, and a host of specially trained counselors. Children have their own pools, hot tubs, and open deck area at the stern of the ship, thankfully away from adult areas. There are good netted-in areas; one section has a dip pool, while another has a mini-basketball court.

Gamers should enjoy the Grand Casino, with more than 260 slot machines; there are blackjack, craps and roulette tables, plus newer games such as Let It Ride Bonus, Spanish 21 and Caribbean Draw Progressive. But the highlight could well be the specially linked slot machines that provide a combined payout.

Other features include a decent library/CD-Rom computer room, and a separate card room. Ship lovers should enjoy the wood-paneled Wheelhouse Bar, finely decorated with memorabilia and ship models tracing part of parent company P&O's history; this ship highlights the 1950-built cargo ship *Ganges*. A sports bar, Shooters, has two billiard tables, as well as eight television screens.

A high-tech hospital is provided, with live SeaMed telemedicine link-ups with specialists at the Cedars-Sinai Medical Center in Los Angeles available for emergency help.

The ship is a stunning, grand resort playground in which to roam when you are not ashore. Princess Cruises delivers a consistently fine, well-packaged vacation product, with a good sense of style, at an attractive, highly competitive price, and this ship will appeal to those that really enjoy a big city to play in, with all the trimmings and lots of fellow passengers. The ship is full of revenue centers, however, designed to help part you from your money. As cruising aboard large ships such as this has become increasingly an onboard revenue-based product, you can expect to be subjected to a stream of flyers advertising daily art auctions, "designer" watches and other promotions, while "artworks" for auction are strewn throughout the ship.

The dress code has been simplified – reduced to formal or smart casual, which seems to be translated by many as jeans and trainers. Gratuities to staff are added to your account, at $10 per person, per day (gratuities for children are charged at the same rate). If you want to pay less, you'll need to go to the reception desk to have these charges adjusted; this could mean lining up with many other passengers wanting to do the same. The onboard currency is the US dollar.

Whether this really can be considered a relaxing holiday is a moot point, but with so many choices and "small" rooms to enjoy, the ship has been extremely well designed, and the odds are that you'll have a fine cruise vacation.

If you are not used to large ships, it will take you some time to find your way around, despite the company's claim that this vessel offers passengers a "small ship feel, big ship choice." The cabin bath towels are small, and drawer space is very limited. There are no butlers – even for the top-grade suites (which are not really large in comparison similar suites aboard some other ships). Cabin attendants have too many cabins to look after (typically 20), which does not translate to fine personal service.

The automated telephone system is frustrating, and luggage delivery is inefficient.

ACCOMMODATION. There are six principal types of cabins and configurations: (a) grand suite, (b) suite, (c) mini-suite, (d) outside-view double cabins with balcony, (e) outside-view double cabins, and (f) interior (no view) double cabins. These come in 35 different brochure price categories (the price you pay will depend on the grade, location and size chosen). The choice is quite bewildering for both travel agents and passengers; pricing will depend on two things, size and location.

(a) The largest, most lavish suite is the Grand Suite (B748, which is located at the ship's stern – a different position to the two Grand Suites aboard *Grand Princess*). It has a large bedroom with queen-sized bed, huge walk-in (illuminated) closets, two bathrooms, a lounge (with fireplace and sofa bed) with wet bar and refrigerator, and a large private balcony on the port side, with a hot tub that can be accessed from both balcony and bedroom.

(b/c) Suites (with a semi-private balcony) have a separate living room with sofa bed and bedroom, with a TV set in each. The bathroom is quite large and has both a tub and shower stall. The mini-suites also have a private balcony, and a separate living and sleeping area, with a TV set in each. The differences between the suites and mini-suites are basically in the size and appointments, the suite being more of a square shape while mini-suites are more rectangular, and have few drawers. Both suites and mini-suites have plush bathrobes, and fully tiled bathrooms with ample open shelf storage space. Suite and mini-suite passengers receive greater attention, including priority embarkation and disembarkation privileges. What is not good is that the most expensive accommodation has only semi-private balconies that can be seen from above and so there is little privacy (Suites C401, 402, 409, 410, 414, 415, 420, 421, 422, 423, 424 and 425 on Caribe Deck in particular). Also, the suites D105 and D106 (Dolphin Deck), which are extremely large, have balconies that are overlooked from above.

(d/e/f). Both interior (no view) and outside-view (the outsides come either with or without private balcony) cabins are of a functional design, although almost no drawers are provided. They are quite attractive, with warm, pleasing decor and fine soft furnishing fabrics; 80 percent of the outside-view cabins have a private balcony. Interior (no view) cabins measure 160 sq. ft (14.4 sq. meters), while the standard outside-view cabins measure 228 sq. ft (21 sq. meters).

The 28 wheelchair-accessible cabins measure 250–385 sq. ft (23.2–35.7 sq. meters). Surprisingly, there is no mirror for dressing, and no full-length hanging space for long dresses – yes, some passengers in wheelchairs do also use mirrors and full-length clothing. Additionally, two family suites consist of two suites with an interconnecting door, plus a large balcony. These can sleep up to 10 (if at least four are children) or up to eight people (if all are adults).

All passengers receive turndown service and chocolates on pillows each night, bathrobes (on request), and toiletry amenity kits (larger for suite/mini-suite occupants). A hairdryer is provided in all cabins, sensibly located at the vanity desk unit in the living area. All bathrooms have tiled floors, and there is a decent amount of open shelf storage space for personal toiletries, although the plain beige decor is very basic and unappealing. Princess Cruises typically carries CNN, CNBC, ESPN and TNT on the in-cabin color television system (when available, depending on cruise area).

Most outside cabins on Emerald Deck have views obstructed by the lifeboats. There are no cabins for singles. Your name is placed outside your suite or cabin in a documents holder – making it simple for delivery service personnel but also making it intrusive as far as privacy is concerned. There is 24-hour room service (but some items on the room service menu are not available during early morning hours).

Some cabins can accommodate a third and fourth person in upper berths. However, in such cabins, the lower beds cannot then be pushed together to make queen-sized bed.

Almost all balcony suites and cabins can be overlooked both from the navigation bridge wing, as well as from the port and starboard sections of the ship's discotheque – located high above the ship at the stern. Cabins with balconies on Dolphin, Caribe and Baja decks are also overlooked by passengers on balconies on the deck above. They are, therefore, not at all private. However, perhaps the least desirable balcony cabins are eight balcony cabins located forward on Emerald Deck, as the balconies do not extend to the side of the ship and can be passed by walkers and gawkers on the adjacent Upper Promenade walkway, so occupants need to keep their curtains closed most of the time. Also, passengers occupying some of the most expensive suites with balconies at the stern of the vessel may experience considerable vibration during certain ship maneuvers.

CUISINE. As befits the size of the ship, there is a variety of dining options. For formal meals there are three principal dining rooms (Amalfi, with 504 seats; Capri, with 486 seats; and Portofino, with 486 seats), and seating is assigned according to the location of your cabin. There are two seatings in one restaurant (Amalfi), while "anytime dining" (where you choose when and with whom you want to eat) is typically offered by the other two. All three are non-smoking and split into multi-tier sections in a non-symmetrical design that breaks what are quite large spaces into many smaller sections, for better ambiance. Each dining room has its own galley.

While four elevators go to Fiesta Deck where the amalfi and Portofino restaurants are located, only two elevators go to Plaza Deck 5 where the Capri Restaurant is located (this can cause long wait problems at peak times, particularly for anyone in a wheelchair).

Specially designed dinnerware and high-quality linens and silverware are used in the main dining rooms; by Dudson of England (dinnerware), Frette Egyptian cotton table linens, and silverware by Hepp of Germany. Note that 15% is added to all beverage bills, including wines.

Alternative (Extra Charge) Dining Options: There are two: Sabatini's and Tequila's. Both are open for lunch and dinner on days at sea. Sabatini's is an Italian eatery, with colorful tiled Mediterranean-style decor; it is named after Trattoria Sabatini, the 200-year old institution in Florence (where there is no cover charge). It has Italian-style pizzas and pastas, with a variety of sauces, as well as Italian-style entrées including tiger prawns and lobster tail – all provided with flair and entertainment from by the staff of waiters (by reservation only, with a cover charge of $15 per person, for lunch or dinner on sea days only).

Tequila's has "southwestern American" food; by reservation only, with a cover charge of $8 per person, for lunch or dinner on sea days only. However, do note that Tequila's is spread over the whole beam (width) of the ship, and two walkways intersect it, which means that it's a very open area, with people walking through it as you eat – not a very comfortable arrangement. The cuisine in both of these spots is decidedly better than in the three main dining rooms, with better quality ingredients and more attention to presentation and taste.

A poolside hamburger grill and pizza bar (no additional charge) are dining spots for casual bites, while extra charges will apply if you order items to eat at either the coffee bar/patisserie, or the caviar/champagne bar.

Other casual meals can be taken in the Horizon Court, which is open 24 hours a day. It has large ocean-view on port and starboard sides and direct access to the two principal swimming pools and lido deck. There is no real finesse in presentation, however, as plastic plates are provided.

ENTERTAINMENT. The Princess Theater (showlounge) is the main entertainment venue; it spans two decks and has comfortable seating on both main and balcony levels. It has $3 million in sound and light equipment, plus a nine-piece orchestra, and a scenery loading bay that connects from stage to a hull door for direct transfer to the dockside.

The Vista Lounge is a second entertainment lounge. It has cabaret acts (magicians, comedy jugglers, ventriloquists and others) at night, and lectures, bingo and horse racing during the day. Explorers, a third entertainment lounge, can also host cabaret acts and dance bands. A variety of other lounges and bars feature live music, and Princess Cruises has a number of male dance hosts as partners for women traveling alone.

SPA/FITNESS. The Lotus Spa has Japanese-style decor, and surrounds one of the swimming pools (you can have a massage or other spa treatment in an ocean-view treatment room). It is unfortunate, however – perhaps a lack of knowledge or respect on the part of the interior designer – that the Japanese symbol on the door of the steam inhalation rooms means insect, not a nice thing to call passengers. Note that some of the spa (massage) treatment rooms are located directly underneath the jogging track.

● **For more extensive general information about the Princess Cruises experience, see pages 148–51.**

Statendam
★★★★

Size: ....Mid-Size Ship	Passenger Decks: 10	Cabins (with private balcony): 150
Tonnage: 55,451	Total Crew: 557	Cabins (wheelchair accessible): 6
Lifestyle: ....Premium	Passengers	Wheelchair accessibility ....Good
Cruise Line: ......Holland America Line	(lower beds/all berths): 1,266/1,627	Cabin Current: ....110 and 220 volts
Former Names: ....none	Passenger Space Ratio	Elevators: 8
Builder: ....Fincantieri (Italy)	(lower beds/all berths): 43.8/34.0	Casino (gaming tables): ....Yes
Original Cost: ....$215 million	Crew/Passenger Ratio	Slot Machines: ....Yes
Entered Service: ....Jan 1993	(lower beds/all berths): 2.2/2.9	Swimming Pools (outdoors): 1
Registry: ....The Netherlands	Cabins (total): 633	Swimming Pools (indoors): 1
Length (ft/m): 719.4/219.3	Size Range (sq ft/m): 186.2–1,124.8/	(sliding glass dome)
Beam (ft/m): 101.0/30.8	17.3–104.5	Whirlpools: 2
Draft (ft/m): 24.6/7.5	Cabins (outside view): 502	Self-Service Launderette: ....Yes
Propulsion/Propellers: .....diesel-electric	Cabins (interior/no view): 131	Dedicated Cinema/Seats: Yes/249
(34,560kW)/2	Cabins (for one person): 0	Library: ....Yes

OVERALL SCORE: 1,403 OUT OF A POSSIBLE 2,000 POINTS

OVERVIEW. *Statendam* is the first of a series of four almost identical ships in the same series – the others being *Maasdam, Ryndam* and *Veendam*. The exterior styling is rather angular, although it is softened and balanced somewhat by the fact that the hull is painted black.

There is a full walk-around teakwood promenade deck outdoors – excellent for strolling, and, thankfully, there's no sign of synthetic turf. The sunloungers on the exterior promenade deck are wood, and come with comfortable cushioned pads, while those at the swimming pool on Lido Deck are of white plastic. Holland America Line keeps its ships clean and tidy, and there is good passenger flow throughout the public areas.

In the interiors of this "S" -class ship, an asymmetrical layout helps to reduce bottlenecks and congestion. Most of the public rooms are concentrated on two decks, Promenade Deck, and Upper Promenade Deck, which creates a spacious feel to the ship's interiors. In general, a restrained approach to interior styling is taken, using a mixture of contemporary materials combined with traditional woods and ceramics. There is, fortunately, little "glitz" anywhere.

What is outstanding is the array of artworks throughout the ship (costing about $2 million), assembled and nicely displayed to represent the fine Dutch heritage of Holland America Line. Also noticeable are the fine flower arrangements throughout the public areas and foyers.

Atop the ship, with forward facing views that wrap around the sides is the Crow's Nest Lounge. By day it makes a fine observation lounge, with large ocean-view windows, while by night it turns into a nightclub with extremely variable lighting. The atrium foyer is three decks high, although its sculptured centerpiece (*Fountain of the Sirens*, a late 17th-

BERLITZ'S RATINGS		
	Possible	Achieved
Ship	500	372
Accommodation	200	150
Food	400	247
Service	400	280
Entertainment	100	72
Cruise	400	282

century bronze piece by Willem de Groat) makes it look a little crowded, and leaves little room in front of the purser's office (called the Front Office). A hydraulic glass roof covers the reasonably sized swimming pool/ and whirlpools and central Lido area (whose focal point is a large dolphin sculpture) so that this can be used in either fine or inclement weather.

The ship has a large, relaxing library. There's also a cardroom, an Explorer's Lounge (good for relaxing in, for afternoon tea, and after-dinner coffees), a Crows Nest (the ship's observation lounge that doubles as a late-night spot and discotheque), an intimate Piano Bar, and, of course, a casino.

As part of HAL's "Signature of Excellence" program, the ships have received a new "Mix" lifestyle area. The trendy, upbeat space combines three specialty theme bars: Champagne (serving champagne and sparkling wines), Martinis (in individual shakers), and Spirits & Ales (a sports bar – beer and baseball/ basketball for the boys). Microsoft Surface touch-screen technology is available for playing checkers and chess, air hockey, and other sports games

Statendam is a fairly well-built ship, and has reasonably decent interior fit and finish. HAL is constantly fine-tuning its performance as a cruise operator and its regular passengers (almost all of whom are North American – there are few international passengers) find the company's ships very comfortable and well-run. The company continues its strong maritime traditions, although the present food and service components let down the rest of the cruise experience. Perhaps the ship's best asset is its friendly and personable Filipino and Indonesian crew, although communication can be frustrating. The onboard currency is the US dollar.

An escalator travels between two of the lower decks (one of which was originally planned to be the embarkation point), but it is almost pointless. The charge to use the washing machines and dryers in the self-service launderette is petty, particularly for occupants of expensive suites. The men's urinals in public restrooms are unusually high.

ACCOMMODATION. There are 17 cabin price grades. The price you pay will depend on the grade, location and size you choose. Cabins range from small interior (no view) cabins to a large penthouse suite (with ocean views). All cabin televisions carry CNN and TNT.

The interior (no view) and outside-view standard cabins have twin beds that can be converted to a queen-sized bed, and there is a separate living space with sofa and coffee table. However, although the drawer space is generally good, the closet space is very tight, particularly for long cruises (although more than adequate for a 7-night cruise). The bathrooms are tiled, and compact but practical. Bathrobes are also provided for all suites/cabins, as are hairdryers, and a small range of personal amenities (soap, conditioning shampoo, body lotion, shower cap, vanity kit). The bathrooms are quite well laid out, but the tubs are small units better described as shower tubs.

On Navigation Deck, 28 suites have accommodation for up to four persons. These also have in-suite dining as an alternative to the dining room, for private, reclusive meals. These are very spacious, tastefully decorated and well laid-out, and have a separate living room, bedroom with two lower beds (convertible to a king-size bed), a good size living area, dressing room, plenty of closet and drawer space, marble bathroom with whirlpool tub.

The largest accommodation of all is a penthouse suite. There is only one, located on the starboard side of Navigation Deck at the forward staircase. It has a king-sized bed, television and video player, and vanity desk. A large walk-in closet has superb drawer space. There is an oversize whirlpool bath (it could seat four) and separate shower enclosure, and a separate washroom with toilet, bidet and washbasin. The living room has a writing desk, a large television and a full set of audio equipment. The dressing room has a large private balcony (with teak lounge chairs and drinks tables, dining table and four chairs). The pantry has a large refrigerator, toaster unit, and full coffee/tea making facilities and food preparation area, and a separate entrance from the hallway.

There's a mini-bar/refrigerator, a guest toilet and floor to ceiling windows. Note that there is no bell push.

Passengers in accommodation designated as suites and mini-suites have the use of a private concierge club called the Neptune Lounge, where light breakfast and snacks throughout the day can be taken.

CUISINE. The Rotterdam Dining Room, a no-smoking venue, spans two decks. It is located at the stern of the ship, is quite dramatic, and has two grand staircases to connect the two levels, panoramic views on three sides, and a music balcony. Both open seating and fixed (assigned tables and times) seating are available, while breakfast and lunch are open-seating – you'll be seated by restaurant staff when you enter. There are tables for two, four, six or eight note that the waiter stations in the dining room are very noisy for anyone seated adjacent to them. Fine Rosenthal china and cutlery are used.

Alternative Dining Option: A small restaurant was added in 2002. Called the Pinnacle Grill, it is located just forward of the balcony level of the main dining room on the starboard side. The 66-seat dining spot has Pacific Northwest cuisine (Alaska salmon, halibut and other regional specialities, plus a selection of premium steaks). The new venue (reservations are necessary, and a cover/service charge of $20 applies) was created out of the the former private dining wing of the main dining room, plus a slice of the Explorer's Lounge. A Bulgari show plate, Rosenthal china, Riedel wine glasses, and Frette table linen are used. The Pinnacle Grill is a much better dining experience than the main dining room, and worth it for that special celebration.

For more casual evening eating, the Lido Buffet is open for dinners on all except the last night of each cruise, in an open-seating arrangement. Tables are set with crisp linens, flatware and stemware. A set menu is featured, and this includes a choice of four entrées.

The dual-line, self-serve Lido Buffet (one side is for smokers, the other side for non-smokers) is also the place for casual breakfasts and lunches. There is much use of canned fruits (good for dentally challenged passengers) and packeted items, although there are several commercial low-calorie salad dressings. The choice of cheeses and accompanying crackers is poor. The beverage station also lets it down, for it is no better than those found in family outlets ashore in the USA. Each night, a section of the venue is transformed into Canaletto using glass screens; the cuisine is Italian-flavored (but the Italian wine list is poor). There's no additional charge, although reservations are requested.

Passengers will need to eat in the Lido Cafe on days when the dining room is closed for lunch (typically once or twice per cruise, depending on the itinerary). A poolside grill provides basic American hamburgers and hot dogs.

ENTERTAINMENT. The Showlounge at Sea, located at the forward part of the ship, spans two decks, with banquette seating on both main and upper levels. It is basically a well-designed room, but the ceiling is low and the sightlines from the balcony level are quite poor.

SPA/FITNESS. The Ocean Spa is located one deck below the navigation bridge at the very forward part of the ship. It includes a gymnasium (with all the latest muscle-pumping exercise machines, including an abundance of treadmills) with ocean views, an aerobics exercise area, large beauty salon with ocean-view windows to the port side, several treatment rooms, and men's and women's sauna, steam room and changing areas.

● **For more extensive general information on what a Holland America Line cruise is like, see pages 139–42.**

Sun Princess
★★★★

Size: . . . . .Large Resort Ship	Passenger Decks: 10	Cabins (with private balcony): 410
Tonnage: 77,499	Total Crew: 900	Cabins (wheelchair accessible): 19
Lifestyle: . . . . .Standard	Passengers	Wheelchair accessibility . . . . .Good
Cruise Line: . . . . .Princess Cruises	(lower beds/all berths): 1,950/2,250	Cabin Current: . . . . .110 and 220 volts
Former Names: . . . . .none	Passenger Space Ratio	Elevators: 11
Builder: . . . . .Fincantieri (Italy)	(lower beds/all berths): 39.7/34.4	Casino (gaming tables): . . . . .Yes
Original Cost: . . . .$300 million	Crew/Passenger Ratio	Slot Machines: . . . . .Yes
Entered Service: . . . . .Dec 1995	(lower beds/all berths): 2.0/2.5	Swimming Pools (outdoors): 4
Registry: . . . . .Great Britain	Cabins (total): 975	Swimming Pools (indoors): 0
Length (ft/m): 857.2/261.3	Size Range (sq ft/m): 134.5–753.4/	Whirlpools: 5
Beam (ft/m): 105.6/32.2	12.5–70.0	Self-Service Launderette: . . . . .Yes
Draft (ft/m): 26.5/8.1	Cabins (outside view): 603	Dedicated Cinema/Seats: . . . . .No
Propulsion/Propellers: . . . . .diesel-electric	Cabins (interior/no view): 372	Library: . . . . .Yes
(28,000kW)/2	Cabins (for one person): 0	

OVERALL SCORE: 1,489 OUT OF A POSSIBLE 2,000 POINTS

OVERVIEW. In November 2007, *Sun Princess* moved its permanent base to Australia, operating cruises from Sydney, Melbourne, and Freemantle. The onboard currency became the Australian dollar, the entertainment was geared to Australian tastes, and other aspects of the cruise operation modified accordingly. Note that, for long voyages (such as a Grand Circle Pacific cruise), the cabin closet space is extremely small.

Although large, this all-white ship has a good profile, and is well balanced by its large funnel, which contains a deck tennis/basketball/volleyball court in its sheltered aft base. There is a wide, teakwood wrap-around promenade deck outdoors, some real teak steamer-style deck chairs (complete with royal blue cushioned pads), and 93,000 sq. ft (8,600 sq. meters) of space outdoors. An extensive glass area on the upper decks provides plenty of light and connection with the outside world.

The ship, while large, absorbs passengers well, and has an almost intimate feel to it, which is what the designers intended. The interiors are very pretty and warm, with attractive colors and welcoming decor that includes some very attractive wall murals and other artwork. The signs around the ship could be improved, however. There is a wide range of public rooms, with several intimate rooms and spaces so that you don't get the feel of being overwhelmed by large spaces. The interior focal point is a huge four-deck-high atrium lobby with winding, double stairways, complete with two panoramic glass-walled elevators.

The main public entertainment rooms are located under three decks of cabins. There is plenty of space, the traffic flow is good, and the ship absorbs people well. There are two showlounges, one at each end of the ship; one is a

BERLITZ'S RATINGS

	Possible	Achieved
Ship	500	415
Accommodation	200	162
Food	400	257
Service	400	278
Entertainment	100	80
Cruise	400	297

superb 550-seat, theater-style show-lounge (movies are also shown here) and the other is a 480-seat cabaret-style lounge, complete with bar.

The library is a very warm room with ocean-view windows, and has six large buttery leather chairs for listening to audio CDs. There is a conference center for up to 300, as well as a business center, with computers, photocopiers and fax machines. The collection of artwork is good, particularly on the stairways, and helps make the ship feel smaller than it is, although in places it doesn't always seem co-coordinated. The casino, while large, is not really in the main passenger flow and so it does not generate the "walk-through" factor found aboard so many ships.

The most traditional (many say the nicest) room aboard is the Wheelhouse Lounge/Bar, which is decorated in the style of a late 19th-century gentleman's club, complete with wood paneling and comfortable seating. Its focal point is a large ship model from the P&O archives.

At the end of the day, as is the case aboard most large ships today, if you live in the top suites, you will be well attended; if you do not, you will merely be one of a very large number of passengers. One nice feature is the captain's cocktail party; it is held in the four-deck-high main atrium so you can come and go as you please – and there's no standing in line to have your photograph taken with the captain if you don't want to.

There are a number of dead ends in the interior layout, so it's not as user-friendly as a ship this size should be. The cabin numbering system is extremely illogical, with numbers going through several hundred series on the same deck. The walls of the passenger accommodation decks are very plain (some artwork would be a distinct improvement).

The swimming pools are quite small for so many passengers, and the pool deck is cluttered with white, plastic sunloungers, which do not have cushioned pads.

ACCOMMODATION. There are 28 different cabin grades: 20 outside-view and 8 interior (no view) cabins. Although the standard outside-view and interior (no view) cabins are a little small, they are well designed and functional in layout, and have earth tone colors accentuated by splashes of color from the bedspreads. Proportionately, there are quite a lot of interior (no view) cabins. Many of the outside-view cabins have private balconies, and all seem to be quite well soundproofed, although the balcony partition is not floor to ceiling type, so you can hear your neighbors clearly (or smell their smoke). Note that the balconies are very narrow, only just large enough for two small chairs, and there is balcony light.

A reasonable amount of closet and abundant drawer and other storage space is provided in all cabins – adequate for a 7-night cruise, as are a television and refrigerator. Each night a chocolate will appear on your pillow. The cabin bathrooms are practical, and come complete with all the details one needs, although they really are tight spaces, best described as one person at-a-time units. They do, however, have a decent shower enclosure, a small amount of shelving for your personal toiletries, real glasses, a hairdryer and a bathrobe.

The largest accommodation can be found in six suites, two on each of three decks located at the stern of the ship, with large private balcony (536–754 sq. ft./49.8–21.3 sq. meters, including balcony). These are well laid-out, and have large bathrooms with two basins, a Jacuzzi bathtub, and a separate shower enclosure. The bedroom has generous amounts of wood accenting and detailing, TV sets in both bedroom and lounge areas. The suites also have a dining room table and four chairs.

The 32 mini-suites (374–536 sq. ft./34.7–49.7 sq. meters) typically have two lower beds that convert into a queen-sized bed. There is a separate bedroom/sleeping area with vanity desk, and a lounge with sofa and coffee table, indented ceilings with generous amounts of wood accenting and detailing, walk-in closet, and larger bathroom with Jacuzzi tub and separate shower enclosure.

There are 19 wheelchair-accessible cabins, which measure 213–305 sq. ft (19.7–28.2 sq. meters.), and are a mix of 7 outside-view and 12 interior (no view) cabins.

CUISINE. There are two main dining rooms of asymmetrical design: Marquis, and Regency. Both are non-smoking, as are all dining rooms aboard the ships of Princess Cruises. They are located adjacent to the two lower levels of the four-deck high atrium lobby. Each seats around 500, has its own galley, and is split into multi-tier sections, which help create a feeling of intimacy, although there is a lot of noise from the waiter stations adjacent to many tables. Breakfast and lunch are provided in an open-seating arrangement, while dinner is in two seatings.

On any given 7-day cruise, a typical menu cycle will include a Sailaway Dinner, Captain's Welcome Dinner, Chef's Dinner, Italian Dinner, French Dinner, Captain's Gala Dinner, and Landfall Dinner. The wine list is reasonable, but not good, and the company has, sadly, dispensed with wine waiters. Note that 15% is added to all beverage bills, including wines.

Alternative Dining (Extra Charge) Option: For some really good meat, however, consider the Sterling Steakhouse; it's for those that want to taste four different cuts of Angus beef from the popular "Sterling Silver" brand of USDA prime meats – Filet Mignon, New York Strip, Porterhouse, and Rib-Eye – all presented on a silver tray.

There is also a barbecue chicken option, plus the usual baked potato or French fries as accompaniments. This is available as an alternative to the dining rooms, between 6.30pm and 9.30pm only, at an additional charge of $8 per person. However, it is not, as you might expect, a separate, intimate dining room, but is located in a section of the Horizon Buffet, with its own portable bar and some decorative touches to set it apart from the regular Horizon Buffet.

The Horizon Buffet is open 24 hours a day, and, at night, has an informal dinner setting with sit-down waiter service; a small bistro menu is also available. The buffet displays are, for the most part, quite repetitious, but better than they have been in the past few years (there is no real finesse in presentation, however, as plastic plates are provided, instead of trays). The cabin service menu is very limited, and presentation of the food items featured is poor.

There is also a pâtisserie (for cappuccino/espresso coffees and pastries), a wine/caviar bar, and a pizzeria (complete with cobblestone floors and wrought-iron decorative features), and excellent pizzas (there are six to choose from).

ENTERTAINMENT. There are two showlounges (both theater and cabaret style). The principal showlounge, the Princess Theater, has a sloping floor, with aisle-style seating (as typically found in shore-side movie houses) that is well-tiered, and with good sightlines to the raised stage from most of the 500 seats.

The second showlounge (Vista Lounge), located at the aft end of the ship, has cabaret entertainment, and also acts as a lecture and presentation room. Princess Cruises has a good stable of regular cabaret acts to draw from, so there should be something for almost all tastes.

SPA/FITNESS. A glass-walled Lotus Spa complex is located high atop ship and includes a gymnasium with high-tech machines. One swimming pool is "suspended" aft between two decks (there are two other pools, although they are not large for the size of the ship).

Sports facilities are located in an open-air sports deck positioned inside the ship's funnel and adaptable for basketball, volleyball, badminton or paddle tennis. Joggers can exercise on the wrap-around open Promenade Deck.

● **For more extensive general information about the Princess Cruises experience, see pages 148–51.**

Superstar Aquarius
★★★

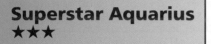

Size:	Mid-Size Ship	Total Crew:	889
Tonnage:	50,760	Passengers	
Lifestyle:	Standard	(lower beds/all berths):	1,529/1,607
Cruise Line:	Star Cruises	Passenger Space Ratio	
Former Names: *Norwegian Wind, Windward*		(lower beds/all berths):	33.1/31.5
Builder: .Chantiers de l'Atlantique (France)		Crew/Passenger Ratio	
Original Cost:	$240 million	(lower beds/all berths):	1.7/1.8
Entered Service:	June 1993/May 2007	Cabins (total):	765
Registry:	The Bahamas	Size Range (sq ft/m):	139.9–349.8/
Length (ft/m):	754.0/229.8		13.0–32.5
Beam (ft/m):	93.5/28.5	Cabins (outside view):	611
Draft (ft/m):	22.3/6.8	Cabins (interior/no view):	154
Propulsion/Propellers: diesel (18,480 kW)/2		Cabins (for one person):	0
Passenger Decks:	10	Cabins (with private balcony):	74

Cabins (wheelchair accessible):	11)
Wheelchair accessibility	Fair
Cabin Current:	110 volts
Elevators:	10
Casino (gaming tables):	Yes
Slot Machines:	Yes
Swimming Pools (outdoors):	1
Swimming Pools (indoors):	0
Whirlpools:	2
Self-Service Launderette:	No
Dedicated Cinema/Seats:	No
Library:	Yes

BERLITZ'S OVERALL SCORE: 1,232 OUT OF A POSSIBLE 2,000 POINTS

OVERVIEW. The exterior design emphasizes a clever and extensive use of large windows that help create a sense of open spaces, but the interior design has many smaller public rooms (better for Asian passengers). There is no big atrium lobby, as one might expect, and the ceiling height is low.

Public rooms include several bars and lounges, Skyline Karaoke (with five private karaoke rooms), mahjong/ card room, childcare center, video arcade, Genting Club (for invited gaming guests), three small business meeting rooms, an internet-connect center/library, cigar lounge, and a small boutique. There is a blue rubber-covered wrap-around promenade deck outdoors.

This ship was transferred from Norwegian Cruise Line to the Star Cruises fleet in 2007 to operate overnight and short cruises from Hong Kong. The dress code is strictly casual. Some lounges were converted into a large Star Club, for casino gamers. The onboard currency is the Hong Kong dollar, and all gratuities for staff are included.

Outdoor stairways are numerous and confusing, while the carpeted steel interior stairwell steps are tinny. Standing in line for embarkation, disembarkation, and for buffet meals is inevitable aspect when cruising aboard large ships.

ACCOMMODATION. There are 16 cabin price grades, depending on grade, location and size). Most cabins have outside views and wood-trimmed cabinetry and warm decor, with multi-colored soft furnishings, but there is almost no drawer space (the closets have open shelves, however), so take minimal clothing. All cabins have a sitting area. The bathrooms are small but practical, although there is little space for storage of personal toiletry items.

BERLITZ'S RATINGS

	Possible	Achieved
Ship	500	331
Accommodation	200	124
Food	400	216
Service	400	249
Entertainment	100	64
Cruise	400	248

There are 18 suites (12 of which have a private entrance and a small, private balcony), each with separate living room and bedroom, and plenty of closet and drawer space. Occupants of suites receive "concierge" service. In addition, 16 suites and 70 cabins have interconnecting doors. Several cabins are specially equipped for the hearing-impaired.

CUISINE. Freestyle Dining venues include the 280-seat Dynasty Restaurant, for Chinese family-style food; Spices Restaurant, an Asian specialty buffet venue with 180 seats; Oceana Barbeque, an outdoor buffet venue; Blue Lagoon, a 24-hour bistro, with 80 seats; Mariner's Buffet, international self-service buffet.

The Dynasty Restaurant, the largest sit-down dining spot, has some prime tables at ocean-view window seats in a section that extends from the ship's port and starboard sides in half-moon shapes.

ENTERTAINMENT. The 700-seat Stardust Lounge is the ship's only venue for production shows and cabaret acts. It is two decks high (but the banquette and individual tub chair seating is only on the main level) and is located not in the forward part of the ship as is normal, but almost in the center.

High-volume razzle-dazzle shows are presented each cruise, to a pre-recorded track (there is no live showband), as well as special individual cabaret acts.

SPA/FITNESS. A gymnasium has high-tech muscle-toning equipment, reflexology lounge, and Oscar Hair and Beauty Salon. Therer's a ping pong table, basketball/volleyball court, golf driving range, and a jogging track.

SuperStar Libra
★★★ +

Size:...................... Mid-Size Ship	Passenger Decks:.................9	Cabins (with private balcony):.........0
Tonnage:......................... 42,276	Total Crew:......................700	Cabins (wheelchair accessible):.......4
Lifestyle: ....Standard	Passengers	Wheelchair accessibility ....Fair
Cruise Line:..............Star Cruises	(lower beds/all berths): 1,472/1,800	Cabin Current: ....110 volts
Former Names: ...*Norwegian Sea, Seaward*	Passenger Space Ratio	Elevators:.........................6
Builder: ....Wartsila (Finland)	(lower beds/all berths): 28.0/23.5	Casino (gaming tables): ....Yes
Original Cost: ....$120 million	Crew/Passenger Ratio	Slot Machines: ....Yes
Entered Service: ......June 1988/Oct 2005	(lower beds/all berths): 2.1/2.5	Swimming Pools (outdoors): 2
Registry: ....The Bahamas	Cabins (total): 732	Swimming Pools (indoors): 0
Length (ft/m): 708.6/216.0	Size Range (sq ft/m): 109.7–269.1/	Whirlpools: 2
Beam (ft/m): 95.1/29.0	10.2–25.0	Self-Service Launderette: ....No
Draft (ft/m): 22.9/7.0	Cabins (outside view): 501	Dedicated Cinema/Seats: ....No
Propulsion/Propellers: ....diesel	Cabins (interior/no view): 231	Library:...........................No
(21,120 kW)/2	Cabins (for one person): 0	

OVERALL SCORE: 1,286 OUT OF A POSSIBLE 2,000 POINTS

OVERVIEW. This is an angular yet reasonably attractive ship that has a contemporary European cruise-ferry profile with a sharply raked bow and sleek mast and funnel added. The ship (the first to be totally geared to passengers from India) is quite well designed, with generally sound passenger flow. The interior decor, stressing corals, blues and mauves, reminds you of sea and sky.

The lobby, two decks high, is pleasing without being overwhelming. There is a decent selection of public rooms, bars and lounges, including an inviting wood-paneled Admiral's Lounge and Star Club (casino), a discotheque (Boomer's), and The Bollywood (karaoke lounge). The onboard currency is the Indian rupee, and gratuities are included in the cruise fare.

The open decks are cluttered, and badly dented and scuffed panels in the accommodation hallways are unattractive. The steps on the stairways are quite tinny. The constant background music in the hallways is irritating. There is too much use of synthetic turf on the upper outdoors decks – this gets soggy when wet.

SUITABLE FOR: *SuperStar Libra* is suited specifically for passengers from the Indian continent seeking a short cruise experience in surroundings tailored for them.

ACCOMMODATION. There are 16 suite/cabin price categories. This ship was built before balcony cabins came into vogue – so there aren't any. The cabins are of average size (which translates to "a bit cramped for two") although they are tastefully appointed and comfortable, with warm, pastel colors, bright soft furnishings and a touch of art deco styling; however, the walls and ceilings are plain and sim-

BERLITZ'S RATINGS

	Possible	Achieved
Ship	500	327
Accommodation	200	124
Food	400	250
Service	400	260
Entertainment	100	62
Cruise	400	263

ple. Audio channels are available via the TV set, although the picture cannot be turned off. The bathrooms are efficient units that are well designed but basic; hairdryers (they are weak) are included.

If you book a suite or one of two upper-grade cabins, you'll get a little more space, a lounge area with table and sofa that converts into another bed (good for families), European duvets, and a refrigerator (top categories only). The bathrooms also have a bathtub, shower and retractable clothesline.

CUISINE. There are no assigned dining rooms, tables or seats, but some eateries cost extra. All restaurants and eateries are non-smoking. They include: Four Seasons Restaurant (the principal dining room, serving Continental Cuisine); The Saffron (Indian vegetarian and Jain buffet, located aft with fine ocean views); Two Trees Restaurant (exclusive lounge/restaurant); Taj by the Bay (Indian family-style restaurant, with aft-facing ocean views); Blue Lagoon (24-hour casual refreshments); and Coconut Willy's (poolside refreshment center).

ENTERTAINMENT. The 770-seat Stardust Lounge is the venue for shows and major cabaret acts, although 12 thick pillars obstruct many sightlines. The Galaxy of the Stars Lounge, is located aft, and is for cabaret acts. A number of bands and solo entertaining musicians provide live music for listening and dancing in several lounges and bars.

SPA/FITNESS. There's a good gymnasium/fitness center, located around the mast and accessible only from the outside deck – not good when it rains.

SuperStar Virgo
★★★★

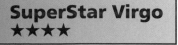

Size: . . . . .Large Resort Ship	Total Crew: .1,225	Cabins (wheelchair accessible): 4
Tonnage: 75,338	Passengers	Wheelchair accessibility . . . . .Good
Lifestyle: . . . . .Standard	(lower beds/all berths): 1,804/2,800	Cabin Current: . . . . .240 volts
Cruise Line: . . . . .Star Cruises	Passenger Space Ratio	Elevators: 9
Former Names: . . . . .none	(lower beds/all berths): 41.7/26.9	Casino (gaming tables): . . . . .Yes
Builder: . . . . .Meyer Werft (Germany)	Crew/Passenger Ratio	Slot Machines: . . . . .Yes
Original Cost: . . . .$350 million	(lower beds/all berths): 1.4/2.2	Swimming Pools (outdoors): 2
Entered Service: . . . . .Aug 1999	Cabins (total): .902	Swimming Pools (indoors): 0
Registry: . . . . .Panama	Size Range (sq ft/m): 150.6–638.3/	Whirlpools: 4
Length (ft/m): 879.2/268.0	14.0–59.3	Self-Service Launderette: . . . . .No
Beam (ft/m): 105.6/32.2	Cabins (outside view): 575	Dedicated Cinema/Seats: . . . . .No
Draft (ft/m): 25.9/7.9	Cabins (interior/no view): 327	Library: . . . . .Yes
Propulsion/Propellers: diesel (50,400kW)/2	Cabins (for one person): 0	
Passenger Decks: 10	Cabins (with private balcony): 390	

OVERALL SCORE: 1,502 OUT OF A POSSIBLE 2,000 POINTS

OVERVIEW. *SuperStar Virgo* (sister to *SuperStar Leo,* now renamed *Norwegian Spirit*) was the second new ship ordered for the Asian market. The all-white ship has a distinctive red/blue funnel with gold star logo. There are three distinct classes of passengers. As you check-in, you will be issued with a colored boarding card to denote Admiral Class passengers (yellow), Balcony Class (red), or World Cruisers (blue).

There is a walk-around promenade deck outdoors, good for strolling. Inside are two boulevards, and a stunning, larger two-deck-high central atrium lobby, with three glass-walled elevators and ample space to peruse the shops and cafés that line its inner sanctum.

The casino complex is at the forward end of the atrium boulevard on Deck 7. This includes a large general-purpose, brightly lit casino, called Oasis, with gaming tables and slot machines. There's a smaller "members only" gaming club, as well as VIP gaming rooms, one of which has its own access to the upper level of the showlounge. The 450-seat Galaxy of the Stars Lounge is an observation lounge by day and a nightclub at night, with live music.

The interior decor has some distinctly European touches in its design, taste and color combinations, and the layout was modified and improved slightly from that of the sister ship (for a slightly different market). The lobby, for example, has become an Italian Piazza, with a stunning *trompe l'oeil* and multi-colored stained-glass ceiling. The decor mixes east and west, and public room names have been chosen to appeal to a mixture of Australian, European and Asian passengers. Three stairways are each carpeted in a different color, which helps new cruise passengers find their way around easily.

Other facilities include a business center (with six meet-

BERLITZ'S RATINGS

	Possible	Achieved
Ship	500	417
Accommodation	200	156
Food	400	289
Service	400	284
Entertainment	100	66
Cruise	400	290

ing rooms), a large library and writing room, plus private mahjong and karaoke rooms, and a smoking room. A shopping concourse includes a wine shop.

Teens have their own huge video arcade, while younger children get to play in a wet 'n' wild aft pool (complete with pirate ship and caves) and two whirlpool tubs. Plus there's all the fun and facilities of Charlie's childcare center (open 24 hours a day), which includes a painting room, computer learning center, and small cinema. There's a room full of cots for toddlers to use for sleepovers, and even the toilets are at a special low height. About 15,000 sq. ft (1,400 sq. meters) is devoted to children's facilities. On deck, children will find the world's first stainless-steel water slide. Installed in 2009, it cost $550,000, and, at 100 meters long, you can zoom along at up to 22 feet per second, due to its steep incline, from 35 feet above the deck.

Star Cruises has established a Southeast Asian regional cruise audience for its diverse fleet. *SuperStar Virgo* is good for the active local market, and is the most comprehensive ship sailing year-round in this popular region. The passenger mix is international, although the local (regional) market is now developed, so you can expect to find lots of families with children, who are allowed to roam around the ship uncontrolled – particularly on the weekend cruise.

Lots of choices, more dining options, and Asian hospitality all add up to a very attractive holiday package particularly suitable for families with children, in a very contemporary floating resort that operates from Hong Kong (Apr–Nov) and Singapore (Nov–Mar). The dress code is ultra-casual (no jacket and tie needed), and the ship operates under a "no-tipping" policy. While the initial cruise fare seems very reasonable, the extra costs and charges soon mount up if you want to indulge in more than the basics. Although service levels and finesse are inconsistent, hospitality is very good.

There are many extra-cost items (in addition to the à la carte dining spots), such as for morning tea, afternoon tea, most cabaret shows (except a crew show), and childcare. Finding your way around many areas blocked by portable "crowd containment" ribbon barriers can prove frustrating.

SUITABLE FOR: *SuperStar Virgo* is best suited to couples, singles, and families with children of all ages who want to cruise aboard a real contemporary floating resort with decent facilities and many dining spots that are really dedicated to Asians, at a very attractive price.

ACCOMMODATION. There are seven types of accommodation, in 15 price categories. Three entire decks of cabins feature private balconies, while two-thirds of all cabins have an outside view. Both the standard outside-view and interior (no view) cabins really are very small (particularly since all cabins have extra berths for a third/fourth person), so take only the very smallest amount of clothing you can – there's almost no storage space for luggage.

All cabins have a personal safe, 100% cotton towels and duvets or sheets. Bathrooms have a good-sized shower enclosure, and include personal toiletries such as Burberry soap, conditioning shampoo and body lotion.

For more space, choose one of 13 suites. Each suite has a separate lounge/dining room, bedroom, and bathroom, and an interconnecting door to an ocean-view cabin with private balcony (with light). All cabinetry features richly lacquered woods, large (stocked) wet bar with refrigerator, dining table with a top that flips over to reveal a card table, and four chairs, sofa and drinks table, and trouser press.

The bedroom is small, completely filled by its queen-sized bed; there is a reasonable amount of drawer space (but the drawers are very small), and the closet space is rather tight – it contains two personal safes. A large en-suite bathroom is part of the bedroom and open to it – as is the trend in high-cost, interior architect-designed bathrooms ashore, and has a gorgeous mosaic tiled floor, kidney bean-shaped whirlpool bathtub, two basins, separate shower enclosure (with floor-to-ceiling ocean-view window) and separate toilet (with glass door). There are TV sets in the lounge, bedroom and bathroom.

For even more space, choose one of the six largest suites (Boracay, Nicobar, Langkawi, Majorca, Phuket, and Sentosa) and you'll have a generous amount of private living space, with a separate lounge, dining area, bedroom, large bathroom, and private balcony (with light). All cabinetry features richly lacquered woods, large (stocked) wet bar with refrigerator, dining table with a top that flips over to reveal a card table, and four chairs, sofa and drinks table, and trouser press. The bedrooms and large en-suite bathrooms are similar to those in the suites already described. There are TV sets in the lounge, bedroom and bathroom.

A small room service menu is available, with a 15% service charge plus a gratuity.

CUISINE. There is plenty of choice, with eight venues (all non-smoking). Plan your venue in advance, or you may be disappointed. These eateries are included in the cruise price:
● **Bella Vista** seats over 600 in an open-seating arrangement, although, in effect it operates two seatings. The aft section is two decks high, and huge cathedral-style windows are set in three sections overlooking the stern.
● **Mediterranean Buffet:** this is a large self-serve buffet restaurant with indoor/outdoor seating for 400.
● **The Pavilion Room:** has traditional Cantonese Chinese cuisine, including dim sum at lunchtime.
The following are à la carte (extra-cost) dining spots:
● **Noble House:** a Chinese Restaurant, with traditional Hong Kong-themed decor and items such as dim sum (there are also two small private dining rooms).
● **Palazzo:** a beautiful, if slightly ostentatious Italian restaurant. It has fine food, and a genuine Renoir painting (well protected by cameras and alarms).
● **Samurai:** a Japanese restaurant and sushi bar (for sashimi and sushi). There are two teppanyaki grills, each with 10 seats, where the chef cooks in front of you.
● **The Taj:** an Indian/Vegetarian dining spot that offers a range of food in a self-serve buffet setup.
● **Blue Lagoon:** a casual 24-hour street cafe with noodle dishes, fried rice and other Southeast Asian dishes.
● **Out of Africa:** a casual karaoke cafe and bar, where coffees, teas and pastries are available.

ENTERTAINMENT. The Lido showlounge, with 934 seats, is two decks high, with a main and balcony levels (the balcony level is reserved for "gaming club" members only). The room has almost no support columns to obstruct the sightlines, and a revolving stage for revues and other production shows (typically to recorded music – there is no live showband). "Kingdom of Kung-Fu," with a cast of 30, features the power and form of the Shaolin Masters in an action-packed martial arts show. The showlounge can also be used as a large-screen cinema, with superb surround sound.

In addition, local specialty cabaret acts are brought on board, as are revue-style shows (complete with topless dancers). Bands and small musical units provide plenty of live music for dancing and listening in the various lounges.

SPA/FITNESS. The Roman Spa and Fitness Center is located on one of the uppermost decks, just forward of the Tivoli Pool. It has a gymnasium full of high-tech muscle-toning equipment, and aerobics exercise room, hair and beauty salon, and saunas, steam rooms, and changing rooms for men and women, as well as several treatment rooms, and aqua-swim pools that provide counter-flow jets. There is an extra charge for use of the sauna and steam rooms.

Although there are several types of massages available, Thai massage is a specialty of the spa – you can have it in the spa, outdoors on deck, in your cabin or on your private balcony, space permitting. Sports facilities include a jogging track, golf driving range, basketball and tennis courts, and there are four levels of sunbathing decks.

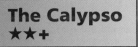

The Calypso
★★+

Size: . . . . .Small Ship	Passenger Decks: 8	Cabins (wheelchair accessible): 2
Tonnage: .11,162	Total Crew: 220	Wheelchair accessibility . . . . .None
Lifestyle: . . . . .Standard	Passengers	Cabin Current: . . . . .110 volts
Cruise Line: . . . . .Louis Cruises	(lower beds/all berths): 486/740	Dining Rooms: 1
Former Names: . . . . . .*Regent Jewel, Sun*	Passenger Space Ratio	Elevators: 2
Fiesta, Ionian Harmony, Canguro Verde	(lower beds/all berths): 22.9/15.0	Casino (gaming tables): . . . . .Yes
Builder: . . . . .Fincantieri (Italy)	Crew/Passenger Ratio	Slot Machines: . . . . .Yes
Original Cost: .n/a	(lower beds/all berths): 2.2/3.3	Swimming Pools (outdoors): 1
Entered Service: 1968/July 2000	Cabins (total): 243	Swimming Pools (indoors): 0
Registry: .Cyprus	Size Range (sq ft/m): .135–244/12.5–22.6	Whirlpools: 0
Length (ft/m): 444.2/135.4	Cabins (outside view): 158	Self-Service Launderette: . . . . .No
Beam (ft/m): 62.9/19.2	Cabins (interior/no view): 85	Dedicated Cinema/Seats: . . . . .No
Draft (ft/m): 20.6/6.3	Cabins (for one person): 0	Library: . . . . .Yes
Propulsion/Propellers: .diesel (9,000kW)/2	Cabins (with private balcony): 0	

OVERALL SCORE: 990 (OUT OF A POSSIBLE 2,000 POINTS)

OVERVIEW. *The Calypso*, a former Mediterranean ferry, was extensively reconstructed in 1999. Although its profile is a little bit unusual, one nice aspect is its enclosed wooden promenade deck – good for strolling, or just sitting and reading. There is a decent selection of public rooms, bars and lounges, considering the ship's size. The interior decor is very pleasant; there's a cozy and unpretentious ambiance, and the dress code is relaxed, with formal attire not required. The onboard currency is the Cyprus pound.

This is a high-density ship, so it is very crowded when full, and there may be a large number of smokers. There are very steep, narrow stairways on the outer decks. The ship formerly operated under charter to Thomson Cruises.

SUITABLE FOR: The ship is best suited to adult couples seeking a low-priced, but comfortable ship for a first short cruise experience, with unpretentious and unstuffy surroundings and acceptable food and service.

ACCOMMODATION. There are four suites, seven semi-deluxe, 147 outside-view cabins and 85 interior (no view) cabins. The price you pay depends on grade, size and location (cabins on higher decks command higher prices). No matter which cabin you choose, however, all have double or twin beds, television set, telephone, personal safe, and bathrooms have a shower enclosure, toilet and washbasin.

The cabins have warm pastel decor, although the artwork

BERLITZ'S RATINGS

	Possible	Achieved
Ship	500	195
Accommodation	200	95
Food	400	209
Service	400	241
Entertainment	100	55
Cruise	400	195

is minimal, and the fabrics and other soft furnishings could be of better quality. Some cabins have a third and fourth upper berth (there is only one personal safe), and drawer and storage space is very limited – in other words, take as little clothing as possible.

Those designated as suites also have a refrigerator/ minibar. There is a limited cabin service menu.

CUISINE. L'Orchidee dining room, in the aft section of the ship, is reasonably attractive and decorated, although its layout is somewhat awkward, as it is positioned on two slightly different levels. There are two seatings, and tables are for four, six or eight persons.

The menu choice is quite good (it includes a vegetarian option), and the food has plenty of taste. The service comes with a smile. Breakfast and lunch buffets are quite attractive, with plenty of variety. The wine list is very small, but prices are reasonable (don't expect vintage wines, though).

ENTERTAINMENT. The showlounge is a single-level room, and several pillars obstruct the sightlines from many seats. The entertainment consists mainly of cabaret acts. Several bands and musical units provide live music for dancing and listening.

SPA/FITNESS. Apart from a small gymnasium and sauna, there is little else. Massage, however, is available (the massage room is tiny), as are beauty/hair treatments.

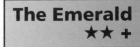

The Emerald
★★ +

Size:	Mid-Size Ship	Passenger Decks:	10	Cabins (wheelchair accessible):	2
Tonnage:	26,428	Total Crew:	412	Wheelchair accessibility	None
Lifestyle:	Standard	Passengers		Cabin Current:	110 and 220 volts
Cruise Line:	Louis Cruises	(lower beds/all berths):	990/1,198	Elevators:	3
Former Names:	Regent Rainbow,	Passenger Space Ratio		Casino (gaming tables):	Yes
	Diamond Island, Santa Rosa	(lower beds/all berths):	26.6/22.0	Slot Machines:	Yes
Builder: Newport News Shipbuilding (USA)		Crew/Passenger Ratio		Swimming Pools (outdoors):	1
Original Cost:	$25 million	(lower beds/all berths):	2.4/2.9	Swimming Pools (indoors):	0
Entered Service:	June 1958/Apr 1997	Cabins (total):	500	Whirlpools:	2
Registry:	Cyprus	Size Range (sq ft/m):	124.8–304.6/	Self-Service Launderette:	No
Length (ft/m):	599.0/182.57		11.6–28.3	Dedicated Cinema/Seats:	No
Beam (ft/m):	84.0/25.60	Cabins (outside view):	338	Library:	Yes
Draft (ft/m):	27.5/8.38	Cabins (interior/no view):	162		
Propulsion/Propellers:	steam turbine	Cabins (for one person):	10		
	(16,400kW)/2	Cabins (with private balcony):	0		

BERLITZ'S OVERALL SCORE: 1,063 (OUT OF A POSSIBLE 2,000 POINTS)

OVERVIEW. This solid, American-built, former ocean liner benefits from a strong, riveted hull; all new ships are seam-welded. The open deck and sun-bathing space is quite limited when the ship is full, although there are a good number of sunloungers. There is, however, a good wrap-around promenade deck outdoors, with plenty of chairs.

The ship's interiors are quite pleasant and surprisingly comfortable, and have a warm decor that is contemporary without being at all brash. Many of the public rooms have high ceilings, and the ship has a spacious ocean-liner feel. There are some fine wrought-iron railings on the stairways. The artwork, unfortunately, is low-budget stuff.

For its short cruises from Cyprus, this ship provides a range of public spaces that, in turn, promote good ambiance and a number of bars for drinking in (five, actually). The casino is quite large, and has a high ceiling.

SUITABLE FOR: *The Emerald* is best suited to adult couples and singles who want a first cruise providing very good value-for-money vacation in unpretentious, old-style surroundings (typically 80 percent of passengers are over 45).

ACCOMMODATION. There are six main categories: Premier, Superior Outside Plus, Superior Outside, Superior Inside (no view), Standard Outside, and Standard Inside (no view).

Cabins are assigned at embarkation check-in unless you pay a supplement of £30 per cabin to pre-book (you can choose your preferred cabin from the deck plan. This method of assigning cabins means that those who book first, and those who arrive first at the embarkation port,

BERLITZ'S RATINGS

	Possible	Achieved
Ship	500	243
Accommodation	200	107
Food	400	210
Service	400	238
Entertainment	100	50
Cruise	400	215

probably will get the best cabins. It's better to pre-book.

Many of the original cabins are quite spacious, with good closet and drawer space, while newer ones are a little more compact, and have poor insulation. Continental breakfast in your cabin will cost about $7.50 (£4.50) extra per person (each time). There is also a 24-hour cabin service menu for snacks, all of which cost extra.

CUISINE. The Chanterelle Dining Room (non-smoking) is in the center of the ship. It has large ocean-view windows. A second restaurant, Le Bistro (non-smoking), is also in the center of the ship, but two decks above the Chanterelle.

While it won't win any awards, the food quality and its variety and presentation are actually quite decent considering the cost of a cruise. That there is always a vegetarian entrée for lunch and dinner (as well as vegetarian appetizers and soups). The service is friendly and quite attentive, but don't expect grand hotel-style service.

ENTERTAINMENT. The sight lines in the showlounge are poor, particularly from port and starboard side seating areas. The shows, although not of top professional quality, are fun and entertaining for the whole family. In addition, there is plenty of music for dancing, both live and recorded.

SPA/FITNESS. There is a small, windowless fitness center, located low down in the ship. There's also a sauna, while the ship's beauty salon is located on another deck – again in an interior position. There is no natural light, which makes tinting and coloring difficult.

Thomson Celebration
★★★ +

Size: ....Mid-Size Ship	Passenger Decks: 10	Cabins (with private balcony): 0
Tonnage: 33,930	Total Crew: 520	Cabins (wheelchair accessible): 4
Lifestyle: ....Standard	Passengers	Wheelchair accessibility ....Fair
Cruise Line: ....Thomson Cruises	(lower beds/all berths): 1,254/1,350	Cabin Current: ....110 and 220 volts
Former Names: ....*Noordam*	Passenger Space Ratio	Elevators: 7
Builder: .Chantiers de l'Atlantique (France)	(lower beds/all berths): 27.0/25.1	Casino (gaming tables): ....Yes
Original Cost: ....$160 million	Crew/Passenger Ratio	Slot Machines: ....Yes
Entered Service: .....Apr 1984/May 2005	(lower beds/all berths): 2.4/2.6	Swimming Pools (outdoors): 2
Registry: ....Dutch Antilles	Cabins (total): 627	Swimming Pools (indoors): 0
Length (ft/m): 704.2/214.66	Size Range (sq ft/m): 150.6–296.0/	Whirlpools: 1
Beam (ft/m): 89.4/27.26	14.0–27.5	Self-Service Launderette: ....Yes
Draft (ft/m): 24.2/7.40	Cabins (outside view): 413	Dedicated Cinema/Seats: Yes/230
Propulsion/Propellers: ....diesel	Cabins (interior/no view): 194	Library: ....Yes
(21,600 kW)/2	Cabins (for one person): 0	

OVERALL SCORE: 1,307 (OUT OF A POSSIBLE 2,000 POINTS)

OVERVIEW. *Thomson Celebration* (formerly Holland America Line's *Noordam*) and sister to *Thomson Spirit* (formerly Holland America Line's *Nieuw Amsterdam*), has a nicely raked bow and a contemporary transom stern, but overall the ship's angular exterior superstructure design makes it look rather squat. There is a good amount of open deck space, and the traditional teakwood decks outdoors include a wrap-around promenade deck. The ship, however, is now quite dated and occasionally suffers from some vibration. Perhaps its best asset is its friendly and personable international crew.

The ship has a spacious interior design and layout, with most public rooms located aft in a vertical arrangement, while accommodation is positioned in the forward section, which keeps noise away from the accommodation areas. The soothing color combinations do not jar the senses; although they are rather dark and somber, with some new color splashes added during the ship's refurbishment in 2005. There is much polished teakwood and rosewood paneling throughout the interiors. Horizon's observation lounge, atop the ship, is a pleasant retreat, with fine views forward. The main lounge, which has a small balcony level, is reminiscent of those found on former ocean liners, and is really more suited to cabaret entertainment, and not full production shows. While children are also catered to, with their own play areas and hosts, the majority of passengers are adults.

The ship is exclusively chartered by Thomson Cruises, so your fellow passengers are likely to be mostly British, and typically about 90 percent of passengers will be over 55. Refreshingly, all gratuities are included, and the onboard currency is the pound sterling. Thomson Celebration oper-

BERLITZ'S RATINGS		
	Possible	Achieved
Ship	500	332
Accommodation	200	137
Food	400	235
Service	400	261
Entertainment	100	64
Cruise	400	278

ates a wide variety of cruises, and, for part of the year, is based in the UK.

Thomson Cruises' ships are non-smoking, although smoking areas are provided in most public rooms. Note that there are many interior (no view) cabins, and standing in line for embarkation, disembarkation, shore tenders and for self-serve buffet meals is an inevitable aspect of cruising aboard all large ships.

SUITABLE FOR: *Thomson Celebration* is best suited to adult couples and singles taking their first or second cruise, seeking a modern (but not glitzy) ship with a wide array of public lounges and bars, and a middle-of-the-road lifestyle, with food and entertainment that is quite acceptable rather than fancy.

ACCOMMODATION. There is one suite grade, four grades of outside-view cabins (one designated Deluxe), two grades of interior (no view) cabins. There are four cabins for the disabled – these are large, and have great forward-facing views. You can pre-book your preferred cabin for a per cabin fee of £39 (around US$65).

In general, most cabins have a reasonable amount of space, although they are small when compared with those of many other ships. In general, they are adequately appointed and practically laid out, with some wood furniture and fittings, wood paneling, good counter and storage space (although there is very little drawer space), a large mirror, and a private bathroom very modest in size.

The top three categories of cabins – which are only marginally larger and should not really be called suites or mini-suites – have bathtubs while all others have shower enclosures only. Several cabins have king- or queen-sized beds, although most have twin beds (some, but not all, can be pushed together). In many cabins, particularly those that are interior (no view), the bed configuration is L-shaped, and the beds cannot be pushed together.

A number of cabins also have additional upper berths for a third/fourth person. Room service is provided 24 hours a day. All cabin televisions receive live news via satellite. Note that the cabin insulation is really quite poor, and bathroom towels are small. In addition, some cabins on Mariner and Bridge Decks have lifeboat-obstructed views.

CUISINE. The Meridian Restaurant, which sits in the center of the ship, is a reasonably large and attractive room, with warm decor, and ample space. Breakfast and lunch and dinner (6pm–10.30pm) are served in an open-seating arrangement, so you may get a different table and different waiters for each meal. Although there are a few tables for two, most are for four, six or eight. Dinners typically include a choice of four entrées; a vegetarian entrée is also available daily.

Children have their own menu, with "home-from-home" dishes and small portions. Dessert and pastry items will usually be of good quality, and made specifically for British tastes, although there is much use of canned fruits and jellies.

A small à la carte restaurant, called Zilli's after celebrity chef Aldo Zilli, is an alternative dining spot; reservations are required and there's a per-person cover charge. It seats up to 45 and has superior food and service plus a quieter, more refined atmosphere. It is adjacent to the Meridian Restaurant, but is best entered from the aft stairway.

Instead of the more formal dining room, there is also a Lido Restaurant for a more casual setting. This is open 24 hours a day in an open-seating arrangement. Tables are set with crisp linens, flatware and stemware for dinner, when a set menu includes a choice of four entrées. Each week a themed buffet (Chinese, Indian or Mexican, depending on the cruise itinerary) may be featured for dinner. However, self-serve buffets are quite repetitive and not as creative as aboard *Thomson Destiny* or *Thomson Spirit*. On Lido Deck, the outdoor Terrace Grill provides fast-food grilled items and pizza during the day. All dining venues are non-smoking.

ENTERTAINMENT. The 600-seat Broadway Showlounge, two decks high (with a main and balcony level), is the principal venue for production shows and cabaret entertainment. Note that there are many pillars in the show lounge, so sightlines are obstructed from some seats.

Thomson presents an array of production shows that are colorful, lively, and entertaining (aboard other Thomson charters, the young entertainment/cruise staff enthusiastically provide the shows), while cabaret acts provide entertainment on evenings when there are no production shows.

A second entertainment venue (Hemingway's) is a multifunctional room for quizzes, dancing, and for use as a late-night discotheque. A number of bands and musical units provide live music for dancing and listening in several lounges and bars.

SPA/FITNESS. Oceans Health Club is atop the ship at the aft end. It has good ocean views, and overlooks the aft pool. Facilities include an aerobics exercise room, a decent size gymnasium with plenty of treadmills, exercycles, and other body-toning and muscle-pumping equipment, sauna (there is no steam room), and four body treatment rooms. You can have massages, aromatherapy facials, body wraps, manicures, pedicures, and hair beautifying treatments.

Note that the beauty salon is located in a completely different area (close to the Reception Desk on the port side) to the health and fitness facilities.

Sample treatment prices: Swedish Classic Massage/ Indian Head Massage £30 (30 minutes) or £44 (45 minutes) or £52 (60 minutes); Cleansing Facial £36; Pedicure and Foot Massage £22; Exfoliating Body Polish £34.

Thomson Destiny
★★★ +

Size: .... Mid-Size Ship	Total Crew: .... .540	Cabins (wheelchair accessible): 0
Tonnage: .... .37,773	Passengers	Wheelchair accessibility .... .Fair
Lifestyle: .... Standard	(lower beds/all berths): 1,450/1,611	Cabin Current: ....110 volts
Cruise Line: .... Thomson Cruises	Passenger Space Ratio	Elevators: 7
Former Names: *Sunbird, Song of America*	(lower beds/all berths): 26.0/23.4	Casino (gaming tables): .... .Yes
Builder: .... Wartsila (Finland)	Crew/Passenger Ratio	Slot Machines: .... .Yes
Original Cost: ....$140 million	(lower beds/all berths): 2.6/2.9	Swimming Pools (outdoors): 2
Entered Service: ... .Dec 1982/May 2005	Cabins (total): .... .725	Swimming Pools (indoors): 0
Registry: .... The Bahamas	Size Range (sq ft/m): 118.4–425.1/	Whirlpools: 0
Length (ft/m): 705.0/214.88	11.0–39.5	Self-Service Launderette: .... .No
Beam (ft/m): 93.1/28.40	Cabins (outside view): .... .425	Dedicated Cinema/Seats: .... .No
Draft (ft/m): 22.3/6.80	Cabins (interior/no view): .... .300	Library: .... .Yes
Propulsion/Propellers: diesel (16,480kW)/2	Cabins (for one person): 0	
Passenger Decks: .... .11	Cabins (with private balcony): 9	

OVERALL SCORE: 1,303 (OUT OF A POSSIBLE 2,000 POINTS)

OVERVIEW. Originally built for Royal Caribbean International, the ship was sold in 1999 to My Travel/Sun Cruises, which pulled out of cruise vacations and ship ownership in 2004. It is now the largest ship in the Thomson Cruises fleet (on charter until 2011). The all-white ship, now refurbished, is smart-looking, with nicely rounded lines, sharply raked bow, and a single funnel with a cantilevered, wrap-around lounge called the Chart Room – a fine place from which to observe the world around and below you.

There is a decent amount of open deck and sunbathing space (but it will be crowded when the ship sails full, which is most of the time), and some nicely polished wooden decks and rails. There are two swimming pools – the aft pool designated for children, the forward pool for adults.

The interior decor is bright and breezy. There is a good array of public rooms, most of which have high ceilings, and are one deck above the dining room. These include the main show lounge, casino and nightclub. There is also a small conference center for meetings, as well as an internet café which has six computer terminals – but no café.

Thomson Cruises provides a consistent, well-tuned and well-packaged, fun product, in comfortable surroundings. As part of Thomson Holidays, it uses its own Thomson Airways and is therefore able to offer complete cruise-air-stay packages at such attractive rates. The company does a good job of getting you and your luggage from aircraft to ship without having to go through immigration (depending on itinerary) in foreign countries whenever possible – so your cruise holiday is relatively seamless. The company offers airlift from almost a score of UK airports via Britannia Airlines. You can pre-book a window seat for an extra cost,

BERLITZ'S RATINGS		
	Possible	Achieved
Ship	500	340
Accommodation	200	125
Food	400	241
Service	400	261
Entertainment	100	66
Cruise	400	270

including a premium seat (more space than standard seats), while pre-booked meals also cost extra.

The company's brochures tell it like it is – so you know before you go exactly what you will get for your money. Like other ships in the Thomson Cruises fleet, the space per passenger, particularly on the open decks, is very tight when the ships are full. There is little choice of tea and coffee. There are no cushioned pads for the sunloungers.

Standing in line for embarkation, disembarkation, shore tenders and for self-serve buffet meals is an inevitable aspect of cruising aboard all large ships.

Your fellow passengers are likely to be British (typically about 80 percent of passengers will be over 45). During the summer a lot of families with children go cruising, so you can expect to find them everywhere. Perhaps the best part of cruising aboard *Thomson Destiny* lies in the destinations, and not the ship (although it is perfectly comfortable). Hotel add-ons can extend a cruise vacation, and Thomson has a fine collection, depending on your needs, budget, and whether you are traveling with children (or grandchildren). The onboard currency is the British pound. All Thomson Cruises' ships are non-smoking, although smoking areas are provided in most public rooms.

Passenger niggles include some serious vibration in the Clipper Bar, and the tired look of the ship's interiors.

SUITABLE FOR: *Thomson Destiny* is best suited to adult couples, singles, singles taking their first or second cruise, and families with children, all seeking a modern (but not glitzy) ship with a wide array of public lounges and bars, a middle-of-the-road lifestyle, with food and entertainment that is quite acceptable rather than fancy, and a British ambience. The company does not actively market or specialize in cruises for families with children because the children's and youth facilities are limited – there is also no evening babysitting service.

ACCOMMODATION. This is provided in five categories and nine price bands: Interior (no-view) Cabins (parallel or L-shaped bed arrangement), Outside View Cabins (parallel or L-shaped bed arrangement), Deluxe Cabins (with parallel twin beds that can be converted to a queen-sized bed), Suites and Grand Suites. You can pre-book the exact cabin and location you want if you pay an extra charge of £39 per cabin (roughly US$60), which also lets you choose whether to dine at the early or late evening seating.

Most cabins are of a similar size (actually very small compared to today's newer ships) and the insulation between them is quite poor. The cabins also have mediocre closets and very little storage space, yet somehow everyone seems to manage. They are just about adequate for a one-week cruise, as you will need only a small selection of mainly casual clothes (you'll probably have to put your shoes – and luggage – under the bed).

Most bathrooms typically contain a washbasin, toilet, and shower, with very little space for your toiletry items. Although they are reasonably cheerful, the shower enclosure is small, and has a curtain that you will probably end up dancing with. Towels are 100% cotton.

In some cabins, twin beds are fixed in a parallel mode (some are moveable and can be made into a queen-sized bed), while others may be in an L-shape. Note that in almost all cabins there is a "lip" or threshold (of about 9 inches/23 cm) at the bathroom door to step over.

You can get more space and a larger cabin if you book one of the 21 slightly more expensive deluxe-grade cabins on Promenade Deck. These have twin beds that convert to a queen-sized bed, set diagonally into a sleeping area adjacent to outside-view windows. There is more drawer space, more closet space, and the bathroom has a half-size tub and shower combination – bathrobes are also provided. The largest of these deluxe-grade cabins is Cabin 7000.

For even more exclusivity, you can book one of nine Suites. All are located in a private area, have fine wood paneling and trim, and come with additional space and better, more personalized service.

The additional space includes a lounge area with sofa (this converts to a double bed – making it ideal for families with children), coffee table and two chairs, a vanity desk, combination TV/VCR, an abundance of drawers, illuminated closets (with both hanging space and several shelves), excellent storage space, king-sized bed, and bathrobes. The bathroom is fully tiled, and has a full-sized enamel bathtub (rare in ships today) with shower, pink granite-look washbasin, and plenty of storage space for toiletry items. Suite occupants also get a semi-private balcony – the door of which is extremely heavy and hard to open – with drinks table and two teak chairs. Book one of the two Grand Suites,

and you'll get even more room – plus views over the ship's bows and a larger balcony (these can be overlooked from the open deck above), more floor space, and a walk-in closet. Missing are a bedside telephone and a bathroom telephone.

The cabin voltage is 110 volts, so British passengers will need to take a US-style adapter for any electrical appliances such as a hairdryer. Note that the accommodation deck hallways are also very narrow on some decks.

CUISINE. The Seven Seas Restaurant, a large room, consists of a central main section and two long, narrow wings (the Magellan Room and Galileo Room) with large, ocean-view windows. The low ceiling creates a high level of ambient noise. There are two seatings, both no-smoking. There are tables for two (but only 14), four, six or eight (window tables are for two or six). The service is average.

The cuisine is basic, no-frills food. There is plenty of it, though; indeed, it is quantity, not quality, that prevails, but do remember that it is all provided at a low cost. Presentation is a weak point, and there are no fish knives. If you enjoy going out to eat, and enjoy being adventurous with your food and eating habits then you could be disappointed. The menus are standard and deviation is difficult. Bottled water is offered, and costs extra; the ship's drinking water (for which there is no charge) is adequate.

There is an adequate, but limited, wine list, and the wines are almost all very young – typical of supermarket bottles. Wine prices are quite modest, as are the prices for most alcoholic beverages.

For casual, self-serve breakfasts and lunches, the Veranda Cafe is the alternative choice, although the tables and seats outdoors are of metal and plastic, and the buffets are basic and old-fashioned. The low cruise price dictates the use of plastic cups and plastic stirrers – teaspoons are unheard of. At night you can "dine" under the steel and canvas canopy, where the café becomes a pleasant, outdoors alternative to the dining room – and includes waiter service.

ENTERTAINMENT. The Can Can Lounge is the venue for all entertainment events and social functions, and has a stage and hardwood dance floor. It is a single-level room, designed more for cabaret acts than for large-scale production shows. The revue-style shows are typically the end-of-pier variety type, with an energetic, well-meaning cast of young people who also double as cruise staff during the day, together with some professional cabaret acts.

Another, smaller room, the Oklahoma Lounge, has a stage and dance floor, and is often used to present late-night comedy and other acts.

SPA/FITNESS. Although the spa facilities are not exactly generous, there is a gymnasium, sauna (no steam room), changing rooms for men and women, and a beauty salon. Spa and beauty services are provided by Harding Brothers, who operate similar beauty services for a number of cruise lines. You can book a massage, an aromatherapy facial, manicure and pedicure, among other treatments.

Thomson Dream
NOT YET RATED

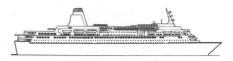

Size: ....Mid-Size Ship	Passenger Decks: 9	Cabins (with private balcony): 6
Tonnage: 53,872	Total Crew: 650	Cabins (wheelchair accessible): 4
Lifestyle: ....Standard	Passengers	Wheelchair accessibility ....Fair
Cruise Line: ....Thomson Cruises	(lower beds/all berths): 1,506/1,756	Cabin Current: ....110/220 volts
Former Names: .... *Costa Europa,*	Passenger Space Ratio	Elevators: 7
Westerdam, Homeric	(lower beds/all berths): 35.7/30.6	Casino (gaming tables): ....Yes
Builder: ....Meyer Werft (Germany)	Crew/Passenger Ratio	Slot Machines: ....Yes
Original Cost: ....$150 million	(lower beds/all berths): 2.4/2.7	Swimming Pools (outdoors): 2
Entered Service: ....May 1986/Dec 2010	Cabins (total): 753	(1 with magrodome)
Registry: ....Italy	Size Range (sq ft/m): 129.1–425.1/	Swimming Pools (indoors): 0
Length (ft/m): 797.9/243.23	12.0–39.5	Whirlpools: 2
Beam (ft/m): 95.1/29.00	Cabins (outside view): 501	Self-Service Launderette: ....Yes (5)
Draft (ft/m): 23.6/7.20	Cabins (interior/no view): 252	Dedicated Cinema/Seats: Yes/237
Propulsion/Propellers: diesel (23,830kW)/2	Cabins (for one person): 18	Library: ....Yes

BERLITZ'S OVERALL SCORE: NYR (OUT OF A POSSIBLE 2,000 POINTS)

OVERVIEW. *Thomson Dream* was originally *Homeric* for the now long-defunct Home Lines, and was given an $84 million "chop and stretch" operation in 1990 when bought by Holland America Line. You don't even have to look closely to tell where the mid-section was inserted, because the windows are larger than the fore and aft sections. The ship was moved to Costa Cruises (owned by Carnival Corporation) in 2002, and then acquired by Thomson Cruises in 2009, when it was sent for an extensive refurbishment to cater to Thomson's mainly British passengers.

The ship has good teak outside decks and a walk-around promenade deck, plus a decent amount of open deck space for sunbathing. There is also a swimming pool deck, which can be covered by a sliding glass dome, although this is rather small for the number of passengers carried.

The ship has a functional, restful interior decor, mainly with pastel tones and some added color accents. The ship absorbs passengers well, and the passenger flow is good, although the layout is a little awkward to learn at first. However, many of the public entertainment rooms are located on one deck, which makes access simple. There are several bars and lounges, some small and intimate, others larger and noisier. However, there are, fortunately, lots of nooks and crannies – much nicer than the warehouse-style public rooms of the latest ships.

Thomson Dream has a good amount of space allotted to children's facilities, suiting the increased number of families who will choose this ship. Other facilities include an internet lounge, library, card room and shops.

It's a reasonably modern ship – comfortable, but certainly not luxurious. The largest in the Thomson fleet, it

BERLITZ'S RATINGS		
	Possible	Achieved
Ship	500	NYR
Accommodation	200	NYR
Food	400	NYR
Service	400	NYR
Entertainment	100	NYR
Cruise	400	NYR

provides the setting for a satisfactory family cruise experience.

Passenger gripes incluse irritating, repetitious announcements, expensive shore excursions, and noticeable vibration in some areas. The onboard currency is the British pound.

SUITABLE FOR: *Thomson Dream* is best suited to adult couples and singles taking their first or second cruise, families with children of all ages, all seeking a modern but not glitzy ship with a wide array of public lounges and bars, and a middle-of-the-road lifestyle, with food and entertainment that is quite acceptable rather than fancy.

ACCOMMODATION. There are several cabin price grades, including suites, mini-suites, outside-view cabins, and inside (no view) cabins, priced according to grade, size and location. You can pre-book your preferred cabin for a per cabin fee of £39 (around US$60).

Except for suite category cabins – there are five suites, each with king-sized beds, separate lounge area and bathroom with full size bathtub – almost all other cabins are of a similar size. In general, they are generously proportioned, well appointed, and equipped with almost everything you need. Features include ample closet, drawer and storage space, hairdryer, and good-sized bathrooms. The towels are quite small, however. Unfortunately, there are far too many interior (no view) cabins – over 50 percent of all cabins – and cabin soundproofing is rather poor, so you really can hear your neighbors brushing their hair. All cabin TV sets receive European news channels.

Most cabins have twin beds, although a number have the old-style upper and lower berths, so do make sure when you book that you request – and get – the kind of cabin with the sleeping arrangements you want. Some larger cabins also have a sofa that turns into a bed – good for families with small children. There are four cabins for the disabled, suitably located, on higher decks, close to lifts.

CUISINE. There are several eateries to choose from, depending on your taste and budget.

The Orion Restaurant (enlarged by 345 sq.ft/32 sq. meters in 2006) is a traditional dining room that has a raised central, cupola-style dome, and port and starboard side portholes are highlighted at night by pleasing lighting. Open-seating dining is the norm, so you can sit with whomever you wish. The restaurant is open for breakfast, lunch and dinner, but note that the tables are extremely close together, and, except for the center section, the ceiling is quite low – just one deck high – so the noise level can be extremely loud. The service is decent enough, but communication can sometimes be frustrating, and smiles from the waiters and assistants can do only so much. The cuisine is British-Continental in nature, but, although there is plenty of food, its quality and presentation are disappointing when compared to other cruise products on the market.

The Grill is a steak and seafood (including surf 'n' turf) extra-cost restaurant, with food cooked to order. Reservations are required.

The 24-hour Andromeda Restaurant and a smaller Sirens Restaurant, both in the aft section, provide breakfast, lunch and dinner in a self-serve buffet style, but lines and a crowded environment make these noisy eateries. Twice during each cruise, there's a theme night.

The Terrace Grill, open for lunch, serves fast-food such as BBQ items, pizzas and salads.

ENTERTAINMENT. Facilities include the Atlante Theater, the ship's two-decks-high showlounge, with seating on both main and balcony levels. However, several pillars obstruct sightlines from a number of seats. A resident troupe of singers and dancers provides the cast members for colorful, high-energy production shows. For nights when there is no production show, the showlounge presents cabaret acts such as singers, comedy jugglers, magicians, ventriloquists, and so on.

A number of bands and small musical units provide live music in many of the lounges and bars – so there is always plenty of music to dance to or listen to, from light classical in the Argo Lounge to jazz to pop, dance and rap. In addition, there is a discotheque for the young at heart and hard of hearing.

SPA/FITNESS. The Nereidi Fitness Center, located on an upper deck, aft of the ship's mast, includes a gymnasium, saunas and massage rooms, although there is no steam room. The facility is really small, considering the number of passengers carried – although, to be fair, such facilities were not very popular when the ship was built.

The spa is operated by Harding Brothers, a specialist concession. Some fitness classes are free, while some, such as yoga, cost extra.

However, being aboard will give you an opportunity to try some of the more exotic treatments, particularly some of the massages. Massages, including Aroma Stone massage, Chakra Balancing massage and other well-being massages, facials, pedicures, and beauty salon treatments cost extra. Do make appointments as early as possible – aboard a ship of this size, time slots go quickly, so the day you board is the best time to book your treatments.

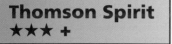

Thomson Spirit
★★★ +

Size: ....Large Resort Ship	Passenger Decks: 10	Cabins (with private balcony): 0
Tonnage: 33,930	Total Crew: 520	Cabins (wheelchair accessible): 4
Lifestyle: ....Standard	Passengers	Wheelchair accessibility ....Fair
Cruise Line: ....Thomson Cruises	(lower beds/all berths): 1,254/1,350	Cabin Current: ....110 and 220 volts
Former Names: ......Nieuw Amsterdam,	Passenger Space Ratio	Elevators: 7
Patriot, Nieuw Amsterdam	(lower beds/all berths): 27.0/25.1	Casino (gaming tables): ....Yes
Builder: .Chantiers de l'Atlantique (France)	Crew/Passenger Ratio	Slot Machines: ....Yes
Original Cost: ....$150 million	(lower beds/all berths): 2.4/2.6	Swimming Pools (outdoors): 2
Entered Service: ...July 1983/May 2002	Cabins (total): 627	Swimming Pools (indoors): 0
Registry: ....The Bahamas	Size Range (sq ft/m): 150.6–296.0/	Whirlpools: 1
Length (ft/m): 704.2/214.66	14.0–27.5	Self-Service Launderette: ....Yes (3)
Beam (ft/m): 89.4/27.26	Cabins (outside view): 413	Dedicated Cinema/Seats: Yes/230
Draft (ft/m): 24.6/7.52	Cabins (interior/no view): 194	Library: ....Yes
Propulsion/Propellers: diesel (21,600 kW)/2	Cabins (for one person): 0	

OVERALL SCORE: 1,316 (OUT OF A POSSIBLE 2,000 POINTS)

OVERVIEW. *Thomson Spirit* was originally built for and operated by Holland America Line. It has a nicely raked bow and a contemporary transom stern, but overall the ship's angular exterior superstructure design makes it look squat and quite boxy. The ship's exterior has an all-white hull and superstructure. There is a good amount of open teakwood deck space, particularly at the aft section of the ship, and the traditional outdoors teakwood decks include a wrap-around promenade deck. Unfortunately, the ship has always suffered from poor build quality (it was built in a French shipyard) and excessive vibration, particularly at the stern, since new.

As *Patriot*, the ship had a disastrous, short-lived liaison with United States Lines, following its sale by Holland America Line to the publicly funded United States Lines in 2000. That venture was short-lived, and United States Lines collapsed in a sea of debt owed to US taxpayers in October 2001. Carnival Corporation (owners of Holland America Line) repurchased the ship for the amount outstanding ($79.8 million), and then chartered it to Louis Cruises, which in turn has sub-chartered it to Thomson Cruises. *Thomson Spirit* has a sister ship in the slightly newer, 1984-built *Thomson Celebration* (formerly Holland America Line's *Noordam*).

Thomson first operated cruises in the 1970s, then abandoned them, only to start cruises operations again in the mid-1990s using chartered, rather than wholly-owned ships. It has proved a highly successful venture, offering extremely good value for money, particularly for adult couples, and occasionally families with children.

Thomson Spirit has quite a spacious interior design and layout, with little crowding and almost no points of con-

BERLITZ'S RATINGS

	Possible	Achieved
Ship	500	330
Accommodation	200	137
Food	400	245
Service	400	262
Entertainment	100	64
Cruise	400	278

gestion, and most public rooms are on a single deck. The color combinations do not jar the senses – most are pretty non-descript, though there are many splashes of color – and the decor was greatly changed and brightened by its new owners. There is much polished teakwood and rosewood paneling throughout the interiors. For quieter moments, try the Horizon Lounge, atop the ship; it has a wooden dance floor.

The main lounge, with a small balcony level, is reminiscent of the ocean liners of yesteryear.

Children are well catered to, with their own play areas at the aft of Bridge Deck. There are several children's clubs: Tots is for 3–5 year-olds, Team is for 6–8 year-olds, while Tribe is for 9–12 year-olds. The clubs operate five days a week (not on embarkation or disembarkation days), and are supervised by qualified "Children's Hosts."

It's good to see a tour operator like Thomson Cruises charter and operate this ship, especially since competition in the cruise industry is increasing. This ship is quite acceptable for passengers wanting pleasant surroundings and an all-British ambience. However, many newer ships have more space, better facilities and more options, and these leave this ship losing a few points in relation to the increased competition in the international marketplace.

Perhaps the best part of cruising aboard *Thomson Spirit* lies in the destinations and not the ship – although it is perfectly comfortable. Hotel add-ons can extend a cruise vacation, and Thomson has a fine collection, depending on your needs, budget, and whether you are traveling with children or grandchildren. The ship is exclusive to Thomson Cruises, so your fellow passengers are likely to be British (typically about 80 percent of passengers will be over 45).

Thomson owns its own airline, Thomson Airways, and has much experience in operating fly-cruises to the Mediterranean – the company offers airlift from almost a score of UK airports. With Thomson, you pay only for what you want. You can pre-book a window seat or a premium seat (more space than standard seats) for an additional cost.

All Thomson Cruises' ships are non-smoking, although smoking areas are provided in most public rooms. Standing in line for embarkation, disembarkation, shore tenders and for self-serve buffet meals is inevitable aboard all large ships.

SUITABLE FOR: *Thomson Spirit* is best suited to adult couples and singles taking their first or second cruise, families with children of all ages, all seeking a modern (but not glitzy) ship with a wide array of public lounges and bars, and a middle-of-the-road lifestyle, with food and entertainment that is quite acceptable rather than fancy.

ACCOMMODATION. There is one suite grade, four grades of outside-view cabins (one designated Deluxe), two grades of interior (no view) cabins. There are four cabins for the disabled (these are large, and have great forward-facing views). You can pre-book your preferred cabin for a per cabin fee of £39 (around US$60).

Most of the cabins are quite small (below the industry standard of 170 sq. ft/15.7 sq. meters). They are reasonably well appointed and practically laid out. Some have wood furniture, fittings, or accenting, good counter and storage space (but little drawer space), a large dressing mirror, and private bathrooms that are adequate, but no more. The top cabin categories (which are only marginally larger and should not really be called suites), have full-sized bathtubs while all others have showers. Several cabins have king- or queen-sized beds, although most have twin beds.

The largest accommodation is in the Presidential Suite (on Eagle Deck). Small by comparison to suites aboard many other ships, it measures 464 sq. ft (43.1 sq. meters) and is located on the uppermost accommodation deck. There is a king-sized bed, walk-in closet, wet bar, study and dining areas, television, VCR, and stereo system. The bathroom includes a whirlpool tub, double sink unit, and a separate powder room.

A number of cabins also have additional berths for a third/fourth person. Room service is provided 24 hours a day. All cabin TVs carry live news channels (when available). The cabin insulation is extremely poor, and the bathroom towels are small.

CUISINE. The Compass Rose Restaurant is reasonably large and attractive, with warm decor and ample space. Breakfast, lunch and dinner (6pm–10.30pm) are served in an open-seating arrangement, so you may get a different table and different waiters for each meal. Although there are a few tables for two, most are for four, six or eight. Dinners typically include a choice of four entrées; a vegetarian entrée is also available daily. Children have their own menu, with "home-from-home" dishes and small portions.

Dessert and pastry items will typically be of good quality, and made specifically for British tastes, although there is much use of canned fruits and jellies.

Sirocco's A La Carte Restaurant is the ship's alternative dining spot (reservations are required and a per-person cover charge applies). It seats only 45 and has superior food and service as well as a more refined, quieter atmosphere. It is located adjacent to the Compass Rose Restaurant, but is best entered from the aft stairway.

Instead of the more formal dining room, there is a more casual Lido Restaurant. This is open 24 hours a day, with open-seating. Tables are set with crisp linens, flatware and stemware for dinner, when the set menu includes a choice of four entrées. Each week a themed buffet (Chinese, Indian or Mexican, depending on the cruise itinerary) may be featured for dinner. On Lido Deck, the outdoor Terrace Grill provides fast-food grilled items and pizza during the day. All dining venues are non-smoking, except outdoor areas.

ENTERTAINMENT. The 600-seat Broadway Showlounge is two decks high (main and balcony levels) and is the ship's principal venue for production shows and cabaret entertainment. Although Thomson is not generally known for high-quality shows, they are, in fact, good fun, and are professionally produced (aboard other ships chartered by Thomson the young entertainment/cruise staff enthusiastically provide the shows), while cabaret acts provide entertainment on evenings when there is no production show.

A second entertainment venue, High Spirits, is a multi-functional room for quizzes, dancing, and late-night discotheque. A number of bands and musical units provide live music for dancing and listening in several lounges and bars.

SPA/FITNESS. Oceans Health Club is atop the ship at the aft end. It has good ocean views, and overlooks the aft pool and hot tub, on Bridge Deck. Facilities include an aerobics exercise room, a decent size gymnasium (there are plenty of treadmills, exercycles, and other body-toning and muscle-pumping equipment), sauna (there is no steam room), and several treatment rooms.

You can have massages, aromatherapy facials, body wraps, manicures, pedicures, and hair beautifying treatments. Note that the beauty salon is located in a completely different area (close to the Reception Desk on the port side) to the health and fitness facilities.

Sample prices: Swedish Classic Massage/Indian Head Massage £30 (30 minutes) or £44 (45 minutes) or £52 (60 minutes); Cleansing Facial £36; Pedicure and Foot Massage £22; Exfoliating Body Polish £34.

Veendam
★★★★

Size: ....Mid-Size Ship	Passenger Decks: 10	Cabins (with private balcony): 150
Tonnage: 55,451	Total Crew: 561	Cabins (wheelchair accessible): 6
Lifestyle: ....Premium	Passengers	Wheelchair accessibility ....Fair
Cruise Line: ......Holland America Line	(lower beds/all berths): 1,266/1,627	Cabin Current: ....110 and 220 volts
Former Names: ....none	Passenger Space Ratio	Elevators: 8
Builder: ....Fincantieri (Italy)	(lower beds/all berths): 43.8/34.0	Casino (gaming tables): ....Yes
Original Cost: ....$215 million	Crew/Passenger Ratio	Slot Machines: ....Yes
Entered Service: ....May 1996	(lower beds/all berths): 2.2/2.9	Swimming Pools (outdoors): 1
Registry: ....The Bahamas	Cabins (total): 633	Swimming Pools (indoors): 1
Length (ft/m): 719.3/219.3	Size Range (sq ft/m): 186.2–1,124.8/	(magrodome)
Beam (ft/m): 101.0/30.8	17.3–104.5	Whirlpools: 2
Draft (ft/m): 24.6/7.5	Cabins (outside view): 502	Self-Service Launderette: ....Yes
Propulsion/Propellers: .....diesel-electric	Cabins (interior/no view): 131	Dedicated Cinema/Seats: Yes/249
(34,560kW)/2	Cabins (for one person): 0	Library: ....Yes

OVERALL SCORE: 1,420 (OUT OF A POSSIBLE 2,000 POINTS)

OVERVIEW. *Veendam* is one of a series of four almost identical ships in the same series – the others being *Maasdam, Statendam,* and *Ryndam.* The exterior styling is rather angular (some would say boxy – the funnel certainly is), although it is softened and balanced somewhat by the fact that the hull is painted black. A new ducktail sponson stern was added in 2009 for better stability and ride characteristics. There is a full wrap-around teakwood promenade deck outdoors – excellent for strolling, and, thankfully, no sign of synthetic turf anywhere. The sunloungers one the exterior promenade deck are wood, and come with comfortable cushioned pads, while those at the swimming pool on Lido Deck are of white plastic.

In the interiors of this "S" -class ship, an asymmetrical layout helps to reduce bottlenecks and congestion. Most of the public rooms are concentrated on two decks, Promenade Deck, and Upper Promenade Deck, which creates a spacious feel to the ship's interiors. In general, a restrained approach to interior styling is taken, using a mixture of contemporary materials combined with traditional woods and ceramics. There is, fortunately, little "glitz" anywhere.

What is good is the array of artworks throughout the ship (costing about $2 million), assembled and displayed to represent the fine Dutch heritage of Holland America Line and to present a balance between standard itineraries and onboard creature comforts. Also noticeable are the fine flower arrangements throughout the public areas and foyers – used to good effect to brighten up what to some is rather dull decor.

Atop the ship, with forward-facing views that wrap around the sides is the Crow's Nest Lounge. By day it makes a fine

BERLITZ'S RATINGS		
	Possible	Achieved
Ship	500	372
Accommodation	200	150
Food	400	254
Service	400	287
Entertainment	100	72
Cruise	400	285

observation lounge, with large ocean-view windows; by night it is a nightclub with extremely variable lighting.

A three-deck high atrium foyer is quite appealing, although its sculpted centerpiece makes it look a little crowded, and leaves little room in front of the purser's office. A hydraulic glass roof covers the reasonably sized swimming pool/whirlpools and central Lido area so that it can be used in good or bad weather. The focal point here is a large dolphin sculpture.

There is a large, relaxing reference library. The company keeps its ships very clean and tidy, and there is good passenger flow throughout. As part of its "Signature of Excellence" program, the ships have received a new "Mix" lifestyle area. Mix is a trendy, upbeat space combining three specialty theme bars in one central area: Champagne (serving champagne and sparkling wines), Martinis (in individual shakers), and Spirits & Ales (a sports bar – beer and baseball/basketball for the boys). Additionally, Microsoft Surface touch-screen technology is available for playing checkers and chess, air hockey, and other sports games.

Veendam is fairly well-built, with decent interior fit and finish quality. Holland America Line is constantly fine-tuning its performance, and its regular passengers, almost all North American, find its ships very comfortable and well-run. The company continues its strong maritime traditions, although the present food and service components still let the rest of the cruise experience down.

The service staff is Indonesian, and, although they are mostly quite charming, communication often proves frustrating, and service is spotty and inconsistent.

An escalator travels between two of the lower decks

(one was originally planned to be the embarkation point), but it is almost pointless. The charge to use the washing machines and dryers in the self-service launderette is petty, particularly for suite occupants, who pay high prices for their cruises. The men's urinals in public restrooms are unusually high.

ACCOMMODATION. The accommodation ranges from small interior (no view) cabins to a large penthouse suite, in 17 price categories, the price depending on the grade, location and size chosen. All cabin televisions normally carry CNN and TNT programming.

The interior (no view) and outside-view standard cabins have twin beds that convert to a queen-size bed, and there is a separate living space with sofa and coffee table. However, although the drawer space is generally good, the closet space is actually very tight, particularly for long cruises – although more than adequate for a 7-night cruise. The bathrooms are tiled, and compact but practical. Bathrobes are also provided, as are hairdryers.

Bathrobes are also provided for all suites/cabins, as are hairdryers, and a small range of personal amenities (soap, conditioning shampoo, body lotion, shower cap, vanity kit). The bathrooms are quite well laid out, but the bathtubs are small units better described as shower tubs. Some cabins have interconnecting doors.

On Navigation Deck, 28 suites have accommodation for up to four. These also have in-suite dining as an alternative to the dining room, for private, reclusive meals. These are very spacious, tastefully decorated and well laid-out, and feature a separate living room, bedroom with two lower beds (convertible to a king-sized bed), a good-sized living area, dressing room, plenty of closet and drawer space, marble bathroom with Jacuzzi tub.

The largest accommodation of all is a penthouse suite. There is only one, located on the starboard side of Navigation Deck at the forward staircase. It has a king-sized bed (TV and video player) and vanity desk; large walk-in closet with superb drawer space, oversize whirlpool bath (it could seat four) and separate shower enclosure, separate washroom with toilet, bidet and washbasin; living room with writing desk, large TV and full set of audio equipment); dressing room, large private balcony (with teak lounge chairs and drinks tables, dining table and four chairs), pantry (with large refrigerator, toaster unit, and full coffee/tea making facilities and food preparation area, and a separate entrance from the hallway), mini-bar/refrigerator, a guest toilet and floor-to-ceiling windows. There is no bell push.

CUISINE/DINING. The Rotterdam Dining Room spans two decks. It is located at the stern of the ship, is quite dramatic, and has two grand staircases to connect the two levels, panoramic views on three sides, and a music balcony. Both open seating and fixed (assigned tables and times) seating are available, while breakfast and lunch are open-seating (you'll be seated by restaurant staff when you enter). There are tables for two, four, six or eight. The waiter stations in the dining room are very noisy for those

seated near them. Fine Rosenthal china and good-quality cutlery are provided.

Alternative Dining Option: The intimate Pinnacle Grill, added in 2002, is located just forward of the balcony level of the main dining room on the starboard side. The 66-seat dining spot has Pacific Northwest cuisine (fresh Alaskan salmon and halibut, and other regional specialties, plus a selection of premium steaks such as filet mignon from Black Angus beef). The venue (reservations are necessary, and a cover/service charge of $20 applies for dinner, $10 for lunch) was created out of the former private dining wing of the main dining room, plus a slice of the Explorer's Lounge. A Bulgari show plate, Rosenthal china, Reidel wine glasses, and Frette table linen are featured. The Pinnacle Grill is a much better dining experience than the main dining room and worth it for that special celebration.

Instead of the more formal dining room or Pinnacle Grill, the Lido Buffet is open for casual dinners on all but the last night of a cruise, in an open-seating arrangement. Tables are set with crisp linens, flatware and stemware. A set menu includes a choice of four entrées.

For more casual evening eating, the Lido Buffet is open for casual dinners on all except the last night of each cruise, in an open-seating arrangement. Tables are set with crisp linens, flatware and stemware. A set menu is featured, and this includes a choice of four entrées.

The dual-line, self-serve Lido Buffet is also the place for casual breakfasts and lunches. At night, a section is transformed into Canaletto for casual Italian meals. It is open 5.30–9pm and reservations are requested.

There is much use of canned fruits – good for dentally challenged passengers – and packeted items, although there are several commercial low-caloric salad dressings. The choice of cheeses and crackers is poor. The beverage station also lets it down, for it is no better than those found in family outlets ashore in the USA. In addition, a poolside grill provides basic American hamburgers and hot dogs.

Passengers will need to eat in the Lido Cafe on any days when the dining room is closed for lunch (typically once or twice per cruise, depending on the ship's itinerary).

ENTERTAINMENT. The Showlounge at Sea, located at the forward part of the ship, spans two decks, with banquette seating on both main and upper levels. It is basically a well designed room, but the ceiling is low and the sightlines from the balcony level are quite poor.

SPA/FITNESS. The Ocean Spa is located one deck below the navigation bridge at the very forward part of the ship. It includes a gymnasium (with all the latest muscle-pumping exercise machines, including an abundance of treadmills) with ocean views, an aerobics exercise area, large beauty salon with ocean-view windows to the port side, several treatment rooms, and men's and women's sauna, steam room and changing areas.

● **For more extensive general information on what a Holland America Line cruise is like, see pages 139–42.**

Ventura
★★★★

Size: ....Large Resort Ship	Passenger Decks: 15	Cabins (with private balcony): 880
Tonnage: 116,017	Total Crew: 1,239	Cabins (wheelchair accessible): 25
Lifestyle: ....Standard	Passengers	Wheelchair accessibility ....Good
Cruise Line: ....P&O Cruises	(lower beds/all berths): 3,092/3,574	Cabin Voltage: ....220 volts
Former Names: ....none	Passenger Space Ratio	Elevators: 12
Builder: ....Fincantieri (Italy)	(lower beds/all berths): 37.5/32.4	Casino (gaming tables): ....Yes
Original Cost: ....€535 million	Crew/Passenger Ratio	Slot Machines: ....Yes
Entered Service: ....April 2008	(lower beds/all berths): 2.4/2.8	Swimming Pools (outdoors): 3
Registry: ....Bermuda	Cabins (total): 1,546	Swimming Pools (indoors): 0
Length (ft/m): 951.4/290.0	Size Range (sq ft/m): 134.5–534.0/	Whirlpools: 6
Beam (ft/m): 118.1/36.0	12.5–49.6	Self-Service Launderette: ....Yes
Draft (ft/m): 27.8/8.5	Cabins (outside view): 1,101	Dedicated Cinema/Seats: ....No
Propulsion/Propellers: .....diesel-electric	Cabins (interior/no view): 445	Library: ....Yes
(42,000kW)/2	Cabins (for one person): 0	

BERLITZ'S OVERALL SCORE: 1,509 (OUT OF A POSSIBLE 2,000 POINTS)

OVERVIEW. *Ventura* is the P&O version of Princess Cruises' Grand-class ships, and, together with sister ship *Azura*, is the largest cruise ship yet built specifically for UK passengers. With its flat stern, it looks a bit like a giant hatchback, but the ship's side profile is softer and more balanced. Promenade walking decks are to port and starboard sides, underneath the lifeboats. You can't walk completely around, however; it's narrow in some places, and you have to negotiate past a number of deck lounge chairs. There are three pools: two on the pool deck, one at the stern. The center pool can be covered by a glass-roofed skydome. If your cabin is towards the front of the ship, it's a long walk to get to the pool at the stern. Considering the number of passengers carried, there's not a lot of outdoor deck space.

Inside the ship, a three-deck atrium is the focal point. Designed on a gateway theme, central to which are four towering black granite archways specially sourced from India, it's the place to see and be seen, and the best location to arrange to meet friends. The ship's upper-deck public room layout, however, is challenging because you can't go from one end of the ship to the other without first going down, along and up – so, not so good for those with mobility problems. In other words, you'll need to plan your journey and use the most appropriate of three elevator banks.

Other public rooms include a surprisingly small, rather open-plan library (Chapter One) that is not at all intimate, a Cyb@center for internet connections, an overly large Cruise Sales Centre, Fortunes Casino, and several bars, including The Exchange (an urban warehouse bar), and Metropolis (set high atop the ship with great aft views and views along the sides of the ship – over everyone's balcony), a Cuban

BERLITZ'S RATINGS		
	Possible	Achieved
Ship	500	425
Accommodation	200	166
Food	400	249
Service	400	286
Entertainment	100	77
Cruise	400	306

bar, and a Spanish bar with tapas. It's all rather multi-cultural and not so British. But, do check out the train that runs around the upper part of the upper bar of The Exchange.

There are 7,000 pieces of art on board, from 55 British artists, and there's an art gallery so you can buy "artwork." Niggles include the constant push for onboard revenue; low passenger space ratio; mediocre self-service buffet food; and a charge for shuttle buses in many ports.

Ventura is targeted at families and children. Indeed, children will be pleased to find that, for 2–4-year olds, Noddy is on board. There are children's clubs for the under-2s up to 17 years, plus a rock 'n' roll school. Youngsters can also enjoy Scalextric at sea with Grand Prix-style track, 3D cinema, and interactive art classes. Family shore programs feature aqua and "theme parks." There's a useful Night Nursery for the under-fives. It's possible to get married on board, with the captain officiating.

Active types can take instruction and participate in Cirque Ventura's activities, including juggling, acro-balancing, tight-wire walking, stilt walking, and clowning. Also, the area has four bungee trampolines and a flying trapeze – all up high on Deck 19.

Smoking is not permitted in the ship's interior, but it is on cabin balconies and in designated spots on the open decks. The onboard currency is the British pound. Gratuities are recommended at £3.75 per person, per day.

SUITABLE FOR: *Ventura* is best suited to families with children and adult couples who want to spend time together, and are seeking a big-ship environment with comfortable but unstuffy surroundings and lots of options.

ACCOMMODATION. There are 31 accommodation price grades, according to size and location chosen, although there are really just five types of accommodation: suite with balcony; family suite with balcony; outside-view twin/queen with balcony; outside-view twin/queen; interior no-view cabin. More than one-third of all cabins are of the interior no-view variety. Some cabins have extra third/fourth berths that fold down from the ceiling. While the suites are quite spacious, they are quite small when compared to suites aboard some other cruise lines, such as Celebrity Cruises or NCL.

Standard in all cabins: bed runners, 10.5 tog duvets, Slumberland 8-inch sprung mattresses, Egyptian cotton towels and robes, and extensive Nick Munro-designed stainless steel tea/coffee making facilities (including water kettle, coffee pot, proper teapot, milk jug, two glass mugs), all on a bespoke silver tray. The tea-making set-up is excellent, but getting fresh milk can sometimes be a problem.

Open closets are new for P&O Cruises, however (no doors – save money), and actually provide easier access. Balcony cabins have teak patio furniture, and an outside light. Decent-quality personal toiletries are by Temple Spa, an upgrade from what was previously provided aboard the ships of P&O Cruises (with larger bottles and more selection choice provided for suite occupants).

Wheelchair-accessible cabins have a shower enclosure, except one (R415) that has a bathtub with integral shower. Wheelchair-accessible cabins are mostly in the front section of the ship, but the Bay Tree restaurant is aft – so be prepared for lots of wheeling time and waiting time at elevators. Wheelchair users should note that breakfast in the three main restaurants typically ends at 9.30am on sea days (9am on port days). To take breakfast in the self-serve Waterside casual eatery, wheelchair users need to wheel across the decks containing the Beachcomber and Laguna pools and lots of deck chairs – not easy. Alternatively, they can order room service breakfast (typically cold items only). Note that there is no room service breakfast on disembarkation day, when the company wants you out of your cabin by 8am.

CUISINE/DINING. P&O's marketing blurb claims that there are 10 restaurants. There aren't. There are five genuine restaurants (Bay Tree, Cinnnamon, Saffron, The White Room, and East); the rest are eateries.

The three principal dining rooms, Bay Tree, Cinnamon, and Saffron, have standard à la carte menus. The Bay Tree offers fixed seating dining, with assigned tables (typical seating times: 6:30pm or 8:30pm). In the other two, you can dine when you want, with whom you want, at any time between 6pm and 10pm – P&O calls it "Freedom Dining" – although at peak times there can be long waiting times for a table.

Once or twice per cruise, additional special dinners are served in the main dining rooms, one being a Chaîne des Rôtisseurs event. The ship's wine list is ho-hum average.

Alternative dining venues include the following:
● *The White Room* is located high up on the ship, above the children's play area, with a quarter of the tables on deck. It serves modern European dishes by celebrity chef Marco Pierre White in an environment which is intimate and atten-

tive but not stuffy and is particularly suitable for families. Reservations are necessary, and the cost to dine here is about £20 per person. The food is good because it's cooked to order, unlike in the main dining rooms. Occasionally, Marco Pierre White will sail aboard the ship, and private cooking classes for up to eight participants in one of the ship's galleys; the cost is £75, including a tasting of the finished product.
● For complete privacy, private balcony dining, with selections from the Marco Pierre White menu, is also available as a rather pricey (but perhaps worthwhile) extra-cost option.
● *The Waterside* is a large, self-serve buffet "seaside chic" dining spot, with indoor-outdoor seating, but the seating is rather poorly designed and cramped).
● On the same deck, adjacent to the forward pool, are *Frankie's Grill* and *Frankie's Pizzeria*.
● *Tazzine*, a coffee lounge by day, turns into a cocktail bar in the evening.
● *The Beach House* is a casual dining spot for families, open 24 hours. Marco's roof-side café serves gourmet pizzas, grills and original ice cream flavors, such as chocolate truffle and prune and Armagnac. Children's cutlery, bibs and beakers are available.
● *Ramblas* is a tapas and wine bar (some items at extra cost).
● *East*, an Asian fusion eatery on the main indoor promenade.
In addition, 24-hour room service is available in cabins.

ENTERTAINMENT. P&O claims the 785-seat Arena Theatre, located at the front of the ship and spanning two decks, is the largest showlounge aboard a UK-based cruise ship, but in fact the showlounge aboard *Queen Mary 2* is bigger, with 1,094 seats, as is the Showlounge aboard *Independence of the Seas*. Havana, the main nightclub and entertainment venue, where movies are sometimes shown, is an activities room by day and a sultry Cuba-inspired club by night, but sightlines to the stage area are extremely poor from many seats.

A video wall in the Cosmopolitan club lounge screens real-time footage of the world's seven most famous city skylines – Sydney, Paris, New York, Rio de Janeiro, Las Vegas, Hong Kong and London. It's neat.

SPA/FITNESS. The Oasis Spa is located forward, almost atop the ship. It includes a gymnasium, aerobics room, beauty salon, separate male and female sauna and steam rooms, and 11 treatment rooms. An internal stairway connects to the deck below, which contains an extra-charge Thermal Suite. Harding Brothers provide the spa staff and services.

Treatments include special packages for couples, and the SilverSpa Generation, as well as a whole range of individual treatments. Examples of prices: Swedish Massage is £66 for 60 minutes; a Hot Stones massage is £77 for 60 minutes; Couples massage is £220 for 100 minutes; Oriental Massage Ritual is £99 for 90 minutes; and a holistic facial is £45 for 75 minutes. A manicure is £22 for 30 minutes, while a pedicure is £28 for 30 minutes.

● **For more extensive general information on what a P&O cruise is like, see pages 147–48.**

Vision of the Seas
★★★★

Size: . . . . .Large Resort Ship	Passenger Decks: 11	Cabins (with private balcony): 229
Tonnage: 78,491	Total Crew: 765	Cabins (wheelchair accessible): 14
Lifestyle: . . . . .Standard	Passengers	Wheelchair accessibility . . . . .Good
Cruise Line: Royal Caribbean International	(lower beds/all berths): 2,000/2,435	Cabin Current: . . . . .110 and 220 volts
Former Names: . . . . .none	Passenger Space Ratio	Elevators: 9
Builder: Chantiers de l'Atlantique (France)	(lower beds/all berths): 39.2/32.2	Casino (gaming tables): . . . . .Yes
Original Cost: . . . .$275 million	Crew/Passenger Ratio	Slot Machines: . . . . .Yes
Entered Service: . . . . .May 1998	(lower beds/all berths): 3.0/3.6	Swimming Pools (outdoors): 1
Registry: . . . . .The Bahamas	Cabins (total): 1,000	Swimming Pools (indoors): 1
Length (ft/m): 915.3/279.0	Size Range (sq ft/m): 135.0–1,270.1/	(inside/outside)
Beam (ft/m): 105.6/32.2	12.5–118.0	Whirlpools: 6
Draft (ft/m): 24.9/7.6	Cabins (outside view): 593	Self-Service Launderette: . . . . .No
Propulsion/Propellers: . . . . .diesel-electric	Cabins (interior/no view): 407	Dedicated Cinema/Seats: . . . . .No
(50,400kW)2	Cabins (for one person): 0	Library: . . . . .Yes

---

OVERALL SCORE: 1,491 (OUT OF A POSSIBLE 2,000 POINTS)

OVERVIEW. This contemporary ship, sister to *Rhapsody of the Seas*, shares design features that make all Royal Caribbean International ships identifiable, including a Viking Crown Lounge (which is also the ship's disco). The Viking Crown Lounge is just aft of the center of the ship (above the central atrium lobby), with the funnel located well aft – a departure from all other RCI ships to date. The ship's stern is beautifully rounded. There is a reasonable amount of open-air walking space, although this can become cluttered with sunloungers (which, incidentally, do not have cushioned pads).

Inside, the ship provides RCI's interpretation of a floating contemporary hotel, and presents the nicest mix of colors and decor of any of the Vision-class ships, with lots of warm beige and pink tones, particularly in the expansive atrium.

The artwork (which cost $6 million) is plentiful, colorful and very creative, with more previously blank wall space covered with interesting artworks of differing shapes and sizes. Most noticeable is the extensive use of glass. Two beautiful glass sculptures stand out: one in the atrium, at the entrance to a Champagne Bar, and one on the upper level of the Viking Crown Lounge. There are plenty of public rooms, bars and lounges, as well as a large, well-lit casino.

The Viking Crown Lounge is a multi-level nightspot. The music can be loud and overbearing, however, and so can cigarette smoke around the bar – one of few places where smokers can light up. Perhaps the best atmosphere is in the nautical-theme Schooner Bar. The Library has an excellent array of hardbacks, and a neat wooden sculpture of some-

BERLITZ'S RATINGS		
	Possible	Achieved
Ship	500	425
Accommodation	200	166
Food	400	240
Service	400	287
Entertainment	100	81
Cruise	400	292

thing that looks like the Tin Man from *The Wizard of Oz*.

ACCOMMODATION. There are 18 cabin categories, in 11 pricing unit, the price you pay depending on the grade, location and size chosen.

The standard interior (no view) and exterior view cabins are of an adequate size, and have just enough functional facilities to make them comfortable for a one-week cruise, but longer might prove confining. The decor is bright and cheerful, although the ceilings are plain; colorful soft furnishings make one's home away from home look like the inside of a modern Scandinavian hotel – minimalist, yet colorful. Twin lower beds convert to queen-sized beds, and there is a reasonable amount of closet and drawer space, but there is little room to maneuver between the bed and desk/television unit.

The bathrooms are small but functional, although the shower units are small, and there is no cabinet for personal toiletry items. The towels could be larger and thicker.

Choose a "C" grade suite if you want spacious accommodation that includes a separate (curtained-off) sleeping area, a good-sized outside balcony (with part, not full, partition), lounge with sofa, two chairs and coffee table, three closets, plenty of drawer and storage space, television and VCR. The bathroom is large and has a full-size tub, integral shower, and two washbasins/two toiletries cabinets.

For the ultimate accommodation aboard this ship, choose the Royal Suite, which resembles a Palm Beach apartment, and comes with a white baby grand player piano. It has a separate bedroom with king-sized bed, living room with queen-size sofa bed, refrigerator/mini-bar, dining table, entertainment center, and vanity dressing area. The decor is simple and elegant, with pastel colors, and wood accented ceiling treatments. Located just under the starboard side navigation bridge wing, it has its own private balcony.

CUISINE. The no-smoking Aquarius Dining Room is set on two levels with large ocean-view picture windows on two sides (rectangular windows on the upper level, large circular windows on the lower level) and a large connecting stairway. Choose one of two seatings, or "My Time Dining" (eat when you want, during dining room hours).

The Windjammer Cafe is the casual dining spot for self-serve buffets. The area is well-designed, with contemporary decor and colors, but the food is really basic fare and disappointing; the four-sided self-service buffet area is small for the number of passengers that use it. More money needs to be spent for better-quality ingredients and more variety is needed. Each evening, the room offers an alternative to the dressier dining room. The evening buffets typically feature a different theme, something this company has been doing for more than 25 years – perhaps the time has come for more creativity.

A hamburger/hot dog grill counter in the Solarium, but typically you don't get a choice of how you like your hamburgers cooked – everything appears to be well done.

The company has introduced a drinks package (available at all bars, in the form of cards or stickers) that enables you to pre-pay for a selection of standard soft drinks and alcoholic drinks. The packages are not easy to understand.

ENTERTAINMENT. The Masquerade Theatre is the ship's principal showlounge, located in the forward section of the ship (accessed by the forward stairway/elevators), for production shows and other major cabaret shows. It is a large, but a well-designed room with main and balcony levels, and good sightlines from most of the banquette seats.

Other cabaret acts are featured in the Some Enchanted Evening Lounge, located aft, and these include late-night adult (blue) comedy, as well as live music for dancing. A number of other bars and lounges have live music of differing types.

The entertainment throughout is upbeat (in fact, it is difficult to get away from music and noise). There is even background music in all corridors and elevators, and constant music outdoors on the pool deck. If you want a quiet relaxing holiday, choose another ship.

SPA/FITNESS. The spa, with its solarium and indoor/outdoor dome-covered pool, Inca- and Mayan-theme decor, sauna/steam rooms and gymnasium, provides a haven for the health-conscious and fitness buff, although there is a pizza bar forward of the pool area. A lovely "Mayan Serpent" sculpture is featured in the solarium.

For more sporting passengers, there is activity galore – including a rock-climbing wall, with several separate climbing tracks. It is located outdoors at the aft end of the funnel.

● **For more extensive general information about the Royal Caribbean cruise experience, see pages 151–6.**

WATERTIGHT CONTRACTS

Cruise lines are masters of small print when it comes to contracts. A clause in the ticket typically reads: "The Carrier's legal responsibility for death, injury, illness, damage, delay, or other loss or detriment of person or property of whatever kind suffered by the Passenger will, in the first instance, be governed by the Athens Convention relating to the Carriage of Passengers and their Luggage by Sea, 1974, with protocols and amendments, together with the further provisions of the International Convention on Limitation of Liability for Maritime Claims, 1976, with revisions and amendments (hereinafter collectively referred to as the "Convention"). The Carrier shall not be liable for any such death, injury, illness, damage, delay, loss, or detriment caused by Act of God, war or warlike operations, civil commotions, labor trouble, interference by Authorities, perils of the sea, or any other cause beyond the control of the Carrier, fire, thefts or any other crime, errors in the navigation or management of the Vessel, or defect in, or unseaworthiness of hull, machinery, appurtenances, equipment, furnishings, or supplies of the Vessel, fault or neglect of pilot, tugs, agents, independent contractors, such as ship's Physician, Passengers or other persons on board not in the Carrier's employ or for any other cause of whatsoever nature except and unless it is proven that such death, injury, illness, damage, delay, loss resulting from Carrier's act or omission was committed with the intent to cause such loss or with knowledge that such loss would probably result therefrom and in that event the Carrier's liability therefore shall not exceed the specified limitations per Passenger in Special Drawing Rights (S.D.R.) as defined in the applicable conventions or in any further revision and/or amendment thereto as shall become applicable."

Vistamar
★★ +

Size: .Small Ship	Passenger Decks: 6	Cabins (with private balcony): 11
Tonnage: 7,478	Total Crew: 114	Cabins (wheelchair accessible): 0
Lifestyle: . . . . .Standard	Passengers	Wheelchair accessibility . . . . .None
Cruise Line: . . . . .Plein Cap	(lower beds/all berths): 299/320	Cabin Current: . . . . .220 volts
Former Names: . . .Santa Cruz de Tenerife	Passenger Space Ratio	Elevators: 1
Builder: . . . . . . .Union Navale de Levante	(lower beds/all berths): 25.3/23.3	Casino (gaming tables): . . . . .No
(Spain)	Crew/Passenger Ratio	Slot Machines: .No
Original Cost: . . . .$45 million	(lower beds/all berths): 2.7/2.9	Swimming Pools (outdoors): 1
Entered Service: . . . . .Sept 1989	Cabins (total): 152	Swimming Pools (indoors): 0
Registry: . . . . .Italy	Size Range (sq ft/m): 129.1–150.6/	Whirlpools: 0
Length (ft/m): 396.9/121.00	12.0–14.0	Self-Service Launderette: . . . . .No
Beam (ft/m): 55.1/16.82	Cabins (outside view): 126	Dedicated Cinema/Seats: . . . . .No
Draft (ft/m): 14.9/4.55	Cabins (interior/no view): 26	Library: . . . . .Yes
Propulsion/Propellers: .diesel (3,900kW)/2	Cabins (for one person): 5	

OVERALL SCORE: 1,061 (OUT OF A POSSIBLE 2,000 POINTS)

OVERVIEW. *Vistamar* has a moderately smart, reasonably contemporary, but rather squat small ship profile. The ship, which has an ice-hardened hull, also carries six inflatable rubber landing craft for close-up landings during certain itineraries that include the Amazon, Arctic and Antarctic.

An "open bridge" policy means you can join the captain and other navigation officers at almost any time except during difficult maneuvers. There is a good open observation deck at the forward-most part of the ship – atop the navigation bridge, although the other open deck and sunbathing space is a little limited, particularly on the aft open deck around the small outdoor pool (really only a "dip" pool, though it has a large splash surround).

The interior layout has all the public rooms located aft, in a "cake-layer" stacking, with a single, central staircase that takes up most of the space in an atrium lobby that spans three decks (with a glass elevator shaped like half a cable car). Features include wood-trimmed interior decor, which is quite jazzy, attractive and warm, although the mirrored metallic ceilings are somewhat irritating.

A four-deck high atrium with a "sky dome" has a glass-walled elevator and a wrap-around staircase, and is the focal point of the ship's interior. The library has comfortable high wingback chairs, but there aren't many books. There is also a Card Room, and board games are available.

The ship's main lounge, Don Fernando, is named after Senor Don Fernando Abril Martorell, the president of the Union Navale de Levante shipyard that constructed *Vistamar* in 444 days (perhaps if more time had been taken, the ship would have been built better). Additionally, there is a rather jazzy nightclub/disco, with acres of glass, set around

BERLITZ'S RATINGS		
	Possible	Achieved
Ship	500	232
Accommodation	200	107
Food	400	210
Service	400	237
Entertainment	100	56
Cruise	400	219

the base of the funnel, with a long bar, and dance floor, for the late-night set.

Since 1991 the ship has been operated by Plantours & Partner for German-speaking passengers. However, from January 2011 it will operate under charter to French Riviera-based Plein Cap for the French-speaking market.

The product is aimed at the inexpensive end of the market. The dress code is ultra-casual (no tuxedos, no ties). There is an abundance of greenery, which provides a warm, comfortable and less clinical ambiance.

The ship is quite small, enabling passengers to enjoy interesting destination-intensive cruises, with many port calls that larger ships simply can't get into. Plein Cap's focus is on its lecture and enrichment programs, and its convivial staff and atmosphere.

Plein Cap cruises includes drinks, table wines, and mineral water with meals. Tipping is recommended at 5–6 euros (the onboard currency) per person, per day.

The tiny "dip" swimming pool is virtually useless. There is a distinct odor of diesel fuel at the upper level of the lobby, where there is also a complete lack of air-conditioning. The ship's hotel operation is rather sloppy and needs streamlining. There is no walking track or walk-around promenade deck outdoors. The fit, finish and maintenance of this ship are all quite poor. Sightlines in the single-level showlounge are very poor, and there is a lack of good stage lighting.

SUITABLE FOR: *Vistamar* is best suited to French-speaking couples and single travelers looking for a first cruise in the comfortable, contemporary, but not luxurious or pretentious surroundings of a small ship featuring interesting itineraries, and all at a low price.

ACCOMMODATION. Passenger accommodation areas are located forward, while the public rooms are positioned aft, which means there is a minimal amount of noise in the cabins – good if you're having an early night.

There are 11 cabin grades, but in just two different sizes: suites with private (covered) balcony and queen-sized bed; outside-view or interior (no view) cabins for two, three or four persons, all with fixed, wide single beds. All of the cabins are reasonably comfortable, although the bathrooms are extremely small and tight (there is a considerable "lip" to step over to access the bathroom), and both closet and drawer space is limited.

Cabins have twin beds with wooden headboard, small vanity/writing desk, color television, climate-control, telephone, and hairdryer. Most of the cabinetry is made with a wood finish.

There are 11 suites, each of which has a small, narrow, private, covered balcony outdoors. The suites are: Alboran, Algarve, Almeria, Armador, Cadiz, Cordoba, Granada, Huelva, Jaen, Malaga, Seville – all regions of Andalucia. They also have a more spacious bathroom, with a large bathtub and integral shower. The living area s also larger, and comes with a sofa, coffee table, vanity/writing desk, and a larger color television. Note that Armador is the owner's suite, and comes with a circular bathtub with integral shower, set against large picture windows – wonderful for the Arctic and Antarctic cruises that this company typically operates in the appropriate season. Petit fours and mineral water are provided for suite occupants.

No matter what accommodation grade or location they choose, all passengers get personal amenities that include soap, shampoo, body lotion and bath/shower gel, and shoeshine mitt. Accommodation hallways are provided either in hospital green, powder blue, or hot pink.

CUISINE. The Andalucia Restaurant is quite warm and inviting, with contemporary colors and decor, and large picture windows, although the six pillars detract from the otherwise attractive room. The room's focal point is a model of a sailing vessel with an emerald green hull – about the same color as the fabrics on the dining room chairs. There is one seating for all passengers, so meals are leisurely, with assigned tables for four, six or eight (there are no tables for two). Window-side tables are for six, and chairs have armrests. Some dinners are themed.

The food is reasonably adequate, and quite sound, and dinners typically come with a choice of three entrées plus a vegetarian selection. The selection of cooked green vegetables, breads, cheeses and fruits is limited, and the overall cuisine really is of quite a low standard – it could be said to be quite similar to that found aboard other ships operated for German-speaking passengers, such as *Albatros* and *Astor*, which have two seatings for dinner. The service is adequate, no more, as is the wine list. Sekt (sweet sparkling wine) is provided for breakfast, while white and red table wines are provided for lunch and dinner. Breakfast and lunch buffets are available on the Lido deck.

ENTERTAINMENT. There is little entertainment apart from some cabaret acts and live music for dancing and listening.

SPA/FITNESS. There is no spa to speak of, although there is a fitness room, a sauna, a massage treatment room, and a small beauty salon.

Volendam
★★★★

Size:	Mid-Size Ship	Passenger Decks:	10
Tonnage:	61,396	Total Crew:	561
Lifestyle:	Premium	Passengers	
Cruise Line:	Holland America Line	(lower beds/all berths):	1,440/1,850
Former Names:	none	Passenger Space Ratio	
Builder:	Fincantieri (Italy)	(lower beds/all berths):	42.6/33.1
Original Cost:	$300 million	Crew/Passenger Ratio	
Entered Service:	Nov 1999	(lower beds/all berths):	2.5/2.5
Registry:	The Netherlands	Cabins (total):	720
Length (ft/m):	781.0/238.00	Size Range (sq ft/m):	113.0–1,126.0/
Beam (ft/m):	105.8/32.25		10.5–104.6
Draft (ft/m):	25.5/7.80	Cabins (outside view):	581
Propulsion/Propellers:	diesel-electric	Cabins (interior/no view):	139
	(37,500kW)/2	Cabins (for one person):	0

Cabins (with private balcony):	197
Cabins (wheelchair accessible):	23
Wheelchair accessibility	Good
Cabin Current:	110 volts
Elevators:	12
Casino (gaming tables):	Yes
Slot Machines:	Yes
Swimming Pools (outdoors):	2
Swimming Pools (indoors):	1
	(magrodome cover)
Whirlpools:	2
Self-Service Launderette:	Yes (2)
Dedicated Cinema/Seats:	Yes/205
Library:	Yes

OVERALL SCORE: 1,540 (OUT OF A POSSIBLE 2,000 POINTS)

OVERVIEW. The ship's name is derived from the fishing village of Volendam, located north of Amsterdam, Holland. The hull is dark blue, in keeping with all Holland America Line ships. Having been built to approximately the same size as the company's newest *Rotterdam*, the same layout and public rooms have been incorporated into the interiors. This carries on the same flow and comfortable feeling so that repeat passengers will quickly feel at home aboard almost any ship in the Holland America Line fleet.

Volendam has three main passenger stairways, which is so much better than two stairways, particularly the viewpoints of safety, accessibility and passenger flow. There is a magrodome-covered pool on the Lido Deck between the mast and the ship's funnel. The main interior design theme is flowers, from the 17th to the 21st centuries. The interior focal point is a huge crystal sculpture, *Caleido*, in the three-deck-high atrium, by one of Italy's leading contemporary glass artists, Luciano Vistosi. Health spa facilities include more treatment rooms (each has a shower and toilet).

In the casino bar (also known as the ship's sports bar), a cinematic theme presents visions of Hollywood, and includes a collection of costumes, props, photos and posters of movies and the actors who starred in them.

At the Lido Deck swimming pool, leaping dolphins are the focal point. The pool itself is also one deck higher than the Statendam-class ships, with the positive result being the fact that there is now direct access between the aft and midships pools (not so aboard the S-class ships).

There is a charge to use the washing machines and dryers in the self-service launderette, although it really should be included for the occupants of high priced suites. Although

BERLITZ'S RATINGS

	Possible	Achieved
Ship	500	429
Accommodation	200	165
Food	400	282
Service	400	276
Entertainment	100	77
Cruise	400	311

room service is adequate, it remains a weak point.

ACCOMMODATION. The range is similar to that found aboard the similarly sized *Rotterdam*, and comprises 17 different categories. The price you pay will depend on the grade, location and size you choose. There is one penthouse suite, and 28 suites, with the rest of the accommodation a mix of outside-view and interior (no view) cabins, and many more balcony cabins ("mini-suites") aboard this ship than aboard the slightly smaller *Statendam*-class ships.

All standard interior and outside cabins are tastefully furnished, and have twin beds that convert to a queen-sized bed, but space is tight for walking between beds and vanity unit. All cabin televisions carry CNN and TNT. The bathrooms (fully tiled) are disappointingly small (particularly for long cruises) and have small shower tubs, utilitarian personal toiletries cupboards, and exposed under-sink plumbing. Storage space is also small for long cruises.

There are 28 full Verandah Suites (Navigation Deck), and one Penthouse Suite. All suite occupants share a private Concierge Lounge (the concierge handles such things as special dining arrangements, shore excursions, private parties and special requests). Strangely, there are no butlers for these suites. Each Verandah Suite has a separate bedroom, dressing and living areas. Suite passengers get personal stationery, complimentary laundry and ironing, cocktail hour hors d'oeuvres and other goodies, as well as priority embarkation and disembarkation.

For the ultimate in accommodation and living space aboard this ship, choose the Penthouse Suite. It has a separate steward's entrance, a large bedroom with king-sized bed, separate living room (with baby grand piano) and a dining room, dressing room, walk-in closet, butler's pantry, and private balcony – though the balcony is no larger than that of any other suite. Other facilities include an audio-visual center with television and VCR, wet bar with refrigerator, large bathroom with Jacuzzi bathtub, separate toilet with bidet, and a guest bathroom with toilet and washbasin.

With the exception of the penthouse suite, located forward on the starboard side, the bathrooms in the other suites and "mini-suites" are a little disappointing – neither as spacious nor as opulent as one would expect. All outside-view suites and cabin bathrooms feature a bathtub/shower while interior (no view) cabins have a shower only. Also, note that the 23 cabins for the mobility-limited have a roll-in shower enclosure for wheelchair users – none have bathtubs, no matter what the category.

CUISINE. There is one main dining room, and one alternative dining spot (dinner only). The 747-seat Rotterdam Dining Room, a no-smoking venue, is a traditional, grand room, spread over two decks, with ocean views on three sides and an imposing staircase connecting upper and lower levels.

Both open seating and fixed (assigned tables and times) seating are available, while breakfast and lunch are open-seating (you'll be seated by restaurant staff on entry). Fine Rosenthal china and good-quality cutlery are provided (but no fish knives). Tables are four two, four, six or eight.

Alternative Dining Option: The casual-dress Marco Polo Restaurant seats 88, and there is no charge, although reservations are required. It is created in the style of a California artists' bistro and provides Italian cuisine (this has a set menu together with nightly specials). Passengers thus have more choice and an occasional change of venue (anyone booking suite-grade accommodation get priority reservations).

The Lido Buffet is a self-serve cafe for casual breakfasts and luncheons. There is also an outdoor grill for those who enjoy hamburgers, hot dogs and other grilled fast-food items. The Lido Buffet is also open for casual dinners on each night except for the last one, in an open-seating arrangement. Tables are set with crisp linens, flatware and stemware. A set menu includes a choice of four entrées.

ENTERTAINMENT. The Frans Hals Showlounge spans two decks, with banquette seating on both main and upper levels. It is basically a well-designed room, but the ceiling is low and the sight lines from the balcony level are poor.

SPA/FITNESS. The health spa facilities are quite extensive, and include a gymnasium with good muscle-toning equipment, separate saunas and steam rooms for men and women, and more treatment rooms (each has a shower and toilet). Practice tennis courts can be fund outdoor, as well as the traditional shuffleboard courts, jogging track, and a full wrap-around teakwood promenade deck for strolling.

The Ocean Spa and onboard fitness classes are operated by Steiner, a specialist concession.

● **For more extensive general information on what a Holland America Line cruise is like, see pages 139–42.**

Voyager of the Seas
★★★★

Size: . . . . .Large Resort Ship	Passenger Decks: 14	Cabins (with private balcony): 757
Tonnage: .137,280	Total Crew: .1,176	Cabins (wheelchair accessible): 26
Lifestyle: . . . . .Standard	Passengers	Wheelchair accessibility . . . . .Best
Cruise Line: Royal Caribbean International	(lower beds/all berths): 3,114/3,838	Cabin Current: . . . . .110 volts
Former Names: . . . . .none	Passenger Space Ratio	Elevators: . . . . .14 (6 glass-enclosed)
Builder: . . .Kvaerner Masa-Yards (Finland)	(lower beds/all berths): 44.0/35.7	Casino (gaming tables): . . . . .Yes
Original Cost: . . . .$500 million	Crew/Passenger Ratio	Slot Machines: . . . . .Yes
Entered Service: . . . . .Nov 1999	(lower beds/all berths): 2.6/3.2	Swimming Pools (outdoors): 3
Registry: . . . . .The Bahamas	Cabins (total): 1,557	Swimming Pools (indoors): 0
Length (ft/m): 1,020.6/311.1	Size Range (sq ft/m): 151.0–1,358.0/	Whirlpools: 6
Beam (ft/m): 155.5/47.4	14.0–126.1	Self-Service Launderette: . . . . .No
Draft (ft/m): 28.8/8.8	Cabins (outside view): 939	Dedicated Cinema/Seats: . . . . .No
Propulsion/Propellers: . . . . .diesel-electric	Cabins (interior/no view): 618	Library: . . . . .Yes
(42,000 kW)/3 pods (14 MW each)	Cabins (for one person): 0	

OVERALL SCORE: 1,445 (OUT OF A POSSIBLE 2,000 POINTS)

OVERVIEW. The exterior design of *Voyager of the Seas* is not unlike an enlarged version of the Royal Caribbean International's Vision-class ships. Its propulsion is derived from three pod units, powered by electric motors: two azimuthing (rotating), and one fixed at the centerline, instead of conventional rudders and propellers, in the latest configuration of high-tech systems.

With its large proportions, it provides more facilities and options, yet manages to have a healthy passenger space ratio (the amount of space per passenger). It's too large to go through the Panama Canal, thus limiting itineraries almost exclusively to the Caribbean, where few islands have decent enough sized facilities to service it, or for use as a floating island resort. When you step aboard, spend the first few hours exploring all the many facilities and public spaces aboard this vessel; you'll find it to be time well spent.

Although *Voyager of the Seas* is large, the cabin hallways have an extremely warm and attractive feel to them, with artwork cabinets and wavy lines to lead you along and break up the monotony. In fact, there are plenty of colorful, even whimsical, decorative touches to help you avoid what would otherwise be a very clinical environment.

At certain times, passengers may be allowed to stand right at the bows of the ship on an observation platform, perhaps with arms spread in an "eagle-like" position, just like the stars in the film *Titanic*. What a photo opportunity! However, for the best ones, as in the film, you'll need to bring a helicopter. But looking up at the cake-layer stacking of the decks towards the bridge gives you an idea of the size of the ship.

Embarkation and disembarkation take place through two

BERLITZ'S RATINGS		
	Possible	Achieved
Ship	500	414
Accommodation	200	150
Food	400	222
Service	400	272
Entertainment	100	83
Cruise	400	304

stations/access points, designed to minimize the inevitable lines at the start and end of the cruise (that's more than 1,500 people for each access point). Once inside the ship, you'll need good walking shoes, particularly when you need to go from one end to the other – it really is quite a long way.

A four-decks-high Royal Promenade is the interior focal point of the ship, and is a good place to arrange to meet someone. It is 393.7 ft (120 meters) long – the length of two football fields (American football, that is), and has two internal lobbies (atria) that rise through 11 decks, one at each end. There are 16 elevators in four banks of four.

The entrance to one of three levels of the main restaurant, together with shops and entertainment locations are spun off from this "boulevard", while interior "interior promenade-view" cabins, with bay windows, look into it from above. It houses a traditional English "pub" (the "Pig 'n' Whistle, with draft beer and "street-front" seating), a Promenade Café (for continental breakfast, all-day pizzas, sandwiches and coffees), Ben & Jerry's Ice Cream (at extra cost), Sprinkles (for round-the-clock ice-cream and yoghurt), and Scoreboard (a sports bar).

Several shops complete the picture: a jewelry shop, gift shop, perfume shop, liquor shop and a logo souvenir shop. There's also a bright red telephone kiosk that houses an ATM cash machine. Altogether, it's a nice place to see and be seen, and street performers complete the scene. It really is a cross between a shopping arcade and an amusement park (Florida's Aventura meets New York's Coney Island). The chairman of Royal Caribbean International even donated his own beloved Morgan sports car to grace the

Royal Promenade, which is supposedly designed in the image of London's fashionable Burlington Arcade. Actually, by far the best view of the whole promenade is from one of the 138 premium-price cabins that look into it, or from a "captain's bridge" that crosses above it. At the forward end is the showlounge, and a Connoisseur's Club cigar lounge sited on the starboard side between the showlounge and the main section of the Royal Promenade.

Arched across the grand promenade is a captain's balcony, and in the center of the promenade a stairway connects you to the deck below, where you'll find the Schooner Bar (a piano lounge that is a feature of all RCI ships) and the colorful Casino Royale (large and full of flashing lights and noises). Gaming includes blackjack, Caribbean stud poker, roulette (including the world's largest interactive roulette wheel that is activated by a roulette ball tower four decks high), and craps, as well as 300 slot machines.

A second showlounge (Studio B, a regulation-size ice-skating rink that has real, not fake, ice) has arena seating for up to 900, and the latest in broadcast facilities. A number of slim pillars obstruct the clear-view arena stage sightlines, however. An Ice Follies show is presented by a professional ice-skating show team each cruise. If ice-skating in the Caribbean doesn't particularly appeal, you might like to visit the stunning two-deck library; it's the first aboard any cruise ship, and is open 24 hours a day. A total of $12 million was spent on permanent artwork.

Drinking places include a neat Aquarium Bar, with 50 tons of glass and water in four large aquariums (whose combined value is over $1 million), the small and intimate Champagne Bar, and the Connoisseur Club – for cigars and cognacs. Lovers of jazz might appreciate High Notes, an intimate room for cool music atop the ship within the Viking Crown Lounge, or the Schooner Bar piano lounge. Golfers might enjoy the 19th Hole, a golf bar, as they play the Voyager Links.

There is a large TV studio, part of Studio "B", located adjacent to rooms that can be used for trade show exhibit space, with a 400-seat conference center and a 60-seat multimedia screening room. Meanwhile, many decks above, lovers can tie the knot in a "wedding chapel in the sky," the Skylight Chapel – it's located on the upper level of the Viking Crown Lounge, and even has wheelchair access via an electric stairway elevator. Outdoors, the pool and open deck areas (Deck 11) provide a resort-like environment.

Facilities for children and teenagers are quite extensive. "Aquanauts" is for 3–5-year-olds. "Explorers" is for 6–8-year-olds. "Voyagers" is for 9–12-year-olds. Optix is a dedicated area for teenagers, including a daytime club (with computers), soda bar, disk jockey and dance floor. Challenger's Arcade has an array of the latest video games. Virtual Submarine is a virtual reality underwater center for all ages. Computer Lab has 14 computer stations loaded with fun and games. Paint and Clay is an arts and crafts center for younger children. Adjacent to these indoor areas is Adventure Beach, an area for all the family: it includes swimming pools, a water slide and game areas outdoors.

Royal Caribbean International has, since its inception,

always been an innovator in the cruise industry, and will probably remain so with this family-friendly vessel.

In terms of sheer size, this ship presently dwarfs many other ships in the cruise industry, but in terms of personal service, the reverse is the case, unless you happen to reside in one of the top suites. Royal Caribbean International does, however, try hard to provide a good standard of programmed service from its hotel staff. This is impersonal city life at sea, and a superb, well-designed alternative to a land-based resort, which is what the company wanted to build. Remember to take lots of extra pennies: you'll need them to pay for all the additional-cost items. The onboard currency is the US dollar.

Expect some standing in lines for the reception desk, and waiting for elevators, particularly at peak meal times, as well as for embarkation and disembarkation. If you arrange to meet someone, be very specific about the location – for this really is a large ship. My advice is to arrange to meet somewhere along the Royal Promenade.

The theme-park, banquet-style regimentation is well organized, but it's hard to find better value for money, particularly for families with children. You will, however, need to plan your time aboard, otherwise you'll miss out on some of the things that you might like to include in your vacation.

Because the cruise fares are so reasonable, you can expect a big push aboard the ship for extra revenue items, drinks packages, extra-cost dining options, etc. In the end, however, you should have a decent floating vacation. Note that the same comments apply to the other sister ships (*Adventure of the Seas, Explorer of the Seas, Mariner of the Seas*, and *Navigator of the Seas*); their layout and flow are the same, and, although there may be some slight differences, it's mainly in the decor and trimmings.

ACCOMMODATION. There is a wide range of 22 cabin price grades, in four major groupings: Premium ocean-view suites and cabins, interior (atrium-view) cabins, Ocean-view cabins, and Interior (no view) cabins. Many cabins are of a similar size (good for incentives and large groups), and 300 have interconnecting doors (good for families). Price depends on grade, location and size.

A total of 138 interior (no view) cabins have bay windows that look into an interior horizontal atrium – a cruise industry first when the ship debuted. Regardless of what cabin grade you choose, however, all except for the Royal Suite and Owner's Suite have twin beds that convert to a queen-sized unit, television, radio and telephone, personal safe, vanity unit, hairdryer and private bathroom. However, you'll need to keep the curtains closed in the bay windows if you wear little clothing, because you can be seen easily from adjacent bay windows (Bay Watch?).

Royal Suite (Deck 10): The Royal Suite (there's only one), which measuring approximately 1,146 sq. ft (106.5 sq. meters) is the ship's largest private living space, and is located almost at the top of the Centrum lobby on the port side. It is a nicely appointed penthouse suite, whose occupants, sadly, must share the rest of the ship with everyone else, except for access to their own exclusive concierge club. It has a king-sized circular bed in a separate large bedroom that can be fully closed off; a living room with an additional queen-sized sofa bed, baby grand piano (pianist not included), refrigerator/wet bar, dining table and four chairs, expansive entertainment center, and a reasonably large bathroom.

Royal Family Suite: The four Royal Family suites (two aft on Deck 9, two aft on Deck 8, each measuring approximately 574 sq. ft/53 sq. meters), have two separate bedrooms – the main bedroom has a large vanity desk; the second, smaller bedroom also includes two beds and third/ fourth upper Pullman berths. There's also a lounge with dining table and four chairs, wet bar, walk-in closet; and large bathroom with Jacuzzi bathtub, washbasin, and separate shower enclosure. The suites are located at the stern of the ship and have large balconies with views out over the ship's wash.

Owner's Suites: Ten slightly smaller but desirable Owner's Suites (approximately 468 sq. ft/43 sq. meters) are located in the center of the ship, on both port and starboard sides, adjacent to the Centrum lobby on Deck 10. Each features a bedroom with queen-sized bed) or twin beds); lounge with large sofa; wet bar; bathroom with Jacuzzi bathtub, washbasin and separate shower enclosure. There's also a private balcony, although it is not very large.

Standard Outside-View and Interior (no-view) Cabins: All cabins have a private bathroom, as well as interactive TV and pay-per-view movies, including an X-rated channel. Cabin bathrooms really are compact, but at least they have a proper shower enclosure instead of a shower curtain – so you won't have to dance with a curtain.

Some accommodation grades have a refrigerator/mini-bar, although there is no space left because it is crammed with "take-and-pay" items. If you take anything from the mini-bar/refrigerator on the day of embarkation in Miami, Florida sales tax will be added to your bill.

Cabins with "private balconies" are not so private. The balcony decking is made of Bolidt – a sort of rubberized sand – and not wood, while the balcony rail is of wood. If you have a cabin with a door that interconnecting door to another cabin, be aware that you'll probably be able to hear everything your next-door neighbors say and do. Note that bathroom toilets are explosively noisy, based on the vacuum system. Cabin bath towels are small and skimpy. Room service food menus are very basic.

CUISINE. The main dining room is extremely large and is set on three levels, each with an operatic name and theme: Carmen, La Boheme and Magic Flute. A dramatic staircase connects all three levels, and huge, fat support pillars obstruct the sight lines from many seats. All three have exactly the same menus and food. All dining venues are non-smoking. Choose one of two seatings, or "My Time Dining" (eat when you want, during dining room hours).

Alternative Dining Options: Alternative dining options for casual and informal meals at all hours (according to company releases) include:

● *Promenade Café:* for continental breakfast, all-day pizzas, sandwiches and coffees (provided in paper cups).

● *Windjammer Café:* for casual buffet-style breakfast, lunch and light dinner (except for the cruise's last night).

● *Island Grill* (this is actually a section inside the Windjammer Café): for casual dinner, no reservations necessary, featuring a grill and open kitchen.

● *Portofino:* this is the ship's "upscale" (non-smoking) Euro-Italian restaurant, open for dinner only. Reservations are required, and a $6 gratuity per person is charged. The food and its presentation are better than the food in the dining room, although the restaurant is not large enough for all passengers to try even once during a cruise. Choices include: antipasti, soup, salad, pasta, main dish, dessert, cheese and coffee.

● *Chop's Grille*: Aboard all other *Voyager*-class ships, but not *Voyager of the Seas*.

● *Johnny Rockets*, a retro 1950s all-day, all-night diner-style eatery that has hamburgers, malt shakes, and jukebox hits, with both indoor and outdoor seating (all indoor tables have a mini-jukebox; dimes are provided for you to make your selection of vintage records), and all-singing, all-dancing waitresses. There is a charge of $3.95 whether you eat in or take out.

● *Sprinkles:* for round-the-clock ice cream and free yoghurt, pastries and coffee.

ENTERTAINMENT. The 1,350-seat Showlounge is a really stunning space. It is located at the forward end of the ship and spans the height of five decks, with only a few slim pillars and almost no disruption of sightlines from any seat in the house. The room has a hydraulic orchestra pit and huge stage areas, together with sonic-boom loud sound, and some superb lighting equipment.

In addition, the ship has an array of cabaret acts. Although many are not what you would call headliners, they regularly travel the cruise ship circuit. The strongest cabaret acts are presented in the main showlounge, while others appear in the Cleopatra's Needle Lounge, also the venue for late-night adults-only comedy, The best shows, however, are the Ice Spectaculars.

There is also a TV studio that can be used, for example, for trade show exhibit space (good for conventions at sea).

SPA/FITNESS. The ShipShape health spa is large, measuring 15,000 sq. ft (1,400 sq. meters). It includes a large aerobics room, fitness center (with the usual stairmasters, treadmills, stationary bikes, weight machines and free weights), treatment rooms, and men's and women's sauna/ steam rooms. Another 10,000 sq. ft (930 sq. meters) is devoted to a Solarium (with magrodome sliding glass roof).

For the more sporting, there is activity galore – including a rock-climbing wall that's 32.8 ft high (10 meters), with five separate climbing tracks. Other sports facilities include a roller-blading track, a dive-and-snorkel shop, a full-size basketball court and 9-hole, par 26 golf course.

● **For more extensive general information about a Royal Caribbean cruise experience, see pages 151–6.**

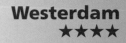

Westerdam
★★★★

Size: . . . . .Large Resort Ship	Passenger Decks: 11	Cabins (with private balcony): 641
Tonnage: .81,811	Total Crew: 817	Cabins (wheelchair accessible): 28
Lifestyle: . . . . .Premium	Passengers	Wheelchair accessibility . . . . .Good
Cruise Line: . . . . . . .Holland America Line	(lower beds/all berths): 1,916/2,455	Cabin Current: . . . . .110 volts
Former Names: . . . . .none	Passenger Space Ratio	Elevators: 14
Builder: . . . . .Fincantieri (Italy)	(lower beds/all berths): 42.6/33.3	Casino (gaming tables): . . . . .Yes
Original Cost: . . . .$400 million	Crew/Passenger Ratio	Slot Machines: . . . . .Yes
Entered Service: . . . . Apr 2004	(lower beds/all berths): 2.3/3.0	Swimming Pools (outdoors): 2
Registry: . . . . .The Netherlands	Cabins (total): 958	+1 children's pool
Length (ft/m): 935.0/285.0	Size Range (sq ft/m): 170.0–1,318.6/	Swimming Pools (indoor/outdoor): 1
Beam (ft/m): 105.6/32.2	15.7–122.5	Whirlpools: 5
Draft (ft/m): 25.5/7.80	Cabins (outside view): 804	Self-Service Launderette: . . . . .No
Propulsion/Propellers . . . .diesel-electric	Cabins (interior/no view): 154	Dedicated Cinema/Seats Yes/170
(34,000 kW)/2 pods (17.6 MW each)	Cabins (for one person): 0	Library: . . . . .Yes

OVERALL SCORE: 1,522 (OUT OF A POSSIBLE 2,000 POINTS)

OVERVIEW. *Westerdam* is another in the series of Vista-class ships (sister ships: *Eurodam, Nieuw Amsterdam, Noordam, Oosterdam* and *Zuiderdam*) designed to appeal to younger, active vacationers. Westerdam has two funnels, placed close together, one in front of the other, the result of the slightly unusual machinery configuration. The ship has, in effect, two engine rooms – one with three diesels, and one with two diesels and a gas turbine. Podded propulsion *(see page 45 for explanation)* is provided, powered by a diesel-electric system, plus a small gas turbine located in the funnel for the reduction of emissions.

There's a complete walk-around exterior teak promenade deck, and teak "steamer" style sunloungers are provided. A jogging track is located around the mast and the forward third of the ship. Exterior glass elevators, mounted midships on both port and starboard sides, provide ocean views. There are two centrally located swimming pools outdoors, and one can be used in inclement weather due to its retractable sliding glass roof. Two whirlpool tubs, adjacent to the swimming pools, are abridged by a bar. Another smaller pool is available for children; it incorporates a winding water slide that spans two decks in height. There is an additional whirlpool tub outdoors.

You enter the ship through an intimate lobby that spans three decks, and is topped by a beautiful, rotating, Waterford crystal globe of the world. The interior decor is interesting; the ceilings are particularly noticeable in the public rooms. In terms of overall decor, the colours are muted, warm. Maintaining its traditions, Holland America Line provides a large collection of artwork, including Dutch exploration, maritime history and art. The focal point of the ship is its soothing midnight blue atrium lobby (like a hotel

BERLITZ'S RATINGS		
	Possible	Achieved
Ship	500	428
Accommodation	200	162
Food	400	269
Service	400	278
Entertainment	100	77
Cruise	400	308

lobby), containing a glass replica of a sailing ship.

There are two whole entertainment/public room decks. The most dramatic room is the showlounge, spanning four decks in the forward section.

Other facilities include a winding shopping street with several boutique stores and logo shops, an internet center, a fine library, card room, an art gallery, photo gallery, and several small meeting rooms. The casino is large (one has to walk through it to get from the restaurant to the show lounge on one of the entertainments decks), and has the usual gaming tables and slot machines.

There's a basketball court, volleyball court, and golf simulator. Club HAL's KidZone is dedicated to kids' facilities and extensive programming for different age groups (5–17), with one counselor for every 30 children. An Explorations Café was added to the Crow's Nest (a HAL trademark observation lounge atop ship) in a 2007 refit.

With this large resort ship, HAL tries hard to be all things to all people, although this reviewer is not convinced that the formula works well for the many loyal repeat passengers used to the smaller ships. However, this vessel does offer a range of public rooms that have a reasonably intimate feel to them and the overall feel of the ship (relative to its size) and its eclectic decor is quite homely and comforting.

The information desk in the lobby is small and somewhat removed from the main passenger flow on the two decks above it. Many pillars obstruct the passenger flow and lines of sight throughout the ship.

There are no self-service launderettes – something families with children might miss, although special laundry packages *are* available. The air conditioning cannot be turned off in cabins or bathrooms.

ACCOMMODATION. There are 24 price categories (16 outside-view/eight interior (no view). Some cabins on the lowest accommodation deck (Main Deck) have views obstructed by lifeboats. Some cabins that can accommodate a third and fourth person have very little closet space, and only one personal safe. Some cabins have interconnecting doors – good for families with children.

Occupants of suites also get exclusive use of the Neptune Lounge and concierge service, priority embarkation and disembarkation, and other benefits – thus, in effect, making this a two-class ship. In many of the suites and cabins with private balconies the balconies are not really very private, as many can be overlooked from various public locations.

Penthouse Verandah Suites: These two suites have the largest accommodation (1,318 sq. ft/122.5 sq. meters, including balcony). These have a separate bedroom with a king-sized bed; there's also a walk-in closet, dressing room, living room, dining room, butler's pantry, mini-bar and refrigerator, and private balcony (verandah). The main bathroom has a large whirlpool bathtub, two washbasins, toilet, and plenty of storage space for personal toiletries. Personalized stationery and complimentary dry cleaning are included, as are hot hors d'oeuvres daily.

DeLuxe Verandah Suites: Next in size are 60 of these suites (563 sq. ft/52.3 sq. meters). These have twin beds that convert to a king-sized bed, vanity desk, lounge area, walk-in closet, mini-bar and refrigerator, and bathroom with full-size tub, washbasin and toilet. Personalized stationery and complimentary dry cleaning are included, as are hot hors d'oeuvres and other goodies.

Verandah Suites: There are 100 of these Verandah Suites (actually they are cabins, not suites, and measure 284 sq. ft (26.3 sq. meters). Twin beds convert to a queen-sized bed; there is also a lounge area, mini-bar and refrigerator, while the bathroom has a tub, washbasin and toilet. Floor to ceiling windows open onto a private balcony.

Outside-view Cabins: Standard outside cabins (197 sq. ft/18.3 sq. meters) have twin beds that convert to a queen-sized bed. There's also a small sitting area, while the bathroom has a tub/shower combination. The interior (no view) cabins are slightly smaller (182.9 sq. ft/17 sq. meters).

CUISINE. Dining options range from full-service meals in the main dining room and à la carte restaurant to casual, self-serve buffet-style meals and fast-food outlets.

The 1,045-seat Vista (main) Dining Room is two decks high, with seating provided on both main and balcony levels, and is located at the stern of the ship. It provides a traditional Holland America Line dining experience, with friendly service from smiling Indonesian and Filipino stewards. Both open seating and fixed (assigned tables and times) seating are available, while breakfast and lunch are open-seating (you'll be seated by restaurant staff when you enter).

There are tables for two, four, six or eight, and both smoking and no-smoking sections. The waiter stations can be noisy for anyone seated adjacent to them. Fine Rosenthal china and decent cutlery are used (but there are no fish knives). Live music is provided for dinner each evening. Once each cruise, a Dutch Dinner is held (hats are provided), as is an Indonesian Lunch. "Lighter option" meals are available for the nutrition-conscious. Holland America Line can provide Kosher meals, although these are prepared ashore, frozen, and brought to the table sealed in their original containers.

Alternative Dining Option: The 130-seat Pinnacle Grill is a more upscale dining spot (with higher quality ingredients, and smarter presentation than in the larger main dining room). It is located on Lower Promenade Deck, and fronts onto the second level of the atrium lobby; a Pinnacle Bar was added in the 2007 refit. Pacific Northwest cuisine is featured with items such as sesame-crusted halibut with ginger-miso, Peking duck breast with blackberry sauce, and an array of premium quality steaks from hand-selected cuts of beef, shown to you at tableside. Fine table settings, china and silverware are provided, as are leather-bound menus. The wine bar offers mostly American wines. Reservations are required and there is a cover charge of $30 per person for service and gratuity.

Informal Eateries: For casual eating, there is an extensive Lido Cafe, which wraps around the funnel housing and extends aft. It includes a pizzeria counter, a salad bar, Asian stir-fry counter, deli sandwiches, and a dessert buffet. Warm green vegetables are hard to come by – as are warm plates. Movement around the buffet area can be very slow.

Additionally, there is an outdoor self-serve buffet, adjacent to the fantail pool, which serves fast-food items such as hamburgers and hot dogs, chicken and fries, as well as two smaller buffets adjacent to the midships swimming pool area, and a Windsurf Cafe in the atrium lobby (open 20 hours a day), for coffee, pastries, snack foods, deli sandwiches and liqueur coffees (evenings only) – all at extra cost.

ENTERTAINMENT. The 867-seat Vista Lounge is the main venue for Las Vegas-style revue shows and major cabaret presentations. It spans three decks in the forward section. The main floor level has a bar in its starboard aft section. Spiral stairways at the back of the lounge connect all levels. The upper levels have better sightlines.

SPA/FITNESS. The Greenhouse Spa, a large, two-decks-high health spa, is directly above the navigation bridge. Facilities include a solarium, hydrotherapy pool, unisex thermal suite – a unisex area incorporating a Laconium (gentle sauna), Hammam (mild steam), and Camomile Grotto (small aromatic steam room). There is also a beauty parlor, 11 massage/therapy rooms (including one for couples), and a large gymnasium with floor-to-ceiling windows on three sides and forward-facing ocean views, and the latest high-tech muscle-toning equipment.

● **For more extensive general information on what a Holland America Line cruise is like, see pages 139–42.**

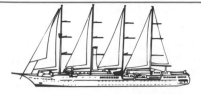

Wind Spirit
★★★ +

Size: . . . . .Boutique Ship	Number of Masts: . . .4/6 self-furling sails	Size Range (sq ft/m): 185.0–220.0/
Tonnage: .5,350	Sail Area (sq ft/m2): 21,489/1,996.4	17.0–22.5
Lifestyle: . . . . .Premium	Main Propulsion: . . . . .(a) engines (b) sails	Cabins (outside view): 74
Cruise Line: . . . . .Windstar Cruises	Propulsion/Propellers: . . . . .diesel-electric	Cabins (interior/no view): 0
Former Names: . . . . .none	(1,400kW)/1	Cabins (for one person): 0
Builder: . . . . .Ateliers et Chantiers	Passenger Decks: 5	Cabins (with private balcony): 0
du Havre (France)	Total Crew: 88	Cabins (wheelchair accessible): 0
Original Cost: . . . .$34.2 million	Passengers	Wheelchair accessibility . . . . .None
Entered Service: . . . . Apr 1988	(lower beds/all berths): 148/159	Cabin Current: . . . . .110 volts
Registry: . . . . .The Bahamas	Passenger Space Ratio	Casino (gaming tables): . . . . .Yes
Length (ft/m): 439.6/134.0	(lower beds/all berths): 36.1/33.6	Slot Machines: . . . . .Yes
Beam (ft/m): 51.8/15.8	Crew/Passenger Ratio	Swimming Pools (outdoors): . .1 (dip pool)
Draft (ft/m): 13.4/4.1	(lower beds/all berths): 1.6/1.8	Whirlpools: 1
Type of Vessel: . . . . . .computer-controlled	Cabins (total): .74	Self-Service Launderette: . . . . .No
sail-cruiser		Library: . . . . .Yes

OVERALL SCORE: 1,394 (OUT OF A POSSIBLE 2,000 POINTS)

OVERVIEW. *Wind Spirit*, when built, was one of three identical vessels (a fourth, *Wind Saga*, was planned but never built). One of the original three sister ships, *Wind Song*, suffered a fire and was declared a constructive total loss in Tahiti in 2002.

Wind Spirit is a long, sleek looking craft that is part-yacht, part-cruise ship, with four giant masts that tower 170 ft (52 meters) above the deck (they are actually 204 ft, or 62 meters) high, and fitted with computer-controlled sails; the masts, sails and rigging alone cost $5 million. The computer keeps the ship on an even keel (via the movement of a water hydraulic ballast system of 142,653 gallons/540,000 liters), so there is no heeling (rolling) over 6 degrees.

There is little open deck space when the ship is full, due to the amount of complex sail machinery. At the stern is a small water sports platform for those who enjoy all the goodies the ship offers – but only when at anchor and only in really calm sea conditions. Water sports facilities include a banana boat, kayaks, sunfish sailboats, windsurf boards, water ski boat, scuba and snorkel equipment, and four Zodiacs. You will be asked to sign a waiver if you wish to use the water sports equipment.

The ship has a finely crafted interior with pleasing, blond woods, together with soft, complementary colors and decor that is chic, even elegant, but a little cold. Note that the main lounge aboard this ship is of a slightly different design than sister ship *Wind Star*.

No scheduled activities help to make this a real relaxing, unregimented "get away from it all" vacation. The Windstar ships help you to cruise in very comfortable, contempo-

BERLITZ'S RATINGS

	Possible	Achieved
Ship	500	361
Accommodation	200	160
Food	400	265
Service	400	270
Entertainment	n/a	n/a
Cruise	500	338

rary surroundings bordering on the luxurious, yet in an unstructured environment. They provide a very relaxing, virtually unstructured cruise experience just right for seven idyllic nights in sheltered areas, but can be disturbing when a Windstar vessel is in small ports alongside several gigantic cruise ships.

This ship is ideal for couples who do not like large ships. The dress code is casual (no jackets and ties), even for dinner – the brochure states casual elegance. There are no formal nights or theme nights.

You will probably be under sail for less than 40 percent of the time (conditions and cruise area winds permitting).

Gratuities are charged at $11 per person, per day, and 15% is added to bar and wine accounts. The onboard currency is the US dollar.

Note that the swimming pool is really only a tiny "dip" pool. Be prepared for the "whine" of the vessel's generators, which are needed to run the air-conditioning and lighting systems 24 hours a day. That means you will also hear it at night in your cabin (any cabin); it takes most passengers a day or two to get used to.

Beverage prices are high. The library is small, and needs more hardback fiction. The staff, though friendly, is casual and a little sloppy at times in the finer points of service.

SUITABLE FOR: *Wind Spirit* is best suited to young-minded couples and singles who want contemporary facilities and some watersports in a very relaxed but chic setting that is different to "normal" cruise ships, with good food and service, but with no entertainment, time-passing parlour games, structured activities, or ship's photographers.

ACCOMMODATION. Regardless of the category you choose, all cabins are nicely equipped, have crisp, inviting décor and a mini-bar/refrigerator (stocked when you embark, but all drinks are at extra cost), 24-hour room service, personal safe, television (with CNN, when available, for news) that rotates so that it is viewable from the bed and the bathroom, video player, compact disc player, plenty of storage space, and two portholes. The cabins all have two portholes with outside views, and deadlights (steel covers that provide a complete blackout at night and can be closed in inclement weather conditions). The decor is a pleasant mix of rich woods, natural fabrics and colorful soft furnishings, and hi-tech yacht-style amenities. However, note that some of the cabinetry is looking a little tired, and has that "I've been varnished many times" look. A basket of fruit is provided, and replenished daily.

The bathrooms are best described as compact units, designed in a figure of eight, with a teakwood floor in the central section. There is a good amount of storage space for personal toiletries in two cabinets, as well as under-sink cupboard space; a wall-mounted hairdryer is also provided. The shower enclosure (no cabins have bathtubs) is circular – like many of today's passengers – and has both a hand-held as well as a fixed shower so you can wash your hair without getting the rest of your body wet. Personal bathroom amenities by L'Occitane are provided, as are a vanity kit and shower cap.

Note, however, that the lighting is not strong enough for women to apply make-up – this is better applied at the vanity desk in the cabin, which has stronger overhead (halogen) lighting. Bathrobes and towels are 100% cotton.

CUISINE. There is one rather chic and elegant dining room (The Restaurant), with ocean views from large, picture windows, a lovely wood ceiling and wood paneling on the walls. California-style nouvelle cuisine is served, with dishes that are attractively presented. Additionally, "signature" dishes, created by master chefs Joachim Splichal and Jeanne Jones, are offered daily. Open seating means you dine when you want and with whomever you wish to.

When the company first started, European waiters provided service with practiced European finesse. However, those waiters have been replaced by Indonesians and Filipinos, whose communication skills at times can prove inadequate, although their service is pleasant enough. The selection of breads, cheeses, and fruits could be better. There is a big push to sell wines, although the prices are extremely high, as they are for most alcoholic drinks (even bottled water is the highest in the industry, at $7 per liter bottle).

There is often casual dinner on the open deck under the stars, with grilled seafood and steaks. At the bars, hot and cold hors d'oeuvres appear at cocktail times.

Fancy something romantic? One nicely introduced in 2006 is a "Cuisine de l'Amour" romantic dinner for two (at no extra charge) served to you in your cabin, complete with candle. The menu, with seductive sounding selections, offers a choice of appetizer, a set soup, choice of salad, and two entrée options, and a set dessert to finish – ideal for that quiet romantic dinner.

ENTERTAINMENT. There is no showlounge, shows or cabaret. However, none are really needed, because a cruise aboard this high-tech sailing ship provides an opportunity to get away from all that noise and "entertainment". The main lounge (a corner of which is dedicated to a small casino) does have a small dance floor, and, typically, a trio is there to play for your dancing or listening pleasure.

The main lounge is also used for cocktail parties and other social functions. Otherwise, it's down to more personal entertainment, such as a video in your cabin late at night – or, much more romantic, after-dinner hours spent outside strolling or simply lounging on deck.

SPA/FITNESS. A gymnasium (with a modicum of muscle-toning equipment, treadmills and exercycles) and sauna are located at the aft of the ship, adjacent to the Watersports platform. Special spa packages can be pre-booked through your travel agent before you arrive at the ship. Well-being massages, aromatherapy facials, manicures, pedicures, and hair beautifying treatments are all at extra cost (massage, for example, costs about $2 per minute, plus gratuity). The spa is operated by Steiner Leisure, a specialist concession, whose young staff may try to sell you Steiner's own-brand Elemis beauty products.

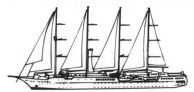

Wind Star
★★★ +

Size: . . . . .Boutique Ship	Number of Masts: . . .4/6 self-furling sails	Size Range (sq ft/m): 185.0–220.0/
Tonnage: 5,350	Sail Area (sq ft/m2): 21,489/1,996.4	17.0–22.5
Lifestyle: . . . . .Premium	Main Propulsion: . . . . .(a) engines (b) sails	Cabins (outside view): 74
Cruise Line: . . . . .Windstar Cruises	Propulsion/Propellers: . . . . .diesel-electric	Cabins (interior/no view): 0
Former Names: . . . . .none	(1,400kW)/1	Cabins (for one person): 0
Builder: . . . . .Ateliers et Chantiers	Passenger Decks: 5	Cabins (with private balcony): 0
du Havre (France)	Total Crew: 88	Cabins (wheelchair accessible): 0
Original Cost: . . . .$34.2 million	Passengers	Wheelchair accessibility . . . . .None
Entered Service: . . . . Dec 1986	(lower beds/all berths): 148/168	Cabin Current: . . . . .110 volts
Registry: . . . . .The Bahamas	Passenger Space Ratio	Casino (gaming tables): . . . . .Yes
Length (ft/m): 439.6/134.0	(lower beds/all berths): 36.1/33.6	Slot Machines: . . . . .Yes
Beam (ft/m): 51.8/15.8	Crew/Passenger Ratio	Swimming Pools (outdoors): . .1 (dip pool)
Draft (ft/m): 13.4/4.1	(lower beds/all berths): 1.6/1.8	Whirlpools: 1
Type of Vessel: . . . . . .computer-controlled	Cabins (total): .74	Self-Service Launderette: . . . . .No
sail-cruiser		Library: . . . . .Yes

OVERALL SCORE: 1,393 (OUT OF A POSSIBLE 2,000 POINTS)

OVERVIEW. *Wind Star* is one of three identical vessels (a fourth, *Wind Saga*, was planned but never built). One of the original three sister ships, *Wind Song*, suffered a fire and was declared a constructive total loss in Tahiti in 2002. *Wind Star* is a sleek-looking craft that is part-yacht, part-cruise ship, with four giant masts that tower 170 ft (52 meters) above the deck (they are actually 204 ft, or 62 meters) high, and fitted with computer-controlled sails; the masts, sails and rigging alone cost $5 million. The computer keeps the ship on an even keel (via the movement of a water hydraulic ballast system of 142,650 gallons/540,000 litres), so there is no heeling (rolling) over 6 degrees. When the masts for *Wind Star* (first of the three original Windstar vessels) were lowered into position, a US silver dollar, dated 1889, was placed under mast number two (the main mast).

There is very little open deck space when the ship is full, due to the amount of complex sail machinery. There is a tiny dip pool. At the stern is a small water sports platform for those who enjoy all the goodies the ship offers – but only when at anchor, and only in really calm sea conditions. Water sports facilities include a banana boat kayaks, sunfish sailboats, windsurf boards, water ski boat, scuba and snorkel equipment, and four Zodiacs. You will be asked to sign a waiver if you wish to use the water sports equipment.

The ship has a finely crafted interior with pleasing, blond woods, together with soft, complementary colors and decor that is chic, even elegant, but a little cold. Note that the main lounge aboard *Wind Star* is of a different design than sister ship *Wind Spirit*.

No scheduled activities help to make this a real relaxing,

BERLITZ'S RATINGS

	Possible	Achieved
Ship	500	359
Accommodation	200	160
Food	400	265
Service	400	270
Entertainment	n/a	n/a
Cruise	500	339

unregimented "get away from it all" vacation. The Windstar ships will cruise you in extremely comfortable surroundings bordering on contemporary luxury, yet in an unstructured environment. They provide a very relaxing, virtually unstructured cruise experience just right for seven idyllic nights in sheltered areas, but can be disturbing when a Windstar vessel is in small ports alongside several huge cruise ships.

This ship is ideal for couples who do not like large ships. The dress code is casual (no jackets and ties required), even for dinner (the brochure states casual elegance). There are no formal nights or theme nights. You will probably be under sail for less than 40 percent of the time (conditions and cruise area winds permitting).

Gratuities are charged at $11 per person, per day, and 15% is added to bar and wine accounts. The onboard currency is the US dollar.

Note that the swimming pool is really only a tiny "dip" pool. Be prepared for the "whine" of the vessel's generators, which are needed to run the air-conditioning and lighting systems 24 hours a day. That means you will also hear it at night in your cabin (any cabin), and takes most passengers a day or two to get used to.

Beverage prices are high. The library is small, and needs more hardback fiction. The staff, though friendly, is casual and can be a little sloppy at times in the finer points of service. Pity about the plastic sunloungers!

SUITABLE FOR: *Wind Star* is best suited to young-minded couples and singles who want contemporary facilities and some watersports in a very relaxed but chic setting that is different to "normal" cruise ships, with good food and service, but with no entertainment, time-passing parlour games, structured activities or ship's photographers.

ACCOMMODATION. Regardless of the category you choose, all cabins are very nicely equipped, have crisp, inviting decor, and a mini-bar/refrigerator (stocked when you embark, but all drinks are at extra cost), 24-hour room service, personal safe, television (with CNN, when available, for news) that rotates so that it is viewable from the bed and the bathroom, video player, compact disc player, plenty of storage space, and two portholes.

The cabins all have two portholes with outside views, and deadlights (steel covers that provide a complete blackout at night and can be closed in inclement weather conditions). The decor is a pleasant mix of rich woods, natural fabrics and colorful soft furnishings, and hi-tech yacht-style amenities. However, note that some of the cabinetry is looking a little tired, and has that "I've been varnished many times" look. A basket of fruit is replenished daily.

The bathrooms are best described as very compact units, designed in a figure of eight, with a teakwood floor in the central section. There is a good amount of storage space for personal toiletries in two cabinets, as well as under-sink cupboard space; a wall-mounted hairdryer is also provided. The shower enclosure (no cabins have bathtubs) is circular – like many of today's passengers – and has both a hand-held, as well as a fixed shower, enabling you to wash your hair without getting the rest of your body wet. Personal bathroom amenities by L'Occitane provided, as is a vanity kit and shower cap.

Note, however, that the lighting is not strong enough for women to apply make-up – this is better applied at the vanity desk in the cabin, which has stronger overhead (halogen) lighting. Bathrobes and towels are 100% cotton.

CUISINE. There is one rather chic and elegant dining room (The Restaurant), with ocean views from large, picture windows, a lovely wood ceiling and wood paneling on the walls. California-style nouvelle cuisine is served, with dishes that are attractively presented. Additionally, "signature" dishes, created by master chefs Joachim Splichal and Jeanne Jones, are offered daily.

Open seating means you dine when you want and with whomever you wish to. Both smoking and no-smoking sections are provided.

When the company made its debut, European waiters provided service with practiced European finesse; those waiters are now from Indonesia and the Philippines, who provide friendly service but with less finesse. The selection of breads, cheeses, and fruits could be better. There is a big push to sell wines, although the prices are extremely high, as they are for most alcoholic drinks (even bottled water is the highest in the industry, at $7 per liter bottle).

There is often casual dinner on the open deck under the stars, with grilled seafood and steaks. At the bars, hot and cold hors d'oeuvres appear at cocktail times.

A nice addition is a "Cuisine de l'Amour" romantic dinner for two (at no extra charge) served to you in your cabin, complete with candle. The menu (with seductive sounding selections) offers a choice of appetizer, a set soup, choice of salad, and two entrée options, and a set dessert to finish – ideal for that quiet romantic dinner.

ENTERTAINMENT. There is no showlounge, shows or cabaret. However, none are really needed, because a cruise aboard this high-tech sailing ship provides an opportunity to get away from all that noise and "entertainment". The main lounge (a corner of which is dedicated to a small casino) does have a small dance floor, and, typically, a trio is there to play for your dancing or listening pleasure. The main lounge is also used for cocktail parties and other social functions. Otherwise, it's down to more personal entertainment, such as a video in your cabin late at night – or, much more romantic, after-dinner hours spent outside strolling or simply lounging on deck.

SPA/FITNESS. A gymnasium (with a modicum of muscle-toning equipment, treadmills and exercycles) and sauna are located at the aft of the ship, adjacent to the Watersports platform. Special spa packages can be pre-booked through your travel agent before you arrive at the ship. Well-being massages, aromatherapy facials, manicures, pedicures, and hair beautifying treatments are all at extra cost (massage, for example, costs about $2 per minute, plus gratuity). The spa is operated by Steiner Leisure, a specialist concession, whose young staff may try to sell you Steiner's own-brand Elemis beauty products.

Size: . . . . .Small Ship	Sail Area (sq ft/m2): 26,910/2,500	Cabins (for one person): 0
Tonnage: 14,745	Main Propulsion: . . . . . .a) engines/b) sails	Cabins (with private balcony): 0
Lifestyle: . . . . .Premium	Propulsion/Propellers: diesel (9,120kW)/2	Cabins (wheelchair accessible): 0
Cruise Line: . . . . .Windstar Cruises	Passenger Decks: 8	Wheelchair accessibility . . . . .None
Former Names: . . . .*Club Med I*	Total Crew: 163	Cabin Current: . . . . .220 volts
Builder: . . . . .Ateliers et Chantiers	Passengers	Elevators: 2
du Havre (France)	(lower beds/all berths): 312/347	Casino (gaming tables): . . . . .Yes
Original Cost: . . . .$140 million	Passenger Space Ratio	Slot Machines: . . . . .Yes
Entered Service: . . . .Feb 1990/May 1998	(lower beds/all berths): 47.2/42.4	Swimming Pools (outdoors): 2
Registry: . . . . .The Bahamas	Crew/Passenger Ratio	Whirlpools: 2
Length (ft/m): 613.5/187.0	(lower beds/all berths): 1.9/2.1	Self-Service Launderette: . . . . .No
Beam (ft/m): 65.6/20.0	Cabins (total): 156	Library: . . . . .Yes
Draft (ft/m): 16.4/5.0	Size Range (sq ft/m): 188.0–500.5/	
Type of Vessel: . . . . .high-tech sail-cruiser	17.5–46.5	
Number of Masts: . . . . . . .5/7 computer-	Cabins (outside view): 156	
controlled sails	Cabins (interior/no view): 0	

OVERALL SCORE: 1,396 (OUT OF A POSSIBLE 2,000 POINTS)

OVERVIEW. One of a pair of the world's largest sail-cruisers, *Wind Surf* is part-cruise ship, part-yacht (its sister ship operates as *Club Med II*). This is a larger, grander sister to the original three Windstar Cruises vessels. Five huge masts of 164 ft/50 meters (these actually rise 221 feet, or 67.5 meters above sea level) carry seven triangular, self-furling sails made of Dacron, with a total surface area of 26,881 sq. ft (2,497 sq. meters). No human hands touch the sails, as everything is handled electronically by computer control from the bridge.

A computer keeps the ship on an even keel (via the movement of a water hydraulic ballast system of 266,800 gallons/1 million liters), so there is no heeling (rolling) over 6 degrees. When the ship is not using the sails, four diesel-electric motors propel it at up to approximately 12 knots.

A large, hydraulic water sports platform at the stern hasn't functioned properly for ages – it's time it was fixed. Swimming from it isn't allowed, but extensive water sports facilities include 12 windsurfers, 3 sailboats, 2 water-ski boats, 20 single scuba tanks, snorkels, fins and masks, and 4 inflatable Zodiac motorized boats for water-skiing, etc, and all at no extra charge (except for the scuba tanks). You must sign a waiver to use the water sports equipment.

There are two saltwater swimming pools – little more than dip pools; one is amidships on the uppermost deck of the ship, while the other is aft, together with two hot tubs, and an adjacent bar. There are no showers at either of the pools, so passengers get into the pools or hot tubs while covered in oil or lotion, an unhygienic arrangement.

BERLITZ'S RATINGS		
	Possible	Achieved
Ship	500	361
Accommodation	200	160
Food	400	264
Service	400	271
Entertainment	n/a	n/a
Cruise	500	340

In 2000, the ship had a further internal redesign. A new gangway improved embarkation and disembarkation. A business center incorporated a computer center (with 10 internet-access terminals, and a meeting room for 30–60 people. In the casino/main lounge (with four blackjack and one roulette table, and 21 slot machines), which has an unusually high ceiling for the size of the ship, the dance floor has been relocated for better access and flow.

In the 2006 refit, a Yacht Club replaced the library; it provides comfortable seating for socializing. An espresso bar offers gourmet coffee drinks; there are eight computers with internet access, and wi-fi access for laptops.

Wind Surf cruises from Barbados (November–March) and in the Mediterranean (May–October). However, the European itineraries are really port-intensive, which means you sail each night and are in port each day. With such itineraries, there seems little point to having the sails, as passengers don't get to experience them.

Don't buy a cigar from the onboard shop – because the air temperature in the shop is high, cigars will be dry and worthless and should be sold from a properly kept humidor. Plastic sunloungers spoil the ship's otherwise elegant image.

Hotel service is provided mostly by Filipino and Indonesian staff. The onboard currency is the US dollar. Gratuities are charged at $11 per person, per day, and 15% is added to bar and wine accounts.

SUITABLE FOR: *Wind Surf* is a good choice for couples seeking the "California Casual" dress code (no jackets or ties required) and informality found aboard this vessel, yet don't want the inconvenience of the workings of a real tall ship. The quality of food and its presentation is a definite plus, as is the policy of no music in passenger hallways or elevators – in other words, it's a delightful, peaceful environment.

ACCOMMODATION. There are just three price categories, simplifying your choice. All cabins are very nicely equipped, have crisp, inviting decor, and a mini-bar/refrigerator (stocked when you embark, but all drinks are at extra cost), 24-hour room service, personal safe, a TV set that rotates so that it is viewable from the bed and the bathroom, DVD player, compact disc player, plenty of storage space, and two portholes. Videos and compact discs are available from the library. There are six four-person cabins; 35 doubles are fitted with an extra Pullman berth, and several cabins have an interconnecting door – good for families. "Spa Suite" packages are available at extra cost.

The bathrooms are compact units, designed in a figure of eight, with a teakwood floor in the central section. There is a good amount of storage space for toiletries in two cabinets, as well as under-sink cupboard space, and a wall-mounted hairdryer. The shower enclosure is circular, and has both a hand-held and a fixed shower, enabling you to wash your hair without getting the rest of your body wet. The lighting is not strong enough for women to apply make-up – this is better applied at the vanity desk in the cabin.

All but one of the 31 suites added to Deck 3 in 1998 have two bathrooms, a separate living/dining area, sleeping area (this can be curtained off), two writing desks, and four portholes instead of two. A further two new suites (approximately 495.1 sq.ft./46.0 sq.m) were added in 2006; each has a bedroom, separate living/dining room, and marble bathroom with Jacuzzi bathtub, and separate toilet/wash room. In the 2006 refit, all bathrooms were refurbished with granite countertops, open glass shelves, new cabinets, and magnifying mirror, making them more contemporary.

There are two TV sets (one in the lounge, one in the sleeping area), VCR and CD player, and Bose SoundDock for iPods. But movies cannot be watched from the bed – only from the sofa in the lounge area. Popcorn is available from room service.

New "Spa Suite" packages were introduced in 2010. These take an existing cabin and provide extras such as a queen-size bed with microfiber bed linen, bathrobes, an orchid flower arrangement, two bathrooms, a flat-screen TV with DVD player, and Bose SoundDock speakers for Apple iPods. Also, a pillow menu provides several choices, including a "snore-no-more" hypoallergenic pillow.

Three tea collections by Tea Forte include well-being, herbal, or exotic teas. Brewing service features contemporary, porcelain teaware and is available from room service 24 hours a day. Berlitz Tip: ask for it to be made with mineral water, not the standard chlorinated ship's water.

CUISINE. The 272-seat Restaurant has tables for two, four or six, and open seating with no pre-assigned tables so you can sit with whom you wish. It is open only for dinner, which is typically between 7.30pm and 9.30pm. Smoking and no-smoking sections are provided. California-style nouvelle cuisine is served, with dishes attractively presented. Additionally, "signature" dishes, created by master chefs Joachim Splichal and Jeanne Jones, are offered daily.

A 124-seat Degrees Restaurant is an alternative venue to the main restaurant for dinner, with menus from around the world as well as Joachim Splichal-developed steakhouse cuisine. Located atop the ship, on Star Deck, it has picture windows on port and starboard sides, an open kitchen, and tables for two, four or six. This is a no-smoking dining spot. Reservations are required for dinner, although there is no extra charge, and passengers are restricted to two visits per seven-day cruise.

The Veranda, amidships (on Star Deck), has its own open terrace for informal, self-serve breakfast and lunch buffets. It really is very pleasant to be outside, eating an informal meal on a balmy night. Do try the bread pudding, available after lunch each day – the ship is famous for it. Additionally, a permanent barbecue is also set up aft of the Veranda, for fresh grilled items for breakfast and lunch.

The Compass Rose, an indoor/outdoor bar, provides snack items plus some pastries and coffee for breakfast.

Windstar Cruises food is generally very good, although highly geared toward American tastes. Europeans and other nationals should note that items such as bacon is fried to death, and the choice of cheeses and teas is poor. Service in the dining room is also quite fast, geared towards those who have not yet learned to unwind.

A nice addition is a "Cuisine de l'Amour" romantic dinner for two (at no extra charge) served to you in your cabin, complete with candle. The menu, with its seductive sounding selections, offers a choice of appetizer, a set soup, choice of salad, and two entrée options, and a set dessert to finish.

ENTERTAINMENT. There is no showlounge, shows or cabaret. However, none are really needed, because a cruise aboard this high-tech sailing ship provides an opportunity to get away from all that noise and "entertainment". The main lounge (a corner of which is dedicated to a small casino) does have a small dance floor, and music typically provided by a trio. The main lounge is also used for cocktail parties and other social functions.

One annoying trend, however, is use of the lounge for art auctions after dinner. How sad that an otherwise pleasant, casual cruise experience is ruined in this way. Better to retire to your cabin and take in a video, or spend it out on deck taking a stroll or lounging under the stars.

SPA/FITNESS. The Health Spa has a unisex sauna (bathing suits required), beauty salon, and several treatment rooms for massage, facials and body wraps. There is also a decent gymnasium – on a separate deck, with ocean views – and an aerobics workout room. Unfortunately, the spa facilities are split on three separate decks, making them rather disjointed. Special spa packages can be pre-booked through your travel agent before you embark. The spa is operated by the UK's Onboard Spa Company.

Zaandam
★★★★

Size: . . . . .Mid-Size Ship	Passenger Decks: 10	Cabins (with private balcony): 197
Tonnage: .60,906	Total Crew: 561	Cabins (wheelchair accessible): 23
Lifestyle: . . . . .Premium	Passengers	Wheelchair accessibility . . . . .Good
Cruise Line: . . . . . . .Holland America Line	(lower beds/all berths): 1,440/1,850	Cabin Current: . . . . .110 volts
Former Names: . . . . .none	Passenger Space Ratio	Elevators: 12
Builder: . . . . .Fincantieri (Italy)	(lower beds/all berths): 42.3/32.9	Casino (gaming tables): . . . . .Yes
Original Cost: . . . .$300 million	Crew/Passenger Ratio	Slot Machines: . . . . .Yes
Entered Service: . . . . .May 2000	(lower beds/all berths): 2.5/2.5	Swimming Pools (outdoors): 2
Registry: . . . . .The Netherlands	Cabins (total): .720	Swimming Pools (indoors): 1
Length (ft/m): 777.5/237.00	Size Range (sq ft/m): 113.0–1,126.3/	(magrodome cover)
Beam (ft/m): 105.8/32.25	10.5–104.6	Whirlpools: 2
Draft (ft/m): 25.5/7.80	Cabins (outside view): 581	Self-Service Launderette: . . . . .Yes
Propulsion/Propellers: . . . . .diesel-electric	Cabins (interior/no view): 139	Dedicated Cinema/Seats: Yes/205
(37,500kW)/2	Cabins (for one person): 0	Library: . . . . .Yes

OVERALL SCORE: 1,541 (OUT OF A POSSIBLE 2,000 POINTS)

OVERVIEW. *Zaandam*'s hull is dark blue, in keeping with all Holland America Line ships. Although similar in size to *Rotterdam*, this ship has a single funnel, and is a sister ship to *Volendam*.

Zaandam has three principal passenger stairways, which is so much better than two stairways, particularly from the viewpoints of safety, accessibility and passenger flow. There is a magrodome-covered pool on the Lido Deck between the mast and the ship's funnel.

The interior decor is restrained, with much traditional ocean liner detailing, wood accenting, and the design theme of music incorporated throughout. Music memorabilia is scattered throughout the ship, in fabrics, posters, and – believe it or not – real instruments.

The musical instruments and other memorabilia were acquired from the "Pop and Guitars" auction at Christie's in London in 1997. They include a Fender Squire Telecaster guitar signed by Mick Jagger, Keith Richards, Charlie Watts, Ronnie Wood and Bill Wyman of the Rolling Stones; a Conn Saxophone signed on the mouthpiece by former US President Bill Clinton; an Ariana acoustic guitar signed by David Bowie and Iggy Pop; a Fender Stratocaster guitar signed in silver ink by the members of the rock band Queen; a Bently "Les Paul" style guitar signed by various artists, including Carlos Santana, Eric Clapton, B.B. King, Robert Cray, Keith Richards and Les Paul. Perhaps the ship should be named *Rockerdam*.

New additions include The Oasis outdoor relaxation areas (aft of the funnel, including a waterfall and family gathering areas), Explorations (an excellent combination coffee/tea café, internet connection center, and library; and children's and teens' play areas. Popcorn is even provided at the Wajang

BERLITZ'S RATINGS		
	Possible	Achieved
Ship	500	430
Accommodation	200	165
Food	400	282
Service	400	276
Entertainment	100	77
Cruise	400	311

Theater for moviegoers (just like ashore), and this location now incorporates a fully equipped kitchen for HAL's "Culinary Arts" program, which involves visiting chefs and interactive cooking and tasting demonstrations.

The casino has blackjack, roulette, stud poker and dice tables alongside the requisite rows of slot machines. Adjacent is a sports bar.

The ship's focal point is a three-deck-high atrium, around which the ship's main offices can be found (reception desk, shore excursions desk, photo shop, and photo gallery). It also houses a real showpiece – a fancy 22-ft (6.7-meter) high pipe organ that comes complete with puppets that move in time with the music. One of the largest such Dutch band organs ever built, it was custom-made in Hilversum in the Netherlands especially for Holland America Line.

As in *Volendam*, the Lido Deck swimming pool is located one deck higher than the *Statendam*-class ships, so that you can now have direct access between the aft and midships pools aboard this ship (not so aboard the S-class ships). This provided more space on the Navigation Deck below for extra cabins to be accommodated.

With one whole deck of suites and a dedicated, private concierge lounge, the company has in effect created a two-class ship. The charge to use the washing machines and dryers in the self-service launderette is petty and irritating, particularly for the occupants of suites, as they pay high prices for their cruises.

Holland America Line's "Signature of Excellence" program, now introduced fleetwide, provides passengers with more choice, and has given a boost to the cabin toiletry amenities provided. Communication (in English) with many of the staff, particularly in the dining room and buffet areas, can be frustrating. Room service is poor. Non-smokers should avoid this ship, as smokers are everywhere. Standing in line for embarkation, disembarkation, shore tenders and for self-serve buffet meals is inevitable aboard large ships.

ACCOMMODATION. The range is comparable to that found aboard the similarly sized *Rotterdam*, and comprises 17 different categories. The price will depend on the grade, location and size you choose. There is one penthouse suite, 28 suites, and 168 mini-suites, with the rest of the accommodation comprised of a mix of outside-view and interior (no view) cabins. However, there are many more balcony cabins (called "mini-suites") aboard this ship than aboard the slightly smaller *Statendam*-class ships (*Maasdam, Ryndam, Statendam*, and *Veendam*). All passenger hallways now include pleasing artwork.

All standard interior and outside cabins are tastefully furnished, and have twin beds that convert to a queen-sized bed (space is tight for walking between beds and vanity unit). There is a decent amount of closet and drawer space, although this will prove tight for the longer voyages featured. All cabin televisions carry CNN and TNT. The bathrooms, which are fully tiled, are disappointingly small, particularly for long cruises, and have small shower tubs, utilitarian personal toiletries cupboards, and exposed under-sink plumbing. There is no detailing to distinguish them from bathrooms aboard the *Statendam*-class ships.

There are 28 full Verandah Suites (Navigation Deck), and one penthouse suites. All suite occupants share a private concierge lounge, called the Neptune Lounge (the concierge handles such things as special dining arrangements, shore excursions and special requests). Strangely, there are no butlers for these suites, as aboard many other ships with similar facilities.

Each Verandah Suite has a separate bedroom, dressing and living areas. Suite passengers get personal stationery, complimentary laundry and ironing, cocktail hour hors d'oeuvres and other goodies, as well as priority embarkation and disembarkation. The concierge lounge, with its latticework teak detailing and private library, is accessible only by private key-card.

The ultimate in living space is the Penthouse Suite. It has a separate steward's entrance, and has a large bedroom with king-sized bed, separate living room (with baby grand piano) and a dining room, dressing room, walk-in closet, butler's pantry, private balcony (the balcony is no larger than the balcony of any of the other suites).

Other facilities include an audio-visual center with television and VCR, wet bar with refrigerator, large bathroom with Jacuzzi bathtub, separate toilet with bidet, and a guest bathroom (with toilet and washbasin).

With the exception of the penthouse suite, located for-

ward on the starboard side, the bathrooms in the other suites and "mini-suites" are a little disappointing – not as spacious or opulent as one might expect. All outside-view suites and cabin bathrooms have a bathtub/shower while interior (no view) cabins have a shower only. Also, note that the 23 cabins for the mobility-limited are very spacious and have a large roll-in shower enclosure for wheelchair users (some also have a bathtub), and ramped access to the balcony.

CUISINE. The Rotterdam Dining Room is a grand, traditional room, and is spread over two decks, with ocean views on three sides with a grand staircase to connect the upper and lower levels. Both open seating and fixed (assigned tables and times) seating are available, while breakfast and lunch are open-seating (you'll be seated by restaurant staff when you enter).

There are tables for two, four, six or eight. The waiter stations are very noisy for anyone seated adjacent to them.

Live music is provided for dinner each evening; once each cruise, a Dutch Dinner is featured (hats are provided), as is an Indonesian Lunch. "Lighter option" meals are available for the nutrition- and weight-conscious. Fine Rosenthal china and cutlery are used, although there are no fish knives.

Alternative Dining Option: The Pinnacle Grill features Pacific Northwest cuisine and seats 88. Reservations are required, and anyone booking suite-grade accommodation qualifies for priority reservations.

In addition, the Lido Buffet is a casual, self-serve cafe for casual breakfasts and luncheons, and a poolside grill (Terrace Café) has hamburgers, hot dogs and other fast-food items. The Lido Buffet is also open for casual dinners on several nights each cruise (typically three nights on a 7-night cruise), in an open-seating arrangement. Tables are set with crisp linens, flatware and stemware. The set menu includes a choice of four entrées.

All dining venues are no-smoking areas.

ENTERTAINMENT. The Mondriaan Showlounge, located at the forward part of the ship, spans two decks, with banquette seating on both main and upper levels. It is basically a well-designed room, but the ceiling is low and the sightlines from the balcony level are quite poor.

SPA/FITNESS. The Greenhouse Spa facilities are quite extensive, and include a gymnasium (with good muscle-toning equipment), separate saunas and steam rooms for men and women, and several treatment rooms, each with a shower and toilet. Outdoor facilities include basketball and shuffleboard courts, a jogging track, and a full wrap-around teakwood promenade deck for strolling.

● **For more extensive general information on what a Holland America Line cruise is like, see pages 139–42.**

Zenith
★★★+

Size: . . . . .Mid-Size Ship	Total Crew: 670	Cabins (wheelchair accessible): 4
Tonnage: .47,255	Passengers	Wheelchair accessibility . . . . .Good
Lifestyle: . . . . .Standard	(lower beds/all berths): 1,378/1,800	Cabin Current: . . . . .110/220 volts
Cruise Line: . . . . .Pullmantur Cruises	Passenger Space Ratio	Elevators: 7
Former Names: . . . . .none	(lower beds/all berths): . . . . . .34.2 /26.2	Casino (gaming tables): . . . . .Yes
Builder: . . . . .Meyer Werft (Germany)	Crew/Passenger Ratio	Slot Machines: . . . . .Yes
Original Cost: . . . .$210 million	(lower beds/all berths): 2.0/2.6	Swimming Pools (outdoors): 2
Entered Service: . . . . .Apr 1992/Jun 2007	Cabins (total): .720	Swimming Pools (indoors): 0
Registry: . . . . .Malta	Size Range (sq ft/m): 172.2–500.5/	Whirlpools: 3
Length (ft/m): 681.0/207.59	16.0–46.50	Self-Service Launderette: . . . . .No
Beam (ft/m): 95.1/29.00	Cabins (outside view): 572	Dedicated Cinema/Seats: . . . . .No
Draft (ft/m): 23.6/7.20	Cabins (interior/no view): 148	Library: . . . . .Yes
Propulsion/Propellers: diesel (19,960kW)/2	Cabins (for one person): 0	
Passenger Decks: 10	Cabins (with private balcony): 110	

OVERALL SCORE: 1,343 (OUT OF A POSSIBLE 2,000 POINTS)

OVERVIEW. *Zenith*, formerly owned and operated by Celebrity Cruises (the sister ship is Island Cruises' *Island Star*, formerly *Horizon*), is now over 15 years old. However, the ship still has a contemporary, though rather sharp, angular profile that gives the impression of power and speed owing to its blue paint striping along the sides, separating the hull from the superstructure (the hull was designed by mega-yacht designer Jon Bannenberg). Pullmantur Cruises took over the ship in 2007, installed 220-volt (European) outlets in all cabins, and started operations in June.

Inside, there is a similar interior layout to its sister ship, *Island Star*, and elegant and restrained decor. The feeling is one of uncluttered surroundings, and the ship benefits from some interesting artwork. Soothing, pastel colors and high-quality soft furnishings are used throughout the interiors.

The ship's art deco-style hotel-like lobby, reminiscent of hotels in Miami Beach, has a two-deck-high ceiling and a spacious feel to it, and is the contact point for the reception desk, shore excursions, and onboard accounts.

The principal deck that houses many of the public entertainment rooms has a double-width indoor promenade. There is a good-sized library, relocated and enlarged in a 1999 refit. Other facilities include Harry's Bar, a cigar smoking lounge complete with fireplace and bookshelves containing leather-bound volumes; a library and internet-connect center; a Plaza Café, for coffee and loud chat. A large, elegantly appointed casino has its own bar.

Pullmantur Cruises has made changes to some of the public rooms and open areas, and has added splashes of bright colors, motifs, and new signage. The hospitality and the range and variety of food have been tailored to its Span-

BERLITZ'S RATINGS

	Possible	Achieved
Ship	500	371
Accommodation	200	147
Food	400	234
Service	400	263
Entertainment	100	63
Cruise	400	265

ish-speaking family clientele. Pullmantur Cruises also has a good programme for children and teenagers, with specially trained youth counsellors, and lots of activities. You will typically find a lot of smokers aboard.

Standing in line for embarkation, disembarkation, shore tenders and for self-serve buffet meals is inevitable cruising aboard large ships. Also, the doors to the public restrooms and the outdoor decks are rather heavy. The public restrooms are clinical and need some softer decor. There are no cushioned pads for poolside sunloungers.

SUITABLE FOR: *Zenith* is best suited to young (and young at heart) Spanish-speaking couples, singles, and families with children of all ages who want a first cruise experience in an elegant ship, with plenty of public rooms and a lively atmosphere, food that is quantity rather than quality, at low cost. The onboard currency is the euro, and gratuities are extra. However, all drinks are included, and that makes it easy for families with children.

ACCOMMODATION. There are 15 price grades, including outside-view suites and cabins, and interior (no view) cabins, but even the smallest cabin is a decent size. Note that many outside-view cabins on Fantasy Deck have lifeboat-obstructed views.

Standard Cabins: The outside-view and interior (no view) cabins have good-quality fittings with lots of wood accenting, are tastefully decorated and of an above-average size, with an excellent amount of closet and drawer space, and reasonable insulation between cabins. All have twin beds that convert to a queen-sized bed, and a good amount of closet and drawer space. The cabin soundproofing is quite good although this depends on location (some cabins are located opposite crew access doors, which can prove to be busy and noisy.

The bathrooms have a generous shower area, and a small range of toiletries is provided, although bathroom towels are a little small, as is storage space for toiletries. The lowest-grade outside-view cabins have a porthole, but all others have picture windows.

Royal Suites: The largest accommodation is in two Royal Suites midships on Atlantic Deck (Deck 10), and forward on Marina Deck. These have a large private balcony, and feature a separate bedroom and lounge, dining area with glass dining table (with CD player and VCR player in addition to the large television). The bathroom is also larger and has a whirlpool bathtub with integral shower.

Another 20 suites (also on Atlantic Deck) are very tastefully furnished, although they are really just larger cabins rather than suites. They do have a generous amount of drawer and other storage space, however, and a sleeping area with European duvets on the beds instead of sheets and blankets, plus a lounge area. They also have good bathrooms. Butler service is standard.

All accommodation designated as suites does suffer from noise generated on the swimming pool deck directly above. No suites or cabins have private balconies – they weren't in vogue when this ship was built.

In early 2005, *Zenith* underwent a major refit and reconstruction program that moved the navigation bridge forward so that additional cabins could be added. Balconies were added to many cabins on Atlantic and Marina Decks, while the spa/fitness area was expanded, the observation lounge was expanded forwards; a new "alternative" restaurant was added, and public rooms and foyers were redecorated. All cabins were refurbished (new furniture was introduced), and bathrooms were renewed.

CUISINE. The Caravelle Dining Room, which has a raised section in its center, has several tables for two, as well as for four, six or eight (in banquettes), although the chairs do not have armrests. There are two seatings for dinner (open seating for breakfast and lunch), at tables for two, four, six, eight or 10. The cuisine, its presentation and service are more quantity rather than quality, and green vegetables are hard to come by.

For informal meals, the Windsurf Buffet (non-smoking) has a traditional single line self-service buffet for breakfast and luncheon, and includes a pasta station, rotisserie and pizza ovens. At peak times, however, the buffet is simply too small, too crowded, and very noisy. The Grill, located outdoors adjacent to (but aft of) the Windsurf Cafe, serves typical fast-food items such as pizzas.

ENTERTAINMENT. The two-level Celebrity Showlounge/theatre, with main and balcony levels, and good sightlines from almost all seats – however, the railing at the front of the balcony level does impede sight lines. It has a large stage for this size of ship, and decent lighting and sound equipment.

The shows consist of a troupe of showgirl dancers, whose routines are reminiscent of high-school shows. Cabaret acts are the main feature; these include singers, magicians, and comedians, among others, and very much geared to the family audience that this ship carries on most cruises. There is also plenty of live (loud) music for dancing to in various bars and lounges, plus the inevitable discotheque. Participation activities tend to be quite amateurish.

SPA/FITNESS. The Belleza Spa, the health and fitness center is high in the ship, aft of the funnel. It has a gymnasium with ocean-view windows and high-tech muscle-pump equipment, an exercise area, several therapy treatment rooms (including a rasul room), and men's/women's saunas.

Zuiderdam
★★★★

Size:	Large Resort Ship	Passenger Decks:	11	Cabins (wheelchair accessible).	28
Tonnage:	81,679	Total Crew:	800	Wheelchair accessibility	Good
Lifestyle:	Premium	Passengers		Cabin Current:	110 volts
Cruise Line:	Holland America Line	(lower beds/all berths):	1,848/2,387	Elevators:	14
Former Names:	none	Passenger Space Ratio		Casino (gaming tables):	Yes
Builder:	Fincantieri (Italy)	(lower beds/all berths):	43.6/34.2	Slot Machines:	Yes
Original Cost:	$400 million	Crew/Passenger Ratio		Swimming Pools (outdoors):	2+1
Entered Service:	Dec 2002	(lower beds/all berths):	2.3/2.9		children's pool
Registry:	The Netherlands	Cabins (total):	924	Swimming Pools (indoors):	1
Length (ft/m):	935.0/285.00	Size Range (sq ft/m):	185.0–1,318.6/		(indoor/outdoor)
Beam (ft/m):	105.6/32.25		17.1–122.5	Whirlpools:	5
Draft (ft/m):	25.5/7.80	Cabins (outside view):	788	Self-Service Launderette:	Yes
Propulsion/Propellers:	diesel-electric	Cabins (interior/no view):	136	Dedicated Cinema/Seats:	Yes/170
	(34,000 kW)/2 azimuthing pods	Cabins (for one person):	0	Library:	Yes
	(17.6 MW each)	Cabins (with private balcony):	623		

OVERALL SCORE: 1,517 (OUT OF A POSSIBLE 2,000 POINTS)

OVERVIEW. *Zuiderdam*, sister to *Eurodam, Noordam, Oosterdam* and *Westerdam*, shares a common platform and hull shape (*Zuiderdam* is pronounced Ziderdam), and is designed to appeal to younger, more vibrant, multi-generational family-oriented passengers. There are two funnels, placed close together, one in front of the other, and not side by side as aboard the smaller *Amsterdam* and *Rotterdam*. This placement is the result of the slightly unusual machinery configuration. The ship has, in effect, two engine rooms – one with three diesels, and one with two diesels and a gas turbine. Pod propulsion *(see page 45 for definition)* is provided, powered by a diesel-electric system, with a small gas turbine located in the funnel for the reduction of emissions.

A complete wrap-around exterior promenade deck is enjoyed by many. Exterior glass elevators, mounted midships on both port and starboard sides, provide fine ocean views. There are two centrally located swimming pools outdoors, and one of the pools can be used in poor weather due to its retractable magrodome (glass dome) cover. Two whirlpool tubs, adjacent to the swimming pools, are abridged by a bar. Another smaller pool is provided for children.

When you first walk into the ship's interior, you'll be greeted by the small size of the lobby space that spans just three decks. It has a stairway, and its focal point is a large, 10-foot high transparent seahorse. In keeping with the traditions of Holland America Line, there is a large collection of artwork. The decor is extremely bright for a Holland America Line ship, and an eclectic color and pattern mix that assails you from all directions.

There are two entertainment/public room decks, the

BERLITZ'S RATINGS		
	Possible	Achieved
Ship	500	426
Accommodation	200	162
Food	400	269
Service	400	277
Entertainment	100	77
Cruise	400	306

upper of which has an exterior promenade deck – something new for this traditional cruise line. Although it doesn't go around the whole ship, it's long enough to do some serious walking on. Additionally, there is also a jogging track outdoors, located around the mast and the forward third of the ship.

The most dramatic public room is the Vista Lounge, the ship's showlounge; it spans three decks in the forward section of the ship. The main floor level has a bar in its starboard aft section. Other facilities include a winding shopping street with boutique stores and logo shops.

The casino is large (one has to walk through it to get from the restaurant to the showlounge), and this is equipped with all the gaming paraphernalia and array of slot machines you can think of – all designed, of course, to entertain you while you are relieved of your money.

Children have KidZone (an indoor/outdoor facility), and Cub Hal for ages 5–12 (sleepovers aren't allowed, though), with dedicated youth counselors. Teenagers get to use WaveRunner, which includes a dance floor, special lighting effects, and booming sound system. There's also a video game room, and big-screen television for movies.

The information desk in the lobby is small in comparison to the size of the lobby. Many of the private balconies are not so private, and can be overlooked from various public locations. Many pillars obstruct the passenger flow and lines of sight throughout the ship.

Communication (in English) with many of the staff, particularly in the dining room and buffet areas, can prove very frustrating. It may be difficult to escape from smokers, and people walking around in unsuitable clothing, clutching plastic sport drinks bottles.

ACCOMMODATION. There are 19 price grades.

Penthouse Verandah Suites: The largest accommodation (1,318 sq. ft/122.5 sq. meters, including balcony) is in two Penthouse Verandah Suites. These have a separate bedroom with a king-sized bed; there's also a walk-in closet, dressing room, living room, dining room, butler's pantry, minibar and refrigerator, and private balcony (verandah). The main bathroom has a large whirlpool bathtub, two washbasins, toilet, and plenty of storage space for personal toiletries. Personalized stationery and complimentary dry cleaning are included, as are hot hors d'oeuvres and other goodies daily.

DeLuxe Verandah Suites: Next in size are 60 DeLuxe Verandah Suites (563 sq. ft/52.3 sq. meters). These have twin beds that can convert to a king-sized bed, vanity desk, lounge area, walk-in closet, mini-bar and refrigerator, and bathroom with full-sized tub, washbasin and toilet. Personalized stationery and complimentary dry cleaning are included, as are hot hors d'oeuvres daily and other goodies.

Verandah Suites: There are 100 of these (actually they are cabins, not suites, and measure 284 sq. ft/26.3 sq. meters). Twin beds can convert to a queen-sized bed; there is also a lounge area, mini-bar and refrigerator, while the bathroom has a tub, washbasin and toilet. Floor-to-ceiling windows open onto a private balcony (verandah).

Outside-view Cabins: Standard outside cabins (197 sq. ft/18.3 sq. meters) have twin beds that convert to make a queen-sized bed. There's a small sitting area, while the bathroom has a tub/shower combination. The interior (no view) cabins are slightly smaller, at 182.9 sq ft/17 sq. meters.

A number of cabins on the lowest accommodation deck (Main Deck) have views obstructed by lifeboats. Some cabins that can accommodate a third and fourth person have very little closet space, and there's only one personal safe. There is no separate radio in each cabin – instead, audio channels are provided in the in-cabin TV system.

Each morning, an eight-page *New York Times* (Times Fax) is provided for each cabin. Fresh fruit is available on request, shoe shine service, and evening turndown service are also provided, as is a small range of bathroom toiletries including shampoo, bath and facial soaps, and body lotion.

Niggles include noisy cabin air-conditioning – the flow can't be regulated or turned off in cabins or bathrooms; the only regulation is for temperature control.

CUISINE. The non-smoking 1,045-seat Vista (main) Dining Room, located at the stern, is two decks high, and is quite stunning. Both open seating and fixed (assigned tables and times) seating are available, while breakfast and lunch are open-seating (you'll be seated by restaurant staff when you enter). It is traditional Holland America Line in its operation, with friendly service from smiling Indonesian stewards, and has Rosenthal china, but no fish knives.

There are tables for two, four, six or eight. The waiter stations in the dining room can be noisy for anyone seated adjacent to them. Live music is provided for dinner each evening; once each cruise, a Dutch Dinner is featured (hats are provided), as is an Indonesian Lunch. "Lighter option" meals are always available for the nutrition-conscious and the weight-conscious.

Alternative Dining Option: The 130-seat Pinnacle Grill is a slightly more upscale dining spot (with higher-quality ingredients and better presentation than in the larger main dining room). Located on Lower Promenade Deck, it fronts onto the second level of the atrium lobby. The cuisine is Pacific Northwest, with items such as sesame-crusted halibut with ginger-miso, Peking duck breast with blackberry sauce, premium quality steaks from hand-selected cuts of beef. Fine table settings, china and silverware are provided, as are leather-bound menus. The wine bar offers mostly American wines. Reservations are needed and there is a cover charge of $30 per person for service and gratuity.

Informal Eateries: For casual eating, there is an extensive Lido Cafe, which forms an eatery that wraps around the funnel housing and extends aft. It includes a pizzeria counter, a salad bar, Asian stir-fry counter, deli sandwiches, and a separate dessert buffet, although movement around the buffet area is very slow – particularly at peak times, such as in the mornings in port before shore excursions – and requires you to stand in line for everything.

Additionally, there is an outdoor self-serve buffet (adjacent to the fantail pool), which serves fast-food items such as hamburgers and hot dogs, chicken and fries. There are two smaller buffets adjacent to the midships swimming pool area, and a Windsurf Cafe in the atrium lobby (open 20 hours a day), for pastries, snack foods, deli sandwiches and liqueur coffees (evenings only).

ENTERTAINMENT. The 867-seat Vista Lounge is the principal venue for Las Vegas-style revue shows and major cabaret presentations. It spans three decks in the forward section of the ship. The main floor level has a bar in its starboard aft section. Spiral stairways at the back of the lounge connect all levels. Stage shows are best seen from the upper levels, from where the sightlines are quite good.

SPA/FITNESS. The Greenhouse Spa is a large, two-decks-high health spa, located directly above the navigation bridge. Facilities include a solarium, unisex thermal suite – a unisex area incorporating a Laconium (gentle sauna), Hammam (mild steam), and Camomile Grotto (small aromatic steam room). There's also a beauty parlor, 11 massage/therapy rooms (including one for couples), and a large gymnasium with floor-to-ceiling windows on three sides and forward-facing ocean views, and the latest high-tech muscle-toning equipment.

● **For more extensive general information on what a Holland America Line cruise is like, see pages 139–42.**

SHIPS RATED BY SCORE

Ship	Score	Rating	Ship	Score	Rating
LARGE (RESORT) SHIPS			Star Princess	1,496	4
(over 1,600 passengers)			Oceana	1,494	4
			Disney Wonder	1,491	4
Queen Mary 2 (Grill Class)	1,702	5	Serenade of the Seas	1,491	4
Queen Victoria (Grill Class)	1,671	4+	Vision of the Seas	1,491	4
Celebrity Eclipse	1,612	4+	Arcadia	1,490	4
Celebrity Equinox	1,611	4+	Disney Magic	1,490	4
Celebrity Solstice	1,611	4+	Rhapsody of the Seas	1,490	4
MSC Fantasia (Yacht Club)	1,570	4+	Sun Princess	1,489	4
MSC Splendida (Yacht Club)	1,570	4+	AIDAblu	1,487	4
Celebrity Constellation	1,568	4+	Norwegian Dawn	1,487	4
Celebrity Millennium	1,568	4+	Norwegian Gem	1,487	4
Celebrity Summit	1,568	4+	Sea Princess	1,487	4
Celebrity Infinity	1,566	4+	Norwegian Jewel	1,486	4
Ruby Princess	1,547	4	AIDAbella	1,485	4
Emerald Princess	1,546	4	AIDAluna	1,485	4
Mein Schiff	1,546	4	Norwegian Pearl	1,485	4
Celebrity Century	1,545	4	Norwegian Spirit	1,485	4
Coral Princess	1,544	4	Norwegian Star	1,485	4
Diamond Princess	1,544	4	AIDAdiva	1,484	4
Sapphire Princess	1,544	4	Queen Victoria (Britannia Class)	1,483	4
Norwegian Epic	1,543	4	Norwegian Jade	1,481	4
Island Princess	1,542	4	MSC Magnifica	1,467	4
Crown Princess	1,541	4	MSC Poesia	1,467	4
Queen Mary 2 (Britannia Class)	1,541	4	MSC Orchestra	1,465	4
Zaandam	1,541	4	MSC Musica	1,462	4
Volendam	1,540	4	Explorer of the Seas	1,461	4
Caribbean Princess	1,539	4	Mariner of the Seas	1,457	4
Rotterdam	1,539	4	Navigator of the Seas	1,456	4
Amsterdam	1,537	4	Adventure of the Seas	1,454	4
Nieuw Amsterdam	1,535	4	Costa Pacifica	1,453	4
Eurodam	1,534	4	Costa Concordia	1,450	4
MSC Fantasia (standard cabins)	1,528	4	Costa Deliziosa	1,450	4
MSC Splendida (standard cabins)	1,528	4	Costa Serena	1,449	4
Dawn Princess	1,527	4	Brilliance of the Seas	1,446	4
Oasis of the Seas	1,524	4	Radiance of the Seas	1,446	4
Westerdam	1,522	4	Costa Luminosa	1,445	4
Jewel of the Seas	1,520	4	Costa Magica	1,445	4
Oosterdam	1,520	4	MSC Opera	1,445	4
Noordam	1,519	4	Voyager of the Seas	1,445	4
Celebrity Mercury	1,518	4	Costa Fortuna	1,444	4
Zuiderdam	1,517	4	MSC Lirica	1,439	4
Azura	1,512	4	Costa Mediterranea	1,437	4
Freedom of the Seas	1,510	4	Costa Atlantica	1,436	4
Independence of the Seas	1,510	4	MSC Armonia	1,431	4
Liberty of the Seas	1,510	4	MSC Sinfonia	1,431	4
Ventura	1,509	4	Splendour of the Seas	1,415	4
Aurora	1,503	4	Legend of the Seas	1,414	4
SuperStar Virgo	1,502	4	Enchantment of the Seas	1,407	4
Golden Princess	1,499	4	Grandeur of the Seas	1,407	4
Oriana	1,497	4	Carnival Dream	1,395	3+
Grand Princess	1,496	4	Carnival Splendor	1,393	3+

Ship	Score	Rating	Ship	Score	Rating
Norwegian Sun	1,393	3+	Regatta	1,572	4+
Carnival Freedom	1,390	3+	Pacific Venus	1,548	4
Carnival Spirit	1,390	3+	Ocean Princess	1,487	4
Carnival Legend	1,388	3+	Pacific Princess	1,487	4
Norwegian Sky	1,388	3+	Azamara Quest	1,466	4
Carnival Miracle	1,387	3+	Azamara Journey	1,465	4
Carnival Pride	1,386	3+	Saga Ruby	1,421	4
Carnival Conquest	1,385	3+	Ryndam	1,420	4
Carnival Liberty	1,383	3+	Veendam	1,420	4
Costa Victoria	1,382	3+	Maasdam	1,412	4
Carnival Glory	1,380	3+	Statendam	1,403	4
Carnival Valor	1,380	3+	Balmoral	1,398	3+
Carnival Triumph	1,379	3+	Bleu de France	1,396	3+
Carnival Victory	1,369	3+	Artemis	1,385	3+
Pacific Pearl	1,364	3+	AIDAvita	1,381	3+
Carnival Destiny	1,361	3+	AIDAaura	1,380	3+
Pride of America	1,268	3+	Astor	1,370	3+
Monarch of the Seas	1,248	3	AIDAcara	1,367	3+
Carnival Ecstasy	1,248	3	Boudicca	1,357	3+
Carnival Fantasy	1,247	3	Pacific Dream	1,344	3+
Carnival Fascination	1,247	3	Zenith	1,343	3+
Costa Romantica	1,247	3	Black Watch	1,339	3+
Majesty of the Seas	1,246	3	Thomson Spirit	1,316	3+
Costa Classica	1,245	3	Braemar	1,315	3+
Carnival Sensation	1,244	3	Grand Mistral	1,315	3+
Sovereign	1,242	3	Grand Voyager	1,314	3+
Carnival Imagination	1,226	3	Thomson Celebration	1,307	3+
Empress	1,226	3	Thomson Destiny	1,303	3+
Carnival Elation	1,225	3	SuperStar Libra	1,286	3+
Carnival Inspiration	1,223	3	Gemini	1,254	3+
Carnival Paradise	1,222	3	Delphin Voyager	1,243	3
Grand Celebration	1,182	3	Louis Majesty	1,242	3
Pacific Dawn	1,181	3	Cristal	1,236	3
Grand Holiday	1,160	3	SuperStar Aquarius	1,232	3
AIDAsol	NYR	NYR	Albatros	1,194	3
Allure of the Seas	NYR	NYR	MSC Melody	1,175	3
Carnival Magic	NYR	NYR	Ocean Countess	1,178	3
Celebrity Silhouette	NYR	NYR	Pacific Sun	1,172	3
Costa Favolosa	NYR	NYR	Discovery	1,111	3
Disney Dream	NYR	NYR	Ocean Dream	1,110	3
Queen Elizabeth	NYR	NYR	Island Escape	1,109	3
			Orient Queen	1,103	3
			Costa Allegra	1,092	2+
MID-SIZE SHIPS			Aquamarine	1,090	2+
(600–1,600 passengers)			Costa Marina	1,090	2+
			Marco Polo	1,082	2+
Crystal Serenity	1,702	5	Ocean Pearl	1,080	2+
Crystal Symphony	1,701	5	The Emerald	1,063	2+
Asuka II	1,685	4+	Bahamas Celebration	1,035	2+
Seven Seas Voyager	1,654	4+	Pacific	1,013	2+
Seven Seas Mariner	1,651	4+	Coral	944	2
Prinsendam	1,642	4+	Adonia	NYR	NYR
Amadea	1,600	4+	Marina	NYR	NYR
Nautica	1,575	4+	Thomson Dream	NYR	NYR
Insignia	1,574	4+			

Ship	Score	Rating	Ship	Score	Rating
SMALL SHIPS *(201–600 passengers)*			**BOUTIQUE SHIPS** *(50–200 passengers)*		
Europa	1,853	5+	SeaDream II	1,788	5
Seabourn Odyssey	1,787	5	SeaDream I	1,786	5
Seabourn Sojourn	1,787	5	Hanseatic	1,746	5
Seabourn Legend	1,774	5	Sea Cloud	1,704	5
Silver Spirit	1,772	5	Sea Cloud II	1,702	5
Seabourn Spirit	1,770	5	Prince Albert II	1,684	4+
Seabourn Pride	1,769	5	Hebridean Princess	1,680	4+
Silver Whisper	1,753	5	Orion	1,612	4+
Silver Shadow	1,750	5	Island Sky	1,562	4
Silver Wind	1,669	4+	Corinthian II	1,546	4
Silver Cloud	1,664	4+	Bremen	1,461	4
Seven Seas Navigator	1,595	4+	Le Levant	1,415	4
Paul Gauguin	1,547	4	Celebrity Xpedition	1,404	4
Royal Clipper	1,540	4	Clelia II	1,404	4
Nippon Maru	1,503	4	Star Clipper	1,402	4
Club Med 2	1,483	4	Star Flyer	1,402	4
C. Columbus	1,398	3+	Wind Spirit	1,394	3+
Wind Surf	1,396	3+	Wind Star	1,393	3+
Minerva	1,324	3+	Le Ponant	1,385	3+
Saga Pearl II	1,319	3+	Clipper Odyssey	1,245	3
Spirit of Adventure	1,249	3	Galapagos Explorer II	1,244	3
Fuji Maru	1,186	3	Spirit of Oceanus	1,222	3
Princess Daphne	1,131	3	Le Diamant	1,219	3
Delphin	1,121	3	Kapitan Khlebnikov	1,144	3
Princess Danae	1,112	3	Independence	962	2+
Athena	1,092	2+	Spirit of Yorktown	949	2
Vistamar	1,061	2+	Spirit of America	948	2
Funchal	1,042	2+	Clipper Adventurer	947	2
Sapphire	1,030	2+	Professor Multanovskiy	947	2
The Calypso	990	2+	Spirit of '98	946	2
The Emerald	990	2+	National Geographic Endeavour	945	2
Arion	902	2	National Geographic Polaris	943	2
easyCruise Life	771	1+	American Star	925	2
Aegean Odyssey	NYR	NYR	American Spirit	922	2
Alexander von Humboldt	NYR	NYR	Spirit of Alaska	920	2
Deutschland	NYR	NYR	Spirit of Discovery	920	2
L'Austral	NYR	NYR	Spirit of Endeavour	920	2
Le Boreal	NYR	NYR	Spirit of Columbia	919	2
Pearl Mist	NYR	NYR	American Glory	835	2
Seabourn Quest	NYR	NYR	American Eagle	830	2
			Grande Caribe	756	1+
			Grande Mariner	747	1+
			National Geographic Sea Bird	743	1+
			National Geographic Sea Lion	743	1+
			50 Years of Victory	NYR	NYR
NYR = Not Yet Rated			Sea Cloud Hussar	NYR	NYR

BOOKING AND BUDGETING

Is it better to book a cruise directly with the operator
or through a travel agent? And what hidden extras
should you look for when calculating costs?

Booking direct
In the 1960s, about 90% of all cruises were booked by passengers directly with cruise lines and about 10% were booked by travel agents. Then along came some enterprising travel agents. They saw a golden opportunity and started to act on behalf of the cruise lines, which were happy to accept such bookings because they could then reduce staff and overheads in their sales offices.

Established companies such as American Express and Thomas Cook booked cruises, as did many others, and received a commission. Today, about 80% of all cruises are booked by travel agents, and about 20% are booked direct (including internet bookings).

When you see newspaper adverts for cruises, check what's included in any heavily discounted offers. Make sure that all port charges, government fees, and any additional fuel surcharges are included in the quote.

The internet
While the Internet may be a good *resource* tool, it is not the place to book your cruise, unless you know *exactly* what you want. You can't ask questions, and most of the information provided by the cruise companies is strictly marketing hype. Most sites providing cruise ship reviews have something to sell, and the sound-byte information can be misleading or outdated. Also, many discounts for senior citizens, military personnel, and alumni groups, or special discounts for various regions and locales are typically not available on the web, but only through cruise-booking agencies

If you do book with an internet-based cruise agency or wholesaler, you should confirm with the cruise line that the booking has been made and that final payment has been received. Be aware that many internet booking agents are unlicensed and unregulated. Some add a "booking fee" – which can be substantial.

The internet vs travel agents
So, you've found a discounted rate for your cruise on the net. That's fine. But, if a cruise line suddenly offers special discounts for your sailing, or cabin upgrades, or if things go wrong with your booking, your internet booking service may prove unfriendly or may even have disappeared. Your travel agent, however, can probably make special discounts work for *you* and perhaps even provide upgrades. It's called personal service.

Large travel agency groups and consortiums, such as American Express, often reserve huge blocks of cabins,

and smaller independent agencies can access extensive discounts not available on the internet. Furthermore, the cruise lines consider travel agents as their distribution system, and provide special discounts and value-added amenities that are not provided over the internet.

Travel agents
Travel agents do not charge for their services, although they earn a commission from cruise lines. Consider a travel agent as your business advisor, not just a ticket agent. He/she will handle all matters relevant to your booking and should have the latest information on changes of itinerary, cruise fares, fuel surcharges, discounts, and any other related items, including insurance in case you have to cancel prior to sailing. Most travel agents are linked into cruise line computer systems and have access to most shipboard information.

Your travel agent should find exactly the right ship for your needs and lifestyle. Some sell only a limited number of cruises and are known as "preferred suppliers," because they receive special "overrides" on top of their normal commission (they probably know their limited number of ships well, however).

If *you* have chosen a ship and cruise, be firm and book exactly what you want, or change agencies. In the UK, look for a member of the Guild of Professional Cruise Agents. ACE (Association for Cruise Education), part of the UK's Passenger Shipping Association, provides in-depth agent training, as well as a full "bonding" scheme to protect passengers from failed cruise lines. In the US, look for a CLIA (Cruise Lines International Association) affiliated agency, or one belonging to the National Association of Cruise Oriented Agencies (NACOA), or the National Association of Commissioned Travel Agents (NACTA).

Questions to ask a travel agent
● Is air transportation included in the cabin rate quoted? If not, what will be the extra cost?
● What other extra costs will be involved? These can include port charges, insurance, gratuities, shore excursions, laundry, and drinks.
● What is the cruise line's cancellation policy?
● If I want to make changes to my flight, routing, dates, and so on, will the insurance policy cover everything in case of missed or canceled flights?
● Does your agency deal with only one, or several different insurance companies?
● Does the cruise line offer advance booking discounts or other incentives?

LEFT: accessing the internet aboard *Carnival Miracle*.

● Do you have preferred suppliers, or do you book any cruise on any cruise ship?
● Have you sailed aboard the ship I want to book or that you are recommending?
● Is your agency bonded and insured? If so, by whom?
● If you book the shore excursions offered by the cruise line, is insurance coverage provided?
● Can I occupy my cabin on the day of disembarkation until I am ready to disembark?

Reservations

Plan ahead and book early. After choosing a ship, cruise, date, and cabin, you pay a deposit that is roughly 10 percent for long cruises, 20 percent for short cruises. The balance is normally payable 45 to 60 days before departure. For a late reservation, you pay in full when space is confirmed (when booking via the internet, for example). Cruise lines reserve the right to change prices in the event of tax increases, fluctuating exchange rates, fuel surcharges, or other costs beyond their control.

When you make your reservation, also make special dining requests known, and any seating preferences. It's useful to keep a note of them.

After the line has received full payment, your cruise ticket will be sent by mail, or as an e-document. Check all documents. Make sure the ship, date, and cruise details are correct. Verify connecting flight times that seem suspiciously short.

Extra costs

Cruise brochures boldly proclaim that "almost every-thing's included," but in most cases you will find this is not true. In fact, for some cruises "all-exclusive" would be a more appropriate term. In the recent credit crisis, many cruise lines cut their fares dramatically in order to attract business. At the same time, the cost of many onboard items went up. So allow for extra onboard costs.

Your fare covers the ship as transportation, your cabin, meals, entertainment, activities, and service on board; it typically does not include alcoholic drinks, laundry, dry cleaning or valet services, shore excursions, meals ashore, gratuities, port charges, cancellation insur-ance, optional onboard activities such as gambling.

Expect to spend about $25 a day per person on extras, plus $10–$12 a day per person in gratuities. Exceptions can be found in some small ships (those with fewer than 600 passengers) where just about everything is included.

Calculate the total cost of your cruise (not including any extra-cost services you might decide you want once on board) with the help of your travel agent. Here are the approximate prices per person for a typical seven-day cruise aboard a well-rated mid-size or large cruise ship, based on an outside-view two-bed cabin:

Cruise fare	$1,000
Port charges	$100 (if not included)
Gratuities	$50
Total per person	$1,150

This is less than $165 per person per day. For this price, you wouldn't get a decent hotel room, without meals, in London, Miami, New York, Tokyo, or Venice.

However, your 7-day cruise can become expensive when you start adding on any extras. For example, add two flight-seeing excursions in Alaska (at about $250 each), two cappuccinos each a day ($25), a scotch and soda each a day ($35), a massage ($125), 7 mineral waters ($28), 30 minutes' access to the inter-net for emails ($15), three other assorted excursions ($150), and gratuities ($50). That's an extra $928 – without even one bottle of wine with dinner! So a cou-ple will need to add an extra $1,856 for a 7-day cruise, plus the cruise fare, of course, and the cost of getting to and from your local airport, or ship port.

Discounts and incentives

Book ahead to get the best discounts (they decrease closer to the cruise date). You may be able to reserve a cabin grade, but not a specific cabin – "tba" (to be assigned). Some lines will accept this arrangement and may even upgrade you. The first cabins to be sold out are usually those at minimum and maximum rates. Note: Premium rates apply to Christmas/New Year cruises.

TYPICAL EXTRA-COST ITEMS	
"Alternative" dining (cover charge)	$15–$100 each
Baby-sitting (per hour)	$5
Bottled water	$2.50–$7 (per bottle)
Cappuccino/espresso	$2–$3
Cartoon character bedtime "tuck-In" service	$20
Wash one shirt	$2–$3
Dry-clean dress	$4–$7.50
Dry-clean jacket	$4–$8
Golf simulator	$20 (30 minutes)
Group bicycling class	$10 per class
Hair wash/set	$25–$50
Haircut (men)	$25
Ice cream	$2–$3.75
In-cabin movies	$6.95–$12.95
Internet connection	$0.50 per minute
Kick-boxing class	$10 per class
Laundry soap	$1–$1.50
Massage	$2-plus a minute (plus tip)
Satellite phone/fax	$4.95–$15 per minute
Send/receive e-mails	$0.50–$0.75 per minute
Shuttle bus in ports of call	$2–$4
Sodas (soft drinks)	$1–$2
Souvenir photograph (8" by 6")	$10–$12
Souvenir photograph (10" by 8")	$20–$27.50
Trapshooting (three or five shots)	$5, $8
Tuxedo rental (7-day cruise)	$85
Use of Aqua Spa (Queen Mary 2)	$25 per day
Video postcard	$4.95–$6.95
Wine/cheese tasting	$10–$15
Wine with dinner	$7–$500
Yoga class	$10 per class

Cancellations and refunds

Do take out full cancellation insurance (if it is not included), as cruises (and air transportation to/from them) must be paid in full before your tickets are issued. Otherwise, if you cancel at the last minute – even for medical reasons – you could lose the whole fare. Insurance coverage can be obtained from your travel agent or from an independent company, and paying by credit card makes sense (you'll probably get your money back if the agency goes bust) or through the internet.

Note that cancellation insurance offered by a cruise line is a "one-size-fits-all" product, so personalization is impossible. It covers only the cruise itself but not any add-ons that you may have arranged on your own – such as non-refundable air tickets.

Cruise lines usually accept cancellations more than 30 days before sailing, but all charge full fare if you don't turn up on sailing day. Other cancellation fees depend on the cruise and length of trip. Many lines do not return port taxes, which are not part of the cruise fare.

Medical insurance

Whether you intend to travel overseas or cruise down a local river, and your present medical insurance does not cover you, you should look into extra coverage for your cruise. The cruise line may offer a "passenger protection program," the charge for which will appear on your final invoice, unless you decline. It is worth every penny, and typically covers such things as evacuation at sea by air ambulance (Medivac), high-limit baggage, baggage transfers, personal liability, and missed departure.

Port taxes/Handling charges

These are assessed by individual port authorities and are usually shown in the brochure. Port charges form part of the final payment, although they can be changed right up to the day of embarkation.

Fuel surcharges

Cruise lines publish their brochures a year ahead. If oil and other fuel costs rise in the interim, a fuel surcharge may be imposed, in addition to the quoted fare.

Air/Sea packages

If your cruise fare includes air transportation (as in a one-way or round-trip air ticket), then airline arrangements usually cannot be changed without paying a premium, as cruise lines often book group space on aircraft to obtain the lowest rates. If you do make changes, remember that, if the airline cancels your flight, the cruise line is under no obligation to help you or return your cruise fare if you don't reach the ship on time. If flying to a foreign country, allow extra time (particularly in winter) for flight delays and cancellations.

Airlines often use a "hub-and-spoke" system, which can prove frustrating. Because of changes to air schedules, cruise and air tickets may not be sent to passengers until a few days before the cruise.

In Europe, air/sea packages generally start at a major metropolitan airport; some include first-class rail travel from outlying districts. In the US, many cruise lines include connecting flights from suburban airports convenient to the traveler. If you fly and want to lock your check-in baggage, use a TSA (Transportation Security Administration)-approved security lock.

Most cruise lines allow you to fly out to join a ship in one port and fly home from another. An advantage is that you only have to check your baggage once at the departure airport and its transfer from plane to ship is handled for you. This doesn't include intercontinental fly/cruises, where you must claim your baggage at the airport on arrival to clear it though customs.

Travel insurance

Note that cruise lines and travel agents routinely sell travel cover policies that, on close inspection, appear to wriggle out of payment due to a litany of exclusion clauses, most of which are never explained. Examples:
● "Pre-existing" medical conditions – ignoring this little gem could cost you dearly.
● "Valuables" left unattended on a tour bus, even if the guide says it is safe and that the driver will lock the door.

Getting the best travel insurance deal:

● Allow time to shop around and don't accept the first travel insurance policy you are offered.
● Read the contract carefully and make sure you know exactly what you are covered for.
● If you purchase your own air transportation, it may not cover you if the airline fails, or if bad weather prevents you from joining your ship on time.
● Beware of the "box ticking" approach to travel cover, which is often done quickly at the travel agent's office in lieu of providing expert advice. Insurers should not, in reality, be allowed to apply exclusions that have not been clearly pointed out to the policyholder.
● Ask for a detailed explanation of all exclusions, excesses, and limitations.
● Check out the procedure you need to follow if you are the victim of a crime, such as your wallet or camera being stolen while on a shore excursion. If anything does happen, *always* obtain a police report as soon as possible. Many insurance policies will reimburse you only for the secondhand value of any lost or stolen item, rather than the full cost of replacement, and you may have to produce the original receipt for any such items claimed.
● Watch out for exclusions for "hazardous sports." These could include things typically offered as shore excursions aboard ships. Examples: horse riding (there goes that horse riding on the beach excursion in Jamaica) or cycling (mountain biking excursions), jet skiing (most beaches), or ziplining.
● If you purchase travel cover over the internet, check the credentials of the company underwriting the scheme. It is best to deal with well-established names, and not to take what appears to be the cheapest deal offered. ❑

DON'T LEAVE HOME WITHOUT...

Cruise ships are well stocked for most people's
everyday needs, but there are certain things
you need to take with you

Baggage

There is generally no limit to the amount of personal
baggage you can take on your cruise (most ships provide towels, soap, shampoo, and shower caps), but airlines do have weight limits. Do allow extra space for
purchases on the cruise.

Tag all baggage with your name, ship, cabin number, sailing date, and port of embarkation (tags are provided with your tickets). Baggage transfers from airport
to ship are generally smooth and problem-free when
handled by the cruise line.

Liability for loss or damage to baggage is contained
in the passenger contract (part of your ticket). Do take
out insurance; the policy should extend from the date of
departure until two or three days after your return home.

Some cruise lines offer fee-based luggage courier
services that collect your luggage from your home and
the next time you see your luggage, it will be in your
cabin (and vice versa at the end of the cruise).

Clothing

Closet space aboard many ships is at a premium. So,
unless you are on an extended cruise, keep your baggage to a minimum. It's a good idea to choose four or
five interchangeable outfits to wear throughout the
week, in two or three color groups and mix-and-match
clothing that can be layered. Black is always a good
neutral color to team with other colors.

For cruises to tropical areas, casual wear should
include plenty of lightweight cottons and other natural
fibers. Synthetic materials do not "breathe" as well and
often retain heat. Clothes should be as opaque as possible to counteract the sun's ultraviolet rays. Take a lightweight cotton sweater or windbreaker for the evenings,
when the ship's air-conditioning will seem even more
powerful after a day in the sun. Pack sunglasses and a
hat. Rainstorms in the tropics don't last long, but they
can give you a good soaking, so take inexpensive, lightweight rainwear for excursions.

The same is true for cruises to the Mediterranean,
Greek Isles, or North Africa, although there will be little or no humidity for most of the year. Certain areas
may be dusty as well as dry. In these latitudes, the
weather can be cool in the evenings from October to
March, so take extra sweaters and a windbreaker.

For cruises to Alaska, the North Cape, or the Norwegian fjords, pack warm comfortable clothing layers,
plus a raincoat or parka for the northernmost port calls.
Cruises to Alaska and the Land of the Midnight Sun

are operated in summer, when temperatures are pleasant. Unless you are going to northern ports such as St.
Petersburg in winter, you will not need thermal underwear. However, you will need thermal underwear, thick
socks – and heavy sweaters – if you take an expedition
cruise to the Antarctic Peninsula or through the Northwest Passage.

In destinations with a strong religious tradition, like
Venezuela, Haiti, the Dominican Republic, Colombia,
and countries in the Middle East and Far East, shorts or
bare shoulders may cause offense, so cover up.

Aboard ship, dress rules are relaxed by day, but in the
evening what you wear should be tasteful. Men should
take a blazer or sports jacket and ties for the dining
room and for any "informal" occasions. Transatlantic
crossings are normally more elegant and require formal attire.

For formal nights (usually two out of seven), women
can wear a long evening gown, elegant cocktail dress,
or a smart pants suit. Gentlemen are expected to wear
either a tuxedo or dark business suit and tie. These
"rules" are less rigid on short and moderately priced
cruises. If you are the athletic type, pack sportswear
and gym shoes for the gymnasium or aerobics classes.

No matter where you are going, comfortable low- or
flat-heeled shoes are a must for women, except for formal nights. Light, airy walking shoes are best for walking. If you are in the Caribbean or Pan-Pacific region
and you are not used to heat and humidity, your ankles
may swell, so tight shoes are not recommended. Rubber
soles are best for walking on the open deck of a ship.
Formal: Tuxedo, dinner jacket or dark suit and tie for
men; evening gown or other appropriate formal attire
for women.
Informal: Jacket and tie for men; cocktail dress, dressy
pantsuit, or the like for women.
Casual (Elegant/Smart): While this is an oxymoron, it
generally means long trousers (no shorts or jeans),
proper collared and sleeved shirt (gentlemen); skirt or
slacks and top for women.
Casual (Relaxed): Slacks over sweater or open shirt
(no tie) for men (no beach wear or muscle shirts); a
blouse with skirt, slacks, or similar comfortable attire
for women. Shoes are required.

Documents

A passport is the most practical proof of your citizen-
ship and identification. Visas are required for some
countries (allow time to obtain these). On most cruises,

you will hand in your passport to the company at embarkation (it would be wise to keep a copy of the main pages with you). This helps the ship to clear customs and immigration inspection on arrival in ports of call. It will be returned before you reach the port of disembarkation.

Flying... and airports

If you purchase anything in Duty Free outlets such as a camera or electronic goods (from a well known high-street chain, for example), note that if the item goes wrong, and you cannot return it to the airport store concerned, any high-street branch store may refuse to help, because the item was not purchased "in the country."

Flying... and jet lag

Several cruise lines have "air deviation" desks that allow you to change your flights and connections, for a fee (typically $25–$50 per person).

Air travel today is fast and efficient. But even experienced travelers find that the stress of international travel can persist long after the flight is over (for long international flights, I recommend the flat beds in Club Class on British Airways or in Upper Class on Virgin Atlantic aircraft). Eastbound flights tend to cause more pronounced jet lag than westbound flights. Jet aircraft are generally pressurized to some 8,000 ft (2,400 meters) in altitude, causing discomfort in the ears and the stomach, and swollen feet.

A few precautions should help. Plan as far in advance of your cruise as possible. Take a daytime flight, so that you can arrive at, or close to, your normal bedtime. Try to be as quiet as possible before flying, and allow for another five hours of rest after any flight that crosses more than five time zones.

Medication

Take any medicine and other medical supplies that you need, plus spare eyeglasses or contact lenses. In many countries it may be difficult to find certain medicines.

FIVE FIRSTS

● In 1903 the British liner *Lucania* acquired wireless equipment which enabled it to keep in touch with both sides of the Atlantic Ocean at the same time.
● The first ship-to-shore wireless telegraphy took place on the American passenger ship *St. Paul* in 1899.
● The first twin-screw passenger ship was the Compagnie Générale Transatlantique's 3,200-ton *Washington*, built in 1863 and converted in 1868.
● The first floating eclipse expedition was led by the US astronomer Ted Pedas in 1972, when 800 passengers sailed to a spectacular rendezvous with a total sun eclipse in the North Atlantic.
● The first passenger ship to exceed 80,000 gross tonnage was the Compagnie Générale Transatlantique's *Normandie* (82,799 gross tonnage in 1936).

Others may be sold under different names. If taking a long cruise, ask your doctor to name alternatives.

The ship's pharmacy will stock certain standard remedies, but do not expect a supply of the more unusual medicines. Remember to take along a doctor's prescription for any medication (required if you join a cruise in Dubai). Also, be advised that if you run out of your medication and you need to get a supply aboard ship, most ships will require that you see the doctor, even if you have a prescription. There is a charge for each visit, plus the cost of any medication.

Let spouses/companions carry a supply of your medicine and medical supplies. Do not pack medicine or medical information in luggage to be checked in when flying; take it in your carry-on.

Money matters

Most ships operate primarily in US dollars, euros or UK pounds, but a few use other currencies (check with your travel agent or supplier). Major credit cards and traveler's checks are accepted on board (few lines take personal checks). You sign for drinks and other services, as part of "cashless cruising." Some large resort ships have ATM cash machines, although a "transaction fee" is assessed.

Pets

Pets are not allowed aboard cruise ships, with one exception: the regular transatlantic crossings aboard Cunard Line's *Queen Mary 2* ocean liner, which has air-conditioned kennels, plus a genuine British lamp-post, New York fire hydrant, and cat containers.

Photography

Users of digital cameras should pack a spare memory card unless they are carrying a laptop onto which they can transfer pictures. Users of film should bring low-speed film for tropical areas such as the Caribbean or South Pacific – heat can damage high-speed film.

Sun protection

Take suncream/sunlotion with a minimum SPF 15 or higher protection factor. Keep reapplying it after you take a dip in the pool or hot tub, and allow for the fact that if you perspire, the suncream/sunlotion dissolves. If you wear a tee-shirt over your swimsuit, its SPF protection factor is between 7 (white tee-shirt), and 10 (dark tee-shirt). While cotton tee-shirts allow more "breathing," unbleached cotton has special pigments that can actually absorb UV rays vs polyester/other synthetic or silk tee-shirts that reflect radiation.

Clothing designated as sun-protective, including swimwear, carries a UPF number. This is similar to the SPF factor, except that the UPT number shows how much UVA and UVB is blocked. Companies specializing in outdoor sports clothing and swimwear now make sun-protective clothing from special microfibers that have a very tight weave to block out the sun. ❑

WHAT TO EXPECT

**Your first cruise? Here is what you need to know
about a typical initial embarkation process**

Taking your first cruise? Make sure you have your passport and any visas required (in some countries – such as the People's Republic of China, or Russia – you might go ashore on organized excursions under a group visa). Pack any medication you may need (in original, labeled containers) in your carry-on hand luggage.

You already have been sent your cruise tickets and documents by the cruise line or your travel agent. Increasingly, e-documents are provided. A typical document package might include:
- Air ticket (or e-ticket boarding pass or reference code)
- Cruise ticket and e-boarding pass (not all lines)
- Luggage tags
- Embarkation/Immigration card (to fill out before you get to the ship)
- Discount coupons for the shops on board
- Bon Voyage gift selection form
- Shore excursion brochure
- Onboard credit account form
- Guide to services on board (including e-mail)
- Ship's telephone and fax contact numbers
- Coupon for tuxedo rental

Assume that you've arrived at the airport closest to your ship's embarkation point, and retrieved your luggage. It is likely that there will be a representative from the cruise line waiting, holding aloft the company's name. You will be asked to place your luggage in a cluster together with those of other passengers. The next time you see your luggage should be in your cabin.

You'll find check-in desks in the passenger terminal. Go to the one displaying the first letter of your surname, wait in line (having filled out all embarkation, registration, and immigration documents, unless these have been done online). If your accommodation is designated as a "suite," there should be a separate check-in facility.

If you are cruising from a US port and you are a non-US citizen or "resident alien," you will go to a separate desk to check in (*Note*: Do not buy duty-free liquor to take on board – it will not be allowed by the cruise line and will be confiscated until the last day of the cruise). You will leave your passport with the check-in personnel. Ask for a receipt – it is a valuable document – and preferably have a photocopy of the main pages to keep with you. If you are cruising from any other port in the world that is not a US port, be aware that each country has its own check-in requirements.

You will then proceed through a security-screening device, for both your body and hand luggage, as at airports. Next, you'll walk a few paces towards the gangway. This may be a covered, airport-type gangway, or an open one (hopefully with a net underneath it in case you drop something over the side). The gangway could be flat, or you may have to walk up (or down) an incline, depending on the location of the gangway, the tide, or other local conditions. As you approach the gangway you will probably be greeted by the ship's photographers, a snap-happy team ready to take your photograph, bedraggled as you may appear after having traveled for hours. If you do not want your photograph taken, say "no" firmly.

HOW TO CHECK IN ONLINE

Several major cruise lines now insist that you check-in online. This helps reduce staff numbers – usually locally sourced part-time retirees – at check-in desks in embarkation cruise terminals. This could be smooth if you are computer-literate or a frustrating nightmare if you are not.

The truth is that the old paper cruise tickets and other documents of most of the major cruise lines have become collectors' items, because these companies have gone to paperless ticketing (at least in their offices), although you will need to print your boarding pass. Expect more cruise lines to follow suit in an effort to cut costs. It typically takes about 15–20 minutes to complete the online check-in process, assuming that you have all your personal details to hand.

Pretty soon there'll be self-serve cruising, where you wait your own tables, and…? Wait a moment, didn't easyCruise try the no-frills style of cruising – and failed? Warning to cruise line accountants: you may soon not be needed.

Depending on the cruise line, there are usually four major steps to complete, each step requesting information before you can actually reach the stage where you can print out your "boarding pass." Before you start the online check-in procedure, however, you'll need to put in your name, reservation number, and any other pertinent personal information requested.
- **Step 1:** Passenger information.
- **Step 2:** Your onboard expense account information (pre-register your credit card).
- **Step 3:** Cruise ticket contract (you'll need to have 20/20 eyesight to read this, or take it to your local optician).
- **Step 4:** Print your boarding pass.

Offer to do the online check-in for your whole family or group, and you could end up spending hours and hours at your computer.

At the ship end of the gangway, you will find a decorated (hopefully) entrance and the comfortable feel of air-conditioning if the weather is hot. The ship's cruise staff will welcome you aboard.

Things to check

The door to your cabin should be open. If it is locked, ask the steward to obtain the key to open the door. Aboard the newest ships, you will probably be handed an electronically coded key card. Once inside the cabin, take a good look. Is it clean? Is it tidy? Are the beds properly made? Make sure there is ice in the ice container. Check the bathroom, bathtub (if there is one), or shower. Make sure there are towels and soap.

If there are problems, bring them to the attention of your cabin steward immediately. Or call the reception desk, explain the problem, and establish how it will be resolved and by whom. Memorize the telephone number for the ship's hospital, doctor, or for medical emergencies, just so you know how to call for help should an emergency arise.

Your luggage probably will not have arrived yet – if it is a ship carrying more than 1,000 passengers – so don't sit in the cabin waiting for it. Put your hand luggage away somewhere, and, deck plan in hand, take a walk. If you're hungry, you may want to head to the self-serve buffet – but, be warned that aboard the large resort ships, it'll probably be a bit of a free-for-all.

Familiarize yourself with the layout of the ship. Learn which way is forward, which way is aft, and how to reach your cabin from the main stairways. This is also a good time to learn how to get from your cabin to the outside decks in an emergency (these are rare, but they do happen).

Control that thirst

You're thirsty when you arrive in your cabin. You notice a bottle of water with a tab around its neck. Be sure to read the notice on the tab: "This bottle is provided for your convenience. If you open it, your account will be charged $4.50."

On deck, you are greeted by a smiling waiter offering you a colorful, cool drink. But, put your fingers on the glass as he hands it to you and he'll also ask for your cruise card. Bang, you've just paid $6.95 for a drink full of ice worth 5 cents.

Drinks costs soon add up. Aboard ships operated by Europe-based companies, mixers such as tonic for gin are usually charged separately.

The safety drill

Regulations dictate that a Passenger Lifeboat Drill must take place within 24 hours after the ship sails from the embarkation port, but typically it takes place before the ship sails. You'll find your lifejacket in the cabin and directions to your assembly station will be posted on the back of the cabin door. After the drill, you can take off the lifejacket and relax. By now, your luggage probably will have arrived. ❑

CRUISE LINES BY MARKET CLASSIFICATION

Although there are three fairly distinctive divisions of cruise lines and their ships, some blurring between these divisions has occurred as companies have responded to more demanding passenger tastes and to the market conditions created by the threat of international terrorism and a harsher economic climate.

LUXURY				
Crystal Cruises **	Regent Seven Seas	Costa Cruises	Mediterranean Classic	TUI Cruises
Cunard Line **	Cruises **	Cruise and Maritime	Cruises	Voyages of Discovery
Hapag-Lloyd Cruises *	Saga Cruises	Voyages	Mitsui OSK Passenger	
Sea Cloud Cruises	Venus Cruise	Cruise West	Line ***	NICHE MARKET OPERATORS
SeaDream Yacht Club	Voyages to Antiquity	Delphin Seereisen	Noble Caledonia	These small expedition-
Silversea Cruises	Windstar Cruises	Disney Cruise Line	Norwegian Cruise Line	market companies
The Yachts of Seabourn		easyCruise.com	P&O Cruises	charter ships for specific
	STANDARD	Fred Olsen Cruise Lines	P&O Cruises (Australia)	voyages or seasons:
	Abercrombie & Kent	Galapagos Cruises	Page & Moy Cruises	Antarctic Shipping
PREMIUM	AIDA Cruises	Hansa Touristik	Phoenix Reisen	Antarpply Expeditions
Asuka Cruise (NYK)	American Canadian	Hapag-Lloyd Cruises *	Plantours & Partner	Arcturus Expeditions (Far
Azamara Club Cruises	Caribbean Line	Happy Cruises	Princess Cruises	Frontiers Travel Ltd)
Celebrity Cruises	American Cruise Lines	Hurtigruten	Pullmantur Cruises	Aurora Expeditions
Hebridean Island	CDF Croisières de	Iberocruceros	Quark Expeditions	G.A.P. Expeditions
Cruises	France **	Island Cruises (part of	Royal Caribbean	Heritage Expeditions
Holland America Line	Canodros	Thomson Cruises)	International	Oceanwide Expeditions
Oceania Cruises	Carnival Cruise Lines	Kristina Cruises	Star Cruises	OneOcean expeditions
Orion Expedition Cruises	Classic International	Lindblad Expeditions	Star Clippers	Polar Star Expeditions
Peter Deilmann Cruises	Cruises	Louis Cruises	Swan Hellenic Cruises	Zegrahm Expeditions
Paul Gauguin Cruises	Club Méditerranée	MSC Cruises ***	Thomson Cruises	
Ponant Cruises (CIP)	Cruises	Mano Cruises	Transocean Tours	

* Europa only   ** This company operates ships that straddle the line between Luxury and Premium.   *** Some of this company's ships straddle the line between Premium and Standard.

WHAT TO DO IF...

Twenty practical tips for a good cruise experience

❶ Your luggage does not arrive at the ship.
If you are part of the cruise line's air/sea package, the airline is responsible for locating your luggage and delivering it to the next port. If you arranged your own air transportation it is wholly *your* problem. Always have easy-to-read name and address tags both *inside* as well as *outside* your luggage. Keep track of claim documents and give the airline a detailed itinerary and list of port agents (usually included with your documents).

❷ *You* miss the ship.
If you miss the ship's departure at the port of embarkation (due to late or non-performing flight connections, etc), and you are traveling on an air/sea package, the airline will arrange to get you to the ship. If you are traveling "cruise-only," however, and have arranged your own air transportation, then *you* are responsible for onward flights, hotel stays, and transfers. If you arrive at the port just as your ship is pulling away, see the ship's port agent immediately (contact details will be included in your documents).

You miss the ship in a port of call. The onus is on you to get back to the ship before its appointed sailing time, unless you are participating in a ship-organized shore excursion. Miss the ship and you'll need to get to its next port at your own cost. It could prove difficult if the ship is going to a different country, and your passport is on board, and it's a Sunday, for example. So, take a copy of your passport with you, just in case. Ships have also been known to leave port early because of impending inclement weather conditions. However, if you do miss your ship, the ship's port agent should be close by to assist you. In case he's not – always take the name and telephone contact details with you (they are normally provided on the daily program for each port).

❸ Your cabin is too small.
Almost all cruise ship cabins are too small (I am convinced that some are designed for packages rather than people). When you book a cruise, you pay for a certain category and type of cabin but have little or no control over which one you actually get. See the hotel manager as soon as possible and explain what is wrong with the cabin (noisy, too hot, etc). If the ship is full (most are nowadays), it will be difficult to change. However, the hotel manager will probably try to move you from known problem cabins, although they are not required to do so.

❹ Your cabin has no air-conditioning, it is noisy, or there are plumbing problems.
If there is anything wrong in your cabin, or if there is something wrong with the plumbing in your bathroom, bring it to the attention of your cabin steward immediately. If nothing gets better, complain to the hotel manager. Some cabins, for example, are located above the ship's laundry, generator, or galley (hot); others may be above the disco (noisy). If the ship is full, it may be difficult to change.

❺ You have noisy cabin neighbors.
First, politely tell your neighbors that you can hear them brushing their hair as the cabin walls are so thin, and would they please not bang the drawers shut at 2am! If that does not work, complain to the purser or hotel manager, and ask them to attend to the problem.

❻ You have small children and the brochure implied that the ship has special programs for them, but when on board you find out it is not an all-year-round program.
In this instance, either the brochure was misleading, or your travel agent did not know enough about the ship or did not bother to ask the right questions. If you have genuine cause for complaint, then see your travel agent when you get home. Most ships generally will try to accommodate your young ones (the large resort ships – those carrying more than 1,600 passengers – have more facilities), but may not be covered by their insurance for "looking after" them throughout the day, as the brochure seemed to promise. Again, check thoroughly with your travel agent *before* you book.

❼ You do not like your dining room seating.
Some "standard" market ships (particularly the large "resort" ships) operate two seatings for dinner (sometimes this applies to all meals). When you book your cruise, you are asked whether you want the first or second seating. The line will make every attempt to please you. But if you want second seating and are given first seating (perhaps a large group has taken over the entire second seating, or the ship is full), there may be little the restaurant manager can do.

❽ You want a table for two and are put at a table for eight.
Again, see the restaurant manager (maître d') and explain why you are not satisfied. A little gratuity should prove helpful.

❾ You cannot communicate with your dining room waiter.
Dining room waiters are probably of a nationality and tongue completely foreign to yours, and all they can do

is smile. This could prove frustrating for a whole cruise, especially if you need something out of the ordinary. See the restaurant manager, and tell him you want a waiter with whom you can communicate. If he does not solve the problem, see the hotel manager.

⑩ The food is definitely not "gourmet" cuisine as advertised in the brochure.

If the food is not as described (for example, whole lobster in the brochure, but only cold lobster salad once during the cruise, or the "fresh squeezed" orange juice on the breakfast menu is anything but), inform the maître d' of the problem.

⑪ A large group has taken over the ship.

Sometimes, large groups have blocked (pre-booked) several public rooms for meetings (seemingly every hour on the hour in the rooms you want to use). This means the individual passenger (that is you) becomes a second-class citizen. Make your displeasure known to the hotel manager immediately, tell your travel agent, and write a follow-up letter to the line when you get home.

⑫ A port of call is deleted from the itinerary.

If you only took the cruise because the ship goes to the place you have wanted to go for years, then read the fine print in the brochure *before* you book. A cruise line is under *no* obligation to perform the stated itinerary. For whatever reason (political unrest, weather, mechanical problems, no berth space, safety, etc.), the ship's captain has the ultimate say.

⑬ You are unwell aboard ship.

There will be a qualified doctor (who generally operates as a concession, and therefore charges) and medical facilities, including a small pharmacy. You will be well taken care of. Although there are charges for medical services, almost all cruise lines offer insurance packages that include medical coverage for most eventualities. It is wise to take out this insurance when you book.

⑭ You have a problem with a crew member.

Go to the hotel manager or chief purser and explain the problem; for single women this could be a persistent cabin steward who has a master door key. No one will do anything unless you complain. Cruise ships try to hire decent staff, but, with so many crew, there are bound to be a few bad apples. Insist on a full written report of the incident, which must be entered into the ship's daily log by the staff captain (deputy captain).

⑮ You leave personal belongings on a tour bus.

If you find you have left something on a tour bus, and you are back on board your ship, the first thing to do is advise the shore excursion manager or the purser's office. The tour operator ashore will then be contacted to ascertain whether any items have been handed in to their office.

⑯ The cruise line's air arrangements have you flying from Los Angeles via Timbuktu to get to your cruise ship.

Fine if your cruise ship is in Timbuktu (difficult, as it is inland). Most cruise lines that have low rates also use the cheapest air routing to get you to your ship. That could mean flights from a central hub. Be warned: you get what you pay for. Ask questions *before* you book.

⑰ You fly internationally to take a cruise.

If your cruise is a long distance away from your home, then it usually makes good sense to fly to your cruise embarkation point and stay for at least a day or two before the cruise. Why? Because you will be better rested and able to adjust to any time changes. You will step aboard your ship already relaxed and ready for a real vacation. As a bonus, you will get to know the port of departure.

⑱ The ship's laundry ruins your clothes.

If any of your clothing is ruined or discolored by the ship's laundry, first tell your cabin steward(ess), and then follow up by going to the purser's office and getting it registered as a proper complaint. Take a copy of the complaint with you, so you can follow up when you get home. Unfortunately, you will probably find a disclaimer on the laundry list saying something to the effect that liability is limited to about $1 per item, which is not a lot. So, although the laundry and dry cleaning facilities generally work well, things can occasionally go wrong just like ashore.

⑲ You have extra charges on your bill.

Check your itemized bill carefully. Then talk to the purser's office and ask them to show you the charge slips. Finally, make sure you are given a copy of your bill, *after* any modifications have been made.

⑳ You're unhappy with your cruise experience.

You (or your travel agent) ultimately choose the ship and cruise. But if your ship does not meet your specific lifestyle and interests, or the ship performs less well than the brochure promises, then let your travel agent and the cruise line know as soon as possible. If your grievance is valid, many cruise lines will offer a credit, good towards a future cruise. But do be sure to read the fine print on the ticket. ❑

HOW SAFE ARE CRUISE SHIPS?

How likely is an accident at sea? What if there's a fire? Can you
fall overboard? How good are are medical facilities aboard?

You can't always stop passengers having too much to drink and falling over balconies. But, as far as maritime accidents are concerned, cruising can claim the travel industry's best safety record, with fewer than 20 passenger fatalities during the past 20 years. Eleven of those happened when the *Royal Pacific* sank off Malaysia in 1992 after colliding with a Taiwanese trawler.

International regulations require all crew to undergo basic safety training *before* they are allowed to work aboard any cruise ship. On-the-job training is no longer enough. And safety regulations are getting more stringent all the time, governed by an international convention called SOLAS (Safety of Life at Sea), introduced in 1914 in the aftermath of *Titanic'* s sinking in 1912.

Can you accidentally fall overboard?

No. All cruise ships have sufficient railings to protect you and your children. You simply can't go overboard unless you really, really want to.

Safety measures

All cruise ships built since July 1, 1986, must have either totally enclosed or partially enclosed lifeboats with diesel engines that will operate even if the lifeboat is inverted.

Since October 1997, cruise ships have had:
● All stairways fully enclosed in self-contained fire zones.
● Smoke detectors and smoke alarms fitted in all passenger cabins and all public spaces.
● Low-level lighting showing routes of escape (such as in corridors and stairways).
● All fire doors throughout the ship controllable from the ship's navigation bridge.
● All fire doors that are held open by hinges capable of release from a remote location.
● Emergency alarms audible in all cabins.

Since 2002, ocean-going cruise ships on international voyages have had to carry voyage data recorders (VDRs), similar to black boxes carried by aircraft).

In October 2010, new SOLAS regulations will prohibit the use of combustible materials in all new cruise ship construction. Some older vessels will either have to be withdrawn or be expensively upgraded.

Crew members attend frequent emergency drills, the lifeboat equipment is regularly tested, and the fire-detecting devices, and alarm and fire-fighting systems are checked. Any passenger spotting fire or smoke is encouraged to use the nearest fire alarm box, alert a member of staff, or contact the bridge.

Lifeboat drill

Few recent incidents have required the evacuation of passengers, although two cruise ships were lost following collisions (*Jupiter* in 1988, and *Royal Pacific* in 1992), one after striking an iceberg near Antarctica (*Explorer* in 2007) and one after foundering on a reef off the Greek island of Santorini (*Sea Diamond* in 2007).

A passenger lifeboat drill, announced publicly by the captain, must be held within 24 hours of leaving the embarkation port. Attendance is compulsory. Learn your boat station or assembly point and how to get to it in an emergency. If other passengers are lighthearted about the drill, don't be distracted. Note your exit and escape pathways and learn how to put on your lifejacket correctly. The drill takes no more than 20 minutes and is a good investment in playing safe – the *Royal Pacific* took less than 20 minutes to sink after its collision.

Medical services

Except for ships registered in the UK or Norway, there are no mandatory international maritime requirements for cruise lines to carry a licensed physician or to have hospital facilities aboard. However, in general, all ships carrying over 50 passengers do have medical facilities and at least one doctor.

The standard of medical practice and of the doctors themselves may vary from line to line. Most shipboard doctors are generalists; there are no cardiologists or neurosurgeons. Doctors are typically employed as out-

IS SECURITY GOOD ENOUGH?

Cruise lines are subject to stringent international safety and security regulations. Passengers and crew can embark or disembark only by passing through a security checkpoint. Cruise ships maintain zero tolerance for onboard crime or offences against the person. Trained security professionals are employed aboard all cruise ships. In the case of the USA, where more than 60 percent of cruise passengers reside, you will be far more secure aboard a cruise ship than almost anywhere on land.

It is recommended that you keep your cabin locked at all times when you are not there. All new ships have encoded plastic key cards that operate a lock electronically; older ships have metal keys. Cruise lines do not accept responsibility for any money or valuables left in cabins and suggest that you store them in a safety deposit box at the purser's office, or, if one is provided, in your in-cabin personal safe.

You will be issued a personal boarding pass when you embark. This typically includes your photo, lifeboat station, restaurant seating, and other pertinent information, and serves as identification to be shown at the gangway each time you board. You may also be asked for a government-issued photo ID, such as a passport.

PIRACY IN THE GULF OF ADEN

The UN Security Council has renewed its authorization for countries to use military force against the pirates operating off Somalia who have been sabotaging one of the world's busiest shipping lanes. There were around 95 pirate attacks in Somali waters in 2008, with over 40 ships hijacked, including a Saudi tanker holding oil worth $100 million.

The pirates rarely harm people – their aim is to take hostages and demand a ransom from a ship's owners. Cruise ships are not immune from attack, particularly smaller ones. But *MSC Melody*, carrying 1,500 passengers, was attacked in 2009; its crew repelled the pirates by firing in the air and spraying water on them.

In 2008, the US Navy created a special unit, called Combined Task Force 151, to combat piracy in the Gulf of Aden.

In February 2009 the Maritime Security Patrol Area, introduced by coalition navies in 2008 as a safe passage corridor, was replaced by two separate 5-mile wide eastbound and westbound, separated by a 2-mile buffer.

side contractors and will charge for use of their services, including seasickness shots.

Regrettably, many cruise lines make medical services a low priority. Most shipboard physicians are not certified in trauma treatment or medical evacuation procedures, for example. However, some medical organizations, such as the American College of Emergency Physicians, have a special division for cruise medicine. Most ships catering to North American passengers carry doctors licensed in the United States, Canada, or Britain, but doctors aboard many other ships come from a variety of countries and disciplines.

Cunard Line's *QM2*, with 4,344 passengers and crew, has a fully equipped hospital with one surgeon, one doctor, a staff of six nurses, and two medical orderlies; contrast this with *Carnival Sensation*, which carries up to 3,514 passengers and crew, with just one doctor and two nurses.

Any ship operating long-distance cruises, with several days at sea should have better medical facilities than one engaged in a standard 7-day Caribbean cruise, with a port of call almost every day.

Ideally, a ship's medical staff should be certified in advanced cardiac life support. The equipment should include an examination room, isolation ward/bed, X-ray machine (to verify fractures), cardiac monitor (EKG) and defibrillator, oxygen-saturation monitor, external pacemaker, oxygen, suction and ventilators, hematology analyzer, culture incubator, and a mobile trolley intensive care unit.

Existing health problems requiring treatment on board must be reported when you book. Aboard some ships, you may be charged for filling a prescription as well as for the cost of prescribed drugs. There may also be a charge if you have to cancel a shore excursion and need a doctor's letter to prove that you are ill.

Shipboard injury

Slipping, tripping, and falling are the major sources of shipboard injury. There are things you can do to minimize the chance of injury.

● Aboard many pre-1980 ships, raised thresholds separate a cabin's bathroom from its sleeping area. Don't hang anything from the fire sprinkler heads on the cabin ceilings.

● On older ships, note how the door lock works. Some require a key on the inside in order to unlock the door. Leave the key in the lock, so that in the event of a real emergency, you don't have to hunt for the key.

● Aboard older ships, take care not to trip over raised thresholds in doorways leading to the open deck.

● Walk with caution when the outer decks are wet after being washed, or if they are wet after rain. This applies especially to solid steel decks – falling onto them is really painful.

● Do not throw a lighted cigarette or cigar butt, or knock out your pipe, over the ship's side. They can easily be sucked into an opening in the ship's side or onto an aft open deck area, and cause a fire.

Surviving a shipboard fire

Shipboard fires can generate an incredible amount of heat, smoke, and often panic. In the unlikely event that you are in one, try to remain calm and think logically and clearly.

When you board the ship and get to your cabin, check the way to the nearest emergency exits fore and aft. Count the number of cabin doorways and other distinguishing features to the exits in case you have to escape without the benefit of lighting, or in case the passageway is filled with smoke. All ships use "low location" lighting systems.

Exit signs are normally located just above your head – this is virtually useless, as smoke and flames rise. Note the nearest fire alarm location and know how to use it in case of dense smoke. In future, it is likely that directional sound evacuation beacons will be mandated; these will direct passengers to exits, escape-ways and other safe areas and may be better than the present inadequate visual aids.

If you are in your cabin and there is fire in the passageway outside, put on your lifejacket. If the cabin's door handle is hot, soak a towel in water and use it to turn the handle. If a fire is raging in the passageway, cover yourself in wet towels and go through the flames.

Check the passageway. If there are no flames, or if everything looks clear, walk to the nearest emergency exit or stairway. If there is smoke in the passageway, crawl to the nearest exit. If the exit is blocked, go to an alternate one. It may take considerable effort to open a heavy fire door to the exit. Don't use the elevators: they may stop at a deck that's on fire, or they may stop working.

If there's a fire in your cabin or on the balcony, report it immediately by telephone. Then get out of your cabin, close the door behind you, sound the alarm, and alert your neighbors. ❑

CHECK YOUR CARBON FOOTPRINT

The good news: sea travel produces an estimated 36 times less carbon dioxide than flying. The bad news: that's still not good enough

An average cruise passenger's carbon footprint is a complicated equation to work out. However, experts agree that, first the distance of any cruise itinerary must be calculated. This is then multiplied by the amount of greenhouses gas emissions that each passenger creates – approximately 0.30kg per passenger per kilometer, based on a typical cruise ship, if there is such a thing.

Thus, for a 7-day cruise of about 2,000 nautical miles, the calculation is 3,200 km x 0.30 = 960 tons (the approximate equivalent of planting four native trees).

Although marine vessels are responsible for almost 3 percent of the world's greenhouse gases, the world's fleet of around 350 ocean-going cruise ships produces just 0.1% of those emissions. But can the cruise industry achieve the proposed international sulphur emissions (NOx) reduction to 0.5%, set to be introduced in 2020?

Cruise companies are already working to achieve an integrated, industry-wide approach to reduce air emissions, to provide more fuel-efficient ships, and to retrofit some existing, older ships with more efficient replacement machinery. New ships also benefit from better hydrodynamic hull design and advanced hull coatings can also improve efficiency. Careful handling of solid and liquid waste also results in lower fuel consumption, and, therefore, CO_2 emissions. Further, flue gas from shipboard incinerators is controlled and ozone-depleting substances are prohibited.

MSC Fantasia and *MSC Splendida*, for example, use only low-sulphur fuels worldwide. *Celebrity Solstice*-class ships have 80 solar panels that help power elevators.

Other eco-friendly measures include the use of LED lighting rather than fuel-guzzling halogen lighting; cabin lights and other electrical devices that are turned on (with the cabin key card) only when the cabin is occupied; water flow reducers fitted to all the faucets (taps) and showers; use of automatic darkness-activated sensors that switch on the ship's external lights at dusk; the use of chilled river

Setting a good example: *MSC Fantasia*.

rocks, which retain low temperatures well, rather than ice for buffet items; heat-deflecting window coatings, and use of the latest wastewater treatment technology. While all these measures help, they must be weighed against the costs involved in implementing them.

The British Isles introduced the very first Emissions Control Areas (ECA) around its shores and in the English Channel, in 2009. This was followed by 10 countries in the Baltic and North Sea region. The IMO subsequently adopted the ECR system to formally establish a North American Emission Control Area – an area ringing the USA/Canada coast with a 200-mile exclusion zone to be brought into force in September 2011. IMO's global air emissions standards call for a progressive reduction of SOx emissions from the current 4.5% to 3.5% effective January 2012, then to 0.5% in January 2020, subject to a review to be completed by 2018. The stricter ECA sulphur limits were reduced from 1.5% to 1% in July 2010 and will be reduced further to 0.1% by 2015.

Blended fuels and even some residual fuels have 1.5% sulphur content but meeting the 0.1% limit will mean a shift to costlier distillate. This means passengers will probably be paying more for cruises, particularly to Alaska and Canada/New England, regions entirely within the new ECA, as operators switch to distillate in 2015.

The IMO also introduced an International Convention on the Management of Ballast Water and Sediments (wastewater discharge) in 2010. MSC Cruises, for example, will have almost completely eliminated the use of plastics by the end of 2010, with no chemical detergents now used in its shipboard laundries.

"Cold Ironing" – plugging a ship into a land-based energy supply capable of running a ship's essential functions while in port – certainly makes sense in areas where electricity can be generated from renewable sources – as is the case in Juneau, Los Angeles, San Diego, Seattle, and Vancouver – rather than being taken from the national grid. Expect more city ports to build this option into their infrastructure. ❑

WHAT IS MARPOL?

Short for "Marine Pollution," the International Convention for the Prevention of Pollution from Ships (MARPOL 73/78 – the dates refer to its adoption) is the convention that all United Nation countries subscribe to. It was designed to minimize pollution of the oceans and seas, including dumping, and pollution by oil and exhaust gases, whether by operational or accidental causes. The original MARPOL Convention was signed on 17 February 1973, but did not come into force then. The present Convention took effect on 2 October 1983. Presently, some 136 countries, representing 98% of the world's shipping tonnage, are signatories to the Convention. Ships flagged under these countries are subject to its requirements, regardless of where they sail.

Ocean Ships to Debut: 2011–2014

This chart, alphabetically by cruise line, shows ships under firm contract. Delivery/debut dates may be subject to change.

CRUISE LINE	NAME OF SHIP	GROSS TONNAGE	COST	LENGTH (feet)	LENGTH (meters)	PASSENGERS (lower bed capacity)	BUILDER	MONTH
2011								
AIDA Cruises	AIDASol	71,300	€380 million	826.7	252.0	2,174	Meyer Werft (Germany)	April
Carnival Cruise Lines	Carnival Magic	130,000	$740 million	1,092.5	330.0	3,652	Fincantieri (Italy)	June
Celebrity Cruises	Celebrity Silhouette	122,000	$641 million	1,033.4	315.0	2,850	Meyer Werft (Germany)	Fall
Costa Cruises	Costa Favolosa	114,000	€510 million	951.4	290.0	3,012	Fincantieri (Italy)	Spring
Disney Cruise Line	Disney Dream	128,000	$900 million	1,114.8	339.8	2,500	Meyer Werft (Germany)	Spring
MSC Cruises	MSC Meraviglia	94,600	$700 million	1,033.4	315.0	2,550	Aker Yards (France)	February
Oceania Cruises	Riviera	65,000	$530 million	823.4	251.0	1,260	Fincantieri (Italy)	July
Pearl Seas Cruises	Pearl Mist	8,700	$50 million	330.0	100.5	214	Irving Shipyards (Canada)	January
Ponant Cruises	L'Austral	10,700	$100 million	459.3	140.0	264	Fincantieri (Italy)	March
The Yachts of Seabourn	Seabourn Quest	32,000	$200 million	650.0	198.0	450	Mariotti (Italy)	Summer
2012								
AIDA Cruises	to be announced	71,300	€385 million	826.7	252.0	2,174	Meyer Werft (Germany)	May
Carnival Cruise Lines	to be announced	130,000	$738 million	1,092.5	330.0	3,690	Fincantieri (Italy)	Spring
Celebrity Cruises	to be announced	122,000	$641 million	1,033.4	315.0	2,850	Meyer Werft (Germany)	Fall
Costa Cruises	Costa Favolosa	114,200	€510 million	951.4	290.0	3,012	Fincantieri (Italy)	Spring
Disney Cruise Line	Disney Fantasy	128,000	$900 million	1,114.8	339.8	2,500	Meyer Werft (Germany)	Spring
MSC Cruises	MSC Favolosa	139,000	n/a	1,093.5	333.3	3,502	STX Europe (France)	June
2013								
Princess Cruises	to be announced	139,000	n/a	1,092.5	330.0	3,600	Fincantieri (Italy)	Spring
MSC Cruises	to be announced	141,000	n/a	1,093.5	333.3	3,502	STX Europe (France)	Spring
Utopia Residences*	Utopia (option)	105,000	$1.1 billion	971.1	296.0	400	Samsung Shipyards (Korea)	tba
2014								
Princess Cruises	to be announced	139,000		1,092.5	330.0	3,600	Fincantieri (Italy)	Spring

* This ship has residences for purchase, and cabins for cruise passengers

Index

Credits

Photography:
A1Vista Cruises 104
ABB Group 45TR
AIDA Cruises 65T, 158
American Safari Cruises 98, 159T
Antigua & Barbuda Tourism 33T
Tom Arban/Quark Expeditions 19T
Azamara Cruises 160
Berlin ITB 100
Blount Small Ship Adventures 97B
Captain Cook Cruises 11B, 41, 95, 108B
Carnival Cruise Lines 3, 10–11, 18, 19B, 20T, 25, 28, 31, 46, 55T, 62, 66B, 71, 76B, 86, 88, 90, 119, 124T, 126B, 127, 128T, 128B, 129, 130T, 130B, 131, 188T, 190–191, 702
Celebrity Cruises 50B, 93B, 94B, 123T, 132, 133T, 133B, 134T, 134B, 185
Corbis 1, 109, 159B
Costa Cruises 24, 63B, 66–67, 111C, 135T, 135B, 136, 137, 157(6), 178
CPTM (Danee Hazama, Julien Aurial) 102, 103B
Cruceros Australis 160–161
Cruise People, The 89T
Cruise West 161
Crystal Cruises 7, 23B, 26–27, 39, 54, 73B, 77B, 115B, 162, 175

Cunard Line 9B, 12–13 (all except 13T), 14, 15B, 23T, 65B, 87T, 99, 110B, 111B, 121, 125, 138, 139, 157(2), 183, 192
Disney Cruise Line 10B, 74T, 78–79, 162–163
easyCruise 9T
Fred Olsen Cruise Line 20B, 30T, 48T, 100T, 120, 163
Glyn Genin/Apa 107
Getty Images 48B, 87B, 126T
Peter Guttman/Quark Expeditions 91, 93T
Hapag Lloyd 27B, 29T, 50T, 72, 164, 182, 184
Hebridean Island Cruises 165
Holland America Line 47, 80, 140, 141T, 141B, 142T, 142B
Ralph Lee Hopkins/Lindblad 166–167
Hurtigruten 97T
iStockphoto 13TR, 79, 118B, 173
Louis Cruises 60, 106B, 166
Meyer Werft 44–45 (all except 45T)
MSC Cruises 21, 22T, 30B, 49B, 51, 52T, 58T, 64, 68, 69B, 85T, 114B, 117, 143, 144, 157(3), 179B, 714
Michael S. Nolan/Lindblad 4–5, 33B
Norwegian Cruise Line 57T, 58B, 114–115, 123B(2), 145T, 145B, 146T, 146B, 180
Orion Expedition Cruises 167
P&O Cruises 55B, 70, 73T, 111T, 147,

148, 157(4)
Ponant Cruises 94T, 116, 168
Princess Cruises 22B, 76–77, 85B, 149T, 149B, 150T, 150B, 151, 157(5), 181, 186
Regent Seven Seas Cruises 53, 112, 169B
Matthew Ross/Quark Expeditions 169T
Royal Caribbean International 6, 8T, 8B, 16–17, 26B, 49T, 52B, 56T, 56B, 63T, 69T, 74B, 75, 81, 82, 84, 113, 118T, 122 (all), 123B(3), 152–153, 152B, 153B, 154–155, 154B, 155B, 157(1), 187
Saga Cruises 83
SeaDream Yacht Cruises 174
Silversea Cruises 57B, 92, 123B(1), 170–171B
Star Cruises 156T, 156B
The Yachts of Seabourn 172T, 176–177, 189
Ayako Ward 106T, 188B
Douglas Ward 2, 16B, 29B, 61, 89, 105, 108T, 124B
Star Clippers 101T, 172B
Peter Stuckings/Apa 179T
Windstar Cruises 170–171B

Cover design: Richard Cooke
Cartography Editor: Zoë Godwin
Map Production Tyne Mapping
Maps © 2010 Apa Publications GmbH & Co. Verlag KG (Singapore branch)

WHERE TO FIND THE CRUISE LINES ONLINE

Abercrombie & Kent
www.aandktours.com

AIDA Cruises
www.aida.de

American Canadian Caribbean Line
www.accl-smallships.com

American Cruise Lines
www.americancruiselines.com

American Safari Cruises
www.amsafari.com

Antarctic Shipping
www.antarctic.cl

Azamara Club Cruises
www.azamaracruises.com

Carnival Cruise Lines
www.carnival.com

Captain Cook Cruises
www.captcookcrus.cm.au

Celebrity Cruises
www.celebrity-cruises.com

Classic International Cruises
www.cic-cruises.com

Club Med Cruises
www.clubmed.com

Costa Cruises
www.costacruises.com

Cruceros Australis
www.crucerosaustralis.com

Cruise & Maritime Voyages
www.cruiseandmaritime.com

Cruise West
www.cruisewest.com

Crystal Cruises
www.crystalcruises.com

Cunard Line
www.cunard.com

Delphin Seereisen
www:delphin-cruises.com

Disney Cruise Line
www.disneycruise.com

easyCruise.com
www.easycruise.com

Fred Olsen Cruise Lines
www.fredolsencruises.com

G.A.P Adventures
www.gapadventures.com

Hansa Touristik
www.hansatourstik.com

Hapag-Lloyd Cruises
www.hlkf.com

Happy Cruises
www.happycruises.eu

Hebridean Island Cruises
www.hebdrideanislandcruises.com

Holland America Line
www.hollandamerica.com

Hurtigruten (Norwegian Coastal Voyages)
www.coastalvoyage.com

Island Cruises
www.thomson.co.uk

Kristina Cruises
www.kristinacruises.com

Lindblad Expeditions
www.expeditions.com

Louis Cruises
www.louiscruises.com

Mano Cruise
www.manocruise.co.il

Mediterranean Classic Cruises
www.mccruises.gr

Mitsui OSK Passenger Line
www.mopas.co.jp

MSC Cruises
www.msccruises.com

MSC Cruises USA
www.msccruisesusa.com

Noble Caledonia
www.noblecaledonia.co.uk

Norwegian Cruise Line
www.ncl.com

NYK Line (Nippon Yusen Kaisha)
www.asukacruise.co.jp

Oceania Cruises
www.oceaniacruises.com

Orion Expedition Cruises
www.orioncruises.com

P&O Cruises
www.pocruises.com

P&O Cruises (Australia)
www.pocruises.com.au

Paul Gauguin Cruises
www.pgcruises.com

Pearl Seas Cruises
www.pearlseascruises.com

Peter Deilmann Cruises
www.deilmann-cruises.com

Phoenix Reisen
www.phoenixreisen.com

Plantours & Partner
www.plantours-partner.de

Ponant Cruises
www.ponant.com

Princess Cruises
www.princesscruises.com

Pullmantur Cruises
www.pullmanturcruises.com

Quark Expeditions
www.quarkexpeditions.com

Regent Seven Seas Cruises
www.rssc.com

Royal Caribbean International
www.royalcaribbean.com

Saga Cruises
www.sagacruises.com

Sea Cloud Cruises
www.seacloud.com

SeaDream Yacht Club
www.seadreamyachtclub.com

Silversea Cruises
www.silversea.com

Star Clippers
www.starclippers.com

Star Cruises
www.starcruises.com

Swan Hellenic Cruises
www.swanhellenic.com

The Yachts of Seabourn
www.seabourn.com

Thomson Cruises
www.thomson.co.uk

Transocean Cruises
www.transocean.de

Travel Dynamics International
www.traveldynamicsinternational.com

TUI Cruises
www.tui.com

Venus Cruise
www.venus-cruise.co.jp

Voyages of Discovery
www.voyagesofdiscovery.com

Voyages to Antiquity
www.voyagesto antiquity.com

Windstar Cruises
www.windstarcruises.com

Zegrahm Expeditions
www.zeco.com

FREIGHTER CRUISE COMPANIES

Andrew Weir Shipping
www.aws.co.uk

Aranui Polynesienne
www.aranui.com

CMA-CGM
www.cma-cgm.com

Grimaldi Freighter Cruises
www.grimaldi-freightercruises.com

Hapag-Lloyd Container Line
www.hapag-lloyd.com

Horn Line Hamburg
www.hornlinie.com

Reederei F. Laeisz
www.laeiszline.de

Rickmers Reederei
www.rickmers.de

RMS St. Helena
www.RMS-St-Helena.com

Senator Line
www.senatorlines.com

Transeste Schiffart
www.transeste.de

DEAR PASSENGER,

You are most welcome to send me your observations concerning any recent cruises taken. Please complete the following basic information when sending comments.

Although I cannot acknowledge receipt of this comment form, or any letters, because of my intensive travel schedule, I do thank you for your input, and for purchasing this book.

Cruise Date . . . . Ship Name . . . .

Cruise Line . . . . Suite/Cabin Number . . . .

Dining Room Seating (tick box): ❑ Open ❑ First ❑ Second

Your Comments . . . .

. . . .

. . . .

. . . .

Your Pet Peeves

(1) . . . .

. . . .

(2) . . . .

. . . .

Your name . . . .

Address . . . .

. . . .

email address: . . . .

Please send to the address below:

Mr Douglas Ward
The Maritime Evaluations Group
Canada House, 1 Carrick Way
New Milton, Hampshire BH25 6UD
United Kingdom

Alternatively, please email these details to:

shipratings@hotmail.com

Sign up now for free updates of this book...

As new ships are launched and cruise lines compete ever more fiercely, it's hard to keep up. Forewarned is forearmed, and you can learn of the latest changes by signing up for Douglas Ward's free quarterly newsletter, available through Berlitz's website. Based on his intensive schedule of ship visits, he will detail the facilities that have changed aboard ships reviewed in this book. He will also keep readers abreast of the latest industry news – cruise lines changing ownership, ships changing their names, new cruise terminals, and money-saving tips.

To sign up for this free service, available during the lifetime of the 2011 edition of this book, simply email your name and place of residence to **cruiseletter@berlitzpublishing.com**